Interviews
Published in
The American Journal of Cardiology
1982–2015

Volume 1: A–K

BaylorScott&White
HEALTH

The compilation was prepared by Baylor Scott & White Health and was published in 2016. All rights reserved.

BaylorScott&White
H E A L T H

Baylor Scott & White Health
3500 Gaston Avenue, Dallas, TX 75246
1-800-4BAYLOR
http://baylorscottandwhite.com/
ISBN: 978-0-9845237-8-8 (hardcover)

Contents

Preface

In the 1960s, Dr. William C. Roberts and I were on the staff of the intramural program of the (then) National Heart Institute in Bethesda, Maryland. Dr. Roberts was chief of pathology, I was chief of cardiology, and we worked shoulder to shoulder with the late Dr. Andrew (Glenn) Morrow, chief of cardiac surgery. Those were the "halcyon days" of cardiology and cardiac surgery, when exciting new developments in these closely related fields occurred almost weekly. Our clinical services were quite active, and while great strides were made in the care of cardiac patients, many critically ill patients did not survive the surgical or medical treatments evolving at the time. Hence, Dr. Roberts and his team were kept quite busy. The collaboration between the three groups was intense, and together we learned a great deal about the natural (and unnatural) history of many congenital, valvular, and cardiomyopathic disorders. Dr. Roberts attended our rounds and clinical conferences, which sharpened his skills as a pathologist and enhanced his contribution to the clinical services.

When Dr. Roberts and I left the National Institutes of Health, we went our separate ways, but we have maintained our friendship and I have tracked his many achievements. Prominent among them has been his editorship of the *American Journal of Cardiology* since 1982. A unique feature since 1996 has been the published transcripts of the detailed interviews that he has conducted with 74 leaders of cardiology and cardiovascular surgery. These interviews make up these two volumes.

Each interview begins with a brief biographical sketch. Dr. Roberts then simply places a microphone on a nearby table and in a friendly manner asks straightforward questions about the interviewee's parents, his/her childhood, and early schooling. What drove them into medicine in the first place? What led them to cardiovascular medicine or surgery? What were their greatest ambitions? Who were their most important mentors? What are their hobbies? How did their professional lives affect their personal lives? He ends the interview by asking whether the interviewee has anything else to add. Several photographs of the interviewee, many taken during childhood or adolescence, are usually included. In one instance there is a photo taken on the day of his birth! This is followed by a list of references to the published papers of which the interviewee is most proud.

This anthology of the 74 mini-biographies makes for enjoyable reading; I have certainly learned a great deal about the lives of colleagues and acquaintances with whom I have had professional relationships for decades. Importantly, it will be of intense interest to the medical historians of the future who will learn something about how the enormous advances in cardiology and cardiovascular surgery occurring in the latter half of the 20th century and the beginning of the 21st century came about, and more importantly, of the people who were responsible for them.

Dr. Roberts deserves enormous credit for devising and successfully completing this novel project. His patience, dedication, hard work, and talent shine through.

—EUGENE BRAUNWALD, MD
Boston, MA

Life Lessons from Modern-Day Greats in Cardiovascular Disease

In July 1996, interviews of prominent cardiovascular specialists began appearing in *The American Journal of Cardiology* (*AJC*). Listed in Table 1 are the names of the 62 cardiovascular internists whose interviews have been published in the *AJC*. One interview was done by Dr. Mark Silverman, 2 by Dr. J. Willis Hurst, 1 by Dr. Charles Stewart Roberts, 1 by Dr. Colin Ku Lo Phoon, and the others by me. Three interviews focused on medical topics rather than on the interviewees, and they are not further considered in this presentation.

Interviews of 8 cardiovascular surgeons also have appeared in the *AJC*, and their names are listed in Table 2.

In addition to the 70 interviews in the *AJC*, 74 others (with me as the interviewer) have been published in the *Baylor University Medical Center Proceedings* (Table 3), but they are not further considered in this piece.

Certain data on the 59 cardiovascular internists and on the 8 cardiovascular surgeons (a total of 67 interviews) are listed in Table 4. Their ages when interviewed averaged 65 and 74 years, respectively. Most were born from 1926 to 1950. Eleven (17%) were born outside the United States. Of the 52 internists who grew up in the United States (1 was born abroad), 26 (50%) grew up in the Northeast, mostly in New York City (15 of 26); 11 grew up in the middle portion of the United States, 15% in the Southeast, and 14% in the West. Seven of these 67 had no siblings. Of those with siblings, the interviewees were most often the first children (>50%). Ten of the 67 interviewees (15%) had lost parents when the interviewees were <20 years of age. More than 1/2 played on ≥1 high school athletic team and >20% on college varsity teams. The interviewees had averages of 2.7 and 3.1 children, respectively. Ten of the 59 cardiovascular internists (16%) and none of the 8 cardiovascular surgeons were divorced. The interviewees' first publications came at relatively early ages (mean 29 years, range 23 to 36). (That finding is of interest, because the present average age of a recipient of his or her first National Institutes of Health research grant is 42 years.) All of these interviewees were highly productive, and 41% had >500 publications in medical journals. A number were presidents of the American Heart Association or the American College of Cardiology, and 7 of the surgeons were presidents of ≥1 national surgical organization. About 1/3 of the interviewees' mothers worked, and also 1/3 of the interviewees' spouses worked. Seven were married to physicians, but only 2 practiced. Fewer than 1/3 were overweight. Six had PhDs in addition to their MDs. Of the 59 cardiovascular internists, 24 (41%) were Jewish, as was 1 of the 8 cardiovascular surgeons. Of the 54 cardiovascular internists who attended college or medical school or did training in the United States, just over half had some training at an Ivy League university or medical center (not including, however, such institutions as New York University, Johns Hopkins University, or any school in the South, Midwest, or West). None of these 67 interviewees could be considered heavy alcohol users: 1+ represents drinking wine at a social event, 2+ usually daily wine, and 3+ includes spirits.

Some characteristics of the parents of the 67 interviewees are listed in Table 5. One or both members of the 25 couples (37%) were born outside the United States. In 42 couples (63%), 1 or both parents attended college; in 8 of the 67 couples, 1 or both were physicians; only 2 (3%) were divorced; the average number of children was 2.8; and the interviewees were the only children of 8 couples (12%).

The major commonalities among these 67 interviewees are listed in Table 6. Without exception, their parents were devoted to their children, love was abundant in their homes, education was heavily stressed by their parents, the home atmosphere provided an enormous curiosity to learn, nearly all were superb students, all had a passion for medicine, and all worked exceedingly hard. Most slept <6 hours per night, and all were incredibly focused on their goals. Writing was a major priority, and they all worked hard at it. Most were good teachers and good mentors. In my view, all were very competitive. They had strong character. Most had a good capacity for friendship, alcohol played little to no major role in their lives, and most maintained healthfulness.

I have selected to reproduce small portions from 2 interviews: those of Dr. Eugene Braunwald,[1] the most renowned cardiologist of the 20th century, and Dr. Michael E. DeBakey,[2] the most renowned cardiovascular surgeon of the past century.

Eugene Braunwald, MD (1929-)

Dr. Braunwald was born on August 15, 1929, in Vienna, Austria, and lived his first 9 years there.

Roberts: *Can you discuss your life in Vienna?*

Braunwald: My memory of that period falls into 2 very distinct phases: before and after March 13, 1938. On that date the Nazis occupied Austria in the so-called *Anschluss*. My childhood was idyllic before that. We lived in one of the elegant areas of Vienna, I went to an excellent school and had private tutors in English and piano. My parents were very interested in opera, and by the time I was 6 they had begun taking me to the Vienna State Opera. Vienna was a gracious city in the 1930s, the cultural capital of central Europe. Then, suddenly, on March 13, 1938, everything changed. I recall vividly the enthusiastic crowds welcoming Hitler and his troops marching into Vienna. My father's and other Jews' businesses were taken over several days later and their liquidation was begun. We lived in constant terror

Table 1

Interviews of cardiovascular medicine specialists published in *The American Journal of Cardiology*, 1996 to 2008 (n = 62)

Eric Jeffrey Topol	Carl John Pepine
James Thornton Willerson	Kenneth Hardy Cooper
Joseph Stephan Alpert	Watkins Proctor Harvey
John Willis Hurst*	Joseph Kayle Perloff
Jesse Efrem Edwards	Charles Richard Conti
Howard Bertram Burchell	William Watts Parmley
William Howard Frishman	Dean Michael Ornish
Robert Ogdon Bonow	Dean Towle Mason
Eugene Braunwald	George Allan Beller
Joseph Cholmondeley Greenfield	Leslie David Hillis
Norman Mayer Kaplan	Douglas Peter Zipes
Robert McKinnon Califf	Nanette Kass Wenger
Bernard John Gersh	Andrew Peter Selwyn
Dean James Keriakes	Arthur Garson, Jr.
Jeffrey Michael Isner	Edward David Frolich
Scott Montgomery Grundy	Robert Alan Vogel
Burton Elias Sobel	Ferid Murad
Robert Anthony O'Rourke	Steven Evan Nissen
Spencer Bidwell King III	William Peter Castelli
Robert Roberts	Wallace Bruce Fye III
Eugene Austin Stead, Jr.†	Anthony Nicolas DeMaria
Bertram Pitt	Barry Lewis Zaret
Christopher John Dillon Packard‖	Franz H. Messerli
Terje Rolf Pedersen‖	Joseph Loscalzo
Valentin Fuster	Donald Carey Harrison
Henry Arthur Solomon	Hollis Bryan Brewer
Harvey Stanley Hecht‖	Barry Joel Maron
Myrvin Harold Ellestad	William Clifford Roberts§
Richard John Bing†	Jean Schlatter Kan‡
Melvin Mayer Scheinman	Robert William ("Bobby") Brown
James Stuart Forrester III	Lawrence Cohen

* Interviewed by Mark Silverman.
† Interviewed by John Willis Hurst.
‡ Interviewed by Colin K.L. Phoon.
§ Interviewed by Charles S. Roberts.
‖ Topic interviews.

Table 2

Interviews of cardiovascular surgeons published in *The American Journal of Cardiology*, 1997 to 2006 (n = 8)

Michael Ellis DeBakey
Denton Arthur Cooley
John Webster Kirklin
David Coston Sabiston, Jr.
David Kempton Cartwright Cooper
Francis Robicsek
Magdi Habib Yacoub
Lawrence Harvey Cohn

Table 3

Interviews by William Clifford Roberts published in the *Baylor University Medical Center Proceedings*

Baylor physicians	
Lloyd Wade Kitchens, Jr.	Robert Peter Perrillo
David Joseph Ballard	David Wesley Barnett
Adrian Ede Flatt	William Clifford Roberts
J.B. Howell	George Kennedy Hempel, Jr.
George Justice Race	Joseph Allen Kuhn
Michael Emmett	Virginia Pascual
Marvin Jules Stone	William Mark Armstrong
Ronald Coy Jones	William Levin Sutker
Jimmie Harold Cheek	Perry Edward Gross
Robert Wilson Jackson	Barry Wayne Uhr
George Marion Boswell, Jr.	Carolyn Michele Matthews
Göran Bo Gustaf Kintmalm	**Baylor nonphysicians**
Robert Pickett Scruggs, III	Luz Remedios Tolentino
Wilson Weatherford	Boone Powell, Jr.
Fred David Winter, Jr.	Joel Tribble Allison
Gary L. Davis	Mark Timothy Parris
Peter Allen Dysert, II	Gary Dale Brock
Zelig ("Zeck") Lieberman	Julie Michelle O'Bryan
Martin Alan Menter	Herman Grant Lappin
Harold Clifton Urschel, Jr.	Albert Julio Alvarez
John Flake Anderson	**Visiting professors**
John W. Hyland	Gerald Bernard Appel
Joyce Ann O'Shaughnessy	Robert William Schrier
Daniel Earl Polter	Larry Harold Hollier
Jonathan Martin Whitfield	Charles Stone Bryan
Andrew Zolton Fenves	Richard Vaille Lee
Glenn Weldon Tillery	Gregory Gordon Dimijian
Clement Richard Boland, Jr.	Peter Emanuel Dans
Elmer Russell Hayes	Donald Wayne Seldin
Robert Lee Fine	Ellen Taylor Seldin
Jay Donald Mabrey	Thomas John (Jock) Murray
Donald Alan Kennerly	Matthew Whitfield Ridley
Barry Cooper	Robert Ogden Bonow
Robert Gary Mennel	David Westfall Bates
Paul Bernard Convery	Robert Steven Galvin
Irving David Prengler	Carolyn Maureen Clancy
Zaven Hogop Chakmakjian	Lynne Anne Marcum Kirk
Priscilla Larson Hollander	Lee Marshall Nadler

from March until the end of July 1938, when we escaped from Austria. Many people in our situation, of course, did not escape.

Roberts: *Before March 13, 1938, you lived next to your father's business? What was your father like? Your mother? What were your day-to-day activities, not only at school, but at home in those more pleasant moments?*

Braunwald: Our apartment was just off the Schottenrink, Vienna's major thoroughfare, close to the University and to the State opera. I saw a good deal of my father because the proximity of our apartment to his business allowed him to have lunch with us quite frequently. In childhood, both of my parents had been too poor to receive an education beyond high school. My father was fifth generation Viennese, and my mother was born in a small town in the east of what was then the Austro-Hungarian empire. Her family fled to Vienna at the end of World War I because of an anti-Jewish pogrom in her town. My father had built a successful wholesale clothing business by the time I was born, and we enjoyed a very pleasant life. The 3 most important things that I learned from those early years were: a central focus on the well being of the nuclear family; a reverence for learning; and an interest in classical music. As I just mentioned, we lived not far from the University of Vienna, and when I was 6 or 7 years old my mother took me for walks in the Stadtpark adjacent to the University. She would point to the University and say to me, "You will be a professor there someday." Because my parents had been deprived of an education themselves, they made my education their highest priority.

Table 4
Data on the interviewees

Variable	Internists (n = 59)	Cardiovascular Surgeons (n = 8)
Age (yrs)	41–91 (mean 65)	59–88 (mean 74)
Years of birth		
1901–1925	9 (15%)	5 (63%)
1926–1950	45 (76%)	3 (37%)
1951–1954	5 (8%)	0
Country of birth		
United States	53 (90%)	5 (63%)
Outside the United States	6 (10%)	3 (37%)
State of childhood residence		
Northeast (26/52 [50%])		
New York	15*	
Pennsylvania	4	
Connecticut	1	
New Jersey	4	
Massachusetts	1	
Maryland	1	
Middle United States (11/52 [21%])		
Indiana	1	
Ohio	4	
Minnesota	0	1
Oklahoma	2	
Texas	4	1
Southeast (8/52 [15%])		
Virginia	1	
Georgia	4	
South Carolina	1	
North Carolina	0	1
Louisiana	1	1
Alabama	1	
West (7/52 [14%])		
California	5	1
Wyoming	1	
Utah	1	
No. of siblings		
None	5 (8%)	2 (25%)
1–5	54 (92%)	6 (75%)
Hierarchy of interviewees in the families with >1 child		
First child	29/54 (54%)	3/6 (50%)
Last child	12/54 (22%)	2/6 (33%)
Middle child	12/54 (22%)	1/6 (17%)
A parent died when interviewee was aged ≤20 years	8 (14%)	2 (25%)
Competitive athlete		
High school only	31 (53%)	7 (88%)
College also	13 (22%)	5 (63%)
Children	157 (2.7%)	25 (3.1%)
0	2 (3%)	1 (12%)
1	2 (3%)	0
2	23 (39%)	1 (12%)
3	21 (36%)	3 (38%)
4	9 (15%)	1 (12%)
5	2 (3%)	2 (25%)
Divorced	10 (17%)	0
Age (yrs) at first publication	24–36 (mean 29)	23–34 (mean 29)
Publications in medical journals¶		
<250	15/58 (26%)	1 (12%)
251–500	19/58 (33%)	2 (25%)
>500	24/58 (41%)	5 (63%)

Table 4
(continued)

Variable	Internists (n = 59)	Cardiovascular Surgeons (n = 8)
President of the American Heart Association, the American College of Cardiology, or a major surgical society	21 (36%)	7 (88%)
Mother worked	21 (36%)	2 (25%)
Spouse worked	19 (32%)	2 (25%)
Married a physician	5[†] (8%)	2[†] (25%)
Overweight	19 (33%)	2 (25%)
PhD	5 (8%)	1 (12%)
Jewish	24 (41%)	1 (12%)
Ivy League education[‡]		
College	13/54[§] (24%)	0
Medical School	12/54 (22%)	1/5[∥] (20%)
Houseofficership	11/54 (20%)	1/5 (20%)
Fellowship	15/54 (28%)	0
At least 1 of the 4	28/54 (52%)	2/5 (40%)
Drinks alcohol (0–3+)		
None	6 (10%)	1 (12%)
1+	16 (27%)	0
2+	24 (41%)	0
3+	7 (12%)	6 (75%)
Uncertain	6 (10%)	1 (12%)

* One interviewee was born outside the United States but grew up in New York City.

† Only 1 practiced.

‡ Brown University, Columbia University, Cornell University, Dartmouth University, Harvard University, Princeton University, the University of Pennsylvania, and Yale University; does not include New York University, Johns Hopkins University, or any school in the South, Midwest, or West.

§ The other 5 had all their training abroad.

∥ The other 3 had all their training abroad.

¶ One interviewee who was not in academic medium was excluded.

Table 5
Data on parents of interviewees

Variable	Value
One or both born outside the United States	25 (37%)
Attended college (1 or both)	42 (63%)
Were physicians (1 or both)	8 (12%)
Divorced (after interviewee was born)	2 (3%)
No. of children	185 (mean 2.8)
1	8 (12%)
2	24 (36%)
3	18 (27%)
4	9 (13%)
5	6 (9%)
6	2 (3%)

Roberts: *Did you have intellectual discussions at the dinner table at night or at lunch time?*

Braunwald: I remember discussions of history, economics and politics at the dinner table. My parents probably did emphasize such discussions because of their own lack of higher education. Of course, there was much talk about music. Actually, my parents had met in the standing room area at the Vienna State Opera!

Table 6
Commonalities among interviewees

Parents devoted to children
Abundant love from parents
Education stressed by parents
Enormous curiosity to learn
Superb students
Passion for medicine
Worked exceedingly hard
Slept little (<6 h)
Incredibly focused on goals
Good writers
Good teachers and mentors
Competitive
Strong character
Good capacity for friendship
Consumed little or no alcohol
Maintained healthfulness

Roberts: *Although your parents were poor initially, your father became quite successful?*

Braunwald: Yes. By the time of the *Anschluss* he had a prosperous business, but the Nazis quickly sent SS officers to liquidate all Jewish businesses. The officer who was assigned to my father's business had, I believe, been imprisoned for the assassination of Chancellor Dolfuss of Austria several years earlier. I got to know this SS officer because sometimes he came over to the apartment for lunch or coffee.

Roberts: *What was he like?*

Braunwald: He was cold and businesslike but always polite, as he went about destroying our livelihood. The liquidators themselves were able to make off with most everything, and therefore he wanted the process to be rapid and complete.

Roberts: *How did it come about that your father was arrested by the Nazis within a couple of months of their invading Austria?*

Braunwald: It was the proverbial knock on the door in the middle of a night in May 1938. I remember being awakened by my parents at about 3:00 A.M. My mother was hysterical, screaming, "They are taking your father away." He had 15 minutes to get dressed and to say goodbye to us. I now recall that he was remarkably stoic about it. Then my mother, my younger brother and I ran to the window and saw him herded into an open truck with 15 or 20 other men. They were then driven off to the railroad station.

Roberts: *How did your mother get him back? I gather he came back the next day?*

Braunwald: Yes. It is incredible what life can hinge on. When "our" S.S. officer came to the business the next morning, he asked for my father. My very upset mother said he had been taken away, presumably to a work camp. He shrugged his shoulders. (My mother and I subsequently talked about this event innumerable times.) Then came the pivotal moment, she said something along the following: "You need him back because you have liquidated only half of the business, and if you get him back you can liquidate the rest. Look how much richer you would be." He replied, "You might be right." He then phoned the depot to find that my father was about to board the train. My mother only

overheard his side of this conversation in which he pulled rank on the officer at the depot, saying, "I don't care if you are a full colonel in the German army, I am a captain in the SS and I want this Jew returned!" So it ultimately became a matter of authority. By 11 A.M. my father was returned to us. He had been gone for only 8 hours, but it was a very close call. If my mother had not acted at that moment, none of our family would have survived, and of course, we wouldn't be having this interview.

Roberts: *From that point it was about 2 months before you escaped? What happened in the interim?*

Braunwald: My father had actually begun preparations for our escape in March immediately after the occupation, but he redoubled his efforts after his brief arrest. There were several opportunities for him to leave Vienna alone and to try to bring us along later, but he refused to allow the family to be separated. He insisted that we stay together even though that made escape more difficult. But he obviously calculated correctly. We left at the end of July 1938, in something that resembled the *Sound of Music* story, except that there was no music. We ended up in London, totally destitute, literally with only the shirts on our backs. We were taken care of by a relief agency. I spoke a little English because of the special tutoring I had received, but my parents did not then speak a word of English. (They later learned English in night school.). . .

Michael Ellis Debakey, MD (1908–2008)

Roberts: *What was it like growing up in your family and in Lake Charles, Louisiana?*

DeBakey: First, Bill, I was blessed with parents who were both highly intelligent and exceedingly kind and generous in their temperament and psyche. They lived almost exclusively for their children. They wanted to give us the best of everything, and they believed education was crucial. They were both first generation immigrants, having come to this country as children. Because they believed that a good education was essential to prepare us for a fulfilling life, they always encouraged us to excel in our studies. For example, they urged us to go to the local library once a week and choose any book we wanted to read. We had a small but very good library in Lake Charles. I came home from the library one day and told my Father that there was a wonderful set of books there, but you could not borrow them; you had to read them in the library. He asked me the name of the book, and I responded, *The Encyclopaedia Britannica*. He said, "Well, we will get it." I don't remember how many volumes there were at that time—not as many as there are today—but he purchased the complete set. All of us, my brother, sisters, and I, before we went to college, had each read that whole set of *The Encyclopaedia Britannica*. That is how important it was to us, not only from an educational standpoint, but mainly because we enjoyed reading. All of us excelled at school; we all led our classes. My sisters all led their classes. They were smarter than I was; at least they were a little more studious. My brother and I wanted to play and do other things. The one thing that I never got an "A" in was deportment. In those days we had a deportment grade, and I had great difficulty with it because I would finish all my studies and would get bored because the teacher was dealing with material I had already mastered. In what we then called grammar school or elementary school—I think I was in the fifth or sixth grade—the classes were divided into 2 sections—A and B—and the same teacher taught both classes. While she was teaching one class, she would give the other class a study period of 30 minutes, after which she would go back to the other side. She noticed I was sitting in the center, paying attention to what she was doing, whether she was in my class or the other one. So near the end of the class, she said to me one day, "I notice that you are paying attention to both classes, would you like to take the exam for both of them?" I said, "Sure." I took both exams and was permitted to skip a grade because I passed the exam. School was fun for me because I enjoyed learning new things. My parents had always emphasized to all of us the joy of learning. I studied, learned, and earned good grades, and I think that became a habit.

Roberts: *Did your parents go to college?*

DeBakey: No, but they were self-educated, read widely, and had remarkably critical minds and retentive memories.

Roberts: *And they pushed education to the hilt.*

DeBakey: Yes, absolutely.

Roberts: *I presume you read the book or books that you got from the library once a week?*

DeBakey: Yes, regularly.

Roberts: *From age 6 through age 17, I calculate that you must have read over 600 books outside of school.*

DeBakey: Yes, at least, plus the encyclopedia. I was a voracious reader. In fact, we had to go to bed at a certain time. We would do our lessons—our parents would make sure we had done our lessons—and then if we had time, we would read the library book or sections of *The Encyclopaedia Britannica*. Often, we were all going to *The Encyclopaedia Britannica* at the same time. Of course we would not read the same thing. Usually by 10:00 o'clock, our parents wanted us in bed, because we had to get up early. Our Father was a very early riser, and we all had assigned chores, to encourage self-discipline and responsibility, even though my parents had a house staff. By 5:00 A.M. we were up. I guess I got habituated to the early rising. That came in handy, because when I first started as a freshman in college, I lived in a dormitory, and the boys were raising cane all night. I wanted to study, but couldn't because of the commotion. I would just go on to bed, and get up at 3:00 or 4:00 in the morning and do all my studying while it was quiet. So I got into the habit of getting up early, and it does not matter what time I go to bed now; I still arise at 5:00 A.M. I read *The New York Times* and *The Wall Street Journal* in about 30 minutes. After that I can get some of the things done that I may not be able to do during the day—work on a manuscript or attend to some other paper work. Getting up early has been of great value not only in my surgical practice, but also in allowing me an additional couple of hours beyond that of the average person. Fortunately, I manage well on 5 or 6 hours of sleep a night, just as my Father did.

Roberts: *So if you get 5 hours sleep a night, and you are 88 years old, you have slept only 14 of your last 68 years?*

DeBakey: You are probably right about that. If you sleep 8 hours a night (one-third of every day) and you live 60 years, you have really lived only two-thirds of that time or 40 years. So whatever you can take from your sleep extends your conscious living.

Roberts: *So you are 88 years and a maximum of one-fifth of your life has been spent sleeping.*

DeBakey: That is about right. And that gives me a tremendous advantage. People ask me, "How in the world could you write nearly 1,500 articles in that period of time?" If you live your life long enough and you have enough time, you can do it.

Roberts: *Yes, but you don't waste a minute. You spend very little time commuting. You live 5 minutes from the hospital.*

DeBakey: In fact, I deliberately chose to live near the College. When I first came to Houston, I rented a house that was also only about 10 minutes from here. . . .

William Clifford Roberts, MD
Baylor Heart and Vascular Institute
Baylor University Medical Center
Dallas, Texas

1. Braunwald E, Roberts WC. Eugene Braunwald, MD: a conversation with the editor. *Am J Cardiol* 1998;82:93–108.
2. DeBakey ME, Roberts WC. Michael Ellis Debakey, MD: a conversation with the editor. *Am J Cardiol* 1997;79:929–950.

JOSEPH STEPHEN ALPERT, MD:
A Conversation With the Editor*

Joe Alpert was born on February 1, 1942, in New Haven, Connecticut, and he grew up there. He attended college at Yale University and went to medical school at Harvard. His training in both internal medicine and in cardiology was at the Brigham and Women's Hospital in Boston, and after a 2-year stint in the Navy he returned to Brigham to head the coronary care unit. In 1978 he went to Worcester to be Chief of the Division of Cardiovascular Medicine at the University of Massachusetts Medical Center. In 1992 he moved to Tucson, Arizona, to be Chairman of the Department of Medicine at the University of Arizona Health Sciences Center. He has won outstanding teacher awards at the Brigham and Women's Hospital in Boston, the University of Massachusetts Medical Center, and at the University of Arizona Health Sciences Center. His publications are numerous and diverse. His books, entitled *Manual of Coronary Care* and *Valvular Heart Disease,* have each gone through multiple editions. He has authored or edited 32 books.

• • •

William Clifford Roberts, MD** (hereafter called WCR): I am speaking with Dr. Joseph S. Alpert in my home in Dallas on September 16, 1996. Dr. Alpert arrived about 15 minutes ago from Tucson, Arizona. We have about 90 minutes before we have dinner with several members of the Baylor University Medical Center staff. Joe, let me start by asking you to speak a bit about your background, where you were born, your parents, what growing up was like in your home and in your city. What early influences shaped you?

Joseph Stephen Alpert, MD*** (hereafter called JSA): I was born in New Haven, Connecticut. My father was a practicing dentist, a very popular clinician in New Haven. I think that many of my clinical skills and attitudes have come from him and from his very relaxed, friendly, and folksy approach to the patients that made him extremely popular. My mother and father met at the University of Pittsburgh during the Depression when he was in dental school and she was an undergraduate. She went on to major in journalism and then worked for some years as a journalist before they were married. In those days you didn't get married right away, you had to wait until things were financially straightened out. They got married toward the end of the Depression. My mother stopped working as a journalist and eventually, when my brother and I were in junior high, went back to school and got a graduate degree in English

and then taught high school English. She was an excellent writer, very articulate, very interested in books and written expression. I think I got a lot of my interest in writing, books, and reading from her. There was one other person who had a lot of influence on my early life and that was my father's sister (Aunt Eva, for whom my daughter is named). She was a very popular first grade teacher in New Haven. She taught me to read long before I went to school. I was already reading by the time I got to kindergarten and books and reading have played an important part in my life from the very earliest point. Therefore, my earliest influences were my clinician father, my journalist mother, and my first grade reading teacher aunt. I have always loved books and school.

Growing up in New Haven, you grow up in the shadow of Yale University. My earliest memories are of being taken to the Yale Peabody Museum to see the dinosaurs and going to Yale football games. From my earliest school years I always wanted to go to Yale University. I think that is not an unusual feeling on the part of people who grow up in New Haven. Doing well in school was strongly emphasized in my family. I can't remember a time when it was not expected that not only would I go to college when I graduated from high school, but that I would go on to graduate school of some kind. I think my father would have loved it if I had gone to dental school and joined him in his very large and successful practice, but it did not work out that way.

There were a number of teachers who influenced me along the way. There were several fine high school English teachers who saw that I liked to write and was reasonably good at it and who really pushed me hard to write as much as I could and to read as much as I could. I could give you a few of their names. There was a woman named Ms. Frazee who was very important as a sophomore English teacher. I had some very good science teachers, too. This was a time when the public school system in New Haven really was very good and we would send 20 or 25 students off to Ivy League schools from the James Hillhouse High School, which was the central high school in New Haven.

When I got to Yale it was as if I had died and gone to heaven. There were so many interesting people. There were so many exciting courses. I remember freshman year thinking there was not enough time in a lifetime to participate in all the interesting things going on. I loved history, English, and various science courses. I took art history courses and psychology courses. There was almost nothing I took that I didn't say, "Oh, this is really interesting, I wish I had more time to study this." I think I was also very fortunate in my roommates at Yale. Yale had a system at that time where nobody was allowed to

*This series of interviews are underwritten by an unrestricted grant from Bristol-Myers Squibb.
**From the Baylor Cardiovascular Institute, Baylor University Medical Center, Dallas, TX 75246.
***From the Department of Medicine, The University of Arizona Health Sciences Center, Tucson, Arizona 85724.

FIGURE 1. Photograph of Dr. Joseph Alpert at the time of the interview with WCR.

live off campus unless you were married and there was hardly anyone married. Essentially, the entire student body lived on campus and lived in residential units known as colleges. Harvard has the same system where the residential units are called houses. Within these residential units there are faculty members who live there including some married faculty members and single faculty members. You ate your meals there; there was a great variety of cultural and academic activities that went on there. I had contact with just a tremendous number of very, very exciting people. I remember to this day telling my wife about things I can remember from lectures. I can remember big chunks of lectures from those first 2 or 3 years at Yale. I remember Charles Garside who taught Introductory European History and Maynard Mack who taught Shakespeare. I was fascinated and I was not alone in this. My roommate was David Gergen, who you know as a political commentator and Washington pundit who has been in 4 different White Houses. He was my roommate for 4 years at Yale and he and I had all kinds of interesting conversations. I would have to say that for me there was great value in my roommates and my friends at Yale. We would stay up until 3:00 A.M. arguing and discussing politics, religion, philosophy, literature, you name it. That to me was as valuable as the courses, even though the courses were wonderful. Dave and I took a number of courses together. I remember very well our taking Introductory European History together

and really getting excited about European history, probably because the teaching was so exciting. The material was interesting, but you know medieval European history was a little bit removed from New Haven, Connecticut, in the early 1960's. Yet, the course was taught in such an exciting way that you could not help but be fascinated by what had gone on 600 or 700 years earlier. There were teachers like that throughout Yale. Of course, Yale had a fabulous library and a wonderful art gallery. The science laboratories were equally interesting.

During my first 3 years at Yale, it was such a very exciting time that I actually had a very hard time deciding what my major would be. I think I changed it about 4 times. For the longest period of time I was going to be an English major, specializing in Elizabethan England. Then I thought for a while that I would be a History major. Then eventually, because of some summer work in the Bingham Marine Biological Laboratories at Yale, I really got excited about biology. I ended up in the beginning of my senior year becoming a Biology major. I took a lot of English courses, a lot of history, a very broad liberal arts education. I think that was terribly important and I feel badly for many of our current medical students who have majored in something like microbiology; not that there is anything wrong with microbiology, but I think they have missed out on a lot of very exciting material in their undergraduate years. It is unfortunate when they focus themselves that tightly, that early in their career. I agree with Lewis Thomas, if it were up to me, I would strongly discourage premed students from majoring in science. I would force people to take a much broader liberal arts background. We will talk about that again because it has continued to play a role in my career.

In any case, the summer before my senior year I worked with a faculty member named Alfred Ebling who needed some extra technicians in his lab during the summer; I worked with him on deep sea fish that were dredged up from a mile down: very interesting animals with lantern lights and big teeth and telescope eyes, and all the adaptations that are required to live at that depth. Of course, almost no light gets down there, the temperature is constantly just barely above freezing, and the pressure is intense. It is a very marginal zone to survive in. Yet, there are a lot of very interesting fish that live down there and obviously do survive. I worked with Ebeling and I got so excited about what he was doing that I ended up deciding that I would be a Biology major and that I would focus on fish biology. At that time, Yale had several programs that encouraged independent study. One of them was an honors program where for 2 of your 5 course credits you did a research project. I started doing this research project with Al Ebeling for 2 of my 5 courses. After about 3 or 4 weeks of the senior year it became clear that this project, if I was going to do it right, was going to take a lot more than just 40% of my time. I was working on the physiology of air breathing fish from southeast Asia, the same family as the Siamese fight-

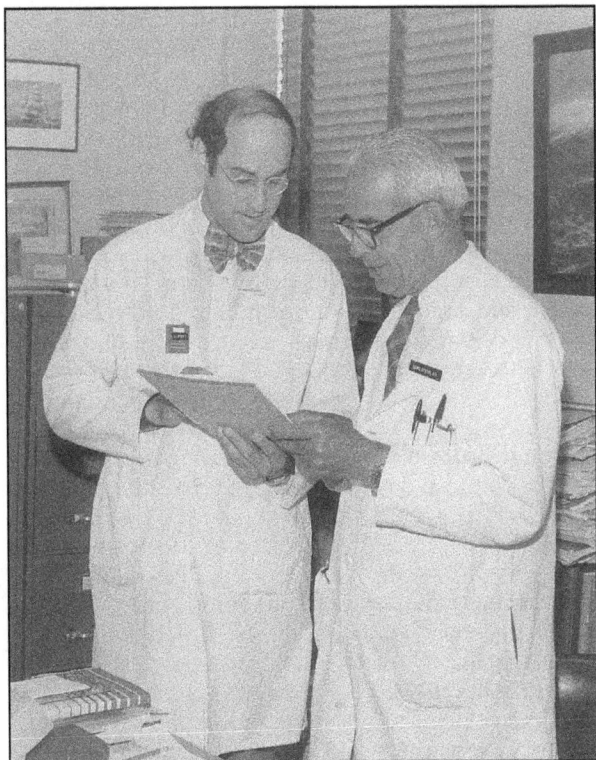

FIGURE 2. Dr. Joseph Alpert *(left)* and Dr. Lewis Dexter *(right)* in 1973.

ing fish. The particular fish I was working on was known as *Macropodis Opercularis* (this work resulted in my first publication), the paradise fish. This is a fish that actually breathes air, so it not only has gills for extracting oxygen from the water, but it also has a little specialized respiratory organ underneath its gill cover, the operculum. It can actually take bubbles of air into that specialized organ, so that during the long dry seasons in Southeast Asia when most of the ponds are dry or nearly dry and the water is very hot so there is very little oxygen in it, this fish can breathe air. Al Ebeling and I got to talking about this and to be honest with you, I can't remember whether it was his idea or my idea, but we sought to learn if changing the oxygen in the environment could speed up or slow down the development of this organ. In any case, after a few weeks of work it became clear that I could not conclude this research project in the time allotted. Fortunately, Yale had a program at that time known as the Scholar of the House in which you basically did full time research during your senior year in addition to a long reading list. In essence, it was like a little Masters' degree done as a senior student. Many other students were in the same program. People were working in English, Sociology, Anthropology, Music, and so forth. There were about 18 or 19 throughout the University. You met once a week for dinner and 1 of the scholars came with their professor and presented what they were doing with discussion afterwards. You can imagine that these were some of the 18 or 19 most interesting people intellectually in the undergraduate college, because each of them had a burning passion for some area. Normally, you were supposed to apply at the end of your junior year. Ebeling gave a very quick call to the fellow who was running the thing and said, ''We have this critical situation here; either this project is only going to get done halfway or we are going to do it right, and the only way to do it right is to get into this program.'' They were very good about it and took me in. I basically spent my whole senior year working very closely with Al Ebeling doing 10 to 12 hours a day of investigation on this fish project as well as a lot of reading on fish biology. By the end of that year when I took my oral exam and presented my thesis, I really felt like I had already done a Masters' degree in fish physiology. Probably, there was a lot less to know in 1963 when I did this than there is today, but nevertheless I thought it was exciting.

I had always thought I would probably go on to medical school and end up being a clinician like my dad, but I got so excited about basic biology that I thought about doing a PhD in fish biology. Ebeling was a graduate of Scripps Oceanographic Institute and he was encouraging me to consider doing a PhD at Scripps. I was really very conflicted at that point. Al became a very good friend. He and his wife did not have any kids and I think I sort of became an adopted son. He said to me, ''You know what you ought to do, you ought to do a year's graduate study and see how it goes. If it is interesting and excites you, you can go into the PhD program. If it doesn't excite you, keep up your applications to medical school, and they will surely accept you.'' Ebeling went on: ''I have a very good friend who runs the Carlsberg Oceanographic Laboratories in Copenhagen, Denmark, and I could arrange for you to do a year's research with him on deep sea fish, because I spent a year there and it was really fun. It is a wonderful place to go. The Danes are just fabulous people, and you will have a year away from New Haven where you grew up and went to college; and here is a chance to get on your own for a year and then you will see what happens. At the end of that year you will know whether you like it or not.''

I applied for a Fulbright Fellowship and got one to Denmark to the Carlsberg Oceanographic Laboratories at the University of Copenhagen. That was a life changing event for me in a variety of ways. I could joke about it and say I went there and met my wife and that changed everything, and to some degree that did happen, but also I discovered that I really wanted more human contact than I would get doing fish physiology, particularly deep sea fish physiology, where much of what you do is sit alone in a laboratory working with specimens from jars. Perhaps it was my dad's clinician influence working on me.

During that year a number of things happened. I ended up living in a Danish *kollegium*, which is sort of like a cross between an American fraternity and a dormitory. I was the only foreigner there, so it became sort of the game of the *kollegium* to teach me to speak Danish. About half way through the year I met my wife at the University of Copenhagen and she also thought it would be a good idea for me to learn the language, which I did. Suddenly, I found myself at the end of that year in this culture where I could not quite pass for a Dane because people could hear my accent, but where people thought I was from some other Scandinavian country. It gives you a whole different perspective on life because suddenly you are seeing things from other people's viewpoint and with other people's attitudes as opposed to the ones that you have always grown up with. It was a very maturing experience. I went home that year committed to figuring out how to get my future wife, Helle Mathiasen, over to the US so we could get married and be together. I also decided I would go to medical school and try that out, since after a year of basic biology I felt that I was not cut out for a full-time life in the laboratory.

I went back to Harvard Medical School and kept corresponding with my fiancee. I went over at Christmas time and visited her, and we got married the summer of 1965. During medical school, I had a lot of help from people at Harvard Medical School, specifically Dr. Clifford Barger, Professor of Physiology, and subsequently Head of the Department of Physiology at Harvard Medical School. He had very good friends in Denmark, particularly a fellow named Niels Lassen, who is still one of the world's great clinical circulatory physiologists. Lassen was one of the first investigators to come up with a way to measure blood flow in various organs, for example, the kidney, skeletal muscle, and the heart, using radioactive tracer gases. He subsequently won many prizes for his work and is very well known. Barger had spent time in Lassen's laboratory and was able to arrange for me to get summer support from the Harvard Medical School, money that I believe originated from the National Institutes of Health (NIH) Those were the good old days of the NIH, when there was lots of money to support student projects. I went over that summer, worked with Niels Lassen, and actually wrote my first medical scientific paper with him. We used Xenon-133 gas dissolved in saline and injected it into skeletal muscle in normal people and patients with peripheral vascular disease in order to demonstrate flow deficits when they walked on a treadmill. The extent of the deficit depended on the severity of the vascular disease. This project got me absolutely excited about circulatory physiology. Basically, at that point, the rest of my life was determined. That was 1965. The die was cast: I married Helle and that has meant an ongoing and continued relationship with Danes. I have a very warm and loving relationship with my Danish family and many friends. I have a close relationship with many Danish cardiologists as well as many European cardiologists and feel like I have close to a second home in Denmark.

Niels Lassen really got me excited about clinical physiology, and I went back to Harvard Medical School in the second year determined to be a circulatory clinical physiologist. Of course in the USA that means you are going to be a cardiologist. After my second year in medical school, my attitude about clinical research was totally different. Two or 3 times each semester, the Dean of Students would come into our class both during the first and second year and say things like, ''I have money for every single one of you students to spend the summer in somebody's laboratory.'' Can you imagine anyone saying that today? During the second year he came and said, ''I have a substantial amount of money to send a large number of you to somebody's laboratory for a whole year between the second and third years, and I really want to see a lot of you come to my office and tell me you want to do that.'' These days we have to scrounge to find a pittance for someone to do research. In those days they were literally twisting everybody's arm, ''Come talk about this.'' There were probably 16 or 18 of our class of 100 that did do that. I went back to Niels Lassen's laboratory for a year, where I published a number of papers and actually wrote a gold medal thesis, which is a competition that the University of Copenhagen has every year in a number of different areas. I was fortunate that year since the question fell in the area of circulatory physiology and actually related to some of the studies I was already doing. I wrote a thesis on that and was awarded a gold medal from the University of Copenhagen for that year's work. Basically, my career was established by the time I started my third year in medical school.

Our first child, a daughter, Eva, was born at the end of that year, 1967, and we returned to the USA to do the third and fourth years of medical school. My wife, an English major and Master's Degree recipient at the University of Copenhagen, entered Tuft's University to do a PhD in English. Again, the influence that I had had from Yale, a strong liberal arts influence, continued right throughout my medical school career, because my wife was coming home talking about Kafka, Shakespeare, Chaucer and so forth, some of which I had read, some of which I had not, and when I found a little time I would try to read and talk to her. I had saved some of my notes from some of my best Yale English classes and we would get those out and look at them and talk about them. I was able to maintain at least a little bit of contact with the world of literature, literary criticism, and philosophy. Our son, Niels, was born one and half years after our daughter.

Meanwhile, Helle finished her PhD and I finished my MD, and then we stayed on in Boston because I stayed at Brigham to do internal medicine residency. During my medical student years I met 2 more people who had particular influence. My first attending, when I did third year medicine, was Lewis Dexter, one of the first people to do a cardiac catheterization, and perhaps the first person to put a catheter in the pulmonary artery, which he did by accident. It is a wonderful story. His laboratory was where the pulmonary wedge pressure was first worked on and where Dick Gorlin was a fellow. Gorlin, of course, also worked out the Gorlin formula for valve area calculations. Many other developments also came out of that laboratory. In any case, Lew was my attending the first month I did medicine at Brigham, which would have been February 1968.

Within a few days, it was clear to me that this was the kind of doctor I wanted to be. This was a man who was both a circulatory physiologist, a fine clinician, a wonderful teacher, and a fabulous human being. Literally, one of the nicest people I had ever met. He died in December 1995 and was widely mourned by the cardiology community.

Subsequently, I took a fourth year elective in Dexter's laboratory and met Lew's first lieutenant, Jim Dalen, a very young faculty member at that time. He had been an Assistant Professor for a couple of years when he and I met and there was just a definite "click." Even though I was still a medical student and he was a junior faculty member, there was a sense of meeting somebody you immediately like and they immediately like you. You just know you are on the same wave length. We started working together on some projects, so that when I graduated from medical school it was clear I was going to be a cardiology fellow in Lew and Jim's laboratory as soon as I finished internal medicine training. In those days internal medicine was only 2 years, so you had to make up your mind reasonably quickly because by the middle of internship you had to apply for cardiology fellowship. I only applied to Dexter's program and, of course, they took me. That was also a very exciting time at Brigham in cardiology. I don't know if we will ever come to a time when one has as much going on in a single institution.

• • •

WCR: You started your cardiology fellowship July 1971?

JSA: Right. I was an intern in 1969 to 1970 and a junior resident in 1970 to 1971. Beginning July 1, 1971, I was a cardiology fellow with Dexter and Dalen.

The exciting thing at Brigham at that time was that there were 4 separate cardiology fellowships, 4 separate groups in this 320-bed hospital. You might say that does not make any sense at all: people must have torn each others throats out, but somehow though there was competition, everybody got along with everybody else. Dexter was a special person. When Dick Gorlin finished training with Lew, Dexter went to George Thorn, the Chief of Medicine, and said, "Hey, this guy Gorlin is too good to lose. He is interested in things like the coronary circulation that I am not interested in." (Dexter was interested in valves, congenital heart disease, pulmonary embolism, right ventricular function.) "Why don't you give him his own cath lab and let him go after the coronary circulation." Remember, this was a time when cath labs were very different from what they are today. They were basically clinical physiology laboratories and you did few "studies" for clinical purposes. Almost every patient was studied to learn something about circulatory physiology. No one anticipated the huge growth in coronary arteriography and percutaneous transluminal coronary angioplasty (PTCA). Remember, Sones started to do coronary angiography in the 1960s, and Favaloro did the first saphenous vein bypass only a few years before I became a fellow. It was not yet clear whether any of that was going to turn out to be important. In any case, Gorlin had his own lab and he had his own fellows, and they mainly focused on patients with chronic coronary disease. Now, you might think they also ran the coronary care unit since they were interested in coronary disease, but that was not the case. Dr. Bernard Lown ran the coronary care unit. He also had his own fellowship program and his own people, and they were totally separate. Lown had a very noninvasive approach; he was generally opposed to cardiac catheterization and surgery. Edmund Sonenblick also had a basic science laboratory that was very loosely affiliated with Gorlin, but basically he ran his own show as well. Thus, there were 4 different groups. Sonnenblick's group consisted of fellows who had already finished their clinical fellowship and wanted to spend a couple of years in the lab. At the time, Bill Parmeley, Michael Lesch, and Michael Herman were also there, and Lown had interesting people in his group as well. Many of the people that were fellows or junior faculty when I was there have ended up as chiefs of cardiology or chiefs of medicine. It was a very interesting and exciting time, because these 4 cardiology groups would compete to have papers at the meetings and articles in the *New England Journal of Medicine*. It was a golden era. Of course, the NIH was supporting the training grants and research for all 4 of these programs. It was just a remarkably fruitful and exciting time for cardiology, and many people launched their careers at that time.

I did 2 years of cardiology fellowship. I had a Navy deferral on the old Berry plan, named after Dean Berry of the Harvard Medical School who devised this plan. The Vietnam War was going on then and I had friends who actually were drafted out of fellowship and internship and were sent to Vietnam. I had a full 5-year deferment just by the luck of the draw. At the end of 4 years I had to choose what to do with that fifth year, whether I should think about trying to be a chief resident in medicine or whether to stay in Dexter's lab. Lew and Jim came to me and said, "Why don't you be our junior associate in the lab?" Jim was the 1st lieutenant and Dexter was the General; then I became the corporal. I accepted their offer and published a number of papers. I was involved in a lot of exciting projects and was not anxious to leave, but I knew I had this 2-year commitment to the military.

Then, another fortunate thing happened. During my second year of cardiology fellowship, George Thorn retired after 25 years as Chief of Medicine at Brigham. The new Chief of Medicine was a cardiologist, Eugene Braunwald. Braunwald took an interest in me. He came to Brigham in 1972 or 1973. (He retired this year after more than 20 years as the

Hersey Professor at Brigham.) Braunwald found out that I owed time in the Navy. You may remember that Braunwald had been Chief of Medicine at the University of California, San Diego, before coming to Brigham. He had worked on clinical research projects with the Balboa Navy Hospital in San Diego, which was one of the premier hospitals in the Navy. They had very good people on staff, and a lot of fellows would have given anything to get there. It was about a 1,200-bed hospital, so it had a lot of clinical material. We had about 15 cardiologists there and a good cardiac surgery program. We basically did all complex cardiology for all the services from the western United States and the Pacific. You can imagine how many patients we saw: one fascinating patient after another, plus the connection to the University meant that we were doing a lot of teaching and were heavily involved with the University. Braunwald did me a tremendous favor by recommending me to the Head of Cardiology at Balboa, a fellow named Art Hagan, who was a superb cardiologist and one of the pioneers of 2-dimensional echocardiography. I came as a hemodynamic cardiologist, but after arriving they told me they had lots of people in the cath lab, but needed someone to run the coronary care unit. I quickly went to the library and read everything I could find on coronary care. Of course, I had had some time with Bernard Lown in the coronary care unit at Brigham. During the next 2 years I did a lot of work in coronary care. There were more than 800 patients per year with acute myocardial infarction going through that coronary care unit. At the time there were almost a million people in San Diego County eligible for care at the Naval Hospital. In addition, we were involved in some of the early myocardial infarction (MI) intervention trials that were going on.

Just as I was concluding my service with the Navy, Michael Lesch, the person who had been running the coronary care unit at Brigham, (the Samuel A. Levine Cardiac Unit) left to go to Northwestern to be Chief of Cardiology. I got a phone call from Tom Smith, who was the Chief of Cardiology at Brigham, and he said, "I understand you have been doing a lot of coronary care. Would you like to come back to Brigham to run the coronary care unit?" For me that was just a dream come true. Jim Dalen, Dexter's lieutenant with whom I had a very close personal relationship, had just moved to the new University of Massachusetts Medical School in Worcester to be its Chief of Cardiology and he wanted me to join him. But the chance to run the Levine Cardiac Unit, or "the LCU" as we called it, was just more fun than I could have thought possible. I accepted the job at Brigham and went back to Boston. That was the year (1976) when we were just starting up the Milis Trial. Again, there were a lot of exciting people at Brigham. Tom Smith was a wonderful person to work for, a superb academic cardiologist, and a great human being as well. Braunwald, of course, knew more cardiology than almost anybody I had ever met. It was another exciting time. I

would have been perfectly happy to stay there for the rest of my career.

However, an interesting thing happened at that point as so often occurred in my career: suddenly a door opens and somebody says "here is an opportunity for you, would you like to do this?" The opportunity that happened then was that Jim Dalen became Chief of Medicine at the University of Massachusetts Medical School and that left the job of Chief of Cardiology open. He called me up at Brigham where I was running the CCU and said, "Why don't you come here to be Chief of Cardiology?" I did that and it led to many events in my life. The University of Massachusetts hospital had opened only about 18 months earlier. Things were just starting up, and I got to be involved with Jim Dalen in building the Department of Medicine and the Division of Cardiovascular Medicine nearly from its inception to where it is today, one of the better cardiology sections in the country.

Then, about 7 years ago, Jim, who is an excellent investigator, a very good clinician, a superb teacher, and an outstanding administrator (perhaps one of the best physician/administrators in the country) was offered several deanships of medical schools. He accepted the job at the University of Arizona, which he thought would be the most exciting and interesting. He went there approximately 7 years ago. About 4 years ago, the Chief of Medicine at Arizona, who had been there for a long time, retired, and Jim asked me to apply for his position. I went there as Chief of Medicine and continued our working relationship that had begun when I was a medical student.

I would have to say that the most important factors influencing my career besides my childhood and early schooling and the influence of my wife, have been a number of outstanding people in academic circles in high school, college, and medical school. Influential people who said to me, "I like you and I can see that you like working with me and let's work on some things together." Each time that happened it has been a very positive experience for me and has influenced the direction in which I have gone.

• • •

WCR: What were you most pleased with as your accomplishments as Chief of Cardiology at the University of Massachusetts in Worcester, looking back on it?

JSA: The thing I'm most proud of is my mentoring of young physicians. I have written a lot of papers and done a lot of research but I don't think any of that is going to win the Nobel Prize. Perhaps 100 years from now some of my contributions will be mentioned in various footnotes along with a lot of other people. I have done some good solid work, but if you ask me what was the most important thing I have done, I would say it was mentoring and developing the careers of young people: medical students, house officers, cardiology fellows, and junior faculty members. What I am most proud of at Worcester is that when I first went there there we were only 4 faculty, all trained in the Dexter lab and all picked by Jim Dalen to start off his cardiology program. We went from that faculty of 4 people to a total of 16 or 17 faculty members by the time I left in 1992. When I went to Worcester they were doing essentially no research and the quality of the fellows was not great. Yet, over that period of 15 years we ended up getting wonderful cardiology fellows and house officers. The internal medicine program took off and really became one of the most competitive in the Northeast. The faculty blossomed. Many faculty members who are there now were trained at the University of Massachusetts as fellows. They have been able to get grants; they have published articles in first rate journals. My greatest satisfaction was mentoring and developing these young people, many of whom have become senior faculty members and have developed substantial and solid careers.

• • •

WCR: Was it hard for you when you became Chairman of Medicine in Tucson to give up exclusive cardiology? When you had this opportunity to be Chairman of Medicine at the University of Arizona was that a difficult decision? Had you always wanted to be a Chairman of Medicine somewhere?

JSA: I considered all of that, but what went through my mind was "wouldn't it be wonderful to work with Jim Dalen again, because so many of the good things that had happened in my professional life had happened when we had been working together." When I thought about giving up cardiology and going to be Chief of Medicine, I said, "Well I'll still be a cardiologist." I could still attend in the coronary care unit, which I do. I can still see a lot of cardiology patients, which I do. I had always liked internal medicine. In fact, I remember during my first year as a fellow when I used to do consults, Jim Dalen used to say to me, "There is too much internal medicine in this consult. Just give me the cardiology. They are not asking us to manage the electrolytes and the acid base. They just want to know how to deal with the heart problem here." In fact, it was pleasant for me going back to part-time internal medicine.

What has been less than pleasant is the current environment in which one is a Chief of Medicine. I thought Chiefs of Medicine were people like Braunwald, George Thorn, etc. When I got to Tucson, managed care was galloping along in Arizona, and it was an extraordinarily tough first year because of the impact of managed care. We really had to completely redesign how the faculty did medicine with the amount of protected time markedly reduced and the amount of clinical time increased, because we had to compete with the community for managed care contracts. I know this is an issue that is going on throughout the country. It was not difficult for me to decide to be a Chief of Medicine, but once I became one, I had the difficult challenge of dealing with an academic department of medicine in the midst of this managed care revolution. That was, and still is, a major challenge. I spend a lot of time thinking about and dealing with economic and organizational problems. We are completely revamping the way the hospital and the group practice work together. Therefore, a lot of time has to be spent with these issues and a lot of time is spent supporting the faculty and reassuring them about the outcome of all of these changes. This is a revolutionary time. The faculty grew up as did I in what I call "the golden era," the era when there was lots of NIH and American Heart Association support. If you wanted a grant there was probably a 40% chance you were going to get it. If you got turned down the first time, you kept at it and if you were persistent and people saw you were serious, there was a very good chance that you would get funded. The NIH pay line now is no more than 10% and in some instances less. This is discouraging for both junior and senior faculty members. The amount of money we are being reimbursed for our clinical activity is also markedly less than formerly. The profit, if you will, in our enterprise has essentially vanished. We used to use that profit to cover people's free time so you could do half-time clinical, or sometimes even less if you had a grant, and have a lot of protected time paid for by the department to do investigation and to teach. There is much less of that free time now. People have to do academic activity on weekends and evenings and steal a little time here and a little time there. It is a lot tougher than it used to be.

• • •

WCR: How many faculty members do you have in medicine?

JSA: We have 76 or 77 full-time faculty members in the Department of Medicine at the University Hospital, and then at the Veterans Administration Medical Center, which is part of our system, there are about another 20. We have about 100 full-time faculty members.

• • •

WCR: How many house officers, interns, residents, fellows, in the various divisions?

JSA: The total number of house officers is 52. There is a far smaller number of fellows, probably 23 or 24.

• • •

WCR: When you add up secretaries, lab technicians, and other personnel, the total number of people in your department of medicine is approximately what?

JSA: There are over 400 people that I am, in a sense, ultimately responsible for. Of course, I can't possibly micromanage all the daily routines of those 400. There are a number of section heads who are involved and a number of laboratories with heads and so forth, but ultimately I am responsible for a little over 400 people.

• • •

WCR: As a cardiologist who is chairman of a department of medicine, could you sort of go through your typical day? What time do you get up in the morning? What do you do first during the day? How does your day go? What time usually each day do you leave the hospital? What are your evenings at home like? What time do you go to bed?

JSA: I was expecting this question because you asked Eric Topol the same question. It was interesting how much my life resembles Bruce Fye's life and Eric's life in terms of sleep. I don't get a lot of sleep. Maybe that is what is going to come out of this whole series, Bill, is how little sleep your interviewees get. I usually get up about 5:00 A.M., I go out and run or run/walk, depending on how sleepy I am, for about 60 to 70 minutes. It is almost a 5 mile hilly route. I have been doing that for years, although not necessarily in the mornings. Sometimes, if I have a day where I have some time at noon, I will go out and run instead of eating lunch. I call it "the negative calorie lunch." I have been doing this for about 10 years. In the late 80s and early 90s I ran the Boston Marathon 5 times, which was an instructive event, an experience. The first twenty miles were great and the last 6 miles were pure pain. Not that I was very fast, but it was fun and we had a group I would run with. After exercise, I come in, have a little breakfast, shower, dress, and get to the hospital about 8:00 A.M. When I am on the Coronary Care Unit, where rounds start at 7:00, then I get up about 4:15 or 4:30 so I can get my exercise in before getting to work at 7:00. I do 3 months of attending a year, 2 months of medicine, and 1 month of coronary care. Three months is actually a lot, but, as I told you, we are going through this managed care revolution and I felt like I could not just sit in my office and tell everybody else to increase their clinical load, I had to increase mine, too. I am doing more clinical work now than I have ever done, because I also have 3 half afternoons a week when I see outpatients, so I carry a pretty heavy clinical load. I believe in the Patton theory of leadership: "if you are not in the front tank that is heading towards the enemy, then you have not earned the responsibility or the right to lead the people." Sitting back behind the lines and telling other people what they ought to be doing somehow never appealed to me.

Besides those 3 months when I have to be there at 7:00 A.M. and when I am up at 4:00 to 4:30 A.M. to get my run in, most days I get to work about 8:00 A.M. Then, I will look at the mail that comes in or answer the phone calls from the East coast (Arizona is Pacific time in the summer and Mountain time in the winter). We don't do daylight savings time so we are either 2 or 3 hours behind the East coast depending on the time of year. Then, I go to morning report many mornings which is 9:00 to 10:00 A.M., unless there is some meeting with the head of the hospital or the head of the group practice to deal with urgent or emerging economic or administrative issues. That probably happens 40% of the time, so 60% percent of the time I get to morning report. That ends at 10:00 A.M. Then, from 10:00 A.M. until noon I will again go back to my office. There will be a huge stack of mail to answer, and there are always people that just have to see me right away. It could be from our cancer center, or the arthritis center, or

the cardiologists. The latter are pretty easy to work with because they know that somehow they can get to me at one point or another, and I usually go to their section meeting on Tuesdays at noon. Most of the other sections want to talk to me as well. These days, the Head of Infectious Disease is one of my major clinical right-hand people and so he often comes by to talk about how we are reorganizing. The office for our house staff program is right next to mine and the Head of the House Staff program and his associate director may want to grab me about an issue. Administrative activity usually will wind down about noon time. Then, there are noon conferences. Wednesday from 12:00 to 1:00 is grand rounds; Tuesday is the cardiology section meeting. There are often a variety of administrative conferences at noon. Thursday, for example, is the medical group practice executive committee, of which I am a member. From 1:00 to 2:00 P.M. I usually do paperwork, see people, make decisions, phone calls, etc. I go to the clinic from 2:00 to about 4:30 on Tuesdays, Wednesdays, and Thursdays. Mondays and Fridays I have appointments: any student, any house officer, any fellow, any faculty member that wants to talk to me. My door is always open. In general, I prefer that people make appointments; otherwise it gets unmanageable. I have superb secretarial and executive assistants who help in terms of the business aspects, the paperwork, and the phone calls. I have built this team over the 4 years that I have been in Tucson. Many of them are new people who have come on board to be with me, and we work very well together. Generally, when I come back from the clinic, there will be people waiting to see me or I will have other appointments.

Starting at 5:00 P.M., there are either group practice meetings or other administrative meetings. Then, I am involved in 2 courses that meet in the late afternoon. One I have been teaching with my wife for almost 20 years. I call it "Medicine and Literature." She calls it "Literature and Medicine." As I mentioned earlier, she has a PhD in English literature. She teaches on the main campus at the University of Arizona. She taught for many years at Boston College. We started back in 1978 to teach this seminar called "Literature and Medicine." The course picks works of literature that relate to medicine in some way. We might do a Camus novel, *The Plague*, in which the main character is a physician, Dr. Rieux, or we might do Graham Greene's novel *A Burnt Out Case*, which takes place in a leper colony and also has a prominent physician in it. We might read Chekhov, the famous Russian author of short stories, plays, and so forth, who was a physician. Many of his stories have a lot of medical material in them. We might talk about the Pulitzer Prize winning poet, William Carlos Williams, who was a practicing pediatrician and a writer of poems, novels, and short stories or Simone deBeauvoir's recollection of her mother's death from cancer, *A Very Easy Death*. The course runs in the fall semester for undergraduates on the main campus from 5:00 to 7:15 P.M. on

Wednesdays, and in the spring semester we run it for medical students and that generally runs from 4:00 to 6:30 P.M. twice a week for 6 weeks. In addition, this year the Chief of Surgery, Bruce Jarrell, and I have been running a course in intensive care medicine, surgery, and pathophysiology for fourth year medical students, which meets on Mondays from 3:00 to 5:00 P.M.. I get back to my office after that and I finish the day's paperwork, letters, and so forth. Generally, I finish work between 6:30 and 7:00 P.M., except when I am on the clinical service. If I am on the coronary care unit or the ward service, then I have to go back and see the residents and patients. Those days I might not leave the hospital until about 7:30 P.M. On weekends during the 3 months I am on a clinical service, I do rounds on both Saturdays and Sundays. When I am not on service, I may have meetings on Saturday mornings. I try and keep as much as possible of the weekends free for my wife. We travel a fair amount when we can. I also try to take a month's vacation every summer. We usually try to take a substantial trip. When we left Massachusetts we had a small house on Cape Cod, which we still keep. We try to get back to that periodically and it is very curative and restorative. The long trip this past summer was to Alaska and western Canada.

• • •

WCR: What do you do on your vacations? Is that when you and your wife have more time to develop new material for your course the following year or how does that work out?

JSA: We are always talking about our course. One of the nice things about living in Arizona is that the weather is always good, so we talk about the course when we go for a walk together or over dinner, now that our kids are grown. Besides our 2 cats, there is just my wife and I at home, and the cats are not big conversationalists, so we might discuss topics from the course over dinner. When we take a vacation, we are always talking about things that come up in the course as well as new books we run across. We tend to be energetic tourists. We are often out hiking or roaming around. In Alaska, we were doing a lot of hiking and touring, looking at the animals, and seeing the wonderful natural environment there is up there. My wife says, ''Medical issues are life issues, every person on this planet at some time or another has a medical issue.'' For example, recently we discussed assisted suicide. That is the sort of issue that comes up in our class. Often Helle and I have a dialog going on, which continues in the classroom when we teach the class.

• • •

WCR: When you get home on weekdays, what are your evenings like?

JSA: My wife and I will have dinner together. Usually the Wednesday night in the fall when we are teaching the Med Lit class we don't finish until 7:30, then we usually will not cook. At that point we have both been going for about 12 plus hours. We might order food in or we might stop at a restaurant on the way home. Sometimes we prepare food on the week-

ends that we will just heat up in the microwave. On the days when we get home at reasonable times, my wife still likes to cook and I occasionally cook. Most nights she cooks, although I like to cook. We have a fairly simple meal together, and a glass of wine. If we have work to do, then we will work for 1 or 2 hours or so. Occasionally, we watch TV or a VCR movie. Last night, for example, we watched Ken Burn's new series, *The West*, which was excellent. Some nights we go to the movies when we need to relax. Most weekday nights and on the weekends we will do some work. We try to get together with friends, often for dinner, or go hiking with friends or to the movies on weekends. My wife is on the board of the Tucson Symphony, so we have a certain number of nights when we go to the symphony or the Chamber Concert series or the theater.

• • •

WCR: So you do it all? What time do you go to bed?

JSA: It depends on how exhausting the day has been. When I am on the wards and up at 4:00 in the morning, usually I will try to get to bed by 9:00 or 9:30 P.M., otherwise 10:00 or 10:30 P.M.

• • •

WCR: So you can go pretty well on 6 hours sleep?

JSA: Yes, 6 hours is fine.

• • •

WCR: People are pulling at you all the time. With this number of people on your house staff, your full-time faculty, it must be a real pleasure to get away sometime. You are 54 years old now? Do you want to continue being Chairman of Medicine for another 11 years or what do you see on the horizon?

JSA: I think the days of trying to be Chief of Medicine for 20 or so years, as was common in the past, would not be realistic in the current environment. Today, in order to stay that long in this position would require someone made not of iron, but made of diamond to withstand the constant problems. The house officer problems are the least difficult. The economic problems, the constant pressure from the business side are, however, energy draining. I believe these days that 10 to 12 years would be a reasonable term of office for a chairman of medicine in a university setting. That should be more than enough. Maybe when I get to 10 to 12 years I will change my mind, but at least from this vantage point, 4 years in, it seems to me that 10 to 12 years would be more than reasonable. By then, I would be over 60 years of age and I would like to go back into the section of cardiology and continue to teach, write, and see patients. I would be more than happy to continue the level of clinical activity I have now, more than happy to continue to teach, do my books, be involved in clinical research projects the way I have been; in other words, continue to do everything, except the heavy administrative load. I would perhaps even be willing to take a small administrative load. I don't think I want to be a Dean, at least not as seen from this vantage point. If there is any job that is more political, more administrative than the Chief of Medicine, it is the Dean. The Dean's job is very difficult. I see how beautifully Jim Dalen does it, and he is a superb administrator with just the right sense of where people are coming from and what his vision is and where he wants to go. At least at this vantage point, I don't think I would like to do that. I think I would like to stay in an arena where I am heavily involved in clinical medicine, teaching, clinical investigation, and my books.

• • •

WCR: You obviously are a wonderful teacher. You have won a number of awards while at Worcester, San Diego, and Tucson. You obviously work hard at that. It takes a lot of energy to be a really good teacher. You must be worn out when you get home at night. Does the running give you more energy or less energy?

JSA: I have always been a high energy person. You know some people are born with high energy and some people are not. I have always been a high energy person and I have always had a lot of enthusiasm for things. Somebody comes to me and tells me something new and different and I am always interested in that. I can pick up a *National Geographic* or another magazine, open any issue, and say ''Oh, that is interesting'' and get myself engrossed in it. I think that is just something I am genetically endowed with — high energy. However, I do think the running helps. For many years when I was in Worcester and did not have such a heavy administrative load, I tried to keep the 12:00 to 1:30 P.M. period open and run 5 miles. In those days, I ran with friends. I found that I came back and had more energy in the afternoon having done that. These days, because of the administrative load, my 12:00 noon to 2:00 P.M. period gets eaten up, so I generally run in the morning, but I think it still helps increase my energy.

• • •

WCR: You grew up in the Northeast corridor, namely New Haven, had Ivy school college and medical and postgraduate training there, and then all of a sudden you are in Tucson, Arizona, a striking contrast. How did you adjust to the new environs?

JSA: It was, of course, a major cultural change. Probably you would have a hard time finding a greater cultural difference in the USA than the Boston area versus southern Arizona. The Boston area is Anglo, New England, long tradition, Ivy League, and the Southwest is Hispanic, Native American, and more of a sun culture. On the other hand, the patients' illnesses are the same. The medical students are just as bright in Arizona and just as interested. The house officers are just as involved. The faculty members are the same. At least within my work environment it is not much different. It is when I leave work that suddenly things are different. That is why my wife and I have built up around us a lot of the cultural things that we did in Boston, the symphony, concerts, theater. Our Lit Med course continues. We still get the Sunday *New York Times* each week. We

maintain a number of our Northeastern habits. But remember, we lived in San Diego from 1974 to 1976, and I have always taken that 1 month summer vacation (a Lew Dexter tradition). He always insisted that everyone have a 1 month vacation in the summer and I think it is a good idea. When we lived in Boston, my wife and I spent a lot of time in the West, hiking, white water rafting, being out in the environment. We spent a couple of summers on the Zuni Indian reservation as volunteers. I was a volunteer physician and my wife was involved in the hospital and also in some of the other community activities. So we had been to the Southwest a lot before moving to Tucson and had lived there for 2 years if you count San Diego as the Southwest. After Phoenix, San Diego is the closest big city to Tucson. We sort of knew what we were getting into. Despite that, it was a cultural change. I think moving after age 50 takes a lot of strength and energy. Fortunately, our son moved to Los Angeles this year, so we can see more of him now.

• • •

WCR: You have continued to write your books, several of them, but you are not working as you did when you were exclusively in cardiology on publications for peer review journals. You are an editor of a cardiology journal. Do you miss the article publishing?

JSA: Absolutely, that is what I had to sacrifice, unless I did not want to sleep at all at night when I moved into the heavy administrative load that goes with being the Chief of Medicine. What I had to sacrifice was clinical investigation. I am involved in some of the clinical studies that are going on in cardiology, heart failure, and angina trials. So I keep a little finger in. I am on a couple of data safety and monitoring boards for some big trials. I would say I keep my pinky in the investigative waters. I will continue to do that because I envision at the end of my time as Chief of Medicine that I will have time to go back and be more heavily involved in those activities again. But I definitely miss that! It is exciting doing research, looking at the data. I get a little of that flavor on a data safety and monitoring board because you see the data when nobody else is seeing it and that is fun. I feel that I have to put heavy investigative involvement on hold until I am no longer Chief of Medicine.

• • •

WCR: It sounds like your wife is your best friend. Is that correct?

JSA: Absolutely! Even though I have many other very close friends; for example, Jim Dalen the Dean of the Medical School, is like an older brother to me. We have that kind of older brother–younger brother relationship that is very special to me. I also have other family and friends with whom I am very close, but the first 3 people on the list of most important friends are all my wife.

• • •

WCR: You have 2 children?

JSA: We have 2 children. I have a daughter, Eva, who is a tax attorney in Boston, which also keeps the Boston connection for us. We get back and see her periodically. I have a son, Niels, who is a film maker and lives in Hollywood.

• • •

WCR: Is academic medicine going to survive as we have known it in the past?

JSA: I would say, Bill, we are going through difficult times for medicine in general in the USA and for academic medicine in particular at the present time. The message I constantly repeat to younger physicians is not to get too depressed and discouraged. It is easy to get down when nothing is working right: there is no grant money, there is no money for clinical activities, people are being squeezed for time. It is a frightening era. What I keep telling everybody is that we just have to hang in there. We have to do whatever it takes, even if that means we have to write on the weekends or in the evenings, or do our research after hours. Somehow or other we have to keep the enterprise going. I am convinced that the pendulum will swing back. Things will get better, but we may have to go through a half dozen more years of difficult times to do that. I don't want to see us lose a whole generation of young, exciting academic cardiologists or gastroenterologists, rheumatologists, infectious disease people, and so forth. I don't want to see them disappear and get discouraged and depressed and leave academics. My message is it is still the best job in America.

• • •

WCR: Do you think all 125 USA medical schools are going to survive?

JSA: I think there will be some downsizing of faculty just as we are downsizing our fellows now. I suspect you will continue to see medical schools amalgamating, like the combining of Hahnemann and Medical College of Pennsylvania into a single medical school. New York University and Mt. Sinai have just formed a somewhat similar relationship, and one could envision that maybe they will downsize their medical school classes. Columbia and Cornell in New York City are also coming closer to a relationship. Whether that means some medical schools will totally close or whether everybody will just amalgamate and downsize, I can't say, but I think we will be training fewer medical students 10 years from now than we are training today.

• • •

WCR: What excites you most right now in cardiology?

JSA: There are a number of exciting things. I am going to be giving a talk next month, the Diggs lectureship at the University of Tennessee, in which they have asked me to discuss the most exciting things that are going on in cardiology. The advances in coronary care continue to be very exciting. We have had a 10-year period of tremendous advance, and I don't think we are finished there. I am very excited by some of the new heart failure research. There is a new surgical procedure that we have just started to do at the University of Arizona to try to shrink down some of these dilated huge ventricles and actually salvage them short of having to do a heart transplantation. The third area that is really exciting is what is going on in basic science, in molecular cardiology. Cardiology basic science when I was a fellow was predominantly physiology, but now basic research is mostly molecular biology. I think over the next 10 years a lot of exciting information is going to come out of the molecular biology labs. I think we'll see many more advances in our understanding of pathophysiology as well as therapeutics.

• • •

WCR: How do you view cardiac surgery in the future?

JSA: Coronary bypass is not going to disappear no matter how good we get at doing stents and all these little interventional tricks. There is still going to be a substantial number of patients at some point that are going to need coronary bypass. Coronary bypass will continue although perhaps not in a volume as great as today. Valve disease is not going to disappear. Mitral stenosis is disappearing, but at the same time we are getting lots of older folks with aortic stenosis. Congenital lesions are going to continue to be produced at the same rate as before. The major issue is going to be how to deal with heart failure. Can we come up with medical or surgical therapy short of heart transplantation, since it looks like we are not ever going to be able to get enough hearts? Cardiomyoplasty is one possibility. However, if I had to bet, I wouldn't bet on cardiomyoplasty. I would bet more on the new procedure, ventricular reduction surgery, the remodeling of the dilated ventricle. Perhaps we will come up with some molecular biology technique in conjunction with surgery to help the remaining heart muscle hypertrophy. I believe there is still going to be a lot that is going to have to be fixed by cardiac surgery.

• • •

WCR: Do you push lipid lowering aggressively?

JSA: As so many things in medicine, you are either a believer or not a believer. I am a believer in lipid lowering and I am very aggressive. I must say I have been influenced in that regard by one of my former colleagues at the University of Massachusetts, Dr. Ira Ockene, who received a cardiology preventive award from the NIH. He and I were fellows together in Dexter's lab and 30-year friends since then. He has convinced me with data that the cholesterol hypothesis is true and that the lower we can get people's cholesterol, the more likely it is that we will stem the huge volume of coronary artery disease that we have in the US. I think the cholesterol guidelines should be to get individual patients' cholesterol well under 200 mg/dl; closer to 150 mg/dl.

• • •

WCR: You are on salary I presume? Everybody on your faculty is on salary? Do you believe in salary scales for physicians in general?

JSA: I do. I think one of the problems we have had in the last 30 years has been that in some areas physicians have started to make too much money. They have gotten to the point where they are making high 6 and 7 figure incomes, and what happens then is that it is very easy to lose sight of why they went to medical school to become totally tied up with making money. I believe in the salary system. We need to have incentives and rewards for those people who are very clinically productive as opposed to those people who feel they need to spend more time contemplating or reflecting or doing research. The disparity between what people make in private practice and what people make in academics is too great. I know that this is changing rapidly. Managed care is leveling the playing field. However, I think academics will always receive a lower salary and that is fine. Many of the managed care companies put physicians either on salary or within a salary range based on incentives that seem quite reasonable to me. I bet we will see more and more of that control. Fee for service medicine is dying and may be gone in 10 more years.

• • •

WCR: I understand you had an acute myocardial infarction about 3 years ago. Could you describe that? Would you mind doing that?

JSA: As you know Bill, I have written about it in an editorial and in a review article on acute myocardial infarction with normal coronary arteries (*Archives of Internal Medicine*). Writing that piece helped me intellectually heal myself. It occurred at the end of the first year in my new job as Chief of Medicine. That was a very difficult and stressful year in large part because of managed care, but in part because it was and still is difficult to move after age 50, and to pull up stakes after 30 years in Boston. That clearly contributed to it. I was out running one day in Denmark on vacation after a very strenuous meeting, a very vigorous week, where I was doing a lot of lecturing and had received an award. It was a very emotional and exciting week. My wife and I had gone off to a Danish beach in the far north of Denmark and I was out running one morning in just a T-shirt and shorts. It was very cold and windy and I was running up a hill into the cold wind and noticed this sense of indigestion in my epigastrium. I attributed the discomfort to all the coffee and the red wine and partying that had gone on for the previous 4 or 5 days. I slowed down and walked for a while and the indigestion went away. I started to run again and the indigestion came back. I said to myself, "I don't like that symptom related to exertion." I decided to walk. I continued to walk for a while. Then, I began to run again and the indigestion didn't come back and I completed the last 2.5 miles of the 5 mile run. I then had breakfast with my wife and after breakfast this discomfort came back again. I said to my wife, "You know I am not happy about this and I really think I should have an electrocardiogram. It is probably just hysterical on my part, but I don't like the sensation." It was more severe than any indigestion

I had ever had before. We went and found a small hospital in this resort town. They did an electrocardiogram and it was normal, but the physician on call that day said, "You are a cardiologist. You would not have come in here for nothing, and I think we should ship you down to the nearest coronary care unit and get you monitored for 24 hours." I said, "Hey, you're the doctor. Whatever you say." At that point I was feeling very embarrassed and very sheepish because I was sort of pulling the fire alarm for no fire. We got down to the CCU and I was put in the bed. You can imagine all the excitement in this little regional Danish coronary care unit because once they learned who I was, cardiologists started calling in from different parts of Denmark. I was really getting progressively more and more embarrassed about the whole thing when that night, about 3:00 A.M., the indigestion came back again. I called the nurse and got an electrocardiogram and that showed ST elevations in leads 2, 3, and aVF. There was a resident on call and he came quickly. We read the electrocardiogram together and I was treated with thrombolytics, aspirin, a β blocker, and heparin. The next morning a friend of mine, Kristian Thygesen, arrived from Aarhus, the second largest city in Denmark where he is Chief of Cardiology. By now everything was fine again. The electrocardiogram showed a small myocardial infarct. An echocardiogram showed a small apical area of akinesis. My course thereafter was completely benign. About 9 days later when I got back to the University of Arizona, Sam Butman, the head of our cath lab did a coronary angiogram on me and it was normal. There was still this apical area of akinesis. In subsequent echos (I get an echo every year now), a little area of hypokinesis is still present at the apex. My electrocardiogram still shows small Q-waves in leads 2, 3, and aVF. Thus, I had a small, successfully treated acute myocardial infarct. It was probably spasm related. My total cholesterol at that time was about 200 mg/dl; now I take a statin drug and keep my cholesterol around 150 mg/dl. Today, when I go out to run I keep myself well clothed.

• • •

WCR: You don't think about it anymore?

JSA: Once in a while. You know it was kind of a funny thing. Even when I was in the midst of having it, I was saying to myself, "Well this can't be a big myocardial infarction because I don't have much in the way of risk factors, and really it has to be single vessel disease or distal disease or something minor. Maybe that sort of intellectualization kept me from thinking to myself, "Wow, this is a heart attack; you are liable to die from this." Somehow that thought never crossed my mind. I was always sure I was going to survive. I knew that I just needed to get the right treatment and this was not going to be a major problem. I don't think much about it now, but when I am out running I don't push myself quite as hard as I used to. I make sure I get that 1 month's vacation every year and I'm pretty careful to take my medicines and aspirin everyday.

• • •

WCR: Does your wife run with you?

JSA: No, she does not run, but we often walk together on the weekends; at other times we go swimming or bicycle riding together.

• • •

WCR: Do you ever talk about the myocardial infarct anymore?

JSA: Once in a while. Sometimes people will bring it up and most people say we can't believe you had a heart attack. I think it proves that first of all even with minimal to no clinically evident coronary disease you can have a myocardial infarction. I believe that psychological factors, the stresses of that year, played a role as well as the cold.

• • •

WCR: The angiogram was 9 days after onset. So whatever had been there could have been lysed?

JSA: I am sure. I got treated with 2 thrombolytics: I got both streptokinase and tissue plasminogen activator (t-PA), as well as heparin and aspirin. Even if there had been residual clot there initially, 7 to 10 days later you could certainly dissolve it all.

• • •

WCR: Do you have any thoughts about what you were feeling when you were receiving that thrombolytic therapy?

JSA: I was very grateful that I was in a coronary care unit when the ST elevation was coming on, that I was actually getting thrombolytic treatment well under an hour after the onset of the symptoms. I think what probably happened was I must have had a spastic event when I was out on the cold run. That ruptured a little intramural plaque leading to coronary thrombosis, either in the distal right or the distal left anterior descending where it wraps around the apex. When I stopped running and came inside I got warm, and the artery dilated a little bit so enough blood flow was getting by for the muscle to survive. Then, later that night as I was lying quietly in bed, the flow decreased a little. Maybe the thrombus built up again because there was not such rapid flow past it. Then the thrombus eventually built up to the point where it occluded the artery.

• • •

WCR: Were you on the track team in high school? Were you an athlete? At 54 years of age you run about 30 miles a week?

JSA: I was a swimmer from either the eighth or ninth grade. I swam everyday, trained, and swam for the high school swim team, and swam in college. When I was in the Navy in San Diego, I was on the Navy swim team. Today, I exercise one hour everyday: running, swimming, or bicycling.

• • •

WCR: You swam for Yale University?

JSA: The Yale University team at that time had basically 4 teams. The first team was Olympic champions; the second team NCAA champions; the third

team Ivy league champions; and the fourth team were guys who were good in high school. I was on the fourth team, but it was fun swimming with those guys anyway.

• • •

WCR: What did you swim?

JSA: In high school I swam freestyle and butterfly. In college I swam breast stroke. I still swim. In Arizona we have a pool and we belong to a racket and pool club and I still swim all the time.

• • •

WCR: You are a pretty tall fellow. How tall are you?

JSA: Six foot, three inches.

• • •

WCR: Can you dunk?

JSA: No, I can't jump very high. I never was very good at jumping. I started running when I got to my 40th birthday when I was starting to gain a little weight. I said to myself, "I don't like this. My clothes are tight on me." I started running with some friends at noon time at Worcester.

• • •

WCR: It is awfully cold up there in the wintertime.

JSA: I wore a Gortex suit and dressed warmly. I used to run in the snow, too. When I got to Arizona I started running in quite warm weather and that felt fine.

• • •

WCR: Do you ever see any snakes while you are running in Arizona?

JSA: Sometimes, and actually I do a lot of hiking in the mountains where there are lots of snakes. Just this past summer a friend and I were hiking and almost stepped on a rattlesnake. Fortunately, the snake was heading uphill and we sort of froze and he kept going uphill. Most rattlesnakes are not interested in having anything to do with human beings.

• • •

WCR: Joe, many thanks.

BEST PUBLICATIONS OF JSA AS SELECTED BY JSA

1. Alpert J, Garcia del Rio H, Lassen NA. Diagnostic use of radioactive xenon clearance and a standardized walking test in obliterative arterial disease of the legs. *Circulation* 1966;34:849–855.

2. Alpert JS, Larsen QA, Lassen NA. Evaluation of arterial insufficiency of the legs: a comparison of arteriography and 133-xenon walking test. *Cardiovasc Res* 1968;2:161–169.

3. Alpert JS, Coffman JD. The effect of intravenous epinephrine on skeletal muscle, skin and subcutaneous blood flow. *Am J Physiol* 1969;216:156–160.

4. Alpert JS. The mechanism of the increased maximum work performance of small muscle groups resulting from "diverting work" with other muscle groups. *Acta Physiol Scand* 1969;77:261–157.

5. Alpert JS, Larsen QA, Lassen NA. Effect of daily training on muscle blood flow in patients with occlusive arterial disease of the legs. *Circulation* 1969;39:353–359.

6. Alpert JS, Coffman JD, Balodimos MC, Koncz L, Soeldner JS. Capillary permeability and blood flow in skeletal muscle of patients with diabetes mellitus and genetic prediabetes. *N Engl J Med* 1972;286:454–460.

7. Alpert JS, Haynes FW, Dalen JE, Dexter L. Experimental pulmonary embolism: effect on pulmonary blood volume and vascular compliance. *Circulation* 1974;49:152–157.

8. Alpert JS, Rickman FD, Howe JP, Dexter L, Dalen JE. Alteration of systolic time intervals in right ventricular failure. *Circulation* 1974; 50:317–323.

9. Alpert JS, Bass H, Szucs MM, Banas JS, Dalen JE, Dexter L. Effects of physical training on hemodynamics and pulmonary function at rest and during exercise in patients with chronic obstructive pulmonary disease. *Chest* 1974;66:647–651.

10. Alpert JS, Smith RE, Ockene IS, Askenazi J, Dexter L, Dalen JE. Treatment of massive pulmonary embolism: is embolectomy ever indicated and feasible? *Am Heart J* 1975;89:413–418.

11. Alpert JS, Smith RE, Carlson CJ, Ockene IS, Dexter L, Dalen JE. Mortality in documented pulmonary embolism. *JAMA* 1976;236:1477–1480.

12. Alpert JS, Krous HF, Dalen JE, O'Rourke RA, Bloor CM. Pathogenesis of Osler's nodes. *Ann Intern Med* 1976;85:471–473.

13. Alpert JS, Francis GS, Vieweg WVR, Thompson SI, Stanton KC, Hagan AD. Left ventricular function in massive pulmonary embolism. *Chest* 1977;71:108–112.

14. Alpert JS, Dexter L, Vieweg WVR, Haynes FW, Dalen JE. Anomalous pulmonary venous return with intact atrial septum; diagnosis of pathophysiology. *Circulation* 1977;56:870–875.

15. Alpert JS, Godtfredsen J, Ockene IS, Anas J, Dalen JE. Pulmonary hypertension secondary to minor pulmonary embolism. *Chest* 1978;73:795–797.

16. Pape LA, Haffajee CI, Markis JE, Ockene IS, Paraskos JA, Dalen JE, Alpert JS. Fatal pulmonary hemorrhage after use of the flow directed balloon-tipped catheter. *Ann Intern Med* 1979;90:344–347.

17. Alpert JS, Sloss JL, Cohn PF, Grossman W. The diagnostic accuracy of combined clinical and non-invasive cardiac evaluation—comparison with findings at cardiac catheterization. *Cath Cardiovasc Diag* 1980;6:359–370.

18. Mathiasen H, Alpert JS. Medicine and literature in the medical curriculum. *JAMA* 1980;244:1491.

19. Ockene IS, Shay MJ, Alpert JS, Weiner BH, Dalen JE. Unexplained chest pain in patients with normal coronary arteriograms. A follow-up study of functional status. *N Engl J Med* 1980;303:1249–1252.

20. Dalen JE, Ockene IS, Alpert JS. Coronary spasm, coronary thrombosis, and myocardial infarction: a hypothesis concerning the pathophysiology of acute myocardial infarction. *Am Heart J* 1982;104:1119–1124.

21. Haffajee CI, Love JC, Canada AT, Lesko LJ, Asdourian G, Alpert JS. Clinical pharmacokinetics and efficacy of amiodarone for refractory tachyarrhythmias. *Circulation* 1983;67:1347–1355.

22. Love JC, Haffajee CI, Gore JM, Alpert JS. Reversibility of hypotension and shock by atrial or atrioventricular sequential pacing in patients with right ventricular infarction. *Am Heart J* 1984;108:5–13.

23. Pape LA, Rippe JM, Walker WS, Weiner BH, Ockene IS, Paraskos JA, Alpert JS. Effects of the cessation of training on left ventricular function in the racing greyhound. *Basic Res Cardiol* 1984;79:98–109.

24. Bianco JA, Pape LA, Alpert JS, Zheng M, Hnatowich D, Goodman MM, Knapp FF. Accumulation of radioiodinated 15-(p-iodophenyl)-6-tellurapentadecanoic acid in ischemic myocardium during acute coronary occlusion and reperfusion. *J Am Cardiol* 1984;4:80–87.

25. Bianco JA, Elmaleh DR, Leppo JA, King MA, Moring A, Livni E, Espinoza E, Alpert JS, Strauss HW. Effect of glucose and insulin infusion on the myocardial extraction of a radioiodinated methyl-substituted fatty acid. *Èur J Nucl Med* 1986;12:120–124.

26. Gold RL, Haffajee CI, Charos G, Sloan K, Baker S, Alpert JS. Amiodarone for refractory atrial fibrillation. *Am J Cardiol* 1986;57:124–127.

27. Goldberg RJ, Gore JM, Alpert JS, Dalen JE. Recent changes in attack and survival rates of acute myocardial infarction (1975 through 1981). *JAMA* 1986;255:2774–2779.

28. Pape LA, Price JM, Alpert JS, Rippe JM. Hemodynamics and left ventricular function: a comparison between adult racing greyhounds and greyhounds completely untrained from birth. *Basic Res Cardiol* 1986;81:417–424.

29. Goldberg RJ, Gore JM, Alpert JS, Dalen JE. Non-Q wave myocardial infarction: recent changes in occurrence and prognosis: a community-wide perspective. *Am Heart J* 1987;113:273–279.

30. Chipkin SR, Frid D, Alpert JS, Baker SP, Dalen JE, Aronin N. Frequency of painless myocardial ischemia during exercise tolerance testing in patients with and without diabetes mellitus. *Am J Cardiol* 1987;59:61–65.

31. Goldberg RJ, Gore JM, Haffajee CI, Alpert JS, Dalen JE. Outcome after cardiac arrest during acute myocardial infarction. *Am J Cardiol* 1987;59:251–255.

32. Gore JM, Goldberg RJ, Spodick DH, Alpert JS, Dalen JE. A community wide assessment of the use of pulmonary artery catheters in patients with acute myocardial infarction. *Chest* 1987;92:721–727.

33. Bianco JA, Bakanauskas J, Carlson M, Jones S, Moring A, Alpert JS. Augmented uptake of 2-C-14-D-deoxyglucose in reversibly-injured myocardium. *Eur J Nucl Med* 1988;13:557–562.

34. Held AC, Cole PL, Lipton B, Gore JM, Antman EM, Hochman JS, Corrao J, Goldberg RJ, Alpert JS. Rupture of the interventricular septum complicating acute MI: a multicenter analysis of clinical findings and outcome. *Am Heart J* 1988;116:1330–1336.

35. Goldberg RJ, Gore JM, Gurwitz JH, Alpert JS, Brady P, Strohsnitter MS, Chen Z, Dalen JE. The impact of age on the incidence and prognosis of initial acute myocardial infarction: the Worcester Heart Attack Study. *Am Heart J* 1989;117:543–549.

36. Goldberg RJ, Seeley D, Becker RC, Brady P, Chen Z, Osganian V, Gore JM, Alpert JS, Dalen JE. Impact of atrial fibrillation on the in-hospital and long-term survival of patients with acute myocardial infarction: a community-wide perspective. *Am Heart J* 1990;119:996–1001.

37. Sanabria T, Alpert JS, Goldberg R, Pape LA, Cheeseman SH. Increasing frequency of staphylococcal infective endocarditis: experience at a University Hospital, 1981 through 1988. *Arch Int Med* 1990;150:1305–1309.

38. Goldberg RJ, Gore JM, Alpert JS, Osganian V, DeGroot J, Bade J, Chen ZD, Dalen JE. Cardiogenic shock after acute myocardial infarction: incidence and mortality from a community-wide perspective, 1975-1988. *N Engl J Med* 1991;325:1117–1122.

39. Gurwitz JH, Goldberg RJ, Chen Z, Gore JM, Alpert JS. β-Blocker therapy in acute myocardial infarction: evidence for underutilization in the elderly. *Am J Med* 1992;93:605–610.

40. Chiriboga DE, Yarzebski J, Goldberg RJ, Chen Z, Gurwitz J, Gore JM, Alpert JS, Dalen JE. A community-wide perspective of gender differences and temporal trends in the use of diagnostic and revascularization procedures for acute myocardial infarction. *Am J Cardiol* 1993;71:268–273.

41. Goldberg RJ, Gorak EJ, Yarzebski J, Hosmer DW, Dalen P, Gore JM, Alpert JS, Dalen JE. A community-wide perspective of sex differences and temporal trends in the incidence and survival rates after acute myocardial infarction and out-of-hospital deaths caused by coronary heart disease. *Circulation* 1993;87:1947–1953.

GEORGE ALLAN BELLER, MD:
A Conversation With the Editor*

George Beller was born in New York City on December 23, 1940, and grew up mainly in the borough of Queens. He graduated from Dartmouth College in 1962 and from the University of Virginia School of Medicine in 1966. His internship and first-year residency in internal medicine was at the University of Wisconsin Hospitals in Madison, Wisconsin. His second year of residency in internal medicine and his first year of cardiology fellowship were at the Boston City Hospital. He then went into the United States Army and was stationed in Natick, Massachusetts. After 3 years as a research internist at the physiology laboratory of the US Army Research Institute of Environmental Medicine, he completed his cardiology fellowship at the Massachusetts General Hospital in June 1974 and remained on the faculty there until 1977 when he returned to the University of Virginia Health System as the Donald C. Barnes Professor of Cardiology and the Chief of the Cardiovascular Division. In 1992, he became the Ruth C. Heede Professor of Cardiology and Professor of Internal Medicine.

Dr. Beller has been highly productive his entire professional career despite his many administrative responsibilities. He is the author of nearly 350 articles in peer-reviewed medical journals, 4 books, and nearly 300 abstracts. He also has been the visiting professor once or more at all the major university medical centers in the United States and many abroad, and he has received many honors for his work.

While I was a visiting professor in Dr. Beller's division recently, I had the opportunity to spend time with several of his faculty members. Several of them described him as: "a wonderful, wonderful man; very supportive of his colleagues; he's made a big difference for a lot of us; he is a splendid physician and he takes very good care of his patients; he is humble; he has time for everyone; he is one of us; he's very involved; he considers himself not more important than any of his people; he is extremely supportive of our efforts; he never fails to acknowledge a kind deed; he answers every e-mail; we all love him; he is simply a wonderful, fabulous guy, amazing actually; he not only meets with his faculty at length twice a year, but he is available for interaction almost daily; he is extremely good to the fellows as well as to all of the house staff; he meets with the fellows regularly." It's no wonder George Beller has prospered in his position for so long and so effectively.

William Clifford Roberts, MD[†] (hereafter, WCR): *This is February 13, 2001. I am in the office of Dr. George Beller at the University of Virginia Medical Center in*

FIGURE 1. GAB during the interview.

FIGURE 2. GAB in his office in Charlottesville.

Charlottesville, Virginia. Dr. Beller has agreed to talk to me and therefore to the readers of The American Journal of Cardiology. *George, could we start by your describing your early upbringing in New York City, and a bit about your parents and siblings?*

*This series of interviews is underwritten by an unrestricted grant from Bristol-Myers Squibb.
†Baylor Heart & Vascular Center, Baylor University Medical Center, Dallas, Texas 75246.

15

George Allan Beller, MD[‡] (hereafter, GAB): I was born in New York City. When I was 5 years old, we moved to Queens and I went to elementary school and high school in Forest Hills. My father grew up in Vienna, Austria, and when the Germans invaded Austria, he and the family left almost at midnight on a train to get out of Vienna. After several months going through various countries, he and his family arrived in Belgium. They settled in Antwerp where my father then met my mother. After a courtship, they were married and 2 months later the Germans invaded Belgium and they had to leave. My mother had a visa, so she got out quickly with her parents and made it to Portugal, which was neutral. My father was arrested with his brother at the border, because he carried an Austrian passport, and was put into a French internment camp, which was not yet controlled by the Germans. Finally, they got out by securing some money from relatives and bribing a guard. This surely saved their lives, because Jewish residents of these camps were ultimately sent to Nazi concentration camps. For about 4 months my father was escorted with the Catholic underground from one monastery to another dressed as a monk, until he was delivered to partisans in Spain over the Pyrenees. This is a story of World War II that is not well known. There were many in the Catholic Church who helped Jews escape. My mother and father finally hooked up in Oporto, Portugal, 4 months after they were separated. My mother was pregnant with me. She wanted me to be born in the USA, but there were no passages on a ship at that time to the USA.

WCR: *What year are you talking about?*

GAB: This was September 1940. My mother being young (in her mid-20s) pleaded with the US immigration officers to allow her to go. There was only 1 passage on the next ship to America, so she went by herself to the USA. She knew few people in the USA—only a few relatives on my father's side. She went to live in a hotel room in New York City, and about 3 months later (December 23, 1940) I was born. My father didn't arrive for another 2 months after that.

WCR: *How did you father get to the USA?*

GAB: He came by boat on a subsequent passage to New York. He wanted to do something to contribute to the war effort once he arrived in the USA. So, from 1941 until 1944 we lived in Vineland, New Jersey, where my father ran a chicken farm to help the war effort. All eggs hatched there were sold to the government for food for the soldiers. I have a wonderful picture of my father, a university educated, very well informed and sophisticated European gentleman, and my mother, who had a master's degree, who spoke 5 languages, with our dog and a horse on that farm. As soon as the war was over, we moved back to Manhattan and then, 1 year later, to Forest Hills, Queens.

WCR: *How old was your father when you were born? Your mother was 24.*

GAB: My father was 29. He was 5 years older than my mother was. My father was born in 1911 and my mother in 1916.

FIGURE 3. GAB as a young child living on a chicken farm in Vineland, New Jersey.

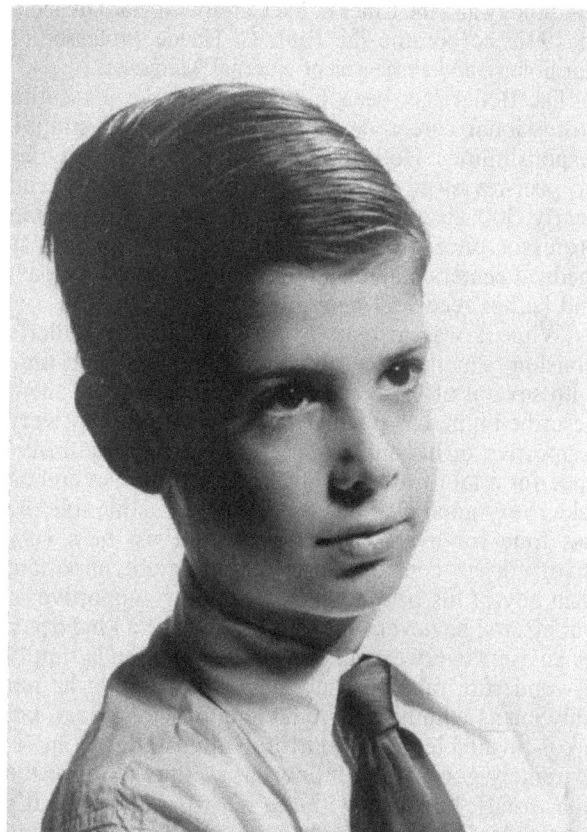

FIGURE 4. GAB as a young child in New York.

WCR: *Is your father still alive?*

GAB: No. My father died just short of his 89th birthday in April 2000.[§]

WCR: *What was it like growing up in Queens?*

[‡]Cardiology Division, University of Virginia Health System, Charlottesville, Virginia 22908.

[§]Dr. Beller's mother died in April 2002.

FIGURE 5. GAB at a summer camp as an early teenager.

GAB: With time, my parents became completely assimilated to the American life. My youth was predominantly taken up with schoolwork, sports, and the arts. Starting in elementary school and all through high school, I was a very avid participant in multiple sports (mostly basketball and baseball). Each summer I went to camp in upstate New York, which was mostly oriented around athletics. In addition, my parents exposed me very early to the arts. They took me to the theater, to orchestra performances, and to recitals in Carnegie Hall. My mother was a musician. She was a pianist and probably could have been a professional pianist had she decided to pursue that, but it was more of a hobby. I had a very typical urban upbringing where you went to school, did homework, played basketball in organized leagues and pickup games in the local schoolyard, and traveled to Manhattan to the theater and museums, even during the weekdays. My parents took me to see art exhibitions at a very early age. I developed a life-long interest in the arts and, in turn, I tried to convey that to my own children. I think the earlier you are exposed to music, the visual arts, and theater, the more you have a lifelong appreciation of those arts. Today, I serve on

the board of a Charlottesville repertory theater company.

WCR: *Did you have siblings?*

GAB: I have a brother who is 4 years younger and a sister who is 7 years younger than I am.

WCR: *Where did you live in Queens?*

GAB: We lived in a typically middle-class neighborhood with attached houses that were not very large. As a young child, everything was focused on the neighborhood. Most every afternoon, after school and on weekends, kids rode bikes up and down the street. We had stoopball and stickball games. We drove our bikes to the schoolyard to play basketball, softball, and handball (against a large cement wall). It was like the classic pictures you see of suburbia back in the 1950s. I have very fond memories of going to Yankee Stadium to see the New York Yankees, to Ebbets Field to see the Dodgers, and to the Polo Grounds to see the Giants' games. I still remember seeing Bobby Thompson hitting his legendary home run, on our small black and white television set, when the Giants won the pennant in 1951. I frequently saw the New York Knickerbockers play in the old Madison Square Garden. When showing a school ID card, you could get in to watch the Knickerbockers play for 50¢ and sit in the upper balcony. I went to New York Ranger hockey games and college basketball tournaments. I followed all major sports religiously. That was one of the joys of my youth. I was never bored between sports, cultural events, and music lessons. I started playing the violin in the fourth grade, and there was always a tension between having to practice and getting out of the house to play ball.

WCR: *Was money something you worried about growing up?*

GAB: No, except for the fact that we had lots of restrictions on our spending. We had strict allowances like all kids did in those days. I didn't get my first car until I was a sophomore in college. I had summer jobs from age 16 on. We took only a few family vacations. My father bought a farmhouse in rural Connecticut in the early 1950s. That was his and my mother's passion—to get away on the weekends. During the summer he would commute by train back and forth to New York. It took 1-1/2 hours each way. It was a nice, quiet place, with a brook and a pond. It was a way to escape New York City in the summer while the children were in summer camp.

WCR: *Your parents pushed education as you were coming along?*

GAB: Yes. It was very important that all of us valued our education. I also recall reading a great deal of fiction while in high school, both for school assignments and for pleasure. I think I read all the Hardy Boys novels and the *Kipling* adventure stories. The subject I disliked the most was math. I was never good at it. I still like to read a great deal for relaxation, predominantly fiction.

WCR: *Were there a lot of books around the house?*

GAB: Yes. We had quite a few books, ranging from best sellers to very eclectic art books. My uncle was one of the foremost art publishers in the world. He was the owner of Phaidon Press in London, which produced beautiful books of paintings by *Michelangelo*, *Renoir*, *Van Gogh*, and others. He was married to my father's older sister. We had a huge number of these art books in our house, many of them gifts from my uncle when he visited our home on his frequent trips to New York.

WCR: *What had your father studied in college?*

GAB: He studied chemistry. Before the war, he and his brother owned a chemical factory in Vienna that manufactured chemicals for perfumes. When his brother came to New York he continued in that arena.

WCR: *What was it like when you came home from school? Did you have intellectual discussions at the dinner table at night when you were growing up? Did your father get home in time for dinner?*

GAB: My mother insisted that the whole family be together at dinner on weekday nights. Sometimes, when my father worked late, we might have soup or something else to eat early because we were hungry. During dinner we talked about all kinds of things—from current events to what we did that day. The children wanted to eat as quickly as possible because we still had homework to do and there were sporting events to listen to on the radio, and later on television.

WCR: *Did you play sports on the high school teams?*

GAB: I was not good enough to play on the varsity teams in high school. Our high school had more than 5,000 students, and the basketball team was about the second or third best public high school team in New York City at that time. I was barely 6-feet tall. I had friends, who like me, were not good enough to play on our high school team, so we played in various leagues in the area. We could play as often as 3 or 4 nights a week and most weekends during the season. Many boys who were in those leagues and who played in those pickup games in schoolyards could have played in most high schools outside of New York City in those days.

WCR: *Did you have your own room growing up?*

GAB: I shared a room with my brother until I was 14 years old. We then moved within Forest Hills to a larger house; I got my own room. The house was situated not far from the tennis stadium where they used to play the US Open. I recall one of the best things about having my own room was the ability to listen to the radio or read all hours of the night without disturbing my younger brother.

WCR: *Was it safe around your house?*

GAB: It was pretty safe. Police cars patrolled the area. That was also the time of gangs in New York. We would hear about some potential "rumbles" that were going to occur after school between various groups. I witnessed a few pretty good fights.

WCR: *You didn't fear going to school? How far was school from home?*

GAB: It was about a 30-minute walk to my high school. The elementary school—Public School (P.S.) 144—was about 5 blocks away. We didn't have junior high or middle schools until later. I went through to the eighth grade in elementary school and then to high school as a 9th grader. Back in the 1950s I could ride the subways of New York day or night and feel safe. I often got on the subway in Forest Hills as a 16- or 17-year-old and went to New York City for the evening. On Saturdays we would come back sometimes at 1:00 to 2:00 A.M. and not think anything of it. Today, you couldn't do that.

WCR: *What languages did your mother speak?*

GAB: She spoke French, German, Flemish, Dutch, and English. She took Italian lessons in her 70's.

WCR: *What did your brother and sister do?*

GAB: My brother became an independent filmmaker, producing predominantly documentaries. Some have appeared on public television (PBS). One won an Emmy Award. In recent years he developed an interest and expertise in doing projects in medicine. He currently has a contract with the American Heart Association to produce video clips that are distributed to the national TV networks.

WCR: *Where is he?*

GAB: He's in New York City.

WCR: *You mentioned that your sister lives in Italy?*

GAB: My sister has been in Italy for about 27 years. She met her husband, who lived in Rome, when she was in her 20s, and they fell in love. After they married she moved to Rome where she has raised 2 children and has worked as a music instructor in the Italian public school system. She also gives private piano lessons and occasionally plays recitals.

WCR: *Was there a fast track in your high school? Did everybody take the same subjects?*

GAB: I don't recall, but I think we had just 1 curriculum. We had about 40 students in a class. Because the school was overcrowded we had triple sessions during my senior year. As a senior, I went to school from 8:00 A.M. to 12:30 P.M. The sophomores arrived at 12:30 P.M. and didn't finish until 5:00 P.M. The juniors went from 9:30 A.M. to 3:30 P.M. because there wasn't enough classroom space. *Paul Simon* and *Art Garfunkel* were in my high school class. We had a lot of interesting people of all backgrounds who lived in Forest Hills. It was a pretty crowded place but a very good school. Eighty percent of our graduating class went on to college.

WCR: *What did you do in the summers in high school? Did you work?*

GAB: The first job I had, and I was 16 years old, was as a waiter in the same summer camp that I had gone to as a camper for 9 years. I was a waiter for 2 years and then a counselor for 1 summer.

WCR: *What about religion as you were growing up? Were your parents active in the synagogue?*

GAB: Moderately so, and less so as they got older. I attended what was called "Hebrew School" one afternoon a week, and I went to services at the temple on most Saturday mornings with my parents when I was young. By high school, I went less frequently but we still always celebrated the Jewish holidays. Perhaps the most memorable religious-associated activity of not only my youth, but also my entire adult life, was the Passover Seder at our home, which ushers in the Passover holidays. Throughout my adult life I would

FIGURE 6. GAB holding a beer in his dorm room at Dartmouth College, 1958.

FIGURE 7. GAB with his father on graduation day from Dartmouth College, June 1962.

go with my own family to New York for the annual Seder. My brother continued this tradition after my father died.

WCR: *How did it come about that you went to Dartmouth to college?*

GAB: Having grown up in New York, I wanted to get out and see more of the country. I had heard from a friend of the family that Dartmouth was a very good school and well balanced with respect to academics, athletics, and extracurricular activities. It was located in a beautiful part of the country. When visiting Hanover for my interview, I fell in love with the town and the college. I also was anxious to learn how to ski. I was fortunate enough to get accepted.

WCR: *How did Hanover, New Hampshire and Dartmouth hit you? You had never lived outside of New York City until this point. How did you react to college?*

GAB: It was a fantastic 4 years! I thoroughly enjoyed it. I'll never forget the first day I was there after my parents had driven me, brought all my belongings to my dorm room, and left for home. This was the freshman orientation week before classes started. There was an upper classman on the first floor of my dorm who had helped me unload my possessions from my parent's car. Within a few minutes after my parents had left he offered me a beer. That was characteristic about Dartmouth College back then. It had quite a reputation for being a drinking school. I had many more beers over the next 4 years. Dartmouth was great academically. I majored in philosophy with a minor in comparative literature while taking the prerequisite premed studies. My premed advisor told us that we should major in a non-science area in college because we would get plenty of science in medical school. I took the minimum science requirements for medical school, like physics and organic chemistry. I had taken an introductory survey philosophy course as a freshman and enjoyed it immensely.

I decided then to become a philosophy major. I took many art history courses. Overall, I had a wonderful academic and social experience at Dartmouth. I also learned to ski.

WCR: *How did you get interested in becoming a physician? Were there any physicians in your extended family?*

GAB: No. I had not decided to pursue a medical career when in high school. I thought about medicine as a future career because I liked the idea of helping people and caring for them. Many of us were very idealistic. I still feel that way. One great joy in being a physician is encountering people you can help. At the end of my sophomore year in college, I decided that I would pursue medicine as a field. I was initially interested in psychiatry because it merged science with psychology and philosophy. I continued to be interested in psychiatry as a specialty through my first year in medical school until 2 things happened. The first was that my initial exposure to psychiatry was rather negative. This was in 1963 when not much could be done for people with mental illness except psychoanalysis for those with neuroses. For the more severe forms of mental illness, like schizophrenia, not very much could be done. This was the era before the advent of psychopharmacology. I just didn't connect with psychiatry, in general. I then became exposed to cardiac physiology in our physiology course and really "connected" with the subject matter. Then when encountering physiology of the cardiovascular system something just lit up in me and I said to myself, "I really like this." I liked trying to comprehend the mechanism of cardiac contraction, Starling's Law, the autonomic nervous system, the concepts of cardiac output, peripheral resistance, and autoregulation. When I finally was exposed to physical diagnosis of the heart and started to see patients with cardiovascular disease, I subjectively felt more inner satisfaction than when seeing patients with noncardiac illnesses. Hence, my decision to become a cardiologist was made very early in medical school. What really iced it was the series of articles (about 7 of them) in *The New England Journal of Medicine* entitled "The Mechanism of Contraction of the Normal and Failing Heart" by *Eugene Braunwald, John Ross, Jr., Edward Sonnenblick*, and others who were then at the National Heart Institute in Bethesda. Those articles conveyed a new level of sophistication of cardiac physiology (the ultrastructural basis of Starling's Law, the sarcomere length–tension relationship, and the force–velocity relationship). It really connected with me. Once when John Ross came to UVA as a visiting professor, I showed him the original *New England Journal of Medicine* articles that I had clipped together, with underlines on virtually every page and comments in the margins. I think this series of papers came out at either the end of my fourth year of medical school or during my internship. The reading of those articles on cardiovascular physiology was the major turning point for me. I decided that I definitely wanted to be a cardiologist. Even before that I used to go and watch open-heart operations from a glass dome over the heart surgery operating room at UVA. *Dr. William Muller*, head of the UVA department of surgery, performed most of these open-heart operations. I would sneak away from the library to watch him replace an aortic valve. I volunteered to work in the cardiac intensive care unit one summer during medical school and spent another part of a summer in the cardiac surgical animal laboratory working with cardiac surgical fellows on their research projects.

WCR: *How did you do at Dartmouth from the academic standpoint? Did you feel well prepared after having come from Forest Hills High School?*

GAB: I was well prepared. I was a good student in college, but not outstanding. I didn't care that much about grades. I didn't like studying for exams. I never have. I became immersed in other activities and spent many hours in dorm rooms with friends discussing "the meaning of life" or at the fraternity house enjoying myself. I was a sports reporter for the *Daily Dartmouth* during my first year. I covered the freshmen sports teams. I thought I had achieved a nice balance between classroom work and extracurricular activities that included periodic afternoons of skiing. Many of my college courses required a great deal of reading. For example, one course in Russian civilization was comprised of reading most of the novels by *Tolstoy* and *Dostoevsky*. I completed "War and Peace," one of the longest novels ever published, over a period of 1 week—sitting every afternoon and evening in the Tower Room of the Dartmouth library in a huge comfortable easy chair with a window in front of me looking out on the campus. I recall trying to comprehend the logistics of the battles between *Napoleon* and the Russians. Reading such novels took me away from studying for an organic chemistry examination. I was lucky to get into medical school, since my grades in premed science courses were rather mediocre.

WCR: *You grew up in New York City. You went to Hanover, New Hampshire, to college. And then lo and behold you came to Charlottesville, Virginia, for medical school. How did that come about?*

GAB: It is an interesting story. At the beginning of my senior year at Dartmouth I was ready to go back to New York City to medical school. I had applied to the usual New York schools. At that time I was on a student–faculty committee that was organized to recommend to Dartmouth the installation of a student honor system. One day I saw on a bulletin board that a physician from the admissions office of the University of Virginia was coming to Dartmouth to interview potential medical school applicants. I had learned from the work of this committee that the University of Virginia had one of the most distinguished college honor systems in the country. I said, "I'm going to sign up so I can talk to this physician about how the honor system works at the University of Virginia." I had no intention of applying to medical school there. When I arrived at the interview session, the first thing I said was, "By the way, I just want to let you know I have not applied to the University of Virginia. I don't know anything about it, but I would like to have the opportunity to talk to you about how the student honor system works at UVA." The interviewer was very gracious and didn't get upset. Toward the end of our discussion about how the honor system functions at UVA, he said, "Have you ever been to Charlottesville? Do you know anything about the University of Virginia?" I said, "I know a little about it. I knew that the school had a good reputation and that they had a great law school." He proceeded to tell me more about Charlottesville and the School of Medicine. He said, "Do you like Hanover? Do you like a college community and the atmosphere of a college town?" I said, "Yes, very much." He said, "Then, why are you going back to New York City? Why don't you think about applying to the University of Virginia?" He invited me to come and visit Charlottesville and see the medical school. I went several weeks later and had a wonderful visit. I ended up applying and was admitted. I subsequently decided that I would rather go to Charlottesville than back to New York City. It was one of the best decisions I ever made.

WCR: *How did Charlottesville really hit you after you got there for medical school?*

GAB: Right from the very first day I arrived in Charlottesville I thought it was a great place. It was a wonderful atmosphere. It was a small school at that time, and had 75 medical students per class. More than 50% were non-Virginians. One of the legacies of *Thomas Jefferson* was that although he wanted the University of Virginia to be a state university, his desire was that it also be a national university. Even today, the University of Virginia admits a significant percentage of its class from outside the state. Medical school was actually fun. I enjoyed the classes, my classmates, and the town. It was a great experience. My roommate during my second year, who is still one of my best friends, was *Delos (Toby) Cosgrove*, who is currently Chairman of Cardiac Surgery at The

FIGURE 8. GAB during his medical school days at the University of Virginia in the early 1960s.

Cleveland Clinic. We became very close. I was the best man at his wedding. We both trained in Boston at about the same time.

WCR: *Who had a major impact on you while in medical school?*

GAB: The 2 individuals who had the most profound impact on me in medical school were *Dr. Julian Beckwith*, Chief of Cardiology, and *Dr. Francis (Frank) Dammann,* Chief of Pediatric Cardiology. Dr. Dammann introduced cardiac catheterization to Charlottesville. He trained with *Helen Taussig* at Johns Hopkins. Dr. Beckwith was the quintessential bedside cardiologist. He had tremendous skills in electrocardiography and vectorcardiography. He wrote a textbook on vectorcardiography. I took an elective in cardiology with him during my fourth year. I accompanied him on rounds, saw patients with him in the clinic, and read electrocardiograms while under his tutelage. He was a wonderful role model as a diagnostician, as a caring physician, as a person with superb clinical judgment. He had a wonderful personality. Dr. Dammann was a visionary physician who was years ahead of his time. He was one of the first to computerize hemodynamic data, which is now common in digital catheterization laboratories. He had a keen understanding of hemodynamics and cardiac physiology. He was a master at diagnosing the most complex of congenital heart lesions, using his stetho-

scope, the electrocardiogram, and the chest x-ray. He devised the pulmonary artery banding procedure for ventricular septal defects. Julian Beckwith and Frank Dammann complemented each other very well. I considered them as role models. When I returned to the University of Virginia, I had the privilege of working with both of them as colleagues.

WCR: *It sounds like it was relatively easy for you to pick cardiology. You must have been glad that you chose cardiology early. It made it easier.*

GAB: It really did. I now see interns and first-year residents trying to make decisions whether to go into primary care or to specialize and, if the latter, which specialty to choose. I was focused on cardiology from the end of my first year in medical school. One reason I never wanted to become a chairman of a department of medicine or a dean is that it would take me away from cardiology. My whole professional life has been geared toward remaining close to cardiology, even though in recent years I've spent more and more time involved in administration.

WCR: *How did you decide to go to the University of Wisconsin in Madison for medical internship?*

GAB: I got married in the middle of my second year in medical school. I had 2 children by the time I graduated. Neither my wife nor I had ever been in the midwest. She was from Georgia and had attended Randolph Macon Women's College in Virginia. I had heard a lot about Madison, Wisconsin, as a nice place to live, and Dr. Beckwith thought highly of the cardiologists there.

WCR: *How did it work out? Were you happy there?*

GAB: Yes, I was. It was very cold in the winter, which was 1 aspect of living in Madison I wasn't thrilled about. It was at Wisconsin that I decided to go into academic medicine. I was ready to stay there for all 3 years and then again something else fortuitously happened in my life. I was on a general medical rotation at the Veterans Administration Hospital. My attending was *Dr. Robert Donaldson*, the Chief of Gastroenterology, who had come to Madison from Boston. In a conversation on rounds one day I told him that I was interested in pursuing a career in academic medicine. I told him I wanted to engage in research training during my fellowship. He said, "I've just decided to take a job in Boston. Why don't you come with me? I'll speak to *Dr. Arnold Relman*, Chief of Medicine at Boston City Hospital's Boston University service to see if he has an open position for another third-year resident. In Boston you will have the opportunity to acquire your cardiology training at one of the Boston programs that are geared to training academic cardiologists." I told my wife about this conversation and we agreed to move to Boston if I was accepted for the residency position at Boston City Hospital. Later that week I asked Dr. Donaldson to pursue the position on my behalf. A few weeks later he called me after his return from a trip to Boston and told me I could have an interview for a third-year residency position at Boston City. I then flew to Boston, had the interview, and was accepted. We moved to Boston that June and remained there for 9 years.

FIGURE 9. The cardiac unit in the Ether Dome of the Massachusetts General Hospital in about 1974. GAB is on the last row, fourth from the right. Dr. Edgar Haber, chief of the unit, is in the middle of the first row.

WCR: *How did Boston and Boston City Hospital hit you? In the 1960s, Boston City Hospital changed a good bit. How did it go?*

GAB: It was a fantastic and exciting experience. When I arrived at the Boston City Hospital in 1968, there were still 3 medical services there: Boston University, Harvard, and Tufts. All beds were open at that time. (They subsequently downsized the hospital.) The patient mix was incredible. The house staff had major responsibility for the care of patients. We didn't have a great deal of technology, but whatever we had, we used. I applied for a cardiology fellowship position on the Harvard Medical Service and the Thorndike Memorial Laboratory, and was accepted.

During the fellowship year that began in July 1968, I encountered another one of my lifelong mentors, *Dr. William B. Hood, Jr.* Bill was the faculty supervisor of my first research project. I had observed as a resident what seemed to be a high incidence of digitalis toxicity in patients admitted to the hospital. I told Dr. Hood and my chief, *Dr. Walter Abelmann*, that I wanted to undertake a prospective study on the epidemiology of digitalis toxicity. My idea was to see how often it was observed in patients taking digitalis, the manifestation of toxicity, the contributing risk factors for toxicity, and the outcomes of toxic patients. Dr. Abelmann suggested I contact *Drs. Edgar Haber* and *Tom Smith* at the Massachusetts General Hospital, who had just developed a serum assay for digoxin and digitoxin. He suggested I meet with them to see if they were interested in performing assays on the Boston City Hospitals' patients that I enrolled in my study. I met Drs. Haber and Smith, who agreed to perform the digoxin and digitoxin assays to see if they were useful

clinically. Every morning I screened the admissions to the medical service to see who had been admitted the previous day. I gathered data from all patients who were receiving digoxin, digitoxin, or digitalis leaf. I screened 931 patients, of whom 15% were taking digitalis. I found a high incidence of definite or possible digitalis intoxication (29%). We correlated the clinical and electrocardiographic data on patients judged to be toxic by electrocardiographic criteria with the serum levels.

Collaborators in this study were 4 cardiologists who were or ultimately became chiefs of cardiology in Boston: Edgar Haber, who was at that time chief of the Cardiac Unit at Mass General; Tom Smith, who became chief of cardiology at The Brigham and Women's Hospital; Bill Hood, who subsequently became chief of cardiology at Boston City Hospital, and then at the University of Rochester; and Walter Abelmann, who was my chief of cardiology at the Boston City Hospital. I was a first-year fellow conducting a study with 4 very distinguished academic cardiologists. When we finished the study I wrote the first draft of the manuscript. I sent this draft to the 4 collaborators. The drafts were returned with countless editorial changes and suggestions for revisions. I made the appropriate changes and sent the second draft for their review. Again, they were returned with additional suggestions for revisions. Finally, a third draft sent to them was returned with even more changes. I said to Bill Hood, "Can't we send it in? Let's submit it for review." We sent the manuscript in to *The New England Journal of Medicine* and it was accepted without any revision. (That didn't happen again to me for about another 20 years!) This experience shows you the importance of the senior people with whom you train and do research with.

I then began doing experimental research with Dr. Hood in the animal laboratory in the area of experimental myocardial infarction. We would often start our experiments at 6:00 P.M., after evening rounds. Those experiments usually ended by 11:00 P.M. or midnight. I'll never forget that experience. The senior investigator was present throughout the entire experiment. We did the animal surgery together, acquired the data, and analyzed it. I spent that year of fellowship getting training in clinical cardiology, conducting the prospective digitalis study, and doing experimental infarction studies at night.

WCR: *Your cardiology fellowship lasted 2 years?*

GAB: My first year of cardiology fellowship (1969 to 1970) was at the Boston City Hospital, as I described. The next year I went into the military for 3 years, after which I undertook my second year of fellowship at the Massachusetts General Hospital (1973 to 1974).

WCR: *Tell me about your military service.*

GAB: I learned that there was an Army research laboratory in Natick, Massachusetts, called the US Army Research Institute of Environmental Medicine. They were undertaking research in cardiac physiology related to high altitude stress, heat stroke, and hypothermia. I was able to get assigned to this laboratory to fulfill my military obligations. It was most convenient. I merely headed from my home in the opposite direction from Boston each day and drove against the rush hour traffic. I spent parts of 2 summers in Fort Polk, Louisiana, where I worked in the Heat Ward and did observational studies on heat stroke and heat exhaustion. Fort Polk was an infantry training camp where drafted recruits would go through basic training and then be sent to Vietnam. We cared for soldiers with heat stroke and heat exhaustion and wrote up some of our observations in the literature. During the non-summer months, I worked predominantly in the area of high altitude physiology. I was also permitted to continue my cardiology research work in Boston. I spent 1 day a week doing collaborative research at Harvard Medical School, mostly with Bill Hood and Tom Smith. We published some papers on the effect of hypoxia on digitalis toxicity.

WCR: *Your military experience turned out to be useful for your academic advancement?*

GAB: Yes, it did. I also was permitted to keep my outpatient clinic at Boston City Hospital, which I attended 1 afternoon each week.

WCR: *Did you wear a military uniform?*

GAB: Yes, we had to every day.

WCR: *After the 3 years in the Army you went to the Massachusetts General Hospital. You needed 1 more year of cardiology fellowship.*

GAB: Yes, I needed 1 more year of fellowship training, and Ed Haber saved a position for me in his program. During that second year of training, I worked with Tom Smith on a basic research project in cardiac biochemistry. We investigated the effects of ischemia on Na^+, K^+-ATPase activity in the myocar-

dium. We were interested in why patients with acute myocardial infarction had increased sensitivity to digitalis and why they often developed digitalis-toxic arrhythmias. Using a canine model of acute ischemia, we found that myocardial ischemia alone inhibited the sodium pump. Digoxin further inhibits the pump that may set up the conditions for digitalis-toxic arrhythmias. We published our findings in the *Journal of Clinical Investigation*. That year I also worked on some clinical research projects based in the coronary care unit.

WCR: *After you finished your cardiology fellowship year at Mass General you were offered a position to stay. You stayed there an additional 3 years.*

GAB: Yes. I was an instructor for 1 year, and then I spent 2 years as an assistant professor until 1977.

WCR: *Once you hit Boston your academic career really took off. Would that be appropriate?*

GAB: I had a good start. I had the good fortune to work with a number of superb people who took the time to train and mentor me. During my 3 years on the faculty I developed an interest in nuclear cardiology and collaborated with *Dr. Gerald Pohost* in introducing myocardial perfusion imaging with thallium-201 at the Massachusetts General Hospital.

WCR: *How did it come about that you were offered the chiefship of cardiology at Charlottesville?*

GAB: I was contacted by someone on the search committee who asked me if I was interested in looking at a position. I came down and talked to *Dr. Ed Hook*, who was chairman of medicine. I decided, after some deliberation and talking to various colleagues in Boston, that I would not accept the job. Then, certain personal events occurred in my life, including separation from my first wife. We wanted to try to get together again, and returning to Charlottesville where we started seemed attractive. In April 1977, I called Ed Hook and asked him if the job was still open. Within 3 or 4 days, he flew up to Boston. I reserved a room in the Countway Library at the Harvard Medical School, where we had a negotiating session that lasted about 6 hours. After the session was over, I accepted the position with a handshake. The recruitment package included 9 new faculty positions, 8 fellow positions, and new research laboratory space. Charlottesville was a wonderful place to return to. It was a difficult first year since my wife and I separated again 4 months after the move. We subsequently divorced.

WCR: *When you came in September 1977, how many full-time faculty members were there in the division of cardiology?*

GAB: I was the sixth person.

WCR: *How many are on your faculty in the cardiology division now?*

GAB: Thirty-two full time and 4 part time. This does not include non-MD research faculty.

WCR: *George, it was 7 months ago when we talked before, and I would like to continue in the same vein as previously. We ended just as you were coming to Charlottesville to be chief of the Cardiovascular Division, and you had mentioned that when you came you were the sixth person in the division. That was*

FIGURE 10. GAB as a faculty member at the University of Virginia in the early 1980s.

September 1977. Now you have 32 full-time clinical faculty in your division and 25 fellows. How did it actually work out after you came back to Charlottesville as chief of the division? How did it develop? What are the things you are most proud of during your 20+ years as division chief?

GAB: When I came back to Charlottesville it was obvious to me that the major strength of the cardiology division then was its clinical and teaching accomplishments. Dr. Julian Beckwith, my predecessor as division chief, was a beloved clinician/teacher and was a wonderful role model. *Dr. Lockhart McGuire* was the next senior person in the division. He and *Dr. Carlos Ayers*, the head of the hypertension program, had been at UVA for quite a while and were outstanding. The other divisional members were doing an excellent job but they needed help. The research program was minimal. Dr. Ayers was the only faculty member with an extramural research grant. My goal as the division chief was to substantially expand the research program as well as the subspecialty disciplines that were emerging in cardiology. Electrophysiology was just emerging and so was coronary angioplasty. In the noninvasive area, we needed to introduce nuclear cardiology and 2-dimensional echocardiography to the program. When I arrived in Charlottesville, we didn't have clinical services in any of these new areas.

Over the next 5 to 10 years, my goal was to recruit outstanding individuals, as well as retain some of our own fellows to build up the division so it would have a higher research profile and also offer a greater variety of clinical services. I believe we have successfully accomplished this goal and built the division with superb individuals who have become internationally recognized for their accomplishments in their own right. In fact, that is what I am most proud of. I am most proud of the faculty who work in the division in a collegial and collaborative manner. They are devoted to excellence in clinical service and committed to training the next generation of cardiologists. Along the way, they have contributed immensely to the academic reputation of the division.

WCR: *George, despite your heavy administrative activities in your own division and your responsibilities to your medical center outside your division, plus your national responsibilities in leadership positions you've held, how have you been able to continue your own productivity so strongly despite these other activities?*

GAB: I've always told myself that no matter how much I became immersed in administrative activities, both within and outside the University of Virginia, I wanted to sustain my own research program. Throughout the years, I've been fortunate in working with 2 research faculty members in my laboratory— *David Glover*, a biomedical engineer, and *Mirta Herrera*, a research physician, who have been my collaborators and colleagues for many years. We've been fortunate in sustaining our extramural funding from the NHLBI, the American Heart Association, and industry sponsors. In addition, we've had gifted research fellows from all over the world who have contributed to our productivity, particularly in the field of nuclear cardiology research.

WCR: *How did you get interested initially in the nuclear aspects of cardiology? You've been a leader in that worldwide for years now.*

GAB: My interest in nuclear cardiology was spawned in Boston when I was a fellow at the Massachusetts General Hospital. I was working with Dr. Thomas Smith on the effect of ischemia on the sodium potassium ATPase pump. We found that severe ischemia injures the sodium pump because of injury to the sarcolemmal membrane. Monovalent cations such as potassium-43 and thallium-201, new imaging agents being investigated for possible noninvasive detection of myocardial blood flow abnormalities, are actively transported intracellularly via the sodium potassium ATPase pump. Our group at the MGH predicted that such radiolabeled cations therefore would be useful to assess not only blood flow, but also myocardial viability with gamma camera imaging. Decreased myocardial uptake of such cations reflects the integrity of the sarcolemmal membrane, and viability is predicated on an intact cell membrane with preserved monovalent cation transport function.

Down the hall from my experimental laboratory at the MGH was a prototype positron camera built by *Dr. Gordon Brownell*. I began imaging other monovalent cations like ^{13}N-ammonia, potassium-38, and rubidium-82 and found that these positron emitters were also taken up by the myocardium in proportion to blood flow and viability.

Dr. Gerald Pohost, another MGH faculty member, was introducing gated cardiac blood pool scanning to evaluate left and right ventricular function, and we began talking about jointly developing nuclear cardiology in the cardiac unit at the MGH. We designed

FIGURE 11. The cardiovascular division at the University of Virginia, 1986 (some faculty are missing). GAB is in the first row, third from the right.

basic research protocols to validate nuclear cardiology techniques and conducted clinical nuclear cardiology research protocols. Some of the first experiments we performed were to determine the uptake and clearance kinetics of thallium-201 in a canine ischemia model. This work led to the discovery of what was later called "thallium redistribution." We found that when thallium was given intravenously in animals under conditions of transient myocardial ischemia, initial defects filled in over time as long as no irreversible injury existed. That translated to the concept of serial gamma camera imaging after a single dose of thallium injected under stress conditions using exercise or dipyridamole administration. Hence, my lifelong interest in nuclear cardiology was derived from several directions: my basic research on the sodium pump with the late Dr. Tom Smith, my early exposure to positron scintigraphy, and my association with Dr. Gerald Pohost.

WCR: *When you and Gerry Pohost started working in what became nuclear cardiology, some others around the country were also involved in that aspect of cardiology at that time. Could you comment on that?*

GAB: Yes, other very talented academic cardiologists had already begun to apply the principles of nuclear medicine to cardiology in the early 1970s. They included *William Strauss, Bertram Pitt, Barry Zaret, Dan Berman, Frans Wackers, Jim Willerson, Jim Ritchie,* and others. Dr. Willerson and his group were imaging myocardial infarcts with technetium-99m-pyrophosphate, another new imaging technology under investigation at that time.

WCR: *How do you view nuclear cardiology today*

particularly in comparison to stress echo, to MRI, and to CT?

GAB: The field of nuclear cardiology has matured a great deal over the last 30 years. It has a major role today in both detecting coronary disease using either exercise stress or pharmacologic stress and simultaneously evaluating left ventricular function with gated-SPECT technology. Its major role is in the detection of stress-induced ischemia, in assessing prognosis, and in determining myocardial viability in patients with coronary artery disease. MRI (magnetic resonance imaging) is a very promising technique for noninvasive cardiology, since its resolution is better than either nuclear cardiology or echocardiography. It has the capability of identifying subendocardial scar and quantitating the extent of transmural myocardial injury after infarction. This is not currently possible with nuclear cardiology or echocardiography. However, contrast echocardiography using microbubbles holds great promise for evaluating perfusion and imaging certain biologic targets like damaged endothelium. *Drs. Sanjiv Kaul, Jonathan Lindner,* and *Kevin Wei* are conducting pioneering research in the field of contrast echocardiography at the University of Virginia. *Dr. Chris Kramer* is leading a very exciting MRI clinical and research program here, as well.

WCR: *You read these nuclear images every week. Some private cardiology groups have nuclear capabilities in their offices. How good do you think those images are being read?*

GAB: Many community cardiologists are highly skilled in interpreting images and can easily distinguish true defects from artifacts. Then there are some individuals who are not as well trained and whose interpretive skills could be improved. The American Society of Nuclear Cardiology has introduced many CME programs and self-learning tools that have had a profound effect on improving the quality of nuclear cardiology interpretation worldwide.

WCR: *In the last 20 years, your research endeavors have broadened a good bit. Of the original investigations, which ones are you most proud of or pleased with, or do you think will have the most long-term impact?*

GAB: The work outside the basic experimental animal research that I'm most pleased about relates to the development of quantitative perfusion imaging in collaboration with my colleague of 25 years, *Dr. Denny Watson.* Applying quantitation algorithms to our everyday nuclear cardiology interpretation of perfusion images improved sensitivity and specificity of the technique. I am proud of the work we did in contributing to the body of knowledge regarding the prognostic value of stress perfusion imaging. Together with another colleague, *Dr. Robert Gibson,* we demonstrated that submaximal exercise thallium imaging was useful for risk stratification after acute myocardial infarction. I am proud of the work *Dr. Michael Ragosta* in our group did to show that resting thallium-201 imaging could accurately assess myocardial viability in patients with ischemic cardiomyopathy, and assist in identifying which patients with coronary artery disease and left ventricular dysfunction benefited most from revascularization surgery. I think this latter observation has had long-term impact. I am very pleased about all the research work we've done in the basic laboratory, defining the kinetics of new imaging tracers in animal models of ischemia and infarction. David Glover and Mirta Herrera have done a great job in overseeing this basic research program.

More recently, our laboratory has been engaged in research pertaining to the investigation of novel adenosine A_{2A} agonists for vasodilator imaging and for cardiac protection against inflammatory injury after coronary reperfusion during acute myocardial infarction. *Dr. Joel Linden* has been the leader in this area of research at UVA and nationally, and I was fortunate to be given the opportunity to collaborate with him. We've recently shown that when you infuse an adenosine A_{2A} agonist in a canine ischemia–reperfusion model, myocardial infarct size can be reduced by >50% following reflow, compared to just reflow alone. These agents also attenuate myocardial stunning that occurs with transient ischemia.

WCR: *You have a large division and nearly every faculty member in your division is doing some type of research. You've supported those endeavors, and you haven't hooked on to their work except when you were actively involved in it. Most publications coming out of your division do not have your name on them.*

GAB: That's correct, and that is by design. I never felt that the research output of an academic division had to be centered around the division chief's research interests and everything interrelated with that. What I have tried to do at UVA is to develop diverse areas of research in the fields of vascular biology, cellular and

clinical electrophysiology, experimental echocardiography, MRI investigation, cath lab-based physiologic research, and other areas. Although the division chief is a nuclear cardiologist, I have always advocated a balance in our clinical and research programs. I have never felt that just because I am the division chief that my name should appear on papers published by our faculty, especially if I had no substantive contribution to the studies.

WCR: *George, you've been chief of this cardiovascular division for 25 years now. I gather Bob Myerburg (Miami) is the only cardiovascular chief at a USA university institution with a longer tenure in his position. When I was here before, I talked to a number of your faculty members, and they love you. What are your secrets of success as a cardiovascular chief? You seem to love the position. You flourish in it. Your faculty members and fellows seem happy and enormously supportive of you. What recommendations do you have for new chiefs of cardiology or other chiefs of cardiology with, thus far, short tenures?*

GAB: Bill, thanks for those kind words. I am grateful that members of my division appreciate what I'm doing. I've always felt that the major role of the division chief is to be a mentor, advocate, and friend to faculty members and fellows working in the division. I always felt a strong responsibility to make sure that a new faculty member starts off his or her career on the right track and with proper resources and emotional support. For researchers, that means protecting their time (difficult in today's environment), providing them with startup funds to get their research work going until they can get their own funding, and working hard on their behalf to get them promoted when the time comes. I spend many hours putting together my promotion letters and supporting documents for faculty seeking promotion to the next academic level. One of the things I'm most proud of is that almost 95% of the faculty I've put up for promotion have been promoted to the next rank on the first try. I hold the belief that you must earn the trust and loyalty of those who commit so much time and energy to making an academic cardiology division productive, collegial, and fun. Young faculty members are the future of a program, and they need to know that you're behind them, that you're defending them, and that you're an advocate for their well-being. That means often fighting for more resources and money for their professional growth and satisfaction.

Another piece of advice is to foster good interdisciplinary collaboration within and outside the division. One of the major strengths at UVA is that our cardiovascular division has extremely good working relationships with our cardiac surgeons, our interventional radiologists, our cardiovascular basic scientists, our molecular biologists, and our biomedical engineers, among others. Whenever possible, I have tried to foster these collaborations. As a result, the UVA Heart Center is well represented by these multiple groups who work closely with us on a daily basis. Our most recent successful collaboration is with our endocrinology colleagues in the field of diabetes. We recently were awarded an NIH Program Project Grant in cardiovascular disease and diabetes in which *Drs. Ian Sarembock* and *Coleen McNamara* from our division are major participants.

Another recommendation I have for a new chief is to leave good people alone and let them flourish without micromanagement or interference. If you have people with tremendous talent in either research or clinical disciplines, don't micromanage them. Empower them, delegate authority to them, and give them the resources needed to build up their own program. Our invasive cardiology laboratories, our electrophysiology laboratories, our noninvasive laboratories, and our heart failure and our preventive cardiology programs are all headed by superb people who have been at UVA for a long time. They are given the responsibility to run those labs or clinical programs, but they know they can come to me for help and support, and I will be a strong advocate for them in negotiations with the Department of Medicine, the hospital, or the dean's office. I think they know I trust them and don't second guess their decisions. In return, I hope I earned their trust and loyalty. A cardiology division is only as good as its faculty. If they are happy and productive, a division stays healthy and is not plagued by a high turnover rate.

WCR: *George, I spent a year at Hopkins as a house officer in medicine. I was intrigued by watching Richard S. Ross, who was then chief of cardiology there. What a wonderful relationship he had with the cardiovascular surgeons! He instilled that into his fellow faculty members. That relationship was the best I had ever observed. In many places there is an unwritten rule of antagonism between the cardiologists and cardiovascular surgeons. You seem to be in Dick Ross' tract.*

GAB: Well, I hope so. I have very high respect for *Dr. Irving Kron*, the chief of thoracic and cardiovascular surgery at UVA. We served as co-directors of our heart center for 9 years. We worked very hard to maintain good working relationships between surgeons and cardiologists, and do a great deal of problem solving together with our heart center administrator, *Ms. Karen Forsman.*

WCR: *I gather that you have no interest in being chairman of a department of medicine anywhere. Is that correct?*

GAB: I've never desired to become a chair of medicine or a dean. I love cardiology. I always wanted to maintain my identity as a cardiologist. I still have a wonderful patient practice, and I will never give that up. I see patients either 2 or 3 half-days a week when I'm in town, and I've done that for years. I still attend on the wards 6 weeks a year, cover the stress test laboratory 4 days a month, and read nuclear cardiology scans 1 day a week. My only other major administrative role at UVA is that I've been president of the clinical staff of the hospital for 4 years and have a seat on the Medical Center Operating Board, which oversees all aspects of our medical center.

WCR: *The fact that you have no desire to go on to another position like chairman of a department of medicine must be helpful in your relationship with the chairman of medicine. Is that appropriate or fair? How much dealing do you have with the departmental chairmen?*

GAB: The chair of the Department of Medicine has delegated virtually all of the administrative responsibility for running the cardiology division to me. I have few interactions with him since our clinical activities are integrated into a service line designated as the Heart Center, and our research activities are integrated into the Cardiovascular Research Center that comprises cardiovascular researchers from multiple departments. My main involvement with the Department of Medicine relates to the residency teaching program in internal medicine.

Because I've been at UVA a long time, I've been able to develop close working relationships with the administrators and deal with them on a one-to-one basis in planning and negotiations. The one significant issue I've had with the 3 chairs of the Department of Medicine whom I've worked with these past 25 years is my desire to keep more of our clinical revenue in cardiology.

WCR: *How many fellows in cardiology do you have in total and how many per year?*

GAB: We have 5 fellows a year in our basic 3-year program, but we have fellows who stay here for up to 5 years because of advanced training in research or clinical subspecialties, or both. We have fellows who come here just for research training, and those who are here from the outside for specialized training in areas such as clinical electrophysiology, noninvasive imaging, or interventional cardiology. If I counted them all, we probably have 25 to 30 fellows in the program at any one time.

WCR: *If you take the 15 3-year fellows and 2 or 3 specialty clinical fellows, how many applications do you actually get for those positions? I guess you'd take 5 that first year of fellowship?*

GAB: We get more than 450 applications for those 5 fellowship positions. We usually interview about 50 to 60 applicants from which we match 5. I've been blessed with 2 outstanding fellowship directors, *Dr. David Haines* and, starting this year, *Dr. Amy Tucker.*

WCR: *You are very much involved in selecting the fellows. What are you looking for in these applicants?*

GAB: I've always felt it important to seek fellowship applicants who have shown outstanding qualities as students, interns, and residents. I rely a great deal on the recommendations from their department heads and their record of achievements. We look for diversity and balance. We don't want 5 fellows to all track in 1 subspecialty or 5 fellows who all want to become molecular cardiologists. We look for excellence in prior educational and training experiences. The interviews at UVA are very important. For the past 25 years, I've interviewed all the applicants invited to UVA and have always participated in the generation of our rank list prior to the match.

WCR: *When I went to Baylor University Medical Center 8 years ago, Baylor had a cardiology fellowship program, at that time 3 new cardiologists a year*

FIGURE 12. GAB receiving the Distinguished Achievement Award from the American Heart Association's Council on Clinical Cardiology at the annual scientific sessions in 1993. To the right of GAB is *Dr. Joseph Alpert* and to his left, *Dr. Gerry Pohost.*

and then it went to 2 a year. I wondered at that time whether or not we were training too many cardiologists. And yet, every one of these fellows when he or she finishes gets several offers for cardiology positions. Do you think training 5 cardiologists a year is too many now or too few, and do we have too many cardiologists in this country or too few?

GAB: Bill, you are bringing up some interesting points with that question. Ten years ago, The American College of Cardiology came out with a position statement that we were training too many cardiologists, and it was felt at that time that fellowship programs should be cutting back. There was a fear that managed care would transform the referral patterns, and that access to a cardiovascular specialist would be limited. At that time, people were concerned with the gatekeeper issue, feeling that primary care physicians would not refer patients to cardiovascular specialists. That led to fellowship programs like our own cutting back. We had cut back to 4 fellows a year as a result of those fears, and other programs were cut back as well. Today, we recognize that a shortage of cardiologists exists, and our predictions of too many cardiologists in the workforce were erroneous.

There are private practice groups who are desperate to expand personnel, but there are not enough fellows around to fill those positions, particularly in general cardiology. There are medium-sized hospitals in smaller cities that don't have any cardiovascular specialists. With the marked increase in our elderly population and the epidemic of obesity and diabetes in this country, more and more patients with cardiovascular disease will be encountered. Even though the mortality rate for cardiovascular disease is falling, its prevalence is increasing. The number of patients with heart failure is rapidly increasing. Management of patients with atrial fibrillation has become so complex that most primary care physicians refer patients with this arrhythmia to cardiologists. In fact, many general cardiologists aren't comfortable with treating atrial

fibrillation patients and refer them to electrophysiologists. Thus, I believe we're heading for a potential shortage of cardiologists in the US. *Dr. Bruce Fye*, who is president of The American College of Cardiology, is taking on the workforce issue as one of his major priorities during his presidency.

WCR: *George, you have been an elected president of several major organizations in this country, including the American College of Cardiology, the Association of University Cardiologists, and the Association of Professors of Cardiology. You were president of the Council of Clinical Cardiology of the American Heart Association. Some ACC presidents have taken leave of their regular professional position during their presidency. You seem to handle these outside activities without losing too many steps. How have you handled the presidencies of these organizations, particularly the ACC, without a huge disruption of your usual responsibilities?*

GAB: The time commitment was greatest for the American College of Cardiology. I was fortunate to have tremendously supportive colleagues at UVA who covered for me when I had to be away, and who were able to address acute problems of my patients and see them in the emergency room, if necessary, in my absence. I also worked out my inpatient attending responsibilities such that they were fulfilled before March of the beginning of the ACC presidency year to March of the following year when I finished. Thus, from March 2000 to March 2001, I did not cover any inpatient attending rotation.

During my presidency, I didn't go to any overseas meetings. The reason was that my wife, Emily Covric, was diagnosed with metastatic pancreatic cancer 4 months into my ACC presidency. I also only attended meetings in the US or visited ACC chapters if I could leave my home and return the same day. The same was true for meetings at the Heart House in Bethesda. I often left home at 5:00 A.M. to arrive in Bethesda for ACC business by 8:00 A.M. and then returned the same day. With respect to travel in the earlier years, I always tried to catch up on my UVA-related work by devoting an average of 12 hours of work on weekends when in town.

WCR: *You mentioned that Bruce Fye in his presidency of the ACC decided to tackle the issue of too few cardiologists. What did you try to do during your ACC presidency?*

GAB: I was involved with several initiatives, including laying the groundwork for the ACCardio initiative which provides comprehensive web-based learning and scientific information, the creation of a new 501(c)(6) entity to permit more resources devoted to advocacy on the federal and state level and establishment of a PAC, the funding and organization for a quality improvement tool for cath labs, the implementation of the GAP (Guidelines Applied in Practice) project in Michigan originally planned by my predecessor, *Dr. Tim Garson*, and the implementation of the recommendations of the Task Force for the 2first Century. Prior to my presidency, I headed up the effort that led to the ACC's 5-year strategic plan.

WCR: *Although you are president of the ACC for just for 1 year, you have the year before you actually take office and the year after you actually serve where you still have a number of responsibilities. How much time did you spend on it during your presidency and those other 2 years?*

GAB: I started getting involved to a significant extent with the ACC when I became chair of the Board of Governors. I was the governor for Virginia at that time. As you know, the College has both a Board of Trustees and a Board of Governors. The Board of Governors represents the states in the governance of the College. When you chair the Board of Governors, you serve on the ACC Executive Committee. Then, a few years later, I was nominated to be vice president, which meant 4 more years on the Executive Committee. During this leadership experience, I served on many committees and task forces. I participated in almost weekly conference calls of one sort or another, engaged in reviewing many documents (e.g., guidelines), and participated in a group of e-mail list serves. Of course, I reduced the time devoted to these duties when my wife, Emily, became ill.

One of the most gratifying experiences I had as a volunteer for the ACC was working with *Chris McEntee* and her superb staff at Heart House. Chris has been a truly outstanding CEO for the College, and she assisted me greatly when I was president.

WCR: *George, can you describe what your private practice is like? You have mentioned that you are a practicing cardiologist and that you see patients 2 or 3 half-days a week. How many patients do you generally see a week? How does your private practice work?*

GAB: I have 3 half-days where I see patients myself with a cardiovascular nurse specialist, and 1 afternoon when I see patients with fellows. Usually, I try to schedule 7 to 8 office patients in a half-day in the office.

WCR: *Are most of those new patients?*

GAB: I have about 3 new patients a month. Since I've been at UVA for so long, I have a group of patients I've followed for many years. I try to follow my patients in the hospital when they need to be admitted, but often one of my colleagues who is attending on one of our cardiology inpatient services covers them for me. None of our attending faculty attends on general medicine wards. We cover 3 inpatient services and a cardiology consult service.

WCR: *It's my understanding, George, that a lot of your colleagues who are chiefs of cardiovascular divisions in university centers in the USA don't have any private practice. Have you thought that having a practice has helped you be a better division chief?*

GAB: Sustaining a clinical practice helps me stay

FIGURE 13. GAB in his office signing his *Nuclear Cardiology* book for a visiting professor, 1995.

current with clinical cardiology. It may or may not have made me a better chief, but I think it has forced me to at least stay knowledgeable on how to care for patients with coronary disease, hypertension, heart failure, and so forth. I am closer to my colleagues by having a practice since, when I'm in the clinic, I see them and we have a chance to talk and catch up. Perhaps that has helped me the most because not being clinically active would have made me isolated. I never wanted to be in an "ivory tower" and be invisible to colleagues, fellows, and nurses. I might also say that some of my patients became good friends whom Emily and I saw socially. Another advantage of having a practice was that I had the opportunity to persuade many of my patients to vote for my wife when she ran for the state senate. She won both of her elections!

WCR: *George, I know you've been on the editorial board of* The American Journal of Cardiology *since 1982 and have reviewed numerous manuscripts. You have reviewed them in a timely fashion, and always your reviews have been quite thorough. I realize that you are on the editorial board at one time or another of probably 20 medical journals. You obviously take on these non-divisional responsibilities in an extremely responsible fashion. You must get several manuscripts to review every week plus the manuscripts that your staff produces, that you, I'm sure, go over. How do you handle all of that?*

GAB: Bill, I review on the average about 1 manuscript a week. I always considered it one of my academic responsibilities. I must say, I always learn something when reviewing, particularly when I've written accompanying editorials. Today, I can no longer review every manuscript that is requested of me.

WCR: *You've received a number of awards and honors for your contributions through the years. Which ones are you most proud of?*

FIGURE 14. GAB receiving the James B. Herrick Award from the president of the American Heart Association, *Dr. Rose Marie Robertson*, on November 14, 2000. To his right is *Dr. Robert Bonow*, who was chair of the Council on Clinical Cardiology at that time.

FIGURE 15. GAB receiving a plaque commemorating his having given the Bishop Lecture at the 4first Annual Scientific Sessions of the American College of Cardiology, 1992. *Dr. Bernard Gersh*, now at the Mayo Clinic, is also in the picture.

GAB: I am grateful for the awards I've received throughout the years. The James B. Herrick Award of the American Heart Association was particularly meaningful for me since it permitted me to give a lecture regarding my vision for the future of cardiovascular medicine in the next 30 years. Perhaps most gratifying are the young investigator awards that fellows who worked in our laboratory received at the various annual meetings of national cardiology societies.

WCR: *George, you've been a visiting professor at nearly 150 university medical centers around the country and around the world. That's a lot of traveling and it's a little more difficult, I suspect, to travel out of Charlottesville, Virginia, than it is out of Dallas, Texas, because the number of direct flights you have to cities out of Charlottesville is limited. How have you been able to manage all of that travel to other centers and continue to carry out your responsibilities in Charlottesville so well?*

GAB: I don't know the number. Many were for just 1 day. I did more traveling earlier in my career—too much as I look back on it—than I do now. Traveling was hard, and I was away longer than I should have been. This meant having to devote a lot of time trying to catch up when I got back. In recent years, I've tried to leave on the last possible flight after work and return as soon as I could and almost always taking the red-eye flight when returning from the West Coast. During my wife's 15-month illness in 2000-2001, I was away overnight perhaps only 4 or 5 nights.

WCR: *What is your budget for the division of cardiology? Is that appropriate to ask?*

GAB: We have a total revenue stream amounting to about $16 million a year. Of this amount, approximately $9 million comes from clinical revenue. The remainder comes from research grants, endowed chairs, state teaching dollars, and other sources. At the end of the year, we have enough of an overage to put money in our reserve account and to pay bonuses to faculty members after all expenses are paid. We have

a superb fulltime business administrator, *Mr. James Carnes*, who has an MBA and does a great job in administering the finances and personnel.

WCR: *Are your entire faculty in the division of cardiology on salary?*

GAB: Everyone has a base salary. We have an incentive plan that provides supplements to faculty based on formulas that relate to financial performance and productivity.

WCR: *Do you think it would be ideal if every cardiologist in the country were on salary?*

GAB: I've really never thought of that possibility. I'm a big believer in incentives and having people know that they will be financially rewarded for increased productivity.

WCR: *George, do you have some non-professional hobbies or interests? Your time commitments professionally are enormous. Do you have time to read non-medical books?*

GAB: I enjoy reading. I read mostly fiction for relaxation and follow the works of authors like *John Irving, Philip Roth, John Grisham*, and others. I like mysteries and can read them rapidly. I read 3 newspapers a day whenever I can. I awake early in the morning to peruse *The New York Times*, the *Washington Post*, and the local Charlottesville paper. I love sports now, just like I did earlier in life. I have season tickets to the UVA football and basketball games. I enjoy watching sports on television, enjoy skiing and hiking, and just acquired a liking for fly-fishing. I continue to have an interest in and am a supporter of the arts. Emily and I acquired a collection of art from local painters, as well as pieces of aboriginal art from Australia. I'm on the board of directors of our local repertory theater group, LIVE ARTS.

WCR: *George, I remember talking to you years ago and you mentioned meeting your wife, Emily, on an airplane. It must have been very exciting through the*

FIGURE 16. GAB and his wife *Emily* in the early 1990s.

member of the Charlottesville School Board. She then became chairwoman of the school board. In 1993, the sitting governor of Virginia, *George Allen*, proposed to cut hundreds of millions of dollars from the education budget so that the state would have more funds to build additional prisons. Emily and other supporters of public education and higher education were very upset about cutting the education budget in order to build more prisons. Somebody suggested to my wife that she run for political office to advocate for public education funding. After meeting with local Democratic leaders, she mounted a grass-roots campaign for the state senate, which lasted 2 years. It was successful, and she unseated an incumbent who backed the governor's fiscal policies. Four years later, in 1999, she ran for re-election and won every precinct in every county by large margins. In the spring of 2000, she began her campaign as the Democratic candidate for lieutenant governor of Virginia. She was favored to win and was predicted to eventually become the first woman governor of Virginia. In July of that year, she was diagnosed as having cancer of the pancreas and had to withdraw from that race. She continued serving in the state legislature, and despite vigorous chemotherapy regimen, she never missed a vote in the 2001 legislative session. In January 2001, she also took on the responsibility of the chair of the state Democratic Party.

WCR: *You have how many children?*

GAB: A total of 5 children, 3 from my former marriage and 2 stepsons. Two live in Los Angeles, 1 in Chicago, 1 in New York City, and 1 in Philadelphia. They are all very close.

WCR: *Any physicians in there?*

GAB: *Ray Wadlow*, Emily's oldest son, is now a resident in medicine at the University of Pennsylvania. He is going to Dana Farber in Boston for his oncology fellowship in July 2002.

WCR: *Any television personalities in there?*

GAB: *Jeff Wadlow*, my youngest stepson, finished graduate school at the University of Southern California film school. He is now a director and actor in Hollywood. He just signed a contract to make his movie, *Living the Lie*, for Universal Pictures. My eldest son, *Michael*, has worked for NBC and ABC in marketing and advertising sales for television series. My daughter, *Amy*, is a lawyer in Manhattan, and my other daughter, *Leslie*, is CEO of a nonprofit foundation in Chicago.

WCR: *George, could you describe a bit about your sleep habits? What time do you wake up in the morning? What time do you get into work? What time do you leave the hospital at night? What time do you get*

years to discuss her career with her. Could you talk about Emily and your relationship?

GAB: We, indeed, met on an airplane. I was coming back from Salt Lake City where I was participating in a CME course. The plane stopped in Chicago. Emily was a journalist at that time in Washington and was covering the American Bar Association convention in Chicago for her newspaper, *The Legal Times* of Washington. I was sitting on the aisle seat and she sat in the window seat. No one sat between us in the middle seat. We started a casual conversation; 3 weeks later I called her for a date, and we went to the Kennedy Center in Washington, DC, to see a *Tennessee Williams'* play. We dated over the next year and then married. I had been divorced for about 3-1/2 years, and she had been separated and divorced for about a year.

WCR: *You got married when?*

GAB: We were married in August 1981.

WCR: *Your wife is the sister of a prominent television person.*

GAB: Emily is the oldest of 4 siblings. Her youngest sister is *Katie Couric* who is the co-host of *The Today Show*.

WCR: *How did Emily get into politics?*

GAB: After we married, Emily moved to Charlottesville and began her career here by writing freelance articles for newspapers and magazines and writing books. She wrote 2 books that were published, *The Trial Lawyers* and *The Divorce Lawyers*.

WCR: *Is she a lawyer?*

GAB: No, she wrote freelance articles and books related to the legal profession for *The Washington Post*, *Washingtonian Magazine*, and other publications. She also edited newsletters related to the practice of law. I suppose you would call her a legal journalist. Her first foray into public service was as a

FIGURE 17. GAB, his wife Emily, and family during the Thanksgiving holiday, 1998.

FIGURE 18. GAB congratulating *President George W. Bush* after President Bush's speech at the 2001 annual meeting of the American College of Cardiology. Also shown from left to right are *Governor Jeb Bush*, *Dr. Douglas Zipes*, and Dr. Bruce Fye.

home? What time do you go to bed? What are your evenings usually like?

GAB: I usually wake up about 6:00 A.M. I am at work by 7:00 A.M. or 8:00 A.M. For many years, I wouldn't get home until 8:00 or 8:30 P.M. Because I only live 5 minutes from the hospital, I would often go home for dinner with the family when the children were at home, and then return to my office at the hospital to work a few more hours. I go to bed by 11:30 P.M.

WCR: *In general you try to get 7 hours sleep?*

GAB: I try to get a minimum of 6-1/2 to 7 hours of

sleep. I never get 8 hours of sleep, even on the weekend.

WCR: *Of all your activities, and let's limit it to your professional activities, what are you most proud of?*

GAB: It's hard to pinpoint the 1 single thing I'm most proud of. I guess the achievement I'm most proud of is watching the members of my division, particularly those whom I recruited to UVA, become professionally successful and receive recognition for their own accomplishments. I'm glad that their success was attained with my support and encouragement. This has meant more to me than my own academic accomplishments. I'm pleased to have played a role in the transformation of our division from a very strong clinical division to one that has now also been recognized for its contributions to science and the body of medical knowledge in cardiology. A second area I'm proud of is my research group's contributions to advancing the field of nuclear cardiology. A third area I'm proud of was the opportunity to contribute in my role as president of the American College of Cardiology and being given a chance to represent the profession on a national level.

WCR: *What about non-professional activities?*

GAB: On a personal level, what gave me tremendous happiness was the close partnership and loving relationship I had with my wife. We were best friends and mutually supportive of each other in every way. During her illness, I spent countless hours researching with her oncologist the most current scientific advances in pancreatic cancer therapy to determine what treatment might be best for her. We battled this dreadful cancer as a team. Emily was the most courageous person I've every known. Throughout her illness, she remained upbeat and optimistic and continued working full time. She devoted much of her time helping other cancer patients and raising money for the UVA Cancer Center.|| I also derive great satisfaction when all 5 children, spouses, and grandchildren spend time together. We are all quite close.

WCR: *George, is there anything that we haven't discussed that you think you would like to discuss?*

GAB: I think this is a very exciting time for car-

||Senator Emily Couric, George's wife, died on October 18, 2001, after gallantly fighting her disease for 15 months.

diovascular medicine. The disciplines of molecular genetics and proteomics will have a major impact in our field. The field of imaging will continue to advance with the emergence of molecular and targeted imaging. Stem-cell technology will be exploited in cardiology, and some day damaged myocardium will be repopulated with new myocytes. When I was in medical school in 1962, 40% of admitted patients with acute myocardial infarction died. Today, 95% will survive. This improved survival is the result of the discovery of new drugs and new technology. Patients with heart failure can live much longer and with a far better quality of life than 40 years ago. One major concern I have for the future is the increase in premature coronary artery disease we will encounter with the current epidemics of obesity and type 2 diabetes in the country. We need to do a better job in primary prevention and getting our children to have better nutrition and exercise more.

WCR: *George, not only on my behalf, but also on the behalf of the readers of* The American Journal of Cardiology*, I want to sincerely thank you for pouring your soul out so to speak so that we all get to know you better.*

GAB: Thank you.

GAB's Best Publications as Selected by GAB

1. Beller GA, Smith TW, Abelmann WH, Haber E, Hood WB Jr. Digitalis intoxication: a prospective clinical study with serum level correlations. *N Engl J Med* 1971;284:989–997.

19. Beller GA, Conroy J, Smith TW. Ischemia-induced alterations in myocardial (Na$^+$ + K$^+$)-ATPase and cardiac glycoside binding. *J Clin Invest* 1976;57:341–350.

23. Khaw BA, Beller GA, Haber E, Smith TW. Localization of cardiac myosin-specific antibody in experimental myocardial infarction. *J Clin Invest* 1976;58:439–446.

24. Pohost GM, Zir LM, Moore RH, McKusick KA, Guiney TE, Beller GA. Differentiation of transiently ischemic from infarcted myocardium by serial imaging after a single dose of thallium-201. *Circulation* 1977;55:294–302.

25. Beller GA, Khaw BA, Haber E, Smith TW. Localization of radiolabeled cardiac myosin-specific antibody in myocardial infarcts: comparison with technetium-99m stannous pyrophosphate. *Circulation* 1977;55:74–78.

27. Beller GA, Hood WB Jr, Smith TW. Effects of ischemia and coronary reperfusion on regional myocardial blood flow and on the epicardial electrogram. *Cardiovasc Res* 1977;11:489–498.

29. Nichols AB, Cochavi S, Moore RH, Beller GA. Detection of experimental pulmonary emboli in dogs by sequential positron imaging of ^{15}O-carbon-dioxide. *Circ Res* 1978;42:53–63.

41. Berger BC, Watson DD, Burwell LR, Crosby IK, Wellons HA, Teates CD, Beller GA. Redistribution of thallium at rest in patients with stable and unstable angina and the effect of coronary artery bypass surgery. *Circulation* 1979;60:1114–1125.

49. Beller GA, Watson DD, Ackell P, Pohost GM. Time course of thallium-201 redistribution after transient myocardial ischemia. *Circulation* 1980;61:791–797.

51. Berger BC, Watson DD, Taylor GJ, Burwell LR, Martin RP, Beller GA. Assessment of the effect of coronary collaterals on regional myocardial perfusion using thallium-201 scintigraphy. *Am J Cardiol* 1980;46:365–370.

57. Watson DD, Campbell NP, Read EK, Gibson RS, Teates CD, Beller GA. Spatial and temporal quantitation of plane thallium myocardial images. *J Nucl Med* 1981;22:577–584.

58. Berger BC, Watson DD, Taylor GJ, Craddock GB, Martin RP, Teates CD, Beller GA. Quantitative thallium-201 exercise scintigraphy for detection of coronary artery disease. *J Nucl Med* 1981;22:585–593.

60. Grunwald AM, Watson DD, Holzgrefe HH Jr, Irving JF, Beller GA. Myocardial thallium-201 kinetics in normal and ischemic myocardium. *Circulation* 1981;64:610–618.

61. Gibson RS, Taylor GJ, Watson DD, Stebbins PT, Martin RP, Crampton RS, Beller GA. Predicting the extent and location of coronary artery disease during the early post-infarction period by quantitative thallium-201 scintigraphy. *Am J Cardiol* 1981;47:1010–1019.

68. Gibson RS, Watson DD, Carabello BA, Holt ND, Beller GA. Clinical implications of increased lung uptake of thallium-201 during exercise scintigraphy 2 weeks after myocardial infarction. *Am J Cardiol* 1982;49:1586–1593.

73. Gibson RS, Crampton RS, Watson DD, Carabello BA, Holt ND, Beller GA.

Precordial S-T segment depression during acute inferior myocardial infarction: clinical, scintigraphic and angiographic correlations. *Circulation* 1982;66:732–741.

80. Gibson RS, Watson DD, Taylor GJ, Crosby IK, Wellons HL, Holt ND, Beller GA. Prospective assessment of regional myocardial perfusion before and after coronary revascularization surgery by quantitative thallium-201 scintigraphy. *J Am Coll Cardiol* 1983;1:804–815.

83. Gibson RS, Watson DD, Craddock GB, Crampton RS, Kaiser DL, Denny MJ, Beller GA. Prediction of cardiac events after uncomplicated myocardial infarction: a prospective study comparing predischarge exercise thallium-201 scintigraphy and coronary angiography. *Circulation* 1983;68:321–336.

87. Beller GA, Holzgrefe HH, Watson DD. Effects of dipyridamole-induced vasodilation on myocardial uptake and clearance kinetics of thallium-201. *Circulation* 1983;68:1328–1338.

89. Nygaard TW, Gibson RS, Ryan JM, Gascho JA, Watson DD, Beller GA. Prevalence of high-risk thallium-201 scintigraphic findings in left main coronary artery stenosis: comparison with patients with multiple- and single-vessel coronary artery disease. *Am J Cardiol* 1984;53:462–469.

99. Beller GA, Holzgrefe HH, Watson DD. Intrinsic washout rates of thallium-201 in normal and ischemic myocardium after dipyridamole-induced vasodilation. *Circulation* 1985;71:378–386.

101. Pamelia FX, Gibson RS, Watson DD, Craddock GB, Sirowatka J, Beller GA. Prognosis with chest pain and normal thallium-201 exercise scintigrams. *Am J Cardiol* 1985;55:920–926.

105. Haines DE, Beller GA, Watson DD, Nygaard TW, Craddock GB, Cooper AA, Gibson RS. A prospective clinical, scintigraphic, angiographic and functional evaluation following inferior myocardial infarction with and without right ventricular dysfunction. *J Am Coll Cardiol* 1985;6:995–1003.

109. Granato JE, Watson DD, Flanagan TL, Gascho JA, Beller GA. Myocardial thallium-201 kinetics during coronary occlusion and reperfusion: influence of method of reflow and timing of thallium-201 administration. *Circulation* 1986;73:150–160.

114. Gibson RS, Beller GA, Gheorghiade M, Nygaard TW, Watson DD, Huey BL, Sayer SL, Kaiser DL. The prevalence and clinical significance of residual myocardial ischemia 2 weeks after uncomplicated non-Q wave infarction: a prospective natural history study. *Circulation* 1986;73:1186–1198.

118. Granato JE, Watson DD, Flanagan TL, Beller GA. Myocardial thallium-201 kinetics and regional flow alterations with 3 hours of coronary occlusion and either rapid reperfusion through a totally patent vessel or slow reperfusion through a critical stenosis. *J Am Coll Cardiol* 1987;9:109–118.

124. Gheorghiade M, St. Clair J, St. Clair C, Beller GA. Hemodynamic effects of intravenous digoxin in patients with severe heart failure initially treated with diuretics and vasodilators. *J Am Coll Cardiol* 1987;9:849–857.

125. Haines DE, Beller GA, Watson DD, Kaiser DL, Sayer SL, Gibson RS. Exercise-induced ST segment elevation two weeks after uncomplicated myocardial infarction: contributing factors and prognostic significance. *J Am Coll Cardiol* 1987;9:996–1003.

127. Sellers TD, Beller GA, Gibson RS, Watson DD, DiMarco JP. Prevalence of ischemia by quantitative thallium-201 scintigraphy in patients with ventricular tachycardia or fibrillation inducible by programmed stimulation. *Am J Cardiol* 1987;59:828–832.

134. Wilson WW, Gibson RS, Nygaard TW, Craddock GB, Watson DD, Crampton RS, Beller GA. Acute myocardial infarction associated with single vessel coronary artery disease: an analysis of clinical outcome and the prognostic importance of vessel patency and residual ischemic myocardium. *J Am Coll Cardiol* 1988;11:223–234.

137. Kaul S, Lilly DR, Gascho JA, Watson DD, Gibson RS, Oliner CA, Ryan JM, Beller GA. Prognostic utility of the exercise thallium-201 test in ambulatory patients with chest pain: comparison with cardiac catheterization. *Circulation* 1988;77:745–758.

138. Gascho JA, Flanagan TL, Jennings CF, Beller GA. Mechanism for remote myocardial ischemia after coronary occlusion in open-chest dogs. *Cardiovasc Res* 1988;22:398–406.

141. Touchstone DA, Beller GA, Nygaard TW, Watson DD, Tedesco C, Kaul S. Functional significance of predischarge exercise thallium-201 findings following intravenous streptokinase therapy during acute myocardial infarction. *Am Heart J* 1988;116:1500–1507.

143. Huey BL, Beller GA, Kaiser DL, Gibson RS. A comprehensive analysis of myocardial infarction due to left circumflex artery occlusion: comparison with infarction due to right coronary artery and left anterior descending artery occlusion. *J Am Coll Cardiol* 1988;12:1156–1166.

149. Reed DC, Beller GA, Nygaard TW, Tedesco C, Watson DD, Burwell LR. The clinical efficacy and scintigraphic evaluation of post-coronary bypass patients undergoing percutaneous transluminal coronary angioplasty for recurrent angina pectoris. *Am Heart J* 1989;117:60–71.

152. Wackers FJT, Berman DS, Maddahi J, Watson DD, Beller GA, Strauss HW, Boucher CA, Picard M, Holman BL, Fridrich R, et al. Technetium-99m hexakis 2-methoxyisobutyl isonitrile: human biodistribution, dosimetry, safety, and preliminary comparison to thallium-201 for myocardial perfusion imaging. *J Nucl Med* 1989;30:301–311.

155. Sinusas AJ, Beller GA, Smith WH, Vinson EL, Brookeman V, Watson DD. Quantitative planar imaging with technetium-99m methoxy-isobutyl isonitrile: comparison of uptake patterns with thallium-201. *J Nucl Med* 1989;30:1456–1463.

156. Varma SK, Watson DD, Beller GA. Quantitative comparison of thallium-

201 scintigraphy after exercise and dipyridamole in coronary artery disease. *Am J Cardiol* 1989;64:871–877.

161. Sinusas AJ, Watson DD, Cannon JM Jr, Beller GA. Effect of ischemia and postischemic dysfunction on myocardial uptake of technetium-99m-labeled methoxyisobutyl isonitrile and thallium-201. *J Am Coll Cardiol* 1989;14:1785–1793.

164. Moore CA, Cannon J, Watson DD, Kaul S, Beller GA. Thallium 201 kinetics in stunned myocardium characterized by severe postischemic systolic dysfunction. *Circulation* 1990;81:1622–1632.

169. Sinusas AJ, Trautman KA, Bergin JD, Watson DD, Ruiz M, Smith WH, Beller GA. Quantification of area at risk during coronary occlusion and degree of myocardial salvage after reperfusion with technetium-99m methoxyisobutyl isonitrile. *Circulation* 1990;82:1424–1437.

170. Gasperetti CM, Burwell LR, Beller GA. Prevalence of and variables associated with silent myocardial ischemia on exercise thallium-201 stress testing. *J Am Coll Cardiol* 1990;16:115–123.

171. Marieb MA, Beller GA, Gibson RS, Lerman BB, Kaul S. Clinical relevance of exercise-induced ventricular arrhythmias in suspected coronary artery disease. *Am J Cardiol* 1990;66:172–178.

173. Granato JE, Watson DD, Belardinelli L, Cannon JM, Beller GA. Effects of dipyridamole and aminophylline on hemodynamics, regional myocardial blood flow and thallium-201 washout in the setting of a critical coronary stenosis. *J Am Coll Cardiol* 1990;16:1760–1770.

175. Villanueva FS, Kaul S, Smith WH, Watson DD, Varma SK, Beller GA. Prevalence and correlates of increased lung/heart ratio of thallium-201 during dipyridamole stress imaging for suspected coronary artery disease. *Am J Cardiol* 1990;66:1324–1328.

192. Pollock SG, Abbott RD, Boucher CA, Beller GA, Kaul S. Independent and incremental prognostic value of tests performed in hierarchical order to evaluate patients with suspected coronary artery disease. Validation of models based on these tests. *Circulation* 1992;85:237–248.

193. Edwards NC, Sinusas AJ, Bergin JD, Watson DD, Ruiz M, Beller GA. Influence of subendocardial ischemia on transmural myocardial function. *Am J Physiol* 1992;262:H568–H576.

194. Villanueva FS, Smith WH, Watson DD, Beller GA. ST-segment depression during dipyridamole infusion, and its clinical, scintigraphic and hemodynamic correlates. *Am J Cardiol* 1992;69:445–448.

196. Beller GA, Granato JE, Cannon JM, Belardinelli L, Watson DD. Effects of intracoronary dipyridamole infusion on regional myocardial blood flow and intrinsic thallium-201 washout in dogs with a critical coronary stenosis. *Am Heart J* 1992;124:56–64.

200. Watson DD, Smith WH, Beller GA, Vinson EL, Taillefer R. Blinded evaluation of planar technetium-99m-sestamibi myocardial perfusion studies. *J Nucl Med* 1992;33:668–675.

205. Haber HL, Beller GA, Watson DD, Gimple LW. Exercise thallium-201 scintigraphy after thrombolytic therapy with or without angioplasty for acute myocardial infarction. *Am J Cardiol* 1993;71:1257–1261.

206. Desmarais RL, Kaul S, Watson DD, Beller GA. Do false positive thallium-201 scans lead to unnecessary catheterization? Outcome of patients with perfusion defects on quantitative planar thallium-201 scintigraphy. *J Am Coll Cardiol* 1993;21:1058–1063.

207. Beller GA, Glover DK, Edwards NC, Ruiz M, Simanis JP, Watson DD. 99mTc-sestamibi uptake and retention during myocardial ischemia and reperfusion. *Circulation* 1993;87:2033–2042.

210. Ragosta M, Beller GA, Watson DD, Kaul S, Gimple LW. Quantitative planar rest-redistribution 201Tl imaging in detection of myocardial viability and prediction of improvement in left ventricular function after coronary bypass surgery in patients with severely depressed left ventricular function. *Circulation* 1993;87:1630–1641.

217. Sinusas AJ, Bergin JD, Edwards NC, Watson DD, Ruiz M, Makuch RW, Smith WH, Beller GA. Redistribution of 99mTc-sestamibi and 201Tl in the presence of a severe coronary artery stenosis. *Circulation* 1994;89:2332–2341.

221. Taylor AJ, Sackett MC, Beller GA. The degree of ST-segment depression on symptom-limited exercise testing: relation to the myocardial ischemic burden as determined by thallium-201 scintigraphy. *Am J Cardiol* 1995;75:228–231.

222. Glover DK, Ruiz M, Sansoy V, Barrett RJ, Beller GA. Effect of N-0861, a selective adenosine A1 receptor antagonist, on pharmacologic stress imaging with adenosine. *J Nucl Med* 1995;36:270–275.

223. Glover DK, Ruiz M, Edwards NC, Cunningham M, Simanis JP, Smith WH, Watson DD, Beller GA. Comparison between 201Tl and 99mTc sestamibi uptake during adenosine-induced vasodilation as a function of coronary stenosis severity. *Circulation* 1995;91:813–820.

225. Glover DK, Ruiz M, Bergmann EE, Simanis JP, Smith WH, Watson DD, Beller GA. Myocardial technetium-99m-teboroxime uptake during adenosine-induced hyperemia in dogs with either a critical or mild coronary stenosis: comparison to thallium-201 and regional blood flow. *J Nucl Med* 1995;36:476–483.

229. Sansoy V, Glover DK, Watson DD, Ruiz M, Smith WH, Simanis JP, Beller GA. Comparison of thallium-201 resting redistribution with technetium-99m-sestamibi uptake and functional response to dobutamine for assessment of myocardial viability. *Circulation* 1995;92:994–1004.

237. Kauffman GJ, Boyne TS, Watson DD, Smith WH, Beller GA. Comparison of rest thallium-201 imaging and rest technetium-99m sestamibi imaging for assessment of myocardial viability in patients with coronary artery disease and severe left ventricular dysfunction. *J Am Coll Cardiol* 1996;27:1592–1597.

238. Koplan BA, Beller GA, Ruiz M, Yang JY, Watson DD, Glover DK. Comparison between thallium-201 and technetium-99m-tetrofosmin uptake with sustained low flow and profound systolic dysfunction. *J Nucl Med* 1996;37:1398–1402.

240. Glover DK, Ruiz M, Yang JY, Koplan BA, Allen TR, Smith WH, Watson DD, Barrett RJ, Beller GA. Pharmacological stress thallium scintigraphy with 2-cyclohexylmethylidenehydrazinoadenosine (WRC-0470): a novel, short-acting adenosine A2A receptor agonist. *Circulation* 1996;94:1726–1732.

242. Taillefer R, DePuey EG, Udelson JE, Beller GA, Latour Y, Reeves F. Comparative diagnostic accuracy of Tl-201 and Tc-99m sestamibi SPECT imaging (perfusion and ECG-gated SPECT) in detecting coronary artery disease in women. *J Am Coll Cardiol* 1997;29:69–77.

245. Boyne TS, Koplan BA, Parsons WJ, Smith WH, Watson DD, Beller GA. Predicting adverse outcome with exercise SPECT technetium-99m sestamibi imaging in patients with suspected or known coronary artery disease. *Am J Cardiol* 1997;79:270–274.

246. Sansoy V, Watson DD, Beller GA. Significance of slow upsloping ST-segment depression on exercise stress testing. *Am J Cardiol* 1997;79:709–712.

250. Fenster MS, Feldman MD, Camarano G, Johnson WH, Ellis M, Linden J, Beller GA. Correlation of adenosine thallium 201 perfusion patterns with markers for inducible ischemia. *Am Heart J* 1997;133:406–412.

256. Pagley PR, Beller GA, Watson DD, Gimple LW, Ragosta M. Improved outcome after coronary bypass surgery in patients with ischemic cardiomyopathy and residual myocardial viability. *Circulation* 1997;96:793–800.

260. Vanzetto G, Calnon DA, Ruiz M, Watson DD, Pasqualini R, Beller GA, Glover DK. Myocardial uptake and redistribution of 99mTc-N-NOET in dogs with either sustained coronary low flow or transient coronary occlusion: comparison with 201Tl and myocardial blood flow. *Circulation* 1997;96:2325–2331.

261. Glover DK, Ruiz M, Yang JY, Smith WH, Watson DD, Beller GA. Myocardial 99mTc-tetrofosmin uptake during adenosine-induced vasodilatation with either a critical or mild coronary stenosis: comparison with 201Tl and regional myocardial blood flow. *Circulation* 1997;96:2332–2338.

262. Calnon DA, Glover DK, Beller GA, Vanzetto G, Smith WH, Watson DD, Ruiz M. Effects of dobutamine stress on myocardial blood flow, 99mTc sestamibi uptake, and systolic wall thickening in the presence of coronary artery stenoses: implications for dobutamine stress testing. *Circulation* 1997;96:2353–2360.

263. Smanio PEP, Watson DD, Segalla DL, Vinson EL, Smith WH, Beller GA. Value of gating of technetium-99m sestamibi single-photon emission computed tomographic imaging. *J Am Coll Cardiol* 1997;30:1687–1692.

264. Smith WH, Kastner RJ, Calnon DA, Segalla D, Beller GA, Watson DD. Quantitative gated single photon emission computed tomography imaging: a counts-based method for display and measurement of regional and global ventricular systolic function. *J Nucl Cardiol* 1997;4:451–463.

265. Calnon DA, Kastner RJ, Smith WH, Segalla D, Beller GA, Watson DD. Validation of a new counts-based gated single photon emission computed tomography method for quantifying left ventricular systolic function: comparison with equilibrium radionuclide angiography. *J Nucl Cardiol* 1997;4:464–471.

270. Shanoudy H, Raggi P, Beller GA, Soliman A, Ammermann EG, Kastner RJ, Watson DD. Comparison of technetium-99m tetrofosmin and thallium-201 single-photon emission computed tomographic imaging for detection of myocardial perfusion defects in patients with coronary artery disease. *J Am Coll Cardiol* 1998;31:331–337.

283. Glover DK, Ruiz M, Koplan BA, Watson DD, Beller GA. 99mTc-tetrofosmin assessment of myocardial perfusion and viability in canine models of coronary occlusion and reperfusion. *J Nucl Med* 1999;40:142–149.

286. Yang JY, Ruiz M, Calnon DA, Watson DD, Beller GA, Glover DK. Assessment of myocardial viability using 123I-labeled iodophenylpentadecanoic acid at sustained low flow or after acute infarction and reperfusion. *J Nucl Med* 1999;40:821–828.

289. Calnon DA, Ruiz M, Vanzetto G, Watson DD, Beller GA, Glover DK. Myocardial uptake of 99mTc-N-NOET and 201Tl during dobutamine infusion: comparison with adenosine stress. *Circulation* 1999;100:1653–1659.

291. Brown KA, Heller GV, Landin RS, Shaw LJ, Beller GA, Pasquale MJ, Haber SB. Early dipyridamole 99mTc-sestamibi single photon emission computed tomographic imaging 2 to 4 days after acute myocardial infarction predicts in-hospital and post-discharge cardiac events: comparison with sub-maximal exercise imaging. *Circulation* 1999;100:2060–2066.

296. Petruzella FD, Ruiz M, Katsiyiannis P, Watson DD, Pasqualini R, Beller GA, Glover DK. Optimal timing for initial and redistribution technetium-99m-N-NOET image acquisition. *J Nucl Cardiol* 2000;7:123–131.

299. Beller GA. President's page: convocation address. *J Am Coll Cardiol* 2000;35:1694–1696.

300. Takehana K, Ruiz M, Petruzella FD, Watson DD, Beller GA, Glover DK. Response to incremental doses of dobutamine early after reperfusion is predictive of the degree of myocardial salvage in dogs with experimental acute myocardial infarction. *J Am Coll Cardiol* 2000;35:1960–1968.

302. Vanzetto G, Glover DK, Ruiz M, Calnon DA, Pasqualini R, Watson DD, Beller GA. 99mTc-N-NOET myocardial uptake reflects myocardial blood flow and not viability in dogs with reperfused acute myocardial infarction. *Circulation* 2000;101:2424–2430.

305. Beller GA. President's page: geographic variations in delivery of cardiovascular care: an issue of great importance to cardiovascular specialists. *J Am Coll Cardiol* 2000;36:652–655.

313. Beller GA. Noninvasive assessment of myocardial viability. *N Engl J Med* 2000;343:1488–1490.

316. Beller GA. President's page: the epidemic of type 2 diabetes and obesity in the U.S.: cause for alarm. *J Am Coll Cardiol* 2000;36:2348–2350.

318. Takehana K, Ruiz M, Petruzella FD, Watson DD, Beller GA, Glover DK. Tc-99m sestamibi defect magnitude predicts the amount of viable myocardium after coronary reperfusion despite the presence of severe residual stenosis. *J Nucl Cardiol* 2001;8:40–48.

319. Beller GA. President's page: patient satisfaction: a personal perspective. *J Am Coll Cardiol* 2001;37:687–688.

322. Ragosta M, Powers ER, Samady H, Gimple LW, Sarembock IJ, Beller GA. Relationship between extent of residual myocardial viability and coronary flow reserve in patients with recent myocardial infarction. *Am Heart J* 2001;141:456–462.

326. Beller GA. Coronary heart disease in the first 30 years of the 2first Century: challenges and opportunities: the 3third Annual James B. Herrick Lecture of the Council on Clinical Cardiology of the American Heart Association. *Circulation* 2001;103:2428–2435.

329. Beller GA. Presidential address: quality of cardiovascular care in the U.S. *J Am Coll Cardiol* 2001;38:587–594.

330. Takehana K, Beller GA, Ruiz M, Petruzella FD, Watson DD, Glover DK. Assessment of residual coronary stenoses using ^{99m}Tc-N-NOET vasodilator stress imaging to evaluate coronary flow reserve early after coronary reperfusion in a canine model of subendocardial infarction. *J Nucl Med* 2001;42:1388–1394.

331. Soto JR, Watson DD, Beller GA. Incidence and significance of ischemic ST-segment depression occurring solely during recovery after exercise testing. *Am J Cardiol* 2001;88:670–672.

332. Glover DK, Ruiz M, Takehana K, Petruzella FD, Riou LM, Rieger JM, Macdonald TL, Watson DD, Linden J, Beller GA. Pharmacological stress myocardial perfusion imaging with the potent and selective A(2A) adenosine receptor agonists ATL193 and ATL146e administered by either intravenous infusion or bolus injection. *Circulation* 2001;104:1181–1187.

333. Calnon DA, McGrath PD, Doss AL, Harrell FE Jr, Watson DD, Beller GA. Prognostic value of dobutamine stress technetium-99m-sestamibi single-photon emission computed tomography myocardial perfusion imaging: stratification of a high-risk population. *J Am Coll Cardiol* 2001;38:1511–1517.

339. Riou LM, Ruiz M, Sullivan GW, Linden J, Leong-Poi H, Lindner JR, Harris TD, Beller GA, Glover DK. Assessment of myocardial inflammation produced by experimental coronary occlusion and reperfusion with ^{99m}Tc-RP517, a new leukotriene B4 receptor antagonist that preferentially labels neutrophils in vivo. *Circulation* 2002;106:592–598.

342. Riou LM, Ruiz M, Rieger JM, Macdonald TL, Watson DD, Linden J, Beller GA, Glover DK. Influence of propranolol, enalaprilat, verapamil, and caffeine on adenosine A_{2A} receptor-mediated coronary vasodilatation. *J Am Coll Cardiol* 2002;40:1687–1694.

BOOKS

1. Zaret BL, Beller GA, eds. Nuclear Cardiology: State of the Art and Future Directions. St. Louis: Mosby-Year Book, 1993.

2. Beller GA. Clinical Nuclear Cardiology. Philadelphia: WB Saunders, 1995.

3. Beller GA, ed. Chronic Ischemic Heart Disease. In: Braunwald E, ed. Atlas of Heart Diseases, Volume V. St. Louis, MO: Mosby, 1995.

4. Zaret BL, Beller GA, eds. Nuclear Cardiology: State of the Art and Future Directions. second Ed. St. Louis: Mosby, 1999.

WILLIAM EDWARD BODEN, MD: A Conversation With the Editor

William E. Boden, MD[a],* and William Clifford Roberts, MD[b]

Bill Boden was born in Rochester, New York, on June 21, 1948, and he grew up there. He graduated from the McQuaid Jesuit High School in 1966, from LeMoyne College in Syracuse with honors in 1970, and from SUNY Upstate Medical School in Syracuse, New York, in 1974. His internship and 2-year residency in internal medicine was at the Boston University (BU) Hospitals. Between his resident years, he was a research fellow in the Cardiology Section also at Boston University Hospitals. His clinical fellowship in cardiology was at Tufts-New England Medical Center in Boston. His first staff position was at the Miriam Hospital of Brown University in Providence, Rhode Island, where he was director of the coronary care unit. In 1986, he moved to Detroit as director of the coronary care unit and codirector of the cardiovascular clinical trials, and he was associate professor of internal medicine at Wayne State University School of Medicine. In 1989, he returned to Boston as chief of the section of cardiovascular medicine at the Boston VA Medical Center and professor of medicine at Tufts University School of Medicine. In 1994, he became professor of medicine at Boston University School of Medicine, and in 1996, he returned to Syracuse as professor and associate chairman of the Department of Medicine of the State University of New York Health Science Center. In 2000, he moved to Hartford, Connecticut, as director of cardiology and as program director of the Henry Low Heart Center and professor of medicine at the University of Connecticut School of Medicine. In 2006, he moved to Buffalo as chief of cardiology at the Buffalo General and Millard Fillmore Hospitals and professor of medicine and preventive medicine at the University of Buffalo, State University of New York School of Medicine. In late 2011, he assumed a new position as chief of medicine at the Albany Stratton VA Medical Center and vice chairman of the Department of Medicine at the Albany Medical Center, where he will be a professor of medicine.

Dr. Boden's research interests have focused primarily on myocardial infarction, stable and unstable angina pectoris, heart failure, and dyslipidemia, particularly in patients with coronary disease. He has worked extensively in the clinical trials arena, including as a project director or study chairman or co-chairman for several multicenter major clinical trials, including the Diltiazem Reinfarction Study, the Veterans Affairs Non-Q-Wave Infarction Strategies In-Hospital (VANQWISH) trial, the Incomplete Infarction Trial of European Research Collaborators Evaluating Prognosis Post-Thrombolysis (INTERCEPT), the Clinical Outcomes Utilizing Revascularization and Aggressive Drug Evaluation (COURAGE) trial, and the Atherothrombosis Intervention in Metabolic Syndrome With Low HDL/High Triglycerides: Impact on Global Health Outcomes (AIM-HIGH) trial. Dr. Boden has published >350 peer-reviewed articles, in addition to chapters in books. He has been selected for inclusion in the Best Doctors in America listing continuously since 2003. And finally, Bill Boden is the father of 5 offspring and an all-around good guy. He is one of the better speakers among the cardiology community.

William Clifford Roberts, MD (hereafter Roberts*): *Dr. Boden, I appreciate your willingness to allow me to interview you and particularly your willingness to do this while in Dallas and in my home. We are here on 4 August 2011, and it's approximately 110 degrees outside. Bill, could we start with your describing your early childhood, where you were brought up, some of your early memories, your parents and your siblings?*

William Edward Boden, MD (hereafter Boden): First, thank you for the privilege of coming today to spend some time with you in your home. I was born in 1948, and my parents, Edward and Mary, brought us up in a middle-class working neighborhood in Rochester, New York, where for the first 10 years of my life we lived in the same house with my maternal grandparents. They lived on the second floor and we on the first. I have 1 sister, Nanci, who is 3½ years older than I am. She still lives in Rochester, New York. In my current location in Buffalo, I have reunited more with my sister over the last 5 years than I have over the last 25 years. A benefit of returning to New York is to have more time with her. I came from a very much working-class family, and that includes my extended family. My dad was a machinist at a local tool and die maker, and he also worked for a time at a division of General Motors called Delco. He worked the day shift. My mother was a secretary at Taylor Instruments Company, which made precision instruments. Neither my mom nor dad went beyond high school. My sister also did not go to college, which was not uncommon in the 1960s for young women. She started work in the mortgage division of M&T Bank, and she still works there. My father had 3 sisters and 2 brothers, so we had a large extended family. My mom had 2 brothers. They all lived in the Rochester area. My cousin Ronald, on my

[a]Department of Medicine, Albany Medical College, Samuel S. Stratton VA Medical Center, Albany, New York; and [b]Baylor Heart and Vascular Institute, Baylor University Medical Center, Dallas, Texas. Manuscript received and accepted 22 March 2012.

*Corresponding author: Tel: 518-626-6386; fax: 518-626-6511.
Email address: william.boden@va.gov (W.E. Boden).

father's side, was the only other member of my extended family who attended college, and he also went to medical school and became a physician. He was 15 years older than me. He had a strong influence on my career, and I admired him. I was very impressed that he was the first one in our entire extended family, on either side, to go to college. He trained in ob-gyn, moved to Tulsa, Oklahoma, and practiced there until his death in 2010.

My grandparents came from Poland and the Ukraine. My maternal grandfather came over from the Ukraine around 1910 and went to work for the Baltimore and Ohio Railroad Company in Rochester. He worked for about 10 years and saved enough money so that he could bring his family to the States. Shortly after he arrived in Russia in 1919, the Bolshevik Revolution occurred, and he and his family were trapped there for 9 years. My mother was born in the Ukraine in 1920. My grandparents were farmers. With the Russian revolution, however, they essentially lost any land and possessions they had. Fortunately, my grandfather had deposited money in an American bank, so he had a means to return to the USA. They returned in 1929 and settled in Rochester.

My father was born of Polish descent in Winnipeg, Canada. In his early 20s, he and his family moved to Rochester, where my parents met and married in 1941. My sister was born in 1944, while my dad was serving in the Army during World War II. He was away for nearly 4 years. He returned in late 1944. They settled in Rochester, and he went to work for Delco. My mother worked the evening shift (5 PM to 11 PM), and my dad worked the day shift (7 AM to 3 PM). When I came home from school, we had roughly an hour to go out and play, and then we had dinner around 4:30 PM. Fortunately, we lived only 3 minutes from the plant.

I loved living with my grandparents. They spoke very little English, and despite my best efforts to teach my grandmother to read, I rarely succeeded. She tried mightily to learn English but never mastered it. Conversely, typical of that era, the émigrés to the USA wanted to be "Americanized," so that they made a conscious decision that we would only speak English in the house. As much as they were fluent in both Polish and Ukrainian, I never picked up the language. I missed an opportunity to have a greater appreciation for my own heritage.

I loved to use the phonograph. I would sit for hours listening to 78-rpm and 45-rpm records. I very much admired Eddie Fisher and Perry Como, and I memorized their songs (Figure 1). I became quite a good singer as a youngster. Whenever there was any kind of family get-together, I would almost invariably be asked to go on stage and sing. I would be bribed for a paltry sum of 25 cents to go and sing some songs. I was delighted. This was when I was 5 to 7 years old. I enjoyed mimicking the 1950s singers. My family was delighted and loved to hear "Billy" sing. Children in that era spent a lot of time outside playing, and we were no different. At least an hour before dinner and then after

Figure 1. Eddie Fisher protégé, 1955.

dinner I would listen to the phonograph or read. We got a black-and-white TV in the mid-1950s. I liked to watch the evening news with John Cameron Swayze. TV revolutionized what we did, I think, relative to an earlier era, when there was only radio. In 1957, my father had a medical illness, and I was told he had a "stomach ulcer." He was admitted to the hospital, and had surgery, which, I presumed at the time, was removal of the gastric ulcer. I thought nothing further of it until 2 or 3 months later, when we moved out of the duplex we shared with my grandparents to the suburbs. We moved, when I was about 10 years old, to a middle-class neighborhood in a western suburb of Rochester. It was a residential neighborhood with single-family homes. Thereafter, we made new friends and neighbors. We had a very enjoyable time. In 1958, my father had to be rehospitalized for what I thought was recurrent ulcer surgery. As it turns out, and I found this out only many years later, he had been diagnosed with gastric carcinoma in 1957, and that was the precipitant for his wanting to move our family to a house of our own. My parents never disclosed the nature of his illness. But I watched his gradual demise over the course of a year, where he progressively lost weight, became weaker, and ultimately when I was 12, he died. This was in 1960. I was devastated, and the thing I regret is that I never knew he was dying, or if I did, I repressed it. I found myself withdrawing from my dad during those months, because it was hurtful for me to see him in such pain. Years after, I lamented the fact that my sister knew he was terminal, but everyone felt it would be too traumatic for me to know the truth. I was fearful of what would happen to us. My mother didn't have a well-paying job. My father's death forced me to grow up quickly. I had in my mind that I wanted to be a physician. In 1953, at the age of 5, I had a ruptured appendix. One evening, I was incredibly sick. I had severe vomiting, and the pediatrician came to see me at home, noted that I had a boardlike abdomen, and immediately rushed me to the hospital for surgery. This wasn't long after penicillin became commercially available in the private sector. I remember the nurses and physicians commenting on the fact that this was touch and go, because I had severe peritonitis. There was no guarantee that I would make it through the surgery, much less have no complications. A very young skilled surgeon, Dr. Harry Phillips, did the surgery. I came home after a 2- to 3-week hospitalization. During the time in the hospital, I got first-hand exposure to medicine: to orderlies, nurses, and physicians. At that period, I decided that I wanted to be a doctor when I grew up. That, coupled with my physician cousin, reinforced in my mind that I wanted to pursue a career in medicine. I became completely focused on that goal. When my dad passed away, I was concerned that my goal would be unattainable.

I worked hard and was accepted to McQuaid Jesuit High School. It was a very important step in my life, because I became exposed to very rigorous educators. The Jesuits really challenged students, both in high school and college, to become excellent thinkers. We were required to read voraciously. As a freshman, I read 25 books, all required reading. I was encouraged by the faculty to pursue the "Greek honors" curriculum as opposed to the "science honors" curriculum, despite the fact that it made sense to me, since I wanted to me a physician, to track in the science honors program. During high school, I took 4 years of Latin, 3 years of classical Greek, and innumerable other courses, but remained focused on becoming a physician. In my sophomore and junior years, I made the football team, although I didn't play very much, because I wasn't fast. In my senior year, I decided I would be the manager of the team. I was involved in other extracurricular activities: student council, yearbook. I also was on the debate team for 2 years, and really got an opportunity to engage in public speaking and the rigors of learning to defend a particular position. I graduated in 1966 and was seventh or eighth in my class.

Roberts: *How many were in your class?*

Boden: One hundred forty. I had my heart set on going to Boston College. I was inspired by Jesuit education and how they challenged me—the dialectic was thesis, antithesis, synthesis—which was drilled into our heads from the beginning. Every step in life, one had to be a rigorous thinker and to challenge conventional wisdom. (Now that I am saying this, it immediately becomes apparent to me how I've tracked in the professional career that I have, challenging conventional wisdom in a lot of the clinical research work that I have done.) I began looking for college interviews after my junior year of high school. My mother remarried when I was 16, in 1964. We then had a blended family of 5 new siblings and my sister and me. The 2 older stepsiblings were already out of the house, We had 3 stepbrothers—John, Jim, and Chris—still at home. We went from a family of 3 to a family of 7. What immediately became apparent to me when they moved in with us is that I had absolutely nothing in common with my stepbrothers. All they could do was sit and watch TV endlessly, eat ice cream, and not do anything that was in any way intellectual. They all went to public schools. I got home from football

practice or an extracurricular activity around 6 or 6:30 PM and had dinner, often after the rest of the family had already eaten, and then go to my room and study for 3 hours. I was never a good test taker. I never figured out how to take the PSATs, SATs, or the MCATs. I'm convinced you are either a neurotic or a paranoid when it comes to taking tests, and I was always a paranoid. I kept looking for the curveball rather than the fastball down the center. I was an average test taker.

I was so thrilled to get an invitation to interview at Boston College. I met with the dean of admissions, Father Brady, who upon reviewing my scholastic achievement noted that I was a very good student, finishing high in my class but that I didn't score very well on the SATs. He told me that they would offer me admission to Boston College but only in a liberal arts curriculum, because they didn't think I had an aptitude to succeed in premed. I thanked him and said goodbye.

I was offered a scholarship to attend a small Jesuit liberal arts college in Syracuse, LeMoyne College, which was a relatively new school with a matriculation of about 2,000 students. Again, recognizing that I had to help my mother as much as I could, I jumped at the opportunity to get a scholarship to go to college. My major was biology/premed, and I did exceedingly well. I was involved in a lot of extracurricular activities: student government (I was vice president of my class during 2 separate years), the yearbook, and the debate team, which I thought was quite a prize. I graduated from LeMoyne in 1970. The previous year, I submitted applications to medical schools. I don't remember how many I applied to, but I received only 1 interview invitation, which was at SUNY Upstate Medical Center in Syracuse. I think my not receiving other interview invitations was because I had gone to a small college and had only so-so MCAT scores (150 range). In the fall of my senior year, I was accepted to SUNY. In September/October 1969, President Nixon reinstituted the military draft for the Vietnam War, and it was a lottery system based on birthdays. There was random selection of birthdates starting from 1 to 365, and my day of June 21 was number 60. I was destined for Vietnam had I not gotten into medical school. As fate would have it, the individuals in college who partied the most and were the worst students ended up getting the higher draft numbers and didn't get drafted. I was pretty anxious for several months, knowing that I only had 1 interview for medical school and knowing that I would be going to war if I didn't get in that following spring. I got a military deferment.

I started medical school in 1970 and graduated in 1974. My cousin, David, who was a year younger than me, was drafted to go into the Army, and he sadly died in Vietnam when he came upon a landmine in his jeep. I remember how sad I was being a pallbearer at his funeral when I was a freshman in medical school, recognizing, Why him and not me? It took a toll on me to see my cousin die in the war and

Figure 2. Dr. Boden and his mother, 1992.

made me very grateful that I had been given the opportunity to pursue a career in medicine.

Roberts: *What was your father's full name?*

Boden: Edward John Boden, born in 1912 and died in 1960. He was 47 when he died.

Roberts: *What was your mother's full name?*

Boden: Mary Ann Babey, born 1920 and died in 1994. She had an acute myocardial infarct during my internship year. She survived and lived another 20 years.

Roberts: *Were you close to your father? Did you have a lot in common?*

Boden: We did until he got sick. We took a summer vacation every year to the Adirondack Mountains or to the Thousand Islands in upstate New York. We went camping and fishing. One summer, we drove to Prince Edward Island in Canada. We got hit by Hurricane Hazel, and we were stuck in our cabin for a week. When his health began to deteriorate, I tended to withdraw from him. I never thought he would die.

Roberts: *What about your relationship with your mother?*

Boden: I was very close with my mom (Figure 2). I felt badly for her because she was only 39 when my dad died. She was young, attractive, and vivacious woman, who lost her husband too young. For a period of 2 or 3 years, she dated quite a bit. My sister and I hoped she would meet somebody that she could have a happy life with. She met a man who also worked at Taylor Instruments as a metallurgist, Herb Miller. Herb was a couple years older than she. They married in 1964. I believe they had a very happy relationship. There was a lot of stress in the house, because my sister and I didn't have anything in common with his kids. I would feel tension because there were differences in how we were brought up and that created some conflict. I very much wanted to go away to college so I wouldn't have to be in that environment daily.

At age 16, I went to St. Mary's Hospital and asked for a summer job. I was hired as an orderly and assigned to an orthopedic floor with a demanding head nurse, Miss Marie Fink. She was a terror. Everything I did or said, in her eyes, was wrong. I stuck it out, and by the end of the summer, she valued what I could do, and I became one of her "favorites." I made $1.47 an hour, the minimum wage in 1964. President Johnson increased the minimum wage to $1.62, which I felt was a windfall. In 8 hours, I made $10 to $12. But it was a wonderful way for me to see medicine from the nursing perspective, and I was able to save money for school and spending. Throughout both high school and college, I worked summers and holiday breaks as an orderly. When I was in college, I was routinely assigned to the emergency room. It gave me an opportunity to shadow an emergency medicine physician and watch what they did. I think I absorbed medical information through my skin. I observed very intently, to the point where as a medical resident, I moonlighted in the emergency room and became proficient at taking care of almost any problem.

Roberts: *How did you and Nanci get along?*

Boden: We got along reasonably well. My sister was very independent. She did not get along with our stepbrothers. Within 6 months of their moving into our house, Nanci left home at age 17 and got her own apartment. It bothered me that she bailed out of the household. In the subsequent years, we have become very close. We get together at least every month or so, if not more often, and it has been a real bonus being close to her again.

Roberts: *Does she have children?*

Boden: No. She was married for about 5 years, got divorced, and never remarried.

Roberts: *It seems to me that your father, if he sensed he was dying, would have been pleased to have your family stay in the duplex with your grandparents?*

Boden: I think his reasoning would have likely been "I don't know how long I have to live but if we don't move now, we'll never have to opportunity to move." He wanted to move the family while the getting was good. Years after I completed my residency, I unearthed his medical records. From the beginning (1958), his diagnosis was gastric carcinoma, and he kept it to himself. I believe he didn't even tell my mother. He was told by the physicians that there was little they could do for him. He eventually had both liver and bone metastases and was miserable his last several months. I was struck by his silence in dealing with his cancer. It took courage on his part to move us to the suburbs under such difficult circumstances (Figures 3 and 4).

Roberts: *Do you remember any of those family dinners before his illness? What did you talk about at the dinner table?*

Boden: We talked about school, things going on in the neighborhood. Dinner was relatively brief, maybe 25 minutes, and then my mother had to go to work. The rest of the evening would be spent with my dad, watching a little bit of TV, doing homework. We were a very religious family and went to church every Sunday. I loved sports and was an avid fan of the Rochester Red Wings and the Triple AAA base-

Figure 3. Mom, Nanci, and Bill, Easter 1958.

Figure 4. Dad, Nanci, and Bill, Easter 1958.

ball team and would try to go to as many games as possible. I listened to the away games on my transistor radio at night.

Roberts: *It sounds like your parents would have almost certainly gone to college if they had grown up in another era.*

Boden: I think so. My father was the glue that held our family together. He had 3 sisters and 2 brothers, and he was the youngest of the boys. He was the person to reach out to his siblings. Once or twice a week, we would go visit my uncles or aunts. He was the catalyst. I remember my uncle Stanley wanting to build a summer house in Canandaigua. My father was a very proficient carpenter. He built that house almost by himself. Not only would dad work his day job but whenever he could in the evenings or weekends, he would go help out at this summer cottage. He was a very outgoing, giving individual. After he died in 1960, the family sort of fell apart.

Roberts: *Were there books or newspapers or magazines around your house?*

Boden: Yes.

Roberts: *Who did the reading?*

Boden: I did. I read a lot of books during grade school and high school. We had either *Time* or *Newsweek*. I had a subscription to *Sports Illustrated* when in high school (I

liked the Buffalo Bills, only 60 miles away, and the New York Giants). My parents were not college grads, and there was some void in having not been exposed to literature. My mother insisted that my sister and I take piano lessons, which lasted until high school. I was pretty good. We had piano recitals. In high school, I got busy in other things and discontinued playing the piano.

Roberts: *What position did you play in football?*

Boden: Receiver, but I couldn't get down the field fast enough to separate myself from the defenders.

Roberts: *Were there any teachers in grammar school, junior high, high school, or college that had a particular influence on you?*

Boden: The nuns in grammar school were notorious for riding herd on the student body in ways that would never be permissible in 2011. Discipline was very much in evidence in school. I remember my seventh and eighth grade teacher, Sister John Joseph. She was the person who probably most saw my potential. That was the year that my dad died. The other person who became very prominent in my life was a young priest in our parish, Father Leo Inglis. He had just been ordained a priest, and St. Helen's Church was his first parish assignment. When my dad died, he took me under his arm. He took me to ballgames, taught me how to play little league ball. He was in a Friday-evening bowling league. He would pick me up, and I would go watch him bowl. He adopted me as a son. I was an altar boy for 4 years (fifth grade to eighth grade) in the church. There were 2 morning Masses, 7 AM and 7:45 AM. I would get up at 6:30 AM and walk to the church and let myself in the rectory and prepare the 7 AM Mass. We had assignments whether it was a weekday or weekend Mass. I got so attached to Father Inglis that during my eighth grade year, I considered becoming a priest. I had a lot of discussions with him and others about whether I should consider entering the priesthood. We had 2 seminaries in Rochester. Priesthood is a 12-year path: St. Andrew's for the first 6 years and then St. Bernard's seminary for the last 6 years. When it got to the final crunch, I wanted to be a physician. Then I thought maybe I could be a priest and a physician.

In high school, there were 2 individuals: Father O'Malley, my English teacher, and Father Hoegenkamp, my Greek teacher. They were young, late 30s. Both were incredibly charismatic teachers. They were so involved with the students. Many of us students considered them to be amazing role models. These priests were the reason I wanted to go to a Jesuit college. Those 4 years of high school were the ones that gave me a solid foundation to be a hardworking and challenging student.

Roberts: *Were the fathers at your high school the ones who suggested LeMoyne College to you?*

Boden: I applied to several other Jesuit schools: Boston College, as I said before, Creighton University in Nebraska, Wheeling College in West Virginia, plus about 3 or 4 others. I was offered a scholarship by LeMoyne, and that sealed the deal. I realized that I would never have a good educational pedigree because of that, but I reasoned that if I worked hard, I could get into medical school. In retrospect, it was a long shot. I only got 1 interview to medical school, the one located in the same city. There was a track record of Upstate Medical Center having known that the students who came through LeMoyne College in premed and that the undergraduate curriculum was very good. The priest who was the science educator at LeMoyne, Francis X. Flood, was cut from the same cloth as Ms. Fink. And Father Flood made it abundantly clear that he would—and he alone—would decide who did and who did not get into medical school. He was tough! Some of my classmates, who were very good premed candidates, did not make the cut with Father Flood. He decided who he would give a good recommendation to and who he wouldn't. He played a major role in my getting into medical school.

Roberts: *Was college an enjoyable experience?*

Boden: It was great. I was only 80 miles from home. I met my first wife, Barbara, between my freshman and sophomore years in college.

Roberts: *What's her full name?*

Boden: Barbara Ann Murphy. We met in 1967, and we dated throughout college. In that era, many couples got married right after graduating from college. Quite a few of my classmates actually got married before their senior year of college. I was actively involved in extracurricular activities, but not any sports. I had a lot of good friends and many from my hometown. A couple of us worked together at the hospital. I remember the drinking age was 18 years old. We all made fake college IDs. I got into a bar with a fake Holy Cross ID at the age of 16. That was another school I applied to. Barbara and I got married in June 1970, almost 3 months before I started medical school. I had just turned 22 and felt I was pretty mature for my age. We lived in our first apartment in Syracuse for 1 year. The rent was $100 a month. My wife had gotten a BA in sociology. She then went on to get a masters of social work. She worked during the time I went to medical school. I worked the summer before the second year at the blood bank. During my sophomore, junior, and senior years in medical school, I worked in the clinical pathology lab at night. I was called a "night boy," and I worked from 11 PM to 7 AM. I was able to do everything that came to the lab. That experience was invaluable. Before I got to be an intern or resident, I knew how to look at peripheral blood smears. I'd seen leukemia under the microscope. I had used the flame photometer to do sodium and potassium assays. I analyzed cerebrospinal fluid. I swabbed blood agar plates with infected fluids. The "night boy" on a bad night would never sit down. I ran from one end of the corridor, chemistry, to the other, hematology. I needed roller skates. On a good night, I got an hour or 2 of sleep in a little on-call room. Then, I'd go to med school the next day and try to stay awake. I worked on average of 1 night a week to generate some income to pay rent.

Roberts: *What was it about Barbara Ann Murphy that made you take a second look?*

Boden: She was attractive and had a good personality. We fell in love during college. She was in sociology. She was from New Jersey. I met her parents between my first and second year of college. I loved her parents. Her dad, Bob, became my Father Ingles when I got into medical school. We had a very good relationship. It was a struggle being married and going through medical school. I totally underestimated the work required during medical school, both in the rigors of medical school and in marriage. I thought I was a mature 22 years old, but I had no idea. Our personal relationship suffered during the time I was in medical school. I never made the time to be a good spouse, spending all my time studying. I always regarded myself as being "average," so I felt almost compelled to be an overachiever. I was fixated: nothing was going to deter me from that goal of being a physician.

Roberts: *Were there any surprises in medical school for you? You had worked on the wards as an orderly, so you knew your way around.*

Boden: I knew my way around incredibly well. I was probably in the top half of my class the first 2 years. Once I got into the third year of medical school and into the wards, I flourished. Because I had worked for years as an orderly, as a "night boy," I was far ahead of my classmates. They would come to me to ask me to look at something or to show them how to do a test. I was good clinically with patients. I did very well during my junior and senior years. Early in my senior year, I got selected for AOA (Alpha Omega Alpha), a shock to me. I didn't think that based on performance during the first 2 years of medical school that I would ever offset that even with a strong performance during the third or fourth years. AOA was a real honor.

Roberts: *How many were in your class?*

Boden: One hundred twenty.

Roberts: *When you finished, how do you think you came out?*

Boden: Probably top 10% of the class. I think that was a requirement for AOA. I remember getting a letter my last year from the dean congratulating me on being elected by my peers and faculty to AOA.

Roberts: *Were there any faculty who had a particular impact on you?*

Boden: Yes. Two pathologists had a big impact on my life: Dr. Rolla Hill and Dr. Robert Rohner. Pathology was a yearlong course during medical school. It went in parallel with anatomy. I really enjoyed it. Dr. Hill took me under his wing. I did a couple of research projects with him. As mentioned earlier, during the summer months in college, I worked in the blood bank, and in medical school, I worked during the week as a night boy. After the first year of medical school, I worked with 2 pulmonary physicians. We wrote a paper, my first publication. They had come up with the "magnetometer," a device placed on the chest wall and abdomen, and it could discern the respiratory and abdominal components of the respiratory cycle. I worked with them for 2 summers. The third summer, I worked in the Cardiology Department. Dr. Robert Eich was the chief of cardiology as SUNY Syracuse, was a special man, an incredible clinician, and a wonderful mentor. He was a midwestern fellow, tall, wiry, self-deprecating, and disarming. One couldn't help but love the guy. I did a summer research project on the anginal syndrome with normal coronary arteriograms. He believed that one explanation for angina pectoris was what he termed "hyperdynamic ventricular contraction." I had a series of 20 patients with the anginal syndrome, angiographically clean epicardial coronary arteries, and supernatural ejection fractions (80%). I did a planimetric analysis of their ventriculograms in both peak systole and in end-diastole. We submitted an abstract the summer before my senior year, and it got accepted. Thus, as a senior medical student in 1974, I attended the Annual Scientific Sessions of the American College of Cardiology (ACC), held in New York City. (Carl Pepine was also there as a presenter, dressed in Navy whites. I was struck with awe at his appearance.) I gave an oral presentation to a huge, packed room. I got some questions fired at me. Somebody asked me if there had been epinephrine in the lidocaine. I said there hadn't been. Ultimately, that paper was published in *Catheterization and Cardiovascular Diagnosis*. My senior year, I was one of the few medical students who ever presented at medical grand rounds at SUNY Syracuse. That was quite an honor. The chair of medicine, Dr. William Williams, was a hematologist. He was one of the other individuals who were important in my life. Bill Williams had just published the *Williams' Textbook of Hematology* and had moved from the University of Pennsylvania during my freshman year. I went into his office, introduced myself, and said that I wanted to go into internal medicine. We probably chatted for about 45 minutes and developed a very good relationship in the years going forward. He wanted me to stay in Syracuse for my residency. But after getting into AOA, I thought I could shoot a little higher. My first choice was Penn, second was Tufts, and third Boston University. I only applied to 6 residency programs. The other 3 were Georgetown, University of North Carolina, and University of Virginia.

Roberts: *Did you have any difficulty in deciding that internal medicine was truly the area for you?*

Boden: I didn't like surgery. My sense was that surgeons were just more interested in getting to the operating room and didn't really like taking care of patients. I thought surgical morning rounds were superficial. Even though I did very well in surgery, I didn't want to do that. The only other specialty that appealed to me was pediatrics, which is essentially internal medicine with a younger clientele. I found it emotionally difficult, however, to see the really sick young kids. I didn't want a career dealing with pediatric catastrophes. I got inspired by cardiology. The physiology fit. After my fourth year of medical school and having completed a clinical research project ending with a publication, I was sure that cardiology was what I wanted to do.

Figure 5. William Edward Boden: internship, 1974.

Roberts: *You must have been thrilled to get an internship at Boston University. How did it work out?*

Boden: I was thrilled. BU was a very demanding training program (Figure 5). We spent 6 months at University Hospital, 3 months at the Veterans Administration Hospital, and 3 months at Boston City Hospital. It was a beautiful blend of training, and we saw everything rotating among those 3 institutions. That was an era that the American Board of Medicine tried an experiment. They allowed residents to fast-track into a fellowship program after the second year of residency training. At that time, I had already decided to go into cardiology, so I did an internship and junior residence at BU, then I decided I wanted to do basic research. I took a year of research and worked both in a cardiology fellowship as well as doing basic research with Dr. William B. Hood, Jr., the chief of cardiology at Boston City Hospital. During my third year, I worked with him and 2 other individuals, Carl Apstein and Chang Liang. We got 3 publications out of doing work on open-chest anesthetized dogs, where we looked at segmental ventricular function using strain gauges attached to myocardium. I asked Bill Hood about submitting the work to the Young Investigators' Award competition at the Annual Scientific Sessions of the American College of Cardiology. He thought it was a great idea. No one had ever done that from BU. I submitted it and got selected as 1 of the 5 finalists in 1978. I didn't win, but it was a thrill to go to the ACC and present. Dr. Sandy Williams, the dean at Duke, won that year. After my research and clinical fellowship at BU, I returned for a year of chief residency in medicine in 1977. There were 2 chief residents. Each served in that role worked for 6 months, and the other 6 months were electives. I did a clinical fellowship at Tufts Medical Center in 1978 to 1979. I had 2 years of cardiology sandwiched around 3 years of medicine. In 1979, I had my first professional job, assistant professor of medicine at Brown University and director of the coronary care unit at Miriam Hospital, a 250-bed medical/surgical hospital. That was my first opportunity to do clinical research. That was during the early 1980s, when calcium channel blockers came on the scene. At a symposium in Mexico, I met Robert Roberts, who at the time was at Barnes Hospital, Washington University, and got involved in my very first clinical trial. It was the Diltiazem Reinfarction Study, and I was the second leading enroller. It was a 2-week trial. That trial got me set on a path of doing clinical research. It was an opportunity for me to get exposed to the industry-academia interface, which provided young aspiring academic cardiologists to work with more established investigators. In addition to Bob Roberts, I had the good fortune to meet, early in my career, Bob O'Rourke, John Schroeder, Dick Conti, Carl Pepine, and Rick Walsh, among others, all involved with calcium channel blocker research. Then I was able to get involved in a long-term outcomes trial involving diltiazem study (Multicentre Diltiazem Post-Infarction Trial) with Arthur Moss. Miriam Hospital was the lipid core lab for that trial. All the lipid analyses were done there, and we got a couple of papers out of that. I collaborated with Arthur Moss considerably during that era. (Parenthetically, Arthur took care of my mother for 20 years in Rochester. When she had her myocardial infarction, she had bypass surgery [in 1978]. Paul Yu took care of her initially, but he stepped down. Since I had gotten to know Arthur, I asked him if he would take care of my mom. He did a wonderful job. She not only had bypass surgery but developed conduction disease, got a pacemaker, and had terrible left ventricular function [ejection fraction about 20%]. Despite that, she did remarkably well for 20 years after her large anterior infarct.).

During my internship at BU, I had a 3-week vacation, and mine that year corresponded with the last 2 weeks of December and the first week in January. My father-in-law, Bob Murphy, who had had systemic lupus erythematosus for years, had intermittent remissions and exacerbations. He had gotten progressively worse during my internship year and during my Christmas vacation, and he was virtually bedridden. Being a pure Irishman, he was incredibly stubborn and did not want to leave the house. The day after Christmas, I told him that he had to go to the hospital. We took him to a small community hospital in northern New Jersey. He was admitted to the intensive care unit, received peritoneal dialysis, developed a catheter infection, and then infective endocarditis. He died mid-January the year of my internship. Two things happened within a 4-week period: my mom had the heart attack and my father-in-law died. I returned to do my coronary care unit rotation, which was every other night. I didn't have time to feel sorry for myself with such a rigorous schedule.

Roberts: *You've made a few moves in your career. How long were you at Brown?*

Boden: Seven years, 1970 to 1976. The chief of cardiology after a falling out with the administration at Miriam left, as did 2 other cardiologists. For me, it was a signal that it was time to go. It was an unstable professional situation. At that time, I had 15 to 20 publications, so Josh Wynne, who was selected to be the chief of cardiology at Harper Hospital Wayne State University in 1984, invited me to join his division, along with 9 others in a 2-year period. I came in 1986 to run the coronary care unit. But Detroit was a tough adjustment for my east coast–based family, who loved Rhode Island. For personal and professional reasons, there was a lot of dissatisfaction with the way the division was going during that time period. Bill O'Neill moved from the University of Michigan to Beaumont Hospital. Harper Hospital and Henry Ford Hospital were the 2 competing tertiary hospitals that had gotten most of the percutaneous coronary intervention referrals, but when Bill O'Neill and later Cindy Grines followed him, that ended our referrals coming from Oakland County. Our cath and coronary care unit volumes plummeted. Nine of the staff that Josh Wynne had recruited left by 1989. I returned to Boston in 1989 as chief of cardiology at the Boston Veterans Administration Medical Center. I was there for 7 years (until 1996), and then another unfortunate event transpired. There had been a struggle going on for almost 15 to 20 years about which VA hospital would emerge as the dominant tertiary VA in Boston. There was the Boston VA, affiliated with BU in Jamaica Plain, and the West Roxbury VA Hospital, affiliated with Harvard. The Boston VA was a huge building, 17 stories, clearly had far more outpatient and in-service facilities than West Roxbury. The VA program, trying to consolidate in the mid-1990s, considered it too duplicative to have 2 tertiary VA hospitals so close together. The decision was made that the West Roxbury VA would become the tertiary site and the Jamaica VA would become a largely ambulatory facility. I didn't want to stay in that type of setting.

The individual who had been the associate director at the Boston VA had a year earlier been recruited to Syracuse to be the director, and he recruited me in 1996 to be the chief of medicine. I was there for 4 years. The other reason I went to Syracuse was that Alan Jaffe was now chief of cardiology at SUNY Syracuse, having moved from Washington University in 1995. I thought this was a nice opportunity for me to step up to be a chief of medicine and associate chair of medicine at the Syracuse VA and also to develop a collaboration with Alan. The chair of medicine at Syracuse, for some reason, never really supported cardiology. (He was an oncologist.) Several cardiology faculty left, including Alan who went to the Mayo Clinic in 1999 or 2000. It was another sign for me that what I had thought was the perfect place wasn't. My coming back to Syracuse was coming full circle back to the environment where I had started medical school. I had the best of intentions of giving back to the institution where I had received my medical training. It was a good place, just too many factors conspired against it becoming the place I thought it could be.

Thereafter, I became chief of cardiology at Hartford Hospital and the director of the cardiovascular service line. It was the principal teaching affiliate for the University of Connecticut, an 800-bed hospital. I was there from 2000 to 2006. We doubled the size of the cardiology faculty, expanded the fellowship training program, inaugurated the Henry Low Heart Institute (an iconic cardiac surgeon) as a legacy to Dr. Low, and developed a robust preventive cardiology program and women's heart disease program under Paul Thompson's leadership. We established an interventional electrophysiology program, expanded the noninvasive and novel imaging capability and, all in all, developed a first-rate cardiology program.

In the meantime, the COURAGE trial had stated. The VANQWISH trial was my first trial in Boston. There were 2 trials I was involved with at the VA: the VA-HIT (Veterans Affairs High-Density Lipoprotein Intervention Trial) trial, which was the high-density lipoprotein (HDL) intervention trial where we looked at gemfibrozil versus placebo in 2,500 men with low HDL. I was on the planning and steering committees and one of the investigators. I submitted my own cooperative study proposal, which was the VANQWISH trial, a study of non-Q-wave myocardial infarction, which ultimately got approved and funded. It started up right around the time I was at the Boston VA and concluded when I was in Syracuse in 1997 to 1998. Around the same time, in 1996, I submitted the COURAGE trial. I was involved with 3 VA collaborative studies, which were all very similar trials. The VA-HIT study was the very first one to prove the HDL hypothesis that one could reduce coronary deaths in myocardial infarction without influencing low-density lipoprotein (LDL) cholesterol at all, just by modulating HDL and triglycerides, and VANQWISH showed that the conservative strategy was the equivalent of the invasive strategy in non-Q-wave myocardial infarction patients. This study was not well accepted by the interventional community. It attacked one of the sacred cows: the importance of the routine invasive strategy in non-Q-wave myocardial infarction or unstable angina patients. VANQWISH differed in that it was all in non-Q-wave myocardial infarction patients, most of the other preceding studies were a mixture of unstable angina pectoris and non-Q-wave myocardial infarction. For that reason, we thought VANQWISH a bit different. COURAGE actually began in Syracuse, where it got approved and funded. That was a herculean effort, because we only received $12 million from the VA to support the VA enrollment, and I was told that I had 18 months to find the remainder of funding either from the NIH (National Institutes of Health), Canadian government, or industry. There was a full-court press for about 18 months to pull together funding for COURAGE. We approached the Medical Research Council, now known as the Canadian Institutes of Health Research (CIHR), and we formulated the first ever VA-CIHR collaborative study. The CIHR funded the Canadian enrollment in COURAGE. Salim Yusuf played a big role in helping to get that approved and funded. Koon Teo was the principal investigator (PI) to the Canadian sites. Ultimately, we got $20 million from pharmaceutical companies to help support COURAGE. It ended up being a $35 million trial that we cobbled to-

gether from multiple sources, largely from Merck, Pfizer, and Sanofi. COURAGE has become a landmark trial.

Roberts: *Of your professional accomplishments, which ones are you most proud of?*

Boden: I would frame it a bit differently than that. I've been involved with complex strategy trials or, broadly speaking, "comparative effectiveness research" before that phrase became a buzzword. The VA-HIT study challenged the hypothesis that the only way to reduce atherosclerotic events was to reduce the LDL cholesterol. If we use a drug that doesn't affect LDL, can we modulate outcomes with gemfibrozil? We proved the answer to be "yes." VANQWISH was a strategy trial looking at a routine invasive versus elective invasive strategy in non-Q-wave myocardial infarction. COURAGE was a strategy trial looking at percutaneous coronary intervention (PCI) plus optimal medical therapy versus optimal medical there alone in 2,287 patients with stable coronary heart disease, inducible myocardial ischemia, and significant multivessel coronary disease. It showed no incremental benefit of PCI on top of a background of optimal medical therapy. More recently, the AIM-HIGH trial, which unfortunately was stopped several months ago prematurely by the NHLBI (National Heart, Lung, and Blood Institute) for a lack of efficacy. It was a comparative effective research trial looking at a combination of simvastatin plus Niaspan versus simvastatin alone in 34,014 patients with established coronary heart disease and low HDL cholesterol. Lastly, the International Study of Comparative Health Effectiveness with Medical and Invasive Approaches (ISCHEMIA) trial, a sequel to COURAGE in which we plan to test the hypothesis that, in patients with moderate to severe baseline myocardial ischemia and stable ischemic heart disease, "revascularization of choice" with PCI (largely using everolimus stents) or bypass surgery will be superior to an optimal medical therapy strategy alone strategy where coronary anatomy is not defined in the latter group. This will be an ambitious, multinational trial of close to 400 international sites and 8,000 randomized patients in order to determine if a strategy of more "complete revascularization" strategy in chronic angina patients with high risk will provide incremental clinical benefit over and above intensive medical therapy and lifestyle intervention. Judy Hochman from NYU (New York University) is the study chair, David Maron from Vanderbilt is PI, and I will be 1 of 4 co-PIs, along with Gregg Stone, David Williams, and Bob Harrington.

All of these trials have tested strategies of what therapies are better, or can we demonstrate whether one strategy or approach is better or comparable to another strategy or approach. I am proud of having been a major player in these trials, which have a consistency or theme to them. It may trace all the way back to my contrarian roots as a youngster. During high school, in debates, I always took the antagonist side. Challenging conventional wisdom is what drives me.

Returning to the VA health care sector would give me an opportunity to reconnect with the VA Cooperative Studies

Figure 6. Lisa, Audra, Wolfie, and Ryan, 1990.

Program. It's going to be necessary going forward in American medicine to develop a more effective approach to reign in health care expenditures. We cannot continue to sustain the current model of spending 17% of the GDP (gross domestic product) on health care. This is the whole essence of comparative research: finding effective and cost-effective approaches to managing chronic disease. Maybe in the VA system, I will have a platform where I will not be as constrained by the institutional needs and demands of continually expanding procedural cardiology, which hospitals rely on increasingly for generating larger revenues and contribution margins. Chiefs of cardiology in tertiary, academic centers face complex challenges to enhance referral and increase procedural volumes to offset declining reimbursements from payers, which has become increasingly

like running in place on a treadmill. Perhaps, back in the VA health care sector, I can become a more effective spokesperson to confront head on the challenges we face in health care delivery and practice. In the private sector, I would probably get run out of Buffalo if I were to preach that "less is more." That we need to be more selective and evidence based in doing catheter-based revascularization on the coronary, carotid, and peripheral arteries is a difficult philosophy to espouse and sell in a reimbursement system that rewards "doing more, not less." That view also completely contradicts the building of a $200 million heart and vascular institute on the Buffalo Niagara medical campus with an almost singular focus on procedural activity, and where there appears to be only a passing interest in the importance of risk factor intervention and prevention. Do I want to spend the remaining years of my professional life in conflict with what I believe? I think there will be an opportunity for me to have more of an effective role in perhaps changing health care in this country by virtue of returning to the health care sector of the VA system.

Roberts: *What about your personal life—your wife and family? What are the things you enjoy doing outside of medicine and cardiology?*

Boden: As I mentioned earlier, I initially married after graduating from college in 1970 and, with my first wife (Barbara), had 3 wonderful children (Ryan, Lisa, and Audra) (Figure 6). None have gone into medicine, though Ryan aspired to do so earlier in his career. All of our children have grown up and have gone on to higher education and successful careers (public service, publishing, and education). I went through a divorce in 1996 and ultimately remarried a wonderful woman and life partner (Judy Hurstak) in 2002. Judy had likewise transitioned out of a

Figure 7. Surprise 60th birthday party.

long-term marriage and has 2 grown children (Kelly and Jack) who, along with Audra and her new husband (Steve Kenny), all live in the greater Boston area, as do our 4 grandchildren. Judy has been my very best friend and has taught me a great deal about what is really important in life. She is my most ardent supporter: kind, generous, patient, loving, and eternally optimistic. These are qualities I both admire and cherish. Judy and I love doing things together: taking long walks with our 2 Westies, exploring the many fine vineyards in southern Ontario, Canada (and, of course, collecting wine from there and elsewhere), gardening (she amazingly with flowers, me with vegetables), and enjoying our second home in coastal Rhode Island, which has been our "home away from home" and where we generally find it easier to rendezvous with our children and grandchildren (Figures 7 and 8). Rhode Island has become our magnet and safe haven to gather with family. Living and working in Albany will bring us 4 hours closer to New England than living in Buffalo and will put us within 2½ hours of most of our family and our Rhode Island home. I love football and have, since 1993, been a New England Patriots season ticket holder. I'll now be able to take in more games with a far easier commute. I also love to play golf but just haven't found as much time as I would like to play in the past few years, but I'm hoping I'll find a way to make more time. When I lived in Rhode Island, I used to enjoy sailing and saltwater fishing. Judy's dad, who is in his late 80s and slowing down, has been living in East Greenwich, Rhode Island, for the past several years, has had an old O'Day 25-foot sailboat that we will soon inherit, and is one of the things I really look forward to when we can put this in the water in the spring off the mooring adjacent to our home on Duck Cove in Wickford, Rhode Island. Again, I think we will once again find it easier have more time to spend in Rhode Island by being so much closer than we could have been living in Buffalo.

Roberts: *Bill, is there anything else you would like to add?*

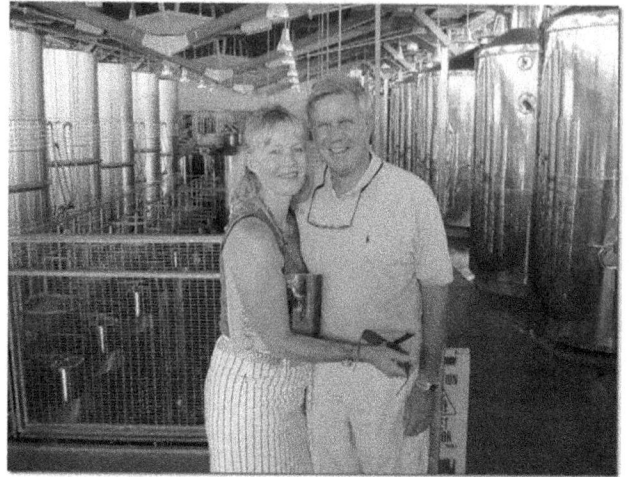

Figure 8. Judy and Bill, Canadian vineyard, 2011.

Boden: I really don't think so. We have really covered an enormous amount of terrain over the last few hours, and I have thoroughly enjoyed this opportunity to meet with you in your home, where the 2 of us could chat so openly and freely without other distractions. In reflecting on all that we've discussed, I really think this interview has given me a renewed perspective of how very thankful and blessed I have been in both my professional and personal life. As I'm sure you would agree, it has been a privilege to have been able to develop a fulfilling career in academic cardiology, to have engaged in the training and education of countless residents and fellows over the past 33 years, to have contributed, I hope, in advancing the management of cardiac patients through clinical research activities, and lastly, to have had the opportunity to have met, worked with, and collaborated with so many remarkably talented mentors and colleagues for almost 4 decades. Thanks so very much for giving me this special opportunity to meet with you today. Now, I want to get back outside and see if it's still 110 degrees on this otherwise sunny Dallas summer day!

BEST PUBLICATIONS OF WEB SELECTED BY WEB

1. Gilbert R, Auchincloss JH Jr, Brodsky J, Boden WE. Changes in tidal volume, frequency and ventilation induced by their measurement. *J Appl Physiol* 1972;33:252–254.

5. Boden WE, Liang C, Apstein CS, Hood WB Jr. Experimental myocardial infarction: XVI. The detection of inotropic contractile reserve with postextrasystolic potentiation in acutely ischemic canine myocardium. *Am J Cardiol* 1978;41:523–530.

8. Boden WE, Liang CS, Hood WB Jr. Postextrasystolic potentiation of regional mechanical performance during prolonged myocardial ischemia in the dog. *Circulation* 1980;61:1063–1070.

11. Sherman LG, Liang CS, Boden WE, Hood WB Jr. Effect of verapamil on mechanical performance of acutely ischemic and reperfused myocardium in the conscious dog. *Circulation Res* 1981;48:224–232.

12. Boden WE, Bough EW, Korr KS, Benham I, Gheorghiade M, Caputi A, Shulman RS. Exercise-induced coronary spasm with S-T segment depression and normal coronary arteriography. *Am J Cardiol* 1981;48:193–197.

15. Boden WE, Bough EW, Benham I, Shulman RS. Unstable angina pectoris with S-T segment elevation and increased creatine kinase activity culminating in extensive recurrent myocardial infarction. *J Am Coll Cardiol* 1983;2:11–20.

19. Bough EW, Boden WE, Korr KS, Gandsman EJ. Left ventricular asynergy in electrocardiographic "posterior" myocardial infarction. *J Am Coll Cardiol* 1984;4:209–215.

20. Boden WE, Bough EW, Korr KS, Gandsman EJ, Shulman RS. Inferoseptal myocardial infarction: Another cause of precordial ST-segment depression in transmural inferior wall myocardial infarction? *Am J Cardiol* 1984;54:1216–1223.

22. Boden WE, Korr KS, Bough EW. Nifedipine-induced myocardial ischemia in refractory angina pectoris. *J Am Med Assoc* 1985;8:1131–1135.

23. Boden WE, Bough EW, Reichman MJ, Rich V, Young PM, Korr KS, Shulman RS. Beneficial effects of high-dose diltiazem in patients with persistent effort angina on beta-blockers and nitrates: A randomized, double-blind, placebo-controlled crossover trial. *Circulation* 1985;71:1197–1205.

28. Gibson RS, Boden WE, Theroux P, Strauss HD, Pratt CM, Gheorghiade M, Capone RJ, Crawford MH, Schlant RD, Kleiger RE, Young PM, Schechtman K, Perryman MB, Roberts R, and The Diltiazem Re-Infarction Study (DRS) Group. Diltiazem and reinfarction in patients with non-Q wave myocardial infarction: Results of a double-blind, randomized multicenter trial. *N Engl J Med* 1986;315:423–429.

31. Kohl DW, Boden WE, Kleiger RE, Gibson RS, Schechtman KB, Capone RJ, Roberts R, on behalf of the Diltiazem Reinfarction Study Group, Brown University, Providence, RI. Electrocardiographic evolution of posterior myocardial infarction: importance of early precordial S-T segment depression. *Am J Cardiol* 1987;59:782–787.

34. Bough EW, Boden WE, Korr KS, Gandsman EJ. Left ventricular asynergy in electrocardiographic "posterior" myocardial infarction. *J Am Coll Cardiol* 1987;4:209–215.

35. Gibson RS, Young PM, Boden WE, Schechtman K, Roberts R. Prognostic significance and beneficial effect of diltiazem on the incidence of early recurrent ischemia after non-Q wave myocardial infarction. *Am J Cardiol* 1987;60:203–209.

38. Moss AJ, Abrams J, Bigger JT, Boden WE, Bodenheimer MM, Case R, et al. The effect of diltiazem on mortality and reinfarction after myocardial infarction: Results of the multicenter diltiazem post-infarction trial (MDPIT). *N Engl J Med* 1988;319:385–392.

41. Boden WE, Kleiger RE, Schechtman KB, Capone RJ, Schwartz DJ, Gibson RS. The clinical significance and prognostic importance of left ventricular hypertrophy in non-Q wave acute myocardial infarction. *Am J Cardiol* 1988;62:1000–1004.

50. Boden WE, Gibson RS, Schechtman KB, Kleiger RE, Schwartz DJ, Capone RJ, Roberts R. ST-segment shifts are poor predictors of subsequent Q-wave evolution in acute myocardial infarction: Natural history study of early non-Q-wave myocardial infarction. *Circulation* 1989;79:537–548.

52. Boden WE, Kleiger RE, Gibson RS, Reddy BR, Schechtman KB, Schwartz DJ, Capone RJ, Roberts R. Favorable long-term prognosis of acute non-Q-

wave myocardial infarction associated with absent or nonspecific electrocardiographic changes. *Br Heart J* 1989;61:396–402.

55. Boden WE, Gibson RS, Kleiger RE, Schechtman KB, Capone RJ, Schwartz DJ, Roberts R, and the Diltiazem Reinfarction Study Research Group. Importance of early recurrent ischemia on one-year survival after non-Q-wave acute myocardial infarction. *Am J Cardiol* 1989;64:799–801.

56. Schechtman KB, Capone RJ, Kleiger RE, Gibson RS, Schwartz DJ, Roberts R, Young PM, Boden WE, and the Diltiazem Reinfarction Study Research Group. Risk stratification of patients with non-Q-wave myocardial infarction: The critical role of ST segment depression. *Circulation* 1989;80:1148–1158.

58. Kleiger RE, Boden WE, Schechtman KB, Gibson RS, Schwartz DJ, Geiger BJ, Capone RJ, Roberts R, and the Diltiazem Reinfarction Study Group. Frequency and significance of late evolution of Q-waves in patients with initial non-Q-wave acute myocardial infarction. *Am J Cardiol* 1990;65:23–27.

59. Kleiman NS, Schechtman KB, Young PM, Goodman DA, Boden WE, Pratt CM, Roberts R. Lack of diurnal variation in the onset of a non-Q-wave infarction. *Circulation* 1990;81:548–555.

60. Schechtman KB, Capone RJ, Kleiger RE, Gibson RS, Schwartz DJ, Roberts R, Boden WE, and the Diltiazem Reinfarction Study Group. Differential risk patterns associated with 3 month as compared with 3 to 12 month mortality and reinfarction after non-Q-wave myocardial infarction. *J Am Coll Cardiol* 1990;15:940–947.

61. Boden WE, Krone RJ, Kleiger RE, Oakes D, Greenberg H, Dwyer EJ Jr, Miller JP, Abrams J, Coromilas J, Goldstein R, Moss AJ and the Multicenter Diltiazem Post-Infarction Trial Research Group. Electrocardiographic subset analysis of diltiazem administration on long-term outcome after acute myocardial infarction. *Am J Cardiol* 1991;67:335–342.

63. Boden WE. Electrocardiographic correlates of reperfusion status after thrombolysis: Is the "incomplete" or "interrupted" infarction a non-Q-wave infarction? *Am J Cardiol* 1991;68:520–524.

64. Boden WE. Moss AJ, Oakes D. Hypolipidemic effect of Type IA antiarrhythmic agents in post-infarction patients. *Circulation* 1992;85:2039–2044.

66. Schechtman KB, Kleiger RE, Boden WE, Capone RJ, Schwartz DJ, Roberts R, Gibson RS. Relationship between 1-year mortality and infarct location in patients with non-Q-wave myocardial infarction. *Am Heart J* 1992;123:1175–1181.

67. Pepine CJ, Kern MJ, Boden WE. The ischemic myocardium: Strategies for preservation and protection. *Am J Cardiol* 1992;69:41B–46B.

69. Boden WE. Meta-Analysis in Clinical Trials Reporting: Has a tool become a weapon? *Am J of Cardiol* 1992;69:681–686.

71. Krone RJ, Greenberg H, Dwyer E, Kleiger RE, Boden WE. Long-term prognostic significance of ST-segment depression during acute myocardial infarction. *Am J Cardiol* 1993;72:361–367.

73. Boden WE, Moss AJ, Herbert PN, Saritelli A, Oakes D, Eberly S, and the Multicenter Diltiazem Post-Infarction Trial Research Group. Effect of long-term diltiazem administration on serum lipids in post-myocardial infarction survivors. *Am J Cardiol* 1994;73:513–515.

78. Boden WE, Brooks WW, Conrad CH, Bing OHL, Hood WB Jr. Incomplete delayed functional recovery after reperfusion following myocardial infarction: "Maimed Myocardium". *Am Heart J* 1995;130:922–932.

80. Boden WE, Ziesche S, Carson PE, Conrad CH, Syat D, Cohn JN, and the V-HeFT-III Research Study Group. Rationale and design of the Third Vasodilator-Heart Failure Trial (V-HeFT-III): Felodipine as adjunctive therapy to enalapril, digoxin and loop diuretics in chronic congestive heart failure. *Am J Cardiol* 1996;77:1078–1082.

81. Cohn JN, Ziesch S, Smith R, Anand I, Dunkman WB, Loeb H, Cintron G, Boden WE, Baruch L, Rochin P, Loss L. Effect of the calcium antagonist feldipine as supplementary vasodilator therapy in patients with chronic heart failure treated with enalapril: V-HeFT III. Vasodilator-Heart Failure Trial (V-HeFT) Study Group. *Circulation* 1997;96:856–863.

82. Ferry RD, O'Rourke RA, Blaustein AS, Crawford MH, Deedwania PC, Carson PE, Pepine CJ, Thomas RG, Hlatky MA, Leppo JA, Iwane MK, Kleiger RE, Zoble RG, Dai H, Chow BK, Lavori PW, Boden WE. Design and baseline characteristics of the Veterans Affairs Non-Q-Wave Infarction Strategies In-Hopital (VANQWISH) Trial. *J Am Coll Cardiol* 1998;31:312–320.

83. Boden WE, O'Rourke RA, Crawford MH, Blaustein AS, Deedwania PC, Zoble RG, Wexler LF, Kleiger RE, Pepine CR, Ferry DR, Chow BK, Lavori PW. Outcomes in patients with acute non-Q-wave myocardial infarction randomly assigned to an invasive as compared with a conservative management strategy. *N Eng J Med* 1998;338: 1785–1792.

84. Boden WE, Pearson TA. Raising Low Levels of High-Density Lipoprotein Cholesterol Is an Important Target of Therapy. *Am J Cardiol* 2000;1:85–89.

106. Boden WE, Pearson TA. Raising low levels of high-density lipoprotein cholesterol is an important target of therapy. *Am J Cardiol* 2000;85:645–650.

107. Boden WE, van Gilst WH, Scheldewaert RG, Starkey IR, Carlier MF, Julian DG, Whitehead A, Bertrand ME, Col JJ, Pedersen OL, Lie KI, Santoni JP, Fox KM. Diltiazem in acute myocardial infarction treated with thrombolytic agents: a randomized placebo-controlled trial. Incomplete Infarction Trial of European Research Collaborators Evaluating Prognosis post-Thrombolysis (INTERCEPT). *Lancet* 2000; 355:1751–1756.

108. Gibson RS, Hansen JF, Messerli F, Schechtman KB, Boden WE. Long-term effects of diltiazem and verapamil on mortality and cardiac events in non-Q-wave acute myocardial infarction without pulmonary congestion: post hoc subset analysis of the multicenter diltiazem post-infarction trial and the second Danish verapamil infarction trial studies. *Am J Cardiol* 2000;86:275–279.

112. Heggunje PS, Wade MJ, O'Rourke RA, Kleiger RE, Deedwania PC, Lavori PW, Boden WE, VANQWISH trial investigators. Early invasive versus ischemia-guided strategies in the management of non-Q wave myocardial infarction patients with and without prior myocardial infarction; results of Veterans Affairs Non-Q Wave Infarction Strategies in Hospital (VANQWISH) trial. *Europ Heart J* 2000;21: 2014–2025.

116. Wexler LF, Blaustein AS, Lavori PW, Lehmann KG, Wade M, Boden WE. Non-Q-wave myocardial infarction following thrombolytic therapy: a comparison of outcomes in patients randomized to invasive or conservative post-infarct assessment strategies in the Veterans Affairs non-Q-wave Infarction Strategies In-Hospital (VANQWISH) Trial. *J Am Coll Cardiol* 2001;37:19–25.

118. Boden WE, McKay RG. Optimal treatment of acute coronary syndromes--an evolving strategy. *N Eng J Med* 2001;344:1939–1942.

125. McKay RG, Boden WE. Small peptide GP IIb/IIIa receptor inhibitors as upstream therapy in non-ST-segment elevation acute coronary syndromes: results of the PURSUIT,PRISM, PRISM-PLUS, TACTICS, and PARAGON trials. *Curr Op Cardiol* 2001;16:364–369.

127. Barnett PG, Chen S, Boden WE, Chow B, Every NR, Lavori PW, Hlatky. Cost-effectiveness of a conservative, ischemia-guided management strategy after non-Q-wave myocardial infarction: results of a randomized trial. *Circulation* 2002;105:680–684.

129. Kerensky RA, Wade M, Deedwania P, Boden WE, Pepine CJ. Revisiting the culprit lesion in non-Q-wave myocardial infarction. Results from the VANQWISH trial angiographic core laboratory. *J Am Coll Cardiol* 2002;39:1456–1463.

130. Goyal A, Samaha FF, Boden WE, Wade MJ, Kimmel SE. Stress test criteria used in the conservative arm of the FRISC-II trial underdetects surgical coronary artery disease when applied to patients in the VANQWISH trial. *J Am Coll Cardiol* 2002;39:1601–1607.

134. Boden WE. Is it time to reassess the optimal timing of coronary artery bypass graft surgery following acute myocardial infarction? *Am J Cardiol* 2002;90:35–38.

136. Samaha FF, Kimmel SE, Kizer J, Goyal A, Wade MJ, Boden WE. Usefulness of the TIMI Risk Score in predicting both short and long-term outcomes in the Veterans Affairs Non-Q-Wave Infarction Strategies In-Hospital (VANQWISH) Trial. *Am J Cardiol* 2002;90: 922–926.

137. Januzzi JL, Cannon CP, Theroux P, Boden WE. Optimizing glycoprotein IIb/IIIa receptor antagonist use for patients with non-ST-segment elevation acute coronary syndrome. *Am Heart J* 2002;146: 764–774.

140. Yarlagadda RK, Boden WE. Cardioprotective effects of an early invasive strategy for non- ST-segment elevation acute coronary syndromes: are we all becoming 'Interventional' Cardiologists? *J Am Coll Cardiol* 2002;40:1915–1918.

147. Januzzi JL, Cannon CP, Theroux P, Boden WE. Optimizing glycoprotein IIb/IIIa receptor antagonist use for the non-ST-segment ele-

vation acute coronary syndromes: risk stratification and therapeutic intervention. [Review] *Am Heart J* 2003;146:764–774.

153. Boden WE. Surgery, angioplasty, or medical therapy for symptomatic multivessel coronary artery disease: is there an indisputable "winning strategy" from evidence-based clinical trials? *J Am Coll Cardiol* 2004;43:1752–1754.

154. Elkoustaf RA, Boden WE. Is there a gender paradox in the early invasive strategy for non ST- segment elevation acute coronary syndromes? *Eur Heart J* 2004;18:1559–1561.

157. Mehta SR, Cannon CP, Fox KA, Wallentin L, Boden WE, Spacek R, Widimsky P, McCullough PA, Hunt D, Braunwald E, Yusuf S. Routine vs selective invasive strategies in patients with acute coronary syndromes: a collaborative meta-analysis of randomized trials. *J Am Med Assoc* 2005;293:2908–2917.

158. Boden WE. Acute coronary syndromes without ST-segment elevation--what is the role of early intervention? *N Engl J Med* 2005;353: 1159–1161.

161. Bhatt DL, Fox KAA, Hacke W, Berger PB, Black HR, Boden WE, Cacoub P, Cohen EA, Creager MA, Easton JD, Flather MD, Haffner SM, Hamm CW, Hankey GJ, Johnston CJ, Mak K-H, Mas J-L, Montalescot G, Pearson TA, Steg PG, Steinhubl SR, Weber MA, Brennan DM, Fabry-Ribaudo L, Booth J, Topol EJ: Clopidogrel and aspirin versus aspirin alone for the prevention of atherothrombotic event. *N Engl J Med* 2006;354:1706–1717.

163. Boden WE, O'Rourke RA, Teo KK, Hartigan PM, Maron DJ, Kostuk WJ, Knudtson M, Dada, M, Casperson P, Harris CL, Chaitman BR, Shaw L, Gosselin G, Blaustein AS, Booth DC, Bates ER, Spertus JA, Berman DS, Mancini GBJ, Weintraub WS. Design and rationale of the Clinical Outcomes Utilizing Revascularization and Aggressive DruG Evaluation (COURAGE) Trial. *Am Heart J* 2006;151:1173–1179.

166. Diercks DB, Roe MT, Mulgund J, Pollack CV, Kirk JD, Gibler WB, Ohman EM, Smith SC, Boden WE, Peterson ED: The obesity paradox in non-ST-segment elevation acute coronary syndromes: Results from the CRUSADE Quality Improvement Initiative. *Am Heart J* 2006;152:140–148.

169. Favarato ME, Hueb W, Boden WE, Lopes N, Nogueira CR, Takiuti M, Gois AF, Borges JC, Favarato D, Aldrighi JM, Oliveira SA, Ramires JA. Quality of life in patients with symptomatic multivessel coronary artery disease: a comparative post hoc analyses of medical, angioplasty or surgical strategies - MASS-II trial. *Intl J Cardiol* 2007;116:364–370.

170. Boden WE, O'Rourke RA, Teo KK, Hartigan PM, Maron DJ, Kostuk WJ, Knudtson M, Dada, M, Casperson P, Harris CL, Chaitman BR, Shaw L, Gosselin G, Blaustein AS, Booth DC, Bates ER, Spertus JA, Berman DS, Mancini GBJ, Weintraub WS: The evolving pattern of symptomatic coronary heart disease in the United States and Canada: Baseline characteristics of the Clinical Outcomes Utilizing Revascularization and Aggressive Drug Evaluation (COURAGE) Trial. *Am J Cardiol* 2007;99:208–212.

171. Boden WE, O'Rourke RA, Teo KK, Hartigan PM, Maron DJ, Kostuk WJ, Knudtson M, Dada, M, Casperson P, Harris CL, Chaitman BR, Shaw L, Gosselin G, Nawaz S, Title LM, Gau G, Blaustein AS, Booth DC, Bates ER, Spertus JA, Berman DS, Mancini GBJ, Weintraub WS. Optimal medical therapy with or without PCI in stable coronary disease. *N Engl J Med* 2007;356:1503–1516.

172. Bhatt DL, Flather MD, Hacke W, Berger PB, Black HR, Boden WE, Cacoub P, Cohen EA, Creager MA, Easton JD, Flather MD, Haffner SM, Hamm CW, Hankey GJ, Johnston CJ, Mak K-H, Mas J-L, Montalescot G, Pearson TA, Steg PG, Steinhubl SR, Weber MA, Brennan DM, Fabry-Ribaudo L, Booth J, Topol EJ: Patients with prior myocardial infarction, stroke, or symptomatic peripheral arterial disease in the CHARISMA trial. *J Am Coll Cardiol* 2007;49:1982–1988.

174. Boden WE, Eagle K, Granger CB: Reperfusion strategies in acute ST-segment elevation myocardial infarction: a comprehensive review of contemporary management options. *J Am Coll Cardiol* 2007;50: 917–929.

179. Shaw LJ, Berman Ds, Maron DJ, Mancini GBJ, Hayes SW, Hartigan PM, Weintraub WS, O'Rourke RA, Dada M, Spertus JA, Chaitman BR, Friedman J, Slomka P, Heller GV, Germano G, Gosselin G, Berger P, Kostuk WJ, Schwartz RG, Knudtson M, Veledar E, Bates ER, McCallister B, Teo K, Boden WE for the COURAGE investigators: Optimal medical therapy with or without percutaneous coronary intervention to reduce ischemic burden. Results from the Clinical Outcomes Utilizing Revascularization and Aggressive DruG

Evaluation (COURAGE) Trial Nuclear Substudy. *Circulation* 2008;117:1283–1291.

180. Boden, WE, Hoekstra J, Miller CD: ST-elevation myocardial infarction: the role of adjunctive antiplatelet therapy. *Am J Em Med* 2008; 26:212–220.

181. Taggart DP, Kaul S, Boden WE, Ferguson TB Jr, Guyton RA, Mack MJ, Sergeant PT, Shemin RJ, Smith PK, Yusuf S. Revascularization for unprotected left main stem coronary artery stenosis stenting or surgery. *J Am Coll Cardiol* 2008;51:885–892.

182. Boden WE, Shah PK, Gupta V, Ohman EM: Contemporary approach to the diagnosis and management of non-ST-segment elevation acute coronary syndromes. *Prog Cardiovasc Dis* 2008;50:311–351.

183. Boden WE, Maron DJ: Reducing post-myocardial infarction mortality in the elderly: The power and promise of secondary prevention. *J Am Coll Cardiol* 2008;51:1255–1257.

184. Boden WE, Diamond GA: DTCA for PTCA–Crossing the line in consumer health education? *N Engl J Med* 2008;358:2197–2200.

185. Alexander KP, Chen AY, Wang TY, Rao SV, Newby LK, LaPointe NM, Ohman EM, Roe MT, Boden WE, Harrington RA, Peterson ED; CRUSADE Investigators. Transfusion practice and outcomes in non-ST-segment elevation acute coronary syndromes. *Am Heart J* 2008; 155:1047–1053.

189. O'Donoghue ML, Boden WE, Braunwald E, Cannon CP, Clayton TC, de Winter RJ, Fox KA, Lagerqvist B, McCullough PA, Murphy SA, Spacek R, Swahn E, Wallentin L, Windhausen F, Sabatine MS. Early invasive vs conservative treatment strategies in women and men with unstable angina/ non-ST-segment elevation myocardial infarction: A meta-analysis. *J Am Med Assoc* 2008;300:71–80.

191. Weintraub WS, Spertus JA, Kolm P, Maron DJ, Zhang Z, Jurkovitz C, Zhang W, Hartigan PM, Lewis C, Veledar E, Bowen J, Dunbar SB, Deaton C, Kaufman S, O'Rourke RA, Goeree R, Barnett PG, Teo KK, Boden WE; COURAGE Trial Research Group, Mancini GB. Effect of PCI on quality of life in patients with stable coronary disease. *N Engl J Med* 2008;359:677–687.

194. Mehta SR, Boden WE, Eikelboom JW, Flather M, Steg PG, Avezum A, Afzal R, Piegas LS, Faxon DP, Widimsky P, Budaj A, Chrolavicius S, Rupprecht HJ, Jolly S, Granger CB, Fox KA, Bassand JP, Yusuf S; for the OASIS 5 and 6 Investigators. Antithrombotic therapy with fondaparinux in relation to interventional management strategy in patients with ST- and non-ST-segment elevation acute coronary syndromes. an individual patient-level combined analysis of the fifth and sixth organization to assess strategies in ischemic syndromes (OASIS 5 and 6) randomized trials. *Circulation* 2008;118:2038–2046.

195. Weintraub WS, Boden WE, Zhang Z, Kolm P, Zhang Z, Spertus JA, Hartigan P, Veledar E, Jurkowitz C, Bowen J, Maron DJ, O'Rourke RA, Dada M, Teo KK, Goeree R, Barnett PG. Cost-effectiveness of percutaneous coronary intervention in optimally treated stable coronary patients. *Circ Cardiovasc Qual Outcomes* 2008;1:12–20.

198. Boden WE, O'Rourke RA, Teo KK, Maron DJ, Hartigan PM, Sedlis SP, Dada M, Labedi M, Spertus JA, Kostuk WJ, Berman DS, Shaw LJ, Chaitman BR, Mancini GBJ, Weintraub WS. Impact of optimal medical therapy with or without percutaneous coronary intervention on long-term cardiovascular endpoints in patients with stable coronary artery disease from the COURAGE Trial. *Am J Cardiol* 2009;104:1–4.

199. Mancini GBJ, Bates ER, Maron DJ, Hartigan P, Dada M, Gosselin G, Kostuk WJ, Sedlis SP, Shaw LJ, Berman DS, Berger PB, Spertus JA, Mavromatis K, Knudtson M, Chaitman BR, O'Rourke RA, Weintraub WS, Teo KK, Boden WE. Quantitative results of baseline angiography and percutaneous coronary intervention in the COURAGE Trial. *Circ Cardiovasc Qual Outcomes* 2009;2:320–327.

202. Maron DJ, Spertus JA, Mancini GBJ, Hartigan PM, Sedlis SP, Bates ER, Kostuk WJ, Berman DS, Shaw LJ, Teo KK, Weintraub WS, Boden WE. Impact of an initial strategy of medical therapy without percutaneous coronary intervention is high-risk patients from the COURAGE Trial. *Am J Cardiol* 2009;104:1055–1062.

206. Teo KK, Sedlis SP, Boden WE, O'Rourke RA, Maron DJ, Hartigan PM, Dada M, Gupta V, Spertus JA, Kostuk WJ, Berman DS, Shaw LJ, Chaitman BR, Mancini GBJ, Weintraub WS. Optimal medical therapy with or without percutaneous coronary intervention in older patients with stable coronary disease; a pre-specified subset analysis of the COURAGE Trial. *J Am Coll Cardiol* 2009;54:1303–1308.

210. Mehta SR, Granger DB, Boden WE, Steg PG, Bassand JP, Faxon DP, Afzal R, Chrolavicius S, Jolly SS, Widimsky P, Avezum A, Rupprecht HA, Zhu J, Col J, Natarajan MK, Horsman C, Fox KA, Yusuf S, for the TIMACS investicators. Early versus delayed invasive intervention in acute coronary syndromes. *N Engl J Med* 2009;360:2165–2175.

211. Boden WE, Taggart DP. Diabetes with coronary disease – a moving target amid evolving therapies? *N Engl J Med* 2009;360:2570–2572.

212. Jolly SS, Faxon DP, Fox KAA, Afzal R, Boden WE, Widimsky P, Steg PG, Valentin V, Budaj A, Granger CB, Joyner CV, Chrolavicius S, Yusuf S, Mehta SR. Efficacy and safety of Fondaparinux versus enoxaparin in patients with acute coronary syndromes treated with glycoprotein IIb/IIIa inhibitors or thienopyridines. Results from the OASIS 5 (5th Organization to Assess Strategies in Ischemic Syndromes) Trial. *J Am Coll Cardiol* 2009;54:468–476.

215. Maron DJ, Spertus JA, Mancini JB, Hartigan PM, Sedlis SP, Bates Er, Kostuk WJ, Dada M, Berman DS, Shaw LJ, Chaitman BR, Teo KK, O'Rourke RA, Weintraub WS, Boden WE for the COURAGE Trial Research Group. Impact of an initial strategy of medical therapy without percutaneous coronary intervention in high-risk patients from the clinical outcomes utilizing revascularization and aggressive drug evaluation (COURAGE) Trial. *Am J Cardiol* 2009;104:1055–1062.

221. Chaitman BR, Hartigan PM, Booth DC, Teo KK, Mancini GBJ, Kostuk WJ, Spertus JA, Maron DJ, Dada M, O'Rourke RA, Weintraub WS, Berman DS, Shaw LJ, Boden WE. Do major cardiovascular outcomes in patients with stable ischemic heart disease in COURAGE differ by healthcare system? *Circ Cardiovasc Qual Outcomes* 2010;3:476–483.

222. Cannon CP, Rhee K, Califf R, Boden WE, Hirsch A, Alberts M, Cable G, Shao M, Ohman EM, Steg PG, Eagle K, Bhatt D for the REACH Registry Investigators. Current use of aspirin and antithrombotic agents in the United States among outpatients with atherothrombotic disease (from the Reduction of Atherothrombosis for Continued Health (REACH Registry). *Am J Cardiol* 2010;105:445–452.

223. Maron DJ, Boden WE, O'Rourke, RA, Hartigan PM, Calfas KJ, Mancini JBJ, Spertus JA, Dada M, Kostuk WJ, Knudtson MK, Harris CL, Sedlis SP, Zoble RG, Title LM, Gosselin G, Nawaz S, Gau GT, Blaustein AS, Bates ER, Shaw LJ, Berman DS, Chaitman BR, Weintraub WS, Teo KK for the COURAGE Trial research group. Intensive multifactorial intervention for stable coronary artery disease. *J Am Coll Cardiol* 2010;55:1348–1358.

230. Williams DO, Vasaiwalda SC, Boden WE. Is optimal medical therapy "optimal therapy" for multivessel coronary artery disease? Optimal management of multivessel coronary artery disease. *Circulation* 2010;122:943–945.

238. Zhang Z, Kolm P, Boden WE, Hartigan PM, Maron DJ, Spertus JA, O'Rourke RA, Shaw LJ, Sedlis SP, Mancini GBJ, Berman DS, Dada M, Teo KK, Weintraub WS. The cost effectiveness of PCI as a function of angina severity in patients with stable angina. *Circ Cardiovasc Outcomes* 2011;4:172–182.

239. AIM-HIGH Investigators. The role of niacin in raising high-density lipoprotein cholesterol to reduce cardiovascular events in patients with atherosclerosis cardiovascular disease and optimally treated low-density lipoprotein cholesterol rationale and study design. The Atherothrombosis Intervention in Metabolic syndrome with low HDL/high triglycerides: Impact on Global Health outcomes (AIM-HIGH). *Am Heart J* 2011;161:471–477.

242. Maron DJ, Boden WE, Spertus JA, Hartigan PM, Mancini GBJ, Sedlis SP, Kostuk WJ, Chaitman BR, Shaw LJ, Berman DS, Dada M, Teo KK, Weintraub WS, O'Rourke RA. Impact of Metabolic Syndrome and Diabetes on Prognosis and Outcomes with Early Percutaneous Coronary Intervention in the Clinical Outcomes Utilizing Revascularization and Aggressive DruG Evaluation (COURAGE) Trial. *J Am Coll Cardiol* 2011;58:131–137.

243. Mancini GBJ, Hartigan PM, Sedlis SP, Maron DJ, Spertus J, Berman DS, Kostuk WJ, Bates ER, Shaw LJ, Weintraub WS, Teo KK, Dada M, Chaitman BR, O'Rourke RA, Boden WE. Angiographic changes and residual risk of cardiovascular events while on optimal medical therapy: observations from the COURAGE trial. *Circ Cardiovasc Interv* 2011;4:545–552.

244. Maron DJ, Stone GW, Berman DS, Mancini GBJ, Scott TA, Byrne DW, Harrell FE, Shaw LJ, Hachamovitch R, Boden WE, Weintraub WS, Spertus JA. Is cardiac catheterization necessary prior to initial management of patients with stable ischemic heart disease? Results from a web-based survey of cardiologists. *Am Heart J* 2011;162: 1034–1043.

245. Shaw LJ, Mieres JH, Hendel RH, Gulati M, Veledar E, Boden WE, Hachamovitch R, Arrighi JA, Merz CN, Gibbons RJ, Wenger NK,

Heller GV. Comparative Effectiveness of Exercise Electro-cardiography With or Without Myocardial Perfusion SPECT in Women with Suspected Coronary Artery Disease: Results from the What's the Optimal Method for Ischemia Evaluation in Women (WOMEN) Trial. *Circulation* 2011;124:1239–1249.

246. Boden WE. Is myocardial perfusion imaging an important predictor of mortality in women with suspected ischemic heart disease in developing countries - and, if so, is this likely cost-effective? *JACC Cardiovasc Imaging* 2011;4:889–893.

247. Boden WE, Probstfield JL, McBride R for the AIM-HIGH Trial investigators: Niacin in patients with low HDL cholesterol levels receiving intensive statin therapy. *N Engl J Med* 2011;365:2255–2267.

248. Boden WE. Mounting evidence for lack of PCI benefit in stable ischemic heart disease: What more will it take to turn the tide of treatment: *Arch Intern Med*; 2012;172:319–321.

249. Gosselin G, Teo KK, Tanguay J-F, Gokhale R, Hartigan PM, Maron DJ, Mancini GBJ, Bates ER, Chaitman BR, Spertus JA, Kostuk WJ, Dada M, Sedlis SP, Berman DS, Shaw LJ, O'Rourke RA, Weintraub WS, Boden WE. Effectiveness of percutaneous coronary intervention in patients with silent myocardial ischemia (Post hoc analysis of the COURAGE trial). *Am J Cardiol* 2012; (in press, April 1, 2012)

254. Boden WE. Weighing the evidence for PCI decision-making in patients with stable CAD. *Circulation* 2012; (in press, April 17, 2012)

255. O'Donoghue ML, Vaidya A, Afsal R, Alfredsson J, Boden WE, Braunwald E, Cannon CP,Clayton TC, de Winter RJ, Fox KAA, Lagerqvist, McCullough PA, Murphy SA, Spacek R, Swahn E, Winshausen F, Sabatine MS. An invasive or conservative strategy in patients with diabetes mellitus and non-ST-segment elevation acute coonary syndromes: A collaborative meta-analysis of randomized trials. (in press, *J Am Coll Cardiol*, June, 2012).

ROBERT OGDEN BONOW, MD:
A Conversation With the Editor*

Bob Bonow was born in Camden, New Jersey, on 11 March 1947, and grew up in New Jersey in the suburbs of New York City. He graduated from Lehigh University magna cum laude in chemical engineering in 1969, and from the University of Pennsylvania School of Medicine in 1973. His medical internship and residency were at the Hospital of the University of Pennsylvania. In 1976 he went to the National Heart, Lung, and Blood Institute in Bethesda, Maryland, where he remained until 1992 when he moved to Chicago to be the Goldberg Distinguished Professor of Cardiology and Chief of the Division of Cardiology in the Department of Medicine of Northwestern University Medical School. Dr. Bonow is one of the world's outstanding cardiologists. He is a superb clinician, splendid clinical investigator, and marvelous teacher. He is also a nice guy and a good friend. I had the privilege of interviewing Dr. Bonow in his office at Northwestern University Medical Center in Chicago on 31 October 1997.

William Clifford Roberts, MD† (Hereafter, WCR): *Dr. Bonow, I would like to talk primarily about you as a person rather than about the work. I wonder if you could start by talking about your upbringing, where you were born, where you grew up, your family, your mother and father, your siblings.*

Robert Ogden Bonow, MD‡ (Hereafter, ROB): I was born in New Jersey and grew up in the 1950s in a New York suburb. We originally lived in a little town called Wood Ridge, New Jersey. This same town produced several other cardiologists who have done quite well, including Raymond Gibbons at the Mayo Clinic. Ray and I played baseball in the same little league. My father was a chemical engineer and my mother was a homemaker. Both of them spent a lot of time with their kids and were very nurturing parents. There were a lot of things we did as a family. My father was very much involved in little league, Boy Scouts, and sports with his children. I have a brother, Tom, who is 2 years older and is now living in Dallas. I have a sister Kathryn who is 4 years younger and she lives in New Jersey. I came away from my childhood with the feeling from my parents that family is very important and spending time with children and nurturing them is a very important part of what being an adult is all about.

WCR: *What was it like around the dinner table at night when you would come home from school? Did you have a lot of discussions, was it an intellectual*

type of environs? What was it like on a day-to-day basis?

ROB: As youngsters, we dealt with the usual day-to-day things kids do and kids remember. I would not say it was terribly intellectual until perhaps when we were teenagers and could talk in a more adult style. We had a true family relationship, which I find very difficult to maintain in my own career. Sometimes I feel I am not giving to my family what I should, based upon what my parents gave me. My father traveled and had business obligations. He was not home every night, but when he was not traveling he was home for dinner. Even when he was traveling he somehow made it possible to be there when I had a baseball or basketball game. I played basketball in high school and college. He would travel sometimes hundreds of miles to get to the game, despite his own busy professional life. He was always there. I can't say our dinner conversations were always on the most intellectually fascinating things regarding finance, culture, politics or what was happening at that point in time in world history, but we were pretty much together as a family.

WCR: *You were an athlete. You played both basketball and baseball. What did you play in baseball?*

ROB: I played baseball (first baseman) up through high school and then dropped out when I was a junior. I was pretty good in the field, but not that good at batting. I stuck with basketball instead. As a high school student and college student I wound up practicing basketball almost every day of my life, maybe 6 or 7 years straight.

WCR: *Dr. Bonow, you went to Lehigh University in Bethlehem, Pennsylvania to college. Were you planning to be an engineer?*

ROB: Lehigh has a rich tradition in engineering. Initially, I was more or less following in the footsteps of my father. I did very well academically in science and math in high school, and engineering seemed like a rather natural and comfortable field for me to gravitate into. Three-quarters of the way through with my chemical engineering training I realized that I was not going to feel very gratified in that career. I had enough of the basic requisites through the engineering curriculum to be eligible to apply to medical school with a little extra biology and biochemistry in my senior year. Initially, I considered going into biomedical engineering, but with a little more experience in biomedical sciences, I realized that what I really wanted to be was a doctor.

WCR: *Did you go to college on a basketball scholarship?*

ROB: No, I was a walk-in candidate. Lehigh has a great tradition in wrestling, but it did not have much of a tradition in basketball. However, we competed among some of the better schools in the East, such as

*This series of interviews was underwritten by an unrestricted grant from Bristol-Myers Squibb.

†Executive Director, Baylor Cardiovascular Institute, Baylor University Medical Center, Dallas, Texas 75246.

‡Chief, Division of Cardiology; Goldberg Distinguished Professor, Northwestern University Medical School, Chicago, Illinois 60611.

FIGURE 1. ROB during the interview (photo by WCR).

the Ivy League schools and the big 5 schools in Philadelphia. We played Army, and I played against Mike Krzyzewski when Bobby Knight was the coach at Army and against Jim Valvano when he played at Rutgers. Pete Carril was our coach at Lehigh before he went to Princeton, and so among many mentors there is one who is now in the basketball Hall of Fame. Coach Carril was like another father to me and instilled in me a sense of discipline, competitiveness, and goal orientation. He was only with us for a year at Lehigh before he went on to great success for 30 years at Princeton, but I remember many aspects of that year vividly, in almost minute-to-minute detail.

WCR: *You were on the varsity team all 4 years?*

ROB: Back then the NCAA had a freshman rule that permitted only 3 years of varsity eligibility. The same rule kept Lew Alcindor, who became Karem Abdul Jabbar, from playing 4 years of varsity ball at UCLA. They also had a rule about dunking. You could not dunk in college and you could only spend 3 years on the varsity team. The former rule affected Lew Alcindor more than me, but the latter rule affected both of us. I played on the freshmen team and then 3 years on the varsity. I was a co-captain my senior year.

WCR: *What position did you play on the basketball team?*

ROB: I was not big enough to play up front, so I was a shooting guard. I usually guarded someone a few inches taller than me. I could not handle the ball well enough to be the point man, but I had a pretty good outside shot. I would get out there in what is now 3-point territory. Unfortunately, the 3-point shot was not in effect at that time. If the 3-point shots were

credited as such at the time, I would have had a hefty increase in my total field goal scoring.

WCR: *You scored a lot of points?*

ROB: Of course, not as many as I would have liked to. I had a couple of 20-point games, but my average was in single figures. The 3-point shot would have been a big help.

WCR: *Were you first team all 3 years on the varsity?*

ROB: I started about 50% of the games. I probably was on the starting team in more games as a sophomore under Pete Carril. Then we started winning some games, and they began recruiting some talented underclassmen to better the team.

WCR: *You mentioned your basketball coach as a mentor. Was there anybody in your family who had been a physician? Were there other mentors in high school that had an influence on you?*

ROB: I am the first physician in the family, although my father had a major influence in helping me decide my ultimate career goals. I had several important mentors in high school. My basketball coach in high school, Bob Sanislow, is a wonderful guy, and he still keeps in contact. I went to high school in Westfield, New Jersey. Bob still lives in Westfield and we exchange notes around Christmas time. He was a true mentor on and off the court. He taught me enormously about how to get along with people in life, work as a team, work for common goals. He had great faith in me and in my potential and I hope I delivered. I remember many other teachers very fondly from high school—English, science, math—all of whom had a formative effect on me but are too numerous to mention here.

WCR: *You went to public high school?*

ROB: Yes.

WCR: *Who influenced you at Lehigh University?*

ROB: There were a number of people, most notably the basketball coaches, and my classmates. The Chairman of the Chemical Engineering Department, *Leonard Wenzel*, had a major influence on me. I remember having a meeting with him when I made the decision that engineering was not the field I wanted to pursue as a career. He was not disappointed in my decision and helped my plans to attend medical school. He was a very good advisor, very good at pointing me in the right direction. He recognized that I was setting my sights too low. I had done very well scholastically in the engineering curriculum, but as I was not in the premed curriculum, I did not believe that I would be a competitive applicant for the better schools. When I showed him my list of possible medical school applications, he quickly x'd out about 75%, because I was not shooting high enough.

WCR: *You played on the varsity basketball team in college as a walk-on, you made the team, and you made all A's in your studies. Was college a wonderful experience for you?*

ROB: I think most people look back at college as being a kind of wonderful time of life because this is a time when you have a lot of opportunities, a lot of time to think and dream, and not a whole lot of responsibility. Having said this, I should point out that I was an undergraduate during the era of the Vietnam War when there was tremendous turmoil and unrest on college campuses, enormous social changes, a large number of thought-provoking issues. I was caught up in all of it at that time, along with everyone else. The climate on the college campuses was unique during that era and shaped the lives of everyone in my generation.

WCR: *That was 1965 to 1969?*

ROB: That's right.

WCR: *Then you went to the University of Pennsylvania to medical school? That is the one you wanted to go to?*

ROB: Yes, Penn ended up being top on my list. Both of my parents were from Philadelphia. My mother's family had been there for generations going back to the Quaker settlement of Pennsylvania. My father had grown up there as well. Even though I grew up in the suburbs of New York City, most of my family roots were in Philadelphia. That was one of the reasons why I wanted to go to Penn, along with its terrific ranking among medical schools. I was delighted to be accepted there. I really enjoyed that experience.

WCR: *You were accepted there after a major in chemical engineering in college?*

ROB: That is correct.

WCR: *As you look back on medical school, how does that hit you now? Who had a major impact on you in medical school?*

ROB: I think more so than the professors I had as an undergraduate, the professors I had in medical school are the people I think of as the individuals who really shaped me. There were so many it is really hard to be fair in naming any, but I will name a few. I encountered *Darwin Prockop* on my first day of medical school when he gave a lecture that captivated me on the metabolic basis of inherited disease. I knew something about biochemistry before entering medical school, but he put some biochemical concepts in context with patients, and I was really captivated by the whole idea that learning on the scientific front could be directly translated to disease of patients. I spent 2 summers doing biochemical genetics in the laboratory of *William Mellman*, Chief of the Genetics Department. We developed a close relationship. Along the way, I encountered *Sam Thier* and *Arnold Relman*; Sam was the Associate Chairman and Arnold Relman was the Chairman of Medicine. They had recently come to Pennsylvania. I remember as a second-year medical student shaking in my boots because I had to present a case of mitral stenosis to Sam Thier who was legendary for being a great teacher, but also for being an intimidating figure. Somehow I survived the case presentation with Sam, learned a lot about one-on-one roundsmanship, and Sam, even though he is not a cardiologist, also taught me a lot about mitral stenosis. I remember to this day how that case presentation went. Drs. Relman and Thier were my Chairman and Associate Chairman during my residency in medicine before Dr. Relman went on to become Editor of *The New England Journal of Medicine* and Dr. Thier went on to become Chairman of Medicine at Yale, President of the Institute of Medicine, President of Brandeis University, and, currently, Director of the Partners Hospitals in Boston.

In cardiology there were some notable figures also. *Stan Briller* was at Penn before he moved to Pittsburgh. I spent a summer in his laboratory with Gary Gerstenblith who is now a Professor of Medicine in the Cardiology Division at Johns Hopkins. *Richard Helfant*, I think, is a person who ultimately was the single most important individual in making me choose cardiology as a subspecialty career focus. Dick recently had come from the Peter Bent Brigham Hospital to the University of Pennsylvania and he was the Chief of Cardiology at Presbyterian Hospital. He and *Steve Miester* had at that point the premier cardiology rotation for the medical students. I went there to do 1 month with them and liked it so much I ended up doing 2 months. I saw in Dick Helfant the possibility of being a triple threat, taking care of patients and doing procedures, doing research and teaching. Until that point, I was uncertain regarding my career focus and whether I was going to be in practice or academics. Dick Helfant made it clear to me that cardiology was an exciting subspecialty and that an academic career could be rewarding; he also had the knack of making learning cardiology enjoyable and exciting. My fourth year, *Joe Perloff* came to Penn as the Chief of Cardiology and Joe, of course, is a master teacher. I already knew I was going to be a cardiologist, but Joe's arrival was wonderful for me; I spent hours listening to his lectures and making rounds with him. I stayed at Penn for my internship and residency and was able to continue learning from Joe and the faculty he brought to Penn, most notably *Doug Rosing, Nat Reichek*, and *John Hirshfeld*. I should not leave out *Jim Shelburne* and *Joel Manchester* who made the cath lab and the coronary care unit an exciting and entertaining environment.

WCR: *What about your classmates in medical school? Did they have much impact on you? Did some of your classmates go on to prestigious positions?*

ROB: I have several good friends from medical school, most of whom are currently in practice. I know they are still enjoying their medical careers even though they are under the same enormous pressures that are facing everyone right now. I have several good friends who have done quite well in academics as well. *Al Buxton*, a classmate, is now Professor of Medicine and Associate Chief of Cardiology at Temple University; *Jerome Strauss* is Professor of Obstetrics and Gynecology at the University of Pennsylvania; *Neil Goldman* is a Professor of Physiology at Penn; *Stephen Parnes* is Chief of Otolaryngology at the State University of New York at Albany; and *Frank James* is on the faculty in Cardiology at Temple. I think the individuals who had the biggest impact on me as colleagues were not so much my medical school classmates but the medical residents I trained with after medical school. As you know, residency is an intense experience and one develops close bonds with other residents in the middle of the night taking

FIGURE 2. ROB during the interview (Photo by WCR).

care of sick patients. You also get to know who you can trust and whose judgment you can respect. I trained at a time when residents were on call every other night or every third night. I have a number of very close friends from my residency days. Again, many of them have wound up in practice settings but several are doing very well in academic circles also. *Irwin Klein*, a very close friend, is Professor of Medicine at New York University and Chief of Endocrinology at North Shore University Hospital, Long Island. Irwin's cutting edge research on hormonal regulation of myocyte growth makes him far more of a cardiologist than an endocrinologist. *Al Buxton*, already mentioned, was also a resident with me. Six or 7 members of our residency class went into cardiology. I keep in touch with them professionally and personally. These include *Eric Michelson* who was Chief of Cardiology at Hahnemann before assuming his current position as Vice-President of Astra Merck; *Arthur Riba*, who was the Chief of Cardiology at the West Haven Veterans Administration Hospital and a faculty member at Yale before taking his current practice position in Michigan; *Taylor Cope* and *Willie Lam*, practicing cardiologists here in Illinois; *Alan Speilman*, an electrophysiologist in Philadelphia; *John Coyle*, practicing cardiology in Tulsa, Oklahoma; and *Leonard Horowitz* was a year ahead of me and was a nationally recognized electrophysiologist at Penn before his untimely death, and *Bill Follansbee* was a year behind me in training and is now Professor of Medicine in the Cardiology Division at the University of Pittsburgh.

WCR: *In medical school you mentioned that cardiology appealed to you relatively early. Did you know you wanted to go into medicine pretty quickly?*

Did you have a problem deciding whether to go into medicine or into surgery? Was that decision relatively easy for you?

ROB: It was not easy. I was grappling with the usual uncertainties many students face. When I first went to medical school I thought I was going to be a pediatrician. I enjoyed the pediatric experience, but I determined I would go into internal medicine around the same time I determined I would go into cardiology.

WCR: *You began your internship in 1973 at the University of Pennsylvania. After the internship you did 2 years of residency in general medicine there.*

ROB: That is correct.

WCR: *Did you do any research in college?*

ROB: I did some research because it was expected as a chemical engineer student. To get my diploma I had to complete a research project. I studied crystal formation as liquid suspensions freeze on metal surfaces and the characteristics of the crystals that were deposited. This is about all I can tell you about it because it certainly did not stick with me. That was my research experience in college.

WCR: *Did that lead to a publication?*

ROB: It led to an in-house piece of work I wrote to pass the course. That research experience also occurred when I was practicing basketball daily and/or was on the road with the team. I can't say this was an intense research experience, because I was not able to devote sufficient time or mental energy to it. On the other hand, I don't want to minimize the importance of that experience, as it instilled the idea that there is a scientific process and there are suitable hypotheses that one can develop and test. It also lead me to understand that doing research was an important part of my education when I was in medical school.

WCR: *What did you do research in in medical school?*

ROB: The summer work with *Stan Briller* dealt with new methods of computerizing electrocardiograms. I spent that summer working with a wall-to-wall computer. That did not lead to a publication but it helped Stan Briller with his work and some of the publications he was preparing at that time. I was not a co-author there and did not deserve to be. The research in the early and midpart of my medical school career was with *Bill Mellman* in the genetics department there. We studied galactosemia and galactokinase deficiency and identified some new familial forms of galactokinase deficiency. That lead to 2 publications and also my first oral presentation at a national scientific meeting as a medical student. That experience paid off later when I applied for a position at the NIH.

WCR: *By the time you graduated from medical school you had how many publications?*

ROB: Two. Actually, both were published when I was a resident, but the work with Bill Mellman was done while in medical school.

WCR: *It seems to me that doing research in medical school is a key element to look at in somebody's*

CV because so many people who go on to successful academic careers have done research early on.

ROB: I agree entirely. That is a topic of discussion here among the faculty and I explore the issue when we are interviewing our fellowship candidates. It is important to capture people early in their careers. They have to get the bug early. A successful career in research requires discipline and extra effort. Research is fun, exciting, and worth the extra time, effort and frustration that is added on to an otherwise very busy complicated life in medicine. However, if you don't attract talented young people in the early stages of their careers, you risk loosing them to the other exciting opportunities medicine has to offer.

WCR: *After the 2 years of residency at the University of Pennsylvania, you went to the Cardiology Branch at the National Heart, Lung, and Blood Institute (NHLBI) of the National Institutes of Health in Bethesda, Maryland, in 1976. You had no cardiology fellowship training before that point?*

ROB: That's right.

WCR: *How did it come about that you went to NIH?*

ROB: I decided as a resident, given the backdrop of my cardiology experience in medical school, that I wanted an academic career in cardiology. I wanted to have a solid research experience. I had some friends in my residency program who had either been at NIH or were going to NIH, and it was apparent that this might be an excellent opportunity for a young person to spend a couple of years of completely protected research time, either in a basic or clinical laboratory and to really get a foothold in a research career. This was at a time right toward the end of the Vietnam War when positions at the NIH were very competitive to get into. I remember that there were 4 of us in my residency class who were applying for 1 of the 6 positions in the Clinical Associate program at the NHLBI. The NHLBI was not necessarily looking for residents interested in clinical cardiology training for, I think, legitimate reasons. The NHLBI was seeking individuals who either had a research background or clearcut research potential. Of the 4 of us, I was the 1 person who had done research in medical school and my research had been in genetics. I think that basic laboratory experience was quite helpful in making me a very competitive candidate for 1 of those 6 positions at the NIH. Of course, I don't know for certain what led to the decision to accept me, but I was accepted and was thrilled with the decision.

WCR: *You came to NIH as a Clinical Associate in the NHLBI. You were not automatically in the Cardiology Branch when you first came so how did it work out that you joined the Cardiology Branch?*

ROB: You know the system there since you were there for so long and had a very important leadership role. The 6 Clinical Associates rotated through all the clinical branches of the NHLBI including the Cardiology, Pulmonary, Hypertension, Hematology, and Metabolic Disease Branches. There were very prominent figures in all of those areas: *Robert Levy, Brian Brewer, Ronald Crystal, Art Neinhaus, Harry Keiser,* and *Fred Bartter.* We had great opportunities in many areas but, again, I went there because I wanted to be involved in cardiovascular research, so on day one, I made it clear to *Steve Epstein,* the Cardiology Branch Chief, that his Branch was where I wanted to be. I did have several months of research time during my first year to begin work with the Cardiology Branch members, and, in my spare time, in the clinical rotation could continue that work. The person I hooked up with initially was *Walt Henry* who was, at that time, one of the leading figures in echocardiography. Walt and I did some work initially in patients with aortic valve disease. I credit Walter early on for stimulating my interest in valve disease and turning it into a more academic focus regarding left ventricular function, prognosis, and timing of aortic valve replacement. I am indebted to Walter Henry for guiding and mentoring me this entire area. However, it was Steve Epstein, who guided me later on in this area of investigation, and I credit Steve for mentoring me in developing deliberate, methodical, hypothesis-driven research pathways.

WCR: *After your 2 years as a Clinical Associate in the NHLBI you moved into the Cardiology Branch and that became very quickly a full time position.*

ROB: That's right. In fact, the Clinical Associateship was a 3-year position. It was a 1-year training position with the clinical rotations and then 2 years of research. The third year and part of the fourth year, *Dr. Lewis Lipson* and I shared the responsibilities of being chief fellow of the clinical cardiology service. In a way, this resulted in a 4-year training period.

WCR: *Then you became a full member of the staff of the Cardiology Branch. You never actually had a fellowship in cardiology?*

ROB: That is true, in a pure sense. However, fellowship requirements for board certification in the subspecialty of cardiology codified at a later point in time. It was around 1980 when I was completing my training and became Board-certified. In today's environment, I would probably do a year or 2 of research at the NIH and then be required to do 2 years of clinical fellowship training somewhere else, because the NHLBI program is not considered an accredited training program. However, the clinical training I received in 4 years at the NHLBI was equivalent to most fellowship programs in the 1970s and superior to many. This was the era before coronary angioplasty and thrombolytic therapy. The training I received from *Steve Epstein, Kenny Kent, Walt Henry,* and *Jeff Borer* occurred at the time the NIH was at the forefront of most areas in clinical cardiology including coronary, valvular, and myocardial diseases. The experience I obtained in echocardiography and nuclear cardiology, these new areas of noninvasive imaging, were clearly equivalent to the best training programs at the time. My experience in the cardiac catheterization laboratory included studies of patients with complex congenital heart disease, valvular disease, and cardiomyopathies. Every patient undergoing surgery at the NHLBI returned at 6 months for repeat cardiac catheterization. Hence, I did many transseptal punctures and percutaneous left ventricular punctures to obtain pressure measurements in patients who had prosthetic heart valves. This was routine. Kenny Kent was among the first cardiologists in this country to perform coronary angioplasty, at a time when I was an attending cardiologist in the cath lab. I don't have any problems regarding my clinical training in cardiology and regarding my ability to take care of patients with many forms of heart disease.

WCR: *Your training in cardiology actually was similar to that of people like Eugene Braunwald, John Ross, Ed Sonnenblick, Dean Mason, Donald Harrison. Those individuals never took official cardiology fellowships. They just learned cardiology along the way in their day-to-day work.*

ROB: That's right and obviously from very good mentors and teachers. I was not going to put it quite in those terms, but I am glad you did. There are many other cardiologists both in my generation and earlier generations who came through the process at the NIH. Cardiologists in many other programs in that era also did not sit through what is now considered the requirements for fellowship training and board eligibility.

WCR: *Dr. Bonow you were at NIH in the Cardiology Branch from 1976 until you came here to Chicago in 1992, a period of 16 years. As you look back at your period at NIH what accomplishments are you most pleased about? How do you fit your NIH experience into your present activities?*

ROB: That is a big question, so it is not possible to answer in a single word or two. There were several things. First, the mentorship I received there was from many individuals, among them *Steve Epstein, Kenny Kent, Walt Henry, Doug Rosing, Barry Maron.* It was very important, not only in developing me, but in allowing me to recognize the importance of mentorship and transmitting it to others. During my time at the NIH I was able to contribute to the development of other individuals who were in the program with me or a year or 2 behind me. *Marty Leon* and *Richard Cannon* were a year or 2 behind me. We became very good friends and, because of my being a few years ahead, I was able to provide some seniority and guidance in the early parts of their careers. *Jim Udelson,* who is now at Tufts-New England Medical Center, and a well known nuclear cardiologist, and *Vasken Dilsizian,* who now directs the nuclear cardiology program at the NIH, are other individuals in the next generation with whom I have a very strong personal connection. One of the values that grew out of the NIH experience is that mentorship is important, both on the receiving end and the giving end.

Second, the NIH, at that point in time and I hope beyond the current time, is a national treasure where young people can develop strong career foundations, where research opportunities are unique regarding protected time—the ability to develop and test hypotheses, and do what is considered high-risk research. I have certainly realized that creating this environment in Chicago or anywhere else in the world, for that matter, outside the NIH is very difficult. There are funding issues and clinical pressures. As a Chief of a

FIGURE 3. ROB during the interview (Photo by WCR).

Division of Cardiology in a major medical school, I also have a large number of other responsibilities that are administrative and academic, so my own ability to do research is limited. However, I can develop a research atmosphere, help to develop research themes, and work to develop funding mechanisms. In addition, I can impart how to ask the questions and how to go about answering those questions. The ability to transmit that information to others is very important. That is something else I owe to my experience at the NIH.

Also, the NIH was one of those rare places 15 or 20 years ago where basic research was done a hallway away from where patient care was provided. Although I can't say that we were as a group any more successful than others in taking basic concepts from the laboratory to the bedside, I think 15 years ago we had our share of success in that area. Steve Epstein was a master of taking ideas and concepts developed in the animal laboratory and thinking of ways of applying them to patients, either in practice or at least in theory. Examples include the use of nitroglycerin and aspirin in acute coronary syndromes and the use of calcium channel blockers in chronic coronary disease. Of course, this translational research is what we are all striving for in the current era of molecular biology and genetics. We obviously still have a long way to go in cardiovascular disease. This concept is nothing unusual or surprising in 1997, but in the 1970s there were very few places in the world equipped to think along these terms.

Finally, what is helping me the most in my current position is the fact that to do good clinical research, you have to be a good doctor. You have to know how to take care of patients and how to explain the details of diseases and the limitations of our current treatments with patients and their families. That has helped me tremendously in moving from 16 years in a scientific institution to what is much closer to the real world. Although a university medical school is not necessarily the real world, we are also part of a very successful and progressive hospital. Here in Chicago we compete with several other medical schools and a large number of community hospitals. We have to be very good clinically to grow our program and develop clinical services, which is the basis of our research and teaching programs. I believe strongly that my 16 years at the NIH have made me a much better physician. I am recognizable here as being a good doctor as much as I am for any other accomplishments I have achieved previously. In fact, I suspect most of the internists inside and outside my institution who refer patients to me don't know much about my research background. They know that I take care of their patients well, that I relate to them professionally as a physician should, and that the patients, hopefully, not only receive good care but are satisfied with me as their physician. The most important thing I learned at the NIH is that you have to be a skilled physician to do high quality clinical research. That is something that will never leave me.

WCR: *In the 16 years at NIH you obviously did a lot of investigations there. You became a world authority in nuclear cardiology. Your work of patients with certain types of valvular disease, particularly valvular regurgitation—when to operate, when not to operate on them—is masterful. As you look back on the work you did, what are you most pleased with now?*

ROB: There are a couple of things. I am certainly proud of the accomplishments in valvular heart disease, particularly aortic regurgitation and mitral regurgitation, and that has helped me as well in my current position. We have great expertise in valvular disease here at Northwestern, both in cardiology and cardiac surgery. I am also pleased with my studies of the impact of myocardial ischemia on left ventricular function, both in defining prognosis of patients with coronary artery disease and in identifying reversible left ventricular dysfunction, myocardial hibernation and stunning. I am pleased with the work I did with Vasken Dilsizian in my latter years at the NIH in the assessment of myocardial viability. Many of the original ideas were Vasken's, not mine, but I provided a great deal of help in formulating the questions and developing the protocols to address them. Together we created a great team. The viability issue is a big item here in the management of patients with coronary disease and impaired ventricular function and in selecting high-risk patients for revascularization to improve prognosis and also improve function. That is something we do essentially every day here both for clinical investigation and clinical care. The valve studies and the viability studies are probably the 2 most important areas in which the research I did has actually had a broad impact on patient care. The other areas of research I pursued at the NIH were fun, including assessment of left ventricular diastolic func-

tion and development of new radionuclide tests and procedures. The relationship I had at the NIH with nuclear medicine physicists and physicians was unique. *Steve Bacharach* and *Mike Green* are world class nuclear physicists. We worked closely together for 15 years. They taught me tremendously, and we remain close friends. I am trying to develop that kind of relationship between cardiology and nuclear medicine. I guess there are several reasons I am proud of my NIH days not only related to research productivity but also to the firm foundation provided for my subsequent career here in Chicago.

WCR: *Dr. Bonow, what was your day-to-day life like at NIH? Let's say 2 or 3 years before you left. How much time were you spending at NIH? Were you working at night on papers, weekends?*

ROB: The last couple of years there were quite different from my first 12 or 13 years. Again, those later years prepared me for my current position rather well. First of all, the cardiac surgery program was discontinued at the NIH, as you know. I won't discuss all the reasons for that because it is not pertinent here, but that had an impact on us as cardiologists both in terms of patient care and also in trying to recruit patients for clinical research protocols. Around the same point in time, Steve Epstein, who had already established himself as one of the nation's great teachers and clinical cardiologists, and whose research had touched patients all over the world, around 1990, determined that he wanted to embark on a new career path in molecular biology. He took a sabbatical for about 18 months during which time I was acting Chief of Cardiology. I took on many more administrative responsibilities in helping to run the program. This was at a time when the Surgery Branch had just been dismantled, and we needed to develop mechanisms to take care of our patients who required surgery. We developed a contracting process to provide care for our patients at 3 of the Washington, DC, area hospitals, each of which had great expertise in cardiac surgery: Georgetown University, the Washington Hospital Center, and Fairfax Hospital. That process, which was a new experience for me, was a difficult and laborious process, dealing with different hospital types, a university hospital on the one hand and 2 private hospitals on the other, dealing with the surgeons who worked in 3 hospitals, and at the same time dealing with the NIH and contracting officers. That experience, in retrospect, was not bad—learning how the world operates outside the NIH, which was helpful to me when I came to Chicago.

My daily life at NIH prior to those last 3 to 4 years was much different. Before that my professional life was busy but enjoyable. It actually was grueling work. We had to care for our patients and communicate with referring physicians regarding the care of their patients with complex heart disease. We had to recruit patients for research protocols, obtain informed consent from them, and discuss the implications of our research findings with them and their families. We had an enormous amount of data that was being generated for numerous ongoing protocols. We were understaffed in terms of nursing support, research nurses, research technicians, and fellows. Therefore, the attending physicians did a lot of the work themselves, work which in most academic institutions is routinely handled by nurses and technicians. This was an accepted part of the daily routine. Therefore, writing manuscripts was not done from 9:00 A.M. to 5:00 P.M. Even in the most austere research environment like the NIH, virtually all of the writing I did was on evenings and weekends. That sort of lifestyle was fine when I was single but created obvious conflict when I became a husband and a father. This went against the grain of what my parents had taught me when I was little about having quality time as a family. My wife, Pat, has been incredibly understanding and supportive and, of course, she has made most of the sacrifices because I would either get home late or, worse, get home and become preoccupied with professional things, trying to get my papers completed, trying to review manuscripts, trying to get my own manuscripts revised and sent back in for publication. Again, almost all of that was being done after hours and on weekends. This is also the way it is here for me now. My day-to-day life is tied up with either clinical issues or administrative issues. The last 4 years at NIH, when I had much more administrative responsibilities, slowed down my hands-on research. The publications, luckily, kept rolling since I had just terrific collaborative projects, proceeding with Vasken Dilsiziam, Richard Cannon, Arshed Quyyumi, and Barry Maron. Luckily, the research activity kept up and I was able to continue contributing. Although I missed the hands-on level of research, I realized that somebody had to mind the shop and provide leadership and administrative stability to keep the rest of the group productive.

WCR: *Dr. Bonow, in 1992, when you were 45 years of age, you had a major decision on your hands. I gather you were offered the Chiefship of the Division of Cardiology at Northwestern, one of the most prestigious medical schools in the world. You had only 4 years or so before you reached 20-year retirement in the Public Health Service at NIH which would be nice change in your pocket for the rest of your life. How did it come about that you came to Northwestern? Once you received the offer, was it easy to say "yes" or was it difficult for you?*

ROB: That is a good point. It is true that a number of people at the NIH worked with an eye on that 20-year clock because of the potential retirement package. That certainly was a factor for me to consider. I had looked at other positions over the course of many years, including some very good positions at very prestigious institutions. For one reason or another, I decided that what I was doing at the time in Bethesda was more important to me and my family, and I turned down the earlier opportunities. The Northwestern offer came at a time when there were changes going on in my life. I was already doing a lot of administrative work, and my own individual research productivity was not where it had been earlier. Although I had more of a leadership role in the Cardiology Branch by then, Steve Epstein had returned from his sabbatical and resumed his role as Branch Chief. I was beginning to wonder where the tide would take from there on out. I certainly could have stayed there. I was still pretty happy there and my relationship with Steve Epstein was good and remains terrific to this day. When the opportunity in Chicago came along it was an opportunity that was only going to stay open for short time. I had to suddenly stop and look. Most of my colleagues over the years at the NIH had an inkling that they were not there forever, and sooner or later they had ventured out to a more real world environment. I had originally planned to spend 3 years at the NIH, but I stayed because it was fun, interesting, exciting, and productive. All along I kept my feelers out for the right situation at the right time to make a move such as the one I ultimately made. Steve Epstein counseled me early on that as long as I was productive in what I was doing, there is no reason to make a premature move, as greater productivity would bring bigger and better opportunities. That was good advice because through my tenure there the job market did not evaporate but only got better and more tantalizing. The Northwestern offer materialized as a great opportunity at the right time. Northwestern is a very interesting institution with enormous potential in a very big and great city, where it is easy to recruit physicians and scientists to work. We are located in one of the best parts of the city where patients are not concerned about the neighborhood. Northwestern Memorial Hospital is a very prestigious and successful institution. It has terrific experience and recognition and reputation in patient care. We are building a new hospital as we speak that will be open in 1999. The medical school is one of the major schools of Northwestern University. It is a very forward-thinking institution with new leadership. The new Chairman of Medicine, *Lewis Landsberg,* had arrived 2 years earlier from Beth-Israel Hospital in Boston and had initiated a search for a new Chief of Cardiology. *Francis Klocke* had arrived here a year earlier to run the Feinberg Cardiovascular Research Institute in the medical school. Fran and I had known each other for years and had similar research interests. It looked like an opportunity worth exploring. The more I developed a relationship with Dr. Landsberg and understood the potential here in cardiology it became apparent that this was an opportunity where, with a little bit of careful thought and maybe a little bit of good luck, one could do very well in terms of recruiting young faculty, developing clinical programs, and developing research programs. And so I decided to accept the Northwestern offer. I could have stayed where I was and might still be at the NIH, and I suspect if I was there my life would be a little easier. I knew I was ending one of the happiest periods of my life leaving Bethesda and venturing out to Chicago. On the other hand, my family and I live in a wonderful community north of Chicago where we love our home and neighbors and the town we live in.

The experience I have had here at Northwestern has actually been terrific. I have learned a tremendous amount about the way clinical programs develop and

FIGURE 4. ROB during the interview (Photo by WCR).

the close relationship required between the faculty and the hospital to develop programs to provide services and attract patients. I think I have also become much more rounded as a clinical cardiologist. I have gotten up to speed with a number of aspects of heart failure, acute coronary care, and interventional cardiology, which were not part of my day-to-day life at the NIH. I am pretty conversant in these areas and have been successful at recruiting individuals who have helped balance out the program I inherited to create a program which is pretty solid in all aspects of the clinical components of cardiology. In addition to covering all the bases, we have considerable depth. We have 2 or 3 people in each aspect of the various subspecialties of cardiology, and this provides depth in terms of clinical care, teaching, and research. We do need greater development in basic science research. When I first arrived, given all the changes that were going on in terms of managed care and the enormous demands initially to turn around some aspects of the clinical programs, I was not able to concentrate on the development of basic research initiatives. Those pressures have not gone away, but at least we have been able to turn things around and be successful in terms of our clinical volume. Our patient volume has increased substantially in everything we do. This has fostered excellent clinical investigation, but it has taken a lot of work. I think now is an opportune time to develop our basic research program.

WCR: *Dr. Bonow, how many physicians do you have in the Division of Cardiology here at Northwestern? What size of division are you talking about?*

ROB: We have both full-time and voluntary faculty (private cardiologists who are part of the division). All cardiologists with hospital privileges at

Northwestern Memorial Hospital are members of the faculty at the medical school; so I am their Chief, whether they are full-time or private cardiologists. I try to do what is best for everybody on both sides, in terms of academic appointments and research as well as clinical privileges and activities. In the total we have 25 full-time cardiologists, in varying degrees devoted to research, teaching, and patient care. We have roughly 20 private cardiologists on the voluntary faculty. Both groups have grown since I have been here and I have done recruitment for both private and full-time cardiologists. I think that is a good balance. I think it is helpful for residents and fellows to see different approaches to patient care. It creates very interesting discussions at our cath conference or cardiology grand round series, just 2 of the many conferences we have every week. Our trainees receive a balance of different approaches for patient care. Our patients, many times, have a preference for a physician who is on the cutting edge of research and new developments in the field, while others prefer physicians taking care of patients in a private practice setting. I think we have a good balance here in terms of what our patients are looking for, and that balance has helped us be as successful as we have been. It is not a huge division. One could certainly find other larger divisions around Chicago, and elsewhere they may be larger.

WCR: *Now you have 25 full-time cardiologists and 20 volunteer cardiologists who are in private practice and they are all members of your faculty. How many full-timers did you have when you came in 1992?*

ROB: We had roughly the same number but there has been some transition and attrition in various areas. Several previous full-timers left to go into practice. Other physicians have left for movement up the ladder academically. One has become Chief of Cardiology at another medical school, and one has become director of an echocardiography laboratory at another medical school. Their career choices left us with important vacancies that needed to be filled. As difficult as it is to lose good people, the loss also represents an opportunity for it allows you to recruit good people to fill their ranks, people who can come in and grow academically. It is a challenge to keep things in balance. I may be missing the numbers by 1 or 2 physicians. I think in general we are about where I started, although it is true in most academic programs that one of the jobs of the Chief is constant recruitment. This year we will add more cardiologists because our clinical volume has risen to the point where we are really stretched thin in several areas.

WCR: *If you add secretaries and lab technicians to your 25 full-time faculty, how many people are you talking about in this division? How many cardiology fellows do you have?*

ROB: The answer to the fellowship issue is quite easy. We used to have 5 fellows per year but we have downsized from 5 to 4 to 3. This was our first year of bringing in only 3 first-year fellows. We have 5 in the third year, 4 in the second year, and 3 in the first. That gives a total of 12 fellows. We also have 2 fourth-year fellows in electrophysiology and interventional cardiology. We have a total of 14 fellows right now with 1 other research fellow. That will continue to get smaller as we continue to evolve into 3 per year for 3 years. At our tightest we will probably be down to 11 total. That has an impact, not so much on the fellows who continue to receive everything they have received in the past, but on the faculty who will have more to do with fewer fellows to support the clinical demands. There are some months in some of the clinical laboratories when an attending cardiologist cannot count on a fellow being present. We do make sure a fellow is always in a rotation where a fellow is necessary. You can't run a cardiac catherization laboratory or a large coronary care unit without a cardiology fellow.

In addition to the fellows, we have technicians, nurses, and secretaries, some of whom are hospital personnel, some of whom are employed by the medical school, and some of whom are employed by the faculty. Depending upon how you analyze this, we could be talking anywhere from 65 to 100 cardiologists and support personnel in the full-time components of the Division.

WCR: *The private practitioners are the volunteer faculty. They are not housed here in Northwestern Hospital quarters, are they? They have their own private offices?*

ROB: Yes, they are for the most part, practitioners who practice only here. Some of the practitioners also have privileges at other hospitals, but their offices are within the immediate area, either on campus or a few blocks away. Many of them have satellite activities going on or may have 2 offices, 1 downtown here, for example, near the university hospital or 1 in the suburbs, and they split their time. Their offices are not housed here in the hospital.

WCR: *Bob, you deal with a faculty of 45 physicians. It seems to me that 30 years ago that was how many people were on the entire faculty of the Department of Medicine. Today, you are equivalent to a Departmental Chairman as of several decades ago. How many physicians and PhDs are in the entire Department of Medicine here?*

ROB: I think it is roughly 120 to 140. It is true cardiology takes up a large percentage of the faculty in the Department of Medicine. Obviously, the things we do are very important for the department in terms of our teaching responsibilities and our clinical revenue. In return, we also receive support back from the department for our ongoing activities.

WCR: *Do you have much contact with the Chairman of the Department of Medicine?*

ROB: Yes, I have a very good, close, and collegial relationship with the department chairman. He has been very supportive. Again, he recruited me and I believe I was the first Division Chief he recruited after his arrival here. I have gone through a number of important agenda items since I have been here that have required his advice and support. He does have some firm ideas many times about the direction the department should be going and luckily most of the time we see eye to eye. At the times we don't, we discuss our differences. Sometimes he wins, sometimes I win, but there has never been a clash of personalities. I can't think really of an incident in which I have not felt supported in moving forward, even in situations where we disagree. Around 1992 when I took this position, the Association of the Professors of Cardiology, APC, which is an organization for the division chiefs of the university-based cardiology programs nationwide, was going through a major revolutionary thought process regarding whether cardiology divisions should remove themselves from the departments of medicine and become their own free-standing departments, which would have altered some of the financial relationships between divisions of cardiology and departments of medicine. As a new recruit here, it would have been suicidal for me to consider doing that. I actually discussed this whole issue with the department chairman. He and I believe that in the current era of evolving managed care, this may not be the best thing for divisions of cardiology. At Northwestern, we are a part of a very large multispecialty practice group in which many of the issues about contracting and referrals from general specialists to subspecialists, capitation, etc., can be handled in a pretty efficient way. I think if our cardiology division was separated out, that would become more problematic. In addition, many of the current breakthroughs in cardiovascular research involve very tight collaboration with hematologists, immunologists, and other specialties. These collaborative interactions can occur interdepartmentally but are more natural and more easily fostered if they develop within the same department.

WCR: *Bob, you are responsible for a broad range of activities: patient care, teaching, research. Each of these activities are in and of themselves full-time activities. You are just one person, you have a family. What is your day-to-day life like? Let's start from the time you wake up in the morning. What time do you wake up? How long does it take you to get to the hospital? What time do you get out of the hospital at night? How long does it take you to get home? What do you do after you get home? Are you exhausted by that time so you don't do anymore professional work once you get home? What time do you go to bed? Can you discuss that in detail?*

ROB: I mentioned earlier that perhaps if I had stayed at the NIH, in some ways my life would be a lot simpler. That is related to your question. This is grueling. I actually enjoy what I am doing and I enjoy the responsibilities, but it is difficult to handle all these various aspects of the job and keep everybody happy, handle the balance of clinical care versus research, and also remain active in professional societies. Even if that balance can be achieved, it is at the expense of something else. This has been the major issue I have. Chicago is a big city. To have a nice home and a yard for your children to play in, good school systems, etc., most physicians live outside of the city, especially those with children. Our 2 boys are 13 and 9, and my wife, Pat, and I decided to move to our current home

FIGURE 5. ROB and his wife Pat and their 2 boys.

because of the school system and the community. However, it is a long way from work. In Bethesda I commuted 1 mile to work and I could be there in 5 minutes. Here in Chicago it is a 30-minute drive when there is no traffic, but the rush hour is a big problem. I usually get up between 5:00 and 5:30 A.M. and hit the road about half an hour later. If I am going in that early I can usually be there in about half an hour. Any later, it may take me an hour. I just can't commit that kind of time to sitting in a car. The same is true about going home at night. I usually end up leaving after the rush hour and getting home around the time to get the kids to bed if I am lucky. Sometimes the children have not seen me for a couple days.

WCR: *So what time do you get home?*

ROB: Average time would be somewhere between 8:30 and 9:30 P.M., but there are times when I have set the record here at Northwestern for leaving late. There are some things, though, that I have built into my commitments. The boys participate in some sports. The last couple of years I have been a coach on the little league baseball team and now the basketball team. I am assistant scout master for the Boy Scout troop that my older son is involved in. I have spent a week camping with the Boy Scouts the last 2 summers, go to the weekly meeting at night, and participate in several weekend activities each year. The Boy Scouts is a great organization. I was an Eagle Scout as

a teenager and my older son is almost there. I try to get home when the boys' activities are going on. I can't say that I am doing this as well as my father did. I am not there for dinner most nights. I am not there to help the kids with their homework as much as I would like. All of this responsibility falls on my wife. Obviously, this creates a lot of struggle internally for me as to whether I am doing the right thing for my family and whether this is the kind of thing I can continue to do. On the other hand, I am not sure it would be much different if I were in a different location or even be in a different job these days in medicine. I know, although I often compare my life now to my life in Bethesda, times have changed. These are not really comparable points in time and most of my colleagues in medicine have very similar stories of the demands they are under, either in practice or in academics.

WCR: *So you wake up about 5:00 A.M. You get to the hospital about 6:30 or 7:00 A.M. You leave the hospital at night, that's variable, but 8:00 or 8:30 and you get home on the average at 9:00. What time do you go to bed?*

ROB: I never answered the earlier part of your question about what I do when I get home. I make sure the kids have not unraveled and have their school work done and try to help get them ready for bed. If I have not had dinner here at the hospital I have some dinner. I try to deal with any of the other home fires that are still burning. I cut the pumpkins last night for Halloween, for example, somewhere around 11:00 P.M. If I am just too burned out, I sit and talk to my wife for awhile and then go to bed, but more likely, that is the time when I have to pick up a manuscript that I am reviewing for the AJC or another journal or try to do some writing. I am still involved with what I think are important aspects of the American Heart Association (AHA) and the American College of Cardiology (ACC), so I have committee work to do there. I am Vice-Chairman of the Scientific Session Program Committee for the AHA and also Vice-Chair of the AHA Council on Clinical Cardiology. I am chairing the ACC/AHA committee to develop guidelines for management of valvular heart disease. I will soon become Chairman of the ACC Extramural Education Committee. I am also serving on the Subspecialty Board on Cardiovascular Disease of the American Board of Internal Medicine. That stuff, again, I am doing after hours for the most part. A lot of it is being done at home once I get home. Many times I go to bed at 12:00 or 1:00 A.M. Average sleep time here is 4 to 5 hours.

WCR: *What about weekends? Do you come into the hospital?*

ROB: I come in when I am on service. I do attend on the clinical cardiology service, but I don't do that as often as many of the other attendings do. I want to be visible and I enjoy seeing patients very much. I wish I could do more of that. When I am on the service I come in both Saturday and Sunday and make rounds. However, on the weekends when I am not involved clinically, I stay home. I take a couple of briefcases home. I usually have more than 1 briefcase full of papers that goes back and forth. I spend the weekends with a lot of hours of work, but I try as much as I can to put that off until the evening or the early morning hours so that during the key hours of Saturday and Sunday I am there with my wife and kids. We go to church every Sunday and we are active in some of the activities in the community, primarily those involved around children.

WCR: *Do you have a social life? Do you go out on Friday or Saturday evenings? Do you have friends over or go to their houses? Do you have time for that?*

ROB: Nothing scheduled. On Friday or Saturday we may go out, go to a ballgame or friend's house, go out to dinner, or have friends over for dinner. We probably do not do as much socializing as we should or would like. We are trying to balance the demands of the family versus the professional demands. My wife is now back at work. She received a master's degree in journalism here at Northwestern and is now working part time so her life has become much more complicated. Having people over can place a lot of extra demands on a situation that is already pretty demanding. We tend to go out more than we have people in, but we do socialize. We have several parties a year for the division members in cardiology in the summer and at Christmas time. We try to get to the symphony occasionally, to plays and museums. I wish we were doing more of that.

WCR: *Bob, what about vacations? How much time do you take off from work? Do you take off a month a year?*

ROB: We probably have a vacation in its truest sense, where I am devoid from work, not traveling because I am going to a meeting, a total of 2 weeks a year. I mentioned that I take a week out with the Boy Scouts. That is good for the 1 son that goes with me but not for the other one or my wife. This year we took a week at the beach. We are going for a week to Orlando next spring for the boys' school break. We usually go skiing for several days in the winter, not for a full week necessarily, and usually surrounding a ski meeting in which I give a lecture or 2. True vacations probably average about 2 weeks a year, not all at one time but spread out.

WCR: *You mentioned professional travels. How many trips do you go on? How many cities do you go to to give talk(s) or as a visiting professor or to committee meetings? Travel is a very tiring thing. I know you limit that some. How do you handle it?*

ROB: I try to limit it. You know how demanding that can be. However, when a good friend asks you up to do something you hate to say no. I enjoy teaching. I was a visiting professor at the Mayo Clinic last year where the fellows created a grueling schedule of rounds, conferences, and bedside teaching with the fellows, and I loved it. It was very tiring, but I really enjoyed it. That was 3 days away in a true professional visiting professor-type setting. I don't do that very often, perhaps once a year. That was kind of a unique and wonderful experience. Usually, as you know, travels consists of going away for 1 day and giving a lecture or participating in a committee meeting. I try

to limit that, but I still do it maybe once or twice a month. There are symposia where I am invited to speak, and I still do that. That probably averages once or twice a month as well. Unfortunately, many of these continuing education activities now occur on weekends, which cuts further into the family time. I go to 3 national scientific meetings each year. There are also a number of committee meetings, but luckily in Chicago a lot of those committee meetings occur at O'Hare Airport at the airport hotel so I don't have to travel as much. Still I am on the road a lot even though I try to keep it under control. Despite my best efforts, though, I tend to get myself over committed. Traveling has to be kept under control because there are not only the family pressures but also the pressures at work. Things have to get done for the medical school and the hospital. You have to be visible and be able to take care of your patients and be a role model for the other faculty. I am not the busiest doctor around, but I see a large number of outpatients, including many new patients. That is demanding also and places limits on traveling. I try to balance those things as best I can.

WCR: *What about trips abroad? Do you take 3 or 4 a year?*

ROB: Probably 2 to 4 a year. This year I was at the European meeting at Stockholm and 2 meetings in Italy. I will be going to Uruguay in December for their national meeting. I know I will be going to the World Congress next spring in Rio and a Congress on Valvular Heart Disease later in London. I try to limit those long trips, and I often do some crazy things like trying to go in overnight, give a lecture, and come back again without spending a lot of time to decompress and enjoy the location. I try to keep time away to a minimum. I may spend an extra day in a foreign city but usually I will not spend a week there.

WCR: *Bob, your schedule is obviously a grueling one, you are pulled in numerous directions by faculty, by fellows, by responsibilities in the medical center outside the division of cardiology, by the national committees you are on, and by the pressures to publish and review manuscripts. You review numerous manuscripts for various editors. You have been an unbelievably good reviewer for* The American Journal of Cardiology, *a very unselfish thing to do. You get very little credit for that. Your colleagues don't know that you are providing these splendid reviews all the time. Your family is pulling on you. You want to see your kids more. You want to see your wife more. You want to spend more time at home. I presume you want to read books other than medicine sometimes. I presume you would like to develop this hobby or that hobby a little better. Do you have hobbies?*

ROB: Photography remains my hobby. I am doing less of that than I used to do. Sports have always been fun and interesting and I can do that with the kids, but you are right, it is hard. I don't have very many other hobbies at the current time because I am caught up in the whirlwind of all you mentioned. The children do provide a nice outlet though because we get involved in their activities, namely sports, scouts, or things they do at school. We do some things together as a family, such as skiing, but I would like to be doing more of that.

WCR: *Did your athletic endeavors as a younger person in a way provide more stamina for you than if you had not been an athlete?*

ROB: Yes. They have given me more stamina so I had the physical energy to accomplish what I was doing, but also sports were very helpful in college in making me budget my time. I had limited time to study and that was it. I did not have time to goof off. I had basketball practice for several hours every afternoon from September until April. We traveled so I would either be reading on the bus to our game or would be getting back late from practice having only an hour or 2 to study. So I am pretty good at turning things off and focusing, which is very helpful at present with my time being very limited. That is the reason why I believe children should really be encouraged to participate in extracurricular activities. It really does heighten their ability to deal better with the other demands that develop later in life. Otherwise, they have all this time on their hands and run the risk of learning how to procrastinate.

WCR: *Are you going to be able to handle this grueling day-to-day schedule for 15 or 20 more years? You are 50 now? Do you have other goals or other things you might like to do for 5 or 10 years during the next 20 years?*

ROB: Yes. It may be just that I am not a good long-range planner, which is true. I think my short-term goals are to continue developing the program here, get the research program on a much more solid base. I do not have a major interest in moving up the ladder to become a Department Chairman. I have not been burned out enough yet. I can keep this going for awhile longer and for the most part I enjoy it and we have been successful. It is not like I have been hitting my head against the wall and not been able to produce. Our clinical and research activities are growing and that keeps me enthused to keep going. If this had been a loosing proposition here I would feel much different, but right now I am still enthusiastic and optimistic that my current position, and academic medicine in general, can still be fun, rewarding, and productive. I enjoy working with young people and developing their talents, and I can continue doing that for a while longer.

WCR: *It seems to me that you are an enormously diplomatic person. You rarely raise your voice. You are very kind to other people, very gracious. Do you think this is an absolute necessity in the environs we live in today, to make sure that we get along with everybody?*

ROB: That is a really good question. I don't know the answer. I think sometimes I might be better at what I do if I were tougher or meaner or raised my voice more. I think it is true that when I do get angry people do sit up and listen. It does not happen often. I think my personality has helped me as a person to be reasonably effective at accomplishing things. For other people it may not work as well. Diplomacy is

one way of doing things, but I don't think it is an absolute necessity.

WCR: *You have very tough environs here in Chicago. Chiefs of Medicine, Chiefs of Cardiology don't last too long historically, and yet you seem to be thriving very well. Is there anything you would like to discuss that we haven't?*

ROB: No, I think you have asked some tough questions that I probably have not discussed in a public forum before. It is fun to think some of these things through with you. I cannot think of anything we have not discussed. You have covered a lot of bases already.

WCR: *Bob, it has been a pleasure. Thank you.*

BOOKS

Most Important Publications Selected by ROB from His 261 Publications

2. Tedesco TA, Bonow RO, Miller K, Mellman WJ. Galactokinase: evidence for a new racial polymorphism. *Science* 1972;178:176–177.

4. Henry WL, Bonow RO, Borer JS, Ware JH, Kent KM, Redwood DR, McIntosh CL, Morrow AG, Epstein SE. Observations on the optimal time for operation for aortic regurgitation. I. Evaluation of the results of aortic valve replacement in symptomatic patients. *Circulation* 1980;61:471–483.

5. Henry WL, Bonow RO, Rosing DR, Epstein SE. Observations on the optimal time for operative intervention for aortic regurgitation. II. Serial echocardiographic evaluation of asymptomatic patients. *Circulation* 1980;61:424–492.

6. Henry WL, Bonow RO, Borer JS, Kent KM, Ware JH, Glancy DL, Redwood DR, Itscoitz SB, McIntosh CL, Conkle DM, Morrow AG, Epstein SE. Evaluation of aortic valve replacement in patients with valvular aortic stenosis. *Circulation* 1980;61:814–825.

9. Bonow RO, Borer JS, Rosing DR, Henry WL, Pearlman AS, McIntosh CL, Morrow AG, Epstein SE. Preoperative exercise capacity in patients with aortic regurgitation as a predictor of postoperative left ventricular function and long-term prognosis. *Circulation* 1980;62:1280–1290.

15. Bonow RO, Lipson LC, Sheehan FH, Capurro NC, Isner JM, Roberts WC, Goldstein RE, Epstein SE. Lack of effect of aspirin on myocardial infarct size in the dog. *Am J Cardiol* 1981;47:258–264.

19. Bonow RO, Borer JS, Rosing DR, Green MV, Bacharach SL, Kent KM. Left ventricular functional reserve in adult patients with atrial septal defect: pre and postoperative studies. *Circulation* 1981;63:1315–1322.

20. Bonow RO, Bacharach SL, Green MV, Kent KM, Rosing DR, Lipson LC, Leon MB, Epstein SE. Impaired left ventricular diastolic filling in patients with coronary artery disease: assessment with radionuclide cineangiography. *Circulation* 1981;64:315–323.

21. Lipson LC, Kent KM, Rosing DR, Bonow RO, McIntosh CL, Condit JS, Epstein SE, Morrow AG. Hemodynamic evaluation of porcine heterografts in the mitral position for more than five years. *Circulation* 1981;64:397–401.

24. Bonow RO, Rosing DR, Bacharach SL, Green MV, Kent KM, Lipson LC, Maron BJ, Leon MB, Epstein SE. Effects of verapamil on left ventricular systolic function and diastolic filling in patients with hypertrophic cardiomyopathy. *Circulation* 1981;64:787–795.

29. Kent KM, Bonow RO, Rosing DR, Lipson LC, McIntosh CL, Epstein SE. Improved myocardial function during exercise after successful percutaneous transluminal coronary angioplasty. *N Engl J Med* 1982;306:441–446.

30. Bonow RO, Leon MB, Rosing DR, Kent KM, Lipson LC, Bacharach SL, Green MV, Epstein SE. Effects of verapamil and propranolol on left ventricular systolic function and diastolic filling in patients with coronary artery disease: radionuclide angiographic studies at rest and during exercise. *Circulation* 1982;65:1337–1350.

33. Maron BJ, Bonow RO, Seshagiri TN, Roberts WC, Epstein SE. Hypertrophic cardiomyopathy with ventricular septal hypertrophy localized to the apical region of the left ventricle ("apical hypertrophic cardiomyopathy"). *Am J Cardiol* 1982;49:1838–1848.

35. Bonow RO, Kent KM, Rosing DR, Epstein SE. Timing of operation for chronic aortic regurgitation. *Am J Cardiol* 1982;50:25–336.

38. Bonow RO, Kent KM, Rosing DR, Lipson LC, Bacharach SL, Green MV, Epstein SE. Improved left ventricular diastolic filling in patients with coronary artery disease after percutaneous transluminal coronary angioplasty. *Circulation* 1982;66:1159–1167.

47. Bonow RO, Frederick TM, Bacharach SL, Green MV, Goose PW, Maron BJ, Rosing DR. Atrial systole and left ventricular filling in patients with hypertrophic cardiomyopathy: effect of verapamil. *Am J Cardiol* 1983;51:1386–1391.

51. Bonow RO, Rosing DR, McIntosh CL, Jones M, Maron BJ, Lan KKJ, Lakatos E, Bacharach SL, Green MV, Epstein SE. The natural history of asymptomatic patients with aortic regurgitation and normal left ventricular function. *Circulation* 1983;68:509–517.

52. Bonow RO, Ostrow HG, Rosing DR, Lipson LC, Kent KM, Bacharach SL, Green MV. Verapamil effects on left ventricular systolic and diastolic function in patients with hypertrophic cardiomyopathy: pressure-volume analysis with a non-imaging scintillation probe. *Circulation* 1983;68:1062–1073.

61. Maron BJ, Bonow RO, Epstein SE, Wyngaarden MK, Hurley YE. Obstructive hypertrophic cardiomyopathy associated with minimal left ventricular hypertrophy. *Am J Cardiol* 1984;53:377–378.

64. Bonow RO, Rosing DR, Maron BJ, McIntosh CL, Jones M, Bacharach SL, Green MV, Clark RE, Epstein SE. Reversal of left ventricular dysfunction after aortic valve replacement for aortic regurgitation: influence of duration of left ventricular dysfunction. *Circulation* 1984;70:570–579.

65. Bonow RO, Kent KM, Rosing DR, Lan KKJ, Lakatos E, Borer JS, Bacharach SL, Green MV, Epstein SE. Exercise-induced ischemia in mildly symptomatic patients with coronary artery disease: identification of subgroups at risk of death during medical therapy. *N Engl J Med* 1984;311:1339–1345.

75. Cannon RO, Bonow RO, Bacharach SL, Green MV, Rosing DR, Leon MB, Watson RM, Epstein SE. Left ventricular dysfunction in patients with angina pectoris, normal epicardial coronary arteries and abnormal vasodilator reserve. *Circulation* 1985;71:218–226.

77. Bonow RO, Vitale DF, Bacharach SL, Frederick TM, Kent KM, Green MV. Asynchronous left ventricular regional function and impaired global diastolic filling in coronary artery disease: reversal after coronary angioplasty. *Circulation* 1985;71:297–307.

78. Bonow RO, Dilsizian V, Rosing DR, Maron BJ, Bacharach SL, Green MV. Verapamil-induced improvement in left ventricular diastolic filling and increased exercise tolerance in patients with hypertrophic cardiomyopathy: short- and long-term effects. *Circulation* 1985;72:853–864.

81. Bonow RO, Picone AL, McIntosh CL, Rosing DR, Maron BJ, Clark RE, Epstein SE. Survival and functional results after valve replacement for aortic regurgitation from 1976 to 1983: influence of preoperative left ventricular function. *Circulation* 1985;72:1244–1256.

83. Bonow RO, Epstein SE. Indications for coronary artery bypass surgery: implications of the multicenter randomized trials. *Circulation* 1985;72(suppl V):V-23–V-30.

91. Betocchi S, Bonow RO, Bacharach SL, Rosing DR, Maron BJ, Green MV. Isovolumic relaxation period in hypertrophic cardiomyopathy: assessment by radionuclide angiography. *J Am Coll Cardiol* 1986;7:74–81.

92. Cannon RO, Schenke WH, Bonow RO, Leon MB, Rosing DR. Left ventricular pulsus alternans in patients with hypertrophic cardiomyopathy and severe obstruction to left ventricular outflow. *Circulation* 1986;73:276–285.

94. Spirito P, Maron BJ, Bonow RO. Noninvasive assessment of left ventricular diastolic function: a comparative analysis of Doppler echocardiographic and radionuclide angiographic techniques. *J Am Coll Cardiol* 1986;7:518–526.

95. Palmeri ST, Bonow RO, Myers C, Sieppe CA, Jenkins J, Bacharach SL, Green MV, Rosenberg SA. Prospective evaluation of doxorubicin cardiotoxicity by serial rest and exercise radionuclide angiography. *Am J Cardiol* 1986;58:607–613.

105. Tracy CM, Winkler JA, Brittain E, Leon MB, Epstein SE, Bonow RO. Determinants of ventricular arrhythmias in mildly symptomatic patients with coronary artery disease and influence of inducible left ventricular dysfunction on arrythmia frequency. *J Am Coll Cardiol* 1987;9:483–488.

106. Bonow RO, Vitale DF, Maron BJ, Bacharach SL, Frederick TM, Green MV. Regional systolic and diastolic asynchrony and impaired global left ventricular diastolic filling in hypertrophic cardiomyopathy: effect of verapamil. *J Am Coll Cardiol* 1987;9:1108–1116.

108. Spirito P, Maron BJ, Bonow RO, Epstein SE. Occurrence and significance of progressive left ventricular wall thinning and relative cavity dilatation in patients with hypertrophic cardiomyopathy. *Am J Cardiol* 1987;60:123–129.

109. O'Gara PT, Bonow RO, Maron BJ, Damske BA, Van Lingen A, Bacharach SL, Larson SM, Epstein SE. Myocardial perfusion abnormalities assessed by thallium-201 emission computed tomography in patients with hypertrophic cardiomyopathy. *Circulation* 1987;76:1214–1223.

111. Bonow RO, Bacharach SL, Green MV, Lafreniere RL, Epstein SE. Prognostic implications of symptomatic vs asymptomatic (silent) myocardial ischemia induced by exercise in mildly symptomatic and in asymptomatic patients with angiographically-documented coronary artery disease. *Am J Cardiol* 1987;60:778–783.

113. Maron BJ, Bonow RO, Cannon RO, Leon MB, Epstein SE. Hypertrophic cardiomyopathy: interrelation of pathophysiology, clinical manifestations and therapy. *N Engl J Med* 1987;316:780–789, 844–852.

116. Bonow RO, Epstein SE. Is preoperative left ventricular function predictive of survival and functional results after aortic valve replacement for chronic aortic regurgitation? *J Am Coll Cardiol* 1987;10:713–716.

119. Bonow RO, Vitale DF, Bacharach SL, Maron BJ, Green MV. Effects of aging on asynchronous left ventricular regional function and global ventricular filling in normal human subjects. *J Am Coll Cardiol* 1988;11:50–58.

122. Dilsizian V, Bonow RO, Cannon RO, Tracy CM, Vitale DF, McIntosh CL, Clark RE, Bacharach SL, Green MV. The effect of coronary artery bypass grafting on left ventricular systolic function at rest: evidence for preoperative subclinical myocardial ischemia. *Am J Cardiol* 1988;61:1248–1254.

124. Epstein SE, Quyyumi AA, Bonow RO. Myocardial ischemia: silent or symptomatic. *N Engl J Med* 1988;318:1038–1042.

127. Bonow RO. Prognostic implications of exercise radionuclide angiography in patients with coronary artery disease. *Mayo Clin Proc* 1988;63:630–634.

130. Bonow RO, Dodd JT, Maron BJ, O'Gara PT, White GG, McIntosh CL, Clark RE, Epstein SE. Long-term serial changes in left ventricular function and reversal of ventricular dilatation after valve replacement for chronic aortic regurgitation. *Circulation* 1988;78:1108–1120.

131. Brush JE, Cannon RO, Schenke WH, Bonow RO, Leon MB, Maron BJ, Epstein SE. Microvascular angina in patients with hypertension without left ventricular hypertrophy. *N Engl J Med* 1988;319:1302–1307.

135. Udelson JE, Cannon RO, Bacharach SL, Rumble TF, Bonow RO. Beta-adrenergic stimulation with isoproterenol enhances left ventricular performance in hypertrophic cardiomyopathy despite potentiation of myocardial ischemia: comparison with rapid atrial pacing. *Circulation* 1989;79:371–382.

139. Mazzotta G, Bonow RO, Pace L, Brittain E, Epstein SE. Relation between exertional ischemia and prognosis in mildly symptomatic patients with single or double vessel coronary artery disease and left ventricular dysfunction at rest. *J Am Coll Cardiol* 1989;13:567–573.

141. Bonow RO. Left ventricular structure and function in aortic valve disease. *Circulation* 1989;79:966–969.

142. Bonow RO. Left ventricular ejection dynamics and outflow obstruction in hypertrophic cardiomyopathy. *J Am Coll Cardiol* 1989;13:1280–1282.

144. Udelson JE, Bonow RO, O'Gara PT, Maron BJ, Van Lingen A, Bacharach SL, Epstein SE. Verapamil prevents silent myocardial perfusion abnormalities during exercise in asymptomatic patients with hypertrophic cardiomyopathy. *Circulation* 1989;79:1052–1060.

145. Dilsizian V, Cannon RO, Tracy CM, McIntosh CL, Clark RE, Bonow RO. Enhanced regional left ventricular function after distant coronary bypass via improved collateral flow. *J Am Coll Cardiol* 1989;14:312–318.

146. Brush JE, Udelson JE, Bacharach SL, Cannon RO, Leon MB, Rumble TF, Bonow RO. Comparative effects of verapamil and nitroprusside on left ventricular function in patients with hypertension. *J Am Coll Cardiol* 1989;14:515–522.

149. Epstein SE, Quyyumi AA, Bonow RO. Sudden cardiac death without warning: possible mechanisms and implications for screening asymptomatic populations. *N Engl J Med* 1989;321:320–324.

154. Cuocolo A, Sax FL, Brush JE, Maron BJ, Bacharach SL, Bonow RO. Left ventricular hypertrophy and impaired diastolic filling in essential hypertension: diastolic mechanisms for systolic dysfunction during exercise. *Circulation* 1990; 81:978–986.

155. Bonow RO. Regional left ventricular nonuniformity: effects on left ventricular diastolic function in ischemic heart disease, in hypertrophic cardiomyopathy, and in the normal heart. *Circulation* 1990;81(suppl III):III-54–65.

157. Hennein HA, Swain JA, McIntosh CL, Bonow RO, Stone CD, Clark RE. Comparative assessment of chordal preservation versus chordal resection during mitral valve replacement. *J Thorac Cardiovasc Surg* 1990;99:828–837.

158. Dilsizian V, Rocco TP, Freedman NMT, Leon MB, Bonow RO. Enhanced detection of ischemic but viable myocardium by the reinjection of thallium after stress-redistribution imaging. *N Engl J Med* 1990;323:141–146.

159. Udelson JE, Bacharach SL, Cannon RO, Bonow RO. Minimum left ventricular pressure during beta-adrenergic stimulation in human subjects: evidence for elastic recoil and diastolic "suction" in the normal heart. *Circulation* 1990; 82:1174–1182.

164. Bonow RO, Dilsizian V, Cuocolo A, Bacharach SL. Identification of viable myocardium in patients with coronary artery disease and left ventricular dysfunction: comparison of thallium scintigraphy with reinjection and PET imaging with ^{18}F-fluorodeoxyglucose. *Circulation* 1991;83:26–37.

169. Perrone-Filardi P, Bacharach SL, Dilsizian V, Bonow RO. Impaired left ventricular filling and regional diastolic asynchrony at rest in coronary artery disease and relation to exercise-induced myocardial ischemia. *Am J Cardiol* 1991;67:356–360.

170. Dilsizian V, Smeltzer WR, Freedman NMT, Dextras R, Bonow RO. Thallium reinjection after stress-redistribution imaging: does 24 hour delayed imaging following thallium reinjection enhance detection of viable myocardium? *Circulation* 1991;83:1247–1255.

171. Cannon RO, Dilsizian V, O'Gara PT, Udelson JE, Bonow RO. Myocardial metabolic and hemodynamic significance of reversible thallium-201 perfusion defects in hypertrophic cardiomyopathy. *Circulation* 1991;83:1660–1667.

173. Dilsizian V, Perrone-Filardi P, Cannon RO, Freedman NMT, Bacharach SL, Bonow RO. Comparison of exercise radionuclide angiography with thallium SPECT imaging for detection of significant narrowing of the left circumflex coronary artery. *Am J Cardiol* 1991;68:320–328.

175. Bonow RO, Lakatos E, Maron BJ, Epstein SE. Serial long-term assessment of the natural history of asymptomatic patients with chronic aortic regurgitation and normal left ventricular systolic function. *Circulation* 1991;84:1625–1635.

176. Perrone-Filardi P, Bacharach SL, Bonow RO. Identification of viable myocardium in patients with chronic ischemic heart disease and left ventricular dysfunction: correlation of flow, metabolic activity, and regional function. *Cardiologia* 1991;36:299–307.

177. Clyne CA, Arrighi JA, Maron BJ, Bonow RO, Cannon RO. Systemic and left ventricular hemodynamic responses to exercise stress of asymptomatic patients with significant aortic stenosis. *Am J Cardiol* 1991;68:1469–1476.

184. Bonow RO. Prognostic applications of exercise testing. *N Engl J Med* 1991;325:887–888.

186. Bonow RO. Radionuclide angiographic evaluation of left ventricular diastolic function. *Circulation* 1991;84 (suppl I):I-208–I-215.

187. Bonow RO. Radionuclide angiography in the management of aortic regurgitation. *Circulation* 1991;84 (suppl I):I-296–I-302.

189. Dilsizian V, Freedman NMT, Bacharach SL, Perrone-Filardi P, Bonow RO. Regional thallium uptake in irreversible defects: magnitude of change in thallium activity after reinjection distinguishes viable from nonviable myocardium. *Circulation* 1992;85:627–634.

191. Dilsizian V, Bonow RO. Differential uptake and apparent thallium-201 "washout" after thallium reinjection: options regarding early redistribution imaging before reinjection or late redistribution imaging after reinjection. *Circulation* 1992;85:1032–1038.

194. Bonow RO. Determinants of exercise capacity in hypertrophic cardiomyopathy. *J Am Coll Cardiol* 1992;19:513–515.

195. Cannon RO, Dilsizian V, O'Gara PT, Udelson JE, Tucker E, Panza J, Fananapazir L, McIntosh CL, Wallace RB, Bonow RO. Impact of operative relief of outflow obstruction on thallium perfusion abnormalities in hypertrophic cardiomyopathy. *Circulation* 1992;85:1039–1045.

197. Perrone-Filardi P, Bacharach SL, Bonow RO. Effects of regional systolic asynchrony on left ventricular global diastolic function in patients with coronary artery disease. *J Am Coll Cardiol* 1992;19:739–744.

198. Quyyumi AA, Panza JA, Diodati JG, Callahan TS, Epstein SE, Bonow RO. Relation between left ventricular function at rest and with exercise and silent myocardial ischemia. *J Am Coll Cardiol* 1992;19:962–967.

200. Perrone-Filardi P, Bacharach SL, Dilsizian V, Maurea S, Marin-Neto JA, Arrighi JA, Frank JA, Bonow RO. Metabolic evidence of viable myocardium in regions with reduced wall thickening and absent wall thickening in patients with chronic ischemic left ventricular dysfunction. *J Am Coll Cardiol* 1992;20:161–168.

201. Bonow RO, Udelson JE. Left ventricular diastolic dysfunction as a cause of congestive heart failure: mechanisms and management. *Ann Intern Med* 1992;117:502–510.

202. Perrone-Filardi P, Bacharach SL, Dilsizian V, Maurea S, Frank JA, Bonow RO. Regional left ventricular wall thickening: relation to regional uptake of ^{18}F-fluorodeoxyglucose and ^{201}Tl in patients with chronic coronary artery disease and left ventricular dysfunction. *Circulation* 1992;86:1125–1137.

209. Dilsizian V, Bonow RO. Current diagnostic techniques of assessing myocardial viability in hibernating and stunned myocardium. *Circulation* 1993;87:1–20.

210. Quyyumi AA, Panza JA, Diodati JG, Callahan TS, Bonow RO, Epstein SE. Prognostic implications of myocardial ischemia during daily life in low risk patients with coronary artery disease. *J Am Coll Cardiol* 1993;21:700–708.

211. Perrone-Filardi P, Bacharach SL, Dilsizian V, Panza JA, Maurea S, Bonow RO. Regional systolic function, myocardial blood flow, and glucose uptake at rest in hypertrophic cardiomyopathy. *Am J Cardiol* 1993;72:199–204.

212. Quyyumi AA, Diodati JG, Lakatos E, Bonow RO, Epstein SE. Angiogenic effects of low molecular weight heparin in patients with stable coronary artery disease. *J Am Coll Cardiol* 1993;22:635–641.

214. Dilsizian V, Perrone-Filardi P, Arrighi JA, Bacharach SL, Quyyumi AA, Freedman NMT, Bonow RO. Concordance and discordance between stress-redistribution-reinjection and rest-redistribution thallium imaging for assessing viable myocardium. *Circulation* 1993;88:941–952.

215. Marin-Neto JA, Dilsizian V, Arrighi JA, Freedman NMT, Perrone-Filardi P, Bacharach SL, Bonow RO. Thallium reinjection demonstrates viable myocardium in regions with reverse redistribution. *Circulation* 1993;88:1736–1745.

216. Dilsizian V, Arrighi JA, Diodati JG, Quyyumi AA, Bacharach SL, Marin-Neto JA, Uddin S, Bonow RO. Myocardial viability in patients with chronic ischemic left ventricular dysfunction: comparison of ^{99m}Tc-sestamibi, ^{201}thallium, and ^{18}F-fluorodeoxyglucose. *Circulation* 1994;89:578–587.

217. Perrone-Filardi P, Bacharach SL, Marin-Neto JA, Dilsizian V, Maurea S, Arrighi JA, Bonow RO. Clinical significance of reduced regional myocardial glucose uptake in regions with normal blood flow in patients with chronic coronary artery disease. *J Am Coll Cardiol* 1994;23:608–616.

219. Arrighi JA, Dilsizian V, Perrone-Filardi P, Diodati JG, Bacharach SL, Bonow RO. Improvement of the age-related impairment in left ventricular diastolic filling with verapamil in the normal human heart. *Circulation* 1994;90:213–219.

220. Mazzotta G, Pace L, Bonow RO. Risk stratification of patients with coronary artery disease and left ventricular dysfunction by exercise radionuclide angiography and exercise electrocardiography. *J Nucl Cardiol* 1994;1:529–536.

221. Bonow RO. Asymptomatic aortic regurgitation: indications for operation. *J Card Surg* 1994;(suppl)9:170–173.

223. Bonow RO. Management of chronic aortic regurgitation. *N Engl J Med* 1994;331:736–737.

232. Bonow RO. The hibernating myocardium: Implications for the management of congestive heart failure. *Am J Cardiol* 1995;75:17A–25A.

233. Ritchie JL, Bateman TM, Bonow RO, Crawford MH, Gibbons RJ, Hall RJ, O'Rourke RA, Parisi AF, Verani MS. Guidelines for clinical use of cardiac radionuclide imaging. Report of the American Heart Association/American College of Cardiology Task Force on Assessment of Diagnostic and Therapeutic Cardiovascular Procedures (Committee on Radionuclide Imaging). *Circulation* 1995;91:1278–1303, *J Am Coll Cardiol* 1995;25:521–547.

235. Bonow RO, Nikas D, Elefteriades JA. Valve replacement for regurgitant lesions of the aortic or mitral valve and advanced left ventricular dysfunction. *Cardiol Clin* 1995;13:73–83.

240. Hendel RC, Chaudhry FA, Bonow RO. Myocardial viability. *Curr Prob Cardiol* 1996;21:145–224.

245. Bonow RO. New insights into the cardiac natriuretic peptides. *Circulation* 1996;93:1946–1950.

248. Bonow RO. Identification of viable myocardium. *Circulation* 1996;94:2674–2680.

249. Davidson CJ, Fishman RF, Bonow RO. Cardiac catheterization. In: Braunwald E, ed. *Heart Disease: A Textbook of Cardiovascular Medicine* 5th Edition. Philadelphia: W.B. Saunders Company, 1996:177–203.

251. Gheorghiade M, Bonow RO. Coronary Artery Disease. In: Kelley W, ed. *Textbook of Medicine* 3rd Edition. Philadelphia: J.B. Lippincott Company, 1996:371–385.

252. Kong TQ, Davidson CJ, Meyers SN, Tauke JT, Parker MA, Bonow RO. Prognostic significance of creatine kinase elevation following elective coronary artery interventions. *JAMA* 1997;277:461–466.

256. Bonow RO. Need more research on heart disease. *Chicago Tribune* Feb 19,1997;1:14.

260. Gheorghiade M, Bonow RO. Chronic heart failure in the United States: a manifestation of coronary artery disease. *Circulation* 1998;97:282–289.

261. Bonow RO, Carabello B, de Leon AC, Edmunds LH Jr, Fedderly BJ, Freed MD, Gaasch WH, McKay CR, Nishimura RA, O'Gara PT, O'Rourke RA, Rahimtoola SH. ACC/AHA guidelines for the management of patients with valvular heart disease. A report of the American College of Cardiology/American Heart Association Task Force on Practice Guidelines (Committee on Management of Patients with Valvular Heart Disease). (submitted for publication).

Eugene Braunwald, MD and the Early Years of Hypertrophic Cardiomyopathy: A Conversation With Dr. Barry J. Maron

There is some uncertainty, and even controversy, as to when hypertrophic cardiomyopathy was first recognized. Dating back to 1868, there are autopsy-based case reports from France, Germany, and the United Kingdom composed of 1 or a few patients who appear to have died suddenly of a disease consistent in its features with hypertrophic cardiomyopathy.[1-8] The 1959 and 1960 reports from London of Brock (clinical)[9,10] and Teare (pathologic)[11] are generally regarded as the first contemporary descriptions of hypertrophic cardiomyopathy. However, it is appropriate at this time to reflect on how and why this important disease was transformed from the subject of a few anecdotal case reports into a robust and treatable clinical entity ultimately regarded as a common genetic heart disease and the most frequent cause of sudden death in young individuals (including trained athletes).[12,13]

In the early 1960s, a number of clinical investigators, largely in North America, most notably Dr. Douglas E. Wigle of Toronto General Hospital,[14] made novel observations regarding outflow obstruction that contributed importantly to this transformation. However, it is undeniably the body of work of Dr. Eugene Braunwald and colleagues, particularly Dr. Andrew Glenn Morrow, at the National Institutes of Health (NIH) from 1958 to 1968, that is most responsible for the initial description of hypertrophic cardiomyopathy as a unique clinical entity (and its treatment, medical and surgical), culminating in the seminal 1964 American Heart Association (AHA) monograph in *Circulation*.[15] That document is the first comprehensive description of hypertrophic cardiomyopathy, presented in 213 pages with 176 illustrative figures, 18 tables, and 191 references.

As part of this program at the NIH, the first patient with hypertrophic cardiomyopathy was diagnosed on clinical examination by Dr. Braunwald,[16] and this disease, initially described in the context of dynamic obstruction of left ventricular outflow,[14,15] was expanded to a broader spectrum to include the nonobstructive form. Also, in a remarkable twist, using only auscultation, Dr. Braunwald diagnosed his close friend and colleague, Dr. Andrew G. Morrow, the very individual responsible for designing the myotomy-myectomy operation that is still used today (referred to in the following discussion as "myectomy"), as having that same disease.

It is now 53 years since Morrow and Braunwald's[17] initial report, and Dr. Braunwald's numerous seminal ac-complishments, authoring more than 1,400 reports in diverse areas of cardiovascular medicine—prominently including coronary atherosclerosis and the pathophysiology of acute coronary syndromes (which continue to this day)[18]—are well recognized and unnecessary to replicate in any detail here. What is particularly relevant to the present discussion is Dr. Braunwald's intellectual attachment to the era at the NIH so early in his professional life, which he regards as perhaps the most creative in his long career, that included the early description of the disease he called idiopathic hypertrophic subaortic stenosis and which we (and he) now refer to as hypertrophic cardiomyopathy.

For these reasons, it seems very appropriate to discuss with Dr. Braunwald his recollections of those unique days when the NIH was a premier clinical cardiovascular research center. The purpose here is not only to formulate recollections but also to gain insights into the mechanisms and circumstances by which novel clinical research discoveries actually occur, in this case the description of a new and complex cardiac disease. Potentially, these principles and lessons will prove useful to future investigators who unexpectedly make observations for which there is no previous context. This conversation took place in Dr. Braunwald's office in the TIMI Study Group at Brigham and Women's Hospital in Boston, Massachusetts, on October 6, 2011.

The Beginning

Dr. Maron: Dr. Braunwald, thank you for allowing me to come here today and help you tell the story of the "birth" of hypertrophic cardiomyopathy in the late 1950s and early 1960s. The place is the Clinical Center at the National Institutes of Health in Bethesda, Maryland. When you started your observations on hypertrophic cardiomyopathy, you were only 28 years old, I guess, and the NIH Clinical Center and the cardiology and surgical branches were brand new. There were really no senior people. In fact, everyone was young, right?

Dr. Braunwald: That's right, and at 28, I was one of the "older" guys. But I was 22 when I graduated from medical school, so I was 6 years postgraduate. Actually, I first came to NIH in 1955 and then went to The Johns Hopkins Hospital to finish my medical residency.

Soon after coming back to NIH in June 1958, the first patient, E.Z.,[16] a 27-year-old man from Saskatoon, was admitted to the Clinical Center. He had moderately severe angina pectoris and a loud holosystolic murmur at the apex of the heart and along the sternal border. Glenn Morrow, the chief of cardiac surgery, carried out a transbronchial left-heart catheterization. I was responsible for balancing the strain gauges that we used for pressure measurements, and for recording the tracings, but to me the most exciting task was analyzing the pressure tracings. The patient had a left

Manuscript received December 16, 2011; revised manuscript received and accepted January 16, 2012.

This work was funded in part by a grant from the Hearst Foundations, San Francisco, California.

intraventricular peak pressure gradient of 74 mm Hg, and we thought that he had a congenital subaortic stenotic membrane. Since his angina had progressed and he had severe obstruction, we scheduled him for surgery. At the time, cardioplegia was inducted with potassium citrate to arrest the heart.

During the operation, Glenn Morrow called me from the catheterization laboratory to come to the OR (operating room) immediately. When I arrived, he was very upset, telling me that the operation was a "royal screw-up." Open-heart surgery was anything but routine in those days. This was one of the early open operations at the Clinical Center. Glenn's voice was high pitched: "I opened the aorta and I stuck my finger into the ventricle and there was *no* obstruction!" He yelled, "Gene, I can't feel anything wrong! I can't see anything. What have you done? What the hell is going on here?" I thought, "How could this be? I didn't know anything about gradients without obstruction. Maybe I made some terrible mistake with the pressure gauges or the multichannel recorder. Did I not balance the gauges properly?" I couldn't imagine. I said, "Glenn, I must go back to the cath lab, because I left a patient on the table with a first-year fellow. *If* you can get his heart started, and take him off bypass, please measure the left ventricular pressure and see if he has a gradient." That was a big "if" at the time. When a patient was placed on bypass, and the heart was arrested and the surgeon didn't fix the problem, the patient was worse off and at high risk of death. Well, fortunately Glenn restarted the heart and got the patient off bypass successfully.

Glenn came down from the OR and walked into my office. I did not yet know the outcome. I was shaking with fear, but he was now very friendly and apologetic about his outburst and said that in fact that there was a high pressure gradient present after he had restarted the heart. He also told me that although there was no palpable or visual obstruction in the arrested heart, he did think that the left ventricle was thickened. Fortunately, the patient recovered uneventfully. We couldn't figure the whole thing out. The patient had a loud heart murmur, and a high pressure gradient in the left ventricular outflow tract, but no obstruction in the arrested heart. After about 2 or 3 weeks of talking about this patient every day, Glenn said "Look, Gene. I've been in medicine longer than you have." He was only 35 at the time. "Sometimes you come across something that you can't explain, and you just have to move on." A couple of months later, we had a similar experience with a second patient, and agreed then that we probably had something new here.

I was rereading this 1959 paper[17] last night in preparation for this conversation, and I think that what I was pleased to see is this paragraph on page 186. I'll let you read it.

Dr. Maron: Yes, you describe obstruction here: "The hemodynamic evidence of obstruction to left ventricular outflow is unequivocal; in the first 2 patients a systolic pressure difference between left ventricle and aorta was demonstrated on 2 separate occasions and was definitely localized to an area within the ventricle. . .none of the usual forms of aortic stenosis were present.. . .In these 2 patients it must be concluded that the obstruction. . .can only be explained by muscular hypertrophy of the left outflow tract of sufficient severity that flow is actually impeded during contraction."

Dr. Braunwald: Yes, I think we pretty much nailed it. We knew there was an obstruction, and that it was due to the left ventricular hypertrophy. We proposed that these patients had muscular subaortic obstruction.

Dr. Maron: Absolutely. The key word is "impedance." That observation was made in what could be regarded as the era of awakening in cardiovascular hemodynamics and pathophysiology. That was the beginning. Now, let me ask you about the original Morrow procedure for obstructive hypertrophic cardiomyopathy (surgical resection of muscle from the upper portion of ventricular septum).[19–21] I assume that the collaboration and design was between you and Andy Morrow.

Dr. Braunwald: Yes, we talked about it a lot. But he led the conversations and developed the procedure. I was an intensely interested spectator in the operating room during the first few cases. Interestingly, Kirklin and Ellis[22] began a surgical program almost simultaneously at the Mayo Clinic.

Dr. Maron: So, it's interesting that the correct operation was designed without knowing the precise mechanism by which impedance to outflow occurred. The true mechanism of obstruction due to SAM (systolic anterior motion of the mitral valve)[23] came along later, perhaps 1969, right?

Dr. Braunwald: Yes, it was after I left the NIH in 1968. But as early as 1960, Glenn felt the muscular obstruction grabbing his forefinger when he inserted it into the left ventricular outflow tract of the beating heart. Often in medicine, we come upon something that works, and we don't really understand it yet, but we gradually understand the mechanism.

Dr. Maron: This is a great example of that principle.

We Are Onto Something Important

Dr. Maron: There was a lot of serendipity in this whole thing.

Dr. Braunwald: Yes, also a lot of luck.

Dr. Maron: We talked about the E.Z. operation and the first 2 patients, but when did you really think you knew? When did you get to that point? Was there anxiety and doubt that maybe this whole thing was not what you thought it is, and maybe that explains why hardly anyone else knew what you knew?

Dr. Braunwald: Over the next 2 years, we began to feel that we were onto something that was much more important—very exciting, but quite infrequent. What we didn't suspect in our early experience was that hypertrophic cardiomyopathy was going to be so common and so important.

Dr. Maron: That's interesting because when I started with hypertrophic cardiomyopathy in about 1975, we also thought of it as rare. Now, we understand it to be the most common of the genetic heart diseases, occurring in 1 in 500 of the general population, with at least 600,000 Americans affected.[24]

Dr. Braunwald: As open-heart surgery developed and became more frequent, we identified an increasing number of cases, and by 1960 we described an additional 12 patients.[25] That is also the paper in which we described the familial nature of the condition. So the pieces gradually

Figure 1. Eugene Braunwald, 1963.

Figure 2. Andrew Glenn Morrow, 1963.

came together. We were energized by the study of these patients and became even more excited as the years went on (Figures 1 and 2). In 1962, we described a group of patients who had left ventricular hypertrophy similar to those with obstructive hypertrophic cardiomyopathy, but without obstruction.[26]

In that year, we also published an editorial entitled: "Hypertrophic Subaortic Stenosis: A Broadened Concept."[27] The idea behind the "broadened concept" was that there are patients with hypertrophic cardiomyopathy who had obstruction *all* of the time. They may have close relatives with left ventricular hypertrophy who *never* had obstruction, and there were patients who had obstruction *some* of the time. In 1963, the editor of *Circulation* invited Glenn and me to prepare the monograph, which was published as a supplement in 1964.[15] More and more patients with hypertrophic cardiomyopathy were being reported from all

over the world. Doug Wigle's group at the University of Toronto[14] and John Goodwin and his colleagues at Hammersmith Hospital in London[28] made the most important contributions.

Dynamic Obstruction

Dr. Maron: One of the most interesting and distinguishing features of hypertrophic cardiomyopathy is the dynamic nature of the outflow obstruction. How did that discovery come about?

Dr. Braunwald: Actually, it was quite serendipitous. We were studying the effects of intravenous ouabain on the hemodynamics of patients with severe valvular aortic stenosis and other patients with hypertrophic cardiomyopathy.[29] We observed intensification of the intraventricular pressure gradient with the glycoside. An important coinvestigator on this study was Bob Frye, who went on to a dazzling career at the Mayo Clinic, first as chair of cardiology and then of medicine. After this observation with ouabain, we immediately went on to study a more powerful inotropic agent, the β-adrenergic agent isoproterenol, and found the same thing. We also studied the α-adrenergic agonist methoxamine, a pure vasoconstrictor, and found that the obstruction could be eliminated transiently.[30]

In addition, we found that in patients with hypertrophic cardiomyopathy, in the beat after a premature ventricular contraction, the arterial pressure fails to show a normal increase in pulse pressure. This phenomenon, which is quite accurate in recognizing hypertrophic cardiomyopathy, is called the "Brockenbrough sign," named for Ned Brockenbrough, a research fellow rotating through the catheterization laboratory, who first authored this paper.[31] We observed and reported the development of sudden cardiac death,[15] a complication that sometimes occurred in patients with little or no obstruction. We also commented on the great variability of the clinical course of hypertrophic cardiomyopathy.[32]

Other hemodynamic observations that led to provocation or intensification of the pressure gradient were reductions of preload with nitroglycerin during the strain of the Valsalva maneuver,[33] during tachycardia,[34] and on assuming the erect posture.[35] We also showed slowed ventricular filling, i.e., diastolic dysfunction, that was presumably due to reduced left ventricular compliance.[36] Putting these and other observations together, we postulated that the reduction of left ventricular volume, however produced, provoked or intensified obstruction, and that increases in ventricular volume have the opposite effect.

Beta Blockade

Dr. Maron: For a long time, β blockers were essentially the only nonsurgical treatment available for hypertrophic cardiomyopathy. It remains a mainstay in the treatment of the disease to this day. I suspect you were responsible for the development of β-adrenergic blockade in hypertrophic cardiomyopathy? Can you elaborate on that?

Dr. Braunwald: In 1962, the late James Black described the first β-adrenergic blocker, pronethalol, and shortly thereafter, I met him in London, where I was participating in one of the first international hypertrophic cardiomyopathy meetings. I described the condition to him and the intensification of obstruction with isoproterenol, as well as with muscular exercise. I asked him if we could get the drug—it was not yet available—and he graciously agreed. Interestingly, in 1988, Black received a Nobel Prize for that discovery. Immediately after my return, we administered intravenous pronethalol to patients with hypertrophic cardiomyopathy, and we noted that, as expected, it blocked the provocation or intensification of obstruction with isoproterenol. We were also excited to note that it also reduced the intensification of obstruction during exercise.[37] The paper's first author was Don Harrison, who went on to become chief of cardiology at Stanford and president of the American Heart Association.

Naturally, we saw β blockade as a potential treatment for patients with hypertrophic cardiomyopathy. When oral propranolol became available, we conducted a placebo-controlled study, which showed that the anginal threshold in these patients (as assessed by treadmill exercise) was markedly increased.[38] We found that symptomatic benefit was sustained on propranolol in some patients with angina and that surgical treatment could be averted, or at least postponed.[39] The lead author of these 2 papers was Lawrence S. Cohen, who went on to become chief of cardiology at Yale.

Dr. Maron: When did you leave the NIH—and hypertrophic cardiomyopathy?

Dr. Braunwald: It was 1968, and in that year, I published my last paper on hypertrophic cardiomyopathy, in which Stuart Frank and I reviewed the natural history in 126 patients.[32]

Dr. Maron: 1958 to 1968, 10 years. What stands out is the confidence and lack of doubt, and maybe that's the message. If you want to be an innovative clinical investigator, great confidence is a requisite.

Dr. Braunwald: How about a dash of youthful arrogance thrown in? No, I wouldn't be as certain today if I made findings like those I made a half century ago. I am much more cautious today, probably because I have been "bitten" a few times. Of course, the whole Criley episode. . .

A Challenge to the Concept of Obstruction

Dr. Maron: Right, that is what I wanted to ask you. There is this great confidence, what you are calling youthful arrogance, and then came a threat to all of this—a very visible and public threat in about 1966—the idea that obstruction really did not exist,[40,41] that you had been fooled by the pressure gradients, and Glenn Morrow was operating on patients to relieve a gradient that did not even exist!

Dr. Braunwald: What troubled Glenn and me was not so much that we could have been wrong, but rather the possibility—unlikely, to be sure, but still the possibility—that we were misleading people by advocating myectomy in seriously symptomatic patients with high gradients, which we interpreted as signifying severe outflow tract obstruction. Cardiac surgeons from all over the world were coming to Bethesda to learn the operation from Glenn! Most patients who were operated on were relieved of obstruction and improved clinically, but we didn't have a randomized controlled trial. Could we have been fooling ourselves be-

cause of a prolonged placebo effect? Were we consigning patients to an operative mortality, which was 5% to 10% around the world at that time, and were we making the "mistake of the century"? I had a number of sleepless nights worrying about it. Glenn was less concerned. He was quite certain from palpation and direct observation of the heart that obstruction was present and that he was able to relieve it by myectomy.

Dr. Maron: So there must have been some doubt then.

Dr. Braunwald: Yes, it was then that I got the nickname "Worrier in Chief," which is one that has stuck to this day. Let's say that it brought me up short. It did not give me a sinking feeling in the pit of my stomach, but it made me wonder what was going on.

I give John Ross credit for answering the question by showing that the intraventricular pressure was high in the left ventricle as the transseptal catheter was withdrawn across the mitral valve, proving that the left ventricular intracavitary pressure was really elevated and that the gradient was not an artifact due to cavity obliteration and/or catheter entrapment.[42] The Criley episode made us realize how very important the reliability of our work was to the care of a huge number of patients worldwide. Not that cavity obliteration or catheter entrapment and other artifacts cannot occur. All of us who have worked in cardiac catheterization laboratories have seen them, but when the catheter tip moves freely in the left ventricular cavity, it measures intracavitary pressure.

Dr. Maron: Fortunately, transseptal catheterization saved the day. Certainly, this was a turning point. It could have been a great loss to the hypertrophic cardiomyopathy patient population, considering how dramatically and long-lasting myectomy relieves symptoms and enhances longevity, as we know now.[43,44] The patients would have been deprived of one of the major innovations in hypertrophic cardiomyopathy management over the last 50 years.

Do you think that you were in a position then, similar to the 1990s with peptic ulcer disease—*Helicobacter pylori* and Barry Marshall? I guess there were many people who didn't believe in obstruction because of the Criley controversy? But, you had some followers. . .

Dr. Braunwald: Yes, we did. You know, some people are professional skeptics, and many people enjoy watching a controversy play out in public. So that's why this controversy attracted so much attention at the AHA meeting in New York in 1966, when *all* the attendees were present for the 90-minute panel at which time the controversy was aired.[43]

Dr. Maron: Trust me, we have "bottom feeders" in this field devoted to attacking other people's work to this day. The nature of the disease seems to promote that.

Dr. Braunwald: I agree.

Goodbye to Bethesda and Hypertrophic Cardiomyopathy

Dr. Maron: Dr. Braunwald, you obviously are a major figure in contemporary cardiology in a multitude of ways and in several key areas of investigation—if not the number 1 guy—that is not a matter of dispute. Do you believe that hypertrophic cardiomyopathy is the best thing you did in terms of creativity and novelty?

Dr. Braunwald: During my time at the NIH, I worked on 5 major topics, mostly simultaneously: (1) determinants of myocardial oxygen consumption; (2) myocardial mechanics and ventricular function; (3) the role of the adrenergic nervous system in heart failure; (4) the hemodynamics of valvular heart disease, especially the effects of valve replacement; and, of course, (5) hypertrophic cardiomyopathy. In looking back on my career, the work on hypertrophic cardiomyopathy was clearly the most exciting that I have ever done.

Dr. Maron: When you left the NIH in 1968, did your work on hypertrophic cardiomyopathy continue?

Dr. Braunwald: I fell off the "hypertrophic cardiomyopathy cliff" and left the field when I changed my career goals and went to the University of California, San Diego. I was going to become the best possible chairman of medicine. I wasn't going to do much research, but I felt that I wanted to do *some* research. So I had to decide whether I could continue to work on hypertrophic cardiomyopathy. What could I do with hypertrophic cardiomyopathy in San Diego? I had lost my most precious resource—my patient base—which was in Bethesda. In San Diego, I began research on limiting infarct size because it was an extension of my studies on myocardial O_2 consumption and ischemia begun at NIH.

Dr. Maron: Right. It is impossible to understand hypertrophic cardiomyopathy without exposure to many patients, because of its inherent heterogeneity. The more patients you see, the more your perceptions evolve and become more precise. And that is a good thing.

Dr. Braunwald: I was referred many patients with hypertrophic cardiomyopathy while in San Diego and then in Boston for diagnosis and clinical care. I have been asked why I didn't set up a hypertrophic cardiomyopathy program when I came to the Brigham as chief of medicine. In retrospect, I probably should have done so. But I was just so extremely busy with the Department of Medicine and so focused on the work on myocardial infarction, and I had become an editor of Harrison's textbook of medicine. I simply didn't have the time. In retrospect, I wish I had picked someone in the division and said, "Establish a program on hypertrophic cardiomyopathy. I will support you."

Dr. Maron: Well, we have to play the cards we are dealt.

Dr. Braunwald: Yes, the cards change. Of course, the Seidmans, Christine and Jon, carried out their seminal work on the genetics of hypertrophic cardiomyopathy at the Brigham and Harvard. I have received some vicarious pleasure from that.

Why the NIH?

Dr. Maron: Let's go back just a moment to the brand-new days of the NIH Clinical Center. What has always struck me is the question, "Why did it happen there?" After all, it was a new place with a lot of smart guys, that's for sure, but it wasn't an institution with a long historical context in cardiology.

Dr. Braunwald: Sometimes, a new institution can break down barriers more easily than a well-established one. You see, in those years, in the late '50s and in the early '60s, when we worked on hypertrophic cardiomyopathy, there was only 1 other "full-service" integrated cardiology/cardiac surgery program in the country besides ours: at the Mayo Clinic. Now we have such centers everywhere. The open relation between cardiology and cardiac surgery also played an important role.

Dr. Maron: So, it was a distinct advantage to be small and focused full time on research with a selected patient population. NIH decided which patients would be admitted. Patients had to have the "right" disease, and hypertrophic cardiomyopathy was one of the right ones then.

Dr. Braunwald: And it was the primary mission of the programs in the Clinical Center to be focused on research. It certainly helped that we didn't get distracted by having to see patients in order to provide the income we needed for our work. As you said, we could select our patients.

Dr. Maron: Yes. NIH was a unique place, but the patients had to show up.

Dr. Braunwald: Yes, they showed up. As we now know, they were pretty frequent, so there was some luck. First, E.Z. showed up, and then many others. We were puzzled by the first 2 patients. Probably a weird anomaly never to be heard of again. But after we saw more and more, we sensed this was going to be a big deal. We had an inside joke: any patient admitted to cardiology in those days had hypertrophic cardiomyopathy until proven otherwise. It helped that we were in the business of studying these patients carefully.

Dr. Maron: Also, let's not forget that at the Clinical Center care was cost free, and health insurance was unnecessary. Reflecting on this time, there was clearly a lot of serendipity and maybe even luck in play. But you guys were smart enough to see the big picture. It is also amazing that the patient that you regard as the first to be diagnosed by simple clinical examination[16] turned out later to develop what is a very rare natural history of the disease, the so-called end stage, with systolic dysfunction and striking remodeling. That subgroup constitutes only about 2% of our current hypertrophic cardiomyopathy cohorts,[45] yet he was the first clinically diagnosed hypertrophic cardiomyopathy patient (by you). He survives to this day, with a heart transplant, 50 years later.[16]

Dr. Braunwald: Yes, and it was gratifying to meet him at a hypertrophic cardiomyopathy patient function a couple of years ago.

Dr. Maron: This is a typical hypertrophic cardiomyopathy story—about its heterogeneity and unpredictability.

The Role of the NIH Group

Dr. Maron: Dr. Braunwald, UK investigators seem to believe this disease is theirs, that somehow it belongs to them as their discovery—an ownership mentality. Of course, there were Teare and Brock, and John Goodwin certainly was a real pioneer. I just thought I would ask you about that to get your reaction. You don't have to answer it if you don't want to.

Dr. Braunwald: No, Barry, I don't have any problem answering you. First of all, I stand in awe of the contributions to this disease by those early UK investigators such as

Figure 3. Eugene Braunwald (left) and Barry Maron (right) at the American Heart Association meeting in Orlando, Florida, 2011.

John Goodwin and his talented team.[28] We learned a lot from them, particularly about the diastolic abnormalities in this disease.

I think that there are 6 key aspects to hypertrophic cardiomyopathy: left ventricular hypertrophy, sudden death, familial heart disease, dynamic obstruction, medical treatment with β blockers, and surgical treatment with myectomy. As you stated, patients with idiopathic left ventricular hypertrophy were described in the 19th century.[8] The next thing that came along was sudden death in patients who were found to have idiopathic hypertrophy at postmortem. Then patients with familial left ventricular hypertrophy. So, were Glenn and I the first to describe idiopathic ventricular hypertrophy? Absolutely not. Were we the first group to describe sudden death in patients with left ventricular hypertrophy? Absolutely not. Were we the first to describe familial ventricular hypertrophy? Absolutely not. Were we the first to describe dynamic obstruction? Yes, I believe that we were.[15,29,30] Were we the first to describe the "package," i.e., all 4 of these features, and put them all together into a single entity? I think so.[15] Were we the first to develop medical treatment with β blockers in hypertrophic cardiomyopathy? Yes.[37–39] Was Glenn Morrow the first to carry out myectomy for those who failed medical therapy?[19–21] Again, I believe that he was. Incidentally, it's surprising and gratifying that these 2 treatments (medical and surgical) described a half century ago are still cornerstones of therapy today. Very few therapies remain unchanged for such a long period nowadays.

Dr. Maron: Yes, I think most would agree with you. In fact, that's why I am here today. There are only a few investigators who have had a disease named after them for putting the package together and perhaps hypertrophic cardiomyopathy should be "Braunwald's disease."

Dr. Braunwald: That's very generous, but I don't believe in eponyms. In any event, Morrow was at the very least an equal partner.

Present State of Hypertrophic Cardiomyopathy Research

Dr. Maron: Let me ask you just a few more questions. You basically left the field in 1968. So, as the father of hypertrophic cardiomyopathy, if I can use that term, are you pleased with what the rest of us have done (Figure 3)? Obviously, there have been many astute investigators working on various aspects of this disease in the US and throughout the world all these years, building on what you and Glenn Morrow started.

Dr. Braunwald: The work that you have done, identifying the patients at risk for sudden death, and doing something about it,[46] demonstrating that hypertrophic cardiomyopathy is often a disease compatible with normal longevity, sometimes even without treatment,[47] and now exploring with MRI (magnetic resonance imaging) patients who are genotype positive and phenotype negative, is very, very important.[48] So, I think you, your son Martin, and the rest of your collaborators deserve a great deal of credit. In fact, I think what you have done is of historic importance, and you should keep on going.

Dr. Maron: Thank you. It does mean a lot to hear this from you. One recent time we spoke, you wrapped that up into 3 simple, but I must say inspirational, words—"keep it up"—which actually made a difference to me. Very important words for investigators over the age of 60. After you've done the same thing for a long time, thoughts periodically come into your mind: what am I really doing here? But, your words resonated because they instill a reminder that what we are doing is in fact important.

Dr. Braunwald: It is *extremely* important. You have built a wonderful resource in addition to your brain. You have connections with patients, that's probably the most important, and connections with colleagues. For example, the work that you have done with the groups in Italy, with Paolo Spirito.[49]

Glenn Morrow's Illness

Dr. Maron: Dr. Braunwald, here is something else I have always wanted to ask you. At a time when diagnostic criteria for hypertrophic cardiomyopathy were just being developed for this completely novel clinical entity, an incredible circumstance arose. Your closest colleague and friend, responsible for designing the myectomy operation for obstructive hypertrophic cardiomyopathy that bears his name (the Morrow procedure), was diagnosed by you as having the very same new disease you were in the process of characterizing for the first time, and he was operating on. Can you tell us about it?

Dr. Braunwald: Barry, looking back on it, it was one of the more unusual events of my life. Let me paint the picture of the time. It was 1964, and at that time I was 34 years old and chief of the cardiology branch, and Glenn was 40 and a world-renowned chief of cardiac surgery. We worked together intensely, and I would say that out of a hospital work week of 60 hours, we would have been in the same room for 10 hours; we saw each other almost daily. Our offices were close together; we were collaborating on various papers and the 1964 monograph in *Circulation*.[15] All the patients that were admitted to the surgery branch were transferred from cardiology. Several hours a week, we saw patients together, but mostly we discussed the work on hypertrophic cardiomyopathy.

One day we were working on a manuscript in his office, and Glenn said, "Gene, would you examine my heart?" And

I said, "Sure." I had my stethoscope in my pocket, and he took off his shirt. I put my stethoscope on his chest, and I did a double take. At the time, we were privately referring to hypertrophic cardiomyopathy as "*the disease*," as in, "We have another patient with *the disease*," or "Did you examine the sister of the patient with *the disease*?" Or he would say, "Next week I am operating on 2 patients with *the disease*."

Remarkably, Glenn's physical findings at that time were classical for *the disease*, just as we were describing it. I felt it couldn't be anything else. I was shocked, and I said, "Glenn, I don't know what to say, but you have the physical findings that we know so well and what we have been talking about almost nonstop for the past 6 years." He didn't show any emotion. It was as if he expected it.

Then I took the history. I asked, "Have you had shortness of breath on exertion?" He said, "Yes, a little." "Have you fainted?" "Almost." Then something very interesting occurred. I said, "Well, tell me about the 'almost,' " and here is an example of a very accurate historian. He said, "It's often in the morning, when I walk from the car to the entrance of the Clinical Center. I often feel faint." So then I said, "I want you to describe exactly what happens." This was a time when thoracic surgeons still smoked, and Glenn smoked at least a pack a day. Glenn said that when he parked his car, and was finishing his second cigarette of the day, he walked to the entrance of the Clinical Center: "I feel like I'm going to faint and I sit down"—and there was a bench at the entrance of the Clinical Center. "Are you aware of arrhythmias or do you get any palpitations?" "No." And that history was strongly suggestive of obstructive hypertrophic cardiomyopathy, because when patients with valvular aortic stenosis faint, it is usually sudden. Patients with transient ventricular fibrillation also collapse suddenly. They don't usually know they are going to faint and prevent it. They just collapse. I had lectured about "graying-out" spells in hypertrophic cardiomyopathy, and he had those spells, not once, not twice, but almost daily.

From the clinical examination, I was certain that he had hypertrophic cardiomyopathy. I asked myself, What else could it be? I wanted to get an electrocardiogram (ECG) and chest x-ray, and I wanted to get him worked up at Toronto or Mayo, and I said that I would make all the arrangements. He adamantly refused. He was stubborn and didn't want to talk about it, although I brought it up repeatedly. Several years after I left NIH, he developed repeated syncope, atrial fibrillation, and unfortunately then a series of strokes that ultimately and tragically led to his death.

I think that if you saw this story on TV or in a movie, you would call it ridiculous—those things just don't happen in real life. There are these 2 men who were very close collaborators, and one of them has the condition they're describing, and the other diagnoses it—it's just too cute to believe.

Dr. Maron: It is amazing, mind-boggling really. But I am struck by "What else could it be?" Your clarity was amazing. A lot of people would have said, "It just can't possibly be" and moved on.

Dr. Braunwald: By the time that this happened, we had obstructive hypertrophic cardiomyopathy down pretty well. I mean, as you know, in the 1964 monograph, we described the physical findings in detail. Glenn's findings were absolutely typical.

Dr. Maron: What did the 12-lead ECG look like?

Dr. Braunwald: I don't know.

Dr. Maron: Oh yes, you said he wouldn't even do an ECG. Well, I'm glad you felt comfortable talking about Glenn.

Dr. Braunwald: Eventually, after I left Bethesda, the diagnosis was confirmed by echocardiography, and then, sadly, at postmortem. Glenn and I had a very close relationship. At various times, he was my boss, then my partner. He was also Nina's (my late first wife's) boss. He was extremely supportive of her. We became personal friends as well as professional colleagues. It was very difficult for me to just stand by.

Reflections

Dr. Maron: Let me ask you something else—let's do it this way. Perhaps the 2 most important scholars of the cardiovascular community in the last half century are yourself and Michel Mirowski, whose vision created the implantable defibrillator.[50] Of course, there have been many, many others as well, but let's just say this for argument sake. We have been talking about many things for the last 90 minutes, including the role of chance in defining events and making discoveries. You and Michel both survived the Holocaust in different ways. I believe Michel was the only one of a large family of more than 20 to survive. But, had the Nazis had their way, there would have been a huge gap in a couple of really big areas of cardiovascular medicine. Would we be where we are today if you and Michel had not survived the Holocaust? That's the question.

Dr. Braunwald: First, Barry, I am honored to be placed in the same category as Michel Mirowski. But to respond to your question, as far as hypertrophic cardiomyopathy is concerned, I believe it would have happened anyway. Many talented clinical investigators in Toronto, Rochester, London, and elsewhere were playing in the same sandbox and would probably have put the pieces together very soon. Michel was a great visionary who left us too early, but the defibrillator also probably would have been developed by someone else a few years later. (Dr. Braunwald pauses.)

You know, I believe in the saying "The graveyards are filled with the bodies of indispensable people." Science has a way of moving forward. Whether it is a disease like hypertrophic cardiomyopathy, a device such as the implantable defibrillator, or the structure of DNA. There will always be a few people who are lucky for one reason or another, with a prepared mind and the right environment, like the NIH in the '50s and '60s, or the Cavendish Laboratory at Cambridge, England, in the '50s, and they will reach the goal earlier. For me and hypertrophic cardiomyopathy, it was being in the right place, i.e., the NIH, at the right time, from 1958 to 1968, and with the right people, Glenn Morrow, John Ross, and others.

Dr. Maron: Okay, but who knows, really? I am not so sure. Your contributions have been vast. Nevertheless, for sure it is an uncontrolled experiment.

Dr. Braunwald: Yes, it's an uncontrolled experiment.

Dr. Maron: Dr. Braunwald, thank you for your time. We

have covered a lot of ground, and your insights have been invaluable and unique, as always. You have established an instructive historical record of those seminal events that took place in the cardiology and surgery branches of the National Institutes of Health over a half century ago, possibly never to be replicated. Thank you for all that you have done for "the disease."

Dr. Braunwald: And thank you, Barry, for allowing me to tell the story.

Barry J. Maron, MD
The Hypertrophic Cardiomyopathy Center
Minneapolis Heart Institute Foundation
Minneapolis, Minnesota

Eugene Braunwald, MD
The TIMI Study Group
Brigham and Women's Hospital
Boston, Massachusetts

1. Vulpian A. Contribution a l'etude des retrecissements de l'orifice ventriculo-aortique. *Arch Physiol* 1868;3:456–457.
2. Liouville H. Rétrécissement cardiaque sous aortique. *Gaz Med Paris* 1869;24:161–163.
3. Hallopeau M. Rétrécissement ventricuo-aortique. *Gaz Med Paris* 1869;24:683–684.
4. Whittle CH. "Idiopathic" hypertrophy of the heart in a young man. *Lancet* 1929;216:1354–1355.
5. Evans W. Familial cardiomegaly. *Br Heart J* 1949;11:68–82.
6. Davies LG. A familial heart disease. *Br Heart J* 1952;14:206–212.
7. Campbell M, Turner-Warwick M. Two more families with cardiomegaly. *Br Heart J* 1956;18:393–402.
8. Braunwald E. Hypertrophic cardiomyopathy: the early years. *J Cardiovasc Trans Res* 2009;2:341–348.
9. Brock R. Functional obstruction of the left ventricle; acquired aortic subvalvar stenosis. *Guys Hosp Rep* 1957;106:221–238.
10. Brock R. Functional obstruction of the left ventricle (acquired aortic subvalvar stenosis). *Guys Hosp Rep* 1959;108:126–143.
11. Teare D. Asymmetrical hypertrophy of the heart in young adults. *Br Heart J* 1958;20:1–8.
12. Maron BJ. Hypertrophic cardiomyopathy: a systematic review. *JAMA* 2002;287:1308–1320.
13. Maron BJ, McKenna WJ, Danielson GK, Kappenberger LJ, Kuhn HJ, Seidman CE, Shah PM, Spencer WH, Spirito P, ten Cate FJ, Wigle ED. American College of Cardiology/European Society of Cardiology Clinical expert consensus document on hypertrophic cardiomyopathy. A report of the American College of Cardiology Task Force on Clinical Expert Consensus Documents and the European Society of Cardiology Committee for Practice Guidelines Committee to Develop an Expert Consensus Document on Hypertrophic Cardiomyopathy. *J Am Coll Cardiol* 2003;42:1687–1713.
14. Wigle ED, Heimbecker RO, Gunton RW. Idiopathic ventricular septal hypertrophy causing muscular subaortic stenosis. *Circulation* 1962;26:325–340.
15. Braunwald E, Lambrew CT, Rockoff SD, Ross J Jr, Morrow AG. Idiopathic hypertrophic subaortic stenosis. A description of the disease based upon an analyses of 64 patients. *Circulation* 1964;30(suppl):3–119.
16. Maron BJ, Bonow RO, Salberg L, Roberts WC, Braunwald E. The first patient clinically diagnosed with hypertrophic cardiomyopathy. *Am J Cardiol* 2008;102:1418–1420.
17. Morrow AG, Braunwald E. Functional aortic stenosis; a malformation characterized by resistance to left ventricular outflow without anatomic obstruction. *Circulation* 1959;20:181–189.
18. Mega JL, Braunwald E, Wiviott SD, Bassand J-P, Bhatt DL, Bode C, Burton P, Cohen M, Cook-Bruns N, Fox KAA, Goto S, Murphy SA, Plotnikov AN, Schneider D, Sun X, Verheugt FWA, Gibson CM. Rivaroxaban in patients with a recent acute coronary syndrome. *N Engl J Med* 2012;366:54–63.
19. Morrow AG, Brockenbrough EC. Surgical treatment of idiopathic hypertrophic subaortic stenosis. *Am Surg* 1961:154:181–189.
20. Morrow AG, Lambrew CT, Braunwald E. Idiopathic hypertrophic subaortic stenosis. II. Operative treatment and the results of pre and postoperative hemodynamic evaluations. *Circulation* 1964;30(suppl):120–151.
21. Morrow AG, Fogarty TJ, Hannah H III, Braunwald E. Operative treatment in idiopathic hypertrophic subaortic stenosis. Techniques and the results of preoperative and postoperative clinical and hemodynamic assessments. *Circulation* 1968;37:589–596.
22. Kirklin JW, Ellis FH Jr. Surgical relief of diffuse subvalvular aortic stenosis. *Circulation* 1961;24:739–742.
23. Shah PM, Gramiak R, Kramer DH. Ultrasound localization of left ventricular outflow obstruction in hypertrophic obstructive cardiomyopathy. *Circulation* 1969;40:3–11.
24. Maron BJ, Gardin JM, Flack JM, Gidding SS, Bild D. Assessment of the prevalence of hypertrophic cardiomyopathy in a general population of young adults: Echocardiographic analysis of 4111 subjects in the CARDIA study. *Circulation* 1995;92:785–789.
25. Braunwald E, Morrow AG, Cornell WP, Aygen MM, Hilbish TF. Idiopathic hypertrophic subaortic stenosis. *Am J Med* 1960;29:924–945.
26. Braunwald E, Aygen MM. Idiopathic myocardial hypertrophy without congestive heart failure or obstruction to blood flow. Clinical, hemodynamic and angiocardiographic studies in 14 patients. *Am J Med* 1963;35:7–19.
27. Braunwald E, Brockenbrough EC, Morrow AG. Hypertrophic subaortic stenosis—a broadened concept. *Circulation* 1962;26:161–165.
28. Goodwin JF, Hollman A, Cleland WP, Teare D. Obstructive cardiomyopathy simulating aortic stenosis. *Br Heart J* 1960;22:403–414.
29. Braunwald E, Brockenbrough EC, Frye RL. Studies on digitalis. V. Comparison of the effects of ouabain on left ventricular dynamics in valvular aortic stenosis and hypertrophic subaortic stenosis. *Circulation* 1962;26:166–173.
30. Braunwald E, Ebert PA. Hemodynamic alterations in idiopathic subaortic stenosis induced by sympathomimetic drugs. *Am J Cardiol* 1962;10:489–495.
31. Brockenbrough EC, Braunwald E, Morrow AG. A hemodynamic technique for the detection of hypertrophic subaortic stenosis. *Circulation* 1961;23:189–194.
32. Frank S, Braunwald E. Idiopathic hypertrophic subaortic stenosis. Clinical analysis of 126 patients with emphasis on the natural history. *Circulation* 1968;37:759–788.
33. Braunwald E, Oldham HN Jr, Ross J Jr, Linhart JW, Mason DT, Fort L III. The circulatory response of patients with idiopathic hypertrophic subaortic stenosis to nitroglycerin and to the Valsalva maneuver. *Circulation* 1964;29:422–431.
34. Mason DT, Cohn LH, Ross J Jr, Braunwald E. Idiopathic hypertrophic subaortic stenosis. Effects of changes in heart rate on the severity of obstruction to left ventricular outflow. *Am J Cardiol* 1967;19:797–805.
35. Mason DT, Braunwald E, Ross J Jr. Effects of changes in body position on the severity of obstruction to left ventricular outflow in idiopathic hypertrophic subaortic stenosis. *Circulation* 1966;33:374–382.
36. Stewart S, Mason DT, Braunwald E. Impaired rate of left ventricular filling in idiopathic hypertrophic subaortic stenosis and valvular aortic stenosis. *Circulation* 1968;37:8–14.
37. Harrison DC, Braunwald E, Glick G, Mason DT, Chidsey CA, Ross J Jr. Effects of beta-adrenergic blockade on the circulation with particular reference to observations in patients with hypertrophic subaortic stenosis. *Circulation* 1964;29:84–98.
38. Cohen LS, Braunwald E. Amelioration of angina pectoris in idiopathic hypertrophic subaortic stenosis with beta-adrenergic blockade. *Circulation* 1967;35:847–851.
39. Cohen LS, Braunwald E. Chronic beta adrenergic receptor blockade in the treatment of idiopathic hypertrophic subaortic stenosis. *Prog Cardiovasc Dis* 1968;11:211–221.
40. Criley JM, Lewis KB, White RI Jr, Ross RS. Pressure gradients without obstruction. A new concept of "hypertrophic subaortic stenosis." *Circulation* 1965;32:881–888.
41. Criley JM, Siegel RJ. Has "obstruction" hindered our understanding of hypertrophic cardiomyopathy? *Circulation* 1985;72:1148–1154.
42. Ross J Jr, Braunwald E, Gault JH, Mason DT, Morrow AG. The mechanism of the intraventricular pressure gradient in idiopathic hypertrophic subaortic stenosis. *Circulation* 1966;34:558–578.

43. Maron BJ, Maron MS, Wigle ED, Braunwald E. The 50-year history, controversy, and clinical implications of left ventricular outflow tract obstruction in hypertrophic cardiomyopathy: from idiopathic hypertrophic subaortic stenosis to hypertrophic cardiomyopathy. *J Am Coll Cardiol* 2009;54:191–200.

44. Ommen SR, Maron BJ, Olivotto I, Maron MS, Cecchi F, Betocchi S, Gersh BJ, AckermanMJ, McCully RB, Dearani JA, Schaff HV, Danielson GK, Tajik AJ, Nishimura RA. Long-term effects of surgical septal myectomy on survival in patients with obstructive hypertrophic cardiomyopathy. *J Am Coll Cardiol* 2005;46:470–476.

45. Harris KM, Spirito P, Maron MS, Zenovich AG, Formisano F, Lesser JR, Mackey-Bojack S, Manning WJ, Udelson JE, Maron BJ. Prevalence, clinical profile and significance of left ventricular remodeling in the end-stage phase of hypertrophic cardiomyopathy. *Circulation* 2006;114:216–225.

46. Maron BJ, Spirito P, Shen W-K, Haas TS, Formisano F, Link MS, Epstein AE, Almquist AK, Daubert JP, Lawrenz T, Boriani G, Estes NAM III, Favale S, Piccininno M, Winters SL, Santini M, Betocchi S, Arribas F, Sherrid MV, Buja G, Semsarian C, Bruzzi P. Implantable cardioverter-defibrillators and prevention of sudden cardiac death in hypertrophic cardiomyopathy. *JAMA* 2007;298:405–412.

47. Maron BJ, Casey SA, Poliac LC, Gohman TE, Almquist AK, Aeppli DM. Clinical course of hypertrophic cardiomyopathy in a regional United States cohort. *JAMA* 1999;281:650–655.

48. Maron MS, Maron BJ, Harrigan C, Buros J, Gibson CM, Olivotto I, Biller L, Lesser JR, Udelson JE, Manning WJ. Appelbaum E. Hypertrophic cardiomyopathy phenotype revisited after 50 years with cardiovascular magnetic resonance. *J Am Coll Cardiol* 2009;54:220–228.

49. Spirito P, Bellone P, Harris KM, Bernabo P, Bruzzi P, Maron BJ. Magnitude of left ventricular hypertrophy predicts the risk of sudden death in hypertrophic cardiomyopathy. *N Engl J Med* 2000;342:1778–1785.

50. Mirowski M, Reid PR, Mower MM, Watkins L, Gott VL, Schauble JF, Langer A, Heilman MS, Kolenik SA, Fischell RE, Weisfeldt ML. Termination of malignant ventricular arrhythmias with an implanted automatic defibrillator in human beings. *N Engl J Med* 1980;303:322–324.

HOLLIS BRYAN BREWER, JR., MD: A Conversation With the Editor*

Bryan Brewer, who was born in Casper, Wyoming, on 17 August 1938, is presently the Director, Lipoprotein and Atherosclerosis Research, Cardiovascular Research Institute, MedStar Research Institute, Washington Hospital Center in Washington, DC. After attending public schools in Casper, Dr. Brewer graduated from The Johns Hopkins University in Baltimore with a BA degree in biological chemistry in 1960 and from the Stanford University School of Medicine in Stanford, California, in 1965. His internship and residency in internal medicine were at the Massachusetts General Hospital in Boston. After 2 years of training, he went to the National Institutes of Health as a clinical associate in what was then the National Heart Institute (later, National Heart, Lung, and Blood Institute) at the National Institutes of Health in Bethesda, Maryland. By 1970, he was head of the section on peptide chemistry of the Molecular Disease Branch in the National Heart Institute, and in 1976 he was appointed Chief of the Molecular Disease Branch. He remained in that position until 2005, when he assumed his present position. During his nearly 36 years at the NIH, Dr. Brewer ran an extremely productive laboratory. His investigations led to publication of 470 articles in peer-review medical journals. His research work has included the elucidation of cholesterol and lipoprotein metabolism in normal subjects and in patients with genetic dyslipoproteinemias; the use of transgenic and knock-out animal models to determine the role of specific genes modulating lipoprotein metabolism and atherosclerosis; and diagnosis and treatment of patients with disorders of cholesterol and triglycerides with the ultimate goal of developing gene specific diagnoses as well as treatment of patients at risk for the development of cardiovascular disease. For his work, he has received several honors, and he has been a featured speaker at numerous medical meetings. Bryan Brewer is also a good guy and fun to be around (Figure 1).

William Clifford Roberts, MD (hereafter, Roberts[†]): *Dr. Brewer, I appreciate your talking to me so that the readers of* The American Journal of Cardiology *will get to know you better. We are in my home in Dallas on 23 January 2006. Dr. Brewer is in town for a roundtable discussion on high-density lipoprotein (HDL) cholesterol tomorrow at Baylor University Medical Center. Let's start by your talking about your early life, early memories, your family, and siblings.*

Hollis Bryan Brewer, Jr., MD[‡] (hereafter, Brewer): I was born and grew up in Casper, Wyoming (Figure 2), a town of approximately 50,000 people. Both my father and mother were pharmacists. They together had a family drug store just across the street from the only hospital in the city. My mother, who had graduated from college in Illinois, came with my father to Casper. She was the first woman pharmacist in the state of Wyoming. I had a very straightforward growing up in terms of the childhood problems, but no major difficulties. I have 2 sisters, one (Virginia Vaughn) who is 7 years older than I am, and one (Karen Kay) who is 2 years younger than I am. My older sister graduated from the University of Wyoming in Laramie and my younger sister, from Duke University. The latter then got a PhD in psychology from University of Wyoming. In Casper, there was only 1 high school. Family life was organized around activities of my parents. They were active both physically and socially in the community. They were very much involved with several organizations in the city for years: the Lion's and the Shriner's Clubs, Elks, and several women's organizations. Over the years, my mother was president of all the major clubs and felt very strongly about participating in community organizations. She did a lot of work for the regional burn center. Both my mother and father worked fairly long hours each day in their small drug store. We also had a small ranch just on the outskirts of town and we spent a lot of weekends there. We had both horses and cattle.

Roberts: *Your basic house was in the city, and it was close to the pharmacy?*

Brewer: Yes. It was on the same block.

Roberts: *How far was the ranch from your house?*

Brewer: Five miles.

Roberts: *How many acres did you have?*

Brewer: 240.

Roberts: *How many horses did you have?*

Brewer: Over the years we had several different numbers of horses, usually about 6 or 7. We did a lot of riding. I also raced horses when I was younger.

Roberts: *How many cattle did you have?*

Brewer: Anywhere from 50 to 250 cattle depending upon the time of year and when they were sold.

Roberts: *Your father was busy running the pharmacy and the ranch. Was someone else on the ranch full time?*

Brewer: There was a limited amount of activity on the ranch. We had help when we needed to haul hay or do something with the cattle.

* This series of interviews was underwritten by an unrestricted grand from Bristol-Myers Squibb.

† Director, Baylor Cardiovascular Institute, Baylor University Medical Center, Dallas, Texas, 75246.

‡ Director, Lipoprotein and Atherosclerosis Research, Cardiovascular Research Institute, MedStar Research Institute, Washington Hospital Center Washington, DC, 20010.

Figure 1. Recent photograph of Hollis Bryan Brewer, Jr., MD.

Figure 2. Dr. Brewer as a young man in Wyoming with his favorite horse.

Roberts: *Is hay the only thing you grew?*
Brewer: Yes.
Roberts: *What was your mother's name?*
Brewer: Virginia Rose.
Roberts: *When was she born?*
Brewer: She was born in 1904 and died in 2005 at 101 years of age! She was a unique person in terms of her energy level. She gave up driving at the age of 92 and was still volunteering at the hospital in the coronary care unit at the age of 95!
Roberts: *Was she always at the ideal body weight?*
Brewer: Yes. She also always had normal lipoprotein levels.
Roberts: *Where was she born?*
Brewer: Matone, Illinois.
Roberts: *How was your relationship with your mother?*
Brewer: I had a very warm relationship with both of my parents. Our family was a very close one. We did a lot of activities on the weekends, such as riding horses. Casper was an ideal place to raise a family.
Roberts: *Were your mother and father able to get home for dinner at night?*
Brewer: Yes. The store and the house were right next to each other, so they could go back and forth. They also had part-time employees who helped run the pharmacy. I had a

great deal of interaction with my parents as a result of having the store so close to the house.
Roberts: *Someone was home when you got home from school?*
Brewer: Yes. I went back and forth between the store and the house several times a day.
Roberts: *You worked at the store, too?*
Brewer: Yes. All my life.
Roberts: *What was your father's name?*
Brewer: Hollis Bryan, Sr. He was born in 1902 in Tyler, Texas, and died in 1979 at age 77.
Roberts: *Your mother was by herself for a good while?*
Brewer: My older sister also lived in Casper near her.
Roberts: *What was your father like?*
Brewer: My father was a very caring individual who had a great interest in education. He had a difficult time during the depression and, as a consequence, was very much focused on his kids' getting a good education and having an opportunity for success. He wanted to provide for his kids so that they could do whatever they wanted to do. He was very supportive of our activities. He was a very compassionate person. He was very involved with civic activities and tried to help those in the community who were less fortunate.
Roberts: *Why did your father go from Tyler, Texas, to Casper, Wyoming?*
Brewer: He was living in Denver. That was where he met my mother. He heard that there was a job opening at that time in Casper for a pharmacist at the drug store in the center of the city. He applied and got the job.
Roberts: *How far is Casper from Denver?*
Brewer: About 280 miles.
Roberts: *Was dinner at night a big deal in your house growing up?*
Brewer: We usually had dinner together. Occasionally, 1 parent was at the store and then, of course, dinner was with only 1. My sisters and I saw our parents a great deal because of the proximity between the house and the drug store.
Roberts: *Do you remember any conversations around*

the dinner table? Do you remember some topics of conversation?

Brewer: School activities, what we children were doing, what our plans for the next weekend were, and what was going on in the city were mostly the conversations. It was usually casual conversations, not much detailed political discussion.

Roberts: *What was your home like physically?*

Brewer: It was a small house. We 3 children each had a room. We had a large yard where my father spent a lot of time planting flowers and developing a garden. That activity was very limited, however, because of the short growing season in Casper.

Roberts: *Did your mother do that, too?*

Brewer: No. She said she killed every plant, so she never did participate in growing the flowers.

Roberts: *It sounds like your mother and dad got along pretty well.*

Brewer: I never heard them argue.

Roberts: *Was there alcohol in the house?*

Brewer: There was alcohol, but it was never a major thing.

Roberts: *Did either parent smoke?*

Brewer: My father smoked cigars. He died of pancreatic cancer. Smoking may have been a risk factor for his development of pancreatic cancer.

Roberts: *The interval between you and your older sister was 7 years, so she was like a second mother in a way?*

Brewer: Yes.

Roberts: *Did your parents push the 3 of you in school or did they expect you to do well and you knew that was your duty, so to speak?*

Brewer: We were always told to do the best we could do. We were expected to work hard, but there was not a great deal of pressure. All of us fortunately got good grades.

Roberts: *When you brought a report card home and it had all A's on it, what would your parents say to you?*

Brewer: They would say that was good. We didn't have a big discussion about grades. High school was a particularly active time with regard to several activities. My younger sister and *Lynn and Dick Cheney* were in the same high school class together. The Cheney's were good friends with my sister and brother-in-law, all of whom graduated from Natrona County High School. My sister's husband later worked with Dick Cheney in the Defense Department on NATO activities.

Roberts: *Was that a public high school?*

Brewer: Yes.

Roberts: *How many people were in that high school?*

Brewer: At that time I was there, it was grades 9 through 12 with about 400 students.

Roberts: *How many were in your senior class?*

Brewer: Probably about 100.

Roberts: *I gather that you graduated first of your class in high school?*

Brewer: I have no idea. They never told us.

Roberts: *Had anyone ever gone from your high school to the Johns Hopkins University before?*

Brewer: Not that I'm aware of.

Roberts: *What were your non-academic activities in high school?*

Brewer: I was very interested in sports, particularly basketball. I wiped out my ankle as a sophomore playing basketball. I also raced horses, and I raced and worked on cars.

Roberts: *Where did you race them?*

Brewer: At local places, such as an old airport.

Roberts: *Were junior high and high school close together?*

Brewer: Yes. Everything in Casper is close together.

Roberts: *How far away were they from you home?*

Brewer: About half a mile.

Roberts: *Did you walk to school?*

Brewer: No. There was a bus.

Roberts: *How cold was it in the winter time?*

Brewer: It was $-10°$ F or $-15°$ F, but the humidity there is very low. Although the temperature was much lower, the winters in Baltimore (when I was at Hopkins) were much colder to me than in Casper because of the high humidity in Baltimore.

Roberts: *You played basketball in high school?*

Brewer: Yes. I still have problems with the ankle I hurt then in basketball.

Roberts: *Were you a football player?*

Brewer: I played football up to high school and then focused on basketball.

Roberts: *What else did you do in high school?*

Brewer: I was involved in a lot of social and academic organizations. There was one in economics and math. We had after school activities related to social academics. I also played the clarinet in the school band.

Roberts: *Do you still play it?*

Brewer: No. I gave that up a long time ago.

Roberts: *Although your older sister went to the University of Wyoming, you went to college at the Johns Hopkins University. How did that come about?*

Brewer: As a little kid I was always going to be a doctor. I dissected rabbits, trying to figure out where the various body organs were located. Hopkins had a prestigious name in medicine, and so I selected it.

Roberts: *Did you apply to several colleges?*

Brewer: Yes, but I was particularly interested in going to Johns Hopkins because of its reputation. I talked with physicians in the community as well.

Roberts: *Did you work with any physicians in the community? Did you get to know them well?*

Brewer: I got to know several physicians very well. There was a doctor's office right behind our house, because we were on the hospital complex. My parents were one of only a few pharmacists in town, so we got to know physicians. I grew up in a medical environment, which stimulated my interest in medicine.

Roberts: *Were there any physicians in your extended family?*

Brewer: No.

Roberts: *Did your mother or father have any family in Casper?*

Brewer: No.

Roberts: *What did your school think when you said you wanted to apply to Johns Hopkins University?*

Brewer: Several students at Natrona County High School had gone to places like that. My younger sister's husband went to Harvard. Dick Cheney went to Yale. They placed their students in some major universities.

Roberts: *What did your older sister study at the University of Wyoming?*

Brewer: Business.

Roberts: *What did she do?*

Brewer: She married a man in the oil industry. They moved a lot. He eventually became a vice president of Shell Oil Company. She did not pursue a career.

Roberts: *Did she have children?*

Brewer: Yes. Two boys and 1 girl.

Roberts: *How did Baltimore and Johns Hopkins strike you after coming from a town of 50,000 people? All of a sudden you are on the East coast of the USA, and Baltimore is 1 of its more prominent cities. How did that hit?*

Brewer: It was a challenge, because Hopkins at that time was still a relatively small school. It was a challenge academically and environmentally. Additionally, it was a very competitive environment, since most students were interested in medicine. I thought I received an excellent education. I had a very science-oriented education. It was not a liberal education at that time. Hopkins was very focused on the biological sciences. I began my research in the McCullum Platt Institute there with *William McElroy*. Some of my first studies focused on what makes the firefly tail light up. We used to gather fire flies and extract their luciferase. That is what makes fire flies tails light up.

Roberts: *And you enjoyed it?*

Brewer: Yes. I was very challenged by it. It was a time when I was trying to figure out what I wanted to do, and that work clearly interested me in research.

Roberts: *Was that right after your first year?*

Brewer: No. That was during my junior year.

Roberts: *Did you stay during the summer to do research or did you do that during the academic term?*

Brewer: During the school year.

Roberts: *That was your first research?*

Brewer: Yes.

Roberts: *When you were in high school did you have to study hard or did the studies seem to come easy for you?*

Brewer: It came easy for me in high school. I didn't study a lot and I still got relatively good grades.

Roberts: *And what about when you were at Hopkins?*

Brewer: I had to study a lot more to maintain a good average because the competition and course matter were significantly more challenging than that in high school.

Roberts: *Initially, did you live in a dorm at Hopkins?*

Brewer: No. They had limited dorms at that time at Hopkins. I lived in a classic Baltimore row house.

Roberts: *How many undergraduate students were at Hopkins in a class in 1960?*

Brewer: Only about 300, I believe.

Roberts: *What did you do during the summer time while you were going to college?*

Brewer: I went back to Casper and worked in the drugstore.

Roberts: *Did you race horses then, too?*

Brewer: By that time I was too big to race horses.

Roberts: *But you were good with cars and knew how to fix them and modify them.*

Brewer: Yes. I was very interested in cars particularly in high school. I souped up and customized a number of different cars. I would change engines and other things like that.

Roberts: *You must have been pleased with yourself coming from a small town to Hopkins and low and behold you found that you could compete with anybody academically. That must have been a confidence boost, not that you needed much confidence.*

Brewer: I guess it was. I didn't ever regard it as such. I just felt that I needed to do what I needed to do to get where I wanted to go.

Roberts: *You were focused on getting into medical school the day you walked into Hopkins undergraduate.*

Brewer: When I was still in high school, I was focused on becoming a doctor.

Roberts: *Did you have any activities in college outside you studies other than the research?*

Brewer: No. There wasn't a lot of extracurricular activities at that time at Hopkins. I was very focused on the academics and research.

Roberts: *How did you like Baltimore?*

Brewer: I thought it was an interesting city. It was near the lowest time in Baltimore. They began to build up the dock area at the time. It was pleasant to see the change in the city.

Roberts: *How did you get from Casper to Johns Hopkins in 1956 initially?*

Brewer: I drove.

Roberts: *You had a car as a freshman? Did you have a car all the way through college? One that you had souped up yourself?*

Brewer: Yes. That's true.

Roberts: *You made Phi Beta Kappa in college. It was not co-ed at that time?*

Brewer: Yes, and it was co-ed. In certain departments there were more women students. But it was predominately male.

Roberts: *Who did you date?*

Brewer: I was married.

Roberts: *When did you get married?*

Brewer: At age 19.

Roberts: *What did your parents think when you told them you were going to get married at 19?*

Brewer: They thought that it was too young.

Roberts: *You married after 1 year at college?*

Brewer: Yes.

Roberts: *You married a high school sweetheart?*

Brewer: There were several high school sweethearts! I married someone I met in high school, let's put it that way.

Roberts: *When did you have the first baby?*

Brewer: Not until I was in medical school.

Roberts: *Did you apply to several medical schools?*

Brewer: Yes. I was particularly interested in Stanford, because it had a 5-year program, which included a year in research. I was very interested in doing research so that's why I focused on Stanford. *Kornberg* and *Letterberg* had come to Stanford, and I was interested in their research programs.

Roberts: *How did you learn of Stanford's program? Did you have advisors at Hopkins? You had always been interested in research? You liked learning new things?*

Brewer: Yes. I like learning new things and also finding out the physiology of things. I was interested in that facet of medicine, and so I decided that Stanford would give me the opportunity to see whether I wanted to go into research or practice medicine. I was intrigued by Stanford's program. I also thought the weather would be just the opposite of Baltimore.

Roberts: *So you and your wife got into this hot rod automobile, and you drive across the country to Palo Alto.*

Brewer: Yes.

Roberts: *What did your wife do those years?*

Brewer: She worked as a secretary.

Roberts: *How did Stanford strike you?*

Brewer: The city, of course, was very different from Baltimore, but it was the same intellectual environment. I thoroughly enjoyed the curriculum and the way it was set up there. It was an excellent program. I enjoyed both the pre-clinical and clinical activities there as well as the opportunity to do research.

Roberts: *What appealed to you so much?*

Brewer: The faculty and the level of science being carried out there.

Roberts: *So you entered Stanford in 1960 and graduated in 1965. Did you do that research during the entire 5 years or did you have a year off?*

Brewer: Research was interdigitated through the year.

Roberts: *How many students were in your class at Stanford?*

Brewer: About 125.

Roberts: *Did any of them other than you become famous?*

Brewer: Yes. *Irv Weissman* at Stanford is an international authority on stem cell research. *Bruce Tune* stayed on there as faculty. I'm sure there are a number of other people that I don't know.

Roberts: *Did any teachers in junior high, high school, college or medical school have a particular impact on you?*

Brewer: In high school, *Ms. Ferris*, an excellent teacher, encouraged me to go to the best college for medicine. She encouraged me to go to both the East and West coasts. In college, *McElroy* influenced me. He was the head of that institute at the time and encouraged me to have a career in research. Interacting with such an extremely well-known scientist was very instructive. I discussed careers in science with him. At that time, I had to make a decision on whether to go to medical school or get a PhD. I considered getting a PhD at Hopkins, and he encouraged me to go into medicine.

Roberts: *He had a PhD himself?*

Brewer: Yes.

Roberts: *As you rotated through the various subspecialties of medicine was it clear to you which area you wanted to go into?*

Brewer: I was fairly intrigued by the research side of the various subspecialties. *Tom Stamey* at Stanford was doing a lot of studies on kidney function and renovascular hypertension. He was a leader in technologies looking at renal function studies. I was interested in that research, but I decided that I didn't want to become a surgeon so I focused more on medicine.

Roberts: *But you knew that you were pretty good with your hands because you replaced engines in automobiles and raced horses. Physically, you were pretty active.*

Brewer: Yes, that's true.

Roberts: *How did it come about that you went to the Massachusetts General Hospital (MGH) for your postgraduate training?*

Brewer: It was because it was such a superb training program. During my time at Stanford, I took about 4 or 5 months off to get more exposure to clinical medicine, since the hospital at Stanford was very specialized and small. I went back to The Johns Hopkins Hospital and was an extern on the medical service. I considered going to Hopkins for my internship and residency. I met *Virgil Brown* there and liked working with him. Because of the reputation of the Harvard system and the MGH, I decided to apply there.

Roberts: *For the internship, you applied to Hopkins, the MGH, and Stanford?*

Brewer: Yes.

Roberts: *But Stanford was probably number 3 on your list because of the small number of patients.*

Brewer: Yes. It is a superb hospital for very detailed analysis of rare diseases, but what I wanted to do was get extensive training in all diseases and Stanford did not supply that.

Roberts: *So you reved up this hot rod with your wife and baby from Palo Alto and headed off to Boston. How did the MGH hit you?*

Brewer: I thoroughly enjoyed the MGH. I thought it was an absolutely spectacular hospital, and the training was superb. The years I was there were a fantastic time. *Joe*

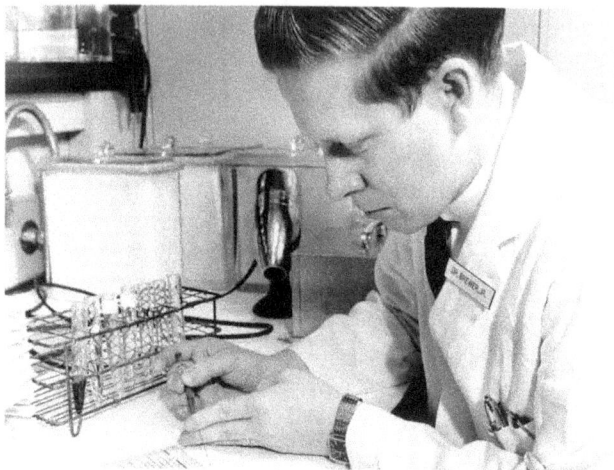

Figure 3. Dr. Brewer during 1980s at NIH doing research in plasma lipoproteins.

Figure 4. Dr. Brewer appointed chief of the Molecular Disease Branch.

Goldstein, David Bilheimer, Fred Murad, Tom Smith, and *Jim Willerson* were all there then.

Roberts: *Why was it such a great training place? Was it because of the colleagues that you were training with or was it because it was loaded with patients and you saw a huge variety of diseases or was it the super quality of the faculty or all 3?*

Brewer: It was all 3. The staff at the MGH was spectacular and the patient population included a spectrum of both rare and common diseases. The fellows and residents were also exceptional individuals, so it was a very exciting and intellectually challenging time.

Roberts: *Where did you live?*

Brewer: Beacon Hill.

Roberts: *How did it work out that you came to NIH?*

Brewer: The draft. I was very interested in cardiology at that time, and I planned to go to NIH for a couple of years and then come back to the MGH.

Roberts: *You were a Clinical Associate in the National Heart Institute? (Later called the National Heart, Lung, and Blood Institute.)*

Brewer: Yes.

Roberts: *After your full clinical year as a clinical associate, you chose the Molecular Disease Branch for your research. Were you getting cholesterol and lipid oriented by that time?*

Brewer: Yes. At first I was very interested in peptide chemistry. At that point, I worked with *John Potts* in the National Heart Institute. *Don Fredrickson* asked me if I would be interested in characterizing the newly discovered apoproteins on the plasma lipoproteins since I had been doing peptide amino acid sequencing. I became very interested in the challenge of characterizing the plasma apoproteins because it was clear that they played an important role in determining the clinical phenotype of patients. It also became clear that there were not just 2 but several different proteins attached to the lipoproteins, and one of the keys would be to learn about the structure and function of the individual apoproteins. That's when I decided that I would be interested in that area. That was based on discussions with Don Fredrickson at the time (Figure 3).

Roberts: *You had your choice of which branch or laboratory in the National Heart Institute that you wanted to work in?*

Brewer: Yes. You could interview and then pick the area that you wanted to go into at the time.

Roberts: *How did NIH strike you? That was sort of the beginning of its hay day.*

Brewer: It was an ideal location for me because of the focus on patients. Don Fredrickson had collected a wonderful array of patients with various dyslipoproteinemias. I saw the clinical and research opportunities as unparallel in developing a career as both an experimentalist and as a clinician. What really attracted me to the lipoprotein field was the ability to do research at the basic level and have the findings directly applicable to the lipoprotein disorders that the patients had.

Roberts: *Were you always interested in chemistry?*

Brewer: Chemistry and pathophysiology.

Roberts: *What was your major in college?*

Brewer: Biological chemistry.

Roberts: *What does that mean?*

Brewer: Chemistry courses.

Roberts: *You were at MGH for how long?*

Brewer: For 2 years.

Roberts: *You started at NIH in 1967 and you left NIH in 2005?*

Brewer: Correct.

Roberts: *What was your branch called when you were first there?*

Brewer: It was called the Metabolism Branch. *Dan Steinberg* was the initial Chief and then Don Fredrickson, who changed its name to the Molecular Disease Branch.

Roberts: *You are now living in Bethesda? Your family is expanding?*

Brewer: Yes. My son was born in Bethesda.

Roberts: *You have 4 kids?*

Brewer: No. I have 2 offspring of my own, and my second wife, Silvia, has 2 offspring.

Roberts: *What do they do?*

Brewer: My biologic son is a partner in a law firm in Washington. He worked in my lab at NIH, and I think I cured him of wanting to be a physician.

Roberts: *What does your daughter do?*

Brewer: She is in business. She owns a printing company. She was trained as an accountant and lives in Colorado.

Roberts: *When did you decide that you would stay at NIH and make it your career?*

Brewer: Every year I decided that the next year I would leave! In 1976, *Jack Orloff* named me the Branch Chief, and at that point I decided that I wanted to stay there permanently (Figure 4).

Roberts: *I am sure you have had a number of offers through the years, and you didn't leave until 2005. You must have loved what you were doing.*

Brewer: Yes, that's true. It was the unique opportunity to do what I wanted to do. I did studies ranging from basic protein chemistry to clinical characterization and treatment of the patients. It was a unique opportunity to be able to have that spectrum of activities.

Roberts: *You were Branch Chief for essentially 30 years.*

Brewer: Yes.

Roberts: *In 1976 when you were made Branch Chief, you were 38 years old. How big of a lab did you create eventually?*

Brewer: About 30 people with different areas of expertise. As the technology developed over the years, I tried to apply the new technology to the characterization of patients with dyslipoproteinemias. As the lab developed, we initially focused on protein chemistry as we characterized the proteins and developed a number of the metabolic techniques for looking at the metabolism of the lipoproteins. Later, we looked at the molecular defects in patients as the molecular biology techniques became applicable to clinical disorders and then focused on gene function. The laboratory changed over the years as we incorporated people with new expertise

Figure 5. Dr. Brewer doing studies related to low HDL and Tangiers disease.

as techniques became available. My interest in high-density lipoprotein (HDL) cholesterol began in the 1980s.

Roberts: *You have published extensively. Of all the work you have done, what are you the most proud of?*

Brewer: There are 4 areas that the lab made contributions. One was the isolation and characterization of the apoproteins. We sequenced and determined the initial structures of several of the apoproteins, so that we really began to understand the protein part of the lipoproteins. Another major contribution was in the metabolism of the lipoproteins. We developed techniques to do kinetic studies with the apoproteins. We characterized lipoprotein metabolism in normal individuals and then in patients with various dyslipidemic defects. The third area that was fun in terms of science was the identification of the molecular defects of some of the patients with dyslipoproteinemia, such as genetic deficiencies of lipoprotein lipase and lecithin cholesterol actyltransferase (LCAT). Another area that I think was a very productive one was the utilization of transgenic and knockout animal models to study gene functions. We were able to create a number of genetic defects seen in patients in mice and correct the genetic defect using adenovirus gene transfer. Underlying a lot of these studies was my interest for years in HDLs–both in understanding how it worked and using it as a potential therapy for treatment of cardio-vascular disease.

HDL has been the major focus of my research (Figure 5). In the 1980s, there was a great deal of interest in the low-density lipoproteins (LDL) and the LDL receptors. Goldstein and Brown developed knowledge about the LDL receptor and how it was defective in patients with familial hypercholesterolemia. Most of the research was focused on lowering LDL as a potential therapeutic target. In the early 1980s, HDL was not of great interest to many investigators. I became very interested in it mainly because of the epidemiological studies that suggested that HDL was inversely correlated with cardiovascular disease based on the hypothesis that HDL took cholesterol out of the cell. I studied in detail the clinical disorders associated with HDL, such as LCAT deficiency and the clinical pathophysiology of their genetic defects. I became very interested in learning if raising HDL would be an effective therapeutic target. For a long time, most investigators thought that if we lowered LDL enough that we wouldn't have to worry about the role that HDL might have as a potential therapeutic target. Only in the last few years has HDL really begun to be a focus of the pharmaceutical industry as well as the biomedical research community. Much of the work we did over the years was focused in one way are another on the structure and function of HDL.

Roberts: *You left NIH in March 2005? You are now 66 years old, and at the Washington Hospital Center. You have 35 more years if your mother's longevity applies to you. What are your objectives and goals now after changing courses after 3 decades at NIH?*

Brewer: The goal that I have right now is to see if we can develop the technology to effectively raise HDL and determine if elevated HDL levels will have a significant protective effect on cardiovascular disease. One reason I left NIH was to have an opportunity to pursue the potential of HDL as an effective therapeutic target for the treatment of patients with cardiovascular disease. I want to see if infusions of HDL in the patient with the acute coronary syndrome will be an effective way to reduce their risk of recurring cardiovascular events. Thus, my current research activities now focus on developing technologies and clinical trials that will allow us to definitively answer the question of whether HDL therapy will be effective in helping to reduce the risk of cardiovascular disease.

Washington Hospital Center is an ideal location to pursue HDL therapy in acute coronary syndrome patients because it's the largest cardiac center in the world with 18,000 cardiac catheterizations each year. It provides the ideal center to test the question whether HDL therapy will be useful in these patients.

Roberts: *In your hay day at NIH—when your lab was the most productive—what were your work habits? What time would you get up in the morning, what time would you get to the NIH, what time would you leave, get home, what did you do in the evening, and what time did you go to bed?*

Brewer: I used to get up about 6:30 A.M and get to NIH at about 8 A.M. I would leave about 6 to 8 P.M. I would eat dinner, then work until about 1 or 2 A.M.

Roberts: *You didn't need much sleep?*

Brewer: No. I have been lucky in that regard.

Roberts: *How much sleep do you get?*

Brewer: I usually go to bed between 1 and 2 A.M. and get up at 5 to 6 A.M.

Roberts: *What about Saturdays and Sundays during that period?*

Brewer: I continued to work writing papers or traveling. When the kids were younger, I participated in activities with them. My son is an extremely talented basketball player. He was the starting point guard at his high school when he walked on as a freshman. I never missed virtually any one of his basketball games.

Roberts: *Do you have non-medical hobbies?*

Brewer: I am still interested in cars and electronics. I like building computers. I have a gun collection.

Roberts: *Did you hunt?*

Brewer: Yes. I hunted some on the ranch.

Roberts: *What did you hunt?*

Brewer: Deer, antelope, rabbits, and prairie dogs.

Roberts: *Did you fish?*

Brewer: I did some fishing but not as much as hunting, because there were not any good fishing areas where we lived.

Roberts: *How much do you take off each year? Do you take vacations?*

Brewer: I take working vacations.

Roberts: *So you go to a meeting and sometimes stay an extra day or 2.*

Brewer: Yes. The last few years Silvia and I have tried to go to different places for vacation, though I continue to bring my computer along and work.

Roberts: *How have you worked in travel throughout your career? You have given a lot of talks and participated in a number of meetings, etc. How do you fit that in to your life pattern? Have you enjoyed the travel?*

Brewer: I enjoy the travel and the scientific exchange that meetings provide. I enjoy the intercollegiate aspects of the meetings.

Roberts: *Did you have family vacations when you were growing up?*

Brewer: Yes. We went to places in Wyoming, Colorado, and Louisiana (New Orleans).

Roberts: *Had you been on the East coast before attending Hopkins?*

Brewer: Yes.

Roberts: *When you went to Hopkins and Stanford did you have scholarships?*

Brewer: I had a scholarship to medical school.

Roberts: *That came about because you were in the research program?*

Brewer: Partly. Because there is no medical school in Wyoming. The state had scholarships for its students for medical school.

Roberts: *What do you think is the biggest problem right now at NIH?*

Brewer: In my opinion, NIH's current greatest challenge is how to resolve its conflict of interest policy and prevent the isolation of its scientific staff as well as retain and attract new outstanding investigators. It remains to be seen if this can be accomplished.

Roberts: *What did your mother, who lived 101 years, think about your research and the cholesterol thesis of atherosclerosis?*

Brewer: She was not really convinced that high cholesterol was going to be a major risk factor for cardiovascular disease, and more importantly, whether lowering it would really change the risk of cardiovascular disease. She watched with great interest my career over the years. However, she asked me periodically when I was going to get a real job.

Roberts: *What is the story that each of us has a different percent of cholesterol in our intestinal tract that we absorb?*

Brewer: Yes. There is a different degree of intestinal absorption of cholesterol for each of us. There was a major breakthrough in our understanding of cholesterol absorption with the discovery of the Niemann-Pick C1-like1 (NPC 1L1) protein. That protein clearly influences the absorption of cholesterol, and the new drug, ezetimibe (Zetia, Merck/Schering-Plough, West Point, Pennsylvania), specifically blocks intestinal cholesterol from being absorbed. We now have a lot of additional new biochemical information to let us begin to really understand from a molecular level the difference in absorption that people have, because we now have a much greater appreciation for the molecular mechanism of how cholesterol is absorbed into the enterocyte. We also now understand that cholesterol is taken into the cell and then a significant fraction of it is removed out of the enterocyte back into the gastrointestinal tract. There was controversy for years whether there was a gate keeper that kept cholesterol out of the body in terms of absorption. It turned out that there is a significant amount of absorption into the enterocyte via the NPC1L1 protein and then a significant fraction is secreted back into the gastrointestinal tract by the ABCG5 and G8 transporters.

Roberts: *Does this explain why the 95-year-old who eats 3 eggs and 2 strips of bacon each day can live that long? Is that person absorbing 25% of the cholesterol in the intestinal tract versus the person who absorbs 85% and has the same serum levels but dies much earlier?*

Brewer: The discovery of the NPC1L1 protein that is involved in the uptake of the cholesterol into the enterocyte and the G5 and G8 transporters that secrete the cholesterol on back out will now help us to understand much better the 25% versus the 85% cholesterol absorber. We will now be able to look at the functionality of those 2 parts of the

Figure 6. Dr. Brewer and colleagues at NIH in honor of Don Fredrickson, MD.

pathway that we really didn't know about until the last few years.

Roberts: *Whether one is a high or a low intestinal absorber of cholesterol is genetically determined?*

Brewer: Yes.

Roberts: *Do you take a cholesterol-lowering drug?*

Brewer: No.

Roberts: *What are your numbers?*

Brewer: My HDL is in the 40s and my LDL is 110 mg/dl.

Roberts: *Why don't you take a statin?*

Brewer: I will probably start taking one soon and lower my LDL cholesterol down to about 70 mg/dl.

Roberts: *I remember a Fredrickson publication in 1972 in which he indicated his worry level for serum total cholesterol. It was 300 mg/dl for patients >50 years of age.*

Brewer: That was because there was limited data at that point for doing anything about it (Figure 6). The problem was that we really couldn't test the effectiveness of lowering cholesterol cardiovascular risk because there were no good cholesterol-lowering drugs until the statin drugs appeared. With the advent of the statin drugs, we have really been able to lower the LDL cholesterol and see the effects of that on cardiac events. Without that class of drugs we still would not have the data to make definitive scientific conclusions because we just couldn't lower the LDL cholesterol levels enough.

Roberts: *I was at NIH for 32 years and then moved to Baylor University Medical Center, which is a medical center very much like the Washington Hospital Center where you are now. I had to re-adjust to the new world, but I like it very much. How has your adjustment been these 8 months to this change after 35 years at NIH?*

Brewer: It is a significant change. A large hospital focused on clinical care and patients is an entirely different environment than that of a purely research institute like the NIH. I am enjoying the change. The other facet that is particularly important to me is having the opportunity at the

Washington Hospital Center and Medstar Research Institute to see if we can change the risk of cardiovascular disease with HDL raising therapy. We learned by the end of the 1990s that the reduction in atherosclerotic events by the statin drugs even when the LDL was lowered to <70 mg/dl, was about a maximum of 50%. As high as 50% of the patients were still going to have an atherosclerotic event. My interest at this particular point in my career is whether the CETP inhibitor such a torcetrapib will be able to decrease atherosclerotic events another 40% to 50%. In addition, the acute coronary syndrome patients might potentially be treated with infusions of HDL, and non-acute patients, with some sort of oral therapy such as a CETP inhibitor or something of that nature that can significantly raise the plasma HDL.

Roberts: *Do you think that the ideal would be to have the serum HDL higher than the LDL?*

Brewer: We don't know the answer to that. What we don't know is how low do we need to go for LDL, and we don't have any data to know what the ideal level of HDL should be. We don't know if you raise your HDL to 50, is that enough or will we have additional benefits by going to 80? We don't have any good clinical data to know how high we should raise HDL.

Roberts: *How successful do you believe the new Pfizer HDL raising drug torcetrapib, a CETP inhibitor, will be?*

Brewer: The CETP inhibitor torcetrapib prevents cholesterol transfer from HDL to LDL, which is the normal function of the cholesterol ester transfer protein. A program is now set to address the question of safety and efficacy of torcetrapib as a way to raise HDL. Raising HDL may have potential benefits for decreasing the risk of cardiovascular disease, but a big question is how best should we raise the HDL level. One way to raise the HDL is to inhibit the CETP transfer protein, which raises HDL and increases the size of the mature HDL particles. A program at Pfizer has now been initiated to address the question whether the addition of torcetrapib to statin therapy will decrease surrogate end points of cardiovascular disease. In 1 group of patients, the intima-media thickness (IMT) of carotid arteries will be measured at baseline and after 24 months therapy with a atorvastatin versus atorvastatin plus torectapid. Another study will use intravascular ultrasonic (IVUS) imaging to study regression of plaques in the coronary arteries before and after 24 months of therapy with atorvastatin versus atorvastatin plus torcetrapib. The cardiovascular field has limited data on whether changes in either IMT or IVUS are associated with decreased clinical events, and therefore, it will be the decision of the Federal Drug Administration whether there is sufficient data with torcetrapid to warrant approval of a new drug. In parallel to these 2 studies, Pfizer has developed a large-scale morbidity and mortality trial to evaluate the clinical end points (outcomes) using torcetrapid plus atorvastatin versus atorvastatin alone. That data won't be available for another 3 or 4 years.

Roberts: *The plan is for torcetapib to come out in combination with atorvastatin.*

Brewer: Yes, initially. Since this is a new class of drug, both safety and efficiency questions must be answered. The clinical program is developed to look at safety combined with atorvastatin 10 to 80 mg. It's a very large clinical trial and database to see if the addition of 60 mg of torcetapib is safe and efficacious. If this drug proves both safe and efficacious in Phase III studies, then Pfizer plans to consider at that point the development of a CETP inhibitor as monotherapy.

Roberts: *Dr. Brewer, thank you for talking to me and therefore to the readers of* The American Journal of Cardiology.

Brewer: It's been an honor and a pleasure.

Best Publications as selected by Hollis Bryan Brewer, Jr., MD

19. Brewer HB Jr., Shulman R, Herbert P, Ronan R, Wehrly K. The complete amino acid sequence of an apolipoprotein obtained from human very low density lipoprotein (VLDL). *Adv Exp Med Biol*1972; 25:280–281. (*Dr. Brewer's comment: First report of a sequence of a human plasma apolipoprotein, apo-C-III.*)

22. Brewer HB Jr., Lux SE, Ronan R, John KM. The complete amino acid sequence of a human plasma high density apolipoprotein, apoLp-gln-II (A-II). *Proc Natl Acad Sci USA* 1972;69:1304–1308. (*Dr. Brewer's comment: First amino acid sequence of a HDL apolipoprotein, apoA-II.*)

34. Assmann G, Brewer HB Jr. A molecular model of high density lipoproteins. *Proc Natl Acad Sci USA* 1974;71:1534–1538. (*Dr. Brewer's comment: Molecular model of HDL apolipoprotein-lipid interaction illustrating that the characteristic feature of the apolipoprotein was an amphipathic helix with 1 surface hydrophobic and 1 surface hydrophilic.*)

44. Osborne JC, Palumbo G, Brewer HB Jr., Edelhoch H. The self-association of the reduced apoA-II apoprotein from the human high density lipoprotein complex. *Biochem* 1975;14:3741–3746. (*Dr. Brewer's comment: Demonstration that human apolipoproteins self associate into discrete oligomeric complexes with marked increases in secondary and tertiary structure with association.*)

56. Osborne JC Jr., Brewer HB Jr. The plasma lipoproteins. In: Advances in Protein Chemistry. Vol. 31, Academic Press, New York, 1977. (*Dr. Brewer's comment: Detailed review that summarized the discovery that the human plasma apolipoproteins, in contrast to classical proteins, could change from a random coil to a globular protein when interacting with lipids or during self association.*)

60. Brewer HB Jr., Fairwell T, LaRue A, Ronan R, Houser A, Bronzert TJ. The amino acid sequence of human apoA-I, an apolipoprotein isolated from high density lipoproteins. *Biochem Biophys Res Commun* 1978;80:623–630. (*Dr. Brewer's comment: Amino acid sequence of the major HDL apolipoprotein, apoA-I which is the major ligand for cholesterol efflux from cells.*)

63. Schaefer EJ, Blum CR, Levy RI, Jenkins LL, Alaupovic P, Foster DM, Brewer HB Jr. Metabolism of high density lipoproteins in Tangier Disease. *N Engl J Med*1978;299:905–910. (*Dr. Brewer's comment: First demonstration that the low plasma HDL in Tangier disease was due to increased HDL catabolism and changed the prevailing concept that the low HDL was due to decreased HDL production.*)

76. Schaefer EJ, Zech LA, Schwartz DS, Brewer HB Jr. Coronary heart disease prevalence and other clinical features in familial high density lipoprotein deficiency (Tangier disease). *Ann Int Med* 1980;93:261–

266. (Dr. Brewer's comment: Initial report of a review of the cases of Tangier disease establishing that low HDL in Tangier disease was associated with an increased risk of cardiovascular disease.)

84. Schaefer EJ, Anderson DW, Zech LA, Lindgren FT, Bronzert TJ, Rubalcaba EA, Brewer HB Jr. The metabolism of high density lipoprotein subfractions and constituents in Tangier disease following the infusion of high density lipoproteins. J Lipid Res 1981;22: 217–228. (Dr. Brewer's comment: Metabolic study in a Tangier disease patient following an infusion of normal HDL to increase the plasma HDL to control levels. HDL catabolism was increased despite the normal plasma level of HDL, establishing that the increased catabolism of radiolabeled HDL observed in the kinetic studies in Tangier disease patients was not due to a decreased HDL pool size.)

87. Gregg RE, Zech LA, Schaefer EJ, Brewer HB Jr. Type III hyperlipoproteinemia: defective metabolism of an abnormal apolipoprotein E. Sci 1981;211:584–586. (Dr. Brewer's comment: Clinical study which established that the genetic defect in type III hyperlipoproteinemia [dysbetalipoproteineima] was due to a structural defect and loss of function of apolipoprotein E.)

90. Ghiselli G, Shaefer EJ, Gascon P, Brewer HB Jr. Type III hyperlipoproteinemia associated with apolipoprotein E deficiency. Science 1981;214:1239–1241. (Dr. Brewer's comment: Initial identification of a kindred with a mutation in apo-E resulting in apo-E deficiency and type III hyperlipoproteinemia.)

98. Schaefer EJ, Zech LA, Jenkins LL, Aamodt RA, Bronzert TJ, Rubalcaba EA, Lindgren FT, Brewer HB Jr. Human apolipoprotein A-I and A-II metabolism. J Lipid Res 1982;23:850–862. (Dr. Brewer's comment: Analysis of HDL metabolism in humans using radiolabeled apolipoproteins A-I and A-II. A new approach to lipoprotein kinetics using radiolabeled apolipoproteins reassociated with plasma lipoproteins.)

111. Zech LAS, Schaefer EJ, Bronzert TJ, Aamodt RL, Brewer HB Jr. Metabolism of human apolipoproteins A-I and A-II: compartmental models. J Lipid Res 1983;24:60–71. (Dr. Brewer's comment: Compartmental model of HDL metabolism in humans based on apolipoprotein kinetics in control subjects. Model served as a basis for analysis of HDL kinetic studies in patients with genetic defects in lipoprotein metabolism.)

112. Law SW, Gray G, Brewer HB Jr. cDNA cloning of human apoA-I: amino acid sequence of preproapoA-I. Biochem Biophys Res Commun 1983;112:257–264. (Dr. Brewer's comment: Nucleotide sequence of preproapoA-I. Identification that apo-A-I was synthesized as a preproapolipoprotein.)

113. Brewer HB Jr., Zech LA, Gregg RE, Schwartz D, Schaefer EJ. Type III hyperlipoproteinemia: diagnosis, molecular defects, pathology, and treatment. Ann Int Med 1983;98:623–640. (Dr. Brewer's comment: Review of the data on the clinical, biochemical, and genetic defect in patients with type III hyperlipoproteinemia.)

123. Gregg RE, Ghiselli G, Brewer HB Jr. Apolipoprotein E: a new variant of apolipoprotein E associated with type III hyperlipoproteinemia. J Clin Endocrinol Metab 1983;57:969–974. (Dr. Brewer's comment: Characterization of the apo-E2 isoform of apoE associated with type III hyperlipoproteinemia.)

126. Hospattankar A, Fairwell T, Ronan R, Brewer HB Jr. Amino acid sequence of human apolipoprotein C-II from normal and hyperlipoproteinemic subjects. J Biol Chem 1984;259:318–322. (Dr. Brewer's comment: Amino acid sequence of human apoC-II, the apolipoprotein which is the co-factor for lipoprotein lipase.)

138. Fojo SS, Law SW, Sprecher DL, Gregg RE, Baggio G, Brewer HB Jr. Analysis of the apoC-II gene in apoC-II deficient patients. Biochem Biophys Res Commun 1983;124:308–313. Dr. Brewer's comment: Initial report of a structural defect in apo-C-II resuling in hypertriglyceridemia and type I hyperlipoproteinemia [familial hyperchylomicronemia syndrome].

141. Fojo SS, Law SW, Brewer HB Jr. Human apolipoprotein C-II: complete nucleic acid sequence of preapolipoprotein C-II. Proc Natl Acad Sci USA 1984;81:6354–6357. (Dr. Brewer's comment: Complete genomic sequence of preapoC-II. Sequence used in the characterization of patients with apo-C-II deficiency and type I hyperlipoproteinemia [familial hyperchylomicronemia syndrome]).

145. Sprecher DL, Taam L, Brewer HB Jr. Two-dimensional electrophoresis of human plasma apolipoproteins. Clin Chem 1984;30:2084–2092. (Dr. Brewer's comment: Initial report utilizing 2-dimensional gel electrophoresis in the characterization of the human plasma apolipoproteins.)

147. Gregg RE, Zech LA, Schaefer EJ, Brewer HB Jr. Apolipoprotein E metabolism in normal lipoproteinemic human subjects. J Lipid Res 1984;25:1167–1176. (Dr. Brewer's comment: Detailed review of the metabolism of apo-E in humans.)

156. Lackner KJ, Law SW, Brewer HB Jr. The human apolipoprotein A-II gene: complete nucleic acid sequence and genomic organization. Nucleic Acids Res 1985;13:4597–4608. (Dr. Brewer's comment: Characterization of the gene of preproapoA-II, a major HDL apolipoprotein.)

158. Edge SB, Hoeg JM, Schneider PD, Brewer HB Jr. Apolipoprotein B synthesis in humans: liver synthesizes only apolipoprotein B-100. Metabolism 1985;34:726–730. (Dr. Brewer's comment: Analysis of the tissue distribution in humans of the synthesis of the apoB-100 and apoB-48 isoforms.)

159. Bojanovski D, Gregg RE, Ghiselli G, Schaefer EJ, Light JA, Brewer HB Jr. Human apolipoprotein A-I isoprotein metabolism: proapoA-I conversion to mature apoA-I. J Lipid Res 1985;26:185–193. (Dr. Brewer's comment: Kinetic study in man establishing that apo-A-I was synthesized and secreted as a proprotein and converted in plasma by a protease to mature apo-A-I.)

163. Law SW, Brewer HB Jr. Tangier disease: the complete mRNA sequence encoding the preproapoA-I. J Biol Chem 1985;260:12810–12814. (Dr. Brewer's comment: Analysis of the nucleotide sequence of apo-A-I, establishing that the molecular defect in Tangier disease was not due to a structural mutation in apo-A-I.)

192. Law SW, Grant SM, Higuchi K, Hospattankar A, Lackner K, Lee N, Brewer HB Jr. Human liver apolipoprotein B-100 cDNA: complete nucleic acid and derived amino acid sequence. Proc Natl Acad Sci USA 1986;83:8142–8146. (Dr. Brewer's comment: Elucidation of the amino acid sequence of human apoB-100, the major structural apolipoprotein of LDL.)

198. Schaefer EJ, Gregg RE, Ghiselli G, Forte TM, Ordovas JM, Zech LA, Brewer HB Jr. Familial apolipoprotein E deficiency. J Clin Invest 1986;78:1206–1219. (Dr. Brewer's comment: Clinical and metabolic characterization of the patient with apo-E deficiency.)

206. Fojo SS, Law SW, Brewer HB Jr. The human preproapolipoprotein C-II gene. Complete nucleic acid sequence and genomic organization. FEB 1987;213:221–226. (Dr. Brewer's comment: Complete genomic sequence of the C-II apolipoprotein.)

210. Fairwell T, Hospattankar AV, Brewer HB Jr., Khan SA. Human plasma apolipoprotein C-II: total solid-phase synthesis and chemical and biological characterization. Proc Natl Acad Sci USA 1987;84: 4796–4800. (Dr. Brewer's comment: Total synthesis and characterization of a human plasma apolipoprotein, apo-C-II.)

216. Hospattankar AV, Higuchi K, Law SW, Meglin N, Brewer HB Jr. Identification of a novel in-frame translational stop codon in human intestine apoB mRNA. Biochem Biophys Res Commun 1987;148: 279–285. (Dr. Brewer's comment: Identification of the stop codon in the apo-B mRNA identifying the novel molecular RNA editing mechanism responsible for the synthesis of 2 apolipoproteins, apoB-100 and apoB-48, from a single gene.)

242. Tennyson GE, Sabatos CA, Higuchi K, Meglin N, Brewer HB Jr. Expression of apolipoprotein B mRNAs encoding higher- and lower-molecular weight isoproteins in rat liver and intestine. Proc Natl Acad Sci USA 1989;86:500–504. (Dr. Brewer's comment: Study that established that RNA editing in the rat liver resulted in the synthesis of both apo-B-100 and apo-B-48, which was in contrast to the human liver which synthesized only apo-B-100. The rapid catabolism of

plasma apo-B in the rat was due to the increased synthesis of the rapidly catabolized apoB-48 isoform of apo-B.)

264. Beg OU, Meng MS, Skarlatos SI, Previato L, Brunzell JD, Brewer HB Jr., Fojo SS: Lipoprotein lipase$_{Bethesda}$: A single amino acid substitution (Ala^{176}→Thr) leads to abnormal heparin binding and loss of enzymic activity. *Proc Natl Acad Sci USA* 1990;87: 3474–3478. (*Dr. Brewer's comment: Intial report of a molecular defect in lipoprotein lipase resulting in hypertriglyceridemia and type I hyperlipoproteinemia [Familial Hyperchylomicronemia Syndrome]).*

265. Schaefer JR, Rader DJ, Gregg RE, Fairwell T, Zech LA, Kindt MR, Benson MD, Brewer HB Jr. In vivo protein metabolism utilizing stable isotopes and mass spectrometry: a new approach to the study of mutant proteins in humans. *Association of American Physicians* 1990;CIII:187–194. (*Dr. Brewer's comment: Description of the development of the stable isotope technique to study lipoprotein metabolism in humans.)*

270. Nichols WC, Gregg RE, Brewer HB Jr., Benson MD. A mutation in apolipoprotein A-I in the Iowa type of familial amyloidotic polyneuropathy. *Genomics* 1990;8:318–323. (*Dr. Brewer's comment: Discovery that a structural mutation in apo-A-I was the genetic defect in a kindred with family amyloidosis establishing that structural changes in the A-I apolipoprotein could result in the cellular accumulation of the abnormal protein leading to amyloidosis.)*

274. Santamarina-Fojo S, Brewer HB Jr. The familial hyperchylomicronemia syndrome: new insights into underlying genetic defects. *JAMA* 1991;265:904–908. (*Dr. Brewer's comment: Review of molecular defects in lipoprotein lipase resulting in hypertriglyceridemia and type I hyperlipidemia.)*

282. Rader DJ, Castro G, Zech LA, Fruchart JC, Brewer HB Jr. In vivo metabolism of apolipoprotein A-I on high density lipoprotein particles LpA-I and LpA-I, A-II. *J Lipid Res* 1991;32:1849–1859. (*Dr. Brewer's comment: Analysis of the metabolism of the 2 major lipoprotein particles in HDL, LpA-I and LpA-I,A-II in humans.)*

295. Emmerich J, Beg OU, Peterson J, Previato L, Brunzell JD, Brewer HB Jr., Santamarina-Fojo S. Human lipoprotein lipase. Analysis of the catalytic triad by site-directed mutagenesis of Ser-132, Asp-156, and His-241. *J Biol Chem* 1992;267:4161–4165. (*Dr. Brewer's comment: Identification of the amino acid residues in the catalytic site modulating lipoprotein lipase activity.)*

296. Klein H-G, Lohse P, Pritchard PH, Bojanovski D, Schmidt H, Brewer HB Jr. Two different allelic mutations in the lecithin-cholesterol acyltransferase gene associated with the fish eye syndrome. Lecithin-cholesterol acyltransferase (Thr^{123}→Ile) and lecithin-cholesterol acyltransferase (Thr^{347}→Met). *J Clin Invest* 1992;89:499–506. (*Dr. Brewer's comment: Identification of the molecular defects in the LCAT gene resulting in Fish eye disease.)*

299. Dugi KA, Dichek HL, Talley GD, Brewer HB Jr., Santamarina-Fojo S. Human lipoprotein lipase: the loop covering the catalytic site is essential for interaction with lipid substrates. *J Biol Chem* 1992;267: 25086–25091. (*Dr. Brewer's comment: Analysis provided evidence that lipoprotein lipase contains a loop of amino acids that covers the active site of the enzyme and is a primary site of interaction with lipids.)*

301. Rader DJ, Gregg RE, Meng MS, Schaefer JR, Zech LZ, Benson MD, Brewer HB Jr. In vivo metabolism of a mutant apolipoprotein, apoA-I$_{Iowa}$, associated with hypoalphalipoproteinemia and hereditary systemic amyloidosis. *J Lipid Res* 1992;33:755–763. (*Dr. Brewer's comment: Metabolic study that established that the mutant A-I apolipoprotein, apo-A-I$_{Iowa}$, which accumulates in this form of amyloidosis, was rapidly catabolized, resulting in low plasma HDL levels.)*

303. Mautner SL, Sanchez JA, Rader DJ, Mautner GC, Ferrans VJ, Fredickson DS, Brewer HB Jr., Roberts WC. The heart in Tangier Disease: severe coronary atherosclerosis with near absence of high-density lipoprotein cholesterol. *Am J Clin Pathol* 1992;98:191–198. (*Dr. Brewer's comment: Detailed analysis of the coronary atherosclerosis in a patient with Tangier disease.)*

316. Klein H-G, Santamarina-Fojo S, Duverger N, Clerc M, Dumon M-F, Albers JJ, Marcovina S, and Brewer HB Jr. Fish eye syndrome: a molecular defect in the lecithin-cholesterol acyltransferase (LCAT) gene associated with normal α-LCAT-specific activity. *J Clin Invest* 1993;92: 479–485. (*Dr. Brewer's comment: Clinical and biochemical analysis that established that the different clinical features of classical LCAT deficicany and Fish eye disease were due to differences in residual LCAT acitivity in the individual patient rather than a defect in 2 separate genes coding for the LCAT enzyme.)*

320. Roma P, Gregg RE, Meng MS, Ronan R, Zech LA, Franceschini G, Sirtori CR, Brewer HB Jr. In vivo metabolism of a mutant form of apolipoprotein A-I, apo A-I$_{Milano}$ associated with familial hypoalphalipoproteinemia. *J Clin Invest* 1993;91:1445–1452. (*Dr. Brewer's comment: Pivotal metabolic study in Italian patients providing evidence that the low plasma HDL levels in apo-A-I Milano were due to increased catabolism of the mutant A-I apolipoprotein.)*

329. Rader DJ, Schaefer JR, Lohse P, Ikewaki K, Thomas F, Harris WA, Zech LA, Dujovne CA, Brewer HB Jr. Increased production of apolipoprotein A-I associated with elevated plasma levels of high-density lipoproteins, apolipoprotein A-I, and lipoprotein A-I in a patient with familial hyperalphalipoproteinemia. *Metab* 1993;42: 1429–1434. (*Dr. Brewer's comment: First reported kindred with high plasma HDL levels due to increased synthesis of apo-A-I.)*

331. Ikewaki K, Rader DJ, Sakamoto T, Nishiwaki M, Wakimoto N, Schaefer JR, Ishikawa T, Fairwell T, Zech LA, Nakamura H, Nagano M, Brewer HB Jr. Delayed catabolism of high density lipoprotein apolipoprotein A-I and A-II in human cholesteryl ester transfer protein deficiency. *J Clin Invest* 1993;92:1650–1658. (*Dr. Brewer's comment: HDL kinetic study in Japanese patients with CETP deficiency, establishing that the increase plasma HDL levels were due to decreased HDL catabolism.)*

332. Rader DJ, Ikweaki K, Duverger N, Schmidt H, Pritchard H, Frohlich J, Clerc M, Dumon M-F, Fairwell T, Zech LA, Santamarina-Fogo, Brewer HB Jr. Markedly acclerated catabolism of apolipoprotein A-II (apoA-II) and high density lipoproteins containing apoA-II in classic lecithin: cholesterol acyltransferase deficiency and fish-eye disease. *J Clin Invest* 1994;93:321–330. (*Dr. Brewer's comment: HDL metabolic study that indicated that the low plasma HDL levels in LCAT deficiency and Fish eye disease were due to rapid catabolism of a poorly lipidated HDL.)*

348. Duverger N, Rader D, Ikewaki K, Nishiwaki M, Sakamoto T, Ishikawa T, Nagano M, Nakamura H, Brewer HB Jr. Characterization of high-density apolipoprotein particles A-I and A-I: A-II isolated from humans with cholesteryl ester transfer protein deficiency. *Eur J Biochem* 1995;227:123–129. (*Dr. Brewer's comment: Detailed characterization of the very large HDL particles that are present in patients with CETP deficiency.)*

355. Vaisman BL, Klein H-G, Rouis M, Berard A, Kindt MR, Talley GD, Meyn SM, Hoyt RF Jr., Marcovina SM, Albers JJ, Hoeg JM, Brewer HB Jr., Santamarina-Fojo S. Overexpression of human lecithin cholesterol acyltransferase leads to hyperalphalipoproteinemia in transgenic mice. *J Biol Chem* 1995;270:12269–12275. (*Dr. Brewer's comment: Overexpression of LCAT leads to marked increases in plasma HDL in mice that lack CETP, indicating that modulation of LCAT activity can significantly effect plasma HDL levels.)*

359. Kashyap VS, Santamarina-Fojo S, Brown DR, Parrott CL, Applebaum-Bowden D, Meyn S, Talley G, Paigen B, Maeda N, Brewer HB Jr. Apolipoprotein E deficiency in mice: gene replacement and prevention of atherosclerosis using adenovirus vectors. *J Clin Invest* 1995;96:1612–1620. (*Dr. Brewer's comment: First report of the correction of a genetic defect in lipoprotein metabolism using adenovirus delivery of the normal gene.)*

360. Ikewaki K, Nishiwaki M, Sakamoto T, Ishikawa T, Fairwell T, Zech LA, Nagano M, Nakamura H, Brewer HB Jr., Rader DJ. Increased catabolic rate of low density lipoproteins in humans with cholesteryl ester transfer protein deficiency. *J Clin Invest* 1995;96:1573–1581. (*Dr. Brewer's comment: Kinetic study in Japanese patients with*

CETP deficiency that revealed that the composition and metabolism of LDL was abnormal and the explanation for the low LDL levels in CETP deficiency was increased catabolism of abnormal LDL.)

364. Applebaum-Bowden D, Kobayashi J, Kashyap VS, Brown DR, Berard A, Meyn S, Parrott C, Maeda N, Shamburek R, Brewer HB Jr., Santamarina-Fojo S. Hepatic lipase gene therapy in hepatic lipase deficient mice: adenovirus-mediated replacement of a lipolytic enzyme to the vascular endothelium. J Clin Invest 1996;97:799–805. (Dr. Brewer's comment: First evidence that a deficiency of an endothelial bound plasma lipolytic enzyme, hepatic lipase, in a hepatic lipase deficient animal model could be replaced by the delivery of the normal gene using adenovirus vectors directed to the liver.)

365. Hoeg JM, Vaisman BL, Demosky SJ, Meyn SM, Talley GD, Hoyt RF, Feldman S, Berard AM, Sakai N, Wood D, Brousseau ME, Marcovina S, Brewer HB Jr., Santamarina-Fojo S. Lecithin-cholesterol acyltransferase overexpression generates hyperalphalipoproteinemia and nonatherogenic lipoprotein pattern in transgenic rabbits. J Biol Chem 1996;271:4396–4402. (Dr. Brewer's comment: First report of the development of transgenic rabbits for the analysis of genes that modulate lipoprotein metabolism.)

367. Brousseau ME, Santamarina-Fojo S, Zech LA, Berard AM, Vaisman BL, Meyn SM, Powell D, Brewer HB Jr., Hoeg JM. Hyperalphalipoproteinemia in human LCAT transgenic rabbits: in vivo apolipoprotein A-I catabolism is delayed in a gene dose-dependent manner. J Clin Invest 1996;97:1844–1851. (Dr. Brewer's comment: Metabolic study indicating that the marked increase in plasma HDL levels with overexpression of the LCAT gene was due to decreased catabolism of apo-A-I.)

371. Hoeg JM, Santamarina-Fojo S, Bérard AM, Cornhill JF, Herderick EE, Feldman SH, Haudenschild CC, Vaisman BL, Hoyt RF Jr., Demosky SJ Jr., Kauffman RD, Hazel CM, Marcovina SM, Brewer HB Jr. Overexpression of lecithin:cholesterol acyltransferase in transgenic rabbits prevents diet-induced atherosclerosis. Proc Natl Acad Sci USA 1996;3:11448–11453. (Dr. Brewer's comment: Pivotal study that established that overexpression of LCAT resulted in increased HDL levels and decreased atherosclerosis. These results indicated that modulation of LCAT activity is an attractive target for the development of new agents to treat atherosclerosis in man.)

376. Sakai N, Vaisman BL, Koch, Hoyt RF, Meyn SM, Talley GD, Paiz JA, Brewer HB Jr., Santamarina-Fojo S. Targeted disruption of the mouse lecithin: cholesterol acyltransferase (LCAT) Gene. J Biol Chem 1997;272:7506–7510. (Dr. Brewer's comment: Development of a LCAT knockout mouse model to study the effects of the LCAT gene on lipoprotein metabolism and atherosclerosis.)

381. Foger B, Santamarina-Fojo S, Shamburek RD, Parrot CL, Talley GD, Brewer HB Jr. Plasma phospholipid transfer protein: Adenovirus mediated overexpression in mice leads to decreased plasma HDL and enhanced uptake of phospholipids and cholesteryl esters from HDL. J Biol Chem 1997;43:27393–27400. (Dr. Brewer's comment: Results indicated that overexpression of phospholipid transfer protein decreased HDL levels, increased cellular uptake of lipids, and induced heterogeneity of the size of HDL ranging from smaller to larger HDL particles.)

384. Remaley AT, Shumaker UK, Stonik JA, Farsi BD, Nazih H, Brewer HB Jr. Decreased reverse cholesterol transport from Tangier disease fibroblasts. Acceptor specificity and effect of brefeldin on lipid efflux. Arterioscler Thromb Vasc Biol 1997;17:1813–1821. (Dr. Brewer's comment: In vitro cell culture study showing that cholesterol efflux from Tangier disease fibroblasts was decreased, which is consistent with the concept that the molecular defect in Tangier disease was a cellular defect in cholesterol efflux.)

394. Hammad SM, Stefansson S, Twal WO, Drake CJ, Fleming P, Remaley A, Brewer HB Jr., Argraves WS. Cubilin, the endocytic receptor for intrinsic factor-vitamin b_{12} complex, mediates high density lipoprotein holoparticle endocytosis. Proc Natl Acad Sci USA, 1999. (Dr. Brewer's comment: Studies suggest that the cubilin system

present in the kidney may play an important role in the metabolism of HDL.)

395. Rust S, Rosier M, Funke H, Real J, Amoura Z, Piette JC, Deleuze JF, Brewer HB Jr., Duverger N, Denefle P, Assmann G. Tangier disease is caused by mutations in the gene encoding ATP-binding cassette transporter 1. Nat Genet 1999;22:352–355. (Dr. Brewer's comment: Analysis revealed the genetic defect in Tangier disease was a defect in the ABCA1 transporter that regulates cellular cholesterol efflux.)

396. Remaley AT, Rosier M, Knapper C, Peterson KM, Koch C, Duverger N, Assmann G, Dinger M, Dean M, Santamarina-Fojo S, Fredrickson DS, Denefle P, Brewer HB Jr. Human ATP-binding cassette transporter 1 (ABC1): genomic organization and identification of the genetic defect in the original Tangier disease kindred. Proc Natl Acad Sci USA 1999;97:12685–12690. (Dr. Brewer's comment: Identification of the molecular defect in the first kindred with Tangier diease that presented to the NIH with low HDL levels in the 1960s. In addition, the complete genomic sequence of the ABCA1transporter was reported.)

398. Foger B, Chase M, Amar MJ, Vaisman BL, Shamburek RD, Paigen B, Fruchart-Najib J, Paiz JA, Koch CA, Hoyt RF, Brewer HB Jr., Santamarina-Fojo S. Cholesteryl ester transfer protein corrects dysfunctional high density lipoproteins and reduces aortic atherosclerosis in lecithin cholesterol acyltransferase transgenic mice. J Biol Chem 2000;274:36912–36920. (Dr. Brewer's comment: LCAT transgenic mice were shown to have increased atherosclerosis due to a large dysfunctional HDL. Expression of CETP in this model reduced the abnormal HDL and decreased atheroscslerosis. Results from this study indicated that increased HDL may not always protect against atherosclerosis, and an analysis of the function as well as the level of HDL is necessary to determine the potential protection of HDL in the development of atherosclerosis.)

399. Dugi KA, Amar MJA, Haudenschild CC, Shamburek RD, Bensadoun A, Hoyt RF Jr, Fruchart-Najib J, Madj Z, Brewer HB Jr., Santamarina-Fojo S. In vivo evidence for both lipolytic and nonlipolytic function of hepatic lipase in the metabolism of HDL. Arterioscler Thromb Vasc Biol 2000;20:793–800. (Dr. Brewer's comment: In vivo studies that showed that hepatic lipase could function both as a lipolytic enzyme as well as a ligand for the cellular uptake of lipids and lipoproteins.)

402. Santamarina-Fojo S, Lambert G, Hoeg JM, Brewer HB Jr. Lecithin Cholesterol Acyltransferase (LCAT): role in lipoprotein metabolism, reverse cholesterol transport and atherosclerosis. Curr Opin Lipidol 2000;11:267–275. (Dr. Brewer's comment: A review that summarized the new concept that plasma enzymes can function both as enzymes modulating lipoprotein metabolism as well as ligands for the cellular uptake of lipids and lipoprotein particles.)

406. Lambert G, Sakai N, Vaisman BL, Neufeld EB, Chan C-C, Paigen B, Lupia E, Thomas A, Striker LJ, Blanchette-Mackie J, Costello R, Brewer HB Jr., Csako G, Striker GE, Santamarina-Fojo S. Analysis of glomerulosclerosis and atherosclerosis in lecithin cholesterol acyltransferase-deficient mice. J Biol Chem 2001;4:276:15090–15098. (Dr. Brewer's comment: LCAT transgenic mouse model used to demonstrate the absence of LCAT activity was responsible for the renal defect in LCAT deficiency.)

408. Vaisman BL, Lambert G, Amar M, Joyce C, Ito T, Shamburek RD, Cain WJ, Fruchart-Najib J, Neufeld ED, Remaley AT, Brewer HB Jr., Santamarina-Fojo S. ABCA1 overexpression leads to hyperalphalipoproteinemia and increased biliary cholesterol excretion in transgenic mice. J Clin Invest 2001;108:303–309. (Dr. Brewer's comment: First description that overexpression of the ABCA1 transporter resulted in high HDL levels.)

409. Neufeld EB, Remaley AT, Demosky SJ, Stonik JA, Cooney AM, Comly M, Dwyer NK, Zhang M, Blanchette-Mackie J, Santamarina-Fojo S, Brewer HB Jr. Cellular localization and trafficking of the human ABCA1 transporter. J Biol Chem 2001;276:27584–27590. (Dr. Brewer's comment: Analysis of the cellular trafficking of the ABCA1 transporter revealed that the transporter was present not

only on the cell surface but also trafficked to the late endocytic compartment within the cell.)

413. Santamarina-Fojo S, Remaley AT, Neufeld EB, Brewer HB Jr. Regulation and intracellular trafficking of the ABCA1 transporter. *J Lipid Res* 2001;42:1339–1345. *(Dr. Brewer's comment: A review that summarized the data to support the concept that the ABCA1 transport had a surface as well as intracellular pathway involved in the efflux of cellular cholesterol.)*

416. Remaley AT, Stonik JA, Demosky SJ, Neufeld EB, Bocharov AV, Vishnyakova TG, Eggerman TL, Patterson AP, Duverger NJ, Santamarina-Fojo S, Brewer HB Jr. Apolipoprotein specificity for lipid efflux by the human ABCAI transporter. *Biochem Biophys Res Commun* 2001;280:818–823. *(Dr. Brewer's comment: Pivotal result that established that several of the apolipoproteins, including apoA-II and apoE in addition to apoA-I, were able to bind to the ABCA1 transporter and facilitate cholesterol efflux.)*

417. Berard AM, Clerc M, Brewer HB Jr., Santamarina-Fojo S. A normal rate of cellular cholesterol removal can be mediated by plasma from a patient with familial lecithin-cholesterol acyltransferase (LCAT) deficiency. *Clin Chim Acta* 2001;314:131–139. *(Dr. Brewer's comment: LCAT deficient plasma was able to stimulate cellular cholesterol efflux, providing a reason for the lack of increased atherosclerosis in LCAT deficient patients. The lipidated nacent HDL is unable to form a mature HDL due to the deficiency of LCAT, which esterifies free cholesterol to cholesteryl esters. The partially lipidated nascent HDL particles are filtered by the kidney and catabolized, resulting in the low plasma HDL levels in LCAT deficient patients.)*

421. Joyce CW, Amar MJA, Lambert G, Vaisman BL, Paigen B, Najib-Fruchart J, Parks JS, Hoyt Jr RF, Neufeld ED, Remaley AT, Fredrickson DS, Brewer HB Jr., Santamarina-Fojo S. The ATP binding cassette transporter A1 (ABCA1) modulates the development of aortic atherosclerosis in C57Bl/6 and apoE-knockout mice. *PNAS* 2002;99:407–412. *(Dr. Brewer's comment: Atherosclerosis in ABCA1 transgenic mice was increased and associated with increased plasma LDL levels suggesting that overexpression of the hepatic ABACA1 transporter was associated with increased HDL as well as LDL in these experimental mouse model systems.)*

426. Neufeld EB, Demosky SJ Jr., Stonik JA, Combs C, Remaley AT, Duverger N, Santamarina-Fojo S, Brewer HB Jr. The ABCA1 transporter functions on the basolateral surface of hepatocytes. *Biochem Biophys Res Comm* 2002;297:974–979. *(Dr. Brewer's comment: The ABCA1 transporter was shown to be localized to the basolateral side in the liver. Increased expression of hepatic ABCA1 would result in increased HDL in the plasma rather than increased delivery of cholesterol to the bile.)*

428. Hannuksela ML, Brousseau ME, Meyn SM, Nazih H, Bader G, Shamburek RD, Alaupovic P, Brewer HB Jr. In vivo metabolism of apolipoprotein E within the HDL subpopulations LpE, LpE:A-I, LpE:A-II and LpE:A-I:A-II. *Atherosclerosis* 2002;165:205–220. *(Dr. Brewer's comment: The subpopulation of HDL containing apoE had markedly increased catabolism when compared to the apoE–free LpA-I and LpA-I,A-II particles.)*

429. Basso F, Freeman L, Knapper C, Remaley A, Stonik J, Tansey T, Amar MJA, Fruchart-Najib J, Dugerger N, Santamarina-Fojo S, Brewer HB Jr. Role of the hepatic ABCA1 transporter in modulating intrahepatic cholesterol and plasma HDL-cholesterol concentrations. *J Lipid Res* 2003;44:296–302. *(Dr. Brewer's comment: Pivotal study that demonstrated that increased expression of the hepatic ABCA1 transporter resulted in increased HDL and, in addition, LDL levels due to transfer of HDL cholesterol to LDL. These studies suggest that increased ABCA1 expression in the liver may not result in protection against the development of atherosclerosis due to the increased LDL cholesterol levels.)*

434. Remaley AT, Thomas F, Stonik JA, Demosky SJ, Bark SE, Neufeld EB, Bocharov AV, Vishnyakova TG, Patterson AP, Eggerman TL, Santamarina-Fojo S, Brewer HB Jr., Synthetic amphipathic helical peptides promote lipid efflux from cells by an ABCA1-dependent and an ABCA1-independent pathway. *J Lipid Res* 2003;44:828–836, 2003. *(Dr. Brewer's comment: Detailed analysis of structure–function requires for the binding and efflux of cholesterol from the ABCA1 transporter.)*

445. Neufeld EB, Stonik JA, Demosky SJ, Knapper CL, Combs CA, Cooney A, Comly M, Dwyer N, Blanchette-Mackie J, Remaley AT, Santamarina-Fojo S, Brewer HB Jr. The ABCA1 transporter modulates late endocytic trafficking: insights from the correction of the genetic defect in Tangier disease. *J Biol Chem* 2004;279(15):15571–15578. *(Dr. Brewer's comment: Correction of the genetic defect in Tangier disease resulted in a decrease in the intracellular pool of cholesterol in the late endocytic compartment characteristic of Tangier disease and restoration of cellular cholesterol efflux. These results substantiated the important role and intracellular trafficking of the ABCA1transporter in cellular cholesterol metabolism.)*

447. Brewer HB Jr. High-density lipoproteins: a new potential therapeutic target for the prevention of cardiovascular disease. *Arterioscler Thromb Vasc Biol* 2004;24:387–391. *(Dr. Brewer's comment: Review of HDL function, metabolism, and developing role as an important therapeutic target for the treatment of the high-risk patient with cardiovascular disease.)*

449. Brewer HB Jr. Increasing HDL cholesterol levels. *N Engl J Med* 2004;350(15):1491–1494. *(Dr. Brewer's comment: Conceptual view of the potential role of HDL in the treatment of patients at risk for cardiovascular disease. HDL therapy can be divided into acute therapy to reduce vulnerable plaques by IV infusion in patients with the acute coronary syndrome and oral chronic HDL therapy to reduced the risk of cardiovascular disease.)*

454. Stonik JA, Remaley AT, Demosky SJ, Neufeld EB, Bocharov A, Brewer HB Jr., Serum amyloid A promotes ABCA1-dependent and ABCA1-independent lipid efflux from cells. *Biochem Biophys Res Comm* 2004;321:936–941. *(Dr. Brewer's comment: Serum amyloid A is increased on plasma HDL during acute inflammation. Serum amyloid like apo-A-I and other plasma apolipoproteins was shown to facilitate cellular efflux.)*

455. Brewer HB Jr., Remaley AT, Neufeld EB, Basso F, Joyce C. AHA Scientific Sessions 2002 George Lyman Duff Memorial Lecture. Regulation of HDL metabolism by the ABCA1 transporter and the emerging role of HDL in the treatment of cardiovascular disease. *Arterioscler Thromb Vasc Biol* 2004;24:1755–1760. *(Dr. Brewer's comment: Invited lecture that summarizes the role of the ABCA1 transporter in cholesterol efflux and the potential use of HDL to treat patients at risk for cardiovascular disease.)*

ROBERT WILLIAM ("BOBBY") BROWN, MD, Cardiologist, Major League Baseball Player (New York Yankee), and American League President: A Conversation With the Editor*

Bobby Brown (Figure 1) was born in Seattle, Washington, on October 25, 1924. His grew up in Seattle; East Orange and Maplewood, New Jersey; and San Francisco, California. He was president of the student body at Maplewood Junior High School in New Jersey and president of the student body in Galileo High School in San Francisco, from which he graduated in June 1942. His freshman year in college was at Stanford University (1942 to 1943). He enlisted in the United States Navy at age 18 and was assigned to the Navy's V12 program at the University of California, Los Angeles (UCLA), where he completed his premedical studies. He entered the Tulane University School of Medicine on December 1, 1944, and graduated on June 6, 1950. He interned at the Southern Pacific Hospital in San Francisco (1950 to 1952) and did a residency in internal medicine at the San Francisco County Hospital (July 1954 to June 1957). Dr. Brown was chief resident during his final year there. He did a fellowship in cardiology at the Tulane University School of Medicine from July 1957 to June 1958. He was in private practice in cardiology in Fort Worth, Texas, from August 1, 1958, until January 31, 1984.

Bobby Brown, nicknamed "The Golden Boy," was a star baseball player in junior high school, high school, and 3 different colleges, namely, Stanford, UCLA, and Tulane. At each college, he hit between .450 and .500 as a shortstop. After completing 1.5 years of medical school, he signed a baseball contract with the New York Yankees, receiving a signing bonus of $52,000, only 1 of 2 baseball players to receive a signing bonus of that magnitude at that time. During the 1946 season, Brown played for Newark (the Yankees' Triple A affiliate in the International League), and he led the league in hits, with a batting average of .341. He was called up to the Yankees in late September of that year and hit .333 during the 7 games in which he played. Dr. Brown was the first person to play a complete major league schedule while attending medical school. He played with the Yankees, mainly as a third baseman, from the last month of the 1946 season to June 30, 1954, when he retired from baseball to begin his residency in internal medicine.

Attending medical school and playing professional baseball at the same time was not an easy journey. Tulane initially was not particularly sympathetic to Brown's desire to play professional baseball and simultaneously attend medical school. Attending medical school also made it difficult for Brown to compete equally with his teammates and competitors in professional baseball, because he usually missed most or all of spring training, which put him behind the 8-ball when the season started, although he trained an hour a day to keep in shape during his time at medical school. During the 1947 season, in which he platooned at third base (playing against right-handed pitchers), he was hit by a pitched ball, which fractured his index finger. When Brown returned to play after several weeks out, the Yankees were winning, the lineup was set, and he spent the rest of the season filling in and pinch-hitting. On another occasion (in 1949 or 1950), he ruptured some ankle ligaments while hitting and was on crutches for about 4 weeks. In 1952, just after finishing his internship, he was eligible for the Doctor's Draft (Korean War) and enlisted in the United States Army. He was called to active duty on July 1, 1952, and as a consequence missed the remainder of that baseball season and all of the 1953 season. He returned to the Yankees on May 1, 1954. Soon he was back in the lineup, but he retired from baseball so that he could begin his residency in internal medicine in San Francisco. During Brown's 8 years (minus 20 months) with the Yankees, they won the World Series on 6 occasions, and he played in 4 of those series (during the other 2, he was in Korea). During those 4 series, Brown had 41 official at-bats and 18 hits, for a lifetime World Series average of .439, the highest average ever recorded for someone with $\geq$20 official at-bats.

Almost certainly, Bobby Brown's baseball average during the regular season would have been higher had he had an opportunity to attend spring training (Table 1). Also, he was a member of the best team in the majors virtually every year during his entire professional career. Beginning in 1949, he platooned at third base and therefore was considered a regular player. A number of his teammates, including Joe DiMaggio, Mickey Mantle, Yogi Berra, Phil Rizzuto, and Whitey Ford among others, became Hall of Fame members, and others are deserving of such status.

Dr. Brown practiced cardiology for 25 years, retiring in January 1984 to become president of the American League of Professional Clubs. He served in that capacity until August 1, 1994. In addition to his duties as league president, he instituted and supported youth baseball programs throughout the United States. Through his influence and guidance, a ban was initiated in the minor leagues against the use of smokeless tobacco. Its dangers led to the production of a video distributed to 22,000 high schools throughout the country.

Dr. Brown has received a number of awards for his athletic and medical abilities. He is in the athletic halls of fame at Stanford, UCLA, and Tulane, where he played varsity baseball (and captained the UCLA team), and he is also a member of the Prep or High School Hall of Fame of San Francisco. He also was captain of his Galileo High School baseball team in his senior year. In 1946, he received

---

* This series of interviews was underwritten by an unrestricted grant from Bristol-Meyers Squibb.
† Director, Baylor Cardiovascular Institute, Baylor University Medical Center, Dallas, Texas, 75246.
‡ Retired.

Figure 1. Dr. Robert W. Brown during the interview.

the Outstanding New Jersey Professional Athlete of the Year Award. Other awards and honors include Outstanding Alumnus, Tulane School of Medicine (1985); the Stanford University Athletic Board Distinguished Achievement Medal (1991); the Presidential Citation of Otolaryngology (1991); Distinguished Alumnus, Tulane University (1993); the American Medical Association ERF Award for Health Education (1994); the Exchange Club of Fort Worth Golden Deeds Award as Fort Worth's Outstanding Citizen (1996); the All Saints Health Foundation Truman C. Terrell Award, Fort Worth (2004); Honorary Doctor of Science, Trinity College, Hartford, Connecticut (1994); Honorary Doctor of Science, University of Massachusetts, Worcester (1995); and Honorary Doctor of Humanitarian Service, Hillsdale College, Hillsdale, Michigan (2002).

Bobby Brown is a delightful human being, a great storyteller, a natural leader, and a very popular after-dinner speaker. He and his lovely wife, Sara (Figures 2 and 3), each have a tremendous capacity for friendship, and they are enormously popular in Fort Worth and Dallas as well as in many other areas of the country. They are the proud parents of 3 children and have 10 upstanding and delightful grandchildren. It was truly a pleasure to spend 6 hours talking to this outstanding individual.

William Clifford Roberts, MD (hereafter Roberts[†]): *Dr. Brown, it is a privilege for me and I am sure for the readers of The American Journal of Cardiology to be able to get to know you a bit better. Could we start by your*

describing *your early life in Seattle, your parents, and your siblings?*

Robert William Brown, MD (hereafter Brown[‡]): I was born October 25, 1924, in Seattle, Washington. I started school there when I was 5. School opened the day after Labor Day in those days, and I went to John Muir Elementary School in the Mount Baker district of Seattle. After 3 or 4 days in class, the teacher found out that I was 5. I was told to leave school until I was 6, and fortunately, on October 25 I turned 6, and they accepted me again in first grade. I stayed in that school for my first 3 years. The school had separate play areas for the girls and the boys. They wouldn't let us mix. At recess we played softball. I could hit better than my other classmates in the first grade class. When the Depression hit, we lost our house. As a consequence, we moved from Mount Baker to Puget Sound on Alki Point in Seattle. A carpenter built us a house on the beach for $900. It was wonderful. We had a row boat and later, a motorboat, with the biggest motor made at the time—an Evinrude 24-horsepower motor.

I started the fourth grade at Alki Grammar School. I spent 3 delightful years there. The first team I played on was a 90-lb basketball team at the Alki Field House. We had 5 or 6 kids on that team, all of us in fourth grade. We would get up on Saturday mornings at 5:00 or 5:30, catch the first streetcar at 6:30, and travel into Seattle and then out to wherever we were going to play. Nobody bothered kids in those days. We traveled on our own all over the city.

Roberts: *This was when you were 9?*

Brown: Yes, I was in the fourth grade and 9 years old. I weighed about 65 lb when playing in the 90-lb league. I stayed at Alki through the sixth grade. During that time, I skipped half a grade and entered junior high school in February 1937—the beginning of the seventh grade. I finished that half semester. In the spring of that year, the Seattle Indians, the Coast League team, had a school for kids who wanted to play baseball. When filling out the application, both my brother and I listed infield and pitchers, but we spelled it "pictures." At this school we ran through various drills. After taking batting practice the coach, Bill Grader, came up to me and asked if I would like to be on his team. He had an American Legion team consisting only of high school kids, and I was just starting junior high. My dad said, "Do it." Although I did not play in the games, I worked out with the team. That was my first real team with a uniform.

Roberts: *Although you were in the seventh grade, how old were you?*

Brown: Twelve. At Alki, semipro teams played on the high school field, and I watched them. I told them I would be the batboy if they would let me take batting practice with them. They agreed. Once I got a nickel for being the batboy. (Nickels were big in those days.) After I finished that spring semester and the first half of the seventh grade, my folks moved back to Mount Baker. Times had gotten better and my dad had gotten a good job ($400/month). He had a job all during the Depression. Mount Baker was near my grandparents, and my mother was anxious to be close to them.

I had a brother who was 2 years younger and a sister 4 years younger. My brother is William Charles Brown, Jr, and he was born in 1926. My dad was William Christopher

Table 1
William Robert ("Bobby") Brown*: career baseball statistics

Season	Team	G	AB	R	H	2B	3B	HR	RBI	TB	BB	SO	SB	CS	OBP	SLG	AVG
1946	New York Yankees	7	24	1	8	1	0	0	1	9	4	0	0	0	.414	.375	.333
1947	New York Yankees	69	150	21	45	6	1	1	18	56	21	9	0	2	.383	.373	.300
1948	New York Yankees	113	363	62	109	19	5	3	48	147	48	16	0	1	.380	.405	.300
1949	New York Yankees	104	343	61	97	14	4	6	61	137	38	18	4	3	.359	.399	.283
1950	New York Yankees	95	277	33	74	4	2	4	37	94	39	18	3	1	.356	.339	.267
1951	New York Yankees	103	313	44	84	15	2	6	51	121	47	18	1	1	.363	.387	.268
1952	New York Yankees	29	89	6	22	2	0	1	14	27	9	6	1	1	.320	.303	.247
1954[†]	New York Yankees	28	60	5	13	1	0	1	7	17	8	3	0	1	.304	.283	.217
Career totals		548	1619	233	452	62	14	22	237	608	214	88	9	10	.363	.376	.279

* Dr. Brown played third base, batting left-handed and throwing right-handed.

[†] When the season began, Dr. Brown had been out of baseball for 20 months serving our country in Korea and Japan.

AB = at-bats; AVG = batting average; BB = bases on balls; CS = caught stealing; G = games; HR = home runs; OBP = on-base percentage; R = runs; RBI = runs batted in; SB = stolen bases; SLG = slugging percentage; SO = strikeouts; 3B = triples; TB = total bases; 2B = doubles.

Figure 2. Dr. Brown and his wife, Sara, at the time of the interview.

Figure 3. Dr. and Mrs. Brown at the Fort Worth, Texas, Exchange Club, 2006.

Brown, born in 1894 in Newark, New Jersey, and my mother, Myrtle Kathryn Berg, was born in 1900 in Seattle, Washington (Figure 4). My mother was Norwegian, and my dad was of German extraction. My sister's name was Beverley Jane Brown, born in 1928.

Roberts: *What were your parents like?*

Brown: They were just good people, good middle-class Americans. My maternal grandmother and grandfather were full-blooded Norwegian. My dad's mother had emigrated from Germany, and his father, although born in the USA, also was full-blooded German. I was German-Norwegian extraction. My dad was a first lieutenant in World War I and stationed at Fort Louis in Tacoma, Washington (Figure 5). He met my mother, who was then working in a bank in Seattle, and after he was discharged, they got married.

Roberts: *What year did they get married?*

Brown: I believe 1920.

Roberts: *What was your father like?*

Brown: My dad was a very good athlete for those days. He ran track and he was also a very good baseball player. He was good enough to be a professional player, but there was no money in professional baseball in those days. When he was in Newark, he could work and play on a semipro team. He could make more money playing baseball as a semi pro than as a professional. He never played professional baseball, but he knew how to play, and of course he taught me. He had me playing ball before I could remember. My parents were just good solid people who were anxious for their children to get good educations and be good athletes too.

Roberts: *Had your father gone to college?*

Brown: No. My dad went to a technical school. He had to quit regular school when he was about 14, and then he

Figure 4. Dr. Brown's mother, Myrtle Kathryn Berg.

Figure 6. The Brown family: Robert W. Brown (6 years), William, Beverley Jane (2 years), Myrtle, and William Charles ("Billy"; 4 years).

Roberts: *What about your mother?*

Brown: My mother was a high school graduate and then went to work. She never entered college either.

Roberts: *But your parents pushed all 3 of you toward education?*

Brown: Always! My dad wanted me to hit .500 and get straight A's. That's what he wanted, and it never changed.

Roberts: *It sounds as though you and your father were quite close.*

Brown: Very. My dad was amazing. He was a very good athlete. I played all sports until I got to the ninth grade, and then he insisted that I quit football and basketball, although I could play both well. He wanted me to concentrate on baseball. After the seventh grade, we moved to Maplewood, New Jersey, where I entered the eighth grade. When the physical education teacher learned that I was going to quit football and basketball, he was incensed. He just couldn't believe it and got mad. Instead of playing football and basketball, I'd swing the bat in the cellar during the winter. My dad worked on my running to get me ready for baseball.

Roberts: *What did your father run in track?*

Brown: He ran sprints and the broad jump. He did not have world-class speed. He worked at that time for the Prudential Life Insurance Company, and he got the job there because he was a good athlete. Large companies at that time had some sports teams. I've got pictures of the Prudential relay team, and he was on that team.

Roberts: *Did you ever run track in high school?*

Brown: No. I was just a baseball player. I had only average speed.

Roberts: *What was your mother like?*

Brown: Mother was a beautiful lady and a great mother. She followed along with what my dad felt was right. She would put her 2 cents in every so often. She was strictly a homemaker. She was a great cook. We never had maids.

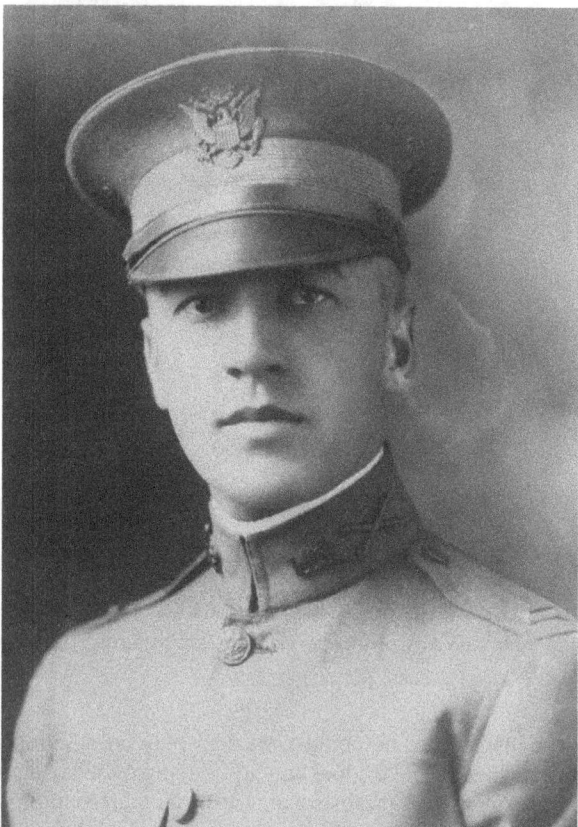

Figure 5. Dr. Brown's father, William Christopher Brown, during World War I.

finished high school by going to classes at night. Then he took some business training at Pace & Pace, either in New York City or New Jersey. He never went to a formal 4-year college.

Whenever my brother and I played ballgames, she and my dad were there. My dad was really the decision maker in the family. She was very instrumental in our moving from the beach back to Mount Baker.

Roberts: *What was your home life like during grammar school, junior high, and high school? Was the evening meal a big deal in your home?*

Brown: All the meals were attended by all family members (Figure 6). It was a routine. We did our homework after the evening meal. There was a 15-minute program at 8:00 or 8:15 P.M.—Lum and Abner or maybe Fibber McGee and Molly, and after it we went to bed, usually by 9:00. In Seattle, I could look out the window and see the Black Ball Ferry coming from Bremerton to dock about a block from where we lived. I could always tell it was about 9:00 P.M. because the ferry would show up every night about that time.

Roberts: *What time did you get up in the morning?*

Brown: We got up early. School began in those days at 8:00, so we were up between 6:00 and 6:30 A.M.

Roberts: *Did your studies in school come easy for you, or did you have to work hard for your grades?*

Brown: I worked hard, but I was always a reasonably good student, one of the better students in the class, at least through high school. It wasn't that it came easy. I worked hard.

Roberts: *Did you go by "Bobby" all through school?*

Brown: I was "Bob Brown" mostly through high school, but as I entered college, the sportswriters began to call me "Bobby."

Roberts: *You mentioned that your coach couldn't believe that you were giving up basketball and football. Did your classmates push you to play those other 2 sports also?*

Brown: No. In junior high in those days, nothing was really organized. We had intramural games until the ninth grade. There wasn't any real pressure, because they knew I was a baseball player, and that was good enough. The coaches, once I got into high school, didn't push me either, because they knew I was going to try out for the baseball team.

Roberts: *You were president of the student body when you were in junior high school in Maplewood, New Jersey.*

Brown: Yes.

Roberts: *Was baseball a little more strenuous in New Jersey than it was in Seattle?*

Brown: No. I was on an American Legion team in Seattle, and when in the ninth grade in New Jersey, I also played on the American Legion team in Maplewood–South Orange, which was a combined team from 2 towns. When I completed the ninth grade, I played on a man's team in the Maplewood Twilight League. I was the only kid not in high school, or in college or working full-time. We played on Sundays in the Lackawanna League, comprised of towns in the vicinity—Morristown, Madison, Milburn, Summit, and Maplewood–South Orange. After the games, the men would all head for the bar. They would sit me down at the end of the bar and tell the bartender to give me sarsaparilla, and they would all have a beer.

When I got to Columbia High School in the 10th grade, I had worked hard all winter. Maplewood and South Orange had excellent school systems. I was gung-ho to make the baseball team in the spring. We worked out in the gym in March because it was so cold outside. When it came time to go outside, the coach put me on the junior varsity team, and that was a bitter blow to me. My dad at that time had a job offer in San Francisco from a friend who was a distributor in the liquor business. He wanted my dad to join him. My dad was doing quite well, however, in New Jersey, in business for himself. We loved Maplewood and New Jersey. I told my dad that I was on the junior varsity and didn't get a chance to compete for the varsity team. The previous summer, I had been on a man's team. We didn't have any high school kids in the whole league. I was the only kid playing in the league, and then I'm put on the junior varsity! My dad asked the coach what he was going to do with me, and he said that he was going to keep me on the junior varsity all year. That edict convinced my dad that we would go to California, and we did. It's ironic, because later when I joined the Yankees, I was the first kid in that high school to ever get to the major leagues, and I was not allowed to play on the varsity team! To this day I dislike that coach. That episode, it was a stimulus for me to really bust my fanny every time I played!

Roberts: *Did you get back to San Francisco in time to play during your 10th grade year?*

Brown: No. We drove through Seattle to see my grandparents and then got to San Francisco just as the baseball season was ending. But they had an American Legion team from that high school, and I tried out for it. At the beginning of the first game we played, I was sitting on the bench. My dad was there and asked me if I wanted to go home. I said I would stick around. The manager put me in to hit about the fourth inning, and I hit one to right centerfield for a home run, and from then on, I played every game, every inning, and it didn't stop until I got to the Yankees.

Roberts: *You must have been pretty quick to play shortstop.*

Brown: Yes. I was a good fielder, but I could really hit. I wasn't the fastest guy, but I wasn't the slowest either, and that's how it went even into the major leagues.

Roberts: *The next year, your junior year in high school in San Francisco, you played on the high school team?*

Brown: Yes. We had a terrific team. To this day, I don't think I've ever seen a high school team as good as that one. We won the city championship both my junior and senior years, and it was not because the other teams were not good. As a junior, I hit .583, the highest in the league. My senior year, I hit .375. I also had a great summer with the American Legion team. I played on the American Legion team in San Francisco (the Galileo American Legion Post). Galileo was the name of the high school that I went to. We not only won our city championship, but we also won the region when we played in Oakland for the bay area championship. A New York Yankee scout came up after the game and gave me his card and told me that they were really interested in me.

I had attended a tryout camp in Newark when in junior high (ninth grade) by the Newark Bears. They were in the Triple A league. For the tryouts, you were supposed to be at least 18 years of age. I put down that I was 18 and got into the mix of things. My dad came down to see how I was doing and visited with the Yankee scouts who were running the team. They said that I looked pretty good, but that I did not have a very good arm for an 18-year-old. My dad told

BACK ROW: McKie, Graham, Miller, Provost, J. Miller, Brownson, Merriman, Pinion, Cunha
MIDDLE ROW: Wellington, Hammett, Brown, Flatland, Wakefield, Holmes, Grau, Stephenson
FRONT ROW: Shipkey, Washburn, Stromsmoe, Walkup, Wolter, Tibbetts, Woody, Ferrari

Figure 7. Stanford University team, April 1943 (Dr. Brown, middle row, third from left).

them that I was only 13. That got them interested. I got a letter afterwards that they were impressed. That letter was the very first I ever got from a professional team.

Before the summer was over after my junior year in high school, I was contacted by scouts from the Cleveland and Brooklyn teams. At that time, freshman in college were ineligible to play on varsity baseball teams. Stanford and the University of California at Berkley had freshman baseball teams, and we would play them. We obliterated them. The games were 7-inning games. We beat the University of California at Berkley 13 to 2. After the game, a man came out of the stands and grabbed me and said he was a professor there at the university. His name was Professor Chapman. He said he had never seen a high school team take apart a college freshman team like we did. He asked me if I would be interested in working out with the Cincinnati Reds. He was a scout for the Reds. He told me that he would like to take me to Cincinnati if I'd like to go. I told him, "You bet I would like to go." Consequently, during the summer after my junior year, I spent nearly 14 days with the Reds, working out every day taking batting and fielding practice with them. Then they took me to Chicago for games there. I also worked out at Wrigley Field. A photographer there took pictures of the players. There I was at 16 in a Cincinnati uniform. To this day, every once in a while, I get a copy of that picture to autograph. That was a great summer. Wherever I played thereafter, the major league scouts were there following me.

The next year, I was a senior in high school and the student body president during 1 semester. I got good grades.

Roberts: *How many were in your high school class?*

Brown: Just over 300. The high school (10th, 11th, and 12th grades) had about 950 students. I was in the school in the Marina District on the border of Marina and North Beach. North Beach was basically the Italian district, so maybe 50% of the student body was Italian, 25% was Chinese, and about 25% everything else. On my starting high school baseball team there were 7 Italians, 1 Irishman, and I was Norwegian-German.

Roberts: *How many were on the team?*

Brown: Probably 18. Eight guys played every game, and we had 2 or 3 pitchers. All the managers knew who could play. There were never any announcement of tryouts for the team. There were no tryouts. Another high school in town, Mission High School, also had a very good team. Both my junior and senior years, we played them for the championship. We had split the regular season (1 and 1), and we won the championship game, which was played on a Thursday afternoon at Seals Stadium, the Pacific Coast League Park. About 10,000 fans saw the high school championship game. Every time we played, there were 4 or 5 major league scouts in the stands watching us play ball.

Roberts: *When you hit .583 as a junior, how many at-bats did you get?*

Brown: I can't remember now. We played, I believe, 16 games in high school. There were 8 high schools, and we played each school 2 games each.

Roberts: *How many home runs did you hit?*

Brown: I can't remember.

Roberts: *But you were the power guy back then?*

Brown: No. I was one of the guys who could really hit, but there were others who could really hit well.

Roberts: *Did any of them make the majors?*

Brown: Yes. Dino Restelli made it with Pittsburgh, and Frank Lucchesi with the Texas Rangers.

Roberts: *After graduating from high school in June 1942, what happened next?*

Brown: I wanted to go to Stanford. At that time, both Stanford and Cal played semipro teams to fill in their schedule. (Baseball in the San Francisco Bay area was just outstanding. Many guys could really play.) The summer after my junior year in high school, I played on a semipro team, which played Stanford on their campus. I loved the campus and stadium and decided that I wanted to go to there for college. When playing with the semipro team, a Stanford student when learning I was just a high school kid invited me to his fraternity house for a meal. I went and thought it unbeatable. From then on every time I saw in the newspaper where 1 of the semipro baseball teams was going to play Stanford (they used to print the schedule on the sports pages of the paper), I'd call the manager and asked if I could play. "Of course" was always the answer. (I was well known in San Francisco by that time. All the high school kids who could really play were well known.) I'd show up at Stanford maybe 2 or 3 times a year. I told the Stanford baseball coach that I'd like to come there for college.

Roberts: *Did you get a baseball scholarship?*

Brown: Stanford at that time had what they called "grant-in-aids." Students had to be in a certain economic level to get a scholarship. They were the only college that had that stipulation. I filled out the form and told them my dad's income. They wrote back that I didn't qualify, that my dad was making too much money. We were not wealthy, but he had a good job. I told the coach, "You know I can go to any school to play. I want to come here." He said, "We'll take care of you." In those days, things were a little loose. They didn't have the NCAA (National Collegiate Athletic Association) looking over their shoulder. The coach said, "I'll get somebody to take care of your tuition. I'll get you a job waiting on tables and then you will get your food for free. You will have to pay for a room"—and that was $90 a quarter—"and you will have to buy your books." I said I could handle that. I found out later that the father of the catcher on the baseball team was a wealthy guy. He took care of my tuition. I waited on tables in the freshman dorm, got free food, bought used books, and paid the $90 a quarter for a room. I got by on $5 a week (Figure 7).

Roberts: *Where did your family live in San Francisco?*

Brown: We lived in the Marina District, which was near the bay between the Golden Gate Bridge and North Beach and next to the Presidio and the Palace of Fine Arts. The earthquake in 1989 hit that area badly.

Roberts: *That was a lot of landfill.*

Brown: Yes.

Roberts: *You were president of the student body during high school.*

Brown: Yes. I was also captain of the baseball team my senior year. Both my junior and senior year the football coaches were also the baseball coaches, and they knew nothing about baseball. They would sit in the corner of the dugout and never say a word. We had no signs, no nothing, but everybody knew how to play. In the spring of 1942, the war was on, and the services took over our ball park where we played our games and practiced. The coach told us that we didn't have a place to practice, but that we should just practice on our own and show up for the games. We did and we won!

Roberts: *Did your father smoke cigarettes?*

Brown: No, never.

Roberts: *Was there alcohol in your home growing up?*

Brown: Yes. He was a distributor in the liquor business in San Francisco. Later he became the regional manager for Shenley Distillery, a large distillery in those days. We always had whiskey in the house.

Roberts: *Did he have a drink every night?*

Brown: No, not every night. A lot of times, he had to go around to the bars and check on how sales were going. I'm sure he would have a drink there. He never had a drinking problem.

Roberts: *Were your mother and daddy pretty close?*

Brown: Yes.

Roberts: *It was a pleasant home?*

Brown: Always. No problems, none. Great home.

Roberts: *Your childhood was splendid?*

Brown: Utopian.

Roberts: *Could you read fast?*

Brown: Yes. Pretty fast, and I loved to read. I read everything I could get my hands on. A lot of times it was a sports book, but I love novels.

Roberts: *Was your brother a good athlete?*

Brown: Yes, but at a college level. He had a scholarship to St. Mary's College and played baseball for 4 years. He was a very good semipro player, but not good enough to play professionally.

Roberts: *What did he play?*

Brown: Outfield. He couldn't run very well, but he could hit.

Roberts: *Did he bat left-handed?*

Brown: Yes. My dad taught us both to hit left-handed, but we are both right-handed throwers. We do everything right-handed.

Roberts: *What about a golf club?*

Brown: My dad made me swing a golf club, but I never played much. He told me to play right-handed, because in those days it was tough to get left-handed clubs. I can swing a golf club right-handed. I can't swing a bat right-handed. At the end of my senior year, I had so many scouts after me that my dad decided to send me east on our own. I went and worked out with Cincinnati again.

Roberts: *Right after graduation?*

Brown: Yes. I worked out for 3 or 4 days with Cincinnati Reds, Detroit Tigers, the New York Yankees, the Brooklyn Dodgers, and the Philadelphia Athletics. I worked out with 5 major leagues teams before I got to college.

Figure 8. University of California, Los Angeles, April 1944.

Roberts: *You really knew how the major leagues operated before you got there?*

Brown: That's right.

Roberts: *Did many other eventual major leaguers have that kind of experience?*

Brown: Probably not. Some of the better prospects I would run into occasionally. In Detroit, there were 2 other kids who worked out with them: Rex Barney, from Omaha, Nebraska, and Art Houtteman, from Detroit. Art was 15, and both Rex and I were 17. I ended up playing against both of them in the major leagues: against Rex Barney in the World Series (Dodgers), and we were lifelong friends.

Roberts: *What happened when you went to Stanford? You enrolled in September 1942.*

Brown: I turned 18 in October 1942. I was eligible for the draft at that point. I started out as a chemical engineer. One month into freshman chemistry, however, convinced me that I did not want to be a chemical engineer. I wanted to do something where I could deal with people. I thought medicine would be my best shot to do that. I changed to premed. The Navy, Army, and Marine recruiters came to the colleges looking for potential officers. We all listened to them. I went with the Navy. All the premed students who enlisted in the Navy were called up the following July 1, 1943, and put into uniform. All of the premeds at Stanford who went into the Navy were sent to UCLA, which had a

large naval unit (>3,000) there called V12. Many were from the naval ROTC (Reserve Officer Training Corps) units in different colleges. All the premeds were placed in 2 buildings. They gave us 5 semesters to do all our premed work. I had had the equivalent of 2 semesters at Stanford, which was on the quarter system. We went year round, starting in July 1943. From July 1943 until June 1944, I did 3 semesters. Then, if your grades were satisfactory and you were eligible for medical school, they put you on temporary duty to wait for medical school to open. Tulane opened in December 1, 1944, and I was assigned there. Except for 1 other person who was a year ahead of me, I was the only one assigned to Tulane.

Roberts: *What kind of grades did you make during that year at Stanford?*

Brown: All A's or B's except for 1 C in analytical geometry. I got 2 C's at UCLA: 1 in quantitative analysis and 1 in organic chemistry. The spring semester (1944), I had 5 labs—2 quantitative analyses, 2 organic chemistry, and 1 zoology. I told the baseball coach that I didn't see how I could play, because I was carrying 19 or 20 hours and had to get it all in that semester. I had labs every day except Wednesday, and I was in school until 5:00 P.M. The coach told me that he would schedule all our games on Wednesdays and Saturdays, which he did. I practiced with the team when I got out of the labs, but, of course, most of the team had already practiced. The whole team was service guys. We had guys who were 30 years old in school. UCLA had a meteorology school, and the Navy sent some of its officers there to become meteorologists. Three of them played on the UCLA baseball team, of which I was captain (Figure 8). I virtually never practiced with the team. I saw them at the games. The coach would keep a batting practice pitcher, and I would get on the field about 5:15 P.M. and would work out until 6:00 P.M. I'd hit and take infield practice and then would get up to the mess hall just before it closed. I practiced all by myself except for a pitcher and a batter for infield practice. Almost every day there was 1 guy sitting in the stands wearing a hat. He was a scout for the St. Louis Browns.

Roberts: *How did you do in baseball your year at Stanford?*

Brown: I hit between .450 and .500 at Stanford, at UCLA, and at Tulane.

Roberts: *How many games did you have, for example, at Stanford?*

Brown: About 30. Now they have maybe 80. Because of travel restriction and gas rationing, we couldn't travel much at that time. Each of the 5 colleges in the bay area had teams: University of San Francisco (USF), St. Mary's, Santa Clara College, Stanford University, and University of California at Berkeley. It was a 5-team league. As a freshman, I hit .463, second highest in the league.

Roberts: *You played 3 years in college, and each year at a different school?*

Brown: Correct.

Roberts: *How did you do that year at UCLA in grades? You mentioned you were taking 20 hours, 5 labs, you made 2 C's. The other grades must have been mostly A's?*

Brown: That's right, mostly A's.

Roberts: *Did you have to study a great deal?*

Figure 9. Medical student, Tulane University Medical School, 1946.

Brown: Sure did. I studied and played ball. I also played ball every Sunday with a semipro team.

Roberts: *You played baseball every Wednesday, Saturday, and Sunday. You went to Tulane Medical School in New Orleans beginning December 1, 1944?*

Brown: Correct.

Roberts: *What happened at Tulane? How did medical school work out?*

Brown: There were quite a few service guys in the medical school class of 125 (Figure 9). Some classmates had gone to Tulane as undergraduates, but most of the class was strangers. No one knew that I was a ballplayer. When I first got there, I went to a boarding house adjacent to the campus run by 2 unmarried sisters, the Donovan sisters. They had 1 vacancy, but I would have a roommate. They told me to go up and meet him before I decided whether I wanted to live there. He was a little guy with a toothpick in his mouth wearing glasses. He was only 17 and had graduated early from Millsaps College. His dad was a physician. His name was Clarence Denser. I had a sea bag with all my Navy stuff. He watched me unpack: I took out my Navy uniforms and then my bat and baseball equipment (shoes, gloves, jock strap and cup, sliding pads). And he said, "Are you really going to med school?" I said, "Yes."

Like all freshman medical students, it was an avalanche. All the students fought for their lives. The anatomy professor, Dr. Wilbur Smith ("the Bull"), was a Tulane institution. He absolutely terrified every freshman in his anatomy class. He convinced all the students that they would flunk. All the students studied every minute of the day. He also was the athletic director of the university and had been there for years. We had anatomy virtually the whole year. They didn't have air conditioning in New Orleans during the war, and we were upstairs on the uptown campus, with 2 giant fans at both ends of the building. The professor allowed only 1 window to be opened because the air would dry out the cadavers. All the male students were stripped down to the waist. The class also had 8 girls.

Roberts: *Do you require a lot of sleep, or can you get along pretty well on 5 or 6 hours a night? What do you need to feel good the next day?*

Brown: Four to 6 hours.

Roberts: *Have you always been that way?*

Brown: Yes. Until college I got plenty of sleep, but once I got to college, I didn't sleep as much. In medical school, I slept very little. If I sat down during the day for 10 or 15 minutes, I slept.

Roberts: *By the time you got to medical school, how tall were you?*

Brown: I was 6'1".

Roberts: *How much did you weigh?*

Brown: When I finished with the Yankees in 1954, I weighed 185 lb. The first year in the majors—1946—I weighed between 175 and 180 lb.

Roberts: *When you entered medical school, had you known any doctors, or had you had any injuries during your playing time up to that point where you had contact with physicians? Were there any physicians in your extended family?*

Brown: None in the family. I lived next door to a physician, Dr. Clarence Porter, in San Francisco. He was in family practice. He was our doctor and he also was the doctor for the Del Monte Food Company. We knew him quite well. I also had a family doctor, Dr. Burge, in Seattle and another in New Jersey.

Roberts: *Were there any big surprises for you early on in medical school?*

Brown: The thing that surprised me was the volume of information. I never felt totally prepared for any examination. There was always the feeling that I needed more time to prepare. I studied a lot of time for exams until 2:00 A.M. I never had had to do that before. I also studied hard at Stanford and UCLA, but there was not the volume as in medical school. Also, none of the 125 medical students were dumb. Everybody was there for a reason, and all had been screened pretty vigorously. Tulane was not trying to flunk anyone. The faculty felt that everybody ought to be able to get through if they went through the admission process correctly. They didn't grade on the curve. They graded each of us numerically, but we were not told our numerical grades, because they didn't want us to be studying just for grades. We got "pass," "low pass," "condition," or "fail." Those were the 4 grades we knew about. The numbers put in the books the students never saw. I got all "passes" in med school. I was not the smartest guy in the class, but I was the best hitter!

Roberts: *You played ball for Tulane University your freshman year in medical school?*

Brown: Yes. I got there 2 or 3 days before December 1, 1944. I read in the *Times-Picayune* that the semipro baseball championship game was being played that day at Audubon Park, located on St. Charles Avenue, across the street from the Tulane University campus. I walked over there in my Navy uniform. A guy came up to me and asked me if I played baseball. I said I did. He said that they were short a player and needed 1 player. "What are you doing here? Are you in the service?" I told him I was starting med school on Monday. He asked me if I wanted to play. I said, "Yes." He asked if I had any equipment. I said that I did and ran home and got it. I played and got a few hits. After the game, he said that this was the last game of the season but asked me if I ever played softball. I told him that I didn't play softball. He said, "They have a real fast slow-pitch softball league in town, and its run by the gamblers. The gamblers sponsored the team so they can bet on the teams. Would you like to play?" I asked him when they played. He replied that they played every Sunday afternoon. I said, "I might do that." He said, "We play at Taylor Park." I played shortstop for the softball team, and after about 4 or 5 games, they knew that I had played before. Mel Ott, the manager of the Giants, who was in the Hall of Fame, was from Louisiana. He was born and raised in Gretna, across the river from New Orleans. Someone called him and said, "You gotta come look at this guy play shortstop." He said, "I don't want to come see a softball player." He said, "This guy plays hard ball. He's in med school. You gotta come see him." Ott came. He saw me play, and afterwards, this was in December 1944 or January 1945, he said when it got a little warmer, would I take batting practice? He would come up and pitch batting practice. I said, "Fine." At that time, the Tulane baseball field was adjacent to McAlister Hall. He came out that spring before the Giants went to spring training and pitched batting practice to me. After I hit batting practice, he said that he would keep in touch with me, and he did.

In the spring 1945, when taking physiology and anatomy, I read in the school paper, *Hullabaloo*, that the Tulane baseball team was going to start practicing. Although usually not getting out of class until 5:00 P.M. or so, I decided to try out. I went to my room and changed into baseball clothes, walked to the field, and met with the head baseball coach, Claude "Little Monk" Simons, who was also the head football coach. He asked if I was in school here. I said, "Yes, med school." He asked, "What year?" I said, "Freshman." He said, "You taking anatomy?" I said, "Yes." He knew that the athletic director was the professor of anatomy. He asked if I was taking physiology too. I said, "Yes." He asked if I wanted to play baseball too. I said I thought I would come and work out. He said, "You are crazy. You don't have time to play. I don't want to fool with you. It would be a waste of time. There is no way you can play." I said, "Okay." I am playing on Sundays for a semipro team (Joe's Jungle), getting paid $15 a game, which was almost as much as the Navy was paying me so at least I was playing somewhere. I did not tell the coach about this Sunday activity, however. He said, "Where do you play?" I said, "I play shortstop." "Well, go on out there and they'll hit you some ground balls, and when you are tired, you can go home," he said. I said, "Okay." So I fielded about 15 or 20 balls. He said, "Hey, you want to hit a few?" I said, "Yeah." I hit about 5 screaming line drives all over the field, and everything stopped. Guys stopped playing in the field, and they all started watching. So I hit about 20, 1 right after the other, and suddenly the coach grabbed me by the shoulders, and said, "Man, let me tell you, we'll work something out, we will work something out. . . ." The only school they could play was Louisiana State University (LSU), because of travel restrictions, and none of the colleges around there had enough service people to play. As a consequence, we played all service teams plus LSU. He would tell the opposing teams that we would start our games between 4:30 and 5:00 P.M. They would question why, and the coach

would tell them that his shortstop was in medical school, and when he got here we will start the game. When we had a traveling game, the team would come over on a bus and park right in front of the med school, which at that time was uptown. The bus would wait there until I got out of school. Every once in a while, they would send somebody up there to look through the window to see how I was doing in the physiology experiment, and they would have my uniform on the bus, and I would change clothes on the bus.

Roberts: *How many games did you play?*

Brown: Probably 30 to 35.

Roberts: *How many did you play on Sunday?*

Brown: I played every Sunday. We played in a little dinky ballpark—Franklin Stadium—and the gamblers loved it. We played only baseball (hardball), but the stadium was used for both baseball and softball. Pete Reiser (Brooklyn Dodgers) at that time was stationed at Camp Polk, near Shreveport, and 2 or 3 other major leaguers were in nearby Army camps, and they all came to play. They would pay the major leaguers, and nobody would know it. I rode the St. Charles streetcar downtown and transferred to another streetcar that let me out right in front of the ballpark. I studied my anatomy book during the 45-minute ride coming and going.

Roberts: *You played baseball in the spring and summer of 1945 while attending medical school. What also was happening with you during this time?*

Brown: Sometime during 1945, the first year of medical school was finished and the second year started. The war ended in August 1945, and I got out of the Navy in January 1946. Once I got out of the Navy, baseball scouts began to descend on me. The Giants offered me $25,000 to sign with them, the Cincinnati Reds $25,000, and the St. Louis Browns $30,000. (In contrast, the dean of Tulane Medical School was making a $1,000 a month!) That was a lot of money in those days. My dad had gone east to the 1945 World Series (Chicago Cubs vs Detroit Tigers) to talk to some of the big league teams that were interested in me. He met with Horace Stoneman (owner of the New York Giants), Mel Ott (manager), Carl Hubbell (farm director), and Honus Lobert (head scout). Horace Stoneman asked my dad how much he wanted for me to sign. My dad said, "$52,000." Horace Stoneman said he wouldn't pay that kind of money for an amateur player. My dad said to him, "Well, suppose you had a big league bona fide player, would you pay him that much?" Horace said, "Yeah, I'd pay a big league player that much." My dad said, "Why don't we do this. Why don't we make it double or nothing? If he makes the major leagues, you pay him $100,000. If he doesn't, you don't owe him a cent!" Horace said, "I might do that." Mel Ott said, "Don't do that, Horace. He's going to make it."

My father later met with Colonel Larry MacPhail, 1 of the 3 owners of the Yankees. (He had put together a deal during the war where Dan Topping, Del Webb, and he had bought the Yankees from Colonel Jacob Ruppert. Dan Topping was an heir to his family's fortune in tin. MacPhail got a third of the interest for putting the deal together.) MacPhail, while still in the Army, had met my dad earlier in San Francisco. MacPhail now asked how much my dad wanted for his son. My dad said, "$52,000." (Only 1 other major league player had ever received this large a signing bonus, and that was Dick Wakefield in 1941.) MacPhail said, "You got it." And they shook hands, and that was it. My dad then called and told me. I said, "Why did you do that? They have Phil Rizzuto, an all-star shortstop; Billy Johnson, who was the rookie of the year; George Sternweiss, who led the league in hitting last year; and Joe Gordon, an all-star second baseman. What chance have I got there?" He said, "You will be all right."

At that time, Tulane had started spring training, and the coach said if I didn't go professional and stayed in school, they would give me a full scholarship through medical school. I started spring training at Tulane, but then I signed the contract with the Yankees. Now I had a dilemma. I was about 2/3 through the sophomore year and within 3 weeks of taking the exams in pathology and pharmacology. I had already taken the final exam in bacteriology. The whole class was taking a clinical lab course that lasted from January until June, doing blood sugars, blood counts, urinalyses, et cetera. I was probably 1/4 through that too. I went to Dean Lapham and told him that I had gotten this chance to play baseball professionally. He was flabbergasted. He said, "You are in med school here?" I said, "Yes." He asked, "What year?" I said, "I'm a sophomore." He called his secretary and asked for my grades. I was probably the bottom of the top 25% in a class of 125 students. He said, "Why would you want to play professional baseball? Have you been playing here?" I said, "Yes." He said, "Who did you play for?" I told him "Tulane." He said, "You played for Tulane when?" I said, "Last year." He said, "When you were in anatomy and physiology?" I said, "Yes." He shook his head and said, "Why do you want to play now?" I said, "They had offered me a lot of money to play." He asked, "How much?" I said, "$52,000." He said, "$52,000. What for?" And I told him to play baseball. He sat there and looked at me and said, "You think if you played well, those fools might want to endow a chair in surgery here?" I said, "I didn't think so." He said, "Let him think about it."

By then, the anatomy professor (Dr. Smith), who had terrorized all the students but was really a wonderful guy, had retired from Tulane and became, for a year, the dean of the medical school at LSU. I went to see him because he knew that I played baseball for Tulane. I told him that I had the offer to play professionally but that I really wanted to continue in medical school. I told him that I think I can do both. I said that I had talked to Dr. Lapham and had another conference scheduled with him. He is thinking about it. I asked if he would come down with me and visit with the dean. He said he would. I was also lucky that I was assigned in anatomy to the same cadaver as Alton Ochsner, Jr, son of the professor of surgery, Dr. Alton Ochsner, Sr. I had also played intramural football and ran track at Tulane against Dr. Ochsner's second son, John. John's sister, Sis, at that time was in Newcomb College with my sister, Beverley, and they were friends. So I knew Dr. Oschner and his family well. The professor of anatomy, Dr. Smith, and I met with the Tulane dean. Dr. Smith told the dean that he should let me play ball, and he raved about how terrific a student I was. I looked at him, not believing that he was saying all this nice stuff about me. (Dr. Smith called all his med students "freshman." It didn't make any difference whether they were fourth-year students or new graduates.

It was just "freshman.") When I got out of that room, he looked at me and said, "Freshman, there is just a time or 2 in life when you have to lie." Anyway, the dean decided that he would let me try. I went off to play baseball! That was March 1946.

Roberts: *You went to spring training with the Yankees?*
Brown: Correct.
Roberts: *Where was training camp?*
Brown: St. Petersburg, Florida. Joe McCarthy was the manager. He had been the manager when I worked out with the Yankees right after graduating from high school. At that time, the Yankee scout (Joe Devine) had given me a letter to the Yankees telling them to let me work out. When I showed the letter to the clubhouse man, Mr. Logan, a cranky old man who had worked in the Yankee clubhouse 50 years or so, he told me to go to Newark and work out with the Newark Bears. I said, "No, I don't want to work out in Newark. If I wanted to work out there, I'd have stayed in San Francisco. I'm supposed to work out here with the Yankees." He told me that I couldn't work out here. I said, "You show that letter to Mr. McCarthy and then come tell me." He came back and said that I could work out. He gave me a pair of pants that were too short. I told him that I needed a bigger pair of pants. He said, "That's all you get, kid." I told him they were too short and that I didn't want to go out there looking like a clown. He said that that was it and if I wanted to work out I'd have to wear those pants. I was really steamed when I got out there. The coach, Art Fletcher, asked me where I played. I told him shortstop. He said, "You hit with the extra men. Just tell them that you are supposed to hit with them." Joe Gordon, the second baseman, a terrific player, was pitching batting practice. They told me to go ahead and hit. Although still really steamed, I borrowed a bat and the first ball I hit, a line drive, missed Joe Gordon's ear by about 6 inches. I hit 5 line drives (you only got 5 swings in those days) all over the field. And the guy said, "Keep hitting kid." I hit 5 more, and after 10 hits, I quit. When I walked off the coach, Art Fletcher said, "Mr. McCarthy wants to talk to you over there on the bench." I went over, and he asked me where I was from. I told him, "San Francisco." He asked if I was 1 of Joe Devine's boys, who was the scout. I said I was. He said that I could work out with them anytime I wanted, on the road or at home, just let him know. They would be glad to have me. "Now go in and tell Mr. Logan to give you a pair of pants that fit." I went into the clubhouse and gave Mr. Logan back the pair of pants I had been wearing and told him that Mr. McCarthy said to give me a pair of pants that fit. He never said a word as he gave me the pants!

Roberts: *Now you are 21 years old?*
Brown: Correct. There was lots of publicity about a medical student trying out with the Yankees. There were not a lot of scouts going to medical schools looking for players! Also the fact that I got $52,000 to sign was big news. It was all over the newspapers. But Mr. McCarthy was a smart guy. Rather than playing me right off, I just worked out. Finally toward the end of spring training he put me into a game to hit. I got a base hit.

At the time, many players from the war had come back from the service; 1946 was the first year that they all got back. We had an all-veteran team coming out of the service.

Some of them hadn't touched a baseball in 4 years. Training camp was filled with war veteran players. They divided the players into Yankee A team and Yankee B team. I was placed on the B team. The Dodgers had a B team too. I played every day at shortstop, and we played against the Brooklyn B team and toured all the way up the East Coast to New York. We first played the Kansas City team, which was in Lake Wales; then we went to Waycross, Valdosta, and Savannah, Georgia; then to Columbia, South Carolina; then Charlotte, North Carolina, and then to Virginia. We played the Dodger B team 8 or 10 games all the way to New York City. I played awfully well. I hit really well. When we got to Norfolk, Virginia, I hit a home run with the bases loaded against Norfolk, which was their Class C team—a minor league team. The general manager, George Weiss, came to me and said they were going to put me in Binghamton, part of the AA Eastern league. I said that I gotta start higher than that, and that I wasn't going to Binghamton. He said, "Okay," they would put me in Newark. I said, "Fine." I joined Newark, which was an AAA team. I had worked out there as a 14-year-old kid. I had a great year, hitting .341 in the International League, but I also led the nation in errors (50). Near the end of September 1945, they brought me up to the Yankees, also with Yogi Berra, Vic Raschi, and Frank Coleman. We all played the last 10 days of that season. In 1946, Boston had won the pennant by a large margin, and by the time we 4 got to the Yankees, the pennant had already been decided. The remaining games weren't of any great importance, so I played every game at shortstop except for a couple of games at third base. Yogi Berra also played every game. Vic Raschi pitched a couple of games. I finished that year with the Yankees and hit .333.

Then, I went back to medical school. It was a heck of a year! I had started spring training with Tulane and ended playing for the Yankees. During the 1946 baseball season, I studied pathology and pharmacology because I knew I would take exams in those subjects as soon as I got back to New Orleans.

Roberts: *You came back to Tulane in October 1946?*

Brown: Yes. The season ended around October 1 for the Yankees because they weren't in the World Series that year. I was back in medical school 3 days later. I had to make up the remainder of the sophomore year. The professor of the lab course that I had missed, Georgia Van Langerman, arranged to give me the course by myself. I would show up at 8:00 A.M., I'd spend all morning in the lab. She would outline the work I needed to do; once or twice she would help me. I swallowed that long tube for the gastric analysis and then ran the experiments, did the blood sugars, the blood counts, urinalysis, et cetera. I took the whole course and then the final examination.

The pathology textbook was *Boyd's Pathology*. I had studied that book all during the season, but I couldn't lug the microscope and slides around. I got 1 of the students or instructors to help me with the slides. After about 3 or 4 weeks, I went to the pathology professor, Dr. Charles Dunlap, and told him I was ready to take the exam. I passed it. Then I took the pharmacology exam after studying another 3 or 4 weeks for that one. Then I had the big courses out of the way but was still taking the lab course. Then there were maybe 7 or 8 introductory courses for the clinical years.

There was only 1 lecture a week in each subject—pediatrics, surgery, internal medicine, ob-gyn, urology, preventive medicine, psychiatry, and then 1 final exam on each. I got notes from my classmates and studied them. When I thought I had learned enough to take the medicine exam, I went to see the professor and took the exam. I worked off all the exams of those preclinical courses, with 2 exceptions—preventive medicine and pediatrics. Both professors said they didn't want to give me a special exam. What they would do is mail me the exam in the spring when the class took it. I said, "Okay." I asked if they wanted me to take the exams at either New York University or Columbia and see if someone in the dean's office could monitor it, but they said, "No. When you are ready to take it, just take it and mail it in." I got those 2 exams in the spring of 1947 after joining the Yankees, getting to spring training on time the only time during my 8-year professional baseball career.

Roberts: *When you got back to medical school after playing with the New York Yankees in 1946, what was the reaction of your medical school classmates?*

Brown: They knew who I was. I had been with them for almost 2 years. I was just another med student. Nobody ever treated me any differently.

Roberts: *It's now March 1947. You are 22 years old. What happened?*

Brown: We trained in Puerto Rico for 10 days; then 7 days in Venezuela; then 7 days in Havana, Cuba; and then we returned to St. Petersburg, Florida. I was playing third with Billy Johnson, who also was a terrific player, and we started off the season platooning. I was a little slow getting started, and I was just beginning to loosen up and hit when I was hit by a pitched ball. Mel Parnell, who was pitching for the Boston Red Sox, hit me in the hand and broke a finger. I was out for 3 or 4 weeks. By the time I was ready to play again, the team was on a winning streak, and I never got back in. I had to fill in for the rest of the year pinch-hitting and playing when guys were hurt or sick. I played the whole year that way and hit .300, but wasn't a regular. In the World Series, we played the Dodgers, and I did most of the pinch-hitting. I was up 4 times in the series. The first time was in game 1, with the bases loaded, and I walked. I got credit for a run batted in. The next time I came up, I hit a double. The ball hit the little screen that was attached to the foul pole in Ebbets Field (Brooklyn). The ball hit the screen 10 or 15 feet above the fence, and I assumed it was a home run. As I was trotting around, I saw the right fielder retrieve the ball, and then I sped to second base. I asked what was going on, and the umpire said the ground rule was that the ball was in play. Branca, the pitcher, had thrown 2 fastballs down the middle of the plate, and I hadn't wiggled. I backed out of the box and said to myself that I must swing before rigor mortis sets in. The next pitch I hit went over the fence. I pinch-hit again in game 6 and got another base hit. After 6 games, we were tied 3 games apiece, and our pitching staff was shot. Frank Shea and Bill Bevens, 2 of our best pitchers, each had bad arms. Shea started and pitched 1 and 2/3 innings, and then Bevens got through the third and fourth innings. At the end of the fourth inning, I pinch hit for Bevens. There were 2 men on base when I came up, and we were down 2 to 1. I hit a double, and that scored the tying run and put the go-ahead run on third base. I was on second. We scored the run on third.

Roberts: *Did you score?*

Brown: I got to third base but didn't score. We went up 3 to 2. Then we got 2 more runs and won 5 to 2. Joe Page pitched from the fifth inning on and shut them out. A picture on my living room wall shows my hitting the double. That picture was in the *Washington Post* in 2000 and the Ft. Worth representative in Washington, DC, Pete Geren, now secretary of the Army and who lives across the street from me, saw it. Shirley Povich, a sportswriter, had written an article on the history of the World Series, starting with the first World Series in 1903. Pete Geren, my son's best friend, got the photo from the paper and sent it to me. I had it blown up and mounted with a caption underneath the picture when it was taken in 1947. I never saw it back then. You can see the guys running and I am at home plate just leaving the bat. I can still see the pitch that I hit because it was on the outside part of the plate. I said that it could be a ball, but it's good enough to hit, and I had a line drive down the third base line for a double. There were over 72,000 fans there that day. It was the only time I ever really listened to the crowd, and that was when I was standing on second base. It was a tremendous roar. I knew where my folks were sitting. My dad had on old beat-up hat (everybody wore hats in those days), a good luck hat, and I saw him throwing it up in the air and catching it. That was a heck of a thrill for me. Then I came back to med school and that was my toughest year.

Roberts: *Did the Yankees know that you were a medical student when they gave you that $52,000 bonus?*

Brown: Yes.

Roberts: *Was there any discussion that you might not be able to make all the spring trainings?*

Brown: That came as a surprise to them.

Roberts: *Most of your baseball games were in the afternoon?*

Brown: Yes. We played 7 to 14 night games a year, and they were big events in Yankee Stadium at that time. We had a full house every time we had a night game.

Roberts: *You returned to med school immediately after winning the World Series?*

Brown: Yes. It was October 12. The series started October 1. That's a crucial date. Medical school started September 1. At Tulane, the junior class took physical diagnosis in September. They spent the whole month doing blood pressures, pulses, listening to the heart, lungs, palpating the abdomen, doing ophthalmologic exams, et cetera. The clinical blocks (courses) began October 1 in the third year. I got back 2 weeks after the clinical rotations had started, and I had not had physical diagnosis. I knew my classmates were taking physical diagnosis while I was trying to finish the season. I found a resident at Lincoln Hospital in the Bronx, and he helped me. I tried to go there after games to learn physical diagnosis. It was a big typical charity hospital. I learned something about physical diagnosis, but not enough. I went to see the dean, Dr. Max Lapham, when I got back to med school when my classmates were 2 weeks into the clinical courses. He said, "I don't see how you are going to be able to start since you hadn't had physical diagnosis. What was I going to do? I don't know how I am going to let

you back in?" "You've got to let me back in," I said. "You've got too much invested in me now." He told me to go talk to the professor of medicine.

Roberts: *Was this the same dean?*

Brown: Yes. Dr. Max Lapham, my savior. Dr. John Musser was the professor of medicine when I went off to play baseball, but he had died during the summer I was in New York. Dr. Roy Turner was now the acting head, and I was to see him. He didn't see how I could start either, since I hadn't had physical diagnosis. He suggested that I go to the University of Tennessee Medical School, because they were on the quarter system. I told him that I didn't want to go to Tennessee. "I'm a Tulane guy." He wanted to know how I was going to get physical diagnosis. I said, "Why can't I hire tutors to give me the course while I'm in the medicine block? I can catch up in the medicine block. Put me in with the regular class and let me start even though I'll be 2 weeks behind. I can catch that up and take physical diagnosis in the off hours when I am through with my duties during the day." He asked how I was going to get the tutors? How much would I pay them? I said I would pay them anything they wanted. (At that time, the residents were getting at the most $100 a month.) He said, "All right, let me talk to some of the residents. Come back and see me tomorrow." I came back and he said that he had some residents who would give me the course, but they want $100 apiece to give me the course. I said, "That was easy. I've got the $100."

When I got that huge hit in game 7—it was the thing that turned the series around for us—I came into the clubhouse afterwards, and Colonel MacPhail, who was roaring drunk, put his arms around me, and said, "If you never get another hit, you've earned your money"—meaning the bonus. I had paid him in full with that hit. "You come by the office tomorrow and I'll give you another $500 for getting these hits in the series". I said, "That's great." That night, we had our victory banquet at the Commodore Hotel downtown, and he got into a tremendous fight with the general manager and with the other 2 owners. The next day, I read in the newspaper (we didn't know about this at the banquet) that he has resigned and had sold his third interest to the 2 other owners. I said, "There goes my $500!" I drove by Yankee Stadium before going to New Orleans to see if the $500 was there. I told the gal in the office that Colonel MacPhail had said for me to come by and pick up an envelope: "I know that he's sold his interest so I don't know if the envelope is here." She said, "It's here." She gave it to me and I had 5 $100 postal money orders in there. Thus, when the professor of medicine told me that the residents wanted $100 apiece, I said, "I've got it." I had $500 sitting at the fraternity house.

One of the instructors, Dr. Oscar Creech, later became the professor of surgery at Tulane. I went to the lectures during the day with the regular class, then worked up my assigned patients on the ward, doing the histories and physicals, lab work, et cetera, and after 5:00 P.M., I would meet with the resident until 8:00 or 9:00 P.M. and learn physical diagnosis. One resident would take me to the tuberculosis ward and do auscultation. I would listen to lungs and learn how to percuss the chest and listen for rales. There were maybe 700 patients with tuberculosis in the hospital, and they had every form of lung disease you could think of:

Figure 10. New York Yankee, 1947.

plural effusions, abscesses, infiltrates, et cetera. An ophthalmologist worked with me with eye rounds. Thus, over the next 2 and 1/2 months, I got the physical diagnosis course.

Roberts: *You probably got the best physical diagnosis course of any of your classmates?*

Brown: Yes, it was terrific. In December 1947, I took the exam on the medicine block and the exam on physical diagnosis and caught up with the class. From then on, it became simple, because the clinical years were divided into thirds, and the thirds were divided into sixths. A student could take a 6-week urology course, or a 12-week medicine course, or a 6-week ob-gyn course. I could then return to medical school during the middle of October, and I could pick up a class that was starting then. I always worked Christmas vacations so I could get off a bit earlier in the spring. At the Christmas "vacation," I would go to the surgery clinics, or maybe get all my baby deliveries in. Every student had about 30 deliveries. I would just live in the ob-gyn ward and deliver babies. I also worked during the Thanksgiving vacation and Mardi Gras holiday, so I could pick up about 2 and 1/2 weeks with those extra times. I would leave medical school usually late March or early April and join the team the last 7 to 10 days of spring training, and then the season would start. When I interned, I missed spring training completely but got to New York by opening day of the season. My late arrival was a tremendous handicap for me (Figure 10).

After the 1947 baseball season, I didn't do any physical training or work out during that winter or spring. I was carrying the double academic load, trying to catch up with my class, so physical exercise did not fit into the schedule. I was really out of shape when I reported for spring training

in late March. My dad was really mad at me for getting fat and not doing any physical work. He made me put on a heavy wool shirt and I would get in 1 of those hot metal cinder block garages and throw a baseball off the wall, field it, and throw it over and over again. I would move back and forth for about an hour. I would report to Miller Huggins Field (the Yankees' training site) at 7:30 A.M. and take extra batting and fielding practice to get into shape. After that experience, I never got out of shape again while playing baseball. Back at school, I'd work out 1 hour every day. I would swing the bat and throw the ball so that I'd never have to worry about my arm. I would throw hard every day. I would run, and I would try to find somebody who could pitch to me a little bit, and they would hit ground balls to me. I tried to do that all during the winter. Then, when I would join the team in the spring or early in the season, they would ask when I could play and I could tell them "today."

Roberts: *What happened in the 1948 season?*

Brown: We finished third. The Boston Braves, the Cleveland Indians, and the New York Yankees the last week were all within 2 games of each other, and we lost the series in Boston. We lost either 2 of 3 or all 3 games of that series. I can't remember. Boston finished tied with Cleveland and lost the tie game to Cleveland, who played the Boston Braves in the 1948 World Series. I was back in med school, and went through the clinical rotations (6, 12, and 6 weeks) without any trouble.

Roberts: *How about the 1949 season? What happened?*

Brown: We won that year in Yankee Stadium on the last day of the season against Boston. We were 1 game behind Boston with 2 games to play against them. We won both games and thus won the pennant by a game.

In September 1949, Lois DeBakey, Dr. Michael DeBakey's sister and secretary to Dr. George Burch, called me to say that Dr. Burch would be in New York City the first of October and would like to see a game. (Dr. Burch had become chairman of the Department of Medicine at age 37 after Dr. Musser died. Dr. Burch grew up in Edgard, Louisiana. His dad was a country doctor. Dr. Burch was a brilliant guy. He was a researcher, a good clinician, and although he had played baseball as a kid, he really didn't know much about baseball.) I told Lois DeBakey, a tough lady but always really good to me, that if we were playing in the World Series that I would be glad to get him tickets. We won our division on Sunday, which meant that the World Series would start on Wednesday. We were going to play Wednesday and Thursday at Yankee Stadium (games 1 and 2) against the Dodgers and then play Saturday, Sunday, and Monday at Ebbets Field in Brooklyn. I called Lois and told her when we would be playing. I got Dr. Burch tickets for the Saturday game. On Friday, I called him at the hotel and said, "Dr. Burch, I've got your tickets. How many do you want? Two, four?" (World Series tickets at Ebbets Field, which only had 33,000 seats, were very hard to get.) He said, "I'm going to try and find a friend to go with me? So, I think 2."

I went to his hotel room after phoning from the lobby. I knocked on the door, and he opened it. He didn't invite me into the room. "I've got your tickets, Dr. Burch. Do you need 2 or 4?" He said, "I think I have a friend who will go with me. I just need 2." I said, "Okay." He took his wallet out. It was wrapped with a piece of inner tube rubber from car tires. (They would cut them and get those big elastic bands out of the inner tube. He had 1 of those things wrapped around his wallet, because he was in New York City.) He tried to get this thing off his wallet but I told him that he didn't have to pay. "These are my tickets that I'll just give them to you." He asked me, "Where are you playing?" I told him we were playing in Brooklyn. He said, "How do I get there?" I told him we were playing at Ebbets Field. "All you have to do is go down to the doorman and tell him that you want a cab. Tell the cab driver that you want to go to Ebbets Field. He will take you." He asked me, "Will he know how to get there?" I said, "He will know how to get there." That is the last that I heard of it. It was a heck of a game—game 3. The first 2 games were 1 to 0. The Yankees won the first game 1 to 0 with Reynolds pitching. Don Newcomb pitched for the Dodgers and Tommy Henrich, our right fielder, hit a home run in the bottom of the ninth with no one on base to win the game. The next day, Preacher Roe pitched for the Dodgers and won 1 to 0. I pinched hit in the ninth, and he struck me out on a bad pitch that was called a strike. It was never a strike. In game 3, we were behind 2 to 1 in the ninth inning. The first guy up was Yogi Berra, who got on base. DiMaggio, hitting fourth, made an out. Then I hit fifth with Yogi on first. I got a big hit "in the hole." The next hitter, Woodling, got a base on balls and loaded the bases with 1 out. John Mize pinched hit for Cliff Mapes and hit a double off the right field wall, scoring both Yogi and me, so we were up 3 to 2. Then, my longtime friend and teammate, Jerry Coleman, hit a long fly ball to the outfield that scored the runner from third base, and we went on to win the game 4 to 2. We won the series in 5 games. I had a great series, hitting .500.

When I got back to med school, I went to see Lois DeBakey. I asked her how Dr. Burch liked the game. She said, "You wouldn't believe it! He called his friend and asked him to go to the baseball game with him. I've got 2 tickets." His friend said, "You've got 2 tickets to a baseball game today? Are you talking about the World Series?" He said, "I don't know, there is a game in Brooklyn?" His friend said, "George, you've got 2 tickets to the World Series. How in the world did you get 2 tickets? Nobody has tickets. There are only 33,000 seats!" Dr. Burch said he had a student who plays for 1 of those teams! After I talked to Lois, I asked Dr. Burch, "Did you enjoy the game?" He said, "Yes." I said, "Did you get there okay?" He said, "Fine." I said, "Did you stay for the whole game?" "Oh no," he said, "We left in the seventh inning to beat the traffic." He never knew that I got a big hit in the ninth inning, and I never told him. I just let it go at that. Dr. Burch became a real ally of mine and a very valuable friend. I now have his life story by his daughter on my coffee table. She is trying to get the book published. I've gotten with a couple of publishers trying to get it edited.

Roberts: *You went back to New Orleans in mid-October 1949. What happens then?*

Brown: I was then in my senior year with 2/3 of it to go. I did a 6-week session, a Christmas vacation session, and a 12-week session finishing in early April 1950. The last 6 weeks was a surgery session with Dr. Ochsner. I'll never forget it. The most traumatic thing about the senior surgery

Figure 11. Graduation day from Tulane University Medical School, June 6, 1950.

block was that the student had to do the "bullpen." This was a Saturday morning conference in 1 of the amphitheaters at Charity Hospital. Two senior students had to be there 30 minutes before the session started, and each 1 was assigned a patient never seen before by the student. After doing a 30-minute history and physical examination, the patient was wheeled into the amphitheater, and Dr. Ochsner would quiz the patient and the medical student. The amphitheater was always filled because Dr. Ochsner was outstanding. That was my last class that I had to take to finish. I was petrified. The patient assigned to me was a very obese black lady with obvious exophalmos. Her thyroid gland was going wild. I just wanted to hug her. I got through that session with Dr. Ochsner and then was finished with medical school! I saw Dr. Lapham, the dean, and told him that I had finished all medical school requirements and was returning to the Yankees. He asked about graduation in June, and I told him I would be there. The Yankees had a night game with Cleveland the night before. I played in the game and got in a plane for New Orleans around midnight at LaGuardia Airport. It was a prop plane (no commercial jets then) and it had to refuel in either Memphis or Birmingham. I arrived in New Orleans around 8:30 A.M., and my parents, who had driven to New Orleans earlier, met me. My sister Beverley was already there at Newcomb as a student. My brother Billy was still in school in California. Dr. Lapham had arranged for my gown to be at McAlister Hall where we were graduating. The graduation ceremony started at 10:00 A.M., and

I graduated (Figure 11). When Dr. Lapham handed me that diploma, it was the greatest thrill of my life. (Family events not included.) After the graduation ceremony, my parents drove me back to the airport for my flight back to New York, and I was in the ballgame the next day.

In 1950, the Yankees were in the World Series again, this time against the Phillies. I had a good series. I hit .333. I scored the only run in game 1. I hit a triple in game 4 that knocked in a big run. That was a great year, having graduated from med school and winning the World Series!

I had tried to get Dr. Lapham to come to a World Series. I called him in 1947 and asked him to come. He said that he couldn't do it then but would like to come up some time. In 1949, we played against Brooklyn, and I called him again. He said he couldn't. I told him that I wasn't going to be playing forever and we were not going to be in the series every year. I told him that he needed to come up. He promised that if we got in next year, he'd come. In September 1950, it looked like we are going to be in the series. I called him at the season's end and told him we were playing Philadelphia and this is the year he had to come up. He said, "I think I can come up later in the week." I said, "Okay, we are playing Wednesday and Thursday in Philadelphia, Friday is an off day, and then we play Saturday, Sunday, and Monday in New York." He said, "I'll be up for the New York games." We won the first 2 games in Philadelphia: the first game 1 to 0, and the second 2 to 1 in 10 innings. I then called him and said, "Dr. Lapham, we've won 2 games. This thing could be over on Sunday. He said, "I'll be up there for the Sunday game." We played on Saturday and won. I was put in to hit during the seventh inning when we were behind 2 to 1 and the bases were loaded. I fouled off 4 or 5 balls, and then I hit a tough ground ball into deep short. The shortstop bobbled it a second and DiMaggio, who was a tremendous base runner and on first base, beat the throw to second base. A run scored to tie the game. (They gave the shortstop an error, which it probably was.) We went on to get another run and won that game. We were then up 3 to 0. The dean came in that night for game 4. My mother, dad, and brother were there, and I told my dad that I was going to have the dean sit with them. I said, "If by chance we win, bring him down to the clubhouse so he can see what's going on." I hit a triple right up against the right center field wall late in the game to score another run. We won that final game 5 to 2. In those days, no women, of course, could get into the clubhouse. In the clubhouse some guys would be naked, some had only their jock shorts on, some still had their uniforms on, and some were showering. The press and cameramen with the old-fashion cameras that had the hoods on them were all over the place. The dean looked at all of this going on—squirting champagne all over everybody—and he was bug-eyed. I said, "Dr. Lapham, I want you to meet some of my teammates." I spied Yogi Berra across the room. (In those days we would get long winter underwear and cut the pants off just above the knees and they fit tightly. Those would go on first and then we would put the jock strap and cup on, and then the rest of the uniform.) I took Dean Lapham over to Yogi Berra, who was 5'8", 198 pounds, 1 muscle from his neck down to his toes. I said, "Dr. Lapham, I want you to meet Yogi Berra. Yogi, this is Dr. Max Lapham. He is the

dean of my medical school." Yogi looked at him and said, "You really the dean?" Dr. Lapham said, "Yes. I am the dean of Tulane Medical School." Yogi said, "Listen here, dean, I'm going to tell you something. You've got some shitty school down there if this dope can pass!" as he was pointing at me. I'll never forget that. The 2 of them just thought it was hilarious and I just shook my head. I didn't think it was all that funny. I took Dr. Lapham to the big party that night. Later that night, my brother took him around to the bars in Manhattan. He and my brother felt no pain afterwards. The dean had saved me in medical school, and I knew it.

Roberts: *After that 1950 season, you had to think about where you were going to intern? Had you decided as you rotated through all the various subspecialties at Tulane what subspecialty appealed to you? When did you focus on internal medicine?*

Brown: My hands never worked too well. I wasn't the guy to take apart a watch or operate on cats in the physiology laboratory. I always felt a surgical specialty wasn't going to be right for me. I could catch a ball, and I could throw it, but I never felt that doing stuff with my hands was very good. I couldn't carve something out of a bar of soap very well.

Roberts: *Or surgery just didn't appeal to you too much?*

Brown: Both. I loved surgical problems as far as diagnosing them and trying to figure out what was going on, but the actual operating was not my thing.

Roberts: *Pediatrics and gynecology also were ruled out pretty quickly?*

Brown: I liked ob and delivering babies, but I would not have done well with gyn and the surgical part. I enjoyed pediatrics, but I thought internal medicine would be the best specialty for me. The internships were all rotating at that time.

Roberts: *You didn't have a choice?*

Brown: Correct. I had to find a place that would let me do only 6 months during each of 2 years rather than a continuous 12-month internship. The best friend of the baseball coach at Stanford was the president of the Southern Pacific Railroad (SPR). It was an unusual friendship. The president of SPR came to all the Stanford games. The SPR head office was in San Francisco, but the president lived down in Palo Alto. And, of all things, the president was a Tulane graduate. His name was Mercier. I met him when playing at Stanford. The end of the SPR line was New Orleans. Periodically, he would come to New Orleans in a special car and call me. He'd say, "Bring another med student and come eat with me." He had a special dining car. Another buddy and I would have the best steak you could imagine in his dining car. Thus, I saw him on occasion during all my college and med school careers. The SPR had a 500-bed hospital in San Francisco. SPR had over 80,000 employees. All of their problem medical cases from their entire network came to San Francisco. (They did not have pediatrics, and they had few female employees.) The SPR president said that he would be glad to arrange for me to take a 6-month internship there. The head of the hospital surgery department was a Tulane graduate. He always had 3 to 5 interns from Tulane. I went there and did 6 months 1 year and another 6 months the next year (Figure 12).

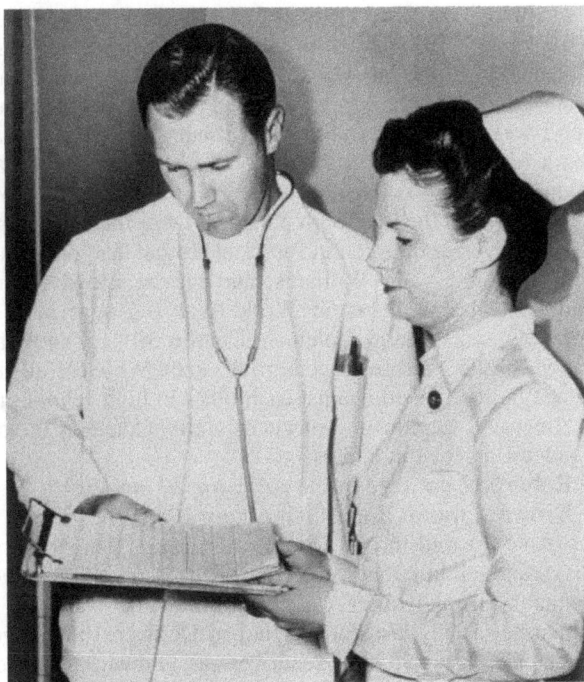

Figure 12. Southern Pacific Railroad Hospital, San Francisco, California, October 1950.

Figure 13. Wedding day, October 16, 1951.

Roberts: *Life sort of eased up a little.*

Brown: That's right, except for arranging my schedule. I got out to San Francisco immediately after the World Series against Philadelphia in 1950. It took me 4 days to drive out, and I got there about the middle of October, and I started the internship. The first rotation was gastroenterology. The internist (Dr. Calloway) running that service was an ex-Stanford football player who had played in the Rose Bowl. He was a big guy and a terrific physician. After a short period with him, he asked me if I was interested in internal medicine. I said, "Yes." He said, "If you are interested in it, the place to go is the county hospital in San Francisco. The Stanford service has half the hospital. The chief of the internal medicine department is Dr. J.K. Lewis. If you are interested, I can arrange for you to go over and visit with him." The following year (1951), I contacted Dr. Calloway and told him that I had to go back into the Army but that I would like to talk with Dr. Lewis, and I did. Dr. Lewis told me he would have a place for me when I wanted to do a residency.

Roberts: *You got married in 1951. What is Sara's maiden name?*

Brown: Sara Kathryn French.

Roberts: *You met your future wife when?*

Brown: It was after the World Series in October 1949, and after my birthday on October 25. She had gone to Randolph Macon College, an all-girl school, the first 2 years, and because she wanted to be in a co-ed college, she transferred to Newcomb, a part of Tulane, but all girls, for the last 2 college years. The girls had their own student council and their own president. The Newcomb girls could take any Tulane course, and Tulane students could take any Newcomb course. When students graduated, they got both Newcomb and Tulane diplomas.

Roberts: *How did you happen to meet?*

Brown: My sister, who is 4 years younger than I, was in Newcomb while I was in medical school. Because I was older than most female college students—medical school took 6 years for me—I asked my sister to keep her eye peeled for possible dates for me with juniors or seniors at Newcomb. She identified Sara. I eventually got a date with Sara, but it took a while to break into the lineup.

Roberts: *What were the characteristics of Sara that attracted you to her?*

Brown: She was a great girl, beautiful, great personality, very much a people person. I was a lousy dancer, and she was terrific. We didn't do much on the weekends. She danced on the weekend with the guys that could dance. But I had the weeknight dates. We would go to the library and study. That was our dates. She was a terrific girl. Always has been.

Roberts: *It must have been very disappointing when you were called back into the service? When were you actually called back in?*

Brown: The Korean War broke out in 1950. After the 1950 World Series, I did 6 months of internship beginning in October 1950. We won the World Series again in 1951, and immediately thereafter, Sara and I got married (Figure 13). Our honeymoon included the drive from New York City to San Francisco before beginning the last 6 months of my internship. We also spent a few days in Carmel before continuing the internship. During both 6-month internships, I missed the entire spring training, arriving on opening day of the season.

The premeds who had gone to med school under the Navy and had been mostly in medical school during World War II were called back into the service. I was registered in the draft board in Long Branch, New Jersey, and there were 3 or 4 other doctors in that category, but I was the only 1 not practicing in Long Branch. They picked me number 1 to go. I got a postcard stating that I was going to be called up and

Figure 14. 160th Field Artillery Battalion Aid Station, Korea, January 1953.

that I either had to enlist or I would be called up as a private. In 1952, I was in my internship at Southern Pacific Hospital. I called Dr. Heaton, the general who was head of Letterman Hospital in San Francisco (he operated on President Eisenhower eventually for regional ileitis) and asked him what I should do. He told me that reenlistment in the Navy would be a 3-year commitment but that reenlistment in the Army was for 2 years. I picked the Army. He said, "After finishing your internship, I will arrange for you to go to Governor's Island when you get to New York, and you can enlist there and they will put you right in. They will probably call you up in July." When I got back to New York, the first thing I did was go to Governor's Island and enlisted in the Army. I knew I was going to be called back up on July 1. Of course, I had to tell the Yankees that I was getting called back up July 1, so I didn't play very much. On July 1, 1952, I was called to report to Fort Sam Houston in San Antonio, Texas.

I was a marked man. My being the third baseman of the Yankees, a physician, and also being drafted into the Army was in every newspaper in the country. I was the only physician in the country playing major league ball. When the new drafted doctors lined up that first day, I had never seen a sadder looking group. We were all in civilian clothes, holding umbrellas because of a rain shower. The captain asked, "Is Lieutenant Brown here?" I raised my hand. He said, "The general wants to talk to you." I went in to see the general at Brooke Army Medical Center. That medical center had a terrific baseball team: all pro players, mainly soldiers. All the professional ballplayers that had been drafted were in the service playing on these teams. None of them got sent abroad. The Brooke Army team had 2 guys, at least, from the major leagues, and at least 6 or 7 from the AAA and AA leagues. There were no amateur players on the team. The general told me, "We'd love to keep you here, but I've got orders from the surgeon general to send you to the Far East. We want you to play here while you are in basic training. But when training is over, you go to the Far East. You don't have a choice." Everybody filled out forms to indicate where they wanted to go, and the most popular choices were Tripler, Hawaii, and Stuttgart, Germany.

Roberts: *How long were you in Korea?*

Brown: I got there October 1, 1952, the day the World Series opened. We landed in Inchon on a troop ship, and I was there until the last week of July 1953. I spent a month in a MASH (Mobile Army Surgical Hospital) hospital, and then I was transferred to the 45th Infantry Division, when I was a battalion surgeon for the 160th Field Artillery Battalion (Figure 14). I had a battalion aid station, and our division was in the line (38th parallel). I was the only major league player in the ground forces in Korea! The only one! Jerry Coleman, Ted Williams, and maybe Lloyd Merriman—all Marine flyers in World War II—were sent to Korea as flyers. (Jerry Coleman, Charlie Silvera, and I all played on the Yankees together for years. We were all the same age and played against each other in high school and in American Legion on weekends. Jerry Coleman is still broadcasting for the Padres.)

Roberts: *You were in the Army for 20 months?*

Brown: I was in Korea until August 1953. The general in San Antonio told me he would call General Shambora in Tokyo and tell him that I was coming. Incidentally, Sara got pregnant a month after we got married and was due in September 1952. We got married in October 1951. I got called up in July 1952 and sent overseas, and while I was en route overseas, our son was born. From Tokyo, I went to a big relocation camp—Camp Drake—where all service personnel coming into the Far East went and then were dispersed from there. I was met by either the United Press or International News Service, and they showed me a radiogram of Sara and my son. To this day, I can't remember if he was born on the 21st or the 23rd of September, because I was crossing the Pacific Ocean at the time. I was sent to Seoul, Korea. I was in a MASH hospital located about 10 to 15 miles behind the line. They gave me a 2-day course in anesthesia. I gave anesthesia to the wounded soldiers during operations. The worst of the wounded were sent to evacuation hospitals either in Seoul, Korea, or in Japan. Each officer in a MASH hospital got 2 points a month, and a certain number of points were needed either to rotate to Japan or rotate back to the States. I was in a MASH hospital located about 12 to 15 miles behind the demilitarized zone. After I was there for about a month, I decided the situation was untenable. The artillery at that time got 3 points a months; the infantry got 4 points a month, and they did not stay on the line all the time. The soldiers were on the line maybe 2 months and got 8 points, and then they'd be put in reserves for a month or 2 and get 2 points for each month. But the artillery got 3 points a month. I said that's where I would like to go. I flew back to Seoul and asked the commanding general to transfer me to an artillery battalion. He sent me to the 160th Field Artillery Battalion, which was attached to the 45th Division. We directly supported an infantry regiment right in front of us with the Chinese a bit further north. From November 1952 to August 1953, I amassed enough points to go on "rest and relaxation." I flew to Tokyo and found out that most of the doctors I was with at Fort Sam Houston were at the Tokyo Army Hospital. They lived in Tokyo, had regular hours, and considered it great duty. It was a hospital with 400 to 500 beds. The hospital personnel took care of all of the wounded arriving from Korea. I decided I would rotate to Japan and get Sara and our son Pete over. General Shambora honored my

Figure 15. Arrival in San Francisco from Korea, April 1954.

Figure 16. Dr. Brown, May 1954.

Figure 17. General McArthur and Dr. Brown, 1952.

request to be stationed at the Tokyo Army Hospital. I was assigned to the orthopedic service! He phoned General Ginn in Seoul, and I returned to Seoul, where General Ginn informed me that I would be out of Korea in 7 to 10 days. At that time, all replacements coming to Korea were called "turtles" because they took so long to get there. When I got back to my division and my Captain, Sam Tashima, informed me that guys usually stay 3 to 6 months waiting for their "turtle." About a week later, he called me and said, "I can't believe it. Your turtle is here! Are you ready to go?" I called the general of the 45th Infantry Division (General Ginder) to say goodbye, and he offered his helicopter to get me back to 1 of the airbases where I could fly back to Seoul. (The jeep ride to Seoul was 8 hours, 120 miles away. There were only dirt roads and many mountains.) His helicopter flew me to a place where they had a Piper Cub, which flew me to Seoul. From there I got on 1 of those big Globe Master airplanes, which could carry 250 guys, plus trucks, crates, and automobiles in the fuselage. We sat up on the side looking down at some 3 and 1/2 ton truck. It was like being in a 4-story building, you were so high up. We took off from Gimpo International Airport (formerly Kimpo International Airport). The plane had 4 big motors. On take-off, the whole plane and everything on it would shake. It took "forever" to leave the land.

In Japan, I phoned Sara and talked, then the phone company would do something to the line, she would call back. I told her to get her passport. Rather than wait 6 months for dependents to arrive via troop ship, I told her to buy a plane ticket. A telephone call from Japan to the USA was difficult in those days because a 2-way conversation was not possible. I phoned and talked; then the phone company had to do something, so she could phone back. A conversation was impossible, the reception was poor. She informed me that she was waiting for her passport. I told her to call our representative to the House of Congress, which

she did, and she got her passport in 2 days. She and Pete, our son, flew over on the Panama Clipper.

Roberts: *When did your father die?*

Brown: It was in 1982, just short of his 87th birthday. My mother, who was born in 1900, died in 1987, also just short of her 87th birthday.

Roberts: *How did you like orthopedics?*

Brown: I was an expert on managing the distal fragment, which meant that I held the arm or leg while the cast was being applied. I did the menial work of orthopedics. I didn't get a chisel and hammer and fix broken legs. I told Camp Drake it had a chance to assign me there when I came

Figure 18. Yankee infield: Coleman, Rizzuto, Tommy Henrich, Dr. Brown, Johnston.

through on my way to Korea. Now I wish to remain on the orthopedic service at Tokyo Army Hospital. I had my residency lined up starting July 1, 1954. I had been away from baseball almost 2 solid years and hadn't played. I didn't play much in 1952 the 2 months before I left to go into the service, so that year was pretty much wasted. I hadn't played in 1953 and missed spring training in 1954. I figured I couldn't afford to stay out of medicine any longer. My Army service certainly didn't enhance my knowledge of internal medicine. I thought that I'd almost have to start over if I went back to playing baseball again. And I didn't think I could go on the 6-month basis anymore. I thought I had to get back into medicine if I was really going to do it. I made up my mind to quit baseball on July 1, 1954, and go back into my residency.

Sara had gotten pregnant with our second child, and although I was due to be released from the service on July 1, 1954, I was discharged in April so that Sara would not have to cross the Pacific Ocean in a troop ship while 8 months pregnant (Figure 15).

Roberts: *What happened after arriving back in the USA in April 1954?*

Brown: I had 2 months off after being discharged in April. My residency was to start July 1, 1954. I went to see the professor at the County Hospital in San Francisco, who was in charge of the Stanford service: the University of California had half and Stanford the other half of the medical service. I told Dr. Lewis that I was scheduled to report July 1 and intended to do that, but I got discharged early and was going to go back and play ball for a couple of months with the Yankees (Figures 16 to 18). I asked if it would be possible for me to start the residency in October instead of July. He said that he didn't think so. He had counted on me to begin in July but if I wanted to play ball that he would release me and that he would have to try to find somebody else. He didn't want me to start in October. I told him the only reason I wanted to try and play the whole season was that it would be another $20,000 or $25,000 for me. He said,

"In 20 years you won't need that $25,000. You won't know whether you have it or not." I said, "You are probably right. I'll be here the first of July." I went back to New York and told the Yankees that I had to quit at the end of June 1954 because I was starting my residency in July. They weren't too happy to see me, because they thought I was going to fiddle around for 2 months and collect my salary. They were obligated to take me as a service man for a while at least. (Servicemen at that time on the baseball teams didn't count as eligible people on the roster.) In other words, they could carry servicemen and not be over the limit. They weren't too anxious to have me play. I called up Commissioner Ford Frick. In the spring 1953, Ford had come to Japan with the New York Giants, and I had dinner with him at the Officers Club in Tokyo with Leo Durocher and his wife, Laraine Day, the movie actress, and my wife Sara. Thus, I knew Ford Frick and he knew me. I called him, and he told me to come right on down and talk to him. I told him I had a problem with the Yankees and I needed to visit with him. I told him the Yankees were reluctant to take me, and he said that he needed to make a phone call. He called George Weiss, the general manager. Frick told Weiss that I was in his office and he told me that he is having trouble getting put on the Yankee roster. He told him, "You put him on today and make sure he gets taken care of." When I saw George Weiss, of course he was mad. He said, "According to rules, we can make you take 10 days of spring training at your own expense." That's what they made me do. I said, "Okay," I would do that. I worked out at the stadium, and instead of their thinking I was just going to fool around, I got out there at 7:00 or 7:30 A.M. and I started running, hitting, and throwing (because I really hadn't played in 2 years). After 4 or 5 days, they saw that I was really serious about training. They were due to take a road trip, and they were still requiring me to take the rest of my spring training time. Nevertheless, they took me on the road trip to Detroit. In Detroit, 3 of our left-handed hitters got hurt—John Mize, Gene Woodling, and Joe Collins—and in the late innings,

Figure 19. Dr. Brown and team manager, Casey Stengel, May 1954.

they needed a left-handed pinch hitter. Casey Stengel, the manager (Figure 19), wanted me to hit and told Coach Frank Crosetti to send me in. Crosetti told Stengel that I couldn't be used because I wasn't on the active players list and that I was supposedly in spring training. Casey was shocked and wanted to know why I was in spring training. Crosetti said that George Weiss was making me pay my own expenses and take spring training. Crosetti said to get me on the active list. That night they put me on the active list for the next day. From that day on, I played. I filled in for anybody who was hurt, or I pinch-hit. I hadn't played in so long, I was really rusty and my timing was off badly. I played in 20 to 30 games during those 2 months. On June 30th, when I was just starting to hit again, I had to quit, since I was due to start my residency on July 1. I played in Fenway Park on June 30 and caught the plane out of Boston about 10:00 P.M., flew all night, got into San Francisco about 8:30 A.M., and went right to the hospital to report in.

Roberts: *As you look back over your baseball career, in retrospect, it seems to me that breaking your finger was a major deficit, because you were right there in major competition for the first team. You were in 4 World Series in 6 years. That means the Yankees were an extremely powerful team, so that on almost any other team in the league you would have played full-time.*

Brown: I was in 4 World Series. I missed 2 while I was in Korea. I would have been in 6. We won all 6. I think I would have done well. I probably would have played a lot more on nearly any team other than the Yankees. My big regret, baseball-wise, is that I never had a regular baseball life, where I could get to spring training on time and work in the winter on the things that needed to improve, which I could have done. I really would have liked to have played under those circumstances for a year or 2 just to see how well I could have played. And at the same time, I suffered in medical school. I was always trying to catch up. I really would have liked to have spent my life in medical school, like any medical student. Fortunately, I did as a resident. I would have really liked to have seen what I could have done as a full-time medical student. I could have been both a better medical student and a better baseball player if I had done either one singly. To do both was a tremendous strain.

I get teary talking about some of these things. I had some huge thrills in the World Series and playing for the Yankees, but the biggest thrill I ever had in my life (other than personal stuff, like getting married and having children) was graduating from medical school. I never got an undergraduate degree: never even bothered after I got into medical school. I can't tell you what it meant to me to graduate from med school!

Roberts: *Why do you think that was such a heart-rending feeling?*

Brown: I had to work so hard!

Roberts: *You never had any time off?*

Brown: Correct. And everybody was saying that I couldn't do it. The only people who said I could achieve this were my folks and maybe the dean. Even 50 years later, it still gets me. I was fortunate to get into Tulane.

Roberts: *But you had done well in college?*

Brown: Yes, I had. It wasn't a question of getting in. It was trying to figure out how I could do both. I asked my dad to talk to the dean of Stanford Medical School in San Francisco because Stanford University was on the quarter system. (The school later moved to the campus in Palo Alto.) I thought that before talking to Tulane, I could work something out with Stanford. The dean told my dad that he had a nut for a kid. He's crazy to try to do something like this. I came up against that kind of attitude everywhere, even inside baseball. It had never been done before. There had never been a person in medical school play full major league baseball schedules. Subsequently, there was one other guy who did it. I told him how to do it and he did. He was a pitcher and he successfully did it.

Roberts: *Who was that?*

Brown: George Medich. He graduated from Pitt, and he wrote to me as an underclassman at Pitt and asked me how I did it, and I told him. We stayed in touch. The only team that drafted him was the Yankees, because they had had someone who had done it. He was a good prospect and he pitched in the major leagues. It was a little easier for him to do it because he could report late. Pitchers can get in shape easier than infielders. He went through Pitt med school and considered transferring to a New York University medical school. I strongly urged him not to leave Pitt.

Roberts: *Among the major league ballplayers whom you met through the years, could you speak a bit about the most talented players you encountered and those who had an impact on your career and/or life?*

Brown: When I reported to spring training out of medical school, I met with Joe McCarthy, the manager. He asked me after I first got to spring training out of med school to ride with him to Clearwater, Florida, for the game. This contact was very unusual. The other players couldn't understand it. He told me that they didn't have any rats on this team. I knew what he was talking about. He said, "We have all good people. We don't keep bad people." The whole time I was with the Yankees, we never had a bad guy. If we got someone who didn't fit in, he didn't stick. They got rid of them within a week or 2. We had guys who got along, guys from every part of the country, all from different social strata, all areas of education. They were all good people. Teammates didn't have to worry about finding someone to go to the movies with or out to eat. Everyone was an equal.

Figure 20. Reception in Tokyo: O'Doul, Joe DiMaggio, Marilyn Monroe, Dr. Brown, and host.

Figure 21. Lotus Club, New York City: Dr. Brown, Sara, and Joe DiMaggio.

Figure 22. Opening day, Yankee Stadium: Bill White, General Colin Powell, and Dr. Brown.

Besides having people who could really play, they were good people.

When I retired from baseball, my teammates often called me about medical problems. That goes on to this day. Most of them are dead now. I still stay in contact with a lot of those guys. That was the thing about the Yankees. We had Joe DiMaggio, Mickey Mantle, Phil Rizzuto, Yogi Berra, Whitey Ford—all Hall of Famers, all great players—and we had 4 or 5 others who were Hall of Fame caliber but just got overshadowed by the others. All could really play, and they could play in big games. We played better in the big games than any of our opponents. It was a joy to play with them. It was an education for me. I played with the best! I got an education in big league baseball that stood me in good stead ever since (Figures 20 to 22).

Roberts: *To show what winning really means?*

Brown: In all-out effort and how to get along and operate under extreme pressure. They cultivated the people who could play under extreme pressure. In every game during the season, the opposing team used their best lineup against us. We were really tough the last third of every game. The concentration developed to operate under those circumstances with tremendous crowds and enormous pressure to win helped me in medicine. Seeing patients with acute myocardial infarction or acute heart failure required my focus as in baseball. One could not make a mistake.

Roberts: *Were the Yankees the first team that ever platooned (putting a left-handed batter against a right-handed pitcher and vice versa)?*

Brown: We platooned because we had so much talent. We had 4 guys on the bench who could play as well as the 4 guys on the field. Fortunately, the 4 guys on the bench hit opposite the 4 guys on the field. That allowed the manager options that other teams didn't have. Our manager could get down to the fourth substitute, for example, in a tight game, and that player was a heck of a player. Other teams would get down to the fourth player sitting on the bench and wouldn't have much. Our manager could throw in 4 or 5 left-handed hitters if a left-hander started the game for the other team. Casey Stengel had great flexibility with his personnel. The Yankees during the 1920s and 1930s didn't do much substituting, because they had 8 guys who were very good. The subs were okay but not equal to the guys who were playing. We had an unusual array of top-notch players.

Roberts: *You still have the World Series record of batting averages for players who appeared at the plate over 30 times, isn't that correct?*

Brown: Yes, that is correct. Of players with 20 or more legitimate at-bats, I have the highest average in World Series play. I was up 41 times and got 18 hits, plus 3 or 4 walks. In slugging average, I'm fourth all time behind Babe Ruth, Lou Gehrig, and Reggie Jackson. When people ask me how good a baseball player I was, I'd say "I was pretty darn good for a medical student!" I am often asked about awards I have. I say I got the award for being the best player in my medical school class.

Roberts: *What was life like off the field from 1946 through 1952? What did you do? Who did you room with?*

Brown: I had several roommates. I roomed with Yogi Berra when I was in Newark. With the Yankees, the first couple of years, I roomed with Ralph Houk, who was 1 of the reserve catchers. After that, I roomed with whomever was available when I got there in the spring, so that changed from year to year. I had different roommates for short periods of time. Because I was late to spring training or missed it entirely, all roommates were paired up by the time I got there.

Roberts: *What did you do when you were off the playing field? I know you were studying a good bit when you were still in medical school.*

Brown: My original medical school class was 1948. I spent part of the time with the class of 1949 and graduated with the class of 1950. I had classmates in every city that I played in, and I would see them. I gave them tickets many times for the games, and I would visit with them. A lot of my time on the road would be with former classmates. We actually didn't have much extra time. If there was a day game and we were playing at 2:00 P.M., we would have to be at the ballpark by 11:30 A.M., and if it was a night game, we had to be there by 4:00 P.M. There wasn't as much free time as one would think. The focus also had to be on the game. I would not want to take a walking tour around town all day and then go try to play a night game. There was relatively little time for sightseeing. I had a baseball teammate from Tulane, Courtney Owens, who worked for the Un-American Activities Committee of the U.S. House of Representatives or U.S. Senate. He took me all over Washington, DC—Mt. Vernon, the Smithsonian Institution, Supreme Court, Congress—the whole gamut. I visited classmates at their hospitals, or I would go to the movies. I didn't socialize much where there was drinking because it wasn't fun for me. I went to dinner with different guys all the time, but most of the time, we ate in the hotels because we were not given meal money. We could eat anything we wanted in the hotels. Management was afraid if they gave us meal money we would eat a hamburger and pocket the extra money. In the hotel we ate all we wanted.

Roberts: *You returned to San Francisco on July 1, 1954. How did the residency work out?*

Brown: It was wonderful. I struggled initially, obviously, because I had graduated from medical school 4 years earlier. Medicine in the service did not help me much. In actuality, I essentially started from scratch. The other residents were good to me. I was on a fast track to catch up, and I worked hard. The professor also was wonderful. By about 6 months, I was rolling along in great fashion. We rotated through the different services; female wards, male wards, emergency room. I was in the emergency room for 4 of the 36 months of residency. It was a 2,000-bed county hospital, and all kinds of acute disease were seen, including much alcoholism, cirrhosis, and delirium tremens. The residency at the county hospital under Dr. Lewis was top flight. Then I took a year of cardiology back at Tulane with my friend

Dr. George Burch, and that was wonderful too. By the time I got out to practice, I thought I was well geared.

Roberts: *How did that cardiology fellowship go? That was in 1957?*

Brown: That was from July 1957 through June 1958. There was nothing formal in those days about cardiology. There were no official cardiology programs at that time. Dr. Burch was very astute, but a peculiar guy. He loved cardiology more than anything else. He assigned me and the brother of 1 of my classmates from the class of 1949 to cardiology at the Veterans Hospital. We had no specific assignments over there. I wondered initially what we were supposed to do. We had certain requirements, such as meeting him in the morning for review of electrocardiograms, and once a week we dissected hearts. Most of the physicians at the Veterans Administration left at 5:00 P.M. The 2 of us then took over. We spent most of our time working nights with the acutely ill patients. We read the hundreds of feet of electrocardiograms with arrhythmias with Dr. Burch. We had few medications then—quinidine and digitalis. We gave quinidine intravenously to stop ventricular tachycardia, but we had no way of doing blood levels of the drugs. When the QRS complex began to widen, we would stop the quinidine. We treated all kinds of arrhythmias that way. We also treated all patients with heart failure or acute myocardial infarction in shock after 5:00 P.M.—the 2 of us.

Roberts: *Who was the other guy?*

Brown: Dan Bullington. His brother, Bob Bullington, also is a cardiologist. Both eventually practiced in Phoenix. New Orleans was an excellent experience. The 2 of us also saw patients in the cardiac clinics in Charity Hospital. I did some pediatric cardiology with a pediatrician who was interested in pediatric cardiology.

Roberts: *Did you really get a lot of time with Dr. Burch?*

Brown: Yes. We went to his rounds. He spent as much time as possible with us. There was a close association with him. Unfortunately, coronary arteriography was just starting. I would have liked to have gotten some training in cardiac catheterizations, but the staff people were just learning themselves, and a fellow couldn't get in there. By the time I got into clinical practice, I had had very little in the way of training in coronary angiography. Cardiology changed enormously during my 25 years in private practice.

Roberts: *How did you decide to come to Fort Worth after your cardiology fellowship?*

Brown: After the 1947 baseball season, I was in my clinical years at Tulane in the medicine block. After working up patients following my sessions with the tutors in physical diagnosis, I would get around to doing my patients' lab work. This was around 10:30 P.M. The chief resident, who was a baseball fan, began showing up in the lab. He wanted to talk to me about big league players. His name was Albert Goggans. He asked me what I thought about Luke Appling. I said, "He was a heck of a player." He hit about .340 that year. (He was the shortstop for the White Sox and in the Hall of Fame.) He said, "He actually hit .347." I said, "You are probably right." Then he would ask me about some other ballplayers, and I would give my opinion and he would correct me on the stats. I realized that this guy was a real baseball freak. He helped me and tutored me in medicine. We became very close friends. After his chief residency in 1950, he came to Fort Worth to practice. I communicated with him thereafter when playing ball. In 1951, he decided that he wanted to do only cardiology. He went to Philadelphia and spent time with Drs. Glover and Bailey, who were operating on patients with mitral stenosis without a heart/lung machine, and some internists who were specializing in cardiology. Then he came back to Fort Worth and specialized in cardiology while I was still in medical school. He told me that Dr. Glover also was a baseball fan. Albert told Dr. Glover that I was Albert's friend and that I played for the Yankees and that I would like to come watch him operate. He told me to call Glover when I went to Philadelphia. So I did. He told me that he was operating the next day at 7:00 A.M. at Jefferson Hospital. I went. I was told to scrub up, which I did. They must have had at least a dozen doctors from all over the world there to watch the operation. Glover opened the heart while it was beating. He had some kind of a well that he sewed on the atrium. The blood would bubble up. I was at his elbow. I could hear the doctors in the back who had come from all over Europe and the US asking who I was. They were told that I was a medical student. They wanted to know what a medical student was doing at the operating table. They were told that I played third base for the Yankees and Dr. Glover wanted to see the game that night.

When I finished my training in 1958, Albert had been practicing in Fort Worth working for about 8 years, and he was looking for a partner. I was interested. When I finished my residency in San Francisco, 1 of the top clinics in town was run by a Dr. Wilbur, who visited at the county hospital and made rounds with us. His father, Dwight Wilbur, had been the president of Stanford University. Dr. Wilbur asked me if I would like to join their clinic, but I wanted to get a year in cardiology, and I wasn't too happy about living in San Francisco. Two young doctors who also had trained at the San Francisco County Hospital (Dr. Sam Bonar and Dr. Wheeler) had a private practice in Palo Alto, and they also asked me to go into practice with them. I was leery, however, about raising a family in California. I told them that I just didn't think so. I wanted to go to Tulane for a year. When I got to Tulane, I talked with Dr. Lapham, who was still the dean. During my fellowship he told me when I was through that they would like for me to either join the faculty at Tulane or head the medical service at Tulane University and take care of the students. Even though I loved New Orleans, the real estate values in the uptown section were high, even though I had enough money to get through my training and put a down payment on the house and be debt free. A good friend from the service, a surgeon in Jacksonville, wanted me to come there, but I would have had to be in solo practice, and I didn't want to do that. When Dr. Goggans asked me about coming to Fort Worth, I came, visited with him, and decided to come. We were in practice together for over 25 years, and we have been close friends forever. We were the only 2 doctors in Fort Worth doing cardiology initially. Within the next 3 or 4 years, we were joined by Drs. David Cristol and Andrew Megarity. By the time I went off to be president of the American League in 1984, our group consisted of 6 physicians.

Roberts: *What was a typical day like after you had been in practice 5 or 10 years? What time did you get up in the morning, what time would you get to the hospital, how was your day spent?*

Brown: I got up at 6:00 A.M. if I didn't get disturbed during the night, and if I wasn't on call. I was usually at the hospital by 7:00 A.M. and made rounds till 9:00 A.M. I would usually have maybe 15 to 20 minutes for coffee with some of the doctors at the hospital. I was in the office from 9:00 A.M. until 5:00 P.M., using lunchtime to answer phone calls. At 5:00 P.M., I would go back to the hospital to see my patients and do consults. It was rare to get home before 8:00 P.M., and most of the time it was after that. We would have dinner anywhere from 8:00 to 11:00 P.M.

When on call I was awfully busy. Cardiology of course is an emergency service. When on call and a patient with a heart attack is in the emergency room, they don't ask if you can get there tomorrow. You have only 15 minutes to get there.

Roberts: *How often were you on call?*

Brown: During the first 5 years, it was every other day and every other weekend. It was tough. As we grew the number of physicians, each of us was on call less, but when on call, we were taking care of 5 practices. It wasn't a question of getting a good night's sleep when on call; most of the time we were up 2 or 3 times. It was not an easy life. The thing that was so tough was that we could never really count on being free. We were always at the mercy of the phone, and if it's 5 minutes to 5:00 P.M. and a patient called, and you were going off at 5:00, you might be hung up for 2 or 3 hours. It wasn't a question of telling your partner to take care of the patient because you were going home. You just didn't do that. You could never predict during the day if you were going to be involved in some acute emergency. I put up with that and did it. By the time I had been doing that for 25 years, I was tired. I thought I could hang in there for another 5 years, but I didn't think I could continue after I hit age 65. Besides, the practice had changed, with all the new technology; I just felt that I was not able to keep up.

Before I turned 60, however, the baseball thing came up. In 1983, Bowie Kuhn, who was the current commissioner of baseball, was not rehired, and the board was looking for a new commissioner. The owner of the Texas Rangers, Eddie Childs, who was an oil and gas man in Texas, asked me if I would be interested in being interviewed to be the commissioner of baseball. I thought about that for a while. (There are very few things physicians can do if they quit practicing. They don't want to sell suits in a tailor shop or clothing store or sell houses.) I knew baseball. They didn't have to tell me what a waiver was or what it was to be released. I knew the rules. I talked to this committee, and they called me back for a second interview. I was asked a lot of questions, but after the second interview, they said that they were looking for a businessman to be commissioner because they were involved with TV contracts, advertising, et cetera. I said I wasn't a businessman. But they told me that the American League president, Lee MacPhail, the son of the owner of the Yankees who had signed me, was retiring. Lee called me and asked about my being president of the American League. He said, "It is a much better job than the commissioner's because it's a baseball job." You hired the umpires, did the schedules, and dealt with stuff that happened on the field. "It's something you would really

Figure 23. Dr. Brown, 1982.

enjoy. The other job was awful." I thought that would be good. I accepted. I started February 1, 1984. He was right. I didn't need a refresher course. We had only 8 employees, but they were competent people. It was all baseball stuff, and I knew it. During my practice in 1974, my next-door neighbor, Brad Corbett, bought the Texas Rangers, and he knew nothing about baseball. He was in the pipe business. He asked me to help him. The Rangers were floundering indeed, they were about to go broke. He asked me initially how much he should offer to buy the club. I suggested $6 million. He finally bought the team for $8 million. Then he asked me if I would help run the team until he figured out what he was supposed to do. I talked to my partners and got a 6-month leave. That was when I had been in practice for about 15 years. I took leave from May 1 to November 1, 1974. I was the interim president of the organization. I did not fire anybody, but got their pension plan started and a few things like that. I attended the major league meetings as a representative of the Rangers, so I met a lot of the guys, now in executive jobs, that I had played ball with. When I became president of the American League, I never really had any significant problems (Figure 23).

Roberts: *The office was in New York City?*

Brown: Yes, we had to move to New York City.

Roberts: *Where did you live there?*

Brown: We lived on West 54th between 5th and 6th Avenues. It was 3 blocks from the office. We had a great apartment. Our 3 kids were all married by then. One daughter and son-in-law lived in our house in Fort Worth, another

daughter and son-in-law lived in Dallas. Our son is a family practice physician. He had graduated from the University of Texas and Tulane University School of Medicine and lives with his wife and family in Graham, Texas. He has been in practice in Graham for over 25 years.

Roberts: *When you were in practice those 25 years, did you ever take a vacation?*

Brown: Oh, sure.

Roberts: *How much time did you take off each year?*

Brown: My office staff forced me, because I would get tight. I had to go away for a week every 3 or 4 months. When I'd start to get upset and mad, my nurse would tell me that I had to get out of town for a while. We have a family vacation place in Destin, Florida, that we have gone to for the last 49 years. We always would meet the weekend after Memorial Day with 3 or 4 families that we were very close to during my school and training, Newcomb girlfriends of Sara's, 3 or 4 families from New Orleans, and my sister and her family, and our family, and then we added another family from here. One of my best friends died of acute myologous leukemia at age 45. We took his widow and his kids there and every year since. At our 45th year, we had about 75 people there over 3 generations. We started with the 3 families.

Roberts: *You took a little more vacation when you were president of the American League?*

Brown: Actually, that was the first item written in my contract when I went to New York. I had 2 items written in: (1) my wife has to go on any trip that I want to take her on (because as a doctor's wife we just didn't see enough of each other), and (2) the weekend after Memorial Day I had to be off that week to go to Destin. Often when in Destin I would have to leave because of a riot in a baseball game, and I would have to talk to the umpires, and suspend some players as a rule. It's always tough.

Roberts: *You did a good bit of traveling during that job.*

Brown: Oh, yeah. During those 10 years, I was on the road a third of the time. But it was easy. Others did the travel arrangements for me—air, car, hotel. We often had the presidential suite in the hotel. Usually, I would get the presidential suite during the World Series as the president of the league. I always traveled in great style. I could do anything I wanted, so long as I didn't abuse any expense account. I always figured that George Steinbrenner was always going to screw me somehow. I tried to stay within my budget, and everything was always documented.

Roberts: *Those were 10 enjoyable years.*

Brown: Yes.

Roberts: *Why did you retire?*

Brown: I had 5 years, then extended for 2, and then again for 2 more, and then for 1 more. I was going to turn 70, and I didn't want to hang around. I am going to be 83 soon. I said to myself, "I've done this job for 10 and 1/2, years and it's gone fine. We haven't had any big problems. It is time to get out." I had enough money to get out. I was well paid; a whole lot more than I ever made in practice. A classmate and close friend from Stanford, who went into the brokerage business, invested my first bonus money and managed it until he died 6 or 7 years ago. Even though I couldn't put much in each year because expenses were about the same as income, I never took any out, and the

Figure 24. Golden Deed "Man of the Year" Dinner at the Exchange Club.

Figure 25. Brown family, Destin, Florida (approximately 1994).

money in my account just multiplied. He told me that I had enough money to retire without going back into practice. So I did. As a major league ballplayer I had over 7 years of service and therefore was in the baseball pension plan, which started my first year. My first year I paid $260 to get into the pension plan.

Roberts: *Did you have to have 5 years in the plan?*

Brown: At that time, yes, but now the ballplayers are invested after 1 game. I have actually 3 pension plans, so I am fine.

Roberts: *What do you do these days? You've been "retired" for 12 years?*

Brown: It took me a day to get used to it. I never had time to work in my yard. Now I do. The thing about working in the yard is that there is never a bad day. No one dies on you. I don't make decisions that are read about in

Tacoma, Washington, or some other place. Every day I can see what I did the previous day. Every day is a good day in the yard! When I retired from playing baseball, I tried to play golf twice. The Wilson Company gave me some Sam Snead clubs, tees, balls, and shoes. After the second attempt at playing, I realized that I had never done anything athletically that helped me with golf. I wanted a sport I could really do. I had hit a tennis ball when I was in the fourth or fifth grade, waiting for the baseball activities to start on the playground, and I had always enjoyed watching tennis. It was hitting a moving ball, which I could do. Sara's roommate in New Orleans was married to the head of the otolaryngology department, and he loved to play tennis. I went to the New Orleans Country Club with him every Thursday, Saturday, and Sunday and played tennis. I learned to play fairly quickly. After coming to Fort Worth and joining a county club, I started playing a lot. Tennis was a perfect type of recreation for me. There were no beepers in those early days. I had to be near a phone. I played for 90 minutes, and that was it. I usually played from 6:00 until 7:30 P.M. and got home by 8:00 to eat dinner.

Roberts: *Do you still play tennis?*

Brown: Oh, sure.

Roberts: *How much you play a week?*

Brown: Four or 5 days a week. I play both singles and doubles.

Roberts: *Do you have hobbies other than your gardening and tennis?*

Brown: No, none. Sara and I travel some, mainly short trips.

Roberts: *Do you go on cruises?*

Brown: No, because I get out of shape on a 10- to 14-day cruise, and then it is tough to get back in shape for tennis.

Roberts: *Do you run now?*

Brown: Only in tennis.

Roberts: *I see you've got a sizable scar on your knee.*

Brown: I ruptured my quadriceps tendon in 1989 playing tennis.

Roberts: *Did you ever have any major injuries during your baseball career other than the broken finger?*

Brown: I had 1 other one that was disastrous. I had a freak accident. I was on second base, and the batter faked a bunt, and I had to quickly scamper back to second base. When I slid back into the base I turned my ankle and ruptured several ligaments. At the time, I was hitting .350.

Roberts: *What year was this?*

Brown: It was either 1949 or 1950. I knew I had a chance at that time, if I kept hitting well, of getting into the All-Star Game. My left ankle was wrapped in a cast, and I was on crutches for 3 to 4 weeks. It was 6 weeks before I could start playing again. Once an injury like that happens in the middle of the year, it's tough to get going again. Those were the only 2 injuries I had.

Roberts: *What about your children?*

Brown: We have 3 children—1 son and 2 daughters—wonderful kids. The great thing about them is that they married people who were as good as they were. We've got 3 solid kids, 1 solid daughter-in-law, and 2 solid son-in-laws, plus 10 grandchildren, all healthy, bright and without problems (Figures 24 and 25). It's a miracle.

My son, Peter Stanley Brown, was an average athlete growing up. He didn't like baseball much. I made him play tennis because I thought he could do that all his life. He quit playing tennis, however, as soon as he went away to college. He loved to hunt, fish, and camp out. My sister, Beverley, married a doctor (Rayford A. Smith, MD), who graduated from Tulane Medical School a year after me. He joined his father in family practice in Monroeville, Alabama, the place where *To Kill a Mockingbird* took place. He and his father practiced there for over 50 years. My son identified with my brother-in-law, because he would have a shotgun and fishing rod in the trunk of his car and during the noon hour would either shoot birds or fish for bass. My son thought that was great. He took a family practice residency at John Peter Smith Hospital in Fort Worth. He chose Graham, Texas, a location that fits all his requirements: <10,000

people, without a major freeway, and where he can hunt and fish.

Roberts: *How far is Graham from Fort Worth?*

Brown: Eighty-five miles northwest. All 5 doctors in his office trained at John Peter Smith Hospital. He loves Graham. He has 4 kids: 3 sons and a daughter.

My second child is Beverly. She lives in Dallas and is married to Larry Dale, who is in the oil and gas business and is very successful. They have 4 children: 3 boys and 1 girl.

My youngest daughter is Kaydee (Kathryn Dawson). She is married to Bill Bailey. He is in the family grain business. They live around the corner from us here in Fort Worth. They have 2 kids: a daughter and a son.

One grandson is soon to start law school, another medical school. Seven are now in college and 3 in high school.

We've got great kids, great spouses, and great grandchildren, and I've got the greatest wife in the world!

Roberts: *Yes, she seems like it. Any regrets at all?*

Brown: My only regret was that I would have liked to have had a couple of years where I only had to play baseball. I would have liked to see what I could have done. Also, I would have liked to have had several years in medical school where I could have been like the other students. Another minor regret is that none of my grandchildren went to Tulane.

When I took the pediatric and preventive medicine exams to finish my sophomore year in medical school, Tulane mailed them to me. I asked if they wanted me to take the exams in the dean's office at either Columbia or New York University. They said I could take them wherever I wanted. I went to Yankee Stadium around 8:00 A.M. and took the pediatric one in the clubhouse and took the preventive medicine test in the Book Cadillac Hotel in Detroit. I am sure that was the only medical exam ever taken in the clubhouse of Yankee Stadium!

Roberts: *I noticed that you were president of the student body when you were in junior high school and in high school and also captain of several baseball teams. You obviously have great capacity for both leadership and friendship with many friends both locally and in various parts of the country. You have won numerous awards, including honorary doctor degrees, et cetera. Of the various honors you have received, which ones are you most proud of?*

Brown: The one that means the most occurred when I was a freshman at Stanford. On Sunday, May 6, 1943, several other students and I went to San Gregorio beach on the Pacific Ocean. The water was very cold (between 55°F and 59°F), so we didn't do much swimming. At that time, the Coast Guard had surveillance planes looking for Japanese submarines. (It was during World War II.) A Coast Guard plane was flying toward us on the beach at a very low altitude, and we were sitting next to a promontory about 200 feet high that extended out toward the ocean. The plane turned out over the ocean and attempted to turn back in the direction from which it had come. It lost air speed and crashed into the ocean right in front us. After a minute or so, we saw a figure floating in the ocean next to the crash. We figured that it was the pilot or somebody else in the plane. It was about 400 yards from shore. (I had done a lot of ocean swimming in the Atlantic Ocean when I was in New Jersey.

I was familiar with waves, and I was a good swimmer. The water was awfully cold, and the waves were high.) I asked the other students if anyone could swim out with me and 1, Bob McClain, said, "Yes." It took us 20 to 30 minutes to get to the floating survivor, who couldn't move. He apparently was paralyzed from the waist down, but fortunately, that turned out to be temporary. We pulled him back in. It took us about 45 to 60 minutes to get him back to shore, but he survived. He was the radio man on the plane. The pilot washed up on the shore a couple of days later. Both Bob McClain and I received the Silver Lifesaving Medal for the rescue. A later book on Coast Guard exploits mentioned this rescue. The rescued man, Henry Kind, recovered in 4 or 5 months, returned to active Coast Guard duty, and later was a policeman in San Francisco. The Coast Guard award has meant more to me than any other one.

I have given 3 commencement exercises at medical schools—Tulane, Southern Illinois, and Southwestern. I'm in 3 hall of fames—Stanford, University of California at Los Angeles, and Tulane. I'm the only person in the hall of fame in 3 different colleges. In 1946, I was named New Jersey's Professional Athlete of the Year for my season with the Newark Bears (International League). That was a big deal for me. I got that during my first year in professional baseball when playing in New Jersey.

Roberts: *Sir, it's been an honor and a pleasure.*
Brown: My honor.

HOWARD BERTRAM BURCHELL, MD:
A Conversation With the Editor*

Howard Burchell was born in Canada in November 1907 and came to live in the United States 26 years later when he went to Pittsburgh to continue his training in medicine. He never returned to Canada thereafter on a permanent basis. A fellowship at the Mayo Clinic in 1936 eventually led to his permanent position at the Clinic in Rochester in 1946. In 1968, he moved to the Minneapolis/St. Paul area where he headed the Section of Cardiology for several years at the University of Minnesota.

Dr. Burchell is a scholar and a lover of medicine. He was a major force in cardiology in the early years at the Mayo Clinic immediately following World War II. He has always been a student of cardiovascular information and a splendid teacher of medicine. His scholarship, creativity, and teaching abilities have brought him many honors, including the Gold Heart Award and the James B. Herrick Award of the American Heart Association, The Gifted Teacher Award of the American College of Cardiology, and the Outstanding Achievement Award of the University of Minnesota. Dr. Burchell was Editor-in-Chief of *Circulation* from 1965 to 1970. At age 90, he still is an avid reader of cardiovascular publications and attendee of cardiovascular conferences. His scholarship goes beyond medical writings, and his medical writings extend to historical vignettes and biographical sketches. Dr. Burchell has great capacity for friendship. His friends cherish his many handwritten letters. He remains the epitome of what a cardiologist or any physician should strive to be.

I spoke with Dr. Burchell in his home in St. Paul, Minnesota, on October 18, 1997.

William C. Roberts, MD[†] (hereafter, WCR): *Dr. Burchell, what I would like to try to do here is to learn more about you. I gather you were born in Ontario, Canada. Could you tell a bit about your upbringing, who your parents were, what they did, your siblings, and what your growing up was like?*

Howard B. Burchell, MD[‡] (hereafter, HBB): Both of my parents came from an agricultural background from farms on either side of the St. Lawrence River. They had come over as immigrants from Ireland in the 18th century. My father left the farm very early, became a school teacher, and then principal of a high school. I had 4 brothers and 1 sister. My father was very interested in our athletic development in school as well as pushing us in our education. We were kind of "proud poor" at that time. After high school, I had doubts that I could get into medical

school and finance it, but my father said, "oh, we can do that." I had been interested in being a physician since a grade school child. I remember wanting to be a medical missionary. I ended up going to the University of Toronto, where I graduated in 1932. My 65th reunion was just last year, and I received a videotape for being one of the survivors of our class.

WCR: *You said you had 4 brothers and 1 sister. Where are you in the hierarchy?*

HBB: My sister was the oldest and she was kind of a second mother. I was right in the middle. My first brother became an actuary and my second brother, a school teacher. Then there was me. My next brother became an engineer. My youngest brother went into the British Navy where he became somewhat of a hero in World War II as Radar Officer to Admiral Cunningham in the Mediterranean fleet.

WCR: *Where is Athens, Ontario, located?*

HBB: If one can visualize the St. Lawrence River going out of Lake Ontario into the gulf, it is about half way along. Maybe some people remember Kingston, which is the place where Lake Ontario empties into the St. Lawrence, and then about 100 miles further along there is a little town by the name of Brockville, then Gananoque, and then Athens is just 10 miles north of Brockville.

WCR: *Neither your mother nor father went to college, and all of your siblings did?*

HBB: My mother never went to college. My father went for 1 year to what was called "normal school" before receiving his teaching certificate. Then, over the next 10 years he finally got a college degree by going intermittently in the summers to Queens University.

WCR: *You were the only one who became a physician? Do you remember what turned you onto medicine? You mentioned that even in grade school you thought about medicine.*

HBB: It always seemed interesting. I had no particular idol at that time as a physician.

WCR: *Were there any particular teachers in high school or junior high school that had a particular influence on you? Did you have any particular mentors who took a particular interest in you and that influenced you a good bit?*

HBB: Actually, my father did, though I was not cognizant of it at the time. He taught science in high school where he was principal, and I was there. I was kind of a "nerd," a good little boy, and did not misbehave.

WCR: *Did you play sports?*

HBB: I was very active in hockey, in particular, and this was supported by the whole community. I remember at the time we were winners in our little local area. The team was scouted by the New York

*This series of interviews are underwritten by an unrestricted grant from Bristol-Myers Squibb.

†Baylor Cardiovascular Institute, Baylor University Medical Center, Dallas, Texas 75246.

‡Division of Cardiology, Department of Medicine, University of Minnesota, Minneapolis, Minnesota 55417.

FIGURE 1. Photograph of H.B. Burchell taken by W.C. Roberts during the interview.

Rangers and I was terribly disappointed that I was not offered a job on one of their farm teams.

WCR: *Where did you go to college?*

HBB: The University of Toronto.

WCR: *What was college like? What do you remember about college?*

HBB: I found it very pleasant. There were no ups or downs at that time. I was particularly interested in the opening up of the tremendous vastness, you might say, of the knowledge that might be attained. Even at that time, I was an avid library patron.

WCR: *You stayed at the University of Toronto for medical school? How was medical school? Did you enjoy it?*

HBB: I did indeed. It was a lot of work, but I liked it. Perhaps, in medical school the person who influenced me the most was *Dr. Charles Best.* When I was in medical school he was made a Professor of Physiology and he was the youngest professor ever appointed. I think he was only 28 or 29. For some reason, he became interested in me and gave me an encouraging word once in a while.

WCR: *This was the* Best *of insulin fame?*

HBB: Yes.

WCR: *When it came time to pick an internship, did you have a hard time deciding what you wanted, medicine or surgery or something else?*

HBB: I think it was a general aspiration of most medical students at the University of Toronto Medical School to apply for a general medicine internship. I applied for that and was accepted. In this particular

track, a person after the first year often went into the laboratory for awhile. I suppose this is partly the pattern of Sir William Osler, though I didn't recognize it at the time. I applied for an internship in pathology for a year and did that at the Toronto General Hospital in the Department of Pathology and Bacteriology. The next step would ordinarily be to go to a senior internship in the same institution, but the Professor of Pathology, *Dr. Oskar Klotz,* had a friend at the University of Pittsburgh who wanted someone to continue work on what I had been doing at the University Toronto. So I went to Pittsburgh. I was expecting to stay there a year, but I stayed 2 years. They wanted me to continue, but after 3 years in the laboratory I wanted to go back into clinical medicine. *Dr. Maclacklan,* my mentor, along with the people at the Mellon Institute, who were producing various types of chemotherapeutic reagents which I had been testing, suggested that if I wanted to be in clinical medicine I should go to Rochester, Minnesota. I applied to the Mayo Clinic and was accepted. The curious thing about that was that as soon as I arrived there my particular mentor was *Dr. Arlie Barnes* who looked at my background and said, "well, I think you should go up to the institute," so I went back into the laboratory and worked on coronary flow with *Dr. Hiram Essex* for a year.

WCR: *You had a rotating internship which included both medicine and surgery. Then you had a year in pathology. Then, for the next 2 years you were really doing research.*

HBB: Right. I also had clinical teaching duties at the University of Pittsburgh at the Mercy Hospital, where there was a ward which was dedicated to the study of patients with pneumonia. At that time, the coal miners in the Pittsburgh area had practically epidemic pneumonia in the winter. There was a ward with 8 to 10 patients in it. The mortality rate of pneumococcal pneumonia at that time was about 25%. I introduced the typing of the pneumococcus. The mortality rate of type I pneumonia was around 20%, and type II, almost 40%.

WCR: *So you did spend 3 years at the Mayo Clinic?*

HBB: That started a long period at the Mayo Clinic. That was when I was I oriented toward cardiology with Dr. Arlie Barnes.

WCR: *He was considered a cardiologist at that time?*

HBB: Yes. All the people at the Mayo Clinic at that time kept their basic interest in internal medicine, but he spent most of his time in cardiology. He had one landmark article on the electrocardiographic localization of myocardial infarcts. He was very interested in getting people to work in the laboratory.

WCR: *A cardiologist in 1939 to 1949 really meant that you knew something about electrocardiography?*

HBB: That is right. I thought, if I were going to be a cardiologist that I should work with other cardiologists at the time, and obtained a position at the University of Minnesota, Minneapolis, campus to work with *Dr. Maurice Visscher.* I was there for about 6 months. Then I went to England for 6 months.

WCR: *What was it like studying in England?*

HBB: The English system of graduate teaching at that time was interesting because you could go to various open clinics, such as the Heart Hospital and the London Hospital and see patients. There would be a discussion of them afterwards. *Dr. John Parkinson* was particularly helpful. He was a gentleman and a cardiologist right on the top of the pedestal. I also studied with *Dr. Bedford* who was interested in the history of cardiology. I suppose that he was an authority on the development of cardiology in France. He became a close friend of mine. Later in life, when I became editor of *Circulation* (many years afterwards), he contributed articles on the history of cardiology.

WCR: *What did Dr. Parkinson have to say about Sir James MacKenzie?*

HBB: He was an admirer of MacKenzie, and MacKenzie's first assistant in London.

WCR: *When you went to London for those 6 months, was it understood that you would come back to the Mayo Clinic and join the faculty there?*

HBB: Not definitely. I told Dr. Barnes that I wanted to go to England, and at that time I had no idea where I was going to be afterwards. Being unmarried, I did not feel any particular responsibility, but after I was over there for about 3 months, Dr. Barnes wrote me and asked when I was going to come back, indicating I had a place at the Mayo Clinic.

WCR: *You joined the Mayo Clinic as a full time faculty person in 1940?*

HBB: It was kind of understood that I would be soon. Initially, I was a first assistant. Even before the Pearl Harbor bombing, I had indicated to the people in Canada that I might go back to its army services, but they said they did not need doctors in 1940. So then I became an American citizen. Right after Pearl Harbor, I volunteered and entered the US Army. Since I had been working at that time at the Mayo Clinic with the low-pressure chamber with *Randy Lovelace* and *Walter Booth,* it was apparent that where I might be most useful, which was at Randolph Field, Texas.

WCR: *How long were you at Randolph Field?*

HBB: Two years. Then I was in the European theater for 2 years.

WCR: *What did you learn in your investigations?*

HBB: I was teaching physiology. We had a course for the flight surgeons, and I started a course for aviation physiologists. I just taught that for the one session. There were people in that first group who were much more knowledgeable than I was. The new trainees were then scattered all over the world to run the low-pressure chambers.

WCR: *What did you do in Europe for the 2 other years you were in the Armed Services?*

HBB: I went to the Central Medical Establishment, which was just a temporary organization formed by the Headquarters of the 8th Air Force for the study of people with various medical problems. My duties over there were threefold: (1) working with individuals

FIGURE 2. Photograph of H.B. Burchell taken by W.C. Roberts during the interview.

who had physiological problems, disorientation, psychological stresses, and combat fatigue; (2) consulting in the surrounding hospitals where the Air Force personnel might have been hospitalized; and (3) working on the criteria for injuries, psychological and physical, that might require the soldier's being discharged from duty.

WCR: *Did you enjoy your tour over there?*

HBB: Yes, very much.

WCR: *It sounds to me like your 4 years in the Air Force really furthered your medical career a good bit.*

HBB: It forwarded my medical career from the understanding of people with general problems. It did not forward my career very much from the point of view of cardiology, though at Randolph Field, I was closely associated with *Dr. Charles Kossmann,* a cardiologist from New York who had trained with Dr. Wilson at Ann Arbor, Michigan, and we talked quite a bit about cardiology. We were the referring center for individuals where there would be a question of a cardiac disability or a murmur.

WCR: *After World War II you returned to the Mayo Clinic? That was 1946?*

HBB: Yes, January 1946.

WCR: *What was it like on a day-to-day basis at the Mayo Clinic in 1946?*

HBB: One worked in a section which took all

types of medical cases, but the cardiac cases were concentrated in 2 sections.

WCR: *At that time were you seeing patients in both mornings and afternoons 5 days a week?*

HBB: The system there was that you had a period in the hospital and during that time you were full time in the hospital. That was somewhat more enjoyable than working in what would be the equivalent of the outpatient clinic. Full time in the hospital then was for about 3 months of the year.

WCR: *It was not long before most of the patients you were seeing had cardiac conditions?*

HBB: I always had a continued interest in diagnosis of general medical problems. Even in the last years I had many referrals and consultations, I was probably seeing 20% of people with problems which were not cardiac.

WCR: *How did you develop your relationships with Earl Wood, John Kirklin, Jesse Edwards, Jim DuShane? Here, they are, these magnificent magnets for attracting patients with heart disease. How did you folks interact? Did you have a lot of conferences? Were you seeing a lot of patients with heart disease that had not been properly diagnosed or someone had given up on? How did it go?*

HBB: My interest in electrocardiography continued. In England during the last year of the war, I used to drop by various English hospitals. I saw a cardiac catheterization done by Sharpey-Schafer and thought that this was the coming thing, relatively easy, relatively safe, and it opens the window to understanding. One of my first objectives when I got back to the Mayo Clinic was to initiate cardiac catheterizations. When I got back in January 1946, the first thing was to sell the idea. The background I had had in the metabolic laboratory gave me the knowledge to get someone to do the oxygen intakes. At that time, there was *Dr. John Pender* in anesthesiology who was putting catheters in veins to introduce an anesthetic in a more efficient way. He had established a reputation of being able to get into any vein. The first group was John Pender, myself, and a technician from what was called the metabolic laboratory, and we did the first catheterization at the Mayo Clinic. In a way, it was a demonstration case to indicate its feasibility within a large institution as well as a diagnostic procedure. A patient came along with an atrial septal defect. At the time, we were pretty certain of our diagnosis from the point of view of the ausculatory findings and the chest x-ray. This patient of *Dr. Charles Mayo* also had gallstones. I suggested that we might catheterize this patient before surgery, indicating it might give me an even better ability to appraise the cardiac risk. I was exaggerating a little bit. It was done and it went very smoothly. We established the fact that there was a big shunt at the atrial level, and that helped to convince my colleagues that the procedure was feasible, safe, and diagnostic. At that time, it so happened that *Dr. Earl Wood*, who had been very busy during the war years on research of the physiology of ''blackout'' on the human centrifuge at the Mayo Clinic, was beginning to look for something else to do. When I suggested that he might take on the cardiac catheterization laboratory, he did. He revolutionized the way cardiac catheterization was done by the development of oximeters so that the blood oxygen content could be determined without having to send a sample to the laboratory. Then he improved techniques to measure the intravascular pressures.

At the time, *Raymond Pruitt,* a medical fellow about 8 years my junior, had developed an interest in electrocardiography and I suggested he might go to study electrocardiography under Frank Wilson, which he did. When he came back, he and I worked together on recording intracardiac electrograms.

Jesse Edwards was recruited in early 1946 when he got out of the Army. He came to the clinic with the idea that he might do cancer research, but somehow Dr. Arlie Barnes, in concert with *Dr. Kernohan* of the Department of Pathology, got him interested in the collection of congenital hearts that were there.

WCR: *You actually got the cardiac catheterization laboratory up and running after you came back to the Mayo Clinic in January 1946?*

HBB: That gives me a little bit too much credit. I arranged the first catheterization and got it running on a regular schedule.

WCR: *Where was the catheterization laboratory first located?*

HBB: In the Medical Science Building, which was connected by a tunnel to the downtown hospital. It was in a nonclinical building. You had to bring the patient from the hospital, perhaps from the Clinic, and then back. It had some disadvantages, particularly when we were doing very young children. The second laboratory was established later in the St. Mary's Hospital and *Dr. Jim DuShane* and others were responsible for that.

WCR: *When was the first cardiac catheterization at the Mayo Clinic?*

HBB: It was the first week of November 1946.

WCR: *So it took awhile to get this going? You left the Mayo Clinic in 1969? How many cardiac catheterization laboratories were present at the Mayo Clinic when you left?*

HBB: There were 2. When I left, the one in the Medical Science Building was still running for adult catheterizations and the one at St. Mary's Hospital was largely, if not entirely, for pediatric cases. *Jeremy Swan* was instrumental in expanding St. Mary's hospital catheterization activities. *Kincaid* and *George Davis* added intracardiac angiocardiography, and *Robert Frye* expanded the coronary arteriography. Many others including *Sabu Rahimtoola* and *Ben McCallister* were wonderful collaborators.

WCR: *When you came back to the Mayo Clinic in 1946, the only intrathoracic cardiovascular operations being done at that time, I gather, were closure of patient ductus arteriosus, resection of coarctation of aorta, pericardial resection, and mitral valvulotomy? Rapid developments occurred. What happened early on?*

HBB: Dr. Wood and Dr. Code had their PhD's from the University of Minnesota, and even in 1939 we were dreaming of direct-vision intracardiac repair. One of the projects I did with Dr. Visscher before the war was to look at a new type of oxygenator and he said, "what can you do here to make this work better?" I worked with it for awhile, but I was not very successful. The main problem was to prevent blood frothing. Even in the mid 1940s cardiopulmonary bypass was kind of a dream, and when I was in the service, people I met from Sweden, France, and Belgium were thinking along the same lines. At the forefront were the surgeons at the University of Minnesota. The cross circulation procedure pioneered by *Dr. Walton Lillehei* was a tremendous advance. The development of the bubble oxygenator thereafter was good, too. There was some competition between who might do the first cardiopulmonary bypass operation with an artificial heart–lung machine, either Rochester, Minnesota, or Minneapolis, Minnesota. Interest in doing this existed also in Detroit, Stockholm, and Paris and probably in other centers.

WCR: *But the first one was actually done in Philadelphia?*

HBB: Yes.

WCR: *But it spread immediately. The Mayo Clinic pump was simultaneously being developed?*

HBB: Right, it was patterned after the Gibbon machine. This is where *Dr. John Kirklin* came prominently into the picture. An engineer who came from Minneapolis, *Richard Jones,* contributed tremendously to the project. The first open heart operation with the heart–lung apparatus in Rochester, I remember very well, on March 22, 1955. That was over 2 years after the first one was performed in Philadelphia.

WCR: *What cardiac condition did that first patient have?*

HBB: It think it was a ventricular septal defect.

WCR: *What was it like on a day-to-day basis by 1950 at the Mayo Clinic? What were your activities like? Were you seeing patients primarily? How many conferences did you have a week?*

HBB: I was seeing patients primarily. We had a number of conferences. I had an informal electrocardiographic conference during the noon hour several times a week. I would be reading electrocardiograms and people who were interested would drop in and we would discuss them. We had a weekly clinicopathological conference with Dr. Jesse Edwards. Then, we had a review of catheterizations with Earl Wood once a week.

WCR: *Those were taking place primarily at noon time?*

HBB: Yes. We also had one cardiac conference that started at 8:00 A.M.

WCR: *What was your actual schedule with patients? When did you see patients, 9 to 12, 1 to 5? How did it actually work?*

HBB: The people at the desk would arrange for patients to come in at certain hours, but it was a very loose schedule. There would be some patients that would be put in a room for a consultation and the signal was right there and those lights indicated that that patient was waiting for you.

WCR: *So it was a very efficient system of seeing patients?*

HBB: The patients might not say that because there were often quite long waiting periods, but it was efficient from the point of view of the fact that the patient was satisfied because when they were seen, they were not hurried.

WCR: *How many cardiologists were at the Mayo Clinic in the early 1950s? You mentioned Ray Pruitt.*

HBB: There were 2 sections. I think there were 5 physicians in each section. Then, there was also a section in hypertension which was headed by *Ed Allen, Nelson Barker,* and *Edgar Hines.* There were 5 in that section also. They took care of those patients who had special problems in high blood pressure. I regarded them as circulation specialists, even though they were not specialists in hearing the heart sounds and murmurs.

WCR: *After surgery on patients with cardiopulmonary bypass was begun in 1955, I assume the number of patients coming to the Mayo Clinic with cardiovascular disease must have skyrocketed. Was that the situation?*

HBB: I don't know if it would be equivalent to the influx of patients with congenital heart disease that occurred at The Johns Hopkins Hospital, for instance, after the Blalock-Taussig shunt, but certainly there were more and more patients coming for a diagnosis. The numbers increased rapidly; "skyrocketed," would be an exaggeration.

WCR: *In 1965, you became editor of* Circulation *and were editor for 5 years? You were required to step down after 5 years. As you look back over your editorship, did you enjoy it, was it a pleasant experience?*

HBB: Very much so. One reason it was acceptable, you might say, "to step down" was the fact that for me it was a 7-day business. When offered the editorship, I discussed it with administration at the Clinic. I told them that I would like to continue doing clinical work, but wished that to be half time. Thus, I had the mornings for *Circulation* and the afternoons for patients. It turned out that I was working evenings and weekends rather constantly with *Circulation* affairs, but that was enjoyable. I developed contacts with many physicians around the country. When I went to the University of Minnesota in 1968, I asked an epidemiologist (*Henry Blackburn*) and a pediatric cardiologist (*Ray Anderson*) to join me as Associate Editors.

WCR: *You left the Mayo Clinic in 1968 for the University of Minnesota in Minneapolis?*

HBB: After early retirement from the Mayo Clinic in 1968 at age 60, I went to the Department of Medicine to work with *Richard Ebert.* At that time, there was no separation of specialties in the Department of Medicine. There were people in the department, of course, in various subspecialties, but there were no administrative sections. After I came, Dr. Ebert instituted the separation of sections. I was there about a year when sections were established in the subspecialties. Then I became Head of the Cardiac Section in the

Department of Medicine. During this time I had some periods of study abroad—sabbaticals. I had one in Scotland and one in Holland. In Holland, in particular, I became very close to *Dr. Dirk Durrer.* He established a heart institute in Amsterdam.

WCR: *What did you do in Scotland?*

HBB: Teaching and research conferences.

WCR: *Where was that?*

HBB: That was at St. Andrews University. The clinical work was done across the river in the city of Dundee.

WCR: *Why did you decide to take early retirement from the Mayo Clinic and move to Minneapolis?*

HBB: I was interested in undergraduate education and just curious. I thought people in Rochester did not need me particularly.

WCR: *How did it work out?*

HBB: It worked out well. I was very lucky in 2 ways: first, in respect to my health and also my family. I wondered what might happen if I became sick or disabled. I took some financial loss coming to Minneapolis.

WCR: *Both you and John Kirklin left the Mayo Clinic about the same time?*

HBB: Yes. He was tempted to go to Birmingham because it was going to be "the Harvard of the South," and I understood that he was offered practically anything he wanted. He established an outstanding cardiac surgery program there.

WCR: *Jesse Edwards had left the Mayo Clinic in 1960?*

HBB: Yes.

WCR: *After you resigned as Chief of the Section of Cardiology at the University of Minnesota, you remained active in teaching and writing?*

HBB: At the time I accepted the position, it was not a division, it was a section. Initially, I thought someone else would be coming soon. The one who finally came was *Jay Cohn.* He really made the group a division instead of a section. He developed a terrific program.

WCR: *How do you now compare the atmosphere at the University of Minnesota with the atmosphere at the Mayo Clinic?*

HBB: They are certainly different. At the time I was leaving the Clinic, a visitor came and when he had learned I was going he said "why are you leaving here? It's like taking off from a beautiful cruise ship into a large working freighter," indicating that I would find things different. Things at the University were not as well organized, perhaps did not go so smoothly in regard to patients. The emphasis at the University of Minnesota was on laboratory research; at the Mayo Clinic the emphasis was on the care of the patients. I was comfortable, however, in both places. I liked them both; they were just different.

WCR: *As you look back over your career, what activities brought the greatest pleasure to you? What are you most pleased with in what you have done professionally?*

HBB: I suppose it is my associations and perhaps making some minor contributions to new approaches.

I have been long interested in electrocardiography. I think maybe I made some little contributions in the diagnosis of arrhythmias and myocardial injuries. When I was in Amsterdam in about 1960, Dick Durrer and I were particularly interested in the Wolff-Parkinson-White syndrome which, as you know, is a type of electrocardiographic abnormality associated with arrhythmias, and caused by "bypass" across the atrioventricular groove or some area close to the bundle. We were thinking at that time of ablation techniques. We theorized that we could do this with an ablation by recording simultaneously from the atrial side and the ventricular side, and ablated where we had identified the location of the bypass tract.

WCR: *I presume that you always were on salary both at the Mayo Clinic and at the University of Minnesota? What is your view about cardiologists and cardiac surgeons being on fee-for-service compensation? In other words, when you can charge x-dollars to do a cardiac catheterization and you get paid a good bit for that, there might be an added incentive to do the catheterization, whereas if you are on salary, whether you do a cardiac catheterization or not, you are going to get the same salary. Do you think money is too influential now in cardiovascular judgments?*

HBB: That is a difficult question to answer "yes" or "no." I believe in a fee-for-service system, as a philosophy, but I really think it would be better if physicians were on salary. I have a daughter now who is in internal medicine and she is on a fee-for-service. She does all right. Actually, she has a business head, which probably I never had. I have always thought myself very, very lucky because I was doing the things I wanted to do and did not have to worry about how I was getting my living. I liked being on a salary. I was looked at benevolently, you might say, by the people who were paying my salary.

WCR: *When did you marry?*

HBB: In 1941. When I went into the Army, I more or less said goodbye to my girlfriend, the person who was closest to me. I told Margaret: "Well, I am going into the Army and therefore you had better put off any ideas of getting married until after this confrontation is over." She had different ideas and said she would like to get married and came down to visit me in Texas. We were married in the chapel at Randolph Field.

WCR: *You had how many children?*

HBB: Four.

WCR: *What do your children do?*

HBB: Of the 4 girls, the oldest went to Radcliffe and studied genetics. As a senior, she was married, graduated from Barnard. She had 2 children, and then she went to medical school and is practicing internal medicine in New Jersey. The second one went to Smith College in Massachusetts and left in her senior year. That was a time of the Vietnam war problems. She became a potter, an artist, and is doing very well, but different. The third one went to Stanford University. Her husband, Richard Patterson, is a Professor of Philosophy at Emory University, and she also teaches history there. They both have tenure at Emory. The last one went to Stanford University also, studied botany, and ended up at the University of Virginia, where she is now. She is not teaching, but she has a family and is married to a biologist, Henry Wilbur.

WCR: *So you have very scholarly offspring?*

HBB: Yes.

WCR: *How did you meet your wife?*

HBB: A blind date in Rochester, Minnesota.

WCR: *Is she a scholarly person?*

HBB: Yes, I think so. She went to Smith and majored in sociology and then became a nursery school teacher. She established a nursery school in Rochester.

WCR: *I have always thought of you as a very scholarly physician and one who enjoyed medicine for the enjoyment of it, in addition to what you do for people. You have written a number of articles on important figures in medicine. You have been interested in the history of medicine for many years. How did that come about?*

HBB: I guess I just drifted into it. I remember in medical school going to one class where the Professor of Pathology had said that King George II had syphilitic aortitis and then went into another class where the professor said he had ruptured his heart. That was my first case study in history. I found that King George II did indeed rupture his heart, his right ventricle, and he also had a dissecting aneurysm. At that time, *Mr. Thomas Keys* worked in the History of Medicine Department at the Mayo Clinic, and we reported that story together. I became very interested in eponyms and wondered who the person was from whom a disease might have been named.

WCR: *I noticed that you wrote a piece on William Ernest Henley. Who was he?*

HBB: He wrote the poem about the problems of having a disability, probably a tuberculous infection of his foot and ankle. He was in the Edinburgh Infirmary for a long time as a patient of Dr. Lister. Henley then became a poet, a literary man at the time of Sir Walter Scott.

WCR: *The piece entitled, "The Other Wise Man." What is that about?*

HBB: It was a story by Henry Van Dyke about an individual who started out to find Christ by following the stars. But during his search he had many diversions and those diversions were caused by his doing his duty to his fellow man. He was delayed in his search for Christ, arriving only at the crucifixion ending. I compared that story to the general practitioner who often did not get to the medical meetings and things like that because he was looking after patients at home.

WCR: *What about the piece on "Hedgehog and Foxes"?*

HBB: This caught my attention because of a little book Isach Berlin had written by that title, based on Tolstoy, a story of war and peace. This was an attempt to sort out individuals with a different approach to life. It goes something like this: the fox knows many things, the hedgehog but one. Which would be better, the one who had many little approaches to things or an individual who is motivated by a single principle.

WCR: *Which side did you come down on?*

HBB: I couldn't decide.

WCR: *You wrote a piece on "Osler: In Quest of the Gnostic Grail in Morbid Anatomy"? What does that mean?*

HBB: What was it that "drove" Osler in his professional life? Pathology was the prime basis of Osler's knowledge. As you and probably everyone else knows, after Osler graduated from medical school, he studied pathology and did literally hundreds of postmortems. It was from this source of information I think that he became so knowledgeable in disease processes and the clinical manifestations of those diseases.

WCR: *You wrote a piece on Sir Thomas Lewis. Do you consider Sir Thomas Lewis a great man?*

HBB: Oh, I do indeed. I went to some of his clinics when I was in England in 1939. Lewis was a tremendous individual and he said of himself, "I am not a clinician primarily," though he said he could do that, but he was "a clinical investigator." The very first clinic of Lewis' that I went to, he had actually discussed cases. He picked me out for some reason. I think it was the fashion of many of the top medical teachers in England to try "to pick on" Americans, maybe because Americans were thought of as not being real scholars. He said, "Well, Burchell, as an American, what do you know about this?" I answered, "not much." He was talking about the auscultatory findings in mitral stenosis, that old story. Lewis said, "People really can't say this person has a presystolic murmur. It *is* a presystolic murmur, but they don't know that. All they know is that they hear that noise complex of the first sound and they know from phonocardiographic records that it is presystolic; however, when they listen to the patient they don't know that is a presystolic from listening."

WCR: *You have encountered a number of important figures in cardiovascular disease in the past 60 years. You must have met most of them. Who strikes you in these last 60 years of men and women that you have encountered as way above the pack?*

HBB: There are a number, of people, of course, who were exceptionally good. With my early laboratory background, I was initially more active in the American Physiological Society than the American Heart Association. I got to know *Paul White* pretty well because he and I were on the Heart Council together. I never met or got to know *Samuel Levine*. Many people from Boston say that Dr. Levine was the greatest cardiologist, but I never knew him. I liked and admired *Howard Spraque* and *"Coke" Andrus*. An individual who stands out from Philadelphia, who I thought was exceptionally good from a clinical point of view, was *Francis Wood*. Then, from serving on various research committees, I was privileged to get to know *Louis Katz*. I had a tremendous respect for him. There were so many who were leaders. I suppose Paul White would the person in this country who stands out predominantly in my mind. *Arlie Barnes* from the Mayo Clinic was an individual with tremendous insight and a great supporter of research. They were all Presidents of the American Heart Association.

WCR: *What characteristics of Paul Dudley White made him stand out so much in your mind now?*

HBB: He was one of the first persons who said as a young man, ''I am going to be a heart specialist.'' Early in his career, White did basic research work as a student with Sir Thomas Lewis. Many of his articles were case reports with unusual things enlightening the physiological and pathological background of those conditions. He was very public-health oriented. That particular activity may have stemmed from his knowledge of the work of the New York Heart Association. That Association started cardiac clinics for the poor, and then from those clinics, particularly those focusing on rheumatic fever, the concept emerged that certain cardiac diseases could be prevented. Paul White gave great support to *Ancel Keyes* at the beginning of the now famous 7 country study. *Frank Wilson* in Ann Arbor was outstanding in electrocardiography.

WCR: *What do you do most of the time now?*

HBB: You can see I am surrounded by books. I read a great deal. I cannot keep up with the cardiological literature, of course. I go to the History of Medicine Library a couple of times a week, look for various things, and I still go to grand rounds if it is on a cardiac subject. I go to the clinicopathologic correlation conferences. I am as addicted to clinicopathological conferences as some people are to opera, because one can really see life played out there.

WCR: *Did you enjoy the year you spent entirely in pathology?*

HBB: Yes.

WCR: *What did you do mainly? Autopsies?*

HBB: I spent most of the time doing autopsies.

WCR: *That background made working with Jesse Edwards a given, almost.*

HBB: You could say that. I could recognize which was the right and left ventricle. I mentioned that because with the more or less complete disappearance of postmortems, I don't think students know what the heart is like, and this came up in relation to what the candidates knew when they came for the accreditation examination for cardiology. When I took that accreditation cardiovascular discourse in 1939, pathology was something you could choose to do. You were able to coast through it pretty well. When I later came on the accreditation board, we really established a thorough examination with 2 cases and 2 examiners, one of whom was just a ''standby'' and supporter of the students to a certain extent when the other man was quizzing. Then there were short tests of about 15 minutes each in separate rooms. Routine electrocardiograms were passed out. Then heart specimens were shown. Then there were radiographs, pharmacology, and cardiac catheterization data. Some candidates would not be able to tell anything about the heart specimen. Most knew how the heart worked but most did not know what it looked like.

WCR: *As you look back is there anything professionally you would have liked to have done that you were not able to do?*

HBB: Of course, I would have liked to have done things better. Maybe developed better electrocardiographic equipment for the study of arrhythmias at the time of surgery. The people at Duke really did this so well, and they had the equipment and knowledge that surpassed my abilities back in the 1960s.

WCR: *Do you have hobbies other than medicine? I presume the history of medicine is a hobby to you.*

HBB: That is right.

WCR: *Do you have other hobbies?*

HBB: I used to care about fishing and hunting. Earl Wood is a great hunter. I never went deer hunting with him, but many times we went game hunting and duck hunting together. I had a dog ordinarily. In fact, one time I had one of the outstanding retrievers in Minnesota. I used to go to hunting trials.

WCR: *How much time off did you take off, as a rule, when you were at the Mayo Clinic? Did you get a month a year off?*

HBB: It depended upon the length of service. I think you started when you went on staff, getting 3 weeks' vacation, and 2 weeks travel time for meetings. Then, after a certain period of time, maybe it was 10 years on the staff, you got a month off. After 20 years, I think you got 6 weeks off. I was extremely fortunate. When I got up to having 4 to 6 weeks off a year, I used to go back to the laboratory for about half of that time. For 2 or 3 weeks, Ray Pruitt and I would get clinical experiments done in relation to excitation patterns.

WCR: *Did your whole family go on family vacations when your kids were growing up?*

HBB: Yes, we used go on skiing vacations as a family practically every year. One year we saved up to go to a ranch for a couple of weeks one summer.

WCR: *You have had a happy life?*

HBB: Yes. I have been very fortunate.

WCR: *You see your daughters very much now?*

HBB: No, not very much. They have their own things to do and they shouldn't come to see me. They have too many things to do.

WCR: *How many grandchildren do you have?*

HBB: Nine. Three have graduated from college and 2 have just begun.

WCR: *Is your wife healthy?*

HBB: Yes.

WCR: *So you are 90?*

HBB: I will be 90 in November 1997.

WCR: *What is your wife's age?*

HBB: She is 80, so a 9- to 10-year difference depending on the time of year.

WCR: *Do you ever go south in the wintertime to get warm?*

HBB: I was again fortunate in being offered opportunities to take a period at Stanford and for 7 years I went out there for the winter quarter. Donald Harrison invited me. What I did out there was have open-room discussions with the cardiac fellows. Occasionally, I made rounds. For 2 years I went to the University of Arizona for a period, so that was nice also.

WCR: *You must have gotten many invitations to go here and there to speak. I gather you had to limit* *that a good bit, particularly when you were at the Mayo Clinic. Is that right?*

HBB: I did not have to limit it a great deal. I made choices of course. I was able to go where I really wished to go.

WCR: *Do you enjoy traveling?*

HBB: I did. I don't enjoy it any more. I am happy at home with a familiar environment. I have a hearing problem and it is so much easier being at home.

WCR: *Dr. Burchell, it has been a pleasure. I have been privileged to have this opportunity to talk with you.*

HBB'S BEST PUBLICATIONS AS SELECTED BY HBB

2. Burchell HB, Barnes AR, Mann FC. The electrocardiographic picture of experimental localized pericarditis. *Am Heart J* 1939;18:133–144.

3. Burchell HB. Adjustments in coronary circulation after experimental coronary occlusion with particular reference to vascularization of pericardial adhesions. *Arch Int Med* 1940;65:240–262.

8. Barnes AR, Burchell HB. Acute pericarditis simulating acute coronary occlusion, a report of fourteen cases. *Am Heart J* 1942;23:247–268.

12. Burchell HB. Observations on additional instances of a supernormal phase in the human heart. *J Lab Clin Med* 1942;28:7–11.

17. Pruitt RD, Burchell HB, Barnes AR. The anoxia test in the diagnosis of coronary insufficiency, a study of 289 cases. *JAMA* 1945;128:839–845.

21. Burchell HB, Glagett OT. The clinical syndrome associated with pulmonary arteriovenous fistulas, including a case report of a surgical cure. *Am Heart J* 1947;34:151–162.

22. Burchell HB. Cardiac manifestations of anxiety. *Proc Staff Meet, Mayo Clin* 1947;22:433.

32. Burchell HB, Pritt RD, Barnes AR. The stress and the electrocardiogram in the induced hypoxemia test for coronary insufficiency. *Am Heart J* 1948;36:373–389.

42. Burchell HB. An evaluation of esophageal electrocardiograms in the diagnosis of healed posterior myocardial infarction. *Am J Med Sc* 1948;216:492–500.

57. Burchell HB. Sino-auricular block, interference dissociation, and different recovery rates of excitation in the bundle branches. *Br Heart J* 1949;11:230–236.

67. Burchell HB, Taylor BE, Knutson JRB, Wood EH. Circulatory adjustments to the hypoxemia of congenital heart disease of the cyanotic type. *Circulation* 1950;1:404–414.

70. Burchell HB, Taylor BE, Knutson JRB, Wakim KG. Coarctation of the aorta with hypotension in the left arm. Physiologic observations on direct intra-arterial pressures and flow of blood. *M Clin N Am* 1950:1177–1185.

101. Bartholomew LG, Burchell HB. Wolff-Parkinson-White syndrome associated with situs inversus, report of case simulating myocardial infarction electrocardiographically. *Proc Staff Meet, Mayo Clin* 1952;27:98–104.

107. Burchell HB, Essex HE, Pruitt RD. Studies on the spread of excitation through the ventricular myocardium II. The ventricular septum. *Circulation* 1952;6:161–171.

120. Burchell HB, Essex HE, Lambert EH. Action potentials supporting the presence of specialized conduction pathways in the dogs ventricle. *Circulation Res* 1953;1:186–188.

129. Burchell HB, Swan JHC, Wood EH. Demonstration of differential effects on pulmonary and systemic arterial pressure by variation in oxygen content of inspired air in patients with patent ductus arteriosus and pulmonary hypertension. *Circulation* 1953;8:681–694.

300. Atwood RM, Burchell HB, Tauxe WN. Pulmonary scans achieved with macroaggregated radioidinated albumin, use in diagnosis of pulmonary artery agenesis. *Amer J Med Sci* 1966;252:84–88.

313. Burchell HB, Frye RL, Anderson MW, McGoon DC. Atrio-ventricular and ventriculoatrial excitation in Wolff-Parkinson-White syndrome (type B): temporary ablation at surgery. *Circulation* 1967;36:663–672.

321. Burchell HB. A cardiologist's view of modern cardiovascular surgery. *Dis Chest* 1969;55:323.

323. Burchell HB, Merideth J. Management of cardiac tachyarrhythmias with cardiac pacemakers. *Ann New York Acad Sci* 1969;167:546.

366. Burchell HB, Tuna N. The interpretation of gross left axis deviation in the electrocardiogram. *Eur J Cardiol* 1979;10:259–277.

368. Burchell HB. Potassium and the cardiologist—1980 close encounters. *Cardiovasc Rev Rep* 1980;1:316–324.

Historical Pieces

9. Burchell HB, Keys TE. The heart of George II of England. *Bull Med Libr Assn* 1942;30:198–202.

249. Burchell HB. Stephen Hales, September 17, 1677–January 4, 1761, (editorial). *Circulation* 1961;23:1–6.

259. Burchell HB. William Ernest Henley (1849–1903), medical frame of reference for the poem invictus. *Ad Med* 1961;30:510–515.

269. Burchell HB. Henry Van Dyke and his angina pectoris, a note on the story of the other wise man and an analogy to the practitioner. *JAMA* 1962;182:1029–1030.

286. Burchell HB. The other wise man. *New Physician* 1964;13:459–470.

297. Burchell HB. Hedgehog and foxes, renascent reflections of a tyro editor. *JAMA* 1966;195:285–286.

349. Burchell HB. Osler: In quest of the gnostic grail in morbid anatomy. *J Hist Med* 1975;30:235–249.

351. Burchell HB. Hutchinson's ''Don'ts'' for diagnosticians. His principles of diagnosis revisited. *Geriatrics* 1975;30:105–111.

ROBERT McKINNON CALIFF, MD:
A Conversation With the Editor*

Dr. Rob Califf is Professor of Medicine, Associate Vice-Chancellor for Clinical Affairs, and Director of the Clinical Research Institute of Duke University Medical Center in Durham, North Carolina. He was born in Anderson, South Carolina, in 1951. He graduated from Duke University in 1973, having been elected to Phi Beta Kappa, and from Duke University School of Medicine in 1978, having been elected to Alpha Omega Alpha. He was president of his senior class in medical school. His internship and residency in internal medicine were at the University of California, San Francisco, from 1978 to 1980, and his fellowship in cardiology was at Duke University Medical Center from 1980 to 1983. As a resident he received the Distinguished Resident Teaching Award from the University of California Medical School. His first publication was in 1978 as a medical student and since that time he has had over 400 publications in various peer-reviewed medical journals. Nearly all of his publications have focused on coronary artery disease. Along with Dr. Eric Topol, Rob Califf has been the world's leader of multicenter cardiologic studies during the past 15 years. He has established the world's finest databank in cardiovascular disease and the data generated has had a major impact on management of patients with heart disease. I believe it fair to say that Dr. Califf, along with Dr. Topol, are the fathers of evidence-based information for cardiovascular decision making.

William Clifford Roberts, MD†(Hereafter, WCR): *I am talking with Rob Califf in my office at Baylor University Medical Center on April 7, 1998. Dr. Califf just gave a beautiful presentation at our medical grand rounds. Dr. Califf, I would like to talk to you primarily about your upbringing, where you were born, where you grew up, what your home life was like, what your parents and siblings were like.*

Robert McKinnon Califf, MD‡ (Hereafter, RMC): I was born in Anderson, South Carolina, at a hospital that is still standing and does a great job with clinical trials. My dad was a teacher in the architecture school at Clemson University at the time. Anderson was the closest hospital. Both my parents are native South Carolinians. They grew up in the low country, Charleston and St. George, South Carolina, which is steeped in historical tradition. I lived in Clemson until I was 5. I don't remember much about it except for going to football games and being very happy. We moved to Columbia, South Carolina, when I was 5 and I went to grammar school, junior high school, and

FIGURE 1. RMC during the interview.

high school there. That was also a very pleasant experience.

I had the distinction in 1960, while in junior high school, of being one of only a few students to vote for Kennedy in a mock election in my class of 300 or 400. We lived in an area of Columbia known as Republican Hills. Those following politics in the South since recognize that it was an omen of things to come. I felt fortunate to have a remarkable group of people to go to high school with. Many of them went on to political careers and did things related to those activities. Lee Atwater, who went on to become a famous Republican political campaign manager, was a classmate. Whether one agrees with the politics or not, it certainly was interesting to be so close to a colorful part of American history.

WCR: *How big was Columbia, South Carolina, when you were growing up there?*

RMC: I believe about 100,000. It was the State capital. It was dominated by 3 things: (1) the state government; (2) the University of South Carolina; and (3) Fort Jackson. Fort Jackson was one of the early training grounds for soldiers who were headed to Vietnam. We lived on the side of town with Fort Jackson so I could hear the guns at night.

Columbia was an interesting place to grow up. It was big enough that there was a fair amount of intel-

*This series of interviews are underwritten by an unrestricted grant from Bristol-Myers Squibb.
†Baylor Cardiovascular Institute, Baylor University Medical Center, Dallas, Texas 75246.
‡Duke Clinical Research Institute, Duke University Medical Center, Durham, North Carolina 27710.

lectual activity, but it was also very much at the cross roads of what was happening in the South; not so much as Atlanta, but certainly many changes occurred during the time I was in junior high and high school.

WCR: *When your father left Clemson University, he went into the private practice of architecture in Columbia?*

RMC: He taught me many things in a very quiet sort of way. One of the main things he taught me was integrity—the importance of trying to do what is right, even if it is not popular. I think that is a quality we could use a little more today. Watching him deal with the world of architecture, which is very dependent on contracts and wheeling and dealing to get the big jobs, was a growing up lesson for me. Also, he used to take me on Saturdays to the buildings that were being built after he designed them. It was interesting to watch how subcontractors and architects try to get things done together. That was formative for me in some ways.

My father is a man who does not say a lot. His real focus is on architectural design and history. He had been the editor of the yearbook at Clemson when a student there, and had a lot of interesting experiences related to that. During his student days, Clemson was a military school. His class was called to war and arrived in Europe just in time to be at the Battle of the Bulge, which was a major disaster for the American troops. I think that left a permanent impression on him.

WCR: *You have 3 siblings?*

RMC: Yes.

WCR: *Where are you in the hierarchy?*

RMC: I am the second. I have an older brother who is also a Duke graduate and has spent time working in historical architectural work and computer programming. He is currently spending his time with computer programming. My younger brother is an orthopedic surgeon and a graduate of Duke Medical School. He is Chief of Staff at Alamance Regional Medical Center in Burlington, North Carolina, this year. I have a younger sister who lives in Houston. We have quite a family! Our parents' 50th anniversary is coming up this summer. We are all going to congregate at Myrtle Beach and try to get along together.

WCR: *What is your mother like? Did she have a lot of impact on you when you were growing up?*

RMC: Mothers usually do. My mother was a school teacher. At first she stayed home, then she did substitute teaching, and then full-time teaching. She looked out for us and saw that we did what we were supposed to do. She had a big impression that way. She taught us a lot about persistence. I remember not making it on the Little League team the first year I tried out, her making a phone call, and the next thing I knew I was on the team. It was not a political favor. It was probably the coach saying, "If I don't put this kid on the team, I will never hear the end of it." Sometimes you do find in life if you make it easier for people to do what they should do (or harder to do what they shouldn't do), that they will be more likely to do what you want them to do.

WCR: *You mentioned that you enjoyed school? Did you enjoy your studies in high school? Were they easy for you?*

RMC: For the most part, I enjoyed the reading and thinking part of my studies, but I didn't focus on test taking. I was fortunate to have great teachers. I had classmates who were very intellectually active. Of course, it was an interesting time because as we hit high school the Vietnam War was unfolding. Anybody in that class of 1969 in the USA has distinct memories of political speeches and decisions being made in the face of great uncertainty about what was going to happen in life. It was not as if the problem of war was unique to our generation, but 1969 was perhaps the peak of that kind of concern.

We had a tightly bonded class. Probably the most meaningful social thing I did was to play on the basketball team. Another interesting lesson—I had been on the second team in junior high school and there were a group of us who were really good friends who were on the first and second team in junior high school. Some of us on the second team thought we should be on the first team, but we never got the break. When we got to the 10th grade we were on the Junior Varsity team together and the varsity team was having a rough go of it. The coach got frustrated early into the season and said, "Okay, I am just going to call it quits and we are going to have tryouts including all the Junior Varsity and Varsity players, and whoever plays the best will be on the varsity team." One other guy and I got picked for the varsity team and we both started. I went from second team Junior Varsity to starting on the varsity team in 1 day and got 12 points in my first varsity game. We did not have a great year that year but I learned that if you persist in working towards your goal, sometimes unexpected pleasant surprises do happen. The next year we finished second in the state, and in my senior year we won the AAAA state championship in South Carolina, a tremendous team achievement. It was a group of kids who had been together for several years plus a team flavored by the initial integration of secondary schools in South Carolina. Integration in our schools sort of started with basketball. We had kids who had played together since the 7th grade and 3 minority players who came in and made a big impact.

WCR: *You went to public junior high and high school?*

RMC: Yes, public schools.

WCR: *What did you play in basketball?*

RMC: I was too slow to be a guard and too short to be a forward, so I sort of played in between guard and forward. We were blessed with a real big guy center and really good shooting guards. We had a mixture of about 8 or 9 kids who played well together and got along well.

WCR: *How tall are you?*

RMC: Six foot 1 inch.

WCR: *Did you play other sports in high school?*

RMC: Just for fun I played tennis and golf. My grandfather played golf and I got exposed to that at a young age and really enjoyed it as a 12- and 13-year old. Then I gave it up after high school and picked it up again about 8 years ago.

WCR: *When your family had dinner at night when you were a teenager did you discuss US or world topics? Were there intellectual discussions at the dinner table or how did that go?*

RMC: I think it is fair to say that we had a mixture of the usual family chaos with a fairly intellectual flavor. My parents were both interested in events in the world. They are both very bright. There was always a big emphasis in our family on the importance of education. My maternal grandfather had been a Baptist minister so there was a flavor of religion and doing the right thing in the family was very strong. My paternal grandfather had been in the military as an engineer and had been all around the world, so we had the world influence. We had a lot of intellectual discussions. But we also had the usual squabbling and sibling rivalries that most families go through.

One thing I did not learn that I should have was that we *did* have family meals together. I did not understand the importance of this until a little later with my own wife and children. It is something I really try to emphasize with trainees and junior faculty now. I think it is a missing ingredient in many medical families.

WCR: *To be home before dinner?*

RMC: Yes, even if you come back to work later. The discussion time together is important to kids, even if they don't realize it until later on.

WCR: *Did your family go on vacations in the summer time?*

RMC: Yes, but we were not a well-traveled family. We had a lot of relatives in the state so we would gather at the beach. I have fond memories of crabs being thrown in a pot on the beaches in South Carolina. If you have read Pat Conroy, you know that the low country of South Carolina is an unbelievably culturally rich environment and it is mostly oriented towards outdoor family activities. It was a great place to grow up, but we did not travel far. We went to the mountains of Tennessee and we went to the coast of South Carolina and that was pretty much it. I was never on an airplane until I was out of college.

WCR: *Did you have jobs in the summers?*

RMC: I worked most summers. I did bag-boy grocery jobs, and then made prefabricated siding for apartments in a lumber yard. The first summer after college was probably one of the most intense summers of discussion and reflection I ever had. I worked in a rock quarry with 4 or 5 of my friends, including Lee Atwater. Our job was to service the trussels that the big machines dropped the rocks into. Lee had gone to Newberry College (he had barely made it through high school) and gotten involved in Republican politics, and I had been at Duke and gotten very involved in anti-Vietnam War activities. We spent the summer in fairly intense political discourse about the future. He went on, of course, to run campaigns for Republicans, including George Bush's successful run for the Presidency, and I went on into medicine. The discussions we had then were quite formative in terms of thinking

about our future conduct. Not that we were all that wise at the time, but we were listening to a lot of people, reading, discussing, and coming to different conclusions about things.

WCR: *In junior high and high school were there teachers who had a major impact on you?*

RMC: There were in different kinds of ways. In the eighth grade, I had a science teacher who made us do presentations and I was a fairly shy kid. I liked to do things by myself. I had friends but I was fairly shy. She made us give presentations and encouraged me and I learned that I actually liked to talk about things that I knew something about, and that I could do it. That really made a lasting impression on me. Beyond that there was no individual teacher in high school, but it was a great environment where there was always something to do in our high school. When I look at high schools now in our community and others, I often wish the kind of environment we had could be recreated. It was relatively open and stimulating. People got along. We had our problems, but there were no significant physical threats and we had a pretty good time in high school.

WCR: *Were you valedictorian of your class?*

RMC: No. Nowhere near it. We ended up with about a dozen kids going to Ivy League schools. I did not study to make grades. I was sort of interested in certain things and worked on those and did not work as hard on others. I was very interested in sports.

WCR: *How many in your graduating high school class?*

RMC: Around 550.

WCR: *Where were you among those 550?*

RMC: I might have been 40th.

WCR: *How did you decide to go to Duke University?*

RMC: My brother had gone there and I thought it was kind of a neat place. I wanted to get away from home but not too far from home. I had never traveled much. The other college I really thought about was Clemson, because I still loved the town of Clemson and I think it is a great school. I decided to give Duke a shot. It was an interesting experience. I learned a lot. We have our 25th reunion coming up this year.

WCR: *What did you major in in college?*

RMC: Last night I was talking to Joe Mitchell, one of my old roommates who lives here in Dallas and is an attorney, about how we came along at a time where to show your outrage about the Vietnam War you signed a paper saying you were not going to take exams and they still nevertheless passed you. It was an odd time for academics. There were a lot of other issues on campus at the same time—fairness to racial minorities in the workforce, and wages.

I ended up majoring in psychology. My goal was to work in the prison system and try to improve it. I basically took courses I thought were interesting, which was an advantage I had. The thing about the university that was most important to me was that I met a lot of people from places I had never been. They came from different backgrounds with different expe-

FIGURE 2. RMC as a senior in high school. His beloved car (the "Savoy") is in the background just to the left of the basketball hoop.

riences and I learned a heck of a lot from that. It was a great experience. I enjoyed just about all of it.

WCR: *Who had a significant influence on you in college? Was it primarily your classmates? Did any teachers stand out?*

RMC: As opposed to high school where my classmates dominate my memory (we were a pretty self-directed high school group) with modifying influences by teachers, I would say in college I had a lot of intense relationships with professors. One of the things I joke about with my kids now is that at the time I started the freshman year they actually had Saturday morning English tutorials where you had to bring in your writings and sit there with the professor and have your writing critiqued.

I am sure you see the same problems I see with writing, Bill. In editing a cardiology journal right now, I find it amazing how many bright people cannot write. Having to expose your writing and thoughts to a teacher in a one-on-one session was a tremendous experience. There was a psychology professor named Richard Kramer who had a way of teaching about the human brain that was fascinating. He had an influence on me, not that I admire some of the things that were done with psychotropic experimentation at that time, but it was fascinating to see people begin to understand better the capacity of the human mind and how it can be changed, sometimes for the worse.

WCR: *How did you decide to major in psychology in college?*

RMC: I thought I wanted to do something that was socially meaningful. I came from a Baptist sort of mentality that you need to do something that improves the world. My mother made me take all these achieve-

ment and vocational tests. They kept saying I should be a lawyer, and I did not want to be a lawyer. The psychologist position came up high on the list. I was not particularly interested in biological science at that time. It seemed dealing with the human mind would be a good thing to do.

WCR: *When did you decide that you wanted to be a physician?*

RMC: It was very specific. I got a job in the State prison in South Carolina during college one summer. That was a phenomenal experience. They put me in the work-release program. I worked at a facility over in West Columbia. There were 30 to 40 inmates who had done well enough that they were nearing release, and they got jobs out in the communities but had to live in the facility. My job was to help them and make sure they stayed on the premises. We had a basketball team, which I coached. I did not have a gun or anything like that. If there was a problem, I just had to make a phone call and things would be taken care of. I found it to be frustrating, and although I admire people who can work in that environment and struggle with it, it almost seemed like by the time people had gotten into prison there was very little one could do to change behavior.

My ultimate moment of frustration came during one of the Friday nights when I escorted them to the speedway or to the bowling alley (the allowed recreation). A couple of fellows on work release were guys I had played high school ball against. This particular night at the bowling alley, they picked my pocket! Here I was helping these guys and they took my wallet right out of my pants. I didn't even know it was gone until I got back. No one would say who did it. At that point, I thought, this field is not far enough along for me to do what I want to do to improve it. I probably needed some more tangible rewards. I thought maybe I should go into something more physical, like medicine. I had taken no science courses until the summer of my junior year.

WCR: *So you took all your premedical science courses during the summer after your junior year and during your senior year in college?*

RMC: Yes, but also during the summer after my senior year. I had to wait out a year to apply to medical school because I did not get to take organic chemistry in time.

WCR: *That is why you had 5 years between the beginning of college and medical school? What did you do during the rest of the year?*

RMC: Lydia and I got married right after my graduation from Duke in May. (Our 25th wedding anniversary is coming up this year.) We had been high school sweethearts, so we have been together a long time. She was in nursing school at the University of North Carolina at Greensboro and had one more year to go, so I had a fabulous year. We lived in Columbia in a little apartment for the summer. I took organic chemistry and she worked in a hospital as sort of a practicum for her nursing training. We had no money, so we were living off her wages with a little help from our parents. We then went up to Greensboro and she finished her undergraduate degree while I worked as an orderly in a local hospital for 9 months.

It was a great experience. I worked 8 hours a day, 5 days a week. I got to know, at a very fundamental level, what happens to people in a hospital. I had a lot of very personal experiences with patients when putting in a Foley catheter and emptying the bed pans. I did a lot of work in the emergency department and got fascinated by defibrillation. I saw some people resuscitated. When I was not working, I was reading books and playing basketball and cooking. We had a great time, probably the most relaxed time ever. After about 6 months of that, I was ready to do something with a broader purpose and was happy to be headed to medical school.

WCR: *You graduated from college Phi Beta Kappa so you had no problem getting into medical school?*

RMC: I wanted to go to the University of Virginia because they had a program where you could design your own curriculum, and I thought that would be the best thing for me. I still to this day cannot stand sitting in classroom sessions. They did not think enough of me to admit me, however. I got into Duke and Tulane. I did not think I would want to go back to Durham. I thought I had spent enough time there. I started to go to Tulane and then at the last minute—I am still not sure why actually—I decided to go to Duke. Tulane still claims 300 precious dollars of ours that we could not get back because we decided too late to attend Duke.

WCR: *Had anybody in your family ever been a physician?*

RMC: I have a picture of a relative on my father's side who practiced as a horse and buggy physician in the low country of South Carolina. My great-great grandfather graduated from the Medical University of South Carolina in Charleston, and I have his diploma hanging on my wall. There is a family tradition of physicians, but it skipped a couple of generations. That was not a main motivating factor for me. I had seen something that I thought I could do and would enjoy doing.

WCR: *When you picked the medical profession, you really had not known what doctors do every day?*

RMC: Only in that one of my best friends growing up, *Ken Graham,* had a father who was a family doctor. We basketball groupees spent much time at his house because he had a nice court outside his garage, and over his garage he had a pool table in a separate room where we could hang out. I spent enough time to know about the personal interactions of a doctor, but I did not have a good feel for the procedural stuff until I did that year as an orderly. Then, I got a good understanding. I did everything from help out with some autopsies to emptying bed pans to setting up defibrillators and doing some cardiopulmonary resuscitation.

WCR: *So when you entered medical school in 1974 you had a pretty good sense what medicine was all about?*

RMC: I had a good sense for that time about what doctors did in the real world. I had very little sense of what medical school was all about.

WCR: *How did you enjoy medical school?*

RMC: Duke is an interesting place for medical school, because it has a very tough, intense first year where you cram 2 years of work into one. In return you get a third year where you can pretty much do what you want to do. I would say that the first year was very colorful and I learned a heck of a lot, but it was incredibly stressful in every way. The payback was phenomenal though. I had an outstanding third year and actually set my career based on that experience.

I was going to be a pediatrician until I got involved more in the cardiovascular research world. I started out the second year just doing a job working with the Duke Cardiology Databank to make some money and ended up spending the whole third year putting Holter monitors on patients and measuring who had sudden death. That really got me excited about developing evidence and understanding whether what we do actually works.

WCR: *When you got a job in the Duke Databank as a sophomore in medical school had you had any previous experience with computers?*

RMC: Absolutely none.

WCR: *What happened that year?*

RMC: My job was to assist in the clinic. Data would be marked down on sheets and somebody would enter it into a computer. I saw that going on, but as I got involved in the third year, where I actually spent a lot of time with *Kerry Lee,* a senior statistician, who has been a very influential person in my career, it was evident that doctors have a hard time remembering or synthesizing all the information that they experience. It did not take a lot of work to see that the computer would come out with answers about the natural history of disease that were far superior to what the individual doctor could recognize from his/her own experience.

WCR: *You have been on a computer ever since?*

RMC: I would not say on a computer. I am actually not very good with computers myself. I am a computer user, but I don't do any of my own programming. I just use what computers can bring and depend on other people to do the things they like to do. I am more of an interface person. I like to try to interface what computers can do with the world of clinical practice.

WCR: *So your junior year in medical school was essentially spent in the Databank?*

RMC: That brings up the question, "What is medical school for, after all?" I went to medical school when most medical schools didn't do a very good job of education. They offered didactic courses, which I don't consider to be the way you really learn. I was unprepared for what medical school was like, and I continue to think much of medical school is wasted the way it is done presently.

WCR: *If you were a Dean of a medical school right now, how would you set up the medical school?*

RMC: If I were a Dean with unlimited authority?

I believe in the university without walls. If you ask the question, "Why do we have medical schools?" the answer probably is "to train doctors." Then you would ask the question, "What do doctors need to know?" It is at least my contention that we have far too much emphasis on rote learning and basic science constructs that doctors will never use and not enough about what they actually need to know to deal with the world they are going into. That has to do with how health systems work, how to supervise people, how to negotiate, how to interact effectively with other human beings, and how to understand evidence, both clinical and financial. There is very little about that in medical school today. Yet, if you look at what doctors are going to be doing, that is what they need to know.

I would say let's make a self-learning curriculum available for the basic sciences that one could pass or be certified in at any point along the way. Let's get rid of all these classrooms of people sitting through dry lectures. Let's make that kind of learning more interactive, based on computer interaction, one-on-one tutorials, or small tutorials for concepts and feedback. Let's really build in a curriculum that teaches people how to evaluate what needs to be done with other human beings in the practice of medicine. I would see more of a blend of what is currently done in business school and what we try to teach housestaff now. I think the time medical students are not seeing patients should be shortened in the medical school curriculum, with a fair amount of infiltration of what is taught in public health school.

WCR: *You would expose medical students to patients right away?*

RMC: Yes, and I think a lot of schools are doing that. But I think the lecture time is not all that well spent. If medical education stops when you graduate, it is not going to work because the jobs that doctors do are going to change substantially, and the things they need to know, looking at the pace that information is increasing, will change enormously. We should be focused on the skills of self-instruction.

WCR: *Who had the most impact on you in medical school?*

RMC: The most impact all together was by my wife, Lydia. She has kept me humble and aware that the small things in life really are important.

In terms of people at the medical school with the most impact on me, *Eugene Stead*, far and away. I think a lot of people who studied the history of modern medicine know that Dr. Stead is someone who has had a profound influence. He sees the world differently than most other people. He tends to see things other people don't see. The kinds of things that he would do would lead you to learn from them. Often you would initially have no earthly idea what it was you had learned; it would slowly come to you later on.

WCR: *What is an example of that?*

RMC: A concrete example is the first time I gave a talk to a group of doctors where he was in the audience. He walked up to me, took my slide carousel, took the top of it off and turned it upside down on the floor. He said, "Pick them back up, don't think about what order they are in, and give the talk." Obviously, at the time, I did not think that was a very nice thing to do and I did not see how that would teach me anything, but by going through a number of exercises like that I learned how to give a talk, whether or not I had the slides or the projector broke or whatever. It was a great lesson. Half the time he would say things that sounded odd, and he would disregard things that we took as fundamental. After we would think about it, we would realize that he was just ahead of his time. The concept of "outcomes-research"—measuring, quantifying the natural history of disease using computers—seems so straightforward now, but when he was proposing it and writing about it in the 1960s he was considered way out in left field.

WCR: *Did Dr. Stead know anything about computers?*

RMC: No.

WCR: *Did he ever use one as far as you know?*

RMC: Not as far as I know.

WCR: *How much contact did you have with him in medical school?*

RMC: A fair amount. He had retired as Chief of Medicine at a young age and he basically did what he wanted to do, which was mostly to get money to support good ideas with grants and contracts and develop this database. He would come by and talk.

WCR: *This was when you were a junior spending the entire year in the databank?*

RMC: Yes, at that time the world was kind of divided into "Stead disciples" and "non-Stead disciples." He had a way of saying things that would make you scratch your head. Some people would say, "This guy is crazy." Other people would say, "There is something here I need to figure out." They would go off and figure it out and generally do better because they had.

Another person, who was hired by Dr. Stead, was *Kerry Lee*, who is still the senior statistician in our group. He was hired from the University of North Carolina at a time when there was no place for a statistician in Duke Medical Center. In fact, no department except Community and Family Medicine would offer Kerry a position. He ended up with a position in the Department of Community and Family Medicine, but he worked on the cardiology database.

I think a lot of people in medical school are taught a view of medical research that when you construct a hypothesis you pretty much rig the experiment to make the answer come out the way you want. You go into the whole experiment with a bias about what the answer will be. I remember taking my first data set to Kerry Lee, and he said, "Okay, let's do a regression model." I said, "What is a regression model?" He had all these computer cards and he punched out some stuff. The result was different from what we expected. I was unhappy with it because we wanted to show that ventricular premature complexes were really the root cause of sudden death. That was our hypothesis, yet every way we analyzed the data it turned out that left ventricular ejection fraction, not ventricular premature complexes, was the key factor. Kerry kept saying,

FIGURE 3. RMC (top row, second from right) with the University of California-San Francisco houseofficer basketball team.

"You don't need to tell the experiment what the answer is. You need to look at the result and try to understand it and put it in perspective." In retrospect, of course, his advice was pretty good. We have learned since that trying to suppress the frequency of ventricular premature complexes is not necessarily a good thing to do. We all know that people with bad left ventricular function are at high risk of sudden death. Therapies that don't necessarily suppress ventricular premature complexes also prevent sudden death in patients.

WCR: *That was your first paper in 1978?*

RMC: Yes.

WCR: *This article was published while you were in medical school? It was the year you graduated that it was published?*

RMC: Right. There was a tremendous emphasis on publishing what you did at Duke, particularly in cardiology. Obviously, I took this to heart.

WCR: *When you were in medical school you got into the Cardiology Databank early as a sophomore, just to get a job. Then you were so fascinated you spent your entire junior year there. By that time, did you know you wanted to be a cardiologist?*

RMC: I spent a lot of time hanging out with the cardiology fellows. I got to work in the catheterization laboratory, in the noninvasive laboratory, in the exercise laboratory; I put Holter monitors on patients. I just found it fascinating. This was something I could intuitively understand and deal with. I think everybody's mind is a little bit different. I learned that I did have a grasp of data, being able to look at it, draw conclusions, and take action. It also seemed to just fit together extremely well.

When it came time for matching on internship, Lydia and I went around to look at internships all over the country. Neither of us previously had ever been out of the Southeast. I decided I wanted to go to the west coast. Lydia was interested but really wanted to

stay in the Southeast. She was pregnant for the first time when the match came out, and when I matched the University of San Francisco she was pretty upset. She was not too thrilled with that opportunity. I was obviously delighted because that was a tough place to get into, and I knew I would meet a lot of people who would be interesting. I guess I had done well enough in that third year that I was able to arrange a fellowship in cardiology to return to back at Duke before I went to California. That also was a time when there was a special deal with the American Board of Internal Medicine, where if you did enough research in your fellowship you could do 2 years of internal medicine and get credit for the third year. We arranged for 2 years in San Francisco and then came back to Duke to start the cardiology fellowship.

WCR: *So that saved you a year? You went to San Francisco for internship in 1978 and stayed for 1 year of residency.*

RMC: Right.

WCR: *How did you enjoy your time in San Francisco?*

RMC: It was a phenomenal experience. Just about every part of it was interesting. We loved it. We lived in Buena Vista Park, which is right in the Haight-Ashbury District, and saw a lot of kinds of people we had not spent time with previously. Culturally, it was an extremely diverse city and that was interesting.

The medical training was superb with *Holly Smith* as Chief of Medicine. He was someone you could easily look up to. Although he had lost his South Carolina accent, he was from Camden, South Carolina. I got to know him fairly well. For a place that had done so well in research, the environment for the housestaff was extraordinarily friendly and personal. The ability to go over to San Francisco General and spend a third of your time there with one of the busiest emergency departments in the country was a great opportunity. Although we had excellent attending physicians, there was more to do than they could do, so as a houseofficer you really got to run the show in the emergency department and that was a fantastic experience.

I could get on my bicycle from home and ride right through the Golden Gate Park and go to the prettiest piece of real estate in the world, the San Francisco Veterans' Administration Hospital, right at the Golden Gate. You can look out the window and see the boats going by. I think it was a great choice for me and I learned a lot. There were things going on at the time which, again, like other times in life, we did not understand at all. This was right in the middle of the gay influx into the San Francisco community. We took care of patients with AIDS and did not know what AIDS was. I distinctly remember several patients who had AIDS. We just did not know what it was.

WCR: *What did you call it?*

FIGURE 4. The Califf clan: left to right top row: Sam, Lydia, Rob, and Tom; kneeling: Sharon.

RMC: We called it whatever the manifestation was. If it was pneumonia, we called it "pneumonia." If they had weird skin lesions we called it "weird skin lesions" and tried to figure out what they were. It was a very rowdy political time, mostly related to the cultural clashes, the Harvey Milk assassination (a city council leader who was murdered in his office).

Also, the year I arrived, Proposition 13 had just been passed under the Reagan leadership and they had promised about $13,000 a year to interns. After arriving in San Francisco, I learned that they were only going to pay me $11,500. They breached their contract, but said there was nothing I could do about it. It was State law and if I didn't like it I could take it up with Ronald Reagan. I learned about the influence of government on medicine.

WCR: *You mentioned Holly Smith. Who had an impact on you during your internship and year of residency in San Francisco?*

RMC: There were a number of people, but the biggest impact was really from several people for different reasons. Although our daughter Sharon had been born in Durham, it was not until 3 weeks after we arrived in San Francisco that we learned she had congenital heart disease and the diagnosis of coarctation of the aorta, atrioventricular septal defect with a cleft mitral valve was made. We had no money, and were living from month to month on this small income. Sharon was in severe heart failure at the time of diagnosis. The surgeon, *Paul Ebert*, who earlier had been at Duke and was world renowned, had a system for taking care of these sick kids that was phenomenal. It was a system obviously built around his expertise, knowledge, and artistic capability in doing these heart operations. We saw him only a few times. All the other care was rendered by a variety of people who seemed to know exactly what they were supposed to do and when they were supposed to do it, ranging from the anesthesiologist, who resuscitated her after a postoperative cardiac arrest, to the pediatric cardiologist who took excellent personal care of her, to the nurses who were very tuned in to our needs.

Sharon spent a month in the hospital postoperatively, and I was a new intern. You can imagine the situation. She had a big operation where they tried to fix everything at one time, something her cardiologist told us could not be done. We learned later that that was a set up. This was a lesson I learned that I have employed in intensive care medicine ever since, which is when you initially meet a family and the situation is serious, it is probably better to tell them to expect the worst and you are going to do everything you can, than to tell them that everything is going to be all right. If things do turn out okay, it is a great sense of positivity, but if you expect everything to be all right and things turn out badly I think it is a worse situation for a family. It is realistic in those circumstances to expect the worst and that way you actually think about what you need to do.

Paul Ebert taught me that you certainly need to build your healthcare around technical competence, but the systematic approach to the management of illness, using a broad range of people with different talents, is something that makes a big difference. His system was in contrast to a lot of other systems at the University of California at San Francisco at the time, which were very good academically, from the point of view of traditional academic medicine, but were really not very efficient. To watch these children come from all over the world, have their families have a place to stay, see them get through the system, and have their needs taken care of, and have the technical competence too, was really something to watch. My daughter did well and she is now a bright and healthy college student.

Even in one of the best of systems, we had the experience of having a pediatric cardiologist who turned out not to be a pediatric cardiologist. This actually got to be a fairly well-known case. This gentleman was assigned to help in her care, and he ended up being her personal physician after surgery. He was a very nice guy, very attentive, but he turned out to be a fake doctor. He had taken his cousin's credentials and had gotten an internship and had risen through the ranks at University of California at San Francisco. When he came up to be head of the neonatal intensive care unit, which was a pretty big job at that time, his credential check flushed him out. We had the experience of hearing on the news that our child's doctor was not a doctor after all. These experiences reinforced a personal view that the physician has a special responsibility because of the trust of patients.

There was a guy named *Jim Naughton* who ran the housestaff program, and the personal attention that we got during this time of crisis, the little things he and his wife did meant so much to Lydia and me. We spent a month in the hospital just about 24 hours a day while Sharon was recovering. People brought us meals and he made accommodations to my responsibilities. I continued to work and we would make rounds on Sharon every day with the team. I was given some leeway to take care of this crisis in the middle of trying to be an intern. Those little things mean a lot to people when they come from those who are in a position of influence. This is probably something that I have not paid enough attention to, but something I think about fairly often and try to correct myself and do it more.

The other big influence was *Kanu Chatterjee*. Rounding with him on the coronary care unit was just a phenomenal experience because he thinks about human physiology in a way that is great to watch and to learn from. In a way, it was a luxury at the time. The hospital was not that busy a place in cardiology. It was not a high volume facility like many other places, so time was taken on rounds to listen to the heart, talk to the patients, and try to put everything together. I think that had an influence on a whole generation of us who went through the system.

WCR: *Were coronary care unit rounds with Dr. Chatterjee a long experience?*

RMC: They were not particularly long. They were sort of medium. We took time with each patient. He did not waste time on frivolous things. Another thing he did, which was a lesson I learned when I came to run my own coronary care unit and I think is a fundamental system, is that he had a rule that if you were on call at night as an intern or resident, and the nurses did not like what you were doing, they called him at home. He did not always agree with the nurses but he did render judgment on whether what you were doing met standards. His concept in medical care, that there should be a basic level of quality that can be recognizable and enforceable by people who are there as permanent employees, has been useful to me.

WCR: *Did anybody else during those 2 years have a significant impact on you?*

RMC: There were a lot of people, but I would not name anyone in particular. There is a lot of dedication in that institution to training.

WCR: *You said Holly Smith was a superb chairman. What were his qualities that made him so?*

RMC: First of all, he seemed to care about the people on his housestaff. He gave you a sense that he knew who you were and he was concerned that you should do well. Secondly, there was a sense of tradition that had developed there. There were certain things that were done. There were annual get togethers and ways of interacting that were comforting, considering you had a conglomeration of people from all over the country. Then lastly, his demeanor when he dealt with you was respectful and positive. He was a man of enough distinction he did not need to be that way, it was just the way he did things. I think when you saw the way he interacted with other people it set a tone that was great for the whole program. This was not an easy time in terms of society and how people got along. There was a lot going on in San Francisco at that time, but he managed extraordinarily well.

WCR: *Did you have much contact with Bill Parmley?*

RMC: Actually, almost none, but I have since gotten to know Bill Parmley and he has had an influence on me the last couple of years in a very positive way. He is a paragon of integrity.

WCR: *What about your fellow housestaff? Who were some of your fellow housestaff and what kind of impact did they have on you?*

RMC: We had a great group of housestaff and the interactions were formative. The two housestaff with whom I have maintained a very close relationship, I was not particularly close to as house officers. We respected each other but just ended up not being on the same rotations together. They were *Eric Topol* and *Dean Kereiakes*. There were many bright people on the housestaff one could learn from and exchange ideas with. Sitting in the on-call room at San Francisco General Hospital at 4:00 A.M. trying to figure out what to do with a patient was a tremendous experience. The friendships made there are still carrying on. *Ralph Brendis*, who was a Chief Resident 2 years ahead of me and is now the head of the cardiac catheterization laboratory at Kaiser San Francisco, had a very positive influence on me in terms of maintaining enthusiasm and positivity. *Mike Clayman*, who went on to be a nephrologist and head of cardiovascular research at Eli Lilly, has remained a collaborator. Of course, I still have a relationship with Dean Kereiakes, who I work with every day in clinical trials and clinical research. Eric Topol and I have had a very close relationship over the years, and we have done a lot of things together and tend to think alike about how things should be done. *Jay Siegal* was a year ahead of me and is one of the leaders in the Bureau of Biologics at the Federal Food and Drug Administration. There were many people in that housestaff program who have gone on to be people I have interacted with on the national scene in the research that we have done.

WCR: *Did you and Lydia enjoy California?*

RMC: We really did. We laugh about it a lot now, because we did not have a lot of money. We rented a U-Haul truck and drove out to San Francisco with our daughter and our dog and cat. Lydia cried all the way to the Mississippi River on the way out there, and then when it came time to come back she did not want to come back and she cried all the way to the Mississippi River on the way back. We made a lot of friends there and had a great experience. Living in a city of such diversity and being able to go out to the Golden Gate Park on any given day and do interesting things or go across the Golden Gate Bridge and hike in Marin County or experience the California coast and the national parks was awesome. We learned a lot and had a great time. Oftentimes, I have wondered whether it would not have been better for me just to stay out there, but I think on balance we made the right move. On a sobering note, we lived in a predominantly gay community and many of the friends we made are now dead. I would say that most have died of HIV-related illnesses.

WCR: *What happened when you came back to Duke to do your cardiology fellowship? How did that work out?*

RMC: I came back and did the usual things that a fellow does the first year. I did research in the Databank and focused on natural history studies of coronary disease. It was a wonderful time because it was still in the era when there was enough money in the academic medical system that people saw patients for a certain number of hours in the day and then they had time to think. There was a guy named *Phil Harris*, who was a fellow who had come from Australia to spend a couple of years. Phil had a positive influence on an entire group of us. There was *Kerry Lee*, and there was *Frank Harrell*, another statistician; to this day Frank is the most creative thinker about data I have ever met. We all spent a lot of time looking at data and thinking about what it meant. It was a great time. I went on to do my clinical rotations and those were fun.

When I finished that second year of fellowship, *Jim Wyngaarden* was leaving to run the NIH. He had been the Chairman of Medicine, and *Andy Wallace*, who had been Chief of Cardiology, left the Division to run the hospital. They picked *Joe Greenfield* to run Cardiology and then eventually to be the Chair of Medicine. Joe called me and said, "We need someone to run the CCU. How would you like to do that instead of your third year of fellowship?" I ended up sort of being a fellow-faculty, which meant a year of being on call every other weekend and every week night for $35,000. It was a privilege to do it. I learned an incredible amount during that time dealing with acute coronary disease. It is hard for young people to understand this. We did not have thrombolytics or anything else to do to improve outcomes in acute MI. We did not even know about the benefits of aspirin.

WCR: *This was 1982?*

RMC: Yes. We basically put Swan-Ganz catheters in people and tried to modify the hemodynamics to try to make things better. We put in temporary pacemakers if someone went into heart block. We saw a lot of people go down the tubes that year, without being able to do a whole lot about it.

WCR: *I presume when Joe Greenfield asked you to take over the coronary care unit, your third year of fellowship, it was assumed you would stay on the faculty thereafter.*

RMC: There was a fair amount of uncertainty, because whenever you have a new Chief of Medicine you are not sure exactly what is going to happen, but that seemed reasonable and Joe had a very personable way of making you feel like if things did not work out he would help you find something that was to your benefit. That is a key quality in leaders that I see missing a lot today. The personal touch of reassuring those who work for you that even if it is not right for you, I will personally see to it that you get something that is right for you. He also never tried to take credit

FIGURE 5. RMC during the interview.

for someone else's idea. Too many medical leaders today thrive on personal power and glory.

WCR: *Who in cardiology had an impact on you during your fellowship?*

RMC: *Bob Rosati*, who ran the Databank. He was a very bright person who had a lot of insight into how to look at data, but he had sort of gotten side tracked into looking at data before he had a chance to flex all his clinical muscles. He taught me a lot, but just as I finished the fellowship and the first year in the coronary care unit, he felt like he wanted to go back to clinical medicine so he decided not to run the Databank anymore. *Galen Wagner* also had a big influence. Galen had looked out for me during my third year of medical school. He is a person who has always had a different point of view about things and has persevered with the institution for many years. At the time, he was helping with the fellowship program.

WCR: *When Bob Rosati decided to go back into clinical medicine, you sort of captured the Cardiovascular Databank. Is that how that worked out?*

RMC: David Pryor was a colleague who was a year ahead of me, and we sort of split things up. David took over the leadership of the Databank and I took over the coronary care unit. The deal was that we would work together, that I would focus on the clinical enterprise and try to integrate that with the Databank, and he would do the more research-specific and administrative tasks, which he was very interested in. Joe Greenfield, when he called us into his office to talk about this, basically said, "This is an interesting idea of Dr. Stead's, but I don't think it is worth anything, and you have 5 years to prove it is worth something or I am turning it off." That stimulated us at a fairly young age to try to figure out how to make it a productive endeavor. Probably the most creative couple of months of my career in terms of thinking about how to do things was when David and I spent a few months on Saturday mornings trying to think about how to diversify the funding for the Databank.

WCR: *That is when you decided to get commercial support?*

RMC: Up until that time, most of the support for the Databank had come from the NIH to fund the computerization of medical records. People were beginning to realize that business was so far ahead of medicine in terms of computer programming and databases that it was pretty clear the funding was going to dry up for that aspect. We also were getting some grants from the National Center for Health Services Research, which was a very small agency at the time, to look at the observational treatment comparisons of bypass surgery and medical therapy. But, as Bob Rosati said when he decided to move on, "Bypass surgery has been around for awhile and I don't think we will make many advances with this comparison." Little did he know that *Gruentzig* was over there in his kitchen about that same time cooking up angioplasty, which cast a whole new light on the field. Basically, what David and I did was really believe in our hearts and minds that quantitation of medical phenomena was going to be important. This belief had been inspired to a large extent by Bob Rosati's influence. We developed a set of domains of funding that we thought would be worthwhile and useful. It included what became Agency for Health Care Policy and Research (AHCPR), which at the time was the NCHSR, and the NIH and the foundation and industry. We talked about clinical trials, but we did not know a whole heck of a lot about clinical trials at the time.

As it turned out, right about the same time, Eric Topol, who had been an intern when I was a resident at UCSF, had come to Duke to interview but had decided to go to Hopkins for his fellowship. I was disappointed by that, because I thought he really had a talent and a knack for thinking about data. We kept in touch through telephone conversations. As he was finishing his fellowship, thrombolytic therapy was just beginning to come on the scene, but none of us knew what it would amount to. I had given a fair amount of streptokinase to a dozen or so patients at Duke with *Richard Stack*, and Eric Topol had really focused on the science of plasminogen activators. We had a connection with Genentech, because the company had been formed by former University of California at San Francisco professors. *Bill O'Neill* and Richard Stack had been residents together and were good friends. Eric joined Bill at the University of Michigan. We thought it would be fun to see what this new recombinant molecule might do in terms of reperfusion of coronary arteries. In talking about it we said, "Why don't we get a group of friends together and do a clinical trial." I was able to leverage our computer facility, and with Eric's incredible energy and leadership, we did the Thrombolysis and Angioplasty in Myocardial Infarction (TAMI-1) study. I'm really proud of what Eric and I have accomplished. Over the years his creativity and insight into the interface between science and medicine have been incredible.

WCR: *That was the first clinical trial where data outside Duke came into your data center? That was the beginning of the huge number of clinical trials that you later managed?*

RMC: Right, and it was just a group of friends working together. Overall we lost money doing the research, but at the time we had core funding at Duke from NIH for statistics and computing. We were able to get the research done. We did 3 cardiac catheterizations on each of 386 patients for about $300 a patient. Times have obviously changed since then.

There was a great lesson in that trial because we thought doing an angioplasty immediately after thrombolytic therapy would be beneficial and it turned out not to be. We were just trying to demonstrate the benefit of a practice we were sure about, and it turned out we were doing the wrong thing in practice. Along with the Thrombolysis In Myocardial Infarction (TIMI)-2 study and the European Cooperative Group, it led to significant changes in the way people managed thrombolytic therapy.

WCR: *After that you saw that clinical trials were the way to go?*

RMC: I would not put it that way. I think what we saw was that randomization is a powerful tool. When it comes down to deciding if one treatment is better than another, a randomized trial is the best evidence one can get. Chances for bias are so great if you don't employ randomization. Besides that, trials were fun and, in those early days, we had meetings with people who enjoyed spending time with each other. We would all bring our cans of film from the cases we had done. We would see things nobody had ever seen before and try to figure out what to do about them in clinical practice. It was a very exciting time. Everyone wanted to do a series of TAMI studies all the way to TAMI-9.

WCR: *How many clinical trials are you now involved with?*

RMC: The word "involved" is a dangerous word in this regard, but today we have something like 40 clinical trials in which I have involvement on some aspect or another.

WCR: *That data is fed into your Databank?*

RMC: No. The ones we handle the data for are more in the order of 15 or 16, but we work as partners with collaborators on a number of other clinical trials.

WCR: *So you are involved in the design and in the carrying out of 15 to 40 clinical trials?*

RMC: Yes. Some involvement in the design of maybe 30 or 40. In some cases, I might be on a data and safety monitoring committee, and in other cases I may be on a steering committee but our center may not be handling the data.

WCR: *You remained head of the coronary care unit at Duke until when?*

RMC: Until about 2 years ago.

WCR: *When you were head of the coronary care unit, how much of your time was spent in that activity?*

RMC: Until about 4 years ago I was spending over 50% of my time there making rounds and caring for patients. We have a very busy clinical practice. We went through an exciting period before catheterization laboratories proliferated in the state of North Carolina, where we had a helicopter service and brought in a lot of patients who needed revascularization from small hospitals. We developed a lot of innovative approaches to providing care in the region, ranging from outreach clinics with cardiology fellows to catheterization laboratory trucks which brought an experienced crew of cardiologists to outlying hospitals to do the cases. *Harry Phillips* and I instituted the first "modern" group practice at Duke. Harry continues to amaze me with his attunement to the needs of the clinical practice. Those who provide first class patient care in academic centers don't get enough credit—Harry has contributed greatly to Duke over the years.

WCR: *Has that worked out well?*

RMC: Yes, very well. Over the years we have evolved to a practice of 18 cardiologists, and we have set up a clinical model to integrate evidence-based medicine into our practice. The practice that Harry developed has contributed huge amounts of money to the teaching and research mission of the institution.

WCR: *How many trucks do you have?*

RMC: We have 2 trucks and they are busy all the time.

WCR: *You have how many helicopters now?*

RMC: Two helicopters in service at a time, and we've developed a sophisticated ground transport system.

WCR: *They go all over the state?*

RMC: There is a network with other tertiary referral centers, and they pretty much cover the state. We did some interesting things. We were involved in the early digitalis toxicity studies at a time when there was a limited supply of the antibody to reverse the toxicity. We had some helicopter relays that were pretty exciting. At one point, we had a child in South Carolina who was in and out of sustained VT and really sick, and we met the helicopter from there halfway and handed off the Digibind and got the kid treated and the kid did fine from digitalis toxicity. We had a lot of high volume clinical experience.

During the last couple of years, I have spent less time seeing patients and more time with administrative responsibilities.

WCR: *How many people do you have in the Duke Clinical Research Institute?*

RMC: This is a little tricky because we have a lot of "parts" of people. There are many people who see patients or work as nurses and who handle clinical research work part time as well. The total would be 650. We also have people who don't live in Durham who monitor data in outlying regions.

Our hope is to serve as a training facility for those who will develop the evidence for better medical practice in addition to a center for performing research. The support of the Duke Health System lead-ership, *Bill Donelan* and *Ralph Snyderman*, has made a huge difference. The DCRI now includes faculty from 10 other areas of medicine including primary care, otolaryngology, and psychiatry.

WCR: *How big a budget do you have to run this operation?*

RMC: It is somewhere around $40 million a year.

WCR: *How much of that comes from NIH or foundations or pharmaceutical companies?*

RMC: About 20% from NIH or foundations and 80% from industry. The large clinical trials require extensive clinical research networks and that accounts for a fairly large portion of the funding that we get. We also now work with professional societies and managed care organizations in measurement of outcomes and quality improvement.

WCR: *Your activities have evolved since 1983 in just an incredible way. It has been 15 years since you took over the coronary care unit. What do you think you will be doing 15 years from now?*

RMC: I wish I knew the answer to that question. I think that probably what I am destined to do for the foreseeable future is push this concept of evidence-based medicine and try to help make that happen in the best way that I can. I hope I will continue to see patients. I still consider it a privilege to see patients, but I don't do it enough now to consider myself to be a real contributor to the patient-care enterprise the way I used to in those early years on the Duke CCU.

I really believe that given the advances of science and the societal issues concerning what we pay for and what we don't pay for and what is valuable and what is not, that we are going to need to take a quantum leap in terms of developing the evidence for evidence-based medicine.

WCR: *As I understand it, you were one of the finalists in 1995 to be Chairman of the Department of Medicine at Duke. It seems to me that being a Chairman of such a large department is not something that you need quite yet at age 46. With the tremendous amount of data you are generating and the contributions you are making to management of cardiovascular disease through that data, would you still be interested in a departmental chairmanship? Is that something on your horizon?*

RMC: I think there are people wiser than me who made that selection, but I think the path I am going down is something that I am better suited for than being a Chairman of a Department of Medicine. It is such a big job helping people to put together systems to generate the data we need that this endeavor is a better way for me to spend my time. In my institutional role, which has evolved, I feel like an intern. I am working with experts in the neurosciences and all different varieties of medicine, pediatrics, surgery, and trying to help the faculty set up programs that will develop the evidence to help them know how to treat patients more effectively.

WCR: *You are spreading out from coronary disease?*

RMC: I have been for a while.

FIGURE 6. RMC during the interview.

WCR: *It seems to me that about 95% of your publications have been on coronary disease thus far.*

RMC: When we think about cardiology in today's times, such a high portion of it is ischemic heart disease. It is still the world's number one killer, and the recent World Health Organization report points out that it will be even a more dominant health problem in the future. I think that is where a lot of attention needs to be focused, but it is obviously not the only disease in the world. I think one of the issues that we have to come to grips with, and we haven't yet even within cardiology, are the many therapeutic areas that go undeveloped because there is no commercial driver to do the study. I think we need some wisdom here about how to approach the problems for which there is no commercial market.

WCR: *You obviously deal with a lot of different pharmaceutical companies getting support to do many of the studies you do. What have you learned from your relationship with all these companies, the motive of which is profit?*

RMC: First of all, I am a believer in the American profit motive as a driver of innovation. I think on average it is a great system. I think having pharmaceutical companies that are driven by profit is a good thing. It causes people to take routes that they would not otherwise take because of the possibility that it may pay off in a big way and particularly now with the globalization of everything we do, it is a real fundamental advantage that the US has. The pharmaceutical industry, the biotechnology industry, and the devices industry have created drugs and medical devices with creativity and ingenuity.

I have also learned that there are a lot of bright people in industry. The feeling some academic leaders and physicians have that industry is not of the same quality is just not the case. In fact, when it comes to research, I think a lot of the best clinical research is done totally within industry without any academic involvement at all and done to very high standards. Increasingly, our plans at Duke include an interchange of people between industry and academia with a focus on how to do better clinical research and get the answers to the questions that we need answered. If we just look at the statistics, in the US population we see the benefits. For every year that has gone by in the last 20 years, the proportion of disabled but alive people over age 65 years has dropped by 0.6%. Most of that in the older population is due to better lifestyles and better medical care for chronic diseases. I think that is a tremendous tribute to the system.

On the negative side, the problem that continuously arises is that as corporations become global, there are many medical problems and illnesses that are not amenable to generating a large profit. Relying on industry's profit motive may be great for a problem like ischemic heart disease, where if one develops a better way to lower lipids one will make a lot of money and do a lot of good. It is not a very good way to deal with rare diseases or uncommon illnesses in which you can't generate profit for those who develop the therapy.

In addition, there is a worry that the fundamental ethical basis of human experimentation is being sacrificed by the profit motive. I don't regard this problem as the fault of industry—the fault is with the academic and practice communities. Pharmaceutical and device companies cannot do clinical studies on their own; they must work with doctors and nurses. We should be more demanding that when we do medical research, the questions are fairly posed, they are relevant to improving health, and the result is published, whether it is favorable or unfavorable to the sponsor. Patients believe that when we do research, the information will be used to better medicine, and this cannot happen if the result is not published.

WCR: *If you were setting up a medical school would you have separate departments of medicine, surgery, pathology, etc? Would you set it up by the organ systems or how would you do it?*

RMC: Today, obviously, you have to have those departments because that is how people get their credentials to practice. I think that to the extent that they create unnecessary barriers to collaboration, shared resources, and reward for merit, departments need to be deemphasized. If you look at the way medicine is practiced today you can pretty easily see the people who need to work together and who share a common body of knowledge. This would be organized according to what would be called "service lines" in the nonacademic world, so you would have the cardiologists and cardiac surgeons and the cardiac anesthesiologists together in a cardiovascular center, and you would have oncology, which would include surgeons, internists, and radiation experts. You would have orthopedics and rheumatology working together. I think people function better when there is an alignment between what they do in their everyday lives and who their boss is. I would advocate more of a practice-oriented alignment for clinicians in medical schools. And that is beginning to happen at Duke and in a number of places, and I think that trend is going to continue and that is good.

Similarly, those who do basic research increasingly are not, or should not be, limited by departmental lines. If you are interested in a particular type of cellular signaling it should not matter whether you are a biochemist or a microbiologist by your initial training; this is really what you are interested in. Artificial departmental boundaries can be very restrictive. In clinical research, the methodology is common to all diseases, and I think there needs to be more of a focus on good methodology in clinical research. By the same token in a clinical practice plan, which is trying to stay alive in a very competitive world, if your salary is set by someone who is not primarily interested in the practice plan, for that part of your work that is clinical you have a misalignment, which can lead to a lot of difficulties. I think people who are primarily interested in clinical medicine have a lot in common and should hang together.

WCR: *You became editor of the* American Heart Journal *in July 1996? What are your plans for that journal? Are you enjoying it? How much time do you spend on it?*

RMC: I cannot say exactly how many hours I spend on it. *Dan Mark* has been a tremendous driving force and does much of the hands-on editorial work. He is very good at it. We have *Penny Hodgson* as managing editor; she has managed a lot of journals in the past. Our goal is to turn it into a journal devoted to clinical investigation. We are very interested in trying to stimulate research in clinical trials, health policy, and outcomes in cardiovascular disease. I don't think there is enough of that being done. I think we will begin to see some progress in that regard.

Although it is the *American Heart Journal*, we encourage non–US-based studies and are happy to give them the same priority as US-based studies. However, I believe that the potential in the USA to turn out good clinical research has not been met. We would like to be a stimulus to help make that happen.

WCR: *How much teaching do you do, Rob?*

RMC: When I was around the coronary care unit more, that was an everyday teaching experience. Now I spend only a month a year on that activity, and my teaching about individual patient care is less. I do a lot of teaching about clinical research. We have started a master's level course. We have had a course in biometry for over a decade, which has been very successful. We have recently reconfigured it to be very specifically oriented to clinical investigators. That has been an extremely good experience this year. In addition, we have a large number of fellows and junior faculty who spend time in the Clinical Research Institute. I spend a lot of time with them trying to help them sort through issues that they are dealing with as they do their research. Some of the most interesting teaching is continuing medical education. This is most fun when we are reviewing findings from a clinical study with the investigators who participated in the trial. The thirst for knowledge about how to improve practice is substantial in the practice community.

WCR: *You are involved in a lot of different professional activities? How do you do all this? Do you sleep? Maybe you could go through a typical day. What time do you wake up, what time do you get to the hospital, what time to you get home at night, what time do you go to bed?*

RMC: I usually get up around 6:00 A.M. or a little before, have a cup of coffee, read the paper. I go into work a little bit before 7:00 A.M. and start out the day by answering a bunch of e-mails I need to figure out what to do with. On a bad day, I will have meeting after meeting, talking about administrative issues or financial issues. On a good day, I will have a bunch of meetings where I am looking at data with people or going over a new study or thinking about an analysis. I am striving to have more of those good days and fewer of those bad days. I generally will have some kind of meeting or research conference during lunch. I will eat lunch on the fly and then work until between 6:00 and 7:00, usually closer to 7:00, and then head for home and have dinner with the family.

I have a very nice computer setup at home so I can sit at home and get my work done there. I used to have to go back to work at night, but I don't have to do that anymore unless I am on call for the coronary care unit.

WCR: *You finish dinner about 8:00? Are you much good to work after that now?*

RMC: It depends on the situation. There is always some kind of work I can do. That is a good time for me to review manuscripts or talk on the phone or answer e-mails. My best creative time is early in the morning, no doubt about that. If I want to work on something new, I will try to get up early in the morning and work on it, but early for me is 6:00 A.M. At night, by about 11:00, I have had it.

WCR: *What about weekends?*

RMC: I get most of my creative work done on weekends. I get up early in the mornings before the family does. I have a bunch of late sleepers in my family. I put on a pot of coffee, put on some classical music, and go to work. That is a very productive time for me. We are churchgoers on Sunday. We go to the Duke Chapel, which is a beautiful place for worship. It has a lot of traditions and a phenomenal choir and organ. Then the family will go out to lunch and review the situation for the week, whatever it may be.

WCR: *You have 3 children?*

RMC: Right.

WCR: *How old are they?*

RMC: Sharon will be 20 next week. She is at Elon College and doing great. She had her heart surgery at a young age and has done extremely well. I am really proud of her and she is enjoying college. Sam is 15.

He is a musician. He plays the electric guitar. He has a big concert tomorrow at school. He enjoys golf as I do. He is just a good guy to be around, and very bright. Tom, who is 13, is the athlete in the family. He plays on the basketball and soccer teams. He is very good with computers, much better than I am. I feel confident that each of the three will make a positive contribution to the world. It is fascinating how different each one is. We are enjoying the family life. My biggest regret is not spending more time at home when the children were little.

WCR: *You are trying to make up for that now?*

RMC: To some extent, as best I can. It is a struggle.

WCR: *Are you a pretty good daddy?*

RMC: You would have to ask them. I feel like I am. I think our children feel loved and cared for at home. Maybe that is something we don't see enough of these days.

WCR: *Do you take family vacations?*

RMC: We do. Lydia's parents have a beach house at Long Beach just south of Wilmington, North Carolina, and we go there every summer. We, at times, have gone to the mountains of North Carolina. We tend to spend a lot of time at home during the summer, even some vacation times just around the house.

WCR: *How much time do you take off a year, as a rule?*

RMC: Not enough. A couple of weeks.

WCR: *You obviously do a lot of traveling. These multicenter studies require meetings outside Durham; you go places to give talks, participate in educational meetings, visiting professorships. How much time are you gone?*

RMC: We just went over this on the homefront. I am gone about 60 days a year.

WCR: *So that is 60 nights away from home?*

RMC: If you average it out, it is probably a bit fewer than that because a lot of my trips these days are to Washington, and I can go back and forth in the same day. I am away probably about 40 nights a year (not including vacations). Face to face meetings are critical, and I really enjoy the relationships I have developed with clinicians and researchers around the world.

WCR: *For somebody who did not do any traveling when growing up you certainly have made up for it now. Are you going to be able to continue this pace for the next 20 years?*

RMC: I hope not. I hope that I will now settle into a lifestyle that is a little less frenetic but intellectually just as challenging. There are a lot of people in our research group now who are more skilled than I am at things I used to do myself. My goal is to have them develop even further, and I would like to focus on the background work to make the systems more effective.

WCR: *Do you have any ambitions to get other titles, seek other challenges? Would you look at opportunities outside of Duke?*

RMC: No, I think Duke is a great place to be right now. We are busy developing an integrated health system where we can actually try to use evidence as best we can to guide us to practice better medicine. This concept of evidence-based medicine is something people have talked about for a long time. We all know that much of managed care has failed because the financial pressures have been so great. Perhaps the time has come for academic health systems to step forward. The ability to have people who are cared for by your healthcare system over time, and to have information about how they are doing so that you can try to provide the best system of care is an exciting opportunity, and Duke is making an effort to be a leader in that category.

The support for the Clinical Research Institute has been great. The university built a new building that we are getting ready to move into. It will have the latest telecommunications and computer equipment. I might be able to cut out some more of my traveling just by being beamed out and talking with people that way. That would be greatly advantageous to me. I don't really enjoy sitting in airplanes and when I travel I generally don't get time to do things that would be fun. Travel for me is just a way to exchange knowledge and information.

The goal of the DCRI is to improve the practice of medicine and therefore the outcomes of patients through the use of quantitative principles. We hope to facilitate the chain of evidence from translational research to therapeutic trials to outcomes studies. I am grateful to our many collaborators and employees who have made the DCRI successful.

WCR: *Cardiology obviously has become a technology driven specialty. Do you think 12 years from now that there will be as many angioplasties and bypass operations done as there are today?*

RMC: If I had to bet, I would say there probably will be just as many, but it might not be much longer than 12 years that cardiology is going to be so technology driven. As we develop new ways to grow new blood vessels and use biological means to change pathophysiology, we may not need to do nearly as many invasive procedures as we are doing now. In 20 years, the procedures that we will be doing will be very different from today. I think they will be much more biologically oriented.

WCR: *Do we have too many physicians, too many medical schools? What should we be doing?*

RMC: I am not an expert on the number of medical schools, but it is my impression that we are probably training too many doctors right now. I don't think we are training too many healthcare providers. We need a somewhat different positioning of what people do. We are going to need an army of people to deal with the ravages of chronic disease and the aging population. It may not be that the technologically oriented physician is the right person to do that. If I had to bet, the best system would be one in which there is a physician who is trained not only in medicine, but also in management who is the leader of a squad of healthcare delivery people, including nurse practitioners, physician's assistants, and others, who provide most of the hands-on patient care. For example, in heart failure, we already know that you need a good diagnosis, and that needs to be done by someone who is highly trained, and serious effort needs to be put into the design of a treatment plan. But follow-up on that plan can be much more efficiently done by nurse practitioners and physician assistants than by physicians. We will need systems of calling people at home and interacting on the internet. A lot of patients come back once a month to the doctor's office for management of chronic medical problems and this could be done better by nonphysicians. I think the world will change substantially. The question of how many medical schools are needed may be supplanted by a question of how many places do we need for training and re-training of people who are providing medical care.

WCR: *Whether physicians or non-physicians?*

RMC: Right.

WCR: *It sounds to me like you and your wife Lydia have a very close relationship.*

RMC: We do and she has tolerated a lot over the years. She and I are sort of bookends. She frequently says I have no right brain and she doesn't like to use the left side of her brain as much. She really has an incredibly intuitive sense of what needs to be done, how to deal with people, how to notice small things and take care of them, and a tremendous sense of responsibility. I am burdened with often times thinking about the big picture, but missing really obvious things right in front of me that need to be dealt with, so she plays the key role in keeping me straight on those things. I'm often dealing with people who want to be important, and she keeps reminding me that most people are just trying to get through the day. She's been great for me. We are getting ready to celebrate 25 years of marriage and hopefully another 25 or so after that.

WCR: *Both of you were 21 when you got married?*

RMC: Right.

WCR: *Do you have hobbies?*

RMC: I like to play golf.

WCR: *Do you play much?*

RMC: I am playing a lot now. I am not getting any better, but I get out and hit maybe 3 or 4 times a week.

WCR: *Nine holes each time?*

RMC: I joined a golf club. It is not very crowded. I can walk 9 holes in an hour and a half. I can do that at the end of the day, particularly now that we have daylight savings time back. This year for the first time, I go to the driving range, which might improve my game. Both my boys play golf now.

WCR: *Do you have other hobbies?*

RMC: I like to listen to music, but I don't play an instrument. I love to watch basketball, but everybody in North Carolina loves to watch basketball. We've had season tickets to Cameron Indoor Stadium for Duke home games since 1982. I still like to get out and shoot baskets a little bit. I exercise. I finally got some equipment at home so I can ride the bicycle at home and watch television while doing it. I like to follow politics, which I find interesting.

WCR: *Do you do much reading outside of medicine?*

RMC: Not really at this point. I keep thinking I will go back to reading, but I am not doing a lot of reading outside of news magazines, newspapers, and medical stuff.

WCR: *It is pretty hard with your schedule. Who do you admire in cardiology or in medicine in general? You have mentioned Eugene Stead, Holly Smith. Who are medical heroes to you?*

RMC: I am not much of a hero worshiper. What I tend to see are attributes that people have that are admirable that are worth emulating. For example, Joe Greenfield had the personal touch of being able to meet with people and sort of know what they needed. One of our junior faculty once said he had calculated that working for Joe was worth $40,000 in salary. And most of us gave up more than that to work for Joe. Eric Topol's ability to see through data and draw a conclusion is tremendously effective. I aspire to be as good at that as he is. Gene Braunwald's ability to assimilate information and put it together in a way that can be explained to people is phenomenal. If you look at his career, the writing and lecturing he has done, it has transmitted a tremendous amount of information. I think Kanu Chatterjee's ability to see the patient and put things together has been great. If you asked me the one person who I just want to be like more than anybody else, I really would tend to see parts of people, but no single individual I would aspire to copy myself after.

WCR: *Do you think leadership is something neglected when committees get together to pick a chairman of this or that department in medical schools?*

RMC: I think leadership is hard to quantify, but it is something tangible when you look for it, and I don't think it is looked for enough. Of course, leadership, the ability to get people to follow, can be good or bad depending on what your underlying ideas are, but I think it is absolutely critical. We just saw *Primary Colors* over the weekend and that sort of quality that causes people to stop what they are doing and reorient themselves is an important attribute. I think that on balance, we need more emphasis on leadership because life is not a process. We need processes. We need methods of doing things, but the thing that draws the best out of people is when they figure out a way to do it differently and have the inspiration to accomplish a goal. We need more game plans—doing something for a purpose—not just processes. I think leaders bring out those qualities in people.

WCR: *When you are gone, when you cross the river, so to speak, what do you want to be remembered for?*

RMC: I don't really care if I am remembered, except by my family. I want my family to remember that I was a good person and that I had qualities that were passed on to them that they would want to emulate. Where I had qualities that were not admirable—like not coming home for dinner often enough or not paying attention to the little thing that a child did—I would hope to have recognized my deficiency and discussed it with the family so that they would try to do better than I did. I think that in the end these are the only things that really matter in terms of memory.

On a more general level, it is not important that I am remembered as a person, but I would hope to leave behind a better (I have gotten very focused on this issue) method of quantifying medicine so that we can know what we are doing when we treat people. I think if I can leave behind an improvement in the system of evidence-based medicine, I will feel I have done what I was intended to do. It really does not matter to me that I am the one who is remembered. But it does matter to me that the medical care system is better and that it works and that people are closer to getting what they need in the way of medical care. No matter what we do in medical care, if we get people to live longer or not be as ill, they can do something that is enjoyable and worthwhile in the time they have. The medical part is only a part of the equation. I think creating the circumstances to give others opportunity is very good use of one's time.

WCR: *Is there anything you would like to discuss that we haven't? Anything you would like to leave to your grandchildren to read about 25 years from now?*

RMC: I think probably that last part I said is what the grandchildren ought to listen to. You have pretty well exhausted me and I think I said pretty much what is on my mind.

WCR: *Rob, thank you. It has really been a treat. Thank you for sharing your thoughts and your career with the AJC readers.*

RMC PUBLICATIONS SELECTED BY HIM AS HIS BEST

1. Califf RM, Burks JM, Behar VS, Margolis JR, Wagner GS. Relationships among ventricular arrhythmias, coronary artery disease, and angiographic and electrocardiographic indicators of myocardial fibrosis. *Circulation* 1978;57:725–732.

3. Califf RM, McKinnis RA, Burks J, Lee KL, Harrell FE Jr, Behar VS, Pryor DB, Wagner GS, Rosati RA. Prognostic implications of ventricular arrhythmias during 24 hour ambulatory monitoring in patients undergoing cardiac catheterization for coronary artery disease. *Am J Cardiol* 1982;50:23–31.

7. Califf RM, McKinnis RA, McNeer JF, Harrell FE Jr, Lee KL, Pryor DB, Waugh RA, Harris PJ, Rosati RA, Wagner GS. Prognostic value of ventricular arrhythmias associated with treadmill exercise testing in patients studied with cardiac catheterization for suspected ischemic heart disease. *J Am Coll Cardiol* 1983;2:1060–1067.

8. Califf RM, Tomabechi Y, Lee KL, Phillips H, Pryor DB, Harrell FE Jr, Harris PJ, Peter RH, Behar VS, Kong Y, Rosati RA. Outcome in one-vessel coronary artery disease. *Circulation* 1983;67:283–290.

11. Pryor DB, Harrell FE Jr, Lee KL, Califf RM, Rosati RA. An improving prognosis over time in medically treated patients with coronary artery disease. *Am J Cardiol* 1983;52:444–448.

13. Roberts KB, Califf RM, Harrell FE Jr, Lee KL, Pryor DB, Rosati RA. The prognosis for patients with new-onset angina who have undergone cardiac catheterization. *Circulation* 1983;68:970–978.

19. Hlatky MA, Lee KL, Harrell FE Jr, Califf RM, Pryor DB, Mark DB, Rosati RA. Tying clinical research to patient care by use of an observational database. *Statistics in Medicine* 1984;3:375–384.

21. Komrad MS, Coffey CE, Coffey KS, McKinnis R, Massey EW, Califf RM. Myocardial infarction and stroke. *Neurology* 1984;34:1403–1409.

27. Califf RM, Hlatky MA, Mark DB, Lee KL, Harrell FE Jr, Rosati RA, Pryor DB. Randomized trials of coronary artery bypass surgery: impact on clinical practice at Duke University Medical Center. *Circulation* 1985;72:136–144.

28. Califf RM, Phillips HR III, Hindman MC, Mark DB, Lee KL, Behar VS, Johnson RA, Pryor DB, Rosati RA, Wagner GS, Harrell FE Jr. Prognostic value of a coronary artery jeopardy score. *J Am Coll Cardiol* 1985;5:1055–1063.

35. Hlatky MA, Haney T, Barefoot JC, Califf RM, Mark DB, Pryor DB, Williams RB. Medical, psychological and social correlates of work disability among men with coronary artery disease. *Am J Cardiol* 1986;58:911–915.

37. Lee KL, Pryor DB, Harrell FE Jr, Califf RM, Behar VS, Floyd WL, Morris JJ, Waugh RA, Whalen RE, Rosati RA. Predicting outcome in coronary disease: statistical models versus expert clinicians. *Am J Med* 1986;80:553–560.

38. Papanicolaou MN, Califf RM, Hlatky MA, McKinnis RA, Harrell FE Jr, Mark DB, McCants B, Rosati RA, Lee KL, Pryor DB. Prognostic implications of angiographically normal and insignificantly narrowed coronary arteries. *Am J Cardiol* 1986;58:1181–1187.

41. Blackshear JL, O'Callaghan WG, Califf RM. Medical approaches to prevention of restenosis after coronary angioplasty. *J Am Coll Cardiol* 1987;9:834–848.

44. Mark DB, Hlatky MA, Harrell FE Jr, Lee KL, Califf RM, Pryor DB. Exercise treadmill score for predicting prognosis in coronary artery disease. *Ann Intern Med* 1987;106:793–800.

46. Pryor DB, Harrell FE, Rankin JS, Lee KL, Muhlbaier LH, Oldham HN, Hlatky MA, Mark DB, Reves JG, Califf RM. The changing survival benefits of coronary revascularization over time. *Circulation* 1987;76:13–21.

48. Topol EJ, Califf RM, George BS, Kereiakes DJ, Abbottsmith CW, Candela RJ, Lee KL, Pitt B, Stack RS, O'Neill WW, and the Thrombolysis and Angioplasty in Myocardial Infarction Study Group. A randomized trial of immediate versus delayed elective angioplasty after intravenous tissue plasminogen activator in acute myocardial infarction. *N Engl J Med* 1987;317:581–588.

53. Bounous EP, Mark DB, Pollock BG, Hlatky MA, Harrell FE Jr, Lee KL, Rankin JS, Wechsler AS, Pryor DB, Califf RM. Surgical survival benefits for coronary disease in patients with left ventricular dysfunction. *Circulation* 1988;78:151–157.

54. Califf RM, Harrell FE Jr, Lee KL, Rankin JS, Mark DB, Hlatky MA, Muhlbaier LH, Wechsler AS, Jones RH, Oldham HN Jr, Pryor DB. Changing efficacy of coronary revascularization: implications for patient selection. *Circulation* 1988;78:185–191.

56. Califf RM, Mark DB, Harrell FE Jr, Hlatky MA, Lee KL, Rosati RA, Pryor DB. Importance of clinical measures of ischemia in the prognosis of patients with documented coronary artery disease. *J Am Coll Cardiol* 1988;11:20–26.

57. Califf RM, O'Neill W, Stack RS, Aronson L, Mark DB, Mantell S, George BS, Candela RJ, Kereiakes DJ, Abbottsmith C, Topol EJ, and TAMI Study Group. Failure of simple clinical measurements to predict perfusion status after intravenous thrombolysis. *Ann Intern Med* 1988;108:658–662.

58. Califf RM, Topol EJ, George BS, Boswick JM, Abbottsmith C, Sigmon KN, Candela R, Masek R, Kereiakes D, O'Neill WW, Stack RS, Stump D, and the TAMI Study Group. Hemorrhagic complications associated with the use of intravenous tissue plasminogen activator in treatment of acute myocardial infarction. *Am J Med* 1988;85:353–359.

59. Califf RM, Topol EJ, George BS, Boswick JM, Lee KL, Stump D, Dillon J, Abbottsmith C, Candela RJ, Kereiakes DJ, O'Neill WW, Stack RS, and the TAMI Study Group. Characteristics and outcome of patients in whom reperfusion with intravenous tissue-type plasminogen activator fails: results of the thrombolysis and angioplasty in myocardial infarction (TAMI) I trial. *Circulation* 1988; 77:1090–1099.

62. Hlatky MA, Califf RM, Harrell FE Jr, Lee KL, Mark DB, Pryor DB. Comparison of predictions based on observational data with the results of randomized controlled clinical trials of coronary artery bypass surgery. *J Am Coll Cardiol* 1988;11:237–245.

70. Stack RS, Califf RM, Phillips HR, Pryor DB, Quigley PJ, Bauman RP, Tcheng JE, Greenfield JC Jr. Interventional cardiac catheterization at Duke Medical Center. *Am J Cardiol* 1988;62:3F–24F.

71. Stack RS, O'Connor CM, Mark DB, Hinohara T, Phillips HR, Lee MM, Ramirez NM, O'Callaghan WG, Simonton CA, Carlson EB, Morris KG, Behar VS, Kong Y, Peter RH, Califf RM. Coronary perfusion during acute myocardial infarction with a combined therapy of coronary angioplasty and high-dose intravenous streptokinase. *Circulation* 1988;77:151–161.

78. Califf RM, Harrell FE Jr, Lee KL, Rankin JS, Hlatky MA, Mark DB, Jones RH, Muhlbaier LH, Oldham HN, Pryor DB. The evolution of medical and surgical therapy for coronary artery disease: a 15-year perspective. *JAMA* 1989; 261:2077–2086.

82. Gersh BJ, Califf RM, Loop FD, Akins CW, Pryor DB, Takaro TC. Coronary bypass surgery in chronic stable angina. *Circulation* 1989;79:46–59.

84. Hlatky MA, Boineau RE, Higginbotham MB, Lee KL, Mark DB, Califf RM, Cobb FR, Pryor DB. A brief self-administered questionnaire to determine function capacity (the Duke Activity Status Index). *Am J Cardiol* 1989;64:651–654.

86. Kereiakes DJ, Topol EJ, George BS, Abbottsmith CW, Stack RS, Candela RJ, O'Neill WW, Anderson LC, Califf RM, and the TAMI Study Group. Favorable early and long-term prognosis following coronary bypass surgery therapy for myocardial infarction: results of a multicenter trial. *Am Heart J* 1989;118:199–207.

92. Stump DC, Califf RM, Topol EJ, Sigmon K, Thornton D, Masek R, Anderson L, Collen D, and the TAMI Study Group. Pharmacodynamics of thrombolysis with recombinant tissue-type plasminogen activator: correlation with characteristics of and clinical outcomes in patients with acute myocardial infarction. *Circulation* 1989;80:1222–1230.

94. Topol EJ, George BS, Kereiakes DJ, Stump DC, Candela RJ, Abbottsmith CW, Aronson L, Pickel A, Boswick JM, Lee KL, Ellis SG, Califf RM, and the TAMI Study Group. A randomized controlled trial of intravenous tissue plasminogen activator and early intravenous heparin in acute myocardial infarction. *Circulation* 1989;79:281–286.

97. Abbottsmith CW, Topol EJ, George BS, Stack RS, Kereiakes DJ, Candela RJ, Anderson LC, Harrelson L, Califf RM. Fate of patients with acute myocardial infarction with patency of the infarct-related vessel achieved with successful thrombolysis versus rescue angioplasty. *J Am Coll Cardiol* 1990;16:770–778.

99. Bengston JR, Mark DB, Honan MB, Rendall DS, Hinohara T, Stack RS, Hlatky MA, Califf RM, Lee KL, Pryor DB. Detection of restenosis after elective percutaneous transluminal coronary angioplasty using the exercise treadmill test. *Am J Cardiol* 1990;65:28–34.

103. Hlatky MA, Califf RM, Harrell FE Jr, Lee KL, Mark DB, Muhlbaier LH, Pryor DB. Clinical judgement and therapeutic decision making. *J Am Coll Cardiol* 1990;15:1–14.

104. Hlatky MA, Lipscomb J, Nelson C, Califf RM, Pryor D, Wallace AG, Mark DB. Resource use and cost of initial coronary revascularization: coronary angioplasty versus coronary bypass surgery. *Circulation* 1990;82:208–213.

105. Honan MB, Harrell FE Jr, Reimer KA, Califf RM, Mark DB, Pryor DB, Hlatky MA. Cardiac rupture, mortality, and the timing of thrombolytic therapy: a meta-analysis. *J Am Coll Cardiol* 1990;16:359–367.

112. Ohman EM, Califf RM, Topol EJ, Candela R, Abbottsmith C, Ellis S, Sigmon KN, Kereiakes D, George B, Stack R, and the TAMI Study Group. Consequences of reocclusion after successful reperfusion therapy in acute myocardial infarction. *Circulation* 1990;82:781–791.

117. Ohman EM, Califf RM, George BS, Quigley PJ, Kereiakes DJ, Harrelson-Woodlief L, Candela RJ, Flanagan C, Stack RS, Topol EJ. The use of intraaortic balloon pumping as an adjunct to reperfusion therapy in acute myocardial infarction. *Am Heart J* 1991;121:895–901.

118. Califf RM, Topol EJ, Stack RS, Ellis SG, George BS, Kereiakes DJ, Samaha JK, Worley SJ, Anderson JL, Harrelson-Woodlief L, Wall TC, Phillips HR, Abbottsmith CW, Candela RJ, Flanagan WH, Sasahara AA, Mantell SJ, Lee KL. Evaluation of combination thrombolytic therapy and timing of cardiac catheterization in acute myocardial infarction: results of thrombolysis and angioplasty in myocardial infarction-phase 5 randomized trial. *Circulation* 1991;83:1543–1556.

121. Kereiakes DJ, Topol EJ, George BS, Stack RS, Abbottsmith CW, Ellis S, Candela RJ, Harrelson L, Martin LH, Califf RM, and the TAMI Study Group. Myocardial infarction with minimal coronary atherosclerosis in the era of thrombolytic reperfusion. *J Am Coll Cardiol* 1991;17:304–312.

122. Kirklin JW, Akins CW, Blackstone EH, Booth DC, Califf RM, Cohen LS, Hall RJ, Harrell FE Jr, Kouchoukos NT, McCallister BD, Naftel DC, Parker JO, Shelden WC, Smith HC, Wechsler AS, Williams JF Jr. Guidelines and indications for coronary artery bypass graft surgery: a report of the American College of Cardiology/American Heart Association task force on assessment of diagnostic and therapeutic cardiovascular procedures (subcommittee on coronary artery bypass graft surgery). *J Am Coll Cardiol* 191;17:543–589.

123. Mark DB, Shaw L, Harrell FE Jr, Hlatky MA, Lee KL, Bengston JR, McCants CB, Califf RM, Pryor DB. Prognostic value of a treadmill exercise score in outpatients with suspected coronary artery disease. *N Engl J Med* 1991;325:849–853.

128. Sane DC, Stump DC, Topol EJ, Sigmon KN, Clair WK, Kereiakes DJ, George BS, Stoddard MF, Bates ER, Stack RS, Califf RM, and The Thrombolysis and Angioplasty in Myocardial Infarction Study Group. Racial differences in responses to thrombolytic therapy with recombinant tissue-type plasminogen activator, increased fibrin(ogen)olysis in blacks. *Circulation* 1991;83:170–175.

130. Smith LR, Harrell FE Jr, Rankin JS, Califf RM, Pryor DB, Muhlbaier LH, Lee KL, Mark DB, Jones RH, Oldham HN, Glower DD, Reves JG, Sabiston DC Jr. Determinants of early versus late cardiac death in patients undergoing coronary artery bypass graft surgery. *Circulation* 1991;84:245–253.

134. Bengtson JR, Kaplan AJ, Pieper KS, Wildermann NM, Mark DB, Pryor DB, Phillips HR III, Califf RM. Prognosis in cardiogenic shock after acute myocardial infarction in the interventional era. *J Am Coll Cardiol* 1992;20:1482–1489.

135. Bickell NA, Pieper KS, Lee KL, Mark DB, Glower DD, Pryor DB, Califf RM. Referral patterns for coronary artery disease treatment: gender bias or good clinical judgement? *Ann Intern Med* 1992;116:791–799.

138. Mark DB, Lam LC, Lee KL, Clapp-Channing NE, Williams RB, Pryor DB, Califf RM, Hlatky MA. Identification of patients with coronary disease at high risk for loss of employment: a prospective validation study. *Circulation* 1992;86:1485–1494.

142. Pryor DB, Shaw L, McCants CB, Lee KL, Mark DB, Harrell FE, Muhlbaier LH, Califf RM. Value of the history and physical in identifying patient's at increased risk for coronary artery disease. *Ann Intern Med* 1993;118:81–90.

143. Topol EJ, Califf RM, Vandormael M, Grinds CL, George BS, Sanz ML, Wall TC, O'Brien M, Schwaiger M, Aguirre FV, Young S, Popma JJ, Sigmon KN, Lee KL, Ellis SG, and the Thrombolysis and Angioplasty in Myocardial Infarctions-6 Study Group. A randomized trial of late reperfusion therapy for acute myocardial infarction. *Circulation* 1992;85:2090–2099.

144. Williams RB, Barefoot JC, Califf RM, Saunders WB, Peterson BL, Haney TL, Pryor DB, Hlatky MA, Siegler IC, Mark DB. Prognostic importance of social and economic resources among medically treated patients with angiographically documented coronary artery disease. *JAMA* 1992;267:520–524.

145. Chapman GD, Ohman EM, Topol EJ, Candela RJ, Kereiakes DJ, Samaha J, Berrios E, Pieper KS, Young SY, Califf RM. Minimizing the risk of inappropriately administering thrombolytic therapy (thrombolysis and angioplasty in myocardial infarction [TAMI] study group). *Am J Cardiol* 1993;71:783–787.

148. Granger CB, Califf RM, Young S, Candela R, Samaha J, Worley S, Kereiakes DJ, Topol EJ, and the TAMI Study Group. Outcomes of patients with diabetes mellitus and acute myocardial infarction treated with thrombolytic therapy. *J Am Coll Cardiol* 1993;21:920–925.

155. O'Connor CM, Meese R, Carney R, Smith J, Conn E, Burks J, Hartman C, Roark S, Shadoff N, Heard M III, Mittler B, Collins G, Navetta F, Leimberger J, Lee K, Califf RM, for the DUCCS Group. A randomized trial of intravenous heparin in conjunction with anistreplase (Anisoylated Plasminogen Streptokinase Activator Complex) in acute myocardial infarction: The Duke University Clinical Cardiology Study (DUCCS) Group. *J Am Coll Cardiol* 1994;23:11–18.

160. Tenaglia AM, Fortin DF, Frid DJ, Nelson CL, Gardner L, Miller M, Navetta FI, Smith JE, Tcheng JE, Califf RM, Stack RS. Predicting the risk of abrupt vessel closure after angioplasty in an individual patient. *J Am Coll Cardiol* 1994;24:1004–1011.

165. Krucoff MW, Croll MA, Pope JE, Granger CB, O'Connor CM, Sigmon KN, Wagner BL, Ryan JA, Lee KL, Kereiakes DJ, Samaha JK, Worley SJ, Ellis SG, Wall TC, Topol EJ, Califf RM, for the TAMI 7 Study Group. Continuous 12-lead ST segment recovery analysis in the TAMI 7 Study: performance of a noninvasive method for real time detection of failed myocardial reperfusion. *Circulation* 1993;88:437–446.

167. Newby KL, Rutsch WR, Califf RM, Simoons ML, Aylward PE, Armstrong PW, Woodlief LH, Lee KL, Topol EJ, Van de Werf F, for the GUSTO-I Investigators. Time from symptom onset to treatment in the outcomes after thrombolytic therapy. *J Am Coll Cardiol* 1996;27:1646–1655.

168. Simoons ML, Maggioni AP, Knatterud G, Leimberger J, de Jaegere P, Van Domburg R, Boersma E, Grazia M, Califf RM, Schroder R, Braunwald E. Risk factors for intracranial hemorrhage during thrombolytic therapy. *Lancet* 1993; 342:1523–1528.

170. Tenaglia AN, Califf RM, Candela RJ, Kereiakes DJ, Berrios E, Young SY, Stack RD, Topol EJ. Thrombolytic therapy in patients requiring cardiopulmonary resuscitation. *Am J Cardiol* 1991;68:1015–1019.

172. Mark DB, Nelson CL, Califf RM, Harrell FE Jr, Lee KL, Jones RH, Fortin DF, Stack RS, Glower DD, Smith LR, DeLong ER, Smith PK, Reves JG, Jollis JG, Tcheng JE, Muhlbaier LH, Lower JE, Phillips HR, Pryor DB. Continuing evolution of therapy for coronary artery disease: initial results from the era of coronary angioplasty. *Circulation* 1994;89:2015–2025.

174. Ohman EM, Topol EJ, Califf RM, Bates ER, Ellis SG, Kereiakes DJ, George BS, Samaha JK, Kline E, Sigmon KN, Stack RS, and the Thrombolysis Angioplasty in Myocardial Infarction Study Group. An analysis of the cause of early mortality after administration of thrombolytic therapy. *Coron Art Dis* 1993;4:957–964.

176. Granger CB, Hirsh J, Califf RM, Col J, White HD, Betriu A, Woodlief LH, Lee KL, Bovill EG, Simes RJ, Topol EJ, for the GUSTO-I Trial. Activated partial thromboplastin time and outcome after thrombolytic therapy for acute myocardial infarction: results from the GUSTO-I Trial. *Circulation* 1996;93:870–878.

183. Gore JM, Granger CB, Sloan MA, Van de Werf F, Weaver WD, Califf RM, White HD, Barbash GI, Simoons ML, Aylward PE, Topol EJ, for the GUSTO Investigators. Stroke after thrombolysis: mortality and functional outcomes in the GUSTO-I Trial. *Circulation* 1995;92:2811–2818.

184. Knaus WA, Harrell FE, Lynn J, Goldman L, Phillips RS, Connors AF Jr, Dawson NV, Fulkerson WJ, Califf RM, Desbiens N, Layde P, Oye PK, Bellamy PE, Hakim RB, Wagner DP, for the SUPPORT Investigators. The SUPPORT prognostic model: objective estimates of survival for seriously ill hospitalized adults. *Ann Intern Med* 1995;122:191–203.

186. GUSTO IIa Investigators. Randomized trial of intravenous heparin versus recombinant hirudin for acute coronary syndromes. *Circulation* 1994;90:1631–1637.

191. Califf RM, Adams K, McKenna W, Gheorghiade M, Uretsky B, McNulty SE, Darius H, Schulman KA, Zannad F, Handberg-Thurmond E, Harrell FE Jr, Wheeler W, Soler-Soler J, Swedburg K. A randomized controlled trial of epoprostenol therapy for severe congestive heart failure: the Flolan international randomized survival trial (FIRST). *Am Heart J* 1997;134:44–54.

196. O'Neill WW, Brodie B, Ivanhoe R, Knopf W, Taylor G, O'Keefe J, Weintraub R, Sickinger B, Berdan LG, Tcheng JE, Woodlief LH, Strzelecki M, Hartzler G, Califf RM. Primary coronary angioplasty for acute myocardial infarction (the primary angioplasty registry). *Am J Cardiol* 1994;73:627–634.

201. Topol EJ, Califf RM, Weisman HF, Ellis SG, Tcheng JE, Worley S, Ivanhoe R, George BS, Fintel D, Weston M, Sigmon K, Anderson KM, Lee KL, Willerson JT, for the EPIC Investigators. Randomized trial of coronary intervention with antibody against platelet IIb/IIa integrin for reduction of clinical restenosis: results at 6 months. *Lancet* 1994;343:881–886.

204. Tcheng JE, Jackman JD, Nelson CL, Gardner LH, Smith LR, Rankin JS, Califf RM, Stack RS. Outcome of patients sustaining acute ischemic mitral regurgitation during myocardial infarction. *Ann Intern Med* 1992;117:18–24.

215. Granger CG, Miller JM, Bovill EG, Gruber A, Tracy RP, Krucoff MW, Green C, Berrios E, Harrington RA, Ohman EM, Califf RM. Rebound increase in thrombin generation and activity after cessation of intravenous heparin in patients with acute coronary syndromes. *Circulation* 1995;91:1929–1935.

219. Califf RM, Fortin DF, Frid DJ, Harlan WR, Bengston M Jr, Nelson CL, Tcheng JE, Mark DB, Stack RS. Restenosis after coronary angioplasty: an overview. *J Am Coll Cardiol* 1991;17:2B–13B.

220. Mark DB, Shaw L, DeLong ER, Califf RM, Pryor DB. Influence of gender on referral to cardiac catheterization: physician bias or appropriate management. *N Engl J Med* 1994;33:1101–1106.

221. Hillegass WB, Jollis JG, Granger CB, Ohman EM, Califf RM, Mark DB. Intracranial hemorrhage risk and new thrombolytic therapies in acute myocardial infarction. *Am J Cardiol* 1994;73:444–449.

225. The GUSTO Investigators. An international randomized trial comparing 4 thrombolytic regimens consisting of tissue plasminogen activator, streptokinase, or both for acute myocardial infarction. *N Engl J Med* 1993;329:673–682.

229. The EPIC Investigators. Use of a monoclonal antibody directed against the platelet-glycoprotein IIb/IIa receptor in high risk coronary angioplasty. *N Engl J Med* 1994;330:956–961.

235. The GUSTO Angiographic Investigators. The effects of tissue plasminogen activator, streptokinase, or both on coronary-artery patency, ventricular function, and survival after acute myocardial infarction. *N Engl J Med* 1993;329:1615–1622.

242. White HD, Barbash GI, Califf RM, Simes RJ, Granger CB, Weaver WD, Kleiman NS, Aylward PE, Gore JM, Vahanian A, Lee KL, Ross AM, Topol EJ, for the GUSTO-I Investigators. Age and outcome with contemporary thrombolytic therapy: results from the GUSTO-I Trial. *Circulation* 1996;94:1826–1833.

244. Mark DB, Talley JD, Topol EJ, Bowman L, Lam LC, Anderson KM, Jollis JG, Cleman MW, Lee KL, Aversano T, Untereker WJ, Davidson-Ray L, Califf RM, for the EPIC Investigators. Economic assessment of platelet glycoprotein IIb/IIa inhibition for prevention of ischemic complications of high-risk coronary angioplasty. *Circulation* 1996;94:629–635.

245. Wall TC, Califf RM, Blankenship J, Talley JD, Tannenbaum M, Schwaiger M, Gacioch G, Cohen MD, Sanz M, Leimberger JD, Topol EJ, and the TAMI-9 Research Group. Intravenous fluosol in the treatment of acute myocardial infarction: results of the thrombolysis and angioplasty in myocardial infarction 9 trial. *Circulation* 1994;90:114–120.

249. O'Connor CM, Meese RB, McNulty S, Lucas KD, Carney RJ, LeBoeuf RM, Maddox W, Bethea CF, Shadoff N, Trahey TF, Heinsimer JA, Burks JM, O'Donnell G, Krucoff MW, Califf RM, for the DUCCS-II Investigators. A randomized factorial trial of reperfusion strategies and aspirin dosing in acute myocardial infarction. *Am J Cardiol* 1996;77:791–797.

250. Mark DB, Naylor CD, Hlatky MA, Califf RM, Topol EJ, Granger CB, Knight JD, Nelson CL, Lee KL, Clapp-Channing NE, Sutherland W, Pilote L, Armstrong PW. Use of medical resources and quality of life outcomes after acute myocardial infarction in Canada versus the United States. *N Engl J Med* 1994; 331:1130–1135.

252. Granger CB, White HD, Bates ER, Ohman EM, Califf RM. A pooled analysis of coronary arterial patency and left ventricular function after intravenous thrombolysis for acute myocardial infarction. *Am J Cardiol* 1994;74:1220–1228.

256. Kleiman NS, White HD, Ohman M, Ross AM, Woodlief LH, Califf RM, Holmes DR Jr, Bates E, Pfisterer M, Vahanian A, Topol EJ, for the GUSTO Investigators. Mortality within 24 hours of thrombolysis for myocardial infarction: the importance of early reperfusion. *Circulation* 1994;90:2658–2665.

257. Tcheng JE, Harrington RA, Kottke-Marchant K, Kleiman NS, Ellis SG, Kereiakes DJ, Mick MJ, Navetta FI, Smith JE, Worley SJ, Miller JA, Joseph DM, Sigmon KN, Kitt MM, du Mée CP, Califf RM, Topol EJ, for the IMPACT Investigators. Multicenter, randomized, double-blind, placebo-controlled trial of the platelet integrin glycoprotein IIb/IIa blocker integrelin in elective coronary intervention. *Circulation* 1995;91:2151–2157.

261. Lee KL, Woodlief LH, Topol EJ, Weaver WD, Betriu A, Col J, Simoons M, Aylward P, Van de Werf F, Califf RM, for the GUSTO-I Investigators. Predictors of 30-day mortality in the era of reperfusion for acute myocardial infarction: results from an international trial of 41,021 patients. *Circulation* 1995;91:1659–1668.

266. Simes RJ, Holmes DR Jr, White HD, Rutsch WR, Vahanian A, Simoons ML, Morris D, Betriu A, Califf RM, Ross AM, for the GUSTO Investigators. The link between the angiographic substudy and mortality outcomes in a large randomized trial of myocardial reperfusion: the importance of early and complete infarct vessel reperfusion. *Circulation* 1995;91:1923–1928.

270. Califf RM, Woodlief L, Harrell FE Jr, Lee KL, White HD, Guerci A, Barbash GI, Simes RJ, Wever WD, Simoons ML, Topol EJ, for the GUSTO-I Investigators. Selection of thrombolytic therapy for individual patients: development of a clinical model. *Am Heart J* 1997;133:630–639.

272. Holmes DR Jr, Topol EJ, Califf RM, Leya F, Berger PB, Talley JD III, Kellett MA Jr, Shani J, Gottlieb RS, Whitlow PL, Adelman AG, Pinderton CA, Lee KL, Pieper K, Keeler GP, Ellis SG, for the CAVEAT-II Investigators. A multicenter, randomized trial of coronary angioplasty versus directional atherectomy for patients with saphenous vein bypass graft lesions. *Circulation* 1995;91: 1966–1974.

280. Newby LK, Califf RM, Guerci A, Weaver WD, Col J, Horgan JH, Mark DB, Stebbins A, Van de Werf F, Gore JM, Topol EJ, for the GUSTO Investigators. Early discharge in the thrombolytic era: an analysis of criteria for uncomplicated infarction from the global utilization of streptokinase and t-PA for occluded coronary arteries (GUSTO) trial. *J Am Coll Cardiol* 1996;27:625–632.

284. Mark DB, Hlatky MA, Califf RM, Naylor CD, Lee KL, Armstrong PW, Barbash G, White H, Simoons ML, Nelson CL, Clapp-Channing N, Knight JD, Harrell FE Jr, Sims E, Topol EJ. Cost effectiveness of thrombolytic therapy with tissue plasminogen activator as compared with streptokinase for acute myocardial infarction. *N Engl J Med* 1995;332:1418–1424; erratum appears in *N Engl J Med* 1995;333:267.

285. Mahaffey KW, Granger CB, Collins R, O'Connor CM, Ohman EM, Bleich SD, Col JJ, Califf RM. Overview of randomized trials of intravenous heparin in patients with acute myocardial infarction treated with thrombolytic therapy. *Am J Cardiol* 1996;77:551–556.

291. Califf RM, Karnash SI, Woodlief LH. Developing systems for cost-effective auditing of clinical trials. *Control Clin Trials* 1997;18:651–660.

292. Puma JA, Sketch MH Jr, Tcheng JE, Gardner LH, Nelson CL, Phillips HR, Stack RS, Califf RM. Percutaneous revascularization of chronic coronary occlusions, an overview. *J Am Coll Cardiol* 1995;26:1–11.

297. Betriu A, Califf RM, Bosch X, Guerci A, Stebbins AL, Barbagelata NA, Aylward PE, Vahanian A, Van de Werf F, Topol EJ, for the GUSTO-I Investigators. Recurrent ischemia after thrombolysis: importance of associated clinical findings. *J Am Coll Cardiol* 1998;31:94–102.

301. Selker HP, Griffith JL, Beshansky JR, Schmid CH, Califf RM, D'Agostino RB, Laks MM, Lee KL, Maynard C, Selvester RH, Wagner GS, Weaver WD. Patient-specific predictions of outcomes in myocardial infarction for real-time emergency use: the thrombolytic predictive instrument (TPI). *Ann Intern Med* 1997;127:538–556 with corresponding editorial.

304. The SUPPORT Investigators. A controlled trial to improve care for seriously ill hospitalized patients: the study to understand prognoses and preferences for outcomes and risks of treatments (SUPPORT). *JAMA* 1995;274:1591–1598.

306. Peterson ED, Shaw LK, DeLong ER, Pryor DB, Califf RM, Mark DB. Racial variation in the use of cardiac revascularization procedures: are the differences real? Do they matter? *N Engl J Med* 1997;336:480–486.

307. Puma JA, Sketch MH Jr, Tcheng JE, Gardner LH, Nelson CL, Phillips HR, Stack RS, Califf RM. The natural history of single-vessel chronic coronary occlusion: a 25 year perspective. *Am Heart J* 1997;133:393–399.

310. Pilote L, Sapp S, Miller DP, Mark DB, Weaver DB, Gore JM, Armstrong PW, Ohman EM, Califf RM, Topol EJ, for the GUSTO Investigators. Regional variation across the United States in the management of acute myocardial infarction. *N Engl J Med* 1995;333:565–572.

315. Ohman EM, Armstrong PW, Christenson RH, Granger CB, Katus HA, Hamm CW, O'Hanesian MA, Wagner GS, Kleiman NS, Harrell FE Jr, Califf RM, Topol EJ, for the GUSTO-IIa Investigators. Risk stratification with admission cardiac troponin T levels in acute myocardial infarction. *N Engl J Med* 1996;335:1333–1341.

316. Califf RM, White HD, Van de Werf F, Sadowski Z, Armstrong PW, Vahanian A, Simoons ML, Simes J, Lee KL, Topol EJ, for the GUSTO-I Investigators. One-year results from the global utilization of streptokinase and TPA for occluded coronary arteries (GUSTO-I) Trial. *Circulation* 1996;94:1233–1238.

322. Fuster V, Califf RM, Chesebro JH, Cohen M, Comp PC, Gheorghiade M, Hall J, Halperin J, Khan S, Kopecky S, and the Coumadin Aspirin Reinfarction Study (CARS) Investigators. Randomized double-blind trial of fixed low-dose warfarin with aspirin after myocardial infarction. *Lancet* 1997;350:389–396.

327. Connors AF Jr, Speroff T, Dawson NV, Thomas C, Harrell FE Jr, Wagner D, Desbiens N, Goldman L, Wu AW, Califf RM, Fulkerson WJ, Vidaillet H, Broste S, Bellamy P, Lynn J, Knaus WA, for the SUPPORT Investigators. The effectiveness of right heart catheterization in the initial care of critically ill patients. *JAMA* 1996;276:889–897.

329. Berkowitz SD, Granger CG, Pieper KS, Lee KL, Gore JM, Simoons M, Armstrong PW, Topol EJ, Califf RM, for the Global Utilization of Streptokinase and Tissue Plasminogen Activator for Occluded Coronary Arteries (GUSTO-I) Investigators. Incidence and predictors of bleeding after contemporary thrombolytic therapy for myocardial infarction. *Circulation* 1997;95:2508–2516.

331. Pilote L, Miller DP, Califf RM, Rao JS, Weaver WD, Topol EJ. Determinants of the use of coronary angiography and revascularization after thrombolysis for acute myocardial infarction in the United States. *N Engl J Med* 1996;335: 1198–1205.

335. Hathaway WR, Peterson ED, Wagner GS, Granger CB, Zabel KM, Pieper KS, Clark KA, Woodlief LH, Califf RM, for the GUSTO-I Investigators. Prognostic significance of the initial electrocardiogram in patients with acute myocardial infarction? *JAMA* 1998;279:387–391.

337. Topol EJ, Califf RM, Van de Werf F, Simoons M, Hampton J, Lee KL, White H, Simes J, Armstrong PW, for the Virtual Coordinating Center for Global Collaborative Cardiovascular Research (VIGOUR) Group. Perspectives on large-scale cardiovascular clinical trials in the new millennium. *Circulation* 1997;95: 1072–1082.

342. Jollis JG, DeLong ER, Peterson ED, Muhlbaier LH, Fortin DF, Califf RM, Mark DB. Outcome of acute myocardial infarction according to the specialty of admitting physician. *N Engl J Med* 1996;335:1880–1887.

353. Califf RM, Armstrong PW, Carver JR, D'Agostino RB, Strauss WE. Task Force 5, stratification of patients into high, medium, and low risk subgroups for purposes of risk factor management. *J Am Coll Cardiol* 1996;27:1040–1047.

362. Ohman EM, Kleiman NS, Gacioch G, Worley SJ, Navetta FI, Talley JD, Anderson HV, Ellis SG, Cohen MD, Spriggs D, Miller M, Kereiakes D, Yakubov S, Kitt MM, Sigmon KN, Califf RM, Krucoff MW, Topol EJ, for the IMPACT-AMI Investigators. Combined accelerated tissue-plasminogen activator and platelet glycoprotein IIb/IIIa integrin receptor blockade with integrilin in acute myocardial infraction: results of a randomized, placebo-controlled, dose-ranging trial. *Circulation* 1997;95:846–854.

364. Barefoot JC, Helms MJ, Mark DB, Blumenthal JA, Califf RM, Haney TL, O'Connor CM, Siegler IC, Williams RB. Depression and long-term mortality risk in patients with coronary artery disease. *Am J Cardiol* 1996;78:613–617.

371. Tcheng JE, Lincoff AM, Sigmon KN, Lee KL, Kitt MM, Califf RM, Topol EJ, Juran N, Worley S, Tuzi J, et al, and the IMPACT II Investigators. Randomized placebo-controlled trial of effect of eptifibatide on complications of percutaneous coronary intervention—IMPACT II. *Lancet* 1997;349:1422–1428.

387. Topol EJ, Califf RM, Granger C, Van de Werf F, Aylward P, Simes J, Col J, Armstrong P, Vahanian A, Neuhaus K, et al, and the Global Use of Strategies to Open Occluded Coronary Arteries (GUSTO) IIb Investigators. A comparison of recombinant hirudin versus heparin for the treatment of acute coronary syndromes. *N Engl J Med* 1996;335:775–782.

392. Califf RM, Abdelmeguid AE, Kuntz R, Popma JJ, Davidson CJ, Cohen EA, Kleiman NS, Mahaffey KW, Topol EJ, Pepine CJ, Lipicky R, Granger CB, et al.

Myonecrosis after revascularization procedures. *J Am Coll Cardiol* 1998;31:241–251.

404. Peterson ED, Shaw LJ, Califf RM. Clinical guideline: Part II. Risk stratification after myocardial infarction. *Ann Intern Med* 1997;126:561–580.

410. Betriu A, Phillips H, Ellis S, Topol E, Califf RM, Van de Werf F, Ardissino D, Armstrong PW, Aylward P, Bates E, et al, and the GUSTO-IIb Angioplasty Substudy Investigators. A clinical trial comparing primary coronary angioplasty with tissue plasminogen activator for acute myocardial infarction. *N Engl J Med* 1997;336:1621–1628.

413. BARI (The Bypass Angioplasty Revascularization Investigators) Investigators. Comparison of coronary bypass surgery with angioplasty in patients with multivessel disease. *N Engl J Med* 1996;335:217-225.

414. Thel MC, Armstrong AL, McNulty SE, Califf RM, O'Connor CM, for the Duke Internal Medicine Housestaff. A randomized trial of magnesium in in-hospital cardiac arrest (MAGIC). *Lancet* 1997;350:1272–1276.

419. Topol EJ, Weisman HF, Tcheng JE, Ellis SG, Kleiman NS, Ivanhoe RJ, Wang AL, Miller DP, Anderson KM, Califf RM, for the EPIC Investigators Group. Protection from myocardial ischemic events in a randomized trial of brief integrin $\beta 3$ blockage with percutaneous coronary intervention. (EPIC 3-year results). *JAMA* 1997;278:479–484.

420. Topol EJ, Califf RM, Lincoff AM, Tcheng JE, Cabot CF, Weisman HF, Kereiakes D, Lausten D, Runyon JP, Howard W, et al, and the EPILOG Investigators. Platelet glycoprotein IIb/IIIa receptor blockade and low-dose heparin during percutaneous coronary revascularization. *N Engl J Med* 1997;336:1689–1696.

429. Ross AM, Coyne K, Moreyra E, Reiner JS, Walker P, Simoons ML, Draoui Y, Califf RM, Topol EJ, Van de Werf F, Lundergan CF, for the GUSTO-I Angiographic Investigators. Impact of early reperfusion on long term survival after myocardial infarction. *Circulation* 1998;97:1549–1556.

431. Ryan TJ, Anderson JL, Antman EM, Braniff BA, Brooks NH, Califf RM, Hillis LD, Hiratzka LF, Rapaport E, Riegel BJ, Russell RO, Smith EE III, Weaver WD, and the ACC/AHA Task Force on Practice Guidelines (Committee on Management of Acute Myocardial Infarction). ACC/AHA Guidelines for the management of patients with acute myocardial infarction. A report of the American College of Cardiology/American Heart Association Task Force on Practice Guidelines (Committee on Management of Acute Myocardial Infarction). *J Am Coll Cardiol* 1996;28:1328–1428.

433. Cohen M, Demers C, Gurfinkel EP, Turpie AGG, Fromell GJ, Goodman S, Langer A, Califf RM, Fox KAA, Premmereur J, Bigonzi F, for the Efficacy and Safety of Subcutaneous Enoxaparin in Non-Q-Wave Coronary Events (ES-SENCE) Study Group. A comparison of low-molecular-weight heparin with unfractionated heparin for unstable coronary artery disease. *N Engl J Med* 1997;337:447–452.

454. The GUSTO III (The Global Use of Strategies to Open Occluded Coronary Arteries) Investigators. A comparison of reteplase with alteplase for acute myocardial infarction. *N Engl J Med* 1997;337:1118–1123.

REVIEWS

19. Califf RM. Why are large-scale trials needed? *Coron Art Dis* 1992;3:92–95.

39. Califf RM, Bengtson JR. Cardiogenic shock. *N Engl J Med* 1994;330:1724–1730.

EDITORIALS

1. Califf RM, Rosati RA. The doctor and the computer. *Western J Med* 1981;135:321–323.

2. Califf RM, Pryor DB, Greenfield JC Jr. Beyond randomized clinical trials: applying clinical experience in the treatment of patients with coronary artery disease. *Circulation* 1986;74:1191–1194.

10. Califf RM, Harrelson-Woodlief L, Topol EJ. Left ventricular ejection fraction may not be useful as an endpoint of thrombolytic therapy comparative trials. *Circulation* 1990;82:1847–1853.

12. Topol EF, Armstrong P, Van de Werf F, Kleiman N, Lee KL, Morris D, Simoons M, Barbash G, White H, Califf RM, on behalf of the Global Utilization of Streptokinase and Tissue Plasminogen Activator for Occluded Coronary Arteries (GUSTO) Steering Committee. Confronting the issues of patient safety and investigator conflict of interest in an international clinical trial of myocardial infarction. *J Am Coll Cardiol* 1991;19:1123–1128.

28. Califf RM, Jollis J, Peterson E. Operator-specific outcomes: a call to professional responsibility. *Circulation* 1996;93:403–406.

WILLIAM PETER CASTELLI, MD:
A Conversation With the Editor*

Bill Castelli was born on November 21, 1931 in New York City, but grew up in Teaneck, New Jersey. In 1953, he graduated from Yale College with a BS degree in zoology and he received his MD from the Catholic University of Louvain, Belgium, in 1959. He did a rotating internship at Kings County Hospital in Brooklyn, New York, and his residency in internal medicine was at Lemuel Shattuck Hospital and Faulkner Hospital in the Boston area. He also had a fellowship in rheumatology at the Massachusetts General Hospital. After a research fellowship in the Department of Preventive Medicine at Harvard Medical School, he joined the Framingham Heart Study sponsored by the National Heart, Lung, and Blood Institute (NHLBI) as director of its laboratories. In 1979, he became director of the Framingham Heart Study and stayed in that position until 1995, when he formed the Framingham Cardiovascular Institute. Through the years he has had lectureships at Boston University School of Medicine, at Harvard Medical School, and the University of Massachusetts Medical School in Worcester. He has written extensively and probably given more medical presentations than any physician in history. He is married to the former Marjorie Irene Fish and they are the proud parents of 3 children and 8 grandchildren. He is also a good guy and fun to be around (Figure 1).

William Clifford Roberts, MD[†] **(hereafter WCR):** *Dr. Castelli has just given a beautiful grand rounds presentation at Baylor University Medical Center and he will speak again, this time to the medical residents after this interview. We are in a conference room near my office. Bill, I appreciate your willingness to talk to me and therefore to the readers of* The American Journal of Cardiology. *Could we start by my asking you to describe your early life, some of your earliest memories, your parents and siblings, and what it was like growing up in the New York City area?*

William Peter Castelli, MD[‡] **(hereafter WPC):** I was the third child in my family. My father was a physician who had been raised on a little farm in the lower Connecticut River valley in Chester. He was the only boy in his high school class who worked himself through Colby College, a small Ivy League college in New England. He served in World War I and returned to start medical school at the Bowdoin Medical School about 1920. (The Flexnor Report gave Bowdoin a B ranking.) After his first year there, Bowdoin closed because it would only continue with an A ranking. My father then went to Yale Medical School and gradu-

FIGURE 1. WPC at time of interview.

ated. He interned at the City Hospital of New York on Welfare Island. There he met my mother, a nurse from Brownville Junction, Maine. Her father, *William McNeil*, an old Scotsman from Nova Scotia, ran the railroad yard for the Canadian Railroad in Brownville Junction for many years. It was the only place in Maine that you could board a Canadian train to go to Montreal or the Maritimes.

My father started practice as a pediatrician. He worked with 1 of the physicians who came out with 1 of the first vaccines for diphtheria. My father helped run some of the vaccine trials in New York City. But he went into practice during the depression and nobody came to a pediatrician. He became the physician for a lot of famous companies in New York—Heidi Candy Company, JP Stevens (textiles), Waterman Pen Factory (I have had free Waterman pens most of my life), and the Gallo Winery in the Sky. He had about 50 companies. He commuted every day to New York from Teaneck, New Jersey. I was born in New York City but grew up in Teaneck. I went to public schools. In high school I was a good student in the sense that I was always on the honor roll, but my father could

*This series of interviews is underwritten by an unrestricted grant from Bristol-Myers Squibb.
†Baylor Heart & Vascular Institute, Baylor University Medical Center, Dallas, Texas 75246.
‡Framingham Cardiovascular Institute, Framingham, Massachusetts 01720.

FIGURE 2. WPC, right halfback, Teaneck High School, Northern New Jersey Interscholastic League, and State Champs 1948.

never figure out how I made it because my grades were lousy. The honor rolls were based on major subjects and one had to have a Bs or better. I always managed ≥2 Bs but I had 5 major subjects. (Most students had 2 major subjects.)

In high school I was the class president and played on the football team (Figure 2). I was very small, however. In the ninth grade I wrestled at 103 pounds. That toughened me up and I went out for football the next year. They weren't going to take me and then I ran after the coach and told him I could beat the crap out of half the guys he gave a uniform to. He looked at me like I was crazy. "Who the hell are you?" he asked. I told him I was a varsity wrestler. I made the football team because I was very fast and I could tackle. I was so little I could hide in the legs of those defensive tackles. When the guy came through the hole, I'd dive into his ankles and wrap him up. They had a few sprained ankles from that and the coaches in the league actually had a complaint out against me. We won the state championship!

WCR: *What did you play?*

WPC: I played a right halfback in the single wing formation, which was the wide receiver. I was a blocking back. If we played a fast halfback, I was the backer up. There was no halfback in the league who could outrun me on an end run.

WCR: *Did you play any other sports?*

WPC: I was always playing some kind of sport, but I didn't play on any other varsity team. I stopped the wrestling because it gave me terrible boils on the back of my neck. I couldn't live with that.

WCR: *What did you do the 100-yard dash in?*

WPC: There were 2 guys in my high school who could beat me in the 100-yard dash by a half step. I don't know what my times were, but they were fairly fast. I was fast and I never dropped a pass in my high school football career. Our final game we had to win was on Thanksgiving Day, the Hackensack game. Our favorite play was when I would go out in the flat, catch the pass, and then lateral to our fullback who was the best runner I ever saw in high school football. We had 2 touchdowns like that and won the championship game. It was "smash mouth" football. We had no face masks. We had a tough coach, *Charlie Knapp*. If you complained about anything, you were out of the game. You could have a broken leg and you wouldn't tell Charlie.

Then I went up to Yale where I was 1 of the last of the playboys of the western world my first few years at Yale. I joined Beta Theta Phi. I played intramural sports. We had great intramural teams in those days. It was tackle football. We had what was called the "college system." Each college had their own football team. It was great. We made up our own plays in the game. We had a lot of fun. On the Harvard-Yale weekends, we played the houses at Harvard. The college that I played for at Yale, Saybrook College, was named after the town at the end of the Connecticut River where Yale was first founded, Saybrook, Connecticut. Later, Yale moved to New Haven. Our team played the Adams House at Harvard. This was the literary house. They had a terrible football team, so we always won that game. We'd come to the game with a couple of cases of beer and had a lot of fun playing.

What turned me around at Yale was *John Courtney Murray*, who taught a course in scholastic philosophy and that caught my interest. I was a zoology major and thought everything was material. He got me interested in the "realm of ideas." For example, there's a chair. Yes, there is a chair (material), but the idea of a chair is not material. It doesn't have size, weight, color, or molecules. It's part of a whole realm of ideas that is the basic you. Plato told us the real you comes down to this realm and grabs onto this body and you participate in this life. Aristotle and Aquinas enlarged on this concept. The other concept I learned in that course was the idea whether there is chaos in the world. The order in the world, of course, is the grand eternal laws of the universe. I thought, "What is that? Who generates all of that power to keep things in order?" When one looks at a hand, there are all these molecules not flying off into space. What's holding them together? It's the grand internal laws of the earth. A religious person will tell you it's the hand of God in your hand holding that all together and that God is the eternal law of the universe. That requires an act of faith. In philosophy, unlike theology, one reasons to these things from public experience. In theology you actually believe that God sent a message. I turned my grades around at Yale and my last year I went almost from last in my major to almost first.

I had to wait a year to get into an American medical school, so I went to Europe. I picked a university in Belgium, Louvain, because it had one of the most famous institutes of philosophy in the world. I studied philosophy and medicine, but never took the exams in philosophy. I was more serious than the other kids. In Europe it's easy to get into the medical schools, but it's tough to succeed. Two-thirds of my class flunked the first exam in Louvain. I was never near flunking. I always was one of the better students. I had to learn French. I took all my exams in French. I used to tutor classmates in the medical subjects to practice my French. The Belgians were wonderful to me. They treated me like a son because they knew I was helping their kids. Because Belgium is a small country, everyone went home for the weekends. All of the social activities took place in the hometowns. I would be invited home to these families. They would make me part of their family. If I went on a trip, I probably wouldn't send my parents a card, but I would damn sure send my Belgian parents cards because they would find out that I went on the trip and didn't send them a card. I was looking after their sons trying to straighten them out and get them to work harder, etc. They really appreciated that. Belgium was also a place where you could not date girls. People thought, "Oh boy! Wild! Going to Europe. It's going to be a wild time with the women." That isn't true in Belgium. You could invite a young lady once to the movies and probably get away with it. Maybe twice, but on the third time you'd be home meeting her family declaring your general intent to get married.

The Belgians translate your name. I was told I was a lucky guy. I asked, "Why?" "Because of your name." These kids in Belgium all took Latin and Greek in high school. My last name is straight out of the Latin. It's the ablative of *castellum*, "a fortress." The people in Europe, even though they have gotten rid of the aristocracy, think that there are still people from the aristocracy living among them. If you have a name that is named after a castle or a fortress, they are going to think you are a part of the aristocracy. In French, if you put an "i" at the end of a word, it's sort of the diminutive. They called me *petit chateau*, "little chateau." That meant that they considered me part of a dynamic aristocracy. It's crazy. When I went to Italy to find the village where my grandfather came from in the 1800s, the whole village was named Castelli. It would be like having a name and the translation to English would be castle. They treated me with great deference. It was a lot of fun.

After I was at Louvain for about a year I got accepted into an American medical school, but decided to stay at Louvain. My father was pretty upset

about that. My father probably had the first nickel that he ever made. He was a very prudent man. I said, "Dad, the tuition here is $65 a year for the medical school. Because I'm in 2 schools, medicine and philosophy, I have to pay $110." You could live like a king in those days in Belgium for $100 a month.

WCR: *When did you go to Louvain?*

WPC: In 1953. I was there until 1958. I had to go back in 1959 and take the final exam after my internship. To pay the Belgians back, I organized 50 or so internships for members of my class and members of the Flemish medical school class who wanted to do their internship in America. That was good for them to do that. I wrote all the letters and made all the arrangements. They had to pick internships where they paid a lot of money because they didn't have enough money. They didn't get into the better internships. Nonetheless, it was really a great experience for them. Some stayed in America and I still see some of them.

It was a great time in my life. I told my father, "Look Dad. Don't worry. When I come back I will do a residency and I won't miss anything." Towards the end of medical school I started returning to the USA in the summer. By then my father had retired. We had a second home on the Connecticut River about 5 miles up the river from where my father grew up. My father's father came over from Italy in the 1800s and bought 200 acres on the Connecticut River in Chester, Connecticut. If we still had that in the family, we'd be rich. He brought his brother to America and gave half of the land to him. Chester is still one of the well-to-do, unspoiled areas of the lower Connecticut River. We had a house in Haddam with 30 acres on the river. It was a big old mansion that some sugar magnate had built. I came to that place one summer and worked at the local hospital (Middlesex Hospital) in Middletown. Connecticut, the home of Wesleyan University and a big shopping center for the lower Connecticut River valley. I went in to ask the chief of medicine if I could go to grand rounds and use the library. His first question to me was, "Do you speak French?" I said, "Yes." He said, "We have 3 new interns—2 from Belfast, Ireland, and 1 from Paris, France. The guy from Paris says he can speak English, but nobody can understand a word he says and we're not sure he understands us." I got the job of getting him up to speed. Then they said, "What do you want us to give you?" I said, "All I want you to give me is 1 patient per week to myself in medicine to work up with your supervision." It was great training for Framingham. I ordered every test on all of my patients. I had all week to work on the patient. I used to write 70-page work-ups on my patients. Nobody wanted to read them. The chiefs of medicine in those days at Middletown were junior faculty from Yale. It's funny how these things play out. The first chief was *Harold Kahn*. By ordering all these tests, I would find things that nobody suspected. It would change the diagnosis. They'd say, "How the hell can that guy, who is not even an intern, come up with this diagnosis or even think that the patient might have had this?" It was no great mystery.

FIGURE 3. The folks from the Lemuel Shattuck Hospital, with *Thomas Chalmers* and *Hugo Muench* in the *middle.*

I was ordering all the tests to get practice. I got the French intern up to speed.

Edgar Cathcart, one of the interns from Belfast, Ireland, and I used to go home every third night because we were off together. My parents adopted Edgar. When I left to go back to Belgium, he continued to come to my home every third night. Edgar went to Boston and became a rheumatologist. We'd meet when I came home on vacation.

My father asked me to do a rotating internship in a big city hospital. That was all he asked me to do. I picked the Kings County Hospital in Brooklyn, New York. Kings County was the largest city hospital on the east coast at that time. Kings County Hospital was where the Downstate University of New York did their clinics. This was (1958 to 1959) before the University Hospital was built across the street. I saw every disease there was in that year. I set a record in neurosurgery in my second month. A guy went into Prospect Park in Brooklyn with a baseball bat and snuck up behind people on the benches, knocked them out, and robbed them. I got all 17 as patients. I delivered 21 babies in 1 day in obstetrics. Someone beat me with 22 a month later. I was able to experience everything.

I went to Boston the next year to become a rheumatologist on the advice of my friend, Edgar Cathcart. I had a joint appointment at the Lemuel Shattuck Hospital (Figure 3) and Massachusetts General Hospitals. The Shattuck was a special place then because the chief of medicine, *Tom Chalmers*, ran the entire hospital as though it was a clinical pharmacology unit. Chalmers is the father of meta-analysis. I arrived at the Shattuck and my first grand rounds was taught by *Hugo Muench*, the retired professor of biostatistics of the Harvard School of Public Health. When he gave his first lecture I was sitting there wondering what the heck this had to do with medicine. We soon learned the Shattuck attitude. If you got a diagnosis at the Shattuck, we had a protocol. For me, the most important thing Chalmers said was, "You randomize the first patient." His favorite lecture in life was bleeding in medicine. He'd say, "They had bleeding for hundreds of years. Why? Nobody did a trial. Had they done a trial, they probably would have found out it didn't work. At least they wouldn't have bothered bleeding anyone." We had the largest metabolic ward in the history of Boston. We did many trials of everything.

One day a week I went to the Massachusetts General Hospital to work with *Marian Ropes*, one of the best rheumatologists in the history of this country. She was a very good clinician. I'd been trained in Europe and I was big into physical diagnosis because of that. To pick up little effusions in joints, you have to be very thorough. She liked me and let me see all her private patients. Here's rheumatoid arthritis, an incurable disease about which we really don't know the cause. I could spend 45 minutes working up the patient. Many of her patients were very wealthy and they had been to every hospital. One patient would almost give you the history of rheumatology by taking a single history. It was a great education for me. Tom Chalmers came to me 1 day and asked me if I would help a professor, *Dave Rutstein*, at Harvard with a tissue culture model of atherosclerosis. He didn't have a clinical liaison and he needed a research dietitian. We had a couple at the Shattuck. He asked me if I would help organize some studies for him feeding these patients. Dave made his mark in preventive medicine by campaigning against strep throats and preventing rheumatic heart disease. He was part of those committees. He had a tissue culture of atherosclerosis. I started organizing the studies for him and he asked me if I would do a postdoctorate fellowship at Harvard. I did. That got me into all the exotic lipids. It was in the medical school, not the School of Public Health. We taught preventive medicine to the medical students at Harvard. That was a rich experience. *Bill Kannel*, a member of our department at Harvard, came in to talk about Framingham. He used to poke his head into the laboratory and find out what the latest stuff was. He asked me if I would come to Framingham when I finished my postdoctorate fellowship to reor-

FIGURE 4. The Framingham Heart Study.

ganize the laboratory (Figure 4). The only way they could pay me was to make me a commissioned officer in the Public Health Service. I was assigned to the NHLBI. I had to go to *Robert I. Levy's* laboratory to learn to do the β quantification. I spun the blood in a preparative ultracentrifuge, did some cuts, measured high-density lipoprotein (HDL), and eventually calculated low-density lipoprotein (LDL). I measured the triglycerides and did electrophoretic strips. I had to learn how to do the paper electrophoretic strips from *Betty Masket*. That was a finicky thing because, if the humidity changed, it could louse up the run. It was an art as well as a science. We had gone from thinking that the only serum total cholesterol you had to know in the early 1960s was 300. Patients with lower numbers were ignored. With today's therapies, I could have cured most of those patients. If I had done that, the heart attack rate in the USA would have fallen about 5%! In the late 1960s, we went to the various lipoprotein types in the Fredrickson, Levy, Lee's classification. If your LDL fell into the upper 5 to 10 percentiles, then half of your brothers and sisters and half your parents were also were in the upper 5 to 10 percentiles. That taught us the big genetics. Those high LDLs are a dominant trait. Worse than that though was high LDL and high triglycerides, which we called the type 2B. Type 2A was characterized by just high LDL. The type 4s made it to the upper 5 to 10 percentiles in triglycerides. We also did type 3s, but there were only about 4 dozen laboratories in the

USA that could do them. We would look for the chylomicrons on the electrophoretic strips. We'd also inspect the blood after it stood overnight in the refrigerator. Bob Levy was my guide if I had any questions. One Saturday, when we first set up this laboratory, we did 3 electrophoretic strips. One was the total blood, 1 was the top fraction, and 1 was the bottom fraction. In the top fraction you would have the chylomicrons and the pre-βs and the bottom fractions contained the LDLs and HDLs. Then I noticed a pre-β band show up in the bottom fraction. I thought initially that somehow our ultracentrifuge was not working well. I called the company to check out our ultracentrifuge. They said it was fine. The electrophoretic machine was also fine. Finally, I called Bob Levy, and said "Bob. We're getting a pre-β band in the bottom fraction. I thought the ultracentrifuge wasn't working well, but it is working well. I don't know what that is." He said, "It is called sinking pre-β. It is lipoprotein(a) [Lp(a)]." That sinking pre-β predicted dynamite in the Framingham Study. It's worse in women than in men. In the Heart and Estrogen/Progestin Replacement Study (HERS) study, where they fed that phony estrogen at the wrong dose, the only women who did well in the HERS study after a heart attack on estrogen were the women who had an elevated Lp(a). They were the only group who had a fall in their heart attack rate. There are only 2 drugs that lower Lp(a) well: estrogen and niacin. Fenofibrate does just a little. We don't have any good trials showing that when the

FIGURE 5. One of the *Masters of Cardiology*.

ham from Duke to serve as a commissioned officer in the Public Health Service. We set up a coagulation laboratory, and he and I did platelet adhesiveness and aggregation. We bought a Bryston aggregometer. We put platelets in the aggregometer and added different things to make them clump and we studied the clumps. Adhesiveness was shown by drawing blood through the glass beads. I bought all this machinery through the National Institutes of Health (NIH) by finding a way around all of the red tape. I finally learned which guy to go to and he could get me anything. I got machines to do platelet counts automatically. Patrick and I set the lab up in the clinic and started doing studies on adhesiveness, aggregation, and fibrinogen. We learned some new risk factors. The aggregation and adhesiveness studies never played out very well. Bob Levy, who by then was head of the NHLBI, went over what we were spending. He was amazed at all the equipment that I had. He came up to me at a meeting to say, "What the hell have you been measuring? What are you buying at Framingham?" I told him we were doing this, that, and the other thing. He was okay with it. To me he was a great guy for what I wanted to do and what he wanted to do. He helped us a lot. Our overhead in the NHLBI was high I suppose but not as bad as the group developing the artificial heart. Bob Levy and *Claude Lenfant* rescued us.

Manning Feinlieb and I got the second generation at Framingham going in 1970. Some NHLBI advisors had recommended to the director that Framingham should be shut down. It was supposed to last only 20 years. The NIH was trying to eliminate all of the population studies at that time. *Bob Berliner*, who advised them to do that, eventually became the dean at Yale. He was a nephrologist, and to him real science was toad bladders and basic science. We had a big fight about epidemiology. Eventually, we were able to overcome that kind of nonsense. Last year, we started the full recruitment of the third generation, which has been the work of *Dan Levy*, who replaced me as the Framingham director.

Thomas Royal Dawber ("Roy") went to Boston University after he retired from Framingham. He was there the first few years I was at Framingham. Having gone there in 1951, he reorganized the study from a volunteer study to a random sample of the town. He laid down all the diagnostic rules and put us on a sound scientific foundation. He is the most unsung of all the investigators who have worked at Framingham. We owe him one of the biggest debts. When the crisis

Lp(a) was lowered, the heart attack rate was lower. That is going to be hard to do because these drugs have many other effects. We don't have a specific enough drug that treats Lp(a) levels. Nonetheless, the sinking pre-β predicts adverse events well in Framingham.

I reorganized the labs in Framingham (Figure 5). I also worked in the clinics. As long as I put my 8 hours in at Framingham, they let me do 4 hours of research with Dave Rutstein. That research showed that after the "trigs" went up and fell after a high-fat meal, the deposition continued to rise even after the trigs had fallen. That got us into a new issue, free fatty acids. Free fatty acids are one of the most atherogenic particles we know. I had invented some techniques for adding free fatty acids to plasma without denaturing the protein. The method before that was overlaying the plasma with methanol, putting the free fatty acid into the methanol, and then getting them into the plasma. However, a big layer of denatured protein separated the methanol from the plasma. We did not like that. By then, I was at Framingham virtually full time and we were setting up new measuring tests. About that time *Patrick McKee* arrived at Framing-

came and they were going to shut us down, he went to Boston University and got the insurance companies around this country to support us for a year until we were again picked up by the NHLBI. We worked it out that the offspring study would give us enough money, so we could continue the original cohort at the same time. This satisfied the personalities at the NHLBI. That allowed us to continue everything.

When first joining the study, Roy Dawber would go into the clinic with you to explain that Framingham was not a city hospital clinic, that the people who came here were doing us a favor, and that you had to treat them as though they are the finest people in the world. They were. They were giving up of themselves. Every 2 years they put up with the bloody exams. In the later years they realized how important this was. They realized that the Framingham Study was making them famous, that the Framingham Study was their great gift to the world. We've had studies in children, *Curt Ellison's* studies, in the 1980s. We had a family study. I think if you wanted to do Framingham over again, you wouldn't take a random sample of people in a town; you would take a random sample of families in a town. Then you would get all the members of the family and could get into genomes.

In Framingham, you made a measurement and about 10 years later, you had enough data to see how it played out. One of the first big surprises in the lipid area occurred about 1975, 10 years after we started measuring the various lipoproteins. We saw the startling effect of HDL cholesterol. The higher the HDL at Framingham, the lower the heart attack rate! *Tavia Gordon*, a statistician, was one of the real moving lights in the Framingham Study. No one could write a paper in Framingham without the help of a statistician. No statistician, theoretically, could write a paper without the help of a physician. There was always that very important mix.

HDL played out to be a very important risk factor. These particles of LDL, HDL, and very low-density lipoprotein (VLDL) are not single particles; there are 7 LDLs; there will soon be 20 HDLs. We eventually are going to get into some of these subgroups. Basically, in its simplest way; the smaller HDL particles don't protect. The small LDL particles are far more atherogenic than the large LDL particles. We have laboratories, like LipoMed in North Carolina, Val in Birmingham, and Superko's in Berkley, which will now allow you to send the blood to them and allow you to look at all these different particles. If your patients, their insurance, and Medicare will support some of this, it allows you to learn what your particle sizes are. *Melissa Austin* and *Ron Krauss* did a big study on triglycerides in San Francisco. They divided the LDLs into 2 groups and showed that, if the triglycerides went to 90 or so, you started to shift the size of the LDL from large to small. When the triglycerides hit 150, only the small more atherogenic kinds of LDL were present. Almost the same principle holds with the HDLs.

In primary prevention we want the triglyceride levels (<100 mg/dl) so that we'll have all of the good kinds of LDL and most of the good kinds of HDL. How do you use HDL? Our guideline writers have made the big mistake of making these cuttings of 40 and 60 mg/dl. We need to use HDL as a continuous variable. That is where the ratios are. *Tavis Gordon* and *Robert Abbott* did studies using primarily the likelihood ratios, showing that the best predictor were these ratios. They out-predicted LDL, HDL alone, triglycerides alone, any of the single risk factors alone. Our problem with the total cholesterol is that, when the total cholesterol is between 150 and 300 mg/dl, I can't tell if you're on a curve to get a heart attack or on the curve to stay well. There has to be a better way to separate that out. The total cholesterol to HDL ratio does a better job.

Lately, some investigators have proposed apoprotein B/apoprotein A would be even better predictors. I think it would be better simply because the total to HDL ratio has the HDL as both a numerator and a denominator. A better ratio would probably be the non-HDL over HDL. That would be better than LDL over HDL because LDL over HDL can be normal in people with the metabolic syndrome, and they have very atherogenic VLDL. About 70% of the fasting triglycerides, according to *George Steiner* and *Ron Krauss*, are in small, dense β VLDL, one of the most atherogenic particles known. These patients are very responsive to therapy. We could prevent their heart attacks by treating those triglycerides more aggressively.

The sizes of the lipoprotein particles have recently taken on another tack. *Ernie Schaefer*, who has by far the best lipid laboratory in Boston, was recruited by *Peter Wilson* to analyze all the different LDL and HDL particles for the Framingham Study. Ernie collaborated with a group from New York to study the sizes of the LDL and HDL particles in some subjects who lived into their late 90s and early 100s. Their study had no control group. The Framingham Study didn't have enough people in the 90- to 100-year age range, so we studied their children, who were in their 60s and 70s. Their children had large LDL and large HDL particles compared to the Framingham control group. One of the more interesting aspects of this study is the fact that, when the Framingham participants go from 80 to 85 years of age, their LDLs reach the size of the families that live a long, healthy life. How can one increase their lipoprotein particle size? The best way is to get the serum triglycerides very low, and niacin is the best drug to do that. Statins also decrease triglycerides but not as good as niacin.

Roy Dawber introduced the concept of 3 kinds of risk: average, normal, and ideal. We call average normal in the USA but we need to think more about ideal where atherosclerotic events do not occur. There are billions of people on Earth who have ideal numbers, and they do not have atherosclerotic events. Our guidelines are from studies done in the USA.

When I retired from the Framingham Heart Study after 30 years (Figure 6), I started a wellness clinic because I wanted to get into "How do you manage risk?" I modeled the clinic after a study by *Robert*

FIGURE 6. WPC being installed in France as a *Chevalier du Tastevin*.

DeBusk at Stanford. His study showed that patients after heart attacks had lower LDL cholesterol when managed by nurse practitioners than by internists/cardiologists (LDL 104 vs LDL 132). That impressed me. The cardiologists got 53% of their patients to quit smoking; the nurse management group got 70%.

Every time a patient comes to my clinic, he/she has to see the nurse manager, the dietitian, and me. I make out a scorecard with the patient's numbers. Next to the numbers is the goal we want them to achieve. I go over the numbers; I pick the first strategy. The first 3 months in my clinic, patients are sent home on diet, exercise, and 3 fish oils. We want to find out what kind of mileage we're going to get out of diet and exercise. It's not very good. Even if the patient succeeds in the first 3 months, they can't keep it up. That's been the disappointing part of this clinic. It is hard to convince patients. In primary care it is difficult taking someone who feels well and convincing them to go on a diet, to exercise, and to take medicines. It doesn't get done. The guidelines advocate that diet and exercise should be used to treat these people. The guidelines obviously are written by physicians who have never worked in a clinic doing diet and exercise. If they did, they'd say try it for 3 months, but if they aren't getting any mileage in 3 months, you have to add drugs. Physicians know that the patients are going to have to use these drugs.

In this clinic I decided that the National Cholesterol Education Program guidelines weren't good enough if you had a vascular event and that we were going to make the numbers a lot lower: LDLs <80 (triglycerides <90). Many patients lost their angina pectoris. Many patients normalized their treadmills and thalliums. With magnetic resonance imaging, we are now seeing the narrowings disappear in their carotids and renal arteries and other areas. Restoring

patients to a normal quality of life has been a real joy in the clinic.

We are always looking for new stuff. I think the world is divided into 2 kinds of people: "the problem-oriented people" and "the personality-oriented people." The latter ask, "How am I doing? Am I popular? Am I handsome or pretty or rich?" None of which is enough. They are always going to be unhappy. The problem-oriented guys and gals work on a problem. It's like climbing the mountain. The climber gets to the top of the mountain and solves the problem. That is a great joy in life. Then they see all the other peaks that have to be climbed and off they go.

Right now I work in the clinic 2 days a week and every Wednesday I go out to convince the physicians all over America to lower their cholesterol numbers. Thanks to the people at Framingham, I can measure a few simple numbers on peoples' bodies and tell which ones will likely get a heart attack or a stroke or some type of vascular problem. Better still, I can treat all those numbers and prevent the attacks. Physicians are not doing a good job in lowering our cholesterol numbers.

WCR: *Bill, let me go back a little. You mentioned that you grew up in Teaneck, New Jersey, across the George Washington Bridge from New York City. What was your home atmosphere like growing up?*

WPC: I was the youngest and my brother and I shared the top floor of our house. It was a fairly decent-sized house in a nice neighborhood. It was a very happy life in a way. I played all kinds of sports.

WCR: *What was your father like? When was your father born?*

WPC: My father was born in 1895 and died in 1968 at age 73.

WCR: *And your mother?*

WPC: My mother was born in 1902 and died in 1965 at the age of 63.

WCR: *It sounds like your growing-up home was a pleasant one.*

WPC: It was a very pleasant home.

WCR: *What was your father like?*

WPC: My father was a fairly strict sort of a guy. He pushed education for his kids. Education in our family was free as long as you wanted to go. He always encouraged us to get more education. My brother and I had chores to do around the house. I had to cut the grass with an old reel mower. When we bought a vacation place in Haddan, Connecticut, I installed 4 acres of lawn there. I used to go up there in the summer and paint the fences and do the lawns. One of my father's brothers, who earlier had gone out west to find gold and didn't find any, came back and lived at the vacation house for a while. He and I fixed the place up. Eventually, the vacation house became the main house.

My father was the twelfth child in his family. I had uncles that did all kinds of things up and down the Connecticut River valley. There was a castle called Gillette Castle at the state park. My father almost bought Gillette Castle, but the state bought it. Gillette was an actor in New York who built a castle on the river. It was in Hadlyme. It had all these funny door handles and stone awnings. One of my uncles made all the stone awnings. It was an interesting place. Connecticut River Valley was a lovely place. That part of Connecticut is still unspoiled.

My father died when I was still a research fellow. I was in my third year at Framingham. I didn't have the money to buy out my brother and sister so that house passed out of the family.

WCR: *What was your father like in your interaction with him?*

WPC: He was a very serious guy. He was very kind to all of us kids. He didn't play sports with us the way some parents do today. By the time I came along, my parents were worn out from my brother and sister. They left me alone. I had a pretty easy time. The only time my father would get upset was when the grades came in. He couldn't figure out why I was on the honor role with such a lousy report card, I'd tell him, "Oh no Dad. I got Bs in 2 major subjects." The teachers in my high school were very tolerant. I think the mistake that was made in my high school years was they did an IQ test on us when we were young. If you had a high IQ, they babied you. They didn't want to give you a low grade, I guess. I never learned how to do any homework while in high school. The mathematics came automatically. The hard part was the Latin and French. I had to study some of that. I had an instant memory.

WCR: *What was your IQ? Did you know what it was?*

WPC: I think it was around 150. It wasn't that high. They were treating me with great deference. I was a good kid. I was the class president. If I was in a class and somebody acted up, I would help the teacher put the student down. I wasn't a tattletale. I never did anything very bad. When I was in grammar school, I was in the safety patrol. The head of the safety patrol had me working at the back door where the kids were going to be admitted. I had to keep the kids quiet. We had safety patrol guys on all the corners. A couple of bullies came by and shoved a kid into the street. The next day I was assigned to that corner because the teacher knew I was not going to tolerate that conduct. The guy shoved me into the street and I turned around and punched him in the nose. He had a bloody nose. He never pushed anyone after that. She put me on another corner and the same thing happened. I didn't give him a bloody nose, but I gave him a fat lip. Both of those guys were bigger than I. I was a nasty little kid when I got in a fight. It was crazy. I was a very sweet kid. I didn't seek fights.

WCR: *What was your mother like?*

WPC: My mother was an interesting lady because she thought she was an Irish mystic. She had this great following of ladies who came to the house. She read tea leaves. I was sort of her critic of the tea leaves because she would tell these women, "You're going to get a letter." They would call her on the phone and say, "Mac, the letter came today." I had an uncle, *Roy McNeil* (on my mother's side) who was a well-known lawyer in Washington, DC.

WCR: *How many siblings did your mother have?*

WPC: About 10 or so.

WCR: *Just like your father.*

WPC: People had big families in those days. Roy was head of the Washington Bar Association at one time. Back in those days they had lived in Washington, DC, and you couldn't vote there. They would come to Teaneck and vote at our house. One November my uncle Roy came up and told my mother solemnly that they were Scottish, not Irish. My mother went into a fugue, but fortunately I was reading McCawley's *History of England* at the time. I went to her and said, "Ma, you're really still Irish because there were 3 Irish kings and one of them went out and founded Scotland. Don't tell the Scottish this because I don't think they are too happy about that. You're still Irish, mom." She went back to reading tea leaves.

My father was more of a disciplinarian. My mother was the soft spot between us. If I needed money, it was hard to get any from my father. My mother would sneak around and get me some money. If we were wise enough when she read our tea leaves to leave sugar in the bottom of the cup, we were going to get money. We had ladies running up our front lawn, holding out the money. "Mac, the money came today." My mother had a good time. She didn't work. She raised her children.

WCR: *Was dinner at night a big deal in your family?*

WCP: Yes, it was. We all sat down together. Every Sunday also was a big deal. We had lots of relatives around who would come over. It was a happy time. I was a very happy child.

WCR: *What did you talk about at dinner?*

WCP: Just about everything under the sun. My mother took us all to church on Sunday. I had to go through catechism and was raised as a Catholic. My father never quite made it to church, but was still religious in a sense. Religion became a much bigger part of my life when I went to medical school in Europe. I helped organize a mass for the Americans there on Sundays. The Belgians went home, but we foreigners always stayed behind at school. I used to have a coffee on Sunday mornings in Belgium and the Americans there would come to find out what the news was. People from many different religions came to have coffee. There was a big American college at Louvain for training priests. At Egenhoven there were some Jesuits who I would recruit to give the masses. We didn't have any money. We would take the priests out to dinner because the food at their monastery at Egenhoven was terrible. They looked forward to it. It was inexpensive for me. It cost me maybe $1.50 to take them to a big Sunday dinner. It was great interaction. That became a big part of my life. I was in a boy scout–type troop at Louvain. They didn't have fraternities. They had groups called *routiers*. We went into France at Easter. We went to the little villages that had a church, but no priest. We'd hold games for the kids and visit the elderly shut-ins. We gave catechism to the kids. On the Friday before Easter we had the Stations of the Cross in the town. The farmers liked us because we were 8 or 9 able-bodied men and they saved projects for us. We helped them put up barns. We visited with all the shut-ins and the elderly who had no family. I was the cook. It was a great experience.

WCR: *Did you read a lot growing up?*

WPC: I was a fairly good reader. I didn't read my schoolbooks. I used to love poetry. Many times, if I could just read a poem, I'd have it memorized. I still have some of those poems in my head. Life was pretty easy for me in a way. We had high school fraternities. I was the head of my fraternity. I was the president of my class. I was the big man on campus.

WCR: *How big was your high school?*

WPC: There were 250 students in a class.

WCR: *How did you finish?*

WPC: I was ranked pretty high. For the college boards, I had to take the advanced exams because I had taken many major subjects. I did pretty well on the college boards.

WCR: *Did you find Yale difficult?*

WPC: No. Yale was pretty easy. I did not work hard until halfway through my junior year at Yale. That is when my grades started to take off. I did very well thereafter. I came in second in zoology, my major. In my senior year, there were 11 students in zoology and 11 professors. We met 3 times a week. We had to present papers to them. We got into all kinds of arguments and discussions. One of my professors, who I'm convinced had this non-material aspect to his life, called me at 2 A.M. asking, "Where does that go when you die, that realm?" I answered, "Professor, you asked where. Where is an attribute of the physical world? It's not an attribute in the nonphysical world. I've been trying to tell you, it's not that easy to understand."

WCR: *Were there any professors or teachers in high school or college that had a major impact on you?*

WPC: The guy in college who had the most impact on me was *John Courtney Murray*. In medical school it was *Ernest van Campenhout*. The rumor was that he had been kicked off the faculty at Yale because he flunked too many students. My class in medical school started out with 450 students and we graduated 150. There was a big attrition rate. I was very serious so I was never in danger. The first exam I took at Louvain, 2/3 of the class flunked. But they could repeat the exams in September and not miss a year. About 1/2 of the students flunked that exam. There was a very high failure rate the first few years, but when we got to what they called the "doctor years"—the clinical years—there was only a 10% to 15% failure rate.

The other teacher who influenced me a lot was *Christian De Duve* who shared the Nobel prize in the late 1970s for his work on the *lysosomes*. He also got me interested in the *peroxisomes*.

WCR: *What kind of impact did they have on you?*

WPC: Van Campenhout was responsible for so many failures. Students had to know his stuff backwards and forwards. I was always going to the library and getting additional information. I had stretched out my exams the first year so that I had him last. The only problem was that it was the last day of exams and I showed up in the morning for my exam and none of the other students showed up. They were probably told that they would flunk by another professor. Usually an exam would last about 20 minutes. I got in there and von Campenhout started asking questions. I got all the answers right. He yelled out, "Anybody out there?" No other students showed up. He kept asking me questions. Then he tried to stump me. I never bluffed on those exams. You knew the answer or you didn't know. I had to pick a thing that was so minor just to get out of there. I was going to say, "I don't know." And he said, "Take a guess." I guessed and gave him the right answer. He decided to let me go. I was there for 90 minutes. I no sooner got out of there and was walking down the street when one of my classmates came along and asked, "How's it going with van Camp?" I told him, "Listen. There were no other students there, my friend. You'd better get there because he's looking for the next student."

My best exam was my last year. We had a new professor return to Louvain from the USA to teach minor surgery. The professors in Europe publish their own notes and sell them to the students. This professor didn't have any notes. The students had to pick a note taker and I was picked. I used to read, not only the French books, but also the American and British and some German books. I embellished his notes and he loved it. I used to prepare questions for the exams. I would read every paper written about the subject. I really did well on this exam.

The other major aspect of my Louvain education was what I learned in the school of philosophy. It was a course on epistemology. This is the study of how you know what you say you believe in. It starts you out with the basic measures, how reliable are these measurements. Then you evaluate the logic you use to tie these basic measures together. How good is that logic? Finally you add up all this and make a conclusion. However, how valid is that conclusion given the errors in measurement and logic you used? For example, some biostatisticians in San Francisco say they looked at the relationship of triglyceride to cardiovascular risk in an epidemiology study. There was a significant association in the univariate analysis but it disappeared in the multivariate analysis after adjustment by HDL cholesterol and they told us and the American College of Physicians not to measure triglycerides. What was their mistake? Obviously, they must have cut Biostatistics 101 in about the fifth lecture, when we teach you the difference between a marker in medicine and an independent risk factor. Of course, using the combination of the major epi studies, Melissa Austin and her friends in Seattle showed us that, after adjustment by HDL, triglycerides are an independent risk factor. But for a moment, consider the original errors in San Francisco from the standpoint of epistemology. Start with the measure of triglycerides. Had they consulted the "lipid" group at their university in San Francisco, one of the best lipid groups in the country (Havel, Kane, etc.), they would have realized that fasting triglyceride is ≥ 4 major different groups of particles. Two of which, chylomicron remnants and the small, dense β VLDL are among the most atherogenic particles we know of, except we rarely measure them directly. The other 2 particles, chylomicrons and the fluffy, puffy VLDL, are not atherogenic, but if the chylomicrons hit 1,000 or more you may likely die from acute pancreatitis. This should have told these statisticians that the β coefficient based on just the triglyceride measure was watered down. Then they adjusted the triglyceride by HDL but the 2 particles have a very close metabolic relation; as 1 rises, the other falls. This is not the same as adjusting a measure by another measure that is independent from it. All in all, we know that ~30% of the heart attacks in America are caused by the metabolic syndrome, characterized by a triglyceride of ≥ 120 when the HDL is <50, which the statisticians in San Francisco misled us about the danger of such a problem because they lacked both the lipid and epistemological expertise!!

One summer when I was in Middletown, I spent time with a gastroenterologist from Yale working in Spiro's department. They had worked out a new test for blood ammonia. I started reading everything there was to know about it. I virtually read every paper on the subject in the world, including all the papers from Strausbourg in France. My last exam was in minor surgery and was the only exam I took in English in Belgium. He knew I spoke French very well but asked, "As a favor to me, I want you to take the exam in English. I'm only going to ask you 1 question. Ammonia?" I knew far more about it than he did. I'd been to Yale and looked at their laboratories. I gave him a 45- to 50-minute lecture on ammonia. All the students were listening to my exam. He started taking notes. The highest grade you can get in France is when they kiss you on each cheek. It's called *embrassment de la jurie*. He got up and gave me a kiss on each cheek. My fellow students gave me a standing ovation. That was a great shock for me.

WCR: *How did you happen to get interested in blood ammonia?*

WPC: Harold Kahn (he was the gastroenterologist from Yale who started me on the trail of blood ammonia) was the acting chief of medicine in Middletown Memorial Hospital one summer when I was there getting the French student up to speed with his English. He needed help so that he could become an intern. The following year when I returned, they gave me my job back working with patients. I didn't have Pasqual or anybody to get up to speed. I had my 1 patient a week in medicine to work up. I had a lot of fun with that and it was good for me.

WCR: *What do your siblings do?*

WPC: My brother went into business and was the comptroller for a big helicopter company. They made special attack helicopters for the navy. He got into a fight with *Charlie Command,* one of the directors; he had arranged to have them service all the helicopters in Brazil. Charlie didn't want to do it. He left and joined General Dynamics making atomic submarines.

They were going to buy the Quincy boatyard in Massachusetts but my brother *Rudy* told him not to do it because it was a disaster. He left to work at Todd's Shipyard south of Los Angeles in Long Beach, California. They made frigates. He retired from there. My brother developed angina pectoris when in his early 40s and my father had severe claudication. My father eventually had his leg amputated when he was in his early 50s. He had to retire.

WCR: *Did he smoke?*

WPC: Both my brother and my father smoked. My brother, who I couldn't get off cigarettes, kept saying, "No. You have to discover something that prevents this." I told him, "No. You have to quit." My brother ended up with an abdominal aortic aneurysm and died when he was 68. I've outlived my brother. My father retired from New York and then moved to Haddam. He died at 73. If I make it through this year, I'll have at least equaled my father in longevity. But I beat him by 30 years on the clinical disease side. I've got a bad LDL from my Scottish grandfather who died at 57. All the McNeils also had terrible hypertension.

WCR: *That's your mother's side?*

WPC: Yes. They got wiped out early on from hypertension. We didn't have good therapy for it in those years. I have bad hypertension from the McNeil side, but I think I got my grandfather's high LDL.

WCR: *This is your mother's father?*

WPC: Yes. I ran 20 to 30 miles a week for 20 years and I took my HDL cholesterol from the low 40s to 70 mg/dl. Then, my knees gave out so I couldn't run anymore. I can't get enough biking in so my HDL has fallen. I went to crystal niacin because I know all about the flushing and itching. It doesn't bother me. Niacin took my HDL cholesterol back up to 77.

WCR: *How many milligrams of niacin?*

WPC: A 1,000 daily. I did an experiment. I always liked niacin in my clinic. It taught me which of my patients were faithful in taking their drugs. Why? If one skips a day on niacin, the flushing and itching come back for the next day or 2 or 3. Once up and running, the flushing and itching go away. A breakthrough is very unusual. I decided to take niacin on Tuesday, Thursday, and Saturday and my HDL cholesterol rose to 90 mg/dl. This finding is called the first-pass effect. My LDL cholesterol fell from 200 to 130 with only diet and exercise. Now, I take atorvastatin 10 mg on Mondays, Wednesdays, and Fridays, and that schedule has brought my LDL cholesterol to 83 mg/dl. My serum triglycerides are now 50 mg/dl.

WCR: *What's your blood pressure now?*

WPC: I have my blood pressure down to 118/74 with my triple therapy.

WCR: *What do you take?*

WPC: I take hydrochlorothiazide (12.5 mg), amlodipine (5 mg), and quinapril (40 mg). That has really nailed my blood pressure pretty well, considering that all my aunts and uncles were wiped out in their 50s and early 60s by hypertension. I had only 1 uncle and 2 aunts who made it to their 80s on that side of the family.

WCR: *What did you sister do?*

FIGURE 7. The Castelli clan at Christmas 2003.

WPC: Like my father, both my brother and sister went to Colby College. I was the black sheep in the family and went to Yale. My sister had a summer hotel in Asbury Park. She retired from that. My sister, unfortunately, has severe Alzheimer's disease and doesn't know anybody. She is about 74, 2 years older than I am. She is still alive and looks okay, but doesn't even recognize her husband.

WCR: *When did you meet your wife?*

WPC: I was a resident in medicine in my first year at the Shattuck Hospital in Boston. We rotated through Faulkner Hospital for 3 months. The medicine chief nurse on the medical ward was a legend. We called her "Ma Hamilton." Ma had an intuitive feeling about patients and she was always right. She knew when something was wrong or not going right. I would come on duty and Ma would beckon me with a finger like this and I knew something was happening. I had to work it out. It usually worked out okay. I was away for a week's vacation when I came back to work on the ward and we went into this room. There was a patient in the bed, and I could make the diagnosis as we were walking towards the bed: the patient had a moustache "urea frost." "Ma, the guy is in renal failure." She said, "I know that. I have a feeling about this patient. They are screwing up." I said, "Let me see the urine." One of the beauties of that internship at King's County Hospital was that we had to do all our blood counts and urines. We had a little lab on each ward to do that. We had to read the tests, do the counts, and look at the urine sediments. When I was in pediatrics, I had 3 kids a week with acute glomerulonephritis. I knew what a red cell cast looked like. I'd take the patient's urine, take it down to the lab, and spin it myself. I said, "Ma, I thought the patient was in for nephrosclerosis, but he has acute glomerulonephritis." I knew how to treat this condition. I allowed him daily 2,000 calories, ≤1,000 ml water, and no potassium. He could swallow so I wrote the order. Down comes

this new dietitian who looked at this order and said, "Ma, who is the idiot who wrote this order?" This was *Marjorie Irene Fish* from Eatonville, Washington, in the foothills of Mt. Ranier. She grew up on Clear Lake. There was something called Controlyte that we could give in those days. That's what we gave the patient.

WCR: *What is it?*

WPC: It was a solution of calories with no potassium. We gave him 2,000 calories to stop the breakdown of cells in his body. Ten days later, his kidneys opened up and 2 weeks after that he was okay.

WCR: *What happened with Marjorie?*

WPC: We went on a date and from there to marriage.

WCR: *What were the characteristics of your future wife that appealed to you?*

WPC: She was a dietitian and we were both involved in some aspect of medicine. It was love at first sight, I guess.

WCR: *That was what year?*

WPC: We met in 1960 and married in 1961.

WCR: *You have 3 children? What do they do?*

WPC: Our 2 sons are lawyers in the Washington, DC, area. One works for the old Customs Department, which is now part of Homeland Security. The other son is a lobbyist for the real estate board in Annapolis, Maryland. They live in Cheverlee and Silver Springs. They have 5 of our grandchildren (4 girls and 1 boy). My daughter became a coronary care unit nurse. She went to Catholic University in Washington, DC. They have one of the best nursing degree programs anywhere in this country. We sent her there. My kids all went to private schools. They went to the famous Fay School. Fay is probably the oldest boarding grammar school in the country. They were day students there. From there they went to St. Mark's, which is an old prep school that was 3 miles from our house. My oldest son went to Union College in Schenectady, New York, and then to the American University Law School in Washington. My younger son went to Colby College and then to the University of Maryland School of Law. My daughter married Lance Larsen, a cardiologist, on the North Shore of Boston, in Beverly, Massachusetts. They live in Danvers and have 3 of our grandchildren (1 boy and 2 girls). We see them a lot more than the other kids (Figure 7).

WCR: *What hobbies do you have? What do you do in your spare time?*

WPC: My main hobby has been reading everything that Winston Churchill ever wrote or was written about him. Churchill got me interested in World War II. I used to make models of every tank (German, Japanese, and American), plane, and ship. I could recapitulate virtually any battle, tank by tank, in World War II. I was a great student of history. It was

Churchill's 6-volume history of World War II that turned me on to all of that. Then I read all the stuff written about him. I read Samuel Elliott Morrison's 17-volume *Naval History of World War II*. I was big into history, especially that concerning World War II. I have read most books about World War II.

WCR: *Are you a fast reader?*

WPC: I'm fast on certain things.

WCR: *What is your home like? Do you have a lot of bookcases?*

WPC: Yes. I have an office that you can't get into because there are too many books. I've got to throw them out and clean it out. I can never throw anything away. I know where every piece of paper is in my office. I spend time trying to clean it up when my grand kids are coming or they will say, "Grandpa, you're going to be in 'time out' out. Look at the mess in this room."

WCR: *What do you do on the weekends now?*

WPC: On the weekends I usually putter around with my computer. I used to build all my own computers. I'd buy the latest motherboard, chips, video board, hard drive, and system. I had the first desktop PC as my computer at Framingham. I let some of the people there use it. We eventually computerized all the data and studies from Framingham. Now it's much cheaper to buy computers than build them. I would build a terrific computer, the fastest one on the block, and 2 months later the companies would bring out a new motherboard, new chips, etc. My wife cut off my allowance.

WCR: *I presume that when you were in medical school, you traveled around Europe a good bit?*

WPC: I did. I got to see all of Europe. I think the beauty of living in another country was that I learned that everybody is the same around the world. A lot of tourists think that the Belgians are not warm, but they are very family oriented. They make you a member of their family and then treat you like a member. They will do anything for you. When students got our grades in Belgium, they had to file into the auditorium with their parents. The professors would read off your name and your grade before God and everybody else. In the years I was there, a Belgian family would stand with me. It was crazy. It was always, "My little boy Billie is having his grades read." The way they treated me was a wonderful thing.

WCR: *How many miles do you put on airplanes every year?*

WPC: It's terrible. I travel 3 days every week.

WCR: *Do you leave on Wednesday?*

WPC: I leave every Wednesday, and occasionally I might even leave on a Tuesday night to get there for grand rounds at 8:00 A.M. on Wednesday. I usually average 5 or 6 lectures a week: 1 on Wednesday, 3 on Thursday, and 1 or 2 on Friday. Then I go home. The good weeks I'm home by Friday afternoon, and the bad weeks I don't get home until Friday night. In the summer, I have to cut the grass. We have a little shack down on the cape. I have 2 houses to maintain and I don't hire anybody. The rule is that I have to do all the

work. It helps me keep in shape. I've got to do something physically demanding.

WCR: *I bet you've given more talks than any physician who ever walked on planet Earth.*

WPC: You think? Maybe.

WCR: *Who would be your competitor then?*

WPC: There is you and Bill Kannel. Maybe not. Bill Kannel has been a big writer and I have been the lecturer. If you have a message in medicine, you'd better be willing to go out and talk to the doctors. It's hard to get some of these people to believe.

WCR: *I understand.*

WPC: You have to be able to talk to them face to face to convince them that there is another side of an issue that they need to address. That's what I'm trying. If I can convince them to measure these numbers and treat them, that will really be the payoff. There are a lot of people out on the lecture circuits. In any major medical school in this country, you have $\geq 1/2$ dozen. I'm sure there is more than that going out periodically to lecture. The thing is, they are all sponsored by drug companies. You have to find a drug company that will let you say anything you want. There are only a couple of them that work that way for me. They organize these lectures for me. Even grand rounds are often sponsored by drug companies. In a way, I feel that they are using me, but I'm using them to get my message out. It works okay.

WCR: *Do you sleep much?*

WPC: I get close to my 8 hours of sleep each night.

WCR: *Do you go on vacations?*

WPC: We have a little house on the cape. The beauty of that is that all the grand kids come there in the summer. We get together and swim and boat, etc. It's on a dirt road. It's way out on the cape in Eastham. It's a nice refuge to get away to.

WCR: *Do you slow down on your speaking engagements in the summertime?*

WPC: I haven't, but this coming summer I am. I'm not going to do any lectures. I will work the clinic Mondays and Tuesdays and the rest of the week I'll be at the cape with my grand kids. The beauty of owning a house on the cape is that you are not limited to the coming and going of the renting season. I can miss all the traffic. I know how to avoid the traffic there.

WCR: *What sort of foods do you eat? What do you eat for breakfast as a rule?*

WPC: Oatmeal.

WCR: *That's it?*

WPC: When you eat as much oatmeal as I do and you get to my age, you are going to have the cleanest colonoscopy they ever saw. I do the oatmeal with fat-free yogurt with fruit on the bottom. I don't stir up the fruit; I just put the top on or I use plain yogurt. I've been using a lot of soy type things. Occasionally, I'll use soy milk.

WCR: *What do you eat for lunch?*

WPC: A salad usually with vinaigrette dressing. We have a nice salad bar at the hospital where I make up a salad with humus and lots of peas and beans. I have a pure vegetarian lunch. I would like to avoid drug company lunches in my clinic. I'll have 1/2 a tuna salad sandwich and a salad for those lunches. Supper is usually some kind of fish. My wife is very good at cutting the calories back. If I could only get Americans just to eat like the French. I give lectures on what you should eat. The attendees say, "Oh, you're going to take away everything I like to eat." I say, "No, I'm going to have you eat like the French. I'm going to have you take your 10 favorite recipes and eat 1/2 what you have been eating." When I go to France to give a lecture, who is the fattest guy in the auditorium? It's me. The French are all skinny as a rail. When I went back to the school in the fall in Belgium, I would lose weight in fall, winter, and spring. Why? Food there was expensive, the portion sizes were small, and you had to walk everywhere. Why? Gasoline was $5 a gallon. We couldn't afford anything else. I would lose weight. They didn't have McDonald's or any of the fast food chains. They didn't have ice cream stores. You didn't eat between meals. It was much healthier. All the European countries are way ahead of us in longevity.

WCR: *How tall are you? How much do you weigh?*

WPC: I am 5 ft, 9 in;. I weigh about 165. I'm about 10 pounds overweight.

WCR: *What do you do for exercise now?*

WPC: On the cape, I bike because we have great biking trails. I maintain the yard. I'm going to get a bike from my home in Marlborough. When the weather clears up, I'll start biking every night. I had an elliptical machine, but I didn't use it very much. I'm not in great shape presently.

WCR: *Is there anything you'd like to talk about that we haven't touched on?*

WPC: No.

WCR: *On behalf of* The American Journal of Cardiology *and its readers, I want to thank you for doing this interview and being so open and frank.*

WPC: Thank you.

SELECTED ARTICLES

1. Castelli WP. Making practical sense of clinical trial data in decreasing cardiovascular risk. *Am J Cardiol* 2001;88:16–20.

24. Castelli WP, Nickerson RJ, Newell JM, Rutstein DD. Serum NEFA following fat, carbohydrate and protein ingestion and during fasting as related to intracellular lipid deposition. *J Atheroscler Res* 1966;6:328–341.

59. Castelli WP. Cholesterol and lipids in the risk of coronary artery disease—the Framingham Heart Study. *Can J Cardiol* 1988;4:5–10.

111. Hubert HB, Feinleib M, McNamara PM, Castelli WP. Obesity as an independent risk factor for cardiovascular disease: a 26-year follow-up of participants in the Framingham Heart Study. *Circulation* 1983;67:968–977.

125. Castelli WP, Garrison RJ, Dawber TR, McNamara PM, Feinleib M, Kannel WB. The filter cigarette and coronary heart disease: the Framingham Study. *Lancet* 1981;2:109–113.

150. Gordon T, Castelli WP, Hjortland MC, Kannel WB, Dawber TR. High density lipoprotein as a protective factor against coronary heart disease. The Framingham Study. *Am J Med* 1977;62:707–714.

LAWRENCE SOREL COHEN, MD: A Conversation With the Editor*

Lawrence Sorel Cohen, MD, and William Clifford Roberts, MD

Larry Cohen was born on 27 March 1933 in Brooklyn, New York, and that is where he grew up. After finishing public schools in Brooklyn in 1950, he went to Harvard College in Cambridge, Massachusetts, graduating in 1954. From there, he returned to New York City to New York University School of Medicine, where he finished in 1958. He completed his internship and his first 2 years of medical residency at Yale-New Haven Medical Center in New Haven, Connecticut. In 1962, he went to Boston, Massachusetts, as a research fellow in cardiology at the Peter Bent Brigham Hospital, completing that training in June 1964, and the next month he returned to New Haven as a senior assistant resident at the Yale-New Haven Medical Center. From 1965 to 1968, Dr. Cohen was senior investigator and head of the clinical service of the cardiology branch at the National Heart Institute in Bethesda, Maryland. After 2 years, he moved to Dallas, Texas, to be chief of clinical cardiology and associate professor of medicine at the University of Texas (Southwestern) Medical School. Two years later in 1970, he returned to New Haven as professor of medicine and chief of cardiology at Yale University School of Medicine. In 1978, he stepped down from the chief of cardiology position. In 1981, Dr. Cohen was made the Ebenezer K. Hunt Professor of Medicine at Yale University School of Medicine. He has served as acting deputy dean, deputy dean, special advisor to the dean, and the research integrity officer at Yale University School of Medicine. Through all the years, he has taught medical students, houseofficers, and cardiology fellows, plus continues to see private patients with various cardiovascular conditions. Dr. Cohen is a well-loved teacher and mentor and has received the Francis Gilman Blake Award for Outstanding Teaching of the Medical Sciences. In 1989, the Connecticut Heart Association named its auditorium in Wallingford, Connecticut, the Lawrence S. Cohen Auditorium. Larry Cohen has been President of the Association of University Cardiologists and also of the Inter-Urban Clinical Club. He was a founding member of the Yale University School of Medicine Society of Distinguished Teachers. He has been involved in numerous clinical trials during the last 20 or so years. He has been a visiting professor at 31 university medical centers in the USA and in 25 cities in non-US countries. He has been on the editorial boards at one time or another of all the major US cardiovascular journals. His investigations have led to over 125 publications in peer-reviewed medical journals, 34 chapters in various books, 9 editorials, and the editorship of 3 books. He and his lovely wife, Jane, are the proud parents of 2 very fine and successful daughters. Larry Cohen is a good friend, a great guy, and a true gentleman (Figure 1).

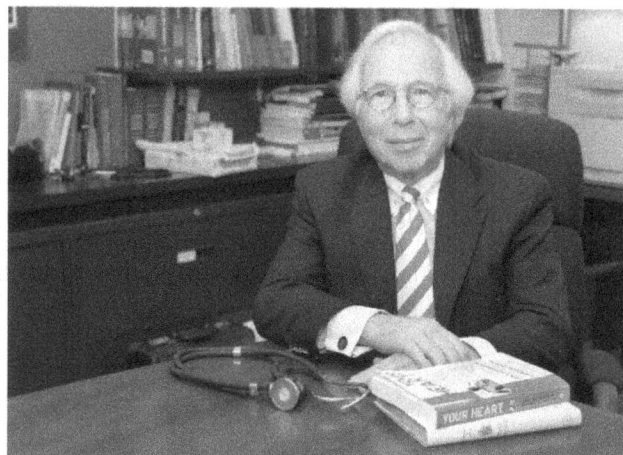

Figure 1. LSC in 2007 at age of 74.

William Clifford Roberts, MD (hereafter WCR[†]): *Dr. Cohen, thank you for honoring Baylor University Medical Center by your visit on 20 February 2007. (Dr. Cohen earlier today spoke at medical grand rounds, and we are now in my office. We have a couple of hours before he is talking to the medical housestaff conference.) May we begin by your discussing your early childhood, your parents and siblings, and what was it like growing up in Brooklyn, New York?*

Lawrence Sorel Cohen, MD (hereafter LSC[‡]): I was the third child in my family. I have a sister, who is 9 years older than I am, and a brother, who is 5 years older. My father was born in 1899 in Eastern Europe. Depending upon who was the Czar at the time, it was sometimes part of Poland and sometimes part of Russia. My father and his parents came to the USA around 1903. His family settled in Brooklyn, where his father started to work. My mother was born in 1904 in the same general area of Poland or perhaps Russia. She also came to the USA at a very young age. My parents were married when my mother was 18 and my father, 22. In the 1920s, my father entered the clothing business. He owned a number of small retail clothing stores in Brooklyn. He was financially stable. My mother was a very smart woman. Although she didn't go to college, she had very good people "smarts." She was the glue that held the family together. She had 5 older brothers, all of whom came to the USA from Europe. She was the youngest, kept her side of the family together, and was the matriarch.

WCR: *Did her siblings all live in Brooklyn?*

* This series of interviews was underwritten by an unrestricted grant from Bristol-Myers Squibb.

† Director, Baylor Cardiovascular Institute, Baylor University Medical Center, Dallas, Texas, 75246.

‡ Special Advisor to the Dean, The Ebenezer K. Hunt Professor of Medicine, Yale University School of Medicine, New Haven, Connecticut.

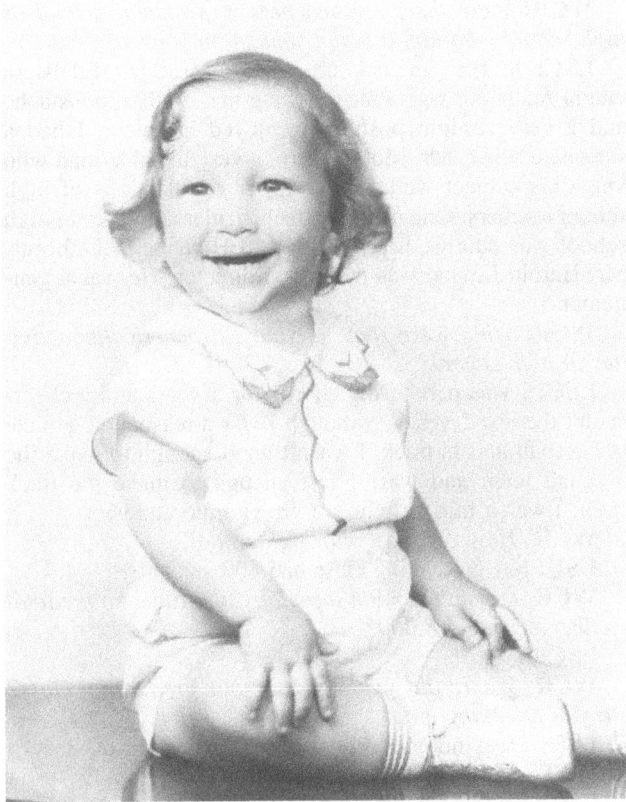

Figure 2. LSC at about the age of 2.

Figure 3. LSC and his mother, about 1939.

Figure 4. LSC in his backyard garden, about 1940.

LSC: They all initially lived in the New York area, most of them in Brooklyn. Later, some moved to North Carolina and Virginia. I grew up with a nuclear family and had tons of cousins as I was growing up. By the time I was born my parents traveled a lot. We had a live-in housekeeper, an African-American woman named Lillie (Figure 2). She treated me like her own child, and she was a second mother to me. In the late 1930s, I would get on the trolley car and go to Lillie's house and have Sunday dinner with her family. She had one child, Paul, a policeman. Lillie was very important to me as I was growing up. When I was 4 years of age, we moved from an apartment house to a single-family dwelling, where I lived until I graduated from high school. I walked to public school located around the corner from our house (Figures 3 and 4). There was never any issue of safety. A favorite sport was Stoop Ball, played with a rubber ball that was thrown at a corner of the front step of a house. You would try to catch it as it came back to you. Stoop is a derivation from step. It was played with a Spalding (pronounced Spaldeen) rubber ball. Another game called Stick Ball was played on the street between manholes. The distance between 2 manholes was 120 feet. Stick Ball was played with a broom stick: there was a pitcher, catcher, batter, and one guy in the "outfield". We would see how far we could hit the ball straight down the street and count how many manholes we could hit on the fly. I have pleasant memories of growing up in Brooklyn in the 1930s and 1940s. Each summer for 4 or 5 weeks, my parents vacationed at a resort hotel in the Catskill Mountains. There was plenty to do at the resort—swimming, games, horseback riding, and other leisure activities. My life changed dramat-

ically in September 1941, when I was 8 years old. My father, who was only 41 years old at the time, had a heart attack. He was treated at home. I remember the doctor coming to the house with a portable electrocardiographic machine. After 3 weeks, my dad was finally allowed to get out of bed. That was the treatment for a heart attack at that time. His heart attack changed my life, because the second phase of his treatment was prolonged rest. In November 1941, my whole family moved to Miami Beach, Florida, to be in a warm climate. I remember clearly the apartment where we lived in Miami Beach. My sister, who had been a freshman at New York University, transferred to the University of Miami and my brother and I went to a public school in Miami. We spent a year in Miami Beach. My father just rested. That was part of the recuperation period.

WCR: *Your family kept the house in Brooklyn?*

LSC: Yes. We moved back into the same house after a year in Miami Beach. We were in Miami Beach when the Japanese attacked Pearl Harbor on December 7, 1941. I remember listening to the radio about the attack on Pearl Harbor, and I remember clearly the events of D-Day, the invasion of Europe, Franklin Roosevelt's radio talks, and his death. World War II was very much a part of my growing up

WCR: *How did you do in grade school, and how many were in your class?*

LSC: I did well in grade school, which was a K to 8th grade at that time. I think I was 1st in my class. I went to public school 193 and each grade was divided into A, B, C, and D. The students with the best aptitude were in the A section and then it moved down from there. There must have been about 800 students at PS 193.

WCR: *About 100 in your class?*

LSC: Yes, but only 25 in my section with an equal number of boys and girls. I then went to a new high school, Midwood High School. I used to walk 20 minutes to school each day. Midwood was one of the better high schools in Brooklyn. Depending on which grade one was in, there were 3 different sessions: 8:00 am to 1:00 P.M., 1:00 P.M. to 6:00 P.M., or 11:00 A.M. to 4:00 P.M. It was a very crowded school. There were some excellent teachers, and I received a good education.

WCR: *What was the actual street address of your house?*

LSC: We lived at 1123 E. 27th Street, the Flatbush section of Brooklyn, between Avenues K and L. Brooklyn was set up as a grid with vertical avenues having letters and streets having numbers. When in high school, I also worked for my allowance as a counselor at a day camp. My older brother was an entrepreneur, and he and his friends organized the Saturday day camp. With a rented bus, we would pick up children, aged 7 to 11, and take them out for the day. We would go to the park, or a ballgame, or Brooklyn Museum, etc. We'd pick the kids up at 10:00 A.M. and have them home around 4:00 or 5:00 P.M. My brother, even at a young age, was a good business person.

WCR: *Did school studies come easy for you or did you really have to work at it?*

LSC: In high school, studies came relatively easily. I found mathematics to be relatively easy. I took Spanish and French.

WCR: *Did you read fast?*

LSC: No, I am a slow reader even now. I was not a voracious reader in high school.

WCR: *Were there any teachers in grammar school or high school who had a major impact on you?*

LSC: In the 7th and 8th grades, Mr. Max Edelstein taught math. He was a nice looking man with a moustache and a very straight posture. I enjoyed his class. I had a science teacher, Mr. Morgenstern, a very likeable man who knew his subject well. I have fewer recollections of high school teachers. One of my extracurricular activities in high school was singing in the Midwood High School Chorus. Mr. Harold Levine was the choral director. He was a gentleman.

WCR: *What were some of your extracurricular activities in high school?*

LSC: I was part of the chorus for 3 years and a cheerleader the last 2 years. Although I was a reasonable athlete in baseball and in track, I wasn't good enough to make the baseball team and wasn't fast enough to make the track team. I was a fairly slight kid growing up and short.

WCR: *How big was your high school?*

LSC: My graduating class had 800 students.

WCR: *It went from 9th through 12th grade. So the total number was over 3,000?*

LSC: Yes.

WCR: *Where did you stand in your graduating class? Do you have any idea?*

LSC: I was number 4 or 5 in the graduating class.

WCR: *How did you decide to be a cheerleader?*

LSC: I wasn't good enough to make the sports teams, but always liked sports, so the closest I could come to being on the field was as a cheerleader. I had a couple of friends on the cheerleading squad. I could do simple gymnastics. I could line up 6 cheerleaders on their hands and knees so that the height would be about 2 feet. I would run and take a dive over them and land on my hands, tuck in my chin and do a roll. I was able to do that so that qualified me as a cheerleader.

WCR: *What was your mother's name? Is she still alive?*

LSC: My mother was Fannie Cooper. She was born in 1904 and died in 1979 at age of 75.

WCR: *What was your father's name?*

LSC: Max Cohen. He was born in 1899 and died September 12, 1950, of a second heart attack.

WCR: *In 1950 you were a senior in high school?*

LSC: He died a couple of days before I was to leave for college.

WCR: *How did your father do during those 10 years between heart attacks?*

LSC: He seemed to get along very well. I don't ever remember his taking nitroglycerin. He did work full-time, 5 days a week. The pace of his life, however, slowed down during those 10 years. Everything was done in slow motion. His walking was a bit slower. We couldn't get excited in the house. We didn't instigate any trouble in the house. We didn't get into arguments in the house. We respected Dad, and we did not want to aggravate him in anyway.

WCR: *Your older siblings were who?*

LSC: The oldest is my sister, Miriam. She was married when she was 21. Her married name is Fogelman. She was born in 1924, and is in good health. She lives 6 months of the year on Long Island and 6 months in Florida.

WCR: *And your older brother?*

LSC: His name is Norman.

WCR: *Does he have a middle name?*

LSC: He adopted one—J. He is alive and very active. Years ago he and his wife bought a second house in Vermont in the ski district near Mount Snow. He spends about 6 months of the year at that house and does a lot of skiing.

WCR: *You said he was a businessman?*

LSC: He retired about 8 years ago. He sold his business.

WCR: *What was his business?*

LSC: He and his brother-in-law were manufacturers of polyethylene bags. Their business was quite successful because they were in the polyethylene bag business as the super grocery stores, Stop-N-Shops started to grow. Many other items got packaged in polyethylene. They had several good decades manufacturing polyethylene bags.

WCR: *Did they live in New York?*

LSC: Yes. My brother lived in Long Island around the corner from my sister.

WCR: *Did your sister work?*

LSC: My sister was a teacher for over 20 years. Her husband was in the Air Force during WWII. He was discharged in 1945 and became a successful wholesale buyer for men's clothing in Manhattan. He survived several illnesses, including colonic cancer, a heart attack, and lymphoma.

WCR: *How many children did your siblings have?*

LSC: My sister has 2 girls, my brother has 2 sons and 1 daughter, and my wife and I have 2 daughters. We are all a very close family.

WCR: *Were you and your father close growing up? I gather that he did not go further than high school?*

LSC: That's correct. We weren't close. Part of it was a natural reticence that he had. He was a quiet man. After his heart attack, he kept relationships at an arm's distance. But he knew the value of education. When I would come home from school and say I got a 93 on whatever test it was, he would say, "What happened to the other 7 points?" That was the level of joking that went on in our family. I was not close to my father. He was a strong figure, but not a person I would confide in. I was much closer to my mother.

WCR: *Did you do any fishing or hunting? You mentioned vacationing with your family? Was he active before his first heart attack? Did you play together?*

LSC: No. As I look back it was very structured. We didn't camp together or play together. He didn't know anything about sports. His life was his work and his family, but nothing interactive in terms of playing together.

]WCR: *Did he smoke cigars or cigarettes?*

LSC: He smoked 2 or 3 cigars a day, but no cigarettes.

WCR: *Was there alcohol in your home growing up?*

LSC: There was always alcohol available in our home but mostly for ceremonial occasions. I don't ever remember my parents drinking just to have a drink. If it was a festive meal, they would have a glass of wine, and we always had a full-array of liquor in the house. It was just there and part of life. It never was a forbidden thing and was available if one wanted it. I didn't drink at all when I was much younger and drank very little even when in high school and college. It wasn't a mystery to me, so I didn't feel the need to indulge.

WCR: *Did your mother smoke cigarettes?*

LSC: No.

WCR: *There was a strong urge for you and your siblings to do well in school?*

LSC: That clearly was a norm. It was a family expectation.

WCR: *When you would bring home your report card and it had all A's on it, would your parents say much about it? Would they congratulate you or what would happen?*

LSC: They would say, "That's good. It's what we expect." There was not a big deal made of it.

WCR: *What about your evening meal at night? Was that a big deal?*

LSC: It was an expectation that we would all be there. There wasn't a lot of dialogue. I don't remember political conversations at dinnertime. We didn't talk about politics very much. We talked about the progress of the war, about what had happened at school that day, and about people. But dinner was something we all participated in at the same time, close to 6:00 pm daily. Friday night dinner was more special because that was the Sabbath. But it wasn't a time of deep philosophical or political discussion.

WCR: *Did you and your family go to Synagogue each week? Were you a deeply religious family?*

LSC: Both my father and mother were reasonably but not extremely religious. My father went to synagogue most Saturday mornings. My mother and my sister stayed home. I went to the local synagogue (Hebrew school) for religious training 3 days a week for 2 hours in the afternoon after public school let out. From age 11 to 14, I was very observant. When I had my confirmation (my Bar Mitzvah), I ran the whole service. I studied very hard for that. A year or 2 later, I gave up the orthodoxy that I was practicing. Culturally, I have never given up being Jewish, but the ritual of being Jewish has left me. I don't observe the rituals anymore.

WCR: *You mentioned that your mother was the glue holding your family together. How did you and your mother interact?*

LSC: We had a very warm and close relationship. She was the person I went to with issues or problems. She was a wise woman, and had the benefit of bringing up 2 older children before I came along. I could talk to her and felt very comfortable doing so.

WCR: *Your father must have been very proud when you got into Harvard College? Fortunately, he knew that before he died.*

LSC: Correct, and he was proud.

WCR: *How did it come about that you went to Harvard? Did you apply to a number of colleges?*

LSC: I applied to Harvard, Columbia, Cornell, and Franklin & Marshall. I applied to Harvard because it was Harvard, and I had heard very good things about it. Columbia was close by, and it, too, was Ivy League. Cornell was not too far away. Franklin & Marshall was a good small college. I didn't visit any of them. I was interviewed locally by alumni. I got into Harvard, Columbia, and Cornell. I was rejected by Franklin & Marshall. I always found that interesting. I chose Harvard because it seemed it was the ultimate college to go to. The first time I was in Cambridge was when I entered college as a freshman.

WCR: *Why didn't your mother and sister go to synagogue?*

LSC: I think that ritual observance was much more a male than female expectation. Only the ultra-orthodox women went to our synagogue. Most wives of the orthodox men were not expected to go to synagogue. They would go to synagogue with the men only on the Holy Days—the New Year and the Day of Atonement.

WCR: *What was your house in Brooklyn like?*

LSC: It was a single-family dwelling. When growing up, it seemed to be very large. When I visited years later, it seemed to have shrunk in size. It was on a plot of maybe 60 x 120 feet with the houses on either side separated by driveways. It had a finished basement, which was our playroom with a ping-pong table. The main level was quite nice with a living room, dining room, and kitchen. The upstairs had 4 bedrooms. At the time I thought it was a very nice house, and it certainly accommodated us quite well.

WCR: *Were there books and magazines around? Did your parents read much?*

LSC: No, they didn't read much, and there were no shelves with lots of books on them. We had encyclopedias and a couple of books, but it wasn't a house where there was a great amount of either reading or learning being done.

WCR: *Do you think that your father had heterozygous familial hypercholesterolemia?*

LSC: Yes. When I was in my 20s, my serum total cholesterol, even when on a good diet with exercise, was about 280 mg/dl. I suspect that my father had a similar cholesterol level, and I think he also had hypertension.

WCR: *What about some of his blood relatives? Did any of them die young or have atherosclerotic events at a young age?*

LSC: Yes. He had a brother, very close in age to him, whose cardiac profile was very similar, in that his brother had a heart attack in his late 40s and died in his late 50s of a heart attack. Perhaps another of my father's brothers also had cardiac disease.

WCR: *How old were your paternal grandparents when they died?*

LSC: My paternal grandfather died about age 63. I never knew my maternal grandparents.

WCR: *Did you have a high school advisor who told you that you should apply to Harvard, Columbia, and Cornell? Your parents having not gone to college probably couldn't give you the advice that you needed at that time. How did it work exactly? Were you the initiator of sending in your applications or were you encouraged by your school advisors?*

LSC: My recollection is that there was very little guidance. I never visited a guidance counselor, and I don't remember having a college advisor. If you wanted to stretch when growing up in Brooklyn, you applied to good Ivy League colleges. That was a simple process. No one had to tell you to do it.

WCR: *Out of your class of 800 seniors in high school, how many got into college?*

LSC: I guess about 75% went to college. Three or 4 were accepted to Harvard. A good number of students went to other Ivy League schools.

WCR: *Were there a lot of bright students in your high school?*

LSC: Nowadays, it would be called a *magnet high school* because we had some students who came quite a distance by subway to go to Midwood High School because their neighborhood schools weren't good.

WCR: *During your growing up, you walked around Brooklyn to get most places. Did you have a bicycle?*

LSC: Yes, that was one way to get around. I used to get around quite a bit on a bicycle. In teenage years, I took the subway everywhere, and it was a very good system. One line was called the IRT and another, the BMT. The BMT went from Coney Island to Manhattan.

WCR: *Did you go into Manhattan very much?*

LSC: Yes, quite frequently with friends on Saturdays and often on Sundays. We would go to a movie, a Broadway show, a concert, and to Carnegie Hall. Growing up in Brooklyn in those days, I had a great sense of freedom and safety. I didn't worry at all about my personal safety. It was an uplifting feeling to be able to go anywhere at any time. It was a good time of life.

WCR: *How did Harvard and Boston work out?*

LSC: Starting at Harvard was like jumping into a cold pool. It was a shock.

WCR: *In what way?*

LSC: My entry was a shock in that my dad died a couple of days before I was supposed to start college, and so I stayed at home for 1 week and missed orientation. I took a midnight train out of Penn Station in New York City and arrived in Boston at 6:00 am. I stayed awake for every stop that the train made: Bridgeport, New Haven, New London, Westerly, Providence, and finally South Station in Boston. I got into a cab and told the cabbie to take me to Harvard Yard. He asked me, "How do you get there?" I said I didn't know because I had never been there. But the cab driver finally found Harvard yard. I found my dormitory, getting there around 7:30 am, and introduced myself to my 3 roommates. That was my introduction to Harvard College (Figure 5).

WCR: *Had classes already started?*

LSC: No. I arrived a day or so before classes started. I registered on that first day.

WCR: *Did you go to college thinking you were going to be pre-med? Already desiring to be a physician? What did you think you wanted to do eventually?*

LSC: I didn't really know. If I had been asked at that time what I thought I would end up doing, I would have said I'd probably enter law. I began college majoring in government, figuring that would be a good introduction if I wanted to be a lawyer. At that point, I had not considered medicine or science.

WCR: *How did the Harvard student body and classes hit you? In high school you went to school with a lot of bright people. When you got to Cambridge, did you see that you were at another level of intelligence?*

LSC: It was a shock in several ways. The student body was different in many ways from any student body I'd ever known, in that half the students came from private schools, like Andover, Exeter, Choate, or Groton. Students from those schools were better prepared than I was. Their education was much more preparatory for Harvard than was

Figure 5. ROTC uniform in Harvard Yard.

mine. Suddenly, I was surrounded by extraordinarily bright people, and it was a shock to me. I received a "C" on the first essay I wrote in my English class. I had never gotten a C in high school. I realized that college was not going to be a cake walk. I studied very hard my freshman year and did little other than study. I didn't enjoy my freshman year very much because I was always walking around feeling somewhat anxious about how I was doing (Figure 6).

WCR: *Then what happened?*

LSC: By the second year I had learned how to learn and things started falling into place. I started to enjoy the courses more, and the whole experience lightened up a bit. I still worked very hard. I did not feel that I was in anyway outstanding in terms of my intellectual activities. I also started making some friends and started to enjoy the college scene.

WCR: *How did medicine come along? How did you switch from law to science or medicine?*

LSC: I had 2 new roommates my second year, and one of them was pre-med. He and I used to talk about his courses and what he was taking. I found that his courses sounded very interesting. At the end of my second year I made the decision to become pre-med. For me to do that, I had to take all the pre-med courses my third and fourth year. I found that I really enjoyed them. Although I had a hard time with organic chemistry, I thoroughly enjoyed general chemistry. I struggled with physics but by the second semester I also mastered that.

WCR: *What did you major in at Harvard?*

LSC: I majored in a field called Social Relations. That was a discipline combining anthropology, social psychology, and psychology.

Cambridge Police Okay Square Football Rallies

Cheerleaders Schedule Princeton Rally for Evening of Nov. 6

By DAVID L. HALBERSTAM

Friday night football rallies—which last year were forced off the Cambridge streets and into the Harvard Yard—will be held in the Square again, it was learned yesterday.

But there will be only one rally this season, on Nov. 6, the night before the Princeton game.

Plans originally called for a rally this Friday night before the Colgate game, but a conflicting Varsity Club dinner forced cancellation. Head cheerleader Lawrence Cohen '54 had arranged for backfield coach Harold "Josh" Williams and backs John Culver and Bob Hardy to speak, but all three will attend the dinner.

Cohen had already received permission from Associate Dean Robert Watson and University Police Chief Matthew Touhey to let the band, cheerleaders and students march through the Square to the traditional spot in front of the Indoor Athletic Building.

Last year, cautious Cambridge police refused the cheerleaders permission, and the Yale rally was held in front of the Widener steps.

No Dartmouth Rally

Cohen said last night that no rally will be held before the Dartmouth game because of a conflicting band concert.

There will probably not be a rally before the Davidson or Brown games, since these come either right before or right after the Princeton game and the cheerleaders don't want to hold rallies two weeks in a row.

Rallies ordinarily start in front of the statue of John Harvard, move across Massachusetts Avenue to the Houses, and

LAWRENCE COHEN

Council Upholds Plan For Joint Film Shows

Approval of the agreement made by Ivy Films, the Liberal Union, and the U.N. Council to show one film, jointly, each week seemed certain last night when the plan was passed by the Student Council. It will go to Associate Dean Watson for his approval today.

The Council also passed a resolution stating that there is no unfair monopoly involved in the film combination, and that any other groups wishing to exhibit pictures could still do so on evenings not already scheduled by the three. The Council still has made no effort to contact other groups who showed films last year. The combination was formed to eliminate competition of the three organizations among themselves.

The entire Council will lunch with Dean Watson today to discuss administrative reasons for the recent parietal rules change prohibiting late permissions on

Figure 6. Article in the Harvard Crimson written by David Halberstam when Cohen was Head Cheerleader.

WCR: *That major probably is a good background for medicine in general?*

LSC: It was invaluable, because medicine is so much an interaction psychologically with patients, peers, trainees, and students. I look back on my major in college as an extraordinary launching pad for life.

WCR: *Let's go back a bit. Your father died just as you were entering Harvard College. How did your family situation work out from there? How did your mother get along? Did she stay in the same house? Were finances adequate after your father was gone?*

LSC: My father left my mother pretty well off. She was not wealthy, but her lifestyle did not change after his death. She lived in the same house and, as far as I could tell, she didn't have to alter her lifestyle in any way. She remarried 4 years later to a widower. She had a 20 plus marriage before her second husband died. He also worked in the wholesale clothing business. They lived in our original house for sometime. Then, perhaps 5 years into the marriage, they moved into an apartment in Long Island and stayed there until his death.

WCR: *Back to Harvard and the start of your junior year. What did you do during the summers while in college?*

LSC: I worked at that same resort hotel in the Catskill Mountains for 3 different summers. I was a bellhop one summer, a busboy the next, and a waiter the third summer.

WCR: *Those must have been fun summers?*

LSC: Yes they were. They were valuable growing up experiences because in each of those different jobs I met and worked with a lot of different people—some with no education, some with a little education, and some like myself. I found that quite enjoyable. It was a good way to spend the summer and gain some income. This relieved some of my guilt about being away at college and being a big expenditure for my mother.

WCR: *Your family paid all the tuition while you were in college?*

LSC: Yes. I never applied for a scholarship but remember, when I started college, the tuition was $600.00 and rose to only $800.00 by the time I graduated.

WCR: *What happened during your junior year? Here you are taking all those science courses. Did you feel good about the switch to medicine? In your extended family in New York City and Long Island, were there any physicians?*

LSC: No. I was the first physician in my entire family.

WCR: *Did you have any interactions with physicians growing up? Were you healthy growing up? You mentioned that a physician lived across the street from you, and you saw physicians at the time of your father's first heart attack, although you were quite young. What was your impression of "doctoring"?*

LSC: My impression was that doctors in those days, almost always men, were a very special cadre of people in our society. Their "calling" or their being able to take care of patients was a very special niche to them. When I was growing up, doctors were on a pedestal.

WCR: *Where did you live during your senior year at Harvard College?*

LSC: We lived in large student housing called "houses." I lived in Kirkland House.

WCR: *How many students were in your class at Harvard?*

LSC: About 1,100 graduated.

WCR: *Were they all males?*

LSC: Yes. Radcliff had a separate campus, and they had their own courses.

WCR: *Were there any teachers or professors at Harvard College who had a particular impact on you?*

LSC: I remember some of them very well: McGeorge Bundy taught government; Thornton Wilder the author; John Finley, a classicist; Louis Fieser, taught organic chemistry and wrote the organic chemistry textbook; Clyde Kluckhohn, taught anthropology and specialized in the Navajo Indians; Albert Guerard, taught comparative literature. They were outstanding teachers at Harvard.

WCR: *Did you have an advisor for medical school?*

LSC: No. I knew what I had to do—2 years of chemistry, 1 year of physics, 1 year of biology, and I knew I had to apply. There was no pre-med advisor.

WCR: *Which medical schools did you apply to?*

LSC: I applied to a small number, and I was admitted to New York University (NYU) and George Washington.

WCR: *You and Eugene Braunwald had very similar paths in a way. Braunwald's from Brooklyn, and went to New York University College and Medical School. How did medical school work out? Where did you live while in medical school?*

LSC: Braunwald and I did have similar backgrounds. The difference is he is brilliant. I lived at home when in medical school. I drove into Manhattan each day.

WCR: *You started medical school in September 1954?*

LSC: Yes.

WCR: *Were there surprises for you in medical school? How many were in your medical school class?*

LSC: My class had 100 students. Surprises for me centered on the difficulty of some of the basic science courses, such as pharmacology and biochemistry. I worked hard. At least initially in medical school, it was almost a throw-back to my freshman year at Harvard. I found myself surrounded by very bright colleagues, and the course work was very challenging.

WCR: *Did NYU in 1954 limit the percentage of Jews in the class?*

LSC: I think not. If anything, NYU brought to it very bright Jewish students from the New York area who might not have had the financial wherewithal to go out-of-town for college or medical school. NYU was, in large part, a meritocracy. About half of my class was Jewish, and a large number were from New York City.

WCR: *Was medical school overall an enjoyable experience for you?*

LSC: The first year was not terribly enjoyable. The second year became more enjoyable, as we started to deal with patients. I really blossomed in the third year during clinical clerkships. I loved every clerkship that I took. Internal medicine was the right choice for me. I never looked back once I started my third year of medical school. I said to myself, "How could I ever have even thought about doing something different than what I am doing?"

WCR: *Your mother must have been quite pleased to have you back in New York. Why did you choose to live at home, since she had just remarried? You were living there the first year of her new marriage?*

LSC: I had a very good study situation at home. I had my own room, which was large. My brother and sister had already moved out. I also had a car. Life was relatively simple.

WCR: *How long did it take you to drive into Manhattan in the morning?*

LSC: About 30 minutes.

WCR: *What professors and/or teachers had a major impact on you during medical school?*

LSC: There were a number of individuals in the basic sciences. We had a Nobel Prize winner, *Severo Ochoa*. In anatomy, we had a *Dr. Pick* and *Dr. Bergman*, both of whom were émigrés from central Europe at the time of the war. In the clinical years, there were a number of role models. By this time, I was starting to gravitate toward cardiology. There was *Charlie Kossman, Bertha Rader, Sherwood Lawrence,* and *Saul Farber*. NYU Medical School was a very rich place in terms of having a long tradition in medicine and having some very good teachers.

WCR: *What convinced you that internal medicine or cardiology was the thing for you?*

LSC: It became clear to me that a vital component of what I did in medicine was interaction with people. Surgery doesn't have that and realistically, although I liked surgery, I didn't have a lot of manual dexterity. I wasn't very good at tying knots. I gravitated toward the specialty where I could interact with people, and of all of the internal medicine subspecialties I liked the cardiology patients and their problems and their care most of all.

WCR: *When it came time to apply for internship, what was your thought process?*

LSC: I did very well in medical school. I was class president and made Alpha Omega Alpha. I was advised to stretch and reach high, so I applied to the Harvard hospitals, Johns Hopkins, and Yale. I was accepted at Yale for internship. I was accepted to a number of other places, but I really liked the Department of Medicine at Yale when I went there for an interview. *Paul Beeson*, Chief of Medicine, was an outstanding leader. It was a small service with only 12 interns. I liked what I saw, I liked the hospital, and when I was accepted at Yale, I decided that was the place I wanted to be.

]WCR: *How big was the Grace New Haven Hospital at that time?*

LSC: In 1958, Grace New Haven Hospital had about a 500 to 600 beds. It was a full service hospital with every specialty and subspecialty.

WCR: *How many were on the faculty in internal medicine in 1958?*

LSC: About 20.

WCR: *What about today?*

LSC: Today, there are 280 full-time medicine faculty members.

WCR: *How did the internship work out?*

LSC: As I look back on it, it was one of my happiest years. I had no responsibilities outside of medicine. I wasn't married. I lived in the hospital. I thoroughly enjoyed the internship. It was very rigorous. We worked all day long, and either Monday and Wednesday nights and all of the weekend or alternately Tuesday, Thursday and Friday nights. It was essentially an every other day, every other weekend on call schedule. That was my life. The camaraderie was fantastic. We had good teachers and wonderful patients.

WCR: *Who had a particular impact on you?*

LSC: *Paul Beeson,* of course, *Frank Epstein* in nephrology, *Howard Spiro* in gastroenterology, *Alan V. N. Goodyer* in cardiology, *Gerald Klatskin* in hepatic disease.

WCR: *Who were some of your fellow interns?*

LSC: *Jerry Burrow* went on to an outstanding career as chair of medicine at Toronto, Dean at UCSD and then back to Yale in the early 1990s as dean. *Paul Rudnick* went into practice (endocrinology) in Los Angeles. *Jay Kislak* went into infectious diseases at NYU. *Steve Malawista* has had an outstanding career at Yale in rheumatology.

]WCR: *What was your thinking at Yale by the time you were a junior assistant resident? Did you think that you wanted to stay in academia or was private practice entering your mind? When did you go into Public Health Service?*

LSC: I joined the Public Health Service in 1960 after my first year of residency. I went into the Center for Disease Control (CDC), the Epidemiology Intelligence Service. In those days, one had to be in a uniformed service or non-uniformed military service. I chose the Public Health Service as an alternative to going to Vietnam. I was stationed, after spending a month in Atlanta, at The Johns Hopkins Hospital as a fellow in the Division of Allergy and Infectious diseases.

WCR: *You were getting armed services credit for that?*

LSC: Yes. That was my 2-year tour of duty in the armed service.

WCR: *Did you choose that division of medicine—Allergy and Infectious Disease—or were you assigned there?*

LSC: I was assigned there. About 30 of us entered the CDC's Epidemiology Intelligence Service in 1960, and about 10 of us were assigned to different hospitals around the country. My job at Hopkins was to be the hospital epidemiologist, specifically to look at nosocomial infections. Hopkins in those days had segregated wards: male, female; medicine, surgery; Caucasian, Black. On a given morning, if I found a clustering of staphylococcal infections in the bacteriology laboratory from a given ward, I knew immediately, for example, that it was male, Caucasian, and surgical. It was an epidemiologist's delight to be able to pinpoint breakouts of nosocomial infections by such precise demographics.

WCR: *Were you interested in infectious disease? Did you consider it as your subspecialty career?*

LSC: I enjoyed it, but I knew I was not going to have a career in infectious diseases. I enjoyed it because I respected Dr. Paul Beeson, and he was an icon in infectious diseases. I worked with *Bob Fekety* at Hopkins, who was a research fellow in infectious diseases. I enjoyed thoroughly working with him. He was a mentor, even though he was only 2 years older. I had already decided by that time that cardiology was where I wanted to be.

WCR: *You had several publications during those 2 years at Hopkins with Lee Cluff and Bob Fekety?*

LSC: Yes I did. It was a good environment. Lee Cluff was a good division chief. When I first came, he gave me a project that I wasn't terribly interested in. After a couple of weeks, I went to him and told him that I didn't really enjoy that particular research project, and he asked me what I would like to do. I told him I would like to extend what I was doing as the hospital epidemiologist. I wanted to do some basic investigations in staphylococcal infections. To his credit, he agreed. Fekety and I worked hand-in-hand and were very productive. We discovered some new strains of staphylococcus and were able to identify them by phage typing.

WCR: *Where did you live in Baltimore?*

LSC: When I first came to Baltimore, I lived in a nice apartment building not far from Hopkins. After that first year, I met my future wife, Jane Abramson. Her family is from Baltimore. We got married in August 1961 and we lived in our first apartment in the suburbs from August 1961 until the time that I left Hopkins in July 1962.

WCR: *What were the characteristics of Jane that attracted you to her and how did you meet?*

LSC: Jane was a senior at the University of North Carolina at the time. We met in December 1960 through mutual

Figure 7. His wife Jane's engagement picture.

friends. I'm usually not a man who makes decisions very quickly, but I knew very early on that she was the woman I wanted to marry. She was a senior in college, and we had only about 10 dates (either in Baltimore or in North Carolina) throughout our courtship. We got married 8 months after first meeting. We celebrated our 45th wedding anniversary in August 2006. It was a good decision (Figure 7).

WCR: *What were the features of Jane that allowed you to come to the marriage decision so quickly?*

LSC: There was a certain commonality. I respected her values. She valued education and family, and so did I. I liked her family. I got to know them very well. We had the same idea about size of family and how we wanted to raise children. Then there was the intangible without which all of the commonality won't go anywhere. There was a physical attraction that we both felt. She was young, only 20, and I was 28. Our union just seemed right.

WCR: *Did she finish college?*

LSC: She was 20 when she graduated. She had skipped along the way. She graduated in June 1961.

WCR: *The Baltimore period sounds to me like it was a wonderful time in your life after the 2 hard-working but rewarding years at Yale. I gather in Baltimore that you had no night work?*

LSC: That's correct. It was a 9 to 5 day essentially. I was able to really enjoy the cultural life of Baltimore. During the second year, I got very close to Jane's parents. Her father was a dentist, the very first endodontist (root canal specialist) in Baltimore. Although he always had a private practice, he was also chair of the department of endodontia at the University of Maryland. We always had a very rich relationship. He died about 5 years ago. Her mother is still alive. In some ways Jane's father was a surrogate father for me.

WCR: *You couldn't say anything nicer about your in-laws. Finishing up your required service at Baltimore, now married, and you had a chance for the first time to take a deep breath and relax a little bit. Where did you apply for cardiology fellowships, and how did it work out that you went to the Brigham and Women's Hospital?*

LSC: I only applied to *Richard Gorlin's* program at the Peter Bent Brigham Hospital. For many reasons, it was the right one for me. I had read some of Gorlin's work on valve area formulas. I was attracted to cardiac catherization, to cardiovascular physiology, and to Boston. I wrote to Gorlin asking him if I could come up to be interviewed. He interviewed me and offered me the job.

WCR: *Just like that?*

LSC: In those days, that was how it was done. In July 1962, we moved to Boston, and I started working in Dick Gorlin's lab.

WCR: *Was it what you expected? How did it go?*

LSC: It was a wonderful fellowship. I learned how to do cardiac catheterizations, which were only diagnostic in those days. I really loved the physiology of the cardiac catheterization laboratory. It was a small program. We had 2 fellows in the first year of the program and 2 fellows in the second year. The work itself was thrilling. Gorlin was extraordinarily bright. On Mondays we would do animal studies, and on Tuesday, Wednesday, and Thursday we would have patients in the same laboratory. On Friday, we would have a conference going over the data from the whole week. On Mondays, the other first year fellow and I we would get to the hospital early, go to the kennel of Harvard Medical School (across the courtyard), select an abandoned dog, and inject the dog with morphine and atropine: (1) to sedate him/her, (2) have him/her evacuate their bowels before we took them to the lab. After the injection, we had a certain amount of time before the dog started going to sleep. We would start walking the dog across the campus and the high school students (who were going to Boston Latin) would ask us what we were going to do with the dog. After awhile the dog would defecate and start to falter. We then placed him/her in a cart and took him/her up the same elevator that the patients used. (It is unthinkable in today's world to do this!) By this time, the cart would be shaking 60 times a minute as the dog was hyperventilating from the atropine. We spent Mondays doing the hemodynamic and physiological studies on the dog. Late in the day, we'd clean up the lab completely and get it ready for the patients on Tuesday, Wednesday, and Thursdays. The catheterization lab was an active one but not by today's standards. On the 3 patient days, we would usually study 2 patients each day in the lab. In those days, every patient participated in a hemodynamic protocol. Every patient had a right-sided heart cath, a left-sided heart cath, and a coronary sinus cath. Many patients had infusions of pressor agents or inotropic agents. Early on in my fellowship, we visited *Dr. Mason Sones* in Cleveland. We learned how to do coronary arteriography through the Sones technique. That became a very active part of every catheterization in 1963 and 1964. Dick Gorlin was a rigorous task master, but he asked nothing of us that he didn't do himself. I began, continued, and ended up with a very high regard and a very positive friendship with Dick Gorlin.

WCR: *How did you get recruited to the NIH?*

LSC: One of my fellow medical school graduates was *Jack Braunwald*, who was taking a hematology fellowship at the Beth Israel Hospital in Boston at the same time I was doing the cardiology fellowship at the Brigham. He was a bachelor, and my wife, Jane, sort of adopted him. We often had Jack over for dinner on Friday nights. When I returned to New Haven on July 1, 1964, I thought I would end up in the private practice of cardiology, because I always liked patient contact. Nevertheless, I was weighing academics against practice. About January, 1965 while in the second half of the second year of residency, I got a call from *Gene Braunwald* at the NIH. Gene said, "My brother Jack thinks a lot of you, and he says you have had some good training in cardiology. Would you consider coming down and working at the National Heart Institute in my branch?" I went down, interviewed with him, liked what I saw, and signed on right away. On July 1, 1965, I traveled with my very young family to Bethesda, and started working in Gene Braunwald's cardiology branch. I was head of the clinical service. I was responsible for the day-to-day care of patients admitted for cardiac catheterization and other clinical research protocols. I had the best and the brightest Clinical Associates working with me; younger doctors who were spending their 2 years in the Public Health Service, as I had done 5 years previously at Hopkins. The 3 years with Braunwald were wonderful. NIH at that time got the most complex and interesting patients ever. Patients could go there free of charge if they had any kind of valvular or congenital heart disease. They would have cardiac catheterization if that were appropriate, and they would be operated upon if that were appropriate. I stayed at the NIH for 3 years (Figure 8).

WCR: *When you were at NIH those 3 years, you wrote a lot of papers. What went through your mind as to what you wanted to do on a life-time basis?*

LSC: Sometime within those 3 years at NIH I decided that academic cardiology was where I wanted to be and private practice receded from my consideration. I knew sometime in those 3 years that the intense training that I had and the interesting patients that I was able to follow and the teaching that I was able to do set me on the academic medicine road. I thoroughly enjoyed the clinical research, and I enjoyed writing papers. It was very intoxicating and it became very clear that I wanted an academic career. I was head of the clinical service from July 1965 on. One of the brightest Clinical Associates who came that same month was *Burt Sobel*. He and I became friends immediately. There was something about him that was very endearing. One day, we got a phone call that a very prominent cardiac researcher, who worked at the NIH, was coming in with chest pain. Gene Braunwald asked Burt Sobel and me to go down to the emergency room at NIH and take care of this patient. This researcher came in with a blood pressure of about 90/60 mm Hg, and the electrocardiogram showed a right bundle branch block. We gave him inotropes and vasopressors to raise his blood pressure. Looking back ,we recognized that that was the wrong thing to do and that we almost killed him. We did not know in those days about

Figure 8. Daughters Melanie and Wendy at a playground in Bethesda, Maryland near National Institute of Health.

right ventricular infarcts where the best thing to do is to give volume loading and the worst thing to do is to give vasopressors. This researcher survived in spite of Sobel and me.

WCR: *To summarize your experience at NIH was enlightening to say the least.*

LSC: It was invigorating working with so many investigators my own age: *Dean Mason, Steve Epstein, Peter Frommer, Jim Gault, John Ross, Ed Sonnenblick, Jim Spann, Bill Parmley, Andy Wechsler, Gerry Glick, Neil Coleman, Bob Buccino, Bob Zelis, Bob Levy, Bill Friedman, Tony Gotto, Virgil Brown,* and, of course, yourself. That's just a few of those who populated the Cardiology Branch in those days.

WCR: *How did it come about that you came to Dallas, Texas, in 1968?*

LSC: I was at the NIH in late 1967 or early 1968. *Jere Mitchell*, a previous researcher at the National Heart Institute came up for a visit. Jere and I talked a bit, and he asked me to consider coming to the University of Texas (Southwestern) Medical School. *Carlton Chapman* had just retired as Chief of Cardiology. Jere Mitchell was Chief of Cardiovascular research. Jere asked me if I would consider joining the faculty as Chief of Clinical Cardiology. He and I would be co-chiefs of the cardiology section in *Donald Seldin's* Internal Medicine Department. I had never been to Dallas. I visited and decided that it was a very good place for me to be. The medical school was young and vigorous. I thought Donald Seldin was a charismatic department chair. I thoroughly enjoyed working with Jere Mitchell. We were to get along extremely well as co-chiefs. I put my family in the car, and drove to Dallas, and I joined the faculty as Chief of Clinical Cardiology beginning July 1968.

WCR: *Had you ever been west of the Mississippi?*

LSC: I had visited for short periods both San Francisco and Los Angeles.

WCR: *Until you went off to Harvard College, you essentially had never left the State of New York?*

LSC: That's true.

WCR: *How did Dallas, Texas, work out? This was a major change in your lifestyle. You had been in Baltimore, Boston, Brooklyn, Bethesda—4 B's and all that essentially in the Northeast corridor of the USA. Now you are in cowboy land. What did Jane think about it?*

LSC: It was a total surprise for all of us. Jane and I loved living in Dallas. There was a friendliness and acceptance that we had never seen before. The first day we got there and moved into our house in Dallas, I looked out my window and there was a man mowing my lawn. I went out and introduced myself. He said, "I'm your next door neighbor. I see you just moved in so why don't I mow your lawn for you the first time just to give you a head start?" It was an interesting time for Dallas. It was 1968, and as far we could put together, the State of Texas and Dallas itself, was still reeling from John Kennedy's assassination. The fact that Kennedy's assassination occurred in Dallas ignited a spirit, as far as I could tell, of liberalism and friendliness. People wanted to change the image of Dallas. We found it an extraordinarily exciting place to be. We made a number of friends very quickly. Jane got a job in television as an associate producer of a TV news program. She loved the work. I was very happy at the school. We found warmth, and acceptance, and friends in Dallas that were unknown to us before. We loved it there (Figure 9).

WCR: *How did it turn out that you went back to New Haven when you were offered the Chief of Cardiology there? Just 2 years later, right?*

LSC: Yes, 2 years later. As often happened in those days, at the annual May meetings of the American Society of Clinical Investigation and the American Federation for Clinical Research, the Chief of Medicine at Yale suggested that I return to Yale-New Haven.

WCR: *That was Phil Bondy?*

LSC: Yes. The conversation, however, was a very peripheral one and not substantive. Nevertheless, it was a conversation. Then, in the early part of 1970, Phil Bondy asked me to return as Chief of the Section of Cardiology at Yale in order to build it up. I was 37 years old at the time. He offered me a tenured professorship. Although I had very fond feelings for New Haven, the decision was very difficult for me and even more difficult for Jane. Left to her own choice, Jane would have stayed in Dallas, but she was a supportive wife and agreed to move. I'll never forget driving from Dallas to New Haven. We had a Ford mustang at the time. Jane sat in the front seat and Melanie and Wendy, aged 5 and 3, in the back seat. None of them could stop crying! I almost turned around and drove back to Dallas.

WCR: *Back in New Haven, how did it go? After being back there a few months, were you glad to be back there? Did you make the right decision?*

LSC: It was a busy time. I did think that I had made the right decision. Cardiology had a tremendous void in New

Figure 9. In the laboratory at the University of Texas (Southwestern) about 1969.

Haven at that time. I had a big job to do then in turning around the clinical program and establishing a teaching program. I enjoyed that. It was an exciting time.

WCR: *When you went back in July 1970, how many full-time cardiologists were there before you started recruiting?*

LSC: Other than me, only 2: Alan Goodyer and a junior faculty member.

WCR: *What was your life like during that period of time when you were head of cardiology at this major medical center?*

LSC: It was at the same time extremely good and extraordinarily exacting, because I was at the hospital every day and I frequently got called at night. We had a nascent fellowship program. An attending had to be at the hospital if there was anything happening at night. I'd find myself going to the hospital at night at least once or twice a week. Any progress we made in terms of the clinical program or the teaching program was a giant step compared to what was there before. I recruited faculty in the first couple of years, and we started to broaden and grow. The climate was receptive to what I was trying to do. Those first couple of years, when I worked very hard, I did not spend as much time with my family as I should have.

WCR: *How many full-time members in the cardiology division were there when you left the chiefship in 1978?*

LSC: We had 11 full-time faculty.

WCR: *What was your day like during that time? What time did you get up in the morning, and what time did you get to the hospital? What time did you leave at night and when did you go to sleep?*

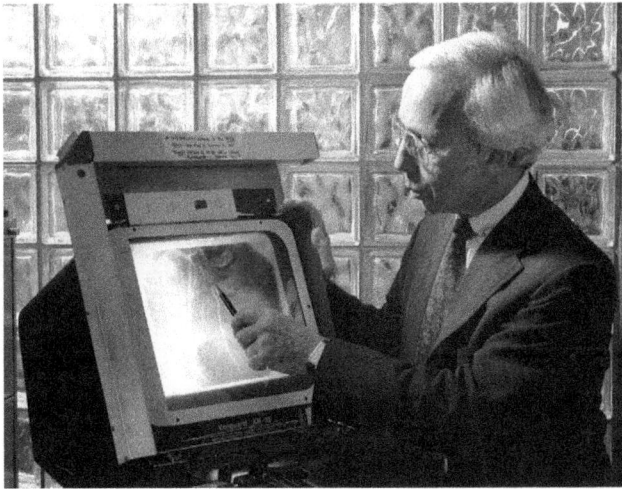

Figure 10. Yale University about 1975.

LSC: I have always been blessed with not needing a lot of sleep. I get up at 5:30 or 5:45 A.M. I feel refreshed. Back in those days, I stayed up later than I do now, so I'd get up, read the newspaper and generally be at the hospital by 7:15 or 7:30. The morning would be spent either rounding or working in the cardiac catheterization laboratory. Afternoons, I would teach or work in the cath lab. There was a lot of in-hospital work in those days. I rounded every day for about 2 hours. As a member of the department of medicine, I had month blocks at a time where I would be the general medical attending. I was responsible for a housestaff team, and I would supervise general medicine, not just cardiology. And then the usual meetings with hospital administrators and staff (Figure 10).

WCR: *Eight years as chief of cardiology—10 years if including Dallas— is long enough and above average. Tell about the offer to be chairman of the department of internal medicine here at Baylor University Medical Center.*

LSC: About 1980. I had maintained many contacts in Dallas, and I can't recall exactly when the offer came, but I was asked to come down to look at the chairmanship of the department of internal medicine at Baylor. Baylor back then, as it is now, was a very good hospital. It did not have much of a research base, but it did have many very good internists and a strong cardiology division. I had to make a decision about getting back into administration, which admittedly also allowed teaching, but which meant giving up cardiology in a significant way. I had a lot of respect for Baylor University Medical Center, and I certainly liked its staff. I also liked living in Dallas. Nevertheless, I made the decision that I was happy at Yale, that I was enjoying what I was doing, and that it would probably be best long term to stay at Yale. I never looked back on that decision. I'm the type of person who thinks about something, makes a decision and moves forward. In the early 1980s, I decided to stop doing cardiac catheterizations, and not get into coronary angioplasty. In the mid-1970s and mid-1980s, I took on a number of national responsibilities. I was on the Subspecialty Board of Cardiovascular Disease. I did that for 10 years, and we had 3 or 4 meetings a year. That took up a sizeable amount of time. In the late 1970s, I was program chairman for the annual meeting of the American Heart

Figure 11. In Russia with Thomas Killip, Richard Kronmal, Richard Russell, Peter Frommer, Ed Alderman, and Michael Mock, 1978.

Association. I was governor for the State of Connecticut of the American College of Cardiology (ACC), and I was on the board of trustees of the ACC. In the early 80s, I became secretary-treasurer and then ultimately president of the Association of the University of Cardiologists. At about the same time, I became secretary-treasurer and ultimately President of the Interurban Clinical Club, a group of academics from Baltimore, Philadelphia, New York, New Haven, and Boston that was actually founded by *William Osler*, and has met continuously twice a year since the early 20th century. I also developed an interest in clinical trials. In the late 70s and early 80s, I was principal investigator on a number of NIH sponsored clinical trials: The Coronary Artery Surgery Study being one, the Thrombolysis and Myocardial Infarction (TIMI) trials, TIMI 1, 2 and 3. were some others. I also became quite involved at the NIH, where I chaired the Clinical Trials Review Committee for the National Heart, Blood, Institute for 8 years. Thus my out-of-Yale activities expanded a lot in the late 1970s and 1980s (Figures 11 to 13).

WCR: *Have you spent the last 36 years continuously at Yale?*

LSC: No. In 1985, we spent a year in London at the Brompton Hospital. I worked in the Echo Laboratory and taught at the Medical School. It was an outstanding year in which I learned a lot, and I also was able to see much of England, Scotland, and Ireland.

WCR: *What have been your activities in the Dean's office? You have been involved there at Yale for nearly 15 years?*

LSC: In 1989, the current dean asked me to become deputy dean, and I agreed to do so. Deputy Dean at that time was essentially dean of the faculty, for all issues of appointment, promotion, tenure, career development, and tracks in the school of medicine. My office handled all of those issues. The associate dean for clinical affairs and the associate dean for financial affairs reported through me to the dean. That position occupied 50% of my time. The deputy dean is also the individual at the medical school who is the

Figure 12. At the Pavlov Institute, St. Petersburg, Russia, 1985.

Figure 13. At the Great Wall of China, 1991.

Figure 14. Melanie and Wendy at Melanie's wedding 1990.

Figure 15. Wendy and son-in-law, Haider, at their wedding in Karachi, Pakistan, 1999.

Research Integrity Officer. All inquiries or investigations or allegation of possible scientific misconduct, such as plagiarism, falsification, fabrication, or egregious authorship issues ran through my office. My plate was full. In 1996, I became Special Advisor to the Dean. That's a position that I have had ever since. My unique responsibility is for those issues of possible academic misconduct or scientific fraud. I also teach a number of times a year on the Responsible Conduct of Research and other ethical issues.

WCR: *What is your life like now? I know every day is not the same, but describe a week anyway.*

LSC: I see cardiology outpatients every Wednesday and Thursday under the aegis of the faculty practice plan. I have a large academic practice of about 400 patients whom I

follow. I see most of them at least twice a year. They all have primary care physicians but see me as their cardiologist. I've followed some patients for over 30 years. I see the children of some of the patients I follow. It's a very rich and satisfying core of what I do and as a spin-off, of course, I always have a couple of patients in the hospital. I'll make rounds on them at the end of the day 5 days a week.

WCR: *Are those full days or half days in the clinic?*

LSC: Full days. I have 4 sessions where I see patients. They are busy sessions. I enjoy it fully and feel very privileged to be able to have a practice of medicine. I often have a resident with me, and we see patients together. Monday, Tuesday, and Friday are very varied. My scientific misconduct work often is done on those days. No week is the same. I keep Wednesday and Thursday sacrosanct. I rarely, if I can help it, am out of town (Figures 14 and 15).

WCR: *Tell me about your two girls. What are their lives like?*

LSC: We have two girls, Melanie and Wendy. Melanie was brought up in New Haven and was always extremely well motivated in terms of school. That has not changed. She has good instincts and wants to do good for people. Melanie went to Harvard College and then Stanford Law School. She was in corporate law for 1 year but didn't like

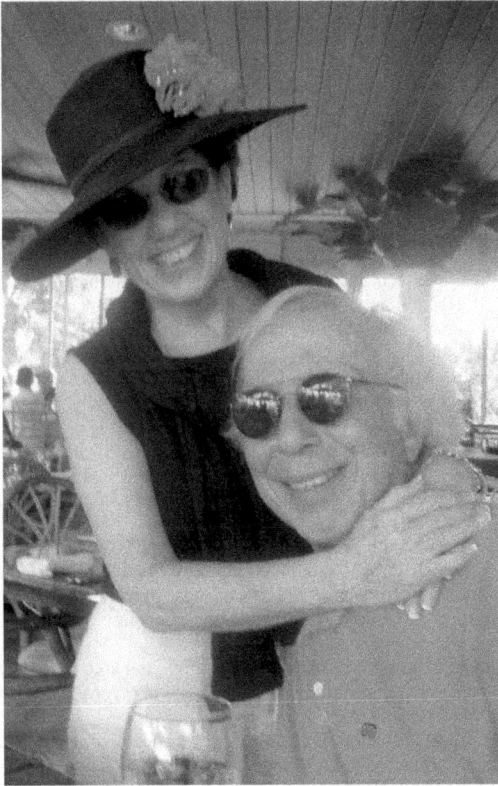

Figure 16. LSC and Jane on a Caribbean vacation.

Figure 17. Daughters, sons-in-laws, and grandchildren, 2006.

Figure 18. At a Yale graduation as Deputy Dean, 1995.

to litigate. While living on the West Coast, she became executive director of a think tank called The Stanford Center on Conflict and Negotiation. That was a perfect fit for her. She was able to use her mediation/arbitration skills of bringing people together to very good advantage. Her husband, Lawrence, who she met at Harvard, went to Stanford Law School also. He went into the corporate sector for awhile and then about 6 years ago, they moved to Washington, DC, where he is general counsel for an internet company. Melanie for a number of years was head of a division in the Hewlett Foundation awarding grants to groups furthering the global peace process. That particular program got disbanded, and she currently, has started a foundation named the Cypress Fund for International Peace and Security. They have 2 children, ages 13 and 10. My daughter Wendy grew up in New Haven and went to Boston University. She met her future husband, Haider at Boston University. His family is from Pakistan and is still living there. His father was chief of staff to a former prime minister of Pakistan, Benizer Bhutto. Haider's father was trade minister to Kashmir and tourist minister. He spent his whole life in government. Haider got his MBA at BU, where he met Wendy. Wendy is an entrepreneur. She is a wonderful sales person and has gotten her real estate agent license. They have 2 young girls, and she is a working mom out of the house. Her children are 6 and 3 (Figures 16 and 17). I'm very proud of both girls. They are both very family-oriented and they have very close relationships.

WCR: *You have been a cardiologist for 40 years. Would you change anything or do anything differently if you were starting now?*

LSC: I don't think so. In spite of all of the changes in our health care delivery system, I remain very positive about the choices I have made. In retrospect, I cannot imagine a more fulfilling specialty than Cardiology. I recently gave a lecture chronicling the growth of Cardiology in the 20th and 21st centuries. The privilege of teaching, practicing, and investigating in Cardiology over these past 40 years is in my opinion not able to be matched. If asked by someone starting out about whether to consider Cardiology I would enthusiastically tell him/her that it is a wonderful career opportunity. With all the advances we have made, there is still much to be done (Figure 18).

WCR: *Larry, on behalf of not only me, but also the*

American Journal of Cardiology, *I want to thank you for allowing the AJC readers to get to know you.*

LSC: Thank you Bill. I have enjoyed talking with you, and I feel very honored to join the ranks of outstanding cardiologists whom you have interviewed for the *AJC*.

Selected Publications of LSC as Selected by LSC

1. Cohen LS, Freedman LR. Damage to the aortic valve as a cause of death in subacute bacterial endocarditis. *Ann Intern Med* 1961;55:562–564.
4. Cohen LS, Fekety FR, Cluff LE. Studies of the epidemiology of staphylococcal Infection: IV. The changing ecology of hospital staphylococci. *N Engl J Med* 1962;266:367–372.
5. Cohen LS, Fekety FR, Cluff LE. Studies of the epidemiology of staphylococcal infection: V. The reporting of hospital-acquired infection. *JAMA* 1962;180:805–808.
6. Cohen LS, Cluff LE. A study of the intestinal flora in a closed pediatric community. *Am J Hyg* 1962;76:262–266.
7. Cohen LS, Fekety FR, Cluff LE. Treatment of a nasal carrier of staphylococcus aureus with oxacillin (5-methyl-3-phenyl-4isoxazolyl penicillin). *Bull Johns Hopkins Hosp* 1962;111:315–320.
9. Cohen LS, Fekety FR, Cluff LE. Studies of the epidemiology of staphylococcal infection: VI. Infections in the surgical patient. *Ann Surg* 1964;159:321–334.
10. Cohen LS, Elliott WC, Gorlin R. Measurement of myocardial blood flow using krypton 85. *Am J Physiol* 1964;206:997–999.
12. Tafur E, Cohen LS, Levine HD. The normal apex cardiogram. *Circulation* 1964;30:381–391.
13. Tafur E, Cohen LS, Levine HD. The apex cardiogram in left ventricular outflow tract obstruction. *Circulation* 1964;10:392–399.
15. Cohen LS, Elliott WC, Rolett EL, Gorlin R. Hemodynamic studies during angina pectoris. *Circulation* 1965;31:409–416.
17. Klein MD, Cohen LS, Gorlin R. Krypton[85] myocardial blood flow: precordial scintillation versus coronary sinus sampling. *Am J Psychol* 1965;209:705–710.
19. Cohen LS, Elliott WC, Klein MD, Gorlin R. Coronary heart disease: clinical, cinearteriographic and metabolic correlations. *Am J Cardiol* 1966;17:153–168.
21. Cohen LS, Mason D, Braunwald E. The significance of an atrial gallop sound in mitral regurgitation: a clue to the diagnosis of ruptured chordae tendineae. *Circulation* 1967;35:112–118.
22. Cohen LS, Buccino RA, Roberts WC. Acquired cor triventriculare, a rare complication of cardiomyopathy. *Am Heart J* 1967;73:538–541.
24. Cohen LS, Braunwald E. Amelioration of angina pectoris in idiopathic hypertrophic subaortic stenosis with beta-adrenergic blockade. *Circulation* 1967;35:847–851.
26. Morrow AG, Cohen LS, Roberts WC, Braunwald NS, Braunwald E. Severe mitral regurgitation following acute myocardial infarction and ruptured papillary muscle: hemodynamic findings and results of operative treatment in four patients. *Circulation* 1968;37 and 38(suppl II);II:124–132.
27. Strober W, Cohen LS, Waldman TA, Braunwald E. Tricuspid regurgitation: a newly recognized cause of protein losing enteropathy, lymphocytopenia and immunologic deficiency. *Am J Med* 1968;44:842.
29. Cohen LS, Simon AL, Whitehouse WC, Schuette WH, Braunwald E. Heart motion video-tracing (radarkymography) in the diagnosis of congenital and acquired heart disease. *Am J Cardiol* 1968;22:678–684.
30. Cohen LS, Braunwald E. Chronic beta adrenergic receptor blockade in the treatment of idiopathic hypertrophic subaortic stenosis. *Prog Cardiovasc Dis* 1968;113:211–221.
34. O'Brien KP, Cohen LS. Hemodynamic and phonocardiographic correlates of the Austin Flint murmur. *Am Heart J* 1969;77:603–609.
37. Cohen LS, Porterfield D, Mitchell J, Mullins C. Sequenced external pulsation in the therapy of cardiogenic shock. Proceedings of Artificial Heart Program Conference, June 9–13, 1969. Washington, D.C. Ed. By R. J. Hegyeli, Washington, D.C., U.S. Government Printing Office, 1969;495–504.
38. Cohen LS, Roberts WC. Tetralogy of Fallot, its unusual variants and its simulators. *Chest* 1970;57:266–274.
40. Cohen LS, Mitchell JH. Sequenced pulsation in the therapy of cardiogenic shock. *Dallas Med J* 1970;56:208–209.
41. Cohen LS, Wechsler AS, Mitchell JH Glick G. Depression of cardiac function by streptomycin and other antimicrobial agents. *Am J Cardiol* 1970;26:505–511.
44. Cohen LS, Rosenthal JE, Horner DW, Atkins JM, Matthews OA, Sarnoff S. Plasma levels of lidocaine after intramuscular administration. *Am J Cardiol* 1972;29:520–523.
46. Roberts WC, Cohen LS. Left ventricular papillary muscles: description of the normal and a survey of conditions causing them to be abnormal. *Circulation* 1972;46:138.
50. Kisslo J, Wolfson S, Ross AM, Pasternak R, Hammond GL, Cohen LS. Ultrasound assessment of left ventricular function following aorto-coronary saphenous vein bypass grafting. *Circulation* 1973;(suppl 3)48:156–161.
52. Cohen LS, Mullins CB, Mitchell JH. Sequenced external counterpulsation and intraaortic balloon pumping in cardiogenic shock. *Am J Cardiol* 1973;32:656–661.
58. Zaret BL, Vlay SC, Freedman GS, Wolfson S, Cohen LS. Quantitative relationships between potassium-43 imaging and left ventricular cineangiography following myocardial infarction in man. *Circulation* 1975;52:1076–1085.
60. Zaret BL, DiCola VC, Donabedian RK, Puri S, Wolfson S, Freedman GS, Cohen LS. Dual radionuclide study of myocardial uptake of potassium-43, technetium-99m stannous pyrophosphate, regional myocardial blood flow and creatine phosphokinase depletion. *Circulation* 1976;53:422–428.
66. Cannom DS, Levy W, Cohen LS. The short- and long-term prognosis of patients with transmural and nontransmural myocardial infarction. *Am J Med* 1976;61:452–458.
69. Pasternak RC, Cannom DS, Cohen LS. Echocardiographic diagnosis of large fungal verrucca attached to the mitral valve. *Br Heart J* 1976;38:1209–1212.
70. Langou RA, Cohen LS. The sequential external counter pulsator: a circulatory assist device. *Yale J Biol Med* 1977;50:59–65.
75. Zaret BL, Cohen LS. Cardiovascular nuclear medicine I: evaluation of cardiac performance. *Mod Concepts Cardiovasc Dis* 1977;46:33–36.
76. Schrumpf JD, Sheps DS, Wolfson S, Aronson AL, Cohen LS. Altered hemoglobin-oxygen affinity with long-term propranolol therapy in patients with coronary artery disease. *Am J Cardiol* 1977;40:76–82.
87. Langou RA, Wiles JC, Cohen LS. Coronary surgery for unstable angina pectoris. incidence and mortality of perioperative myocardial infarction. *Br Heart J* 1978;40:767–772.
99. Langou RA, Van Dyke C, Tahan SR, Cohen LS. Cardiovascular manifestations of tricyclic antidepressant overdose. *Am Heart J* 1980 Oct;100:458–464.
100. Langou RA, Huang EK, Kelly MJ, Cohen LS. Predictive accuracy of coronary artery calcification and abnormal exercise test for coronary artery disease in asymptomatic men. *Circulation* 1980 Dec;62:1196–1203.
102. Lesser RL, Heinemann MH, Borkowski H.Jr, Cohen LS. Mitral valve prolapse and amaurosis fugax. *J Neuroophthalmol* 1981;1:153–160.
104. Levy W, Cannom DS, Cohen LS. The nontransmural myocardial infarction in perspective. *Cardiovasc Rev Rep* 1981;2:1285–1294.
110. CASS Principal Investigators. Myocardial infarction and mortality in the Coronary Artery Surgery Study (CASS) randomized trial. *N Engl J Med* 1984;310:750–758.
112. Brush JE, Cabin HS, Wohlgelernter D, Hammond GL, Cohen LS. Ventricular septal rupture following a clinically unrecognized myocardial infarction. *Am Heart J* 1985;110:667–670.
120. Kirklin JW, Adkins CW, Blackstone EH, Booth DC, Califf RM, Cohen LS, et al. ACC/AHA Guidelines and indications for coronary artery bypass graft surgery. A report of the American College of Cardiology/American Heart Association Task Force on assessment of diagnostic and therapeutic cardiovascular procedures (Subcommittee on Coronary Artery Bypass Graft Surgery). *Circulation* 1991;83:1125–1173.
121. Cairns J, Cohen LS, Colton T. Issues in the early termination of the aspirin component of the Physicians' Health Study. *Ann Epidemiol* 1991;1:395–405.
123. Levy W, Cannom DS, Cohen LS. The nontransmural myocardial infarction in perspective. *Cardiovasc Rev Rep* 1992;Apr:10–15.
124. Marmor A, Jain D, Cohen LS, Nevo E, Wackers FJT, Zaret BL. Left

ventricular peak power during exercise: a noninvasive approach for assessment of contractile reserve. *J Nucl Med* 1993;34:1877–1885.

125. The TIMI IIIB Investigators. Effects of tissue plasminogen activator and a comparison of early invasive and conservative strategies in unstable angina and non-Q-wave myocardial infarction. Results of the TIMI IIIB Trial. *Circulation* 1994;89:1545–1556.

126. Mueller HS, Forman SA, Menegus MA, Cohen LS, Knatterud GL, Braunwald E., for the TIMI Investigators. Prognostic significance of nonfatal reinfarction during 3-year follow-up: results of the Thrombolysis In Myocardial Infarction (TIMI) Phase II Clinical Trial. *J Am Coll Cardiol* 1995;26:900–907.

127. Waxman M, Cohen LS. Authorship in Academia: A challenge for the Ombuds. In *J California Caucus College University Ombuds* (CCCUO), 2001;3:15–20.

Chapters

17. Leon MB, Cohen LS. Hypertrophic cardiomyopathy. In: Cotsonas NJ, Jr., ed. Disease-a-Month. Chicago: Year Book Medical Publishers, Inc., 1981;28:1–86.

18. Leon MB, Cohen LS. Guidelines for patient management. In: Wenger, Hellerstein, eds. Rehabilitation of the Coronary Patient. 2nd Ed. Wiley Medical, 1983:67–95.

24. Cohen LS. Results of coronary bypass surgery. In: Annual Review Med 1987: 38:457–465.

25. Cohen LS. Management of patients after myocardial infarction. In: Hospital Practice 1987:22:149–174.

27. Cohen LS. Diseases of the aorta. In: Cecil's Textbook of Medicine. 18th Ed. 1988:370–374.

30. Kolansky DM, Cohen LS. Immediate postoperative management. In: Frankl, Brest, eds. Valvular Heart Disease: Comprehensive Evaluation and Treatment. 2nd Ed. Philadelphia: F.A. Davis, 1993:277–291.

34. Cohen LS. Hypertrophic Cardiomyopathy. In *Conn's Current Therapy*, Edited by Rakel, R.E. Elsevier Science (USA), 2003:328–332.

Books

1. Cohen LS, Mock MB, Ringqvist I, eds. Physical Conditioning and Cardiovascular Rehabilitation. John Wiley and Sons, 1980:324.

2. Zaret BL, Moses M, Cohen LS, eds. Yale University School of Medicine Heart Book, William Morrow Publishing Co., April 1992: 432.

3. Elefteriades JA, Geha A S, Cohen LS, eds. House Officer Guide to ICU Care. 2nd Ed, Raven Press, 1994:286.

4. Elefteriades JA, Cohen LS. Your Heart: An Owner's Guide, Promethius Books, 2007:415.

LAWRENCE HARVEY COHN, MD: A Conversation
With the Editor*

Larry Cohn was born in San Francisco, California, in 1937 and that is where he grew up. He received a BA in history from the University of California at Berkley in 1958 and his MD degree in 1962 from Stanford University School of Medicine. His internship and junior assistant residency in surgery was on the Harvard Surgical Service at Boston City Hospital from 1962 to 1964. He then was at the National Institutes of Health in Bethesda, Maryland, for 2 years as a surgical associate in the Surgery Branch of the National Heart Institute. In 1966, he returned to San Francisco for a 3-year residency in general surgery including chief resident at the University of California. From 1969 to 1971 he was resident and chief resident in cardiothoracic surgery at the Stanford University School of Medicine. In July 1971, he and his family moved to Boston, Massachusetts, where he initially was assistant professor of surgery at the Harvard Medical School and a member of the division of cardiothoracic surgery at the Brigham and Women's Hospital. By 1980 he was full professor of surgery and in 1999 he became the Virginia and James Hubbard Professor of Cardiac Surgery at Harvard Medical School. From 1987 to 2005, Dr. Cohn served as Chief of Cardiac Surgery at the Brigham and Women's Hospital. During his nearly 35 years at the Brigham and Women's Hospital, Dr. Cohn has published extensively, mainly in peer reviewed medical journals. He has evaluated a number of prosthetic and bioprosthetic heart valves. He has been a major force in simplifying cardiac surgery and making it safer and more effective. He has always been on the forefront of mitral valve repair operations and has personally performed over 2,000 of these operations. His contributions to coronary bypass procedures and those for patients with heart failure have been extensive. He continues to be an extremely active and busy cardiac surgeon. His publications in medical journals number over 400; his invited articles, editorials and reviews number nearly 100; his chapters in books number just over 100, and he has authored or edited 11 books, including the 2nd edition of *Cardiac Surgery in the Adult*, a major textbook in his field. His editorial activities have been extensive. For 6 years he was editor of *Modern Techniques in Surgery*, the founding editor of *Journal of Cardiac Surgery* (1985 to 1995) and presently he is editor of *Operative Techniques in Cardiothoracic Surgery*. He has lectured at >600 medical centers and postgraduate courses throughout the world.

His contributions at the Brigham and Women's Hospital have extended far outside his own surgical activities. From 2000 to 2004 he was Chair of the Brigham and Women's Physician Organization and for 5 years (1998 to 2003) was Director of Partner's HealthCare System Cardiovascular Service Line.

For his many contributions he has received many honors, including an honorary Master's Degree from Harvard University School of Medicine, Distinguished Alumni Award from the University of California at Berkley (1998), an Honorary Doctor's Degree from the University of Paris (1992); and Presidency of the American College of Chest Physicians (1986 to 1987) and the American Association for Thoracic Surgery (1998 to 1999). In 2005 he received the Paul Dudley White Award from the American Heart Association. He and his lovely wife, Roberta, are the proud parents of 2 daughters and the grandparents of 2 granddaughters. His many accomplishments have not gone to his head. Larry is a great guy and he has a wonderful capacity for friendship.

William Clifford Roberts, MD[†] **(hereafter WCR):** *Larry, I sincerely appreciate your willingness to talk to me and therefore to the readers of* The American Journal of Cardiology. *We are in my home in Dallas, Texas, and it is 12 November 2005. The Annual Scientific Sessions of the American Heart Association are taking place at this time in Dallas so it makes our getting together quite convenient. Larry, can we start by your describing your growing up in San Francisco, your parents, your siblings, and some of your earliest memories (Figure 1).*

Lawrence Harvey Cohn, MD[‡] **(hereafter LHC):** My family were native San Franciscans. San Francisco is a fairly young city, with its modern era dating back to 1850, just after the California gold rush. My paternal grandparents came from Lithuania and settled in San Francisco after sailing from Europe around the Cape of Good Hope. My grandfather was not born in San Francisco but came in the 1880's when he was quite young. San Francisco in the late 1800 seconds was a rough town, having begun just after the gold rush, but there were lots of opportunities with a very open entrepreneurial society. My father was born in San Francisco in 1905 one year before the great earthquake and fire of 1906. He, as a 1-year-old boy, was taken in my grandfather's horse and buggy wagon to Golden Gate Park to escape the fire. My mother was born in San Francisco in 1909. She was a concert pianist as a child and played the piano on the "new" radio in 1920s and 1930s. My father

* This series of interviews was underwritten by an unrestricted grant from Bristol-Myers Squibb.

† Executive Director, Baylor Cardiovascular Institute, Baylor University Medical Center, Dallas, Texas, 75246.

‡ Virginia and James Hubbard Professor of Cardiac Surgery, Harvard Medical School, Division of Cardiac Surgery, Brigham and Women's Hospital, Harvard Medical School, Boston, Massachusetts 02115.

Figure 1. LHC at the time of the interview. (Photo taken by WCR).

with his father started the City Wrecking Company, a building materials business, in San Francisco in the heart of the depression (1935). They wrecked old houses, took the materials out, and sold them, along with new building materials. During the depression they would sell a cast iron bath tub for $5. The business was quite successful. I think I got my work ethic from my father. He always enjoyed working. He worked the day before he went to the hospital and died at the age of 83. In the 1950s, he converted his depression-type business where they sold new and used materials, to new materials only what today would be like a small Home Depot. I worked in his business when growing up. I remember going with my father to his business at the age of 12 and help on a job on South Vaness near Mission. (That area was much different then; now high rise apartments are there.) In high school and in college I worked at my father's business during the summers, made extra money, learned to deal with the public and I learned a lot about business. (Whatever you want to say about medicine, it is a business and it is helpful to know the business aspects of it.) I would unload wallboard from railroad cars in the hot summer sun, drive truck, and make deliveries. Physicians have to relate to every kind of person and by meeting the public early I learned to relate to just about every kind of person you come in contact with today. Working with my father was a good experience from many aspects.

WCR: *Do you have siblings?*

LHC: I have 2 sisters who still live in San Francisco.

WCR: *Where are you in the hierarchy?*

LHC: I am the oldest.

WCR: *What year were you born?*

LHC: I was born in 1937. One sister was born in 1940 and the other, in 1947.

WCR: *What was your father like?*

LHC: My dad was a great guy. He was very hard working, sharp and devoted to his family. Work was his life. He wasn't the kind of guy who would take us out to play golf. (It's good to work hard but you have to have diversions and other things to get your mind and body refreshed.)

WCR: *Were you and your father close?*

LHC: Yes. I worked with him all of the time.

WCR: *Was he easy to get a long with?*

LHC: For me he was. He was very supportive. I had an unusual family memory. My mother was upset when I said I was going to be a physician because she wanted me to go into business with my father. I knew his business well and she wanted me to do that. My dad, however, supported my going into medicine 100%.

WCR: *What was your mother like?*

LHC: She was an only child. Her mother was my favorite relative of all time. My mother was a bit tough. She had very high expectations of everybody and she cracked the whip. My father was a bit more lenient in terms of discipline. She wanted me to go into my father's business because she wanted him to take more time off. He was going to work as hard as he wanted to anyway so it didn't matter. She also expected me to be a musician. I took piano when I was 6 years old because she was a pianist but gave it up after my first recital at age 11. I had never been so nervous in my life. (Now I can speak in front of 10,000 people and it's no problem.)

WCR: *Why do you think you were so nervous? Was it because of your mother?*

LHC: Because my mother had such high expectations of me. I did a recital at the Marines Memorial Auditorium in San Francisco at Sutter and O'Farrell. I played perfectly, but when I came home I told her I would never play the piano again, ever! I think things should be enjoyable. I quit that day and never played again.

WCR: *You practiced an hour plus per day for 5 years and then that was it?*

LHC: Yes.

WCR: *Did your father or mother go to college?*

LHC: Neither did.

WCR: *Did they not have the money?*

LHC: They didn't have the money. My family were hard working people who worked hard to make a living during the depression.

LARRY COHN
Editor Lowell

Figure 2. Larry Cohn, age 17, as pictured from the Lowell High School class of 1955 Year Book, indicating he has been elected the Editor of the school newspaper.

WCR: *Did your mother push education on you and your sisters more than your father?*

LHC: Yes, and my father also encouraged us a great deal. We went to the best public high school Lowell High in San Francisco, a magnet school for the entire city. We moved in 1949 when I was about 12 to a neighborhood called Seacliff San Francisco. My father paid $35,000 for the house. It has been sold a few times since for multiple millions of dollars. In those days if you went to a private school in San Francisco there was usually something wrong with you—either you couldn't get along or you weren't smart enough. Lowell High School was the oldest high school west of the Mississippi, started in 1856. It was essentially an academic prep school and 95% of our class went to college (Figure 2).

WCR: *How far was the school from your home?*

LHC: Probably 5 miles. It was in the middle of San Francisco and we were on the edge near the water.

WCR: *Did school come easy for you or did you have to work hard?*

LHC: School was important to me but I did sports and service organizations as well. I was editor of the school newspaper. I liked journalism. School came fairly easy for me. I got a California Federation Scholarship, which was the highest academic honor one could achieve in high school.

WCR: *Does that mean you graduated number 1 in your high school class?*

LHC: No. I was in the top 25.

WCR: *How many were in your senior class?*

LHC: About 150 students. At my high school, you could graduate mid-year, a hangover from World War II. My class graduated in February 1955 and another class graduated in June 1955.

WCR: *What did you do after graduation?*

LHC: I went to college the next month.

WCR: *What kind of sports did you participate in in high school?*

LHC: I played basketball and track. At 12 years of age I learned how to play golf.

WCR: *Were you on the golf team in high school?*

LHC: No. I didn't join the golf team because I was into basketball and track. I was a high hurdler.

WCR: *Did you run the 240 also?*

LHC: No. I did the 120 highs and occasionally broad jumped and occasionally ran the 440.

WCR: *How good were you at basketball?*

LHC: Fair. I played on the junior varsity, and then had to make a choice between basketball and track. I was better at track than basketball so I discontinued basketball. I played golf a lot and am very glad I took up that activity.

WCR: *What was your lowest handicap?*

LHC: I shot in the high 70 seconds and low 80 seconds in high school. I can still do that occasionally. Two years ago I had a 76 in Palm Springs.

WCR: *When did you pick up tennis?*

LHC: I did not start tennis until I was a resident in surgery at the University of California San Francisco (UCSF).

WCR: *What was your home like after you moved to Seacliff? Were there a lot of books around your house?*

LHC: I was a bit more intellectual than other members of my family. I liked to read, particularly history. My parents mainly worked: they read mainly newspapers and magazines.

WCR: *Was dinner at night a big deal in your home when growing up?*

LHC: My father was home for dinner most every night. My father was a big sports fan just like I am. The one activity we did together was attend baseball and football games. He used to take me to a lot of baseball and football games in San Francisco and Oakland. One game we saw was between the Oakland Oaks and the San Francisco Seals; Casey Stengel was the manager, Billy Martin played second base, and Cookie Lavagetto played centerfield. Those were great days. There were not so many teams back then so we took the minor league teams very seriously.

WCR: *When you would eat together at night, what was the conversation like? Did your parents quiz you about what you and your sisters were doing at school or did you talk about current events?*

LHC: My father was too old (late 30 seconds) to go into World War II. Early in the War there was a lot of concern about Japan's bombing San Francisco. There were black-outs and my father was involved with that as an air raid warden. There was much conversation about the War and President Roosevelt. (In September 2005 I visited Hiroshima. On a block on the street near a drug store a granite block read, "Above this block the fire ball erupted". That was awesome.) At the dinner table we talked about lots of things, school, activities, family and business.

WCR: *Since neither your mother nor father were able to go to college, I presume you did not have a lot of advice on where to go to college from them?*

LHC: The magnet high school in which I attended was very tuned in to colleges. Because I graduated in the mid-term, I applied to both the University of CaliforniaFrancisco and to Stanford. I got accepted to Stanford to start in September but decided to go to the University of California at Berkley since I could start in February. I enjoyed it at Cal and decided to stay. In college I lived in a fraternity house all 4 years. I declined the undergraduate invitation to go to Stanford because I was happy at UC Berkeley.

WCR: *What was your major in college?*

LHC: American history.

WCR: *When did you decide that you wanted to become a physician?*

LHC: The summer after the first 6 months of college. That summer my father's brother-in-law, who was also in the same business, after learning that my parents wanted me to go into the family business said, "Don't do that. You are too bright to do that. You should go and do what you want." At the time, physicians had a wonderful image and I told him that I really liked the idea of being a doctor. I liked science in high school. He said, "You have to do this. Otherwise you are going to be unhappy and waste a lot of time and your life." I said, "O.k., I'll try premed". It worked out. I did well in the premed studies. It was very competitive in the undergraduate years.

WCR: *Did you have to study hard in college?*

LHC: In the chemistry courses I did. They were wicked!

WCR: *You said you liked science in high school. Do you mean biology or chemistry?*

LHC: I liked the biologic sciences. Chemistry I did bare minimum. Because I got accepted early to Stanford School of Medicine I never took quantitative analysis because I didn't have to.

WCR: *What were your extracurricular activities during college?*

LHC: I tried out for the track team my freshman year but that was not meant to be. I saw that it was hopeless. The guys were running 14 flat in the hurdles. I was on the UC Berkley Rally Committee, which was a spirit group that helped set up rally material at the football games. It involved school spirit, cheerleading, and organizing card tricks. I was in some scholarship organizations. I worked some on the college newspaper, but that was also too big a commitment of time. I did some independent research when in college. Professor Bern, a zoology professor, asked, "What do you think about doing some research?" I said, "Great." I worked in the cancer research laboratory on breast cancer in mice while a senior student. I enjoyed it. I almost decided to stay in zoology as a PhD. (Mentors are very important in what you do, and this guy was a very exciting guy.)

WCR: *Exciting in what way?*

LHC: Having a protocol, doing experiments, and going to a lab conference was a lot of fun and very exciting. He encouraged independent thinking.

WCR: *Did you finish the University of California Berkley in 3-1/2 years?*

LHC: Yes.

WCR: *How many seniors were there in your class?*

LHC: The graduating class was about 3,000. They had the graduation ceremony in the football stadium.

WCR: *Did you have a scholarship to college?*

LHC: No.

WCR: *At this time your father must have been doing well financially?*

LHC: He was upper middle class. He had a solid business and supported his family very well.

WCR: *When did you decide for sure to go to medical school?*

LHC: Once I got an A in freshman chemistry, I knew I could do it.

WCR: *Did you apply to a medical school other than Stanford?*

LHC: Yes. I also applied to University of California in San Francisco, the University of California at Los Angeles (UCLA), and Harvard. I was asked to interview at Harvard.

WCR: *Do you remember who interviewed you at Harvard?*

LHC: Yes. It was a psychiatrist. He was brutal. He psychoanalyzed me and looked at me with all the psycho-tricks. I said to myself, "I'm not going here." And, I was right. Another doctor that really stimulated me to go into medicine was a dermatologist who treated me in high school. He was Eugene Farber, a Professor of Dermatology at Stanford in San Francisco and brother of Eugene Farber of the Brigham Farber Cancer Center of Boston. He told me that I should go into medicine and that I should go to Stanford Medical School. So I did.

WCR: *Had you ever been East before you went to the Harvard interview?*

LHC: Yes. When I was a freshman in college, some of the guys in the fraternity, and I went to New York and saw the "Damn Yankees" play in 1955.

WCR: *Did you take family vacations growing up?*

LHC: My father didn't like to take long vacations, but we did take some. About a month ago the American College of Surgeons was in San Francisco and they asked me to give a talk on the future of cardiac surgery. My wife and I decided to stay at the Sonoma Mission Inn, where my family went when I was 8 years old. We went there every summer. My mother, grandmother, sisters, and I would go there. We would also go to Santa Cruz for a month, and my father would come down on the weekends.

WCR: *What was the attraction of your maternal grandmother? Why did she appeal to you so much?*

LHC: She was a very sweet, sharp, and loving woman. (Do you know why grandparents and grandchildren are so close? Because they have a common enemy.) (Just kidding.) She made good suggestions about all sorts of things, and she was a very supportive person in everything I did.

WCR: *Did your father have siblings?*

LHC: Yes. He had 1 brother and 1 sister.

WCR: *Did they live in San Francisco?*

LHC: Yes.

WCR: *So you had a fairly extended family.*

LHC: Yes. In fact, his younger brother came into the business that my father started.

WCR: *I gather your father wasn't too disappointed that you didn't go into the business?*

LHC: No. He was proud that I did what I did. He thought, "You do what you have to do and that's wonderful."

WCR: *Did you have teachers in junior high or high school who had a major impact on you?*

LHC: There were a couple of teachers who were role models. One was a basketball coach. He taught work habits to me through basketball. My Spanish teacher was a good guy, as was our principle. The principle of our high school, Edith Pence, about 60 inches tall, was tough as nails. She often said something that I have used and has been successful for me. She would say, "You have a lot of things to do; budget your time." I think a lot of people need that lesson. Particularly busy guys like us.

WCR: *Although you studied hard, it sounds like you had a good time in college.*

LHC: Yes. I took the minimum number of premed courses and concentrated on American history. I like history a lot.

WCR: *You got a BA when you graduated?*

LHC: Yes.

WCR: *How did medical school strike you?*

LHC: It was good, but different.

WCR: *How many were in your medical school class?*

LHC: Sixty students.

WCR: *How many were girls?*

LHC: Ten. When entering medical school in 1958, the basic science courses were at Palo Alto, and then the third and fourth years were done in San Francisco at the hospital there. During my attending medical school, the Stanford Hospital in Palo Alto was being built. It was completed in 1959. My class had a part of the old curriculum and a part of the new curriculum. The old curriculum included the longest numbers of hours of anatomy of any other medical school in the country. In our first quarter we had 4 mornings of anatomy. There were 2 people per cadaver. My friend, and roommate Don Doty, was my partner. An interesting thing happened in my freshman year. I had a very bad time with a physiology instructor and I received an "incomplete" in the course. I thought of going back to my father's business, because I believed and considered it like a failure. I had to retake an examination for which I received an A. It was one of those courses where the teacher was so bad that I couldn't understand what he was talking about.

WCR: *What were some surprises that you experienced in medical school?*

LHC: Most of my fellow students had had a lot more science in college than I did, because I took the minimum of science and the maximum of history. The first year was hard. I struggled with biochemistry. The second year I had clinical diagnosis, and I enjoyed that a great deal. I had an interesting living situation. I was 1 of 4 men who lived together, we were all from California, and we all became surgeons!

WCR: *How many of your 60 classmates had grown up in the San Francisco area?*

LHC: A fair number had gone to Stanford, UC Berkley, and schools in California. At least half grew up in San Francisco.

WCR: *As you rotated through the clinical services, did you decide early on that surgery was the thing for you? Did you have a hard time deciding on a specialty?*

LHC: Because it was a new hospital things were still a bit disorganized. The surgeons were not the best teachers at that early period. Most of my classmates gravitated toward medicine. *Halsted Holman* was the chief of medicine. His father (*Emile Holman*) was one of Halsted's last residents in surgery at The Johns Hopkins Hospital. One surgeon, *Roy Cohn* (no relation), impressed our class enormously. Originally from Portland, he had been a chief resident in surgery at the Massachusetts General Hospital in Boston and had come back to Stanford as a Professor. He had boards in general surgery, thoracic surgery, and in neurosurgery. He did everything except heart surgery. He helped *Norman Shumway* get started when he came from Minneapolis to Palo Alto. *Frank Gerbode* in San Francisco did not give Shumway the time of day. Roy Cohn got Shumway started at Stanford. Roy Cohn instilled an interest in surgery for many in my class. I was mainly interested in medicine before encountering the surgeons. The summer after my sophomore year, I did an externship at the Mt. Zion Hospital in San Francisco in surgery and found that I really enjoyed it. That fall I told *David Rytand*, a wonderful Professor of Medicine, that I liked medicine, but that I really had a great time in surgery that summer. I told him that if I went into academic medicine, I wanted to go into something where I could really do something for people. Dr. Rytand said, "You need to go into surgery." I walked out of his office, and that was it. I was going to be a surgeon.

WCR: *How did you and Roberta get together?*

LHC: Roberta was the best friend of my favorite girl cousin. I met her when she was 11 years old. She grew up on Russian Hill at Lombard (the crooked street) in San Francisco. I met her at a party when I was 12, and she was 11. We went to the same high school. We started dating in high school, but that was interrupted (for a couple of years) when I went to college. She later went to UC Berkley and we started dating again when I was a senior in college. It was common in those days to get married before finishing medical school.

WCR: *What attracted you to Roberta?*

LHC: She was cute, vivacious, smart, and we hit it off very well. She has been enormously supportive to my career.

WCR: *You were married after your sophomore year in medical school?*

LHC: Yes. I was 23 years old, and Roberta was 21.

WCR: I gather that medical school was very successful for you?

LHC: Yes. I was Alpha Omega Alpha (AOA). When a senior, I started hearing about cardiac surgery. I had already gravitated toward surgery and now started to meet many surgeons. One day a publication on the medical center board stated that Shumway had operated upon a dog who had survived an entire year with a heart transplant. He was hot stuff. I sought him out and asked him if I could work on his service. *Richard Lower*, an excellent resident surgeon, was working with Shumway and together they invented heart transplantation. I helped in their lab a couple of times, and then one spring day in 1962 they said I could be a subintern on their service. I started on a Monday and didn't leave the hospital for 8 straight days. I was mesmerized. Shumway was a bit of a Maverick in terms of training, and I said to him, "What should I do?" He said, "I think you should go around the world, get all of your training and boards, and then come back and train with me." That's what I did. He recognized that I desired the more formal training of the era, and I left Stanford in 1962.

WCR: *How did you decide on Boston and Boston City Hospital and the Harvard service for your surgical internship? Where did you apply?*

LHC: After deciding on surgery, I went back to talk to Roy Cohn who had trained as a resident and as chief resident at the Massachusetts General Hospital. He told me there was a good program at Boston City Hospital's Harvard Service as well as at the Massachusetts General Hospital. He didn't have too much good to say about the Peter Bent Brigham Hospital at the time. I applied to Mass General and Boston City Harvard Service and got final interviews at both places. The final Mass General Hospital interview had 30 surgeons in a room and me. I didn't make the internship at Mass General, but I did make it at Boston City Harvard and decided to go there. I wanted to go East

because Stanford still was not good for the formalized general surgery training that I wanted. I wanted to "see the world." In July 1962, we moved to Boston (Cambridge).

WCR: *How did Boston and Boston City Hospital strike you?*

LHC: It was like stepping back into a time machine. Almost all of my graduating class at Stanford sought internships at big public hospitals because the Stanford hospital was new and not overwhelmed with patients.

WCR: *How was your internship? Were you pleased with it?*

LHC: At that stage of my medical career, it was perfect. It was a big and very busy general hospital. I did everything from being a scrub nurse to doing some extensive colon resections. This was pre-Medicare. At that time, there really was a 2-tier healthcare system in the US. One was private care, such as the Deaconess Hospital or Mass General Hospital. At the Boston City Hospital, it was entirely public (the patients did not have health insurance) with a totally resident-run service with attending supervision. It was a good experience.

WCR: *You worked every other night there?*

LHC: Yes. Every other night, every other weekend.

WCR: *When you got off, what time did you get home?*

LHC: It varied depending on the service I was on. Frequently, I would come home, after midnight, open the front door, lie on the floor of the living room, and fall asleep.

WCR: *There was a lot of alcohol drunk in Boston, Massachusetts, by patients who went to the Boston City Hospital. Did you encounter a lot of DTs after operations there?*

LHC: Yes, fairly frequently. When I came back to San Francisco, it was at the height of the drug overdose era. It was just something we dealt with.

WCR: *How did you adjust to those cold winters there after having lived in California all of your life?*

LHC: It was very different. California also was a much more open society. There seemed to be more of a class structure in Boston at the time. It was really quite different from California.

WCR: *It sounds to me like the connections that you made in Boston during those 2 years determined your fate later on.*

LHC: I didn't make any great personal connections, but I did see that Boston medicine was the best in the world. Once at Boston City Harvard Service, I took *Ed Churchill*, former Chair of MGH surgery and *William Castleman*, who had won a Nobel Prize, for medicine on rounds. On rotations at the New England Deaconess Hospital, a very private hospital with elegant surgeons, I met the McKittreck brothers, *Frank Weelock* and *George Starkey*, and all of them were extraordinarily nice to me. It was an elegant type of medicine. "Boston Medicine has got to be the best," I thought so then, and I still think it is today.

WCR: *How did Roberta adjust to Boston?*

LHC: That was harder. We were used to California and getting things done easily. She worked for a couple of physicians and did well with them, but it was tough on her.

WCR: *When was your first child born?*

LHC: In 1963. Her name is Leslie Ann Bernstein. My wife stayed in the hospital for a week. She was overdue, so on Labor Day, September 3, 1963, she was 9-1/2 months pregnant. I said, "Today is Labor Day and I'm off so let's take a canoe and go out on the Charles River." We did. I did all the canoeing while she just laid back. Early the next morning she gave birth to Leslie Ann (on the 4th).

WCR: *How did you break into the Surgery Branch at the National Heart Institute?*

LHC: Shumway and *William McDermott*, the Chief of the Harvard Surgery Service at the Boston City Hospital, wrote terrific letters for me. McDermott was a good guy and was prominent because of his work with the porto-caval shunt. I was surprised that I got the position.

WCR: *How did the NIH strike you?*

LHC: The greatest. It was a life-altering super experience.

WCR: *In what way?*

LHC: It set my intellectual academic sights on the right track. There were some superb academic people there. Some of the people I met there, like yourself, have been life long friends.

WCR: *What was the best thing about NIH from your standpoint?*

LHC: Early on I had decided that I enjoyed writing medical papers. My first study was written as a medical student. I had gotten some residents to come on board with it. I wrote my third study as a medical student working in the emergency room. When I came to NIH and saw all of these hot-shot academic people like *Eugene Braunwald*, *Bill Roberts*, *Dean Mason*, and others, it was exciting, and I enjoyed it. The 6 months in the NIH cath lab were superb as well.

WCR: *When you were at NIH, I gather that you stayed in contact with Shumway regarding training with him eventually.*

LHC: Yes. I knew I did not want to do general surgery at Stanford, but I did talk to him and also to *John Kirklin* in Alabama, who accepted me in his program. The hot program in general surgery at the time was at the University of California at San Francisco. The chief there was *Englebert ("Bert") Dumphy*. He was a very good general surgeon with a tremendous personality and he was a superb leader. He was the best.

WCR: *When you left NIH, you did 3 more years of general surgery at San Francisco General?*

LHC: Yes. They were good years and they helped me become a good cardiac surgeon because I did a lot of vascular surgery. Vascular surgery was the strong point of that program. It had *Jack Wylie*, *Ron Stoney*, and *Bill Blaisdelle*. They were fantastic mentors and great surgeons. They made me a good surgeon. Those were the days when there was a tremendous amount of actual surgery to do as opposed to now, where we have a lot of laproscopic surgery. One day I did 5 carotid endarterectomies with Jack Wylie, who helped to who invent the procedure. He did more to

help me then just about anyone else. He was also a wonderful guy and a great leader, and he did it in a quiet way.

WCR: *What was it like training under Shumway?*

LHC: From the time I got there, he had the finest cardiac training program in the world. I got there in 1969, and I was chief resident in 1970 to 1971. His service had the lowest mortality in heart surgery in the world at that time. We did then everything that we do now. We did over 1,000 cardiac cases a year at that time. There were 2 services, so I was involved in 500 cases and did 300 of them. That was the thing about Shumway that was totally unique. In most programs at that time the way you learned cardiac surgery was to watch—apprenticeship. Shumway was the only residency trainer who allowed his residents to do surgery! He had simplified cardiac surgery to the point where it was simple and easy to teach.

WCR: *Someone once said to me that Shumway was the best surgical assistant ever.*

LHC: That's true. I tell people that I'm the second best.

WCR: *Does it frustrate you at all that you don't do every case yourself? If you did every case, it would be easier, I presume, than assisting.*

LHC: Not really. It's pretty easy because if you have done enough surgery, and you are a good surgeon there is no reason why you can't help somebody do most of the cases and at the same time be in *total control* of the flow of the case. As an assistant, I don't just stand back. Recently, I helped a resident, who had been with us for about 3 months, do an aortic valve replacement, and it took us 51 minutes. The patient is perfect, because I know what needs to be done, he knows the routine that I use, and I happen to be the world's current best first assistant. I'll do parts of some case and let trainees do parts of the case. If you are a good surgeon and a good teacher, you can do that 100% of the time, assuming that the trainee has the basic skills. That role was one of the best things I learned from Shumway. If you had done enough cases yourself, and if you are totally confident in your technique, then you can totally control the flow of the operation. Assisting does not frustrate me at all. Obviously, if a case is very unusual or difficult, I'll do every stitch myself.

WCR: *During the 2 years that you were a fellow under Shumway, how many cases did you do yourself?*

LHC: Five hundred.

WCR: *Your cardiac surgery fellows today have 2 years. How many cases are they doing as primary surgeons?*

LHC: They will probably end up doing 300 or 400. We have a lot of cases, and they do a lot of cases. The number is a little less now because of the 80-hour work week.

WCR: *In summary, you were enormously elated with your cardiac surgery training under Shumway. How did it come about that you went from that fellowship immediately into the second position in cardiac surgery at the Brigham and Women's Hospital in Boston?*

LHC: Sometimes a little luck plays a role. There had been a big change at the Brigham and Women's Hospital in

1970. *Dwight Harken* had been the chief of cardiothoracic surgery at the Brigham from 1948 to 1970. He never got along with *Frannie Moore*, who was chief of the department of surgery. Harken made an ultimatum to Frannie Moore and ultimately Dwight left. During the year that I was co-chief resident in general surgery at UCSF, the other co-chief was *George Sheldon*, who later became the Chair of Surgery at the University of North Carolina. We were very close friends. After being co-chief resident at the UCSF, he went to Boston to work in Frannie Moore's lab at the Brigham. He kept me informed about the big shake up going on at the Brigham. He told *Jack Collins*, the new chief of cardiac surgery at the Brigham, that I was available. I was then asked to give a talk at the Brigham on replacing the aortic valve with homografts. Having trained at Stanford, a very high profile program, this put me in a position as a resident to present our data elsewhere, and I did so at the Brigham in the fall of 1970. I then got a call in December from the chief of cardiac surgery at Boston University, who had a position available at Boston University. I went back in January 1971 and told my friend George Sheldon at the Brigham that I was coming back to Boston. Then Jack Collins at the Brigham called. As a result, I interviewed with BU and the PBBH. I had about 30 publications on my CV at the time. The Stanford program was enormously innovative at the time, particularly using homografts and porcine valves for aortic valve replacement, and the cardiac surgery program was one of the most prominent in the world at that time. My final visit to Boston was April 1971. My wife was pregnant with our second daughter at the time. I came back to Boston to meet with Frannie Moore. As I walked from the hotel to his office, it started snowing. I thought to myself, "What am I doing here?" I'm coming from Palo Alto, California, were it was 75 degrees, and it is snowing in Boston on April 15! Frannie Moore was as nice as he could be and said, "This is a very good CV and we would like to have you here." Afterwards, I talked to Jack Collins and said, "There is one thing I've got to know. I'm coming from Stanford where we do things completely differently. How are the Stanford techniques going to fit into the Brigham?" He said, "I want you to bring in all the Stanford techniques here. We are going to change everything." I said, "That's great. That's all I needed to hear." We didn't finalize the deal until May 15. Shumway was elated because he thought I was going to go back to San Francisco to start a program at the Mt. Zion Hospital or at the University of California at San Francisco.

WCR: *How did Roberta respond?*

LHC: She couldn't believe it. We had a newborn girl, an 8-year-old girl, and a dog, and we moved to Boston.

WCR: *What did your mother and father think of you going back to Boston on a permanent basis?*

LHC: They were surprised and a bit sad, but they knew it was a good career move.

WCR: *After you got to the Brigham Hospital, how long did it take you to get the parking place right next to the entrance door?*

LHC: That happened the first month. One Christmas Eve my car was stolen from that parking place.

WCR: *How did things progress at the Brigham? Did you have no interference as promised?*

LHC: The first thing I did there was talk with the nurses. We completely re-did the entire operating room protocol; we changed the instruments and sutures; we stopped using coronary perfusion and started using local cardiac hypothermia. The biggest reaction came from the cardiologists— *Lew Dexter*, *Richard Gorlin*, and *Bernie Lown*. In January 1972 at a conference at the Brigham, I suggested that a presented patient would be perfect for a pig valve in the aortic valve position. I thought Lew Dexter was going to faint dead away. He hardly knew what I was talking about. It was an interesting interchange. Richard Gorlin had many coronary artery patients. One of his cases had a terrible right coronary artery. Because of my vascular training, which included doing many endarterectomies, I did a right coronary endarterectomy plus triple bypass grafts in the patient. Afterwards, I saw Gorlin in the hall and after telling him what I had done, he was furious at me. I asked him what the problem was and he said, "You didn't tell me you were going to do that. If you don't discuss things with me, you will not ever again get another case from me." I was bringing in a new technique and the cardiologists simply were not used to innovation!

WCR: *When did you become chief of cardiac surgery?*

LHC: 1987.

WCR: *Did he continue to do heart surgery after that?*

LHC: Yes.

WCR: *You must have had a lot of offers to go elsewhere during the last 34 years? How have you handled these other opportunities?*

LHC: I never looked at an opportunity that I thought I had no interest in at all. It depends mainly on your working environment, what you are doing every day, and what you want to do or don't want to do. The best thing you can do is be in a good place. Just to say you are chief of something isn't much fun unless you enjoy the place you work at.

WCR: *In 2004, how many cases did you do?*

LHC: Three hundred twenty-five.

WCR: *How many of those are cardiac valves?*

LHC: Over 300 were valves each year.

WCR: *I understand that the average cardiac surgeon does about 10 valves per year.*

LHC: I didn't know that. That's pretty low. I would have thought more. About a year ago, an article appeared indicating that only 50% of patients ≥65 years (the Medicare population) having aortic valve replacement in the US received a biologic or tissue valve. (The American Heart Association guidelines recommend that patients ≥65 years of age should generally have biologic or tissue valves.) The article indicated that surgeons who do relatively few valve replacements tend to use mechanical valves because it is easier to put in a mechanical prosthesis than a bioprosthesis. Even in smaller hospitals, patients >80 years of age were receiving mechanical prostheses rather than bioprostheses. At the Brigham, about 90% of patients ≥65 years of age receive a bioprosthesis.

WCR: *In most hospitals the frequency of coronary artery bypass grafting is decreasing, and, of course, that is the most common cardiac operation in most centers. Have you decreased the number of cardiac surgical fellows in your program as a consequence?*

LHC: No. We have actually increased the number by 1 because the volume of general thoracic surgery has increased. The general thoracic trainees still have to do the cardiac training, so we now have 4 residents for each of 2 years rather than 3 residents.

WCR: *Will some of them thereafter limit their practice to lung and esophageal problems?*

LHC: Absolutely.

WCR: *You are 68 years of age. What time do you wake up in the morning when you are in Boston?*

LHC: 5:15 A.M.

WCR: *What time do you leave your house to go to the hospital?*

LHC: 6:00 A.M.

WCR: *What time to you arrive at the hospital?*

LHC: 6:10 A.M. My house is 2.8 miles from the hospital.

WCR: *What do you do when you first get to the hospital?*

LHC: I get a cup of coffee and read *The Wall Street Journal*. I then check my e-mail and at 6:30 A.M. I go to the preoperative holding area and see the 1 to 3 patients I will operate on that day. I will say "hello" and let them know I'm there. That gesture I think is very important. I then go upstairs and make rounds on the patients who I operated on the previous day. Then I come back to my office. I go to the operating room by 8:30 A.M.

WCR: *You do about 2 cases per day now?*

LHC: Two or 3 cases.

WCR: *What time do you leave the hospital at night?*

LHC: It depends whether or not I have an evening meeting. If I do 2 cases back-to-back, I usually can leave by 6 or 6:30 P.M.

WCR: *So you are home by 7 P.M.? What time do you go to bed?*

LHC: Yes. I go to bed at 11 P.M.

WCR: *You live comfortably on 6 hours of sleep each night?*

LHC: Yes. I may take a nap after dinner every now and then.

WCR: *What happens if 1 of your patients bleeds at 1 A.M.?*

LHC: I will get a call.

WCR: *Do you go in?*

LHC: No. Board-certified surgeons at the hospital take care of that problem. It happens rarely, about once every 6 months.

WCR: *What about weekends? Do you go in on Saturdays?*

LHC: Yes. I go in on Saturday mornings and Sunday night.

WCR: *What time do you go in Saturday morning?*

LHC: I go in at about 8 A.M., and leave just in time to get to my tennis game at 10 A.M.

WCR: *When do you go in on Sunday night?*

LHC: Usually after dinner to see the patients who are going to be operated on the next day.

WCR: *When you came to the Brigham in 1971, how old were you?*

LHC: I was 34 years old.

WCR: *You are exactly twice that age now. Are you technically as good now as you where then?*

LHC: I'm better now.

WCR: *I presume that is because you have had so much experience.*

LHC: Yes.

WCR: *You were always technically good, though. That is your reputation.*

LHC: That's safe to say. I'm better because I've seen so much more. I do certain procedures so much more quickly than I could earlier because I have seen it 1,000 times.

WCR: *You recently relinquished the chair of cardiothoracic surgery at your institution.*

LHC: I stepped down in June 2005 and another chief was hired.

WCR: *But that change doesn't interfere with what you do?*

LHC: Correct.

WCR: *Actually, you are relieved in certain ways?*

LHC: Yes. There are a lot less meetings I have to go to.

WCR: *You have been at Harvard now for 34 years. Your contributions to Harvard and to the Brigham and Women's Hospital are more than those involving just the department of surgery. You have been involved in a lot of nonsurgical activities at your institution. Can you discuss them a bit?*

LHC: One activity that is still related to the department is the training of other surgeons. We have trained about 150 cardiothoracic surgeons from all over the world. That endeavor has been quite satisfying. I have been on the admissions committee of the Harvard Medical School. In 1994, the Partner's Healthcare was formed, a conglomerate between the Massachusetts General and the Brigham and Women's Hospitals, and in 1997 I was asked to organize the cardiac service line involving all of the hospitals. We tried to develop common protocols and common clinical research studies. I was asked by *Sam Their*, the CEO of Partner's. It was a lot of fun trying to bring all the cardiologists and cardiac surgeons together to reach common ground, to solve common problems, and to decrease costs by ordering similar devices, and so forth. In 2000, I was named the Chair of the Brigham Physician's Organization, which involved governance economically over 15 departments, each with its own set of by-laws and Boards of Trustees. That activity did

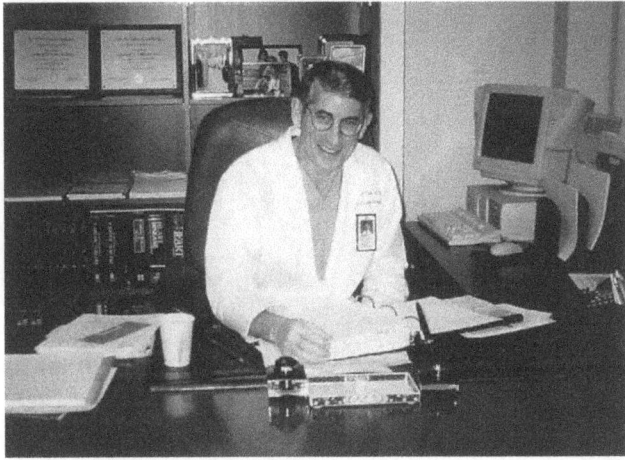

Figure 3. Dr. Lawrence Cohn, Cardiac Surgeon, Brigham and Women's Hospital, Boston, Massachusetts.

not mean I ran the BWPO every single day but, I was in charge over all as the Chair of the Board. That was for 4 years, and it was very important to do improved economic efficiency.

WCR: *How many days per week do you operate?*

LHC: I operate Monday, Tuesday, and Thursday. I often have 2 or 3 cases each day (Figure 3).

WCR: *It appears to me that one of your major surgical contributions was to make things simpler. Is that a proper assessment?*

LHC: Yes. Making things simpler surgically is one of the things I try to do.

WCR: *You have made a lot of contributions involving biologic valves, when to operate in mitral regurgitation, when to operate in acute myocardial infarction, and what to do with the papillary muscles. If you could make a list of the things you have done or contributed to, what would be your top 3 or 4?*

LHC: Simplistic surgery is 1 of the things. I try to innovate. In this field, like any other field, nothing ever stays the same. Innovation has always been a goal. Simplicity of operations, innovation, and always trying to make things easier and better.

WCR: *You are always looking for a better way?*

LHC: Yes. A better way technically or conceptionally. I think that is a fair statement. I have tried to change things and make things simpler and better in a lot of different ways.

WCR: *The point is you tried never to stay static. You kept asking the question, "Could this be done in a better way?"*

LHC: Yes and I'll give you an example. I used cryo-preserved homografts for aortic valve replacement for dysfunctioning congenitally abnormal aortic valves. The operation was effective but later, after long-term evaluation, we found that the bovine pericardial bioprosthesis was as effective and a much simpler procedure, so I changed. That's the kind of thing I always want to do. Use something,

evaluate it clinically, and change if something better comes along.

WCR: *I gather that you have had a precordial murmur most of your life? When did you discover that you had aortic valve disease?*

LHC: In 1985. That was the first time the murmur was heard.

WCR: *Did you ever listen to yourself?*

LHC: Of course.

WCR: *In 1985, you were 48 years old. What happened after that?*

LHC: At that time, the pressure gradient across the valve was small. My father also had aortic valve replacement and my mother had aortic stenosis!

WCR: *Did your father have a bicuspid valve?*

LHC: He had a tricuspid valve. He was operated on in 1975.

WCR: *Did he have coronary narrowing?*

LHC: No. He had angiographically normal coronary arteries.

WCR: *When did you have an aortic valve replacement?*

LHC: In 1997.

WCR: *Did you have a bicuspid valve?*

LHC: It was congenitally abnormal but not a classic bicuspid valve. My coronary arteries were normal.

WCR: *Did you see your operatively-excised aortic valve?*

LHC: No. I had no interest in seeing it.

WCR: *I gather you like the pericardial bioprosthesis better than the porcine bioprosthesis?*

LHC: Yes, because the results with the pericardial bioprosthesis have really been good, and they fail only by 1 mechanism and that is calcification.

WCR: *Do you take a statin drug?*

LHC: Yes. I take atorvastatin 10 mg daily.

WCR: *Do you put all of your patients on statin drugs?*

LHC: Yes, every one that can tolerate the drug.

WCR: *Were you symptomatic before you had the aortic valve replacement?*

LHC: I was a little tired. I was still playing tennis.

WCR: *What was your peak systolic pressure gradient?*

LHC: About 75 mm Hg.

WCR: *You have been fine ever since?*

LHC: Yes.

WCR: My son Charles tells me that he is not aware of any surgeon who has had aortic valve replacement who didn't have a tissue valve substitute.

LHC: I believe that is true.

WCR: *How many mitral valve repairs do you have to do for mitral valve prolapse before you are really good at it?*

LHC: It's hard to say. I've probably done 2,000 mitral valve repairs. It does take a fair bit of experience. A trap is trying to do mitral valve repair as a minimally invasive technique or by robotic surgery before really understanding fully how the mitral regurgitation is produced and repaired.

WCR: *Are you involved in robotic surgery?*

LHC: Yes. We have done several different projects in our hospital.

WCR: *Do you think it is going to sell?*

LHC: I don't think it is going to be the ultimate answer for mitral valve repair. I did 6 cases that way and then I stopped it, because of inadequate flexibility. The robot technique will be useful on other type procedures, such as atrial fibrillation. We have used the robot to take down a mammary artery without sternotomy and then do an off-pump coronary bypass. That is a super operation.

WCR: *What about on-pump versus off-pump coronary bypass?*

LHC: It's variable. Our group does maybe 5% off-pump and 95% of bypass cases on pump. Some surgeons do off-pump bypass very well and do it on almost every case, but it is very tough. The results of on-pump bypass are better.

WCR: *You are one of the most innovative and busy cardiac surgeons in the last 40 years. There are not many cardiac surgeons who themselves have had an aortic valve replacement. Did that make you a better doctor or surgeon? What effect did that procedure have on you?*

LHC: I discussed that topic in my presidential address to the American Association of Cardiothoracic Surgery in 1999. I said, "Cardiac surgeons have a terrible reputation of not seeing their patients. Whether you spend a minute or 2 minutes with a patient, saying "hello" or touching them on the head is very important. It is gratifying to see your surgeon just for a few moments." It is humanism that we all should practice.

WCR: *Earlier you said that physicians meet all levels of the population.*

LHC: Yes. I knew how to be a good patient, and I put that into effect on how to become a good physician. There are patients who moan and moan about things and they are unpleasant to work with. So I said that if I was ever a patient, I would be a good patient. The way to be a good patient is first of all thank the day-to-day nurses and aides as they take care of you. As soon as they know you are really grateful for what they do, the entire team blossoms, and they will want to do the best they can for you. I have mentioned this to patients as well as to their families.

WCR: *You give a lot of talks at various places. You are on national committees and you have been president of major professional societies. How do you handle the traveling and still do nearly 400 cases a year?*

LHC: I go back to my old high school principle: I budget my time. I don't spend huge amounts of time away on any single trip. I went to Japan on a Sunday and came back on Friday. I don't like to be away for huge lengths of time. I can go away for 2 days, and if I'm doing something that refreshes me, I come back to work feeling fabulous. If I go play golf, fish, or ski for 2 days, I come back totally refreshed. I don't go away for a month at a time.

WCR: *You play tennis each week?*

LHC: Twice a week. During the summer, I play golf on Fridays.

Figure 4. Dr. Cohn's family *(left to right)*, Jennifer Cohn, Roberta Cohn, LHC, Carly Bernstein (granddaughter), Leslie Cohn Bernstein, Stephen Bernstein and Rachel Bernstein (granddaughter).

WCR: *You have 2 daughters. What do they do?*

LHC: Leslie is a science teacher at Winsor School for girls. Jennifer lives in San Francisco and works for a museum consulting business (Figure 4).

WCR: *Do you see them often?*

LHC: Yes. I'm currently trying to teach my 14-year-old granddaughter how to play golf. I have 2 granddaughters and both are very good athletes.

WCR: *What do you do at night when you get home?*

LHC: I usually have 1 single malt scotch. I go through the mail and usually bring some work home like manuscripts. I watch television news and sports.

WCR: *Do you read much outside of medicine?*

LHC: I read every night. I like world history and political books. I'm now reading *The World is Flat* by Thomas Friedman. I like books on sports history and on current events.

WCR: *Where in Boston do you live?*

LHC: Chestnut Hill in a house. It's a "grown up" house.

WCR: *Is there anything you would like to discuss that we haven't?*

LHC: The only thing I would say is that there seems to be some downers on cardiac surgery today. If all cardiac surgeons tried to make things better, not just be satisfied, we would have a better specialty. There will soon be a big change in cardiac surgery. There is going to be much more rigorous training and fewer training programs. The newer trainees are going to be able to do a lot more procedures than we have been able to do up to now. One of our fellows who recently finished his formal cardiothoracic residency is now doing halftime in the cardiac cath lab and halftime in surgery.

WCR: *Your career has spanned the hay day of cardiac surgery (45 years since cardiac surgery was developed). Take yourself out of the picture and tell me who are the great cardiac surgeons in the last 50 years?*

LHC: Certainly Norman Shumway because of his incredible mentorship of me, his training program, his ability to simplify many cardiac procedures and the true father of cardiac transplants. *Denton Cooley* is a giant and a master surgeon and has been innovative his entire life. *Michael DeBakey* has been an unbelievable force in the history of cardiac and thoracic surgery, developing devices and operations and still intellectually powerful. *John Kirklin* was a brilliant and innovative surgeon and a tremendous clinical scientist, pioneering outcomes studies. I think *Dwight McGoon* at the Mayo Clinic was a great surgeon, who also started outcomes research. *Floyd Loop* and *Toby Cosgrove* have made notable contributions to the Cleveland Clinic. *Carpentier* and *Duran* have been leaders in mitral valve repair and tissue valve engineering, and Carpentier has had the most major influence on the development of biologic bioprosthesis. Finally, *Walt Lillehei*, who 50 years ago did some very innovative and courageous things, which really got cardiac surgery off the ground.

WCR: *What are your goals from here on?*

LHC: I think retirement is a bad thing to do. I think that bright, active, and energetic people should keep working and do things they like to do and are good at doing. There are some other organizational things that I would like to do. The Thoracic Surgical Foundation for Research and Education and the AATS are big items. The American Heart Association and The American College of Cardiology are tremendously important organizations that have a lot of clout on heart disease. I'm working on a couple of new devices for the nontransplant treatment of heart failure, a huge problem. I'm going to stay active in all of my current organizations and continue to mentor and teach trainees. I had a job offer last year at a major hospital to be primarily an administrator, and I looked at it carefully. It had its own set of rules and problems as well as advantages and disadvantages. Surgery is a lot of fun and it is certainly nice to be able to keep doing it.

WCR: *Larry, it has been a terrific treat talking with you. Thank you for pouring your soul out, so to speak to the readers of* The American Journal of Cardiology. *I'm sure they will be delighted to get to know you better.*

LHC: Thank you.

Original Articles by LHC

5. Cohn LH, Roberts W, Rockoff D, Morrow AG. Bacterial endocartitis following aortic valve replacement. Clinical and pathologic correlations. *Circulation* 1966;33:209–217.

8. Mason DT, Cohn LH, Ross J, Braunwald E. Effects of changes in heart rate on the severity of obstruction to left ventricular outflow in idiopathic hypertrophic subaortic stenosis. *Am J Cardiol* 1967;19:797–805. (*Dr. Cohn's comment: First to suggest that ventricular fibrillation causes decreased left ventricular function.*)

9. Reis RL, Cohn LH, Morrow AG. The effects of induced ventricular fibrillation on ventricular performance and cardiac metabolism. *Circulation* 1967;36:234–243.

11. Vetter WR, Cohn LH, Reichgott M. Hypokalemia and electrocardiographic abnormalities during acute alcohol withdrawal. *Arch Int Med* 1967;120:182–186.

12. Cohn LH, Reis RL, Morrow AG. Left ventricular function following

mitral valve replacement. The effect of excision of the chordae tendineae and papillary muscles. *J Thorac Cardiovasc Surg* 1968;56:11–15. (*Dr. Cohn's comment: First to document importance of papillary muscles.*)

22. Cohn LH, Powell M, Seidlitz L, Hamilton WK, Wylie EJ. Fluid requirements and shifts in patients undergoing aortic reconstruction. *Am J Surg* 1970;120:182–186.

24. Cohn LH, Angell WW, Shumway NE. Body fluid spaces following cardiopulmonary bypass. Effects of cardiac failure and hemodilution. *J Thorac Cardiovasc Surg* 1971;62:423–430. (*Dr. Cohn's comment: References 24, 26, and 45 document body fluid spaces in patients with coronary artery disease for the first time and in 2 hospitals.*)

27. Cohn LH, Kosek J, Angell WW. Pulmonary arteriosclerosis produced by hyperoxemic normotensive perfusion. *Surgery* 1971;70:723–729.

29. Cohn LH, Fogarty T, Daily P, Shumway NE. Emergency coronary artery bypass. *Surgery* 1971;70:821–829. (*Dr. Cohn's comment: One of the first papers at a national meeting documenting that emergency coronary artery bypass grafting could be done with good results.*)

34. Cohn LH, Gorlin R, Herman M, Collins JJ Jr. Surgical treatment of acute coronary occlusion. *J Thorac Cardiovasc Surg* 1972;64:503–513.

45. Cohn LH, Klovekorn P, Moore FD, Collins JJ Jr. Intrinsic plasma volume deficits in patients with coronary artery disease. Effects of myocardial revascularization. *Arch Surg* 1974;108:57–60.

48. Cohn LH, Collins JJ Jr. Local cardiac hypothermia for myocardial protection. *Ann Thorac Surg* 1974;17:135–140.

49. Fujiwara Y, Cohn LH, Adams D, Collins JJ Jr. The use of Gortex grafts for replacement of the superior and inferior vena cava. *J Thorac Cardiovasc Surg* 1974;67:774–779.

50. Cohn P, Gorlin R, Collins JJ Jr, Cohn LH. The left ventricular ejection fraction as a prognostic guide in the surgical treatment of coronary and valvular heart disease. *Am J Cardiol* 1974;34:136–141.

60. Cohn LH, Boyden CM, Collins JJ Jr. Improved long-term survival following aorto-coronary bypass for advanced coronary artery disease. *Am J Surg* 1975;129:380–385. (*Dr. Cohn's comment: One of the first papers documenting improved survival after coronary artery bypass grafting.*)

66. Cohn LH, Anderson W, Fosberg A, Collins JJ Jr. The effects of phlebotomy, hemodilution and autologous transfusion on blood utilization in open-heart surgery. *Chest* 1975;68:283–287. (*Dr. Cohn's comment: Program for blood conservation in heart surgery.*)

72. Sanders JH Jr., Cohn LH, Dalen Je, Collins JJ Jr. Emergency aortic valve replacement. *Am J Surg* 1976;131:495–498.

74. Florian A, Cohn LH, Dammin FG, Collins JJ Jr. Small vessel replacement with Gore-Tex (expanded polytetrafluoroethylene). *Arch Surg* 1976;111:267–270. (*Dr. Cohn's comment: One of the first papers using Gortex in blood vessels.*)

80. Koster JK, Cohn LH, Collins JJ Jr., Muller J, Young E. Continuous hypothermic arrest versus intermittent ischemia for myocardial protection during coronary revascularization. *Ann Thorac Surg* 1977;24:330–336.

87. Koster KJ, Cohn LH, Mee RB, Collins JJ Jr. Late results of operation for acute aortic dissection producing aortic insufficiency. *Ann Thorac Surg* 1978;26:461–467.

94. Cohn LH. Thomas Jefferson's contributions to American medicine. *Am J Surg* 1979;138:286–292. (*Dr. Cohn's comment: History interest.*)

105. Cohn LH, Mudge GH, Pratter F, Collins JJ Jr. Five to eight year follow up of patients undergoing porcine bioprosthetic valve replacement. *N Engl J Med* 1981;304:258–262.

113. Cohn LH, Koster JK Jr., Van Devanter S, Collins JJ Jr. The in-hospital risk of re-replacement of dysfunctional mitral and aortic valves. *Circulation* 1982;66:153–156.

119. Schoen FJ, Collins JJ Jr., Cohn LH. Long-term failure rate and

morphologic correlations in porcine bioprosthetic heart valves. *Am J Cardiol* 1983;51:957–964.

125. Nunn GR, Dance G, Peters J, Cohn LH. Effect of fluorocarbon exchange transfusion on myocardial infarction size in dogs. *Am J Cardiol* 1983;52:203–205.

137. Cohn LH, Allred EN, DiSesa VJ, Sawtelle K, Shemin RJ, Collins JJ Jr. Early and late risk of aortic vlave replacement. A 12-year concomitant comparison of the porcine bioprasthetic and tilting disc prosthetic aortic valves. *J Thorac Cardiovasc Surg* 1984;88:699–705.

140. Cohn LH, Allred EN, Cohn LA, DiSesa VJ, Shemin RJ, Collins JJ Jr. Long-term results of open mitral valve reconstruction for mitral stenosis. *Am J Cardiol* 1985;55:731–734.

148. DiSesa VJ, Gold JP, Mark JB, Kidwell F, Shemin RJ, Collins JJ Jr., Cohn LH. Respiratory and hemodynamic effects of nitrous oxide. A dose response study in patients following cardiac surgery. *Surg Forum* 1985;36:243–245.

149. Stone JJ, Piccione W Jr., Berrizbeitia LD, Dance GR, Schoen FJ, Shemin RJ, Cohn LH. Hemodynamic, metabolic and morphologic effects of cardiopulmonary bypass with a fluorocarbon priming solution. *Ann Thorac Surg* 1986;41:419–424. (*Dr. Cohn's comment: A simple way to handle a tough problem.*)

150. Gold JP, Cohn LH. Operative management of the calcified patent ductus arteriosus. *Ann Thorac Surg* 1986;41:567–569.

163. Adler DS, Goldman L, O'Neil A, Cook EF, Mudge GH Jr., Shemin RJ, DiSesa VJ, Cohn LH, Collins JJ Jr. Long-term survival of more than 2,000 patients after coronary artery bypass grafting. *Am J Cardiol* 1986;58:195–202. (*Dr. Cohn's comment: Indicates residual mitral regurgitation is a very negative long-term risk factor.*)

168. Gharagozloo F, Melendez FJ, Hein RA, Austin RE, Shemin RJ, DiSesa VJ, Cohn LH. The effect of oxygen free radical scavengers on the recovery of regional myocardioal function after acute coronary occlusion and surgical reperfusion. *J Thorac Cardiovasc Surg* 1988; 95:631–636.

174. DiSesa VJ, Allred EN, Kowalker W, Shemin RJ, Collins JJ Jr., Cohn LH. Performance of a fabricated trileaflet porcine bioprosthesis. Midterm follow-up of the Hancock modified orifice valve. *J Thorac Cardiovasc Surg* 1987;94:220–224.

176. Knight JL, Cohn LH. Left thoracotomy and femoro-femoral bypass for reoperative revascularization of the posterior coronary circulation. *J Cardiol Surg* 1987;2:343–349.

180. Cohn LH, Kowalker W, Bhatia S, DiSesa VJ, Shemin RJ, St. John Sutton M, Collins JJ Jr. Comparative morbidity of mitral valve repair versus replacement for mitral regurgitation with and without coronary artery disease. *Ann Thorac Surg* 1988;45:284–290.

185. Cohn LH. The paradox of high tech health care. Has our technology outstripped our ability to be ethical, cost effective and timely in its delivery? *Chest* 1988;93:864–867. (*Dr. Cohn's comment: American College of Chest Physicians, Presidential Address.*)

189. Edmunds LH, Clark RE, Cohn LH, Miller DC, Weisel RD. Guidelines for reporting morbidity and mortality after cardiac valvular operation. Published Simultaneously. *Ann Thorac Surg* 1988;46:257–259; *J Thorac Cardiovasc Surg* 1988;96:351–353. (*Dr. Cohn's comment: This has become the standard terminology for the statistical results of valve data.*)

196. Raza ST, Tam SKC, Sun SC, Laurence R, Berkovitz B, Shemin R, Cohn LH. Sequentially paced heterotrophic heart transplantation in the left chest provides improved circulatory support for the failed left ventricle. A potential biologic bridge to orthotopic transplantation. *J Thorac Cardiovasc Surg* 1989;98:266–274.

199. Cohn LH, DiSesa VJ, Couper GS, Peigh PS, Kowalker W, Collins JJ Jr. Mitral valve repair for myxomatous degeneration and prolapse of the mitral valve. *J Thorac Cardiovasc Surg* 1989;98:987–993.

200. Cohn LH, Peigh PS, Sell J, DiSesa VJ. Right thoracotomy, femoro-femoral bypass and deep hypothermia for re-replacement of the mitral valve. *Ann Thorac Surg* 1989;39:53–55.

201. Cohn LH, Collins JJ Jr., DiSesa VJ, Couper GS, Peigh PS, Kowalker W, Allred EN. Fifteen-year experience with 1678 Hancock porcine bioprosthetic heart valve replacements. *Ann Surg* 1989; 210:435–443.

209. Cohn LH, Couper GS, Kinchla NM, Collins JJ Jr. Decreased operative risk of surgical treatment of mitral regurgitation with or without coronary artery disease. *J Am Coll Cardiol* 1990;16:1575–1578.

245. Cohn LH, Aranki SF, Rizzo RJ, Adams DH, Cogswell KA, Kinchla NM, Couper GS, Collins JJ Jr. Decrease in operative risk of reoperative valve surgery. *Ann Thorac Surg* 1993;56:15–21.

252. Cohn LH, Couper GS, Aranki SF, Rizzo RJ, Kinchla NM, Collins JJ Jr. Long-term results of mitral valve reconstruction for regurgitation of the myxomatous mitral valve. *J Thorac Cardiovasc Surg* 1994; 107:143–151.

257. Cohn LH. Tricuspid regurgitation secondary to mitral valve disease. When and how to repair. *J Cardio Surg* 1994;9:237–241.

261. Savage EB, Cohn LH. "No touch" dissection, antegrade-retrograde blood cardioplegia, and single aortic cross-clamp significantly reduce operative mortality of reoperative CABG. *Circulation* 1994;90:140–143. (*Dr. Cohn's comment: Marked reduction in reoperation coronary artery bypass grafting mortality.*)

269. Cohn LH, Anderson RP, Loop FD, Fosburg RG, Cunningham JN, Laks H. Thoracic surgery workforce report. The fourth report of the thoracic surgery workforce of the American Association of Thoracic Surgery and the Society of Thoracic Surgeons. *J Thorac Cardiovasc Surg* 1995;110:570–585.

270. Horvath KA, Mannting F, Cummings N, Shernan SK, Cohn LH. Transmyocardial laser revascularization: operative techniques and clinical results in two years. *J Thorac Cardiovasc Surg* 1996;111:1047–1053. (*Dr. Cohn's comment: One of the first series of transmyocardial laser revascularization patients.*)

285. Edmunds LH Jr., Clark RE, Cohn LH, Grunkemeier GL, Miller DC, Weisel RD. Guidelines for reporting morbidity and mortality after cardiac valvular operations. Published Simultaneously. *Ann Thorac Surg* 1996;62:932–935; *Eur J Cardiothorac Surg* 1996;10:812–816; *J Thorac Cardiovasc Surg* 1996;112:708–711.

290. Horvath KA, Cohn LH, Cooley DA, Crew JR, Frazier OH, Griffith BP, Kadipasaoglu K, Lansing A, Mannting F, March R, Mirhoseini MR, Smith C. Transmyocardial laser revascularization: results of a multi-center trial with transmyocardial laser revascularization used as sole therapy for end stage coronary artery disease. *J Thorac Cardiovasc Surg* 1997;113:645–654.

317. Sayeed-Shah U, Mann MJ, Martin JS, Grachev S, Reimold S, Laurence RG, Dzau V, Cohn LH. Complete reversal of ischemic wall motion abnormalities by combined use of gene therapy with transmyocardial laser revascularization. *J Thorac Cardvasc Surg* 1998;116:763–769.

328. Cohn LH. What the cardiothoracic surgeon of the 21st century ought to be. *J Thorac Cardiovasc Surg* 1999;118:581–587.

329. Byrne JG, Aranki SF, Couper GS, Adams DH, Allred EN, Cohn LH. Reoperative aortic valve replacement: Partial upper hemisternotomy vs. full sternotomy. *J Thorac Cardiovasc Surg* 1999; 118:991–997.

337. Cohn LH. Becoming a surgical leader. *J Thorac Cardiovasc Surg* 2000;119:S42–44.

342. Linden PA, Cohn LH. Medium term follow-up of pulmonary autograft aortic valve replacement: Technical advances and echocardiographic follow up. *J Heart Valve Disease* 2001;10:35–42.

347. Byrne JG, Cohn LH. The preferred approach for mitral valve surgery after CABG: Right thoracotomy, hypothermia and avoidance of LIMA-LAD graft. *J Heart Valve Dis* 2001;10:584–590.

360. Greelish JP, Cohn LH, Leacche M, Mitchell M, Karavas A, Fox J, Byrne JG, Aranki SF, Couper GS. Minimally invasive mitral valve repair suggests earlier operations for mitral valve disease. *J Thorac Cardiovasc Surg* 2003;126:365–371.

365. Byrne JG, Karavas AN, Mihaljevic T, Rawn JD, Aranki SF, Cohn LH. The role of the cryopreserved homograft in isolated elective AVR. *Am J Cardiol* 2003;91:616–619.

370. Farivar RS, Cohn LH. Hypercholesterolemia is a risk factor for bioprosthetic valve calcification and explantation. *J Thorac Cardiovasc Surg* 2003;126:969–975.

374. Mihaljevic T, Paul S, Leacche M, Farivar RS, Soltesz EG, Rawn JD, Byrne JG, Cohn LH. Robotic mammary takedown and off-pump bypass surgery for single vessel disease of the left anterior descending artery. *Am J Cardiol* 2003;92:I222–224.

381. Yacoub MH, Cohn LH. Novel approaches to cardiac valve repair: from structure to function: Part I. *Circulation* 2004;109:942–950.

382. Yacoub MH, Cohn LH. Novel approaches to cardiac valve repair: from structure to function: Part II. *Circulation* 2004;109:1064–1072.

389. Mihaljevic T, Cohn LH, Unic D, Aranki SF, Couper GS, Byrne JG. One thousand minimally invasive valve operations: early and late results. *Ann Surg* 2004;240:529–534.

396. Byrne JG, Leacche M, Unic D, Rawn JD, Simon DI, Rogers CD, Cohn LH. Staged initial percutaneous coronary intervention followed by valve surgery ("hybrid approach") for patients with complex coronary and valve disease. *J Am Coll Cardiol* 2005;45:14–18.

404. Gogbashian A, Sepic J, Soltesz EG, Nascimben L, Cohn LH. Operative and long-term survival of elderly is significantly improved by mitral valve repair. *Am Heart J*, in press.

CHARLES RICHARD CONTI, MD:
A Conversation With the Editor*

Dick Conti was born in Allentown, Pennsylvania, on October 26, 1934; he grew up in Bethlehem, Pennsylvania, where he graduated third in his high school class of 350 students. He graduated from Lehigh University in 1956, having achieved membership in Phi Beta Kappa, and in 1960 he graduated from the Johns Hopkins University School of Medicine as a member of the Alpha Omega Alpha Honorary Society. His training in internal medicine was on the Osler Medical Service of The Johns Hopkins Hospital and his training in cardiology was at the same institution. His training was interrupted by 2 years of service in the United States Army. Upon completion of his cardiology fellowship in 1968, he stayed on the full-time Hopkins faculty and by 1972 had risen to the rank of Associate Professor of medicine and Medical Director of the cardiac catheterization laboratory. In 1974, at age 39, he became Professor of Medicine and Director of the cardiovascular division at the University of Florida. He remained in that position until 1999 when he stepped down as division director, but he has remained at the same institution and continues his teaching, research, and editing activities. Dr. Conti's clinical, investigative, and teaching interests are primarily in the area of coronary artery disease. His investigative efforts have led to the publication of nearly 650 articles, most of which are in refereed medical journals, to 4 authored or co-authored books, and to 5 edited books. Since 1988 he has been Editor-in Chief of *Clinical Cardiology* and since 1999, the Editor-in-Chief of *ACCEL*.

For his many contributions, Dr. Conti has been the recipient of a number of honors. He was President of the American College of Cardiology in 1989 to 1990. He is an elected member of the Southern Society for Clinical Investigation, the American Clinical and Climatological Association, the Association of University Cardiologists, and the Association of Professors of Cardiology. In 1986, he received the Council on Clinical Cardiology of the American Heart Association's Teacher of the Year Award in Cardiovascular Diseases. In 1995, he received the Distinguished Graduate Award of Allentown Central Catholic High School. In 1996, he was elected to the Johns Hopkins Society of Scholars. In 1998, he became a Master of the American College of Cardiology with the right to use the Master Designation (MACC). In 1999, he received the Gifted Teacher Award of the Florida Chapter of the American College of Cardiology. Dr.

FIGURE 1. CRC at age 67 (2001) during the interview.

Conti for many years has been a major international statesman of cardiology and he has many friends who are cardiologists throughout the world. He and his lovely wife (the former *Ruthie Ellen Wursta* of Allentown, Pennsylvania) of 44 years are the parents of 4 children and the grandparents of 5. Dick Conti is an outstanding guy, a friend, and one who is fun to be around.

William C. Roberts, MD† **(Hereafter, WCR):** *Dick, I appreciate your willingness to talk to me and therefore to the readers of* The American Journal of Cardiology. *Dr. Conti and I are on board a ship called the Crystal Harmony, and we are now traveling between the States and Nassau. This is Wednesday, October 17, 2001. Dr. Conti gave 5 talks this morning at a medical conference and despite talking for nearly 3 hours, he's willing to talk a bit more and I'm grateful*

*This series of interviews are underwritten by an unrestricted grant from Bristol-Myers Squibb.

†Baylor Heart & Vascular Institute, Baylor University Medical Center, Dallas, Texas 75246.

FIGURE 2. CRC at age 1.5 years (1935).

for that. Dick, could we begin by my asking you to speak about your early life, some of your early memories, what your parents were like?

Charles Richard Conti, MD[‡] (Hereafter, CRC): I was born in Sacred Heart Hospital in Allentown, but my home was in Bethlehem, Pennsylvania. I was there for 21 years. My earliest memories are probably when I was in the second grade. I remember the nice, little nun who taught me. The next memory I have was in the third grade and that was of plaster falling down from the ceiling hitting a nun on the head. I attended Catholic school through the 12th grade. I went to St. Simon and Jude until 8th grade and finished second in my class. I played baseball (second base) and basketball in grade school in a league. I made the all star baseball team.

My dad was born in Latrobe, Pennsylvania, the home of Arnold Palmer and of Rolling Rock beer. He had moved from western Pennsylvania to the Bethlehem area, where he met my mom, who was born in Palmerton, Pennsylvania. She was 1 of 4 daughters. Her mother was born in Ireland; her father in Gothenberg, Sweden. I knew her mother well, but I never knew her father. He was killed falling off a girder while working for Bethlehem Steel when my mother

‡University of Florida College of Medicine, Gainesville, Florida, 32610.

was 5 years old. My dad's dad came from the Como area of Northern Italy in 1902. I knew his father well because he lived with us. I never knew my father's mother. She died in the 1918 flu epidemic. My mom and dad met in Bethlehem when my mother was 20 or so, and they got married. We lived in 3 places in Bethlehem. My dad went to St. Vincent's College in Latrobe. He went to work during the depression for a factory called SARCO, which stands for Steam and Regulator Company. (It played an important role in World War II because it made things for ships.) My dad taught me a lot of things, including how to play baseball. But my mother played a very special role in my life. She taught me how to pay attention to details, how to study, how to dance, and why learning things was important. My mother really influenced me to do the things that I've eventually done. We didn't have a lot of money. When I was older, my mother worked as a secretary in the same place as my dad. They both were hard working people. They instilled in me a work ethic that I think still is with me. I worked every summer since I was 12 years old. My first job was caddying at Saucon Valley Country Club. That is where I first thought about playing golf. We used to have a "Caddy's Day," when a club member would lend a caddy his clubs. The clubs were always too long for me as a little kid. I did all kinds of jobs; once, as a janitor in the school system; once, for the telephone company putting in the new dials (that were just then being introduced); once, for Bethlehem Steel Company working in a 110° setting. I said to myself: "This is not the life for me." I learned how to work. I learned from my parents. I thought it was important to work during the summers. I needed money for college. When in college, I worked in the bacteriology laboratory cleaning up bacteriology specimens and things like that.

WCR: *Do you have a sibling?*

CRC: Yes. I have a sister who is 4 years younger than I am. Another thing I remember when 6 years old was my mother's finding a white spot in one of my sister's eyes. I remember my mother's testing her. It turned out that she couldn't see out of that eye. Mother took her to an ophthalmologist, and he found that she had a retinoblastoma. My sister had that eye operatively excised when she was 2 years old. She is still alive and well, has 3 boys of her own, and none of them and none of their children have retinoblastoma. Apparently it wasn't hereditary in her. That was a traumatic experience for the family. My sister went to the same schools I did.

WCR: *How many were in your class?*

CRC: We had about 350 kids in each class in my high school. We had a great basketball team. I played baseball, but we didn't have a great baseball team. Our football team was mediocre. It was a really good school run by nuns and priests. The girls wore uni-

FIGURE 3. CRC at age 2 with his dad.

forms; the boys wore coats and ties. I had a wonderful time there. I thought it was a good education. I was well prepared for college. One of my daughters nominated me for a distinguished graduate award from Central Catholic High School, and 6 years ago I got it. I was 1 of 2 in my class who got it.

In my teenage years I was like a lot of kids in those days. I played sports. Every summer I played baseball in a league. We'd go to the playground practically every day to play basketball and hard ball. I was a fairly good athlete. I wasn't a big guy, but I could handle myself in those 2 sports. We played football without pads. It was a great time. I was in a lot of activities in high school. I was a member of the "Key Club," an honorary student association connected with the Kiwanis Club. I was president of the National Honor Society in high school. I did some acting in the school plays. I loved Latin. I was a star in Latin for some reason. Maybe it was because I heard my grandfather speak Italian. No one ever spoke Italian in my home because we all grew up during World War II. Eastern Pennsylvania had ethnic German/Italian people there. Everyone wanted to speak English, so I never learned to speak Italian, but I have an ear for it. I think if I spent 6 months in Rome I could probably speak the language, but I have never done that. I was a star in 2 things in high school. One was Latin. One semester I got 100 as a score. The same thing happened in chemistry. I had a wonderful chemistry teacher, *Sister Christopher Hogan*, from the Bethlehem/Allentown area. I really looked up to her. She

also made me think about precision and accuracy in what one said and did. For some reason chemistry came easy to me in both high school and college. I walked through organic chemistry like nothing. Before she died in her 90s, I heard that Sister Hogan had been ill, and I wrote her a letter to thank her for everything. My mother knew her family. High school was a lot of fun for me. That's where I met *Ruthie*, my wife. I've known Ruthie since 1948.

WCR: *Was she in the same class?*

CRC: Yes. We started in 1948 and graduated in 1952. We became boyfriend-girlfriend in 1950 and we've been that way ever since.

WCR: *You mentioned that you moved 3 times in Bethlehem. You were moving to bigger houses or what was the scenario?*

CRC: Both a bigger house and a better location.

WCR: *The grandfather who lived in your home was your father's father?*

CRC: Yes. My grandmother, my mother's mother, lived close by and she had 3 daughters and a son. There were 2 daughters older than my mother and her brother was a bit younger. The oldest sister died in her 90s. The brother died at age 77. My mother, now 88, is still alive and well.

WCR: *Your mother was born what year? And your father was born what year?*

CRC: My mother was born in 1913. My father was born in 1908 and died at age 65, in 1974, of sudden cardiac arrest.

WCR: *What was your home like? Were there many books around?*

CRC: No, there were not many books around. I was never a big reader. Neither were my mother or father. I've become a big reader and I think it's because Ruthie is a voracious reader. She reads everything in sight and so do all our kids. I don't read nearly as much as Ruthie, but I'm reading the things I have to read in medicine and cardiology and then some. I have an interest in World War II, and I read a lot about it. I remember vividly when we were bombed at Pearl Harbor. I was 7 years old at the time. I also remember the day when Franklin Roosevelt died. I have some vague memories of D-Day. The houses we lived in were nice and located in decent places. They were all attached to another house. They were not individual homes. The first one was at 317 West Street and the second one was at 434 First Avenue. The West Street house is still there. The First Avenue house is now gone. Then we moved to 1202 West Union Boulevard, a major access way from Bethlehem to Allentown. That's where we lived until my dad died. I was in Baltimore when he died. Then my mother and her sister moved into a little apartment together.

WCR: *What did your father do?*

CRC: He was sort of an engineer.

WCR: *He was a college graduate?*

CRC: He graduated from St. Vincent's in Latrobe. St. Vincent's was not a big-time college. My mother never went past high school. My dad had a brother (*John*) who also went to St. Vincent's. They both lived in Bethlehem. Several of John's family still are in the Bethlehem area.

WCR: *What did your father do at SARCO?*

CRC: He was a supervisor. They made many things for ships during World War II, such as blenders for steam engines. I don't know if they were secret or not. He never did anything with Lehigh University, a big engineering school. He was a hard working man. Both he and my mother supported me fully even though we did not have a lot of money. I got a scholarship to Villanova University. (They gave only 3 or 4 scholarships.) I decided, however, that I didn't want to go there; I wanted to go to Lehigh University. I paid tuition for the first year and then I got a scholarship for the last 3 years. Then I went to Hopkins, which cost money. That was a burden for my family. When I married Ruthie, she supported me during medical school.

WCR: *Do you remember conversations at the dinner table at night? Did you have special occasions around the house that you remember?*

CRC: We always had dinner together. That spilled over to me when I was a house officer at Hopkins. Although I worked day and night at Hopkins, I was home for dinner every night with my wife and kids. It was one of those things that I thought was important to do—for a father to be there when the kids were having dinner. Our conversations were pretty much what my sister and I did in school. We had few intellectual conversations. Both my parents expected me to do well in school. Both my mother and dad were first-generation Americans, born in the USA, but both came from families that weren't. Every one of those families in that generation wanted their kids to be better educated than they were and to do things they didn't have opportunities to do. My parents were very proud of both my sister and me.

WCR: *They obviously were curious about what was going on in your world on a day-to-day basis. You certainly got the idea that not only were they interested, but that they supported your endeavors vigorously.*

CRC: Yes. There's no question about it. My dad died 6 months before we moved to Florida. My mother has seen all the things that have happened to me and I think she thinks it paid off what they did. I certainly do. I was the first physician in my family. My role model as a physician was my family doctor, *Paul Badura, MD*. He was a family doctor in Bethlehem; he treated our whole family. When I first decided to consider medicine (while I was in high school), he's who I wanted to be like. I thought I'd probably come back to Bethlehem and do general practice and be an upstanding member of the community. Dr. Badura was highly respected at our church. He probably had more money than anybody else in the church. He was a nice man. I remember him well. He set me off on the idea of being a doctor. My parents never said I ought to be a doctor or a lawyer or I ought to do this or that. They wanted me to succeed. They wanted me to do well in high school and college, and then do what I thought was important. Another thing that some people wanted me to do, particularly the priests who taught us, was to go into the seminary. For a fleeting moment I considered that. *Harry Strassner*, who later became the principal of the school, took a few of us, who he thought might have potential, to Philadelphia to visit his parents, who were great people. He had trained at St. Charles Borromeo, a Catholic seminary across from Lankenau Hospital. He was trying to influence us, not push us toward priesthood. I think he wanted to be a role model for us. Two of my classmates went into the seminary and became priests. One worked for 10 years and then decided he didn't want to do it anymore. The other fellow is still in the priesthood.

WCR: *The church was very important in your early life.*

CRC: Very important to me. I was an altar boy for 12 years. I served Mass even when I was in high school. I'd serve Sunday Mass at home. At the school we'd have Mass every Friday morning. I served there too. When I was in grade school at High Masses there

FIGURE 4. CRC as an altar boy at age 11 (1946).

was a position called "Master of Ceremonies" and I was that. That's about as high as you can go as an altar boy. Maybe that is why I liked Latin so much, because I knew the liturgy. I had to respond to the priest in Latin and I was pretty good at it. I still remember a lot of the liturgy. (I sometimes think that the changes made in our church to accommodate the English language for the people who didn't understand Latin were wrong. I think the Jewish religion has it right in that they stuck with tradition over the years. Some traditions in Roman Catholicism are not there now in the USA. If you go to the Vatican it is just like the old days that I remember as a young person. It hasn't bothered me a lot, but I sometimes wonder about it.) I was a very devout Catholic when I was a young boy and stayed that way through my early years.

WCR: *You mentioned that you played a lot of sports. You played baseball in high school? Did you stay a second baseman?*

CRC: No. I played shortstop.

WCR: *You were a star?*

CRC: I hit okay. I didn't hit a long ball, but I could get on base. Redding, Pennsylvania, had a very good baseball team. *Stu Gahris* pitched for them. He went on to play professional baseball. He was never a big star in the major leagues, but he was good enough to get into professional baseball. I got a hit off him. It was the first hit we got off him in that game. We lost the game but at least I got a hit off him.

WCR: *I gather you were fairly fast?*

CRC: I was pretty fast. We didn't have a track team at that time in high school. Running became something I did later. Running when practicing for baseball was generally a punishment—taking laps around the field. Baseball is a very skilled sport. I had to learn how to keep my eye on the ball so it didn't hit me. When the ball is coming at you 80 miles an hour (not 100 miles an hour like today), it took something to hit the ball. I wasn't a major base stealer, but I was not bad.

WCR: *Do you remember what you batted?*

CRC: It was in the high 200s in my senior year.

WCR: *You said you played a lot of basketball. Did you play on the basketball team in high school?*

CRC: No. We had a gym. We played intramural basketball. There was a freshman and a sophomore team, and I was on the sophomore team. We played "club" basketball in and around the Allentown area. I never went out for the team because I thought I was too small. We had some fairly good players. Allentown Central Catholic High School had an excellent basketball team. They won the state championship once in the Catholic league. In the public league, they came very close many times. Baseball was my sport, not basketball. It was the one I really liked, and I was definitely too small to play football.

WCR: *How much did you weigh as a senior in high school?*

CRC: About 140.

WCR: *How tall are you?*

CRC: A little over 5 feet, 9 inches.

WCR: *After school, when baseball season wasn't going on, what did you do? How far was your high school from the house?*

CRC: Six miles.

WCR: *How did you get back and forth?*

CRC: Bus or hitchhike.

WCR: *The school bus or a regular bus?*

CRC: A regular transport company. A lot of the time I hitchhiked because it was almost a straight shot from home to school. In those days hitchhiking was safe.

WCR: *That was the best Catholic high school in town? Or was it the only one?*

CRC: It was the only one in Allentown. There was 1 in Bethlehem called Bethlehem Catholic High School, where my mother went. It was a much smaller school and it wasn't at the same level as Allentown Central Catholic.

WCR: *You lived in Bethlehem and went to Allentown High School. Were there other teachers in high school who influenced you?*

CRC: Yes. There was *Sister Ilene* who taught world history in my second year in high school. She was tough. The reason she was tough is that she had a quiz almost every day on what we were supposed to have learned the previous day. I found world history tough, but I did okay. I had to get into the habit of studying all the time. When I went home after school, the first thing I did was my homework and then I did other things. I never did other things before doing my homework. I'm still that way. Stuff on my desk gets done before I do something else. She may have set the tone for that. She also was a drama teacher. I worked with her and a bunch of other people in the school plays that we did. An older nun taught me Latin, and she was a wonderful person, too. They were strict but fair and convinced me that I had to learn all that stuff. I never was an English scholar. I guess it was because I wasn't a big reader when I was in grade school or in high school. I never was encouraged to do a lot of reading. I did okay in English. I was on the honor roll every time one could be on the honor roll, but I never felt comfortable with it. I got better at it as I became an academic physician.

WCR: *Tell me a little more about your mother and daddy. What was your mother like? You said she had a particular influence on you. She seemed to be sensitive to your potential and she wanted to make sure you lived up to your potential. I gather that if you didn't quite do your best, she had something to say about it.*

CRC: She was not strict at all. She was very easy going and but made it clear that I was supposed to do my studies when I had homework to do. My dad never got involved with that. He obviously wanted me to do well, but my mother was the driving force, but not to the point of cracking the whip.

WCR: *She was pleasant then?*

CRC: She was very pleasant. Schoolwork was not hard for me. I guess I liked doing it because I didn't complain about it.

WCR: *It sounds to me like you were the chosen one in your immediate family. You were older than your sister. Your granddaddy was in your house. Your grandmother was not very far away. Your mother's sisters were not far away. Did they have children? Or were you and your sister about the only youngsters around?*

CRC: We were the only ones. My mother's brother was married, but he had no children. One of my mother's sisters was married, but her husband died prematurely and they had no children. She never remarried. Her other sister basically took care of my grandmother. She never married. She's now 91, living with my mother.

WCR: *You had quite a few eyes cheering for you. Did all of the family get together at Christmastime and Thanksgiving?*

CRC: You bet, because we all lived close by and it was easy to do. Now it's a little more complicated because everybody is scattered. The thing that we always did as a family (the 5 of us) was to have an annual vacation at the seashore. We all looked forward to it, and we had a great time. Early on we went to Seaside Heights, New Jersey, north of Atlantic City, which I have vague memories of. We finally decided on Wildwood, New Jersey, and went there at least 15 times. That was always a 2-week vacation, which my sister and I loved. There was a long boardwalk there. I remember walking the boardwalk every night with my family.

WCR: *That was a yearly tradition to look forward to. What about travels outside of the relatively near environs to Allentown and Bethlehem? Did you ever go to New York City or Boston?*

CRC: We went to New York City, to the 1939 World's Fair, but I have vague recollections of that. We didn't travel much. When I was a kid it was during World War II. Gasoline was rationed. Everybody tended to stay home. I went to Pittsburgh to visit relatives there with my grandfather and he had a heart attack while we were there. He recovered and lived another 45 years!

WCR: *Dick, when you got home from high school there was nobody there. You came in, did your homework, and then went out and played.*

CRC: When I was 16, I got my driver's license. My parents allowed me to drive to school, providing I drove them to work in the morning and picked them up at night. I didn't do that every day, but I did it a lot. It worked out pretty well; it saved the bus transportation money. When in high school and college I'd spend some time at Ruthie's house. She lived in Allentown. I never went if I hadn't finished my homework. I'd help her with her homework. We were both in the same classes, so it was pretty easy. I'd come home on an 11:00 bus at night. It was the last bus out of Allentown to Bethlehem. It was a 20-minute ride.

WCR: *What did you do at night? Your family had dinner together and you had already done your homework. What would you do at night?*

CRC: I'd watch television if I was at home. It depended on the time of the year. If it was summertime, I'd be out playing at the local park. I did that until college. I did what other kids did. A couple of guys had cars and we'd get together and talk about things. We went to Betz Restaurant in Allentown. We'd all truck in there and spend 10¢ each for a cup of coffee.

WCR: *You mentioned Dr. Badura who played a major role in your deciding to go into medicine. What was it about him that appealed to you? Was it the fact that he was quite respected in the community and in your church? You saw him in church as well as when you'd go to see him as a patient.*

CRC: I think that's probably it. Everybody wanted to make a good living, but money wasn't an obsession with my family or me. My parents wished me to be somebody of importance in whatever I did. Badura struck me as a leading guy in our little community built around our church.

WCR: *What was the name of the church?*

CRC: Sts. Simon and Jude. That also was the name of the grade school I went to. It was attached to the church. Dr. Badura had a nice house right across the street from the church. We had a nice house, too, but he had a nicer house. Who knows what influences you when you're that young? I wasn't driven by money. I guess prominence. I wanted to be somebody like him. If I remember correctly, he went on to be president of the family practice association nationally. He was a good family practitioner. He definitely influenced me in terms of what I wanted to do. I wanted to be a family doctor. That stayed with me until I got to Hopkins. Then I changed my mind.

WCR: *Did you have any hobbies as a youngster?*

CRC: Mostly they were sports. I wasn't a builder or anything like that.

WCR: *It sounds to me like your home was very pleasant. There was not much fussing or arguments. You and your sister, I gather, got along pretty well.*

CRC: I think you're right. It was pretty relaxed. I never said "God, I don't want to go home again" or that kind of thing. My family always welcomed my friends. Friends spent time at our house. *Timothy Mahoney*, *Jackie Shive*, and I went to grade school and high school together. In grade school we'd go to each other's house every Saturday and play. During the war we played war games together. We played sports together. Those 2 fellows were very close friends of mine. They are both dead. Timmy died as a senior in college from encephalitis. Jackie Shive died 2 years ago after a coronary bypass grafting operation.

WCR: *Had your father retired by the time he died suddenly?*

CRC: Yes, he had. He retired at age 62. Before that, when I was at Hopkins running the cath lab, he told me he was having what sounded like angina pectoris. It wasn't limiting him greatly. I brought him to Hopkins and had *Bud Freisinger* see him. Bud said, "Yeah, I think it is angina. We probably ought to do a cardiac catheterization on him." I did the cardiac catheterization. Whether that was the right thing to do or not, I don't know, but it turned out that it was the right thing to do. My dad thought I'd cured him after that cardiac catheterization. He didn't have angina again for another 3 years. This was before coronary angioplasty. He had a mid-right coronary stenosis and not much else. It wasn't severe. Bud made the decisions. If Bud thought it was severe, I don't know if he would have recommended surgery at that time or not. This was around 1970. Bypass surgery was just getting started and was generally being done only in persons with multivessel coronary disease. My father did very well. In January 1974, while Ruthie and I and our children were skiing in Vermont, I got a call from

FIGURE 5. CRC at graduation from Lehigh University at age 21 (1956).

Ruthie's mother that my father had just died suddenly. My mom and dad were dressing one morning before a planned drive to visit my sister in Cape Cod; he sat down in a chair, sat back, and died. My mother didn't have any idea what to do. She called the ambulance and by the time they got there he had died. If you have to die, I guess it's a blessing to die that way. He was only 65.

WCR: *Your father was healthy until that point.*

CRC: Absolutely.

WCR: *And your mother has been healthy.*

CRC: My mom's been amazing. I talked with her last week. She's doing fine. She had some GYN surgery, but that's about it.

WCR: *And your sister, except for the retinoblastoma, has been healthy?*

CRC: She's been healthy and her children are all healthy. She lives in Hyannis.

WCR: *Dick, how did you choose Lehigh University? Was it because it was local and relatively easy to get to?*

CRC: It's a first class school, particularly noted for engineering, and located in Bethlehem, Pennsylvania. It was heavily supported by the Bethlehem Steel Company. A lot of the graduating mechanical engineers went to work for the Bethlehem Steel, which provided many endowments. It was on South Mountain, a nice campus, and all male. It's no longer an all-male school. There were maybe 2,500 students there, so it

FIGURE 6. CRC and Ruthie on August 24, 1957, having just married.

was a relatively small school. At that time, Ruthie was in the big picture for me. Her being there influenced me somewhat to stay at Lehigh at home. Although my parents never mentioned it, I knew it would be less expensive for me to stay home than to go away. Even if I'd gone to Villanova or LaSalle with a scholarship, it would have probably been more expensive. I think the annual tuition at Lehigh was $800. It was my decision alone to go there. I've never been sorry about that decision. Lehigh was a tough school. Although I got a good education at Allentown Central Catholic, it was not quite the same as going to a secular school. I was hurting for the first 6 months. I think I had a 3.0 grade point average that first year. I graduated, however, with a 3.67 average, and made Phi Beta Kappa. I had some learning to do—English literature, composition, and writing. Writing was tough for me. I didn't do well in that. I don't know when people learn how to write, but I didn't learn how to write until later.

WCR: *You lived at home during each of the 4 years at Lehigh University? How far was it from your house?*

CRC: It was about 4 miles. I didn't have a car of my own. I used the family car occasionally, but most of the time I took a bus. The bus stopped right outside my house since we lived on the main access way to Allentown. I'd get on the bus, go downtown, and transfer to get to school. I joined a fraternity there (Kappa Sigma) which was off campus. I could walk to it. I'd have lunch there and, oftentimes, dinner there, but I lived at home.

WCR: *Where did Ruthie go?*

CRC: Ruthie didn't go to college. She had several job opportunities. She considered going to nursing school and then decided against it. She went to work for a dentist and became a dental technologist. She got good at it, too. She worked for them for many years. When we got married and went to Baltimore, she worked in pharmacology as a technician. She did some pretty nice stuff.

WCR: *But she always read?*

CRC: I guess her voracious reading came from her mother, because her mother was the same way. Her father was not a reader.

WCR: *What did her father do?*

CRC: Her father was a truck driver who eventually became president of the teamster's union. He rose quickly.

WCR: *What was his name?*

CRC: *John Wursta.* He's still alive. Her mother died of a lymphoma in 1999.

WCR: *Who influenced you in college?*

CRC: There were 2 professors who stood out. One, *Hope Ritter*, taught zoology, which I took my first year. He was a very approachable, nice, patient, tall guy who was working like crazy to get his PhD, which he eventually got. He took a lot of time with the 15 or 16 of us, who were in the "premed" curriculum (biology and chemistry courses). I subsequently worked with his daughter, a physician assistant at the University of Florida. The other person was *Edward Amstutz*, an organic chemist. He knew I was doing well in his course. The chemical engineers had to take his course and they hated it, believing they had to memorize everything. This was not true. Basic principles had to be memorized, but then you could put it all together. Amstutz came up to me one time in our lab and asked me what I wanted to do with my life. I told him I wanted to go to medical school. He said, "Why don't you try chemistry? You do good in it." He didn't convince me. He was an impressive guy who taught well. At least he taught me well. I really related to him. He was a senior professor. It was a fun course and relatively easy for me, probably because of the way he taught.

WCR: *My sense of Lehigh University is that it's an outstanding engineering school and you have to be pretty good to get in there. There must not have been many students in Bethlehem or Allentown who were day students. Most of those 2,500 must have lived at the university. Is that correct?*

CRC: That is correct.

WCR: *You were in the minority, living at home.*

CRC: There were some "townies," students from the town going to Lehigh. There were 5 or 6 from my high school who went there. Timothy Mahoney was one of them.

WCR: *Even though it is an engineering school, there were a few premeds, such as yourself, who went there. Bob Bonow went there.*

CRC: I did not know that. I'll have to talk to him about that.

WCR: *He played basketball.*

CRC: We didn't have a very good basketball team. Wrestling was the biggest thing at Lehigh University. We had a national reputation in wrestling. They won the national championship occasionally. One of my classmates, *Eddie Eichelberger*, later went on to get his PhD in electrical engineering and engineering physics (probably the toughest engineering course there). He was a national champion for 3 years in a row (Most Valuable Wrestler for 2 years). He never lost a wrestling match. He wrestled from 137 to 177 lbs, wherever they needed him.

WCR: *It sounds like Lehigh University expanded your horizon.*

CRC: Very much so. I met people from elsewhere. Joining the fraternity was an important part of my life, particularly because of my being from the town and living at home. Students don't participate in university life unless they are in some kind of an organization. I thought it was very important. I've never been sorry about that either. I haven't kept up with my Kappa Sig classmates over the years. It helped me get to know a lot of people from a lot of different places. Some of them are still my friends.

WCR: *Did you have to study hard or after a while did it become a lot easier for you?*

CRC: It came a lot easier for me after a while, but there were certain courses that were tough. Biology was really tough. Embryology, histology, comparative anatomy were the 3 toughest biology courses that I've ever taken, including those in medical school. Immunology was nice. Genetics was so-so. There wasn't much known about genetics then. The biology courses were tougher than the chemistry and physics courses. Once I got in the groove and learned how to do it, I did it. When I had something to do, I'd get it done. I would study until I was done and then do something else. I never put studying off. That's been a pattern in my life since I can remember.

WCR: *Back then did you require a lot of sleep or could you go in high school and college never needing a lot of sleep?*

CRC: I never needed a lot of sleep. I'm a morning person. I like getting up early in the morning. In those days it was rare that I went to bed before 11:30 P.M. That's changed. I go to bed a lot earlier now, but I'm still a morning person. I prefer to get up at 6:00 in the morning and go to bed at 9:30 or 10 at night. In those days I could run around and be out a lot. I never went out unless I was done with my class work. Even if it took me until 9 or 10 o'clock at night, then I went out to see a friend or have a beer someplace when I was in college.

WCR: *You and Ruthie went together throughout your college career.*

CRC: That's correct.

WCR: *How did you choose Johns Hopkins for medical school?*

CRC: Being from Pennsylvania, the Philadelphia schools were appealing to me. I applied to the University of Pennsylvania, Jefferson, Hahnemann, and Temple. One of my advisors was important in my decision making for Hopkins. I was interviewed, but didn't get accepted to the University of Pennsylvania. I was interviewed and accepted at Hahnemann and Jefferson and was accepted without interview at Temple. My advisor, a bacteriologist, encouraged me to think about Hopkins. He had been with the Hopkins unit in the South Pacific in the war. He gave me a book about *Popsie Welch*, whom I had never heard of before. I read about what he did when he came to this country and how he set things up at Hopkins. I applied there. Also, a student at Lehigh the year before me went to Hopkins. I applied and got an interview in New York at Goldwater Memorial Hospital with *Murray Steele*. He had written something in Cecil and Loeb's book about laboratory medicine. My dad drove me there. I talked with him. The summer before I had worked as a lab tech in a laboratory at Sacred Heart Hospital in Allentown. We talked about some laboratories tests. I hit it off very well with him. Three or 4 days later I got accepted to Hopkins. In those days they had regional interviewers. I had never even been to Baltimore when I got accepted to Hopkins.

FIGURE 7. CRC at age 26 (1960) at graduation from the Johns Hopkins Medical School.

WCR: *I had forgotten about your working in college. Did you work all 4 years?*

CRC: Every year. After my third year I worked that summer as an operating room orderly. It was sort of a "clean up the place" job. It was fun and I got to know the housestaff and a lot of the surgeons. The next year I worked in the lab. I worked with a pathologist, *Donald Slater*, affectionately known as "The Chief." He was an anatomic pathologist. I did autopsies with him. He started his dictations by saying, "Tisco", which means, "this specimen consists of." That was my first encounter with the dead human body. It was fun. I worked in the blood bank also. I drew blood and got pretty good at putting in IVs and drawing blood with a big needle. I typed and crossmatched for blood transfusions. That was a fun summer. When I went to medical school, I came back and also worked in the hospital in the summer.

WCR: *You didn't work during the academic college year?*

CRC: I did work cleaning up the labs for the microbiology department. I got paid 90¢ an hour.

WCR: *You came in on the weekends?*

CRC: I'd come in on the weekends. I'd bring my books with me, too, because I could study there. I'd go in before classes and after classes. I'd have to put the Petri dishes in the autoclave. One of them was *Serra-tia marcesens*. I made about $100 a month, and that helped a lot.

WCR: *You were putting in how many hours a week during college?*

CRC: At least 15.

WCR: *After you got accepted to Hopkins, without ever having seen the place, what happened then?*

CRC: I went down to see the place with Ruthie's brother and we stayed at a hotel downtown. I met the admissions person who told me about the school in about 30 minutes. I never had a tour of the place. She told me I had to get a place to live. I visited a couple of places and decided on 726 North Broadway, right across the street from the hospital. Meantime, I had met *Jim Jordan* from Macon, Georgia, who was an Auburn undergraduate. He and I were representatives of Alpha Epsilon Delta Honorary Premed Society (AED). We had a national meeting in Milsaps College in Jackson, Mississippi, and he asked me if I were going to Baltimore anytime soon. He asked me to help him get a room there. I got the room and Jim and I stayed in it for our freshman year in medical school. We didn't start classes until October.

WCR: *This was October 1956. How many were in your class?*

CRC: Seventy-five.

WCR: *Most of your classmates at Hopkins must have been from Harvard, Yale, Princeton, and Johns Hopkins University.*

CRC: A lot of them were from Hopkins and Princeton. The "Baltimore track to Hopkins" via Gilman High School and Princeton University.

WCR: *How did Hopkins and medicine in general strike you? You'd already spent some time in a hospital, so you weren't totally naïve to what to expect. How did the atmosphere of this prominent faculty and school with a great reputation hit you?*

CRC: As a freshman I didn't know the prominent faculty. It was impressive for me to meet the professors who taught the basic science—anatomy, physiology, and biochemistry. This was probably the best educational experience I've ever had. It was not hard for me at Hopkins. I really liked it. I studied hard, but I enjoyed it. I remember my roommate saying, "Let's go out." And I'd say, "I've got this work to do." I really sat there and studied. I probably studied 4 hours every night. It was a time in my life when I was studying things I really enjoyed doing more than anything else. Hopkins was not tough for me.

WCR: *You found it easier than college?*

CRC: I did. I found it easier than Lehigh University. No question.

WCR: *Do you remember any major surprises you had in medical school, particularly early on?*

CRC: I don't think I was surprised by much. We had social fraternities then. I joined Phi Chi. It was dismantled a couple of years later. It didn't exist after 5 or 6 years. The only one left is the Pithotomy Club.

WCR: *You obviously excelled right off the bat in medical school.*

CRC: I did pretty well.

WCR: *Did you know what your standing was early or did you have to wait until you became AOA?*

CRC: We weren't graded, but in our third year we were told where we were in the class. I was in the top third of the class. I knew that. That's all they ever told us. I never saw a report card or a grade. I thought this was a wonderful thing. I liked that idea.

WCR: *Everybody had proved themselves as good students before they ever got there.*

CRC: I think for the most part that's true. Bright students in medical school are a dime a dozen, even now. They have to make the cut to get there. The difference between the top students and the bottom students in medical school is motivation, wanting to be there, and wanting to do well. Some medical students don't enjoy being there.

WCR: *How did you enjoy the basic sciences?*

CRC: I loved anatomy and physiology. Biochemistry was so-so with me. I had one of the world's great biochemists, *Albert Lehinger*, who was head of the biochemistry department.

WCR: *You had already had organic chemistry and had excelled at it.*

CRC: I knew the language. Biochem is different than organic, which is industrial kind of stuff.

WCR: *Who had a major impact on you in medical school?*

CRC: Later on, *Leigh Cluff.* In the early days, *Abu Pollack*, a professor of pathology. *Arnold Rich* was chief and Pollack was a professor and did a lot of teaching in the second year. He was an extremely good teacher who worked with a resident, *"Skip" Huntington Shelton.* The 2 of them taught us a lot of pathology, including both histopathology and gross pathology (in the autopsy room). We went to autopsies in those days. I learned a lot about medicine from them. They advised us to read textbooks of medicine when we were in pathology. I remember those 2 very well. (Pollack later died of pancreatic cancer.) We had some really great teachers. *Phil Bard* was head of physiology and had written *Bard's Textbook of Physiology*, which we all used. I was at Hopkins during an incredible era: *Nicholson Eastman* was head of OB/GYN; *Dick Telinde* in GYN; and *Mac Harvey* and *John Edgar Howard* in medicine. The housestaff also influenced me when I was a medical student, particularly *Mike Criley* and *O'Neal Humphries.* They were important to my development as a medical student.

CRC: They were residents when I was a student.

WCR: *Do you attribute your getting interested in cardiology to them?*

CRC: Yes.

FIGURE 8. CRC at age 29 (1963) as a Captain in the US Army.

WCR: *You've always been a pretty good athlete and lots of surgeons tend to be athletes. Did surgery appeal to you?*

CRC: Cardiac surgery did eventually. When I was there, *Alfred Blalock, Henry Bahnson, Dave Sabiston*, and *Frank Spencer* were there. That's a pretty good crew of heart surgeons who led the world for many years. Hank Bahnson actually tried to recruit me into the surgical program when I was a senior student. I had a long talk with him. I was pretty much committed to medicine at that time. I had given it some thought and I actually gave it some thought a little bit later when I was a cardiology fellow. I talked with *Vince Gott* about that. The other person who had a lot of influence on my life was Leigh Cluff. I worked with Leigh as a medical student one summer between my junior and senior years on the relation of Staphylococcal skin infection to endotoxin in rabbits. My first article was published on that in the *Journal of Experimental Medicine.* I got a couple of other papers out of the work with him. During that time *Joe Johnson* and *Dick Reynolds* were in that lab. Both had an influence on my life. Joe Johnson was my chief resident when I was an intern. During my internship, I also worked with those guys and for a while I thought I was going to go into infectious disease. I got pretty good at it. I spent a lot of time with these fellows making rounds. But then I got a letter from John F. Kennedy, inviting me to join the Army.

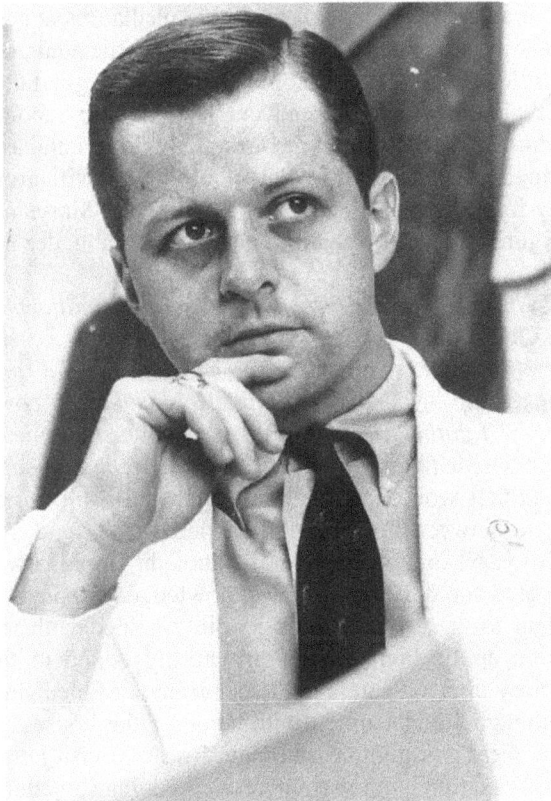

FIGURE 9. CRC at age 33 (1967) as Chief Resident on the Osler Medical Service at The Johns Hopkins Hospital.

WCR: *This was after internship and 1 year of residency.*

CRC: Right. It was when I was in the Army that I made the decision to go into cardiology. I thought a lot about it. I still was going into private practice. I wanted to be a cardiologist, and I talked with several people about it. I came back out of the Army, finished my residency, and then took a cardiology fellowship at Hopkins.

WCR: *For internship did you apply to places other than Hopkins? How did it come about that you did your internship on the Osler Medical Service?*

CRC: I applied to several places. My goal was to get on the Osler Medical Service. Quite frankly, I thought I had a good shot. I was AOA and I knew that others applying from Hopkins weren't necessarily AOA. I was never told that I had the job. This was in the days before matching. I went to Cornell, the University of Pennsylvania, Pennsylvania Hospital, Jefferson, Cincinnati General, and Yale-New Haven. I never went to Boston. Yale was as far north as I went. I thought I did pretty well on the interviews. I really wanted to stay at Hopkins, so I was delighted when accepted. There was a cut line at the assistant resident level then, but it wasn't as severe as it had been in the past.

WCR: *How many interns were on the Osler Medical Service then?*

CRC: My year it was 18.

WCR: *How many first-year residents?*

CRC: Probably about the same. When I was chief resident later on, we had 39 housestaff and me.

WCR: *That was in 1967.*

CRC: Right. We had 18 interns in my class. We always had 2 interns on a ward service of 31 patients or so, and 1, occasionally 2 residents, and usually just 1 assistant resident.

WCR: *You enjoyed your house officership at Hopkins?*

CRC: I loved it. We all lived across the street from the hospital. I was home for dinner every night, but I was back in the hospital every night also. We worked every day, took a little time off on Saturday or Sunday while the other intern covered. We averaged 1.7 admissions a day for each intern. Each ward had 31 patients. There was none of this 11 to 15 admissions a night. Current housestaff are just overwhelmed by this kind of stuff. They have the next day off, but the next day they are paralyzed. They can't even move. I don't think it's good for patient care. I don't think it's good for education. I thought the way we did it was ideal. We got up in the middle of the night if you were next up for a patient. If you were eighth or ninth up, you went to bed and got up when they called you. I thought it was good experience. Times have changed. In those days we didn't have as many diagnostic and therapeutic tools as we have now. Most admissions to the Osler Ward Service were people who were dying or close to dying. They were very sick, and this is still true in most academic hospitals. We still admit very sick people. What I went through was the best thing that could have happened to me.

WCR: *How did you happen to get into the Army? Everybody had to go in the Army back then.*

CRC: Berlin Wall. It went up. I had gone to NIH a couple of years before. I wanted to get a job in the cardiovascular section, but I didn't get one. I had gotten a job with *Vernon Knight* in infectious disease. Leigh Cluff had set that up. That was at a time when I was not sure I wanted to do that. I didn't go into the Berry plan and I didn't go to NIH. There were about 10 of us on medicine and surgery who got drafted during the year the Berlin Wall went up. I was not unhappy, quite frankly. I had 2 kids at the time. Jill and Jamie were born when I was an intern. We were hurting for money. We weren't making any as house officers. I was not unhappy to go in as a captain at a captain's salary. I went in in January 1962. I was drafted in 1961 and had to report to Fort Sam Houston, Texas, in 1962. I took all the family there. We had a good time in the Army. I never regretted it.

WCR: *You were in the Army 2 years. You were in Fort Sam Houston.*

CRC: Just for 6 weeks. We came back to Aberdeen Proving Ground, Kirk Army Hospital.

WCR: *What did you do there?*

CRC: Eventually, I became chief of the outpatient clinic. I worked in the outpatient clinic doing general medicine—taking care of soldiers and civilians, being the on-call person occasionally. After a year, I became the chief and administrated the place, but I also did clinical work. I did a lot of general medicine, including pediatrics and some office GYN. I volunteered to read all the electrocardiograms. (That's something you don't do in the Army!) The internists became good friends of mine. I'd take the electrocardiograms home at night (about 10 of them), read them all, write them out, and give them back to these guys the next day. They'd look at them, sign them, and send them in. It was at this time that I decided I wanted to do cardiology and thought this was a good opportunity to stay in cardiology a little bit. It was a fun time. I did another thing that not many doctors have done in the Army. I volunteered for the airborne infantry school at Fort Benning. To do that in the Army, you have to have at least a year left in the service, but if you were a physician you could do it any time. They think if you are going to do that, you might stay in. All of us drove off to Fort Benning (the 2 children, Ruthie, and me). Every day I went to school and earned my parachute wings. That was a fun thing for me.

WCR: *That was for how long?*

CRC: Four weeks.

WCR: *How many jumps did you make?*

CRC: Five out of an airplane, but many off the 250-foot and the 30-foot towers. The training was wonderful. They train you to react very quickly in circumstances that could be dangerous. The first week is physical training and physical conditioning. The next week is "ground week," when you jump off 3-foot ledges and learn how to fall. The next week is "tower week," when you go out on a 30-foot tower with a harness on you. You leap out down a line and go down maybe 60 yards or so. That gives you the feeling of coming out of an airplane. The final week you go on the airplane. Out you go. I was the second ranking officer in our platoon. The others were 18-year-old kids. I was in pretty good shape to keep up with those young kids running around. In the airborne you don't walk any place. You run everywhere. I was very proud to have been able to do that. I came back and worked in the outpatient clinic. I had a little more respect when I came back.

WCR: *Did you wear a different badge?*

CRC: No. I wore wings on my chest and on my overseas hat.

WCR: *Did you enjoy general medicine? Did you learn a good bit from that?*

CRC: I learned a lot from it. I thought I was pretty good. I'd been an Osler house officer for 18 months and had been exposed to a lot of sick people and knew I could take care of sick people. It was tremendous experience doing general medicine. Pediatrics is general medicine in little persons. It's not a little adult, but a little person. It took some doing, but I got fairly decent at that, too. I subsequently worked for a month almost 11 years straight in Ocean City, Maryland, as a general physician with one of the physicians there to pay for our annual vacation in Ocean City, Maryland. I figure I've got 3 years of general practice under my belt.

WCR: *So you did become a general practitioner?*

CRC: I did.

WCR: *When you were in medical school you hooked up with Leigh Cluff. How did that come about? I gather you did research your last couple of years in medical school? How did that come about?*

CRC: I worked at the Sacred Heart Hospital near home between my first and second and second and third years in medical school. I thought Hopkins was a place for developing new knowledge. I thought I ought to try to do that. It certainly helped with my intern application. It wouldn't hurt. I talked to the various division chiefs in the department of medicine. Although I had worked with some of the housestaff who were going into cardiology, I went to visit Leigh Cluff and told him I was interested in doing something that summer. I didn't have any ideas about what to do, and would he have an opening for a medical student to work in his laboratory. I knew a fair amount about microbiology because of my undergraduate courses in biology. I knew microbiology. I felt I might be able to do something there. He said, "Sure." Leigh had NIH money to support a student for the summer. Leigh got me on a project; he was the driving force behind it. The other person who was on the article we published a few years later was the technician who helped me. Leigh was the idea man and I talked a lot with him. I would go do things and come back and talk to him. While doing the research, I also made rounds with these guys—Leigh Cluff, Joe Johnson, Dick Reynolds, and *Bob Petersdorf.* A lot of their knowledge about infectious disease fell off on me and I learned a lot. That stayed with me. I'm a pretty good infectious disease guy. I don't remember all the drugs anymore, but I learned the basic principles of infectious disease from that experience. I worked there all summer, and then I came back some during the school year. I'd come in occasionally on Saturdays and do some experiments. I did that through my internship, too. We put something together and presented the material at the old Atlantic City meetings. Leigh tells the story about me (I think it's true) every time he gets a chance. When I was a medical student and we published this material, he got a phone call from somebody in infectious disease in Minneapolis asking, "How about this guy Conti? Do you think he could come up here and be an assistant professor?" I was a medical student. He embellishes it every time I hear it.

That was a good experience. I enjoyed working with Leigh and his colleagues. Subsequently, I worked with Joe as my chief resident. Dick Reynolds and Leigh Cluff subsequently came to Florida. Leigh Cluff actually recruited me to Florida. Dick Reynolds was there as chairman of community medicine. It was a nice circle of things that happened because of what I did with Leigh Cluff and what he offered me when I was a medical student.

WCR: *When you were a medical student you didn't have anybody guiding your career, so you had to find all these things out on your own.*

CRC: Absolutely.

WCR: *It's quite remarkable that you figured out that you'd better look into what research is, not only to help you get an internship, but probably self-consciously you may have been giving up that idea of being a family practitioner by then.*

CRC: I had. There's no question about that. I had decided that I was going to at least be an internist. That was my goal at that point. Infectious disease was something I considered.

WCR: *After the Army, you came back to Hopkins, and did another 18 months of medical residency. Then you went into cardiology for 2 years. You said that in the Army you really came to grips with the fact that you wanted to be a cardiologist. When you came back to Hopkins that was firm in your mind.*

CRC: It was very firm.

WCR: *You started talking to Dick Ross right away?*

CRC: I talked with him when I was in the Army. He couldn't guarantee anything, but he more or less said if I wanted to be an Osler house officer, we want you to be a fellow in cardiology. When I came back, there was very little room on the Osler housestaff for another assistant resident. I was doing consult work in cardiology on outpatients with Mike and O'Neal. They smoothed it up for me. Then, I went full time as an assistant resident.

WCR: *After your fellowship in cardiology, you were chief resident in medicine. Why did you do that?*

CRC: At the end of my first-year fellowship in 1965 to 1966 I got a call from Mac Harvey. It was probably Dick Ross that put him up to it. He said, "I'm interested in having you consider the job as chief resident in medicine. I want you to think about it a little bit, go home and talk it over with your wife, and come back and tell me." I said, "Dr. Harvey, I don't have to talk it over with anybody. I want to do it." I was so honored to be asked to be chief resident, because it was a big deal at Hopkins then. By now I was thinking of an academic career. I'd written an article with Bud Freisinger on constrictive pericarditis. I'd put a few other things together and I was getting into some research in the catheterization laboratory with coronary blood flow and some work in the dog lab involving counterpulsation. I thought being chief resident

was a step in the academic door at Hopkins. Dr. Harvey paid a lot of attention to his chief residents in terms of what their careers were going to be. There is a certain amount of ego involved here. I would head a bunch of smart people who were Osler house officers and I would have to be on my toes, make rounds every day, and teach them 3 times a week in the conferences or at least hold a conference and let everybody teach themselves. I thought it was a good opportunity for me, and I jumped at the chance. I never looked back. It was the toughest year I've ever worked in terms of physical demand, but I wouldn't have traded that year for anything.

WCR: *What was it like when you say physical demand? You were in the hospital all the time?*

CRC: I'd go home every night for dinner and come back every night. In those days you did all the consults on the ward service for the other services. If there was a ward service in OB/GYN and they had a problem with surgery, you did all the consults. The chief resident did them. That was one part of the experience. And the other part was to visit all the wards, see how things were going, get an idea what the patient load was, check a few charts every once in a while, see how the interns were coming along, identify some patients that were good for teaching for residents' rounds or for grand rounds. Every Tuesday I met with Dr. Harvey and said, "These are the 4 cases that I think we ought to present." He'd say, "Who do you want talking?" We'd pick out, not only the resident to present the case, but the faculty to discuss it. I'd get on the phone immediately thereafter and tell the faculty that Dr. Harvey wants you to discuss this case on Saturday morning. They'd all say "okay." There was never a question. We did that every Tuesday. It was a good job for me. Mac Harvey had an acute myocardial infarction the spring of 1968. He retired in 1972 at the age of 62. He died in 1999 of a stroke. Dick Ross was his doctor. I was his resident. He was on Myerburg, and I was assigned to watch the monitor because we didn't have a coronary care unit at the time. That year he was the president of the Association of American Physicians. He went to that meeting but gave his talk sitting down. Dick Ross wouldn't allow him to stand up to give the talk.

WCR: *Dick, you mentioned that while you were a fellow in cardiology that you had some second thoughts about not having taken up Henry Bahnson's offer to go into surgery and eventually cardiac surgery. You visited with Vince Gott. What was that about?*

CRC: That may have been while I was an assistant professor from 1968 to 1972. Vince was head of cardiac surgery. I sat down with him and chatted about things. At that time cardiac surgery was taking off. Bypass surgery was just coming in. We'd done a heart transplant in 1968 on my patient. He died 5 weeks later, but it was the first heart transplant at Hopkins. I guess I was musing about things. I felt things that were going on in surgery then were pretty interesting. Vince perked his ears up a little. We left it at that. I didn't go any further than that, but it crossed my mind. I thought back to when Dr. Bahnson talked to me about it and I told Vince Gott that. I don't know if it would have been a good thing or not. What's happened to me has been good for me, and I've been good for what I've done with the people I've worked with. I don't regret not doing that.

WCR: *Now things seem to have swung back toward medicine in so many arenas, particularly coronary artery disease.*

CRC: Do you know about the RAVEL trial? That's a study that's been done outside the USA. The drug Rapamycin, an antibiotic, produces good immune suppression and it has been impregnated in stents. It elutes from the stent over a 10- to 12-day period. The RAVEL Trial compared stents with the drug to those without the drug on about 250 patients. In those without the drug there was a 26% restenosis rate; in those with the drug, a 0% restenosis rate.

WCR: *And that's how long an interval?*

CRC: At least 6 months, but probably more. That is impressive. That data was presented at the European Congress. It's not published yet.

WCR: *I recall that Vince Gott got his job at Hopkins because of impregnating the valve with heparin.*

CRC: Yes. Heparin, benzalkonium graphite. GBH. I think it was a disk valve.

WCR: *Dick, when you finished the chief residency, I gather you were offered a faculty position in cardiology. You started as head of the cath lab immediately? Is that when Mike Criley left or what exactly happened?*

CRC: Mike had gone. Bud Freisinger was still there. Yes, I was head of the cath lab at the time. Initially, it was just me. Eventually, *Larry Griffith* came, and we worked in the cath lab together. Then, Bud left. Bud was there for a year and was very helpful to me as a young guy trying to do a lot of coronary angiography. We were switching over from the Sone's technique, which is what I learned from Bud and others. I had to teach myself how to do the Judkin's technique, which was relatively simple compared to the Sones method, but it too had some problems. One was that it was so easy that you could engage the coronary arteries sometimes too much. You'd intubate the coronary arteries a little bit more than you'd like to. You had to be careful about that. You had to be careful about anticoagulation because this was an end hole catheter and you could get clots in it. If you flushed that clot, it would go right into the coronary artery. This probably was done on several occasions. I had good back up people. We worked pretty hard. Those were the days when we did a

maximum of 10 cases a week—1 in the morning, 1 in the afternoon. Now, we're doing 10 to 12 cases a day. The volume has changed dramatically. I sometimes wonder about research. It's a lot more difficult to do research in the cath lab now because of the large volume of patients. We did a lot of investigation during the Dick Ross, Bud Freisinger, Mike Criley years in the catheter laboratory. A lot of material came out of that laboratory. Times have changed dramatically in the catheterization laboratory. That was what I wanted to do. When I was a fellow, I was basically the only one doing coronary angiography. Whenever there were coronary angiograms to be done, I was the fellow assisting the faculty physician doing it. I had relatively a lot of experience doing that and felt comfortable. I knew this was what I wanted to do. I got good experience with congenital heart disease also. *Helen Taussig* was still there and *Catherine Neal* was there. We studied those patients in their adolescent years. Fourteen was considered an adult in those days and adult cardiologists did the studies. I got a lot of experience with post-op tetalogies, pre-op tets , and post-op shunts. That has really helped me in recent times, because we now see a lot of these patients and few are trained in this area. I feel pretty comfortable in this arena. I can help out with the teaching of our fellows in this area. I spent many hours with Helen Taussig going over the angiograms of patients who she was either taking care of or was sending to surgery.

WCR: *How did it come about that you moved to Gainesville, Florida?*

CRC: I was interested in becoming chief of cardiology someplace. I had looked at a couple of positions. One was at Baylor, where they wanted a chief of a cath lab and not a chief of cardiology. *Henry McIntosh* was chairman of Medicine there and he was not willing to give up the job as chief of cardiology. I talked with Henry and told him that that was not what I wanted. I wanted to be chief. I also went to the Medical College of Ohio in Toledo several times. It was not yet ready for prime time. They didn't have a university hospital. I was in Hopkins where we had all those things and I felt this was not the job for me. The third place I visited was Louisiana State University. The chairman there was *Fred Allison*, a wonderful guy in infectious disease, who knew me from infectious disease times. They did not have a university hospital; they had Charity Hospital, which was a huge hospital with lots of cardiomyopathy and valve disease patients. My interest was ischemic heart disease. I wanted to go to a place where I could see patients with ischemic heart disease. That is what I felt was my future.

I went to one of the old Atlantic City meetings and walked into a lounge where Leigh Cluff and a couple of others were sitting. I had a drink with them. Cluff

FIGURE 10. CRC at age 39 (1973) as an Associate Professor of Medicine at The Johns Hopkins Hospital.

At that time, there were how many cardiologists already there?

CRC: Five: *Jape Taylor, Russ Green, Lamar Crevass, Mahfouz El Shahawy,* and *Charlie Curry.* I brought 3 other people with me: Carl Pepine; *Dan Wise,* a Hopkins fellow to run the echocardiography laboratory, and *Wilmer Nichols,* a physiologist.

WCR: *So you started with 8.*

CRC: Right. We had 2 hospitals, a VA hospital and a university hospital to run. It was a lot of work. We stuck together for a year at least. Dan Wise then left to go back to Charlotte into private practice; Mahfouz El Shahawy went to Sarasota into private practice, and Charlie Curry went to Orlando into private practice. Carl Pepine and Wilmer Nichols are still there.

WCR: *Twenty-four years as chief of cardiology in a university department in the USA is longer than anyone in your era. Isn't that right?*

CRC: I think that's correct. There are people now who may go beyond that. *Bob Myerburg* (Miami) may be beyond it now. *Barry Zaret* (New Haven) is probably going to 25. I talked with him recently and he said he was thinking about stepping down after 25 years. I think *George Beller* (Charlottesville) is past 20 years.

WCR: *When you stepped down as chief in 1999, how many were in your cardiovascular division?*

CRC: About 18 clinical faculty, but we had other researchers and connections with other cardiologists in surrounding areas.

WCR: *Dick, what are the things you are most proud of during your 24 years as chief of the cardiovascular division at the University of Florida?*

CRC: As chief of the division, my thoughts were as follows: nobody works for me; I work for them. I really believe that. I think people in leadership positions need to say that. The President of the United States is paid by us and therefore he works for us. We don't work for him. I felt my job was to promote nationally and internationally the faculty in the division. I tried to get them on appropriate committees in the ACC and AHA—things like that. I worked hard at that, and I think I did a pretty decent job. When I went to Florida I had an RO1 from the NIH. My goal when I went to Florida was not to keep that RO1 up or do research in the cath lab. We published a lot of material

said, "I've been looking for a chief of cardiology for a year now, and I can't find one." I said, "What about me?" He didn't know I was interested. He thought I still wanted to stay at Hopkins. I said, "Hopkins is my life. I love it. I owe it everything I am, but I'm interested in being chief somewhere. I'd like to put my name on something and I think I can do it." I visited him a couple of months later, taking Ruthie and the kids, and they all liked Florida. He said, "Do you know anybody else?" Somebody at Florida mentioned *Carl Pepine* to me. He was in the Navy at the Naval Hospital in Philadelphia. I went to a meeting in New York and Carl and I had lunch together. I said, "Carl, I want to be in the cath lab, but I need somebody to be a cath lab director. You are now running a cath lab. I asked if he would be interested and he said "yes." We went down to Florida together (both families) the next time. Carl and I hit it off, and we have been together ever since. We're close friends. I was chief for 24 years and now he's the chief. My job is to help Carl do good things. I accepted the chief's job in November 1973, and both Carl and I went there in July 1974.

WCR: *You were 39 years of age when you became full professor and chief of the cardiovascular division.*

FIGURE 11. CRC at age 44 (1978) after just finishing a marathon.

which I was a part of, but there were other people leading the way in those areas and my job was to coordinate it and make sure everybody was happy in the sense that they liked being there. I think I did that. That is one reason the division was successful. We had turnover, but we didn't have gross turnover. Five present chiefs of cardiology at university medical centers came out of our program: Carl Pepine at Florida, *Jay Mehta* in Little Rock, *George Abela* in East Lansing, *Danie Marx* in South Africa, and *Filippo Crea* in Rome, Italy.

WCR: *You've been quite productive ever since you've been in academic medicine. How have you done most of your writing? Have you done it at home or at work?*

CRC: In recent years it's both at work and at home. In earlier years it was mostly at home. Now that I am no longer chief, I have a little bit more freedom at work. In the past I've done practically all my writing on weekends or nights or on airplanes. That was the way it was at Hopkins, too. I may not have done it at home when I was at Hopkins as much, but I came back to the hospital at night when I wasn't doing anything else to do that kind of stuff. It took a lot of work. I learned how to write by doing it and by getting criticism from others. I've lots of role models in my life, and Dick Ross was a role model in this respect. He could take the most complicated mess of data and

make sense out of it and put it down on paper so that everybody else could understand it. Some of that rubbed off on me. I have some of that talent. I'm not as good as he was, but he was unique in that regard. He was a master at simplifying very complicated stuff so that you could educate your colleagues and bring new knowledge to the table. I never wanted to be dean or chairman of a department of medicine. I always liked being chief of cardiology and a cardiologist. I wanted to stay visible as a clinical cardiologist, so I didn't follow other paths. I appreciate what I learned from him. It wasn't that we sat down and talked about it a lot. I just watched him.

WCR: *How many fellows have you trained in total?*

CRC: About 120.

WCR: *That's fantastic!*

CRC: We have had an annual reunion the last 2 years. The first year we had about 70 and this year about 50. They were different people each year.

WCR: *Dick, was it hard for you to give up the cath lab?*

CRC: In some ways it was. That's what I did, and I thought I did it pretty well. I looked at my career and said, "I'm getting a lot of radiation. I've been in the cath lab since 1965 and radiation control was not as good in the early days. We never wore glasses or thyroid gland protectors, and therefore the radiation was more than today. We exposed patients and ourselves a lot longer despite not doing angioplasty. Angioplasty is a biggie. I thought it was time for me to get out of the catheterization laboratory for my own safety for one thing. I was still good at what I did. I did transseptal studies a year or 2 ago for our electrophysiology people because they weren't trained to do them. Now we have a person who is very good at it and they don't need me anymore. I don't do anything in the cath lab now. Honestly, Bill, I think I could go in there and do a coronary angiogram tomorrow without any problems. Angioplasty is another story. I never did angioplasty, but I helped Carl with the first 10 or so that were done here. When I left, I felt good about leaving. I felt that the cath lab was in good hands. It's a young man's job. You have a lot of weight on your shoulders literally because of the lead aprons, but also because of the danger associated with cardiac catheterization. Although we joke with our guys about that, you've got to be thinking on your feet all the time. It's like surgery. All these guys have cognitive skills. They need to be thinking. They've got to move fast. Carl did the same thing. Carl came out of the cath laboratory. He doesn't go in there anymore.

WCR: *Dick, you've received a lot of honors for your work. Certainly being president of the American College of Cardiology must have been quite an honor for you.*

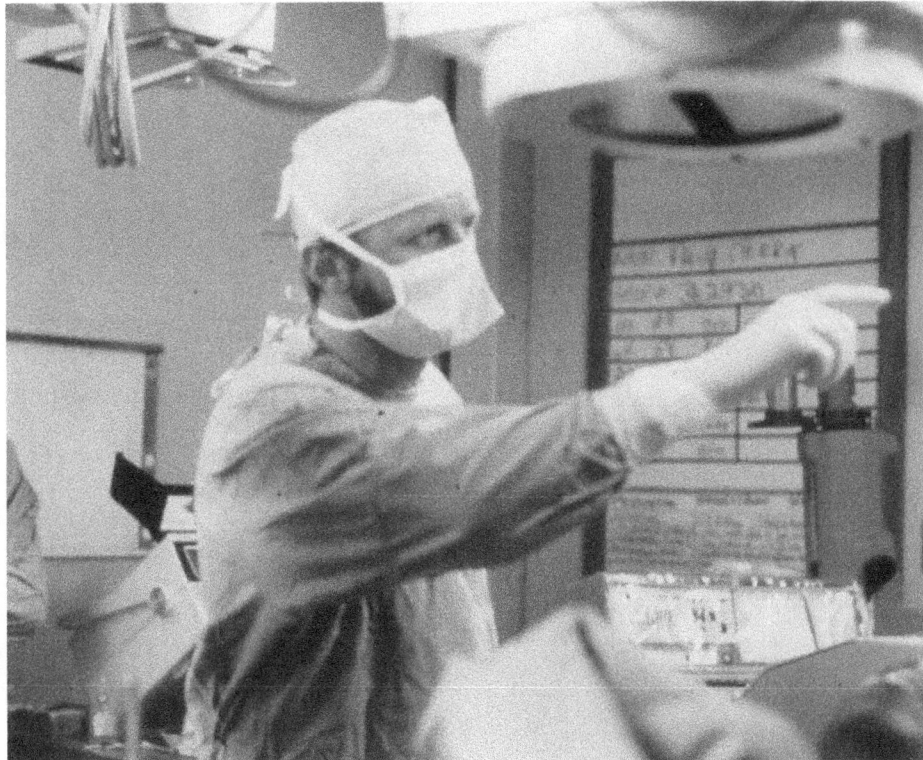

FIGURE 12. CRC at age 50 (1984) working in the catheterization laboratory at the University of Florida.

FIGURE 13. CRC at age 53 (1978) during a ski race at Snowmass, Colorado.

CRC: It really was. I was delighted with that, to say the least. I was very fortunate to be president at a time when education was the major thrust of the American College of Cardiology. We had some private sector and government relations, but we now have tremendous pressure to deal with reimbursement—things that are extremely important for our survival, but not the kind of thing that I enjoy. I enjoyed working with the educational programs and education in general. I was on every education committee of the college. That was important to me. It was a fun year. I really enjoyed it. I worked hard and was away a lot. When I wasn't away, I was on the telephone with *Bill Nelligan*, the executive director, trying to solve little issues for the members of the college. It's one of those things I am glad to have done. I learned the job after about 6 months and then I was gone. It probably would be better if one could do the job for 2 years. You really

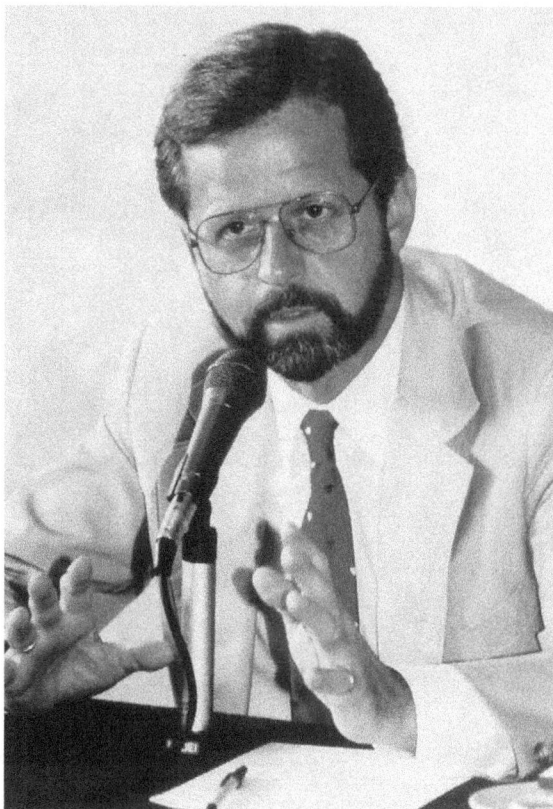

FIGURE 14. CRC at age 53 (1987) during a panel discussion at a meeting in Kyoto, Japan.

FIGURE 15. CRC at age 55 (1989) when President of the American College of Cardiology.

have to stop doing what you're doing, so taking 2 years off would be too much.

WCR: *Tell me about the title you received from the West Palm Beach Heart Association—Eminent Scholar. What is that about?*

CRC: It's sort of a pretentious title, but it's a real one. It's basically an endowed professorship. If the donor donates $600,000 to the University, the State will match it with $400,000. The Palm Beach Heart Association donated $600,000 to the University of Florida. There was a national search for a person to fill that position. The donation is an attempt to attract top-ranked people to the University of Florida. Mine was a clinical professorship for teaching in cardiology. We have another one from the Palm Beach Heart Association for research. We had a search for the clinical professorship and I let it be known that I also was interested in it. After about 18 months, the people in Palm Beach got itchy: "How come we don't have this position filled yet? How come you're not giving us this opportunity? Conti's got the credentials." This was before I was President of the American College of Cardiology. Eventually, the job came to me. I wasn't on the selection committee. Right now it is worth over $2,000,000. A million-dollar endowment today is only $50,000 annually. But $2,000,000 is getting up there. That makes a difference in terms of an annual endowment to your salary. It doesn't add to my salary, it's

instead of some state salary or clinical monies. At the University of Florida we talk with out division chief and department chairman about what salary range we should have and that's it for full-time salaried employees. The "Eminent Scholar" is an academic rank above Professor, which annoys some Professors, but that's the way it is. My ID card says I'm a scholar.

WCR: *Do you think cardiologists ought to be on salary?*

CRC: I like the idea for myself, provided that I can supplement my income with academic things, like giving lectures or grand rounds or being an editor. If I only had my academic salary, I wouldn't be as happy as I am now. I'm not making tons of money, but I'm happy and I'm satisfied. Knowing my own personality, if my salary depended on my hustling all the time clinically, I might not have done some of the things that I've done. I might be out there hustling too much to make income. It's a trade off. Academic faculty tend to forget that our association dues are paid, we've got good insurance, we have no overhead, we've got a paid secretary, and we've got retirement. We don't do a good job of recruiting people from that perspective. Although the physicians in practice have a Mercedes in the front yard, a boat in the back yard, and have a wonderful life, they pay 40% of their income for expenses to practice. I wouldn't trade what I've done for anything. I think I made the right decision and I've never been unhappy about it.

FIGURE 16. CRC at age 55 (1989) when presenting Pope John Paul II with a portable electrocardiogram on behalf of the American College of Cardiology.

WCR: *Dick, I've admired your editorship of* Clinical Cardiology. *Your string of not missing a month of editorials since 1988 is admirable. Nobody else probably has done that in the history of medical editing. I gather that you enjoy this endeavor.*

CRC: My focus is cardiovascular medicine, not problems in medicine, or ethics, or reimbursement or those kinds of things. I'm much more focused on the clinical problems that I see and sometimes don't understand. I want to understand them, so I sit down and work them out. I figure if I don't understand a clinical problem, that there are lots of others who don't understand it either, and I can put it down.

WCR: *How much time does* Clinical Cardiology *occupy for you in a week or a month?*

CRC: On a daily basis, no more than 90 minutes. I talk to the editorial staff at the publisher's office. I send manuscripts out for review and get them back. If the potential reviewer returns the manuscript without review, I send it out again. That takes a lot of my time. Decision-making on manuscripts coming back from reviewers is pretty easy for me. We have a fairly good scoring system. I read what the reviewers say and rarely disagree with them. I go pretty much by what they say. The administrative aspects of it are time consuming. The editorials take my time. I have to think about what I want to say pretty far in advance. I like to have 3 or 4 lined up. I don't do this on a monthly basis at the last minute, worrying about what I'm going to talk about. I know what's coming up for 5 months. I fine-tune them a little bit when I look at

them again. Anytime I go to a major meeting, I'll think "That sounds like an interesting thing." That becomes an editorial or a clinical problem I've seen becomes an editorial. A doctor called me. He said, "I've got this 42-year-old lady. She's had an acute myocardial infarction and she's menstruating. What do I do?" After I had researched the problem, I learned that the mechanism of menstruation is different from bleeding elsewhere. It's a sloughing. The physician administered a thrombolytic and the patient did fine. That was one editorial. How many people have had that happen to them? Few.

WCR: *How are you enjoying your editorship of* ACCEL?

CRC: This is different. This takes a fair amount of time. I go to 3 major cardiac meetings each year: European Congress of Cardiology, American Heart Association, and American College of Cardiology. I also go to *Valentin Fuster's* meeting in New York and *Jack Vogel's* meeting in Snowmass. I get top-of-the-line, brand new stuff, but I have to be away for these 5 meetings and I have to listen to the presentations. At the American College of Cardiology meeting we get about 150 interviews. They range from 10 to 20 minutes apiece. I listen to every one of them. I also have the typed transcripts of every one of them. If I don't like what was said, I edit it on the transcript and send it back. With the digital technology we have now, it's a cut and paste job. I tell the members on the board that my job is to make them sound good. It works out well. I can eliminate some of the extraneous stuff. It's been fun and I've enjoyed it. I now have a much better appreciation of how hard the previous editor of *ACCEL* worked on it. I have a little different approach. I probably edit the stuff a bit more than he did. My editorials there are also clinical and not related to nonclinical things. I've been doing it over 18 months. The job is a 5-year one, just like the editorship of the *Journal of the American College of Cardiology* with an option for another 5 years. I will see how I feel at the end of 5 years.

WCR: *How much time is* ACCEL *taking you now?*

CRC: There are times when I have to do a lot of listening. At the upcoming American Heart Association meeting we will have 100 interviews. After that meeting I spend maybe 20 hours a week, including the weekends. When I'm out walking or jogging, I have the headset and am listening to these interviews. I do it when I'm doing other things. I can't write and do it because I've got to be listening. The average time throughout the year is about 12 hours a week. It's all done at home. I can't do it at work because I've got other things I have to do there.

WCR: *Could you speak briefly about your international statesmanship? It seems to me that you are the USA's no. 1 international spokesman in cardiology. You've been involved actively with the Europeans and Asians for years. Also, how do you manage your travels with your other responsibilities, particularly when you were chief of the division?*

CRC: The last one is tough. Everyone expects attendance at the major meetings. I try to keep it to a minimum. I've never refused a friend (people I have trained, people like yourself, or people who have major meetings someplace else) unless I had something else I had to do at that time. Or if it's someplace I've never been that I'd really like to go with my wife. That doesn't come up often. Since I've taken over *ACCEL*, I have cut back a lot on travel and now go only to national meetings. I'm doing less traveling now than when I was chief of the division. Maybe when you're chief of the division you get more invitations. Those invitations still come, but I have a better ability to say "no" now than I did in the early days. We were allowed about 20 administrative days (working days) a year and about 30 days vacation (working days). A lot of time I used those vacation days for travel. I felt that it was part vacation and part work, so I used that.

WCR: *What about your international trips?*

CRC: In recent years, I have focused mainly on the European Society of Cardiology (ESC). I'm a 1989 fellow of the ESC. No other American received a second fellowship that year. That was the year I was President of the College. I'm a founding fellow of the ESC. During the presidency I spent a lot of time with the leaders of the ESC in trying to develop a relationship with the ACC. *Hans Peter Kraynbeul* was pres-

ident of the ESC when I was president of the ACC. He is Swiss. He and I worked out the ACC/ESC symposium that is now done at each other's meeting. That was the first step. The second step was Merck's funding a 3-week travel for a young cardiologist in the USA with a senior person also going along. I was the first one to do that in Europe. After the ESC meeting in Europe, we went to the Netherlands, England, Germany, and France. That got me in the mode of trying to do things internationally. The Europeans did the same thing the following year in the USA. That's been going back and forth since then. I initiated that, but Merck funded it. We have had, since that time, a meeting of the leadership (president and president-elect of both societies) at each other's meeting to discuss common things. One was electronic publishing. Electronic publishing basically has boiled down to getting Elsevier hooked up with the ESC publisher. Now Elsevier is the ESC publisher. We tried to do it with the American Heart Association, but they weren't interested in having a single website to get to the journals published by these publishers. It took a lot of negotiation. All we could do was recommend it. It was the publishers who had to make the decision. I was the official liaison of the American College of Cardiology to the European Society of Cardiology for a couple of years. Now they have made that the job of the president. I was not president when I was the liaison. There is some advantage to that in that there are fewer people involved. The disadvantage is that the president is there for a year only and there is no continuity. Some presidents are known by Europeans and some aren't. Most of the European presidents have international reputations as academic cardiologists.

WCR: *Could you talk a bit about Ruthie and your family?*

CRC: I met Ruthie when we were children in 1948. The first romantic encounter I had with her was when she invited me to a Sadie Hawkin's Day dance at Central Catholic High School when we were sophomores. It was off and on for a while and then we became very close friends and boy friend/girl friend. We graduated that way from high school and remained that way until we got married in 1957. I was a second-year medical student when we married. During my first year of medical school, I wrote a letter to Ruthie every day and she wrote me one. They were short letters, but 365 of them. When I went home for Christmas I talked it over with my parents, particularly my mom. I told her "I'm lonely. I'd like to be married. I want to marry Ruthie." I bought her an engagement ring for Christmas and we got engaged Christmas day. We married the following August 24, 1957. That's 44 years married to the same person! Our twin girls (identical) were born in 1960 (*Jill and Jamie*) at Hopkins when I was an intern. I was work-

FIGURE 17. CRC and Ruthie in 1990 (both aged 56) with their 4 offspring (Jamie, Richard, Jennifer, and Jill).

ing that Sunday, and they were born about 7:30 P.M. Joe Johnson, the chief resident, said, "Why don't you take a couple of hours off?" I did. Ruthie was in the hospital for a couple of days. They were fine healthy babies. One was 5.5 and the other 5.0 pounds. They grew up in "the compound." They got to know all our friends on the housestaff and their children. We had a good time, and it was a good way to grow up, a lot of young people, people doing the same thing. It was very good for them. *Jennifer*, our middle daughter, was born when I was in the Army, and she was delivered by an Army obstetrician. I gave anesthesia for the delivery. I was there for all of our children's births. I saw every one of them being born. When Jill and Jamie were born 2 obstetricians disagreed; one said there were twins in there and the other said there was just a single baby. I kept saying that it had to be a single baby. It wasn't.

WCR: *You didn't hear 2 heart beats?*

CRC: I don't remember hearing 2 heart beats. With Jennifer, Ruthie had local anesthesia only. I helped the obstetrician with an inhaler. Our son *Richard* was born in 1966 when I was a cardiology fellow. *Jack Johnson* was the faculty person who delivered him. Jack later came to Florida as an obstetrician in the department of OB/GYN and is still there.

WCR: *Your kids have done quite well?*

CRC: Jill is a lawyer, board certified in family law, and lives in Gainesville. She's married to a radiologist, *Ross Zeanah*. Jamie is a cardiologist, an associate professor in our cardiology division, doing electrophysiology. She's married to a doctor, *Robert Yancey*, who has an infectious disease practice. Richard is an airline pilot, something he wanted to do since age 6. He built them, flew remote controlled planes, and took lessons when he was in college. He is now a Delta pilot, flying a 737 out of Orlando. He's loves it. Jennifer, a marketing major who has worked in the pharmaceutical industry, also lives in Orlando and she's married to *Andy Ponseigo*, an airline pilot also.

WCR: *How many grandchildren do you have?*

CRC: We have 5. One is a step grandchild that Ross and Jill have. Jamie has twins (boy and girl). Jennifer has 2 girls.

WCR: *Do you still play golf? How do you fit that in?*

CRC: I live 10 minutes from a golf course. Playing 18 holes takes 4 or 5 hours, so I infrequently play 18 holes. I don't have time to play during the work week. I play in the afternoons on weekends after I do my morning rounds or other responsibilities on Saturday mornings. Often, Carl Pepine and I play a round of

FIGURE 18. CRC while golfing in Hawaii at age 61 (1995).

golf together. We solve some of the problems of the world while we're playing. I play about 100 times a year. If I go on vacation to Hawaii, I'll play 5 days in a row there.

WCR: *Do you get up about 6:00 A.M.?*

CRC: Every day.

WCR: *What time do you leave the house for the hospital?*

CRC: It varies. In chief-of-cardiology days it was 7:00. These days it's 8:00. It takes me 10 to 15 minutes to get to work.

WCR: *What time do you leave the hospital at night?*

CRC: Oftentimes it's after 6:00 P.M. When I was chief, I would say: "I only work half a day—7:00 A.M. to 7:00 P.M. Leaving late avoids some traffic. The traffic from 5:00 to 5:30 P.M. is heavy and it takes almost as long to get home as if I leave at 6:00. With less administrative responsibilities, I can leave the hospital a bit earlier. Most of the time now I get home about 6:00 P.M. or a little later. I still like to go to work early while it's quiet and I can get things done, but I don't go to work at 7:00 A.M. anymore.

WCR: *Do you go in on Saturdays only when you are on the ward duty?*

CRC: Yes, nowadays, only when I'm on ward duty. All of my life I've been going in on Saturday and Sunday, but that's changed since I'm not the chief anymore. I did that when I was at Hopkins when I was running the cath lab. I was in there every weekend and practically every night after dinner. My job was a full-time job, and that's one of the things I am forever grateful to Ruthie about. She thinks her job is a full-time job, too, and it was. There's plenty of credit to go to her for her raising the children, because she was there all the time, there for them, and I wasn't. I was there at dinner. I made sure of that.

WCR: *How many people subscribe to ACCEL now?*

CRC: I'm told it's about 5,000 in the USA, but there's another number out there of industry subscribers in Europe and places like that. They get a break on subscriptions. They don't pay the same thing as ACC members.

WCR: *How many copies of* Clinical Cardiology *go out each month?*

CRC: About 35,000.

WCR: *That's a big impact.*

CRC: Yes. It is a big impact. It goes to everybody with a cardiovascular interest.

WCR: *Is that in the world, or just the USA?*

CRC: Just in the USA. Outside the USA, they have to buy it. In the USA, industry advertisements pay for it. I don't know how they get by with that either, but they do.

WCR: *What are the things you are most proud of in your career?*

CRC: There are a couple of things I'm very proud of. I'm proud of my children for one thing and my wife. Ruthie has done a wonderful job. I'm proud of things I've done. I'm proud of the division. I'm very jealous of the division in that I don't want anybody making it a poor division. I would work hard to prevent that. That's why I said that my job is to help Carl Pepine maintain the status of the division and get it better. It's no longer my division, but it was. Several people here are people I recruited. I'm proud of what I've done with the American College of Cardiology. I'm proud to have been its president. I've enjoyed playing a major role in some of the educational things of the college, particularly the extramural programs.

WCR: *Dick, I know you've had a number of offers through the years and you've had 2 academic appointments, one at Hopkins and one at the University of Florida. How have you been able to stay put, so to speak?*

CRC: I like living in Florida for one. I'm not driven to succeed. I like to take advantage of what's out there so that I can use it. I didn't think our division was where it ought to be for about 10 years. After 10 years we started getting to where we were doing pretty good stuff, we were big enough, and we were seeing a lot of patients referred to us. That has continued to grow. If you had asked me, if you had been offered the job to come back to Hopkins as chief of cardiology, would you have taken it? There's a very good chance I would have. I owe Hopkins everything. Everything I am in cardiology and medicine is related to what I learned as

FIGURE 19. CRC at age 65 (1999) when he stepped down as the Chief of Cardiology at the University of Florida.

a student, house officer, and faculty person there. I love the place and I'm very loyal to it, not only emotionally but also financially. I feel that it's my alma mater. I'm very proud to have come from that place. After 17 years or so in Baltimore, we settled in Gainesville. Our children grew up in Florida. It is not a good time to move when your kids go off to college because they come back and don't know anybody if you've moved. Ruthie entered into it a lot. She said she liked Florida and wanted to live here. When a West Coast program recruited me, she said, "It's okay. You can go there, but it's going to be a long commute." Ruthie has never held me back. She says those things, but she would have done what was best for all of us. I didn't give much thought to being chairman of medicine. That would have been the next step for me. Quite frankly I thought it would be a step backwards for me. I thought I would lose my identity as a clinical cardiologist. There are so few that hold the line. *Gene Braunwald* and *Willis Hurst* are exceptions. I like being admired as a clinical cardiologist, and I want to continue to do it.

WCR: *Dick, is there anything you'd like to discuss that we haven't discussed?*

CRC: No. I think we've covered more than I thought we were going to coverFig. 19. I'm quite happy doing what I'm doing right now. If you made me grade my happiness, it's probably the highest it's ever been right now. I do have a little more time for my wife and my family. Although I now usually go to work at 8:00 A.M., sometimes it is 8:30 because I'm out jogging or walking with Ruthie, something I never did before. I didn't have time to do that. There is going to come a time when I'm going to retire, but it's not around the corner. I think I'm rounding third, heading

for home, but I'm not there yet. I don't look forward to retirement. I love my job. I like going to work. If you ask me what I'd really like to do (and I want you to ask me that), I'd like to do nothing but teach for the rest of my career and not have to be bothered with signing charts and writing notes, which are similar to what the resident writes, the morning of seeing the patient. Some of this is sort of demeaning to senior professors of medicine. Serving almost as a chief resident again is not pleasant. There are ways of making it easier. I don't think this is ego talking here, but I think senior professors should not have to do this kind of stuff to make their salary. I like teaching medical students, residents, and fellows. I'm pretty good at it. I like it in small groups. Patient teaching is fun for me. Right now the pressure is on all of us in academic medicine to teach less and practice more. The pressure now is to make sure you know the intimate details of every patient. I don't mind that. But then having to write about it and to bill for it based on how much time you spent doing it, I don't like that. I wish I could get rid of it. If somebody offered me a job at Florida in the division to say all you have to do is teach, I'd love it. That would be wonderful. I consider writing and editing a form of teaching. When I write an editorial, I'm teaching somebody something, myself for sure. *ACCEL* is a big learning thing for cardiologists.

WCR: *Dick, you've really done a marathon chore today. As mentioned earlier, speaking at least 3 hours this morning and now 3-1/2 more hours straight. That's 6-1/2 hours that I've seen you today talking, and I'm sure you said a few words to some other people today.*

CRC: I took a nap.

WCR: *Nevertheless, on behalf of not just me, of course, but the readers of* The American Journal of Cardiology, *I want to thank you for pouring your soul out, so to speak. I appreciate it.*

CRC's Best Publications as Chosen by Him (each is numbered as in his CV)

2. Conti CR, Cluff LE, Scheder EP. Studies on the pathogenesis of staphylococcal infection: IV. The effect of bacterial endotoxin. *J Exp Med* 1961;113:845–859.
3. Goldfarb D, Conti CR, Brown BG, Gott VL. Treatment of severe cardiogenic shock by diastolic augmentation after ligation and division of the left circumflex coronary artery in dog. *J Thorac Cardiovasc Surg* 1966;51:783–796.
6. Conti CR, Friesinger GC. Chronic constrictive peridarditis—clinical and laboratory findings in 11 cases. *Johns Hopkins Med J* 1967;120:262–274.
12. Dagenais GR, Gundel WD, Conti CR. Peripheral venospasm associated with signs of transient myocardial ischemia. *Am Heart J* 1970;80:544–549.
14. Milnor WR, Conti CR, Lewis KB, O'Rourke MF. Pulmonary arterial pulse wave velocity and impedance in man. *Circ Res* 1969;25:637–649.
16. Conti CR, Pitt B, Gundel WD, Friesinger GC, Ross RS. Myocardial blood flow in pacing induced angina. *Circulation* 1970;42:815–825.
18. Conti CR, Page E, Humphries JO, Pitt B, Ross RS. Objective evaluation of aortic-coronary vein bypass surgery. *Trans Assoc Am Physicians* 1971;84:272–280.
20. Graber JG, Conti CR, Lappe DL, Ross RS. Effect of pacing-induced tachycardia and myocardial ischemia on ventricular pressure-velocity relationships in man. *Circulation* 1972;46:74–83.
23. Griffith LSC, Achuff SC, Conti CR, Humphries JO, Brawley PK, Gott VL, Ross RS. Changes in intrinsic coronary circulation and segmental ventricular

motion after saphenous vein coronary baypass surgery. *N Engl J Med* 1973;288: 589–595.

25. Conti CR, Brawley RK, Griffith LS, Pitt B, Humphries JO, Gott VL, Ross RS. Unstable angina: morbidity and mortality in fifty-seven consecutive patients evaluated angiographically. *Am J Cardiol* 1973;32:745–750.

32. Plotnick GD, Conti CR. Transient ST-segment elevation in unstable angina clinical and hemodynamic significance. *Circulation* 1975;51:1015–1019.

36. Conti CR, Ross RS, Brawley RK, Plotnick G, Gott VL, Donahoo JS, Becker LC. Unstable angina pectoris: National Cooperative Study Group to Compare Medical and Surgical Therapy. I. Report of protocol and patient population. *Am J Cardiol* 1976;37:896–902.

46. Plotnick GD, Conti CR. Unstable angina: angiography, short and long term morbidity, mortality, and symptomatic status of medically treated patients. *Am J Med* 1977;63:870–873.

47. Nichols WW, Conti CR, Walker WE, Milnor WR. Input impedance of the systemic circulation in man. *Circ Res* 1977;40:451–458.

49. Curry RC, Pepine CJ, Sabom MB, Feldman RL, Christie LG, Conti CR. Effects of ergonovine in patients with and without coronary artery disease. *Circulation* 1977;56:803–809.

51. Feldman RL, Nichols WW, Pepine CJ, Conti CR. Hemodynamic significance of the length of a coronary arterial narrowing. *Am J Cardiol* 1978;41:865–871.

52. Conti CR, Pepine CJ, Feldman RL. The angiographic definition of critical coronary stenosis. *Acta Med Scand* 1978;615(suppl):9–17.

54. Pepine CJ, Nichols WW, Conti CR. Aortic input impedance in heart failure. *Circulation* 1978;58:460–465.

57. Feldman RL, Nichols WW, Pepine CJ, Conti CR. Hemodynamic effects of long and multiple coronary arterial narrowings. *Chest* 1978;74:280–285.

68. Curry RC, Pepine CJ, Sabom MB, Feldman RL, Chrisite LG, Varnell JH, Conti CR. Hemodynamic and myocardial metabolic effects of ergonovine in patients with chest pain. *Circulation* 1978;58:648–654.

69. Conti CR, Curry RC, Daicoff G, et al. Unstable angina pectoris: National Cooperative Study Group to Compare Surgical and Medical Therapy, II. In-hospital experience and initial follow-up results in patients with one, two, and three vessel disease. *Am J Cardiol* 1978;42:839–848.

79. Curry RC, Pepine CJ, Sabom MB, Conti CR. Similarities of ergonovine induced and spontaneous attacks of variant angina. *Circulation* 1979;59:307–312.

80. Feldman RL, Nichols WW, Pepine CJ, Conti CR. Hemodynamic significance of the length of a cornoary arterial narrowing. *Am J Cardiol* 1978;41:865–871.

81. Feldman RL, Nichols WW, Pepine CJ, Conetta DA, Conti CR. The coronary hemodynamic of left main and branch coronary stenoses. The effects of reduction in stenosis diameter, stenosis length, and number of stenoses. *J Thorac Cardiovasc Surg* 1979;77:377–388.

83. Feldman RL, Nichols WW, Pepine CJ, Conti CR. Inluence of aortic insufficiency on the hemodynamic significance of a coronary artery narrowing. *Circulation* 1979;60:259–268.

85. Pepine CJ, Nichols WW, Curry RC, Conti CR. Aortic input impedance during nitroprusside infusion. A reconsideration of afterload reduction and beneficial action. *J Clin Invest* 1979;64:643–654.

87. Conti CR, Selby JH, Christie LG, Pepine CJ, Curry RC, Nichols WW, Conetta DA, Feldman RL, Mehta J, Alexander JA. Left main coronary artery stenosis: clinical spectrum, pathophysiology and management. *Prog Cardiovasc Dis* 1979;22:73–106.

101. Conti CR, Curry RC, Diacoff G, et al. Unstable angina pectoris: National Cooperative Study Group to Compare Surgical and Medical Therapy. III. Results in patients with S-T segment elevation during pain. *Am J Cardiol* 1980;45:819–824.

135. Conti CR, Curry RC, Daicoff G, et al. Unstable Angina Pectoris: National Cooperative Study Group to Compare Medical and Surgical Therapy. IV. Results in patients with left anterior descending coronary artery disease. *Am J Cardiol* 1981;48:517–524.

145. Pepine CJ, Feldman RL, Conti CR. Action of intracoronary nitroglycerin in refractory coronary artery spasm. *Circulation* 1982;65:411–414.

153. Conti CR, Feldman RL, Pepine CJ. Coronary artery spasm: prevalence, clinical significance, and provocative testing. *Am Heart J* 1982;103:584–588.

165. Abela GS, Normann S, Cohen D, Feldman RL, Geiser EA, Conti CR. Effects of carbon dioxide, Nd-Yag, and Argon laser radiation on coronary atheromatous plaques. *Am J Cardiol* 1982;50:1199–1205.

177. Abela GS, Conti CR. Laser revascularization: what are its prospects? *J Cardiovasc Med* 1983;8:977–984.

186. Conti CR. Coronary artery spasm and myocardial infarction. *N Engl J Med* 1983;309:238–239.

264. Conti CR. Silent myocardial ischemia: prognostic significance and therapeutic implications. *Clin Cardiol* 1988;11:807–811.

285. Conti CR, Hill JA, Mayfield WR. Unstable angina pectoris: pathogenesis and management. *J Curr Probl Cardiol* 1989;14:549–624.

350. Bertolet BD, Dinerman J, Harke R, Conti CR. Unstable angina: relationship of clinical presentation, coronary artery pathology, and clinical outcome. *Clin Cardiol* 1993;16:167–168.

362. El Timimi H, Mansour M, Wargovich TJ, Hill JA, Kerensky RA, Conti CR, Pepine CJ. Constrictor and dilator responses to intracoronary acetylcholine in adjacent segments of the same coronary artery in patients with coronary artery disease. Endothelial function revisited. *Circulation* 1994;89:45–51.

370. Pepine CJ, Geller NL, Knatterud GL, Bourassa MG, Chaitman BR, Davies RF, Day P, Deanfield JE, Goldberg AD, McMahon RP, Mueller H, Ouyang P, Pratt C, Proschan M, Rogers WJ, Selwyn AP, Sharaf B, Sopko G, Stone PH, Conti CR, for the ACIP Investigators. The Asymptomatic Cardiac Ischemia Pilot (ACIP) Study: Design of a randomized clinical trial, baseline data and implications for a long-term outcome trial. *J Am Coll Cardiol* 1994;24:1–10.

373. Knatterud GL, Bourassa MG, Pepine CJ, Geller NL, Sopko G, Chaitman BR, Pratt C, Stone PH, Davies RF, Rogers WJ, Deanfield JE, Goldberg AD, Ouyang P, Mueller H, Sharaf B, Day P, Selwyn AP, Conti CR, for the ACIP Investigators. Effects of treatment strategies to suppress ischemia in patients with coronary artery disease: 12-week results of the Asymptomatic Cardiac Ischemia Pilot (ACIP) Study. *J Am Coll Card* 1994;24:11–20.

380. Conti CR, Bourassa MG, Chaitman BR, Geller NL, Knatterud GL, Pepine CJ, Pratt C, Sopko G, for the Asymptomatic Cardiac Ischemia Pilot (ACIP). Asymptomatic Cardiac Ischemic Pilot (ACIP). *Trans Am Clin Climatol Assoc* 1994;106:77–83; 83–84.

430. Conti CR, Geller NL, Knatterud GL, Forman SA, Pratt CM, Pepine CJ, Sopko G, for the ACIP Investigators. Anginal status and prediction of cardiac events in patients enrolled in the Asymptomatic Cardiac Ischemia Pilot (ACIP) Study. *Am J Cardiol* 1997;79:889–892.

431. Davies RF, Goldberg AD, Forman S, pepine CJ, Knatterud GL, Geller N, Sopko G, Pratt C, Deanfield J, Conti CR, for the ACIP Investigators. Asymptomatic Cardiac Ischemia Pilot (ACIP) Study two-year follow-up. Outcomes of patients randomized to initial strategies of medical therapy versus revascularization. *Circulation* 1997;95:2037–2043.

452. Campbell RWF, Wallentin L, Verheugt FWA, Turpie AGG, Maseri A, Klein W, Cleland JGF, Bode C, Becker R, Anderson J, Bertrand ME, Conti CR. Management strategies for a better outcome in unstable coronary artery disease. *Clin Cardiol* 1998;21:314–322.

507. Smock AL, Larson B, Brown C, Conti CR. Early prediction of 30-day mortality after Q-wave myocardial infarction by echocardiographic assessment of left ventricular function—a pilot investigation. *Clin Cardiol* 2001;24:191–195.

509. Conti CR. Selective coronary angiography: 42 years later. *Clin Cardiol* 2001;24:269–270.

DENTON ARTHUR COOLEY, MD:
A Conversation With the Editor*

Denton Arthur Cooley was born in Houston, Texas, in 1920. After his surgical training in Baltimore and London, he returned to his beloved Texas by joining the Baylor College of Medicine in Houston in 1951. Since that time he has been a major force in the treatment of cardiovascular disease in the world. He has contributed to the techniques for repair and replacement of diseased heart valves and the aorta and its branches, and he is widely known for his pioneering surgical treatment of cardiac anomalies in infants and children. His publications number nearly 1,200. Dr. Cooley and his team have performed over 90,000 open heart operations at his hospital. In 1962, he created the Texas Heart Institute where he has trained over 600 surgeons who are now members of the Cooley Cardiovascular Surgical Society. Dr. Cooley is a member or honorary member of over 50 professional societies around the world. He has received 68 honors and awards including the Medal of Freedom, the nation's highest civilian award, the Theodore Roosevelt Award given by the National Collegiate Athletic Association to a varsity athlete who has achieved national recognition in his profession, and the Rene Leriche Prize, the highest honor of the International Surgical Society for cardiovascular contributions. He has received honorary degrees from 5 American Universities and from 3 foreign universities. He has been married for 47 years to Louise Thomas Cooley; they have 5 daughters and 16 grandchildren. He enjoys spending time with his family at their ranch and at their Galveston beach house. He has several hobbies and currently is hooked on golf. He also is a nice guy with great capacity for friendship.

• • •

William Clifford Roberts, MD (hereinafter called **WCR**): Dr. Cooley, I appreciate your giving me this time to talk with you. The major purpose is to find out what gave you that passion, that desire to excel the way you have. I would like to begin by asking you about your parents, your siblings, and what your home life was like when you were a youngster. Could you speak a bit about your parents and your grandparents and the atmosphere of Houston when you were growing up?

Denton Arthur Cooley, MD* (hereinafter called **DAC**): I am a native Houstonian. My grandfather moved to Houston with his 3 small sons about 1885. He and one other man developed the Houston

Heights, which at the time was one of the suburban areas of Houston. He built the first impressive home there, which set the standard for future development. My father, who was named Ralph Clarkson Cooley, was 3 years old when the family moved to Houston. I was born on August 22, 1920, about 4 years after my father and mother married. I was named for my father's 2 brothers, Denton and Arthur. When I was born, my father was a young, practicing dentist in Houston. He subsequently became a very prominent dentist, excelling in his profession.

My childhood was spent in a new suburban area of Houston known as Montrose. I attended only public schools: Montrose Elementary School, Sidney Lanier Junior High School, and then San Jacinto High School. We had perhaps 1,200 students in our high school. From high school, I went on to the University of Texas in Austin where I spent 4 years, graduating with a major in zoology.

• • •

WCR: Could I go back just a bit? You had an older brother.

DAC: Yes, I had an older brother named Ralph, Jr.

• • •

WCR: Were there other siblings?

DAC: No, just the 2 of us. Ralph was 16 months older than I, so we were very close— almost like twin brothers.

• • •

WCR: What has he done?

DAC: Ralph went to college with the idea of becoming a dentist, as did I, but his grades were below average. He dropped out of college and spent his life involved with various business activities. Unfortunately, Ralph died about 20 years ago.

• • •

WCR: In high school and earlier you made all A's, I gather, and you were All City in basketball. Is that correct?

DAC: Yes, I was able to blend an excellent scholastic record with some athletic achievements.

• • •

WCR: Did you play sports other than basketball?

DAC: I was a pretty good tennis player. I began to play golf in those days also, but tennis and basketball were my favorite sports back then.

• • •

WCR: What was life like around the house? When you had dinner at night, say when you were in high school?

DAC: My father was a busy dentist. He had a very active practice, but he did get home for dinner almost every evening, usually around 6:30 or 7:00. We sat around the dinner table and exchanged stories and daily experiences. My father was intensely interested

---
* This interview is part of a series of interviews of prominent cardiovascular specialists and the series is underwritten by an unrestricted grant from Bristol Myers Squibb.
** From the Baylor Cardiovascular Institute, Baylor University Medical Center, Dallas, Texas 75246.
*** From the Texas Heart Institute, Texas Medical Center, Houston, Texas 77225-0345.

FIGURE 1. DAC as dressed-up youngster.

in the economics and politics of Houston, and he imparted in me a real feeling that I belonged to Houston and that Houston belonged to us. It was an unusual sort of feeling. Houston really has been an ideal place not only to grow up, but also to enjoy a career.

• • •

WCR: In 1930, when you were 10 years old, what was the population of Houston?

DAC: My recollection is that it was approximately 290,000.

• • •

WCR: There was no air conditioning, a lot of fans?

DAC: That's right. We all lived under ceiling fans or buzz fans. We had no air conditioning. Only in the downtown movie houses could you experience air conditioning, and just a few of them were air conditioned.

• • •

WCR: Your junior high and high school years were very enjoyable periods for you, I presume. You were very successful athletically. You were very successful scholastically. Things went very well?

DAC: Yes, I think they did. I must say that I began to enjoy being above the average in many activities and, even then, I wanted to have a life that was well balanced between scholastic and recreational activities.

• • •

WCR: I gather when you went off to the University of Texas in Austin to college that you really did not consider other colleges very strongly? You sort of made up your mind right quick like. Is that right?

DAC: The only other college that I would have considered was Rice Institute, but that seemed to be too close to home. After my experience in a big high school, I wanted a much more competitive atmosphere, something with a higher profile than our local Rice Institute. I thought nothing would be more challenging than to enter the University of Texas.

• • •

WCR: In high school you were All City in basketball, but when you went to the University of Texas you were not on an athletic scholarship?

DAC: That's true. I had not even aspired to getting an athletic scholarship. When I entered the University of Texas I was just 17 years old. In those days, it was unusual to get a scholarship if you were younger than 19 or 20.

• • •

WCR: You went out for the college basketball team?

DAC: Yes, I was what they called a "walk-on."

• • •

WCR: At that time you were 6 feet, 4 inches tall and weighed 140 pounds?

DAC: I was very thin. The coach looked at me and thought that I was too frail to make the varsity team.

• • •

WCR: What happened? How did it develop?

DAC: I played on the freshman team and did fairly well. As a sophomore, I was a substitute on the varsity basketball squad. In a preseason game against a local school in Austin (St. Edward's University), I got my chance. St. Edward's was beating the great University of Texas varsity team. The coach, I think to disgrace some of the scholarship players, looked down the bench and sent me into the game. Within a very short period, I was able to score 8 or 10 points, and we won the game. From that moment on, I knew that my place on the team was secure. I was offered an athletic scholarship and proceeded on with my varsity career.

• • •

WCR: You played center?

DAC: I played both center and forward. By today's standards, we were not very tall. We had 1 fellow who was 6 feet, 5 inches, about an inch taller than I was. He usually played center, and I played forward. When he was out of the game, I became the center.

• • •

WCR: You did very well in the Southwest Conference?

DAC: We won the conference in my sophomore year, which was quite an achievement in those days. We went on to play in the National Collegiate Athletic Association regional tournament out on Treasure Island in San Francisco Bay. In fact, it was the first regional basketball tournament ever held, and it was quite exciting. I continued to play my junior and senior years.

• • •

WCR: I understand that you made Phi Beta Kappa your junior year. How did you blend in the scholastic achievements with your athletic skills?

DAC: It was a matter of learning how to budget my time. In addition to my studies and sports, I was a member of Kappa Sigma social fraternity, which also demanded my time, particularly as a pledge but also as a member. I was also involved in campus

FIGURE 2. DAC as varsity basketball player at the University of Texas.

politics, and I held an elected office on campus. I found that if I scheduled my time carefully I could accomplish everything I wanted to do. At all times, I kept in mind that my main purpose in being at the University of Texas was to get an education and to make a good scholastic record for my future. It did take hard work, and I was careful to avoid a lot of extraneous influences. I did not play poker or bridge, both of which were big time wasters among fraternity members. I was pretty good at pool and ping pong, neither of which took up a lot of my time.

• • •

WCR: You majored in zoology. When did you decide to switch from pre-dental to pre-med?

DAC: I think my decision was largely influenced by my athletic interests. When I told the coach that I thought I would leave the university after 2 or 3 years to enter dental school, he convinced me that doing so would be disloyal to the team, and that I should go ahead and fulfill my 4 years of athletic eligibility. Originally, I had been somewhat insecure about my ability to compete with some of the more serious intellects taking pre-med courses. In our fraternity, for example, it seemed to me that about 30% of the young fellows were taking pre-med courses. However, none of them finished the standard pre-med major. I found that they were making D's and

F's and that I was making straight A's in the same courses. I realized that maybe I had not given my abilities enough credit. These factors encouraged me to change over to a straight pre-med course of study.

• • •

WCR: Why did you decide on the University of Texas at Galveston for medical school?

DAC: The University of Texas Medical Branch in Galveston was one of the oldest medical institutions in the Southwest. The only other institution I considered in Texas was Baylor University in Dallas, which did not enjoy the reputation of Galveston. Galveston had attracted the most outstanding faculty, and many of the outstanding practicing physicians in Houston had graduated from the Medical Branch. I also applied and was accepted to Tulane and Baylor. When the letter came from the University of Texas Medical Branch in Galveston, I did not hesitate to accept.

• • •

WCR: How did you enjoy it there? You were there, I gather, only 2 years?

DAC: It was in 1941, right at the beginning of the war in Europe. Those of us going to medical school were being prepared to assist in the war. Thus, within 2 weeks of college graduation we were enrolled in medical school. It was a very arduous 2 years of study, although I was able to blend in some of my athletic interests at the time. I played softball for a local church and basketball for a local saloon. I excelled in Galveston and led in my class of 90 students; I was number 1 or 2 in the class with a couple of other fellows who were much more involved in their studies than I.

Something happened while I was at the Medical Branch that made me decide to leave. Whenever there was conflict of any kind during the war years, those involved could be labeled un-American because patriotism was so important. Our dean there, Tom Spies, had a rift with established members of the faculty, and this caused a great deal of concern, not only in local politics but also in the Texas Legislature. The Legislature initiated an investigation to see if a German "bund" was developing in Galveston to disrupt medical education. The Legislature sent a committee down along with about 4 Texas Rangers to look into this "serious" matter. I became rather disillusioned after attending some of these "kangaroo courts" where the heads of departments were pitted against one another. All of this was very discouraging to me because I was interested in seeing my medical school maintain its academic rating. I anticipated that the Medical Branch might be placed on scholastic probation, which did result from this turmoil. I rather quietly decided to leave the University of Texas system and to apply to some other medical schools. I applied to Washington University, Pennsylvania, Harvard, Duke, and, of course, The Johns Hopkins. I was accepted at all of them except Harvard. When I got the Hopkins acceptance, I moved to Baltimore; this was February of 1943.

• • •

WCR: At that time you were 22. You rapidly excelled at Hopkins and, I gather, you met Dr. Blalock not long after you got up there. Is that right?

DAC: The story of my first meeting with Dr. Blalock is somewhat amusing. The weather in Baltimore was miserable in February and early March. I had met another transfer student, a fellow from the University of Michigan named Lester Persky, who has since gone on to a career in academic medicine and a specialty in urology. Lester had played football for the University of Michigan, although as a substitute for Tom Harmon, he didn't play too much. Anyway, I knew he was an athlete, so I asked him to play tennis. There was a tennis court in the compound at Hopkins, and the sun was out that day (a Friday). Lester and I decided to cut Dr. Blalock's Friday clinic, even though attendance at the clinic was considered mandatory, because we had not seen sunshine in some time. After the clinic, Dr. Blalock and his entourage, which included Bill Longmire, Mark Ravitch, and several other people on his surgical staff at the time, came walking across the yard and saw us out playing tennis. Dr. Blalock was going to the Harriet Lane Home, Dr. Taussig's clinic, to see a patient. After they passed by I said to Lester, "I think we're going back home. You're going back to Michigan, and I'm going back to Texas because the professor saw us out here cutting his clinic." When Dr. Blalock came out of the pediatric building, we were still playing tennis. He called me over and said, "Mr. Cooley, may I speak with you?" I was certain that a reprimand was imminent. Instead, he said to me, "You know, Mr. Cooley, you play a good game of tennis. Most tennis players play ping pong. Do you play ping pong?" I said, "Yes sir, I play ping pong." Then he said, "Mrs. Blalock and I have Dr. Rienhoff's house down at Gibson Island, and we are going to go down to spend this weekend there. Would you like to come along and play ping pong with me?" I said, "Oh yes, sir, I would be delighted." I was absolutely flabbergasted at this opportunity.

I went to Gibson Island, a resort close to Annapolis, and I remember very well that Dr. Blalock wanted to play ping pong immediately after we arrived. He said, "Denton, I think I would like to have a little bourbon before we play. You can fix me a bourbon and water." I went back to the kitchen and told Mrs. Blalock. I said, "Mrs. Blalock, the professor would like a bourbon and water. If I make it strong, he will think that I am an imbiber myself; if I make it real weak, he may not respect my ability to make a drink." She said, "Let me tell you that when it comes to drinking, the professor is no ninny." I poured him what I thought was a reasonable mix of bourbon and water and took it to him. We began to play some ping pong. Dr. Blalock soon downed the glass of bourbon and then said, "Denton, let me make the second drink." He brought back a drink so strong that it made my eyes tear every time I took a sip. From then on, formalities disap-

peared, and our friendship commenced. He watched my career, I think, with some interest.

• • •

WCR: I gather that at Hopkins you graduated first or second in your class, is that correct? You finished medical school early? They were moving fast because of the war. You had planned to take a rotating internship?

DAC: In Galveston, I had only heard of rotating internships. When I did not apply to Hopkins for a straight surgical internship, Dr. Blalock called me in and said, "Denton, I noticed that you have not even applied for an internship at Hopkins." I replied, "Dr. Blalock, I think that I may have had as much experience at Hopkins as I need. I am going to move on, maybe to the University of Michigan at Ann Arbor with Dr. Coller." He said, "That surprises me. I want you to know that if you want an internship here, you can have it." Luckily I said, "All right, I'll take it."

• • •

WCR: So when you started your surgery internship, I gather you very quickly went on Dr. Blalock's service. What happened there?

DAC: During the internship, I did work for Dr. Blalock. Also, I knew Vivien Thomas, the remarkable technician who worked in the Hunterian "dog" laboratory. Vivien and I became good friends while I was a medical student, because I was doing some research at the Hunterian. I was involved in and knew something about the development of the Blalock-Taussig operation, the subclavian-pulmonary anastomosis, because of my work at the Hunterian. At the time, Dr. Blalock and Dr. Taussig were studying the effect this anastomosis would have on the pulmonary vascular system, whether it would result in hypertension.

• • •

WCR: You scrubbed on the first "blue-baby" operation?

DAC: Yes, it was November 1944. There was Dr. Blalock with Bill Longmire as the first assistant. I was sort of the junior intern. Vivien Thomas was standing behind Dr. Blalock, and Helen Taussig was at the head of the table with our nurse anesthetist, Olive Burger, who was delivering the anesthesia. It was quite an exciting time, although we did not appreciate the impact it would have on medical history.

FIGURE 3. DAC as a surgical resident at the John Hopkins Hospital. DAC is to the left of Dr. Blalock (in the suit).

WCR: Whose idea was it of creating a ductus? Was that Dr. Taussig's or Dr. Blalock's?

DAC: I think it was basically Dr. Taussig's idea. She, of course, was one of the few really knowledgeable specialists in congenital heart surgery. Dr. Taussig had made the observation that children born with pulmonary stenosis became more cyanotic when their patent ductus closed. She discussed this observation with Dr. Blalock and asked whether a ductus could be created surgically. Dr Blalock replied that he had been doing that same procedure for other purposes in his laboratory. Actually, he had been studying this problem while he was working at Vanderbilt before he even came to Hopkins. Thus, he felt prepared to proceed.

• • •

WCR: You left your surgical training at Hopkins after 2 years. Did you experience the infusion of these huge numbers of patients coming to Hopkins to have this magical shunt procedure done?

DAC: I had only been out of medical school maybe 12 or 18 months when I was assigned as chief resident on Dr. Blalock's cardiac team. I was doing procedures beyond my ability, like closing ductuses and creating subclavian-pulmonary anastomoses. I had done an appendectomy and a couple of inguinal hernias, but I had not even done a gallbladder operation. This was before I joined the Army in 1946.

It may perhaps be of interest to know why Dr. Blalock appointed me as his cardiac resident before I went into the Army. One day, he called me into his office. I was single at the time, of course, and he said, "Denton, you seem to have a reputation around the hospital of getting along well with the women." I replied, "Do I, sir?" He answered, "Yes, that is the rumor. You know, Denton, I am going to make you my cardiac resident. I know it is a little bit premature for you, but I want you to do one thing for me. I want you to get all those damn women out of my hair." I asked, "What do you mean?" He said, "Well, Dr. Taussig, Ruth Whittemore, and Peggy Hanson, (now Peggy Hanlon), and Mary Allen Engle." It seems that Dr. Taussig's staff were hovering over the pediatric patients postoperatively and calling Dr. Blalock with requests at all hours. "That is your assignment. Get those women out of my hair." I could only reply, "I will try, Dr. Blalock."

• • •

WCR: You had 18 months at Hopkins as a surgical house officer, including 9 months in the cardiovascular service and 9 months in general surgery, and then you went into the Army in Europe?

DAC: I went to a town in Austria called Linz, which is on the Danube and is the birthplace of Adolph Hitler. I became chief of surgery in a 200-bed station hospital there.

• • •

WCR: So that is where you really were introduced to general surgery.

DAC: Yes. I mainly did general surgery and obstetrics, but I also did a little neurosurgery. I performed many procedures I certainly was not prepared to do.

• • •

WCR: After those 2 years you came back to Hopkins, and you had 2 more years as a surgical resident. What happened there? Were patients still pouring into Hopkins because of the famous operation?

DAC: Yes, not only patients, but physicians and surgeons were coming from all over the world to see this new surgery. It was very exciting. We were so proud of our professor and, of course, of Dr. Taussig for having started something that seemed to rejuvenate Hopkins at a time when people said the Hopkins had lost its luster—because the days of Halsted and Osler were long since past. The Blalock-Taussig anastomosis really restored interest in The Johns Hopkins Hospital.

• • •

WCR: How good an operator was Dr. Blalock?

DAC: I would say he was sort of average, a deliberate surgeon, who was somewhat insecure in many respects. I never felt as though he was comfortable in the operating room. He was tense, and he tended to complain and whine when things did not go smoothly.

• • •

WCR: He let you and Hank Bahnson do a whole lot right off?

DAC: He did.

• • •

WCR: I gather he sort of enjoyed letting you do this.

DAC: I think so. In the Hopkins program, once a man got to a senior level he was as important as any of the staff surgeons. He had his own set of patients. Surgical programs have, of course, changed significantly since those days. Now, almost all patients are assigned to a staff surgeon. In those days, we had

FIGURE 4. DAC in the Army at age 26.

clinic patients who were the responsibility of the resident staff from admission to discharge. They were our patients, and we only called in Dr. Blalock or a staff member when a problem arose for which we thought we could use some help.

• • •

WCR: What was Dr. Blalock's appeal? It seems to me that he was the father of cardiovascular surgery in this country. Most of you who trained with him and became his chief residents have done extremely well. What were his characteristics that were so special and attractive?

DAC: For one thing, his modesty. He would not take credit for anything that was not his own. I remember one time when he was addressing The Society of Vascular Surgeons in Atlantic City. I had driven up there myself to hear him talk, but he did not know that I was in the audience. I listened from the back of the room as he described some technical aspects of the Blalock-Taussig operation. He said, "My resident, Dr. Cooley, taught me how to do it this way." His acknowledgment made me very proud and meant more to me than I can describe. Such generosity was just part of his nature. Dr. Blalock was a good, honest person who respected the people he was training. He was interested in our development and in our future. We found him to be a very good friend, one who was rarely critical of us. He provided encouragement.

• • •

WCR: He was very well informed medically. You respected his knowledge enormously, I presume?

DAC: Yes, I thought he was very knowledgeable. I know that he read the medical literature. Of course, he also published a lot in those days. He had rather diversified interests. He was, for example, interested in the physiology of myasthenia gravis and pericardial constriction.

• • •

WCR: He was from Georgia. Was he an athlete?

DAC: Yes, he was. He was a tennis player, and he played a pretty good game of golf. I think he and Tinsley Harrison were reputed to have won the doubles tennis championship in Nashville when he was at Vanderbilt.

• • •

WCR: When you finished at Hopkins in July 1950, at age 30, you went to the Brompton Hospital in London. How was that experience?

DAC: Russell Brock from London, a very unusual surgeon, had spent about 2 or 3 weeks with us as a visiting professor at Hopkins. At the time, Brock was the most aggressive and respected cardiac surgeon in the United Kingdom and in western Europe. I was enormously impressed by him. In those days when few surgeons were doing intracardiac operations, Brock was performing some finger-fracture operations on the mitral valve, and he was also perforating the pulmonary valve to treat tetralogy of Fallot, rather than just creating systemic-to-pulmonary shunts. I also needed to learn endoscopy, which was not available to the general or thoracic surgeons

at Hopkins because the otolaryngologists dominated bronchoscopy and esophagoscopy. For both of these reasons, I decided to go to the Brompton Hospital as a senior registrar under Russell Brock. I almost felt as though some divine force led me to the Brompton, as it turned into an incredible and unique opportunity to learn some different surgical methods. Furthermore, one of Brock's associates, Oswald Tubbs, became ill with tuberculosis while I was there, and I took over all of Tubbs' cases as my own. He had a list of about 200 patients waiting for chest surgery. This was in the early days of the National Health Program, and the waiting lists were enormous. Therefore, when I was not operating with Brock, I did Tubbs' cases, which gave me experience in pulmonary surgery that I had not received elsewhere.

• • •

WCR: That year, I gather, at the Brompton was a real growth spurt for you. You met a lot of people, you made a lot of future contacts, and it must have opened your eyes a good bit.

DAC: It did. I also visited several of the best clinics in Europe that year, including clinics in France, Italy, and other countries. From these experiences, I gained an insight into the practice of surgery in western Europe.

• • •

WCR: How did it work out that you came back to Houston after that?

DAC: I had been very much interested in the Texas Medical Center. Actually, the physician founder of the Texas Medical Center was my mother's obstetrician, a man named E. W. Bertner. I had consulted with Dr. Bertner throughout my medical career. He was one of the major reasons I elected to attend the University of Texas in Galveston. I had also consulted with Dr. Bertner about the plans for the Texas Medical Center. My choice for chief of surgery had been William Longmire, who was one of Dr. Blalock's right-hand men. Dr. Michael DeBakey received the appointment. After my residency in Baltimore, I talked to DeBakey and told him that I was considering a year of additional training in England. He agreed that my getting more training in cardiovascular surgery was a good idea, and he assured me of a staff position at Baylor after I completed my year in London. Thus, in July 1951, I joined the full-time faculty at Baylor.

• • •

WCR: Did you start operating immediately? Did you scrub with DeBakey right at first a good bit or how did that actually work out on a day-to-day basis?

DAC: At first I worked with him, assisting on many operations. Mike had limited experience at the time. I had what training was available at the time. I did repairs of aortic coarctation, ductal closures, mitral commissurotomies—any procedure being done at the time. I already had an interest in surgical treatment of aortic aneurysms, as I had repaired a couple of aneurysms while I was a resident at Hopkins. Thus, when I got to Houston, I knew that I also wanted to operate on major vascular lesions. In those days, many of our patients had luetic aneurysms. Although we seldom see a patient with a syphilitic aneurysm today, the aggressive approach needed to treat aortic aneurysms interested me then and remains a major interest of mine today.

• • •

WCR: When you first came back to Houston, which hospital were you operating in?

DAC: I would operate whenever and wherever I could. At the time, Baylor controlled the Jefferson Davis City/County Hospital, which was our major teaching hospital. Private patients could be admitted to Hermann Hospital or to the old Methodist Hospital, which occupied a small building downtown. I also operated at the Riverside Hospital and at St. Elizabeth's Hospital, both of which at the time were for black patients.

• • •

WCR: So you were busy from the very beginning once you came back to Houston. When did your practice expand to the point that you were doing 25 or 30 cases a day? How long did that take?

DAC: That took a long time. Only long after I left Baylor did the volume become enormous. When I came to Houston, I was also very interested in continuing my work in pediatric surgery, which I had begun at Johns Hopkins. St. Luke's Episcopal Hospital opened about that time and was affiliated with Texas Children's Hospital. I began to focus more and more on Children's Hospital. The adjacent St. Luke's Hospital was a convenient place for adult cases, so I soon confined my practice to these 2 hospitals.

• • •

WCR: So long before 1969 when you separated entirely from Baylor, you were essentially moved over to St. Luke's and Childrens?

DAC: Yes.

• • •

WCR: Your contributions obviously in all these different procedures have been enormous. How have you handled this huge amount of operating? In your heyday, I gather, 25 to 30 cases a day were not unusual and not just carotid endarterectomies but transposition of the great arteries, total anomalous pulmonary venous connection, valve replacement, aortic aneurysms, etc. How did you handle this enormous physical activity from an energy standpoint?

DAC: I always say that some of my athletic experiences taught me endurance and competitiveness, with perhaps an emphasis on endurance. I had good health, and I enjoyed what I was doing. Practicing surgery was exciting: there were constant changes and opportunities to do new things. When cardiopulmonary bypass was developed, heart surgery moved into a new era. I began immediately to do open heart cases.

• • •

WCR: That was 1954?

DAC: In 1954, Lillehei first used cross circulation to repair a ventricular septal defect. John Gibbon had done 1 successful closure of an atrial septal defect with his elaborate pump the year before; John Kirklin was working with a Gibbon-type apparatus at the Mayo Clinic. I developed a simpler bubble oxygenator than was available at the time, which we used with 2 sigmamotor pumps, one to pump blood from the caval system to the oxygenator and the other to return oxygenated blood to the systemic arterial system. By the end of 1956, we had done 100 open heart operations, a figure considered unbelievable. From that point forward, we continued to simplify our technique for cardiopulmonary bypass. We proved that hemodilution was a sensible solution to the large volumes of blood required in the early cases. With our pump and our hemodilution technique, we were soon doing 750 to 1,000 open heart operations a year.

• • •

WCR: You went from priming the pump in adults, let's say from 14 units of blood, to much fewer and, finally, to 0?

DAC: We went straight to hemodilution. We would have a couple units of blood on reserve in the blood bank for each patient. However, we used only a crystalloid solution to prime the pump. Even though Zuhdi and some others had shown that nonblood prime was possible, they had not really pushed to make it an accepted method. I think we convinced the world that nonblood prime was a practical solution to the demand that open heart surgery was putting on blood-banking facilities.

• • •

WCR: You really saved a lot of hepatitis cases. Would you put making hemodilution a reality one of your finest contributions?

DAC: I think so, Bill, although I may not be remembered or credited for it. In my mind, I believe that I convinced the world that hemodilution with nonblood prime was a practical method. I personally think my work in simplifying cardiopulmonary bypass and my establishing the Texas Heart Institute are the 2 things for which I may deserve some credit after my life is over.

• • •

WCR: Now in your usual coronary bypass operation, no transfusions are given, with very few exceptions?

DAC: That is true. In all of our patients, we have consistently worked to reduce the amount of blood transfused. We have also operated on about 1,200 Jehovah's Witnesses and, of course, none of them have had blood transfusions before, during, or after their operations.

• • •

WCR: Was it the Jehovah's Witnesses that stimulated you not to use any blood transfusions initially or was that sort of incidental?

DAC: That was more a by-product of our use of nonblood prime. Finally, the Jehovah's Witnesses agreed to surgery under these circumstances. I signed a contract with them, which stated that I would not use blood under any circumstances.

FIGURE 5. DAC standing next to his bust at the Texas Heart Institute.

• • •

WCR: I gather now that you are not doing 25 or 30 cases a day. You are still operating quite a bit. You are 76 years old. How many cases are you doing a week now?

DAC: I think this week I did 15 cases, which is more than I have done in recent weeks, but it has been a big week. I am not, however, the only surgeon at the Institute. I have a team of surgeons, all of whom have trained in this hospital under me, and they are all outstanding surgeons. As happens to any senior surgeon, the younger cardiologists refer to the younger surgeons— those in their own generation. Most of my practice today comes from referrals from former patients or from areas where the cardiologists are not locked into referring to the younger surgeons, as they are here in Houston. Nonetheless, I do get many challenging cases. This week I operated on several patients with very complicated aortic aneurysms.

• • •

WCR: Now at age 76, do you feel yourself to be as good technically as you were when you were 36 or 46? Have you noticed any loss of surgical dexterity?

DAC: No, I have not. I may get a little more tired after doing 5 or 6 strenuous cases, or my back may get sore, but I believe technically I am as good as I ever was. I also think that my many years of experience make me much more comfortable in the operating room and in knowing how to manage complications or difficult situations when they arise.

• • •

WCR: It is a shame that the commercial airline pilots are required to retire at age 60 when they have so much experience. Here you are 16 years later than that, and I gather you have no intention of really slowing down?

DAC: I do not. I think that I would slow down only if something were to happen to my health, like a stroke or a serious heart ailment, both of which can occur when you get to be my age. Luckily, I have not had either of those problems.

• • •

WCR: You are obviously a healthy looking man. What have you done through the years to stay healthy? You are still at ideal body weight.

DAC: My weight is the same as it was when I played varsity basketball in college. Although other factors are important, I believe that the challenge for each of us is to maintain our ideal body weight. Diet and nutrition are certainly important, but I think that a healthful weight can best be maintained by matching caloric intake with body metabolism. You can measure it pretty well if you get a bathroom scale and just step on it in the mornings. Just say, "Look, I didn't know that I gained 3 pounds last week. Today I won't eat any breakfast or lunch."

• • •

WCR: If you pig out today you will be very careful tomorrow?

DAC: Yes. I am anticipating a cruise soon. I am going on the QE II for about 5 days, where the main activity will be eating and drinking. I will compensate for it, and if I come back having gained 3 or 4 pounds, I will promptly lose it.

• • •

WCR: What is your typical diet like? What do you eat generally in the daytime as a rule?

DAC: At breakfast, I have orange juice, probably a bran muffin, and maybe a banana and coffee. Every day at lunch my secretary brings me some clear soup and frozen yogurt. In the evening I have a cocktail and maybe take on about 1,000 to 1,200 calories. That is my usual daily intake.

• • •

WCR: You don't eat between meals, and you don't eat before you go to bed at night. You have always stayed physically active, whether it is tennis, golf, or something. You have never been physically out of shape in 76 years for practical purposes?

DAC: No, I really have not. I have certain ailments. I twisted my knee playing tennis and that gave me phlebitis. I ended up with a pulmonary embolus or 2, but that was 10 years ago. I broke my left hand playing tennis, which has interfered a little with my golf swing. All of those things, however, were due to trauma, not poor health.

• • •

WCR: What about your activities on a typical day? When do you wake up in the morning?

DAC: I set my alarm for 5:00 A.M. every day. I usually leave home just before 6:00 and get to the hospital at 6:15. If I don't make rounds until 6:30, I look over patient records, review items on my desk, or do some correspondence. My patient rounds are either at 6:30 or 6:45 every morning. I make rounds in the intensive care unit, see all the patients who have had operations, talk with the residents about the day's scheduled surgery, and attend brief conferences or lectures that are held before the schedule begins. Usually, the patient's anesthesia begins at 7:00, so we walk into the operating room at 7:45 and get on with the surgery. I stay in the operating room most of the day. Generally, I have finished my operating room schedule by about 4:00 P.M., after which I attend to administrative duties or staff meetings. I make rounds with my residents around 6:00 P.M. and see the postoperative patients and those scheduled for the next day. I get home about 8:00 or 8:30, sometimes 9:00.

• • •

WCR: You are still doing that? That was about the way it was when you were doing even more cases.

DAC: Very much, although in those days I got home a little later than I do today, and I got a couple hours less sleep at night.

• • •

WCR: Let's say you get home at 8:30. Are you ready to have a cocktail and sit down?

DAC: Yes, I relax and watch television or read the newspaper, and have dinner on a TV tray. I am ready for bed by 9:30 or 10:00.

• • •

WCR: What time do you get to sleep?

DAC: I am usually asleep by 10:30 or 11:00.

• • •

WCR: You go pretty well on 6 hours sleep and if you can get 7 you feel very fortunate?

DAC: I have also found that a 15- or 20-minute nap right after that bowl of soup at lunch really is helpful. Even after a light lunch I may get drowsy, and a little nap is a wonderful thing.

• • •

WCR: As you look back over your career, you have made a lot of contributions. You have mentioned hemodilution and the building of the Texas Heart Institute. You have obviously trained an enormous number of surgeons through the years. How does all of that play to you now?

DAC: It is interesting to observe famous people after they are gone, like my professor Dr. Blalock. He has an enduring identification with the Blalock-Taussig operation. I believe, however, that it was his school of surgery that has been his true and lasting legacy. In time, some other surgeon would have done the blood vessel anastomosis. Such things are really not so important. It is what one can inspire in others that counts. I take satisfaction in the performance and success of my students. I am also proud of the Texas Heart Institute. Even the pharaohs wanted to leave something behind. Some of them built pyramids for which they are remembered. I like to think that the Texas Heart Institute may be my pyramid. I have always wanted to live long enough to give the Institute the momentum to prevail in years to come like some of the other great institutions—The Johns Hopkins Hospital, for example, which remains world renowned even though Mr. Johns Hopkins has been forgotten by many. Maybe that would be something I would consider a contribution. I have written or coauthored nearly 1,200 articles, a number of books, this and that, which will be of interest to some historians but not to many. What you pass on to others and what inspiration you give others really counts. I appreciate the inspiration that I received from my 3 medical teachers: Alfred Blalock, Russell Brock, and Mike DeBakey. I learned something from each of them that has helped me in my career and my life.

• • •

WCR: Denton, I have been impressed through the years with your capacity for friendship, your loyalty to your institutions. You were born in Houston, returned to Houston. You went to the University of Texas. All 5 of your daughters, I gather, went to the University of Texas. You have a lot of friends in Houston, in other areas in Texas. This must bring a great deal of satisfaction to you. I am sure through the years that you have had many offers to go to other cities in the United States to set up this institution or that. How have you handled all these types of things?

DAC: At one time, I was imbued with the academic spirit; and, if you are going to be a real academician, say in surgery, you have to be like a circus performer willing to go to the next best level. I was privileged because I had the opportunity to return to my home town of Houston. Houston is a very progressive city with a major medical center that continues to evolve. Returning to Houston gave me an unusual opportunity, not only to have the right venue for a successful career, but also to be involved in a new and exciting specialty, cardiac surgery. I was in the right place at the opportune time. If I had decided to come to the Texas Medical Center as a general surgeon, my life would have been different. I was fortunate enough to be exposed to Blalock, Brock, and DeBakey, all of whom have been leaders in cardiovascular surgery. All these teachers contributed to my professional career.

• • •

WCR: You are still a legend, as I understand it, at the Brompton Hospital. They still talk about you over there. My son is there now and they talk about when you were working with Russell Brock. He wouldn't be in the operating room and you would go ahead and start the case. You called him by his first name? I gather that most—not you—were scared to death of him.

DAC: That is not exactly true. I don't think anyone except possibly Dr. Blalock called Russell Brock by his first name. He was "Mr. Brock" to me. I never called Dr. Blalock by his first name either. He was always "Dr. Blalock" to me. I have always been respectful of people. I was neither invited nor did I want to call either of them by their first names. I did begin to call Mike DeBakey ''Mike'' because other junior staff referred to him in that way. I did get along well with Mr. Brock. He treated me with respect because I had training in cardiovascular surgery at The Johns Hopkins, and Dr. Blalock had informed him that I had been an important member of his team. As a result, he didn't chew on me the way he would a registrar who came up through the ranks in the English schools. I think that I was an enigma to Brock. He was a serious task master and could be a tyrant in the operating room. I had always disciplined myself to play the game and not talk back to my chief. When he complained, I would try my best to do what he wanted, and I always kept my mouth closed at critical times.

• • •

WCR: Dr. Cooley, you have 5 daughters. How were you able to be a good daddy and get home at 9:00 P.M. and leave in the mornings before they were awake? How did you handle that?

DAC: They were all fine, well-behaved young girls and young women, and were never in trouble. They were all good students in school and made good or excellent grades. Although I did not spend a lot of time with them, I tried to do what I could on weekends to be together. I took them on a few summer trips. I have always rationalized that it is not the amount but the quality of time that you spend with children that makes a lasting impression. I wanted my children to grow up in a household with a compatible mother and father and without domestic conflict, which could worry children. I wanted them to appreciate my work ethic and to know that I was not working simply for my own benefit and career, but for theirs as well. My daughters all turned out very well. Children need to know that their mother and father have their interests at heart and that their home, besides being harmonious, is their security now and in the future.

• • •

WCR: That is the way you felt when you were growing up?

DAC: Yes. When I was growing up, my mother and father lived together. When I was off at college, however, my parents got a divorce, which taught me a real lesson. I didn't think either one of my parents achieved as much professionally or socially after the divorce as they had while they were married. In my opinion, their separating handicapped both of them.

• • •

WCR: Do you take vacations or have you through the years? Do you miss work very often?

DAC: I do not miss work often. I do not take structured vacations at all. In the summers when the children were smaller, I would sometimes combine travel to a medical meeting or to a visiting professorship with a family trip, like to Hawaii or Italy. However, I never took off for very long. Dr. Halsted, who set a precedent for faculty at Hopkins, used to leave The Johns Hopkins Hospital on June 1 and return on October 1. I thought that was neglectful. I have always been involved in a surgical practice where I was needed and that I enjoyed very much. I have also wanted to concentrate on the evolution of the Institute.

• • •

WCR: You have been a leader in packaged pricing for various cardiovascular procedures. You must be very pleased that you were in the forefront of that change?

DAC: It does give me some satisfaction. I anticipated 15 years ago that many hospitals, surgeons, and cardiologists were pricing themselves out of the marketplace. In many instances, their fees were excessively high. I predicted a transition to a more realistic economic situation. I was concerned for the

FIGURE 6. DAC with his wife, Louise, and their 5 daughters.

FIGURE 7. DAC during the interview in September 1996.

payers who were not always getting the best return for the dollars they spent for various medical services. Thus, we started a packaged care program called CardioVascular Care Providers. Through this program, we could inform the payers of the costs for certain types of procedures, particularly coronary bypass, so they could properly budget for these medical expenses. We began this program 14 years ago. I don't think that everybody in the profession thought I was wise and, in fact, some may have thought I was a traitor to other surgeons for developing a cost-control program. Actually, I enjoyed being busy and considered surgery as much a hobby as a job. I always wanted to be known as "the Sam Walton of heart surgery."

• • •

WCR: Some of your colleagues smiled a few years ago when it came out in the newspapers that Dr. Denton Cooley had declared bankruptcy. I understand that lasted a very brief period of time. Maybe you could clarify that for the record.

DAC: In the early 1980s Houston was booming, as was my practice. Because I was a native Houstonian, I decided to participate in some of the development of this area. Since my grandfather and father were both involved in Houston real estate, I invested in a number of real estate opportunities. I was not alone in the belief that Houston would have unlimited growth and expansion. In those days, oil was selling for about $35.00 a barrel. Even the best pundits said that by the turn of the century oil would

be at least $100.00 per barrel. At that time, Houston was an oil-based economy. We were almost assured that Houston would be a city of 5 million by the turn of the century, and we were preparing for it. I was overextended, partly because lenders in those days encouraged borrowing money in anticipation of the future. Although I could pay my obligations according to the contracts and mortgages on loans that I had, suddenly the banks reappraised the assets upon which these loans were based, and they wanted enormous cash remittances over a period of a few weeks. Coming up with this amount of cash was just impossible to do. I finally consulted with accountants and lawyers, who said that I could not make such large payments under the present circumstances. I asked, "Well, what do I do?" They responded, "Chapter 11, a form of bankruptcy, in which the debtor ultimately repays his creditors." My case was in bankruptcy court for less than 6 months, considered very brief in comparison to most. Over the next 8 or 9 years, I paid off all my creditors.

I learned a very important lesson from that experience that I probably should have learned from my father, who had gone through the Great Depression. Among the financial failures were a professional office building and hotel, which I built adjacent to the medical center.

• • •

WCR: That was when interest rates were sky high?

DAC: Yes, those were very "heady" times, as people say.

• • •

WCR: Dr. Cooley, where do you see medicine going from here?

DAC: We are now seeing some rather disturbing encroachments upon the way medicine has been traditionally practiced. At present, we are going through a period of transition that will lead to permanent changes in the satisfying way we have practiced medicine. I look back on those early days of my medical training and practice and recall the origins of medical insurance in Blue Cross and Blue Shield, which assured individuals that many basic costs of their medical care would be covered when they became ill. That major change was mostly for the good. But today we are going through a period in which entrepreneurs are dictating how we practice medicine. They are encouraging doctors to become their patients' adversaries. I am seriously concerned about issues such as capitation. HMOs are pretty much in the same category. When doctors invest in HMOs, they become, in essence, their patients' opponents on an economic level. Under these circumstances, it may be more difficult to remain patients' advocates, which I strongly believe is our role. I see so many proposals now that have doctors organizing programs to provide additional income from their practices, sometimes by not working. I think that is dishonest. I don't know what will come of it.

I also think that we are going to see increasing socialization of the practice of medicine. Although

FIGURE 8. DAC During the interview in September 1996.

the Canadian system is far from ideal, it seems reasonably attractive because the public in general seems to approve the plan, even though we hear anecdotal accounts of situations where patients are denied hospitalization or denied treatment because the facilities are overburdened. I think we need to be realistic. I believe the average patient is motivated by economics. If the majority of Americans want a nationalized health program, I think they will ultimately have it. Such systems have endured in other parts of the world. Scandinavia has had socialized medicine for over 100 years. People in countries where it exists have adjusted, although I don't think socialized medicine is ideal.

• • •

WCR: You have designed a couple of artificial heart valves in the past. If you came up with a new design today, you probably would have a problem getting it implemented. That must be disturbing to you.

DAC: No question. I am expecting a visit this week from a group of Russians who have developed a valve that may work better than the mechanical valves available to us now. I am doubtful, however, that they will ever bring it to the marketplace in the United States because of restrictions placed by the FDA and internal review boards, and because of other circumstances that restrict progress in this country. In the early days of open heart surgery, we could develop a new device or technique in the experimental laboratory or even at the armchair and employ it immediately. Of course, there are certain disadvantages with that system, but we would not have made so much progress in those days if we had been under the same extensive restrictions in place today.

• • •

WCR: Do you think that it is ethical for physicians to invest in pharmaceutical or medical device companies?

DAC: Up to a level. I think physicians have to be cautious. I have sold any investment that I had in valve manufacturing companies. When I went through that Chapter 11 scrutiny, I was impressed with a story in *The Wall Street Journal,* which stated that I, as debtor and physician, had stock in tobacco companies and distilleries and that I raised beef on my farm, all of which are "bad for health." After that experience I decided that physicians could just as easily invest in other stocks without these negative connotations. Invest in the oil business, in automobile companies, or communications, but stay away from investments that may reflect on your integrity!

• • •

WCR: Dr. Cooley, you have met many of the more prominent people on planet Earth. Some are friends of yours. Are there any people who just stand out way above the rest to you?

DAC: That is hard to say. I never got very close to any of them. I do admire a number of people who have made outstanding contributions to our way of life, although it is hard for me to single some out.

• • •

WCR: The surgeons you have known—who stands out in your view?

DAC: As a contemporary, I've always admired Henry Bahnson. He is a very skillful surgeon, an academic, and a good person. I admire Walt Lillehei for his intrepidness in getting open heart surgery off the ground. I admire John Kirklin for his many contributions and for the thorough manner in which he has approached so many problems. These are just 3 examples of surgeons I admire; however, there are many others.

• • •

WCR: You have operated on probably more people than any surgeon in history, is that right?

DAC: Heart surgery anyway, probably more than anybody.

• • •

WCR: What is the number now in 1996?

DAC: In our group here, we have done 93,000 open heart operations.

• • •

WCR: That is your whole group, but what would your numbers be?

DAC: I have done maybe 45,000 pump cases here, and, as far as I can tell, maybe another 150,000 other types of operations. I have a long history, dating back more than 50 years to 1944 when I began my surgical career.

• • •

WCR: At the Texas Heart Institute, you have 1 surgery group and you are the leader of that group. When people come here, do they want you to operate on them?

DAC: Not all of them. At one time, say 20 years ago, most patients came here for me, and I would refer some of them to my colleagues. Today, the cardiologists determine which of my surgical colleagues they prefer. All of my associates, however, were trained in my program.

• • •

WCR: You have here 1 surgery group and a lot of different cardiology groups. How does it work? How do you keep so many entrepreneurs, so to speak, under 1 roof?

DAC: I originally planned it that way. In the early days, an institution doing heart surgery had 1 identified surgeon. The real advantage to our Institute's having 75 cardiologists instead of 5 or 6 is obvious. Hopefully, all of our cardiologists are also inclined toward clinical investigation and clinical research. There are, of course, some disadvantages to not having a core group of cardiologists. We do, however, have people like Dr. James Willerson, our medical director and chief of our Cardiology Division, who not only is an outstanding cardiologist but also is the director of our research and educational programs. I am sure Jim would welcome a core group of cardiologists working with him, and I think that may occur in the future. Meanwhile, we enjoy having a large and diversified staff of cardiologists.

• • •

WCR: How do you keep other surgery groups from coming in?

DAC: That is not easy. Many have applied. From a legal standpoint, one is required to accept anyone who wants to come if he or she has adequate credentials. Mostly, I have discouraged new applicants. Ours is a close-knit group, and a new surgeon or group would not flourish in this atmosphere.

• • •

WCR: When you went to college you weighed 140 pounds. You said after that freshmen year you ate a lot, you wanted to weigh more, and by the time you graduated from college you weighed what you do now.

DAC: 185 pounds.

• • •

WCR: Denton, is there any subject you would like to discuss that we haven't discussed?

DAC: I think we covered it all.

• • •

WCR: Denton, I appreciate your sharing your time, your mind, and some of your experiences with me and the AJC readers.

DAC'S MOST IMPORTANT 74 PUBLICATIONS SELECTED BY DAC FROM AMONG HIS 1,172 PUBLICATIONS

Journals

2. Cooley DA. Cardiac resuscitation during operations for pulmonic stenosis. *Ann Surg* 1950;132:930–936.

6. Cooley DA, DeBakey ME. Surgical considerations of intrathoracic aneurysms of the aorta and great vessels. *Ann Surg* 1952;135:660–680.

25. Cooley DA, DeBakey ME. Surgical considerations of excisional therapy for aortic aneurysms. *Surgery* 1953;34:1005–1020.

27. Cooley DA, DeBakey ME. Subtotal esophagectomy for bleeding esophageal varices. *Arch Surg* 1954;68:854–871.

35. Cooley DA, DeBakey ME. Ruptured aneurysms of abdominal aorta: excision and homograft replacement. *Postgrad Med* 1954;16:334–342.

41. Cooley DA, DeBakey ME. Resection of the thoracic aorta with replacement by homograft for aneurysms and constrictive lesions. *J Thorac Surg* 1955;29:66–104.

47. Cooley DA, Dunn JR, Brockman HL, DeBakey ME. Treatment of penetrating wounds of the heart: experimental and clinical observations. *Surgery* 1955;37:882–889.

55. Cooley DA, Mahaffey DE. Anomalous pulmonary venous drainage of the entire left lung; report of case with surgical correction. *Ann Surg* 1955;142:986–991.

65. Cooley DA, DeBakey ME. Hypothermia in the surgical treatment of aortic aneurysms. *Bull Soc Int Chir* 1956;15:206–215.

72. Cooley DA, Al-Naaman YD, Carton CA. Surgical treatment of arteriosclerotic occlusion of common carotid artery. *J Neurosurg* 1956;13:500–506.

76. Cooley DA, DeBakey ME. Resection of entire ascending aorta for fusiform aneurysm using temporary cardiac bypass. *JAMA* 1956;162:1158–1159.

82. Cooley DA, Belmonte BA, Zeis LB, Schnur S. Surgical repair of ruptured interventricular septum following acute myocardial infarction. *Surgery* 1957;41:930–937.

84. Cooley DA, Belmonte BA, DeBakey ME, Latson JR. Temporary extracorporeal circulation in the surgical treatment of cardiac and aortic disease: reports of 98 cases. *Ann Surg* 1957;145:898–914.

96. Cooley DA, Ochsner A Jr. Correction of total anomalous pulmonary venous drainage: technical considerations. *Surgery* 1957;42:1014–1021.

104. Cooley DA, Latson JR, Keats AS. Surgical considerations in repair of ventricular and atrial septal defects utilizing cardiopulmonary bypass: experience with 104 cases. *Surgery* 1958;43:214–225.

115. Cooley DA, Collins HA, Morris GC Jr, Chapman DW. Ventricular aneurysm after myocardial infarction: surgical excision with use of temporary cardiopulmonary bypass. *JAMA* 1958;167:557–560.

119. Abbott JP, Cooley DA, DeBakey ME, Ragland JE. Storage of blood for open heart operations: experimental and clinical observations. *Surgery* 1958;44:698–705.

129. Collins HA, Harberg FJ, Soltero LR, McNamara DG, Cooley DA. Cardiac surgery in the newborn: experience with 120 patients under one year of age. *Surgery* 1959;45:506–519.

132. Cooley DA, Collins HA. Anomalous drainage of entire pulmonary venous system into left innominate vein: clinical and surgical considerations. *Circulation* 1959;19:486–495.

141. Cooley DA, Henly WS, Amad KH, Chapman DW. Ventricular aneurysm following myocardial infarction: results of surgical treatment. *Ann Surg* 1959;150:595–612.

167. Blaisdell FW, Cooley DA. Relationship of spinal fluid pressure and incidence of paraplegia following temporary aortic occlusion: an experimental study. *Surg For* 1960;11:153–154.

184. Cooley DA, Beall AC Jr, Alexander JK. Acute massive pulmonary embolism: successful surgical treatment using temporary cardiopulmonary bypass. *JAMA* 1961;177:283–286.

187. Ellis PR Jr, Cooley DA, DeBakey ME. Clinical considerations and surgical treatment of annulo-aortic ectasia. *J Thorac Cardiovasc Surg* 1961;42:363–370.

191. Beall AC Jr, Morris GC Jr, Cooley DA, DeBakey ME. Homotransplantation of the aortic valve. *J Thorac Cardiovasc Surg* 1961;42:497–506.

196. Cooley DA, Beall AC Jr. Surgical treatment of acute massive pulmonary embolism using temporary cardiopulmonary bypass. *Dis Chest* 1962;41:102–104.

203. Ochsner JL, Cooley DA, McNamara DG, Kline A. Surgical treatment of cardiovascular anomalies in 300 infants younger than one year of age. *J Thorac Cardiovasc Surg* 1962;43:182–198.

206. Blaisdell FW, Cooley DA. The mechanism of paraplegia after temporary thoracic aortic occlusion and its relationship to spinal fluid pressure. *Surgery* 1962;51:351–355.

223. Cooley DA, Beall AC Jr, Grondin P. Open-heart operations with disposable oxgenators, 5 per cent dextrose prime, and normothermia. *Surgery* 1962;52:713–719.

225. Cooley DA, Berman S, Santibanez-Woolrich FA. Surgery in the newborn for congenital cardiovascular lesions: report of 400 consecutive operations. *JAMA* 1962;182:912–917.

235. Cooley DA, Billig DM. Surgical repair of congenital cardiac lesions in mirror image dextrocardia with situs inversus totalis. *Am J Cardiol* 1963;11:518–524.

248. Cooley DA, Hallman GL. Criteria for recommending surgery in total anomalous pulmonary venous drainage. *Am J Cardiol* 1963;12:98–99.

260. Cooley DA, Hallman GK, Henly WS. Left ventricular aneurysm due to myocardial infarction. *Arch Surg* 1964;88:114–121.

290. Cooley DA, Hallman GL. Surgery during the first year of life for cardiovascular anomalies: a review of 500 consecutive operations. *J Cardiovasc Surg* 1964;5:584–590.

320. Hallman GL, Cooley DA, Singer DB. Congenital anomalies of the coronary arteries: anatomy, pathology, and surgical treatment. *Surgery* 1966;59:133–144.

337. Cooley DA, Bloodwell RD, Beall AC Jr, Hallman GL, DeBakey ME. Surgical management of aneurysms of ascending aorta: including those associated with aortic valvular incompetence. *Surg Clin North Am* 1966;46:1033–1044.

344. Cooley DA, Hallman GL, Bloodwell RD, Leachman RD. Two-stage surgical treatment of complete transposition of the great vessels. *Arch Surg* 1966;93:704–714.

350. Cooley DA, Hallman GL, Bloodwell RD. Definitive surgical treatment of anomalous origin of left coronary artery from pulmonary artery: indications and results. *J Thorac Cardiovasc Surg* 1966;52:798–808.

354. Cooley DA, Bloodwell RD, Hallman GL, Jacobey JA. Aneurysm of the ascending aorta complicated by aortic valve incompetence: surgical treatment. *J Cardiovasc Surg* 1967;8:1–15.

357. Cooley DA, Bloodwell RD, Hallman GL, LaSorte AF, Leachman RD, Chapman DW. Surgical treatment of muscular subaortic stenosis. Results from septectomy in 26 patients. *Circulation* 1967;35(suppl. I):124–132.

388. Cooley DA, Bloodwell RD, Hallman GL, Nora JJ. Transplantation of the human heart: report of four cases. *JAMA* 1968;205:479–486.

390. Cooley DA, Bloodwell RD, Hallman GL. Cardiac transplantation for advanced acquired heart disease. *J Cardiovasc Surg* 1968;9:403–413.

394. Cooley DA, Hallman GL, Bloodwell RD, Nora JJ. Human heart transplantation: experience with twelve cases. *Am J Cardiol* 1968;22:804–810.

410. Cooley DA, Liotta D, Hallman GL, Bloodwell RD, Leachman RD, Milam JD. First human implantation of cardiac prosthesis for staged total replacement of the heart. *Trans Am Soc Artif Intern Organs* 1969;15:252–263.

414. Cooley DA, Bloodwell RD, Hallman GL, Nora JJ, Harrison GM, Leachman RD. Organ transplantation for advanced cardiopulmonary disease. *Ann Thorac Surg* 1969;8:30–46.

426. Cooley DA, Liotta D, Hallman GL, Bloodwell RD, Leachman RD, Milam JD. Orthotopic cardiac prosthesis for two-staged cardiac replacement. *Am J Cardiol* 1969;24:723–730.

516. Cooley DA, Reul GJ, Wukasch DC. Ischemic contracture of the heart: ''stone heart.'' *Am J Cardiol* 1972;29:575–577.

532. Cooley DA, Leachman, RD, Wukasch DC. Diffuse muscular subaortic stenosis: surgical treatment. *Am J Cardiol* 1973;31:1–6.

549. Cooley DA, Dawson JT, Hallman GL, Sandiford FM, Wukasch DC, Garcia E, Hall RJ. Aortocoronary saphenous vein bypass: results in 1,492 patients, with particular reference to patients with complicating features. *Ann Thorac Surg* 1973;16:380–390.

618. Reul GJ Jr, Cooley DA, Wukasch DC, Kyger ER III, Sandiford FM, Hallman GL, Norman JC. Long-term survival following coronary artery bypass: analysis of 4,522 consecutive patients. *Arch Surg* 1975;110: 1419–1424.

647. Cooley DA, Angelini P, Leachman RD, Kyger ER III. Intraventricular repair of transposition complexes with ventricular septal defect. *J Thorac Cardiovasc Surg* 1976;71:461–464.

667. Cooley DA, Wukasch DC, Leachman RD. Mitral valve replacement for idiopathic hypertrophic subaortic stenosis: results in 27 patients. *J Cardiovasc Surg* 1976;17:380–387.

670. Cooley DA, Norman JC, Reul GJ Jr, Kidd JN, Nihill MR. Surgical treatment of left ventricular outflow tract obstructions with apicoaortic valved conduit. *Surgery* 1976;80:674–680.

696. Wukasch DC, Cooley DA, Sandiford FM, Nappi G, Reul GJ Jr. Ascending aorta-abdominal aorta bypass: indications, technique, and report of 12 patients. *Ann Thorac Surg* 1977;23:442–448.

734. Ott DA, Frazier OH, Cooley DA. Resection of the aortic arch using deep hypothermia and temporary circulatory arrest. *Circulation* 1978;57,58(suppl. I):227–231.

793. Krajcer Z, Lufschanowski R, Angelini P, Leachman RD, Cooley DA. Septal myomectomy and mitral valve replacement for idiopathic hypertrophic subaortic stenosis: an echocardiographic and hemodynamic study. *Circulation* 1980;62(suppl. I):158–164.

818. Cooley DA, Ott DA, Frazier OH, Walker WE. Surgical treatment of aneurysms of the transverse aortic arch: experience with 25 patients using hypothermic techniques. *Ann Thorac Surg* 1981;32:260–272.

885. Cooley DA, Frazier OH, Painvin GA, Boldt L, Kahan BD. Cardiac and cardiopulmonary transplantation using cyclosporine for immunosuppression: recent Texas Heart Institute experience. *Transplant Proc* 1983;15(suppl. 1):2567–2572.

916. Reece IJ, Cooley DA, Painvin A, Okereke OUJ, Powers PL, Pechacek LW, Frazier OH. Surgical treatment of mitral systolic click syndrome: results in 37 patients. *Ann Thorac Surg* 1985;39:155–158.

930. Cooley DA, Reardon MJ, Frazier OH, Angelini P. Human cardiac explantation and autotransplantation: application in a patient with a large cardiac pheochromocytoma. *Tex Heart Inst J* 1985;12:171–176.

954. Frazier OH, Cooley DA, Heart transplantation at the Texas Heart Institute. *J Heart Transplant* 1986;5:61.

968. Cooley DA, Frazier OH, Van Buren CT, Bricker JT, Radovancevic B. Cardiac transplantation in an 8-month-old female infant with subendocardial fibroelastosis. *JAMA* 1986;256:1326–1329.

997. Colon R, Frazier OH, Cooley DA, McAllister HA. Hypothermic regional perfusion for protection of the spinal cord during periods of ischemia. *Ann Thorac Surg* 1987;43:639–643.

1044. Cooley DA. Ventricular endoaneurysmorrhaphy: results of an improved method of repair. *Tex Heart Inst J* 1989;16:72–75.

1049. Cooley DA. Ventricular endoaneurysmorrhaphy: a simplified repair for extensive postinfarction aneursym. *J Card Surg* 1989;200–205.

1082. Lewis CT, Murphy MC, Cooley DA. Risk factors for cardiac operations in adult Jehovah's witnesses. *Am Thorac Surg* 1991;51:448–450.

1103. Cooley DA, Baldwin RT. Technique of open distal anastomosis for repair of descending thoracic aortic aneurysms. *Ann Thorac Surg* 1992;54:932–936.

1120. Cooley DA, Colosimo LR. Eversion technique for carotid endarterctomy. *Surg Gynecol Obstet* 1993;177:420–422.

1131. Cooley DA. Fifty years of cardiovascular surgery. *Ann Thorac Surg* 1994;57:1059–1063.

1147. Cooley DA. Retrograde replacement of the thoracic aorta. *Tex Heart Inst J* 1995;22:162–165.

Books

Cooley DA, Hallman GL. Surgical Treatment of Congenital Heart Disease. Philadelphia: Lea & Febiger, 1966.

Hallman GL, Cooley DA, Gutgesell HP. Surgical Treatment of Congenital Heart Disease. 3rd Ed. Philadelphia: Lea & Febiger, 1987.

Cooley DA, Wukasch DC. Techniques in Vascular Surgery. Philadelphia: W. B. Saunders, 1979.

Cooley DA. Surgical Treatment of Aortic Aneurysms. Philadelphia: W. B. Saunders, 1986.

Cooley DA. Techniques in Cardiac Surgery. 2nd Ed. Philadelphia: W. B. Saunders, 1984.

DAVID KEMPTON CARTWRIGHT COOPER, MD:
A Conversation With the Editor*

David Cooper is presently an immunologist (Surgery) at the Transplantation Biology Research Center of Massachusetts General Hospital, and an Associate Professor of Surgery (Immunology) at Harvard Medical School in Boston, Massachusetts. He was born in London, United Kingdom, on July 27, 1939. He graduated from Guy's Hospital Medical School of the University of London in 1963 and received a PhD from the Institute of Cardiology of the National Heart Hospital of the University of London in 1973. His training in cardiothoracic surgery continued until 1980 when he went to Cape Town, South Africa, as a faculty member of the University of Cape Town Medical School. In 1987 he went to Oklahoma City where he developed the transplantation program of Baptist Medical Center. In 1996 he joined the faculty of Harvard Medical School and the Transplantation Biology Research Center in Boston. Dr. Cooper is the author of 348 articles published in medical journals, 88 chapters in books, and the editor or author of 7 books. His most recent book, *Outwitting Evolution*, written with Robert Lanza, is currently in press. It is a review of xenotransplantation aimed at both scientists and/or physicians and the lay person. He has received several awards for his contributions to the field of xenotransplantation. He is the co-inventor of 5 patents related to the methods for removing antipig antibodies from potential human recipients of pig organs. He and his group are working intensively to make pig-to-primate transplantation a reality. He is also the author of 5 plays for stage, television or radio, a few short stories and articles, and 1 full-length (unpublished) novel. Two of the plays have been broadcast by the South African Broadcasting Company, and 1 play won a playwriting contest in Oklahoma. Finally, he is a lovely person with a charming personality.

WILLIAM CLIFFORD ROBERTS, MD (hereafter, WCR)[†]: *I am talking with Dr. David Cooper on September 9, 1998. Dr. Cooper is here at Baylor University Medical Center as Visiting Professor of the Baylor Transplantation Institute. Dr. Cooper, we are honored by your presence here at Baylor. Dr. Cooper gave a talk at surgical grand rounds earlier today and he is now in my office sharing a bit of his background. Dr. Cooper, I gather that you were born in London, United Kingdom. Could you talk a bit about your early upbringing?*

*This series of interviews are underwritten by an unrestricted grant from Bristol-Myers Squibb.
†Baylor Cardiovascular Institute, Baylor University Medical Center, Dallas, Texas 75246.
‡Immunologist (Surgery), Transplantation Biology Research Center, Massachusetts General Hospital, and Associate Professor of Surgery, Harvard Medical School, Boston, Massachusetts 02129.

DAVID KEMPTON CARTWRIGHT COOPER, MD (hereafter, DKCC)[‡]: I was born in south London in July 1939, about 6 weeks before the Second World War started. My family lived directly under the route used by the bombers coming from Germany. There was a big ammunition factory not far from where we lived, so we had our full share of the Blitz. I was moved out of London several times with my mother when the bombing got particularly heavy. I went to a local school. In those days, at the age of 11, we took an examination called the "11 Plus" scholarship, and you either then went on to a "grammar school," which was very academic, or you went to a "secondary modern school." (This system was later abolished. Everybody now goes to the same type of school because it was felt you should not discriminate at the age of 11.) Fortunately, I passed the exam and went to a grammar school where the standard of academic work was fairly high, and a large number of us went on to university. However, far fewer went to university than they do today. At age 16, the courses we took were reduced to just 3. My 3 subjects were English, history, and geography. We took an exam at 18 to go on to university. But during those 2 years (ages 16 to 18) I decided that I wanted to do medicine.

I found that I could go to medical school at London University even without having taken science. I did an extra year "crash" course in science and then joined the usual group. It was difficult at first, but I got through. The medical school was at Guy's Hospital in London, which is famous for physicians such as *Thomas Hodgkin* of Hodgkin's disease, *Richard Bright* of Bright's disease, and *Thomas Addison* of Addison's disease. Those 3 were all on the staff at the same time. That was a great period. The medical school also is famous because it is the oldest Rugby football club in the world. The game of Rugby started at Rugby School, but the first actual club to be formed was at Guy's Hospital. It is also famous because *John Keats*, the poet, was a medical student there and graduated in medicine. He never practiced medicine and unfortunately died very young.

I was influenced very much there by 2 cardiac surgeons, *Lord Russell Brock* and *Donald Ross*. Lord Brock was one of the earliest heart surgeons in Britain and Europe. He did the first pulmonic valvulotomy in a child with pulmonary valve stenosis. Donald Ross did the first homograft aortic valve replacement. I went into cardiac surgery because of their influence. I did my general surgical training mainly in Cambridge with *Sir Roy Calne,* of organ transplantation fame. He had also studied medicine at Guy's Hospital, by the way. Sir Roy introduced azathioprine, an early immunosuppressive drug, and really initiated the concept of pharmacologic immunosuppressive therapy. He was also the first to use cyclosporine in transplant patients,

FIGURE 1. DKCC during the interview.

and the first surgeon to perform liver transplantation on a regular basis other than *Thomas Starzl* in the USA. My experience with Sir Roy probably explains my interest in transplantation. I was always interested in research. I did an internship, part of a surgical residency, and then took off for 3 years to get a PhD at the Institute of Cardiology, London University. I ended up with training in general and cardiothoracic surgery, with a PhD in cardiovascular research, and an interest in transplantation. The first heart transplant in England was done at the National Heart Hospital in 1968 while I was a PhD student there, and I was also at Papworth Hospital in Cambridge as a chief resident when heart transplantation began there in 1979.

I left England in 1980 to do 1 year's research with *Chris Barnard* in Cape Town, South Africa. I wanted to stay in academic cardiac surgery and there were few opportunities in Britain at that time. I thought I would spend a year with Chris Barnard and then perhaps go back to Britain and find a suitable post. While I was in Cape Town, I cared for the transplant patients and did some research, and during that first year Barnard offered me a post on the faculty. As a consequence, I stayed there for 7 years, by which time he had retired. He then helped set up a transplant program in Oklahoma City, and they invited me to join him. I spent 9 years in Oklahoma City looking after the transplant patients and doing research. I gave up routine cardiac

surgery for transplantation because that was where my interests lay.

I was then invited to relocate to the Massachusetts General Hospital at Harvard Medical School by *David Sachs,* a leading transplant immunologist. Two years ago I gave up doing clinical work and concentrated entirely on trying to solve the problems of xenotransplantation.

WCR: *Who influenced you to be a physician? Was there any medical heritage in your family?*

DKCC: None whatsoever. No one in either my father's or my mother's families had anything to do with medicine. My father was a businessman. I had thought that my skills were on the arts and humanities side. I was quite good at writing and, therefore, thought I was not really scientifically inclined. However, I was quite good at biology. When I was about 16, I joined a youth group and toured a suburban hospital in London, and then became interested in medicine. There was something about seeing the hospital and what was going on there that made me think that that was what I wanted to do. By this time, however, I was committed at school to the arts. But I made some inquiries and found that one could still get into medical school even without scientific qualifications. There was no influence from my family to go into medicine; they wanted me to do whatever I wanted to do.

WCR: *You started at Guy's Hospital Medical School at age 18?*

DKCC: Yes. We went straight from high school to study medicine.

WCR: *Medical school was 6 years?*

DKCC: It was actually about 5 years, but I had to put in an extra year because of having lacked science courses earlier.

WCR: *Did you enjoy medical school?*

DKCC: Yes, very much. The science was difficult, but I worked very hard at first and did well. The second and third years included anatomy and physiology, and I was not at my best there. I got overconfident after the first successful year. I took life a little bit too easily, and also I did not have particularly good health during those 2 years. I had to re-sit the exams 3 months later. I then picked up healthwise and pulled myself together, and did the 3 years of clinical work and enjoyed those immensely. I did well then. As a result, I got a good internship based on my medical school record.

WCR: *Was it easy for you to decide that you wanted to be a surgeon versus an internist or something else?*

DKCC: I was always attracted to surgery because the surgeon could personally and directly make the patient better. It was just a little more personal than prescribing a drug to make the patient better. It just seemed very satisfying. Also, I never thought of myself as being particularly academic. I thought the internists knew a lot more than the surgeons. Surgery is fairly simple. You chop something out or put something in. The only other area that I actually seriously considered pursuing, apart from surgery, was psychiatry, which is the other extreme. Psychiatry appealed to me because I had never seen patients who suffered so much as psychiatric patients. Their lifestyle was appalling, I thought. Even if you had cancer or heart disease, you enjoyed some moments of the day—music, television—but people with depressive disorders enjoyed nothing, and this had an impact on me. Added to which, I felt there was a great need for some sensible people in psychiatry because psychiatry was still primitive. I believed there was going to be tremendous progress in the treatment of psychiatric diseases. But I thought it was all going to come from new drugs. I was afraid, therefore, that the psychiatrist would actually not be doing very much except prescribing drugs. On balance, I thought I was more suited to surgery, and would be more satisfied with this as a career. General surgery, in contrast to cardiac, was not interesting to me. Cardiac was the thing that really appealed to me, and I think that was because it was a very exciting era. It was new and developing, and newness has always attracted me. No sooner had I gotten into cardiac surgery, I moved into the transplant arena, and that was even newer and more exciting. As soon as that had become routine, I moved into xenotransplantation, which is even more exciting. I always like to be at the cutting edge of the field. A research-type career always appealed to me.

WCR: *After 18 months as a house officer, beginning in 1965, you took 3 years off from your training in surgery to get a PhD. You also came to the States?*

DKCC: I came to the States to teach anatomy at Harvard Medical School. In England, to take what is the equivalent of your "Boards" — the Fellowship of the Royal College of Surgeons—anatomy, physiology, and pathology are included in the first examination. We had to study to get up to the high standard required. In those days, quite a few of us took a year to teach 1 of those subjects to refresh ourselves about them. I did some research at the Peter Bent Brigham Hospital (in *Professor Francis Moore's* department) while in Boston, but my prime aim was to teach anatomy and give myself time to refresh my memory of the subject, particularly as I had not done very well in those exams when in medical school. Luckily, I found I was a good teacher. I found the medical school class at Harvard absolutely outstanding. I was stunned by how quickly the students learned. I was also very impressed by how friendly they were. Some of them remained friends for many years. The most famous of this class has proved to be *Michael Crichton,* the author. Then I went back to England and did a year of junior residency. After that I took the time off to do the PhD.

WCR: *You did your PhD where?*

DKCC: I did it at London University at the Institute of Cardiology, which was the postgraduate teaching center for cardiology and cardiac surgery associated with the National Heart Hospital.

WCR: *So you had decided early on that you wanted to be an academician and a researcher?*

DKCC: Yes.

WCR: *You did your PhD in what?*

DKCC: I studied donor heart resuscitation and storage. I was with a group working on combined heart

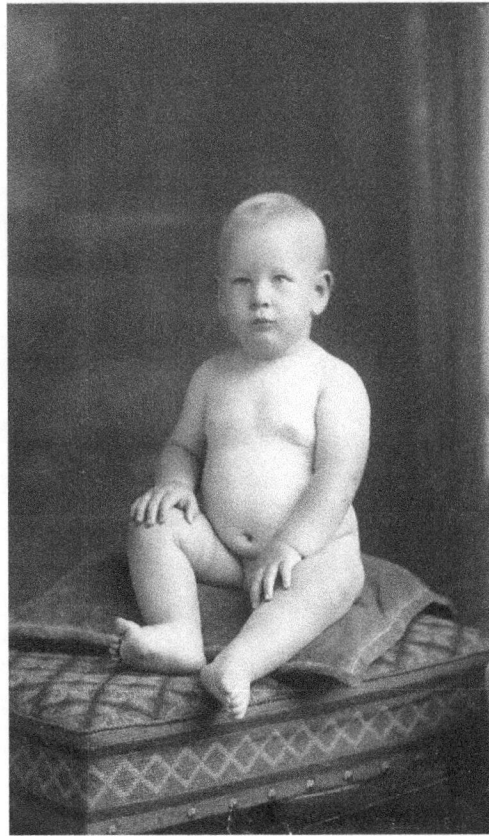

FIGURE 2. DKCC as a baby—first known photograph.

and lung transplantation in the lab. This was in 1967, before any human heart transplants had been done. I believed that this area was the future. My PhD was on methods of storing the heart with a view to later transplantation.

WCR: *Not only had you decided on an academic career, but you had decided on the area of cardiovascular disease you wanted to work in.*

DKCC: I had certainly decided on cardiovascular disease, and I thought that transplantation would be the future. But I did not realize it would be the future so quickly. Within 6 months of starting my PhD research, Chris Barnard did the first cardiac transplant.

WCR: *In the United Kingdom, you can virtually train forever in surgery. Although you finished medical school in 1963, your full training was not completed until 1979!*

DKCC: That is correct. I took a little bit longer than most, partly because I took 3 years off to do the PhD and 1 year off to teach anatomy. I also interrupted my training at different times to experience life as a ship surgeon, help out in a mission hospital in India, and work as a flying doctor in Central Canada. After completing general surgery and a junior residency in cardiac surgery, I still had 4 years more as a senior/chief resident in cardiothoracic surgery. At the end of that time, which was about 1977, I could have gotten a permanent post in the UK, but because I was so keen on staying in an academic environs I went from London back to Cambridge and did another 2 years as a

FIGURE 3. DKCC in his very early teens.

chief resident at Papworth Hospital, under *Sir Terence English* (another Guy's graduate). It was during that time that we initiated the heart transplantation program there—the first fully established program in the UK. Since returning from the USA, I had been teaching anatomy once a week at a Cambridge college—Magdalene College—in addition to doing the surgical residency. I was made a Fellow of the College, which was quite an honor, and which gave me certain privileges in the College. Being a bachelor at that time, it gave me a wonderful lifestyle. I lived in the College. I dined in the College's 17th century hall by candlelight with some very interesting people—the Professors of English and eminent historians, for example. It was a wonderful experience to be part of that group. I wanted to continue doing that, and that is one reason I went back to Cambridge for a couple of years. Toward the end of that 2 years, there was still no obvious academic post coming up anywhere in Britain. I then decided to spend another year in research, hoping something would come up. That was when I went to Cape Town, which was ideal for me because Barnard had a very good research lab and a good transplant program.

WCR: *How did you meet Chris Barnard? Were you already friends?*

DKCC: I had met him a couple of times. After I did my internship, before I came to the States, I spent 3 months as a ship surgeon. Several of us did this at the time, and it was really just to have a vacation. In those days, there were ships that went from Southampton in England to Cape Town, and around to Durban in South Africa every week. I was on a Mediterranean cruise and then I was on 1 of the ships to South Africa. It took 6 weeks to South Africa and back and was a wonderful experience. I lived like a king, having my own table and guests in the first class dining room. I met some very interesting people. I had just finished working with Donald Ross, the cardiac surgeon, in London, who was a South African from the same medical school class as Chris Barnard. Ross knew Barnard well, and said I should see him when I got to Cape Town. He gave me a letter of introduction. I thought Chris Barnard would not be interested in seeing me—a very junior doctor then but, in fact, he was very interested because he was quite isolated in Cape Town. The nearest cardiac surgeons were either in Australia or Europe, and he did not normally meet anybody who had any cardiac surgical experience. Even though I had only been an intern, at least I knew what was going on in London. He wanted to talk to me about my London experience and what Donald Ross was doing. He showed me around the wards. He was very pleasant. Cape Town was beautiful, really spectacular. I met Barnard again when I was doing my PhD. Whenever he was in London, he visited the National Heart Hospital. But meeting him briefly on 2 occasions did not influence my getting a post with him. That is how I came to Cape Town.

WCR: *That was in 1980?*

DKCC: Yes. I went there in February 1980.

WCR: *How did it work out? I gather you did a lot of surgery there other than transplantation?*

DKCC: Yes. We had a busy adult program—largely valve surgery, because the nonwhite population had a high incidence of rheumatic heart disease. We did relatively little coronary surgery compared to that being done in Britain and the States. Some of the valve surgery was in children. We replaced one or more of their valves when they were very young, sometimes aged 7 to 10. It was a busy and varied practice. There was also pediatric congenital heart disease, but this was not my main interest. I did participate in it, but there were a couple of surgeons who did most of it. My main interest was the transplant program. Under Chris Barnard, I actually ran the program the whole time I was there. I also helped run the research lab. We had a PhD biochemist in the lab, *Winston Wicomb*, with whom I spent a lot of time. That is when I first started getting interested in xenotransplantation. The move to South Africa worked out very well for me. First of all, Cape Town was a wonderful place in which to live, with spectacular scenery and a beautiful climate. I could not speak more highly about it. Also, although the apartheid system was bad, in Cape Town there were many liberal people. The University of Cape Town made a great stand against apartheid. In our hospital, we illegally put all races in the same ward. We were supposed to have 1 ward for whites and 1 for nonwhites. I never saw any discrimination at all. We treated all races exactly the same. In fact, to some extent, the South Africans got a bad rap internationally. For ex-

FIGURE 4. DKCC as a ship surgeon in 1965.

ample, if you were a poor black man in a country area, our cardiologist would visit that area once a month and you would be brought in to see him. If you needed surgery, you would be flown to Cape Town free of charge, have exactly the same care in exactly the same unit as the white patients, and then be flown home and followed up in your home area. It would cost you nothing. You cannot get that care in the USA, let alone anywhere else. If you were a child from Zimbabwe or Zambia or Kenya, and if you could get down to Cape Town, you would not pay a penny for your care. The South African government would cover everything. There were many good things about South Africa. I felt to some extent that I was almost a missionary, because most of the patients I operated on were non-white. However, we tended not to transplant nonwhite patients if they were from areas where they could not cope with the immunosuppressive regimen. We could not send them back to a country area 500 miles away and expect them to manage a complex therapy regimen. Many of the so-called "colored" population (mixed race) in Cape Town, however, had transplants, and did very well.

WCR: *When you went to Cape Town in 1980 from Cambridge, by that time Professor Chris Barnard was not operating much anymore?*

DKCC: He was doing about 1 case a week, or he would go in with 1 of our senior surgeons who would help him or do most of the procedure.

WCR: *So when you went there in 1980, you were the "main man" in cardiac transplantation.*

DKCC: Yes, for most of the time. He would nearly always come into the transplant operation and look over with the anesthesiologist and advise, but he was not doing much. Two other surgeons and I essentially did all of the transplants.

WCR: *How many transplants were you doing annually in Cape Town?*

DKCC: We were doing only 10 to 15 a year. When I got there they had done less than 50 altogether since 1967. They did 10 quickly, and then they went on hold for a while because the results were poor. I was involved in about 70 cardiac transplants in Cape Town. Remember, I went there in 1980, and there were not that many groups doing cardiac transplants anywhere at that time. It was before cyclosporine. In England, for example, we had done 3 in the 1968 to 1969 era, and then there were none done until 1979.

WCR: *You stayed in Cape Town 7 years?*

DKCC: Yes.

WCR: *It was 1987 when you moved to Oklahoma?*

DKCC: Yes.

WCR: *How did that come about? I realize that Chris Barnard had a relationship with Oklahoma City.*

DKCC: Chris Barnard retired early (in his early 60s) because he had rheumatoid arthritis. It was not entirely the arthritis; he admitted that he had just lost interest in medicine. The last year he was there we hardly saw him. He came into his office, but never came into the unit. He only stayed on because the hospital asked him to do so. There were 7 faculty and 4 of us were senior enough to be considered for his position as Professor. Two were pediatric surgeons, and 2, including me, did mainly adult surgery. I think the authorities thought that if they gave the job to any 1 of us, the others might leave because we were "competitors." They chose a surgeon from abroad, and we were all disappointed. The 4 of us left. I was the last to do so. I was made the Associate Professor, but I thought "what is the future with another surgeon of my age coming in as the Professor?" I also wondered about the future of the country. The sanctions had made things more expensive. Travel abroad was becoming very difficult because the rand had dropped in value, and therefore getting to meetings abroad was increasingly difficult. I realized I was growing progressively more isolated professionally. Furthermore, we had done some outstandingly good work there, particularly on storage of hearts. In 1981 we had actually stored patients' donor hearts in a perfusion machine for up to 17 hours before we transplanted them. We also did some seminal work on the effects of brain death on the heart. We hardly ever got the opportunity to present this work anywhere outside of South Africa. It was partly because we were in Cape Town, which is a long way to bring somebody just to give a talk. I felt that, from a professional perspective and possibly from a personal perspective, my future was doubtful because of the changes taking place in South Africa and our isolation.

FIGURE 5. DKCC training with the University of London second VIII at Henley Royal Regatta 1969. DKCC is rowing at 7 (second oarsman from left).

Chris Barnard had gone to Oklahoma City to advise. He was not actually practicing surgery because he did not have a license in Oklahoma. One day he phoned me in Cape Town. I asked what he was doing and he said he was working in Oklahoma City. This was the last place I expected Chris Barnard to be! He told me what he was doing, and the salary he was being paid. In South Africa you got paid peanuts compared with the States. I jokingly said to him, "Can't you get me a job?" I was not seriously thinking about it at all. A month later he phoned and asked if I would really like a job. I said I had not thought about it. He asked that I phone a certain Oklahoma surgeon and discuss it. They evidently wanted to bring me and *Dimitri Novitzky* to Oklahoma to put the heart transplant program on a firm basis because they realized it was more work than they had originally thought. Dimitri was keen to go. He had a wife and children and felt the future in South Africa was doubtful for his family. The biochemist with whom we had done all the interesting research on storage of the heart had already left to go to San Francisco. I realized that my close friends and colleagues had either gone or wanted to go. South Africa seemed to be slowly going downhill. I therefore took the opportunity to move to the States. I had no American exams whatsoever. There was a regulation in Oklahoma, however, that if you were licensed in the United Kingdom you could be licensed in Oklahoma. If they had insisted that I take any exams, I would not have gone. I was too old to start studying again.

During my first year in Oklahoma City, I wondered if I had made a mistake. I missed Cape Town enormously. But our transplant program in Oklahoma went very well. We did 32 transplants before we had a death, whereas of the previous 12, 6 had died. We put the program on a firm basis. By the time I left, the 2-year survival was 92%. It worked out very well professionally for me. I made more money than I would have made in South Africa, and had the opportunity to go to meetings. In Oklahoma City, we had a research lab at the University where they had a breeding colony of baboons, so I was able to continue working on baboons. That was very important because it is only baboons, humans, and apes that have antibodies against pigs. Baptist Medical Center supported most of my research so I did not have to apply for grants. I attracted several research fellows, who were very productive. From both clinical and research perspectives, it worked out extremely well for me in Oklahoma.

WCR: *In actuality, Oklahoma City turned out to be a bonanza for you?*

DKCC: Yes. I met my wife there!

WCR: *You did not get married until what age?*

DKCC: I was over 50.

WCR: *You were single for 50 years!*

DKCC: Yes, and I enjoyed every minute of it! I have a lovely wife, and it was the best thing that happened to me.

WCR: *Do you have children?*

DKCC: Unfortunately, we don't.

WCR: *What year did you get married?*

DKCC: We got married in 1991, almost 8 years ago.

FIGURE 6. DKCC in his study at Magdalene College, Cambridge, United Kingdom, in the mid-1970s.

WCR: *It is pretty unusual for Harvard Medical School and Massachusetts General Hospital to pluck a person from Oklahoma City to bring him to Boston. How did that come about?*

DKCC: I decided I wanted to leave Oklahoma City. There were some problems which I was not happy about. It is a long and complicated story. David Sachs, at the Massachusetts General Hospital, had heard that I was looking to move. He had been developing pig-to-primate xenotransplantation, but had run into problems because of the antibodies that reject pig organs. These antibodies had been my main research interest. Our group in Oklahoma had discovered the nature of these antibodies. We had also developed ways of trying to get rid of them. I had met David Sachs at several meetings. One day he phoned and asked if I would be interested in joining him in Boston. He asked if I wanted to do any clinical work once I got there. By that time, I had been in transplantation for almost 17 years and I was getting a bit tired. I had been on call every day both in Cape Town and in Oklahoma City for donors or for problems with transplant patients. I felt I had done my stint. It was getting increasingly difficult to do both research and clinical work. I told him I would do clinical work if I had to, but I preferred not to. He said that sounded fine because they had plenty of clinicians. I joined him 2 years ago to run a group under him. We have a total of 60 or 70 people in the Transplantation Biology Research Center. My group consists of about 10 people working on pig-to-primate organ transplantation. We draw on what the other groups are doing. These groups are studying pig and monkey allografts, and there are rodent groups and a molecular biology group. We draw on all the expertise of these groups and try to put the whole thing together. For a year or so we did not make much progress, but recently we have taken a few steps forward and they are very encouraging. I have enjoyed it very much, and haven't missed clinical work at all. I am very busy, and it has enabled me to fulfill my wish of being in an academic environment. There are many interesting and intelligent people at Harvard and, therefore, a lot of stimuli.

It has given me more time to write, and I get invited to speak more.

WCR: *Where are you actually located? Are you located at the Massachusetts General Hospital?*

DKCC: Yes. The Massachusetts General Hospital has half of its research in the hospital complex and half elsewhere. About 6 or 7 years ago the hospital bought a large building in what was the former Charlestown Navy Yard (about 15 minutes from the main hospital), and converted it into laboratory space. We are in that building. I go to the main hospital for the clinical transplant rounds, in which I participate to keep in touch with what is going on, but our laboratory is actually located in the research facility.

WCR: *What is your title now?*

DKCC: My title is Immunologist (Surgery), and I am also Lecturer on Surgery. I believe they are in the final steps of considering me for an Associate Professorship.

WCR: *You have been doing research in cardiac transplantation since age 27. You have been in that arena a long time and your goal is to make xenotransplantation a reality for human beings?*

DKCC: Yes.

WCR: *What you are working on is to be able to use pig hearts to replace human hearts?*

DKCC: Yes.

WCR: *If you had to predict right now what year that might come about, what would you say?*

DKCC: I think there is a reasonable prospect it may come about within 5 years—but 5 years ago I said the same thing. We are beginning to solve the problems. It will come in stages. It will be ex vivo pig liver perfusion first in patients with acute liver failure, then maybe pig kidney transplantation, and then heart transplantation. There may well be some kidney transplants within a couple of years. How successful they will be, I am not sure. I don't think pig heart transplantation will be a routine procedure in 5 years, but there may be some attempts within that period of time.

WCR: *Will pig lungs be able to replace human lungs, too?*

DKCC: Pig lungs should be able to cope. They primarily exchange gas, and there should be no reason why they should not be able to do that. But pig lungs are very sensitive to even minor rejection changes. This fact is going to delay pig lung transplantation for a while until we really have a solution to the rejection response.

WCR: *Could you discuss why pig hearts are preferred over baboon hearts?*

DKCC: Basically, you can obtain baboons only from the wild. There are not that many in captivity. We are worried about the virus infections they carry in the wild. The AIDS virus is thought to have originated in a primate species. If you breed baboons, they take 9 years to grow to full size. They breed in ones or twos, which means it is going to be a very expensive and time-consuming process to breed them. Even the largest of male baboons rarely get to 40 kg in weight; most females are only 20 to 25 kg, so to get hearts that are going to support the circulation of humans, who may

FIGURE 7. DKCC with Chris Barnard at the time of Barnard's retirement from the staff of the Groote Schuur Hospital, Cape Town, South Africa, in 1984.

weigh 80 or 90 kg, is going to be impossible. You could treat them with growth hormone or implant growth genes, but that is complicated. Also, to try to transgenically manipulate baboons will be difficult.

In contrast, pigs can breed in large numbers and are cheap. They grow quickly, and they can be genetically manipulated. However, a baboon heart placed into a human—a procedure which has been done—with present day immunosuppression would survive at least a few weeks or months. A pig heart in a human, in contrast, survives a few minutes or hours, or maybe, if you are lucky, a few days. There is a much greater rejection response to a pig organ, and that is related to the presence of galactose sugars on the surface of pig cells, against which we have antibodies. Some microorganisms in our gut also have the same sugars on them. We are not born with these antibodies, but within a few weeks we develop them as a protective mechanism against the colonizing bacteria. Unfortunately, they crossreact with pig organs. We have to get over this hurdle if we want pig organs to replace human organs.

WCR: *That has been 1 of your finest contributions, the identification of the surface sugars on the cells of the pigs that make humans reject pig organs?*

DKCC: Yes. That was very important. Several other groups have rediscovered it since then, but we were the first to draw attention to it. To demonstrate how we might get around this problem was also important.

WCR: *Not many surgeons are willing to spend full-time in the laboratory. You have obviously changed professions. You have become a scientist. I don't mean to use the word "technician" to describe what surgeons do in a detrimental manner, but taking out a human heart and putting in another heart is a lot easier than trying to overcome the problem of xenograft rejection, which is what you are challenged by now. What is your life like now? How much time are you in the lab?*

DKCC: I am fortunate in having research fellows and research technicians who do most of the actual work, although I am in touch with them the whole time. We plan everything together, and work closely

with a biotechnology company in Boston called Bio Transplant. I lead a large group that meets each week to review what we have done and what we are planning to do. One nice aspect of the job is that I do have time to think and read. When I was doing clinical work, it was very difficult to find the time to read what other people were doing, and get some ideas from what they were doing. Today, I am able to spend my time with the fellows, supervising, reviewing the results, planning what we should do when things go wrong, meeting with David Sachs, and meeting with the other groups working on related topics. I have always been interested in research. If at any time in my life I had had to choose either research or clinical work, I might have opted for research. It has always been exciting for me to try to do something that will not help just a single patient but might help a generation of patients. If we could solve the problems of xenotransplantation, there are thousands of patients who might benefit. Then you might really feel that you had done something useful with your life.

WCR: *You are on a mission?*

DKCC: Yes, but to some extent it is a selfish mission. I get pleasure and satisfaction out of it, so I would not say it is a wholly altruistic mission. Nevertheless, it would be nice to think you have done something that people value.

WCR: *You are a big guy. How tall are you?*

DKCC: Six feet 5 inches.

WCR: *Were you an athlete?*

DKCC: I was an oarsman when I was at university. I captained the medical school crew. Then I rowed for the University of London second crew. The first crew was the British Olympic crew at the time. They were the best in the UK.

WCR: *What have you done thus far that you are most proud of?*

DKCC: I suppose it is the identification of what these antipig antibodies are directed against. One doesn't always get recognition for it. I have found some people are hesitant to say you discovered it before they did. Once we reported it, everybody wrote about it. But I can remember quite clearly when we were racking our brains to find out what antigen these antibodies were directed against. We hazarded a guess that it was a carbohydrate. We had this link-up with a carbohydrate company in Canada, and I remember going up to them and asking whether, if we provided the antibody, they could tell us what sugar it bound to, and they said "yes." It was a very important step because most people thought there must be hundreds of targets for antipig antibodies. In fact, just this 1 is really crucial. That was an important step forward. That gives me a great deal of satisfaction. I get a little upset when I see a review article, and the author credits the discovery to somebody else, who may have published this fact 2 to 4 years after we did.

WCR: *Who else is focusing full-steam ahead on xenotransplantation?*

DKCC: Our group is working in association with BioTransplant. *Fritz Bach,* who is Professor of Immunology at Harvard at the New England Deaconess

Hospital, has a group working on it. *Jeff Platt,* who was at Duke University and has just moved to the Mayo Clinic, has an active group. There are also 2 groups in Melbourne, Australia, mainly working on genetically engineered mice and pigs. A company associated with the University of Cambridge in England called Imutran, now owned entirely by Novartis, has developed pigs that are protected against human complement. Jeff Platt has worked with a company in the States called Nextran, owned by Baxter, which has a pig similar to the Imutran pig. They are possibly the main players. But there are many others.

WCR: *Dr. Cooper, it has been a pleasure speaking with you. I am sure the readers of this journal will be appreciative also.*

DKCC: Thank you. I have enjoyed it very much.

DKCC's MOST IMPORTANT PUBLICATIONS SELECTED BY DKCC FROM AMONG HIS 436 PUBLICATIONS

Books:

1. Cooper DKC, Lanza RP, eds. Heart Transplantation. Lancaster: MTP Press Limited, 1994.
2. Jackson JW, Cooper DKC, eds. Thoracic Surgery. A Volume of Operative Surgery, 4th ed. London, UK: Butterworths, 1986.
3. Cooper DKC, Novitzky D, eds. The Transplantation and Replacement of Thoracic Organs. 1st ed. . Boston, MA: Kluwer Academic Publishers, 1990.
4. Cooper DKC, Kemp E, Reemtsma K, White DJG, eds. Xenotransplantation. 1st ed. Heidelberg: Springer, 1991.
5. Cooper DKC, ed. Chris Barnard—By Those Who Know Him. Cape Town: Vlaeburg, 1992.
6. Cooper DKC, Miller LW, Patterson GA, eds. The Transplantation and Replacement of Thoracic Organs. 2nd ed. Boston, MA: Kluwer Academic Publishers, 1996.
7. Cooper DKC, Kemp E, Platt JL, White DJG, eds. Xenotransplantation. 2nd ed., Heidelberg: Springer, 1997.
8. Cooper DKC, Lanza RP. Outwitting Evolution. New York: Oxford University Press, New York (In press).

Articles:

1. Cooper DKC. Experimental development of cardiac transplantation. *BMJ* 1968;4:171–181.
2. Cooper DKC. Transplantation of the heart and both lungs: (I) historical review. *Thorax* 1969;24:383–390.
3. Longmore DB, Cooper DKC, Hall RW, Sekabunga J, Welch W. Transplantation of the heart and both lungs: (II) experimental cardiopulmonary transplantation. *Thorax* 1969; 24:391–398.
4. Cooper DKC. A simple method of resuscitation and short-term preservation of the canine cadaver heart. *J Thorac Cardiovasc Surg* 1975;70:896–908.
5. Cooper DKC. The donor heart: the present position with regard to resuscitation, storage, and assessment of viability. *J Surg Res* 1976;21:363–381.
6. Cooper DKC, Charles RG, Fraser RC, Beck W, Barnard CN. Long-term survival after orthotopic and heterotopic cardiac transplantation. *BMJ* 1980;281: 1093–1096.
7. Barnard CN, Barnard MS, Cooper DKC, Curcio CA, Hassoulas J, Novitzky D, Wolpowitz A. The present status of heterotopic cardiac transplantation. *J Thorac Cardiovasc Surg* 1981;81:433–439.
8. Cooper DKC, Lanza RP, Oliver S, Forder AA, Rose AG, Uys CJ, Barnard CN. Infectious complications after heart transplantation. *Thorax* 1981;38:822–828.
9. Wicomb WN, Cooper DKC, Hassoulas J, Rose AG, Barnard CN. Orthotopic transplantation of the baboon heart after 20 to 24 hours' preservation by continuous hypothermic perfusion with an oxygenated hyperosmolar solution. *J Thorac Cardiovasc Surg* 1981;83:133–140.
10. Cooper DKC, Wicomb WN, Barnard CN. Storage of the donor heart by a portable hypothermic perfusion system: experimental development and clinical experience. *J Heart Transplant* 1983;2:104–110.
11. Lanza RP, Cooper DKC, Cassidy MJD, Barnard CN. Malignant neoplasms occurring after cardiac transplantation. *J Amer Med Assoc* 1983;249:1746–1748.
12. Novitzky D, Cooper DKC, Barnard CN. The surgical technique of heterotopic heart transplantation. *Ann Thorac Surg* 1983;36:476–482.
13. Cooper DKC. Orthotopic and heterotopic transplantation of the heart—the Cape Town experience. (Hunterian Lecture, Royal College of Surgeons of England, 1983.) *Ann R Coll Surg Engl* 1984;66:228–234.

14. Cooper DKC, Lanza RP, Barnard CN. Non-compliance in heart transplant recipients: the Cape Town experience. *J Heart Transplant* 1984;3:248–253.
15. Novitzky D, Wicomb WN, Cooper DKC, Rose AG, Fraser RC, Barnard CN. Electrocardiographic, haemodynamic and endocrine changes occurring during experimental brain death in the Chacma baboon. *J Heart Transplant* 1984;4:63–69.
16. Wicomb WN, Cooper DKC, Novitzky D, Barnard CN. Cardiac transplantation following storage of the donor heart by a portable hypothermic perfusion system. *Ann Thorac Surg* 1984;37:243–248.
17. Cooper DKC, Novitzky D, Becerra E, Reichart B. Are there indications for heterotopic heart transplantation in 1986? A 2 to 11 year follow up of 49 consecutive patients undergoing heterotopic heart transplantation. *Thorac Cardiovasc Surgeon* 1986;34:300–304.
18. Cooper DKC, Novitzky D, Rose AG, Reichart B. Acute pulmonary rejection precedes cardiac rejection following heart-lung transplantation in a primate model. *J Heart Transplant* 1986;5:29–31.
19. Lexer G, Cooper DKC, Rose AG, Wicomb WN, Rees J, Keraan M, Du Toit E. Hyperacute rejection in a discordant (pig to baboon) cardiac xenograft model. *J Heart Transplant* 1986;5:411–418.
20. Novitzky D, Cooper DKC, Rose AG, Reichart B. Acute isolated pulmonary rejection following transplantation of the heart and both lungs: experimental and clinical observations. *Ann Thorac Surg* 1986;42:180–184.
21. Novitzky D, Rose AG, Cooper DKC, Reichart B. Histopathologic changes at the site of endomyocardial biopsy: potential for confusion with acute rejection. *J Heart Transplant* 1986;5:79–80.
22. Novitzky D, Wicomb WN, Cooper DKC, Rose AG, Fraser RC, Reichart B. Prevention of myocardial injury during brain death by total cardiac sympathectomy in the Chacma baboon. *Ann Thorac Surg* 1986;41:520–524.
23. Wicomb WN, Cooper DKC, Lanza RP, Novitzky D, Isaacs S. The effects of brain death and 24 hours storage by hypothermic perfusion on donor heart function in the pig. *J Thorac Cardiovasc Surg* 1986;91:896–909.
24. Wicomb WN, Rose AG, Cooper DKC, Novitzky D. Haemodynamic and myocardial histological and ultrastructural studies in baboons three to twenty seven months following autotransplantation of hearts stored by hypothermic perfusion for 24 or 48 hours. *J Heart Transplant* 1986;5:122–129.
25. Novitzky D, Cooper DKC, Brink J, Reichart B. Sequential—second and third—heart transplants in patients with previous heterotopic heart allografts. *Clin Transplant* 1987;1:57–62.
26. Novitzky D, Cooper DKC, Reichart B. Haemodynamic and metabolic responses to hormonal therapy in brain-dead potential organ donors. *Transplantation* 1987;43:852–854.
27. Novitzky D, Cooper DKC, Rose AG, Reichart B. Prevention of myocardial injury by pretreatment with verapamil hydrochloride following experimental brain death: efficacy in a baboon model. *Am J Emerg Med* 1987;15:11–18.
28. Novitzky D, Wicomb WN, Cooper DKC, Tjaalgard MA. Improved cardiac function following hormonal therapy in brain dead pigs: relevance to organ donation. *Cryobiology* 1987;24:1–10.
29. Novitzky D, Wicomb WN, Rose AG, Cooper DKC, Reichart B. Pathophysiology of pulmonary edema following experimental brain death in the Chacma baboon. *Ann Thorac Surg* 1987;43:288–294.
30. Van der Riet F de St, Human PA, Cooper DKC, Reichart B, Fincham JE, Kalter SS, Kanki PJ, Essex M, Madden DL, Lai-Tung MT, Chalton D, Sever JL. Virological implications of the use of primates in xenotransplantation. *Transplant Proc* 1987;19:4068–4069.
31. Cooper DKC, Human PA, Lexer G, Rose AG, Rees J, Keraan M, Du Toit E. Effects of cyclosporine and antibody adsorption on pig cardiac xenograft survival in the baboon. *J Heart Transplant* 1988;7:238–246.
32. Cooper DKC, Wicomb WN, Gould GM, Boonzaier D. Initial experimental experience with a "replaceable" cardiac valve prosthesis. *Ann Thorac Surg* 1988;45:554–558.
33. Novitzky D, Cooper DKC, Morrell D, Isaacs,S. Change from aerobic to anaerobic metabolism after brain death, and reversal following triiodothyronine (T3) therapy. *Transplantation* 1988;45:32–36.
34. Novitzky D, Human PA, Cooper DKC. Inotropic effect of triiodothyronine following myocardial ischaemia and cardiopulmonary bypass: an experimental study in pigs. *Ann Thorac Surg* 1988;45:50–55.
35. Novitzky D, Human PA, Cooper DKC. Effect of triiodothyronine (T3) on myocardial high energy phosphates and lactate following ischemia and cardiopulmonary bypass: an experimental study in baboons. *J Thorac Cardiovasc Surg* 1988;96:600–607.
36. Novitzky D, Cooper DKC, Human PA, Reichart B, Zuhdi,N. Triiodothyronine therapy for heart donor and recipient. *J Heart Transplant* 1988;7:370–376.
37. Rosin MD, Cooper DKC, Morgan JA, Van der Spuy JW. The surgical management of stab wounds of the chest. *J R Coll Surg Edin* 1988;33:78–83.
38. Cooper DKC, Novitzky D, Wicomb WN. The pathophysiological effects of brain death on potential donor organs, with particular reference to the heart. (Arris and Gale Lecture, Royal College of Surgeons of England, 1988.) *Ann R Coll Surg Engl* 1989;71:261–266.
39. Cooper DKC, Human PA, Rose AG, Rees J, Keraan M, Reichart B, Du Toit E, Oriol R. The role of ABO blood group compatibility in heart transplantation between closely related animal species. An experimental study using the vervet monkey to baboon cardiac xenograft model. *J Thorac Cardiovasc Surg* 1989;97: 447–455.
40. Novitzky D, Cooper DKC, Swanepoel A. Inotropic effect of triiodothyronine (T3) following myocardial ischemia and cardiopulmonary bypass: initial experi-

ence in patients undergoing open heart surgery. *Eur J Cardiothorac Surg* 1989; 3:140–145.

41. Cooper DKC, Novitzky D, Schlegel V, Muchmore JS, Cucchiara A, Zuhdi N. Successful management of symptomatic cytomegalovirus disease by ganciclovir following heart transplantation. *J Heart Lung Transplant* 1991;10:656–663.

42. Cooper DKC, Ye Y, Rolf LL, Zuhdi N. The pig as potential organ donor for man. In: Cooper DKC, Kemp E, Reemtsma K, White DJG, eds. Xenotransplanation. Heidelberg: Springer, 1991:481–500.

43. Cooper DKC. Depletion of natural antibodies in non-human primates—a step towards successful discordant xenografting in man. *Clin Transplantation* 1992; 6:178–183.

44. Good AH, Cooper DKC, Malcolm AJ, Ippolito RM, Koren E, Neethling FA, Ye Y, Zuhdi N, Lamontagne LR. Identification of carbohydrate structures which bind human anti-porcine antibodies: implications for discordant xenografting in man. *Transplant Proc* 1992;24:559–562.

45. Muchmore JS, Cooper DKC, Ye Y, Schlegel V, Pribil A, Zuhdi N. Prevention of loss of vertebral bone density in heart transplant patients. *J Heart Lung Transplant* 1992; 11:959–964.

46. Paris W, Woodbury A, Thompson S, Levick M, Nothegger S, Hutkin-Slade L, Arbuckle P, Cooper DKC. Social rehabilitation and return to work after cardiac transplantation—a multi center survey. *Transplantation* 1992;53:433–438.

47. Cooper DKC, Good AH, Koren E, Oriol R, Malcolm AJ, Ippolito RM, Neethling FA, Ye Y, Romano E, Zuhdi N. Identification of α-galactosyl and other carbohydrate epitopes that are bound by human anti-pig antibodies: relevance to discordant xenografting in man. *Transpl Immunol* 1993;1:198–205.

48. Cooper DKC, Koren E, Oriol R. Genetically engineered pigs (letter). *Lancet* 1993;342:682–683.

49. Cooper DKC, Ye Y, Niekrasz M, Kehoe M, Martin M, Neethling FA, Kosanke S, Debault L, Worsley G, Zuhdi N, Oriol R, Romano E. Specific intravenous carbohydrate therapy—a new concept in inhibiting antibody-mediated rejection: experience with ABO-incompatible cardiac allografting in the baboon. *Transplantation* 1993;56:769–777.

50. Koren E, Neethling FA, Richards S, Koscec M, Ye Y, Zuhdi N, Cooper DKC. Binding and specificity of major immunoglobulin classes of preformed human anti-pig heart antibodies. *Transplant Int* 1993;6:351–353.

51. Oriol R, Ye Y, Koren E, Cooper DKC. Carbohydrate antigens of pig tissues reacting with human natural antibodies as potential targets for hyperacute vascular rejection in pig-to-man organ xenotransplantation. *Transplantation* 1993; 56:1433–1442.

52. Cooper DKC, Koren E, Oriol R. Oligosaccharides and discordant xenotransplantation. *Immunol Rev* 1994;141:31–58.

53. Koren E, Neethling FA, Koscec M, Kujundzic M, Richards SV, Ye Y, Oriol R, Cooper DKC. In vitro model for hyperacute rejection of xenogeneic cells. *Transplant Proc* 1994;26:1166.

54. Kujundzic M, Koren E, Neethling FA, Milotic F, Koscec M, Kujundzic T, Martin M, Cooper DKC. Variability of anti-αgal antibodies in human serum and their relation to serum cytotoxicity against pig cells. *Xenotransplantation* 1994; 1:58–65.

55. Neethling FA, Koren E, Ye Y, Richards SV, Kujundzic M, Oriol R, Cooper DKC. Protection of pig kidney (PK15) cells from the cytotoxic effect of anti-pig antibodies by α-galactosyl oligosaccharides. *Transplantation* 1994;57:959–963.

56. Ye Y, Neethling FA, Niekrasz M, Koren E, Richards SV, Martin M, Kosanke S, Oriol R, Cooper DKC. Evidence that intravenously administered α-galactosyl carbohydrates reduce baboon serum cytotoxicity to pig kidney cells (PK15) and transplanted pig hearts. *Transplantation* 1994;58:330–337.

57. Ye Y, Niekrasz M, Kosanke S, Welsh R, Jordan HE, Fox JC, Edwards WC, Maxwell C, Cooper DKC. The pig as a potential organ donor for man. A study of potentially transferable disease from donor pig to recipient man. *Transplantation* 1994;57:694–703.

58. Ye Y, Luo Y, Kobayashi T, Taniguchi S, Li S, Niekrasz M, Kosanke S, Baker J, Mieles L, Smith D, Cooper DKC. Secondary organ allografting after a primary "bridging" xenotransplant. *Transplantation* 1995;60:19–22.

59. Cooper DKC. Ethical aspects of xenotransplantation of current importance. *Xenotransplantation* 1996;3:264–274.

60. Cooper DKC, Koren E, Oriol R. Manipulation of the anti-αGal antibody-αGal epitope system in experimental discordant xenotransplantation. *Xenotransplantation* 1996;3:102–111.

61. Koren E, Milotec F, Neethling FA, Koscec M, Fei D, Kobayashi T, Taniguchi S, Cooper DKC. Monoclonal antiidiotypic antibodies neutralize cytotoxic effects of anti-αGal antibodies. *Transplantation* 1996;62:837–843.

62. Rose AG, Cooper DKC. A histopathologic grading system of hyperacute (humoral, antibody-mediated) cardiac xenograft and allograft rejection. *J Heart Lung Transplant* 1996;15:804-817.

63. Taniguchi S, Neethling FA, Korchagina EY, Bovin N, Ye Y, Kobayashi T, Niekrasz M, Li S, Koren E, Oriol R, Cooper DKC. In vivo immunoadsorption of anti-pig antibodies in baboons using a specific Galα1-3Gal column. *Transplantation* 1996;62:1379–1384.

64. Chae S, Cooper DKC. Legal implications of xenotransplantation. *Xenotransplantation* 1997;4:132–139.

65. Cooper DKC, Oriol R. Glycobiology in xenotransplantation research. In: Gabius H-J, Gabius S, eds. Glycosciences: Status and Perspectives. Weinheim: Chapman and Hall, 1997:531–545.

66. Minanov OP, Itescu S, Neethling FA, Morgenthau A, Kwiatkowski P, Cooper DKC, Michler RE. Anti-Gal IgG antibodies in sera of newborn humans and baboons and its significance in pig xenotransplantation. *Transplantation* 1997; 63:182–186.

67. Taniguchi S, Cooper DKC. Clinical xenotransplantation—past, present and future. *Ann R Coll Surg Engl* 1997;79:13–19.

68. Cooper DKC. Xenoantigens and xenoantibodies. *Xenotransplantation* 1998; 5:6–17.

69. Kozlowski T, Monroy R, Xu Y, Glaser R, Awwad M, Cooper, DKC, Sachs DH. Anti-Galα1-3Gal antibody response to porcine bone marrow in unmodified baboons and baboons conditioned for tolerance induction. *Transplantation* 1998; 66:176–182.

70. Lambrigts D, Sachs DH, Cooper DKC. Discordant organ xenotransplantation in primates – world experience and current status. *Transplantation* 1998;66:547–561.

71. Simon P, Neethling FA, Taniguchi S, Good PL, Zopf D, Hancock WW, Cooper DKC. Intravenous infusion of αGal oligosaccharides in baboons delays hyperacute rejection of porcine heart xenografts. *Transplantation* 1998;65:346–353.

72. Kobayashi T, Cooper DKC. Anti-Gal, Gal epitopes, and xenotransplantation. In: Galili U, Avila J, eds. α1,3 Galactosyltransferase, αGal Epitopes and the natural anti-Gal antibodies. New York: Plenum (In press).

KENNETH HARDY COOPER, MD, MPH:
A Conversation With the Editor*

Ken Cooper was born in Oklahoma City, Oklahoma, on March 4, 1931, and he grew up in nearby Putnam City. After completion of 3 years of college at the University of Oklahoma, he entered the University of Oklahoma School of Medicine, graduating in 1956. His rotating internship was at the King County Hospital in Seattle, the hospital connected with the University of Washington. After internship, he entered the Army in August 1957 and transferred to the Air Force in June 1960 to pursue his interest in aerospace medicine at Brooks Air Force Base in San Antonio. There he got interested in the physiology of conditioning and training and studied maximum oxygen consumption, maximum breathing capacity, and the physical training of astronauts and pilots. In September 1961 he went to the Harvard School of Public Health where he received a Master of Public Health degree. In June 1964 he went to the Lackland Air Force Base where he completed requirements for the aerospace medicine residency program. He then went to Wilford Hall US Air Force Hospital in San Antonio where he developed a conditioning program for the Air Force, which resulted in the publication of his first book, *Aerobics*, in 1968. In 1970 he left the Air Force after 13 years in the military to develop the Cooper Aerobics Center in Dallas, Texas, a preventative medicine center which now has an annual budget of approximately $35,000,000 and employs 450 persons.

Ken Cooper is the recognized leader of the international physical fitness movement. He has probably motivated more people to exercise in pursuit of good health than any other person. He is credited with initiating the jogging boom which reached an estimated 35,000,000 Americans by 1984. In Brazil, running is called "coopering" or "doing the cooper," and in Hungary, the *Coopertezt* is the national fitness test. In Japan, near Tokyo, a 750-acre model of the Dallas Aerobics Center was constructed with Dr. Cooper's council. He has advocated shifting medicine away from disease treatment to disease prevention through aerobic exercise, proper diet, and proper emotional balance. His 18 books have sold >30,000,000 copies and have been translated into 41 languages and Braille. Several titles have spent weeks on best seller lists. From the Cooper Aerobic Center's beginning, Ken Cooper has emphasized the importance of basic and epidemiological research to document the value of exercise in the practice of preventive medicine. His Cooper Institute contains the largest computerized exercise database on record (approximately 750,000 per-

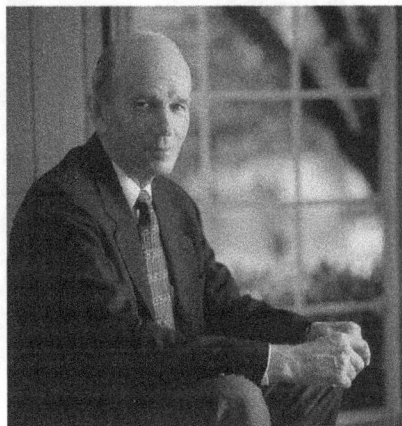

FIGURE 1. Through the window of his office, KHC observes a jogger passing by.

son-years) using the treadmill stress test. He has lectured in over 50 countries. For his work he has received many honors, including 7 honorary doctor's degrees. Dr. Cooper is a straight and honorable man, a good family man, and one with a passion and mission to improve the health of all of us.

William Clifford Roberts, MD[†] (hereafter WCR): *Dr. Cooper, it's a pleasure to be sitting in your office here on Saturday afternoon June 23, 2001. I appreciate your willingness to speak to me and therefore to the readers of* The American Journal of Cardiology. *Could we begin by your describing your early life, your mother, father, siblings, and what it was like growing up near Oklahoma City?*

Kenneth Hardy Cooper, MD, MPH[‡] (hereafter KHC): I was born on March 4, 1931, in Oklahoma City and spent 12 years at the same school, the Putnam City School District, a suburb of Oklahoma City. At that time Putnam was the largest rural consolidated school in the world. There were about 150 in my high school graduating class. I was very active in school, both academically and athletically, and was salutatorian of my high school graduating class. (*Marvene Wycoff* was valedictorian.) As a senior in high school I made All-State in basketball and won the state championship in the one-mile run. I missed setting a new record in the state by 1.1 seconds. I've been honored over the years by Oklahoma City, and in 1993 the Putnam City School District built a new middle school (grades 6 to 8) and named it the Kenneth Cooper Middle School. I go there frequently; recently I helped them dedicate their new quarter-mile track. We are trying to motivate the students attending Kenneth Cooper Middle School to become the most highly conditioned students in America. I've been working with them to achieve this goal and hope to establish a model physical education program for American mid-

*This series of interviews are underwritten by an unrestricted grant from Bristol Myers Squibb.
†Baylor Heart & Vascular Center, Baylor University Medical Center, Dallas, Texas 75246.
‡The Cooper Aerobic Center, Dallas, Texas 75230.

FIGURE 2. KHC in his office during the interview on June 23, 2001.

dle schools. It's been an honor and a pleasure to work with them for the last eight years.

My father was a practicing dentist. He specialized in periodontia most of his career. My mother was a homemaker, a very fine lady who supported me in my athletic endeavors. My father didn't support me in my athletic endeavors because he was convinced that I would get "an athletic heart" from running so much and playing basketball. I played football too. His concern about my athletic activities, however, didn't prevent me from participating. My father never saw me run in a track meet or play in a basketball game. In contrast, my mother didn't miss a game or a track meet. She traveled everywhere, even while I was in college (on a track scholarship), to watch me run. My father, however, was my academic supporter; my mother supported me athletically. My dad always felt that his four children should make top grades. I had a younger brother, a younger sister, and an older sister. Three of us were either valedictorian or salutatorian of our graduating class. My younger brother, by six years, didn't make the grades, but now he's the most successful. He became a dentist, took over our father's practice, and later became a businessman.

My father instilled in me the concept of preventive medicine by being very interested in nutrition, particularly supplementation. Being a periodontist, he noted that following gingivectomies many patients did not respond well unless they changed their diets. He recommended a diet which eliminated white flour and sugar because he felt this aggravated their condition. Many of his patients discovered that this diet also improved their arthritic symptoms. At one time he was so involved in the overall care of his patients that he was accused of practicing medicine. My father was a frustrated physician, even though he was a very successful and competent dentist. He was born in 1897 and died in 1974, at age 77. He lived life to the fullest and died suddenly. He practiced dentistry on a Friday and died on a Monday.

My mother was born in 1902 and died in 1984 at age 82. She also "squared off the curve," that is, "lived a long, healthy life to the fullest and then died suddenly." She was living alone in her own home, driving her own car, totally independent. She voted in the 1984 Presidential elections the day she died. She was home that night watching the election returns on television. We found her there the next morning. The television was still on. She wore a lapel pin that said, "I Voted Today." And I can assure you that what she feared worse than death was losing her independence. That's what I hope for. I want to live life to the fullest, as both my mother and father did, and die suddenly, "squaring off the curve."

My father instilled in me a desire to practice preventive medicine. When I was going to medical school his statement was, "If I'm paying for you to go to medical school to do nothing but treat disease and not change lifestyles, I'm wasting my money." I thought he was crazy at first with all his nutrition and vitamin supplementation recommendations. I later changed my mind and in 1994 dedicated my book, "The Antioxidant Revolution," which encouraged supplementation as a means of counteracting free radical activity, to my father.

My background was one of both athletics and academics, supported by a very close family. My father demanded the best. He had been raised in a rural area in Alabama, one of five children. His father was an itinerant Baptist preacher who preached in small churches in Alabama and usually gave most of his fees back to the church. My father, being the oldest, had to support his family in his early years. He went to dental school at Vanderbilt University in Nashville, Tennessee. He was a member of the next-to-last graduating class before they closed the school in 1931. My family lived in Tulahoma, Tennessee, for a short time. My oldest sister was born there. My mother, father, and older sister moved to Oklahoma shortly afterward, and he practiced dentistry for the next 50 years.

I was raised a Baptist and was always very active in church. I have always believed that if I didn't keep God at the top, family second, and work third, I was going to have problems. When I let work get out of line, I start losing harmony in my life. When I've had problems over the years, that is usually what has happened. I've tried to teach that to young interns and residents on the Internet in a program I'm involved with called "Doctors."

I'm 70 years of age and not even thinking about retiring, even though I've been told that about a third of my medical school graduating class has died, another third have quit practicing, and only a third of us are still practicing. I enjoy it and hope to be able to follow the pattern of my mother and father. My father didn't want to retire. He tried retiring from dentistry two or three times, but he just couldn't do it. He loved his practice and his patients.

During those formative years we lived three miles from school and we had only one car, which my father used to go to work. He had an office in downtown Oklahoma City, about 10 miles from where we lived. Usually, I rode the bus to and from school. Frequently, however, I would play basketball, football, or run track in the afternoons and I'd miss the bus. Not only did I get the physical conditioning associated with athletics, but because of the bus, I had to run the three miles home. During my senior year, I trained for cross-country in the fall (instead of playing football) and later in the year played basketball and ran track. Nearly every morning of my senior year, a friend who lived across the street would take my clothes to school in a paper sack and I'd run to school, take a shower, and go on to class. At the end of the classes, I'd work out, and then run home. I became state champion in the mile probably because I exercised so extensively.

I had a good upbringing. My father gave me responsibilities around the home. Although not a disciplinarian and rather quiet, he had strong feelings. He led by example more than by command. When I got home from school at night, I always had chores to do. We lived in the suburbs on 10 acres, and we had cows and horses. From the sixth to the twelfth grade, I milked a cow twice a day. I had to get up at 6:30 A.M. and milk the cow before I went to school, and again in the evening. My dad always wanted fresh milk. The chores taught me discipline. My dad took over if I went on a date or played basketball or I had to work in the evening. My dad always had a garden because he wanted fresh vegetables. Another one of my "chores" was working in the garden. My evenings were spent studying. We didn't have much to distract us in those days. We didn't have a television set. We did have a radio. Occasionally, I listened to the "Lone Ranger," "Inner Sanctum," or "I've Got a Mystery."

I didn't date until I was a sophomore in high school, and then not much because of a lack of time. I was mainly interested in athletics and academics. From six years of age on, I told my family that I wanted to be a physician. I tried to get interested in dentistry but it never appealed to me. My dad didn't encourage me to go into dentistry, probably because he was a frustrated physician. He was thrilled when I went into medicine. The first time I watched him perform a gingivectomy, seeing blood made me nauseated, and I thought, How could I ever be a physician or a dentist if I can't stand the sight of blood? That response rapidly disappeared once I got into medical school. People have asked me why I wanted to go into medicine. My answer has always been, "So that I will be able to help people when they need help the most."

WCR: *Ken, what was home like when you'd come home from school? Would the whole family have dinner together? What was the conversation like at the dinner table?*

KHC: We had breakfast together every morning because my father insisted on a good breakfast. We always had eggs and bacon, a traditional Southern breakfast. We all left the house about the same time. My mother would take him to work if she needed the car. We always had sack lunches until we got into junior high and we started eating in the cafeteria. In the evening we usually had dinner together. My mother was an outstanding cook. She churned our butter and I was raised on buttermilk! My mother didn't embrace the concept of low sugar and low white flour like my dad did. My dad usually got home from work about 6:30 or 7:00 P.M., I'd do my chores (work in the garden or milk the cow), and then we would have a quiet supper. My father believed in a good breakfast, a good lunch, and a light evening meal because the latter would "enable you to sleep better." We always had breakfast, dinner, and "supper." (One reason we have the obesity problem in America may be due to the way we eat, that is, breakfast, lunch, and "dinner." Now our evening meal is the heaviest of the day. We don't have a chance to burn up the calories before we go to bed.)

The family had good camaraderie and discussions at the table. I had many intellectual discussions with my father regarding his concepts and ideas. There was not a lot of arguing, feuding, or fussing in our family. We had a harmonious relationship. There was very little pressure in my environment. It was nice in those days to be able to leave the house without locking the doors. We never locked our car. We didn't have air conditioning. Our two-story house was on top of a hill with a southern exposure. We always fought to see who got the bedrooms facing south, which was the direction the wind came from, because we didn't use fans. I ended up unfortunately on the north side of the house, where there was very little circulation of air. In the summer months, my brother and I would sleep in a screened-in porch. My early life was one of good times with a very supportive family.

WCR: *You said that you and your father periodically had intellectual discussions. What would you talk about?*

KHC: One thing my father and I disagreed on was my participation in athletics. He was concerned that I would damage my heart. The theory of the athletic heart was that once it enlarged in response to exercise, the heart muscle would convert into fat and you'd die of a heart attack when you stopped participating in athletics. I told him there was no good research to document that theory. Even when I was young, I was interested in research. I even went to my science advisors and teachers at school to see if there was anything to document what they said. I was convinced that exercise wasn't going to hurt me and, indeed, I believed that I was helping myself. It wasn't until later years that I found that to be true. We had many political discussions. My dad was a staunch conservative and against anything that was overwhelmingly government-directed. He tried to educate us in conservatism. He went through the depression and he vividly recalled it. He was always afraid to get overly financially involved in anything because of his experiences in the depression. My dad was a reasonably good investor. I called him a dentist by avocation and a farmer by vocation. He always had farms. When growing up, I spent nearly all my summers on the farm, baling hay, working in the fields, building fences, plowing, and taking care of cattle. It was good training. I loved those times. I loved going to the farm with my dad in college and medical school when we both had days off. He was the "consummate" boss because he'd tell me what to do and then he would go on to supervise something else. I ended up doing a lot of the manual labor. I recall stretching out under a tree after having a box lunch together and taking a nap. My dad and I had a good relationship. We obviously disagreed on athletics. Furthermore, I didn't completely agree with him on his conservative views, although I'm more conservative now than I was then.

We talked a lot about medicine, dentistry, nutrition, and health. One of his idols was *Dr. Francis Pottinger*, a dentist from Florida who was big on vitamins, minerals, and supplementation, particularly in the natural form. We went to St. Petersburg, Florida, for a series of lectures by Dr. Pottinger. My father wanted me to hear those lectures. Once he brought Dr. Pottinger to Oklahoma City to speak to his dental group. My dad always tried to get other people involved in preventive medicine. He was frustrated because he and his dental friends would extend invitations to their physicians, but they would never come. He said, "Dentists are doctors too." He was more of a physician than a lot of physicians. I showed slides when Dr. Pottinger and others spoke on nutrition. My father thought that would be a good way for me to learn about nutrition. I got nothing in medical school on nutrition or exercise physiology. Everything I'm doing in the fields of nutrition and exercise physiology I got from my father or in the postgraduate years. My dad had a real influence on my life. The auditorium here in the Cooper Clinic is dedicated to my father. He instilled in me an overwhelming desire to practice the art and science of preventive medicine.

My mother was born and raised in Nashville, Tennessee, in a very devout Baptist family. She was staunch in her religious beliefs, more so than my father. My father got turned off on religion because of the relatively poor way his clergyman father took care of his family. On Sundays, our family went to church and my mother always fixed a fantastic dinner immediately afterward. My mother, my siblings, and I always went to training union on Sunday night and to the evening worship service. My dad stayed home and read or listened to the radio. At one time, my dad was a deacon at our church, but he slipped away. He didn't lose his beliefs, but he got frustrated with the organized church. Nevertheless, he encouraged us, but not like our mother did. I remember many wonderful Sundays. We'd go to church to our separate Sunday School classes and then to the service where I'd usually sit with my friends. Sunday afternoon was relaxation time. We'd sit around and do things families used to do back then like play athletic games with neighbors and friends.

We lived in only two houses from my first to twelfth year of school. The first couple of years we lived in a little home in downtown Oklahoma City and then we moved to 10 acres in the suburbs where we had horses and cows. I learned to ride a horse when I was six years old. We also had a garden. Later, my dad bought 80 acres in the neighborhood. It turned out to be a good investment. We had a farm north of Oklahoma City and another one south of the city. My father would buy a farm and we'd improve it, then he'd sell it. We raised dairy cattle and beef cattle. We had a beautiful bottom land farm on the Canadian River south of Oklahoma City. It was a 240-acre irrigated farm, and I loved to work there. It was a successful farm. I didn't know it during those formative years, but just about two miles from that farm was where my wife, Millie, was growing up. She was born and raised in Noble, Oklahoma.

WCR: *What was your mother like? Did you two communicate well?*

KHC: I had a wonderful relationship with my mother, even to the extent that some family members accused my mother of being preferential to me. She would often say, "Kenneth can do this. Kenneth can do that." The family members always called me "Kenneth." Millie's family and others today call me "Ken." If my mother called me Ken, I knew she was mad. Now, if my wife calls me Kenneth, I know something is wrong. Mother was a very gracious and wonderful lady. She was always overweight and had high blood pressure. I was always encouraging her to lose weight, particularly when I became a physician. She supported me wonderfully. My father was more of the disciplinarian. My mother would say, "Oh, let him do it." She was that way with all the kids. She was more easygoing. Even though she lived in Oklahoma many more years than she lived in Tennessee, she never lost her Southern accent. She always had that "All right" type of response to telephone calls. After my father died in 1974, she lived by herself. I always called her on Sunday night about the same time from wherever I was around the country. Her response every time I would call her was, "I knew that would be you." My father wasn't the compassionate, warm, and considerate-type individual like my mother. His feelings were more black and white. He would say, "This is the way it is, this is what is going to be done, and if you're going to do this I want to know why." My mother would say, "Oh, let's look at other possibilities and see if we can't do this." The combination of both parents gave me a good upbringing.

WCR: *How was your relationship with your siblings? You were number 2 in the hierarchy?*

KHC: I was number two. We were all three years apart. My older sister is 73, I'm 70, my younger sister is 67, and my brother is 64. My relationship with my brother is outstanding. He lives in Flower Mound, Texas, and has retired from dentistry. Even though he travels a lot to oversee his Sonic Drive-ins located all over the USA, we get together for lunch usually every other Friday. We usually discuss family matters. We had a family reunion this summer. His children live in Dallas and are members of our health club. My nephew and niece live across the street from us and they use the club's facilities.

My younger sister Beverly lives in Albuquerque, New Mexico. She attended medical school for two years and then dropped out because she didn't think she wanted to be both a homemaker and a physician. She's probably the most intelligent one in the family. She made better grades in medical school than I did, at one time being ranked number six in her class. I was in the top 10 percent when I graduated. She later went back to school and got a degree in physiology. She taught for a while, but then married her classmate, *Dr. Charles Key*. He's been in the department of pathology at the University of New Mexico School of Medicine in Albuquerque for over 25 years. At one time he was chairman of the department. He now directs their tumor registry. He has both an MD and a PhD. He's a slow-speaking, brilliant guy. They have three children and they are all geniuses. They have about 15 grandkids. We don't have any yet.

My older sister graduated from Oklahoma A&M with a degree in Home Economics. My dad got her husband into the vitamin business, Alphabet Vitamin Tablets. He did quite well and retired many years ago. My sister taught school for a while. They are not close to the other members of the family. They still live in Oklahoma City.

WCR: *How many kids do you have?*

KHC: We have two, my older sister has two, my younger sister has three, and my brother has three.

WCR: *Did any teachers in your first 12 years of schooling influence you particularly?*

KHC: I remember *Mrs. Overman*, my first grade teacher, *Mrs. Hickey*, my second grade teacher, *Mrs. Tankersly* was my third grade teacher, and my fifth grade teacher was *Mrs. Goodman*. The only high school teacher I recall was *Mrs. Mullinax*, my science teacher. She was one of my greatest supporters. *Leo Mayfield* was the principal and also my track coach. *Mutt Herring* was the coach in football and basketball. Those are the teachers I recall. Mr. Herring was also my physical education teacher before I started competitive athletics in the ninth grade. As was typical of physical education in those days (something I've tried to change as I became a professional in the field), we would go to the gymnasium and the coach would sit up in the bleachers reading a newspaper and smoking a cigarette while we played basketball and entertained ourselves.

I also had a music career in high school, even making the "All-State" band. Wanting us to be well balanced, my father insisted that we all play musical instruments. I started taking clarinet lessons when I was in grade school. From the sixth to the tenth grade, I played in the band, working up to first chair clarinet when I was a sophomore. Although I enjoyed playing, I enjoyed athletics more. Once when selected to the All-State band in Enid, Oklahoma, my track coach wanted me to run in a relay in Weatherford, Oklahoma. Enid and Weatherford were about 60 miles apart. Without the band teacher knowing, I left Enid and took a bus to Weatherford so I could run with my team in the relay (which we won). As a consequence, I got kicked out of the band. As the president of the band in my sophomore year, I had to crown the Band Queen at a band festival in the gymnasium. I was supposed to kiss her (I'd never kissed a girl in my life). My brother and sisters still laugh. I kissed her and the first thing I did before 500 people was to wipe the lipstick off my mouth. To this day people remember that episode. Thus, the first time I kissed a nonfamily lady was in public.

WCR: *How did it come about that you went to the University of Oklahoma to college?*

KHC: Because I had performed well in basketball and track in high school, I got several college scholarship offers. After winning the state championship in the mile run as a senior in high school, a scout from a prominent college came over to congratulate me. He said, "We want you to come to *our school*. We want you to come down for an interview at least." He took my track shoe and put $20 in it. I asked him what he was trying to do. He said, "I want you to have that." I took it out and threw it back at him and said, "And I'll never go to your school either." Apparently, he was trying to bribe me to come for an interview at his school.

When I was a sophomore in high school, a man named *Harold Keith* told me that I had a lot of potential. He was the sports publicity director at the University of Oklahoma (OU). During my high school track career, I didn't have a regular coach. Harold Keith, an outstanding runner himself, worked with *John Jacobs*, the track coach at OU, and developed a training program for me. They sent me weekly schedules to run when I was a junior and senior in high school and that enabled me to win the state championship in the mile. When a senior in high school I ran with the cross-country team at OU. I was ahead of everybody after the first mile but then they all passed me like I was standing still the second mile. As a senior in high school I ran two miles in 10 minutes. That experience of working with the OU coach for two years and actually running with the OU cross-country team convinced me to go to OU, even though I had a chance to go to many other schools.

WCR: *What did you major in at college?*

KHC: I majored in microbiology in premed. I only went three years. For my first 2½ years, my grade point average was 3.8 and I was inducted into Phi Eta Sigma, the honorary scholarship fraternity. After 2½ years I was accepted into medical school. During my final semester in college I "goofed off" and made straight Bs. I enjoyed premed, even though I was always busy running track and studying. I ended up with a 3.67 grade average in college.

WCR: *Who had influence over you in college? Were there any teachers that were standouts?*

KHC: None in particular. I don't remember any names. They were all good. I had many discussions with teachers. One problem I had in taking examinations was that I often read more into a question than the teacher intended. It frustrated me. I would miss a question and I'd go back and discuss it with the professor. He/she would say that that was not considered. Apparently I saw more in the potential answer to the question than they did. I'd win some arguments, but my grades were never changed. I always argued with teachers when I believed I had a reason for missing an answer.

WCR: *Did you enjoy the sciences?*

KHC: Yes, very much. I also enjoyed the sciences in high school. I always did well in the sciences, particularly chemistry. In college and in medical school I had 30 hours of chemistry and made 28 hours of A and 2 hours of B. I also was strong in foreign languages. I took German, Russian, and Greek, and enjoyed it.

WCR: *How did you do in track in college?*

KHC: I ran primarily on relay teams and won watches and gold medals, but as an individual I didn't bring my times down enough. In high school I ran the mile in 4:31 minutes, which was almost a state high school record. My best in college was 4:18 minutes. My college running mate, *Bruce Drummond*, ran 4:18 during the third year too and he dropped to 4:09 during his senior year. I think I would have done the same thing had I stayed for the senior year. We ran side by side in the half mile, mile, and two-mile runs during the first three years. My interest in college was academics first so I could get into medical school and become a physician. My second goal was to make the Olympic track team, which unfortunately I didn't.

During college, I didn't do as well in track as I wanted. I ran both the half mile and two miles. I didn't break 10 minutes for two miles in high school, but in college I ran 9:37 minutes, which isn't fast anymore, but it was pretty good in the late 40s and early 50s. I usually ranked in the top four or five in the events I entered. I didn't win any big meets, but I did run on relay teams that won big meets. I ran the half mile or the three quarter mile distance in the relays. When I was a junior, we won the two-mile relay (where I ran the half mile) in the Kansas and Drake relays. I lettered all three years in cross-country, indoor, and outdoor track.

I wanted to play basketball in college too. During my freshman year, I was on a track scholarship and I tried out for basketball. The OU basketball coach told me later that they thought they could use me and that I could probably make the team, but the track coach, Coach Jacobs, didn't want me to do both. I would have to make up my mind whether I was going to play basketball or run track. I was a better runner than a basketball player. I'm sure that was the appropriate decision. If I could have continued track for that final year, I think I could have brought my times down and may have made my goal of going to the Olympics or at least the Olympic trials.

I thought that my coach *John Jacobs* did not help me in my college track career. When I was in high school I didn't have a coach except *Leo Mayfield*, but I got information from Harold Keith at OU. Yet my view then was that the more you ran, the better you could run. More was better than less running in my view. "No strain or no pain, then no gain." I ran mile after mile in high school. During my senior year in high school, I ran about 60 miles a week. As soon as I got to college, I was told that that was all wrong. Coach Jacobs said I had to cut down to no more than 15 to 20 miles a week. He felt that greater distances would take "the spring" out of my legs. We wouldn't even start running track or cross-country until college started. We didn't run in the summer. The concept was to rest our legs during the summer. We had about six weeks to get into shape before the cross-country season started and then we had about two weeks layoff before indoor track started. Then we had about two week's layoff again before outdoor track started. We never ran more than 25 miles a week. We ran 100-, 220-, 440-, and 880-yard dashes but we never ran distances. I got so frustrated when I was a sophomore at OU that one Sunday afternoon I went out and ran about 12 miles with some friends. The coach chewed me out the next day like I had done the worst possible thing on earth. He said, "What are you trying to do, Coop? You will take all the spring out of your legs." Now competitive athletes run year-round 40 to 60 miles per week. If I had continued what I'd learned on my own in high school when I was in college, I think I could have come close to a four-minute mile. My coach did not help me achieve my goal of making the Olympics, or at least the Olympic trials.

WCR: *Ken, nobody in your family had been a physician? Is that correct?*

KHC: No. I had a cousin, *Walter Rattan*, who graduated from Harvard Medical School. That was my goal. When I applied to medical school after three years, I applied to three places: Harvard, Tulane, and the University of Oklahoma. I got accepted to Tulane and Oklahoma so I didn't pursue Harvard because my dad didn't think we could afford it. He thought it would be better for me to go to OU since he was going to pay for my training. That would keep expenses down. He gave me $3,600 when I enrolled as a freshman in medical school and that was the total amount he spent on me during the entire four years of medical school! During medical school I had good summer jobs and made a lot of money. I worked as a tour escort for two summers, and those jobs paid well! During school, I worked at least 40 hours a month in the anatomy department. Tuition was low. Even with my restricted income, I bought a car, an engagement ring (for a girl I didn't marry), and still had money left after finishing medical school. I lived in a boarding house and ate the boarding house meals. I gained weight too. In college I sold programs and soft drinks at the football games for spending money. I didn't have a car until I was a junior in medical school. I had a bicycle. When I was in college, I usually dated girls who had a car. I'd ride my bicycle to their dorm or house and use their car. On weekends, I would occasionally borrow the family's car. (By then, my family had two motorized vehicles: a pickup for the farm and a car. At times I could borrow the old beat-up pickup.)

WCR: *Did you continue your religious activities in college and in medical school?*

KHC: In college I was very active in the church, and at 18 years of age dedicated my life to full-time Christian work. I thought I was "being called" to be a medical missionary to China. In 1990 when I went to China for the first time, I spoke at two medical schools: one in Beijing and one in Shanghai. I always say something about my religious beliefs in my presentations, and when I spoke to those students in China, I realized that I was a medical missionary. I was a different type than I had envisioned, but I was working in a hospital in China.

Although I could have joined any fraternity in college and medical school and was pressured to join, I had no interest and never joined. I'm glad I didn't. I didn't drink or smoke and I still don't. My lifestyle wasn't compatible with the fraternity lifestyle. I was very active in the Baptist Student Union during my three years of college and at one time was its president. That was an on-campus coeducational program. We had noonday worship services and I spoke many times. I continued that activity in medical school. We established a noonday worship service for students and nurses. That was a very important part of my life. I even helped start a mission in Goldsby, Oklahoma, about five miles south of Norman, Oklahoma. There was a school there where all six grades were in the same one room. We had visitations on Wednesday nights and would encourage people to come to church on Sunday morning at the Goldsby School. I often preached. That developed into a church which is still active today.

WCR: *How did you enjoy the University of Oklahoma Medical School?*

KHC: Oklahoma University was a good medical school. I would have preferred to have gone to Tulane because I like New Orleans and OU wasn't a highly rated academic school at that time. I've not been active as a medical school alumni, nor have I ever been recognized by it. The college, however, has awarded me the "Distinguished Graduate of University of Oklahoma."

WCR: *How many students were in your class in the University of Oklahoma Medical School when you were there?*

KHC: We had about 110 and about 100 graduated.

WCR: *Where were you among that 100 when you graduated?*

KHC: I know I was in the top third, possibly in the top 10 percent. During the first two years in medical school, I studied like crazy and did well, but did better during the last two years, the clinical years.

WCR: *Who influenced you in medical school? Were there any standouts among the faculty?*

KHC: *Dr. Ernst Lachman*, anatomy professor, of the Lachman sign fame. (It involves the knee.) He hired me when I was a freshman to work as an assistant in the anatomy lab. In addition to cleaning out the cadaver pits, I did dissections for the students. I should have been a surgeon. For four years I did demonstration dissections for the freshman students. I did the dissections on weekends in preparation for the Monday class. I spent lots of time in the anatomy lab.

I enjoyed it and thought I was destined to be a surgeon. Surgery did not appeal to me, however, during the clinical years. Maybe I became discouraged by doing so many dissections. Dr. Lachman spoke with a very distinctive German accent as did his wife, Anya. They both became good friends. Anya couldn't drive a car, and Dr. Lachman paid me to teach her. That was before automatic transmissions, and driving required shifting gears. He paid me to teach his wife to drive a car. The first time I took Anya out on a Saturday afternoon in their old four-door Chevy with a "four-on-the-floor type transmission," she hit the accelerator when I told her to press on the clutch. It was frightening. It took me weeks, if not months, to teach her enough so she could pass the driver's license test. Although I finally taught Anya Lachman how to drive a car, it almost cost me my life, if not my health. Dr. Lachman and I became lifelong friends and he was always one of my greatest supporters.

During my senior year, I did a three-month externship in Pauls Valley, Oklahoma, a nice little farming community about 90 miles south of Oklahoma City with *Dr. Ray Lindsay*, a surgeon who was recognized in those days as probably the finest surgeon in the state of Oklahoma. I worked with several other physicians and had a wonderful time. I worked long hours, delivered babies by myself, and scrubbed in surgery with Dr. Lindsay. A big thing in medical school was to get an invitation after graduation to join the physician with whom you did your externship. When I completed the externship and discussed joining Dr. Lindsay's group, he gave me a book on surgery which he autographed, saying, "Ken, don't waste your time in a place like Pauls Valley, Oklahoma. You've got way too much more to offer than that."

WCR: *Were there classmates in medical school who had a particular influence on you?*

KHC: My closest friend in medical school was *Bill Heath*, who became an ophthalmologist in Oklahoma City. We were together during college, medical school, and internship. *Charlie Rockwood*, our class leader, became a world-renowned orthopedic surgeon in San Antonio and Chairman of their department. Most students smoked in those days and most played bridge during noonday breaks. I went to the noonday worship services. I was a "square" as far as my classmates were concerned. My medical school classmates did not accept my concepts and ideas then and I had little to no interest in their extracurricular activities. I didn't drink, I didn't smoke, and I didn't play bridge. I had other interests. I've been to only one class reunion, the twenty-fifth. (It was 1956 when I graduated so it's going to be our forty-fifth this year.)

WCR: *Did you have a hard time picking internal medicine? You were a good athlete. You were good with your hands. You had spent much time in anatomy. You spent a three-month externship in your senior year with a prominent surgeon who detected your talent. Yet you went into internal medicine. Why was that?*

KHC: That's a good question. I went into internal medicine with the encouragement of Dr. Lachman.

Another professor, *Dr. Bob Cranny*, a pediatrician, stands out in my medical school career. I enjoyed pediatrics and he encouraged me to go into research. The first manuscript I ever published was in medical school and it was "Determination of genetic sex in children by peripheral blood smear." We looked at kids with the adrenogenital syndrome, where it was unclear whether they were male or female. He showed that males had drumsticks on the nucleus of the red blood cells. If no drumsticks, the little appendage off the nucleus of the red cell, then the child was a female. I spent hours studying the blood smears. Our manuscript was published in *the American Journal of the Diseases of Children* in 1956. That started my interest in research and it continued when I was in the Air Force. Publishing and trying to get more involved in research led me away from surgery and into internal medicine. I was more of a thinker than a cutter.

WCR: *Why did you do your internship in Seattle?*

KHC: I interned in Seattle at the King County Hospital, the only hospital in Seattle at that time for the University of Washington. It was an outstanding internship. The reason I went there was because when I worked as a tour escort during the first two summers of medical school, I escorted tours out of Chicago that went through Seattle. I fell in love with that city and thought about living there. But let me digress for a moment. After my first year in medical school I worked as a bus driver in Glacier National Park in Montana. I was a "gear jammer," as they called us in those days, driving red buses (the brand name was "White Bus"). They were 18-passenger buses with a canvas top that rolled back. The driver used a microphone to describe the mountains, the flowers, etc. I had to take a two-week educational course to qualify as a bus driver in the Park. The roads were very narrow and steep going through many mountain passes. At times when going up the mountains I had to double-clutch the bus to get it into gear. If I couldn't get into gear I would stop the bus and start talking about something that didn't exist. I'd make up stories while I was trying to get the bus back into gear. That happened several times. I'd look in the rear view mirror and see 18 sets of eyes looking straight ahead. There was this beautiful scenery off to the sides and everyone was looking at the road, "helping me drive." I told them, "I notice you are watching my driving. I've got a deal. I'll watch the road if you watch the scenery. But if you're going to watch the road, I'm going to watch the scenery." That usually opened them up. I learned a lot about teaching and working with people from that experience. I met many tour escorts that summer and that seemed to be an interesting, better paying job.

WCR: *How did you get this job?*

KHC: As I said, when I worked in Montana at Glacier National Park, I met many tour escorts, several who worked with the Cartan Tour Company in Chicago. They hired me and I worked for them for two summers. I worked the Grand Western Circle the first summer and the Sagenay River Cruise the second summer. It was wonderful. Three times that first summer we arrived into Lake Louise in Canada about 5:30 P.M. After getting my people fed and to bed, I'd join some bellhops and waitresses to hike to a glacier at the base of the mountain, and we would talk and roast weenies and marshmallows. Everything was clean and above board. It was good friendship and good times. I met a lot of wonderful people those summers. We'd hike back to the hotel and get in about 3 A.M., then I'd get up at 5 A.M., meet my tour group and hike up to Lake Agnes, which was an hour up the side of the mountain, return by 7:30 A.M. to have breakfast, get on the train, and head back to Chicago. Those nights I'd get about two hours sleep, but I loved every moment of it. During these tours, I kept going through Seattle, and that prompted me to apply for an internship at King County Hospital . . . and I was accepted.

WCR: *What was your internship like?*

KHC: It was a rotating internship. My goal then was to be an orthopedic surgeon or an ophthalmologist. Those were opposite goals. I had always enjoyed ophthalmology and I loved orthopedics because of my interest in fitness, conditioning, and athletics.

WCR: *During your internship you rotated through medicine, surgery, pediatrics, and obstetrics. Which of those did you enjoy the most?*

KHC: I enjoyed internal medicine the most. It was the prime internship in the Northwest. My teachers and instructors were outstanding. They gave us tremendous responsibilities. I wasn't married so I worked more than did the married interns. I averaged four hours sleep a night during the whole internship year.

During that time, I also learned how to snow ski and how to sail on Lake Washington. During the summer months, several other interns and I would camp out on weekends, usually on the Olympic peninsula. One of those interns was *Tom Hornbein*, who was one of the first Americans to climb Mt. Everest. I looked at Mt. Rainier during my internship and vowed someday to climb that mountain. I finally did in 1972 and 1974. I fell in love with Seattle and the Pacific Northwest. I almost settled in Seattle. I dated a girl who originally was from Anchorage, Alaska, during the year I was in Seattle. We were very serious but finally broke up. If I had married her, I may have settled in Seattle or Anchorage.

I then went into the Army to fulfill my two-year military obligation. That was required because I had been in the Berry plan and had been draft deferred. Even before I left Seattle and enlisted in the Army, I'd already made arrangements to have an ophthalmological residency at the John F. Weeks Ophthalmological Institute in Portland, Oregon. It was one of the outstanding ophthalmological residencies on the West Coast. As I was completing my internship at King County, I was losing interest in orthopedics and was leaning towards ophthalmology. I was accepted by the Weeks Institute and was to enter my residency after I had fulfilled my two-year military obligation. That was what I had planned when I went into the military.

WCR: *You went into the military August 1957.*

KHC: Yes. I finished the internship July 1, 1957, and went into the Army August 1, 1957. I went to San Antonio, Texas, and completed the six-week basic training program at Fort Sam Houston. Since I've had a life-long interest in flying, I decided to become an Army flight surgeon. This required participation in the Air Force's Flight Surgeon course at Randolph Air Force Base for nine weeks, and I was sent to Fort Rucker, Alabama, where I went through another nine-week program to become certified as an Army flight surgeon. After completion of my training, I was assigned to Ft. Sill, Oklahoma, in February 1958 and stayed until June 1960. There I met *Millie*, my future wife. She was a civilian employee in the Army's Special Services. Millie and I started dating in late 1958, and after dating for only nine months were married August 7, 1959.

At that time, the U.S. space program (NASA) was accelerating, and I became very interested in aerospace and medicine. After finishing the two-year military obligation, I decided against the ophthalmological residency, and petitioned the Army to let me directly transfer to the Air Force to pursue my interest in aerospace medicine and possibly become a scientist astronaut. Although rarely done, that was consummated in June 1960 and I was immediately assigned to Brooks Air Force Base in San Antonio to the Department of Aviation and Aerospace Physiology under *Major Fritz Holmstrom*. He was a Harvard graduate, very intelligent, an outstanding military physician, and he influenced me greatly. He encouraged me to pursue my interest in the aerospace medicine program and to get my boards in aerospace medicine. I was there until September 1961 when I went to Harvard School of Public Health. During those months, I taught aerospace physiology and aviation medicine. One of my popular lectures was on pressure breathing—what a fighter pilot must do at very high altitudes when cabin pressurization is lost. I enjoyed the teaching and was reasonably successful. All of this was in preparation for what I am doing now, but, of course, I didn't realize it at the time.

WCR: *Who were the students you were teaching?*

KHC: They were both American and young foreign military officers, who were going through various courses at Brooks Air Force Base. I was one of the main teachers in the primary course in aviation medicine. I taught students who would later become flight surgeons at the various Air Force bases throughout the country and around the world. I made a lot of good international contacts during that time. Along with the teaching I did research. I first looked at the ejection seat problems that were occurring in the Air Force, particularly in the high-performance aircraft. During ejection out of an airplane, their coccyx often was fractured. This also occurred with the ejection seat training. The seat was inadequately cushioned and it had a hard shell beneath the thin cushion. With better insulation of the cushion, we conquered the problem.

Probably the person who influenced my life the most during that time was *Dr. Bruno Balke*. Bruno was a German physician who came to the USA (Brooks Air Force Base) after World War II with Werner Von Braun. He was very interested in the physiology of conditioning and training. He developed the Balke treadmill test that we still use. Bruno saw my interest in research and encouraged me. He was interested in studying maximum oxygen consumption, maximum breathing capacity, and physically training astronauts and pilots. I hadn't much interest in exercise physiology until he created in me a desire to pursue this field professionally. He encouraged me to join him in research with pilots and astronauts. During that time, most of my fellow officers would work regular hours from 8:15 A.M. to 4:15 P.M. Even though I wasn't paid extra, I always arrived early and departed late. Almost every day after work, I'd join Bruno Balke or one of his associates in the lab. I'd work for another two or three hours and get home at about 7:30 P.M. I also was learning a lot about exercise physiology under the tutelage of Bruno Balke. Bruno continued to be a close friend until he died a few years ago at 90 years of age.

In September 1961 I went to Harvard for one year to get a masters degree in public health as a requirement of the Aerospace Medicine Residency Program. There I learned statistical analysis, epidemiology, and more about training and conditioning. After obtaining the MPH, I successfully petitioned the Air Force to give me a second year at Harvard to study exercise physiology. I wanted to stay a third year to complete my thesis and get a D.Sc. or Doctorate of Science in Exercise Physiology, but the Air Force said, "No. We need you in the space program." Harvard allowed me seven years to complete a thesis since that is all I lacked in getting the D.Sc. After my first book was published in 1968, they encouraged me to come back and defend it, thus qualifying for the Doctorate of Science. By that time, however, I was so busy that I never did, even though, as mentioned, I had met all the other requirements: the foreign language requirement, the one-year residence, and the oral qualifying exam. In retrospect, if I'd gone the academic route I would have done that. Since I went another route, I decided I didn't need it and spent my time conducting research in the Air Force.

In June 1964, I was assigned to Lackland Air Force Base and during that year I finished the academic requirements for the aerospace medicine residency program. I had already had the necessary basic aviation and space physiology courses. I went through arctic survival training in Alaska, survival training in the swamps in Florida, and through jet pilot training at Randolph Air Force Base. I spent six weeks learning to fly an airplane. (I'd already learned to fly a helicopter when I was in the Army.) I loved to fly. I never did enjoy flying a jet that much. I was used to an approach at 40 miles an hour, not 140 miles an hour. I passed all the requirements, however, for being jet qualified. However, I didn't pursue flying as a pilot. I always felt that flying was a profession, and that you can't be a good flight surgeon and a good pilot. Both are highly skilled professions. You need to concentrate on being a flight surgeon (i.e., physician) or a pilot, but not both. Some of my colleagues tried to do both. It didn't work.

Then I was assigned to Wilford Hall USAF Hospital in San Antonio. That's where I got most of my cardiology training. The first year in the space program I worked on deconditioning, supervising, and evaluating bedrest programs. This required considerable knowledge in cardiology. Early in the mornings I would interpret electrocardiograms and was even taught to perform cardiac catheterizations. I had a lot of training in cardiology during those two years and that enhanced my interest in the whole field.

Later, I was given command of the Aerospace Medical Laboratory Clinic (AMLC) where both human clinical and animal studies were conducted. One of my officers, *Dr. Gene Dong*, was performing heart transplants in dogs. This was in the early days of heart transplants. From 1964 to 1966, I also worked part-time with the NASA space program, studying the effects of weightlessness. Then in 1966 I was asked to work with the Air Force's conditioning program, which resulted in the publication of my first book, *Aerobics*, in 1968. After that, I could see my time in the Air Force was going to be limited because I had already been a Lieutenant Colonel for about two years, and my superiors felt that I needed to take command of a hospital. I'd been involved in research for six years. I traveled all over the world speaking for the Air Force on exercise physiology, cardiology, and aerospace medicine, and thoroughly enjoying a more academic career. I was told that if I ever expected to become a one-star general, then I had to have a command. In August 1970 I was to be transferred to become the commander of a small Air Force hospital. That was the last thing I wanted to do. Administration I didn't want. So after 13 good military years, I resigned.

WCR: *You certainly didn't make much money during that time.*

KHC: No. I didn't make very much at all. When I left the military, I came to Dallas and tried to borrow $1.2 million to buy what became The Cooper Aerobics Center in 1970. The banks and loan companies asked, "What's your financial statement?" I didn't have a "financial statement." "What are you going to use for collateral?" I thought collateral was something around an obstructed coronary artery. "Who is going to cosign your note?" I guess my dad can. "What's he worth?" All these questions I knew nothing about. My financial statement was about $25,000 after being in the military for 13 years!

Let me talk a bit more about leaving the military because that was a major decision. I had been at Lackland Air Force Base for six years and loved San Antonio. I petitioned the Air Force to let me establish, on campus at Lackland Air Force Base, a tri-service physical conditioning and rehabilitation center rather than becoming commander of a hospital. I felt it was "cheaper to rehabilitate than to retire. It was more effective to prevent than treat disease." That was my thesis. I put together a 52-page report that I sent to Headquarters USAF telling them that "I would stay in

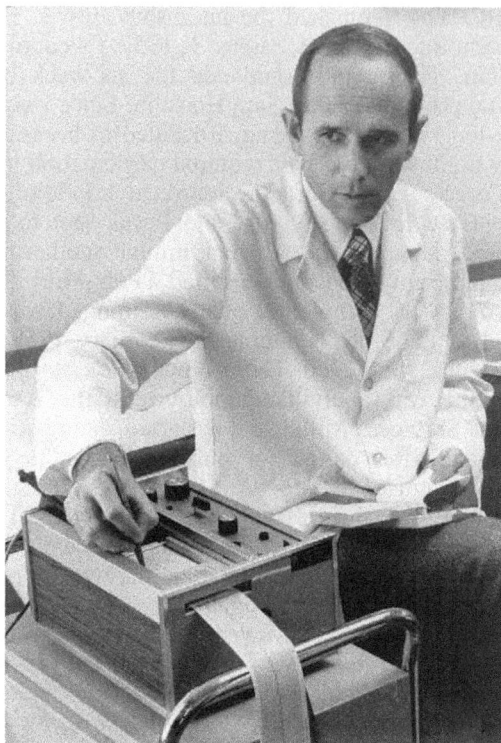

FIGURE 3. KHC conducts analysis of electrocardiogram tracings on a patient during a treadmill stress test in the early 1970s. KHC was the first doctor to use treadmill tests for examinations in Dallas.

the service for at least 20 years and I could care less about military rank." I was to be promoted to Colonel in about six months, and I said, "If I get a full Colonel rank, I'm satisfied. Let me stay in San Antonio and build this tri-service physical conditioning rehabilitation center and I'll spend the rest of my career, and perhaps more than that, building this center and developing this program at Lackland AFB." That 52-page document was sent over to Headquarters at Brooks Air Force Base where one of my superiors endorsed it with "Ha Ha." It was sent up to Headquarters USAF and it was denied. Nothing was done. That was the major factor in my decision to leave the Air Force.

Lieutenant General Dick Bohannan was another person who had a tremendous impact on my life. While Surgeon General, he allowed me to stay at Lackland AFB to continue my research. Others in the Air Force wanted to send me to Vietnam, but General Bohannan liked my work and allowed me to keep my position. I was told that my promotions were slower than I deserved because of my "unfortunate relationship with General Bohannon." It produced controversy among some of the lower ranking officers. I classify my 13 years in the military, particularly my last few years, as being somewhere between "getting a Legion of Merit or a dishonorable discharge." I had problems in those days. They weren't quite sure what to do with me. They gave me a meritorious service medal, however, when I left the Air Force in 1970. I think it was because I left the Air Force that they gave me the medal! Being controversial doesn't bother me. Actually, the Air Force tried to keep me in, but I knew they weren't going to let me build that center.

The plans I had for developing that center are almost exactly what I have now in Dallas. I couldn't believe it. That was divine intervention. People ask me, "Did you worry about leaving the Air Force?" I didn't receive any discharge or separation pay. I had 13 years and with seven more I would have had a nice retirement for the rest of my life. I started a whole new career at 40 years of age. People said, "You're crazy, Cooper. You ought to stay in. If you leave, you need to stay in the active reserves because by the time you are 55, you can still get your retirement pay."

But in building the Aerobics Center, I assumed considerable debt. Therefore, the banks said, "You can't be in the reserves because if they call you up for some military crisis, you aren't going to be able to handle your indebtedness." I came to Dallas with a pregnant wife and no insurance. I had no significant financial statement. I had a five-year-old daughter. I had no place to work or live. And, as you know, I had a very concerned medical society trying to control my practice, which even required an appearance before the board of censors because I was doing treadmill stress testing. Initially, I had only a two-room office and two employees. It was a rough time. If I hadn't had great support from my friends in Dallas, I wouldn't be here today. *Joe McKinney*, then Chairman of the Board of the Tyler Corporation (Saturn Industries at that time) backed me. Joe had been so intrigued with the aerobics book that he asked me to speak to his company presidents. The meeting was at the Lakeway Resort near Austin, Texas. I was still in the military at the time and came over from San Antonio. He was so excited about aerobics and my concept of preventive medicine that he said, "Ken, if you ever decide to leave the service and come to Dallas and need help getting started, let me know." I put that in my "back pocket" and forgot about it. Publication of my first two books was providing some income and recognition. I thought I'd come to Dallas and people would swarm into my office and I'd have all sorts of money available. It didn't happen that way.

WCR: *What did you think you were going to do when you came to Dallas?*

KHC: I wanted to establish a center dedicated to taking care of healthy people, a preventive medicine center, because I felt that the future of medicine was in prevention, not strictly treatment of disease. "We spend too much of our health service dollar on desperate measures which often prolongs death, not life, for a miserable few days." My feeling was that "it's a whole lot cheaper to maintain good health than to regain it once it's lost." What has made The Cooper Aerobics Center successful, a thing we've proven, is that "when people realize they have a need and you provide that service and they get the results they want, they'll make you successful." That's what has made us successful.

WCR: *You had met Joe McKinney but you didn't contact him before you came to Dallas. Is that correct?*

KHC: Yes. But you might wonder why I even selected Dallas? While stationed in San Antonio, my wife and I used to drive through Dallas when going home to Oklahoma. We both liked Dallas not only because it was closer to our homes, but also because it was a good place to live and had excellent airline connections. (By then, I was traveling extensively, giving lectures all over the country.) Also, I thought that I might be able to get some help from Joe McKinney if I needed it. I didn't have much knowledge of business matters at that time and thought I would be able to get together enough financial support to build this first center without his help. That wasn't possible. But then I interviewed at Southwestern Medical School. They wanted me to build the center under the umbrella of the medical school. I declined and decided I could do it better on my own. So then I went back to Joe McKinney . . . and you know the rest of the story.

WCR: *You started in Dallas with how many square feet?*

KHC: I only had two rooms. *Dr. Joe Arends*, a former Navy flight surgeon, was my first associate. It was Joe Arends, a secretary, and me. Joe acted as my assistant, helping with the treadmill stress tests and monitoring the blood pressures and electrocardiograms. It was maximal performance treadmill stress testing that necessitated the appearance before the Dallas County Board of Censors. In the Air Force I had done over 5,000 stress tests and was convinced that it was a safe and valuable test. They were doing bicycle stress testing at the medical school, but no treadmill testing. Yet at the medical school they were doing only bicycle submaximal tests. They were convinced that maximal stress testing was dangerous. I gave a 90-minute presentation to the Board of Censors that night in early 1971 and wasn't censored! That was one of my best presentations.

WCR: *Who was on the Board?*

KHC: It was the Board of Censors for the Dallas County Medical Society. *Dr. Bob Bass* was the chairman, and I heard that he started doing treadmill stress testing after that.

If you had visited my office in Preston Center, you would have seen this beautiful architectural rendering of what the future Aerobics Center was going to look like. It was a plan, a dream, and I didn't have the slightest idea how it was going to be accomplished. I had an architectural rendering of property, but I wasn't sure where it was going to be. I told people that 8215 Westchester was the "temporary offices." I'd tell people not to be too discouraged when they would have to turn sideways to get into the shower after taking a treadmill test. It was crazy. My examining room was so small I had to turn the patient sideways to check the knee reflexes, otherwise they'd kick the wall. You wouldn't believe how bad it was. I didn't see many patients either. I almost went back into the Air Force. It was so difficult being in private practice.

WCR: *When did you contact McKinney?*

KHC: I met the late *Dr. Milford Rouse*, president of the American Medical Association, when I'd consulted with some entrepreneurs to see if they could help me finance this project. The reason I backed out of that, by the way, was that the investors were going to own 80 percent of the operation. I thought there must be a better way. Prior to that time, when I was contemplating leaving the Air Force, I went to San Francisco and met *Dr. Bill Helvy*, who was working for Lockheed. He wanted to start a preventive cardiology center in the shadow of Stanford Medical School with a group of physiologists and physicians. He came to me and said, "Why don't you leave the Air Force and join us?" I made several trips to California and almost joined them. I was so naïve from the business standpoint. His associates were both entrepreneurs and physicians who were going to finance a preventive cardiology clinic. I was the only one who had any reputation and they were depending upon me to make the project successful.

Divine intervention occurred again. I was at the point of signing a contract to join this group and build a center in the Bay area on a beautiful piece of property, but a couple of things made me change my mind: (1) I didn't want to raise my two children in that area. With my Baptist upbringing, I couldn't see raising my children there with all the problems they had back in those days. (2) I would be far down the administrative totem pole and that bothered me. I was being paid for speaking and they said that all honoraria would have to go into a central fund and would be split by everybody. I thought, "Something is not right." We'd been with the attorneys in downtown San Francisco trying to finalize the deal, but I still hadn't made up my mind after being out there on multiple occasions. After a final business meeting in downtown San Francisco, we were driving to the airport and I said to Dr. Helvy, "Bill, I'm not going to join you. I'm going to do this on my own." The next thing I knew he missed the turn and we were going to Oakland on the Bay Bridge. My answer shocked him. They went ahead. They obtained a $1,000,000 loan and started the clinic, and I heard it failed shortly thereafter. I came so close to joining them. I was so naïve after being in the military for 13 years. My business knowledge was nonexistent. I'm sure my not joining them was an act of God.

People ask me if I would have predicted 30 years ago what I'm doing today. I'd have missed it 1,000-fold. My vision was finite but the Lord's was infinite! So many things have happened over the last 30 years that shouldn't have happened. I wanted to go one way, but I went another way. Why? I don't know, but apparently my direction was coming from above. I sincerely believe that.

At one time, I did consider building the center associated with Southwestern Medical School. I went to Dr. Rouse and John Stemmons because he was in charge of capital campaigns for their major projects. This was in 1970 before I left the Air Force. Mr. Stemmons asked, "What's it going to cost to build your center?" I told him, $1.2 million initially. He said, "How much time have you got left in the Air Force before you can retire?" I said, "Seven years." He said, "Son, if you're wise, you'll stay in the Air Force another seven years because it's going to take that long to raise the money. We've got so many projects ahead of yours, so many plans ahead of you, it's going to take that long for us to raise the money. I said, "I don't have that kind of time. I can't do that." So I went to many banks and savings and loan companies. The most money they could loan me was $100,000. They asked me those questions again about collateral and cosigning notes. My back was against the wall. Nobody could help me, so I finally went to Joe McKinney and asked if he could help me. He took it before their board and it was approved by one vote. They said, "We'll give you $1.2 million to make this first investment." They gave me the $1.2 million and didn't charge me any interest for the first eight months. Thanks to Joe McKinney, that gave me a "running head start."

WCR: *And you had the property?*

KHC: I had 8.6 acres. (Today it is almost 30 acres.) I obtained the $1.2 million loan in early 1971. We stayed at Preston Center from December 6, 1970 (when I saw my first patient) until November 29, 1971, when we moved to our present location on Preston Road.

WCR: *What was the first thing built in the aerobics center?*

KHC: The first thing we did was renovate the mansion.

WCR: *What mansion was it?*

KHC: It was the Nichols mansion. It had been there for about 30 years. When I came to Dallas I looked at property with *Harold Dunaway*, my realtor. I thought I needed at least five acres, maybe six or seven acres. We found a place by Presbyterian Hospital that wasn't developed, next to a railroad track. I didn't like it. I looked across the street from the Nichols property and there was the Miller estate with about four acres. I said, "Harold, the Nichols property is what I would like to have." It had two beautiful lakes and an old Southern style mansion. There was a total of 22 acres. I couldn't buy all of it. And he said, "That's the worst property in Dallas you could try to buy." "Why?" "It's come up for zoning a dozen times. Those neighbors are so powerful; they won't let anybody do anything except build individual houses. And we've tried and tried." I said, "But can I try?" He said, "Yes, but you're going to waste your time and money." First of all I had to visit with the owner, Mrs. Nichols. She was a widow who had raised her children on this property. Her husband had died of a heart attack about 10 years earlier. She lived there by herself. Many people had tried to buy her property, but she didn't want to break it up. Her husband had spent a long time putting the property together. The first time I spoke with her, I said, "Mrs. Nichols, I can't afford to buy more than the 8.6 acres, just your major property with the house and the lakes." She said, "I'm not going to sell you my prime acreage and have 14 acres left with no developments."

But a strange thing happened that later influenced her to change her mind: During my last year in the military, I was invited to speak at the Laymen's Leadership Institute in Colorado Springs for Howard Butt, of the HEB grocery chain. It was a group of lay people attending a three-day religious seminar at which both *Millie* and I spoke. I didn't know that Mrs. Nichols was in the audience. She's a wonderful Christian lady. After the initial decline to sell me her property, for some reason I asked my realtor to go back and see her again. She asked Harold, "Is this the Dr. Cooper who spoke in Colorado?" He said, "Yes." And she said, "For him, I'll do it." She had turned down all offers up until that time to break up her property. But she changed her mind (probably due to divine intervention again), so I purchased the 8.6 acres and took an option on the remaining 14 acres. Do you think that was a miracle, an answer to a prayer? I do! A couple of years ago I was having lunch with her at the cafeteria at the Cooper Fitness Center, and I said, "Mrs. Nichols, if you look on the chimney of the old mansion, we still have the initials of your children. We left them up there in honor of you and your children." The city wanted me to drain the lakes to reduce the likelihood of flooding. I had to fight City Hall to keep it as it is today. But, as you know, we've won the Dallas Beautification Award twice. I've spent lots of money keeping this place beautiful. I looked at Mrs. Nichols and said, "Isn't it great how the Lord has blessed The Aerobics Center?" And she said in her Southern accent, "Hon, everybody knows that the Holy Spirit hovers over The Aerobics Center." What a wonderful statement. I just hope it's true.

WCR: *You got that mansion and then what happened?*

KHC: After I obtained the money from Joe McKinney, I purchased the property and the mansion, and within one year I was able to obtain a loan from an insurance company. I paid off the Tyler Corporation relatively quickly, and they have continued to support us over the past 30 years. Unfortunately, Joe McKinney died last year. He was my favorite friend and patient. He was the reason I am here today. In all my books I talk about Joe McKinney's wisdom and insight. We started the annual Tyler Cup, a fitness event for corporate executives, the first year I was here. It's still going on. We have an endowment of $1 million for the Tyler Cup, and that all started with Joe McKinney. Two other top people at the Tyler Corporation have supported me over the years, Fred Meyer and C.A. Rundell. They've made possible what we're doing today.

For two years I tried to sell the other 14 acres because we needed money to expand. I couldn't get anybody to buy it. But by 1984 we needed it plus the adjacent church property, which we succeeded in acquiring. That took us up to the 30 acres that we have today.

WCR: *When you came to Dallas and set up the initial office in Preston Center, you had three people. About a year later, you moved to the mansion. How many people did you have then?*

FIGURE 4. Cooper family running with Millie Cooper leading the Cooper family in a campus run (1983). In 2001, Berkley, *left*, is an occupational therapist at Scottish Rite Hospital and son Tyler is in medical school at University of Texas-San Antonio.

KHC: I still had only two physicians—Joe Arends and me. We started increasing our staff, however, because we put in a lab. I expanded even while I was there at Preston Center. We took over more offices in Preston Center. I had an office on the second floor so at least I had a treadmill room upstairs. I brought along *Jane Counsellor*, my accountant. We had our first laboratory assistant to do urinalysis and complete blood counts. By the time I moved to the mansion there were seven of us.

WCR: *How many people do you have on the payroll at Cooper Aerobics Center now?*

KHC: Over 450, including 23 physicians. We have 19 physicians working in the clinic, 13 who see patients like I do. They do complete examinations. Others are specialists. We have four radiologists, two cardiologists, and one dentist on our staff. And we have four physicians working in the research institute.

WCR: *How many patients have you seen here at The Cooper Clinic?*

KHC: We are seeing about 8,000 per year. Our total database is over 70,000 patients. The database has more than 500,000 person-years of follow-up on those 70,000 patients. We're in our thirteenth year of our Aerobics Center Longitudinal Study (ACLS) and we just received another three-year grant from the National Institutes of Health. The database of patients keeps growing. Some of those 70,000 patients have been coming for as long as 30 years. It's the largest database in the world in which the level of fitness has been measured objectively by time on the treadmill and the people followed prospectively. We've published over 600 articles in the last 30 years.

WCR: *How many patients do you see here a week?*

KHC: As I said, we have 13 physicians seeing patients on a daily basis. A full load is four patients per physician, except me. I see only two or three patients a day. I'm here from 6:30 A.M. until 7:30 P.M. I have the administrative responsibilities. I'll average three, if not four, radio programs a week, in addition to my own. I have interviews all over the country. I still take care of my long-time patients, but I don't take any new patients. Our patients are some of the most well-known people in America. I could give you a very impressive list of people who have come to the Cooper Clinic—even the President of the United States. We see an average of 40 patients a day for complete examinations. Our physicians work 4 ½ days a week with no night or weekend call. It's one of the best positions in America for a physician. It is no problem getting physicians to join our staff.

WCR: *Everybody is on salary. Correct?*

KHC: Yes. We have a sliding scale type of salary based upon years with the clinic, plus a bonus program. Our physicians do very well.

WCR: *How many patients come here to work out in a week?*

KHC: We have seven entities on campus now under the umbrella of The Cooper Aerobics Center. *The Cooper Clinic* is a diagnostic and preventive medicine clinic with 19 physicians. *The Cooper Institute* has at least 12 doctorate-level associates on its staff and is the research center. *The Cooper Fitness Center* is a club with 3,600 members and currently a 96% annual renewal rate. About 800 to 1,000 people exercise here daily, except on weekends. We open at 5:00 A.M. and close at 9:30 P.M. six days a week, on Sunday from noon to 7:00 P.M. The average age of the Cooper Fitness Center member is 46 years. It is a health-oriented club, not a figure-contouring or muscle-building club. Men over 45 or women over 55 must have a stress test to join and be reevaluated every three years to keep their membership. We are a medically prescribed and supervised health club.

The Guest Lodge at The Cooper Aerobics Center is a beautiful four-star hotel patterned after The Mansion in Dallas. It stays full most of the time. Patients stay overnight since half of them come from outside the Dallas-Fort Worth area; 10% come from foreign countries, including Canada and Mexico. About 65% of our patients are return patients. At least 30% of our patients are corporate sponsored. I get requests all the time from corporations. Just a few weeks ago the Fleming Corporation, a grocery distribution firm with about $22 billion in annual sales, wanted to have 70 of their executives go through the clinic as soon as possible. The best we could do was 40 this year and 30 next year.

The Cooper Wellness Program is a 4-day, 7-day, or 2-week wellness program. The average weight loss in two weeks is eight pounds. They drop their cholesterol by 19%, triglycerides by 30%, and blood pressure by 6%. A comment from one patient who spent two weeks on campus was, "These two weeks were the most important two weeks of my life." It is a very successful program. People spend from $2,500 to $3,000 a week to go through our wellness program. We take 20 people per class. We're in the fifteenth year of our wellness program, and many people have drastically changed their lives.

Cooper Ventures is a program in which we work with corporations to establish worksite wellness programs. My staff handles the fitness center and the wellness programs for Nokia and Perot Systems. My staff also operates a very successful program in a residential area in Flower Mound called the Wellington Center.

My Cooper Ventures team recently went to Caracas, Venezuela, to consider setting up a program for a corporation, but we declined. We have a very close association with the Brazilians and the Japanese. We may be helping them establish preventive medicine/wellness centers and programs.

The seventh division, *Cooper Concepts*, is headed by *Todd Whitthorne*, who was the anchor on "Good Morning Texas" for 3½ years before he joined my staff. In that division we have our weekly call-in radio program, "Healthy Living." Todd is outstanding; he's a professional who has been in the business for about 16 years. He's 42 years of age, handsome, gregarious, intelligent, just outstanding. We're tape-delayed in Dallas but live in six Texas cities. Since July 1, 2001, a taped one-minute wellness tip is played two to three times daily on 184 radio stations. We hope to be on up to 250 stations by year-end. Also, daily two-minute wellness tips go all over the world on Yahoo. Todd's responsibilities are the vitamins, the website, and the radio programs.

WCR: *What are the vitamins you mentioned?*

KHC: I've been enthusiastic for years about vitamin supplementation, particularly antioxidants. With them, you can control homocysteine, free radicals, and to some extent the oxidation of low-density lipoprotein (LDL) cholesterol. But we've got only a few data. There have been few large, well-controlled clinical trials using vitamins.

About three years ago, I asked four of the top scientists in America to work with me in a clinical trial evaluating the effectiveness of vitamins. This included *Dr. Walter Willett*, a world authority on vitamins, particularly antioxidants and free radicals. He is the chairman of the department of nutrition at the Harvard School of Public Health. It also included *Dr. Jacob Selhub*, from Tufts Medical School, a world authority on homocysteine, folic acid, B_6 and B_{12}. *Drs. Kenny Jialal* and *Scott Grundy* from Southwestern Medical School in Dallas are also collaborating with us. They are all members of a scientific advisory group which is helping to direct this study.

We first conducted an 18-month observational trial following 151 people. They were placed on the first vitamin product we developed called *Cooper Complete*. Blood samples were taken every three months. There was no placebo. Half the blood was sent to Tufts and the other half to University of Texas Southwestern Medical School. At Tufts, the blood was analyzed for homocysteine, folic acid, B_6, B_{12}, and cystine. The half sent to Southwestern was evaluated for oxidized LDL cholesterol, vitamin C, vitamin E, and β carotene. The results were excellent. First of all, many vitamins purchased over the counter are not guaranteed pure because of the Dietary Supplement

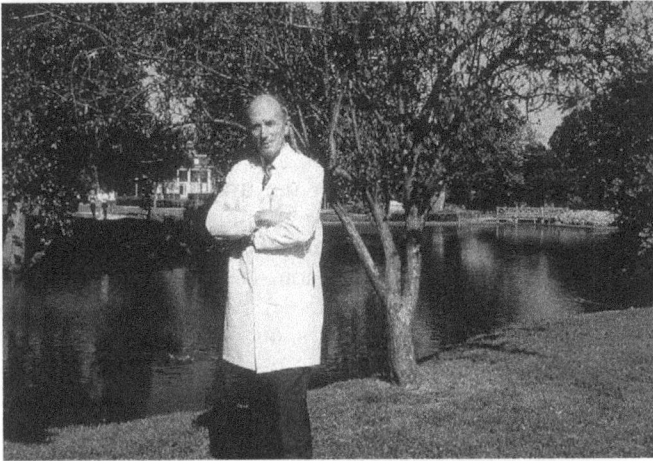

FIGURE 5. In 1970, KHC opened his first office in a Dallas strip mall. Today's 30-acre campus includes a preventive medicine clinic, fitness center, research institute, hotel, day spa, and medical spa.

Health Education Act of 1994. As a result, the Food and Drug Administration has little, if any, control over the vitamin industry. It is estimated that up to one half of the vitamins bought over the counter do not contain what it says on the label. "D Magazine" looked at 40 herbal products bought over the counter in Dallas and had them analyzed by a Food and Drug Administration lab; half the products tested were impure. One of them labeled "ginseng" contained no ginseng. Customers are being taken advantage of by the vitamin industry. In addition, some products may not be absorbed. It is estimated that half the vitamins "go out the same way they come in." What we need is some scientific credibility in this field. In January 1999, *John Cordero*, Director of the Council of Responsible Nutrition, said, "We claim to be a science-based industry. But we are going to have to start putting our money where our mouth is." I'm already doing that.

When we followed 153 people for 18 months, we found that most of them took all of the vitamins, that they were well absorbed, and that even people with normal homocysteine (7.9) still dropped their levels 13% due to the effect of folic acid, B_6, and B_{12} found in Cooper Complete. The oxidation of the LDL cholesterol was blocked by 32%, and both vitamin C and β carotene were well absorbed. We will have spent at the end of this year over $1 million on vitamin research. It's difficult to get money from the government for this type of research. Our support has come from contributors and profits from the vitamins. (No one is making any money on our vitamins.) Yet in the future I hope it will be a source of revenue for our Cooper Institute. Presently, we have 200 people in a clinical trial that will take about two years. *Dr. Tim Church* is supervising this study at our research institute and he is constantly in touch with our consultants. Our consultant committee meets every November to go over the results of the previous year's research and then modifies the vitamin if indicated. As a result, we now have *Cooper Complete Iron Free, Cooper Complete with Iron, Cooper Complete Elite Athlete, Cooper Complete for Kids (5 to 12 years of age),* and *Cooper Complete for Young Adults (13 to 17 years of age)*. Every product is listed on our website along with the scientific references. Last November we increased the dose of vitamin E from 400 to 800 IU in an effort to more effectively block the oxidation of the LDL cholesterol. Also, we doubled the dose of folic acid to further reduce the homocysteine.

I predict that our clinical trial will duplicate the results of the observational trial and perhaps give us even better results. If so, then we will be ready to put the vitamins on the open market. Now, the products are available only at the Cooper Fitness Center, over the Internet (cooperwellness.com), or by calling the Fulfillment Center (1-888-393-2221). We want the name and address of everyone taking the product. We have nearly 10,000 people in our database. Every three months these participants receive a complimentary newsletter bringing them up to date on what's happening with our research. Every six months they get a health questionnaire. The last questionnaire sent out in December 2000 had about 2,000 responses. We discovered that 46% of the people taking our vitamins had either no respiratory illness or had a marked reduction in the frequency of respiratory problems during the previous year.

WCR: *How do you spend your time? You obviously have your paws in many activities. Although I presume that no two days are the same for you, could you comment about what time you get up in the morning, what time you go to bed at night, what time do you get home, what time you get to your office?*

KHC: I have about five full time jobs. Number 1 is *Chairman and CEO of this organization* and the "financial buck stops here." I have a budget of $36 million this year and 450 employees. Number 2, I'm *a practicing physician*, and I still spend the majority of my time working with my patients. I enjoy practicing medicine. I see patients five days a week. Number 3, I'm *a professional lecturer*. I give about 150 lectures a year all over the world. A lot of my presentations now are on campus. I speak every Wednesday from 8:00 to 10:30 A.M. to in-residence patients and students. Also, I'm on the road about 50 percent of the time, lecturing all over the world. Number 4, until recently, I would be considered *a full-time author*. The royalties I've earned from my books have been enough to meet my needs. I've almost stopped writing books. I haven't written one since 1999 because I am concentrating on learning how to educate over the Internet. My lectures, my daily wellness tips on the Internet, my radio program, all take a lot of time. About every five weeks I tape 35 segments for Yahoo. The preparation for that takes a lot of time. That's a major requirement too. My authorship of books has stopped at number 18. Number 5 is *Chairman of the Board of The Cooper Institute* and its major fundraiser. I have been spending many hours visiting potential contributors, trying to raise $22 million to endow chairs for the research institute. I spend a lot of

FIGURE 6. At age 70, KHC still practices what he preaches. He works out 5 or 6 days a week, including jogging or walking most evenings before dinner and often a brisk walk before bedtime with his wife. He does strength training exercise 2 or 3 days a week.

time in research meetings and dealing with administrative problems. Additionally, I work with consultants instituting various projects outside of Dallas. Until last year I was a visiting professor at the National Defense University in Washington, DC, having lectured to the incoming students annually for 25 years. These responsibilities require a great number of hours. I work at least 60 hours a week. I get up at 5:45 A.M., eat a light breakfast, and get to the office by 6:30 A.M. Usually, I go to the fitness center to check operations. I try to get to my desk by 6:45 A.M. That is my time for prayer and Bible study. I'm reading the Bible or religious books every morning. I read professionally in the evening. My favorite religious writers are Max Lucado and Chuck Swindoll. I have a prayer list, which includes friends and patients. By 7:10, I start dictating. That is one of my headaches—dictating charts and letters. I have a tremendous amount of correspondence. I'll see my first patient at 8:15 A.M. I clear the patient (before the technician starts the treadmill stress test), then return to my office to continue dictating. I start patient evaluations in the office by 9:30 A.M. That's solid dictation from 7:15 until about 9:30, except for clearing the patient and starting the treadmill test. I don't take telephone calls during patient time. I take them in the afternoon. I do complete examinations, including 60-cm flexible sigmoidoscopic examinations. I try to finish about 2:30 P.M. I don't like to go over to the cafeteria before 2:30 to 2:45 P.M. It's a little idiosyncrasy because even if I finish early at 12:30 or 1:00 P.M., if I go over there I

get overwhelmed with people asking questions. I don't routinely eat lunch until 2:45 P.M. My lunch is light because I work out in the evening. It consists of a bowl of soup and a glass of unsweetened tea. I return to my office by 3:00 P.M. and I have all sorts of meetings, telephone calls, and conferences. I dictate more correspondence in the afternoon, then try to leave the office by 6:30 P.M., plus or minus 15 minutes. I go to the fitness center where I run and then lift weights. (At the conclusion, I enter my data on the computer. Once a month I download and keep the records in my desk.) At about 7:30 P.M., I leave for home.

WCR: *Describe the data on your exercise chart.*

KHC: At this stage of my life I'm doing as much aerobic walking as I am running. From May 1 through June 15, 2001, I walked or jogged a total of 92 miles. My average workout was 47 minutes. I participated 29 days during that period and averaged 38.5 aerobic points per week. The important thing here is that our studies show that if you average 15 points a week, that translates to a 58% reduction in death from all causes and a six-year increase in longevity. If you average 35 points a week that gives you a 65% reduction in death from all causes and an increase in life span of approximately nine years. During the mentioned time, I averaged 38 points a week. When I work out, I warm up for a few minutes, and I try to walk or jog two to three miles on the track. Two or three days a week I'll spend another 10 minutes lifting weights. I work out at least five to six days a week. Very often I have meetings which last until 7:00 P.M. or later, so I can't work out at the fitness center. I go home and have a light evening meal. About an hour later, I'll walk a two-mile route in the neighborhood starting about 10 P.M. My wife usually goes with me. We walk at least two miles. Until recently we would take our two dogs for a walk. Our dogs are small—a Pekinese and a Maltese. We'd have to carry them because they couldn't walk fast enough. The Coopers are well known in the neighborhood for "taking their dogs for a walk." Our little Pekinese as a result got fat and had a fatal heart attack recently. Occasionally, since it's just my wife and me, we eat the evening meal at a cafeteria or restaurant. That's always my largest meal of the day. I take vitamins, just like I recommend them to my patients. I also take potassium and magnesium aspartate since I sweat a lot. The only other natural thing I take is saw palmetto. My blood pressure is a little elevated so I take atenolol. I've had low-grade hypertension for years, but I didn't take anything until just recently. I keep it under good control. After dinner, if I've worked out at the fitness center, I will stretch out on the sofa, read the newspaper, and drift off to sleep for 30 to 45 minutes. Then I get up at 10:00 P.M. and usually work until midnight. I never get to bed before midnight. This week I prepared my Saturday radio program on Thursday night because I went to the theater Friday night. To keep up to date, it takes me three hours to get ready for the radio program. For the first 30 minutes on the air, I discuss current medical topics. During the second half hour, I answer medical questions. We have a good listening audience and get some outstanding questions. We've been on the air for almost two years.

WCR: *Which station in Dallas?*

KHC: KRLD, CBS 50,000 watts. They've been very good to us. We have all the sponsors we can handle at this time.

I get to bed at midnight Sunday through Friday. My wife and I thoroughly enjoy Friday night together. However, it's been interrupted recently because of the Saturday radio program requirements. I usually prepare on Friday night. Saturday morning I have to get to the office by 8:00 A.M. because I meet with Todd at 8:30 to go over the agenda for the radio program. We leave the clinic at 9:00 and drive to KRLD in Arlington. We get there about 9:30. The radio program goes from 10:00 to 11:00 live in six cities in Texas, including Houston, San Antonio, Waco, Lubbock, Paris, and Midland. We're tape-delayed in Dallas. I get back to the clinic at about 11:45 A.M., unless I visit my patients who are in the hospital. For acute care, I refer patients to one of our consultants. (We have about 160 Dallas physicians who work with us as consultants.) But I still try to see my patients when they need hospitalization.

For years people have come to us for preventive care. That is our specialty. The only time we get involved in acute care is when a patient doesn't have a regular physician. But even then, we try to get them in touch with a local physician. We are preventive medicine physicians. We want to work with the acute care physicians, not replace them. Most of our patients take that well. Many patients start coming to us and then if they aren't sick, they lose touch with their acute care physician. Then a problem occurs when they call their personal physician whom they haven't seen in several years (seems it's always at 3:00 A.M.). He or she might say, "You go see Cooper. He's the one who has been taking care of you." In the past, that was a problem. But now we work closely with several acute care clinics. They take our acute calls. I tell my patients that if you have a medical problem at any time, 24 hours a day, seven days a week, if you can't get in touch with me, call our Cooper Clinic number. We will get you in touch with somebody who can take care of you. For example, one of my patients returned from a business trip on Friday, October 13, 2000. On Saturday at 5:30 A.M. and developed left arm and chest pain. He tried to call me at home, but I was in San Francisco on a speaking engagement. He did what he had been told to do, that is, call the Cooper Clinic. A recorded message gave him instructions as to how he could reach the on-call physician at Presbyterian Hospital. As suggested, he went to the emergency room at Presbyterian Hospital, where an acute myocardial infarction was diagnosed. Immediately he was taken to the catheterization lab, an angioplasty was done, stent inserted, and he was back in a hospital room by 8:00 A.M. There was no damage done to his heart. This all happened between 5:30 and 8:00 A.M. on a Saturday! He was discharged two days later and has had no further problems. It was remarkable how well it worked! That's the way our patients are provided acute medical care if they don't have a regular physician. It's a good system and I believe it is the way medicine will be practiced in the future. Two distinctly different specialties: preventive medicine and acute care medicine.

We ask patients two questions when they come back for their exams: (1) How many days did you miss from work because of illness during the past year? (2) How many times did you see a physician for any reason in the past year? If they follow our guidelines for wellness, including stress management, exercise, and nutrition, those numbers usually approach zero. We pick up disease early. We have 12 patients whose chest x-rays were normal, but the computed tomography showed they had cancer of the lung. We have picked up 64 renal cell carcinomas by electron beam tomography. We send these patients to the appropriate specialist. The specialist will take care of the acute problem and then refer them back to us. When we send a patient to a hospital with an acute medical problem, the physician will see the patient, treat them as indicated, and if not hospitalized, will send them home and contact us the next morning. In essence, I have become their "primary" care physician. I didn't plan it that way, but I am their primary care physician. Primary care should be preventive care. Primary care in medicine is secondary care. You see patients when they are sick. I see patients when they are well. Our whole concept of *health insurance* is *disease insurance*. *Life insurance* is *death insurance*. Primary care is secondary care. My goal is to keep you healthy. When you get sick I'll send you to the specialist who isn't interested in preventive medicine; he's interested in acute care. So it is the best of all worlds.

I stay here on Saturdays until 5:00 or 5:30 P.M., usually dictating. (I'm always behind.) But I still believe in romancing my wife. We have a movie date almost every Saturday night. Then we eat out after the movie. That's our date. We've done that for many years. We celebrated our forty-second wedding anniversary in August 2001.

WCR: *You said that Friday nights were special for you and Millie.*

KHC: That's my number 1. It's at the end of the week and that means that some of the pressure is off. Until recently I could sleep "late" on Saturday morning—until about 8:00 A.M. But this Saturday radio program has changed our Friday evenings. Yet we still have a date on Saturday evening. Saturday evening is my number 2.

WCR: *What about Sunday?*

KHC: Sunday is supposed to be my rest day. We always go to church on Sunday morning. I get up at 6:45 A.M. so that we can go to the early Pastor's class that meets from 8:00 to 9:00 A.M. We then go to the 9:15 worship service so we're out by 10:30. We usually join our friends at a cafeteria for lunch. Ordinarily, I'm home by noon on Sunday. That's one of my big enjoyments. During the week I get by on less than six hours of sleep each night, but on Sunday afternoon I take a two-hour nap. Then I frequently go

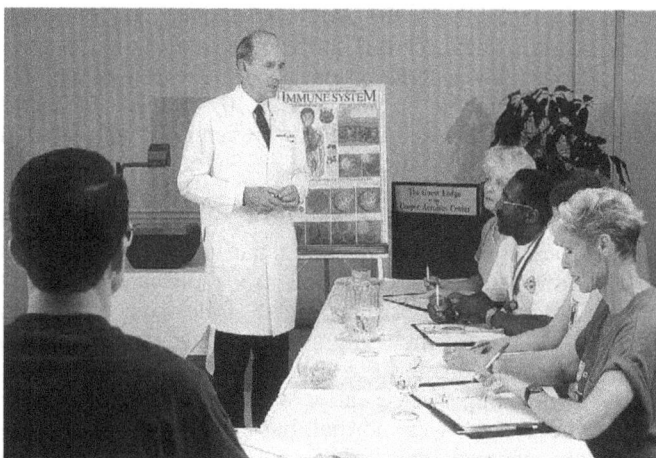

FIGURE 7. Each year KHC lectures to thousands of people all over the world. He enjoys speaking to small groups at the Cooper Wellness Program's lifestyle retreats and other on-campus events in Dallas.

back to the office and dictate for three or four hours. During the week after having dinner with my wife, I do my professional reading. Once I've read the newspaper and taken a short nap, I'll go to my study. I'm always behind in my reading. I read the current literature, either journals or off the Internet. I have to read to keep up. I read books. I study for lectures. I study for my radio program. I'd rather read than sleep. I'm working from 6:30 A.M. until 6:30 P.M. That's 12 hours five days a week. That's when I'm in town.

WCR: *How do you handle the enormous amount of travel that you do each year?*

KHC: The travel gets to be a problem, particularly overseas. But now I make only two or three international business trips per year. In the past, I traveled more. Frequently, I'll give two or three presentations in the same day. If I have a very heavy lecture requirement, I prefer to arrive the night before. However, that interferes with family time, much to Millie's displeasure. I'm now approaching four million American Advantage miles, and that is a lot of traveling!

WCR: *Tell me about your wife. She seems to be quite talented and she does a lot of this work also.*

KHC: My wife is a lovely person. She's an outstanding speaker. She's nationally known. Any speaking ability I have was gained from giving over 3,000 presentations over the years. My wife has given almost that many and she is so relaxed when speaking that she may kick off her shoes as she stands behind the podium. She's an entertaining, educational, and motivational speaker who keeps her audience mesmerized. She's the first person in her family to get a college degree and she paid her own way. I have great respect for her accomplishments, both personal and professional. Her mother is still alive, as are her two sisters. Millie is great! She's the love of my life but also my best friend. We've had ups and downs over the years as most marriages have, but I wouldn't give anything for my wife. Whatever I've done in my career, she may have had reservations, but she always

supported me to the fullest. We moved extensively when I was in the military and she never complained.

In 1968 after publishing my first book *Aerobics*, I received a lot of speaking requests and gained considerable public attention. Millie thought I was having all this fun on the lecture circuits, traveling all the time. I told her, "Millie, it's hard work." Yet I could see that we were splitting apart. I'd just established this new office in Dallas and I was working long hours, trying very hard to establish a practice. It was difficult. We came close to having a problem and it was my fault. I had placed work way up on my priorities, family was secondary. I was miserable. My wife was complaining every night when I got home late. It was frustrating. I was traveling, trying to raise money, trying to solve a myriad of administrative problems, and I could see our lives growing apart. I realized I had to involve my wife in my work. The third book was being considered, "Aerobics for Women." I could have written the book alone; in fact, that is what the publisher wanted. I said, "No, I want to get my wife involved." I wrote the third book adding all of her commentaries. She was listed as the senior author; I was the junior author. That gave her a literary name. All of a sudden she became well known. That opened up doors for her. She has since established her own lecture circuit. Later, she published another book. It gave her a career and brought us back together. She's a wonderful person and she tries to practice and preach what I teach in the field of preventive medicine.

I took a gamble when I married my wife because she comes from a very heavy family. Her oldest sister (six years older) weighs nearly 300 pounds and she's only 5 foot 1 inch in height. Her mother and her other sister are overweight. Millie's very lean and trim. Because of this genetic predisposition, we have a motto in our family. "If you start gaining weight, you start losing or you start looking because I can't afford to drag a fat wife around the country." Millie says in her presentations, "At times I have thought it would probably be easier to look than to lose!" She's now an avid participant in the program. She's enjoying excellent health. She is 66 years of age but she looks 45. She works out at the Cooper Fitness Center in the mornings or walks with me in the evenings. At the fitness center, she usually walks three miles on the indoor track, and at least two days a week she works on weights with her personal trainer. She is completely "Cooperized."

WCR: *You have 2 children. One's in medical school. How have you been able to manage being a father with the numerous activities you are involved in?*

KHC: People ask me all the time, "What is your major contribution to mankind?" They expect me to say "Aerobics, the books, The Aerobics Center." I honestly and sincerely believe it when I tell them, "It's being married for 42 years and having two fantastic

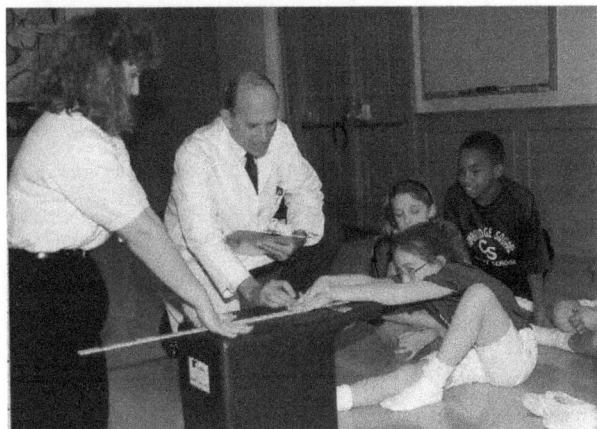

FIGURE 8. KHC promotes exercise and healthy eating for children through his book, *Fit Kids* (1999, Broadman and Holman), and FITNESSGRAM, a fitness assessment program used in approximately 7,000 schools.

kids." That is my major contribution to mankind. I'll be gone in not too many years. Who's going to take over? My kids. That's my greatest contribution.

My son Tyler, an outstanding young gentleman, graduated from Baylor in 1994 with a degree in business. He had no interest in medicine. I used to ask him, "Son, why don't you want to go to medical school?"—although I never tried to coerce him into becoming a physician. His comment was, "Dad, I don't want to work as hard as you do." And I thought, "Thank you, son. You are able to enjoy the necessities and luxuries of life because I worked so hard." He was (and still is) an outstanding runner. He ran a mile in close to 4 minutes when he was at Baylor University. He was the first person from Baylor in 35 years to qualify for the National Cross-Country Championships. He barely missed making All-American in cross-country. After finishing college he wasn't sure what he wanted to do. I thought he'd eventually get a Masters of Business Administration and work as Chief Operating Officer for The Cooper Aerobics Center. I encouraged him to go to Harvard where I have many contacts (and earned my Master's in Public Health). But after graduating, he went to Vail, Colorado, for nine months. Our entire family loves to snow ski (which I have been doing for over 40 years). Also, we've had a home in Beaver Creek, Colorado, near Vail, for 21 years. Tyler thoroughly enjoyed the fall and winter in Colorado, and in the spring of that next year, Millie and I had the chance to go to Australia to promote one of my books, so Tyler went with us. We took an extra five days and went to the Great Barrier Reef. It was a wonderful family time, swimming, snorkeling, and diving. Then a male friend joined him and they spent three months trekking across Australia and New Zealand. They had a great time. He came back and surprisingly said, "I want to go to medical school." I said, "What?" He'd been out of school for a year, had absolutely no premed requirements. I said, "Son, you have an uphill battle." "I don't care, Dad, I want to do it." He worked for me for 2½ years, while going to local schools to get his premed requirements.

He finally got into the medical school at the University of Texas in San Antonio. He is now a senior. His goal is to do exactly what I've done. We hope that after graduating he'll come back to Dallas for a three-year internal medicine residency. He may get his boards in internal medicine or he may take a year of internal medicine and then go to Harvard and get a masters degree in public health, followed by a year of residency, qualifying him for his boards in preventive medicine. Tyler has been dating a very fine young girl for several years. They'll probably get married, but there are no plans yet.

Our daughter Berkley, now 36, graduated from Baylor University in physical education. She works in occupational therapy at Scottish Rite Hospital in Dallas. She is married to *Tommy Estes*, Director of Operations here at our fitness center. They have no children. He's a fine young man. I'm very pleased to have him as a son-in-law. Our children have done well. We have a good relationship. How many fathers can say that their 36-year-old daughter calls every morning at about 7:15 A.M. just to tell him that she loves him?

WCR: *You've received a number of honors for your work. How many honorary doctor's degrees do you have now?*

KHC: Seven. I have one international degree from the University of Budapest in Hungary and six from universities and medical schools in the US.

WCR: *Of all the honors you've received, which one(s) are you most pleased with?*

KHC: Of all the honors I've received, the one I am proudest of is having a middle school in Oklahoma City named after me. Even though I have a presidential citation from Harvard, am a Distinguished Graduate from the University of Oklahoma, and, as mentioned, have been awarded seven honorary doctorate degrees, I am proudest of the Kenneth Cooper Middle School.

WCR: *What do you eat? What does your diet consist of as a rule?*

KHC: I have kept my weight the same plus or minus five pounds over the last 40 years and I do this by exercising and controlling calories. I feel that exercising prior to the evening meal does three things for me: (1) It suppresses my appetite; it makes me thirsty, but not hungry; (2) It tranquilizes me so I can sleep at night. I'm a typical type A, as you've probably guessed by now. Most type As, as I do, tend to awaken at 4:00 A.M. worrying about the day. Yet if I can get my exercise in, I have no trouble sleeping all night. (3) Because the endorphin effect of exercise lasts for several hours after exercising, it makes me feel better and makes me more productive in the evening. I can study much more effectively. Exercise helps me to control stress. My evening meal is customarily my heaviest meal of the day. That might be a problem if I didn't exercise. Let me explain: My resting heart rate is about 42 beats/min. When I work out, it goes up to about 160 beats/min. The first minute after stopping exercising it drops by about 30 beats/min. (Remember, if it doesn't drop at least 12 beats in the first minute, there's an increased risk of heart attack and sudden death over the next six years.) Mine drops to about 130 beats in the first minute. It is less than 100 after five minutes, but it takes about two hours to get back to my pre-exercise resting rate of 42. But during that time is when I consume my evening meal. My metabolism is still up because I'm repaying the slow component of the oxygen debt that I incurred during the run. I've "stoked the furnace!" Consequently, the calories consumed during that time are more effectively metabolized. I'm sure that's a major factor in helping me to control my weight.

I eat very little red meat, consuming almost exclusively fish and chicken. Also, I try to consume about 55% complex carbohydrates, 15% protein and 25% to 30% fat, and less than 300 mg cholesterol a day. My motto is "five is fine, nine is divine." That's consuming five servings of fruits and vegetables a day is fine, but nine is even better. I try to eat five servings a day. I reach that goal by eating at least two servings of fruit. I always have a piece of fruit for breakfast and I try to have fruit before I go to bed at night: nectarines, plums, peaches, pears, oranges, or cherries. I'm following basically an American Heart Association diet.

WCR: *What is your total cholesterol?*

KHC: I check my blood about every six months. My last laboratory studies were January 8, 2001: my total cholesterol was 156, HDL was 51, LDL was 92 (ratio 3.1), and triglycerides were 67 mg/dl. My calcium score on my last EBT scan (February 4, 2000) was 91, which puts me in a very low coronary risk category. The 50 percentile for men aged 70 to 74 is 302. At a calcium score of 91, my arterial age is less than 60; that is 10 years younger than my chronological age. If you used the 75th percentile, my arterial age would be 50 to 53 years.

WCR: *Ken, is there anything that you would like to discuss that we haven't?*

KHC: I think we've covered it well. This is the most extensive interview I've ever had regarding my personal life. I appreciate that. It's been a pleasure visiting with you. I appreciate the opportunity to tell you all these things.

WCR: *I want to thank you, not only for me, but on behalf of the readers of* The American Journal of Cardiology *for pouring your soul out here so we all get to know you better. Thank you.*

KHC: Thank you. I've had a wonderful life. All I regret now is that I'm not about 20 years younger.

KHC's Publications

1. Cooper KH, Cranny RM. Determination of genetic sex in children by peripheral blood smear. *Am J Dis Child* 1956;96:40–42.

2. Cooper KH, Lempert P, Culver JF. Effect of exercise on intraocular tension and its relationship to open angle glaucoma. *Aerosp Med* 1965;36:51–53.

3. Cooper KH, Leverett SD. Physical conditioning vs. +G tolerance. *Aerosp Med* 1966;37:462–465.

4. Cooper KH, Dong E, Beller BM, Ord JW. Effect of a vigorous exercise program on tilt table tolerance, upright and supine working capacity, resting and maximal oxygen consumption. *Aerosp Med* 1966;37:272–273.

5. Cooper KH. A means of assessing maximal oxygen intake: correlation between field and treadmill testing. *JAMA* 1968;203:201–204.

6. Cooper KH, Gey GO, Bottenberg RA. Effects of cigarette smoking on endurance performance. *JAMA* 1968;203:189–192.

7. Cooper KH. Testing and developing cardiovascular fitness within the United States Air Force. *J Occup Med* 1968;10:636–639 and *Journal of the Censeil International du Sport Militaire* 1968;39E.

8. Cooper KH. Exercise prescription—jogging or sprinting? (questions and answers). *JAMA* 1969;208:699.

9. Cooper KH. Quantifying physical activity—how and why? *J SC Med Assoc* 1969;suppl:27–40.

10. Cooper KH. Guidelines in the management of the exercising patient. *JAMA* 1970;211:1663–1667.

11. Cooper KH, Zechner A. Physical fitness in U.S. and Austrian military personnel. *JAMA* 1971;215:931–934.

12. Cooper KH, Pollock ML, Martin RP, White SR. Levels of physical fitness versus selected coronary risk factors—a cross-sectional study. *JAMA* 1976;236:166–169.

13. Cooper KH, Meyer B, Ullman, Blide R, Pollock ML. The important role of stress testing and fitness determination in predicting coronary incidence. *NY Acad Sci* 1977;301:642–652.

14. Gibbons LW, Cooper KH, Meyer BM, Ellison C. The acute cardiac risk of strenuous exercise *JAMA* 1980;224:1799–1801.

15. Cooper KH. Physical training for mass scale use: effect on cardiovascular disease—facts and theories. *Ann Clin Res* 1982;14:25–32.

16. Cooper KH, Gallman JS, McDonald JL Jr. Role of aerobic exercise in reduction of stress. *Dental Clin North Am* 1986;30:S133–S142.

17. Gibbons LW, Blair SN, Kohl HW III, Cooper KH. The safety of maximal exercise testing. *Circulation* 1989;80:846–852.

18. Cooper KH, Blair SN, Gordon NF. Oxygen and athletes. *JAMA* 1989;262:264.

19. Blair SN, Kohl HW III, Paffenbarger RS Jr, Clark DG, Cooper KH, Gibbons LW. Physical fitness and all-cause mortality: a prospective study of healthy men and women. *JAMA* 1989;262:2395–2401.

Books and Chapters

1. Cooper KH. Aerobics. New York: M. Evans and Co, Inc., 1968.

2. Cooper KH. The New Aerobics. New York: M. Evans and Co, Inc., 1970.

3. Cooper M, Cooper KH. Aerobics for Women. New York: M. Evans and Co, Inc., 1972.

4. Cooper KH. Aerobics for Women. New York: M. Evans and Co, Inc., 1977.

5. Cooper KH. The Aerobics Program for Total Well-Being. New York: M. Evans and Co, Inc., 1982.

6. Cooper KH. Running Without Fear. New York: M. Evans and Co, Inc., 1985.

7. Cooper M, Cooper KH. The New Aerobics for Women. New York: Bantam Books, 1988.

8. Cooper KH. Controlling Cholesterol. New York: Bantam Books, 1988.

9. Cooper KH. Preventing Osteoporosis. New York: Bantam Books, 1989.

10. Cooper KH. Overcoming Hypertension. New York: Bantam Books, 1990.

11. Cooper KH. Kid Fitness. New York: Bantam Books, 1991.

12. Cooper KH. Antioxidant Revolution. Nashville, TN: Thomas Nelson Publishers, 1994.

13. Cooper KH. It's better to believe. Nashville, TN: Thomas Nelson Publishers, 1995 (re-released at Faith-Based Fitness in 1997).

14. Cooper KH. Advanced Nutritional Therapies. Nashville, TN: Thomas Nelson Publishers, 1997.

15. Cooper KH. Can Stress Heal? Nashville, TN: Thomas Nelson Publishers, 1998.

16. Cooper KH. Regaining the Power of Youth at Any Age. Nashville, TN: Thomas Nelson Publishers, 1998.

17. Cooper KH. Fit Kids: The Complete Shape-Up Program from Birth through High School. Nashville: Broadman & Holman Publishers, 1999.

18. Cooper KH. Controlling Cholesterol the Natural Way. New York: Bantam Books, 1999.

MICHAEL ELLIS DEBAKEY: A Conversation With the Editor*

Dr. Michael E. DeBakey was born in Lake Charles, Louisiana, on September 7, 1908, and I had the honor of talking with him for over 3 hours in his conference room in Houston, Texas, on September 18, 1996. During the interview, Dr. DeBakey reminisced about his earlier life and a few of his accomplishments. There were only 2 interruptions during the interview and each was a telephone call from President Clinton's physician. Each call concerned President Boris Yeltsin's grave illness and Dr. DeBakey's September 22, 1996, planned trip to Russia to consult about the President's cardiac disease. At the end of the interview, Dr. DeBakey took me into his "manuscript room" where he was working on a paper on 30-year outcomes on about 30,000 patients he had followed after they had had various operative procedures involving the coronary, carotid, renal, and peripheral arteries and the abdominal aorta. For someone who had already published about 1,500 articles plus several books, he was as excited about this latest manuscript as most physicians when seeing their first manuscript published. Furthermore, although Dr. DeBakey did most of the talking during the interview, his stories making me laugh on many occasions, at the end of the nearly 4-hour interview, he appeared to have more energy left than I did and all I did was ask a few questions.

Dr. DeBakey is a great man. In addition to being a masterful surgeon, innovator, and scholar, he is the century's most influential international and national medical statesman. His work in the Surgeon's General Office led to the development of mobile army surgical hospitals (MASH units). He later helped establish the specialized medical and surgical center systems for treating military personnel returning from World War II, which subsequently became the Veterans' Administration Medical Center System. Also, while on active duty during World War II, he proposed a systematic follow up of veterans with certain medical problems, and this initiative subsequently led to the establishment of the Committee on Veterans' Medical Problems of the National Research Council and an extensive Medical Research Program by the Veterans' Administration. He has been the century's best advocate for more dollars for medical research. He was responsible for preserving the Surgeon General's Medical Library. He convinced Congress to provide the new building, now called the National Library of Medicine, and to move it to the Bethesda campus. He was the one most re-

sponsible for making the Texas Medical Center what it is today. Specifically, he single-handedly preserved the Baylor College of Medicine and wove its association with the Methodist Hospital at Houston. He has served as an advisor to almost every President in the last 50 years and to heads of states around the world. For his many accomplishments, Dr. DeBakey has received 50 honorary doctorate degrees from prestigious colleges and universities as well as innumerable awards from educational institutions, professional and civic organizations, and governments throughout the word. These awards include the Legion of Merit, U.S. Army (1945); American Medical Association Hektoen Gold Medal (1954 and 1970); Rudolph Matas Award in Vascular Surgery (1954); International Society of Surgery Distinguished Service Award (1958); Leriche Award (1959); American Medical Association Distinguished Service Award (1959); Albert Lasker Award for Clinical Research (1963); St. Vincent Prize for Medical Sciences (1965); Prix International Dag Hammerskjöld Great Collar with Golden Medal (1967); American Heart Association Gold Heart Award (1968); Eleanor Roosevelt Humanities Award (1969); Yugoslav Presidential Banner and Sash (1971); Union of Soviet Republics Academy of Sciences 50th Anniversary, Jubilee Medal (1973); Independence of Jordan Medal (1980); The Merit Order of the Republic of Egypt (1980); American Surgical Association Distinguished Service Award (1981); Theodore E. Cummings Memorial Prize for Outstanding Contributions in Cardiovascular Disease (1987); Thomas Alva Edison Foundation Award (1988); and the International Platform Association George Crile Award as The Trailblazer in Open Heart Surgery (1988); Presidential Medal of Freedom, 1969; Presidential Medal of Science, 1987.

• • •

William C. Roberts, MD (hereinafter called WCR)**: I am speaking with Dr. Michael E. DeBakey in his office suite in Houston, Texas, on September 18, 1996.

I consider you this century's finest medical spokesman and certainly one of its premier surgeons. I want to try to find where your passion for medicine came from. Where your desire to excel far above the pack came from. What was it like growing up in your family and in Lake Charles, Louisiana?

Michael E. DeBakey, MD (hereinafter called MED)***: First, Bill, I was blessed with parents who were both highly intelligent and exceedingly kind and generous in their temperament and psyche. They lived almost exclusively for their children. They wanted to give us the best of everything, and they believed education was crucial. They were both first-generation immigrants, having come to this country as children. Because they believed that a good edu-

* This interview is part of a series of interviews of prominent cardiovascular specialists and the series is underwritten by an unrestricted grant from Bristol Myers Squibb.

** From the Baylor Cardiovascular Institute, Baylor University Medical Center, Dallas, Texas 75246.

*** From Baylor College of Medicine, Houston, Houston, Texas.

cation was essential to prepare us for a fulfilling life, they always encouraged us to excel in our studies. For example, they urged us to go to the local library once a week and choose any book we wanted to read. We had a small but very good library in Lake Charles. I came home from the library one day and told my Father that there was a wonderful set of books there, but you could not borrow them; you had to read them in the library. He asked me the name of the book, and I responded, *The Encyclopaedia Britannica*. He said, "Well, we will get it." I don't remember how many volumes there were at that time —not as many as there are today—but he purchased the complete set. All of us, my brother, sisters, and I, before we went to college, had each read that whole set of *The Encyclopaedia Britannica*. That is how important it was to us, not only from an educational standpoint, but mainly because we enjoyed reading. All of us excelled at school; we all led our classes. My sisters all led their classes. They were smarter than I was; at least they were a little more studious. My brother and I wanted to play and do other things.

The one thing that I never got an "A" in was deportment. In those days we had a deportment grade, and I had great difficulty with it because I would finish all my studies and would get bored because the teacher was dealing with material I had already mastered. In what we then called grammar school or elementary school—I think I was in the fifth or sixth grade—the classes were divided into 2 sections—A and B—and the same teacher taught both classes. While she was teaching one class, she would give the other class a study period of 30 minutes, after which she would go back to the other side. She noticed I was sitting in the center, paying attention to what she was doing, whether she was in my class or the other one. So near the end of the class, she said to me one day, "I notice that you are paying attention to both classes, would you like to take the exam for both of them?" I said, "Sure." I took both exams and was permitted to skip a grade because I passed the exam. School was fun for me because I enjoyed learning new things. My parents had always emphasized to all of us the joy of learning. I studied, learned, and earned good grades, and I think that became a habit.

• • •

WCR: Did your parents go to college?

MED: No, but they were self-educated, read widely, and had remarkably critical minds and retentive memories.

• • •

WCR: And they pushed education to the hilt.

MED: Yes, absolutely.

• • •

WCR: I presume you read the book or books that you got from the library once a week?

MED: Yes, regularly.

• • •

WCR: From age 6 through age 17, I calculate that you must have read over 600 books outside of school.

MED: Yes, at least, plus the encyclopedia. I was a voracious reader. In fact, we had to go to bed at a certain time. We would do our lessons—our parents would make sure we had done our lessons—and then if we had time, we would read the library book or sections of *The Encyclopaedia Britannica*. Often, we were all going to *The Encyclopaedia Britannica* at the same time. Of course we would not read the same thing. Usually by 10:00 o'clock, our parents wanted us in bed, because we had to get up early. Our Father was a very early riser, and we all had assigned chores, to encourage self-discipline and responsibility, even though my parents had a house staff. By 5:00 A.M. we were up. I guess I got habituated to the early rising. That came in handy, because when I first started as a freshman in college, I lived in a dormitory, and the boys were raising cane all night. I wanted to study, but couldn't because of the commotion. I would just go on to bed, and get up at 3:00 or 4:00 in the morning and do all my studying while it was quiet. So I got into the habit of getting up early, and it does not matter what time I go to bed now; I still arise at 5:00 A.M. I read the *New York Times* and *Wall Street Journal* in about 30 minutes. After that I can get some of the things done that I may not be able to do during the day—work on a manuscript or attend to some other paper work. Getting up early has been of great value not only in my surgical practice, but also in allowing me an additional couple of hours beyond that of the average person. Fortunately, I manage well on 5 or 6 hours of sleep a night, just as my Father did.

• • •

WCR: So if you get 5 hours sleep a night, and you are 88 years old, you have slept only 14 of your last 68 years.

MED: You are probably right about that. If you sleep 8 hours a night (one-third of every day) and you live 60 years, you have really lived only one-third of that time or 40 years. So whatever you can take from your sleep extends your conscious living.

• • •

WCR: So you are 88 years and a maximum of one-fifth of your life has been spent sleeping.

MED: That is about right. And that gives me a tremendous advantage. People ask me, "How in the world could you write nearly 1,500 articles in that period of time?" If you live your life long enough and you have enough time, you can do it.

• • •

WCR: Yes, but you don't waste a minute. You spend very little time commuting. You live 5 minutes from the hospital.

MED: In fact, I deliberately chose to live near the College. When I first came to Houston, I rented a house that was also only about 10 minutes from here. An Associate Dean was living in a place he had built, about 30 minutes away from the hospital. He wanted me to consider that area. Each lot was about an acre or an acre and a half, with a lot of trees, and it was attractive. I simply told him "That means an hour of commuting and that is an hour of wasted time. That is one thing. The second thing is I am a surgeon and if I get a call in the middle of the night, I don't want to use the telephone, I want to see that patient." So I told him, "No, I am not interested." I declined 3 professorships in New York, 2 before I came here, and one after, because at that time I had small children and didn't want to live in an apartment in New York City. One of the physicians in New York who drove me out to Westchester and other places to show me around told me that he spent nearly 3 hours commuting every day. Think of that. I deliberately chose a house in Houston close to the hospital. It has been my home ever since. It takes 5 minutes to get here.

You have to decide early what you want in life. You know that you have a certain time span, whatever God gives you. When you are living, you want to enjoy that. When you are sleeping, you are just dead as far as conscious living is concerned; that's part of your death. So I think you have to set some goals and priorities. I try to use my time as efficiently as I can. Obviously, you can't avoid doing some things. You have to take time to shave, and do the daily chores, but you can control other things. As a surgeon, I could not control a certain amount of time because I had to be in the operating room. When I became Dean of Baylor University College of Medicine in 1968, we had a review for accreditation—I think it was the next year. The accreditation group came to the College, made a thorough review, and gave us its approval. We were sitting at the end of the table, and they were asking a few questions; among them: How do you have the time to be Dean of the Medical School? How do you explain the fact that you are Dean *and* Chairman of Surgery and a very busy surgeon? At that time I was operating every day, including weekends. In a jocular vein, I said, "Well, I do it between cases." This did not go over very well, but the truth of the matter is that is what I did. It was between cases and after I finished the operating schedule for the day that I would go over to the Dean's office and meet with the faculty members who had become associate deans. Actually, we did not have any money to hire a full-time Dean. You remember when you came here in 1973 what the problems were.

So you try to be as efficient as you can with your time. You have to sacrifice some things. For example, I rarely see television, unless there is something of special interest that is called to my attention. If I have a little time at home, I spend it on a manuscript I am working on or some articles I am reviewing for library research, or something like that. I gave up hunting and fishing years ago. I have friends here, for example, who have yachts in Galveston, and they continue to invite me to go fishing or hunting, but I don't do any of that. I go to some College dinners, but I leave as soon as I can. I try to conserve whatever time I can for the things I need to do, most of which are in my professional sphere of interest.

• • •

WCR: May I go back a little bit. I have always been impressed with how beautifully you handle yourself in any situation. When you were growing up at home, what kind of conversation went on at the dinner table?

MED: Most often, my Father or Mother would bring up some topic, for example, my Mother would say to us, "Next Sunday, we are going to the orphanage." Every Sunday morning shortly after church, we would have dinner, and then in the early afternoon, Mother would say, "I want you to help me prepare some things for the orphanage." There might be clothes that needed repair; she had taught me to sew. In those days, young girls were supposed to learn to sew before they were married. About a half dozen girls would come to the house after school, and she would teach them not only crocheting and knitting, but how to cut a pattern and how to use a sewing machine. And I learned all those things as I sat and watched them. I enjoyed it. In fact, I also tatted, using a little bobbin to make lace. Most young people today have never heard of tatting. Of course, neither do most of them know how to sew.

Occasionally, my Father would say we were going to drive to the next parish, Cameron Parish, where some friend of his wanted him to buy some land or obtain a loan from him on it. Our Father would also bring up occurrences at the drugstore that he thought might be of interest to us, perhaps a new pharmacist he was going to hire. Or we would talk about some of the politicians. We were never activists in politics, but state and local politicians always sought my Father's advice and support because he was a successful and highly respected businessman. The governor made him a Louisiana Colonel, and the Sheriff made him an honorary deputy. In addition to the drug store, he had other business interests, including rice farming, real estate, and construction.

We would occasionally also talk about our school work, and if there were any problems, we would discuss those. So the conversation would include topics that were of interest to all of us. If we had read an interesting book, or had read something in the Encyclopedia about a certain country, we would be asked to relate it. Occasionally, one of the children would say "Let me talk" because everyone was speaking, and you could not get a word in edgewise until one of our parents announced who had the floor. It was very stimulating.

My Mother was religiously inclined, but she did not wear her religion on her sleeve. She never tried to convert anyone, but she and my Father lived very Christian lives. My parents had been educated in religious schools. Within the family, religion was very personal. Before we went to sleep at night, we would kneel and say our prayers, beginning with the Lord's Prayer. Before my parents came to America, they had belonged to the Greek Orthodox Church—the church that had split off from the Roman Catholic Church. In Lake Charles, my parents joined the Episcopal Church. We went to church regularly and supported the church; it was an integral part of our lives. My sisters sang in the choir, and we all participated in church activities.

Throughout our childhood, our Mother and Father stressed honesty, self-respect, integrity, probity, compassion, personal independence, and courtesy. They instilled the highest human values not only by example, but also by using various incidents to illustrate and extol those virtues.

I had a boyhood friend and classmate named Pee Wee Hines, so-called because of his smaller size. We both played musical instruments. I played the saxophone, although I actually started with the piano, but because I wanted to play in the band, I got a saxophone. Pee Wee's Father was a Presbyterian minister, and the Presbyterian Church had a small orchestra that would play on Sunday evenings for the congregation. I played with that group and became familiar with the Presbyterian Church. At that time, the Boy Scout Troop that I belonged to (#32) was sponsored by the Baptist Church. I therefore had a broad religious background. I also attended a Catholic School for my first 2 or 3 years before going to public school. In Lake Charles, the public schools had very high academic standards and always ranked high in our State rallies. We lived in a house that was just two blocks from the public school, so I could walk to school.

• • •

WCR: Why did you pick Tulane to go to college?

MED: It was the best college in the South at that time; it was known as the Harvard of the South. I was 23 years old when I graduated from Medical School, because I had only two formal years of college before entering medical school. Since I wanted to get my Bachelor's degree, I told my professors, "I have enough credits to get into medical school, but I also want to get a Bachelor's degree, and I would like to take the additional courses required for my Bachelor's degree while I am in medical school." They said it had never been done, and they would not advise me to do that. I said, "Well if I can do it, would you let me?" They said, "Yes, if you want to try." So I did.

• • •

WCR: So during your first 2 years in medical school you took your last 2 years of college at the same time?

MED: That's right, and I graduated with my freshman Arts and Sciences class at the end of my sophomore year in medical school.

I had also played in the marching band, but then I found out that Tulane had a symphony orchestra. The Professor of Philosophy had been a member of the Philadelphia Symphony Orchestra, and when he came to Tulane, he organized a symphony orchestra among the students. I became interested in this, but when I went to audition, they said "We don't need any saxophones." I said, "Well, what do you need?" They said, "We need a clarinet." I said, "All right, I'll play clarinet." I called my Father that night and told him I wanted to buy a clarinet. He

FIGURE 1. Photograph of Dr. Michael E. DeBakey as a student at Tulane University.

said, "Why?" and I told him, and he approved. My Father was very generous. I went downtown and bought a clarinet and started practicing although I never took formal lessons. I practiced very intensively for 6 weeks. A friend of mine who was in the symphony orchestra and the band helped me. After about 6 weeks of intensive practice, I asked if he thought I could audition. He said, "I will bring some audition music for you." He brought some classical music for the clarinet, and I auditioned for about an hour with him, after which he said, "I think you can make it." That's how I began to play in both the band and the orchestra.

• • •

WCR: So back then you were not sleeping much either. How did you enjoy college?

MED: I had a great time in college; I enjoyed it tremendously. In my freshman year, I took Zoology. One day, the Professor of Zoology asked me, "What are you going to do this summer?" I said, "I am going to go on a vacation." He said, "Why don't you stay here and help me with a course I have to give during the summer?" I said, "Fine." He said he would pay me—I have forgotten what the amount was, but it wasn't a great deal. I called my parents and told them that this was a great opportunity for me. They agreed. He appointed me an Instructor in cat anatomy. I had just finished my Freshman year in college. Most of the summer students were teachers who wanted credit for higher degrees. I found myself teaching young ladies who were older than I was. In addition to that cat course, I was also involved in a course that included a variety of animals. Every Sunday I would go to the marshes to get frogs, snakes, and water moccasins. On one occasion, I was living in a private home, where the only meal on Sunday was at noon, so I would go out early to the land marshes—you didn't have to go very far in New Orleans to get there—get the animals and put them in a gunnysack. One day I rushed to be back in time for lunch, so instead of stopping at the lab, I brought the gunnysack full of snakes with me and put it behind the door. Somehow, the gunnysack opened, and all of a sudden while we were at dinner in the next room, the lady of the house, sitting at the table right in front of the door, saw the snakes come in. She ran, terribly frightened. I had to rush out and catch all the snakes and put them back in the gunnysack.

• • •

WCR: Now in medical school, you met Dr. Alton Ochsner, during your sophomore year, I presume.

MED: In my sophomore year, I worked as an assistant technician in the laboratory of another member of the medical faculty. In my junior year, Dr. Ochsner sought me out, and in my senior year I worked in his lab. The other faculty member was interested in the pulse wave; he wanted to find a pump that could modify the wave. This was *in vitro,* so he asked me to look up "pumps" in the medical library. I could not find much about the kind of pump he wanted. In my college days, one of my closest classmates was studying engineering. I called him and asked, "Do you know anything about pumps?" He said, "Oh sure. We work a lot with pumps in engineering school." I told him what I was trying to do and explained that I could not find much in the medical library. He said, "You have got to go to the School of Engineering library." I went uptown, where the Engineering School was located, across the street from Audubon Park, and in that library I found all kinds of information about pumps, going back more than 2,000 years. I spent days researching it and was fascinated.

In the early 19th century, someone had written an article about the use of rubber tubing (rubber had just been discovered), and about compressing that tubing to force fluid out of it as a possible pump. That is what gave me the idea. So I began to think about a way to make a rubber tube into a pump. I got the idea of some kind of compression. I worked on different ways of compressing, pressing it down, finally rolling something over it as I could with my fingers. I experimented with different ways of doing this. I went to a foundry in New Orleans, and had them make a kind of round cup that I could put the tube in. Then I experimented with different types of rollers, 2 rollers, 3 rollers, 4 rollers. Finally, after a year or 2 years of experimenting, I finally got the 2 rollers and the pump the way I wanted it. At that time I had no idea of using this pump for the heart-lung machine. John Gibbon had been working on a heart-lung machine for some time. This was before World War II. He started as a resident at Massachu-

setts General Hospital, and I ran into him at a meeting where he had an exhibit of his heart-lung machine. He tells the story in an article he published. He was showing his machine to me, and he said, "You know, the problem is the pump. I don't know what to do about this pump." He had what now would be called a Sigma type of pump, but it was not working well. I said, "I have a pump you might be able to use." I told him about it and offered to send him a sample of it, which I did, and he adapted it for his heart-lung machine.

• • •

WCR: But you developed it to get blood in people quickly for transfusions?

MED: No, that came later. I developed it primarily for this faculty member with whom I was working, who wanted to be able to use some kind of pump to modify the pulse wave. I developed the pump for him. If you roll that pump when you have fluid in it, the outlet tube will create a pressure. If you compress the tube, the pressure will go right up. So when you compress the tube and then release it, it will create a wave. Depending on how much pressure you create and how quickly you release it, the wave can be modified. That was what it was for.

When I became a resident, blood transfusion was indirect. The blood from the donor was put in a paraffin-coated glass container, and the collected blood would be brought over to the patient. That is when it occurred to me, "I can do it directly by this roller pump." I must have used the roller pump on a couple of thousand patients for transfusions. This made me an "expert." I would go all around town giving blood transfusions with my pump.

• • •

WCR: When you were a senior in medical school, you worked in Dr. Ochsner's laboratory, I gather you 2 just sort of clicked right away?

MED: Very quickly, I took to him. During my senior year, he came to me one day after a lecture and said, "I want to talk to you. I know you have been working over in the medical lab. How would you like to work in my lab?" I responded, "I would love to." He said, "I need some assistance. We are doing some dog experiments, and if you would like to work, come on over." So I did. He was interested at that time in peptic ulcer. In those days, the concept was that the gastric acid was primarily responsible, so they were doing experiments on modifying it, like transplanting the bile duct from its position in the duodenum to some other place in the ileum. I became a regular dog surgeon. Sometimes I would do 8 or 10 dog operations in an evening, working until midnight. I liked doing this research very much, and I was attracted to the technical aspects of operating. I liked working with my hands. (Both my parents were extremely dextrous.)

One day Dr. Ochsner said to me, "I want you to stay in surgery. You impress me. I want you to be my intern and resident." So I became, from that point on, his student, and he became my mentor. He treated me like a son. We wrote papers together. I would go over to his house and work on a paper in his study at his home and make slides for him. We had to do everything ourselves in those days. It was a great learning experience, and he was a great disciplinarian. He was of Swiss-German origin; as a matter of fact, he traced his ancestry to Paracelsus. He directed my entire early development. He was the one who suggested I study in Europe because he had also trained there. In those days, Europe was the ultimate training ground. My parents were eager to support my study abroad, even though there was a depression, because they wanted all of us to get as much education as we could. I went to Strasbourg, France, because Dr. Rudolph Matas, who was still living at that time, suggested to Dr. Ochsner that I train there with Professor René Leriche. He considered Leriche to be the most advanced surgeon in vascular surgery at the time. I published 3 papers while I was there. It was a wonderful experience.

• • •

WCR: You found Leriche to be technically a very good surgeon?

MED: If he was interested, for example, in sympathectomies, he was technically very good, but if he was doing a gastric resection, he was not very good. He did not have what I would call a surgical temperament either. He was more philosophical, introspective, a great historian, and well versed in art. He was one of those old-fashioned, well-educated Frenchmen, and surgery was almost an avocation. He was interested in the circulation, and if you read some of his articles, you can see how philosophical he was. He wrote beautifully.

• • •

WCR: You learned how to speak French when you were there?

MED: Yes, of course; everyone spoke French. Then I went to Heidelberg, Germany, to be with Professor Martin Kirschner because Dr. Ochsner suggested I go there. I had a great time with Kirschner, too. It was another great experience because Heidelberg in those days was a great university town.

• • •

WCR: So this was 1936?

MED: Yes. This was the beginning of the Nazi regime, and I used to see them marching in the streets in Heidelberg and practicing with brooms instead of guns. I had no idea what was going on. I became close friends with a young man named Ernst, who was a resident with me and spoke English very well. He had an automobile and would drive me around in his car. Every Friday, we would go to Mannheim, a bigger city not far from Heidelberg, because he was a member of a military reserve group. They would all be in uniform when they went to their meetings. I would drive with him to Mannheim, and I would wait in the vestibule until after the meeting. When he came out, everyone would have sausage and beer together. I thought these people were the counterparts of our college students in the R. O. T. C.

FIGURE 2. Photograph of Dr. Michael E. DeBakey as a Research Fellow at the University of Strasbourg, France, 1935.

• • •

WCR: You learned how to speak German when you were over there?

MED: Yes.

• • •

WCR: So you were busy with these languages, in addition, to picking up what you could professionally.

MED: That's right.

• • •

WCR: Kirschner, what kind of surgeon was he?

MED: He was a very good surgeon. He was very kind to me; at least once a month he would invite me to his home for dinner. His wife was also nice, and so was his daughter.

• • •

WCR: What was his expertise? Why did you want to work with him?

MED: Gastroenterology. In those days, there were no medical specialties. I was interested in the circulation, an interest I had acquired when I was working as an assistant technician. There was not much vascular surgery. They were doing sympathectomies, but that was about all. We were doing experimental work. In Strasbourg I became close friends with the chief resident, called a *chef de clinique,* whose name was Jean Kunlin. One day he asked me if I would like to work with him in the laboratory. The research laboratory was a separate building behind the hospital, perhaps twice the size of this room. We operated on dogs. Incidentally, Kunlin was the surgeon who did the first successful femoropopliteal bypass. I remember that we were working experimentally on it at that time. Kunlin died just a couple of years ago. The other research fellow with me—called *Assistant Etranger*—was Cid dos Santos, the son of Renaldo dos Santos, the Professor of Surgery in Portugal, who did the first abdominal aortogram in 1926. Cid, who did the first endarterectomy, and he and I also became very good friends too.

• • •

WCR: How did that come about?

MED: By a kind of serendipity. He wanted to remove an embolus in the femoral artery. It turned out to be a very firmly adherent clot superimposed on an atheroma. When he tried to remove the clot, the underlying plaque suddenly peeled away from the arterial wall. He then observed that there was a cleavage plane between the atheroma and the remaining arterial wall. It is interesting that here were 2 very important contributions to vascular surgery, and they were done by these 2 people at Leriche's Clinic when I was there.

• • •

WCR: Was this the first time you had been abroad, Dr. DeBakey?

MED: No, it was the first time I had been abroad alone. When I was about 12 years old, my Mother and Father decided to take a year off to travel. We went to Lebanon, which, of course, is the country of my parents' families. We took a ship from New Orleans and arrived in Cherbourg, France, about 3 weeks later, having made stops in Cuba and the Canary Islands. We then drove across France to Marseille (my Father had taken our automobile with us), boarded a ship there, stopped off briefly in Naples, and then continued on the ship to Cairo. From there we went to Jedeidet, Lebanon, my grandparents' hometown, which became our base while we traveled all over, staying away 2 or 3 days every week. We visited the Holy Land. I learned to speak Arabic. I don't speak it well now, but when I was there, I was speaking Arabic fluently. I started to read and write in Arabic, and can still write my name in Arabic. The trip was a marvelous experience.

Before I left Lake Charles to go on this trip, I visited the editor of the local newspaper, the *Lake Charles American Press*, and told him that I had a lot of friends and didn't want to write each one individually about the trip. I asked if he would publish a weekly letter from me so all my friends and classmates could read it. He said, "Sure, we'll do that." This set of letters was a diary of my trip. I wrote about what I saw, whom I had met, and something about the history of the places we were visiting.

• • •

WCR: So somebody back in Lake Charles was saving the published letters for you?

MED: Yes, they saved the papers for me. These published letters made it possible for my boyhood friends in Lake Charles to read about what I was doing.

• • •

WCR: Well, that must have given you a confidence boost in your ability to communicate. You were 12 years old?

MED: Yes.

• • •

WCR: Your brother was the next oldest?

MED: Yes. He is a surgeon practicing in Mobile—a very fine surgeon.

• • •

WCR: So when you came back from this yearlong trip abroad, you were pretty sophisticated?

MED: I suppose so for a young boy, mostly about the Middle East.

• • •

WCR: When you came back to New Orleans, after finishing your training with Doctors Leriche and Kirschner, you joined the Tulane faculty?

MED: Dr. Ochsner offered me a full-time job, and I think my yearly salary was $3,000.00. I went home to tell my parents what a great honor it was to get this job. I would be a full-time Instructor in the Tulane Department of Surgery under Dr. Ochsner. I was delighted. When I told my Father the salary, he turned to my Mother and said, "What do you think of that? We spend more than $100,000.00 educating this boy, and now he tells me he is going to make $3,000.00 a year." So they had to support me. They were still supporting me after I arrived in Houston. In fact, I could not buy my home in Houston—the house I am living in now. They bought it for me. I must say I was not a great financial success for a long time. But, you know, it never occurred to me, and somehow I took it for granted that this was the way it ought to be, and I was very happy. So you see how lucky I was to have the parents I had, who fortunately were financially successful and very generous and took great pride in their children. Anything we wanted within reason, we got. I had an automobile while I was in college at Tulane, I had an automobile—in the midst of the Depression. So did my brother.

• • •

WCR: Yeah, but you were not sleeping, you were doing what you are doing now.

MED: That's true, I didn't use the car very much. I had very few dates because I was spending the greater part of my time working.

• • •

WCR: You did get married in the late 30s.

MED: Yes. Shortly after I returned from Germany, I married a young lady whom I had met in New Orleans. We had a very happy time together. We had 4 boys. She died suddenly and unexpectedly in 1972. We had been to Mexico; I had operated on the son of a close relative of the President of Mexico some years before. We were there for a medical meeting, and they insisted we stay with them. We were wined and dined and, as you know, they keep you up pretty late. When we returned, she was complaining of an upset stomach and pain around the lower part of her chest and abdomen. I thought initially it was a gastrointestinal problem. After a couple of days, when she seemed to get worse instead

FIGURE 3. Photograph of Dr. Michael E. DeBakey, 1940.

of better, I insisted that she be admitted to the hospital so we could find out what was going on. Ed Dennis took care of her. It wasn't because Ed Dennis was a cardiologist that I asked him to see her; it was because we were such close friends. Ed was a good internist as well as cardiologist. I was operating, and I got a call that there was an emergency, and was asked to rush over to my wife's room. When I got there, she was gone. She had a profound heart attack. She was relatively young.

• • •

WCR: Could you discuss your experiences in World War II? You appear to have had a major impact on medicine/surgery in World War II.

MED: I had a very interesting experience in World War II, Bill. When Fred Rankin, who was the Chief Surgical Consultant in the Surgeon General's Office of the Pentagon, learned from Dr. Ochsner that I wanted to go into the service, he told Dr. Ochsner that he wanted me in his office. Initially, Dr. Ochsner did not want me to go. He wanted to declare me "essential" at the medical school, but I told him I was very uncomfortable being classified that way. I was healthy, and I felt it was my duty to go into the service. I made so much of it that Dr. Ochsner finally said, "Well, if you feel that strongly, I am going to let you go." Fred Rankin heard this, and Fred knew me too, because of my association with Dr. Ochsner. I had written papers and gone to meetings with him. (I have the longest living service in the American Surgical Association because I was elected at a very young age.) Fred called Dr. Ochsner

and said, "I understand that Mike DeBakey is going into the service. I want him up here." His two associates were Nick Carter, Professor of Surgery at Cincinnati, who had been a resident at Hopkins before that, and I. Kirk was the Surgeon General. I knew very little about military surgery or the military, so I had to learn rapidly. I would go down to the Surgeon General's Library, and I became intensively involved in the Library's activities. I got to know that Library very well. I was given the task of writing virtually every Surgeon General's surgical order. If they had a policy on pilonidal sinus, for example, I had to write that policy.

To give you another example, about the middle of the summer of 1943, I was in the Library, browsing through some old volumes of World War I, both the American and the British (I liked the British volumes better because the prose was better). There was a whole chapter on cold injuries in the military. I didn't know anything about this subject. I knew something about frostbite, but I had never heard the word trenchfoot until I read it there. That gave me the idea that the Surgeon General did not have a policy on any of this and needed one. It was a very important disease in World War I. So I wrote a historical essay of about 10 to 12 pages, describing what it was and what had happened in the past. Then I found from the Library that cold injury was very important and was probably responsible for Napoleon's defeat in Russia. There was considerable historical material. I gave my essay to Fred Rankin, and he called me in one day. He said, "Mike, I think we need to have a policy on this for the Surgeon General. I'd like you to write a policy on it." On that basis, I wrote a policy of about 2 pages, indicating what should be done, what training was needed, and what kind of gear was necessary for prevention of cold injuries. The Surgeon General signed off on it, but since we belonged to the Service of Supply Medical Service, SOS, we had to send anything we wrote there for approval. That was in the middle of the summer, and you know how hot Washington can get. They did not pay much attention to it, I guess, because a good part of what I wrote was dependent on military discipline, training, and equipment. In other words, medical people could not control these factors. They could recommend what should be done; they could recommend socks, boots, and that sort of thing, and how to deal with the cold weather, but they could not tell the soldiers what to do. This was up to the military command. I never thought any more about it.

In 1944, in the middle of the winter, we had a large number of cold injuries as a consequence of the Battle of the Bulge offensive. Various military news correspondents and others criticized us severely. It came out in the *Washington Post* in large letters. So I pulled my cold injuries record out and sent it to the Surgeon General and to Fred Rankin, with a little note saying we had done our job, and it was not the medical people's fault. They were told what might happen if they did not follow our rec-

FIGURE 4. Photograph of Surgeon General Kirk presenting Dr. Michael E. DeBakey the U. S. Army Legion of Merit Award, 1945.

ommendations. The Surgeon General was off the hook right away.

In addition to the experience I had in the Consultant's office, several other experiences proved interesting. One was my relation with Mr. Tracy S. Voorhees in the office of the Adjutant General in SOS, who at that time was also in charge of the classified publication that came out of the medical office of high command. The publication was called *Health,* and I became virtually its medical editor. Some of its publications were classified as Top Secret, because they contained such information as the size of the units that were abroad in certain areas. It was almost always classified, mostly confidential. *Health* went to all the theaters and commands, and included items like the statistics on venereal disease and what we were doing about it. My relation with Mr. Voorhees became very close. When he became Chairman of the Medical Task Force of the Hoover Administration, he asked me to serve as a member of that Task Force and to work closely with him as an executive assistant, which necessitated my going to Washington to work virtually full-time for about 9 months. I had to take a leave of absence from Tulane again. Because of my duties on the Hoover Commission, I was delayed coming to Houston. I had received my appointment to Baylor in July 1948, but I did not arrive in Houston until December of that year, after I finished working on the Medical Task Force report for the Hoover Commission.

Two incidents occurred after that report, one had an effect on the nation, and one had an effect on me. As a consequence of my experience in the Library, I had become convinced that there was a need for a new building for the Surgeon General's Library. When it rained, they had to put tarpaulins over the books. They had a commode outside the building. The stacks were so crowded, in fact, that I wrote an article called "Chaos Among the Stacks." I started making noises about that while I was still in the ser-

vice. The Surgeon General said, "You know, Mike, we have been trying for 30 years to get a new building. We've put in a request every year; we just can't compete with tanks." That convinced me that the Library did not belong in the Army. This was a national treasure, the greatest medical library in the world, and we were not taking proper care of it. It needed to be independent. So I wrote an article about that. It was not very well received, as you can imagine, but I kept raising the issue and recommending its separation from the army. It didn't get very far until I put it in the Hoover Commission Report. I inserted it in there with the approval of Mr. Voorhees, who was my Task Force Chairman. After the report was completed, Mr. Voorhees said to me, "Mike, I'd like you to go with me to meet Mr. Hoover, and to brief him on our report." Hoover was staying in an apartment at the Waldorf Astoria in New York, and we had lunch with him. He was most cordial, and I was very impressed with him. Finally, he said, "Brief me about the recommendations here." He was thumbing through it and said, "You realize how many task forces I've got?" Mr. Voorhees replied, "No, sir, I don't." He said, "Well, we've got about 50 task forces." He said, "If everybody comes in here with 30 recommendations, who do you think is going to read the report? I want you to tell me the one single most important recommendation in here." Before he could say anything, I said "The Library." That became one of the most important medical recommendations in the Hoover Commission Report.

When that report came to the attention of Congress, Senator Lister Hill, who was then very powerful in the Senate and was the Chairman of the Health Subcommittee, picked it up. By that time I had gotten to know him, and one day he called me. He said, "I want you to tell me a little bit about this Library." He was very interested in medicine. His Father was one of the first physicians in this country to use asepsis and the first to repair a wound of the heart. He named his son Lister, and the Senator was very proud of that. He became interested in the Library and developed the bill for it, and I worked with him. His counterpart in the House of Representatives was John Kennedy, and I worked with both committees. Senator Hill called me one day (I was now in Houston) and said, "Mike, we have the votes to pass this bill, but your Congressman down there, the Speaker of the House, Mr. Sam Rayburn, is holding it up because a quarrel developed between the Congressman from Chicago and the other Congressman." The members from Chicago wanted the Library built in Chicago next to the American Medical Association (AMA). The AMA was putting pressure on him to do this. (At that time the AMA published the *Index Medicus.*) I represented those who wanted the Library at the National Institutes of Health (NIH), as an independent institution, because there it would be associated with medical and research activities. There was some discussion about whether it should be in the Library of Congress, but fortunately, the Head of the Library of Congress did not want it. That made it easier for us. Jim Shannon, who was then Head of NIH, did not want it at the NIH. Can you imagine that? He called me and said, "Mike, I don't see why we have to have the library here. It is not a research institution." I responded, "Well, I think it belongs there because all the Institutes need it."

Lister called me one day and said, "I want you and Jim Shannon to meet in my office." When we met in his office, he said, "Now Jim, there is a difference of opinion here. Tell me why you don't want it at NIH." Jim said he just wanted research people at NIH. Mr. Hill turned around to me and said, "Well, Mike, what do you think?" I said, "Dr. Shannon is saying it is not a research institute, but I would like to ask Dr. Shannon one thing. When you were doing research in New York and were working on the kidney—whenever you worked on a new project—what would you do first? You would go to the library to do a little research, wouldn't you?" He said, "Of course." I said, "Then why do you say it is not a research institute?" Lister turned around and said "Jim, I think he's got you." That is how it got to be at the NIH.

Later, Senator Hill called me to say that this quarrel was still going on and that was why the approval for the Library was being held up. That was in 1951, just before the National Democratic Convention, when they nominated Stevenson. Lister asked me: "Does anybody in Houston have any influence on this fellow?" I called around but could find no one who had any influence on Senator Rayburn. After he told me about the National Democratic Convention, it suddenly dawned on me that I had performed an aneurysmal resection on the husband of the Secretary of the National Democratic Party, Dorothy Vredenberg. We became good friends. I called her and said, "Dorothy, I have a favor to ask of you; I think you can make a great contribution to this country." I went on to explain what this Library meant to our nation, what a treasure it was, and how important it was. She said, "Well, Mike let me see what I can do. I will call the Speaker of the House." She called Senator Rayburn, and the next day, she called me back and said, "He is going to let it through." Right after she called me, Senator Hill called me and said, "Mike, I don't know what you did, but we are going to get the Library bill through." That's how we got the Library.

The other important result of the Hoover Commission is related to me here in Houston. I declined the offer to come here twice before finally accepting it. During my first visit to Houston, I learned that the medical school had no university hospital and no affiliated teaching hospital. I was told I would work at the Jefferson Davis Hospital. I said, "I can under-

stand that, but I don't have an appointment there." It was a closed system, almost politicized. Baylor was sending its students there, and the doctors there were making rounds with them. They were all family practitioners at that time. There was not a single board-certified surgeon in Houston. I believe I was the first board-certified surgeon in Houston. So I turned the offer down in a long letter detailing the problems. The second time I came down, they said they would arrange some affiliation with Hermann Hospital, but it was not secured. I told them I couldn't come on that basis. A few months later, Baylor's Dean Moursund came to New Orleans. He said he was going to talk to them about the hospital affiliation. He said, "I think we have it settled. They have promised that you will have a 20-bed surgical service at the Hermann Hospital." So on the basis of his promise, I came.

But when I came, nothing had happened. After a couple of months, I went to the Dean's office and told him that I was getting restless about this. "I can't get a residency program, I can't do anything. I have no service," I said. "Unless I get a service, I am wasting my time here, and I will go back to New Orleans or accept some other offer." He said, "Let me see what I can do." He called Hermann Hospital and told them I was about to leave unless they got that service. They had a special meeting and then the Chief of Staff came to see me. They had just had a meeting of the surgical staff, and I was appointed Chief of Teaching Services. I said, "What does that mean?" "Well," he said, "you are going to be in charge of teaching the students." I said, "Who is in charge of the patients on that service?" He said, "The doctors that are there." I said, "How can that work? Suppose I walk in there and say the operation that was done was wrong, or the patient shouldn't have been operated on." He replied, "That won't happen." I said, "From what I have seen around here, it will happen often." I endeared myself right away, but I didn't care; I was displeased, and I had made up my mind to leave. I went to the Dean and said, "Before I leave, I would really like to talk to Baylor's Chairman of the Board, because I think something has to be done about this, or this school is not going anywhere. You are not going to be able to get anybody worthwhile clinically to come here if he will not have a service." He said, "I will make the appointment." He asked, "Do you want me to come with you?" And I replied, "Of course I want you to come with me."

We went to see the Board Chairman, and I had hardly met him before he lit into me. He had already heard from these people that I was a "revolutionary." He started using clichés, saying you have to do this by evolution, not revolution. I let him talk for awhile. Finally I said, "Are you through?" I was angry and ready to resign. He said, "Yes." I said, "I have been patiently listening to you, without saying a word, and I want you to listen patiently to me now, because you are so ignorant about all this that you don't understand what is going on here. As a consequence, you don't even understand your own responsibilities as Chairman of this Board and a member of the Board of Trustees of Hermann Hospital. Do you realize that a student who graduates from Baylor University College of Medicine has to leave town to get any kind of specialty training, because he can't get any training here? There isn't an approved residency program in the whole city. This school is going to go nowhere; it's going to remain a third-rate medical school as long as it continues this way, and, as Chairman of the Board, you will be responsible for a "third-rate medical school." He turned around to the Dean every once in a while. He asked the Dean, "Is that right?" and the Dean said "Yes." When I got through, his attitude was entirely different. He said, "Dr. DeBakey, I don't think it is quite fair for you to come in and tell me all this and then leave. Why don't you give me a chance to see what I can do?" I said, "I will give you 1 month, because I am wasting your time and money, and wasting my time staying here under these circumstances."

The next week I got a call on a Sunday morning from Paul Magnuson of the Veterans Administration saying, "Mike, we have just been ordered by President Truman to take over the Naval Hospital (at that time it was under the Navy). We don't have personnel to take care of it. Can you organize a faculty group and take it over?" I replied, "Of course." I along with other faculty members just moved into a new hospital, immediately got resident training approval, and the following month I went to see Mr. Ben Taub and persuaded him that the Jefferson Davis Hospital should become a Baylor-affiliated hospital (now called Ben Taub Hospital) over the objection of the whole staff. I was not a very popular man.

Truman had issued the order because of the Hoover Commission Medical Task Force Report. In that report I had spotlighted certain glaring federal deficiencies and examples of wastefulness. I unearthed a memorandum signed by President Roosevelt stating that at the end of the War the Navy Hospital in Houston would be turned over to the VA. It was already 1949 or 1950, and the Navy Hospital still had not been turned over. The Navy wanted to retain the hospital even though they had no active Navy personnel as patients; they were all veterans. The Veterans Administration was going to build another hospital, right next door for 35 million dollars (a huge sum at the time!), and I stated that it was a complete waste of money. When my comments came out in a front page story, Truman ordered the Navy to turn its hospital over to the VA, and that is why I stayed in Houston.

• • •

WCR: How did Baylor University College of Medicine get connected to The Methodist Hospital?

MED: Methodist Hospital, which was about midway downtown, came about later. It was a ramshackled building, mostly made of wood, and they had added to it. They had about 100 beds altogether, but

it was a very warm place, and they had a very nice woman administrator, who was very kind to me. They took an interest in their patients. I was admitting my private patients to both Hermann and Methodist Hospitals. I liked The Methodist Hospital, even though it was not as nice a building as Hermann. I got to know the Methodist people well. In 1953 they decided to move into the Medical Center. Methodist was the first hospital to be built in what later became the Texas Medical Center. By that time, I had a good private service because of my vascular work. In 1952, I had received media attention because I did the first successful aortic aneurysm resection in this country. No one else was performing this operation, so physicians were referring their patients to me. By the time they built the new Methodist Hospital, a private institution, I had already gotten to know the people, the administration, and some of the Board of Trustees — Mrs. Ella Fondren, and others. So I was beginning to have some influence. The staff remained pretty much intact, but I was accepted by the staff, they had no resentment toward me. Also, the physicians began to like the fact that I was bringing some attention to the Hospital, and so did the administration and some of the Board members, like Mrs. Fondren and Mr. Eddy Scurlock.

As my service began to increase, I was using more and more beds; at one time I had a service of about 100 beds. I brought medical students and residents to the new Methodist Hospital, and they liked it much better than the old Jefferson Davis Hospital. I told Dean Olsen "We ought to have an affiliation with The Methodist Hospital." This idea was not very popular with some of the other faculty members who preferred to work at Hermann Hospital. The students and residents expressed increasing interest and enthusiasm for their work at The Methodist Hospital, and Dean Olsen finally approved a formal affiliation with The Methodist Hospital.

• • •

WCR: Is it because your practice was expanding at that time, that the pressure was too much for them to bear?

MED: Yes. I requested an intensive care unit, which did not exist in those days. This idea came out of my military experience, which really arose out of necessity because of the shortage of personnel. I explained to them that I had to have an intensive care unit where my very sick patients could be cared for. Since the private nurses didn't know very much about the care of such patients, I wanted to train some nurses to take care of them. The staff and the Nursing Supervisor did not like the idea, but Mr. Ted Bowen, who by that time had become Chief Administrator of Methodist, said to me, "Mike, let me do this. I will make a 4-bed unit for you." I told him this would not be enough; I needed about 6 beds. Finally, he did get 6 beds on the second floor of the old building for the intensive care unit. The hospital hired the nurses. In those days nurses weren't hired for such duty; they served as private nurses for private patients. I started giving them a little training,

FIGURE 5. Recent photograph of Dr. Michael E. DeBakey in front of the Methodist Hospital Cardiovascular Operating Room.

and I asked our colleagues in Cardiology to give them some training in electrocardiography and other monitoring procedures. These nurses became pretty efficient at caring for these very sick patients. Within less than 6 months, Mr. Bowen said "You know, Mike, some of the other surgeons want to use your intensive care unit for their patients." I said, "Fine, let's get some more beds in there, but don't use my beds. I am having a hard time as it is. By Friday, I can't operate because all the beds are filled." So they expanded the unit. Of course, as time went on, all the doctors wanted to use intensive care. Not a single one later would admit that he objected to it initially.

• • •

WCR: In 1948, at age 40, you must have been the hottest young surgeon in the country. You had had all that experience in World War II, your name was out there a lot, all those papers you had written in the late 1930s with Dr. Ochsner. You must have had options, as you mentioned earlier, to be Chairman of Surgery in a lot of different places?

MED: I did. I had offers from a number of different places. I turned down 3 of them in New York, 2 of them before I came to Houston, 1 after I came here. The one after I came here was from New York University because Mary Lasker was on their Board. This was in the mid-1960s. She said, "You know, New York is the most important city in the world, and we don't have a cardiovascular surgery center." She said, "We need to get Mike DeBakey up here." So she put a lot of pressure on me. I went up and met with the Board at lunch at one of the clubs in New York. During the meeting, Mr. Paley (the Chairman of CBS), a member of the Board, asked me how much I thought it would cost. I said, "I think we need about 15 million dollars." He got up immediately afterwards and said, "We can raise that over night. I will guarantee a million dollars right now." So they all agreed that money was not a problem. They said let's call the Dean at New York Uni-

versity, George Armstrong. George Armstrong was in the Army with me and in the Surgeon General's Office, so I knew him well. When I got there, he greeted me very cordially and warmly. He had gathered several Professors on the faculty together, and they said, "You know we don't have any beds for cardiovascular surgery. We are going to have to build a new building." You couldn't build a new building for 15 million dollars. I said, "What is the possibility of using beds you now have; you have patients who are in cardiology, patients in need of cardiovascular surgery. Why not use the same beds, we would just congregate them in one place." Each one of the professors said, "Oh, we cannot give up any of our beds." I never realized that there was a sort of medical culture in New York based on the old German Herr Professor system. The Herr Professor was a kind of emperor of his empire. You couldn't touch him, and he controlled those beds; they were his, and he used them any way he wanted. I began to learn a little more about that as I read more about its past history. Going back to even the Halsted days, before he went to Hopkins in 1889, the medical professors were greatly influenced by the German system. As you know, the old German system was a very rigid system.

• • •

WCR: How did Tulane let you slip out of there? I gather Dr. Ochsner was only 12 years older than you were?

MED: Yes, but you see he was still very active. When he retired, I was well established here. They did everything they could to get me back. I was very impressed with Oscar Creech, whom I had brought to Houston from New Orleans the year after he had finished his residency, the year after I left. He was with me until Dr. Ochsner retired. I went over and met with the Dean of the Medical School and the Tulane Board of Trustees. I said to them, "Look, I am so involved in Houston that I would feel guilty leaving. I have made commitments with my people there; they are depending on me for a number of things." You have to remember that at that time a not insignificant part of the cost of operating the school and virtually all the cost of the Department of Surgery was met by what I gave them, by what I made from my surgical practice.

In 1968, the Baylor University College of Medicine was about to collapse. An increasing deficit, insufficient financing, and a demoralized faculty placed Baylor in a critical position in the late 1960s. Two deans and seven departmental chairmen had resigned. In 1968 the Baylor Faculty Search Committee and the Board of Trustees asked me to accept the deanship and later the Presidency. Realizing that Baylor required broad nonsectarian support to overturn its financial deficit and demoralization, I proposed that Baylor College of Medicine be established as an independent institution apart from Baylor University. Abner McCall, then President of Baylor University, and the leaders of the Houston Executive Committee on the Board of Trustees all fully supported my proposal, leading to its approval by the Baptist Foundation. The warm and friendly support of Baylor University nurtured the development of the College through this critical period. In 1968 the State of Texas granted Baylor College of Medicine's charter.

I was fortunate, as the newly appointed Dean, to have an independent, committed Board of Trustees, all highly successful community leaders who dedicated considerable time and effort to developing the College. Their initial fund-raising campaign yielded more than $30 million, which cancelled the College deficit.

• • •

WCR: Dr. DeBakey, as I look over your contributions surgically, it seems to me that the great contribution you made was to make the aorta a very treatable entity.

MED: Prior to 1952, the only aortic disease that was treatable was coarctation of the aorta. There was no effective treatment for fusiform aneurysms. Dissection of the aorta was a fatal disease. All studies that were done on the national history of aortic dissection showed that 50% died within 48 hours after occurrence, 90% in 3 months, and rarely did anyone live a year. Treatment of coarctation actually gave me the idea that other problems with the aorta might be treatable. Gross and Hufnagel in Boston presented some experimental work showing that in animals they could bridge an aortic defect with a homograft. That gave me the idea: why not use a homograft for aneurysm? I was in the fortunate position at the time of having access to all the autopsies that the coroner had to do at Jefferson Davis Hospital. All the autopsies were done there by the coroner. He was a very nice person; when I told him that my residents and I would do all his autopsies, because I wanted to train them by this means, he readily agreed. At Charity Hospital in New Orleans, when a patient died, we went to the autopsy room. I considered it a great teaching experience. By doing the autopsies, we had a ready opportunity to obtain homografts. So we started with fresh homografts. The first aneurysm I did, in 1952, was with a fresh aortic homograft for an abdominal aneurysm. At the time we did it, we did not know that in Paris, a few months earlier, Dubost had done the same thing for an abdominal aortic aneurysm. But he did not pursue the rest of the aorta as I did.

I became convinced, after our successful experience with aneurysms of the abdominal aorta, that the thoracic aneurysm could be done as well, but what I did not know at the time was that a few of the patients would develop paresis or paraplegia of the lower limbs after the operation. There was some animal experimental work by Alexis Carrel in 1910–

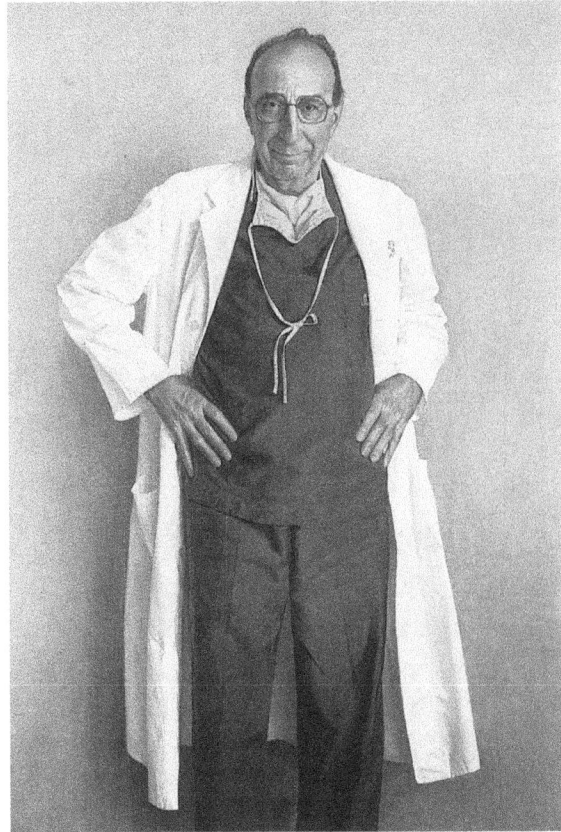

FIGURE 6. Photograph of painting of Aaron Shikler of Dr. Michael E. DeBakey, which hangs in the lobby of the Michael E. DeBakey Center for Education and Research at Baylor College of Medicine, Houston, Texas.

1913 that had pointed this out. In 1953, I had a patient from Arkansas, a very colorful character, a sheriff, who had a huge aneurysm of the descending thoracic aorta that was eroding the vertebral bodies. It was probably of syphilitic origin. He was in constant pain. I told him, ''Nobody has ever done this successfully before in the chest, but we have done a lot of them in the abdomen, and I think we can do it the same way.'' I am sure that because of his pain he was ready for anything. He went through the operation beautifully and had a wonderful result. As you know, it is of great significance to have the first successful case, and you are off and running. It's that first bad case that gives you problems.

That result stimulated us, and I became convinced we could perform resection of aneurysms in the remaining aorta. In January 1954, I had a patient from San Antonio with an aneurysm of the ascending aorta, and I resected it using the heart-lung machine. Gibbon first used the heart-lung machine in the Spring of 1953. By the end of 1953, we were also using it. Like many others, we had been doing experimental work, as he did, on a heart-lung machine that we built in our laboratory, so we were ready with our own heart-lung machine. Also in 1954, I resected an aneurysm of the aortic arch. So I had performed resection and graft replacement for aneurysms in all parts of the aorta. Then in mid-1954 I performed the

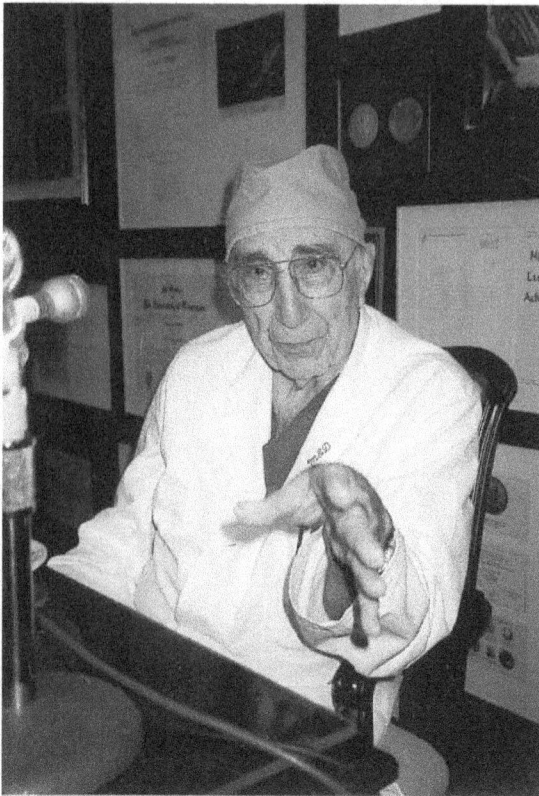

FIGURE 7. Photograph of MED taken by WCR.

first successful operation for an aortic dissecting an-eurysm. From that point on, virtually all diseases of the aorta became amenable to surgical treatment.

• • •

WCR: I have more respect for that aorta than I do for the heart. In other words, to replace an entire aortic arch or descending thoracic aorta, don't you consider that a much bigger operation than, let's say, a valve replacement?

MED: I agree. The technical part of congenital heart surgery, with the exception of a few things like transposition, even the blue baby, is a pretty simple, straightforward technical procedure. You can train a technician to do a valve replacement. The aorta is kind of awesome in a way because it is the main channel of blood to the body. And all the major branches coming off that aorta constitute critical arteries. So you are dealing with a broader area of critical viability of the body.

I am working on a paper right now based on a 30-year follow-up with 1 or more postoperative arteriographic studies. I have divided the data into 4 categories: 1) the coronary arteries; 2) the carotid arteries; 3) the renal arteries; and 4) the peripheral arteries. If you analyze recurrence rates based on the arteriogram, and if you divide those recurrence rates into 3 categories, *rapid* being within 3 years, *moderate* between 3 and 6 years, and *slow* more than 6 years, there is little correlation with any of the lipid levels. The recurrence rates and survival rates with each of the 4 arterial systems are highly significantly different, with p values of 0.0001. The question I

then ask is: if arteriosclerosis is the same disease affecting each one of these arterial beds, why are the recurrence rates and survival rates different between the coronary and peripheral arterial beds, between the coronary and the renal arterial beds, and between the coronary and carotid beds? In other words, there is something in the arterial bed that responds differently to arteriosclerosis, whatever is the cause of the disease.

• • •

WCR: You are saying that if a patient presents with, let's say, peripheral vascular disease, your type 4, and you do an operative procedure on this patient and you see that patient 10 years later, further progression is more likely to occur in the previously operated system than in any of the other 3 systems?

MED: That's right. They can have progression in the other 3 systems, too, but they are more likely to have progression in the same system.

• • •

WCR: What is so different about the mammary arteries?

MED: I was talking recently to one of the members of the Department of Cell Biology, which includes our Department of Anatomy. I showed him these data, and the only explanation he came up with is that probably different genetic factors affect each arterial bed. He said that embryologically each one of these arterial beds has a different origin. I didn't realize that. Isn't that interesting? There is no question about this observation. I now have absolute data. The only reason I have not disseminated the infor-

FIGURE 8. Photograph of MED taken by WCR.

mation earlier (I have had it for a year) is that I know it is going to create a lot of controversy. If you take these patients and divide them into those with total cholesterol levels above 200 mg/dl and below 200 mg/dl, there is no difference in the recurrence rates or survival rates in the coronary group. There is a difference in the peripheral arterial group, so something strange is going on here. There are differences in the arterial beds when you make the various comparisons. They behave differently with the same disease. In fact, a good deal of the publication delay now is due to statistical analysis. I have gone to 4 different statistical analysis groups, the University of Texas, MD Anderson, Rice University, and ours, and they all come out the same. These data have been through all kinds of analyses. These 4 statistician groups have taken all the data, literally thousands of bits of data, and analyzed them in different ways, broken up the data, for example, into 5-year periods, and they all come to the same conclusion. Isn't that interesting?

• • •

WCR: In your life you have done all kinds of surgery with the exception, perhaps, of neurologic and orthopedic. Now today, in most places, cardiovascular surgery is divided into the cardiac and thoracic service and the vascular service. This division is very different from your own mode of operation.

MED: The cardiac and vascular services are separated in many places. I object to that for the simple reason that I consider the cardiovascular system a unified system.

• • •

WCR: You are leaving for Moscow in 4 days? I think that is wonderful. You don't need it, but I think it is wonderful for the USA and a recognition of American medicine. I am sure it hurts their pride.

MED: The person I was talking to just now is President Clinton's physician, Dr. Connie Mariano. She told me that President Clinton made the suggestion that I might need an intensive care specialist. I told her that I would tell my Russian colleagues about the offer.

• • •

WCR: Dr. DeBakey, let me ask you a couple of specific things about surgery. You were the first one to use a saphenous vein for aortocoronary bypass?

MED: No, I was the first one to do it successfully. David Sabiston was the first, in 1962, I think, to do an aortocoronary bypass on a human being. His patient died of a stroke 3 days after the operation. Our patient was operated on in 1964 and lived for about 10 years.

• • •

WCR: You did not report your patient right away?

MED: No. There were a number of firsts that I did not rush to print. There were several reasons for not publishing my case right away. I had written an article in *Circulation* in 1961, in which I described our experimental work on coronary bypass. Experimental work on coronary bypass was being done by

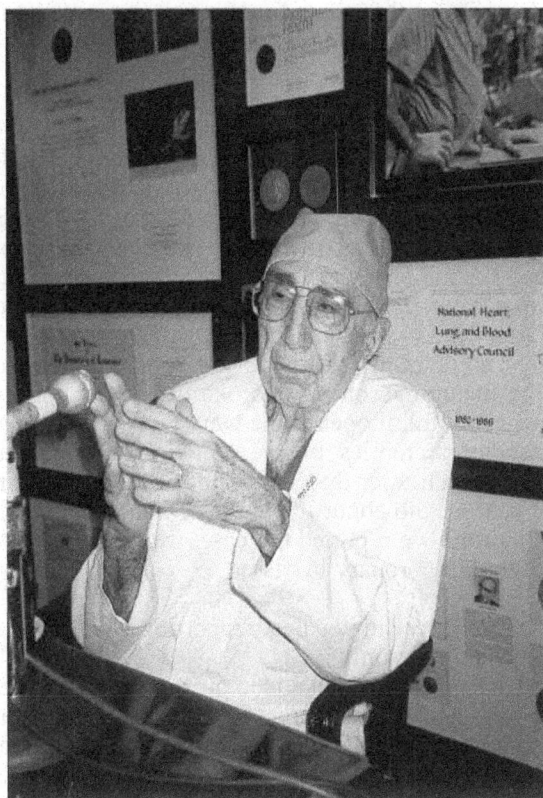

FIGURE 9. Photograph of MED taken by WCR.

a lot of people. Murray in Canada had started in the 1950s. Alexis Carrel in 1910 wrote about performing a coronary bypass on an experimental animal from the descending thoracic aorta to one of the branches of the left circumflex coronary artery. There is a pretty long experimental history on coronary bypass. The concept is not new. The clinical application was delayed for a number of reasons. When we started doing it, we did it virtually on a beating heart, and it was not until we became more adept at stopping the heart that we became a little more assured of doing it properly.

• • •

WCR: Which coronary artery did you put the saphenous vein in?

MED: The left anterior descending coronary artery (LAD). This was an interesting development; we had been doing bypasses experimentally in the laboratory earlier. In 1961, we reported in a paper that we had only about 50% success rate for 6 months after the operation in dogs. More work needed to be done, but we considered this an encouraging trend, and we thought this was the direction in which we should go. We published that in the paper in 1961. We were not the only ones doing it, mind you; it was not original with us. This goes back to 1910, including Murray and quite a few others. In fact, in a paper that I wrote about coronary surgery a long time ago, I reviewed all this and had over 20 references on experimental work.

Our patient was not scheduled for a bypass, but for an endarterectomy. We were performing endarterectomies at that time. In this patient, we tried to do an endarterectomy but couldn't find the cleavage plane because it was so adherent, and pretty soon we had virtually destroyed the artery. That was his vital artery, because he had complete occlusion of his right coronary, and his circumflex artery was small, so we knew we were not going to get him off the table alive unless we did something drastic. That is why we decided to do what we had been doing on dogs. The surgery was successful. We reported him 7 years after the operation because I wanted to get an arteriogram showing that it was patent. When I got the angiogram 7 years later, we reported the case. In the meantime, once we broke that barrier and it was successful, it opened the way. We were still doing endarterectomies, but we started to do bypasses, and each year after that we did more and more. The first year we did about 7, and the next year about 25. By the time we reported the case, we had done 400 or 500 aortocoronary bypasses.

• • •

WCR: Why did you delay reporting your first carotid endarterectomy?

MED: The case is included in some other articles that I wrote before I reported the case alone. The reason I delayed reporting that case is that there was still some question about whether carotid endarterectomy should be performed. When I went to the Neurological Association meeting in New York about 1959 or 1960, we had about 7 years' experience with carotid endarterectomy, and I had accumulated 150 cases with good results. The mortality rate was low, about 3% or 4%. I presented the data there. A man by the name of Baker, a Professor of Neurology at the University of Minnesota, rose and expressed critical comments about the operation. But about 10 or 15 years later, when he was President of the Neurological Association, the first thing he did at their meeting in Houston was to announce to the audience, since he was in Houston, that he wanted to apologize to Dr. DeBakey. He then stated that he had been critical of the procedure of carotid endarterectomy, and that he was wrong, and wanted to pay tribute to my pioneering work.

In 1953, I had a patient from my hometown, Lake Charles, Louisiana. A short time before that, an article by M. Fisher from the Massachusetts General Hospital had been published, indicating that narrowing of the carotid artery could be a cause of stroke. Earlier than that, several pathologists had also contended that carotid arterial narrowing could cause stroke. J. R. Hunt and Fisher did a much more elaborate study in which they correlated it very well. They virtually suggested that if you could eliminate the carotid narrowing, you might prevent stroke.

That is what gave me the idea in the case of the bus driver from Lake Charles. He was having what we now call transient ischemic attacks (TIAs)— transient episodes of sluggish speech and transient paralysis of his right fingers and leg. He had to quit driving the bus because he could not stop it suddenly with his leg. His doctor told me he didn't know what

FIGURE 10. Photograph of MED taken by WCR.

was wrong with the patient. When I examined him, he didn't have any of these manifestations, but he gave a very good history of the transient episodes, and his wife described them beautifully. I heard a little murmur over his neck so we did an arteriogram, and he had almost complete occlusion of the left internal carotid artery. I described to him what I thought should be done, explaining that it had not been done before, but I thought this was what was causing his symptoms. He knew my family in Lake Charles, and for that reason, I am sure, he had more confidence in me. He said, "If you think you can correct the problem, go ahead and do it." He had a beautiful result and never had any more ischemic attacks. I believe he lived 19 years more and died of a heart attack.

• • •

WCR: You have advised virtually every president in the USA since Truman, I gather, Heads of States, and other important officials in various governments around the world. Who have you met that you would say, "This is a great person?"

MED: It is hard to judge greatness. I would say among the persons that you are talking about who are in a governing position, probably Lyndon Johnson insofar as health leadership is concerned. He was very interested in health, and therefore supported health legislation. I was very close to him and was able to relate to him well. In fact, he appointed me Chairman of his Commission on Heart Disease, Cancer, and Stroke. He actually tried to persuade me to be Secretary of Health, Education, and Welfare in his cabinet. I had a hard time convincing him that I did not belong there, because I did not want that job. I explained to him, "I am a surgeon; I am not a bureaucrat." He replied, "Yeah, but you have been running that school down there, haven't you?" I said, "Yes, but that is different." I did not want to go to Washington. I was finally able to get out of it diplomatically. He consulted me about his heart, and I saw him on a number of occasions when he had come down secretly to see me for examinations. I worked with him on health legislation a great deal. He passed more health legislation than any other president. He passed Medicare, after John Kennedy was never able to get anywhere with it.

• • •

WCR: You approved Medicare? You got in trouble with your medical colleagues about that?

MED: Oh *did* I! I went on television with President Kennedy. One of Kennedy's assistants called me and said the President wanted to go on television and wanted me in the background because I believed in Medicare. I thought it was a great idea; it never occurred to me that it would have turned out the way it did. There is no question that bureaucratically it has been a mess, and some in the profession are responsible for some of the abuses. It ought to be done differently. In the final analysis, however, it has been a good thing for older people; there is no question about that. The concept is a good one. Once it became known that I supported Medicare, when the AMA was strongly opposed to it, I became a kind of pariah, and I had telegrams from some physicians saying that they would never refer another patient to me. By that time, however, my name was pretty well known with the public, so many patients came on their own. I rarely got a referral from any doctor in Houston. It concerned me at first because I was sincere in my belief and couldn't understand why anyone would object to Medicare. They thought it was a step toward socialized medicine.

The same was true about the regional medical programs. I would be invited to meet with physicians at society meetings to discuss the regional medical program. Some would get up and say that this is pure socialized medicine. I said, "Well show me where it is in the bill. I have the bill with me; show me where it says anything like that. Show me where the government is going to do anything but provide grants to these institutions. The institutions will run on their own." They couldn't do it, but once they got the idea that it is the road to socialized medicine, that was enough. The profession at that time was far more reactionary than it is today. You just have to accept the fact that if you are going to get out in front on an issue, some are going to shoot you in the back.

• • •

WCR: What about other surgeons. Whom do you consider in your time the best?

MED: In my early days of surgery, I think there were a lot of giants in surgery. There was Evarts Graham in St. Louis, Pete Churchill in Boston, Rudolph Matas and Alton Ochsner in New Orleans, Fred Rankin at the Mayo Clinic, William Halsted and Alfred Blalock at Johns Hopkins, Fred Coller at the University of Michigan, Owen Wangensteen in Minneapolis, Warren Cole, Isadore Ravdin, Loyal Davis, and Allen Whipple. Those were true giants at that time. They were leaders too. I think they set the standard for surgery for this country. Through their training programs, they modified the old German system and expanded surgery. They broadened it, expanded it, and elevated it. They established standards by creating the Boards and the College. To be certified, you had to go through a formal training program. As you remember, prior to that time, in fact when I first came to Houston, all general practitioners were doing surgery and often doing it poorly. The first time I came here they had a meeting over at the old Jefferson Davis Hospital, and one of the doctors there presented a paper on a new technique for hernia operation. You know what it was? Removal of the testicle and sewing of the opening. I was so stunned that when they asked me to comment about it, I said, "I don't know what to say about this." The particular surgeon performed this operation on some patients with bilateral hernias. Think of that! This was just one example. So the giants of American surgery at that time set the standard for the development of high standards in surgery in this country after World War II. There is no question that they had tremendous influence through their training programs and their incorporation of research laboratories into surgery, something which rarely existed before. Today, we have equally good surgeons, but they are not quite as prominent because we have more of them. Virtually every section of our country has prominent surgeons. Thirty-five or forty years ago, there was not a prominent surgeon in Florida, Mississippi, or Arkansas, but now you have very prominent surgeons there. So in addition to setting higher standards, they provided the base for this expansion.

• • •

WCR: As you look back over your career, you have done so many different things—we haven't even talked much about your being a Statesman for medicine in this nation and in the world—what are the things you are the most proud of that you have been able to accomplish?

MED: I have been asked that question before, and I have thought about it. I think probably it is the kind of spirit of surgical endeavor, of surgical standards of excellence, that I have tried to impart, of surgical ethics and integrity that I have tried to reflect in my everyday life with my students and residents. You see, my surgical contributions opened the way for others to refine and perfect them. But when you train people, you are in a sense providing for your immortality, because if you are able to instill these concepts, investigative efforts, ethics, standards, and pursuit of excellence in the new generation, then you have succeeded in continuing your spirit after you leave, because all of us are going to be here for a relatively short period of time. We may make small individual contributions, like aneurysmectomy, end-

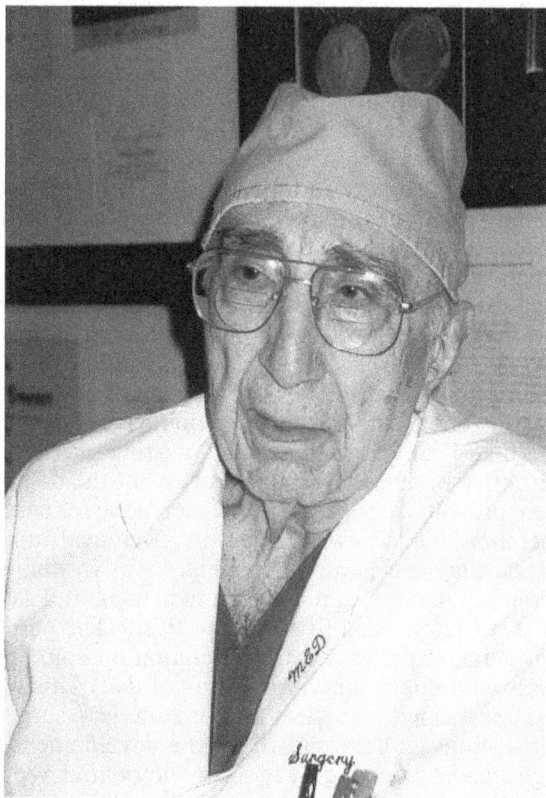

FIGURE 11. Photograph of MED taken by WCR.

arterectomy, or coronary bypass, but in the total scope of things, these are relatively insignificant. It is what you are able to transmit, it seems to me, that matters. Plato is remembered for his ideas and the fact that he was able to transmit them to Aristotle. He is remembered because Aristotle was his student and was able to continue with rational ideas that Plato described and taught. If you transmit to another generation interesting new concepts, whether they are conceptually new ideas, innovations, research, or ethical concepts, then I think you have improved society, especially if the next generation can enhance them.

If you enjoy doing your work, then you have had a satisfying life. People say to me, aren't you proud of your awards? How often do you come and see them? The truth of the matter is the only time I see them is when I am doing an interview like this or at a meeting. Certainly, I am pleased to see my work recognized—everyone is—but I don't dwell on it. You just go on with your activities and interests. I don't mean in any way to diminish their value, but you can't live in the past. You have another day, a new day.

• • •

WCR: Dr. DeBakey, I have been asking you questions here for 3 hours, and you have been talking virtually constantly for 3 hours. It looks like your energy level is such that you could go on for 6 more hours. In other words, you are 88 years old, as of 10 days ago; you are obviously enormously vigorous. What health secrets do you have? Do you have any special diet, or do you do anything that you think is really useful to your health?

MED: I am moderate in my living habits. As far as food is concerned, as you see, we have had this lunch and neither one of us ate very much of it. I am moderate in my eating habits, but when I eat, I try to get a variety of foods, particularly fresh vegetables and fruit, which I like very much. My parents brought us up on a healthful diet long before it became fashionable. I don't eat a great deal of meat, probably once a week at the most. I usually have fish because I like it. I grew up near the Gulf Coast where seafood, including shellfish, is abundant. I like rice, vegetables, and beans. I weigh the same now and can wear the same uniform that I wore in the Army.

• • •

WCR: How much do you weigh?
MED: I weigh 160 pounds.

• • •

WCR: How tall are you?
MED: "5'11." I am relatively thin. I have been that way all my life. All my siblings are thin. It is genetic. I don't deliberately exercise, but I usually walk up and down the stairs instead of taking the elevator, and that provides some exercise. The rest of it is probably genetic. My parents were both thin and highly energetic. They instilled in us early a taste for fresh fruits, vegetables, and other wholesome foods.

I was at a public meeting where I was invited to talk on health habits. They were asking what I do, so I went through the usual things—not smoking, watching your diet, keeping on the low fat side, and so forth. After I had gone through all of it, somebody said what else do you do? I said, "I pray a lot." I don't have any health secrets, but I am moderate, and I think that is the key to it. I don't drink alcohol, I don't smoke, and I was lucky in that regard too, because in my family, growing up as a child, my Father was strongly against alcohol and tobacco, so we never had them in the house. I never thought about smoking a cigarette until I went to college. In fact, in those days during the "fraternity rush week," they called certain parties "smokers." They had tobacco and alcohol on the table. I was odd man out—the only one who didn't smoke or drink. My parents' influence was so strong—we were all exposed to our peers' smoking and drinking when we left home—but not one of us smokes or drinks—neither my brother nor my sisters. When I came under Dr. Ochsner's influence, he was also strongly opposed to it; in fact, he strongly believed that tobacco caused peptic ulcer and, of course, cancer of the lung. We wrote the first article on it when I was his resident, pointing to the relation between smoking and cancer of the lung. Everybody thought we were "wacko" making statements like that. In fact, before Dr. Ochsner went to an American Surgical Association meeting, he asked me to collect some data on the production of tobacco, which I was able to get from the Department of Commerce. We had some data on the increased incidence of cancer of the lung over a 10-

year period. I made a slide of the 2 curves, one showing the incidence of cancer of the lung and the other showing the consumption, and they both rose in parallel. He was delighted with it. At the meeting, Evarts Graham, who at the time was a smoker, arose during the discussion and said if we had taken the trouble to do the same thing with nylon stockings, we would have gotten the same kind of curve. Unfortunately, he was later converted to a non-smoker, but he died of cancer of the lung.

• • •

WCR: You have done over 60, 000 operations, is that right?

MED: Yes. I am not sure it is accurate, but I would say that is the minimal. It is probably more because I have operated elsewhere. I had operated in New Orleans, of course, and none of those operations are on record here.

• • •

WCR: Do you operate any more?

MED: Yes. I don't operate as much as I used to. In fact, I just discharged a patient with a valve replacement I did recently, and I have had some of my old patients come back, who insist on seeing me. I try to turn them over to my associates, but some of them just want to see me.

• • •

WCR: It is my understanding that technically you are a superb surgeon, but some surgeons are not technically superb or even adequate. Do you agree?

MED: Absolutely. No question about that. It is unfortunate because I think if you are not technically adept at using your hands, and some people just aren't, you should not be a surgeon because a great deal of the result of the surgery is dependent on how well and how expeditiously the operation is done. The longer a patient is under an anesthetic, the greater the risk. In my opinion, anesthesia is the biggest risk factor in surgery. You are creating an abnormality when you use an anesthetic, and the patient has to get over it, so the longer you are given enough poison, the more the body has to get rid of it. Technically, I think it is very important to move along quickly. I became interested in surgery from a technical standpoint. I was virtually a technician in a lab doing dog surgery, and I liked it. I liked the way I was doing it, and I practiced doing it. I became adept at tying knots very quickly, and I could tie it with my eyes closed.

I think another factor is that if you can use your hands, let's say, on a musical instrument, somehow I think that helps your neuromuscular coordination. It is why some people can learn to play music well, and some never learn to play well. I was never a superb musician, but I took an instrument like the clarinet, and learned how to play it myself without having any instruction because I already knew how to read music and how to finger and how to play a reed instrument like the saxophone. I just needed to learn the fingering of a clarinet, which is a little different from a saxophone. So it is that kind of neuromuscular coordination with your hands that you

either have genetically, like a good athlete, or you don't. I think a surgeon needs that same quality—athletic coordination. When I operated on the Duke of Windsor, I did his abdominal aortic aneurysm, and he held a conference with the news people just before being discharged. One of the newsmen said, ''How long was the operation?'' He turned around to me, and he said, ''Well, we will ask Dr. DeBakey.'' I said, ''Fifty minutes.'' This is exactly the time it took from making the incision to its closure. The London newspapers asked one of the surgeons in London, and he said he didn't believe it.

• • •

WCR: Most surgeons, it seems to me, are relatively athletic. You played some sports in high school and/or college?

MED: As a matter of fact, I played handball at Tulane. I went out for football, but I was too light. They put me on the scrub team, which the varsity team used to practice with. I didn't want anymore of that. I looked around for some sport where I didn't have to be knocked around. This turned out to be handball, and I loved handball. We won a number of matches with other schools. I also played billiards.

• • •

WCR: As a youngster, you did a lot of hunting and fishing.

MED: I did a lot of hunting. My brother and I used to shoot ducks with a 22-rifle. We could shoot a lot more that way. We would bring back a dozen ducks.

• • •

WCR: You don't go hunting anymore, you don't fish anymore?

MED: I don't have time for it and, secondly, you know, you change. I don't think I could kill an animal now. I couldn't shoot a deer today.

• • •

WCR: Can you speak a bit more about your accomplishments at Baylor?

MED: I had the good fortune of being able to profit from some of the early developments in surgery that gave me a certain amount of recognition, and I was therefore ahead of a lot of people in some of these developments, particularly in aortic surgery. I was getting patients from all over the world and from all parts of the country—mostly private patients. I was able to generate quite a bit of money. The school needed that money, and I was able to put it into both the school and the Department of Surgery. I ran the Department of Surgery after the first year I was here on my own budget from money I had made. The Baylor University College of Medicine never gave me another penny after that. I generated all the money to run my Department and to create everything I did in the research laboratory. I built a beautiful research laboratory.

In many ways, Bill, the development of this medical school from third-rate, when I arrived in 1948, to now, is rather remarkable. We are now 16th in the country in the amount of NIH grant money we receive. When I came in 1948, it was zero. That, in itself, is a very prideful development. Things really got moving in 1968, when I became Dean and further developed after I became President and we became an independent College with a new Board of Trustees whose membership was representative of the business, civic, and philanthropic leadership in Houston. In 1968, I began to realize that the only way we were going to improve the standards was to bring in some new people. We just had to change our faculty. You remember, you were one of the people I tried to bring in. We had to bring in scientists who were capable of doing research—who had the ability, the training and the background, and had that goal. I began to recruit people like you—like Stan Appel in Neurology, Burt O'Malley in Cell Biology, Salih Wakil in Biochemistry, and Tony Gotto and Bill Butler from NIH. That is what made the school, the recruiting of people of that caliber. That is probably my major contribution from the standpoint of the College. This came about largely because of what I did in Surgery, which gave me the basis for doing it. A good many people came because I had a large cardiovascular service, one of the largest in the country, and they were interested. I brought Bill Butler because he was in Immunology, and we were doing heart transplants and needed somebody in Immunology. I realized that what we had was completely inadequate from an institutional standpoint.These are the people who helped build the College.

I keep saying to people concerned about HMO: "If you build a better mouse trap, they will beat a path to your door. Concentrate on excellence. Concentrate on innovation. Concentrate on making advances, and you will get recognition, and you will get patients, no matter what." All this about trying to compete with HMOs, as far as I am concerned, from an academic standpoint, is futile. In my opinion, this is not the right direction to take. I think you should put your money where the track record shows that it works best — in people who pursue excellence in the field, can innovate, and do good research.

• • •

WCR: You won a gardening contest?

MED: Yes, I won the top prize, what was then called the Tri-Parish Gardening Prize, and I still have the watch, a beautiful watch.

• • •

WCR: That is terrific. All these chores you had to do around the house, that you woke up at 5:00 o'clock, what kind of chores are you talking about?

MED: Well, I had to grind the coffee, things like that. My Father was a great gardener, so he put us in the garden, and I liked it.

• • •

WCR: Can we look at some of your pictures?

MED: This picture is when we were students, and this is one of my classmates in medical school.

• • •

WCR: When you grew up there, what was the population of Lake Charles?

MED: About 13, 000. It is now over 100, 000. It grew rapidly during the War because they built an airbase there and then they made it a port.

• • •

WCR: How did your Daddy and Mother happen to go to Lake Charles?

MED: My Father went to Lake Charles to work for a company that needed someone who could relate to the French people there. He spoke French fluently.

• • •

WCR: Did your Daddy or Mother sleep a lot or a little?

MED: They slept very little. My Father slept less than I did.

• • •

WCR: You were a handsome guy. This is about the year you got married?

MED: That shows what a photographer can do. This is about the time I got married.

• • •

WCR: How do you like having a daughter?

MED: She is the joy of my life right now. She just turned 18 and has just started college at Southwestern University in Georgetown, Texas. I have an honorary degree from there. It is a very nice school, still old-fashioned in its curriculum. They still have courses in Latin. I thought she was better off at a college like this, nearby. She can visit on weekends. The college has a good curriculum, and it is well endowed. It has one of the best student-to-faculty ratios in the country, something like 11 to 1. The campus is beautiful; all the buildings are the same style, an academic architectural style. Many of the buildings are named after prominent families in Houston. It is the oldest continuous higher education institution in Texas, going back to 1843.

• • •

WCR: Dr. DeBakey, you are a spectacular man. Thank you very much.

MED: Thank you. It is always a pleasure to be with you.

MED'S MOST IMPORTANT 100 PUBLICATIONS SELECTED BY MED AMONG HIS 1,500 PUBLICATIONS

Books: Kilduffe, RA, DeBakey ME. The Blood Bank and the Technique and Therapeutics of Transfusions. St. Louis: C. V. Mosby, 1942:558.
DeBakey ME, Beebe GW. Battle Casualties: Incidence, Mortality, and Logistic Considerations. Springfield, Illinois:Charles C Thomas, 1952:277.
DeBakey ME, Gotto A. The Living Heart, New York: David McKay, 1977:256.
DeBakey ME, Gotto AM Jr., Scott LW, Foreyt JP. The New Living Heart Diet. New York: Simon & Schuster (A Fireside Book). Paperbound Edition, 1996:414.

Articles:

4. DeBakey ME. A simple continuous-flow blood transfusion instrument. *New Orleans M S J* 1934;87:386–389.
37. Ochsner A, DeBakey ME. Primary pulmonary malignancy: treatment by total pneumonectomy; analysis of 79 collected cases and presentation of 7 personal cases. *Surg Gynecol Obstet* 1939;68:435–451.
69. Ochsner A, DeBakey ME. Carcinoma of the lung. *Arch Surg* 1941;42:209–258.
96. Ochsner A, DeBakey ME. Amebic hepatitis and hepatic abscess. *Surgery* 1943;13:460–493; *Surgery* 1943;13:612–649.
102. DeBakey ME. Section on thrombophlebitis, in Lewis' Practice of Surgery, Hagerstown, Maryland: W. F. Prior, 1943.
109. DeBakey ME, Carter BN. Current considerations of war surgery. *Ann Surg* 1945;121:545–563; *Tr South S A* 1944;56:161–179.

111. DeBakey ME, Simeone FA. Battle injuries of the arteries in World War II: an analysis of 2,471 cases. *Ann Surg* 1946;123:534–579. (Abstracted in *Bull US Army Med Dept* 1946;5:295.)

118. DeBakey ME, Burch G, Ray T, Ochsner A. The ''borrowing-lending'' hemodynamic phenomenon (hemometakinesia) and its therapeutic application in peripheral vascular disturbances. *Ann Surg* 1947;126:850–865.

160. DeBakey ME. The future of the Army Medical Library. *Bull Med Libr Assoc* April,1951;39:122–127.

205. DeBakey ME, Cooley DA. Successful resection of aneurysm of thoracic aorta and replacement by graft. *JAMA* 1953;152:673–676. Reprinted in Stephenson LW, Ruggiero R, eds. Heart Surgery Classics. Part 2, Sect IX. Boston: Adams Publishing, 1994:385–389.

207. DeBakey ME, Cooley DA. Excisional therapy of aortic aneurysms. *Ann Surg* 1953;19:603–612.

208. DeBakey ME, Cooley DA. Surgical treatment of aneurysm of abdominal aorta by resection and restoration of continuity with homograft. *Surg Gynecol Obstet* 1953;97:257–266.

215. DeBakey ME. A critical evaluation of the problem of thromboembolism. *Surg Gynecol Obstet* 1954;98:1–27.

220. DeBakey ME, Cooley DA. Surgical considerations of acquired diseases of the aorta. *Ann Surg* 1954;139:763–777.

227. DeBakey ME, Cooley DA. Successful resection of aneurysm of distal aortic arch and replacement by graft. *JAMA* 1954;155:1398–1403.

228. DeBakey ME, Creech O Jr., Cooley DA. Occlusive disease of the aorta and its treatment by resection and homograft replacement. *Ann Surg* 1954;140:290–310.

242. DeBakey ME, Cooley DA, Creech O Jr. Treatment of aneurysms and occlusive disease of the aorta by resection: analysis of eighty-seven cases. *JAMA* 1955;157:203–208.

251. DeBakey ME, Cooley DA, Creech O Jr. Surgical considerations of dissecting aneurysm of the aorta. *Ann Surg* October, 1995;142:586–612. Reprinted in Stephenson LW, and Ruggiero R, eds. *Heart Surgery Classics,* Part 2, Sect IX. Boston, Adams Publishing Group, Ltd., 1994:398–400.

258. DeBakey ME, Cooley DA, Creech O Jr. Resection of the aorta for aneurysms and occlusive disease with particular reference to the use of hypothemia: analysis of 240 cases. *Trans Am College Cardiol* 1955;5:153–157.

268. DeBakey ME, Simeone FA. Acute battle-incurred arterial injuries. In Elkin DC, DeBakey ME, eds. Vascular Surgery in World War II. Washington, DC:Office of the Surgeon General, Department of the Army, 1955:60–148.

271. DeBakey ME. Dissecting aneurysm of the aorta. *Surg Gynecol Obstet* 1956;102:372–373.

289. DeBakey ME, Creech O Jr., Morris GC Jr. Aneurysm of thoracoabdominal aorta involving the celiac, superior mesenteric, and renal arteries. Report of four cases treated by resection and homograft replacement. *Ann Surg* 1956;144:549–573. Reprinted in Stephenson LW, Ruggiero R, eds. Heart Surgery Classics. Part 2, Sect IX. Boston: Adams Publishing, 1994:401–406.

295. DeBakey ME, Cooley DA, Creech O Jr. Surgical treatment of dissecting aneurysm. *JAMA* 1956;162:1654–1657.

329. DeBakey ME, Crawford ES, Cooley DA, Morris GC Jr. Successful resection of fusiform aneurysm of aortic arch with replacement by homograft. *Surg Gynecol Obstet* 1957;105:657–664. Reprinted in Stephenson LW, Ruggiero R, eds. Heart Surgery Classics. Part 2, Sect IX. Boston: Adams Publishing, 1994:409–412.

352. DeBakey ME, Crawford ES, Cooley DA, Morris GC Jr. Surgical considerations of occlusive disease of the abdominal aorta and iliac and femoral arteries: analysis of 803 cases. *Ann Surg* 1958;148:306–324.

353. DeBakey ME, Cooley DA, Crawford ES, Morris GC Jr. Aneurysms of the thoracic aorta: analysis of 179 patients treated by resection. *J Thorac Surg* 1958;36:393–420.

360. DeBakey ME, Cooley DA, Crawford ES, Morris GC Jr. Clinical application of a new flexible knitted Dacron arterial substitue. *Arch Surg* 1958;77:713–724.

378. DeBakey ME, Crawford ES, Cooley DA, Morris GC Jr. Surgical considerations of occlusive disease of innominate, carotid, subclavian, and vertebral arteries. *Ann Surg* 1959;149:690–710.

381. DeBakey ME. Presidential address: changing concepts in thoracic vascular surgery. *J Thorac Cardiovasc Surg* 1959;38:145–165.

429. DeBakey ME. Some observations on the localizing patterns of arteriosclerosis. *Chicago Med Soc Bull* 1960;63:487–490.

436. DeBakey ME, Henly WS. Surgical treatment of angina pectoris. *Circulation* 1961;23:111–120.

452. DeBakey ME, Morris GC Jr., Crawford ES, Cooley DA. Arterial hypertension of renal origin: analysis of revascularization procedures in 96 cases. *Bull Soc Int Chir* 1961;20:290–301.

457. DeBakey ME, Henly WS, Cooley DA, Crawford ES, Morris GC Jr. Surgical treatment of dissecting aneurysm of the aorta: analysis of seventy-two cases. *Circulation* 1961;24:290–303.

462. DeBakey ME, Crawfrod ES, Morris GC Jr., Cooley DA. Surgical considerations of occlusive disease in the innominate carotid, subclavian, and vertebral arteries. *Ann Surg* 1961;154:698–725.

463. DeBakey ME, Morris GC Jr., Crawford ES, Cooley DA. Surgical considerations of renal hypertension. *J Cardiovasc Surg* 1961;2:435–448.

481. DeBakey ME, Crawford ES, Morris GC Jr., Cooley DA. Patch graft angioplasty in vascular surgery. *J Cardiovasc Surg* 1962;3:106–141.

502. DeBakey ME, Beebe, GW. Medical follow-up studies on veterans. *JAMA* 1962;182:1103–1109.

521. DeBakey ME. Diseases of the arterial wall: concepts of therapy. *Mal Cardiov* 1963;4:377–414.

535. DeBakey ME. A new type of biopsy needle. *Surg Gynecol Obstet* 1963;116:754–755.

549. DeBakey ME. Basic concepts of therapy in arterial disease. (Lasker Award) *JAMA* 1963;186:484–498.

584. DeBakey ME, Henly WS, Cooley DA, Morris GC Jr., Crawford ES, Beall AC Jr. Surgical management of dissecting aneurysm involving the ascending aorta. *J Cardiovasc Surg* 1964;5:200–211.

601. DeBakey ME, Jordan GL, Jr., Abbott JP, Halpert B, O'Neal RM. The fate of Dacron vascular grafts. *Arch Surg* 1964;89:757–782.

609. DeBakey ME. Concepts underlying surgical treatment of cerebrovascular Insufficiency.In Clinical Neurosurgery. Vol 10. Baltimore: Williams & Wilkins, 1964:310–340.

645. DeBakey ME, Crawford ES, Garrett HE, Beall AC Jr., Howell JF. Surgical considerations in the treatment of aneurysms of the thoraco-abdominal aorta. *Ann Surg* 1965;162:650–662.

649. DeBakey ME. Report of President's Commission on Heart Disease, Cancer and Stroke (editorial). *Circulation* 1965;32:686.

663. DeBakey ME, Liotta D, Hall CW. Prospects for and implications of the artificial heart and assistive devices. *J Rehabil* 1966;32(2):106–107.

695. DeBakey ME, Beall AC Jr., Cooley DA, Crawford ES, Morris GC Jr., Garrett HE. Resection and graft replacement of aneurysms involving the transverse arch of the aorta. *Surg Clin North Am* 1966;46:1057–1071.

710. DeBakey ME, Liotta D, Hall CW. Left-heart bypass using an implantable blood pump. In Mechanical Devices to Assist in Failing Heart. Washington, DC: National Academy of Sciences—National Research Council, 1966:223–239.

713. DeBakey ME, Garrett HE, Howell JF, Hallen A. Coronary endarterectomy. In Irvine, WT, ed. Modern Trends in Surgery 2. London: Butterworths, 1966:123–133.

725. DeBakey ME, Garrett HE, Howell JF, Morris GC Jr.Coarctation of the abdominal aorta with renal artifical stenosis: surgical considerations. *Ann Surg* 1967;165:830–843.

746. DeBakey ME. Medical research and the golden rule. *JAMA* 1968;203:574–576.

750. DeBakey ME. Human cardiac transplantation (editorial). *J Thorac Cardiovasc Surg* 1968;55(3):447–451. (Translated as: Transplante del hospital universitario de Caracas Instituto Autonomo, Caracas, Venezuela, 1969;4:99–107.)

752. DeBakey ME. Science and humanism. *Mich Q Rev* 1968;7:85–91.

794. DeBakey ME, Hall CW, Hellums JD, O'Bannon W, Bourland H, Feldman L, Wieting D, Calvin S, Smith P, Anderson S. Orthotopic cardiac prosthesis: preliminary experiments in animals with biventricular artifical heart. *Cardiovasc Res Center Bull* 1969;7(4):127–142. (Abstracted in Excerpta Medica: *CD & CV Surg* 1970;14:248.

799. DeBakey ME, Diethrich EB, Glick G, Noon GP, Butler WT, Rossen RD, Liddicoat JE, Brooks DK. Human cardiac transplantation: clinical experience. *J Thorac Cardiovasc Surg* 1969;58:303–317.

828. DeBakey ME, Diethrich EB. Ventricular assistive devices: present and future. In Burford TH and Ferguson TB, eds. Cardiovascular Surgery, Current Practice. St. Louis: CV Mosby, 1969:225–243.

862. DeBakey ME. Problems involved in the interface between living tissues and Biomaterials. In Engineering and Medicine. A symposium sponsored by the National Academy of Engineering. Washington, DC:Printing and Publishing Office, National Academy of Sciences, 1970:114–124.

866. DeBakey ME. Year Book of General Surgery 1970. Chicago: Year Book Medical Publishers, 1970.

869. DeBakey ME (editor). Left ventricular bypass pump for cardiac assistance: clinical experience. *Am J Cardiol* 1971;27:3–11. (Abstracted in Excerpta Medica: *Surgery* 1972;62:33; also, Excerpta Medica: *CD & CV Surg* 1972;16:76.)

875. DeBakey ME. The artificial heart: total replacement. *Trans Proc* 1971;3:1445–1448.

897. Garrett HE, Dennis EW, DeBakey ME. Aortocoronary bypass with saphenous vein graft. *JAMA* 1973;223:792–794. (Abstracted in Excerpta Medica: *CD & CV Surg* 1973;18:477.)

956. DeBakey ME. Successful carotid endarterectomy for cerebrovascular insufficiency: nineteen-year follow-up. *JAMA* 1975;233:1083–1085.

1009. DeBakey ME, Lawrie GM. Aortocoronary-artery bypass. Assessment after 13 years. *JAMA* 1978;239:837–839. (Abstracted in *J C E Cardiol* 1979;14:36–37.)

1015. DeBakey ME, McCollum CH, Graham JM. Surgical treatment of aneurysms of the descending thoracic aorta. Long-term results in 500 patients. *J Cardiovasc Surg* 1978;19:571–576.

1021. DeBakey ME. Patterns of atherosclerosis and rates in progression. In Paoletti R, Gotto AM Jr., eds. Atherosclerosis Reviews. New York: Raven Press, 1978;3:1–56.

1041. DeBakey ME. The development of vascular surgery. (Great Ideas in Surgery Series) *Am J Surg* 1979;137:697–738.

1044. DeBakey ME, DeBakey L. Relighting the lamp of excellence. *Forum Med* 1979;2:523–528. (Reprinted in *Talent* 1980;87:8.,9,16; 1980;87:10,14)

1047. DeBakey ME. Research related to surgical treatment of aortic and peripheral vascular disease. *Circulation* 1979;60:1619–1635.

1110. DeBakey ME, McCollum CH, Crawford ES, Morris GC Jr., Howell JF, Noon GP, Lawrie GM. Dissection and dissecting anerysms of the aorta: twenty-year follow-up of five hundred twenty-seven patients treated surgically. *Surgery* 1982;92:1118–1134.

1129. Melnick JL, Dreesman GR, McCollum CH, Petrie BL, Burek J, DeBakey ME. Cytomegalovirus antigen within human arterial smooth muscle cells. *Lancet* 1983;2:644–647.

1132. DeBakey ME, DeBakey L. The ethics and economics of high-technology medicine. *Compr Ther* 1983;9:6–16. (Reprinted in *Med Meetings* 1984;11:18–26.)

1139. DeBakey ME, Lawrie GM, Morris GC, Crawford ES, Howell JR. Experience with 366 St. Jude valve prostheses in 346 patients. in DeBakey ME, ed. Advances in Cardiac Valves. Clinical Perspectives. New York: Yorke Medical Books, 1983:14–21.

1151. DeBakey ME, Lawrie GM. Combined coronary artery and peripheral vascular disease: recognition and treatment. *J Vasc Surg* 1984;1:605–607.

1152. DeBakey ME, Lawrie GM, Crawford ES, Morris GC Jr., Howell JF, Noon GP, McCollum CH. Surgical treatment of dissecting aortic aneurysms: 28 years experience with 527 cases. *Contemp Surg* 1984;25:13–23.

1162. DeBakey ME, Lawrie GM, Glaeser DH. Patterns of atherosclerosis and their surgical significance. *Ann Surg* 1985;201:115–131.

1176. Young JB, Short HD III, Noon GP, Lawrence EC, Whisennand HH, Viner SK, Davis FD, DeBakey ME. Clinical experience with heart and heart-lung tranplantation. *J Heart Transplant* 1986;5:84–87.

1181. DeBakey ME. Changing concepts in vascular surgery (and editorial comment). *J Cardiovasc Surg* 1986;27:367–409. (Reprinted from *J Cardiovasc Surg* 1960;1:3–44.)

1188. Bunting A, DeBakey ME, Davies NE, Messerle J, Palmer RA. Medical library assistance act: a twenty-year review,'' In National Library of Medicine Long Range Plan (Report of the Board of Regents), Report of Panel 2: Locating and Gaining Access to Medical and Scientific Literature (Appendix A). Bethesda, Maryland: National Library of Medicine, 1986:32–49.

1208. DeBakey ME. Personal essay.In Manning, Phil R, DeBakey L, eds. Medicine: Preserving the Passion. New York: Springer-Verlag, 1987:15–23.

1211. DeBakey ME, Lawrie GM. DeBakey-Surgitool pyrolite aortic valve: results of isolated replacement in 345 patients followed up to 13 years after operation. In Hilger HH, Homback V, Rashkind WJ, eds. Invasive Cardiovascular Therapy. Dordrecht: Martinus Nijhoff Publishers, 1987:77–93.

1202. DeBakey ME. Holding human health hostage. *J Invest Surg* 1988;1:81–84.

1219. DeBakey ME. Holding human health hostage (editorial). *J Invest Surg* 1988;1:81–84. (Reprinted in: *Baylor Medicine* 1989. Reprinted in Rottenberg

AT, ed. Elements of Argument: A Text and Reader. 3rd ed. Boston: Bedford Books of St. Martin's Press, 1991:383–386.)

1263. DeBakey ME. A surgical perspective. (Presidential address) *Ann Surg* 1991;213:499–531. (Reprinted as: The history of cardiovascular surgery. In Proceedings of the Academy of Athens. Athens, Greece. 1992:346–400.

1272. DeBakey ME. The National Library of Medicine: evolution of a premier information center. *JAMA* 1991;266:1252–1258.

1325. DeBakey ME. Medical centers of excellence and health reform. *Science* 1993;262(5133):523–525.

1326. DeBakey ME. The winds of change in medicine (editorial). *South Med J* 1993;86(11):1316–1317. (Reprinted in *Southern Medicine* 1994;82(1):1,6,9; Shreveport Medical Society, *The Bulletin* 1994;45(4):18–20).

1339. DeBakey ME. Conspectus: Baylor College of Medicine's golden anniversary: historical development in Houston. *Compr Ther* 1994;20(3);145–149.

1343. DeBakey ME, Szilagyi DE, Thompson JE. Special communication: *Journal of Vascular Surgery*: the decennium. *J Vasc Surg* 1994;20:853–854.

1350. DeBakey ME. Review and outlook: prescription for diasater (editorial). *The Wall Street Journal*, June 23, 1994;93(no. 122):A14. (Reprinted in *Texas Medical Center News*, August 1, 1994, 2.)

1356. DeBakey ME, Anlyan WG. Outlook: managed care puts us all at risk. *Houston Chronicle*, June 18, 1995, Sect C, 1, 4.

1358. DeBakey ME. Telemedicine has now come of age (editorial). *Telemed J* 1995;1(1):3–4. (Reprinted as: Telemedicine has come of age. In *The Methodist Times* July 7, 1995;2(14):2. Reprinted as: Reflections on telemedicine's past, present, and future. In the *TMC News* July 15, 1995;17(13):23.

1359. DeBakey ME, Gutterman JU. The Lasker Awards at fifty (editorial). *JAMA* 1995;274(13):1061.

1363. DeBakey ME. The soul of the scientist (address on receiving 1995 Sigma XIX William Procter Prize for Scientific Achievement). In Miller K, ed. Vannevar Bush II: Science for the 21st Century, 1995 Forum Proceedings. Research Triangle Park, North Carolina:Sigma xi, The Scientific Research Society, 1995:173–179.

1368. DeBakey ME. Health care in the '90s: lab coats and legal briefs: is the legal system closing the door on medical research? *The Journal* 1996;14–15.

1377. DeBakey ME. History, the torch that illuminates: lessons from military medicine. *Military Med* 1996;161(12):711–716.

In Press: DeBakey ME, Benkowski R. The DeBakey/NASA axial flow ventricular Assist device. In Heart Replacement, Artificial Heart 6. Akutso, Koyanagi, eds. Tokyo: Springer-Verlag, 1997. Reprinted in: Artificial Organs, Special Issue: ISRP Conference Proceedings, 1997.

ANTHONY NICHOLAS DeMARIA, MD:
A Conversation With the Editor*

Tony DeMaria (Figure 1) was born in Elizabeth, New Jersey on January 12, 1943, and grew up in Bayonne, New Jersey. After public and parochial schools, he went to the College of the Holy Cross, graduating in 1964, and then to the New Jersey College of Medicine, graduating in 1968. His internship in internal medicine was at the St. Vincent Hospital in Worcester, Massachusetts, and his junior and senior medical residency was at the US Public Health Service Hospital in Staten Island, New York. His fellowship in cardiovascular medicine was at the University of California at Davis. Following completion of his fellowship in 1973, he remained on the faculty until June 1981, when he moved to Lexington, Kentucky, to be Professor of Medicine and Chief of the cardiovascular division of the University of Kentucky College of Medicine. In May 1992 he returned to California, this time to San Diego, as Professor of Medicine and Chief of the cardiovascular division of the University of California at San Diego. In October 2001, he was made the Judith and Jack White Chair in Cardiology. Dr. DeMaria has been, for nearly 3 decades, an international authority in cardiology, particularly in the area of echocardiography. His investigations have led to the publication of >450 articles, almost all in peer-reviewed medical journals. He is also the author or editor of 3 books. For his investigative work and teaching abilities, he has received many honors, including several Internal Medicine Distinguished Faculty Teaching Awards, Teaching Scholar of the American Heart Association, Distinguished Alumnus Award of the University of Medicine & Dentistry of New Jersey, and honorary degrees from the Kagawa Medical University and the University of Bordeaux, among others. He was president of the American College of Cardiology in 1988 and president of the American Society of Echocardiography from 1985 to 1987. He became editor in chief of the *Journal of the American College of Cardiology* in January 2002. He has lectured widely, both in the USA and abroad. He and his lovely wife *Lori* are the proud parents of 3 offspring, Christine and Anthony who are now married, and Jonathan. Both Tony and Lori are wonderful people and fun to be around.

William C. Roberts, MD[†] (hereafter WCR): *Dr. DeMaria, I appreciate your willingness to talk to me and therefore to the readers of* The American Journal of Cardiology. *We're onboard the "Silver Whisper" ship traveling around the Italian peninsula. Could we start by my asking you to discuss your parents and siblings, early upbringing, and some early memories?*

FIGURE 1. Anthony Nicholas DeMaria, MD, during the interveiw (photo by WCR).

Anthony Nicholas DeMaria, MD[‡] (hereafter AND): I was born in Elizabeth, New Jersey, but I actually grew up in a town not far away, called Bayonne, New Jersey, which like Jersey City and Hoboken, is in the New York metropolitan area. My dad owned a fruit and vegetable market. He went to the farmer's market very early 5 days a week for produce. He worked extraordinarily long hours, opening the store at 6 A.M. after coming back from the farmer's market, and he closed it at 10 P.M. 7 days a week. He made his own sausage. During Christmas time, we sold Christmas trees. It was in the selling of Christmas trees that I learned that the price for anything was variable and subject to negotiation. We sold flowers at Easter and for Mother's Day. I worked in the store with my dad. My mom was a homemaker (Figure 2). She took care of my 3 younger sisters and me. Bayonne was, and is, a largely an ethnic community. If I knew somebody's address, I could pretty much tell what their nationality was and what church they went to. I went through the local schools and then went off to college in Worcester, Massachusetts.

*This series of interviews is underwritten by an unrestricted grant from Bristol-Myers Squibb.
†Executive Director, Baylor Cardiovascular Institute, Baylor University Medical Center, Dallas, Texas, 75246.
‡Director, Cardiovascular Center, Judith and Jack White Chair in Cardiology Professor of Medicine, University of California, San Diego, California, 92103-8411.

FIGURE 2. AND and his mother and sister.

FIGURE 3. AND's father's grocery store.

WCR: *How big was Bayonne?*

AND: Bayonne had a population of 60,000 packed into a peninsula that was 3 miles long and at its very widest, about 1 mile wide. On one end it was connected to Staten Island, New York, via the Bayonne Bridge, and on the other end, it continued to Jersey City. We could almost see the Statue of Liberty from my house.

WCR: *Did you get to Manhattan or Staten Island very much?*

AND: Not very much. The Verrazano Narrows Bridge, which connects Staten Island to Brooklyn, hadn't been built yet. It was alleged (and I'm sure it's true) that there were people who had been born on Staten Island that never in their lives had left the island, even for 1 day. Going to New York City was an adventure. The traffic was worse, of course, than in Bayonne. The people were a little different. We mostly stayed on the Jersey side.

WCR: *You are the oldest of 4 siblings. You were born in 1943. What's the difference in your siblings' ages?*

AND: Each of us was born roughly 2 years apart. We spanned 8 to 10 years between the 4 of us.

WCR: *What was your daddy's store like?*

AND: It was very small and fascinating. I have a picture of it in my office (Figure 3). When my father died and we went through his things, we found a crumpled up photograph of the store. I had to smooth it out to have it made into a nice big print. The whole store couldn't have been 1,000 square feet. It was mostly fruits and vegetables with canned goods on 1 side and a big freezer in the corner at the back. It

contained a little delicatessen, where we sliced lunch meats. His major business was selling to people who wanted very fresh fruits and vegetables or alternatively, to people who wanted delivery. The latter is what I did most of the time. Customers would call in orders (a pound of this and a sack of sugar) and we'd put together the order and then I'd deliver it to their houses. It was pretty convenient.

WCR: *On a bicycle?*

AND: Remember those bicycles with the small wheels in front? The rear wheel was the usual size and the front wheel was very small with a huge basket above it. I could usually fit 3 or 4 orders in the basket and deliver them. It was a marvelous education in life. My dad died prematurely at 59 years of age from an aortic dissection. My mom is still alive and my sisters Barbara, Carol, and Adele are doing well.

WCR: *When was your father born?*

AND: He was born in 1916 and died in 1976.

WCR: *He worked up to the day he died?*

AND: My father had 2 jobs at the time he died. The store had burned down. The building that the store was in was very old. We were home on a Sunday and somebody came by and told us the store was on fire. The building had kerosene heaters. This was first-generation America. It was not the suburbs. Because my father had records in the store of who owed him money, he ran into the building. I ran to the building, a judgment that compounded the stupidity of the moment, but I convinced him to get out; shortly thereafter the building went up in a blaze.

WCR: *Neither of you got burned?*

AND: Neither one of us got hurt. We got away in time.

WCR: *You were how old then?*

AND: I was 23. My dad then went to work for the city of Bayonne. He was in charge of all their parking meters and helped with zoning issues, etc. He'd do that all day, and then in the evening he went to some truck terminals in Jersey City and loaded trucks until about 2, and then come home and go to bed.(Jersey City was a port.) He died of aortic dissection while loading a truck.

WCR: *Did your father smoke?*

AND: Yes, cigars, continuously. I think he was born with a cigar in his mouth. He'd send me down to the store to get his cigars. I'd get Dutch Master's panatelas. That's all he smoked.

WCR: *How far was the store from your home?*

AND: A block or maybe a block and a half.

WCR: *What was your home like?*

AND: My home was pretty good. We were, by the standards of our neighborhood, well off. We had our own house. It was a small split-level house. My father had it built. There was a lot in the area that was empty. He and my uncle purchased the lot and then contracted out the building of 2 houses next to one another.

WCR: *Did you have a room of your own?*

AND: I did. It was in the attic. The house had 2 bedrooms and an attic. My parents slept in one and my 3 sisters had the master bedroom. That was the only one all 3 could fit in. My parents slept in a smaller bedroom. My dad, who was very handy, put a floor in the attic and plastered the ceiling. You could only stand up in the middle of the room because the roof slanted. But it was mine! I was the only one living in it! It was a different time, Bill. My folks thought it was important for a son to go to college. That was preached to me from day 1. They repeated over and over again that I needed to go to college so that I didn't wind up running a fruit and vegetable market. But my sisters didn't seem to matter so much. If they went to college that was nice; it was icing on the cake. For the first born son, it was absolutely necessary.

WCR: *Were your parents first-generation Americans?*

AND: Yes. Both my parents were born in the USA. Their parents had just come over. I never got to know my grandparents because I couldn't speak their language.

WCR: *Where were they from?*

AND: On my father's side, from Italy (the Naples area), and on my mother's side, Poland. They couldn't speak to one another.

WCR: *How did they meet?*

AND: They met at one of the beaches in Jersey. My father was black-haired with a darker complexion. My mother was blonde with very fair skin. I guess opposites attract. My mother was from Elizabeth, New Jersey. That is why I was born there. My dad was from Bayonne. I was only born in Elizabeth. We always lived in Bayonne.

WCR: *How far is Bayonne from Elizabeth?*

AND: Two stops on the Jersey Turnpike, maybe 10 miles.

WCR: *Where does your mother live now?*

AND: She lives in the same house, in Bayonne, New Jersey. My uncle still lives next door. Two other uncles, my father's brothers, lived across the street until they died. The whole family on my dad's side lived in that area.

WCR: *You had a lot of cousins and family?*

AND: Tons of cousins. There were lots and lots of DeMaria kids in that 3- to 4-block area.

WCR: *It sounds like your father wasn't home very much because he was always at the store or working a second job. But you could always go down to the store and see him. Did you work every day after school after you reached a certain age? How did that work out?*

AND: No. When I got into high school my parents made it clear to me that my job in life was to get to college. They didn't want me to do anything that would interfere with that. I only worked in the store summers and on weekends. During the week, my job was to study and get good grades. My mother did not graduate from high school. My dad did graduate from high school and actually could have gone to college. He had that opportunity, but he had to go into the family business. At that time my paternal grandfather was a peddler. He had 4 sons. He had horses and wagons and as a kid, I often rode the horse and wagon. They'd go up and down the streets of Bayonne with fruits and vegetables. By those standards, my father was a big success. He got his own store! He didn't have to peddle anymore. Frankly, if I didn't want to work weekends, I didn't have to. If I ever went to him and told him that I had to study, he'd say, "That's all right. You do whatever you want. Go study. You don't have to do work here."

In contrast, my kids grew up competitive swimmers and I was the starter of the swim team. Every weekend Lori and I packed up the car and went to a swim meet. I tried to see every little league and soccer game my kids were in. I would make the time. My dad was just too busy. He had to be in the store.

WCR: *What was your father like? Were you and your father close?*

AND: My dad was very smart. He was kind of an overwhelming presence. In our neighborhood, he managed to get his own house. Very few had their own house. Families lived in rooms. He was very facile politically. A lot of Italians in our neighborhood came to the store to seek his advice on various matters. If they had a problem with the city, he knew who to call to get a pothole or whatever fixed. He was active politically. If neighbors needed things done, he knew how to get them done. He spoke Italian fluently, as well as English. He was sought after as a political ally for the elections because a lot of people voted the way he recommended that they should. In our neighborhood, he was a big "chimichanga." I was always quite awed by the respect he was afforded, and by the fact that we lived in our own house and I could go to a private Catholic school.

WCR: *You had to pay tuition?*

AND: Yes. As a kid I thought my dad was about the biggest success in the world. I wasn't sure that I could ever quite achieve what he had achieved. If he had had the opportunities that I had, only God knows what he would have accomplished. He was the real McCoy!

WCR: *It sounds like he was very resourceful and that he was a magnet that attracted people to him.*

AND: Yes. He was the eldest brother and that's why he couldn't go to college. He had to go into the business because the other brothers were a bit younger. He was the glue that held that family together. He was very resourceful and was very handy.

He managed by hook or by crook. I'll never know in a million years where he learned it. I couldn't contract out a house, but my father knew how to hire plumbers and stuff like that. What he didn't know, he knew friends who would provide him with the information he needed. He knew everybody. He was very active in the community.

WCR: *Did you take family vacations?*

AND: Not really. When I was nearly out of high school, my parents rented a bungalow in Seaside for a couple of weeks during the summer, but I worked in the store.

WCR: *What did you do in the summertime other than work at your father's store?*

AND: Nothing. I played the summer sports—Little League, Babe Ruth league.

WCR: *What was dinner like at home? It sounds like your father rarely made it.*

AND: He didn't make it very often. During the summers, he would close the store at noon on Sundays and we'd pack up the car with a picnic lunch and go out to one of the lakes. In those days people swam off Staten Island at a place called South Beach where it was still swimmable. I remember well those excursions to South Beach or to Lake Hopatcong.

WCR: *It sounds like your father was the dominant figure around the house as well as at work with his male colleagues.*

AND: Yes. My father ran the house and everything and my mother ran my father!

WCR: *What was your mother like?*

AND: She was and is a very supportive person. She was a homemaker. She had great aspirations for all her kids. She demanded that we achieve at whatever we did. My sisters took ballet lessons and she'd be with them, making sure that they could dance on their toes. She was a meticulous housekeeper. She had her own circle of friends. Behind the scenes she was the person who took care of the family because my father was always at the store or somewhere. My mother got us ready for school and carted us off to wherever we had to get carted off to.

WCR: *You had a car?*

AND: Yes, our family had a 1948 Mercury, James Dean's car.

WCR: *What about the safety in the neighborhood? Were you safe in the neighborhood where you lived?*

AND: Yes. All of Bayonne was ethnic. It was all shuffled together. There was no real slum. The rich area, so to speak, wasn't all that rich and it wasn't all that big. There wasn't that much that separated the "haves" from the "have-nots." It was all mixed up. That's true of where I lived. Our house was on a nice street. I could go 2 blocks away where my father's store was and there were the low-income "housing projects," consisting of very big box apartment buildings. Bayonne had 2 sets of projects that went on for several city blocks. One of them started on 49th and Broadway and went up to 50th. My dad's store was between 48th and 49th on Broadway. We lived on 48th off Avenue C, which was 1 block up. The projects were the toughest part of town. I can't say that

I ever worried very much about safety. Our house was never burglarized.

WCR: *Your father's store was never robbed?*

AND: Yes, it was a couple times. There wasn't much to rob, however. The robbers could steal salami or something. He didn't have a large amount of money there. Everybody knew everybody. There was no way to commit a crime and not have everybody in the whole damn town knowing it.

WCR: *You spoke English in your home?*

AND: My parents were very adamant about that. My name is mispronounced. The correct pronunciation is not "de Marry A;" it's "day Maria". When my grandfather came over, the Americans called him "DeMaria" and the concept was that you had to assimilate into English as quickly as possible. My mother and father had to speak English to each other because, although my mother was fluent in Polish and my father was fluent in Italian, neither knew the other's language, so they had to communicate in English. That's what we did.

WCR: *What was your mother's name before marriage?*

AND: It was *Tess Kupis*. That's not what the actual name was. It was shortened. It was a long Polish name. When her parents came through Ellis Island, the name had 17 or so vowels and it was shortened. Everyone called her Tess.

WCR: *Do you remember dinner at night in your home when you were growing up? Your daddy was at the store. What was it like? Did you, your mother, and 3 sisters talk about what happened in school or what?*

AND: It wasn't like my father was never there. He occasionally came home for supper. We didn't have a family dinner exactly. It just depended on who was doing what. If one of the kids had a recital or had to go off to Cub Scouts or Girl Scouts or got home late from track practice, then we ate when we got there. My mother, who I hope will never read this, was not a great cook. She has many virtues in this world, but being a great cook was not one of them.

WCR: *But you could always go to the store and get something to eat if you wanted to.*

AND: Yes. We were all skinny as can be. When I was in high school, I became aware of women and things like that. I realized then that I was the "90-pound weakling." I went off to college at 6-feet tall and 122 pounds. I was just skin and bones.

WCR: *What do you weigh now?*

AND: More than that.

WCR: *Are you still 6-feet tall?*

AND: No, I shrunk a little bit. I'm 5 feet 11 inches. My intervertebral disks are desiccating. So are yours.

WCR: *I'm sure they are. Was your family strongly religious? Did you go to mass every Sunday?*

AND: My mother always did. There was a children's mass and we had to go to that one. Those who went to Catholic school sat in one section at mass and those who went to public school in another section. It was fairly regimented. We always went. My dad always ascribed to religion, but he often missed mass until after the store burned down and then he attended mass regularly and indeed became an usher, helping attendees find seats and later passing the collection baskets. He was very active. They were both pretty religious by today's standard.

WCR: *Did you have prayers before you ate meals at home?*

AND: No.

WCR: *Were there books around the house? Did your mother read much?*

AND: She read some but not a lot. It was not a very literary environment.

WCR: *Were there teachers in grammar school, junior high, or high school who had an impact on you?*

AND: Yes. I attended public grammar school. (My father felt very strongly about that.) Bayonne, however, was about 75% Catholic. Every parish had its own school. The concept was that your best chance of getting to college was to go to one of the Catholic schools. My dad, however, insisted that I go to public grammar school because he thought it was very important to learn how to live with people with different cultural backgrounds than our own. After grammar school, my parents switched the children to Catholic private schools, believing they provided a better chance of getting into college than the public schools. It wasn't that kids who went to Bayonne High School didn't get into college, but fewer of them went on to college, whereas most kids who went to the Catholic schools were targeting college. Then the question was, "How do you get into a Catholic high school?" We lived in a town of 75% Catholics and there was only 1 men's and 1 women's Catholic high school, and they couldn't take all the Catholic high schoolers. There were other Catholic high schools in Jersey City, but most were even more competitive. You had to take an entrance exam. I don't know what the acceptance rates of those Catholic high schools were in those days, but it was very competitive to get in.

In the eighth grade I was assigned an elderly teacher named *Mrs. Murphy.* Early on she asked, "How many of you children in this class are going to try to go to Catholic high school and take the entrance exams?" There were about 8 of us in my class of 25 students. Our parents had decided that we were going to try to go to a Catholic high school. She said, "I'm going to come in 1 hour early 3 days a week and we are going to start preparing for the exams." She did. The tests to see if you could qualify were given in the spring. Until April or May she came early 3 days each week to go through vocabulary with us. I don't want to sound like I was in any way disadvantaged, because I wasn't. My parents had a standard vocabulary. They didn't have advanced language skills. Mrs. Murphy went over these things. We practiced taking the test. It was multiple choice, and we hadn't taken one of those to that point. I took the exam. I was not the smartest of those 8, but I got into the Catholic High School in Bayonne and none of the others did. I was very fortunate. I'm convinced that I never would have gotten in if Mrs. Murphy hadn't worked with us. She was at the stage of her life where she had a mission. Her own children were grown. Her life was teaching us kids. She was a spectacular schoolteacher. In seventh grade, sometimes our teacher would come in and say, "Open your book and read this chapter." There was a lot of free study time. Mrs. Murphy was very structured. I never did get a chance to thank her. She was delighted that somebody made it. Only 1 person also made it the year before.

WCR: *You started Catholic high school in the ninth grade. Was there a big change? Was it much harder than the public grammar school and Catholic junior high that you'd gone to?*

AND: Yes. Where I lived it was heavily Catholic. In Bayonne alone there were 7 parish schools. In the Catholic high school, my classmates were on average smarter and often came from families where the parents were schoolteachers, doctors, lawyers, and businessmen. That made it tougher for me. They had a bit of an edge coming in.

WCR: *They also had all come from parish schools?*

AND: Pretty much.

WCR: *Were you active athletically?*

AND: I was a good long-distance runner. In my freshman year in high school I finished second in the conference. I won a lot of races. As I got older, I didn't improve as much as the others. There were a lot I could beat as a freshman, but by the time we were seniors, they had just gotten better than me. I achieved some success at track and I played basketball for a couple of years. It was clear that I was not as good at basketball as I was at track. I never made the starting team.

WCR: *What races did you run?*

AND: Cross-country in the fall and I was a miler or half-miler in the spring.

WCR: *Cross-country was usually how many miles?*

AND: It was 2.5 miles. We'd run it in a park. They would set up a course so that you had to go up and down some hills and through some fields. It wasn't run around a track. In the winter and spring, we ran on the track.

WCR: *You were second in the long-distance run as a freshman.*

AND: That was my pinnacle. That was in our region of the state. In Bayonne, I won the mile and half-mile a couple of times. Once a year there would be a track meet for Bayonne High School, Marist (the Catholic High School I went to), and for other people who went to other schools who lived in Bayonne. Being the champion of Bayonne wasn't that great.

WCR: *How many were in your high school per class?*

AND: About 90.

WCR: *How did you finish in the standings at the end of your senior year in high school?*

AND: I did okay.

WCR: *You were first in your class?*

AND: No. They never gave out a ranking exactly. At my graduation they gave awards to 7 people. To get the top award you had to have gotten an A in every single course for 4 years. To get the second award, you had to get at least a B+ in every course for 4 years. I got the second award. I missed getting the top award by 2.

WCR: *Did you have to study hard for those grades or did they come easy for you?*

AND: I had to study hard.

WCR: *Were there teachers in high school that had a major impact on you?*

AND: Yes, there were a number of them. I had religious brothers. They are like priests, but they don't say mass. One of the brothers was my track coach and he helped me a lot. He was a good friend, but got transferred after a year. In my senior year, I had a brother, *Hugh Arthur*, a French/Canadian guy who scared everybody to death. He ran a tight ship. His field was mathematics. He also taught religion and something else. I was assigned to his homeroom class in my senior year. He was hard as nails, but he was actually a very warm person underneath it all. He gave me a lot of good advice. As seniors in high school, we would get distracted and get into a bit of mischief. I would never claim that I was the best student in the world.

WCR: *Was it a co-ed high school?*

AND: No.

WCR: *All boys. Where were the girls?*

AND: They were down the street at Holy Family.

WCR: *You dated them in high school?*

AND: Yes. I went to mixers and dances.

WCR: *It sounds like high school was a good experience.*

AND: Yes. I enjoyed it.

WCR: *When it came time to go to college, you really couldn't get much advice from your parents or from your father's brothers because they'd never been themselves. Were there many members of your mother's family in the immediate neighborhood? Did you know your mother's family?*

AND: They lived in Elizabeth, New Jersey. We saw them from time to time. She had a brother and a sister. Each of them had 1 child, a boy. We didn't see much of them. We weren't close. My grandmother on my mother's side died relatively young from a subarachnoid hemorrhage. My maternal grandfather lived about 90 years. He couldn't speak English very well, although he worked for decades for Esso (Standard Oil) in Elizabeth. I couldn't communicate with him much, because I didn't speak Polish.

WCR: *You didn't know either of your grandparents on your father's side?*

AND: I did. They lived in Bayonne.

WCR: *You had 4 grandparents.*

AND: Yes. But it was hard to communicate.

WCR: *On your mother's side?*

AND: On my mother's side and my father's side. My paternal grandmother spoke halting English. My paternal grandfather could speak a fair bit, and I could communicate with him.

WCR: *When it came time to pick a college, how did that work out?*

AND: The brothers pushed us toward Catholic colleges. Many of my classmates went to St. Peter's College in Jersey City. A batch went to Seton Hall. Some went to Rutgers. I can't remember anybody going to an Ivy League school. I wanted to get away from home, but not too far. I told the brothers that maybe I'd go to New England or down south. They came back with Holy Cross or Georgetown. I applied to St. Peters and Seton Hall; everybody did. While I was sifting through that, I learned about Dartmouth. That seemed to me like it might fit the bill. I wrote off for their catalog, but I was roundly discouraged from pursuing that by everybody. For whatever reason, they said it wouldn't be a good alternative. I wound up going to Holy Cross.

WCR: *You went to Holy Cross in Worcester, Massachusetts. Your parents must have been extremely proud of you for having gotten into such a good college?*

AND: Yes. It was a good college to get into. Most of my classmates stayed locally. I had a lot of really smart classmates. There was a school called the Stevens College of Engineering in Hoboken. It's still there, but now it's something else. A number of my classmates went there. It too was considered quite a good school.

WCR: *Hoboken? That's where* Frank Sinatra *was from.*

AND: That's right. My dad knew Frank Sinatra. They dated cousins before my father married.

WCR: *What did your father say about Frankie?*

AND: He said he was a nice guy. My father was dating a woman and she had a cousin. Her cousin was dating Frank Sinatra. They double-dated a number of times. They got to be friends. He wasn't anything then, just a skinny Italian kid from Hoboken. My dad lived in Hoboken before his family moved to Bayonne. Frank Sinatra married *Nancy*, but my father didn't go with the other cousin anymore. They drifted apart. By the time my father was dating someone else, Frank Sinatra had started to make it big. He was playing a nightclub in New York City. My father wanted to do something special for New Year's Eve. On a whim he called the nightclub and asked to speak to Frank Sinatra and told them it was Tony DeMaria calling. According to my father, Frank got on the telephone and asked how he was doing? My father asked Frank, "Do you think you can get me a ticket to your show?" And Frank did it; he got him a table for his show on New Year's Eve in a nightclub in New York City. In Bayonne, it just doesn't get any better than that.

WCR: *You are a junior.*

AND: The tradition was that you name the first son after the grandfather. My grandfather's name was Nicolas. My mother just wouldn't abide by naming me Nicholas. They compromised on Anthony, which was my father's name, but Nicolas is my second name, after my grandfather. Of course, I went back to the tradition so my firstborn was named Anthony after my father. The fact that it happened to be my name was a side bonus.

WCR: *Did you go to Holy Cross to interview before you enrolled?*

AND: They didn't have interviews. Maybe they

did, but they didn't call me for an interview. I just applied. I remember that the brothers, when I told them which college I was interested in, advised me to apply to Fairfield in Fairfield, Connecticut, Providence College in Providence, Rhode Island, and at Holy Cross. One weekend my father took off from work. (I'll carry this to my grave because my father never took off from work.) He got one of his brothers to mind the store. We left on a Friday evening and we drove to visit Fairfield, Providence, and Holy Cross in Massachusetts. That drive was the most time I'd ever spent with my father alone. Shortly thereafter, I got a letter of acceptance from all 3 of them. We decided I'd go to Holy Cross, because it had the best reputation at the time.

WCR: *Holy Cross is how far from Bayonne?*

AND: Two hundred miles. It was a 5-hour drive.

WCR: *How many students were at Holy Cross when you were there?*

AND: Sixteen hundred.

WCR: *About 400 in each class. It's a beautiful college.*

AND: It was a nice school. It was on a hill overlooking the city. Surprisingly, for a small steel belt town in the middle of Massachusetts, Worcester had quite a number of colleges: Worcester Poly Tech, Clark University, Anna Maria (the Catholic women's college), Holy Cross, and Assumption College. It was a nice setting, but it was very strict. I had to go to mass every morning for the first 2 years I was there. They took attendance.

WCR: *You started college what year?*

AND: In 1960.

WCR: *You were 17. How did college strike you? That was the first time you'd ever been away from home, right?*

AND: Yes.

WCR: *How did it work out?*

AND: I was nervous. It was like a big filtering process. Going from Washington Public School to Marrist High School, they only took so many into my high school. Going from my high school to college, there were guys from all over the country. The major Catholic colleges in the USA then were Notre Dame, Georgetown, and Holy Cross. There were a lot of valedictorians there. Holy Cross was known for premed education. Even in high school I understood that getting into medical school was tough. One reason I went to Holy Cross was because they had a reputation for getting people into medical schools. When I got there, there were 150 of us who entered as premed (150 of 400 were designated as premed). They called us together at the beginning of school and gave premed orientation in a large auditorium. They told us that of the 150 students who were there, there were lots of valedictorians of their respective high schools. As I got further along, there were fewer guys like me from Bayonne and more who had come from professional families. It was very strict. They told us that, they "never had a person that they gave an unqualified recommendation for medical school that wasn't accepted to an American medical school." They fol-

lowed that up by saying, they "had never recommended more than 55 or 60." You didn't need to be a rocket scientist to realize that there were 150 of us, and the most they ever recommended was 60, so there were a lot of us who would not be recommended. Once that was clear, everybody looked at each other and said, "Who is going to be left standing at the end of 4 years?" That was the atmosphere that permeated the place. Folklore had it that at one time, they had put all the premeds in 1 dormitory on campus that the rest of the student body named "The House of Death." They didn't do that when I was there. It was very competitive as a premed. But it was a good education. It prepared me for medical school. Medical school was quite a bit easier than Holy Cross.

WCR: *It sounds like you had already decided that you wanted to be a physician before you entered college. How did that come about? You had no physicians in your family.*

AND: I'll tell you a true story. My mother and father had been targeting me to go to college from the time I could remember and telling everybody I was going to go to college. They weren't shy about it; they told everybody. It got to be senior year and the whole neighborhood (half of which were my family) was wondering what I would do. Everybody knew each other. Sure enough, I got accepted. My grandmother and my aunts and uncles were asking, "What are you going to take up in college?" I didn't know. How do you know? I liked history. It was easy and I did well in it in school. The first thing I said was, "Maybe I'm going to do history." That drew a blank expression. They didn't know any historians in Bayonne. They were saying, "History. History. What is that?" That bombed. I rummaged around a bit and decided biology was pretty interesting and I had always enjoyed that. So I told them "Biology." That didn't ring any bells either. Honest Bill. This is the truth. I felt the pressure here. One day my grandmother came to me. "Anthony, Anthony. What are you going to take up in college?" And I said, "Maybe I'll be a doctor." "Aahhhh," was her response. All my worries were gone. I just said "doctor" and they were happy. I didn't know if I wanted to be a doctor, but I figured I could change along the way. It got everybody off my back telling them what I was going to do. Nobody would believe for a minute that you would go to college to get an education. What good was that? My dad said to me one time when I was flailing around trying to think what I wanted to do, "Think of college like a train. You are going to get on the train. When you get off you want to be somewhere. That train is going to take you. You have to figure out where it is you want to be when the train stops."

WCR: *That's beautiful.*

AND: Once I got to Holy Cross, the question was no longer what I wanted to do. The question was could I do it? It became a challenge. Was I going to be standing at the end of 4 years to get their recommendation? During orientation week they said, "Everybody needs to go to confession to get in the proper spirit, to take communion, etc." You went to mass every morning so you might as well go to communion, too. I went to confession with one of the Jesuits from New England. I say my thing, "Bless me Father, etc." He said, "What did you say? What did you say?" I said it again. This went on for 3 or 4 minutes. He told me, "Son, I want to tell you something. I can't understand a word you're saying. You're going to waste your money on an education. Nobody's going to understand you. You've got to get rid of this accent." I had a heavy New Jersey accent. There weren't a lot of us there at the time.

WCR: *Did you go on scholarship?*

AND: Partial.

WCR: *Partial scholarship from the very beginning?*

AND: Yes. They didn't offer me a scholarship right off when I was accepted, but my father wrote them a letter. He asked them if there was any chance that I could get some financial help. They sent back an application form where he had to put down his income and expenses. Sure enough, they came back and they gave me a 50% scholarship.

WCR: *That was tuition?*

AND: Maybe room and board and tuition. They also got me a government loan.

WCR: *How did Holy Cross work out? You said it was very rigid. You were scared because the competition was vigorous. You hadn't met all these students who had come from professional households, many of whom, I presume, were fairly wealthy also.*

AND: I can't say it was a wealthy place, but many of the others had more varied experiences than I had. They had often been exposed to more things. However, there were a number of guys like me. Holy Cross wasn't a ritzy school compared to Georgetown. College is a filtering process. To get into the place, nearly everybody was in the top 20% of their high-school class. If you're in the top 20% of your class, you are better than 80% of the other guys. When you get into college, everybody is in the top 20% and things are tougher.

WCR: *You enjoyed the challenge though? You really poured it on from a studying standpoint.*

AND: It was my first time away from home. For the first time I was footloose and fancy free. I goofed off a bit and was slow academically. I caught up. It was a good college life and I've no complaints. I had to work very hard. When I got into medical school, compared with Holy Cross, it was easier.

WCR: *What was your major in college?*

AND: Liberal arts. If you were premed, you either took a bachelor of science in biology or a bachelor of arts. I was a bachelor of arts. I didn't have a major. I took the science courses that I needed for medical school. It was pretty prescribed and I took all liberal arts courses—languages, philosophy, history, etc.

WCR: *Were there any teachers in college that had a major impact on you?*

AND: In my freshman year I had a faculty advisor, *Father Leo McCarthy*. I talked to him. He provided some encouragement. That was really important for me early on to get me through what was a fairly challenging transition. Many of the other students came from elite Jesuit high schools. They had come from an environment that was similar to Holy Cross. Maybe they had a bit of a running start. It took me a little longer to get going. Father McCarthy transitioned me through that pretty well. I did pretty well. I obviously was in the top 50 premeds because I was recommended and got accepted to medical school.

WCR: *Did you enjoy Worcester? Did you go into Boston much?*

AND: You could only go off campus until 11 P.M. If you were leaving the campus, you had to sign out, you had to sign back in, and they did bed check. Somebody came around to make sure you were in your room. (This was a long time ago.) During the week, the lights had to be out at a certain time. That was it. If you had to cram for a test or something, you had to go to the bathroom and get in one of the stalls and sit in there. On the weekends, you had to sign out on Friday and Saturday. I don't think you could go off campus on Sunday. Most of the time students stayed on campus. It was an all-male school; there were no women. We were not allowed to have cars until we were seniors. The first year, all premeds just studied. Taking Saturday night off meant you went to the dining area and watched a movie on campus. If you wanted to go to Boston, you had to hitchhike. You could sign out for the weekend, but you had to give them an address. I didn't have any addresses. It wasn't a big social school.

WCR: *Who did you date up there?*

AND: There was a women's college. There were a lot of students there in Worcester. When you got to Boston, there were even more students. A lot of us had girlfriends back home and we corresponded with our girlfriends. When you got a chance, you'd go back home. That was that.

WCR: *Did you go back home much during the school year? Christmas or Easter?*

AND: Always Christmas and Easter and usually Thanksgiving. That was a long weekend. There was a guy from my hometown of Bayonne who was also at Holy Cross. He was a senior in my first year. He was the son of one of the orthopedic surgeons in Bayonne. Whenever he was going to Bayonne, he'd call me and if I could do it, then I'd ride in his car to Bayonne and give him some money for the cost of the gas.

WCR: *Were you sick much as a child? Did you go to a doctor very often? Do you remember any doctor visits before you went away to school?*

AND: Yes. I used to have a lot of bronchitis. In high school, my mother took me to a chest doctor in Jersey City. He gave me what was the equivalent of puffers in those days and some nose drops. In retrospect, it may have been allergies. In college I had pneumothoraxes. That put me in the infirmary or the hospital.

WCR: *These were spontaneous?*

AND: Yes. I was a skinny kid. It scared the hell out of me the first time I had it.

WCR: *How did you end up in college? Do you have any idea? You mentioned that of the 150 premeds, you finished in the top 50. Did they give you any idea where you stood in your class at Holy Cross?*

AND: I made the Dean's list a number of times. I don't know where I finished, but I would say of the 50 guys who went to medical school, I was probably in the middle of that group.

WCR: *It's also fair to say that those 150 premeds probably finished up higher than the 250 who started freshman year and weren't premed.*

AND: Oh yes. Of course, there were examples of very bright guys in other areas, but, as a group, the premeds were generally at the top of the list.

WCR: *What did you do during the summers when you were in college?*

AND: I worked in my dad's store for a year, I collected tolls on the New Jersey Turnpike for 2 years, and I drove a truck for a dairy distributor.

WCR: *That paid pretty well?*

AND: It paid more than I'd ever made working in the store. If you got a summer job collecting tolls on the New Jersey Turnpike, you got the worst shifts in the worst places. I'd wind up working the Lincoln Tunnel booth on Sunday when everybody was coming back from the Jersey shore. I worked a lot of nights. Those shifts screwed up my summers. My father called me and said that the guy who distributed dairy products to him was looking for a truck driver, somebody to distribute to different stores. I did that for a couple of summers. I worked Monday through Friday, 8 to 5 P.M.

WCR: *When it came time to apply to medical school, did you apply to several medical schools? What happened?*

AND: Everybody was really worried, even the top guys. It has always been competitive to get into medical school and we all had that anxiety. I applied to Seton Hall University, the local medical school in New Jersey. A bunch of my colleagues had applied as well. The Dean of Admissions at Seton Hall actually made a trip to Holy Cross. I'm sure he went to other schools in New England. He was there for 1 day and interviewed 6 of us. This happened in the first couple of weeks we were back in school as seniors. About a week after that, I got a letter in the mail saying that I'd been accepted to medical school. In the first month of my senior year I knew I had a place. My focus thereafter drifted a bit. You asked me about Boston before. I spent a whole lot more time in Boston. I applied to a couple of other places, too, but frankly I couldn't have afforded to go elsewhere. Seton Hall was perfect for me because I lived with my folks again. It was the only sensible thing to do. They didn't give me a scholarship, but they gave me a big loan for school. Between living at home and having a loan, it was financially feasible.

WCR: *How far from home was Seton Hall?*

AND: I didn't have to stop at a red light from my house to there. Seton Hall was at the Jersey City Medical Center. I was in one of the first classes. The medical school didn't last all that long. Ultimately, the state took it over and it became the New Jersey College of Medicine.

WCR: *It was private when you went there?*

AND: Yes. It was run by Seton Hall University, which is a diocesan school. I went there for 2 years. It was too expensive for the diocese to run Seton Hall. The state of New Jersey took it over as a state medical school. I graduated from the New Jersey College of Medicine.

WCR: *You were back living at home after 4 years at very sophisticated (in a way) Holy Cross College. How did you like being back at home even though you were going to medical school at the time?*

AND: It worked out well for me because I was back in my old attic room. I was able to focus. When I was away at college, some of the distractions of college life got to me. The reason I bring up Ned Weyman is that we were very similar. He was 2 years ahead of me. I got to know Ned because his roommate and I were hospitalized together once. I had a pneumothorax and Ned's roommate had a thoracic injury playing lacrosse. Here we were, these 2 college students in this hospital with a bunch of student nurses. That provided some distraction for a good part of the year after that. It seemed like in medical school I'd better not be distracted. Living at home wasn't like being at college, where someone was playing cards all the time or somebody was going down to get a beer or any of those things. It worked pretty well. My mother made all the meals and did all the laundry for me. I must admit, in retrospect, that it was a good thing. I suspect that I had stayed at home for college, I might have wound up at the very top of my class. I didn't mind living at home at all. The first couple of years of medical school were pretty rigorous. I had a girlfriend at the time. It was convenient. I'd call her and we'd go to movies. Living at home worked out well.

WCR: *How many students were in your medical school class?*

AND: One hundred.

WCR: *How many medical schools are in New Jersey?*

AND: There was only 1 then. I think there are 3 now. Rutgers has 1. They are all part of the same system. There's 1 in New Brunswick called Rutgers. There's 1 in Jersey City and there may be 1 in Camden.

WCR: *What is your medical school called now?*

AND: The College of Medicine and Dentistry of New Jersey. It was Seton Hall when I started and the New Jersey College of Medicine when I finished.

WCR: *It moved from Jersey City to Newark. Were there any surprises in medical school for you? When you first entered medical school did anything really strike you that struck you as very unusual?*

AND: Candidly, when I finished grammar school, I was one of the smartest kids. When I finished high school I was one of the smartest, right near the top. I went to college and I didn't finish with the top grades. I dropped down a bit. That shook me up a little. For the first time coming out of college, I wasn't coming out in the top 5% of the premed class. My batteries were a little charged for medical school. I was rip roaring ready to go. I spent the first 2 years of medical school making sure I was in the top 10 or so students in medical school. However, I did go through a period, which started at the end of my first year medical school and hit home in the second year of medical school, when I really wasn't sure that I wanted to study medicine. There were not any counselors at that stage of the game, but I was sent to talk to the Dean by a professor. In medical school, I had been pulled out of the standard classes to be in a special group that was doing special studies on the side. I got to know *Professor Bernard Briody*, another hard-ass kind of guy. Everyone was a little timid around him. He had come up with this idea to pick some medical students and not bother them with the usual day-to-day drudgery of memorizing stuff and put them in some special classes. I was put in that class and got to know him. We had a special relation. I told him that I wasn't sure I wanted to do medicine. He sent me to the Dean. The Dean was a little bit surprised because most of the people he was seeing that weren't sure about going further didn't have good grades. That was not a problem for me. To make a long story short, he said, "Don't do anything dumb. The first 2 years of medical school aren't exactly representative of what medicine is all about. You finish the second year and then take the summer off. Do something totally different and come back in the fall and start again in your clinical training and see what it's like. Take another look at it." That seemed like a reasonable idea.

The question was what was I going to do in the summer. One classmate was a lifeguard at the Jersey shore at one of the state beaches. He said, "There's a lifeguard who has helped with the first aid station who has had the job for a couple of years and he's not coming back this year. He's going to do something else. His name is *Carl Pepine*. Why don't you take his job?" I did. I took Carl Pepine's job on the Jersey Shore. I went down there to work to get away from medicine and to let things sift out. While working there, I met a woman who worked in one of the hamburger stands at the shore.

WCR: *Lori?*

AND: Yes, she's now my wife. We started dating. I returned for my third year of medical school and it was quite a bit different.

WCR: *What were the characteristics of Lori that attracted you to her when you were a lifeguard?*

AND: Here I was on the lifeguard squad in good physical shape. I worked out every day. I was tanned. Most people knew that I was a medical student. Even if you have a bad case of the uglies, you are going to do okay under those circumstances. How many bronzed lifeguard medical students are having trouble finding dates? Not many.

WCR: *Were you living at home?*

AND: No. I was living at the shore with another medical student. When I first got there, I worked on the beach all day and went home at night. I was kind of bored. He was volunteering at some community hospital. I wasn't going to do that. There was a big singles' bar called "The Surf Club," with 14 finger bars. It was enormous. I was having a beer there and asked them if they needed any help. I was anxious to work at night. The owner said, "As a matter of fact, we need a bouncer." By this time I weighed about 165 pounds, but I was still not Gunga Din. I asked the guy

to look at me. He said, "Number one, everyone wears casual clothes except the bartenders and bouncers who wear white shirt and tie. So, people are going to know you are a bouncer, and just that fact alone means no one is going to mess with you even though you don't look like anything. They are going to think you must know karate or something to be a bouncer. Virtually everybody that you are going to need to take care of is going to be drunk." I became a bouncer for about 1 month and then a bartender position opened up. If there's one thing better than being a bronzed lifeguard medical student, it's being a bronzed lifeguard medical student tending bar at the Surf Club with all these singles around. I had all of that going on and here's this woman I'm taking a shine to. I had noticed Lori on the beach and she seemed like a pretty classy lady and a nice person. I tried to chat her up a little bit and she didn't give me the time of day. I wanted to tell her, "Lady, don't you realize? There are 500 women who would drop dead to get a date with me. You don't seem to give a damn." Finally, by hook or by crook (I don't know how I worked it), I got a date with her and we hit it off.

WCR: *How long after that did you get married?*

AND: The next year.

WCR: *You got married after your junior year?*

AND: We got married in the summer between junior and senior year. We got engaged as my junior year in medical school was coming to an end. We thought we would get married when I graduated.

WCR: *Where was Lori going to school?*

AND: She was going to Rider College in the middle of New Jersey. That was the grand scheme. As the summer wore on, we just didn't want to wait for another year. Neither of us wanted a big wedding anyway, so we decided that we would get married and live midway between Newark (where my medical school was) and the Princeton area (where Rider was). The idea was that we were going to live in between the 2, so I'd commute about 45 minutes and she'd commute about 45 minutes. I'd finish medical school; she'd finish college. We went to our families and announced that we were going to get married. We pulled out all the stops and got married in August. The problem was that being good Catholics, Lori got pregnant instantaneously. That screwed everything up. She took a job substitute teaching instead of going back to college during my senior year at medical school. We had *Christine*. (Lori went back and finished college, when I was on the faculty at UC Davis. Her degrees are from UC Davis.) When I started my internship we had a baby already.

WCR: *When you went back to medical school to begin your junior year after the summer of relaxing, meeting Lori, etc., medical school became very attractive to you again. How did that come about?*

AND: The first 2 years of medical school were really like graduate school in biology. It was heavy basic science, the only clinical thing we did, of any kind, was Introduction to Physical Diagnosis, where we examined patients. The rest was biochemistry, physiology, and immunology, etc. After getting to the clinical rotations in the third year, I became very happy with medicine. It came pretty easily to me. I didn't have to work so hard at it. I enjoyed interacting with people. I liked the medicine part of medical school.

WCR: *When going through your rotations, did you have any idea what kind of doctor you wanted to be? As you rotated through surgery, pediatrics, medicine, and all the rest, was your decision to go into medicine easy for you?*

AND: I knew I didn't want to be a surgeon and there was nothing else that appealed to me. The need for dexterity and being in the operating room to fix things up just didn't appeal to me. I flirted a little with orthopedics. I thought orthopedics might be interesting. I got a telephone call from one of the people in medical school asking me what I was interested in. I told them orthopedics. They arranged for me to do orthopedics for one of my very first rotations. That dispelled my interest in orthopedics. I knew I wanted to do medicine, and it was just a question of what kind of medicine to do.

WCR: *Did any clinicians in your last 2 years in medical school have a particular impact on you?*

AND: *Carol Leevy*, Chairman of Medicine, a hepatologist, par excellence, was a world-class investigator. He'd lived in the Hudson County area and was very attached to it. When the medical school made the transition from Jersey City to Newark, there was a lot of disorder as you might imagine. Although a very productive researcher, he was called upon to grab the reins of the Department of Medicine through the transition period and he did.

WCR: *Were you first in your graduating class in medical school?*

AND: No. I'm sure I wasn't first. I wasn't the valedictorian speaker. For the life of me, I can't remember who was. I wasn't too far from first.

WCR: *When it came to picking an internship, how did you reason that out?*

AND: I was married and had a baby. My becoming a physician exceeded everyone's wildest expectations. I not only went to college, I went to medical school. I became a doctor. The entire neighborhood was abuzz. When it came to internship, there was a guy who really was much revered by all the medical students. His name was *Gustave Laurenzi*. He was a pulmonologist. He really made an impression. He was flamboyant, had a big mustache, had a lot of dramatic qualities, and, of course, was very smart. *Harold Jeghers*, Chairman of Medicine at the New Jersey College of Medicine, had been recruited to go to Worcester, Massachusetts, to a hospital called St. Vincent's to participate in the planning of the University of Massachusetts Medical School. He recruited Gustave Laurenzi to be the chairman there. Laurenzi went around to the students that he knew, and made a pitch to consider going to that hospital for internship. It was, to a large degree, the power of his personality coupled with my goal of going into practice. I figured I'd do an internship and residency and open an office and be a practicing doctor. Having a wife and child also was a

significant factor. The idea of going to a hospital where they had a house-staff apartment building next door was fairly attractive. Five of my classmates and I took an internship at that hospital. They filled their internship program. It was the biggest bolus they ever had gotten from 1 medical school. For me, there was a little extra in it because I already knew Worcester. I'd gone to college there. It was like going back to my college town. It was very convenient. I figured for being in private practice, it might even have an advantage because that's what private practice was all about. I made the decision and went with Laurenzi.

From the standpoint of clinical medicine, it was a great internship. We were deluged with patients and worked every other night and every other weekend. The hours were long beyond belief. The "clinical material" was everywhere. They had a solid group of very busy practitioners and they had a full-time faculty of about 12, a full-time staff in every specialty. It was a place where sick people were taken care of. Laurenzi and all the full-time people did some research. The Chief of Cardiology was *Richard Myler*, who subsequently went to San Francisco and coronary angioplasty fame.

At the end of that year, I was drafted. I applied to go into the United States Public Health Service. I initially contacted them because I was going to volunteer for an Indian reservation. I figured that would be an idyllic place. By this time my wife was pregnant again with our second child. I thought that might be an interesting way to spend 2 years because Vietnam was red hot. I had to discharge the service obligation. They came back with an opening for a medical resident in the Staten Island Public Service Hospital. I told them, "You got it." I was a resident at the Public Health Service Hospital. That turned out to be phenomenal. The hospital was busy as could be. There were many junior faculty from medical schools who had joined the faculty before the Vietnam war, but were still eligible for the draft. We were eligible until age 35. They were pulling guys out of junior faculty positions to go back in the service. There were a lot of guys who signed up to do 2 years in the Public Health Service. We had a ton of patients and we had an interesting accumulation of young academic people. We didn't have a lot of grand professors, but there were some lifetime guys who were pretty good. It was a really great experience. Of course, in Staten Island, *Tony Damato* had established a cardiac unit, where they did the first His bundle electrocardiogram. They gave birth to the field of clinical electrophysiology. There were a ton of guys going through there: *Ken Rosen, Mike Rosen, Bruce Goldreyer, John Gallagher* (a classmate of mine at Holy Cross), *Masoud Aktar*, and *Mark Josephson.*

WCR: *You finished your medical residency as a Public Health Service officer, which fulfilled your draft and also paid you reasonably well. When did you decide you wanted to become a cardiologist?*

AND: The pay wasn't great, but that's basically true. There wasn't any way Staten Island was a bonanza! It was good medical training, I was exposed to a lot of new developments going on in medicine, and I met many of the up-and-comers in cardiology. Cardiology was a huge thing at Staten Island because of all the His bundle work and the electrophysiology, etc. That tweaked my interest in cardiology. There was also some thinking that the Public Health Service might need subspecialists, particularly cardiologists. It sounded good to me and I thought maybe that was the way I ought to go.

WCR: *How did it come about that you went to Davis, California, to do your cardiology fellowship?*

AND: Another senior resident and I both decided on cardiology. As fate would have it, we were kind of desirable properties; because of our being at Staten Island, we had a fair bit of exposure to intracardiac electrophysiology when no one else had. My fellow resident interviewed at Indiana with *Charles Fisch* and was accepted into Fisch's program. Later, Fisch mentioned to *Dean Mason*, who had just gone to UC Davis to be the Division Director of Cardiology, that he had hired a senior resident from the Public Health Service and heard that there was another guy looking for a cardiology fellowship. I got a telephone call from Dean Mason who said, "I'm starting a cardiology program out here and I think you might like it. Why don't you come out and take a look?" He even offered to pay my way out. My wife got a baby sitter for the kids and we both flew out to Davis on a cold, rainy New York day in March. When we got to Davis it was sunny and warm. Dean Mason was an impressive person and we said, "Fine." We were there for 36 hours and even rented a house for our coming in July.

Because of being with Damato and all those electrophysiology guys early on, we were pretty desirable. I actually had the opportunity to go to Duke, to Yale, and to Emory. I went to Davis. That was one of the best decisions I ever made. But it was truly uninformed. A knowledgeable person probably would not have turned down the others. *Willis Hurst* also called me and offered me a job on the telephone. He'd written a big cardiology textbook by that time. I was on rounds at the Public Health Service Hospital and a nurse came up to me and said, "Dr. DeMaria, there's a Dr. Hurst from Atlanta on the phone." I thought, Holy Mackerel! But, I said "no" to all of that and went to this fledgling embryonic program in Davis. I was in the first fellowship class. Some of it was the charisma of Dean Mason. A lot of it was the attraction of being in California for the first time. It was just a gut feeling. I sat down with Dean Mason and he said to me, "What do you want to do in cardiology?" I said, "I'm going into practice. I'm going to open an office and practice on the Jersey shore where my wife lives because we like it there. We thought it might be fun to come to California for a couple of years and be trained, before we settled back East and I go into practice." That's exactly what I told him.

WCR: *This was during the interview?*

AND: Yes. It shows you what bad shape he was in; he took me anyway.

WCR: *How did he respond to that?*

AND: He didn't say much of anything. As I say, I had a zero degree of sophistication in terms of what I was doing. I turned down all the prestigious places to go to Davis. No one even knew where Davis was. I had no idea you were supposed to say that you wanted to do research. Nobody told me that. I just told him what I thought. I figured honesty was the best policy.

WCR: *Had you written any papers by that time?*

AND: No.

WCR: *Research hadn't even occurred to you yet?*

AND: Correct, not in the least. I got the intern's award during my internship. There was a competitive test in the Public Health Service Hospital and I finished on top of that also.

WCR: *Who had Dean Mason hired by the time you arrived at Davis?*

AND: He'd hired *Ezra Amsterdam* from Boston, *Rashid Massumi* from George Washington, and *Jim Spann* and *Bob Zelis*, both former colleagues of Dean's at the NIH.

WCR: *Were you the only fellow?*

AND: No. There were 3 of us.

WCR: *Who were the other 2?*

AND: *Richard Miller*, who went on to be chief of cardiology at Baylor College of Medicine in Houston and *Louis Vismara*.

WCR: *How did it work out for you at Davis?*

AND: I went there with the intention of learning how to be a cardiologist for 2 years while enjoying northern California and exploring the West Coast. Of course, the environment I was exposed to was totally research oriented. With Dean setting the agenda, I'd no sooner arrived there than I realized that the most important thing was that in September (a couple of months later) there was a deadline for research submissions to the Annual Scientific Sessions of the American College of Cardiology and what was I going to do to get some research submissions. The next most important thing was a grant deadline. I was entrained by the whole momentum of the place. Zelis and Amsterdam were junior guys who were very ambitious. Massumi, the electrophysiologist, was a very hard-driving individual. I just got swept up in it. I couldn't help but being swept up in it. I enjoyed it.

I got derailed a little bit early on. I had a basic research project where we tried to study the effect of asynchrony of contraction on intrinsic myocardial performance. I'd go to the dog lab every day. It was a brutally difficult protocol to implement. We did cardiopulmonary bypass and put a button in the mitral valve position in the dog and put a balloon in the left ventricle. I didn't like this very much. Dean Mason called me in one day and said, "I've just gotten this machine to work with that I think is going to be an important tool in cardiology. We are one of the few places that have it. I want you to take it on as your project. It's called the radarkymogram." The radarkymogram! Do you remember that? It was a device that could track an epicardial border on fluoroscopy. I had to do a fluoroscopy and get the epicardial border and put a marker on it and it would trace it. From that you were supposed to derive information about cardiac function and everything under the sun. He told me,

"That's your project." I said, "All right, Chief." I worked like crazy for about 3 months on the project. One of my first publications was a review publication on radarkymography, a little known field. I told him that the radarkymography was just a bunch of bologna. It was the epicardial area and I couldn't make much out of it, despite what the manuscript said.

While I was trying to make it work, I read a paper written by *Harvey Feigenbaum* in Indianapolis about trying to do the same thing with ultrasound. I went to Dean Mason, which is a hutzpah kind of thing, and told him that I didn't think the radarkymogram was ever going to make it, but there was a technique with ultrasound that might make it, so that we could see the inside, not the outside of the heart. I wanted to learn that. I wanted to go to Indianapolis where my buddy from the Public Health Service was. I could stay at his house and find out how to do this from Feigenbaum. Dean Mason said, "If I were you, I wouldn't waste my time with this ultrasound thing. I can tell how bad mitral stenosis is and that's all it is used for." I prevailed upon him, telling him I really wanted to do this. I felt it could amount to something. He was going to humor me and said, "I'll make a deal with you. I have a drug study that I need to get done. If you agree to do the drug study for me and get it done, then you can go to Indianapolis and I'll take some of the money from the drug study and I'll buy the echo machine." An M-mode echo only cost $10,000 in those days. I told him we had a deal. The drug study turned out to be perhexiline, which came and died because nobody could figure out how it worked. Subsequently, somebody figured out that it was a calcium channel blocker. The drug was probably a decent drug all the while.

In those days, Harvey Feigenbaum was "the king." He had people come to his lab for 1 week. He claims that I gave the title "1-week wonder" to his training program. *Walter Henry* from the NIH went there. *Rich Popp* had been a fellow under Feigenbaum. Almost anybody who was anybody in echocardiography had made a pilgrimage to Indianapolis. I went for 1 week to learn echocardiography. During the breaks, when we weren't examining patients, I read papers. Harvey had assembled every manuscript that had ever been written on cardiac ultrasound in 1 loose-leaf notebook. There were only about 10 of them plus a big symposium in *Acta Medica Scandinavia*. That was the world's literature on echocardiography! I read the world's literature in 1 week. In addition to that, Harvey had managed to get the first connection of an echo machine with a strip chart recorder. For the first time, instead of taking 1 Polaroid picture and getting a couple of beats on the picture, now he could get a strip chart that he could scan around. Holy mackerel, this was really going to amount to something!

I went back to Davis on fire with all this stuff and talked to Dean Mason. He still thought I was a bit nuts, but he was a man of his word. He got the Smith-Kline echo machine for me. The only place we could find to do echocardiography in the hospital was in physical medicine and rehabilitation. Dean managed to get room in the basement, way down in God's never-never land, to put the machine in to do echocardiography. I felt like the lone ranger. I was trying to find patients to perform echo on to get some examples and to get some practice. Everybody summarily ignored me. One day during professor's rounds, Dean saw a woman in the coronary care unit. This elderly woman had been admitted to the hospital 3 times over the course of about 8 weeks with severe unremitting chest pain, profound ST T-wave changes, and mitral regurgitation. She was old and didn't want catheterization. They were reluctant to catheterize her, because to do a coronary angiogram in 1971 was a big deal. After rounds, I got my echo machine and took it up to the coronary care unit to get an example of what an echo looks like in a patient with mitral regurgitation. Of course she had the most incredible florid flagrant hypertrophic cardiomyopathy. The next day on rounds I showed the echo and told them what she had. Dean Mason became a believer! He said, "My God. This is unbelievable." The echo showed clearly what she had and everybody else had missed. There was still a lot of skepticism. I was struggling to convince people, and 1 day Zelis called me up and said, "I know you are looking for patients. I've got a good mitral stenosis over here. It's not quite classic, but it would be a nice one for you to echo. I've scheduled her for cath." I told him to send her over. She had an atrial septal defect. From that point on, Zelis never catheterized another patient who hadn't had an echo first.

Then we applied for a big grant on disease of the muscle. I was going to do echoes in patients with muscular dystrophy. We got the NIH grant. Now I had enough money to hire a technician. Up to this point I had been everything—the sonographer, the machine washer, everything. *Alex Newman*, a PhD student, was washing glassware in the cath lab. Everybody said he was really good but was just trying to figure out what he wanted to do with his life. I didn't know him very well, but I talked to him saying, "I've got a technician position in ultrasound. It pays more than washing glassware in the cath lab." He immediately became my echo tech. The 2 of us started doing research. We wrote early papers on what nitroglycerin does to the heart, what mitral prolapse does, and Wolff-Parkinson-White, and we performed the first myocardial contrast echocardiography. We were spinning and spinning. Those were magic years. With that, Dean Mason called me and said, "You need to be on the faculty." He got me a full-time faculty position. I went home and talked to Lori, "This is kind of fun. I like this stuff. I think we ought to keep doing it." She said, "I like living here in California." I told her, "Let's keep doing it and if worse comes to worse, I can always go into practice. I'll do it for a couple of years." It was a magic time in Davis. It was a really productive place. Rich Miller was publishing like crazy. Dean was working 24 hours a day. There was a ton of stuff going on. I kept thinking that maybe I ought to go into practice. One day a guy called from Palos Verdes, California, looking for somebody to run cardiology at their hospital and asked if I would be

FIGURE 4. AND receiving a plaque from Dr. Dean T. Mason, at that time President of the American College of Cardiology, for organizing the program of the Annual Scientific Sessions the year that Dr. Mason was the College's president.

interested. I went down and interviewed for the job and they offered it to me. I was very ambivalent. I decided that I would ask for the sky—a high salary, help with my mortgage, all kinds of stuff. I would ask for the moon and if they gave it to me, then of course I couldn't turn it down. If they said they wouldn't do it, I'd stay in academics. That was the way I could resolve my ambivalence. I asked for the moon. After a while they called me to apologize for the time that had gone by. They were pleased to tell me that they would grant me everything I requested, 100% of the things I requested. At that point I realized that practice was just not what I wanted to do. I never looked back after that. I was very lucky, because I got to know Harvey Feigenbaum by being a 1-week wonder. As he taught courses and presided over meetings, I was one of the people he would include. He helped me a lot.

Of course, I owe everything to Dean (Figure 4). He was mentor par excellence. Dean was just spectacular. Harvey helped a lot. Lo and behold, after a time Dean was president of the American College of Cardiology and somebody had to run the Annual Scientific Session. He was going to have Richard Miller run it, but Rich left for Baylor to be Chief of Cardiology. Here he was, a couple of months into his presidency and didn't have anybody to run the meeting. He grabbed me and said, "You've got to be Chairman of the Annual Scientific Session for the American College of Cardiology." What the hell did I know? I was still wet behind the ears. We did it together. That year the whole program was laid out on the floor of my house. I had stacks of papers in different categories. I met a lot of people and got to know them very well. That helped.

WCR: *How did the move to Lexington come about?*

AND: That was kind of a "2 for 1." I was a pretty young guy. I was 37. They were talking to me about being Chief of Cardiology. I liked the man who was recruiting me, *John Thompson*, Chairman of Medicine. I was fascinated by the idea, so I visited there.

Then Davis had a problem with the cardiac surgical program. There was a fair amount of tension in the air at Davis. At some point in time, Dean was no longer Chief of Cardiology and they asked me to take the job. I couldn't do it. I left. Lexington was a good place to go. The Chairman of Medicine was young and energetic. He was rebuilding a department of medicine. They were enormously generous in providing a recruitment package. It was a time for me to see if I could do things my way.

WCR: *That was 1981?*

AND: Yes. Lexington is a nice town, a great place to live. By this time, my wife and I had 3 kids and we liked living in small towns. I had good reason to go there. I was flattered. I was arrogant enough to think at 37 I could run my division. I was too stupid to realize that I was probably too young to do that.

WCR: *You recruited some good people there.*

AND: Yes. I took *Steve Nissen* with me from Davis. He was a resident at Davis and had already signed up for the cardiology fellowship program there. When I left, he came with me. *John Waters* came also. After I got to Lexington, I recruited some really good people—*Tom Wisenbaugh*, a really good hemodynamist *Cindy Grines* and *Jon Elion* who did really well. A guy called me during Christmas vacation. My secretary said, "There's some fellow candidate who wants to talk to you. He happens to be visiting his in-laws in Louisville. He might want to do a fellowship at Kentucky. He wants to know if he can come over." I said, "What the hell. Things are slow. It's Christmas." *Paul Grayburn* came over to visit. I was blown away. I thought he was terrific. I quickly sent him to talk to a couple of other guys who were around. I offered him a job on the spot.

WCR: *He told me you called his home and his wife answered the telephone. She, being from Louisville, accepted for him. When he got home that night she told him where he was going for his cardiology fellowship.*

AND: That's actually the way it went down. He knew darn well when he left that he was getting the fellowship. Usually, after the interview you wait and see all the candidates and make a decision. When he was leaving, I told him not to take any other job unless he talked to me first. He must have known that he was accepted. The way, we selected fellows was that we'd get all of our applications and the faculty would sit around to discuss them at length and offer jobs. In this particular instance, I made it fairly clear to Paul that I was going to have the faculty sit around and deliberate this, but all the votes weren't going to be equal on that.

WCR: *Paul did a little bit like you did. He interned at a private hospital in Dallas, thinking he was going to go into practice.*

AND: He reminded me of myself. The thing about Paul that really gets me is that when he applied to Kentucky, he was exactly the way I was when I applied to Davis. He hadn't done a lick of research. I just knew that there was no way in God's earth he could ever get an interview at University of Texas Southwestern. *Jim Willerson* was running the program

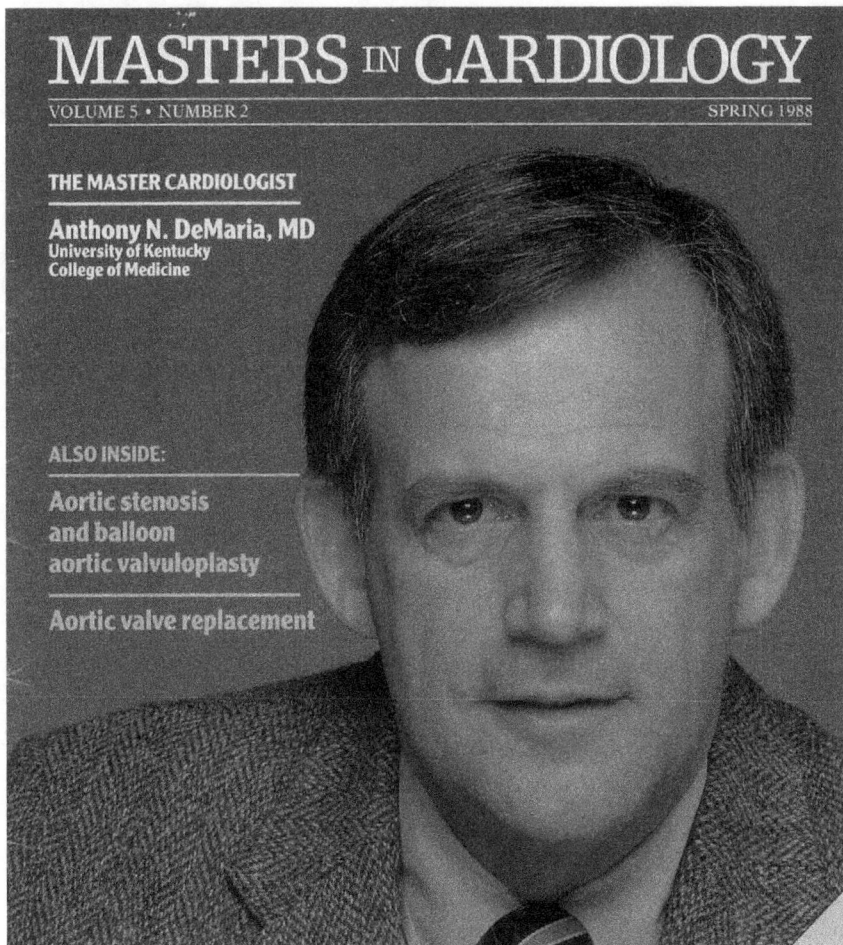

FIGURE 5. AND as a Master in Cardiology in 1988.

there and would have looked at his resume just the way he would have looked at mine. This guy comes to Lexington and I say, "You've got a job here." He comes and he trains and we work with him for 3 years, teaching him everything we knew. I said this guy is going to stay here and he's going to be a star and really build this program. Willerson, with 1 telephone call, recruited him back to Dallas. I thought that Willerson wouldn't have given him the time of day 3 or 4 years earlier. Now all of a sudden Willerson says, "You need to come back to Dallas." Grayburn went back. We lost him.

WCR: *Your experience in Lexington turned out to be a very good one?*

AND: It was a terrific experience (Figure 5). We made a name for ourselves in digital angiography. Steve Nissen started his intravascular ultrasonic imaging career there. He and I worked together very closely for 11 years. In the best tradition of mentor-student relations, the student has now surpassed the mentor. Cindy Grines did a couple of really important studies and then moved on to work with *Bill O'Neill* again. We had a pretty good clinical volume. We trained a lot of good doctors. Many went into academics for only a few years and then drifted off regrettably. That was one of my regrets. It was very hard to leave Lexington.

WCR: *How did the San Diego opportunity come about?*

AND: *John Ross* called me. The institution had recognized that they needed to strengthen the clinical program in cardiology. They were looking for someone to be Chief of Clinical Cardiology. John asked me about it. We liked Lexington, but San Diego was a bigger and more visible program and I admired John very much. The university had a lot of attraction about it, and being back in California, where we had spent 10 years earlier, helped. I went and looked at the position. I was leaning toward not going. I was happy in Lexington and was going to stay put. While I was looking, John made a decision to step down as Chief of Cardiology. That left the division head open and they made me a good offer. It was time. I stayed at Davis for 10 years; I stayed in Lexington for 11 years. It was time to move. So I recruited my assistant *Kate Greathouse*, and my lab manager, *Oi Ling Kwan*, both of whom I have worked with for >20 years and depend on greatly, to go west (Figure 6). Some people move, some people don't. I moved.

WCR: *You went to San Diego in 1992. How many faculty do you have there now in cardiology?*

AND: It's a relatively small program. We have 28 people on full-time faculty.

WCR: *How many fellows do you have?*

FIGURE 6. AND with his wife Lori and devoted assistants.

AND: It varies from year to year. We have 3 regular training positions.

WCR: *Per year?*

AND: Per year. That's 9. Then we have 2 interventional and 2 electrophysiology fellows. We have a number of people who are there just on research fellowships.

WCR: *If you take all the faculty positions and all the fellows, the secretaries, and the technicians, etc., you are talking about 150 people?*

AND: I'd think closer to 125. As of July 1, I've transitioned.

WCR: *You've stepped down as head the division of cardiovascular medicine. You are now director of the Cardiovascular Center. What is that?*

AND: Shortly after I got there, about 7 years ago, *Stuart Jamieson*, *Ken Chien*, and I wanted to have a cardiovascular center that would bring together all the people at our institution who were working in cardiovascular disease. We were spread out all over the place. We are not only in different areas—La Jolla versus the Hillcrest area of San Diego—but even within La Jolla at the Basic Science building and VA Hospital. We had approached the dean about a Cardiovascular Center to make it a comprehensive entity.

WCR: *That's across departments?*

AND: Yes. Along the way, Ken actually became head of the Institute for Molecular Medicine. There's an institute at UCSD dedicated to molecular medicine—all aspects—not only cardiology (Ken is mostly cardiology), but cancer, immunology, the whole ball of wax. He's still associated with the cardiovascular center, but not in a primary position. We formed the group. The triumvirate of *Stuart Jamison*, Chief of Cardiac Surgery and me. As a research director, we have *Kirk Knowlton*. He bridged the gap between Ken Chien and me very nicely. Kirk is an excellent research guy, but he has clinical activities as well. We were working on the center raising money.

About 8 to 10 months ago, *Ed Holmes*, the Dean, called me and said, "Listen, if you can raise $30 million, I can put in $70 million. The hospital will assume debt. Let's build a cardiovascular center and make it inpatient and outpatient. We'll focus on clin-

ical and translational research. We'll house cardiac surgery, adult cardiology, the pulmonary vascular program, pulmonary hypertension of all types a stroke program (*Pat Lyden*), all cardiovascular radiology, preventive cardiology (*Michael Criqui* from the department of preventive medicine), peripheral vascular surgery, and peripheral vascular medicine. The idea was that we would construct a building that would have inpatient and outpatient facilities and clinical research facilities (but not basic science laboratories, not hoods, not even small animals). The catheterization and electrophysiology labs would have adequate backup space so investigators could tie them up doing a research study. It's not just a hospital. It will have all the clinical facilities that you would want to have available to do research projects—appropriate space for noninvasive imaging, cardiovascular, radiology, electrophysiology cath, or whatever you want for clinical research.

Ed Holmes thought it was a full-time job. It's probably close to that. More importantly, this position will oversee adjudication resources—how is space allotted, how are offices allocated, how is priority for hospital beds decided. Those issues on space and money required, in Ed Holmes' opinion, and which I couldn't disagree with, that someone had to be free of a vested interest in those decisions. The question was what did I want to do? I thought it was a neat challenge to build a cardiovascular center, and one that would fit in very well with my lifestyle at this point in time. Being Editor of the *Journal of the American College of Cardiology* obviously occupies a lot of my effort. The Dean and I negotiated a bit and came to an amicable agreement. As of July, I have accepted that responsibility. Kirk Knowlton will assume the duties of Chief of Cardiology. The goal is to have the building up and running in 4 years. It should take us 1 year to plan it out and another 2 to 3 to get it built.

WCR: *How are you enjoying the editorship of the* Journal of the American College of Cardiology?

AND: I love it. It's been a great privilege to have that opportunity. It is a unique opportunity to influence what people read, and therefore, perhaps what they think. We have a sacred responsibility to the authors to treat their work with the respect that they put into it. I feel like I have my finger on the pulse of cardiology. Anything that is going on is being submitted, and usually substantially before it surfaces as something important. It's a learning experience. It's an opportunity to influence my profession. It's gives me a certain creative opportunity in writing editor's pages and making decisions on how to put manuscripts together and organize them in certain ways. It's been a challenge in handling this transition from a purely paper journal to one that's now paper and on-line, and will be progressively on-line.

WCR: *What were some surprises you as you took over the editorship?*

AND: I really hadn't anticipated the degree of serendipity that's involved in what gets accepted for publication and what doesn't. We always joked from my earliest days with Dean Mason that the biggest variable was the reviewer. I fully anticipated that we were going to have to allot for variability on the part of a reviewer, but even with that I have been amazed at the frequency with which critiques are opposite. In addition to reviewer variation are other things that come into play. We went back for a period of 1 year and found that in just <40% of our manuscripts, 1 reviewer ranked it in the top 2 (of 5) categories and the other rejected it. That was in almost 40% of the manuscripts. I was totally unprepared for that much divergence in the way 2 learned clinicians would assess a given manuscript. The reality of the volume and timelines of work have also been striking. Every day, more manuscripts turn up. It's got to be handled in a timely fashion. It's not something you can put on the side. The camaraderie with the associate editors has been an unexpected side benefit. Working with *Ori Ben-Yehuda, Wilbur Lew, Sam Tsimikas, Greg Feld, Kirk Knowlton, and Barry Greenberg* has bonded us closely.

WCR: *I guess you get the question a lot and I've gotten it a lot through the years: How much time do you spend a week on the Journal of the American College of Cardiology?*

AND: About 25 hours a week. It varies up and down. This week I won't spend any. In an average week I usually dedicate 11/2 entire weekend days at least, and usually a bit more to just doing journal things. I dedicate about 1 working day during the week to preparing and handling our weekly meeting, and then there's a couple of hours each day depending on different days. Nobody works a 40-hour week in our business. We're in a competitive business being editors in this day and age. If you and I are competing for the best papers, then one of the things we sell is rapid response. One thing we have not talked about is probably worth talking about. Part of my years in Lexington was being President of the American College of Cardiology. I had come to that position by Dean Mason making me the Scientific Sessions program chairman and then I got involved a lot in the Government Relations Committee and private sector relations. At a relatively young age (I think I was the youngest president ever), I got the opportunity to be president. When they called me and asked me if I was willing to be nominated, I said, "I'm too young for this, but, on the other hand, you may never ask me again." I went and did it.

WCR: *You were how old?*

AND: I was 45 when I was president (1988 to 1989), but I was nominated at age 42. That was a marvelous experience. The year I was president we laid the foundation in a major way for some of the advocacy programs, which I think have been very meaningful to clinical cardiologists, while preserving the important educational mission and the support for scholarship. I had the opportunity to travel for the college. It's a bit of a bully pulpit to tell people what you think cardiology should be like in those President's Pages. I found that thoroughly enjoyable. If you had told me when I sat in front of Dean Mason, or even when I graduated medical school, "You know

what? You're graduating from New Jersey College of Medicine. Someday you're going to be president of the echo society, president of the American College of Cardiology, and the Editor of the *Journal of the American College of Cardiology*." I would have told you, "You've got to be out of your mind. That could never happen."

WCR: *Of all the things you've done professionally, what are you most proud of?*

AND: The people I've trained. Of the people I've had a chance to influence, some are famous—Steve Nissen and Paul Grayburn. Many are important people in medical schools—*Bill Bommer* at Davis, *Michael Smith* at Kentucky, *Ari Ben Yehuda, Ajit Raisinghani, Shami Mahmud,* and *Sam Tsimikas* here at UCSD. I've trained many foreign physicians. I've had the opportunity to have colleagues from countries around the world who've worked in the lab for 1 or 2 years and gone on to be major investigators. Far and away, that's been the thing I've enjoyed the most. I most enjoy when fellows write their first papers and hold them in their hands. It doesn't get much better than that.

WCR: *What happened to your 3 sisters?*

AND: Two are single and still live in New Jersey. Adele is in business and Carol is a schoolteacher. My oldest sister *Barbara Hupe* lives in Houston, Texas now. She's also a schoolteacher. Her husband died an untimely death of a brain tumor.

WCR: *So 2 of the 3 are teachers?*

AND: Right.

WCR: *Did all 3 go to college?*

AND: Yes.

WCR: *That's quite remarkable.*

AND: Especially for my sisters, because the philosophy at the time was men needed to go to college, but for women, it was a luxury. They went.

WCR: *Tell me about your immediate family.*

AND: My wife is the best thing about me. Everybody likes Lori. She's marvelous. We have been partners in everything I've done, including the new UCSD Cardiovascular Center. She's wise, insightful, and a tower of strength.

WCR: *What was her premarital name?*

AND: *Horn.* We've been married 37 years now. I've been very fortunate. That's the best decision I ever made in my life. Going to Davis was the second best. Doing echocardiography was probably my third best decision. Our oldest daughter *Christine* describes herself as a recovering lawyer, who is now getting a PhD in sociology. She and her husband Matt have a son, Jackson, and are having a second child. Christine went to the University of Kentucky Law School. Our middle child *Anthony* is a very successful lawyer in Fresno, California. He and his wife Kim have 3 children, Alec, Blake, and Cameron. He's phenomenally successful. He wins almost all his cases. He did very well in law school at USD Law School. Our son *Jonathan* is involved in a number of different activities. He's very bright but hasn't quite decided where he wants his career path to go yet (Figures 7 and 8).

FIGURE 7. AND and his wife and three offspring.

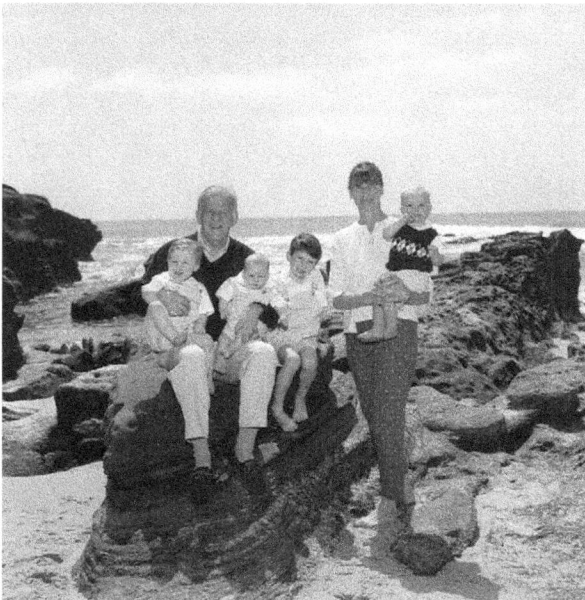

FIGURE 8. AND and his wife with their grandchildren.

WCR: *Is there anything you'd like to talk about that we have neglected to talk about?*

AND: Two of my favorite stories. The first story happened when I was at Davis, my father called me and said, "Anthony, I've got to talk to you man to man. The people around the neighborhood are beginning to ask questions. How come Anthony is hanging around the medical school so long? It's getting embarrassing. They wonder if you haven't finished?" I told him, "Dad, I'm not going to do practice. I'm going to be an academic." He said, "Anthony, you've got a wife and 2 kids. You've got to stop fooling around here. I'm calling you to tell you this very day that *Dr. Fabrielle*, who used to be on 46th and Avenue C, died, and his wife came in to tell me that you can have the practice if you want it." I told him, "Dad, I'm going to stay at the medical school."

The second story. When as President of the American College of Cardiology, I invited my mother to come to the annual meeting. (The College lets the president bring their family to see their child conduct the meeting at the Convocation.) The meeting was in Anaheim. They flew my mother to Los Angeles and put her in a limo, and brought her to the hotel in Anaheim. I got a call that my mother was at the hotel. I went to the lobby to meet her. I said, "Mom, welcome. How're you doing?" She said, "I'm fine. I'm fine." Very soon she asked, "Where's the telephone? I've got to make a telephone call." I was taken aback. She called her best friend, *Rose Yazwinski*, and said, "Rose, you're not going to believe this. They had a car just for me, a very big one! Rose, you could put 4 or 5 people in the car. I was the only one in it." I honestly believe that that limo made my mother think that maybe I'd done all right. And all those years they suspected that I just couldn't quite make it out of medical school!

WCR: *Tony, many thanks for pouring your soul out. It was great.*

MOST IMPORTANT PUBLICATIONS SELECTED BY AND

1. Massumi RA, Mason DT, Amsterdam EA, DeMaria AN, Miller RR, Scheinman MM, Zelis R. Ventricular fibrillation and tachycardia after intravenous atropine for treatmentof bradycardias. *N Engl J Med* 1972;287:336–338.
14. DeMaria AN, King JF, Bogren HG, Lies JE, Mason DT. The variable spectrum of echocardiographic manifestations of the mitral valve syndrome. *Circulation* 1974;50:33–41.
15. DeMaria AN, Vera Z, Amsterdam EA, Mason DT, Massumi RA. Disturbances of cardiac rhythm and conduction inducted by exercise: diagnostic, prognostic and therapeutic implications. *Am J Cardiol* 1974;33:732–736.
16. DeMaria AN, Vismara LA, Auditore K, Amsterdam EA, Zelis R, Mason DT. Effects of nitroglycerin on left ventricular cavitary size and cardiac performance determined by ultrasound in man. *Am J Med* 1974;57:754–760.
18. DeMaria AN, King JF, Salel AF, Caudill CC, Miller RR, Mason DT. Echography and phonography of acute aortic regurgitation in bacterial endocarditis. *Ann Intern Med* 1975;82:329–335.
20. DeMaria AN, Lies JE, King JF, Miller RR, Amsterdam EA, Mason DT. Echocardiographic assessment of atrial transport, mitral movement, and ventricular performance following electroversion of supraventricular arrhythmias. *Circulation* 1975;51:273–282.
21. DeMaria AN, Vismara LV, Miller RR, Neumann A, Mason DT. Unusual echographic manifestations of right and left heart myxomas. *Am J Med* 1975;59:713–720.
31. DeMaria AN. The syndrome of mitral valve prolapse: problems and perspectives. *Ann Intern Med* 1976;85(4):525–526.
32. DeMaria AN, Amsterdam EA, Vismara LA, Neumann A, Mason DT. Arrhythmias in the mitral valve prolapse syndrome: prevalence, nature and frequency. *Ann Interm Med* 1976;84:656–660.
33. DeMaria AN, Miller RR, Amsterdam EA, Markson W, Mason DT. Mitral valve early diastolic closing velocity in the echocardiogram: relation to sequential diastolic flow and ventricular compliance. *Am J Cardiol* 1976;37:693–700.
36. DeMaria AN, Vera Z, Neumann A, Mason DT. Alterations in ventricular contraction pattern in the Wolff-Parkinson-White syndrome: detection by echocardiography. *Circulation* 1976;53:249–257.
59. DeMaria AN, Neumann A, Lee G, Mason DT. Echocardiographic identification of the mitral valve prolapse syndrome. *Am J Cardiol* 1977;62:819–29.
97. DeMaria AN, Neumann A, Lee G, Fowler W, Mason DT. Alterations in ventricular mass and performance induced by exercise training in man evaluated by echocardiography. *Circulation* 1978;57:237–244.
101. DeMaria AN, Oliver LE, Bogren HG, George L, Mason DT. Apparent reduction of aortic and left heart chamber size in atrial septal defect. *Am J Cardiol* 1978;42:545–550.
119. Sahn DJ, DeMaria AN, Kisslo J, Weyman A. Recommendations regarding quantitation in M-mode echocardiography: results of a survey of echocardiographic measurements. *Circulation* 1978;58(6):1072–1083.
125. DeMaria AN, Bommer W, Neumann A, Weinert L, Bogren H, Mason DT. Identification and localization of aneurysms of the ascending aorta by cross-sectional echocardiography. *Circulation* 1979;59:755–761.
129. DeMaria AN, Neumann A, Bommer W, Weinert L, Grehl T, Amsterdam EA, Mason DT. Left ventricular thrombi by cross-sectional echocardiography. *Ann Inten Med* 1979;90:14–18.
130. DeMaria AN, Neumann A, Schubart PJ, Lee G, Mason DT. Systemic correlation of cardiac chamber size and ventricular performance determined with echocardiography and alterations in heart rate in normal persons. *Am J Cardiol* 1979;43:1–9.

148. DeMaria AN, Bommer W, Joye JA, Lee G, Bouteller J, Mason DT. Value and limitations of cross-sectional echocardiography of the aortic valve in the diagnosis and quantification of valvular aortic stenosis. *Circulation* 1980;62:304–312.

150. DeMaria AN, Bommer W, Lee G, Mason DT. Value and limitations of two-dimensional echocardiography in assessment of cardiomyopathy. *Am J Cardiol* 1980;46:1224–1231.

185. Low RI, Takeda P, Lee G, Mason DT, Awan NA, DeMaria AN. Effects of diltiazem-induced calcium blockade upon exercise capacity in effort angina due to chronic coronary artery disease. *Am Heart J* 1981;101:713–718.

195. Woythaler JN, Singer SL, Kwan OL, Meltzer RS, Reubner B, Bommer W, DeMaria AN. Accuracy of echocardiography versus electrocardiography in detecting left ventricular hypertrophy: comparison with post-mortem mass measurements. *J Am Coll Cardiol* 1982;2:305–311.

200. Nissen SE, Booth D, Waters J, Fassas T, DeMaria AN. Evaluation of left ventricular contractile pattern by intravenous digital subtraction ventriculography: comparison with cineangiography and assessment of interobserver variability. *Am J Cardiol* 1983;52(10):1293–1298.

204. DeMaria AN, Bommer W, Kwan OL, Riggs K, Smith MD, Waters J. In vivo correlation of thermodilution cardiac output and videodensitometric indicator-dilution curves obtained from contrast two-dimensional echocardiograms. *J Am Coll Cardiol* 1984;3:999–1004.

207. Johnson GL, Kwan OL, Cottrill CM, DeMaria AN. Detection and quantitation of right ventricular outlet obstruction secondary to aneurysm of the membranous ventricular septum by combined two-dimensional echocardiography: continuous-wave Doppler ultrasound. *Am J Cardiol* 1984;53:1476–1477.

208. Johnson GL, Kwan OL, Handshoe S , Noonan J, DeMaria AN. Accuracy of combined two-dimensional echocardiography and continuous wave Doppler recording in the estimation of pressure gradient in right ventricular outlet obstruction. *J Am Coll Cardiol* 1984;3:1013–1018.

213. Smith MD, Kwan OL, Reiser HJ, DeMaria AN. Superior intensity and reproducibility of SHU-454, a new right heart contrast agent. *J Am Coll Cardiol* 1984;3:992–998.

219. Friedman BJ, Waters JS, Kwan OL, DeMaria AN. Comparison of magnetic resonance imaging and echocardiography in determination of cardiac dimensions in normals. *J Am Coll Cardiol* 1985;5:1369–1376.

221. Smith MD, Dawson PL, Elion JL, Booth DC, Handshoe R, Kwan OL, Earle GF, DeMaria AN. Correlation of continuous wave Doppler velocities with cardiac catheterization gradients: an experimental model of aortic stenosis. *J Am Coll Cardiol* 1985;6:1306–1314.

229. Friedman BJ, Drinkovic N, Miles H, Shih WJ, Mazzoleni A, DeMaria AN. Assessment of left ventricular diastolic function: comparison of Doppler echocardiography and gated blood pool scintigraphy. *J Am Coll Cardiol* 1986;8(6):1348–1354.

230. Grayburn PA, Smith MD, Handshoe R, Friedman BJ, Handshoe S, DeMaria AN. Comparative accuracy of pulsed Doppler, echo and auscultation in the detection of aortic insufficiency. *Ann Int Med* 1986;l04:599–605.

235. Nissen SE, Elion JL, Booth DC, Evans J, DeMaria AN. Value and limitations of computer analysis of digital subtraction angiography in the assessment of coronary flow reserve. *Circulation* 1986;73:562–571.

240. Smith MD, Handshoe R, Handshoe S, Kwan OL, DeMaria AN. Comparative accuracy of 2-D echocardiography and Doppler pressure half-time methods in assessing severity of mitral stenosis in patients with and without prior commissurotomy. *Circulation* 1986;73:100–107.

241. Smith MD, Kwan OL, DeMaria AN. Value and limitations of continuous-wave Doppler echocardiography in estimating severity of valvular stenosis. *JAMA* 1986;255:3145–3151.

244. Wisenbaugh T, Nissen S, DeMaria AN. Mechanics of postextrasystolic potentiation in normal subjects and patients with valvular heart disease. *Circulation* 1986;74:10–20.

248. DeMaria AN, Wisenbaugh TW. Identification and treatment of diastolic dysfunction: role of transmitral Doppler recordings. *J Am Coll Cardiol* 1987;9:1106–1107.

251. Grayburn PA, Handshoe R, Smith MD, Harrison MR, DeMaria AN. Quantitative assessment of the hemodynamic consequences of aortic regurgitation by means of continuous wave Doppler recordings. *J Am Coll Cardiol* 1987;10:135–141.

252. Grayburn PA, Nissen SE, Elion JL, Evans J, DeMaria AN. Quantitation of aortic regurgitation by computer analysis of digital subtraction angiography. *J Am Coll Cardiol* 1987;10:1122–1127.

253. Grayburn PA, Smith MD, Gurley JC, Booth DC, DeMaria AN. Effect of aortic regurgitation on the assessment of mitral valve orifice area by Doppler pressure half-time. *Am J Cardiol* 1987;60:322–326.

260. Nissen SE, Elion JL, Grayburn P, Booth DC, Wisenbaugh TW, DeMaria AN. Determination of left ventricular ejection fraction by computer densitometric analysis of digital subtraction angiography: experimental validation and correlation with area-length methods. *Am J Cardiol* 1987;59:675–680.

263. Rovai D, Nissen SE, Elion JL, Smith MD, L'Abbate A, Kwan OL, DeMaria AN. Contrast echo washout curves application of basic principles of indicator dilution theory and calculation of ejection fraction. *J Am Coll Cardiol* 1987;10:125–134.

273. Gillespie MN, Booth DC, Friedman BJ, Cunningham MR, Jay M, DeMaria AN. fMLP provokes coronary vasoconstriction and myocardial ischemia in rabbits. *Am J Physiol* 1988;254:H481–H486.

274. Grayburn PA, Smith MD, Harrison MR, Gurley JC, DeMaria AN. Pivotal role of aortic valve area calculation by the continuity equation for Doppler assessment of aortic stenosis in patients with combined aortic stenosis and regurgitation. *Am J Cardiol* 1988;61:376–381.

275. Gurley JC, Nissen SE, Booth DC, Harrison M, Grayburn P, Elion JL, DeMaria AN. Comparison of simultaneously performed digital and film-based angiography in the assessment of coronary artery disease. *Circulation* 1988;78(6):1411–1420.

279. Harrison MR, Smith MD, Nissen SE, Grayburn PA, DeMaria AN. Use of exercise Doppler to evaluate cardiac drugs: effects of propranolol and verapamil on aortic blood flow velocity and acceleration. *J Am Coll Cardiol* 1988;1(5):1002–1009.

289. DeMaria AN, Smith MD, Harrison MR. Clinical significance of in-vitro and in-vivo experimental findings regarding Doppler flow velocity recordings. *J Am Coll Cardiol* 1989;13:1682–1686.

291. Grines CL, Nissen SE, Booth DC, Branco MC, Gurley JC, Bennett KA, DeMaria AN, KAMIT Study Group. A new thrombolytic regimen for acute myocardial infarction using half dose tissue plasminogen activator with full dose streptokinase. *J Am Coll Cardiol* 1989;14(3):573–580.

293. Harrison MR, Clifton GD, Sublett KL, DeMaria AN. Effect of heart rate on Doppler indexes of systolic function in humans. *J Am Coll Cardiol* 1989;14(4):929–935.

296. Rovai D, L'Abbate A, Lombardi M, Nissen SE, Marzilli M, Distante A, Ferdeghini EM, DeMaria AN. Nonuniformity of the transmural distribution of coronary blood flow during the cardiac cycle. In-vivo documentation by contrast echocardiography. *Circulation* 1989;79(1):179–187.

297. Smith MD, Kwan OL, Elion JL, McClure R, DeMaria AN. Left heart opacification with peripheral venous injection of a new saccharide echo contrast agent in dogs. *J Am Coll Cardiol* 1989;13:1622–1628.

299. Spain MG, Smith MD, Graybum PA, Harlamert EA, O'Brien M, DeMaria AN. Quantitative assessment of mitral regurgitation by Doppler color flow imaging: angiographic and hemodynamic correlations. *J Am Coll Cardiol* 1989;13:585–590.

300. Wisenbaugh TW, Harlamert EA, DeMaria AN. Relation of left ventricular filling dynamics to alterations in load and compliance in patients with and without pressure-overload hypertrophy. *Circulation* 1989;1(1):101–106.

303 Berk MR, Xie G, Kwan OL, Knapp C, Evans J, Kotchen T, Kotchen JM, DeMaria AN. Reduction of left ventricular preload by lower body negative pressure alters Doppler transmitral filling patterns. *J Am Coll Cardiol* 1990;16(6):1387–1392.

308. Garrahy PG, Kwan OL, Booth DC, DeMaria AN. Assessment of abnormal systolic intraventricular flow patterns by Doppler imaging in patients with left ventricular dyssynergy. *Circulation* 1990;82:95–104.

310. Grines CL, Booth DC, Nissen SE, Gurley JC, Bennett KA, O'Connor WN, DeMaria AN. Mechanism of acute myocardial infarction in patients with prior coronary artery bypass grafting and therapeutic implications. *Am J Cardiol* 1990;65:1292–1296.

312. Gurley JC, Nissen SE, Elion JL, Booth DC, DeMaria AN. Determination of coronary flow reserve by digital angiography: validation of a practical method not requiring power injection or electrocardiographic gating. *J Am Coll Cardiol* 1990;16:190–197.

313. Nissen SE, Grines CL, Gurley JC, Sublett KL, Haynie DP, Diaz C, Booth DC, DeMaria AN. Application of a new phased-array ultrasound imaging catheter in the assessment of vascular dimensions: in-vivo comparison to cineangiography. *Circulation* 1990;81:660–666.

320. Grines CL, Booth DC, Nissen SE, Gurley JC, Bennett KA, DeMaria AN. Acute effects of parenteral beta-blockade on regional ventricular function of infarct and noninfarct zones after reperfusion therapy in humans. *J Am Coll Cardiol* 1991;17:1382–1387.

323. Grines CL, Nissen ST, Booth DC, Gurley JC, Chelliah N, Wolf R, Blankenship J, Branco MC, Bennett K, DeMaria AN, Kentucky Acute Myocardial Infarction Trial (KAMIT) Group. A prospective, randomized trial comparing combination half-dose tissue-type plasminogen activator and streptokinase with full-dose tissue-type plasminogen activator. *Circulation* 1991;84:540–549.

325. Harrison MR, Clifton GD, Pennell AT, DeMaria AN. Effect of heart rate on left ventricular diastolic transmitral flow velocity patterns assessed by Doppler echocardiography in normal subjects. *Am J Cardiol* 1991;67:622–627.

329. Nissen SE, Gurley JC, Grines CL, Booth DC, McClure R, Berk M, Fischer C, DeMaria AN. Intravascular ultrasound assessment of lumen size and wall morphology in normal subjects and patients with coronary artery disease. *Circulation* 1991;84:1087–1099.

330. Smith MD, Harrison MR, Pinton R, Kandil H, Kwan OL, DeMaria AN. Regurgitant jet size by transesophageal compared with transthoracic Doppler flow imaging. *Circulation* 1991;83:79–86.

338. King DL, Harrison MR, King D Jr, Gopal AS, Kwan OL, DeMaria AN. Ultrasound beam orientation during standard two-dimensional imaging: assessment by three-dimensional echocardiography. *J Am Soc Echocardiogr* 1992;5(6):569–576.

339. King DL, Harrison MR, King D Jr, Gopal AS, Martin R, DeMaria AN. Improved reproducibility of left atrial and left ventricular measurements by guided three-dimensional echocardiography. *J Am Coll Cardiol* 1992;20(5):1238–1245.

342. Rovai D, Ghelardini G, Lombardi M, Trivella MG, Nevola E, Taddei L, Michelassi C, Distante A, DeMaria AN. Myocardial washout of sonicated iopamidol reflects coronary blood flow in the absence of autoregulation. *J Am Coll Cardiol* 1992;20(6):1417–1424.

355. Brotheron T, Pollard T, Simpson P, DeMaria AN. Classifying tissue and structure in echocardiograms: hierarchy of fuzzy-logic based neural networks automate analysis. *Engineering Med Bio* 1994;13(5):754–759.

359. Xie GY, Berk MR, Smith MD, DeMaria AN. A simplified method for determining regurgitant fraction by Doppler echocardiography in patients with aortic regurgitation. *J Am Coll Cardiol* 1994;24(4):l041–1045.

360. Xie GY, Berk MR, Smith MD, Gurley JC, DeMaria AN. Prognostic value of Doppler transmitral flow patterns in patients with congestive heart failure. *J Am Coll Cardiol* 1994;24(I):132–139.

368. Nozaki S, DeMaria AN, Helmer GA, Hammond HK. Detection of regional left ventricular dysfunction in early pacing-induced heart failure using ultrasonic integrated backscatter. *Circulation* 1995;92:2676–2682.

378. DeMaria AN, Lee TH, Leon DF, Ullyot DJ, Wolk MJ, Mills PS, Fay SC, Brown JH, Flatau CN, Bodycombe DP. Effect of managed care on cardiovascular specialists: involvement, attitudes and practice adaptations. *J Am Coll Cardiol* 1996;28(7):1884–1895.

379. Giordano F, Ping P, McKirnan MD, Nozaki S, DeMaria AN, Dillman W, Mathieu-Costello O, Hammond HK. Intracoronary gene transfer of fibroblast growth factor-5 increases blood flow and contractile function in an ischemic region of the heart. *Nature Med* 1996;2(5):534–539.

382. Kimura BJ, Russo RJ, Bhargava V, McDaniel M, Peterson KL, DeMaria AN. Atheroma morphology and distribution in proximal left anterior descending coronary artery: in vivo observations. *J Am Coll Cardiol* 1996;27(4):825–831.

386. Yamagishi M, Nissen SE, Booth DC, Gurley JC, Koyama J, Kawano S, DeMaria AN. Coronary reactivity to nitroglyerin: intravascular ultrasound evidence for the importance of plaque distribution. *J Am Coll Cardiol* 1996;25:224–230.

398. Ohmori K, Cotter B, Kwan OL, Mizushige K, DeMaria AN. Relation of contrast echo intensity and flow velocity to the amplification of contrast opacification produced by intermittent ultrasound transmission. *Am Heart J* 1997;134(6):1066–1074.

406. Galiuto L, Ignone G, DeMaria AN. Heterogeneity of contraction and relaxation velocities of normal human myocardium. A quantitative study using pulsed wave tissue Doppler echocardiography. *Am J Cardiol* 1998;81(5):609–614.

415. Yasu T, Schmid-Schonbein GW, Cotter B, DeMaria AN. Flow dynamics of QW7437, a new dodecafluoropentane ultrasound contrast agent, in the microcirculation: microvascular mechanisms for persistent tissue echo enhancement. *J Am Coll Cardiol* 1999;34(2):578–586.

423. Kimura BJ, Scott R, Willis CL, DeMaria AN. Accuracy and cost-effectiveness of single-view echocardiographic screening for suspected mitral valve prolapse. *Am J Med* 2000;108:331–333.

424. Masugata H, Cotter B, Peters B, Ohmori K, Mizushige K, DeMaria AN. Assessment of coronary stenosis severity and transmural perfusion gradient by myocardial contrast echocardiography: comparison of gray scale B-mode with power Doppler imaging. *Circulation* 2000;102:1427–1433.

432. Kimura BJ, Bocchicchio M, Willis CL, DeMaria AN. Screening cardiac ultrasonographic examination in patients with suspected cardiac disease in the emergency department. *Am Heart J* 2001;142(2):324–330.

434. Lafitte S, Masugata H, Peters B, Togni M, Strachan M, Kwan OL, DeMaria AN. Comparative value of dobutamine and adenosine stress in the detection of coronary stenosis with myocardial contrast echocardiography. *Circulation* 2001;103:2724–2730.

435. Laffite S, Masugata H, Peters B, Togni M, Strachan M, Yao B, Kwan OL, DeMaria AN. Accuracy and reproducibility of coronary flow rate assessment by real time contrast echocardiography: in vitro and in vivo studies. *J Am Soc Echocardiogr* 2001;14:1010–1019.

436. Leistad E, Ohmori K, Peterson TA, Christensen G, DeMaria AN. Quantitative assessment of myocardial perfusion during graded coronary artery stenoses by intravenous myocardial contrast echocardiography. *J Am Coll Cardiol* 2001;37:624–631.

437. Mahmud E, Raisinghani A, Keramati S, Auger W, Blanchard DG, DeMaria AN. Dilation of the coronary sinus on echocardiogram: prevalence and signifi-cance in patients with chronic pulmonary hypertension. *J Am Soc Echocardiogr* 2001;14:44–49.

438. Maisel AS, Koon J, Krishnaswamy P, Kasenegra R, Clopton P, Gardetto N, Morrissey R, DeMaria A. Utility of B-natriuretic peptide (BNP) as a rapid, point of care test for screening patients undergoing echocardiography for left ventricular dysfunction. *Am Heart J* 2001;141:367–374.

440. Masugata H, Lafitte S, Peters B, Strachan GM, DeMaria AN. Comparison of real-time and intermittent triggered myocardial contrast echocardiography for quantification of coronary stenosis severity and transmural perfusion gradient. *Circulation* 2001;104:1550–1556.

442. Masugata H, Peters B, Lafitte S, Strachan GM, Ohmori K, DeMaria AN. Quantitative assessment of myocardial perfusion during graded coronary stenosis by rReal-time myocardial cContrast echo refilling curves. *J Am Coll Cardiol* 2001;37:262–269.

443. Ohmori K, Cotter B, Leistad E, Bhargava V, Wolf PL, Mizushige K, DeMaria AN. Assessment of myocardial reperfusion by intravenous myocardial contrast echocardiography: analysis of the intensity and texture of opacification. *Circulation* 2001;103:2021–2027.

458. Kimura BJ, Amundson SA, Willis CL, Gilpin EA, DeMaria AN. Usefulness of a hand-held ultrasound device for bedside examination of left ventricular function. *Am J Cardiol* 2002;90:1038–1039.

460. Lafitte S, Higashiyama A, Masugata H, Peters B, Strachan M, Kwan OL, DeMaria AN. Contrast echocardiography can assess risk area and infarct size during coronary occlusion and reperfusion: experimental validation. *J Am Coll Cardiol* 2002;39(9):1546–1554.

461. Lubien E, DeMaria AN, Krishnaswamy P, Clopton P, Koon J, Kazanegra R, Gardetto N, Wanner E, Maisel AS. Utility of B-natriuretic peptide in detecting diastolic dysfunction: comparison with Doppler velocity recordings. *Circulation* 2002;105:595–601.

464. Raisinghani A, Mahmud E, Sadeghi M, Peters B, Strachan GM, Huynh T, Blanchard D, DeMaria AN. Paradoxical inferior-posterior wall systolic expansion in patients with end-stage liver disease. *Am J Cardiol* 2002;89:626–629.

477. Kimura BJ, DeMaria AN. Time requirements of the standard echocardiogram: implications regarding limited studies. *J Am Soc Echocardiogr* 2003; 16(10):1015–1018.

478. Kimura BJ, Fowler SJ, Nguyen DT, Amundson SA, DeMaria AN. Detection of early carotid arterial atherosclerosis by briefly trained physicians using a hand-held ultrasound device. *Am J Cardiol* 2003;92(2):239–240.

480. Kunichika H, Peters B, Cotter B, Masugata H, Kunichika N, Wolf PL, DeMaria AN. Visualization of risk-area myocardium as a high-intensity, hyperenhanced "hot spot" by myocardial contrast echocardiography following coronary reperfusion. *J Am Coll Cardiol* 2003;42(3):552–557.

482. Masugata H, Fujita N, Kondo I, Peters B, Ohmori K, Mizushige K, Kohno M, DeMaria AN. Assessment of right ventricular perfusion after right coronary artery occlusion. *J Am Coll Cardiol* 2003;41(10):1823–1830.

484. Raisinghani A, Wei K, Crouse LJ, Villanueva F, Feigenbaum H, Schiller NB, Weiss J, Zaqvi TZ, Siegel R, Monaghan M, Goldman JH, DeMaria AN. Myocardial contrast echocardiography with triggered ultrasound does not cause ventricular premature beats: evidence from PB127 studies. *J Am Soc Echocardiogr* 2003;10:1037–1042.

485. Wei K, Crouse L, Weiss J, Villanueva F, Schiller NB, Naqvi TZ, Siegel R, Monaghan M, Goldman J, Aggarwal P, Feigenbaum H, DeMaria A. Comparison of usefulness of dipyridamole stress myocardial contrast echocardiography to technetium-99m sestamibi single-photon emission computed tomography for detection of coronary artery disease (PB127 multicenter Phase 2 trial Results). *Am J Cardiol* 2003;91:1293–1298.

488. Nissen SE, Tuzeu EM, Schoenhagen P, Brown BG, Ganz P, Vogel RA, Crowe T, Howard G, Cooper CJ, Brodie B, Grines CL, DeMaria AN. Effect of intensive compared with moderate lipid-lowering therapy on progression of coronary atherosclerosis—a randomized controlled trial. *JAMA* 2004;291(9): 1071–1080.

JESSE EFREM EDWARDS, MD:
A Conversation With the Editor*

The first time I heard the name Jesse Edwards was in July 1959 shortly after I had come to the National Institutes of Health (NIH) in Bethesda, Maryland. Dr. Louis Thomas, who was in the Laboratory of Pathology of the National Cancer Institute and had trained in anatomic pathology at the Mayo Clinic, recommended that I read some of Dr. Edwards' writings. I was new at the NIH and within a few weeks of arriving found myself doing virtually all of the autopsies on patients from the National Heart Institute. At the time, most cases were either congenital heart disease or valvular heart disease. The Pathology Department of the Clinical Center of the NIH was actually located at that time in the National Cancer Institute, and, therefore, the faculty pathologists focused primarily on cancer, not heart disease. I was interested in the latter. Fortunately, I found the writings by Jesse Edwards to be enormously useful. Before 1959 was out, I had read virtually every one of his publications on cardiovascular disease and also his 1954 *Atlas of Congenital Anomalies of the Heart and Great Vessels* which had been introduced to me by Dr. Andrew Glenn Morrow, who was head of the Surgery Branch of the National Heart Institute and later the person who gave me my first permanent position at NIH. Jesse Edwards had also written the section on congenital heart disease in Gould's *Pathology of the Heart,* which was the most used book on morphologic aspects of heart disease at the time. Dr. Edwards' portion of that book on heart disease occupied nearly 300 pages and it soon became my Bible. Every time I did an autopsy on a patient with tetralogy of Fallot, for example, I reread Jesse Edwards' chapter on tetralogy of Fallot. It was not long before I had most of his chapters nearly memorized. Every cardiovascular subject I encountered for the next several years I first sought Jesse Edwards' writing on the topic before I went elsewhere. Thus, Jesse Edwards became my morphologic tutor in cardiovascular disease. I always found his writings to be logical, straightforward, and well illustrated. He had a wonderful capacity to simplify complicated subjects.

In June 1962, a week or so before leaving the NIH for a year at The Johns Hopkins Hospital, I visited Dr. Edwards at the Miller Hospital in St. Paul, Minnesota, where he had moved 2 years earlier. I was enormously impressed with the efficiency of his cardiovascular registry, with the love and respect that his fellows engendered toward him, and for the kindness he showed me during the visit. Jesse Edwards has trained well over 500 physicians and students. Unfortunately, I was not one among that number in St. Paul or Rochester, but I think no one has studied his publications quite as consistently and thoroughly as I have.

I consider Jesse Edwards a great man. Had he chosen surgery, internal medicine, or pediatrics or a non-medical career he also would have been superb. He has always been good with both his hands and his head. His contributions to our knowledge on virtually every cardiovascular disease is enormous. There are very few cardiovascular conditions that he has not written about. His publications in medical journals number over 700, his chapters in other physicians' books number over 70, and books which he has authored or co-authored number 12. In addition to his contributions to our fund of cardiovascular knowledge, his influence on his students has been widespread. Jesse Edwards is such a good human being, a good family man, a man of high principles. His influence will remain for decades after he is gone. It has been one of the pleasures in my life to know him and to study his contributions.

I am speaking with Dr. Edwards in his home in St. Paul, Minnesota, on October 17, 1997.

William Clifford Roberts, MD[†] (hereafter, WCR): *Dr. Edwards, I would like to discuss your career and try to find out what was it that instilled that desire in you to be such a leader in your profession. Let me start by asking you what was it like growing up in Hyde Park, Massachusetts? What did your parents do? How many siblings did you have? Just discuss your early family life, your early development.*

Jesse Efrem Edwards, MD[‡] (hereafter, JEE): I was born in Hyde Park, Massachusetts, but raised in eastern Connecticut. I grew up on a 150-acre farm and went to school through the eighth grade in a 1-room school. During that time I learned a lot about listening, because when we were in the first grade, we listened to the second grade. When you got to the second grade you knew all about it. In those days, sometimes we skipped a grade, and I skipped grade 6. I went the first year to high school in New London, Connecticut, and here I had a classical experience. Latin was a required subject in those days. I still recall Latin as being very important to me—sentence structure, vocabulary. This has stuck with me. That year was a sad time in my upbringing. My mother died and the family then moved to Boston where I completed high school.

WCR: *Your mother died when you were 13?*

JEE: Yes. She left a memory with me. I have hardly gone through a day without thinking of her even though she died almost 75 years ago. My father never remarried, and he was a great guide to me. One of the things he emphasized to me was never waste anything: "Don't waste things, don't waste time." This advice has stayed with me forever. When I see a specimen, a

*This interview is part of a series of interviews of prominent cardiovascular specialists, and the series is underwritten by an unrestricted grant from Bristol-Myers Squibb.

†Baylor Cardiovascular Institute, Baylor University Medical Center, Dallas, Texas 75248.

‡From the Jesse E. Edwards, Cardiovascular Registry.

FIGURE 1. JEE during the interview in his home on 17 October 1997.

particular condition, I want to see who else I can interest in it to teach, so I constantly think of the days of being taught not to waste anything. If there is something that has teaching value I try to find a student and teach with it. That was maybe the reason eventually why I was put in a position where I collected hearts, first congenital and then acquired conditions, as a symbol that I was taught early not to waste.

WCR: *What did your father do?*

JEE: Basically he was a farmer, with poultry and gardening. He was self-educated. He had a very strong desire for his 3 kids to get educated. Everyone of us went to graduate school.

WCR: *Were your father and mother born in the USA or did they come from Europe? When did your family come to the USA?*

JEE: About 110 years ago. My father was born in the Ukrane. My mother was born in Poland.

WCR: *What year was your father born?*

JEE: In 1875. My mother was born in 1882.

WCR: *Did your father go to college?*

JEE: No, he never went to college, but he had great respect for education. He saw to it that each of his kids had the opportunity for an education.

WCR: *What did your mother die from?*

JEE: She had cancer of the stomach. As the years go by, I wonder, because she did not have an autopsy, if she did not have ovarian cancer.

WCR: *What was her age?*

JEE: She was 42 years old.

WCR: *How old was your father when he died?*

JEE: He was 70.

WCR: *So there were 3 children?*

JEE: I was the youngest, the baby. My sister, the eldest, became a teacher, and my brother became a surgeon at the Harvard Medical School.

WCR: *Your oldest sibling was how much older than you?*

JEE: Seven years.

WCR: *Your brother, who became a surgeon, was 5 years older than you. After high school, you went to Tufts in Boston. What did you major in at Tufts? As you look back over your college career what were the things that influenced you as you think about it now?*

JEE: I had my sights set for medicine. I majored in biology at Tufts. After 3 years, I entered the Tufts Medical School, and after 1 year of medical school, I then graduated from Tufts with a BS degree and had 3 more years of medical school.

WCR: *Because you skipped the sixth grade and then went to only 3 years of college, rather than 4, you entered medical school at age 20.*

JEE: Yes.

WCR: *You graduated from medical school in 1935?*

JEE: Yes.

WCR: *So you graduated from college in 1932, the heart of the depression, and then from medical school in 1935. Were you able to go through college and medical school financially okay?*

JEE: My father and sister helped. During the summers for several years I worked at the postal office to help toward tuition. Then my fourth year, I, along with 2 other classmates, was selected to be an instructor in anatomy for the first-year class, so I had free tuition from medical school that last year. The first half of the year I taught anatomy to the first-year students. This had a great impact on me: one thing was the teaching, which I enjoyed, and the other thing was that you had to love gross anatomy, which I still enjoy, and which plays a part in my day-to-day work.

WCR: *So you were a very good medical student, one of the select chosen during your senior year. You made AOA as a medical student. I presume you did quite well in your studies in college. Is that correct?*

JEE: So-So.

WCR: *Who do you remember in medical school that had an influence on you?*

JEE: The anatomy and physiology professors had great influence on me. The one I remember most was the Professor of Pathology. I got my lowest grade in medical school in pathology! The pathology teacher was Dr. Harold McMann who was superb. He was a young man, only in his second year as a professor. He was a great teacher and covered medicine with pathology. I think that had a great influence on me in my career to correlate pathology with medicine.

WCR: *When you were growing up, your mother had died, there were 3 of you; what was it like sitting around the dinner table at night? Your father must have been working very hard trying to support you 3. What do you recall? Were there active discussions around the dinner table at night? What was the atmosphere like?*

JEE: Not out of the ordinary. We had things to do. First we had to prepare the dinner and do the dishes.

FIGURE 2. JEE during the interview.

WCR: *Each of you had your chores to do. Did you and your brother and sister get along well?*

JEE: Yes, we did. They treated me like a baby. They looked after me. I had no mother, but they participated in mothering me.

WCR: *So you enjoyed medical school a bit more than you enjoyed college. From a scholastic standpoint, you did better in medical school than you did in college. Is that correct?*

JEE: Yes.

WCR: *Why did you choose Tufts for both college and medical school?*

JEE: Tufts was simple. I could get there from home by streetcar.

WCR: *So when you went to college and medical school you lived at home? That saved a lot of money. How many students were in your medical school class?*

JEE: I think 110. We graduated with about 100.

WCR: *Did any of your colleagues in medical school have an illustrous career, even approaching yours?*

JEE: It would be ill-mannered of me to answer the question directly. When the Tufts Medical School celebrated its 100th anniversary the President picked out 7 graduates from the 100 classes and he chose me as one of them.

WCR: *In 100 years, you and 6 others were picked out as the most illustrious to graduate from Tufts Medical School?*

JEE: According to that President.

WCR: *When you graduated from medical school in 1935 you were only 24 years old. You decided to train in pathology and went to the Mallory Institute of Pathology at Boston City Hospital right there in Boston. What was that like? Did you enjoy your training?*

JEE: Yes, it was wonderful. That year we had a lot of deaths from lobar pneumonia. Five or 6 of us did autopsies and each 1 of us did about 20 or 30 cases of lobar pneumonia that year. This was before antibiotics. We all saw the multiple complications of lobar

pneumonia. Also, the histology of lobar pneumonia was very graphic and it got to be an experience of very major proportions. Also, in the general hospital we saw all kinds of things at other autopsies and the surgicals.

WCR: *I noticed that during your training at the Mallory Institute of Pathology you wrote the classic articles with your older brother on morphologic features of varicose veins in the legs. Was your brother training at Boston City Hospital also? How did that come about?*

JEE: At that time he was in practice in Boston. He maintained a connection with the medical examiner where he did some pathology to broaden his surgical experience. We had the opportunity to examine material in the medical examiner's office. From that material we described the pathology of the valves in varicose veins and in deep vein thrombosis in the legs.

WCR: *You are an enormously personable human being, you are easy with people, you are superb with your hands, you could have easily gone into a clinical field, internal medicine, surgery, and you elected to go into pathology. Was that decision easy for you in medical school or did you tustle with that decision a great deal?*

JEE: My first year out of school was pathology. This was intended to be an experience to precede training in medicine or surgery. My first year in pathology, maybe the experience with lobar pneumonia and the experience of teaching students, left me feeling that a career in pathology was very good for me. So during my first year of pathology I began to think that I should stay in pathology and, for that reason, I sought 1 year of clinical medicine my second year out of school. I was very anxious to get into pathology because to me it seemed a natural.

WCR: *At that time, 1935 until about 1940, the Mallory Institute of Pathology was one of the finest centers in the world in that particular specialty. Is that correct?*

JEE: Yes.

WCR: *How did you get interested in cardiovascular disease. I am aware that during that period of your training, roughly 1935 to 1940, you did do that work with your brother on varicose veins, and I consider those papers that you did with him the classic papers on the morphologic aspects of varicose veins and deep vein thrombosis. I am also aware that during the period of your training, that your Chief, Dr. Frederic Parker, wrote a paper on histologic findings in the lungs in patients with mitral stenosis. Did that background, in retrospect, have an impact on you?*

JEE: Yes, it did. Some years later when I was at the Mayo Clinic, I got the assignment of doing cardiac pathology. The experience at that time with congenital heart disease and the background I had had in Boston with the lungs in mitral stenosis led me to continue my interest in the vessels of the lung. Study of the pulmonary vessels turned into an everyday situation in congenital heart disease particularly.

WCR: *Dr. Edwards, I am not sure that everybody is aware of the fact that you were an outstanding re-*

FIGURE 3. JEE at dinner banquet on the evening after his interview.

searcher in cancer. When I was at the National Institutes of Health, Dr. Harold Stewart was the Chief of the Laboratory of Pathology of the National Cancer Institutes. He could not have been more complimentary of you and your cancer work. How did you migrate to the National Institutes of Health in 1940 to do research in cancer?

JEE: In 1940, I had completed my formal training in pathology at Boston. I was interested in doing some work other than day-to-day pathology, so I sought the National Cancer Institute in Bethesda, Maryland. That was fairly new at that time, and I received an appointment as a Research Fellow where I continued for 2 years and then I went into the Army because of World War II.

WCR: *I gather you went into the Army in 1942 when you were 31 years of age. It seems to me that your 4 years in the Army was quite an interesting experience for you. I gather that you were the commanding officer of the Central Laboratory for the U.S. Army in Europe and the European theater. Can you describe your activities during that period and what impact they had on your future career?*

JEE: After having served in a U.S. general hospital and in England, I had a period during 1945, after World War II in Europe had ended, where I was in Europe serving as a pathologist on war crimes. During the summer of 1945 I was doing autopsies in Germany on American and British soldiers and there was the possibility that crimes had been experienced against these people. After the summer of 1945 doing that work, I was given the function of being the Chief Pathologist at the Central Laboratories in the United States theater in Europe. With that I was consultant to the Surgeon General in Europe for laboratory matters.

WCR: *After you got out of the Army in 1946, you went directly to the Mayo Clinic. How did that come about? Here you had spent your entire civilian life in Massachusetts, Connecticut, Maryland; now all of a sudden you are in Rochester, Minnesota.*

JEE: It came about when the Mayo Clinic was looking for a pathologist. The Mayo Clinic in 1946 made contact with the Army asking for potential people coming out of the Army who might be useful to them to fill the vacancy. At that time in Washington the Army knew about me because I had worked as Chief Officer in the laboratories in the European theater. Apparently, I had a good reputation because they offered my name. That is how the Mayo Clinic got interested in me.

WCR: *Do you know who it was at the Mayo Clinic who contacted the Army?*

JEE: Yes. The contact man was Dr. Bryl R. Kirklin, who was in charge of diagnostic radiology at the Mayo Clinic and he was in the Army at that time. His son, John, later became the prominent cardiovascular surgeon at the Mayo Clinic, and I worked closely with him.

WCR: *Rochester, Minnesota, was quite a bit smaller than Boston, Massachusetts, where you had lived for a long time. You were used to farming country since your father was a farmer. How did Rochester, Minnesota, hit you, and how did you get into cardiovascular disease there?*

JEE: I liked Rochester. At that time Rochester had a population of 40,000 people. It was a nice small town. The job I went to fill was in pathology. Quickly, I found I became a cardiovascular pathologist.

WCR: *When you went there, you knew that that was the area of pathology you were going to focus on, or did that not come about until you got there?*

JEE: It did not come about until I got there.

WCR: *You wanted that?*

JEE: No, they said the field was open and I had not done a tour in cardiac work and I had no great preference in one or another field. I was interested in doing human pathology; what field it was did not matter.

WCR: *When you went to the Mayo Clinic you did recognize that the cardiovascular area was open and the Chief of the Department asked you at that time whether you would handle that. That's the way it was?*

JEE: Yes.

WCR: *What was the atmosphere like? Here you are at the Mayo Clinic in 1946, open heart surgery had not started yet. The only cardiac surgery at the time, I gather, included closure of or creation of a patent ductus arteriosus. How did cardiovascular disease develop there?*

JEE: Gradually. When I came there they had operated on patients with patent ductus and constrictive pericarditis. Coarctation of the aorta had not yet been done. I came there in May 1946, and the first coarctation operation at the Mayo Clinic was in November 1946. Catheterization had not been done yet. Catheterization at the Mayo Clinic started a year later. It has been 50 years since the first catheterization was per-

FIGURE 4. At the banquet with his devoted wife Marge.

formed at the Mayo Clinic. They celebrated the occasion this year.

WCR: *Fifty years of cardiac catheterization at the Mayo Clinic was celebrated in 1997. There have been an array of fantastic heart specialists at the Mayo Clinic, Jesse Edwards, Howard Burchell, Earl Wood, John Kirklin, Dwight McGoon, Jim DuShane. How did Burchell come to the clinic? How were these other figures attracted to the Mayo Clinic?*

JEE: Burchell came ahead of me. He was trained in internal medicine but also had experience in pathology and physiology. He was one of the young Mayo Clinic cardiologists when I met him. Wood had been trained at the University of Minnesota by Visiher, a physiologist. He was at the Mayo Clinic during World War II doing work developing and improving a decelerating machine for devices for flying. He was a physiologist but had not done any catheterizations yet. Kirklin came after I did. His fellowship in surgery was interrupted by service in the Army where he worked as a neurosurgeon. When he came back to the Clinic he was told he would be in cardiovascular surgery which developed with time. McGoon had trained at the Hopkins. By the time he came, the field was already established.

WCR: *Could you describe what the atmosphere was like at the Mayo Clinic in the late 1940s? The number of articles you published, almost from the moment you hit the Mayo Clinic, was incredible. What was your day like? What were your day-to-day activities?*

JEE: I had my regular work, along with 4 or 5 other pathologists. I took my turn with the next case, whatever it was, cancer of ovaries, cancer of the stomach, colon, all sorts of things. I participated in the autopsy in all of the congenital heart cases whether or not I was assigned that case. I got to see every congenital heart, even though I was not on duty. In the early days, we had a close connection between pathology and the other fields. We had no turf problems. We did not have the problem of the pathologist only talking about pathology. We could talk about physiology. The physiologist could talk about pathology. In the early days, we had a lot of interplay between the various fields. I would not hesitate in a surgical conference to make a suggestion for the shape of a patch to prevent reste-

nosis. The surgeon did not mind saying something about the autopsy. We had a free play of interest, crossing fields. I think that is what represented the gist of the development of the Mayo Clinic team.

WCR: *How did it work that you would see Burchell and DuShane periodically. Were there one or more adult and pediatric cardiology conferences a week? How did you interact with John Kirklin? When did you do it? How did it work out on a day-to-day basis?*

JEE: We had a lot of conferences. The autopsy conference would deal with all operative cardiac deaths. The surgeons were there, the cardiologists were there, the physiologists were there. When the physiologist held a conference the same people were there. We learned. We thought closely.

WCR: *So you, in essence, became a pretty good physiologist. Burchell became a pretty good cardiac morphologist, etc.*

JEE: Yes.

WCR: *What were your time commitments like in those early days? As a farm boy, so to speak, I gather you always arose early or what time would you get to the Mayo Clinic, what time would you leave home, what time would you wake up in the morning in those days, what time would you leave the Mayo Clinic at night? I gather you were single at the time. Were you working into the night? Can you give me an idea of what your activities were really like?*

JEE: I used to spend a lot of time in the library in the early days, searching the publications way back to the Civil War and beyond, so we could see the development of the field. We could see new developments, and also we could see deficiencies. We did a lot of work on classification of the diseases, for example, the so-called endocardial cushion defect. Burchell and I classified the various types of tricuspid atresia. Some cases have transposition of the great vessels with and without pulmonary stenosis. We also classified truncus arteriosis and even today our classification is used. In those days, every case we saw was something new. For example, I had seen one case of left-sided Ebstein's malformation—a 32-year-old person who had died of a brain abscess. Now with that case I suddenly became a expert on Ebstein's malformation. After that, an 8-year-old boy with Ebstein's had cardiac catheterization. Unfortunately, the patient died and I got on the telephone to Earl Wood and Earl said, ''What did you find''? and I said, ''Ebstein's'', and he said, ''What the hell is an Ebstein's?'' That is how early it was and exciting.

WCR: *Tell me about your work habits then. You didn't have any specific training in heart disease, you trained yourself, and all of your colleagues were sort of learning together at that period of time, I gather, since cardiac catheterization was new, cardiac surgery was new, etc. What time did you get to the Mayo Clinic? What time did you leave home? What were your weekends like?*

JEE: I did most of my extra work at night, at the library or at my desk. I worked very frequently going to bed about 1:00 A.M. and I got up about 6:30 A.M., except when I wrote a 3-volume book, which took me

FIGURE 5. JEE at the banquet with WCR.

18 months, and during that period I worked on it from 6:30 until 8:00 each morning. At 8:00 A.M. the day started.

WCR: *You would go to bed at 1:00 A.M. and you would get up about 6:30 A.M. and that continued for many years? Where did you live in Rochester when you were single. I understand from Larry Elliott that you used to throw some nice parties and have a good number of people over. People liked to come to your house. What were your social activities like? What happened on the weekend?*

JEE: I had normal contacts. Sometimes I would have a group of young fellows over for dinner. It was mixed company. Sometime I would have a date and we would go out.

WCR: *When did you meet Marge and when did you get married?*

JEE: I met Marge 2 years before we were married. We had dates on weekends mostly and we married in 1952. I wish now that we had married earlier. We are proud of our children. One is a newspaper editor and the other is a cardiologist.

WCR: *You were 41 years of age? You had waited a bit long to get married. William Osler was 42 when he got married. I suspect it was quite hard for you to leave the Mayo Clinic. You built up a lot of friends there, you were enormously productive. How did it come about that you moved to St. Paul in 1960?*

JEE: It was hard for me to leave the Mayo Clinic, but the people at the University of Minnesota in Minneapolis were very good about making the cardiac material available to me. My primary hospital was the Miller Hospital in St. Paul, now called United. I wouldn't leave the Mayo Clinic for an ordinary job in pathology. Cardiac material had to be available. When the University said I could have all the cardiac material and the hospital supplied enough people to help me in general pathology, then I moved. I have had a great time working with people who were training at the university. Sometimes we had as many as 12 fellows and graduate students at one time.

WCR: *Your moving to St. Paul was in actuality bringing a university to United Hospital, namely you. Nevertheless, I am sure you must have had some trepidation. That was a bit risky from a professional standpoint. Here you are at the Mayo Clinic. You've published an enormous number of articles in 14 years. You've written a number of books by that time. Your name was associated with the Mayo Clinic. You were one of the big 4, so to speak, and yet you made the St. Paul operation a magnificent success. You acquired a lot of money from NIH grants. As you say, you had a lot of fellows. How do you now look back on those first few years in St. Paul compared to the Mayo Clinic? Did it work out just as you had hoped it would work out?*

JEE: As it turned out, it was a good move. Had I stayed at the Mayo Clinic I am afraid I would have gotten old in the same job. By making the move I had to wake up and make my life here, and I think it worked out very well, but it was a risk.

WCR: *Dr. Edwards, you have published well over 700 articles in medical journals, you have published 12 books, 70 chapters in other people's books. Your name was first among your 726 articles in medical journals only about 100 times, and yet, I gather, you essentially wrote all or virtually all of those articles. In other words, you seem to me to have been an enormously unselfish person. People clammered to work with you. How did you write all these papers? Did you dictate them or did you write with pencil and paper? How did you do your writing work, particularly after you came to St. Paul?*

JEE: Mostly, pencil and paper. The fellows who worked with me usually would write the first draft, and then together we developed many drafts. Many have said to me, "you've taught us a lot more than pathology." I spent a lot of time writing with the young people.

WCR: *As you look back over your illustrious last 40 years (from 1946 to now 1997) what accomplishments are you most proud of?*

JEE: My family and my friends.

WCR: *It seems your capacity for friendship is great. All of your fellows, it seems to me, are still your friends. You stay in touch with your many fellows. How many fellows have you had through the years?*

JEE: Counting medical students, over 500.

WCR: *You have a collection, as I understand it, of approximately 15,000 hearts. These are hearts with heart disease, either acquired or congenital. Autopsies in this country are continually getting fewer and fewer. This material is getting rarer and rarer. Here you can collect 146 cases studied at autopsy with the polysplenia syndrome, or nearly 50 cases of parachute mitral valve syndrome. Nowhere else in the world can anybody come up with this type of collection to study. How can this collection be preserved. Where can the money come from to keep it going?*

JEE: That's tough. We have some funds from the endowment but that is small. We probably have to seek more funds from people who are interested in this collection.

WCR: *You were President of the American Heart Association for 1 year. That was 1969 or something like that. What do you remember about that experience? Was that a good experience?*

JEE: It was a good experience. It's like owning a boat. It's great when you buy it and it's great when you sell it.

WCR: *You enjoyed having the opportunity of being president of the American Heart Association but when it was over you were glad it was over. I have admired you through the years by your ability not to travel too much. You seem to have stuck to your job and you must have had a lot of opportunities to go here and yon, but you seemed to have kept travel down. Could you talk about that a bit?*

JEE: My family was close and my in-laws (who are gone now) lived with us for about 17 years. My wife is an only child and she was very close to her family, and she was not very enthusiastic about travel, so I more or less did it her way. I think the family had a lot to do with it. The kids were raised in part by their grandparents. They had a great influence on the kids. I am happy the way it worked out.

WCR: *I asked you sometime ago to look over your publications and mark those that you thought were the most significant. You have 726 publications in medical journals and you only marked 18 of them. Now I can tell you that you passed over some classic papers. You did not mark enough! I realize you are a modest man but as you look back what are some of your professional accomplishments you are most proud of?*

JEE: First of all, I like young people and I like to help them develop into adults.

WCR: *Do you have any regrets? Were there some things professionally that you wanted to do that you did not do?*

JEE: Not really.

WCR: *As mentioned earlier, you are an extremely personable person. I am sure people have mentioned to you through the years that, "gosh, I wish you had been my doctor." Do you regret at all that you did not have that interpatient contact on a day-to-day basis? Obviously, you would have been very good at that.*

JEE: No, I am happy with the experience I had.

WCR: *It seems to me that you could not have accomplished what you did had you not had good hands. In other words, you were smart, clever, creative, but you also knew how to open the heart and how to illustrate it and how to make it understandable to those who didn't do that every day. Your diagrams have been reproduced by numerous people all over the world. You would have been a superb surgeon. Do you ever regret that you did not go into surgery like your brother did?*

JEE: I sometimes think if I had done something else that I would have prospered. I don't know. I am not dissatisfied with my experience.

WCR: *You have reviewed for cardiology editors and editors for other journals, literally hundreds of manuscripts through the years. You have done that very efficiently, quickly, and promptly. You have always made it a priority if someone asked you to write a chapter or review a manuscript that you got it in by the due date. I guess you get annoyed when people say they are going to do something and yet they don't do it. You seem to always deliver. Can you comment on that?*

JEE: A promise is a promise.

WCR: *Have other physicians or investigators influenced you considerably?*

JEE: I will mention *Bradley Patton*. When I started working at the Mayo Clinic on congenital heart disease, I contacted him and spent some time with him, both at work and some time at home. He taught me some basics of embryology. He gave me some insights that were helpful to me. I would also like to mention *Robert Benassi*. He is a medical illustrator with whom I have worked for the last 30 years or so and he has done most of the illustrations that I have developed. He was a great help to me. If I had a chance to illustrate something, he had the talent to do it. He has made about 5,000 illustrations for me. He worked freelance when I came to St. Paul. I worked with him for quite a few years and one day the Mayo Clinic called me and wanted to know about Bob Benassi. They wanted to give him a job and they did, but he assisted me and to this day he is still available to me.

WCR: *I always thought that you knew a lot about embryology but that you did not mix embryological terms with descriptive terms of congenital heart disease. In other words, you kept the nomenclature simple. You made your nomenclature readily understandable. One of your many contributions was making the nomenclature of corrected transposition of the great arteries reasonable, bringing together the concept of situs, simplifying the concept of detroversion and dextrocardia. I wonder if you could comment on that? I remember when I was a resident in anatomic pathology, one of the first cases that I encountered was a patient who had a large ventricular septal defect, and, in retrospect, both great arteries arose from the right ventricle. I remember keeping that heart in a basin in my office and I looked at it nearly everyday for a couple of months trying to figure it out. During that time, your classic article on the origin of both great arteries from the right ventricle appeared and you had 10 or 12 cases in that first paper. Then I knew exactly what it was, but I had not figured it out myself. Do you want to comment on your relative simplification of nomenclature, particularly in congenital heart failure?*

JEE: Basically I believe in simplicity, call it the way you see it, and I think if you do that people in other fields can understand. Of course, some people with congenital heart disease like to feel that they know it all and no other person can know what they think.

WCR: *Do you have hobbies, Dr. Edwards? What do you do when you are not doing medical things?*

JEE: Before I had my stroke I worked in the garden, and also I love to fish. Once I had my stroke, my son, Brooks, got me a rod and reel that is made for the handicapped. I cast out and then reel it in by pushing a button. The last time I fished, my wife and I caught a 4-pound Northern Pike.

WCR: *Your gardening, I presume, was a continuation of your farming as a youngster. Do you read a good bit? Do you read a lot other than medicine?*

JEE: No, I don't.

WCR: *Time factor, mainly, I presume?*

JEE: I think that also may be my schooling, when you could listen to the second grade when you were in the first grade.

WCR: *I wanted to tell you that I was not one of your 500 or more fellows, but you never had a fellow who read more of your publications than I did. If anybody ever asks me who was my instructor, I say, Jesse Edwards. When I have had fellows through the years, I always tell them, find out what Jess Edwards had to say about this before we go too much further.*

JEE: You are very kind, Bill, thanks.

WCR: *Thank you, Dr. Edwards. It is a real pleasure to see you. I appreciate your spending this time with me. You have a lovely home and it is a pleasure to be here.*

JEE's most important 149 publications selected by JEE among his 721 articles published in journals

1. Edwards EA, Edwards JE. The effect of thrombophlebitis on the venous valve. *SG & O* 1937;65:310–320.
3. Edwards JE, Edwards EA. The saphenous valves in varicose veins. *Am Heart J* 1940;19:338–351.
12. Edwards JE. Hepatomas in mice induced with carbon tetrachloride. *J National Cancer Inst* 1941;2:197–199.
28. Edwards EA, Edwards JE. The venous valves in thromboangiitis obliterans. *Arch Path* 1943;35:242–252.
31. Bartel CM, Edwards JE, Lamb ME. Mycotic and dissecting aneurysms of aorta complicating bacterial endocarditis. *Arch Pathol* 1943;35:285–291.
39. Gates RM, Rogers HM, Edwards JE. The syndrome of cerebral abscess and congenital cardiac disease. *Mayo Clin Proc* 1947;22:401–412.
42. Edwards JE. Retro-esophageal segment of the left aortic arch, right ligamentum arteriosum and right descending aorta causing a congenital vascular ring about the trachea and esophagus. *Mayo Clin Proc* 1948;23:108–116.
47. Rogers HM, Edwards JE. Incomplete division of the atrioventricular canal with patent interatrial foramen primum (persistent common cardioventricular ostium). Report of 5 cases and review of the literature. *Am Heart J* 1948;36:28–54.
48. Edwards JE. Anomalies of the derivatives of the aortic arch system. *Med Clin North Amr* 1948(July):925–949.
50. Edwards JE, Christensen NA, Clagett OT, McDonald JR. Pathologic consideration in coarctation of the aorta. *Mayo Clin Proc* 1948;23:324–332.
51. Edwards JE, Clagett OT, Drake RL, Christensen NA. The collateral circulation in coarctation of the aorta. *Mayo Clin Proc* 1948;23:333–339.
52. Edwards JE. "Vascular rings" related to anomalies of the aortic arches. *Mod Concepts Cardiovasc Dis* 1948 (August);17:1–3.
56. Dahlin DC, Edwards JE. Amyloid localized in the heart. *Mayo Clin Proc* 1949;24:89–98.
58. Ludden TE, Edwards JE. Carditis in poliomyelitis: an anatomic investigation of 35 cases and review of the literature. *Am J Pathol* 1949;25:357–381.
59. Larrabee WF, Parker RL, Edwards JE. Pathology of intrapulmonary arteries and arterioles in mitral stenosis. *Mayo Clin Proc* 1949;24:316–326.
61. Edwards JE, Burchell HB. Congenital tricuspid atresia: a classification. *Med Clin North Am* 1949 (July):1177–1196.
62. Collett RW, Edwards JE. Persistent truncus: a classification according to anatomic types. *Med Clin North Am* (Mayo Clin No) 1949 (August):1245–1270.
68. Edwards JE, DuShane JW. Thoracic venous anomalies. I. Vascular connection of the left atrium and the left innominate vein (levoatriocardinal vein) associated with mitral atresia and premature closure of the foramen ovale. II. Pulmonary veins draining wholly into the ductus venosus. *Arch Pathol* 1950;49:517–537.
75. Civin WH, Edwards JE. Pathology of the pulmonary vascular tree. I. A comparison of the intrapulmonary arteries in the Eisenmenger complex and in stenosis of the ostium infundibuli associated with biventricular origin of the aorta. *Circulation* 1950;2:545–552.
79. Becker DL, Burchell HB, Edwards JE. Pathology of the pulmonary vascular tree. II. The occurrence in mitral insufficiency of occlusive pulmonary vascular lesions. *Circulation* 1951;3:230–238.
80. Civin WH, Edwards JE. The postnatal structural changes in the intrapulmonary arteries and arterioles. *Arch Pathol* 1951;51:192–200.
84. Edwards JE, Chamberlin WB Jr. Pathology of the pulmonary vascular tree. III. The structure of the intrapulmonary arteries in cor triloculare biatriatum with subaortic stenosis. *Circulation* 1951;3:524–530.
85. Edwards JE, DuShane JW, Alcott DL, Burchell HB. Thoracic venous anomalies. III. Atresia of the common pulmonary vein, the pulmonary veins draining wholly into the superior vena cava. IV. Stenosis of the common pulmonary vein (cor triatriatum). *Arch Pathol* 1951;51:446–460.
93. Bahn RC, Edwards JE, DuShane JW. Coarctation of the aorta as a cause of death in early infancy. *Pediatrics* 1951;8:192–203.
96. Williams RR, Kent GB Jr, Edwards JE. Anomalous cardiac blood vessel communicating with the right ventricle. Observations in a case of pulmonary atresia with an intact ventricular septum. *Arch Pathol* 1951;52:480–487.
106. Jordan RA, Miller RD, Edwards JE, Parker RL. Thrombo-embolism in acute and in healed myocardial infarction. I. Intracardiac mural thrombosis. *Circulation* 1952;6:1–6.
107. Miller RD, Jordan RA, Parker RL, Edwards JE. Thrombo-embolism in acute and in healed myocardial infarction. II. Systemic and pulmonary arterial occlusion. *Circulation* 1952;6:7–15.
115. Edwards JE. Malformations of the aortic arch system manifested as "vascular rings." *Lab Invest* 1953;2:56–75.
118. Kelsey JR, Gilmore CE, Edwards JE. Bilateral ductus arteriosus representing persistence of each sixth aortic arch. Report of a case. *Arch Pathol* 1953;55:154–161.
130. Clagett OT, Kirklin JW, Edwards JE. Anatomic variations and pathologic changes in 124 cases of coarctation of the aorta. *SG & O* 1954;98:103–114.
137. Barger JD, Creasman RW, Edwards JE. Bilateral ductus arteriosus associated with interruption of the aortic arch. *Am J Clin Pathol* 1954;24:441–444.
150. Becu LM, Swan HJC, DuShane JW, Edwards JE. Ebstein malformation of the left atrioventricular valve in corrected transposition of the great vessels with ventricular septal defect. *Mayo Clin Proc* 1955;30:483–490.
151. Rogers HM, Waldon BR, Murphey DFH, Edwards JE. Supravalvular stenosing ring of left atrium in association with endocardial sclerosis (endocardial fibroelastosis) and mitral insufficiency. *Am Heart J* 1955;50:777–781.
152. Becu LM, Tauxe WN, DuShane JW, Edwards JE. A complex of congenital cardiac anomalies: ventricular septal defect, biventricular origin of the pulmonary trunk, and subaortic stenosis. *Am Heart J* 1955;50:901–911.
157. Edwards JE, Burchell HB, Christensen NA. Specimen exhibiting the essential lesion in aneurysm of the aortic sinus. *Proc Mayo Clin* 1956;31:407–412, 464.
165. Barger JD, Bregmann EH, Edwards JE. Bilateral ductus arteriosus with right aortic arch and right-sided descending aorta. Report of a case. *Am J Roentgenol* 1956;76:758–761.
169. Kirklin JW, Harshbarger HG, Donald DE, Edwards JE. Surgical correction of ventricular septal defect: anatomic and technical considerations. *J Thorac Surg* 1957;33:45–59.
174. Edwards JE. The Lewis A. Conner Memorial Lecture. Functional pathology of the pulmonary vascular tree in congenital cardiac disease. *Circulation* 1957;15:164–196.
176. Lyons WS, Hanlon DG, Helmholz HF Jr, DuShane JW, Edwards JE. Congenital cardiac disease and asplenia: report of 7 cases. *Mayo Clin Proc* 1957;32:277–286.
177. Edwards JE, Burchell HB. Pathologic anatomy of deficiencies between the aortic root and the heart, including aortic sinus aneurysms. *Thorax* 1957;12:125–139.
183. Dines DE, Edwards JE, Burchell HB. Myocardial atrophy in constrictive pericarditis. *Mayo Clin Proc* 1958;33:93–99.
206. Edwards JE, Burchell HB. Endocardial and intimal lesions (jet impact) as possible sites or origin of murmurs. *Circulation* 1958;18:946–960.
219. Heath D, Wood EH, DuShane JW, Edwards JE. The structure of the pulmonary trunk at different ages and in cases of pulmonary hypertension and pulmonary stenosis. *J Path Bact* 1959;77:443–456.
223. Sommerville RL, Allen EV, Edwards JE. Bland and infected arteriosclerotic abdominal aortic aneurysms: a clinicopathologic study. *Medicine* 1959;38:207–221.
228. Edwards JE. Congenital stenosis of pulmonary veins. Pathologic and developmental considerations. *Lab Invest* 1960;9:46–66.
238. Edwards JE. The problem of mitral insufficiency caused by accessory chordae tendineae in persistent common atrioventricular canal. *Mayo Clin Proc* 1960;35:299–305.
240. Burroughs JT, Edwards JE. Total anomalous pulmonary venous connection. *Am Heart J* 1960;59:913–931.
250. Neufeld HN, DuShane JW, Wood EH, Kirklin JW, Edwards JE. Origin of both great vessels from the right ventricle. I. Without pulmonary stenosis. *Circulation* 1961;23:399–412.
253. Edwards JE. The congenital bicuspid aortic valve. *Circulation* 1961;23:485–488.
254. Neufeld HN, DuShane JW, Edwards JE. Origin of both great vessels from the right ventricle. II. With pulmonary stenosis. *Circulation* 1961;23:603–612.
256. Wagenvoort CA, Neufeld HN, DuShane JW, Edwards JE. The pulmonary arterial tree in ventricular septal defect. A quantitative study of anatomic features in fetuses, infants and children. *Circulation* 1961;23:740–748.

260. Edwards JE. Calcific aortic stenosis: pathologic features. *Mayo Clin Proc* 1961;36:444–451.

266. Lucas RV Jr, Adams P Jr, Anderson RC, Varco RL, Edwards JE, Lester RG. Total anomalous pulmonary venous connection to the portal venous system: a cause of pulmonary venous obstruction. *Am J Roentgenol* 1961;86:561–575.

268. Davignon AL, Greenwold WE, DuShane JW, Edwards JE. Congenital pulmonary atresia with intact ventricular septum: clinicopathologic correlation of two anatomic types. *Am Heart J* 1961;62:591–602.

271. Lucas RV Jr, Lund GW, Edwards JE. Direct communication of a pulmonary artery with the left atrium. An unusual variant of pulmonary arteriovenous fistula. *Circulation* 1961;24:1409–1414.

273. Spiekerman RE, Brandenburg JT, Achor RWP, Edwards JE. The spectrum of coronary heart disease in a community of 30,000. A clinicopathologic study. *Circulation* 1962;25:57–65.

281. Lucas RV Jr, Woolfrey BF, Anderson RC, Lester RG, Edwards JE. Atresia of the common pulmonary vein. *Pediatrics* 1962;29:729–739.

282. Elliott LP, Edwards JE. The problem of pulmonary venous obstruction in total anomalous pulmonary venous connection to the left innominate vein. *Circulation* 1962;25:913–915.

283. Lucas RV Jr, Neufeld HN, Lester RG, Edwards JE. The symmetrical liver as a roentgen sign of asplenia. *Circulation* 1962;25:973–975.

290. Edwards JE. On the etiology of calcific aortic stenosis. *Circulation* 1962;26:817–818.

300. Shone JD, Sellers RD, Anderson RC, Adams P Jr, Lillehei CW, Edwards JE. The developmental complex of "parachute mitral valve," supravalvular ring of left atrium, subaortic stenosis, and coarctation of aorta. *Am J Cardiol* 1963;11:714–725.

306. Titus JL, Daugherty GW, Edwards JE. Anatomy of the atrioventricular conduction system in ventricular septal defect. *Circulation* 1963;28:72–81.

311. Eliot RS, Wolbrink A, Edwards JE. Congenital aneurysm of the left aortic sinus. A rare lesion and a rare cause of coronary insufficiency. *Circulation* 1963;28:951–956.

316. Edwards JE. The direction of blood flow in coronary arteries arising from the pulmonary trunk. *Circulation* 1964;29:163–166.

321. Ruttenberg HD, Neufeld HN, Lucas RV Jr, Carey LS, Adams P Jr, Anderson RC, Edwards JE. Syndrome of congenital cardiac disease with asplenia. Distinction from other forms of congenital cyanotic cardiac diseases. *Am J Cardiol* 1964;13:387–406.

333. Noren GH, Raghib G, Moller JH, Amplatz K, Adams P Jr, Edwards JE. Anomalous origin of the left coronary artery from the pulmonary trunk with special reference to the occurrence of mitral insufficiency. *Circulation* 1964;30:171–179.

335. Eliot RS, Kanjuh VI, Edwards JE. Atheromatous embolism. *Circulation* 1964;30:611–618.

338. Moller JH, Lucas RV Jr, Adams P Jr, Anderson RC, Jorgens J, Edwards JE. Endocardial fibroelastosis. A clinical and anatomic study of 47 patients with emphasis on its relationship to mitral insufficiency. *Circulation* 1964;30:759–782.

341. Eliot RS, Woodburn RL, Edwards JE. Conditions of the ascending aorta simulating aortic valvular incompetence. *Am J Cardiol* 1964;14:679–694.

349. Speckhals RC, Winchell P, Amplatz K, Edwards JE, From AHL. Idiopathic myocardiomyopathy with endocardial fibroelastosis occurring during pregnancy. *Am Heart J* 1965;69:551–558.

357. Todd DB, Anderson RC, Edwards JE. Inverted malformations in corrected transposition of the great vessels. *Circulation* 1965;32:298–300.

358. Ongley PA, Titus JL, Khoury GH, Rahimtoola SH, Marshall HJ, Edwards JE. Anomalous connection of pulmonary veins to right atrium associated with anomalous inferior vena cava, situs inversus and multiple spleens. A developmental complex. *Mayo Clin Proc* 1965;40:609–624.

361. Raghib G, Bloemendaal RD, Kanjuh VI, Edwards JE. Aortic atresia and premature closure of foramen ovale. Myocardial sinusoids and coronary arteriovenous fistula serving as outflow channel. *Am Heart J* 1965;70:476–480.

362. Jue KL, Raghib G, Amplatz K, Adams P Jr, Edwards JE. Anomalous origin of the left pulmonary artery from the right pulmonary artery. Report of 2 cases and review of the literature. *Am J Roentgenol* 1965;95:598–610.

363. Moller JH, Edwards JE. Interruption of aortic arch. Anatomic patterns and associated cardiac malformations. *Am J Roentgenol* 1965;95:557–572.

364. Peterson TA, Todd DB, Edwards JE. Supravalvular aortic stenosis. *J Thorac Cardiovasc Surg* 1965;50:734–741.

371. Jue KL, Noren G, Edwards JE. Pulmonary atresia with left ventricular-right atrial communication: basis for "circular shunt." *Thorax* 1966;21:83–90.

372. Mantini E, Grondin CM, Lillehei CW, Edwards JE. Congenital anomalies involving the coronary sinus. *Circulation* 1966;33:317–327.

375. Jue KL, Adams P Jr, Pryor R, Blount SG Jr, Edwards JE. Complete transposition of the great vessels in total situs inversus. Anatomic, electrocardiographic and radiologic observations. *Am J Cardiol* 1966;17:389–394.

379. Jue KL, Lockman LA, Edwards JE. Anomalous origins of pulmonary arteries from pulmonary trunk ("crossed pulmonary arteries"). Observation in a case with 18 trisomy syndrome. *Am Heart J* 1966;71:807–812.

380. Moller JH, Nakib A, Edwards JE. Infarction of papillary muscles and mitral insufficiency associated with congenital aortic stenosis. *Circulation* 1966;34:87–91.

381. Simmons RL, Moller JH, Edwards JE. Anatomic evidence for spontaneous closure of ventricular septal defect. *Circulation* 1966;34:38–45.

384. Moller JH, Nakib A, Eliot RS, Edwards JE. Symptomatic congenital aortic stenosis in the first year of life. *J Pediatr* 1966;69:728–734.

386. Moller JH, Noren GR, David PR, Amplatz K, Kanjuh VI, Edwards JE. Congenital stenosis of individual pulmonary veins without intracardiac anomalies. *Am Heart J* 1966;72:530–537.

394. Layman TE, Edwards JE. Anomalous mitral arcade. A type of congenital mitral insufficiency. *Circulation* 1967;35:389–395.

396. Levine MA, Moller JH, Amplatz K, Edwards JE. Atresia of the common pulmonary vein: case report and differential diagnosis. *Am J Roentgenol* 1967;100:322–327.

405. Moller JH, Nakib A, Anderson RC, Edwards JE. Congenital cardiac disease associated with polysplenia. A developmental complex of bilateral "left-sidedness." *Circulation* 1967;36:789–799.

413. Stanger P, Benassi RC, Korns ME, Jue KL, Edwards JE. Diagrammatic portrayal of variations in cardiac structure. Reference to transposition, dextrocardia and the concept of four normal hearts. *Circulation* 1968;37,38(suppl IV):IV-1–IV-16.

421. Goor D, Edwards JE. Friction lesions of the right ventricular endocardium. Related to tricuspid chordae in cardiac hypertrophy. *Arch Pathol* 1969;87:100–109.

431. Stanger P, Lucas RV Jr, Edwards JE. Anatomic factors causing respiratory distress in acyanotic congenital cardiac disease: special reference to bronchial obstruction. *Pediatrics* 1969;43:760–769.

435. Koretzky ED, Moller JH, Korns ME, Schwartz CJ, Edwards JE. Congenital pulmonary stenosis resulting from dysplasia of valve. *Circulation* 1969;40:43–53.

458. Becker AE, Becker MJ, Edwards JE. Malposition of pulmonary arteries (crossed pulmonary arteries) in persistent truncus arteriosus. *Am J Roentgenol* 1970;110:509–514.

462. Becker AE, Becker MJ, Edwards JE. Pathologic spectrum of dysplasia of the tricuspid valve. Features in common with Ebstein's malformation. *Arch Pathol* 1971;91:167–178.

476. Vlodaver Z, Edwards JE. Pathologic changes in aortic-coronary arterial saphenous vein grafts. *Circulation* 1971;44:719–728.

477. Schroeckenstein RF, Wasenda GJ, Edwards JE. Valvular competent patent foramen ovale in adults. *Minn Med* 1972;55:11–13.

479. Van Tassel RA, Edwards JE. Rupture of heart complicating myocardial infarction. Analysis of 40 cases including nine examples of left ventricular false aneurysm. *Chest* 1972;61:104–116.

481. Claudon DG, Claudon DB, Edwards JE. Primary dissecting aneurysm of coronary artery. A cause of acute myocardial ischemia. *Circulation* 1972;45:259–266.

500. Edwards JE, McGoon DC. Absence of anatomic origin from heart of pulmonary arterial supply. *Circulation* 1973;47:393–398.

503. Charuzi Y, Spanos PK, Amplatz K, Edwards JE. Juxtaposition of the atrial appendages. *Circulation* 1973;47:620–627.

513. Tandon R, Moller JH, Edwards JE. Communication of mitral valve with both ventricles associated with double outlet right ventricle. *Circulation* 1973;48:904–908.

519. Waller BF, Carter JB, Williams HJ Jr, Wang K, Edwards JE. Bicuspid aortic valve. Comparison of congenital and acquired types. *Circulation* 1973;48:1140–1150.

521. Blieden LC, Randall PA, Castaneda AR, Lucas RV Jr, Edwards JE. The "goose neck" of the endocardial cushion defect: anatomic basis. *Chest* 1974;65:13–17.

526. Marin-Garcia J, Tandon R, Moller JH, Edwards JE. Common (single) ventricle with normally related great vessels. *Circulation* 1974;49:565–573.

529. Tandon R, Edwards JE. Tricuspid atresia. A re-evaluation and classification. *J Thorac Cardiovasc Surg* 1974;67:530–542.

532. Rose AG, Beckman CB, Edwards JE. Communication between coronary sinus and left atrium. *Br Heart J* 1974;36:182–185.

542. Tandon R, Sterns LP, Edwards JE. Thoracopagus twins. Report of a case. *Arch Pathol* 1974;98:248–251.

544. Tandon R, Becker AE, Moller JH, Edwards JE. Double inlet left ventricle. Straddling tricuspid valve. *Br Heart J* 1974;36:747–759.

547. Knight L, Edwards JE. Right aortic arch. Types and associated cardiac anomalies. *Circulation* 1974;50:1047–1051.

561. Vlodaver Z, Edwards JE. Occlusion of coronary grafts-result of injury? *Ann Thorac Surg* 1975;20:719–720.

566. Baldwin JJ, Edwards JE. Rupture of right ventricle complicating closed chest cardiac massage. *Circulation* 1976;53:562–564.

571. Knight L, Neal WA, Williams HJ, Huseby TL, Edwards JE. Congenital left ventricular diverticulum. Part of a syndrome of cardiac anomalies and midline defects. *Minn Med* 1976;59:372–375.

572. Shrivastava S, Tadavarthy SM, Fukuda T, Edwards JE. Anatomic causes of pulmonary stenosis in complete transposition. *Circulation* 1976;54:154–159.

576. Guthrie RB, Edwards JE. Pathology of the myxomatous mitral valve. Nature, secondary changes and complications. *Minn Med* 1976;59:637–647.

581. Arom KV, Edwards JE. Relationship between right ventricular muscle bundles and pulmonary valve. Significance in pulmonary atresia with intact ventricular septum. *Circulation* 1976;54(suppl III):III-79–III-83.

592. Stanger P, Rudolph AM, Edwards JE. Cardiac malpositions. An overview based on study of sixty-five necropsy specimens. *Circulation* 1977;56:159–172.

596. Sotomora RF, Edwards JE. Anatomic identification of so-called absent pulmonary artery. *Circulation* 1978;57:624–633.

600. Edwards WD, Edwards JE. Hypertensive pulmonary vascular disease in d-transposition of the great arteries. *Am J Cardiol* 1978;41:921–924.

603. Sridaramont S, Ritter DG, Feldt RH, Davis GD, Edwards JE. Double-outlet right ventricle. Anatomic and angiocardiographic correlations. *Mayo Clin Proc* 1978;53:555–557.

606. Anderson JL, Durnin RE, Ledbetter MK, Angevine JM, Gilbert EF, Edwards JE. Pulmonary veno-occlusive disease. *Am Heart J* 1979;97:233–240.

615. Zollikofer CL, Vlodaver Z, Nath HP, Castaneda-Zuniga W, Valdez-Davila O, Amplatz K, Edwards JE. Angiographic findings in recanalization of coronary arterial thrombi. *Radiology* 1980;134:303–307.

620. Castaneda-Zuniga WR, Formanek A, Tadavarthy M, Vlodaver Z, Edwards JE, Zollikofer C, Amplatz K. The mechanism of balloon angioplasty. *Radiology* 1980;135:565–571.

622. Scholz DG, Lynch JA, Willerschneidt AB, Sharma RK, Edwards JE. Coronary arterial dominance associated with congenital bicuspid aortic valve. *Arch Pathol Lab Med* 1980;104:417–418.

624. Pritzker MR, Ernst JD, Caudill C, Wilson CS, Weaver WF, Edwards JE. Acquired aortic stenosis in systemic lupus erythematosus. *Ann Intern Med* 1980; 93:434–436.

628. Bramlet DA, Edwards JE. Congenital aneurysm of left atrial appendage. *Br Heart J* 1981;45:97–100.

632. Nath PH, Castaneda-Zuniga W, Zollikofer C, Delany DJ, Fulton RE, Amplatz K, Edwards JE. Isolation of a subclavian artery. *Am J Roentgenol* 1981;137:683–688.

633. Edwards BS, Edwards WD, Edwards JE. Aortic origin of conus coronary artery. Evidence of postnatal coronary development. *Br Heart J* 1981;45:555–558.

644. Castaneda-Zuniga W, Nath HP, Moller JH, Edwards JE. Left-sided anomalies in Ebstein's malformation of the tricuspid valve. *Pediatr Cardiol* 1982;3: 181–185.

647. Braunlin E, Peoples WM, Freedom RM, Flyer DC, Goldblatt A, Edwards JE. Interruption of the aortic arch with aorticopulmonary septal defect. An anatomic review. *Pediatr Cardiol* 1982;3:329–335.

649. Chesler E, King RA, Edwards JE. The myxomatous mitral valve and sudden death. *Circulation* 1983;67:632–639.

653. Peoples WM, Moller JH, Edwards JE. Polysplenia: a review of 146 cases. *Pediatr Cardiol* 1983;4:129–137.

660. Edwards BS, Edwards WD, Connolly DC, Edwards JE. Arterial-esophageal fistulae developing in patients with anomalies of the aortic arch system. *Chest* 1984;86:732–735.

663. Edwards BS, Edwards WD, Edwards JE. Ventricular septal rupture complicating acute myocardial infarction: identification of simple and complex types in 53 autopsied hearts. *Am J Cardiol* 1985;54:1201–1205.

665. Edwards BS, Lucas RV Jr, Lock JE, Edwards JE. Morphologic changes in the pulmonary arteries after percutaneous balloon angioplasty for pulmonary arterial stenosis. *Circulation* 1985;71:195–201.

667. Topaz O, Edwards JE. Pathologic features of sudden death in children, adolescents and young adults. *Chest* 1985;87:476–482.

670. Peterson MD, Roach RM, Edwards JE. Types of aortic stenosis in surgically removed valves. *Arch Pathol Lab Med* 1985;109:829–832.

672. Hanson TP, Edwards BS, Edwards JE. Pathology of surgically excised mitral valves. One hundred consecutive cases. *Arch Pathol Lab Med* 1985;109: 823–828.

674. Feigl D, Feigl A, Sweetman KM, Lobo FV, Moller JH, Edwards JE. Accessory tissue of the tricuspid valve protruding into the left ventricle through a septal defect. *Arch Pathol Lab Med* 1986;110:144–147.

680. Braunlin EA, Moller JH, Patton C, Lucas RV Jr, Lillehei CW, Edwards JE. Predictive value of lung biopsy in ventricular septal defect: long-term follow-up. *J Am Coll Cardiol* 1986;8:1113–1118.

691. Blatchford JW III, Franciosi RA, Singh A, Edwards JE. Vascular ring in interruption of the aortic arch with bilateral patent ductus arteriosi. *J Thorac Cardiovasc Surg* 1987;94:596–599.

692. Edwards BS, Weir EK, Edwards WD, Ludwig J, Dykoski RK, Edwards JE. Coexistent pulmonary and portal hypertension: morphologic and clinical features. *J Am Coll Cardiol* 1987;10:1233–1238.

694. Edwards BS, Edwards JE. Aortico-left ventricular tunnel and aortic insufficiency. *Ann Thorac Surg* 1988;45:5–6.

696. Pierpont MEM, Gobel JW, Moller JH, Edwards JE. Cardiac malformations in relatives of children with truncus arteriosus or interruption of the aortic arch. *Am J Cardiol* 1988;61:423–427.

700. Tveter KJ, Edwards JE. Calcified aortic sinotubular ridge: a source of coronary ostial stenosis or embolism. *J Am Coll Cardiol* 1988;12:1510–1514.

703. Tuna IC, Bessinger FB, Ophoven JP, Edwards JE. Acute angular origin of left coronary artery from aorta: an unusual cause of left ventricular failure in infancy. *Pediatr Cardiol* 1989;10:39–43.

704. Silberbach M, Castro WL, Goldstein MA, Lucas RV Jr, Edwards JE. Comparison of types of pulmonary stenosis with the state of the ventricular septum in complete transposition of the great arteries. *Pediatr Cardiol* 1989;10: 11–15.

708. Gikonyo BM, Jue KL, Edwards JE. Pulmonary vascular sling: report of 7 cases and review of literature. *Pediatr Cardiol* 1989;10:81–89.

709. Kanjuh VI, Katkov H, Singh A, Franciosi RA, Helseth HK, Edwards JE. Atypical total anomalous pulmonary venous connection: two channels leading to infracardiac terminations. *Pediatr Cardiol* 1989;10:115–120.

712. Yomtovian RA, Walley VM, Bollinger DJ, Edwards JE. Isolated valvular amyloid. *Am J Cardiovasc Pathol* 1989;2:365–370.

714. Lobo FV, Heggtveit HA, Butany J, Silver MD, Edwards JE. Right ventricular dysplasia: morphological findings in 13 cases. *Can J Cardiol* 1992;8:261–268.

Books authored or coauthored by JEE

1. Edwards JE, Dry TJ, Parker RL, Burchell HB, Wood EH, Bulbulian AH. *An Atlas of Congenital Anomalies of the Heart and Great Vessels.* Springfield, ILL: Charles C Thomas, 1954:202.

2. Edwards JE. *An Atlas of Acquired Diseases of the Heart and Great Vessels.* Vol. 1–3. Philadelphia: WB Saunders, 1961:1401.

3. Fontana RS, Edwards JE. *Congenital Cardiac Disease: A Review of 357 Cases Studied Pathologically.* Philadelphia: WB Saunders, 1962:291.

4. Wagenvoort CA, Heath D, Edwards JE. *The Pathology of the Pulmonary Vasculature.* Springfield, Ill: Charles C Thomas, 1964:494.

5. Stewart JR, Kincaid OW, Edwards JE. *An Atlas of Vascular Rings and Related Malformations of the Aortic Arch System.* Springfield, Ill: Charles C Thomas, 1964:171.

6. Edwards JE, Carey LS, Neufeld HN, Lester RG. *Congenital Heart Disease. Correlation of Pathologic Anatomy and Angiocardiography.* Vol. 1 and 2. Philadelphia: WB Saunders, 1965:890.

7. Edwards JE, Goot B. *The Illustrated Coronary Fact Book.* New York: Arco, 1973:101.

8. Vlodaver Z, Neufeld HN, Edwards JE. *Coronary Arterial Variations in the Normal Heart and in Congenital Heart Disease.* New York: Academic Press 1975:171.

MYRVIN HAROLD ELLESTAD, MD:
A Conversation With the Editor*

Myrvin Ellestad is one of the best cardiologists anywhere. He was born on 17 August 1921 in Santa Maria, California, and grew up in Auburn, California, a small town in the foothills of the Sierra Nevada Mountains. He graduated from the University of California in Berkeley in 1943 and from the University of Louisville School of Medicine in 1946. His training in internal medicine was at the Jersey City Medical Center and at Seaside Memorial Hospital in Long Beach, California. In 1952 he entered private practice in Long Beach. Despite a busy private practice for nearly 50 years, Dr. Ellestad has published 158 articles in peer-reviewed medical journals, 12 chapters in various books, and he has been the sole author of "Stress Testing: Principles and Practice," the 1st edition of which appeared in 1975 and he is now working on the 5th edition, which will probably appear next year. Myrvin Ellestad was the first to use afterload reduction as therapy for congestive heart failure. He may have been the first to have designed a computerized hospital information system. He is a world-renowned expert in exercise stress testing and has contributed enormously in this area. Since taking anthropology in college, he has continued his interest in that area, having supplemented his knowledge by travels to many famous anthropological locations such as Egypt, Israel, Easter Island, and the Galapagos Islands. Stimulated by one of his granddaughters, he published in 1998 *The World and Its Animals*, an 83-page book written for children but useful to all of us. Nearly 50 years after entering active practice, at age 79 Dr. Ellestad remains a prominent learner and teacher of cardiology and his enthusiasm for learning new things and for always asking questions makes him a very exciting person to be around. He's also a great guy.

William Clifford Roberts, MD† (hereafter WCR): *Myrvin, I appreciate your willingness to speak with me and therefore to the readers of* The American Journal of Cardiology. *We are in my home in Dallas, Texas. Myrvin has been consulting for the Federal Aviation Administration in Oklahoma City, and is stopping in Dallas on his way home. Myrvin, could we start by my asking about your growing up in California? What was that like, what were your parents like, and did you have siblings? What was the general atmosphere of your home?*

Myrvin Harold Ellestad, MD‡ (hereafter MHE): I was born in Santa Maria because my mother's mother lived in Santa Maria, and, as was common in those days, when she was about to deliver she went home to her mother. Then we went back to northern California. I grew up in Auburn, a population of 2,000 people, and located in the foothills of the Sierras, about 35 miles east of Sacramento on the way to Lake Tahoe. It was an idyllic place to grow up. In a town of that size almost everyone knew everybody else. My father was a high school teacher; my mother was a part-time grammar school teacher. It was a very close knit community. The surroundings were very rural. We were within 2 to 3 miles of the American River Canyon, a wild river beautiful canyon. Even though it was in the 1920s and 1930s, there was little poverty and few rich people. It was a seemingly homogeneous community and surrounded by farms and ranches.

My father took the job as a schoolteacher there because of its Norwegian colony. My father was born of Norwegian parents in Minnesota. They had immigrated to Minnesota and lived in East Grand Forks where the Norwegian language was spoken almost exclusively. His first language was Norwegian even though he was born in the USA. He went to a Norwegian school for about 6 grades and worked on his father's farm. When he was 14 his father got drunk (drinking was quite prevalent among the Norwegians) and he ended up in an altercation with his father. My father was beaten up pretty badly by his father and excommunicated from the family. At 14, he didn't know much except farming. He heard about a Norwegian farmer in Oregon, rode the rails to Oregon, and got a job at a ranch. He learned to speak English better. He worked there for a number of years.

My mother, who grew up around the San Francisco Bay area, went to Oregon as a schoolteacher. She taught in a 1-room school. My father was immediately smitten with her, but he felt embarrassed because she was educated and he wasn't. Somehow (this has been a family secret that nobody has ever understood), he got admitted to Oregon State University with only a few grades of elementary school. He got a degree and a teacher's credential there, and after 6 years of dating, they got married. Their marriage was delayed by World War I. He enlisted and was in the service, but never went to Europe. He came back and they were married. They were both in their 30s before I was born.

My mother was from English stock and didn't speak Norwegian. She was a direct descendant of Betsy Ross. There were probably 20 Norwegian families in Auburn. They played an important role in our social life. Several of these Norwegians had been outstanding skiers before they immigrated to California. The US national jumping champion and the national cross-country champion lived in Auburn. A lot of young kids in Auburn started skiing at a very young age. *Roy Mickleson*, who had been the national jump-

*This series of interviews are underwritten by an unrestricted grant from Bristol-Myers Squibb.

†Medical Director, Baylor Cardiovascular Institute, Baylor University Medical Center, Dallas, Texas 75246.

‡Director of Research, Heart Institute, Long Beach Memorial Hospital, Long Beach, California 90801.

FIGURE 1. MHE during the interview.

ing champion, was a close family friend, and he took it upon himself to try to teach me and the kids that I grew up with how to ski and jump. It is a short drive from Auburn up into the higher Sierras where there's good snow. Families were very permissive of their children then but also gave them a lot of responsibilities. Most of us were driving when we were 12 or 13 years old. My parents would allow me to take a car and drive with a carload of kids to the snow when I was very young. Nowadays, that would be almost unheard of. It was a great place to grow up. My father taught auto mechanics in school and wasn't very literary. My mother was very literary and she tried very hard to get me involved in as much classical reading as she could when I was young.

I had a life-shaping experience when I was 7 years old. Auburn in the winter often had snow. It was a very snowy winter and I got a strep throat. Of course in those days there were no antibiotics and there was only 1 doctor in town. The physician *Dr. Russell* examined me and said, "He has Bright's disease" (glomerulonephritis). From my mother's description of my condition (my face was puffy and I had brown urine), I was a classic case. He said, "He's very sick, and he also has a bad heart." I presume he meant rheumatic heart disease. There was no specific treatment so I was put in bed. This was in February and he kept me in bed for months. He'd come back once every week or two and examine me and say; "His heart's still bad. His kidneys are getting better." They set up a bed in the kitchen and I was literally bedridden until July of that year. During this time, because I wasn't allowed to get up out of bed much, my mother spent a lot of time with me. That had a good effect on my interest in reading and academic things. In July a new doctor came to town. He'd just come from the

University of California. His name was *Max Dunovitz*. My father by that time had begun to believe that maybe Dr. Russell, the only other doctor, didn't know what he was doing. He called Dr. Dunovitz and had him come up and examine me. Max said, "I think his heart is okay. That's a functional murmur. Get him out of bed. Forget about his heart." Max became a hero in our family, as you might guess, and a long time family friend. That's about the time I decided I wanted to be like Max. When in college and during breaks at home he would ask me to come to his clinic and see patients with him. That continued when I was in medical school. It was a sort of a preordained thing when I was 7 years old that I would eventually become a doctor.

WCR: *What year was your mother born?*

MHE: She was born in 1890.

WCR: *And your father?*

MHE: They were the same age.

WCR: *Your mother died, what year?*

MHE: Mother died in 1985 at age 95.

WCR: *What year did your father die?*

MHE: My father was 69 when he died. He had had severe hypertension for many years and eventually had a myocardial infarct, and then a stroke, and died.

WCR: *In your home in Auburn, did you speak Norwegian?*

MHE: No, we spoke English. I learned some Norwegian phrases because of the people in town. I remember at church singing "Silent Night" in Norwegian, in German, and in English. I learned Norwegian songs and phrases because they were popular in the community, but I never learned to speak it. Much to my father's unhappiness (he tried very hard to get me to speak Norwegian) I never did.

WCR: *Your father kept speaking Norwegian.*

MHE: Yes, to the Norwegians in town. His school teaching was in English. He always had a Norwegian accent which I didn't really recognize until I went away to college.

WCR: *Do you have siblings?*

MHE: I had 1 sister, 5 years younger, who was adopted. My parents for some reason didn't have any more biologic children so they adopted Elaine.

WCR: *What was growing up in your home like? You mentioned that nobody was rich, but nobody was terribly poor either. There was enough money to do more or less what you wanted to do. Did both your mother and your father work?*

MHE: Mostly my father, mother didn't work much, but schoolteachers had long vacations. We always took a trip somewhere, loaded everything in the car and off we went. One year we took a trip to Minnesota to see where Dad grew up and we visited some of his relatives. We went to Fargo, North Dakota, where he had a cousin, *Hulgar Poulson*, who owned *The Fargo Forum*, the most influential newspaper in North Dakota. He entertained us for several days in his home. I was about 15 at that time. It was a great trip for us because Poulson was quite a political force in that area, and knew a lot of people in Washington. We told him we were going on to visit Washington, D.C. He said, "You have to visit my friend *J. Edgar Hoover.*" We went to the Federal Bureau of Investigation and Hoover met us. He introduced us to one of his secretaries who took us on a tour. And he said, "How would you guys like to shoot machine guns on the machine gun range?" In Auburn, we had done a lot of deer shooting and other hunting. We went down to the machine gun range and got to shoot at the models of people. You can imagine what a big shot I was when I got back home, being able to tell that story.

WCR: *Do you remember much about meeting J. Edgar Hoover? Was he quite a personality?*

MHE: He didn't spend much time with us. He was sort of perfunctory as I remember. I was a little disappointed. He turned us over to his secretary, a man who took us around.

WCR: *What was it like when you sat down to have dinner at night with your family when you were growing up?*

MHE: The discussions were pretty far ranging. My folks liked to talk politics. My father was a very conservative Republican and my mother was a liberal Democrat. They had heated discussions on politics. I was exposed to 2 different political ideologies all the time. It probably was a good idea because I never became very adamant about either side of the political spectrum. It helped me when I went to Berkeley to college because that was a time of radical communist feelings on this campus. Because I'd been exposed to all sorts of ideas I didn't buy into anything hook, line, and sinker like college kids are so likely to do. It was a good experience. Mother always tried to involve me in classical reading and things like that. My father was a very practical guy, very mechanical. During the summers, several times, he built houses that he rented out, and I helped him build houses. I became a reasonable carpenter as a kid.

He believed very strongly that I should have responsibilities. When I was 10 or 11 he bought some rabbits and I raised rabbits. I had 250 rabbits that I had to take care of. I really disliked the job, but it was required. Every day I had to feed and water them. Then on weekends I had to kill rabbits and take them to the local butcher shops and sell them. The year we went on the trip to Washington, D.C., when I was about 15, I talked him into selling the rabbits. I disliked those rabbits, but he felt that I had to have a daily responsibility. I had to do it. As I look back, it was interesting. In some ways they were very permissive about letting me take the car to go skiing and hiking in the mountains (just young kids together without any adults). On the other side, certain jobs around the house, like taking care of the rabbits, etc., were absolutely required. There was never any question whether I should care for them or not.

WCR: *Did you make money on the rabbits?*

MHE: Yes. We sold them for 18 cents a pound. I'd get on my bicycle and I'd go to the various people in town that liked rabbits and I'd sell them to them and to the butcher shops.

WCR: *You'd kill the rabbits, clean them, and then sell them?*

FIGURE 2. MHE skiing in 1939 at a ski meet.

MHE: Killed them, dressed them out, and then I would take them around.

WCR: *They were ready to cook. Why do you think your father picked rabbits? You didn't do that, did you?*

MHE: No, I didn't select rabbits. I don't know why he picked rabbits. He'd grown up on a farm and he knew about animals of course. I guess he figured that was something that was within the grasp of a young kid and was doable. It was just one of the chores. I had other chores around the house like helping my mother in the garden. She was an avid gardener. But there seemed to be enough time to do a lot of other things that I was interested in.

I was always interested in sports. Because our high school was small, I was on the basketball team (despite being short), the ski team, and the track team (a pole-vaulter and 440-yard runner). I was in the school band, and in high school I was part of a dance band that played in the local area. I had a well-rounded childhood. Before high school I was in the Boy Scouts. I became an Eagle Scout.

WCR: *What did you play?*

MHE: The trombone and piano.

WCR: *What was your house and yard like to be able to accommodate 250 rabbits?*

MHE: Our house was built on about a 2-acre parcel. It was at the edge of town, on the top of a hill. There was a grove of oak trees below our house. The rabbit hutches were dispersed down in the oak grove. On weekends my dad and I would go out and buy alfalfa hay and oats to feed the rabbits. Then I would clean out the rabbit manure and we'd haul that out and spread it around. It was quite an operation.

WCR: *It sounds like your dad sort of dominated your home. Is that proper?*

MHE: Yes, he did, although Mother wasn't altogether passive. Once when we were at Pismo Beach my mother went up in a rickety airplane, much against my father's advice. My father was more rigid than my mother. If my father and I had a disagreement, my mother would come to my side. Like most mothers, she did not think her son could do any wrong. Nevertheless, he was very supportive. We never had a new car because father was a good mechanic and he'd buy old cars until I was 15, when he bought a new Pontiac. There was a church program in Sacramento, 30 miles away (we were very active in the Methodist Church). Mother talked Dad into letting me take the new car and a bunch of kids to the church program in Sacramento. Coming back, I wrecked the car. I rolled it. Fortunately, none of the kids were hurt. I swerved because a guy came out of a side road and to miss him I swerved and rolled the car. It was Saturday afternoon when we finally got home. The car would still drive but it was all wrecked. I had to play a dance in Placerville that night. Placerville is about 30 miles down a back road up through the woods. My father, after having a small fit about the car, of course, said, "I don't think you ought to drive to Placerville." We had another old car so he drove me to Placerville that night and waited for me while I played a 3-hour dance and then drove me home. In retrospect, I thought that was pretty nice of him. We had a good relationship.

WCR: *It sounds like you were quite busy as a kid. You were skiing, taking care of rabbits, other chores around the house. You were playing 2 musical instruments. You were on the track team and basketball team. Did you sleep much as a child?*

MHE: Not much. I suppose I slept about 5 hours a night. My mother used to say, "Myrvin, if you would concentrate on one thing, you'd be very good. But you go in so many different directions at once you're never going to do anything right." I think that was common in those days in a little town because in school everybody felt like they wanted to be involved in almost everything.

WCR: *I gather that you were a good student in school.*

MHE: Yes, I was.

WCR: *Did you discuss your studies a lot with your mother?*

MHE: My mother was the strong influence in my studies, particularly in English. She was very involved. My father and mother both said, "If you don't get good grades you are not going to be able to drive the car." That was a strong influence. And they meant good grades. They wouldn't tolerate any Cs and not many Bs. I had to get As. After I got a C in Latin, my father came home from school and said, "I was at a faculty meeting and the Latin teacher told me she was going to give you a C." He was very embarrassed. He grounded me for about a month.

WCR: *Tell me about your hunting. Did you go hunting with your father?*

MHE: I went hunting with my father and his friends. We mostly shot quail and pheasants. A couple of times we went deer hunting. I never shot a deer.

FIGURE 3. Photograph of MHE taken when entering the University of California in 1941.

Hunting and fishing were big in Auburn. In fact, on the opening day of trout season they closed the schools. My father and I did a lot of trout fishing and we hiked in the mountains together and fished. We had a lot of camaraderie in that way. In those days family outings were often camping trips to someplace where we could hike and fish. My father's brother John, who eventually came to California, leeched off of us, living intermittently at our house for several years. John was an excellent fisherman. Father and I and his brother would hike around and fish in the streams around the Sierras.

WCR: *What was your mother's background?*

MHE: My mother's father was a brickyard manager in Richmond, California. His family had originally emigrated from Nebraska where they'd all been farmers. Her mother was a homemaker. She was in the background. Her father was quite a dynamic guy. I always enjoyed visiting the grandparents because he was fun and he made a fuss over me. After mother left home and her parents retired, they moved to Santa Maria where he had worked for some company for a number of years. Mother had a brother, Walter, who was a very bright guy. He went to work for Standard Oil when he was quite young. He was quite a linguist. They sent him to Venezuela to work in one of their oil businesses there. When Aramco Oil (the consortium—Standard Oil and British Oil, and so forth) was formed, he went to the Middle East and learned to speak Arabic. He knew Iben Saud, the old leader of the Saudis, and was instrumental in their negotiations in the Middle East. Walter would occasionally come home from wherever he was. There was always excitement when Walter came home because he had many exotic stories. When in Venezuela he always brought a box of parrots home and usually gave them to Grandma and Grandpa. They had 4 sisters in that family. But Walter, the youngest sibling, and my mother were very close and always kept in touch.

WCR: *Your mother, I gather, encouraged your reading outside of school activities. What did you read primarily when you were growing up?*

MHE: She did. She tried to get me to read almost everything she could. I read Shakespeare. She encouraged me to read *War and Peace*. I never got all the way through it. She was always bringing home some book that she considered to be a classic. I didn't read all of them, but I read parts of them. She liked to discuss what I read and what I thought about it. She did everything she could to make me as literate as possible. It helped me in the sense that English came easy for me and I didn't have much trouble with grammar or expressing myself.

WCR: *How did you choose the University of California at Berkeley to go to college?*

MHE: In those days in northern California, if you were smart you went to Berkeley and if you were rich you went to Stanford. We were certainly not rich. Entrance requirements at Berkeley, even in those days, were strict. It was an honor to be accepted to Berkeley. I didn't go directly to Berkeley. I went to a little junior college in Auburn for the first 2 years to save money for my parents. It wasn't too bad, in retrospect. Academically, it hurt because I was sort of a big shot in Auburn. Everybody thought I was smart and I got good grades in junior college. When I went to Berkeley I was nobody. A kid from a town of 2,000 people suddenly thrust into an environment of 18,000 students was a rude awakening. I didn't excel at Berkeley academically. The only professor I got to know there was *Dr. Hildebrandt* who was head of the Department of Chemistry. I knew him because he coached the California ski team and I'd known him from competing in ski meets before I went to Berkeley. He was a savior for me. When I'd feel lost I'd go and talk to Hildebrandt. He mentored me. The first winter I was there he got me a job working in Yosemite as a ski host. It was an experience that I look back on with a lot of enjoyment.

WCR: *You only spent 2 years at Berkeley.*

MHE: That's right.

WCR: *That was your first exposure really to a large community.*

MHE: Yes. It was sort of a joke. I joined a fraternity on campus. Most of the kids that were in my fraternity (AKK) were from San Francisco and they considered themselves big city boys. They considered me a hillbilly. It was probably accurate.

WCR: *Did studying always come easy for you? In high school did you really have to put out or did it seem easy?*

MHE: It seemed easy. I didn't have to work too hard.

WCR: *But in college, that changed.*

MHE: All of a sudden it was hard. They graded on the curve. You could get a 90 on an exam and still get a C. Not only did we have a lot of smart students from California, but also it was flooded with immigrants from Europe. One of my closest friends was a Polish Jewish immigrant, who had run from Hitler. All the immigrants worked very hard.

WCR: *What years were you at Berkeley?*

MHE: I got to Berkeley in the fall of 1941. I was at Berkeley just 1 semester before Pearl Harbor. I stayed 2 years.

WCR: *Were there any mentors in high school or junior high school who influenced you?*

MHE: Yes, quite a few. My English teacher, *Mrs. Hupe*, was a mentor. I still keep in touch with her son who is in the forest service. There was a biology teacher, a woman that I was very fond of and she was very fond of me, and she encouraged me. I had a good relationship with most teachers, primarily because my father made a big thing of it. He would tell me if you get in trouble in class, it reflects on me. I kept my nose clean; I didn't cut up too much in class.

WCR: *How many students were there in high school?*

MHE: Even though the town was little, it was a bigger school because there were a lot of students bussed in. Most of my classes had about 20 students. My graduating class was about 85.

WCR: *Were you first in the class?*

MHE: No. Possibly in the top 10%.

WCR: *Those 2 years at Berkeley were a good experience.*

MHE: Yes. It was a whole different life for me. The competition in college was entirely different academically. Socially, it was a whole new picture also. At that time we had just formed a partnership with Russia, and communism was rife on campus. There was a communist bookstore right outside the Sather Gate. There were communist clubs. I went to communist meetings frequently and listened to the rhetoric. The members at the fraternity and I would talk about communism. We never really were convinced that it was the answer to the maiden's prayer. Many thought that the establishment was wrong, however. Although there were a lot of kids on campus that were hooked on communism, none of my close friends or associates were. I think it was partly due to the fact that we had a little broader look at life.

Socially things were different in the fraternities. I met a gal in my chemistry class (my chemistry partner in organic chemistry), whom I thought was really cute. I would bring her to the fraternity house for coffee or chocolate after the football games. After I took her home I came back and all the guys jumped all over me because she was Jewish. I didn't know she was Jewish. There was really quite an anti-Jewish feeling in this particular fraternity that I had joined. This bothered me because one of my closest friends *Max Dunovist* at Auburn was Jewish. In Auburn there was absolutely no racial or class distinction. We had 1 black family in the town and 2 or 3 Jewish families. At Berkeley the Gentiles disliked the Jews, and the Jews disliked the Gentiles. It was really a new experience for me and it irritated me. I never really fit into the fraternity like most of the guys. One reason I joined this fraternity was that it gave me a job washing dishes for my house fee.

My father always made a big thing of the fact that he paid his own way through college. I decided when

I was in high school that I was going to do the same thing. I worked part time when I was at Berkeley for the extension division and I washed dishes and waited on tables at the fraternity. In my senior year I took a swing shift job at the shipyard in Richmond. I worked 5 days a week, 8 hours a day on the swing shift so I could have enough money to go to college.

WCR: *In college you really didn't sleep much at all.*

MHE: That's right but it didn't bother me. I didn't require much sleep.

WCR: *What were the swing shift hours?*

MHE: They had a bus pick up students at 2:30 P.M. I had to get all my classes in before that. We'd get there in time to put in 8 hours and then return home.

WCR: *When did you study?*

MHE: After I got home I'd study for about 90 minutes. During the day I would study between classes, and early in the morning.

WCR: *You'd get to bed about 2:00 A.M. and wake up when?*

MHE: I'd get up about 6:00 A.M.

WCR: *Sleep was not something that you required.*

MHE: It didn't bother me. I used to do the same thing in high school. I would play for some of the dances for 5 hours, then sleep for 2 or 3 hours, and get up Sunday morning and drive to ski all day. It didn't seem to bother me.

WCR: *What did you major in at Berkeley?*

MHE: I was a premed, but I took a major in psychology.

WCR: *What courses did you really enjoy in college that have had a subsequent impact on you?*

MHE: The course I enjoyed the most was anthropology, which was not part of my major.

WCR: *Why do you think you got so interested in anthropology?*

MHE: I don't know. I can't explain it. I got "A"s in both psychology and anthropology at Berkeley. There was something about anthropology that just appealed to me. By that time, however, I was headed toward medicine. It never occurred to me that I wouldn't go into medicine. It was something that really intrigued me. I spent a lot of time reading stuff, even what wasn't assigned in my classes.

WCR: *Anthropology today is a lot broader than it was in 1941. What part of anthropology really appealed to you?*

MHE: They were already making discoveries about early man and evolution. My parents were devout Methodists and even in high school I read all sorts of stuff that my mother would recommend or that I would pick out myself. At church we heard classical, Protestant hellfire, and damnation sermons. I'd come home and say, "Mother, I think some of the things he is saying aren't true." And she'd say, "It's allegorical, Myrvin. This is a moral story. Literally, you shouldn't take it seriously at all." I had the feeling that Bible stories were just stories. I guess that interested me in history. Pretty soon I began to find out about early man and it seemed that this might have been my way of developing my individuality. In a sense my interest in anthropology might have been a rejection of the Christian doctrine. I think it is normal for kids to rebel in some way against their parents' beliefs. I used to come home and talk to my mother about all the things I'd learned in anthropology. She never put it down. She would say it was important for me to know those things.

WCR: *So anthropology opened your eyes that teachings in the Gospel are not quite as true as some would like to believe.*

MHE: That's right. In fact, after I started studying anthropology I discussed the topic a lot in our college bull sessions in the evenings. I took a certain pride in trying to discredit someone who took a hard line religious viewpoint. I studied the Bible primarily to pick out areas I thought had been disproved, and I could quote relevant verses to use in discrediting someone. It didn't make me too popular as you might guess.

WCR: *You were well versed in the Bible during your teenage years.*

MHE: Absolutely. I could recite the books of the Bible and many of the Psalms. I was very well versed in Biblical Christianity.

WCR: *Was it difficult for you to get into medical school?*

MHE: Yes, it was because my grades at Berkeley weren't so good and the war had come on. They drafted kids out of Cal right and left. I thought I'd rather go to medical school than go to war. I applied to about 10 different medical schools. One of them was the University of Louisville, because the father of one of my friends in San Francisco had graduated from there and suggested that I go there. I joined a V7 program and it allowed one to complete college and then join the Navy as an Ensign. It was called "a 90-day wonder" preparation at the Great Lakes to become an ensign. My reasoning was—if I join the V7 program I can stay in college long enough to get into medical school and then transfer to the V12 program, which would permit completion of medical school. The first medical school that accepted me was the University of Louisville. I grabbed it.

WCR: *That must have been quite an experience to go across country to the University of Louisville in 1943?*

MHE: Yes. It was. The University of Louisville was an old school and the only one in Kentucky at the time. It was a private school when I went there. It subsequently was taken over by the state. The University of Kentucky Medical School at Lexington started later. Like so many of the schools during the war, it was weakened because many of the faculty of the University of Louisville went off to the war. It was a broadening experience for me. I found out something about the South. I lived in the old fraternity house in medical school and it was in the black district. We had a black cook and housekeepers. Almost all of the patients we had in medical school in the city hospital were black. It was my first experience with blacks. Most of the students in medical school became very good friends and I admired many of them. Most went on to good careers. The competition was good for me. Our freshman class was 100 students. The first day the Dean told us: "I want you to look around you because 1 out every 4 is going to be out of here. We're going to flunk out 25 students." It was a stimulus to study, particularly with the war going on. If you flunked out you went to war. There was much "hands on" teaching in medical school compared to some schools in which almost all teaching was didactic. We had lots of bedside teaching and lots of contact with patients. It was stimulating and it helped us correlate anatomy and physiology with real medicine early in our career. Every year they gave a prize to the student that excelled in surgery, obstetrics, general medicine, and psychiatry. Because I had a degree in psychology and knew the jargon, I always got the psychiatry prize. Everybody in my class thought, for sure, I was going to be a psychiatrist. In my senior year they farmed me out in a mental hospital for 3 months in a clinical clerkship. In those days, mental hospitals and psychiatry were grim. These were people with central nervous system syphilis and catatonic schizophrenia. After that experience I was sure that I was going to have nothing to do with psychiatry.

WCR: *Medical school was quite a different environment than Auburn and Berkeley, California. Many of your patients were very poor and they didn't speak the same English that you spoke. Most of your classmates, I presume, were from Kentucky.*

MHE: Correct, most of them. We had a few from New York and the northern central USA. We had 4 or 5 Jewish students. *Bill Rashkind*, the inventor of the balloon septostomy procedure was there. Bill was my classmate and we were very close friends in medical school.

WCR: *You mentioned that some of your classmates have done quite well.*

MHE: Bill Rashkind is an example. *Tommy Kerns* went on to become a neuro-ophthalmologist at the Mayo Clinic. A couple of my friends became Presidents of the American Medical Association (good medical politicians). Kentuckians are good politicians. Southerners in general are. The academic level of my class was pretty good.

WCR: *How did you get back and forth from California?*

MHE: By train.

WCR: *Was medical school 3 years because of the war?*

MHE: Yes.

WCR: *So you went straight through without vacation.*

MHE: Yes.

WCR: *Did you ever get back home?*

MHE: Yes. Occasionally we had 1 week off and I would take a train home. After the first semester I was inducted into the military and I wore a uniform. I was an apprentice seaman. Twice I got on a Navy transport plane and flew back. At Berkeley, my roommate's father was a big time attorney in San Francisco. His sister was a very pretty girl and I was very attracted to her. We had dated quite a lot when I was at Berkeley.

I would go back to San Francisco and visit them and stay at their place as well as go home. I got back at least twice a year for a few days.

WCR: *You didn't marry that young lady?*

MHE: No.

WCR: *What subjects in medical school really interested you?*

MHE: Probably surgical anatomy the most, partly because I served as an extern at a small Louisville hospital during my last 2 years of medical school. The externs lived in the hospital and started IVs and that sort of thing. The local surgeons that worked there would ask us externs to scrub with them. I'd get up in the morning and scrub on a 7 o'clock case and then leave and get to medical school at 8 o'clock. On weekends, I frequently scrubbed. I got quite interested in surgery. For a long time I thought I would be a surgeon because I was very good in my anatomy class and I was dexterous because of my piano playing. At the end of my second year the private surgeons allowed us externs to take out appendices and uteruses.

WCR: *What brought you back to internal medicine?*

MHE: In my senior year of medical school I became very jaded about our faculty surgeons. Standard practice was for a senior medical student to scrub up as the fourth man (the rest were residents and attendings), work up the patient (history and physical), and then the professor would quiz the medical student about the anatomy which was difficult to see. The faculty surgeons were very critical and would castigate us if we incorrectly described the anatomic relations. I had been scrubbing with the surgeons in the small private hospital and they were very nice guys and they showed me how to do things. I began to think that academic surgeons were sort of four-flushers. They made a big thing of doing surgery, and here I was a medical student and had done quite a bit of it. I thought any trained chimpanzee could do it. Then they would beat on the medical students and I decided against surgery.

WCR: *How did you become interested in internal medicine?*

MHE: Because I was supposed to have had heart disease, I wanted to know more about the heart. When I finished Louisville I wanted to take an internship somewhere in the New York area. One of my classmates knew about the Jersey City Medical Center, which at that time was quite a good teaching hospital. He suggested that I apply there. I also applied to Bellevue and was asked to go for an interview. Since I grew up in California I wanted to get some training in New York. When I got to Bellevue the interview seemed to go well for about 30 minutes. Finally the guy said, "What do you want to do when you finish your internship?" I said, "I want to take a residency in internal medicine and then I'm going into practice." He said, "Going into practice." I told him "yes." He said, "We don't have anybody in our internships going into practice. We only train people for academics. There was some misunderstanding, you shouldn't be here for an interview." I was pretty upset. I went across the river and signed up for the internship at Jersey City. There, a senior medical resident named *Carroll Levy* from the University of Michigan, had a profound influence on me. I admired him intensely and he encouraged me. From that time on I decided that internal medicine was what I wanted to do and possibly later, cardiology. Cardiology was not a specialty at that time. Internists were cardiologists.

WCR: *Was there anybody in medical school that had a major impact on you?*

MHE: Possibly. *Dean John Walker Moore* was the Chief of Medicine. I think all of us looked up to Dean Moore. He was another reason why I was interested in internal medicine. He was really quite an unusual man.

WCR: *What was your internship like?*

MHE: That was at a time when Mayor Haig was a big political force in New Jersey. He had gotten money from the government to build this medical center. I think he was a major supporter of Roosevelt when he ran. The medical center was sort of a payoff. It was a beautiful plant. They had a lot of visiting professors from New York. They had tons of patients, most from Jersey City which was just one big slum. There were immigrants from Poland and Italy and everywhere. It was a very active and busy program. We saw a lot of pathology. We had excellent teaching. The senior resident, Carroll Levy, convinced me that I was going to be a good doctor and I was going to be an outstanding internist. I believed him. I decided in my internship that after I served the 2 years in the Navy, I would continue in medicine.

WCR: *Was that a straight medical internship or rotating?*

MHE: Rotating. We went through obstetrics, orthopedics, and the whole bit.

WCR: *You went into the Navy immediately after your internship. What was that experience like?*

MHE: The war had just finished. Just before I left Louisville I'd gotten married to a Kentucky girl whose father was a preacher. Although I was very attracted to her and she to me, we were a misfit. Our married life was really quite stormy, but we stayed together a long time. She came to Jersey City with me, of course. She got a job as a secretary in the hospital. When we left there I was sent to Washington, D.C., at the Anacostia Naval Air Station for a short time. It was a financial problem for us. We had had a child and my Navy pay just wasn't cutting it. The second month I was there one of the pilots who came through said, "I'll tell you where you can live cheaply. That would be in Guantanamo Bay. They provide housing and everything is practically free." I talked to one of the bureaucrats from the Pentagon who came to the base frequently. He told me he would transfer me to Guantanamo. We moved to Guantanamo Bay after about 3 or 4 months and spent 18 months there.

WCR: *What was that experience like?*

MHE: The hospital at Guantanamo Bay was only about 60 beds. It was run by a Navy command. A urologist, a Navy captain, was in charge of a command. There were just 2 junior medical officers and 8

senior officers who had been in the Navy quite a long time. Most of the outstanding docs who had been in the service had gone back to their business and it left a hiatus of capable people. When I arrived there, there were 2 new guys, both of us with obligated duty. One had taken a straight surgical internship in Boston. I had decided I wanted to be an internist, even though I'd only had a rotating internship. When the Chief interviewed us he said, "So, you're going to be an internist." I said, "That's right." He said, "Well, I'm going to assign you to surgery." The fellow who took a straight surgical internship was assigned to medicine. The fellow who was in charge of the surgical department was the only other surgeon (there were just 2 of us in surgery). He had been a surgeon in private practice. After scrubbing with him a few times I had a low opinion of him. He said to me, "Do you know anything about bones?" I told him I'd had 1 month in orthopedics. He told me I had to take care of the bones. I was assigned to orthopedics. Literally, when people came in with fractures it was my responsibility to take care of them. I had to study the books each time I saw a case. Fortunately, we had a radiologist there who seemed to know a little bit about orthopedics. I would get together with him and we'd figure out what to do with all these fractures. The Navy base was busy. The whole Atlantic Fleet trained there in the winter because it was nice and warm. The harbor always had 8 to 10 big ships in dock. We had sailors coming in with everything under the sun. I got to be a fair orthopedic surgeon in 18 months.

The other thing that was interesting was that they loaned us periodically to the fleet training squadron. They'd put me on a ship during simulated navel battles. I was supposed to go around and evaluate how the corpsmen responded to emergencies. Sometimes I rode submarines. I got to see the big carriers and battleships and learned how they worked. It was a fun experience and one that broadened my outlook. I was on the carrier FDR when the first jet squadron landed on a carrier deck. Academically, I didn't contribute much. I didn't get a chance to do much general medicine since I was involved in surgery all the time.

WCR: *You decided that you didn't want to be an orthopedic surgeon.*

MHE: Yes. In fact, some of the results I had were pretty bad. Particularly difficult patients could be transferred to a big Navy hospital somewhere else, but my boss was reluctant to transfer anybody because it would reflect on him as not having qualified people (which he didn't have). This was before Castro. We frequently visited the cities of Cuba. Guantanamo City was close to the base. Santiago, one of the oldest cities in the Western Hemisphere, was a few miles away. The Cuban people were very cordial to the doctors on the base. It was a nice experience in that sense. The medicine on the base was pretty haphazard. Because there were only 2 junior medical officers, we took calls every other night. The senior men never took calls. We delivered the babies and functioned as all-around general physicians. There was a lot of recreation on the base. The hospital business hours were from 7 A.M. to 1 P.M. We all had afternoons off if we weren't on call at the hospital. We enjoyed golf and sailing. The Navy had a 47-foot auxiliary ketch which we frequently sailed to Jamaica, which was not far away.

WCR: *Then you returned to Jersey City to do a residency in internal medicine in 1949. How did that work out?*

MHE: It worked out well. By now Carroll Levy had been hired as the director of medical services. I was very pleased with his mentoring. He encouraged me to engage in some research projects. That was the first time I'd ever considered doing research. We had a mercurial diuretic named thiomerin. I kept track of the weight loss and the diuresis in the patients. In those days we didn't have a good oral diuretic. The patients consequently came in frequently for injections. I got interested in heart failure. Because he assigned me a lecture every 2 weeks in general physiology, I studied very hard to perform well. That was a good experience. When someone expects you to do well you try to do well. He really stimulated and demanded hard work.

WCR: *Did you live in the hospital?*

MHE: At that time my wife and I had separated. I lived in the staff house which was nice quarters and not far from the hospital. I had another interesting experience there as a resident. In those days electrocardiograms were taken with a string galvanometer, and 1 senior nurse did all of them. She was the only one in the hospital who knew how to work the string galvanometer. I wanted to learn how to take electrocardiograms and she wasn't about to let me learn. I went to great lengths, smoozing her. I took her out to dinner and told her how beautiful she was. Finally, she taught me to take electrocardiograms with the string galvanometer. That gave me status. All of a sudden I was considered to be sort of a cardiologist because I could take electrocardiograms. That stimulated me to study electrocardiography more. That may have been one of the reasons that I eventually got into cardiology. Once you do something like that, people expect you to know more, so you try a little more.

WCR: *Your first marriage lasted how long?*

MHE: We were married about 15 years. We were separated when I went for my residency and then we went back together again and lived in Long Beach for a number of years (even though it was a stormy thing) before we finally divorced.

WCR: *Why did you decide to go back to California to continue your medical residency?*

MHE: For 2 reasons: (1) I wanted to get back to California because I intended to practice there, and (2) the situation in Jersey City was untenable financially if I was going to maintain my marriage. My salary was $50 a month. We didn't have any money. My wife had actually gone out to California and lived with my parents in Auburn. We had 2 children at that time. My wife didn't like my mother very much. That was stormy. I often called from Jersey City. I figured something had to be done to remedy this situation. I got an offer to go to Seaside Hospital in Long Beach because there was a fellow in Jersey City who had been trained at Harvard with *Fred Kellogg* who had gone to Long Beach. He said, "Fred Kellogg was one of the smartest electrocardiographers he had ever met. If you could go there and spend time with Fred Kellogg it would be very good for you." I contacted him and they said they would give me an apartment for my family and $150 a month if I'll come as a medical resident. I left Jersey City at the end of the first year and went to Seaside the second year. I got to know the doctors there. Fred Kellogg turned out to be a fantastic mentor, a very bright guy, and he introduced me to electrocardiography in a serious way. The man I eventually became a partner with, *Elliston Farrell*, was an outstanding scholar who had graduated from Johns Hopkins. He'd gone to England, had been trained in tropical medicine, and then taught tropical medicine at Tulane. When the war came he joined the Air Force and later decided to leave academics and come to Long Beach. He asked me join him in practice. I decided I needed to know more about pathology. I signed up for a year of pathology in San Francisco at San Francisco County Hospital with the option that I could come back to Long Beach if I wanted to. I knew I wasn't going to be a pathologist. When I got there I explained to the chief, *Jessie Carr*, that I would be glad to do autopsies. I did 340 autopsies. I averaged 2 every weekday or more. I figured I could learn the most doing autopsies. I wasn't particularly interested in how 1 exotic cancer was differentiated from another. I tried to learn as much about the heart during that experience as I could.

WCR: *Why did you think you wanted training in pathology? That is a bit unusual.*

MHE: Primarily because internists talked pathology all the time. They talked about how the kidneys looked for example. I felt that we were talking about things we really didn't fully understand. I just felt that it would round me out and make me an outstanding internist.

WCR: *Did you enjoy that year?*

MHE: Yes, very much. It was very stimulating. A fellow named *Warren Bostick* was Chief of Pathology at Cal San Francisco county hospital, and was part of the UC Service. We had rounds weekly together. I got to know Warren Bostick pretty well. He eventually left to become Dean at the University of California, Irvine.

WCR: *So that worked out very much to your advantage.*

MHE: Eventually. Although at the time I enjoyed my experience there. San Francisco County was a zoo with tons of clinical data.

WCR: *Did your family go with you up to San Francisco?*

MHE: Yes. We rented an apartment there.

WCR: *And then you came back.*

MHE: I came back to Long Beach and became partners with Elliston Farrell. He spoke French and Spanish as well as English. Nobody ever discovered his misspelling a word in his life. He was a wonderful guy and he was almost like a father to me. We became very close. He developed infective endocarditis on his aortic valve, had a stroke, retired, and died a few years later. His kids, like most kids, were very much against the Vietnam War. He was very pro-war. He believed we were saving the world from communism. He volunteered and took time off from our practice and left for Vietnam. Because he spoke French he was able to be very effective there. He died about 5 years after the war was over.

WCR: *What was private practice like in the 1950s? You started in 1952.*

MHE: I was in an office with a general internist. Because we had a residency at Seaside Hospital, I was very active in teaching. I tried to take responsibility as much as I could for the teaching because I thought it set me apart from the rest of the staff. There was a children's heart clinic that had been started by the Long Beach Heart Association. I volunteered for that. I tried to enmesh myself as much as I could in the educational part of the hospital.

One of our biggest problems in those days was the emergency room admission of people with pulmonary edema. The old days of using tourniquets and oxygen tents were an unsatisfactory approach and most of these patients had hypertension. I decided that if we could lower their pressure they would improve. Hexamethonium had just come out. I got one of the residents to rotate with me, covering the emergency room at the hospital every other night. If patients came in with pulmonary edema we'd treat them with hexamethonium. The results were dramatic. The pulmonary edema would clear up in 15 to 20 minutes. The standard treatment with oxygen tents and tourniquets would take hours and hours. At that time, UCLA medical school was just beginning and Harbor General Hospital was their only facility. I volunteered there as clinical faculty at Harbor Hospital for the UCLA service.

WCR: *That's how far from Long Beach?*

MHE: It's about a 15-minute drive to Torrance. I got involved in their academic program. After we had treated about 30 patients with hexamethonium, we were ecstatic over the results. I told the Chief of Medicine at Harbor Hospital that I wanted to make a presentation at grand rounds and presented the hexamethonium information. After we finished the Chief of Medicine, Dr. Lawrence got up and said, "Dr. Ellestad, that was a very interesting presentation. If I catch anybody at this hospital using it they'll be fired on the spot." On the other hand George Griffith urged me to present it to the American Heart. I presented it at the first American Heart Association meeting I'd ever been to in 1955. There were probably 1,500 people there. *Stanley Sarnoff* was the chairman of the session. I was pretty well raked over the coals, but Sarnoff supported me. As you remember he was the first chief of cardiology at NIH. After the meeting was over he said, "You know, that's a good idea. You ought to follow up on that." That made me feel good because he was highly respected. It was another 10 years before afterload reduction became popular, although we used it at our hospital on a regular basis.

WCR: *You published that paper in the* Journal of the American Medical Association *in 1956. I gather that by the mid-1950s you were drifting more and more into cardiology.*

MHE: What happened was that *Julian Knutson* came to Long Beach to practice with another internist. Julian was the first cardiac resident with *Earl Wood* at the Mayo Clinic. When he came to Long Beach he also joined the attending staff at Harbor General Hospital, and they decided that they wanted to have a heart catheterization laboratory. Julian wanted somebody to help him and I volunteered so Julian and I started a heart catheterization laboratory at Harbor. We did cardiac catheterization using fluoroscopes and lead aprons. That was long before image intensifiers. Most patients then had valvular or congenital heart disease. We did heart catheterizations at Harbor for several years. I was really caught up in working in the cath lab. I thought it was great. In 1961, I was elected Chief of Staff at Harbor because I'd been out there so much. By that time it was obvious that cardiology was going to be my thing and I tended to spend most of my time in the cardiology laboratory. Also, by that time cardiology was beginning to be recognized as a specialty, although most internists resented the idea because they'd been "cardiologists" for a long time. The fact that I was toting myself as a cardiologist didn't sell too well at Long Beach. I wasn't actually the most popular guy.

WCR: *You started exclusively limiting your practice.*

MHE: I didn't exclusively limit it because I still had many old general internal medical patients. When somebody referred a patient to me I'd send him back. Actually, I didn't get very many referrals from my local environment. I got referrals from outlying areas. If a guy in town wants to send somebody to a specialist, he'd send him/her up to Los Angeles and not to somebody in his own town. In the early days of our cardiology program at Seaside, most referrals came from out of town.

WCR: *When you moved to Long Beach in 1952, what was Long Beach like?*

MHE: Long Beach at that time was a city of about 200,000 people. People called it "Iowa by the Sea." Many people from the Midwest had immigrated there. It was a big small town. The old families that had lived there were very much in control of things, both socially and politically. It was a nice town in the sense that there were a lot of recreational facilities sponsored by the city. Everybody was in everything—the Rotary Club, the Kiwanis Club, and the Junior Chamber of Commerce. When I first came to Long Beach, I joined a number of clubs. It was a nice place to live.

WCR: *You went from 2,000 growing up to 200,000 when you started your practice. You must have been working extremely hard. It sounds like your non-necessity for a lot of sleep always paid big dividends for you. What was it like?*

MHE: It gave me time to study and write. When I first started practice my office visits were $6 and my home visits were $7. I made 15 or 20 house calls a week for years. Also, making house calls took a lot of time.

WCR: *Your first marriage ended in 1963. By that time you were doing a lot of cardiac catheterizations. Did you do your cardiac catheterizations at Seaside in Long Beach?*

MHE: At Seaside Hospital we started a catheterization laboratory about 1958, two years before we moved into the new Memorial Hospital. Julian Knutson and I decided we wanted to do some catheterizations on private patients. We couldn't do them at Harbor because that was only for the County. By that time I was traveling to UCLA in Westwood to help the chief of cardiology, *Al Kattus*. It was a long drive to Los Angeles before the freeways.

WCR: *You didn't get paid for that either.*

MHE: No. There was a new doc that came to Long Beach named *Irv Ungar*, and he'd been trained at Duke under Richard Bing in heart catheterization. He showed up at Seaside (the biggest hospital in town—200 beds). He said that his father, who was a merchant in Long Beach, would put up the money to build a heart catheterization laboratory at Seaside. Fred Kellogg, who was our guru of cardiology at Seaside, took a dislike to Irv Ungar. Irv was very aggressive and quite self-important. Fred said, "No we don't want the catheterization laboratory here." Irv Ungar went to Saint Mary's Hospital (110 beds at that time). They put in a catheterization laboratory there about 1956. I decided that if I wanted to do some private catheterizations, I didn't want to have to take the patients all the way to UCLA (which I had done a few times). I got privileges at St. Mary's. Their chief of radiology was a personal friend and he supported me. One day, about 3 months after I'd done 5 or 6, Irv came into the laboratory as I was finishing up and said, "Myrv, you're not making any contribution to this place. Your privileges are terminated." Pretty soon a Sister came in and asked me into her office. She told me I was fired, that my privileges were terminated at Saint Mary's. The word got out and it stirred up the docs at Seaside. They decided to set up a catheterization laboratory also. Julian Knutson and I set one up at Seaside. At least for a time the internists and general practitioners supported cardiology. We didn't have good imaging at all initially. We made most of our decisions from pressure tracings. We believed that the way to make a diagnosis of mitral valve disease was to have a good atrial pressure. We would stick the left atrium via the back with a Björk needle. Julian Knutson said he was uncomfortable with doing these procedures so he resigned from heart catheterizations, even though he was the one with formal training. He gave it up about the time we got started. I was left as the only invasive person in the area besides Irv at Saint Mary's. Like many places, the competition between the 2 hospitals was intense. You were either Saint Mary's or you were Seaside Memorial. In the meantime we built a new hospital which opened in 1960. We developed the cardiac catheterization lab in a little closet next to the x-ray department. We wheeled our physiological recorder into the x-ray flu-oroscopic room and did heart catheterizations. The chief of radiology accommodated us although he believed that pretty soon this whole business of heart catheterizations would go away and that it was a waste of time.

There was no one at the hospital interested in pulmonary disease. I felt that if we were going to have a catheterization laboratory, we ought to have some pulmonary physiology. I went and spent 3 months with *Julius Comroe* in San Francisco, who at that time was the national guru in pulmonary physiology. We built a homemade helium dilution system for residual volume (see Figure 4). Thus, we had a cardiology-pulmonary department which we called "clinical physiology." When Julius Knutson gave up on catheterizations he took over the ECG lab when Fred Kellog retired. The administration contracted with me to direct the Department of Clinical Physiology.

WCR: *By 1965 you were spending a lot of time in the cath lab?*

MHE: Quite a bit. We didn't do an awful lot until coronary angiograms came along. After *Mason Sones* described coronary angiography, I went to Cleveland and spent a couple of weeks with him and came back with Sones' catheters and started doing coronary angiograms. It wasn't long after that that the Vineberg procedure came along. By that time we had a couple of excellent cardiac surgeons. We were doing a lot. We did several hundred Vineberg operations. After Favolaro introduced coronary bypass, we started that procedure at the new hospital and then things really got busy. We also started our fellowship in 1965.

WCR: *When coronary angioplasty came along, did you get into that yourself?*

MHE: I was at a heart meeting and had a poster. The poster next to me was on angioplasty in dogs. Nobody was interested in my poster and nobody was interested in his poster. I got acquainted with *Andreas Gruentzig*. He told me that he had met *Dick Myler* in San Francisco and that Myler had wanted to do some patients. Gruentzig was in Zurich, Switzerland, at the time, and the surgeons were not very supportive, so he was planning some time with Myler in San Francisco. I went to San Francisco where Myler mentored me on angioplasty and I think I did the first angioplasty in southern California in 1977.

WCR: *You were on the ground floor of angioplasty.*

MHE: I was with the original registry that *Kenny Kent* established. Things were very busy. I had formed an internal medicine group in the late 1950s. There were eventually about 20 doctors, 3 cardiologists, and the rest were general internists, gastroenterologists, etc. The cardiac program was growing and the hospital administrators felt that I was restricting the growth because I was competing with the other cardiologists. They wanted me to get out of private practice and be noncompetitive and were willing to pay me a salary if I would do that. In 1988 I left my group which was about 20+ people and took a full-time job at the hospital as director of the program. I was to continue my research and exercise testing. I had that job for

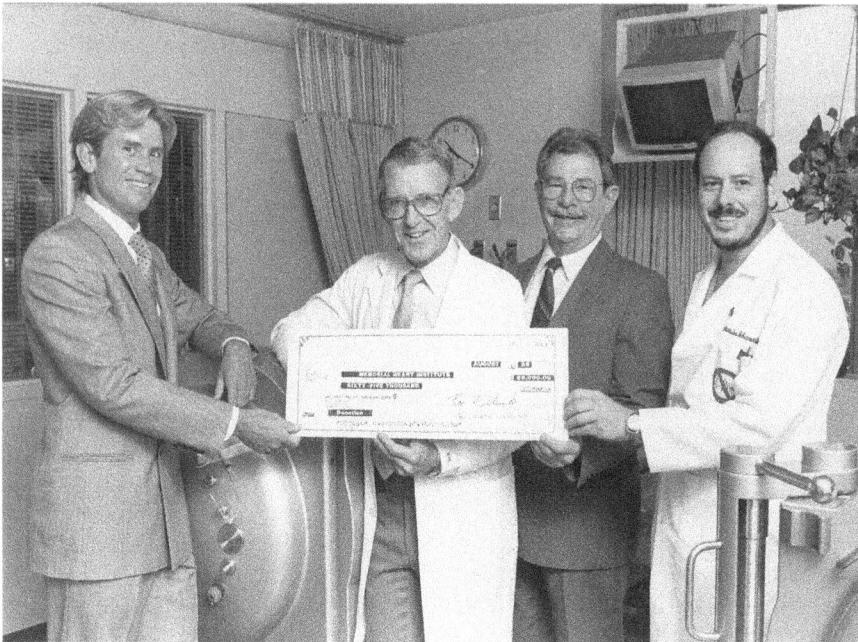

FIGURE 4. MHE receiving a large check from Genentech in 1989 to support a project using hyperbaric oxygen for acute myocardial infarction.

FIGURE 5. Award given to MHE by the National Angiology Society for work in stress testing.

about 3 years when they changed administrators. The next administrator fired me.

WCR: *So you went back with your former group.*

MHE: No. They didn't want me back. They were mad at me for leaving. So when I got fired I had no place to go.

WCR: *What did you do then?*

MHE: I moved in with *John Messenger* who had another cardiology group there and started a small practice. But I stayed on in a teaching capacity at the hospital and I kept up my research projects. Two years after the administrator had fired me he was fired. The next administrator hired me in a new job entitled Care Line Director, which has some of the functions of the

Chief of Cardiology. It doesn't have that title because the Chief of Cardiology is elected from the general staff. Basically, my job is to take care of administrative problems, monitor quality control, and try to keep the department financially solvent, and teach.

WCR: *One of the things, Myrvin, which is so intriguing to me about you is your ability all these years to have been an academic cardiologist. You have published widely in major peer-review journals. You've written a stress-testing book that has gone through 4 editions. How have you been able to incorporate this academic career into your private practice career?*

MHE: You talk to people and ask "Wouldn't you like to do some clinical research" and they say, "they don't have time." What you have time for is what you are interested in. I have time because I make time. It takes some energy. When I get going on redoing the book, I have dinner with my wife and we socialize for a little while and then about 8:00 P.M. I go to work and I work until 11:00 P.M. or midnight or sometimes later. You just have to do it. That's all it takes. I think one of my traits has always been (even when I was very young) that I always look for another answer, another way to solve a problem that doesn't seem to have a solution or a satisfactory solution. I think that's why I started using hexamethonium for heart failure. I have always looked for a unique way to approach or solve a problem. When I'm driving to work, those are the kinds of things I'm thinking about. When I have an idea I

FIGURE 6. MHE's wife whom he married in 1965.

pursue it. A lot of ideas I've pursued, of course, fall through the cracks. Wonderful theories can be destroyed by ugly facts. But quite a few of them have born fruit.

WCR: *How did you get started with the book?*

MHE: *Herman Hellerstein* started a work classification unit around 1955 to evaluate people who had had an acute myocardial infarct to see if they could go back to work or not. He published on this. The Los Angeles County Heart Association sponsored a group of cardiologists in Los Angeles to set up the same thing. *Bert Sobel* was the director of that program in Los Angeles. I knew Bert and he asked me if I had some time to come and help him. That's another thing I did that didn't earn any money. One half day a week I'd go up to Los Angeles and work with Bert Sobel. They were testing the patients on a treadmill. They would put a single-lead electrocardiogram on them, walk them on a treadmill at 1.7 miles/hour on a 10% grade for 10 minutes, and then they would decide if they could go back to work or not.

WCR: *This was after an acute myocardial infarction. How long after?*

MHE: Usually a couple of months afterwards. I went up there once a week for a better part of a year. It seemed to me that they needed to increase the workload to really find out the answer. Sobel was very much opposed to that. In 1960, when we started our new cardiac program at the new hospital I talked them into buying a treadmill and we started doing the same thing at Long Beach, only we increased the workloads. After doing that I discovered that *Bob Bruce*

was doing the same thing in Seattle. I got acquainted with Bruce and he reinforced my belief that you could exercise patients at higher workloads safely. We kept in touch with each other and came up in this business on a parallel course. I was doing a lot of exercising testing along with all these other things. In 1970, our hospital decided to buy a computer for business reasons. They bought a big CDC mainframe computer. I talked the administration into loaning me a programmer and we started a computerized program for heart catheterizations and treadmill. I think it was one of the first "registries." The Long Beach Heart Association was very active socially and raised money. They liked what I was doing and they funded me. I hired some people and we did follow-up studies on all the people who had had the treadmill study. We published in *Circulation* in 1975, the first long-term follow-up on maximum treadmill stress testing. We used that database for a lot of different studies showing the effect of ST depression and discovered the abnormality we named chronotropic incompetence. That database and work we published attracted a lot of attention. I would give lectures on treadmill testing and many docs would say that somebody ought to write a book. I said, "All right. I'll write a book."

WCR: *That was 1975.*

MHE: Yes, 1975 was the first edition.

WCR: *That was a terrific hit. That was the first textbook on stress testing. How many copies did you sell?*

MHE: It sold 5,000 copies the first year. The publisher, F.A. Davis, said, "It's amazing!"

WCR: *How many in the entire first edition did you sell?*

MHE: It trailed off a lot after the first year. The first edition sold about 10,000 copies over a 5-year period.

WCR: *You're revising it about every 5 years.*

MHE: I'm working on the fifth edition now. The fourth edition came out in 1995.

WCR: *How many pages does it have?*

MHE: Now it has about 550. The first edition had 250 pages.

WCR: *That has been a bonanza for you through the years.*

MHE: I don't earn a lot of money on it, but it put my name out there and got me invited to a lot of great meetings. I was able to meet a lot of great doctors all over the world. It was really the frosting on the cake.

WCR: *That's not the only publications you've been doing. You've gotten into a lot of other things through the years.*

MHE: I get interested in something and pursue it and write it up.

WCR: *In your busiest time, 1980, for example, what was your usual day like? What time would you wake up in the morning?*

MHE: I usually get up at 6:00 A.M. For a long time I tried to do some kind of a workout in the morning. I used to live in a house next to a golf course and I'd go out and jog. By 7:00 A.M. I'd have my shower and breakfast and I'd be off to the hospital by 7:30 A.M.

FIGURE 7. Department party in tee shirts to celebrate the first publication of his book in 1975.

WCR: *Would you start your day mainly in the catheterization laboratory?*

MHE: Yes, usually. Some days I would set aside more time for more catheterizations. In 1965, we started a fellowship program. I had 1 or 2 cardiology fellows and I'd meet with them; we'd make rounds. Usually in those days I had 7 or 8 patients in the hospital. I'd have some project to work on. I'd have office hours often in the morning as well as in the afternoon. I'd always have some administrative meetings because I was directing the cardiology program. I'd have sessions with the technicians. We were doing pulmonary function studies, and for a while we even did dialysis out of our department. I finally recruited a pulmonary physiologist and I got rid of that. We hired a nephrologist and I got rid of that. The clinical physiology department was going 7 ways at once for awhile. I became very interested in pacemakers. We were one of the first to do a lot of atrial pacing from the coronary sinus. We published on this in *Circulation* in 1978.

WCR: *What time would you get home at night?*

MHE: I'd always get home for dinner about 6 P.M. because I wanted to have dinner with the kids and sometimes a little before. My oldest boy was quite active in little league and we'd pitch for a while in the evening. I'd have dinner with the family and then I'd go back and work on a manuscript or something at the hospital in the evening until 11:30 P.M. or midnight. In those days I always made rounds on patients twice. I'd go see them in the evening after dinner and then I'd work on something that I was doing at the hospital or come home and work on something.

WCR: *You had a pretty active day. What time would you turn the light out at night?*

MHE: Usually by midnight. I'd get charged up sometimes when I'm working on something and I can't lay it down. I might go on until 1:00 A.M. or 2:00 A.M. That was only occasionally. I always tried to stay active in some sport. On my 35th birthday I gave up

golf and took up tennis. I've played tennis a couple of times a week since that time. During my first few months in tennis, the city had a teacher at one of the parks. I went to this park and enrolled in the tennis class. One of the other people in the class was *Billie Jean King*. She was 10 years old at the time. I learned tennis with Billie Jean and have played tennis ever since. That keeps me active. In the winter I ski. I started skiing as a little kid. My first wife thought skiing was dumb, but *Lera*, my second wife, took it up as soon as we were married. She is now a good skier. We have a group of people in Los Angeles called the Far Western Medical Association (some people call us the "Far Out Medical Association"), and we ski every winter together somewhere—Vail, Aspen, or somewhere in Europe.

WCR: *What's your age now?*

MHE: I'm 78.

WCR: *You're at ideal body weight?*

MHE: Just about.

WCR: *How tall are you?*

MHE: I haven't measured for a long time. I used to be about 70½ inches. I'm probably about 70 inches now.

WCR: *How much do you weigh?*

MHE: One hundred sixty pounds.

WCR: *You've always been about the same. Do you weigh the same as you did in college?*

MHE: I weighed about 170 in college. I probably had more muscle. I haven't ever put on any fat.

WCR: *Your first marriage was 15 years and you had how many children?*

MHE: I had 5 children in a dysfunctional marriage. I look back and I think I must have been out of my mind, but I now enjoy the big family. I love every one of them.

WCR: *In this marriage you separated for the last time in what year?*

MHE: In 1963.

WCR: *And then you met Lera.*

MHE: It was funny how I met Lera. My first wife was the daughter of a preacher. She was quite religious and I went along with it. After I was divorced I was singing in the choir in our church. I used to see this woman sitting down in about the fifth row and I thought she was very pretty. The preacher was a bachelor and he lived in an apartment next to me. Several times I asked who was this gal. He said that she was one of the regulars and a fashion model. Frequently when I came home in the evenings I'd ring the bell and I'd go into the preacher's apartment if his light was on. We would sit and commiserate about philosophy and anthropology. One night he said, "You know that redhead that you remarked about? You know she's a widow. Her husband died. You need a wife; you ought to talk to her. Call her." I asked him,

"How long do you think I should wait?" He said, "Wait 3 months." I wrote down in my little book in 3 months, "Call her." About a year later we were married.

WCR: *And this has been a wonderful marriage.*

MHE: A wonderful marriage. She's a wonderful woman. She's not only very supportive in everything I do but she's at ease in a Munich beer hall or a royal reception.

WCR: *Did she have children?*

MHE: She had 3 children and I adopted them. I really have 8 children.

WCR: *You again had a house full of kids?*

MHE: Well, they never all lived under one roof. Most, but not all of them lived with their mother.

WCR: *You paid for 8 kids to go to college.*

MHE: Well almost.

WCR: *Have they turned out pretty well?*

MHE: Pretty well. I was disappointed, as you might guess, with some of them. Actually, I didn't pay for 8 in college because Lera's youngest daughter dropped out of college very soon. The rest went through and they are all doing pretty well.

WCR: *Do they all live close?*

MHE: Some of them do.

WCR: *How many grandchildren do you have?*

MHE: 7.

WCR: *The book that you wrote, "The World and its Animals" is a wonderful book. Although you wrote it for children I learned an enormous amount from it. Tell me how that came about.*

MHE: I had always wanted to have a little acreage. About 1985 Lera and I had decided that maybe we would try to buy some land out of town. We shopped around and found 22 acres in Temecula, California, located about half way between Los Angeles and San Diego. It's up in a little mountain range. We built a house there. Cheryl, my daughter, and her husband wanted to get out of Long Beach. Her husband is a video marketer and he works from his home. They built a house on the same piece of property. Then Lera's son, Roger, who is a builder, settled down there. Then Debbie, Lera's younger daughter, moved down there. We have one kid in San Diego so there a quite a few of our children in that area. One boy lives in Hawaii. Several of my kids are in the San Francisco Bay area or Santa Cruz. We get together fairly frequently, hardly ever all at the same time. We see them as often as we can. Of course, we see Cheryl and the kids almost every weekend that we are down there.

WCR: *How did your book come about?*

MHE: Cheryl's oldest daughter is very bright, and she was always up at our house quizzing me about things. She'd want to know what the orbit of Jupiter was. We would go dig out some books to find out. She'd want to know what kind of animals do so and so. The subject would come up about why animals are where they are. Pretty soon we got to talking about how animals evolved. By this time she was 10 years old, and she's asking all sorts of questions about where people came from. I said, "Stephanie, we're going to write a book." She said, "I don't want to write

FIGURE 8. MHE in 1990.

a book." I said, "If I write a book, will you help me?" She said, "Well, all right." I started to write this book for Stephanie to read. I'd have her read a chapter and she'd occasionally recommend simpler terminology. I said, "Stephanie, I want you to be a co-author." "No," she said, "I don't want to be a co-author. I didn't write the book, you wrote the book." That's how it happened. Stephanie is now 14.

WCR: *It's a wonderful book.*

MHE: I have a friend who majored in anthropology who reviewed the manuscript. His criticism was quite helpful. We're still arguing about whether birds came from dinosaurs. Anthropology always interested me. I have read all of Darwin's books, and we have traveled to the Galapagos Islands and Easter Island. I've always tried to keep up on what's happening in anthropology.

WCR: *What do you think about the recent discovery of maybe the heart of a dinosaur with 4 chambers and maybe they were actually warm-blooded animals rather than cold-blooded?*

MHE: There's quite a lot of evidence to support that. Probably quite a lot of the dinosaurs were warm-blooded. They weren't like present day reptiles. It's still controversial. There are still a few people who don't think that birds came from dinosaurs either. In general, the anthropology society is beginning to accept that. For a long time there has been a lot of evidence to suggest that dinosaurs, particularly the fast moving predator dinosaurs, were warm-blooded.

FIGURE 9. MHE with his wife at his high school being inducted into the Hall of Fame in 1995.

WCR: *What interests you now? What do you do at night when you get home now?*

MHE: I read journals. I read my anthropology journal. I read biographies. I like history. I'm working on an outline for a novel. There are a couple of good books recently on the history of hospitals. I'm interested in current affairs; I take 2 or 3 magazines. I always try to spend a little time once or twice a week playing the piano. I still enjoy playing the piano.

WCR: *Do you play by ear?*

MHE: Yes. I had classical training when I was young and I still read music and play some classical music. My technique is getting terrible. I have trouble getting through the tough passages of classical pieces and so I play mostly by ear.

WCR: *How much did you practice when you were a kid?*

MHE: My mother stood over me and I practiced exactly 1 hour a day by the clock.

WCR: *Did she play a musical instrument?*

MHE: No.

WCR: *What does your sister do?*

MHE: My sister grew up like most small town girls and she met her husband when she was in junior college. They were married and he became a school administrator in Sacramento. She had 5 children. Because they were close to where my mother lived, after I moved away, they were very much involved in my mother's life. It was great for mother after dad died. About 10 years ago my sister had a cerebral hemorrhage and died.

WCR: *How big is Long Beach now?*

MHE: About 400,000, but it's contiguous with other cities so that you don't know where Long Beach stops and the next city starts.

WCR: *Seaside Memorial Hospital now has how many beds?*

MHE: There are 750 beds. Actually in 1960 they built a new hospital and renamed it Memorial Hospital.

WCR: *You witnessed this huge growth.*

MHE: Our cardiology department has grown and is very successful now. We do about 600 open hearts and about 600 or 700 angioplasties yearly. We are very busy. Last year we admitted over 3,000 patients. In fact, we don't have enough beds and we don't have enough cardiac catheterization laboratory time. We may try to expand further. Keeping cardiology financially sound these days is challenging because of the cost of all the devices we implant. Providers don't like to pay for the devices. I spend considerable time in conferences trying to influence the behavior of some cardiologists and their use of devices. If we can cut down the number of pacemaker providers the pacemaker companies can give a better price. We work closely with the emergency room physicians and try to make sure that the patients with cardiac problems get treated appropriately. We train the nurses. Fortunately, I have a cohort, *Ron Sylvester*, who is a great asset in teaching and research. Ron was on the faculty at the University of Southern California for years and we've always been friends. He's editor of the journal *Electrocardiography*. He joined us over 10 years ago now. He has a constant stream of cardiologists from foreign countries that come and spend a year with him. They help on research projects. We always have 2 or 3 people around who are working on projects. He is very active in our teaching program, a very innovative guy. He has done a lot for our program. Our cardiology fellows were not always very interested in electrocardiography. Now they are very good at it. I think we make a major contribution to the UCI Cardiology Fellowship.

WCR: *How many cardiology fellows do you have at your hospital?*

MHE: In 1982 or 1983 we affiliated with the University of California at Irvine and the program had 12 fellows for a long time. We had 4 of them at any one time. In the last couple of years the number has been trimmed to 9, so now we have 3.

WCR: *How many medicine house staff do you have?*

MHE: There are 7 residents in medicine at any one time. There also are larger programs in obstetrics and pediatrics and other departments.

WCR: *How do you think cardiology is going to evolve in the next 25 years?*

MHE: The invasive people are going to eventually find that there are fewer and fewer patients to work on. Preventive cardiology is going to be big. I foresee a time 20 years from now when interventional kinds of things that we do will be much less common. I don't think it will ever go away because I don't think lifestyle changes are easy to sell. All you have to do is sit in an airport and see how many fat people are there.

In spite of that there will be medical ways to deal with a lot of coronary disease. I don't know about heart failure. It's growing rapidly although there are a lot of good ways (and there's going to be more) to treat it. Whether we can prevent heart failure I'm doubtful, because to prevent heart failure you've got to intervene again in people's lives before they get in trouble and that is hard to pull off. It certainly is going to change dramatically. The other possibility, of course, is that transplants will be xenographs and we won't have to worry about the shortage of donors anymore.

WCR: *If you were graduating from medical school today, what specialty would you lean toward?*

MHE: Still cardiology. It's exciting and will continue to be. You and I have seen these dramatic changes and they will continue.

WCR: *Early on you were very much involved in congenital and valvular heart diseases?*

MHE: That's right. Early on I felt insufficiently trained in congenital heart disease, and I periodically went to the Mexican National Heart Institute in Mexico City because they had an enormous volume of congenital cases. Ron Sylvester used to do the same thing. We used to go down there and spend time with *Sodi Polaris*, the famous electrocardiographer. Then we got a very good pediatric cardiologist from Minneapolis, Minnesota. Eventually, I gave up pediatric cases.

WCR: *You are still working every day.*

MHE: Everyday.

WCR: *Do you ever envision "retirement"?*

MHE: I think there will come a time when it will be pretty obvious to me or to my associates that I probably ought to retire. I don't look forward to it.

WCR: *You are not in private practice. You are paid by the hospital?*

MHE: I do have a small private practice. I work out of another group of doctors' offices. I have a deal where they collect the money, provide the nursing, malpractice and everything, and they take a percent of my billings. It is a small item in my income. I just want to keep my hand in. The hospital pays me for this Care Line Director's job.

WCR: *Where did the name Myrvin come from?*

MHE: My mother's name was *Myrtle* and my father's name was *Melvin*. My parents took "myr" from Myrtle and "vin" from Melvin.

WCR: *Would you choose being a physician if you started today?*

MHE: You bet I would. It's just as exciting to me today as it was when I started. Some doctors, of course, make an awful lot of money. I never expected to make a lot of money. I expected to be comfortable. It's always a challenge. It's always going to be fun.

WCR: *How much time do you take off a year? How many trips do you go on a year?*

MHE: We go on several trips, but they're short—10 days or thereabouts, some years more than others depending on where I get invited. This year I was invited to Athens, Greece, so we took some time in the Greek Islands. The last time I went to Brazil, we also went to Easter Island. You'll remember when we both went to Bombay—we did a lot of traveling that year. We take at least a couple of weeks skiing and we take usually 2 or 3 weeks all told in short trips here and there.

WCR: *When you had a huge load as a private practitioner in the 1970s and 1980s, would you take off much time with family?*

MHE: We always took at least a week or two. We'd usually go camping. That was the days before we did much international travel. We had a lot of weekends together. We didn't take many long trips.

WCR: *Is there anything else that you would like to talk about that we haven't covered?*

MHE: My Federal Aviation Administration experience back in the 1970s was interesting. The Federal Air Surgeon thought that maybe all pilots should have an exercise test so they recruited me as a consultant. Other cardiology consultants, most of them from academics, also would come and spend 2 days or so every 2 or 3 months. The meetings were held in Washington, D.C. The Federal Air Surgeon, the guy that ran it, was usually a political appointee and a retired physician from the military (usually the Navy). They would present cases to us and we would review them, dictate our thoughts, and the Federal Air Surgeon would usually follow our advice. All of a sudden, a new Federal Air Surgeon named *Frank Austin* was appointed. Frank Austin had been a Navy doctor, but he had not practiced medicine for years. He switched and became a line pilot. He flew off carriers in World War II. When he got too old to fly off carriers he went back to being a doctor. He was appointed Federal Air Surgeon of the Federal Aviation Administration. We'd all been consultants by that time for 10 years (*Earl Beard* was one of them and *Marvin Dunn*, another). When Frank met with consultants he told us, "I've flown off carriers. I know more about aviation medicine than all you guys. I just want to tell you that we're not going to need much help from the consultants now that I'm the Federal Air Surgeon."

Shortly after that I started getting calls from the people who worked in the agency saying, "The chief is letting people go back to flying that are a threat to safety." They sent me several cases surreptitiously and wanted to know if I could do anything about it. When we went back to the consultants' meeting I had quite a long discussion with him and explained to him that I thought some of his policies were in error. He didn't respond except to make it pretty clear that he didn't care what I thought. I followed our discussion with a letter of resignation. I got word from the people in the agency that he'd sent a corporate pilot back to flying who shortly thereafter crashed with his boss in a helicopter, and both were killed. Somehow, somebody got a copy of my letter and circulated it in the agency. He had approved a pilot who had had prosthetic valve surgery and the American Airlines people decided they didn't want him flying so the pilot was suing American Airlines. American Airlines people found out about my letter. They called me and asked me to testify. I came to Dallas and my testimony, in effect,

FIGURE 10. MHE's weekend home in Temecula, California.

was that Frank Austin was making a big mistake and he was endangering safety. There were about 30 reporters in the courtroom. The next day what I said about Frank Austin was all over the newspapers. Later, a congressional investigation was held and Frank Austin was fired. A couple of years later they asked me to come back as a consultant.

WCR: *As good as exercise stress testing is and as good as you've made it through the years, if you really want to know the status of the coronary arteries today, you need to inject contrast material or do intravascular ultrasonic imaging or electon beam tomography*

MHE: The trouble with that is, of course, that it doesn't tell us as much as we'd like to know. There is more and more evidence that maybe ST depression is more reliable than we thought. I think that within the next few years we'll evolve some new methods (magnetic resonance imaging probably) and other ways of better evaluating the coronary circulation. I don't think we'll be able to go without the angiogram for a long time. We need to know the anatomy. We're soon going to be able to determine the physiology of it much more accurately than we can now. I think stress testing will still play some role. Just how it will evolve I'm not sure.

WCR: *What is your view on nuclear cardiology? It seems to me that these nuclear tests simply cost too much.*

MHE: They are very expensive and they are not as accurate as they're held out to be. We have a large percentage of physicians in Long Beach who do exercise testing in their office. They find a person with ST depression then they send the patient for a nuclear test. If the nuclear test is negative, they assume that the electrocardiogram was wrong. It's not so. In a study at Memorial Heart Institute we found that 40% of nuclear stress testing studies are false negatives when you compare the result to the coronary anatomy and if you use 70% diameter narrowing as abnormal. If you ask any of the big gurus in nuclear medicine they disagree. I'm not sure why our data are different. We have never published our results because our own nuclear people would rather we wouldn't. Every cardiologist in our group is aware of the high incidence of false negatives. I believe its reliability is overestimated. We can, however, often localize which artery

is important. If the nuclear study is positive, it's pretty reliable.

WCR: *How good is the exercise stress test in asymptomatic people?*

MHE: It depends on just how you use it. If you have a 45-year-old woman with chest pain and you do an exercise test, she has ST depression, we know that women whose coronary arteries are normal have ST depression. I'm not sure that the physiology of their heart is normal. I think that estrogen affects the potassium pump in some way and that causes an abnormal electrocardiogram. There are a lot of people with so-called abnormal exercise who we call false positives who I think may have myocardial ischemia. All ischemia is not due to anatomical changes. The microcirculation must play an enormously important role in the ischemic syndromes.

A 55-year-old patient comes in and tells you that he's as healthy as a horse, and he wants a complete checkup. Why is he here? Maybe his wife sent him in, maybe his best friend dropped dead. There are all sorts of reasons why he is there. If you ask him, "Have you ever had chest pain?" and he says "no," you put him on the treadmill and you see classic ST changes. And you again ask, "Have you ever had chest pain?" He answers, "Well, I have this funny feeling once in a while." It is how you use it clinically that's important. If patients have risk factors it can be useful. We have lots of HMO contracts in our hospital. The hospital, when it writes a contract, provides all sorts of tests as part of that contract. The family practitioners and the general internists, rather than get a cardiology consult, send the patient in for a nuclear stress test that may not be indicated. The hospital is spending a lot of money on nuclear stress tests that are inappropriate.

WCR: *When you do your exercise stress test, what do you do? What does it consist of now?*

MHE: We take a history on the patient. We do a resting electrocardiogram. We now do 15 leads instead of 12 (we do some back leads). Then we exercise the patient to maximum capacity. We don't arbitrarily stop for any heart rate. We analyze a whole host of things besides ST changes—what their recovery blood pressure is, whether they have abnormal septal Q waves, whether they have abnormal T waves in recovery, and a lot of unconventional indicators of myocardial ischemia.

WCR: *What's your view of exercise testing after an acute myocardial infarction?*

MHE: It was pretty well established that it was quite useful at one time, at least before thrombolysis and angioplasty. There are really no good data now as to how useful it is after these treatments. Almost all of our infarct patients now go to the catheterization laboratory and have angioplasty and stents. I don't think there are any good data to show how useful exercise stress testing is after those procedures.

WCR: *You're talking about the hospital patient before they go home?*

MHE: That's right. We already know how useful it is after those procedures. A lot of people with infarcts, of course, have that culprit vessel stented and then they have a lot of other disease. If you do a stress test on those people many of them will have abnormal changes. I think that is important to know.

WCR: *What about a patient that has an infarct and they come back to see you 2 months later in your private office. Do you exercise them?*

MHE: Yes.

WCR: *Virtually routinely? How good are the results of the 2-month study when the patient had coronary angioplasty or thrombolysis at the time of the infarct?*

MHE: We ordinarily believe that the 2-month study is sort of a baseline that we are going to use should the patient become symptomatic or we're concerned about him/her a year later. If the patient has some ST changes at 2 months and he's asymptomatic, we don't necessarily take any action. We tell him that it's like having a risk factor. It's like having a high cholesterol level. It's something we have to check on and use during follow-up. If the ST changes occur at a low workload, however, it has more significance.

WCR: *Myrvin, I can't think of much more to ask you.*

MHE: I hope this has been useful. I must say it's an honor to be here, Bill.

WCR: *Myrvin, thank you very much.*

MHE: You're sure welcome.

Best Publications of MHE Selected by MHE

2. Ellestad MH, Reed J. Circulating eosinophils in cardiovascular stress. *Ann Intern Med* 1952;36:551–561.

3. Ellestad M, Olson W. Use of ganglion blocking agents for acute pulmonary edema. *JAMA* 1956;161:49–53.

6. Roach CJ, Ellestad MH, Lake RB. Medical data processing & computer-automated hospitals. *Datamation* 1962;9:25–28.

8. Liu CK, Piccirillo RT, Ellesta MH. Distensibility of the postmortem human left atrium in nonrheumatic and rheumatic disease. *Am J Cardiol* 1964;13:232–238.

11. Beland A, Jennings E, Cope J, Ellestad M, Monroe C, Shadle O. Citrate intoxication report of laboratory investigation and clinical use of ACD blood for extracorporeal circulation. *Surg Gynecol Obstet* 1965;120:997–1008.

17. Kemp GL, Ellestad MH. The incidence of "silent" coronary heart disease. *CA. Med* 1968;109:363–367.

20. Ellestad MH, Allen WH, Wan MCK, Kemp GL. Maximum treadmill stress testing for cardiovascular evaluation. *Circulation* 1969;17:39:517–522.

28. Ellestad MH. Double-contrast angiography in human internal mammary implants. *Ann ThorAC Surg* 1971;12:428–436.

35. Ellestad MH, Wan MKC. Predictive implications of stress testing follow-up of 2700 subjects after maximum treadmill stress testing. *Circulation* 1975;51:363–369.

38. Ellestad MH, Fox S, Bruce R, Dodge H, Gensini GG, Humphries J, Kannel WB, Levy RI, Mankin HT, McHenry PL, Sheffield TI, Tavel ME. Tast force I. Identification of ischemic heart disease: Bethesda conference in cardiovascular problems associated with aviation safety. *Am J Associated Cardiol* 1975;36:597–608.

39. Stuart RJ, Ellestad MH. Upsloping ST segments in exercise testing: six-year follow-up of 438 patients and correlation with 248 angiograms. *Am J Cardiol* 1976;37:19–22.

43. Sheffield LT, Blackburn H, Ellestad MH, Froelicher VF, Roitman D, Kansal S. The exercise test in perspective. *Circulation* 1977;55:681–683.

48. Greenberg P, Catellanet M, Messenger J, Ellestad MH. Coronary sinus pacing: clinical follow-up. *Circulation* 1978;57:98–103.

53. Bonoris P, Greenberg P, Christison G, Castellanet M, Ellestad MH. Evaluation of R wave amplitude changes versus ST segment depression in stress testing. *Circulation* 1978;57:904–910.

63. Ellestad MH, Blomqvist CG, Naughton JP. Standards for adult exercise testing laboratories. AHA Subcommittee on Rehabilitation. *Circulation* 1979;59:421A–443A.

65. Chin CF, Messenger J, Greenberg PS, Ellestad MH. Chronotropic incompetence in exercise testing. *Clin Cardiol* 1979;2:12–18.

78. Morales-Ballejo H, Greenbert PS, Ellestad MH, Bible M. The septal Q wave in exercise testing. *Am J Cardiol* 1981;48:247–251.

87. Ellestad MH. The mechanism of exercise-induced R wave amplitude changes in coronary heart disease: still controversial. *Arch Intern Med* 1982;142:963–965.

104. Ellestad MH, Kuan P. Naloxone and asymptomatic ischemia: failure to induce angina during exercise testing. *Am J Cardiol* 1984;54:982–984.

111. Ellestad MH. Is exercise harmful in ischemic heart disease? *Am J Noninvas Cardiol* 1987;1:15–17.

118. Ellestad M, French J. Iliac vein approach to permanent pacemaker implantation. *PACE* 1989;12:1030–1033.

131. Myrianthefs MM, Ellestad MH, Startt-Selvester RH, Crump R. Significance of signal-averaged P-wave changes during exercise in patients with coronary artery disease and correlation with angiographic findings. *Am J Cardiol* 1991;68:1619–1624.

132. Saetre HA, Selvester RHS, Solomon JC, Baron KA, Ahmad J, Ellestad MH. 16-lead ECG changes with coronary angioplasty. *J Electrocardiography* 1991;24:153–162.

140. Ellestad MH, Crump R, Surber M. The significance of lead strength on ST changes during treadmill stress tests. *J Electrocardiography* 1993;25:31–34.

147. Ellestad MH. Chronotropic incompetence: the implications of heart rate response to exercise (compensatory parasympathetic hyperactivity)? *Circulation* 1996;93:1485–1487.

149. Shandling AH, Ellestad MH, Hart G, Crump R, Marlow D, Van Natta B, Messenger JC, Strauss M, Stavitsky Y. Hyperbaric oxygen and thrombolysis in myocardial infarction: the "hot MI" pilot study. *Am Heart J* 1997;134:544–550.

155. Stavitsky Y, Shandling AH, Ellestad MH, Hart GB, Van Natta B, Messenger JC, Strauss M, Dekleva MN, Alexander JM, Mattice M, Clarke D. Hyperbaric oxygen and thrombolysis in myocardial infarction: the "hot MI" randomized multicenter study. *Cardiology* 1998;90:131–136.

JAMES STUART FORRESTER III, MD:
A Conversation With the Editor*

Jim Forrester was born on July 13, 1933 in Philadelphia, Pennsylvania. He grew up mainly in
Camp Hill, Pennsylvania, and after public schooling,
went to Swarthmore College in Swarthmore, Pennsylvania, graduating in 1959. His medical school was the
University of Pennsylvania, where he graduated in
1963. He interned in internal medicine at the hospital
of the University of Pennsylvania and did his residency in internal medicine at Harbor General Hospital
in Torrance, California. His 2-year cardiology fellowship was at the Peter Bent Brigham Hospital in Boston, Massachusetts. In July 1969 he then joined the
staff of the Division of Cardiology, Cedars-Sinai
Medical Center, in Los Angeles, California. For 20
years he directed cardiovascular research at that hospital and served periodically as director of the cardiology fellowship program, of the coronary care unit,
of the cardiac stress laboratories, and for 5 years he
was Director of the Division of Cardiology. For nearly
20 years, he was director of the Specialized Center for
Research in Ischemic Heart Disease. He has published
about 275 articles in medical journals, all but 26 of
which were in peer-reviewed journals. Additionally,
he has published 76 chapters in various textbooks. In
addition to being a highly productive clinical investigator, he has been a very popular lecturer and visiting
professor at numerous institutions around the world.
He is the proud father of 3 boys. He and his wife
Barbara, also a physician, are a popular couple and fun
to be around. Both are wonderful human beings and
both are enormous credit to our profession.

William Clifford Roberts, MD[†] (Hereafter WCR): *Jim,
I appreciate your willingness to talk to me and therefore to the readers of* The American Journal of Cardiology. *We are in a hotel adjacent to the Dallas-Fort
Worth Airport on June 22, 2001. Could we start by my
asking you to discuss your early growing up? What
were your parents like? Did you have siblings? Could
you give a feel for that?*

James Stuart Forrester III, MD[‡] (Hereafter JSF): I was
born at Pennsylvania Hospital in Philadelphia, the
oldest hospital in the USA, at the time that Hitler was
starting to rampage through Europe. My early life and
memories were basically of the disruption that was
caused by World War II. My first memory is standing
along the creek behind my parent's house gathering
sticks, running upstream to drop them in the water,
and then throwing stones at the sticks as they came by,
calling them enemy submarines. My next memory
was of my dad, a physician, getting out of our old

FIGURE 1. JSF during the interview (photo by WCR).

Chevy and walking to a train to go to war. That was
when I was about 5. For the next several years, I
moved all over the country. We left Philadelphia and
went to Baton Rouge, Louisiana, where my dad was in
military training, and then back to Philadelphia, and
then to Waterloo, Iowa, where my mom's family
lived. What a trip! There were no seats available on
the train so I slept on the floor of the ladies lounge for
3 days. After the war ended, we returned to Philadelphia, and then went to Albany, New York, where my
dad briefly worked as a pathologist before landing his
permanent position at the Polyclinic Hospital in Harrisburg, Pennsylvania. So in a period of 4 years, I was
in 6 different schools. Totally chaotic.

WCR: *What kind of physician was your dad?*

JSF: A pathologist. My dad was a fascinating character. He was born in 1904 and graduated from high
school when he was 15 as valedictorian. It was probably a great mistake for him to skip 2 years, because
although he was extremely intelligent, he was very
shy. When he finished high school, he went to business school and worked in a bank. That's where he
met my mom, who was a couple of years older. He
then got accepted to the University of Iowa's 6-year

*This series of interviews was underwritten by an unrestricted grant
from Bristol-Myers Squibb.
†Medical Director, Baylor Heart & Vascular Hospital, Baylor University
Medical Center, Dallas, Texas 75246.
‡Director, Cardiovascular Research, Cedars-Sinai Medical Center,
Los Angeles, California 90048.

FIGURE 2. JSF at age 5 and mother.

college-medical school program. When he graduated, he went to Montreal, Canada, for his pathology residency. That was during the depression years, and it was impossible for my mom to get a job because she was married. So she posed as my dad's sister. From that time on my dad referred to my mom as "Sister." After his residency, he returned to the University of Pennsylvania and was a staff pathologist when the war broke out.

WCR: *When did your father die?*

JSF: In 1998 at the age of 94.

WCR: *And your mother?*

JSF: She was born in 1902 and died in 1978 in Harrisburg, Pennsylvania, at the time of Three Mile Island disaster, from giant-cell myocarditis. I always wondered if there was any relationship, since they lived so close to Three Mile Island.

WCR: *Did your father remarry?*

JSF: No. He moved to New Mexico where my mom's 2 sisters lived and stayed there for the rest of his life. But it wasn't the same without my mom. Toward the end of his life, my dad sent me a picture of our Camp Hill home, and underneath it he wrote, "Paradise Lost."

WCR: *Your father was 16 when he decided he wanted to go into medicine. Were there any physicians in his family? How did he make that determination?*

JSF: I'll give you the Forrester family history. The 2 "r's" in the Forrester establishes its Scottish origin. The Forrester family back in Scotland was quite powerful in the 1500s and 1600s. The head of the family was for many years the Stuart Kings' Keeper of the Seal of Scotland. My namesake, James, the second

Lord Forrester in Scotland was quite a rake. After a number of affairs, he ended up having a liaison with his wife's sister's daughter. He jilted her and she stabbed him to death beneath a sycamore tree just outside of Edinburgh. I went back there some years ago and the tree still stands.

From that line of people my great-great-grandfather and his father came from Scotland to the USA in the early 1800s. Subsequently, my dad's father, also James, became a pharmacist and it was through the pharmacy that my dad became interested in medicine.

WCR: *Were there any physicians?*

JSF: No. My dad's brother became a chemist, so there was a scientific bent in the family, but my dad was the first physician.

WCR: *How did your father meet your mother?*

JSF: They both worked in the Waterloo bank. My mom was 1 of 5 children from a dirt-poor family. My mother dropped out of school in the ninth grade and was working in the Waterloo bank when my dad came to work there. She was his first and only girlfriend.

WCR: *How old was your father when he married your mother?*

JSF: They got married when he was 20 and she was 22. They were 2 of the happiest people in marriage that I've ever seen. They had a perfect marriage! I turned out to be the only child, but my mom had a miscarriage both before and after me. They had hoped for more children, but I ended up being the only one.

WCR: *You moved to Harrisburg, Pennsylvania, when you were 8. That was 1945. What was Harrisburg like? How many people lived in Harrisburg in 1945?*

JSF: At that time there were probably 80,000 people. It's grown considerably since then. We moved into an 8-story apartment building, very modest accommodations. We lived there for about 3 years, then one day my dad came home and said, "I've bought some land and we're going to build our own house." My dad and a couple of other doctors bought undeveloped land across the Susquehanna River in Camp Hill. They all built homes in this hilly area that became known as "Pill Hill" because so many physicians lived there.

WCR: *Did your father talk about medicine much as you were growing up? Why did he decide to be a pathologist? You mentioned that he was relatively timid.*

JSF: Not all pathologists are timid, if you get my drift, Bill! Nonetheless, his discomfort in dealing with patients led him toward an interest in intellectual pursuits. He was ideally suited for pathology from the standpoint of loving information and analysis.

WCR: *Where did he train?*

JSF: His medical school was the University of Iowa in Iowa City and his pathology training was at the Montreal General Hospital. He then came back to the US as a staff pathologist at the University of Pennsylvania.

WCR: *Why did he go to Montreal for pathology training?*

JSF: There was a famous pathologist there named George Hansmann. Dad always considered him a mentor.

WCR: *Where was your father born?*

JSF: In Lytton, Iowa, about 100 people. Of course, with the population explosion, it's larger now–320 people in 1990. His parents subsequently moved to Waterloo, where he grew up. He went to grade school and high school there.

WCR: *Where did your mother grow up?*

JSF: My mother also grew up in Waterloo, Iowa. Although they didn't know whether there was going to be food on the table every night, her home was one where there was always laughter. There were 3 sisters and 2 brothers in the family. The 2 brothers became alcoholics and died of alcoholism. My mom and her 2 sisters were all very well adjusted. One sister lived to be 100 and actually lived in 3 different centuries, born in 1899 and living into the 21st century.

WCR: *What did your mother's parents do?*

JSF: The family itself originated in England and came over in the 1750s. My mother's grandfather was a carpenter and served in the Civil War. He was injured in the war and was hospitalized. To wile away the time during rehabilitation, he built ornate wooden picture frames. President Abraham Lincoln visited the injured soldiers in the hospital and gave my granddad a photograph of himself to put into the picture frame that he was constructing. We have still have that picture frame and my great grandfather's Civil War rifle. Framed beside it is the 140-year-old *New York Herald Tribune* published on the day that Lincoln was shot.

WCR: *What did your mother's father do?*

JSF: He was unemployed after an industrial accident. So early in their junior high school years, each one of the kids dropped out of school and went to work so that they could bring money to the family to eat.

WCR: *When you and your parents moved to Camp Hill from Harrisburg— and this was the first time you lived in a home of your own—what was life like? When you would come home and your daddy would come home, what was the flow of conversation and ambiance of your home?*

JSF: Ralph Waldo Emerson liked to say, "The child is father of the man." For me, in a family of 3, my views as an adult were very much influenced by the views of my mom and dad. They had very Midwestern work ethics. From the time I can recall, I always worked, even though it probably was not financially necessary. I had paper route from the third through the sixth grades. When I got older, I worked in the summer laying ties for the railroad. We used to roll barrels of spikes down a ramp. One day I was at the bottom of the ramp with my head turned away when somebody started to roll a barrel down. One of the guys who worked there, a very strong black guy, leapt in front of it and saved me from being crushed by the barrel. He sustained a back injury. Subsequently, I worked in a steel mill. I always worked with "blue-collar" people. The younger guys like me were employed to shovel slag, which is molten rock that results from the separation of ore. At noontime, we would go into these rooms where the slag had accumulated and shovel it all out. It was very tough work, and it was considered the most odious of all the jobs. So the work ethic my parents instilled in me was a major part of my growing up.

Another influence from my parents was an impetus to be the best that I could be. My dad, being very bright, taught me lots of math tricks. For instance, 73×67 is 4,891. It's easy if you recognize that's $X^2 - 9$, where $X = 70$. When I was in the third and fourth grades he decided that after I had learned the 12 by 12 tables for multiplication, that I should learn 18 by 18. That turns out to be quite an undertaking when you have to memorize 14×17 and 13×16, and so forth. One day I just cracked up crying and said, "I can't do this anymore." That was the end of it and I went back to doing multiplication in my head.

He also stimulated me intellectually in other ways. He taught me how to play chess. When I showed an interest, we drove up to Philadelphia and bought books on chess, came back and read them together, and then played. That was something that stayed with me for many years. Some years later, I took up chess by mail where you play 6 people at once. I got to a national rating of over 2000, which is just below a master level. I had to quit because I was spending all my time at the chessboard.

My parents were very strong on family ties. My dad came to every baseball and basketball game I played. Many times when we played our baseball games there would be 1 person in the stands and that would be my dad. My mother and father also sent money every month to our needy relatives—especially the young men who had become alcoholics. Then when my dad's mom became disabled with Alzheimer's disease, she lived in our house quite a few years after she became incontinent and paranoid. There was a strong belief that family takes care of family in our home. I've incorporated many of their beliefs in my own life.

WCR: *You mentioned that your father was extremely bright, and that he graduated from high school when he was 15. He had to wait around a year before he could think about college. And yet your mother didn't get past the ninth grade. Yet their long marriage was one of the happiest that you've ever witnessed. What made your parents' marriage so happy? And secondly, how did the intellectualism of your father and mother match out? In other words, it sounds to me like your mother was quite bright although her formal schooling was not much.*

JSF: That's a fascinating question, Bill. They were sort of interlocking. My mother always described herself as a good listener. She loved people and loved talking to people and everyone loved her back. If she were to be here right now and you asked what did she teach me, I think she would say that the most important lesson that she taught me was to never be judgmental. When my friends from high school came back to Camp Hill, they'd always come by and see my

FIGURE 3. JSF as a basketball player in 10th grade, age 16.

parents. My mom was the most popular parent of any of my friends' parents because she made everybody feel so welcome. Her outgoing personality interlocked with my dad's shyness. He greatly admired her for her personality. And my mom greatly admired my dad's prodigious intellect and deferred to him most decision making within the family. They each recognized a tremendous merit in the other.

You asked me earlier what we talked about at dinner. Since there were only the 3 of us I was often the center of conversation. My dad was particularly interested in politics. Being an Iowa boy, he was a conservative Republican. I can remember (under my dad's influence) naming my first dog "Trooper Republican Forrester." My mom liked to talk about art and literature. Although she left school in the ninth grade, when we moved to Camp Hill she formed a group of ladies who met every month to discuss a topic in art or literature. The group met for 15 to 20 years. My dinner topic was sports. My dad and I would drive the 2 hours to see the Philadelphia Phillies play. The 1950 Phillies, called the "Whiz Kids," went to the World Series when I was 13. I can still name all 23 players on that team.

WCR: *What was your home like? Were there a lot of books around? What was it like going through your house when you were growing up?*

JSF: Our Camp Hill home was a 1-story house on a hill with a huge lawn. I hated mowing that lawn because it would take me 90 minutes, even with a power mower. I used to push the lawn mower along while shouting all kinds of obscenities at the top of my lungs about how I hated mowing the lawn. It was only later that I discovered that my voice was much louder than the motor of the lawn mower.

WCR: *You mentioned that one of the things that you admired in your mother was her ability to listen. I remember that William Osler said one time, "Good doctors are good listeners." What do you mean by saying she was a good listener? How did you come to that conclusion?*

JSF: She connected on an emotional level, empathized with the other person's feelings. She drew them out. I can't say that I understood that at that time. It was perhaps 2 decades later, when I was in my 30s, when I finally came to understand what a good listener is. That occurred when I was getting divorced and saw a psychiatrist for a couple of years. My mother had the ability to genuinely care about other people and other people perceived that. She never put herself first.

WCR: *Did your mother and father have a lot of friends socially? Did they entertain at your house much?*

JSF: Yes. Actually, the entertaining at our house played a major role in my becoming a physician. My dad's 2 best friends were a cardiologist and a surgeon. When they'd come over to the house the conversation would turn to specific patients. I loved to sit silently listening to these dramatic stories of how a patient was helped or saved. Sometimes my dad would talk about how his forensic pathology solved a murder mystery. Someplace along there I began to imagine myself in those same roles. Then when I was in seventh and eighth grades, I began to complain of pain in the middle of my back. X-rays found nothing. For about 6 months I went to physical therapy, where a physical therapist would try to force my neck into a more flexed position. After 6 months they repeated the x-ray and found a mass in my vertebrae, which was thought to be either a malignancy or tuberculosis. It was a devastating diagnosis. I was transferred to the University of Pennsylvania Hospital. There were a lot of very sick kids there! I remember nearly fainting as they hammered a narrow spike into my fourth thoracic vertebrae. Then they took me to surgery. The tumor was a benign osteoid osteoma, which is not commonly found in vertebrae. I was out of school for about 2 months, but I was able to catch up with my class in a matter of weeks. It was those 2 events, listening to physicians talk, and then the personal experience of being in a hospital for quite a while with children who were much more ill than I that set me in the direction of medicine.

WCR: *Let me go back to the books in your home. Did your father do a lot of reading when he came home at night? Were there a lot of books around?*

JSF: My dad brought a lot of medical work home. He had a microscope in the living room and he would dictate pap smears while watching Phillies' games. There was certainly an intellectual tenor to the house. But when I went off to college, I discovered how relatively provincial it was growing up in a town of 5,000 people. I was not well educated at the time I left Camp Hill.

WCR: *Did your father or mother have hobbies?*

JSF: Yes. My mom's principal interest was collecting antiques. We lived right in Pennsylvania Dutch country, so the house was furnished in Pennsylvania Dutch antiques. My dad's hobbies were those I took up. He loved chess and sports. Those became lifelong passions for me as well.

WCR: *I gather you were a good student.*

JSF: I suppose I was in the upper 10% of the class. That's not saying a whole lot. We only had 70 in my high school graduating class. I was a good student, but I wasn't the best. I was very involved in being well rounded. I was president of our student council. I was the editor of our school newspaper. I was the starting guard on a basketball team that won the league championship and went to the district finals. Eisenhower was president, Doris Day was starring in "Pillow Talk," and Gene Kelly was dancing in "Singing in the Rain." It was a tranquil time in the USA, a time of economic expansion following the war and a period of prosperity and tranquility. The important issues to me were less intellectual and more social and athletic.

WCR: *Your pre-college schooling was in public school.*

JSF: School was easy. But even then I was impatient with wasting time. I remember in the steel mill I was spending a lot of time doing nothing, so my mom typed up pages of vocabulary words, probably several thousand. I would walk around in the steel mill, take off my hard hat, and inside it I had these lists of vocabulary words. I memorized all of them. When I graduated from high school, I bet I had the best vocabulary of any kid in central Pennsylvania.

WCR: *Are you a good speller, too?*

JSF: Yes.

WCR: *Who influenced you as a teacher in junior high or high school?*

JSF: I was perhaps most influenced by the basketball coach, but in a strange way. I always saw everything in school, especially basketball, as just being fun. I can recall his pulling me over one time and saying, "Jim, basketball is not a game. It's a business." He built championship teams. I had to learn that my view wasn't always shared by people in authority.

WCR: *You were a good athlete. How tall were you?*

JSF: I was 6 feet, 1 inch. At that time that was a pretty good size for a guard. I played what today is called shooting guard. I was a pretty good shooter. I was the second highest scorer on our team in our championship year.

WCR: *The championship means what?*

JSF: The league of small schools around the Harrisburg area was then called Class B. There were about 10 teams in the league and Camp Hill tradition-ally was a basketball power. Winning that championship was the pinnacle of my high school career.

WCR: *How many points did you average per game?*

JSF: In high school I averaged 12 to 14 points, which was not bad for the scoring in those days, which tended to be in the range of 50 to 60 points a game.

WCR: *You mentioned baseball. Did you play baseball, too?*

JSF: Yes. I also played baseball and football. I was forced to quit playing football when I had the back surgery. I continued to play baseball through high school. When I got to college, I focused only on basketball.

WCR: *What did you play in baseball?*

JSF: Center field.

WCR: *Could you hit?*

JSF: I hit in the range of .280 to .300 and I covered a lot of ground in the outfield. I wasn't an outstanding baseball player. I was much better at basketball.

WCR: *It sounds like you were pretty fast.*

JSF: Above average.

WCR: *As you were growing up did your father or mother smoke cigarettes?*

JSF: No. I never had a drink or smoked until I got to college.

WCR: *Was there alcohol in your home?*

JSF: Yes. My dad would serve liquor when friends came over. But part of my upbringing was that it was not a good thing for high schoolers to drink, so I didn't drink until I got to college.

WCR: *Did your father have an alcoholic drink when he came home at night?*

JSF: Generally not. He had alcohol when friends came over.

WCR: *What about religion in your home?*

JSF: My parents were not religious. They did not go to church at all. Nevertheless, I was sent to church every Sunday. At first, I went with neighbors to the Lutheran Church and then when we moved from Harrisburg to Camp Hill, I went to the Presbyterian Church. So I have a reasonable knowledge of the Bible and I can sing all the great old hymns like "The Old Rugged Cross" and "Onward Christian Soldiers," and "Faith of Our Fathers." I am glad that I got religious training from 2 people who did not care much about religion.

WCR: *You were sent to church every Sunday by parents who would stay home. What did you think about that?*

JSF: Initially it disturbed me greatly because I imagined that I would end up going to heaven and they would end up going to hell. I thought I would miss them. Now as an adult I'm much more like my parents were. So wherever they are, I'll be joining them.

WCR: *Did you and your family go on vacations in the summertime? Or travel much?*

JSF: Yes. Wherever my parents went on vacation, I went along. My granddad had by now moved to Ogden, Utah, where he owned a pharmacy. Every summer we would go to Utah, where my grandparents had built a cabin in the mountains outside of Ogden. When I got older, we traveled in Europe.

WCR: *You were reasonably sophisticated when you went off to college?*

JSF: No. I don't think I was. I went to Swarthmore College, just outside of Philadelphia. This was dumb luck. I wanted to go to a small school where I could play basketball. My best friend's parents had gone to Swarthmore and suggested that I take a look. I got to play with some of their basketball players, and they said I'd make the team. I knew I wouldn't play at the University of Pennsylvania. So I chose Swarthmore.

College challenged everything that I had grown up believing in Camp Hill. Swarthmore is very liberal. Swarthmore was called "the Kremlin on the Crum" because of its very left wing politics. When I got there in the late 1950s, it was the time of Lester Maddox and George Wallace. Civil rights became an extremely important topic to us, and is still a passion for me. When we had the riots in Los Angeles a few years ago, the day after the riots, I took my family into the riot area with brooms and shovels and helped clean up the area, working with the locals who lived there.

Another great influence was the intelligence of my fellow students. I'd come out of Camp Hill thinking I was somebody special, and was thrust into a group where I was average. I had some great classmates. *Michael Oksenberg* became the chief China advisor for the Carter administration and accompanied both Carter and Nixon to China. *Neal Austrian* became president of the National Football League. *David Baltimore* discovered reverse transcriptase and became a Nobel laureate. I wasn't surprised. I played cards with Dave. He cleaned all of us out every time we played for money. He also was the guy who delivered the hoagies (submarine sandwiches) throughout the dormitory. The people I was exposed to at Swarthmore were brighter than any group I've ever encountered.

WCR: *You say it was a small college. How many went to Swarthmore?*

JSF: There were about 300 students in each class. A little over a 1,000 students, so I knew most of them.

WCR: *Did you make the basketball team?*

JSF: Absolutely. Those were the 2 aspects to my years at Swarthmore. One was the intellectual. I became fascinated with "the life of the mind." The other was sports. My best memory from the athletic side is from one game with Johns Hopkins University on their home court. I scored 17 consecutive points for our team. After the 17th point, the coach took me out and said he thought I wasn't playing adequate defense! Of course, they say that about *Alan Iverson*, too.

WCR: *You played first team all 4 years in college?*

JSF: No. I played junior varsity and then varsity. We were a weak team. We played the University of Pennsylvania, Delaware, some very good basketball schools. We always had a losing season.

I also was sports editor for our college newspaper. I have the unique distinction of being the only sports writer who ever actually lost a football game. Ursinus College, one of our opponents, had their homecoming day. We thought it would be fun to go over the night before and lime a big S on the middle of their football field for Swarthmore. A friend of mine and I went to a local hardware store and bought lime. About 2:00 A.M. we put a big S on the field. The football game was played in the downpour. Now what I did not know is that there are 2 kinds of lime. There is the garden lime, which murderers use to decompose bodies, and there is the chalk lime, which marks the yard lines. We bought the wrong kind of lime. The Ursinus players at half time changed their uniforms because they had alternate uniforms there, but the Swarthmore players did not. So many of our players suffered significant skin burns, so that the next week's game had to be cancelled because we didn't have enough players to play!

We were scheduled to play Penn Military College that week. In my weekly newspaper I wrote a story about a PMC football player who was about to be kicked off the team for poor grades. So a test was arranged. He'd be given a word to spell, and if he could get one letter right, he could stay on the team. They gave him the word "coffee." He spelled it "kau-phy," so he was kicked off the team. My article got passed to the dean of PMC, who was outraged because they are quite sensitive about their academic standing. So although they had previously agreed to cancel the game, they now demanded a forfeit. Swarthmore's record was changed from a cancelled game to a loss.

Some months later, our basketball team played at PMC, where the final chapter of the story was played out. At half time, Swarthmore students unfurled a huge banner that spelled out "K-A-U-P-H-Y" and the Penn Military cadets had their first military encounter. They captured the banner, but only after all the folding seats on the Swarthmore side had been slung at their feet as they moved in formation to attack. Needless to say, I was booed lustily at that game, which we won.

WCR: *Jim, what did you major in in college?*

JSF: To me the science courses were not nearly as interesting as English literature and art, so I took the least amount of science that I could and I majored in English literature. I put off taking the required physics until my senior year. Then, rather than go to the physics lectures, I audited a class on the impact of Winslow Homer on American art. I remember I had a make-up laboratory, and asked the physics professor about how long it would take. He said, "For a good student it would probably take about an hour. Why don't you come early and bring your lunch?" I took this as a bad sign. I actually flunked the course, but he gave me a "D." My intellectual passion at Swarthmore was literature and art. I was fascinated with the sounds of language. Edgar Allen Poe's "As I nodded nearly napping, suddenly there came a rapping, as of someone gently tapping, tapping at my chamber door. Only this and nothing more," from *The Raven*. Or Lord Byron's *Prisoner of Chillon*: "My hair is gray, but not with years, Nor grew it white in a single night, As men's have grown from sudden fears: My limbs are bow'd, though not with toil. . . ." Poetry fascinated me much more than comparative anatomy.

WCR: *It sounds like you were quite busy in college. You were playing basketball. You were the sports editor of the newspaper. What else happened? Were you socially active in college?*

JSF: I dated the head cheerleader. I had my first drink of alcohol. And I made lifelong friends. For instance, two years ago, Michael Oksenberg, President Carter's China specialist on the National Security Council, and I toured China together with our wives.

WCR: *You were in a fraternity?*

JSF: Yes. The Swarthmore community broke down into 2 groups, the fraternity brothers and the Bohemians. The Bohos were longhaired, cultured, and much better students. I was part of the fraternity group, but I crossed over quite a bit because of my interest in the humanities.

WCR: *Did you go to Swarthmore on a basketball scholarship?*

JSF: No. They didn't have athletic scholarships at that time.

WCR: *When you told your father that you wanted to go to Swarthmore, how did he react? He was a conservative individual and surely he knew that Swarthmore was quite a liberal institution.*

JSF: My parents were thrilled that I chose a college so near home. A number of weekends I could come home or they could come up and see me. Because I was an only child I remained very much a center of their interest. They'd come and see me play basketball, we'd go out to dinner afterwards, and then they would drive back home. But politics did become a huge issue between my dad and I during the Vietnam War.

WCR: *How far is Harrisburg from Swarthmore?*

JSF: About 90 minutes on the Philadelphia Turnpike. It was not a difficult drive.

WCR: *Were there any teachers at Swarthmore who had considerable influence on you?*

JSF: I would say there were 2. The first was *Gilbert Haight*, one of the best teachers I've ever had. He taught chemistry. He influenced me 2 ways. First, he was unpretentious. Secondly, he brought humor to his lectures. Everyone loved Gil Haight's lectures even though they were on potentially stultifying topics. Gil Haight taught me how to teach.

The second professor was *Hedley Rhys*, who taught fine arts. He also was a great teacher. I don't believe I've ever met a teacher with more enthusiasm for his topic than Hedley Rhys. Hedley's enthusiasm also became a point of reference when I became a teacher myself.

WCR: *How did you decide to go to the University of Pennsylvania for medical school? Did you apply to a number of medical schools?*

JSF: I only applied to 2 medical schools—Johns Hopkins and the University of Pennsylvania. I got accepted to Hopkins first, but my first choice was the University of Pennsylvania. My dad had always referred to Penn as "the University" with a capital U as if there was only the 1 university in the country. So it was Penn.

WCR: *Your academic record in college must have been pretty good to have been accepted in those 2 excellent medical schools.*

JSF: I was upper third of the class. I don't think I was in the upper 10%. I also was considered well rounded because of being in a lot of campus activities.

WCR: *What were some of the other activities? You played on the basketball team; you were the sports editor of the college newspaper.*

JSF: I was an officer in the fraternity.

WCR: *How did medical school hit you?*

JSF: The favorite saying of one of the great intellectuals of that time, Joseph Campbell, was "Discover your passion." In medical school I discovered my passion. I found that as much as I had loved art and literature in college, that human physiology and disease was even more fascinating. I loved medical school. It was a time of learning an entirely new body of information. I look back on it with great fondness.

But during medical school I discovered that I had glaucoma. It was devastating. I thought at that time that I would progressively lose my vision. For the next 8 to 10 years I took daily eye drops of timolol. When President Kennedy established the Peace Corps I tried to join, but I was rejected because of my eyes.

I got married at the beginning of medical school to the head cheerleader and convinced her to go to medical school also.

WCR: *You got married just after graduation from college?*

JSF: A year after graduation from college. Our first year we lived on the Swarthmore campus where I was the proctor in the girl's dorm. Medical school was about a 40-minute drive, which was hard. My colleagues in medical school were not nearly as spectacularly bright as the students at Swarthmore, but they were very hard working. For the first time, I really had to buckle down and study. I studied 3 or 4 hours a night 6 days a week in medical school.

WCR: *How did you do in medical school academically? How many were in your class?*

JSF: We had slightly more than 100 in our class. As usual, I was in the upper third, but I was not the best. I found that I loved internal medicine. In the 1960s, we didn't have the diagnostic tools that we have today (echocardiography, MRI, etc.). You had to do a very careful history and physical examination. You had to do a lot of reasoning to arrive at the correct diagnosis. In some ways this was a return to the chess matches which had fascinated me so much in my youth. I loved internal medicine because of the intellectual challenge. The other topic that I really liked was orthopedics. I liked orthopedics because it was sports-related, and there were quick solutions. I ultimately decided on internal medicine.

WCR: *When did you make that decision?*

JSF: Not until my senior year in medical school.

WCR: *Who influenced you in medical school?*

JSF: I can't point so much to a single professor as to a group of professors. They were the stars of the Clinical Pathologic Conferences of the Massachusetts General Hospital. I read every CPC of the MGH for the 4 years I was in medical school. These doctors were brilliant in the way they looked at each possibility, analyzed it, and then finally came to a conclusion. And after they drew their conclusion, the pathologist showed the specimens that either verified or negated their conclusions. The discussants usually were correct. I found myself fascinated by the brilliance of these men and women.

WCR: *You mentioned that orthopedics had an appeal to you. What about general surgery? You were an athletic person.*

JSF: We had to stand at the operating table for such long periods of time holding retractors. That was boring. To me it wasn't intellectually challenging and it was physically tiring. I really did not have much interest in general surgery.

WCR: *I gather that after your freshman year you and your wife moved to Philadelphia itself.*

JSF: Right. We moved to 34th and Locust, which was about a 10-minute walk from the medical center.

WCR: *Your life was much simplified by that.*

JSF: Yes. She was a year behind me in medical school. So when she started, we moved into Philadelphia.

WCR: *You interned in internal medicine at the University of Pennsylvania. Was that an easy choice for you or not?*

JSF: Yes. It was pretty much an automatic choice because my wife was still in medical school. The subsequent year, however, the choice of residency was a big decision. We decided to go to California. When I got to California and realized that you could be outdoors all day every day, it didn't take long to be convinced that I was not going to spend a lot more time on the East Coast.

WCR: *It must have been a bit disappointing to your parents when you decided to move to California for your residency in internal medicine.*

JSF: Yes, and later there was a much greater disappointment for them. I was offered Chief of Cardiology at Penn State University in Hershey, about 15 minutes from where they lived in the Harrisburg area. I decided to turn it down.

WCR: *When was that?*

JSF: About 1975.

WCR: *Beginning in 1964 you went to Harbor General Hospital in Torrance, California. I presume your wife was at the same hospital. What kind of physician did she become?*

JSF: Yes. When I started my internal medicine residency there, she began her internship.

WCR: *You remained there for 3 years. How did you enjoy that residency academically compared to what you had encountered at the University of Pennsylvania?*

JSF: At Penn Med I discovered my passion. Harbor General Hospital was my evolution into being a good clinician. We had a very strong residency program with very bright guys. We'd admit as many as 20 patients a night. It was a county hospital. We had tremendous responsibility for patient care. During those 3 years, I came to know that I could handle any kind of internal medicine problem that was thrown at me. I felt very confident about handling emergencies. It was a period of wonderful growth: from having an excellent knowledge base to having a broad experience base.

In the middle of my third year of internal medicine residency, I had the opportunity to take a rotation outside the hospital. I chose to go to Cedars-Sinai for cardiology. There I met the new Chief of Cardiology, *Jeremy Swan*, who had just come from the Mayo Clinic. That 2-month rotation led to my decision to become a cardiologist. I loved the idea that cardiology had a very quantitative basis. You measured millimeters of mercury and valve gradients. You measured millimeters of ST-segment depression. With these kind of objective measurements, combined with a good history and physical examination, you could provide reasonable care. Coronary angiography was just beginning. And Jeremy was charismatic. After those 2 months with Jeremy, I knew I wanted to become a cardiologist.

WCR: *And you also were convinced that you wanted to do your cardiology fellowship at Cedars-Sinai Medical Center?*

JSF: I thought that I should get the best cardiology training in the country. In talking to people in Los Angeles, they said you should either go to the National Institutes of Health with *Gene Braunwald* or to Harvard with *Dick Gorlin*. My wife got a residency in radiology at the Massachusetts General Hospital. When she did that, I made the decision to go with Dick Gorlin. I got every darn article that Dick had ever published and read through all of them. When I went to Boston for the interview, I spent most of my time quoting Dick Gorlin's articles back to him. He must have been taken with the young man from California who appeared to know everything about lactate metabolism and the Gorlin formula and all the other great work that he had done, because I was accepted into the fellowship. At Harvard, under the influence of Dick Gorlin and *Ed Sonnenblick*, I decided that I wanted to be a clinical research cardiologist.

WCR: *You were in Boston how long?*

JSF: Two years. The cardiology fellowships in those days were for 2 years.

WCR: *Then you came back to Los Angeles to the Cedars-Sinai Medical Center. What was your status when you came back?*

JSF: When I came back to Los Angeles, I really wanted to go to the UCLA catheterization laboratory. I was tremendously lucky that there was not a position for me. So I went back to Cedars-Sinai. Jeremy made me head of the Myocardial Infarction Research Unit (MIRU), which evolved to become the Specialized Center of Research in Ischemic Heart Disease (or SCOR). That program, which I directed for the next 20 years, ultimately had a budget of $2,000,000 a year. We had the opportunity to do some wonderful research in clinical cardiology.

WCR: *Let me go back to the Harvard experience. You had had that very academic medical school training, your internship was in that same genre, and then* *you had more hands-on care at Harbor General Hospital. You could take care of almost any medical problem. And then you go back to Harvard for the first time and it's a very academic arena. Dick Gorlin is in his heyday. That unit was publishing an incredible amount. How did Gorlin hit you? How did you like that atmosphere?*

JSF: We had a saying at Peter Bent Brigham Hospital that you only come from Harvard once. When you leave Harvard, you had better have done very well. So there was a tremendous amount of stress to produce abstracts and manuscripts. We were all working together, but there was a sense of competition. Who would be the most likely to please Dick and Ed with the research they did? We all strove mightily to produce the most number of abstracts and the best publications. Within that potentially pathologic context, it was a wonderful learning experience. Dick Gorlin and *Harvey Kemp* in particular taught me a great deal about how to write a scientific manuscript. My first manuscripts were flowery, literary gems that read as scientific nonsense. They taught me how to write scientifically.

WCR: *You were around at The Brigham a number of people who really became prominent figures in cardiology in this country and elsewhere. Your connections really broadened a great deal. I guess that Jeremy Swan was very glad to get you back to Cedars-Sinai, particularly after your Harvard experience.*

JSF: What a group at Harvard. I played touch football every weekend in the football season with *Ken Shine*, a burly hard-charging tackle, and playing basketball in the basketball season with *Bill Parmley*, who had a terrific jump shot. And with *Dick Helfant*, who played college basketball and was a superb all-around athlete. A number of others in our fellowship became chiefs of cardiology or well known in academics—*Mike Lesch* in Chicago, *Jay Sullivan* in Dallas, and *Al Most* at Brown, *Ezra Amsterdam* at Davis, and *John Kjeksus* in Europe. Although Jeremy may have been enthusiastic about my coming, it certainly wasn't reflected in the salary that he gave me. I started at $14,000 a year as a full-time staff person. That was 1970. I wondered about academic medicine when others I knew were making 3 or 4 times as much in private practice.

WCR: *Your wife at that time became a radiologist?*

JSF: Debbie trained in radiology at Mass General and then joined the full-time staff at Los Angeles County Hospital. She subsequently published a well-known textbook in orthopedic radiology. But when we returned, one strong aspect of my upbringing, the dedication to family, failed. Our marriage had been unhappy for many years. We really should have terminated it many years earlier. The feeling that one should be committed to a marriage kept me married for far longer than either one of us should have been. To her credit, Debbie would have ended it long before I did.

At that time, I met my future wife, Barbara, who was the chief medical resident at Cedars-Sinai. The most profound change in my life occurred at that time.

Barbara was at that time, and still is, the best doctor I've ever met. She had the great doctor's ability to integrate information. She was a superb diagnostician. But she also had that quality I saw in my mother—empathizing with the emotions and feelings of others. I recognized how much better a doctor she was because of that capacity of bringing out patient's feelings. It wasn't just in the medical area that this happened, it occurred also in our own relationship. Looking back, part of the reason for my failure in my first marriage was I really wasn't in touch with my own feelings.

I spent 2 years in psychotherapy. That was the best experience that I've ever had. I remember after the first meeting I imagined the psychiatrist would say, "Well, you're really quite a normal person. You're just having a problem with your divorce," and send me on my way. Instead he said, "I think you probably should come in and see me 3 times a week." I wasn't quite as normal as I thought I was.

WCR: *Or any of us really. Your first marriage ended as soon as you came back to Los Angeles.*

JSF: It really ended many years before that. But while we were married, we had 2 children, both born while I was in my internal medicine residency at Harbor General Hospital.

WCR: *Do you and Barbara have children?*

JSF: Yes. Barbara's and my son is *Justin*, aged 24.

WCR: *What does he do?*

JSF: He just decided to apply to medical school.

WCR: *What about your first 2 children?*

JSF: Jeffrey is 35 and Brent is 34. *Jeff* tutors college students and designs websites. He works almost entirely at home. He is the best educated of the Forrester family in literature and philosophy. My middle son, *Brent*, is a comedy writer. He has been nominated for 3 Emmys and won 1. He wrote first for the "Ben Stiller Show," "The Simpsons," and "King of the Hill." Currently, he is writing a romantic comedy movie.

WCR: *The kids by your first marriage grew up in Los Angeles, so you were able to see them frequently through the years.*

JSF: When we got divorced, Debbie moved to Malibu, about 45 minutes from Cedars-Sinai Hospital. I very much wanted to be close to my 2 older boys, so Barbara and I moved to Malibu also. We live about 10 minutes apart. This has worked out very well. As the boys grew up, they spent about half their time in our home and half the time in Debbie's house. Debbie is remarried to a physician. We have 4 doctors looking at the 3 children. So naturally neither of the older boys became a physician.

WCR: *Let me ask you a bit about your investigative work. From your CV it looks like your first paper after you got back to Los Angeles was the famous Swan-Ganz-Forrester manuscript on catheterization of the heart in humans via a flow-directed balloon-tipped catheter. Obviously, that's a classic article. I think it should be known as the "Swan-Ganz-Forrester catheter."*

JSF: I'll accept that.

FIGURE 4. JSF, age 29, with first child, Jeffrey.

FIGURE 5. JSF and wife Barbara in Hawaii, January 1, 2000.

WCR: *How did it come about?*

JSF: When I came back to Los Angeles, I was put in charge of the research program. We had a small full-time staff at the time. Three others who joined the staff at Cedars within 6 months included *Bill Parmley, Bill Mandel,* and *Jack Matloff.* Initially, I asked 1 of the young house officers to work with me. *George Diamond* and I began to work on left ventricular compliance. George is the most brilliant person I've ever worked with. He quickly figured out that the relation of pressure to volume was exponential. This became a new finding in cardiology. Just before I arrived, Jeremy Swan had invented a catheter. Ini-

tially, his concept was that you might be able to construct a catheter like a sailboat and sail it out into the pulmonary artery. That concept evolved into a balloon on the catheter. The catheter sat around for some months because nobody was particularly interested in it. One day, when George and I were in the animal lab working on compliance, we took the catheter and put it into a dog's heart. It recorded what we took to be right atrial pressure, but when we stepped on the fluoroscope, we discovered that it wasn't in the right atrium. Initially, we thought it must be far out in the coronary sinus. But as we pulled back the catheter the pulmonary arterial pressure waveform appeared. It took George and I quite a while to figure out what had happened. We had inserted the catheter blindly into the right heart and the catheter had instantly sprung out into the pulmonary wedge position. What we thought was right atrial pressure was actually pulmonary arterial wedge pressure. It was the serendipity of scientific discovery. George and I had been passing catheters in patients with acute myocardial infarction retrograde into the left ventricle. So we immediately took this catheter to the Myocardial Infarction Research Unit. George and I had a large number of difficulties with the catheter. The first few catheters we passed induced ventricular tachycardia because the balloon was placed back on the shaft of the catheter and the tip of the catheter. So we asked Edwards Labs to move the balloon so that it protruded over the tip of the catheter and protected it. We were very fortunate that *Willie Ganz* was a member of our staff. Willie had come from Czechoslovakia. Willie was expert in the thermodilution technique to measure blood flow. After many struggles in which we tried to pass a thermistor wire through the catheter lumen, we asked Edwards to imbed the wire in the body of the catheter. This allowed us then to measure cardiac output. Finally, we had a great deal of difficulty developing a cardiac output computer. I remember traveling around Europe talking about hemodynamic monitoring and discovering that the computer periodically was giving wildly erroneous results. We had to make major changes in the computer algorithm. But over a period of about 6 months, this wonderful coming together of Jeremy with the invention, George with his technical and clinical skills in passing catheters, and Willie with his expertise in thermodilution, we succeeded. To the best of my recollection, neither Jeremy nor Willie ever actually passed the catheter in a patient. That was George's fundamental contribution. If there is one sad aspect about it, it's that George, who contributed so much to the research efforts in those years, never received the amount of credit that he deserved.

Using the catheter, George and I developed the idea of subsets of acute myocardial infarction. We recognized that the cardiac output measurement represented the Y-axis of the Starling function curve and pulmonary arterial wedge pressure represented the X-axis. So we saw that we could assess cardiac function objectively. That led us to quantifying the effect of drugs on cardiac function in patients with acute myocardial infarction. We then chose a cardiac output criterion of 2.2 L/min and a pulmonary arterial wedge pressure of 18 mm Hg, to establish 4 groups of patients who both had vastly different prognoses for survival and very different appropriate therapies. So the balloon catheter ushered in an entirely new approach to treatment of patients with acute myocardial infarction, which was hemodynamic monitoring and management. Cardiac care units (CCUs) were being established about the same time. In the 1960s, prior to the establishment of cardiac care units, the mortality rate from myocardial infarction was 30% and by the end of the 1970s, it had fallen to 15% because of the detection of and new management of arrhythmias and improved management of cardiac function.

WCR: *What is it now?*

JSF: It's down now to about 7%.

WCR: *Do you insert the balloon catheters now in most of your acute myocardial infarction patients?*

JSF: Nowadays, Bill, we don't use the catheter much in management of patients with acute myocardial infarction. I think that's quite appropriate.

WCR: *But a lot of places do.*

JSF: The development of the catheter allowed us to understand how drugs alter left ventricular function. Now its role is predominantly when a patient is unstable and cardiac function is changing rapidly. In a person in shock or a person with significant heart failure the hemodynamic changes can occur well before changes in physical signs appear. The wedge pressure can drop to normal, but you will not hear a difference in rales or see a change in the chest x-ray for 24 hours. Yet at the time the pulmonary arterial wedge pressure falls to normal, you can be reasonably sure that that patient's pulmonary congestion has been relieved. Yes, it still has a role, but now we use echocardiography much more frequently.

WCR: *Jim, you mentioned the probability equations that you and George Diamond developed. Could you discuss this work?*

JSF: In the 1970s and 1980s, my closest professional colleague was George Diamond, to whom I owe much of my professional success. George has the ability to see interesting and profound associations that initially seem unrelated. But he also can go off on nonproductive tangents, so we worked well together. His contribution was his profound intellect, and mine was keeping us on target, keeping our work clinically relevant. In that 15-year period, George and I talked much of the working day and then again on the phone for another hour after we got home. It was intellectually stimulating for both of us. In the early 1980s, I came across a book called, *Beyond Normality.* I've forgotten who gave it to me. The pathologist who wrote it pointed out that the test for phenylketonuria (PKU) had 100% sensitivity and 99% specificity when used to diagnose phenylketonuria in newborns. But the diagnosis was still wrong most of the time, despite the tremendous sensitivity and specificity of the test, and many babies were being mistreated. The author pointed out that the reason was that the antecedent likelihood of the baby's having PKU was so low. So even though the false positive rate was very low, and even though the test never missed a baby who had the disease, there were more false positives than true positives. In a word, we were ignoring pretest likelihood. It clicked with me that the same thing was going on with stress testing. I reviewed all the literature and got values for the diagnostic accuracy of the magnitude of ST-segment depression—1, 2, and 3 mm relative to the likelihood of having coronary artery disease. We collected the same information for age, sex, and symptoms. George then took that body of information and integrated it by Bayesian analysis. In essence, you can lay one probability on top of another, so long as each measurement is independent. We came out with a probability of a person's having a disease based on a diagnostic test. It wasn't that the positive test meant you had disease or that a negative test meant you didn't have disease. It was merely that that diagnostic result altered the probability that existed prior to the test. It seems so obvious now, but at the time it was a profound new insight. We published this study in *The New England Journal of Medicine.* We then worked with *Alan Rosanski* and *Dan Berman* to apply the same kind of Bayesian analysis to nuclear stress testing. The importance of pretest likelihood, the insight that the tests are best applied in people who have an intermediate likelihood of disease, the diminishing incremental value of serial tests, and the relatively ineffectiveness of tests in people with very low or very high probability is now an accepted principle in diagnostic testing. It started with *Beyond Normality* and George deserves a great deal of credit for the evolution of those ideas.

WCR: *You've had 30 years of investigative efforts. You've been involved in a number of different projects. Your focus has been almost entirely on coronary artery disease. What are some other areas that you're most proud of as you look back now?*

JSF: It would be difficult to say whether it was the development of hemodynamic subsets, or probability analysis, or angioscopy. I worked with *Frank Litvak* and *Warren Grundfest*, in the mid 1980s to develop fiberoptic devices that could be inserted into the coronary artery at the time patients were having symptoms of myocardial ischemia. The images were astonishing. We discovered that people with stable angina pectoris almost always had a smooth coronary intima covering their atheroma. In contrast, 95% of the patients who came to coronary bypass surgery with unstable angina had either a torn intimal surface with a thin layering of platelets, or a partially occlusive thrombus. And we found that all the patients with infarction had thrombus. This was the first clinical proof that plaque rupture was the cause of unstable coronary syndromes. The finding with unstable angina was particularly important, because patients with unstable angina rarely died and autopsies were rare. Looking at those coronary images was perhaps the most exciting experience in my research career.

WCR: *Let me ask you more about angioscopy. It seems to me that the unstable plaque or the ruptured plaque is receiving far more recognition in patients with symptomatic myocardial ischemia than quantity* *of plaque ever did. Other than your group, really nobody has looked at the coronary arteries inside with eyeballs. How many patients did you, Litvak or Grundfest actually look at? How positive can you be that what you were seeing by angioscopy was actually a ruptured plaque or a clot on it? You did not see the ruptured plaque, if indeed one was there. You simply say a clot and assumed that the plaque under it had ruptured. What a lot of other cardiologists are talking about now is based to a big degree on what happened in your center.*

JSF: There are a couple of caveats about our observations. First, most coronary angioscopies that we performed were interoperative. So we were seeing a skewed sample of all the people with unstable angina. I said 95% had ruptured plaque. A number of other investigators have felt overall that a more appropriate number would be 75%.

WCR: *And that is based on angiography. Yet, you've got a clot covering it. You are not seeing underneath the clot.*

JSF: You are absolutely right that you either see plaque rupture or you see a partially occlusive thrombus and you have no idea what is beneath that partially occlusive thrombus. Japanese, German, and other Americans have subsequently done a much higher volume of angioscopic investigations than we did. Although there is some variation in what percentage of patients with unstable angina have either plaque rupture with a thin carpet of platelets or partially occlusive thrombus, there is agreement among angioscopers that the range is somewhere between 75% and 95%, depending upon how severely ill the patients are.

WCR: *You are talking about both unstable angina and non–Q-wave acute myocardial infarction?*

JSF: Yes.

WCR: *You make a good point that unstable angina, for example, at necropsy is difficult to study because most patients with unstable angina, if they die, go on to have acute myocardial infarction and then you're not certain that that's what is present in unstable angina versus that which occurs in acute myocardial infarction. Or they go and have coronary angioplasty and angioplasty works by cracking plaques. Or they go on to have a coronary bypass operation and bypass results in plaque fracture when the coronary artery is opened. I think the whole cardiologic community is highly dependent on what you observed. How many angioscopy patients are you talking about?*

JSF: We published in *Circulation* after our first 100 patients. So it was a relatively small population. In the published angiographic literature, there are now at least several thousand patients. Postmortem evaluation in unstable angina is confounded by the intrinsic fibrinolytic system, so in this specific case, I trust angioscopy more than autopsy.

WCR: *How many angioscopies do you have to do to really know what you're looking at?*

JSF: Angioscopy certainly has limitations. You have to flush the catheter, and you may dislodge material. You do not get a complete circular image of the coronary artery unless the catheter is exactly co-

axial with the long axis of the artery. It may be difficult to distinguish clot mass from a hemorrhagic surface.

WCR: *Did you ever at necropsy look in the coronary arteries with the angioscopy technique that you did during life and then make a judgment on this particular area and then process that area in formaldehyde and alcohol and make histologic sections to make sure that what you were seeing by eyeball was what was really there?*

JSF: Yes. My colleague at Cedars-Sinai, *Robert Siegel*, compared angioscopy, ultrasound, and pathology. Robert's results showed that intravascular ultrasound was far better for assessing the vessel wall, and less accurate for detecting thrombus.

WCR: *Let me ask you what your day-to-day life was like in the 1970s and 1980s when your investigative arm was your major focus. How does that compare to what your life is like now? You described that you have to drive 45 minutes into work and 45 minutes back. What time did you and do you get up in the morning? What time do you get to the hospital? What time do you leave the hospital? What time do you get home? What time do you go to bed? What are your evenings like?*

JSF: There were 3 different phases of my career in terms of time commitment. During the first 20 years at Cedars when I was working with George Diamond in clinical research, I worked very hard. During the first 5 years, for instance, I took no vacations. I spent my time in development of the balloon catheter and probability analysis. Then when I was Chief of Cardiology, I became a 9 to 5 person with occasional evenings devoted to major fundraising. Now, since I've stepped down as Chief, I do what many former chiefs do. I run clinical trials, and I am heavily involved in the activities of the American College of Cardiology. I also serve on editorial boards of a number of journals, work on data safety monitoring boards, steering committees, and I lecture extensively. So these years after being Chief seem like the best of all worlds.

But the thing I am most proud of in my career is that for the 15 years that my 3 boys were growing up, I spent every season coaching little league baseball, soccer, and basketball. To do that I often had to leave the hospital early. Although I balanced those early departures with work at home, the balancing of commitment to coaching and profession is one that very few of my colleagues in cardiology have done. One of my best memories is when our Malibu team, from a town of 13,000, went unbeaten in league play, and then won the district championship in a population of 1 million people, with several cities with populations of over a hundred thousand. I loved working with kids and teaching sports.

WCR: *Did you enjoy being Chief of Cardiology at Cedars-Sinai?*

JSF: Yes and no. I loved the first couple of years of being Chief because we were building. But then HMOs emerged in Southern California. Instead of building and expanding a division, I was given the job of sinking the Titanic. Each year the hospital told me

FIGURE 6. JSF, Barbara, and Justin (age 6) at Aspen, Colorado, in 1983.

have medical school appointments? How does it work?

JSF: To understand the structure, which I think comes close to being unique in American medicine, it's worthwhile understanding how Cedars-Sinai evolved. Cedars is the jewel of Beverly Hills and the entertainment community. It is justifiably a source of great pride to the Jewish community. For many years the hospital was simply a private hospital. But community leaders had a strong desire to have it be a center of learning in the Jewish tradition. So in the 1950s, private physicians agreed to have full-time staff to teach house officers and conduct research. The idea was that these professorial types would not engage in clinical practice because that could threaten the livelihood of the private practitioners. Over the years that relationship was strained whenever the academic full-time staff got more involved in consultation. Jeremy did only limited consultation. I did very little consultation, but times change; our new Chairman, P.K. Shah sees many patients. The full-time staff also administers the laboratories (catheterization, echocardiography, electrocardiography, etc.) and that was a source of friction. One of the central issues during my years as chief was the full-time staff control of the revenue from the echo laboratory. The attending staff saw they were bringing in the patients, and were competent to read echos. Yet the income from echo interpretation was going to the full-time staff. The problem was resolved by making the echo lab much more open.

As medical center revenue diminished with the advent of HMOs, the hospital has demanded that every full-time staff member generate his salary from either clinical services or research grants. Consequently, we have much less time for research.

WCR: *How many full-time staff are in Cardiology at Cedars-Sinai?*

JSF: At the peak, we probably had 25 clinical full-time staff physicians. At one point we got down to maybe 60% of that. Similar reductions have affected the entire Department of Medicine. Further, about 5 years ago the hospital removed many of the directors of departments and divisions because they were the highest salaried individuals in the medical center.

WCR: *Cedars-Sinai Hospital, I suspect, is quite a competitive area. I would presume it's quite different from the Polyclinic Hospital that your father worked in. You've come from a Scottish Presbyterian background and yet you're one of the major leaders in a hospital which is the pride of the Jewish community. How have you been able to survive in this community?*

I had to decrease the budget by very large amounts and told me who I had to terminate. The single most painful thing in my professional career was when I was told by the administration that I had to call in my closest professional colleague and tell him that the Medical Center couldn't afford to pay his salary any longer. That finished me psychologically. So I had golden handcuffs: I was very well paid, but not happy. I negotiated a graceful exit with the Chief of Medicine to my current role. The Chief of Medicine also was happy, because I had been pretty intransigent as we battled over each successive termination.

WCR: *Let me ask you a bit about your hospital? There are a number who are Professors of Medicine at UCLA and yet Cedars-Sinai Hospital is a very large private hospital. The chiefs of the various services and some who were not chiefs I presume were on salary from the hospital, not from the medical school.*

JSF: That's right. The salaries of the full-time staff are paid by the Medical Center.

WCR: *I presume also that you do see some private patients. How does it work and what is your relationship to the pure private practitioners in your hospital who have no appointments at UCLA and those who do*

FIGURE 7. JSF with 3 sons, Jeff, Brent, and Justin *(left to right)*.

together, then take a week's vacation after I give my lecture, whether it's in Asia or South America or Europe. We take 5 or 6 of these 1-week trips to some exotic location annually. These escapes have been very important in maintaining the romance of marriage. It's been a successful formula for us.

WCR: *Does Barbara practice?*

JSF: Barbara began in a clinical oncology practice. All her patients were young women with breast cancer. Over a period of about 10 years, she simply couldn't do it emotionally anymore. She went into practice at Pritikin Longevity Center where she supervised diet, exercise, and life style modification. About 3 years ago she retired. Now she takes care of all our friends and relatives, who seem to call about twice a week with some kind of medical problem for her to resolve. It is a very rewarding, very low income job.

WCR: *Although your mother did not have much formal education, it seems to me that she educated herself quite well. When you were home growing up your mother was there when you got home. In other words she was not a professional herself and she did not work outside the home and yet you married 2 physicians. You've come home and they may or may not be there. As you look back, were these just the women you were exposed to and you had no time to recruit outside the professional arena?*

JSF: No. I was always attracted to independent intelligent women. Perhaps what I was looking for early on was somebody who wouldn't be too dependent upon my emotional support. I'm not sure. I know the woman who has always been most attractive to me has been the lady doctor.

WCR: *You mentioned that your mother was quite active in the arts. In college that was the arena that attracted you. Your 3 boys have all been very much involved in the arts. And yet you and Barbara and your boys grew up in Malibu, which is a bit away from the art culture of Los Angeles. How have you worked in these cultural activities in your life?*

JSF: With my first wife, for a number of years we didn't have a television set, so the kids were forced to find entertainment from reading. My second son, now 34, still does not now have a television set. Barbara and I are both avid readers. I read a lot of history, Barbara reads politics. We love discussing what we read. If I read something that I think is interesting, I'll call the kids in and we'll talk about it. And now they come and say ". . . here's a fascinating bit of information about whales, or how are waves formed or here's a great book about how to write short stories." This family is always trading things that they've discovered and found fascinating. We're a "let's discuss it" family.

JSF: I am married to a nice Jewish girl from Brooklyn, which doesn't hurt. But seriously, the Board of Directors is blind to ethnicity. Intellect and performance are their only criterion. There is not a scintilla of advantage or loss for any ethnic group. It's a wonderful environment.

WCR: *Actually, that's been my experience during my training at NIH and through the years. It seems to me that the Jewish community is a more meritorious community than is the non-Jewish community.*

JSF: I agree.

WCR: *Do you and Barbara have hobbies you do together? Or do you have interests different from her? You mentioned that your mother and father had really an idyllic marriage. You and Barbara have been together for a long time now. It seems to me that in my relatively brief contact with you that she's your best friend.*

JSF: Barbara is a very beautiful person, but does have 1 fault. She thinks you are the wittiest person in cardiovascular medicine.

WCR: *That's a major fault.*

JSF: Barbara and I are best friends. Aristotle said, "A life unexamined is not worth living." My great debt to Barbara is that she taught me to examine myself and understand who I am. Yes, we have been fortunate to have a wonderful marriage. We still do something we call "taking a love weekend." We go away to Santa Barbara or some local place and stay in a hotel for the weekend. Even though we have a very nice place on Malibu Beach, we go to recapture the romance that we had when we first met.

In terms of what we do, we try to balance career and other interests. I have been fortunate to be invited to lecture all over the world. Our strategy is to go

WCR: *That in a way is the way your father and you interacted when you were growing up. Is that not correct?*

JSF: Yes. I suppose that in many ways I have tried to recapitulate the house with the white picket fence. I've maintained the Midwestern values that my dad and mom had, even though I'm not much exposed to those values now.

WCR: *Who were the people at Cedars who influenced you particularly?*

JSF: George Diamond was the most influential. In addition to Jeremy, there were at least 2 people who had substantial influence. The first was *Bill Parmley*. Bill is a superb physician who has a second major interest, the Mormon Church. Bill showed me how to balance profession and other commitments. He would arrive every day at 8:30 A.M. and he'd leave every day at 4:30 P.M. He was incredibly efficient and he was very productive. He probably devoted as much time to the Mormon Church as he did to cardiology. But he made both of them successful. It was an important insight for me. It's like Frank Sinatra's song "I Did it My Way." Bill did it his way. I did it my way.

Another person who had a profound effect on me was *Elliot Corday*. Although he had great political power, he was humble, and he was intensely loyal to his people. I found as I got to know Eliot over the years that his quality of loyalty and of giving without expectation of anything in return were qualities I deeply admired and wanted to emulate.

WCR: *You mentioned that your mother and father had several friends in Harrisburg and that they would come to your house and you would go to their house, and that they often included you in those social activities. Do you and Barbara have a number of friends in Malibu that you see a lot and you spend time with? How would you respond to that friendship aspect of your life?*

JSF: I see the friendships as actually in 2 categories, both of which are tremendously important. In the years when the children were growing up, we had a group of friends in Malibu. Many were parents of our children's friends. A group of about 10 of us did every thing together. We played tennis every weekend and we went river rafting together. Many of these friends have now moved out of Malibu in retirement and some have died. There's a second group of friends, Bill, that's enormously important to me. It is the friends that I have made professionally in traveling around the world. I've been very fortunate to be part of a group of people brought together by *Jack Vogel* in his conferences at Aspen and in Hawaii. That would include a group of maybe 10 cardiologists whose wives and husbands know each other and have done many things together. We've literally spent many months of our lives with the wives and kids of Bob Roberts, Bill Spencer, Alan Ross, Bob Vogel, Dick Conti, Spencer King, Peter Block, John Schroeder, Mike Gorman, and Denny Dietz.

WCR: *Jim, is there anything that you would like to discuss that we haven't discussed?*

JSF: Bill, I think you have completely covered my life. There's nothing left. You're a heck of an interviewer.

WCR: *On behalf of* The American Journal of Cardiology *and myself, I want to thank you sincerely for pouring your soul out, so to speak, so that we all can get to know you better.*

JSF: Thank you, Bill. I've thoroughly enjoyed our discussion.

JSF's BEST PUBLICATIONS AS SELECTED BY JSF

2. Swan HJC, Ganz W, Forrester JS, Marcus HS, Diamond GA, Chonette D. Catheterization of the heart in man with the use of a flow-directed balloon-tipped catheter. *N Engl J Med* 1970:283:447–451.

3. Helfant RH, Forrester JS, Hamptom JR, Haft JI, Kemp HG, Gorlin R. Differential hemodynamic, metabolic and electrocardiographic effects in subsets with and without angina pectoris during atrial pacing. *Circulation* 1970;42:601.

4. Forrester JS, Herman HV, Gorlin R. Noncoronary factors in the anginal syndrome. *N Engl J Med* 1970;283:786.

6. Forrester JS, McHugh TJ, Diamond GA, Prakash R, Ganz W, Swan HJC. Rapid assessment of cardiopulmonary hemodynamics in acutely ill patients utilizing a single right heart catheter. *Am J Cardiol* 1970;26:633.

7. McHugh TJ, Adler L, Zion D, Swan HJC, Forrester JS. Simultaneous hemodynamic, radiologic and physiologic evaluation of left ventricular failure in acute myocardial infarction. *Chest* 1970;58:285.

8. Ganz W, Donoso R, Marcus HS, Forrester JS, Swan HJC. A new technique for measurement of cardiac output by thermodilution in man. *Am J Cardiol* 1971;27:392–396.

9. Diamond GA, Forrester JS, Danzing R, Parmley WW, Swan HJC. Acute myocardial infarction in man: comparative hemodynamic effects of norepinephrine and glucagon. *Am J Cardiol* 1971;27:612–616.

12. Diamond GA, Forrester JS, Hargis J, Parmley WW, Danzig R, Swan HJC. Diastolic pressure-volume relationship of the canine left ventricle. *Circ Res* 1971;29:267–274.

13. Forrester JS, Diamond GA, McHugh TJ, Swan HJC. Filling pressures in the right and left sides of the heart in acute myocardial infarction. *N Engl J Med* 1971;285:190–193.

14. Diamond GA, Forrester JS, Danzig R, Parmley WW, Swan HJC. Hemodynamic effects of glucagon during acute myocardial infarction with left ventricular failure in man. *Br Heart J* 1971;33:290–295.

16. Forrester JS, Diamond GA, Freedman S, Allen HN, Parmley WW, Matloff JM, Swan HJC. Silent mitral insufficiency in acute myocardial infarction. *Circulation* 1971;44:877–883.

18. Forrester JS, Diamond GA, Swan HJC. Bedside diagnosis of latent cardiac complications in acutely ill patients. *JAMA* 1972;222:59–63.

20. Forrester JS, Amsterdam EZ, Parmley WW, Sonnenblick EH, Urschel CW. Dissociation of myocardial contractility and pump performance in hemorrhagic shock: correlation of in-vivo measurements with assay of shock plasma in papillary muscle. *Cardiology* 1972;57:333–347.

21. Forrester JS, Diamond GA, Parmley WW, Swan HJC. Early increase in left ventricular compliance following myocardial infarction. *J Clin Invest* 1972;51:598–603.

22. Diamond G, Forrester JS. Effect of coronary artery disease and acute myocardial infarction on left ventricular compliance in man. *Circulation* 1972;45:11–19.

23. Swan HJC, Forrester JS, Diamond GA, Chatterjee K, Parmley WW. Hemodynamic spectrum of myocardial infarction and cardiogenic shock: a conceptual model. *Circulation* 1972;45:1097–1110.

26. McHugh TJ, Forrester JS, Adler L, Zion D, Swan HJC. Pulmonary vascular congestion in acute myocardial infarction: hemodynamic and radiologic correlations. *Ann Int Med* 1972;76:29–33.

27. Forrester JS, Ganz W, Diamond GA, McHugh TJ, Chonette D, Swan HJC. Thermodilution cardiac output determination with a single flow-directed catheter. *Am Heart J* 1972;83:306–311.

28. Chatterjee K, Parmley WW, Swan HJC, Berman G, Forrester JS, Marcus HS. Beneficial effects of vasodilator agents in severe mitral regurgitation due to dysfunction of subvalvular apparatus. *Circulation* 1973;48:684–690.

30. Chatterjee K, Parmley WW, Ganz W, Forrester JS, Walinsky P, Crexells C, Swan HJC. Hemodynamic and metabolic responses to vasodilator therapy in acute myocardial infarction. *Circulation* 1973;48:1183–1193.

32. Forrester JS, Chatterjee K, Swan HJC. Hemodynamic monitoring in patients with acute myocardial infarction. *JAMA* 1973;226:60–61.

33. Crexells C, Chatterjee K, Forrester JS, Dikshit K, Swan HJC. Optimal level of filling pressure in the left side of the heart in acute myocardial infarction. *N Engl J Med* 1973;289:1263–1266.

34. Dikshit K, Vyden JK, Forrester JS, Chatterjee K, Prakash R, Swan HJC. Renal and external hemodynamic effects of furosemide in congestive heart failure after acute myocardial infarction. *N Engl J Med* 1973;288:1087–1090.

35. Abrams E, Forrester JS, Chatterjee K, Danzig R, Swan HJC. Variability in response to norepinephrine in acute myocardial infarction. *Am J Cardiol* 1973; 32:919–923.

41. Wyatt HL, Forrester JS, Tyberg JV, Goldner S, Logan SE, Parmley WW, Swan HJC. Effect of graded reductions in regional coronary perfusion on regional and total cardiac function. *Am J Cardiol* 1975;36:185–192.

42. Nagasawa K, Vyden JK, Forrester JS, Groseth-Dittrich M, Corday E, Swan HJC. Effect of phentolamine on cardiac performance and energetics in acute myocardial infarction. *Circ Shock* 1975;2:5–11.

43. Gray R, Chatterjee K, Vyden JK, Ganz W, Forrester JS, Swan HJC. Hemodynamic and metabolic effects of isosorbide dinitrate in chronic congestive heart failure. *Am Heart J* 1975;90:346–352.

44. daLuz PL, Forrester JS, Wyatt HL, Tyberg JV, Chagrasulis R, Parmley WW, Swan HJC. Hemodynamic and metabolic effects of sodium nitroprusside on the performance and metabolism of regional ischemic myocardium. *Circulation* 1975;52:400–407.

45. Forrester JS, Tyberg JV, Wyatt HL, Goldner SJ, Parmley WW, Swan HJC. Pressure-length loop: a new method for simultaneous measurement of segmental and total cardiac function. *J Appl Physiol* 1975;37:771–775.

47. Forrester JS, Diamond G, Chatterjee K, Swan HJ. Medical therapy of acute myocardial infarction by application of hemodynamic subsets (two parts). *N Engl J Med* 1976;295:1356–1362; 1976;295:1404–1413.

48. Chatterjee K, Swan HJC, Kaushik VS, Jobin G, Magnusson PT, Forrester JS. Effects of vasodilator therapy for severe pump failure in acute myocardial infarction on short-term and late prognosis. *Circulation* 1976;53:797–802.

50. Forrester JS, Wyatt HL, daLuz PL, Tyberg JV, Diamond GA, Swan HJC. Functional significance of regional ischemic contraction abnormalities. *Circulation* 1976;54:64–70.

51. Taylor WR, Forrester JS, Magnusson PT, Takano T, Chatterjee K, Swan HJC. Hemodynamic effects of nitroglycerin ointment in congestive heart failure. *Am J Cardiol* 1976;38:469–473.

52. daLuz PL, Forrester JS. Influence of vasodilators upon function and metabolism in ischemic myocardium. *Am J Cardiol* 1976;37:581–587.

54. Wyatt HL, daLuz PL, Waters DD, Swan HJC, Forrester JS. Contrasting influences of alterations in ventricular preload and afterload upon systemic hemodynamics, function, and metabolism of ischemic myocardium. *Circulation* 1977;55:318–324.

55. Forrester JS, Diamond GA, Swan HJC. Correlative classification of clinical and hemodynamic function after acute myocardial infarction. *Am J Cardiol* 1977;39:137–145.

56. Waters DD, daLuz PL, Wyatt HL, Swan HJC, Forrester JS. Early changes in regional and global left ventricular function induced by graded reductions in regional coronary perfusion. *Am J Cardiol* 1977;39:537–543.

61. Forrester JS, Waters DD. Hospital treatment of congestive heart failure—management according to hemodynamic profile. *Am J Med* 1978;65:173–179.

65. Diamond GA, Forrester JS. Analysis of probability as an aid to the clinical diagnosis of coronary artery disease. *N Engl J Med* 1979;300:1350–1358.

74. Elkayam U, Weinstein M, Berman D, Maddahi J, Staniloff H, Freeman M, Waxman A, Swan HJC, Forrester JS. Stress thallium-201 myocardial scintigraphy and exercise in the detection and location of chronic coronary artery disease: comparison of sensitivity and specificity of these noninvasive tests alone and in combination. *Am Heart J* 1981;101:657–666.

81. Diamond GA, Hirsch M, Forrester JS, Staniloff HM, Vas R, Halpern SW, Swan HJC. Application of information theory to clinical diagnostic testing. The electrocardiographic stress test. *Circulation* 1981;63:915–921.

85. Diamond GA, Forrester JS. Probability of CAD. *Circulation* 1982;65:641.

87. Diamond GA, Forrester JS. Clinical trials and statistical verdicts: probable grounds for appeal. *Ann Intern Med* 1983;98:385–394.

89. Rozanski A, Diamond GA, Berman D, Forrester JS, Morris D, Swan HJC. The declining specificity of exercise radionuclide ventriculography. *N Engl J Med* 1983;309:518–522.

91. Diamond GA, Vas R, Forrester JS, Xiang HZ, Whiting PS, Pfaff MJ, Swan HJC. The influence of bias on the subjective interpretation of cardiac angiograms. *Am Heart J* 1984;107:68–74.

94. Rozanski A, Diamond GA, Forrester JS, Berman DS, Maddahi J, Swan HJC. Comparison of alternative referent standards for cardiac normality: implications for diagnostic testing. *Ann Intern Med* 1984;101:164–171.

101. Forrester JS, Litvack F, Grundfest W. Laser angioplasty in cardiovascular disease. *Am J Cardiol* 1986;57:990–992.

103. Diamond GA, Rozanski A, Forrester JS, Morris D, Pollock BH, Staniloff HM, Berman DA, Swan HJC. A model for assessing the sensitivity and specificity of test subject to selection bias: application to exercise radionuclide ventriculography for diagnosis of coronary artery disease. *J Chron Dis* 1986;39:343–355.

104. Sherman CT, Litvack F, Grundfest W, Lee M, Hickey A, Chaux A, Kass R, Blanche C, Matloff J, Morgenstern L, Ganz W, Swan HJC, Forrester JS. Demonstration of thrombus and complex atheroma by in-vivo angioscopy in patients with unstable angina pectoris. *N Engl J Med* 1986;315:913–919.

108. Forrester JS, Litvack F, Grundfest W, Hickey A. A perspective of coronary disease seen through the arteries of living man. *Circulation* 1987;75:505–513.

116. Forrester JS, Litvack F, Grundfest WS, Mohr F, Papaioannou T. The excimer laser: current knowledge and future. *J Intervent Cardiol* 1988;1:75–80.

119. Forrester JS. Laser angioplasty, now and in the future. *Circulation* 1988; 78:777–779.

121. Forrester JS, Litvack F, Grundfest W, Segalowitz J, Hickey A. Symposium:

intravascular imaging and flow. Cardiac angioscopy in acute ischemic syndromes. *Am J Cardiac Imaging* 1988;2:178–184.

128. Forrester JS, Arakawa K, Barath P, Segalowitz J, Grundfest W, Hickey A, Litvack F. Angioscopic images of the blood vessel surface in man. *Cardiovasc Imaging* 1989;1:4–7.

134. Barath P, Fishbein M, Cao J, Berenson J, Helfant R, Forrester JS. Detection and localization of tumor necrosis factor. *Am J Cardiol* 1990;65:297–302.

135. Siegel R, DonMichael T, Fishbein M, Bookstein J, Adler L, Reinsvold T, DeCastro E, Forrester JS. In vivo ultrasound arterial recanalization of atherosclerotic total occlusions. *J Am Coll Cardiol* 1990;15:345–351.

138. Siegel RJ, Chae JS, Forrester JS, Ruiz CE. Angiography, angioscopy and ultrasound imaging before and after percutaneous balloon angioplasty. *Am Heart J* 1990;120:1086–1090.

139. Barath P, Cao J, Forrester JS. Low density lipoprotein activates monocytes to express tumor necrosis factor. *Am J Pathol* 1990;227:180–184.

142. Forrester JS, Litvack F, Grundfest W. Initiating events of acute coronary arterial occlusion. *Ann Rev Med* 1991;42:35–43.

146. Siegel RJ, Ariani M, Fishbein MC, Chae JS, Maurer G, Forrester JS. Histopathologic validation of angioscopy and intravascular ultrasound. *Circulation* 1991;84:109–117.

147. Forrester JS, Eigler N, Litvack F. Interventional cardiology: the decade ahead. *Circulation* 1991;84:644–653.

148. Forrester JS. A symposium: mechanisms of myocardial ischemia and injury in unstable angina pectoris. *Am J Cardiol* 1991;68:1–2.

149. Forrester JS. Intimal disruption and coronary thrombosis: its role in the pathogenesis of human coronary disease. *Am J Cardiol* 1991;68:69–77.

152. Cercek B, Sharifi B, Barath P, Forrester JS. Growth factors in restenosis. *Am J Cardiol* 1991;68:24–31.

157. Forrester JS, Eigler N, Goldenberg T, Laudenslager J, Grundfest W, Litvack F. Coronary excimer laser angioplasty. *J Invas Cardiol* 1992;4:75–82.

158. Fagin JA, Forrester JS. Growth factors, cytokines and vascular injury. *Trends Cardiovasc Med* 1992;2:90–94.

160. Sharifi B, LaFluer D, Pirola C, Forrester JS, Fagin J. Angiotensin II regulates tenascin gene expression in vascular smooth muscle cells. *J Biol Chem* 1992;267:23910–23915.

174. Bailey WL, LaFleur DW, Forrester JS, Fagin JA, Sharifi BS. Stimulation of rat vascular smooth muscle cell glycosaminoglycan production of angiotensin II. *Atherosclerosis* 1994;111:55.

175. LaFleur DW, Fagin JA, Forrester JS, Sharifi BG. Cloning and characterization of rat tenascin alternatively spliced isoforms: platelet-derived growth factor—BB markedly stimulates expression of spliced variants to tenscin mRNA. *J Biol Chem* 1994;269:20757.

176. Ameli S, Hultgardh-Nilsson A, Cercek B, Shah PK, Forrester JS, Ageland H, Nilsson J. Recombinant apolipoprotein A-1 Milano reduces intimal thickening following balloon injury in hypercholesterolemic rabbits. *Circulation* 1994;90: 1935–1941.

178. Lambert TL, Forrester JS, Litvack F, Eigler N. Localized arterial wall drug delivery from a polymer coated removable metallic stent: kinetics, distribution and bioactivity of forskolin. *Circulation* 1994;90:1003-1011.

180. Litvack F, Eigler N, Margolis J, Rothbaum D, Bresnahan JF, Holmes D, Untereker W, Leon M, Kent K, Pichard A, King S, Ghazzal Z, Cummins F, Krauthamer D, Palacios I, Block P, Hartzler GO, O'Neill W, Cowley M, Roubin G, Klein LW, Frankel PS, Adams C, Goldenberg T, Laudenslager J, Grundfest WS, Forrester JS, for the ELCA Investigators. Percutaneous excimer laser coronary angioplasty: results of the first consecutive 3000 patients. *J Am Coll Cardiol* 1994;23:323–329.

184. Dev V, Eigler N, Fishbein MC, Tian Y, Hickey A, Rechavia E, Kupfer J, Forrester JS, Litvack F. Sustained local drug delivery of dexamethasone and colchicine via biodegradable microspheres does not prevent intimal hyperlasia in rabbits. *Circulation* 1994;90:893.

190. Makkar R, Litvack F, Eigler N, Forrester JS. Treatment of vascular disease with local drug delivery systems. *Cardiologia* 1995;40:651–657.

195. Luo H, Nishioka T, Fishbein MC, Cercek B, Forrester JS, Kim CJ, Berglund H, Siegel RJ. Transcutaneous ultrasound augments lysis of arterial thrombi in vivo. *Circulation* 1996;94:775–778.

200. Makkar RR, Eigler N, Litvack F, Forrester JS. Prevention of restenosis by local drug delivery. *J Cardiovasc Pharmacol Therapeut* 1996;1:177–188.

201. Forrester JS, Merz C, Bairey N, Bush TL, Cohn JN, Hunninghake DB, Parthasarathy S, Superko RH. Matching the intensity of risk factor management with the hazard for coronary disease events: Task Force 4. Efficacy of risk factor management. *J Am Coll Cardiol* 1996;27:991–1006.

203. The Post Coronary Artery Bypass Graft (POST CABG) Trial Investigators. Post coronary artery bypass graft clinical trial: primary results of aggressive LDL-cholesterol lowering and low dose anticoagulation on late obstructive changes in saphenous vein bypass grafts. *N Engl J Med* 1997;336:153–162.

204. Forrester JS, Shah PK. Using serum cholesterol as a screening test for preventing coronary artery disease. The five fundamental flaws of the American College of Physicians Guidelines. *Am J Cardiol* 1997;79:790–792.

207. Bairey Merz CN, Rozanski A, Forrester JS. The secondary prevention of coronary artery disease. *Am J Med* 1997;102:572–581.

208. Nishioka T, Luo H, Fishbein M, Cercek B, Forrester JS, Kim C, Berglund H, Siegel R. Dissolution of thrombotic arterial occlusion by high intensity low frequency ultrasound and dodecafluoropentane emulsion—in vitro and in vivo study. *J Am Coll Cardiol* 1997;30:561–568.

209. Forrester JS, Shah PK. Lipid lowering versus revascularization: an idea whose time (for testing) has come. *Circulation* 1997;96:1360–1362.

211. Frimerman A, Eigler N, Forrester JS, Makkar R, Litvack F. Chimeric DNA-RNA hammerhead ribozyme to CDC-2 Kinase and PCNA reduce stent induced stenosis in a porcine coronary model. *Circulation* 1997; 95:87–91.

212. White CW, Campeau L, Knatterud G, Forrester JS, Gobel F, Har JA, Domanski MH, Hoogwerf B, Canner J, Rosenberg Y, Hunninghake D. Effect of an aggressive lipid lowering strategy on progression of atherosclerosis at the saphenous vein graft (SVG—distal native vessel (NV) anastamoses. *Circulation* 1997;96:65-I.

216. LaFleur DW, Chiang J, Fagin JA, Forrester JS, Shah PK, Sharifi BG. Tenascin-C interacts with aortic smooth muscle cells through its fibrinogen-like domain. *J Biol Chem* 1997;272:32798–32808.

220. Forrester JS, Shah PK. Unstable plaque: pathogenesis and prevention. *J Thrombo Thrombolysis* 1998;5:83.

221. Forrester JS, Kennedy JW, Weinberg SL. External influences on the practice of cardiology. *J Am Coll Cardiol* 1998;31:926–933.

227. Wallner K, Li C, Shah PK, Fishbein MC, Forrester JS, Kaul S, Sharifi BG. Tenascin-C is expressed in macrophage-rich human coronary atherosclerotic plaque. *Circulation* 1999;99:1284–1289.

230. Alaupovic P, Fesmire JD, Hunninghake D, Domanski M, Forman S, Knatterud GJ, Forrester JS, Herd JA, Hoogwerf B, Campeau L, Gobel FL. The effect of aggressive and moderate lowering of LDL-cholesterol and low dose anticoagulation on plasma lipids, apolipotproteins and lipoprotein families in post coronary artery bypass graft trial. *Atherosclerosis* 1999;146:369–379.

233. Hirshfeld JW Jr., Banans JS Jr., Brundage BH, Cowley M, Dehmer GJ, Ellis SG, Ewy GA, Faxon DP, Holmes DR Jr., Jacobs AK, Little WC, Magorien RD, Nocero MA Jr., Oesterle S, Pepine CJ, Taubman M, Tommasco C, Vlietstra RE, Vogel R, Forrester JS, Douglas PS, Faxon DP, Fischer JD, Gregoratos G, Wolk MJ. American College of Cardiology training statement on recommendations for the structure of an optimal adult interventional cardiology training program: a report of American College of Cardiology task force on clinical expert consensus documents. *J Am Coll Cardiol* 1999;34:2141–2147.

234. O'Rourke RA, Brundage BH, Froelicher VF, Greenland P, Grundy SM, Hachamovitch R, Pohost GM, Shaw LJ, Weintraub WS, Winters WL, Forrester JS, Douglas PS, Faxon DP, Fisher JD, Gregoratos G, Hochman JS, Hutter AM Jr., Kaul S, Wolk MJ. American College of Cardiology/American Heart Association expert consensus document of electron-beam computed tomography for the diagnosis and prognosis of coronary artery disease. *Circulation* 2000;102:126–140.

235. Knatterud GL, Rosenberg Y, Campeau L, Geller NL, Hunninghake DB, Forman SA, Forrester JS, Gobel FL, Herd JA, Hickey A, Hoogwerf BJ, Terrin ML, White C, and Post CABG Investigators. The long-term effects on clinical outcomes of aggressive lowering of low-density lipoprotein cholesterol levels and low dose anticoagulation in the Post Coronary Artery Bypass Graft Trial. *Circulation* 2000;102:157–165.

236. Forrester JS. Role of plaque rupture in acute coronary syndromes. *Am J Cardiol* 2000;86:15–23.

239. Forrester JS, Bairey-Merz CN, Kaul S. The aggressive low density lipoprotein controversy. *J Am Coll Cardiol* 2000;36:1419–1425.

WILLIAM HOWARD FRISHMAN, MD:
A Conversation With the Editor*

Dr. Bill Frishman is Professor of Medicine and Pharmacology and Chairman of the Department of Medicine of New York Medical College in Valhalla, New York, and also Chief of Medicine at Westchester County Medical Center in Valhalla, which is located in the northern suburbs of New York City. He was born in the Bronx, grew up in the Bronx, and except for his 6 years in Boston, he has always lived in the Bronx. His father's premature death convinced him that he wanted to be a physician and cardiologist and to work in his beloved Bronx. His career at Albert Einstein stretched from 1976 until 1997 and during this period he published approximately 180 original communications in medical journals; 391 monographs, reviews, and book chapters, and 14 books. His work has involved primarily evaluation of drugs to decrease myocardial ischemia, heart failure, blood pressure, and various arrhythmias. He has been involved in the evaluation of 50 drugs beginning with propranolol in 1973. Bill Frishman is a self-made man devoted to his family, community, country, and medical center. He is also a good guy with a good sense of humor and a good capacity for friendship.

William Clifford Roberts, MD[†] (hereafter WCR): *I am speaking with Dr. Bill Frishman on December 15, 1997, in my office at Baylor University Medical Center. Dr. Frishman has just presented at our Medical Grand Rounds. Dr. Frishman, I would like to find out what it was in you that made it possible for you to stand "above the herd," so to speak. Maybe we could start with your childhood. How was it growing up in the Bronx? Who were your mother and father? Did you have siblings? What do you remember of your young years?*

William Howard Frishman, MD[‡] (hereafter WHF): I was born in the southeast Bronx, a lower middle-class community of New York City, where many first- and second-generation European Americans had settled after moving from crowded neighborhoods in Manhattan to seek greater living space. My great grandparents and grandparents had emigrated from eastern Europe at the turn of the century, and they all worked in the garment industry which was located in lower Manhattan. My father was born in Hoboken, New Jersey, just across the Hudson River from New York City, and my mother was born on the lower east side of Manhattan. Their families moved to the Bronx after World War I.

As a child, I was fortunate to have 2 loving parents and large extended family, all who lived in the same community. My father owned a men's and boys clothing store in the neighborhood, and my mother worked as a bookkeeper for a ceramics factory located in the community. We lived in a small apartment; few people in the neighborhood owned automobiles.

I developed a love of learning from my parents. My father and mother were high school graduates and were reading constantly in their limited spare time. I would go to the local public library every week to borrow books, and I developed from my book browsing a love of history, especially historical biographies.

I attended a local public elementary and junior high school. They were not the easiest places to learn in, with large classes of 35 to 40 students. However, I had many wonderful teachers who were devoted to their work. It was from these experiences, I sought a career as an educator. I was impressed with the impact a teacher can make on a youngster, even in the formative years. The instructor who had the greatest influence on me during these years was a junior high school General Science teacher, Eugene Smolar. I have modeled my teaching style after Mr. Smolar. He made difficult scientific concepts easy to learn, with a sense of humor mixed with firmness. He also had great respect for his students, and I developed a real appreciation for science from him. In subsequent years, I was fortunate to attend the Bronx High School of Science (Figure 1), one of the first specialty science schools in the country. Entry to Bronx Science was based on a competitive examination and grade performance in junior high school. At Bronx Science the student body included young men and women from all over the city, most coming from inner city homes with families struggling to succeed. It was the most competitive school environment I would ever work in, however, an extremely stimulating atmosphere for learning, with the best teachers in the city. Bronx Science has had more Nobel Prize winners than any high school in the U.S., and many alumni would go on to future careers in the physical and biological sciences, medicine, and mathematics. Jimmy Carter's Secretary of Defense, Harold Brown, was a Bronx Science graduate. Some graduates did go on to non-science careers, such as Stokeley Carmichael, William Safire, and Bobby Darin (Walden Cassatto Jr.) who would eventually die from rheumatic heart disease.

My high school years were clouded by the sudden death of my father from an acute myocardial infarction, a great catastrophe for our family, which would ultimately lead to my becoming a cardiologist. My father was a vibrant, active man who worked very hard, 6 days a week from morning until night; unfortunately he had been a heavy cigarette smoker since his teenage years. My mother had also smoked but quit the habit because of migraine headaches. One

*This series of interviews are underwritten by an unrestricted grant from Bristol-Myers Squibb.
†Baylor Cardiovascular Institute, Baylor University Medical Center, Dallas, Texas 75246.
‡Department of Medicine, New York Medical College, Valhalla, New York 10598.

WILLIAM FRISHMAN   SY 2-3115
1366 White Plains Rd., Bx. 62
Ed.-in-Chief of Observatory,
Science Editor Journal of Bio.,
Physical Science Journal, Math
Bulletin, Arista Tutor, Track
Team, ARISTA.

FIGURE 1. Graduation from Bronx High School of Science at the age of 16.

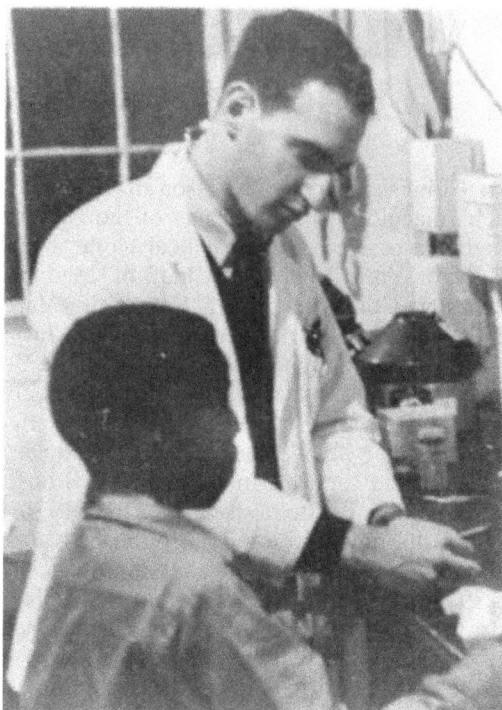

FIGURE 2. Working as a medical student doing my pediatrics rotation at Boston City Hospital, 1967.

childhood remembrance I have is being sent by my parents to buy them cigarettes which in the 1950s sold for 24 cents a pack. A youngster could buy cigarettes during those years without any question from the merchant. My father first suffered myocardial infarction in his 30s and had been warned to stop smoking, but continued after his recovery, right until his death at age 46. My father's death was a tremendous loss, and I learned from this tragedy that an individual with modifiable risk factors for coronary artery disease bears a responsibility not just for his/her own well being, but the well being of their family. Children should not be orphaned by the premature death of a parent from preventable conditions. My father's death occurred just before final exams during my junior year of high school, and I made an immediate decision to become a heart doctor who would work to see that what happened to my family would not happen to other families. I became extremely focused and goal oriented.

I also had more pleasant experiences during my high school years that would influence my future work. First, I was appointed Editor-in-Chief of my high school year book. From my year book work, I learned how to organize a detailed compendium within a defined time limit, since your classmates are counting on the year book being printed before graduation. Second, I worked after classes at a local pharmacy as a stock and delivery boy. I would read the labels on all the medicine bottles. From this experience I developed both a love of pharmacology and an appreciation of the work of pharmacists. Finally, I was awarded a National Science Foundation grant at Cornell Medical School during one of my summer vacations. I worked on my own research project entitled "Cardiac Manifestations of Hyperthyroidism" under the direction of a Cornell physician-biometrician, Dr. Melvin Schwartz. I used the books at the Cornell Medical Library to try to teach myself electrocardiography of the white Wistar rat, a clinical skill I still have not yet mastered.

Following high school, I attended the Boston University 6-year medical program, one of the first such accelerated programs in the U.S. After high school, one was guaranteed admission to medical school after passing all the course work during the 2-year undergraduate portion of the program. For many individuals, this is not the best route for a medical education, but in my eagerness to become a physician, it was just right for me. It was a wonderful experience being a college and medical student in Boston during the 1960s (Figure 2). I had wonderful professors in medical school, and since the class size was relatively small, I was able to know many of the faculty very well, including Stanley Robbins, the editor of the Pathology Text. My chiefs of medicine at Boston University were Franz Ingelfinger and Arnold Relman, who subsequently became editors-in-chief of the *New England Journal of Medicine*, Dr. Norman Levinsky, who would become Chair of Medicine at BU for 25 years, Aram Chobanian, who is now the Dean at Boston University, and John Harrington, who is the Dean at Tufts. An upper classmate at Boston University, Marcia Angell, is now the executive editor of *The New England Journal of Medicine*. The research thrust at Boston University during these years was hypertension and atherosclerosis, a tradition that continues today under Apstein, Gavras, and Loscalzo. Cardiology was beginning to blossom as a scientific discipline during the 1960s, and my experiences at Boston University reinforced my desire to be an academic cardiologist. One experience at BU that had a great impact on my future work as a teacher was the opportunity to work one-on-one with a faculty member in preparation of a required doctoral thesis. This project had to be of such quality that it could stand the light of day if submitted to a peer-reviewed journal. This provided an opportunity to know a faculty member well, something that is lost now in large medical school classes.

WCR: *Dr. Frishman, let me go back just a bit, and put some dates on things. You were born in what year?*

WHF: I was born on November 9, 1946.

WCR: *Your father died in what year?*

WHF: 1961.

WCR: *So you were 15 when your father died. Did you have siblings?*

WHF: Yes, I have a sister who is 2 years younger than I. I picked up other stepsiblings later when my mother remarried, but that was many years later when I was already in medical school. I also had grandparents, many uncles, aunts, and cousins. My entire family was very close and we all lived in the same community.

WCR: *What was your living like? Did you live in an apartment? What was day-to-day situation like? When your father was alive, did you have a lot of discussions at the dinner table at night? Was he home at night? How did that work out on a day-to-day basis?*

WHF: We always lived in an apartment. I shared a bedroom with my sister, while my parents slept in the living room. They never had their own bedroom. That was how we lived until I went away to college and medical school.

My father worked 6 days a week, and came home early only on Tuesday evenings for dinner. Because he had a retail clothing business, he worked Monday thru Saturday and was off only on Sunday. I remember my father, with the little time he had, always reading a book, even during spare moments at work. I had the good fortune to spend time with my father at his business which was close to our home. My mother was one of the first women in the community to go to work, and that was to help the financial situation of the family. Many times during my school vacations, I stayed with my father at his place of work where I had a chance to know him very well. Despite his long work hours, I could always count on his help if I had difficulty in school, where he could always point me in the right direction. My father had also been a great athlete in his youth; a champion handball player. However, because of his work schedule in the later years, he could not get involved in athletic activities, except for playing ball with my sister and me.

WCR: *What did you do in your spare time when you were a youngster in high school? You mentioned*

working in your father's place of work? Was that close? Could you just walk there or ride your bicycle?

WHF: I use to go with my father to his place of work either by bus or car. The Bronx also provided wonderful diversions for a young boy growing up in the 50s and early 60s. Those were the "glory days" of the New York Yankees, the Bronx Bombers. From 1949 to 1964, the Yanks won the American League Pennant 14 times. I used to go to the games with my dad and uncles, usually on Tuesday night. The games we were involved with as children were the New York "street sports." There were few playing fields available, so we spent time playing ball games on the sidewalk and even in the middle of the street, having to dodge oncoming traffic. I was also active in the Boy Scouts. Until my dad's passing, for an inner city youngster, I think I had an idyllic childhood.

WCR: *So you were a happy youngster?*

WHF: Yes

WCR: *How did you get into the Bronx School of Science?*

WHF: The Bronx School of Science was a New York City magnet school that was started in 1938, and the students came from all over New York City. It was a highly competitive school, where admission was based on grades, specifically performance in math and science in elementary and junior high school. We also had to take a competitive entry exam. I entered the school in 1960 in a newly remodeled building in the west Bronx which had a planetarium and other laboratory facilities that few high schools could provide, either public or private. It was a wonderful environment for learning, with very dedicated teachers.

WCR: *Was that close to home? Could you walk to school?*

WHF: My daily commute involved taking 2 subway trains each way. The high school was in the West Bronx, and I lived in the East Bronx. The transportation in the Bronx is only good north to south, not east to west. I had to take a train to Manhattan, and then another uptown to the West Bronx.

WCR: *How long did it take to get to school?*

WHF: An hour by train, each way.

WCR: *You spent 2 hours a day just getting to school and back?*

WHF: Yes. And the train stop was also 5 to 6 blocks from school.

WCR: *Did you think safety when walking around in the Bronx?*

WHF: New York is actually a relatively safe city. However, from the popular press there was always a fear of crime. I think when you live in the inner city you learn how to avoid trouble. At least in the 1950s and 60s young people were not armed with guns. Of course there were a lot of street encounters, most of which were fist fights, but rarely did anyone get seriously hurt. At Bronx Science we did have pressures on us from other neighborhood high schools. They had some tough kids and one always had to defend oneself or learn to run fast. However, I was never fearful for my safety in those situations. You avoided walking alone, especially in a neighborhood you were not familiar with.

WCR: *What floor did you live on in your apartment house?*

WHF: We lived on the 2nd floor and then we moved to a slightly larger apartment on the 1st floor.

WCR: *When you father was not at home, what was it like at dinner time? Your mother was working. When you came home, you came into an empty apartment.*

WHF: I had many relatives in the community, including my grandparents who lived close by. My mother would come home from work around 6 o'clock, and until then my sister and I were on our own. Mom would always prepare dinner, and she did whatever was necessary to get us ready for school the next day. I absorbed a tremendous work ethic from both my mother and father. My mother just kept going, even after my father's death. Although at times with her busy schedule, I think it became a bit overwhelming for her. When my father was alive, he would come home very late on work days. Most often dinner would include just my sister, my mother, and me. My mother would make dinner again for my father when he came home from work.

WCR: *You mentioned your father's reading. Was your mother intellectually inclined?*

WHF: My mother was a bookkeeper. She was a high school graduate and read as much as she could. On Saturday afternoons when my father was at work, my mother would go to the public library. Our entire family always had a reverence for books. Even today in her retirement, my mother can always be found at the public library.

WCR: *Did you have many books in your house?*

WHF: We didn't have space for a library. I would use the encyclopedia in the public library which was located a few blocks from our home. Sometimes I would study there because it was quiet.

WCR: *Did you always feel a bit crowded in the house?*

WHF: Yes, in fact our apartment was really just a place to sleep and eat. I would spend free time on the street with friends. During inclement weather, we congregated in the hallways of our building, went to the movies or to the local bowling alley.

WCR: *You were a reasonable athlete in junior high school and high school?*

WHF: Yes and no. I was a fair athlete but more accomplished in my knowledge of sports trivia.

WCR: *You were always playing some sport, chasing some ball?*

WHF: We played baseball, handball, and stickball during the warm months and basketball and touch football in the winter. If we played with a tennis ball, it was not on a regulation court, but against the outside wall of our apartment building. I also competed on the track team in high school.

WCR: *What did you do?*

WHF: I was a quarter miler.

WCR: *I gather neither your mother nor father went to college.*

WHF: My dad attended the City University as a part-time student for 2 years. My mother would attend college at the City University many years later.

WCR: *You mentioned your grandparents were in the Bronx. You had aunts and uncles. I presume most of them did not go to college either.*

WHF: No, in fact one of my grandmothers could not read or write English; however, she did read the Yiddish newspapers.

WCR: *Where did your mother and father actually come from?*

WHF: My great grandparents and grandparents were born in eastern Europe. My maternal grandmother was from Hungary, my paternal grandmother from Austria, and my two grandfathers were from Russia. My grandparents all married in the U.S. Both my parents were born in the U.S., and I am a second-generation American.

WCR: *Your father was how old when he died?*

WHF: He was 46. He had suffered a previous heart attack while he was in his mid-30s.

WCR: *Your mother is now how old?*

WHF: 79

WCR: *What was the age difference between your mother and father?*

WHF: 3 years

WCR: *You went to Boston University for that 6-year combined liberal arts/medical school program. You came from a family without a lot of financial resources. Did you have a scholarship to Boston University? How did that work out? How did you choose Boston University?*

WHF: I was attracted to the program because of the ability to accelerate in pursuit of a medical degree. I had a partial scholarship and had student loans. I always worked at after-school jobs in college and in medical school. As an undergraduate I worked for room and board as a telephone switchboard operator and as a food server in the dormitory cafeteria.

WCR: *How many hours did you work a week?*

WHF: 10 to 15 hours.

WCR: *You were how old when you went off to college?*

WHF: 16

WCR: *Therefore, you graduated from college and medical school at age 22?*

WHF: Yes. I was in a hurry to get on with a medical career.

WCR: *Your mother and relatives in the Bronx must have been enormously proud of you to have one of theirs go off to college and medical school when they did not have that opportunity to do so themselves.*

WHF: Yes, I was really the first one in my family who went to an out-of-town school. My sister and cousins attended the local public colleges.

WCR: *What about your sister?*

WHF: My sister attended the City University of New York, and she is now a physical education and math teacher in the New York City public school system.

WCR: *Is she back in the Bronx?*

WHF: She teaches in Queens, but she lives on Long Island now.

WCR: *What do you remember about your 2-year liberal arts education at Boston University?*

WHF: The liberal arts program was quite rigorous. We essentially completed 3 years of college by also attending classes through 2 summers. Although we had to take the regular premedical courses, organic chemistry, physics, physical chemistry and biology, there was also time for the humanities. The curriculum was not just concentrated on science. We had very short vacations, 3 weeks at the end of each summer. We eventually received a Bachelor of Arts degree at the time we graduated from medical school.

WCR: *Did any teachers in the liberal arts program have a major impact on you?*

WHF: My physical chemistry professor, Alfred Prock, was an outstanding instructor, and he still teaches in the current 7-year program at Boston University. Physical chemistry was a difficult course for a college freshman, but Dr. Prock made it both enjoyable and easy to understand. In fact, he's another individual whose teaching style I would adopt later. My Western Civilization teacher (I always liked history) also had a great influence on me. I was impressed how teachers could make subject matter come to life through the enthusiasm and dedication they have for their jobs. I consider teaching to be one of the noblest professions.

The 1960s was an interesting time to go to school. John F. Kennedy was assassinated in November of my freshman year of college. In fact he had just visited Boston with his family the week before he went to Dallas. I think individuals growing up at that time (Kennedy was elected when I was in high school) were greatly affected by his assassination, and I don't think the U.S. has ever been the same. I think a lot of the drive and enthusiasm the country had was lost for many years, and of course would be affected more so by the Vietnam War. Many of my former high school classmates at Bronx Science, some of the brightest people I had ever met, were swallowed up by the war. I say "swallowed up" not by being involved in combat, but by the antiwar protests on the college campuses. Many of my friends never pursued their planned scientific careers. I myself was affected greatly by what was going on at the time.

WCR: *You started college in the combined program in September 1963 and Kennedy was shot in November 1963.*

WHF: Most of us looked to Kennedy as the patriarch of the country. He was on television and had a great influence on young people. He was a pro-science, pro-intellectual, pro-athletic type president.

WCR: *I gather from your growing up in the Bronx, you and your family did not go on vacations in the summer time. You didn't travel much outside of New York City.*

WHF: In fact we did. One of the things about living in the New York City in the 1950s was the lack of air conditioners since most of the apartment buildings were not properly wired. The only air conditioners were found in the movie theaters. It was terribly hot and humid during the summer in the 1950s, and our entire family would go to the public beach at Rockaway Peninsula in Queens. In the 1960s our family would go to the Catskill Mountains for the summer, about 100 miles north of the city. I was always in the care of relatives as my parents continued to work through the summer in the city. My family could not afford to send me to camp.

WCR: *Your parents essentially never vacationed?*

WHF: I remember my father having only one weekend off during my early years.

WCR: *When you went to Boston you were, in a way, upgrading your living standards?*

WHF: Well I had my own room for the first time.

WCR: *How did that affect you?*

WHF: It was a wonderful change. I shared a suite of rooms in the dormitory with a group of roommates who today remain my close friends. We were all in the 6-year program together. My 4 roommates were from different parts of the northeast, and we were very supportive and respectful of one another. One became a cardiothoracic surgeon, one became a general surgeon, 2 of us became cardiologists, and one became a psychoanalyst.

WCR: *So you all roomed together the entire 6 years?*

WHF: Yes. We were assigned together at random and not by our choosing. It really worked out well. In fact, George Hines who is now a cardiothoracic surgeon on the faculty of Stony Brook Medical School remains one of my best friends. He and I always sat next to each other during college and medical school final exams for good luck. Even now, when we go out together with our wives, the two of us will sit next to each other. Whoever gets to the restaurant first, saves the place for the other one.

WCR: *What other broadening experiences in college and medical school opened up to you in Boston? After 6 years how did you see yourself compared to when you left the Bronx 6 years earlier?*

WHF: I was a completely different person (Figure 3). Being away from home really helped me in my overall development. First of all, it allowed me to meet people from other parts of the country, particularly other parts of the Northeast. It was also an exciting time to be in Boston, which is a wonderful place to go to school, and a great college town. Overall, it was a mind-expanding experience, but I also worked very hard during these years. Because of the jobs I had and the attention I had to give my studies, I probably had less spare time than most of my peers. However, I still found time to get involved in some athletic activities.

WCR: *Were you a pretty good track man in high school?*

WHF: In the Bronx you learn to run fast.

WCR: *In medical school what kind of jobs did you have? You mentioned those in college.*

WHF: In medical school I worked as a medical technician at the Joslin Clinic because there were no house officers working there at the time. It was a good

FIGURE 3. Graduation from the Boston University 6-Year Liberal Arts-Medicine Program, 1969.

job except I worked through the night. I worked in all the clinical labs—chemistry, blood banking, hematology and bacteriology—and I did this once or twice a week. I also had a job as an attendant in the Boston Garden, where we covered the first aid room during all the sporting events. That was a time when the Boston Celtics were in their "glory days." I also worked during the Boston Bruins hockey games and all the professional wrestling matches.

WCR: *You actually saw the events and you were just called if someone needed you?*

WHF: It was just a wonderful job for someone who enjoyed team athletics as much as I do, and it was a real thrill to be so close to the players, such as Bill Russell and John Havlicek. I was able to go to many games and actually found the time to study during some of the less exciting competitions.

WCR: *Did learning always come easy for you or did you have to bear down a great deal?*

WHF: Learning came easy but I still studied very hard. I always felt it was not enough to study just to pass an exam. I wanted to learn in such a manner that I would retain the information indefinitely. I was never a good note taker in school and relied a great deal on book reading. I was fortunate in that I had a good memory. In those years, especially in medical school, a good memory was important. I was able to perform well because of that, and I could recall facts later on which I would have forgotten if I had only studied to pass examinations.

WCR: *What do you mean you were not a good note taker?*

WHF: I have a bad handwriting. When I got home I often could not read my notes. To take good notes, I

had to write slowly. As a consequence, I would often miss points in the lecture. I attended lectures faithfully but I needed to do more supplementary reading than my peers.

WCR: *While in college and medical school, were you always worried that you did not have enough money?*

WHF: I had real concerns about how I would perform in school because of my outside jobs. Sometimes I would work through the entire night and then have to go to class the next day. However, working did not affect my academic performance. I was able, in those years, as I am today, to balance many different activities. I don't think my medical school instructors realized that I was involved in so much outside work.

WCR: *Did you sleep much? What was your sleeping life like?*

WHF: I slept whenever I could, but even today I can always get around without much sleep. In those years I could get by on 4 to 5 hours of sleep a night.

WCR: *After completing medical school did you return to the Bronx?*

WHF: Yes. That was part of my life plan. I had made a promise to myself that I was going to be a cardiologist and practice in the community where I was raised. I returned to the Bronx to do just that.

WCR: *I gather you had no problem deciding what specialty you wanted to pursue in medical school?*

WHF: I knew I wanted to be a cardiologist in high school. I was so focused. What was still needed to be decided finally was the type of cardiologist. When I finished medical school I was not sure whether I would be a private practitioner or an academician. Because of the wonderful experiences I had in medical school, I was leaning towards an academic career.

WCR: *Although you returned to the Bronx you had not known medicine in the Bronx when you left 6 years earlier. How did you find medicine in the Bronx after having experienced it at Boston University Medical Center, Boston City Hospital, the Boston Veterans Administration Hospital, and some other Boston institutions?*

WHF: One of the interesting things about the Bronx is that it has many similarities to Boston. The Bronx and Boston are the same size, and the types of patients I was caring for in the Bronx really did not differ much from those I cared for in medical school. Because I was used to a rigorous schedule in medical school, I was able to function well working every other night or every third night.

WCR: *What was your living like when you became an intern? Did you live at the hospital?*

WHF: I lived at the hospital in an attached apartment building.

WCR: *You did a year of internship and your first year of residency at Montefiore Hospital. Who influenced you there?*

WHF: Montefiore is an institution with a long and distinguished history. It had initially been an affiliate of Columbia University Medical School during the years that it functioned as a chronic disease hospital. Since so many cardiac diseases were chronic because they could not be treated years ago, Montefiore always had a strong reputation in cardiology. The hospital changed its mission to encompass more acute care in the 1960s, and developed a strong academic affiliation with the newly formed Albert Einstein Medical School. Montefiore would ultimately became the university hospital for the Einstein Medical School and it provided a very good environment for medical training. The faculty included many excellent teachers in both internal medicine and cardiology; the cardiology faculty included Doris Escher and Seymour Furman who had put in the first transvenous pacemaker. Indeed, there was a lot of cardiology history at Montefiore. My Chief of Medicine was David Hamerman who was a gifted teacher and basic scientist in rheumatology. I got to know him quite well. The hospital had a large housestaff that included 48 interns. The Montefiore training program included working at the private hospital and also at an affiliated public hospital in the south Bronx, which was located in an indigent community. The experiences there complimented what we had in the private voluntary hospital. We were exposed to all types of patients one might see in a busy city practice.

WCR: *What do you mean by a "voluntary hospital"?*

WHF: In New York there is a large public hospital system. The voluntary hospitals were private, "not for profit" institutions.

WCR: *How much time did you spend at the south Bronx hospital?*

WHF: Two-thirds of the time were spent at Montefiore Hospital, one-third at the public hospital. One of the bonuses that came with working at Montefiore Hospital was the opportunity I had to meet a very attractive ward nurse who I eventually married.

WCR: *What made you decide to take your final year of medical residency at the Bronx Municipal Hospital?*

WHF: The Bronx Municipal Hospital had an extremely competitive housestaff program, which was located on the Einstein Medical School campus. It was actually closer to my home of origin in the Bronx. In those days physicians in training rarely completed an internal medicine program at one institution and it was not uncommon for people in the middle of internal medicine training to go to another hospital to complete their residency. I was not unhappy at Montefiore; I simply wanted to expand my experiences at another institution.

WCR: *Who influenced you a great deal at the Bronx Municipal Hospital?*

WHF: The Bronx Municipal Hospital is Einstein Medical School's oldest affiliated institution. The clinical faculty at the hospital have a strong research tradition. Many staff physicians who taught on the wards also had basic research laboratories at the medical school. There was more of a focus on research at the Bronx Municipal Hospital than at Montefiore. I was impressed by how many of the staff physicians were able to bring their work from the laboratory directly to the bedside.

WCR: *What made you decide to go to Cornell-New York Hospital to do your cardiology fellowship?*

WHF: Again, it was to get a different experience. Cornell had a superb Chief of Cardiology, Thomas Killip III, and the institution was one of the national leaders in coronary disease research. Cornell had one of the early NIH-sponsored Myocardial Infarction Research Units (MIRU) and had established one of the first coronary care units in the country. The MIRU program was involved in the development of the Swan-Ganz catheter and had pioneered bedside hemodynamic monitoring of myocardial infarction patients. I had the opportunity through the meetings of the various MIRU center faculties to interact with some of the leadership and future leadership of academic cardiology: Charles Rackley (University of Alabama at Birmingham); Jeremy Swan, William Ganz, William Parmley, and James Forrester (Cedars of Sinai); Eugene Braunwald, John Ross, Robert O'Rourke, and Bert Sobel (University of California-San Diego); Richard Ross, Bernadine Healy, Myron Weisfeldt, J. O'Neal Humphries, C. Richard Conti, and Bertram Pitt (Johns Hopkins), and Paul Yu (University of Rochester). This was one of the most exciting times in academic cardiology.

WCR: *Before you started your cardiology fellowship, you had no medical publications? Is that correct?*

WHF: I had written a thesis in medical school but it was not published.

WCR: *In your cardiology fellowship you had several publications during that 2-year span.*

WHF: I had 2 interesting opportunities at New York Hospital. It was a time when the beta blockers were first being introduced in the U.S. for the management of various cardiovascular disorders. I always had an interest in pharmacology. Tom Killip had spoken to some of the senior fellows first to see if they wanted to be involved in an angina project using propranolol as a treatment. I was the third one he spoke with and he did not have to convince me. My research career in cardiovascular pharmacotherapy began with propranolol. Also in the basic laboratory at that time, there was a lot of work being done examining platelet function and its relationship to both acute and chronic coronary disease syndromes. Cornell had a major platelet research effort under Ralpha Nachman, now the Chairman of Medicine at Cornell, and Babette Weksler. I worked with Babette on projects to examine whether or not platelets were activated in chronic or acute coronary syndromes.

WCR: *So your first publication in a medical journal was 1973?*

WHF: I had a case report published in 1973, and an original investigation published in *Circulation* in 1974.

WCR: *How did publishing hit you? I gather that investigation leading to publication, writing up, putting a ribbon around it, turned you on right away?*

WHF: It goes back to my yearbook work in high school, college, and medical school. I really enjoyed taking a research project from the early hypothesis stage and seeing it through to the end: making sure the study is carried out and analyzed properly, being able to do the necessary background research, putting together a manuscript, and seeing it through to publication, being able to present data at national forums. My fellowship experiences had really inspired me to a life in academic cardiology.

WCR: *How did you like New York Hospital? Here is quite a sophisticated hospital in downtown Manhattan, with a lot of private patients who were well off. How did all that phase you at the time?*

WHF: It was a little bit of culture shock at first. I did not live in Manhattan while I trained at Cornell, but continued to reside in the Bronx with my family because it was less expensive and had more living space. Cornell provided me a complimentary experience from what I had encountered from inner city hospitals. New York Hospital was in a very special central academic region of New York, across the street from Memorial Sloan Kettering Hospital and next to the Rockefeller Institute. The intellectual environment was incredible.

WCR: *How long did it take you to get back and forth to the Bronx?*

WHF: About an hour.

WCR: *So you were use to that from high school? I gather you used that time for reading?*

WHF: I would drive and occasionally get stuck in a New York City traffic jam and regret having taken the car. Then I would take the subway and go back to driving. It depended on how I felt each day. Once while trapped in a traffic jam only 2 blocks from the hospital, I had to leave my car to help carry a patient from an ambulance that was directly behind me. The patient was having an acute myocardial infarction. After delivering the patient to the emergency room, I returned to find my car and the ambulance in the same place in the traffic jam.

WCR: *After the fellowship in cardiology, which I gather you completed in June 1974, you went into the service for a couple of years.*

WHF: Because I was so young when I graduated from medical school, I was a prime target for being drafted into the service. I joined the Berry Plan as a way of trying to postpone my military duty, and I was luckily deferred so that I could finish all my internal medicine and cardiology training. In 1974 I entered the military for 2 years.

WCR: *Being in the Berry Plan prevented you from going to the NIH?*

WHF: I had to join the Berry Plan relatively early because I was fearful of being drafted, having been recently married.

WCR: *I gather your 2 years in the armed services actually turned out to be a useful endeavor for you. Could you describe that?*

WHF: I was assigned to a 500-bed military hospital, U.S. Walson Army Hospital in Fort Dix, New Jersey, which was located 1-3/4 hours from where my wife and I lived in the Bronx. I was also able to keep a faculty appointment at Cornell. I was able to balance going to New York Hospital where I was completing some of my research studies, while maintaining a full-time job at Fort Dix where I served as Chief of Cardiology at the hospital. The previous chiefs of Cardiology at Fort Dix included Carlos deCastro and Melvin Marcus who had just preceded me. At Fort Dix there were about 120 physicians like myself, trained in excellent academic programs from different parts of the country. My active duty military experience turned out to be a real opportunity for me.

WCR: *What made it so?*

WHF: First of all, there was great camaraderie in the medical corp and I was always patriotic. My father and uncles had served in the military during World War II. I felt that the soldiers involved in the Vietnam War and their families had made a great personal sacrifice, and the military physician had an obligation to them. I felt privileged to be in the Army, and grateful to the service for allowing me the time to go back to New York Hospital to complete my research studies.

WCR: *Did you enjoy being Chief of Cardiology at Fort Dix?*

WHF: It was a wonderful experience and a unique opportunity. Fort Dix is located in Burlington County, New Jersey, in a rural area close to Philadelphia and Trenton. Surrounding the military camp was a large, retired military population whom we cared for. What was also remarkable about being stationed there for military duty was that outside the gates of the fort, within walking distance, was the Deborah Heart/Lung Institute, one of the leading cardiology specialty hospitals in the U.S. at that time, and an affiliate of Temple Medical School. I was able to present many of our problem military patients at Deborah. Working with the Deborah faculty was comparable to having 2 more years of fellowship, since I had the opportunity to participate in their conferences and other academic functions. There were 3 historical events also that affected me during my military service. First, I entered the Army in July 1974, and in August 1974 President Nixon resigned. That event had a great impact on me with the war winding down and the terrible morale hovering over the military because of feelings of defeatism, especially with the president being brought to his knees. Second, the war officially ended in Vietnam in April 1975 with the evacuation of the U.S. embassy in Saigon. Subsequently many Vietnamese refugees were brought to the U.S. I was pulled out of my unit at Fort Dix for a month and sent to Fort Bragg, North Carolina, to work in a combat hospital during extensive military maneuvers (Figure 4). Although I left the Army in July 1976, I was still on active duty in the military on July 4th when the U.S. Bicentennial was celebrated. This was a very memorable experience for me. I very much enjoyed working with the people in the military, and I was blessed to be able to contribute something to my country.

WCR: *That 2-year experience did indeed have an impact on you?*

WHF: Yes, and I do not think I would have been the same without it.

WCR: *Can you expand on that a little bit?*

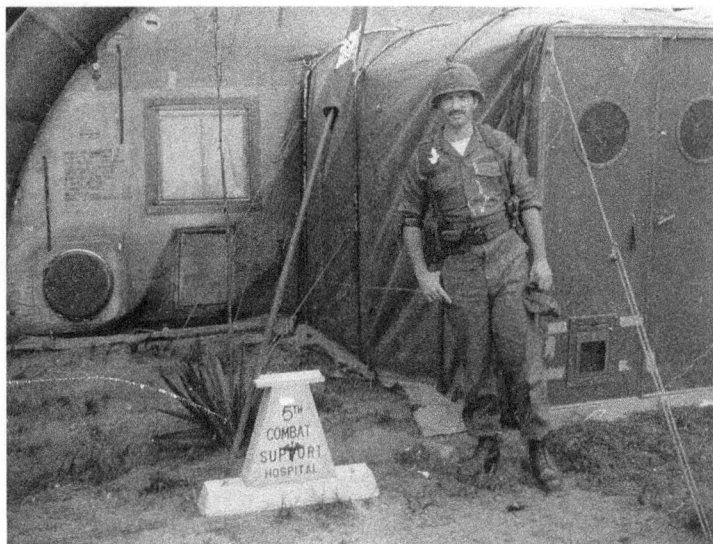

FIGURE 4. At combined Armed Forces war games with the 82nd Airborne Division Medical Corp., Fort Bragg, North Carolina, 1975, just after the end of the Vietnam War.

WHF: I learned to appreciate the many sacrifices the dependents of military personnel actually make. It was not only the soldier and sailor, but their dependents who were making a sacrifice. I felt that what I was doing in the military at that time as a physician actually paled compared to what they were going through. Because of my good experiences in the Army, I joined the Reserves afterwards. Overall, it was a very positive experience for me, and it completed my training as a physician.

WCR: *Are you still in?*

WHF: Not since 1990.

WCR: *Did you actually live in the Bronx when in the Army.*

WHF: Yes, I drove home at night. However, I would stay over when I was on hospital call. My wife would come down to visit at times. We had a small house on the base, but we kept our apartment in the Bronx.

WCR: *How did it come about that you went back to the Bronx?*

WHF: It fulfilled my promise that I would come back as a heart doctor to my community.

WCR: *Did you ever tell your father that, or did you ever have the chance?*

WHF: No I never had the chance, but that was my promise to honor his memory. There was also a great opportunity available at Einstein. Ed Sonnenblick had just come from Harvard and Peter Bent Brigham to be Chief of Cardiology at Einstein. I had the opportunity to work with him.

WCR: *When you joined the faculty, where was your office?*

WHF: I went to work at the Bronx Municipal Hospital and the Einstein College Hospital which was physically attached to the Einstein College of Medicine. I always wanted to be near the medical school. Bronx Municipal Hospital was the public hospital for

the Albert Einstein College of Medicine, and the college hospital was affiliated with Montefiore Hospital.

WCR: *Was Dr. Sonnenblick the one who actually hired you?*

WHF: Right. He recruited me. I also had the opportunity to continue on the faculty at New York Hospital, but my commitment was really to the community where I was raised.

WCR: *When you first went back, what happened? How did you start off when you got back?*

WHF: I started off as Director of the Non-Invasive Cardiac Labs and ultimately became the Chief of Medicine at the hospital and Associate Chairman and Professor of Medicine at the medical school. I also restarted my clinical drug trials. There was a very strong tradition in basic research already at the medical school. Einstein was always a national leader in receiving extramural NIH funding for basic research. What I was able to do was to get the clinical research programs started. Ed Sonnenblick was a basic researcher and had a strong basic cardiac laboratory presence. I realized the possibilities in clinical research with a population that was well-known to me and at the same time was medically underserved. There were not enough physicians in that area of the city. I had the opportunity to carry out the types of trials I had started at Cornell, and I went right to work in this direction.

WCR: *What were the initial trials?*

WHF: They involved the second-generation β blockers. Propranolol was already out, and there was a whole new generation of β blockers that were being introduced, followed later by the calcium blockers, and the ACE inhibitors. It was a gradual progression. I was able to do a great deal of the clinical investigations involving all the new drug breakthroughs that were occurring. In fact, until propranolol appeared, the cardiology pharmacopeia was similar to that in 1930—nitroglycerin, digitalis, isosorbide, and quinidine. The revolution that occurred in human cardiovascular pharmacotherapy began in the early 1970s and is continuing today. I was fortunate to be there at the beginning.

WCR: *You obtained a large number of grants, both from the NIH and from industry. Since you proved yourself rapidly that you could take one of these agents and evaluate it carefully, whether myocardial infarction or congestive heart failure, whether systemic hypertension or arrhythmia, after awhile the pharmaceutical companies must have started coming to you rather than your going to them.*

WHF: Yes, and I also had a very good population of patients to work with, and a wonderful research staff. The patients were individuals I knew from the neighborhood where I grew up. I was very close to them and supportive of their needs. Many of the patients were able to walk to the medical school and hospital. We always had a large cadre of patients that were very reliable and who we could follow carefully in studies.

WCR: *From 1976 to the time you left in 1997, you had 21 years of investigative efforts. You became full professor in 1985?*

WHF: Yes.

WCR: *When did you move to Montefiore Hospital?*

WHF: I always stayed at Montefiore. What happened was that Montefiore had taken over the administrative functions for the Hospital of the Albert Einstein College of Medicine. So technically, I was working at a Montefiore affiliate all the time. I never left the medical school campus.

WCR: *Where you went in 1976 is where you stayed until you left in 1997? What was your life like on a day-to-day basis? Here you were enormously productive. From 1974 until 1997 you published 571 papers in medical journals and 14 books. You were raising a family of 3 children. What was your day-to-day activity like? What time did you wake up in the morning? What time did you get to the hospital? What time did you leave home in the morning? What time did you get home from work? What time did you go to bed? How much sleep were you obtaining during that period? Can you give a flavor of your day-to-day activities?*

WHF: My days were very full. I still wake up early. I do my best work between 4:30 and 7:00 A.M.

WCR: *So you wake up about what time?*

WHF: 4:30 or 5:00.

WCR: *Everyday?*

WHF: For the most part except if I'm on vacation. I work at home in the early morning, and then we always have breakfast as a family. I do not go to work until after the children go to school, which is about 8 A.M. I would get to work about 8:15 or 8:30 after a 20-minute auto commute. We moved out of the Bronx in 1978 to the northern suburb of Westchester, to a town called Scarsdale where we still live.

WCR: *So you moved to a house?*

WHF: Yes, we bought a house.

WCR: *So that was 1978 and you were born in 1946, you were 32.*

WHF: The house was initially too quiet for me. I had trouble sleeping because I was used to the noise of the city. Probably, if it were not for my wife who had grown up in a house, I would have stayed in an apartment in the Bronx.

WCR: *So you would leave home at 8 A.M.? What did you do mainly at work?*

WHF: My work involved a very full day because I combined both my clinical research with clinical practice and large teaching load. I really work nonstop and rarely eat lunch. I always found that by not eating lunch I had an extra hour to get some important work done while other people were eating lunch. I found that was an important hour to have for myself. I work a full day, usually until 6 or 7 o'clock.

WCR: *When you go home, does your family eat together?*

WHF: Yes, we tried. My wife would try to wait until I arrived home. If I cam home really late, she would feed the children first, and we would have dinner together, just as my parents did.

WCR: *Did you try to make your dinners intellectual?*

WHF: We would review what each of us did during the day. We also discussed current events and other things with the children.

WCR: *What then did you do?*

WHF: My wife and I would help the kids with their homework, I would try to read journals or textbooks, and something nonmedical, before I would go to sleep.

WCR: *What time did you go to bed?*

WHF: Usually around midnight.

WCR: *You would wake about around 4:30 or 5 A.M.? What about the weekends?*

WHF: I had to go to the hospital for part of the weekend to care for patients. But mostly I involved myself with the childrens' activities. I was very active in all their team sports. My children say I never missed a game they were involved with or a musical performance. I could not be a full-time coach because of the time commitment, but I would always help out. All my children participated actively in sports throughout the school year.

WCR: *So you and your wife made parenting a major priority?*

WHF: Yes.

WCR: *How old are your kids now?*

WHF: My oldest daughter Sheryl is 26, my daughter Amy is 21, and my son Michael is 16 (Figure 5).

WCR: *What does your older daughter do?*

WHF: She's an attorney that specializes in problems of the elderly. She has always been socially responsive to the needs of people. In fact, she worked with me when she was in college on some of the geriatric research that I was involved with, and that is how she became interested in working with older people. She ultimately married a classmate who is also an attorney. They currently live in Manhattan, but will soon move into a house close to us.

WCR: *Your second daughter?*

WHF: My second daughter is a senior in New York University and she is studying to be a special education teacher, and will be attending graduate school at NYU following completion of her undergraduate studies.

WCR: *And your son?*

WHF: My son is 16 and is a junior in high school. He is a very good student, a class officer, a musician and an athlete, participating in football, baseball, and basketball. He is learning how to balance a very busy work and sports schedule.

WCR: *What do you think he will do?*

WHF: My son is just crossing the line now realizing that he may not make it as a professional football player, to thinking about medicine.

WCR: *Do you keep up well with all your cousins, aunts, and uncles living in the Bronx? Is this still a close-knit family?*

WHF: Yes. I think one of the advantages, or maybe a slight disadvantage, of living around my entire fam-

FIGURE 5. My greatest sources of inspiration: from *left*, my daughter Amy, my daughter Sheryl (seated), and my son-in-law Rob, my wife Esther (seated), and my son Michael, in our living room in Scarsdale, New York.

this course, and received both the Teaching Scholar Award of the American Heart Association and the Preventive Cardiology Academic Award from the NIH for my efforts in this area. I was also involved in the development of an independent scholars program at Einstein where all the students have to prepare a scholarly thesis for graduation. I would mentor 10% to 15% of the class in this activity which involved having a one-to-one relationship with students that provided an experience for them that was similar to mine as a student in Boston. One of the things I am most proud of from all my teaching activities was my ability to mentor hundreds of Einstein students as a thesis advisor. As a result of my efforts in medical education, I was nominated by the medical school to receive the AAMC Distinguished Teacher Award (Figure 6).

WCR: *The only other cardiologist who ever won this national teachers award is W. Proctor Harvey of Georgetown.*

WHF: Yes, and I think that was at the time the award was first presented.

WCR: *Why did you decide to leave the Albert Einstein College of Medicine in 1997 to become Chairman of Medicine at New York Medical College in Valhalla, New York, and Chief of Medicine at the Westchester Medical Center? Was that a difficult decision for you?*

WHF: Yes and no. I have had a wonderful career at Einstein. I had been a hospital Chief and really done all the jobs in the department of medicine, having served as clerkship leader, subinternship leader, and course leader. I was looking for an opportunity to be departmental chairman and make an even greater impact. New York Medical College happens to be located close to where I live. When the Chairman's job became available there, I thought that was an opportunity I could not refuse. The health care mission at New York Medical College, in a way is comparable to Einstein's and New York City's other medical schools. The school has a large hospital network that extends from Staten Island in the southern part of New York City, to just south of Albany, covering almost a 200 mile distance. I was really looking at the chairmanship as an opportunity to grow something new. Although I felt very comfortable at Einstein, I felt I had accomplished what I wanted to do there. I wanted to leave like Jerry Seinfeld, at the top of my form. New York Medical College has particularly great strength in basic cardiology research, which was attractive to me, as well as great expertise in pharmacology, physiology, and medicine. The Open Heart Surgery Program and Interventional Cardiology Program are well known in the region. The medical

ily is that when they have medical problems, I am the first one they call. I am involved with every medical issue that goes on with my aunts and uncles and cousins.

WCR: *Where is your wife from?*

WHF: My wife was born in Israel but was raised in the West Bronx. She is a research coordinator who works with me in the federally funded Women's Health Initiative trial. She is my best friend and a source of great strength for our family. We are extremely devoted to each other and to our children.

WCR: *You have won a number of teaching awards at Einstein School of Medicine. You recently received the Association of American Colleges Distinguished Teacher Award as the nation's outstanding medical educator. That sounds impressive to me. Tell me about it.*

WHF: Because of how I was influenced by my teachers and coming from a family where learning was very important, I always wanted to impart knowledge to students. In almost every activity I was involved with, whether through practice or through research, I always had students with me. I was also involved in teaching at the medical school on all levels, from the first through the fourth year. I have taught basic science, including physiology, epidemiology, pathophysiology, and pharmacology. I always teach on the wards and in the clinics. I also was involved in some innovative course design. We had a course Einstein called the "Return to Basic Science" where students, after being on the ward for a year in their third year of medical school, went back to the classroom for a brief basic science course where we would reinforce a lot of the basic science principles that may not have been appreciated during the first years of medical school. I was involved in directing

FIGURE 6. Receiving the national Distinguished Teacher Award at the 1997 Association of American Medical Colleges, Washington, DC from Dr. David Dale, President of Alpha Omega Alpha and the former Dean of the University of Washington School of Medicine.

FIGURE 7. Giving the 1989 Commencement Address at the Albert Einstein College of Medicine.

FIGURE 8. Bill Frishman (1997), currently the Professor of Medicine and Pharmacology and Chairman of the Department of Medicine, New York Medical College, and Director of Medicine at Westchester University Medical Center, Valhalla, New York.

school is the third largest in the U.S., and sponsors a large graduate medicine program. I felt well qualified for the task, having worked closely with 3 distinguished chairmen of medicine at Einstein, Milford Fulop, Louis Sherwood, and James Scheuer, from whom I learned a great deal.

WCR: *Where is the medical center that you will be working at?*

WHF: Westchester Medical Center, where I am also the Chief of Medicine (Figure 8). This was also an opportunity to become involved in planning health care delivery for a large region. I am very interested in maximizing health care delivery, while trying to make the health care system work better both for patients and their physicians. Again, I was very happy to make

a move, although sad to leave a place where I have had such wonderful memories. However, there is a saying: "You can never really get out of the Bronx." Indeed, I have a visiting faculty appointment at Einstein and continue to participate in collaborative research projects there. I am a co-principal investigator of the national Women's Health Initiative trial in New York City, and will still be working in that capacity while in my new school role.

WCR: *For someone like you who has investigated so many drugs, you will not be able to continue in the investigative arena quite to the same extent that you were before taking on the chairmanship of this large department of medicine medical school. Does that bother you?*

WHF: I may not be able to do all the "hands on work" that I did before, but I will have the opportunity to have a greater impact in helping to train a whole new generation of clinical scientists who will be able to continue the work.

WCR: *It must be a great source of satisfaction to you to receive the Distinguished Alumni Award from Boston University School of Medicine where you went to college and medical school, and an Honorary Alumnus Award from the Albert Einstein College of Medicine where you worked for so many years. You are now 51. What are your goals now?*

WHF: I think there are great opportunities in medicine. I want to rejuvenate the enthusiasm in young people for a career in medicine. I have always enjoyed doing that. Although physicians work hard, there is a tremendous amount of personal gratification that comes from a career in science and health care. There is also an exciting era just beginning in clinical research where many of the discoveries in the basic

FIGURE 9. Photograph of WHF taken by WCR during the interview.

FIGURE 10. Photograph of WHF taken by WCR during the interview.

laboratory are now coming to the clinic. There are new agents being looked at for angiogenesis, and a whole new group of biological agents are being used that potentially could replace the traditional pharmacological approaches that I had investigated in years past. The thrombolytics are a product of that. I see a great opportunity in this area and I always want to remain a part of the drug discovery mission.

WCR: *How have you handled travel through the years? You have been visiting professor at many medical centers around the country. How does traveling fit into your scheme?*

WHF: When traveling, I try to get work done that I cannot do at home. Very often I'm writing a manuscript, correcting, or reviewing a paper. When I come home from a trip, I am able to spend more time with my family rather than less. One of the things I was cautious about all these years, even with my travels, was the time I spent home with my family. I always try to be there for them. Therefore I actually use the time away to get a lot of paperwork done that would not bog me down when I return home. The travel, in a way, complimented my hospital work.

WCR: *What about your vacations in these 22 years with your family? Have you regularly gone away for a period of time?*

WHF: Whenever I was at a meeting, I tried to bring the whole family along, which was an opportunity for them to see what kind of work I was involved with. When our children got older and my wife could not come with me, I would take at least one of the children with me on a trip so we could have a one-on-one experience together. Our family takes 2 one-week vacations during the winter in Florida where we have a home. I always liked being at the beach, since it reminds me of my youth when we frequented the public beach. Our Florida home is in Hallendale, an

area north of Miami, where we have a beachfront view. We have true family vacations. I try to do a lot of my pleasure reading when I am away. I still try to squeeze in, even during a busy day, some reading unrelated to medicine.

WCR: *What are you reading right now?*

WHF: I am reading a new biography of John Quincy Adams. During this past year, I read for the second time, all of Shakespeare's histories. I appreciated these plays a lot more the second time around. Most of my reading is either biography or historical fiction.

WCR: *You do some nonmedical reading every day?*

WHF: Yes. Right before I go to bed. I often wake up with the book open next to me. This was always a very relaxing thing for me to do.

WCR: *So you live by Osler's recommendation of reading the masters the last 30 minutes of each day?*

WHF: I always felt I was a better physician because I did clinical research and therefore had a much better understanding of disease processes and how best to treat them. But also because of my nonmedical reading, I was also able to communicate more effectively with my patients. Knowledge of sports and current events helps you interact closely with patients, relieving the stress they may be under. I also think the lessons of literature help you to become more sensitive and caring when you are at the bedside.

WCR: *Tell me about your private practice. You have always seen a lot of patients. How much time a week, when you were at Einstein, were you spending seeing patients?*

WHF: I would spend a portion of my day teaching and participating in clinical research. My internal medicine and cardiology practice allowed me to take care of many patients in a holistic way. Even though a patient may have come to me with a cardiac problem, I would manage all other medical problems they had on a chronic basis. I have always worked one full day in the office as a practitioner. In actuality, I was practicing 7 days a week while involved in clinical research because I would have to become directly involved with problems that developed in the studies. As a clinical researcher and a principal investigator, you are always "on call." You cannot sign out to a colleague when you are involved in double-blind studies with a sick population; you always have to be available. I have to say that even though I go on vacation, my staff always knows where to get me if there is a problem. Again, I have always enjoyed practice, and would never give it up. In fact at the end of my career, what I would like best to be doing is seeing patients.

WCR: *If you were offered the head of the FDA, would you take that?*

WHF: If I cannot have the opportunity to be involved in direct patient care, I would have problems with such a position.

WCR: *Is there anything you would like to discuss that we have not discussed?*

WHF: The other areas I wanted to discuss relate to my ongoing research work in other disciplines like geriatrics and womens health. One advantage I always had in working in my old neighborhood was I was able to be involved in many large, community-based studies, such as the Bronx Aging Study and the Womens Health Initiative. I am hoping to continue this work, even in my new chairman's role, since my new medical school is also affiliated with many hospitals both in New York City and the surrounding suburbs. I have even begun to enter into new collaborations with my old and my new schools.

WCR: *Of the various activities you do, which do you enjoy the most or do you like the variety?*

WHF: I like the variety and I enjoy all the roles that I'm involved with. I enjoy being a good son, a good brother, trying to be a good parent, a good husband, a good friend, a good teacher, a caring physician for my patients, a good researcher, and a fair-minded administrator. I feel all these roles have been important in rounding me off as a person (Figure 10).

WCR: *You have worked hard at all these various roles. Do you think you will continue to go on 4½ hours sleep from here on?*

WHF: From the way my schedule looks now, maybe 3½. Even during this visit I awoke early this morning to write.

WCR: *Your plane did not arrive until after 11 P.M., so you must not have gotten to the hotel until around midnight?*

WHF: I had my 4½ hours of sleep, and was up at 4:30 this morning.

WCR: *You looked fresh when I picked you up at 7:15 A.M. It has been a pleasure. I appreciate your honoring us with your presence here at Baylor University Medical Center. Speaking for the AJC readers, I appreciate your opening up your life to us so we can all learn from it. Thank you.*

WHF: Thank you Dr. Roberts.

Best Publications of WHF Selected by WHF

2. Frishman WH, Epstein A, Kulick S, Killip T. Heart failure sixty-three years following traumatic arteriovenous fistula. *Am J Cardiol* 1974;34:733–736.

3. Frishman W, Weksler B, Christodoulou J, Smithen C, Killip T. Reversal of abnormal platelet aggregability and change in exercise tolerance in patients with angina pectoris following oral propranolol. *Circulation* 1974;50:887.

4. Frishman W, Smithen C, Befler B, Kligfield P, Killip T. Non-invasive assessment of clinical response to oral propranolol. *Am J Cardiol* 1975;35:635–644.

7. Frishman W, Christodoulou J, Weksler B, Smithen C, Killip T, Scheidt S. Aspirin therapy in angina pectoris: effects on platelet aggregation, exercise tolerance and electrocardiographic manifestations of ischemia. *Am Heart J* 1976; 92:3–10.

9. Frishman WH, Christodoulou J, Weksler B, Smithen C, Killip T, Scheidt S. Abrupt propranolol withdrawal in angina pectoris. Effects on platelet aggregation and exercise tolerance. *Am Heart J* 1978;95:169.

12. Sonnenblick EH, Frishman WH, LeJemtel TH. Dobutamine: a new synthetic cardioactive sympathetic amine. *N Engl J Med* 1979;300:17–22.

13. Frishman WH, Ribner H. Anticoagulation in myocardial infarction: a modern approach to an old problem. *Am J Cardiol* 1979;43:1207.

15. Frishman WH, Kostis J, Strom M, Hosler M, Elkayam U, Davis R, Weinstein J, Sonnenblick EH. Clinical pharmacology of the new beta blocking drugs. Part 6. A comparison of prindolol and propranolol in treatment of patients with angina pectoris. The role of intrinsic sympathomimetic activity. *Am Heart J* 1979;98: 526–535.

19. Frishman WH, Factor S, Jordan A, et al. Right atrial myxoma: unusual clinical presentation and glandular histology. *Circulation* 1979;59:1070.

24. Elkayam U, LeJemtel T, Mathur M, Frishman W, Ribner H, Strom J, Sonnenblick EH. Prazosin therapy in congestive heart failure: importance of prolonged hemodynamic evaluation of vasodilator agents. *Am J Cardiol* 1979; 441:540–545.

25. Becker R, Frishman W, Frater RWM. Surgical management of mitral valve endocarditis: a review of 26 patients. *Chest* 1979;75:314.

31. Davis R, Strom J, Frishman W. Echographic findings of vegetations in bacterial endocarditis: an indication for urgent valvular replacement. *Am J Med* 1980;69:57–63.

35. Matsumoto M, Oka Y, Strom J, Frishman W, Kadish A, Becker RM, Frater RWM, Sonnenblick EH. Application of transesophageal echocardiography to continuous intraoperative monitoring of left ventricular performance. *Am J Cardiol* 1980;46:95–105.

36. Strom J, Frishman W, Davis R, Matsumoto M, Becker R, Frater RWM. Echocardiographic and surgical correlations in bacterial endocarditis. *Circulation* 1980;62:1–164.

38. Frishman W. β-adrenoceptor antagonists. New drugs and new indications. *N Engl J Med* 1981;305:505–506.

39. Frishman W. Nadolol: a new beta-adrenoceptor blocking drug. *N Engl J Med* 1981;305:678.

40. Frishman WH, Strom J, Kirschner M, Poland M, Klein N, Halprin S, LeJemtel T, Kram M, Sonnenblick EH. Labetalol therapy in patients with systemic hypertension and angina pectoris: effects of combined alpha and beta-adrenoceptor blockade. *Am J Cardiol* 1981;48:917–928.

42. Klein N, Siskind S, Frishman W, Sonnenblick E, LeJemtel T. Hemodynamic comparisons of intravenous amrinone and dobutamine in patients with severe congestive heart failure. *Am J Cardiol* 1981;48:170–175.

44. Fein S, Klein N, Frishman W. Exercise testing soon after uncomplicated myocardial infarction. *JAMA* 1981;245:1863.

47. LeJemtel TH, Keung E, Frishman WH, Ribner HS, Sonnenblick EH. Hemodynamic effects of captopril in patients with severe chronic heart failure. *Am J Cardiol* 1982;49:1484–1488.

48. Frishman WH, Klein NA, Strom JA, Willens H, LeJemtel TH, Jentzer J, Siegel L, Klein P, Kirschen N, Silverman R, Doyle R, Kirsten E, Sonnenblick EH. Superiority of verapamil to propranolol in stable angina pectoris: a double-blind randomized crossover trial (abstr). *Circulation* 1982;65 (suppl I):1-51-59.

49. Frishman WH. Antenolol and timolol: two new systemic β-adrenoceptor antagonists. *N Engl J Med* 1982;306:1456–1462.

52. Packer M, Frishman WH. Verapamil therapy for stable and unstable angina pectoris: calcium channel antagonists in perspective. *Am J Cardiol* 1982;50:881.

53. Frishman WH, Klein N, Klein P, Strom JA, Tawil R, Strair R, Wong B, Roth S, LeJemtel T, Pollack S, Sonnenblick EH. Comparison of oral propranolol and verapamil for combined systemic hypertension and angina pectoris: a placebo-controlled, double-blind, randomized, crossover trial. *Am J Cardiol* 1982;50: 1164–1172.

54. Frishman WH, Klein N, Strom J, Cohen MN, Shamoon H, Willens H, et al. Comparative effects of abrupt withdrawal of propranolol and verapamil in angina pectoris. *Am J Cardiol* 1982;50:1991–1195.

55. Frishman WH, Kirsten E, Kates R. Clinical relevance of verapamil plasma levels in stable angina pectoris. *Am J Cardiol* 1982;50:1180.

57. Kostis JB, Frishman WH, Hosler M, et al. The treatment of angina pectoris with pindolol. The significance of intrinsic sympathomimetic activity of β-blockers. *Am Heart J* 1982;104:496.

58. Kugler J, Maskin C, Laragh J, Sealy J, Frishman WH, Sonnenblick EH, LeJemtel T. Regional and systemic metabolic effects of angiotensin converting enzyme inhibition during exercise in patients with severe heart failure. *Circulation* 1982;66:1256–1261.

59. Maskin, C, Forman R, Frishman W, Sonnenblick E, LeJemtel TH. Failure of dobutamine to increase exercise capacity despite hemodynamic improvement in severe chronic heart failure. *Am J Cardiol* 1983;51:177–182.

61. Frishman WH. Multifactorial actions of β-adrenergic blocking drugs in ischemic heart disease. *Circulation* 1983;67(Suppl 1):I-11–18.

62. Frishman WH. Pindolol: a new β-adrenoceptor antagonist with partial agonist activity. *N Engl J Med* 1983;308:940–944.

63. Michelson EL, Frishman WH, Lewis JE, et al. Multicenter clinical evaluation of the long-term efficacy and safety of labetalol in the treatment of hypertension. *Am J Med* 1983;75(4A):68.

64. Jacob H, Brandt L, Farkas P, Frishman WH. Beta-adrenergic blockade and the gastrointestinal system. *Am J Med* 1983;74:1042–1051.

69. Frishman WH, Weinberg P, Peled HB, Kimmel B, Charlap S, Beer N. Calcium-entry blockers for the treatment of severe hypertension and hypertensive crisis. *Am J Med* 1984;77(2B):35.

70. Frishman WH, Furbert CD, Friedewalk WT. β-Adrenergic blockade in survivors of acute myocardial infarction. *N Engl J Med* 1984;310:830–837.

72. Frishman WH, Crawford MH, DiBianco R, Farnham DJ, Katz RJ, Kostis JB, Mohiuddin SM, Sawin HS, Thadani U, Zellner S. Combination propranolol and bepridil therapy in angina pectoris. *Am J Cardiol* 1985;55:43C–49C.

77. Frishman WH, Kirkendall W, McCarron D, et al. Diuretics versus calcium entry blockers in systemic hypertension: a preliminary multicenter experience with hydrochlorothiazide and sustained-release diltiazem. *Am J Cardiol* 1985;56: 92H–96H.

79. Frishman WH, Kimmel B, Charlap S, Saltzberg S, Stroh J, Weinberg P, Moniszko E, Wiezner J, Dorsa F, Pollack S, Strom J. Twice daily administration of oral verapamil in the treatment of essential hypertension. *Arch Intern Med* 1986;146:561–565.

81. Robbins MJ, Frater RWM, Soeiro R, Frishman WH, Strom JA. Influence of vegetation size on the clinical outcome of right-sided infective endocarditis. (Recipient of Grand Prize Award ACP Associates Competition). *Am J Med* 1986;80:165.

84. Goldberger J, Stroh J, Peled H, Cohen M, Frishman WH. The natural history and prognosis of acute pulmonary edema. *Arch Intern Med* 1986;146:489.

87. Frishman WH, Zawada ET, Smith LK, Sowers J, Swartz SL, Kirkendall W, Lunn J, McCarron D, Moser M, Schnaper H. A comparative study of diltiazem and hydrochlorothiazide as initial medical therapy for mild to moderate hypertension. *Am J Cardiol* 1987;59:615.

93. Frishman WH, Garofalo JL, Rothschild A, Rothschild M, Greenberg SM, Soberman J. Multicenter comparison of the nifedipine gastrointestinal system and long-acting propranolol in patients with mild to moderate systemic hypertension receiving diuretics: a preliminary experience. *Am J Med* 1987;83(6B):15–19.

94. Frishman WH, Charlap S, Kimmel B, Teicher M, Cinnamon J, Allen L, et al. Diltiazem compared to nifedipine and combination treatment in patients with stable angina: effects on angina, exercise tolerance and the ambulatory ECG. *Circulation* 1988;77:774–786.

96. Frishman WH, Charlap S. Calcium-channel blockers for combined systemic hypertension and myocardial ischemia (abstr). *Circulation* 1988;75(suppl V): V-154.

103. Frishman WH, Glasser SP, Strom JA, Schoenberger J, Liebson P, Poland M. Effects of dilevalol on left ventricular mass and function in non-elderly and elderly hypertensive patients: double-blind comparisons with atenolol and metoprolol. *Am J Cardiol* 1989;63:69I–74I.

104. Frishman WH, Flamenbaum W, Schoenberger J, Schwartz GL, Vidt DG, Neri GS, Greenberg S, Lazar E, Godrey JC, Stevenson A, Lamon KD, Chang Y, Magner DJ. Celiprolol in systemic hypertension: results of a placebo-controlled double-blind titration study. *Am J Cardiol* 1989;63:839–842.

109. Frishman WH, Giles T, Greenberg S, Heiman M, Raffidal L, Soberman J, Laifer L, Nadelmann J, Lazar E, Strom J. Sustained high-dose nitroglycerin transcutaneous patch therapy in angina pectoris: evidence of attenuation of effect over time. *J Clin Pharmacol* 1989;29:1097–1105.

112. Aronson MK, Ooi WL, Morgenstern PH, Hafner A, Masur D, Crystal H, Frishman W, Fisher D, Katzman R. Women, myocardial infarction and dementia in the very old. *Neurology* 1990;40:1102–1106.

115. Nadelmann J, Frishman WH, Ooi WL, Tepper D, Greenberg S, Guzik H, Lazar EJ, Heiman M, Aronson M. Prevalence, incidence and prognosis of recognized and unrecognized myocardial infarction in persons aged 75 years or older: The Bronx Aging Study. *Am J Cardiol* 1990;66:533–537.

116. Frishman WH, Lazar EJ. Reduction in mortality, sudden death, and nonfatal reinfarction with beta-adrenergic blockers in survivors of acute myocardial infarction: a new hypothesis regarding the cardioprotective action of beta-adrenergic blockade. *Am J Cardiol* 1990;66:66G–70G.

119. Frishman WH, Heiman M, Soberman J, Greenberg S, Eff J, for the Celiprolol International Angina Study Group. Comparison of deliprolol and propranolol in stable angina pectoris. *Am J Cardiol* 1991;67:665–670.

123. Aronson MK, Ooi WL, Geva D, Masur D, Blau A, Frishman WH. Dementia: age-dependent incidence, prevalence and mortality in the old. *Arch Intern Med* 1991;151:989–992.

125. Frishman WH, Heiman M, for the Nisoldipine Multicenter Angina Study Group. Usefulness of nisoldipine for stable angina pectoris. *Am J Cardiol* 1991;68:1004–1009.

126. The SHEP Cooperative Research Group. Prevention of stroke by antihypertensive drug treatment in older persons with isolated systolic hypertension: final results of Systolic Hypertension in the Elderly Program (SHEP). *JAMA* 1991;265:3255–3264.

129. SOLVD Investigators. Effects of angiotensin converting enzyme inhibition with enalapril on survival in patients with reduced left ventricular ejection fraction and congestive heart failure. *N Engl J Med* 1991;325:293–302.

132. Zimetbaum P, Frishman WH, Ooi WL, Derman MP, Aronson M, Gidez LI, Eder HA. Plasma lipid and lipoproteins and the incidence of cardiovascular disease in the old: The Bronx Longitudinal Aging Study. *Arterioscler Thromb* 1992;12:416–423.

133. Guzik H, Ooi WL, Frishman WH, Greenberg S, Aronson MK. Hypertension: Cardiovascular implications in a cohort of old old. *J Am Geriatr Soc* 1992;40:348–353.

135. Frishman WH, Nadelmann J, Ooi WL, Greenberg S, Heiman M, Kahn S, Guzik H, Lazar E, Aronson M. Cardiomegaly on chest x-ray: prognostic implications in a 10 year study of an old old cohort. A report from the BAS. *Am Heart J* 1992;124:1026–1030.

136. Frishman WH. Comparative efficacy and concomitant use of bepridil and beta blockers in the management of angina pectoris. *Am J Cardiol* 1992;69:50D–60D.

137. Gradman AH, Frishman WH, Kaihlanen PM, Wong SC, Friday KJ. Comparison of sustained-release formulations of nicardipine and verapamil for mild to moderate systemic hypertension. *Am J Cardiol* 1992;70:1571–1575.

138. SOLVD Investigators. Effect of enalapril on mortality and the development of heart failure in asymptomatic patients with reduce left ventricular ejection fractions. *N Engl J Med* 1992;327:685–691.

142. Conigliaro J, Frishman WH, Lazar EJ, Croen L. Internal medicine house-staff and attending physician perceptions of the impact of New York State 405 regulations on working conditions and supervision of residents in two training programs. *J Gen Med* 1993;8:502–507.

146. Landau A, Frishman WH, Alturk N, Adjei-Poku M, Fornasier-Bongo M, Furia S. Improvement in exercise tolerance and immediate β-adrenergic blockade with intranasal propranolol in patients with angina pectoris. *Am J Cardiol* 1993;72:995–998.

147. Frishman WH, Bryzinski BS, Coulson LR, DeQuattro VL, Vlachakis ND, Mroczek WJ, Dukart G, Alemayehu D, Koury K. A multifactorial trial design to assess combination therapy in hypertension: treatment with bisoprolol and hydrochlorothiazide. *Arch Intern Med* 1994;154:1461–1468.

150. Frishman WH, Brobyn W, Brown RD, Johnson BF, Reeves RL, Wombolt DG. Amlodipine versus atenolol in essential hypertension. *Am J Cardiol* 1994; 73:50A–54A.

151. Crystal HA, Ortof E, Frishman WH, Gruber A, Hershman D, Aronson M. Serum vitamin B12 levels and incidence of dementia in a healthy elderly population: a report from the Bronx Longitudinal Aging Study. *J Am Geriatr Soc* 1994;42:933–936.

161. Hershman DL, Simonoff PA, Frishman WH, Paston F, Aronson MK. Drug utilization in the old old, and how it relates to self-perceived health and all cause mortality. Results from The Bronx Aging Study. *J Am Geriatr Soc* 1995;43:356–360.

162. Feinfeld DA, Guzik H, Carvounis CP, Lynn RI, Somer B, Aronson M, Frishman WH. Sequential changes in renal function tests in the old old: results from The Bronx Longitudinal Aging Study. *J Am Geriatr Soc* 1995;43:412–414.

163. Frishman W, Pepine CJ, Weiss R, Baiker WM, for the Zatebradine Study Group. Addition of zatebradine, a direct sinus node inhibitor, provides no greater exercise tolerance benefit in patients with angina pectoris taking extended-release nifedipine: results of a multicenter, randomized, double-blind, placebo-controlled, parallel group study. *J Am Coll Cardiol* 1995;26:305–312.

168. Frishman WH, Ram CVS, McMahon FG, Chrysant SG, Graff A, Kupiec JW, Hsu H, for the Benazepril/Amlodipine Study Group. Comparison of amlodipine and benazepril monotherapy to combination therapy in patients with systemic hypertension: a randomized, double-blind, placebo-controlled parallel group study. *J Clin Pharmacol* 1995;35:1060–1066.

169. Pratt CVM, McMahon RP, Goldstein S, Pepine CJ, Andrews TC, Dyrda I, Frishman WH, Geller NL, Hill JA, Morgan NA, Stone PH, Knatterud GL, Sopko G, Conti CR, for the ACIP Investigators. Comparison of subgroups assigned to medical regimens used to suppress cardiac ischemia (The Asymptomatic Cardiac Ischemia Pilot (ACIP) Study. *Am J Cardiol* 1996;77:1302–1309.

170. Kahn S, Frishman WH, Weissman B, Ooi WL, Aronson M. Left ventricular hypertrophy on electrocardiogram: prognostic implications from a 10 year cohort study of older subjects. A report from the Bronx Longitudinal Aging Study. *J Am Geriatr Soc* 1996;44:524–529.

171. Stone PH, Chaitman B, McMahon RP, Andrews TC, MacCallum G, Sharaf B, Frishman W, Deanfield JE, Sopko G, Pratt C, Goldberg AD, Rogerts WJ, Hill J, Proschan M, Pepine CJ, Bourassa MG, Conti CR, for the ACIP Investigators. Relationship between exercise-induced and ambulatory ischemia in patients with stable coronary disease. The Asymptomatic Cardiac Ischemia Pilot (ACIP) Study. *Circulation* 1996;94:1537–1544.

174. Frishman WH, Heiman M, Karpenos A, Ooi WL, Mitzner A, Goldkorn R, Greenberg S. Twenty-four hour ambulatory electrocardiography in elderly subjects: prevalence of various arrhythmias and prognostic implications. A report from the Bronx Longitudinal Aging Study. *Am Heart J* 1996;132:297–302.

176. Bernstein JM, Frishman WH, Chang CJ. Value of ECG PR and QTc interval prolongation and heart rate variability for predicting cardiovascular morbidity and mortality in the elderly: the Bronx Aging Study. *Cardiol in Elderly* 1997;5: 31–41.

178. Frishman WH. Mibefradil: a new selective T-channel calcium antagonist for hypertension and angina pectoris. *J Cardiovasc Pharmacol Ther* 1997;2:321–330.

181. Frishman WH, Gomberg-Maitland M, Hirsch H, et al. Differences between male and female patients with regard to baseline demographics and clinical outcome in the Asymptomatic Cardiac Ischemia Pilot (ACIP) Trial. *Clin Cardiol* 1998;21:184–190.

Books

6. Frishman WH. Current Cardiovascular Drugs, 2nd ed. Philadelphia: Current Science, North American edition, 1995.
7. Goldberg DE, Frishman WH. Beta3 Adrenergic Agonism: A New Concept in Human Pharmacotherapy. New York: Futura Publishing, 1995.
10. Frishman WH, Sonnenblick EH (eds). Cardiovascular Pharmacotherapeutics. New York: McGraw Hill, 1997.
13. Frishman WH, Sonnenblick EH (eds). Cardiovascular Pharmacotherapeutics Companion Handbook. New York: McGraw Hill 1998, in press.
14. Frishman WH (co-editor). Yearbook of Medicine 1998. St. Louis: Mosby 1998, in press.

Monographs, Chapters in Books

6. Frishman WH. Clinical pharmacology of the new beta-adrenergic blocking agents. part I: Pharmacodynamic and pharmacokinetic properties. *Am Heart J* 1979;97:663–670.
49. Spivack C, Ocken S, Frishman WH. Calcium antagonists: clinical use in treatment of systemic hypertension. *Drugs* 1983;25:154–177.
50. Frishman WH, Charlap S. Verapamil in the treatment of chronic stable angina. *Arch Intern Med* 1983;143:1407.
56. Michelson EL, Frishman WH. Labetalol: an alpha-beta adrenergic blocker. *Ann Intern Med* 1983;99:553.
70. Frishman WH, Furberg CD, Friedewald WT. The use of β-adrenergic blocking drugs in patients with myocardial infarction. *Curr Probl Cardiol* 1984; 9:3–70.
111. Frishman WH. Beta-adrenergic blocker withdrawal. *Am J Cardiol* 1987;59: 26F–32F.
114. Maza SR, Frishman WH. Therapeutic options to minimize free radical damage and thrombogenicity in ischemic/reperfused myocardium. *Am Heart J* 1987;114:1206–1215.
118. Kralstein J, Frishman WH. Malignant pericardial disease: diagnosis and treatment. *Am Heart J* 1987;113:785.
133. Schoen RE, Frishman WH, Shamoon H. Hormonal and metabolic effects of calcium-channel antagonists in man. *Am J Med* 1988;84:492–504.
146. Hachamovitch R, Strom JA, Sonnenblick EH, Frishman WH. Left ventricular hypertrophy in hypertension and the effects of antihypertensive drug therapy. *Curr Probl Cardiol* 1988;13:371–421.
153. Frishman WH, Skolnick AE, Strom JA. Effects of calcium-entry blockade on hypertension-induced left ventricular hypertrophy. *Circulation* 1989;80(suppl IV):IV-151–IV-161.
169. Skolnick AE, Frishman WH. Calcium channel blockers in myocardial infarction. *Arch Intern Med* 1989;149:1669–1677.
170. Charlap S, Lichstein E, Frishman WH. Electromechanical disassociation: diagnosis, pathophysiology, and management. *Am Heart J* 1989;118:355–360.
177. Frishman WH, Garofalo JL, Rothschild A, Rothschild M, Greenberg SM, Soberman J. The nifedipine gastrointestinal therapeutic system in the treatment of hypertension. *Am J Cardiol* 1989;64:65F–69F.
182. Frishman WH, Sokol S, Aronson MK, Wassertheil-Smoller S, Katzman R. Risk factors for cardiovascular and cerebrovascular diseases and dementia in the elderly (monograph). *Curr Probl Cardiol* 1998;23:1–68.
188. Frishman WH, Charlap S. The alpha- and beta-adrenergic blocking drugs. In: Parmley WW, ed. Cardiology. Philadelphia: Lippincott, 1990;1–18.
192. Frishman WH. "Something Special". Valedictory Address to the 1989 Graduating Classes of the Albert Einstein College of Medicine and the Sue Golding Graduate Division of Yeshiva University. *Einstein Uart J Biol Med* 1990;8:31–33.
205. Nadelmann J, Frishman WH. Clinical use of β-adrenoceptor blockade in systemic hypertension. *Drugs* 1990;39:862–876.
217. Zimetbaum P, Frishman W, Aronson M. Hyperlipidemia, vascular diseases, and dementia with advancing age: epidemiologic considerations. *Arch Intern Med* 1991;151:240–244.
219. Frishman WH, Lazar EJ, Gorodokin G. Pharmacokinetic optimization of therapy with beta-adrenergic blocking agents. *Clin Pharmacokin* 1991;20:311–318.
222. Frishman WH, Skolnick AE, Miller KP. Secondary prevention post infarc-

tion: the role of β-adrenergic blockers, calcium-channel blockers and aspirin. In: Gersh BJ, Rahimtoola SH, eds. Management of Myocardial Infarction. New York: Elsevier Science, 1991:469–492.
234. Dustan HP, Caplan LR, Curry CL, DeLeon AC, Douglas FL, Frishman W, Hill MN, Washington RL, Steigerwalt S, Shulman N, Taubert K, Champagne B. Report of the Task Force on the Availability of Cardiovascular Drugs to the Medically Indigent. *Circulation* 1992;85:849–860.
237. Frishman WH. Comparative pharmacokinetic and clinical profiles of angiotensin converting enzyme inhibitors and calcium antagonists in systemic hypertension. *Am J Cardiol* 1992;69:17C–25C.
253. Frishman WH. Tolerance, rebound and time-zero effect of nitrate therapy. *Am J Cardiol* 1992;70:43G–48G.
261. Frishman WH. β-Adrenergic blockers. In: Izzo JL, Jr, Black HR, eds. Hypertension Primer of the American Heart Assn. 1993;297–300.
273. Frishman WH, Sonnenblick EH. β-adrenergic blocking drugs and calcium blockers. In: Alexander RW, Schlant RC, Fuster V, eds. The Heart, 9th ed. New York: McGraw Hill 1998:1583–1618.
279. Landau AJ, Gentilucci M, Cavusoglu E, Frishman WH. Calcium antagonists for the treatment of congestive heart failure. *Coron Artery Dis* 1994;5:37–50.
291. Kang PM, Landau AJ, Eberhardt RT, Frishman WH. Angiotensin II receptor antagonists: a new approach to blockade of the renin-angiotensin system. *Am Heart J* 1994;127:1388–1401.
296. Loskove J, Frishman WH. Nitric oxide donors in the treatment of cardiovascular and pulmonary diseases. *Am Heart J* 1995;129:604–613.
298. Schwartz J, Freeman R, Frishman W. Clinical pharmacology of estrogens: focus on their cardiovascular actions and cardioprotective benefits of replacement therapy in postmenopausal women. *J Clin Pharmacol* 1995;35:314–329.
299. Frishman WH, Huberfeld S, Okin S, Wang Y-H, Kumar A, Shareef B. Serotonin and serotonin antagonism in cardiovascular and non-cardiovascular disease. *J Clin Pharmacol* 1995;35:541–572.
301. Katz B, Rosenberg A, Frishman WH. Controlled release drug delivery systems in cardiovascular medicine. *Am Heart J* 1995;19:359–368.
302. Frishman WH, Cavusoglu E. β-Adrenergic blockers and their role in the therapy of arrhythmias. In: Podrid PJ, Kowey PR, eds. Cardiac Arrhythmias—Mechanisms, Diagnosis and Management. Baltimore: Williams & Wilkins, 1995: 421–433.
304. Opie LH, Frishman WH. Lipid-lowering and antiatherosclerotic drugs. In: Opie LH, et al, eds. Drugs for the Heart, 4th ed. Philadelphia: WB Saunders, 1995:288–307.
305. Opie LH, Sonnenblick EH, Frishman WH, Thadani U. β-Blocking drugs. In: Opie LH, et al, eds. Drugs for the Heart, 4th ed. Philadelphia: WB Saunders 1995:1–30.
306. Opie LH, Frishman WH, Thadani U. Calcium channel antagonists. In: Opie LH, et al, eds. Drugs for the Heart, 4th ed. Philadelphia: WB Saunders 1995: 50–82.
309. Patel RC, Frishman WH. Aids and the Heart: Clinicopathologic assessment. *Cardiovasc Pathol* 1995;4:173–183.
310. Cavusoglu E, Frishman WH. Sotalol: a new β-adrenergic blocker for ventricular arrhythmias. *Prog Cardiovasc Dis* 1995;37:423–440.
312. Tamirisa P, Frishman WH, Kumar A. Endothelin and endothelin antagonism: roles in cardiovascular disease and health. *Am Heart J* 1995;130:601–610.
313. Frishman WH, Burns B, Atac B, Alturk N, Altajar B, Lerrick K. Novel antiplatelet therapies for treatment of patients with ischemic heart disease. Inhibitors of platelet glycoprotein IIb/IIa integrin receptor. *Am Heart J* 1995;130:877–892.
317. Frishman WH. Postinfarction survival: role of β-adrenergic blockade. In: Fuster V, Ross R, Topol EJ, eds. Atherosclerosis and Coronary Artery Disease. Philadelphia: Lippincott-Raven, 1996:1205–1214.
321. Frishman WH, Sung HM, Yee HCM, Liu LL, Keefe D, Einzig A, Dutcher J. Cardiovascular toxicity with cancer chemotherapy. *Curr Probl Cardiol* 1996; 21:225–288.
329. Frishman WH, Hotchkiss H. Selective and non-selective dopamine receptor agonists: an innovative approach to cardiovascular disease treatment. *Am Heart J* 1996;132:861–870.
335. Gomberg-Maitland M, Frishman WH. Recombinant growth hormone: a new cardiovascular drug therapy. *Am Heart J* 1996;132:1244–1262.
339. Frishman WH. Faculty practice plan governance and management. Faculty Practice Plans. Florida: *Am Coll Phys Exec*, 1997.
341. Landzberg BR, Frishman WH, Lerrick K. Pathophysiology and pharmacological approaches for prevention of coronary artery restenosis following coronary artery balloon angioplasty and related procedures. *Prog Cardiovasc Dis* 1997;34:361–398.

EDWARD DAVID FROHLICH, MD:
A Conversation With the Editor*

dward Frohlich was born in New York City on
September 10, 1931, and his first few years were
spent in that city. At age 12, he and his family moved
to Washington, DC, where they resided until 1948
when they moved to post-World War II Berlin, Germany. There, Ed graduated in 1948 as salutatorian of
his high school class of American dependent students.
He graduated from Washington and Jefferson College
in Washington, Pennsylvania, cum laude in 1952, and
from the University of Maryland School of Medicine
in Baltimore in 1956. His internship and first-year
residency in internal medicine were at the District of
Columbia General Hospital in the Georgetown program. He then spent a year in cardiovascular research
with Dr. Edward D. Freis in Washington, DC, and
then completed his last year of residency at Georgetown University Hospital in 1960. After 2 years in the
US Army Medical Research Laboratory in Fort Knox,
Kentucky, he moved to Chicago, in 1962, where he
joined the faculty at Northwestern University Medical
School as a Veterans Administration Clinical Investigator and chief of the hypertension clinic at the Veteran's Administration Research Hospital. In 1964, he
joined the staff of the Cleveland Clinic's Research
Division, where he remained until 1969, when he
moved to Oklahoma City, Oklahoma, as Professor of
Medicine, Pharmacology, and Physiology and Bio-
physics and Director of the Hypertension Section of
the Department of Medicine of the University of Oklahoma Health Sciences Center. In 1976, he moved to
New Orleans, Louisiana, as Vice President for Education and Research and head of the section of hypertensive diseases of the Ochsner Clinic. In 1985, he
was named Vice President for Academic Affairs and
Alton Ochsner Distinguished Scientist at that institution.

Ed Frohlich has been an extremely productive researcher and a world leader in hypertension. He has
published over 530 articles in peer-reviewed medical
journals, 127 editorials, 173 invited articles and book
reviews, 153 chapters in various medical books, and
he has written and/or edited 48 books. He has been on
numerous national advisory boards and has been a
consultant to many organizations. He served as Editor-in-Chief of the *Journal of Laboratory and Clinical
Medicine* (1974 to 1976) and of *Hypertension* (1994 to
2002), and he has been on the editorial boards of 38
medical journals. He has received a number of honors
for his achievements, including the Edward D. Freis
Award from the National High Blood Pressure Education Program, National Heart, Lung, and Blood Institute (1989); Lifetime Achievement Award, Council
for High Blood Pressure Research (American Heart

Association) (1993); Master of the American College
of Physicians (1994); Lifetime Achievement Award,
Inter-American Society of Hypertension (1999); an
Honorary Doctor of Science degree from the University of Buenos Aires; Honorary Fellow of the Royal
College of Physicians and Surgeons of Glasgow; and
a number of honorary memberships of national Colleges of Physicians and Colleges of Cardiology. He
and his wife Sherry have 3 children. He is also a nice
and friendly guy.

William Clifford Roberts, MD[†] (hereafter WCR): *I am
in Dr. Frohlich's office at the Ochsner Clinic Foundation in New Orleans, and it is December 5, 2002.
Dr. Frohlich, thank you for talking with me and therefore to the readers of* The American Journal of Cardiology. *Could you describe some of your earliest
memories, your parents and siblings?*

Edward David Frohlich, MD[‡] (hereafter EDF): I was
born in Brooklyn, and lived in New York City for 12
years, and then we moved to Washington, DC. Initially, we lived in Brighton Beach. I remember going
to the beach with my parents and an uncle who lived
nearby. My father, an attorney who practiced in Manhattan, often took me to his office on the 11th floor of
the Times Building. We later lived for 2 years in
Manhattan. I enjoyed going to the country over the
summer vacation with my folks. My mother did not
work until after my brother and I had left home for
college. My brother, 5 years my junior, practiced law
in Washington, DC and now lives in Cape Cod.

In 1942, shortly after the beginning of World War
II, my father joined the Department of Treasury. He
was involved with the control of the foreign funds of
the Germans and Axis countries. A recent book by
Michael Beschloss on the war discusses this activity.
After the war, my father went with the Department of
Army as a finance advisor to General Clay in Berlin,
Germany. Henry Morganthau, President Roosevelt's
Secretary of the Treasury, wanted to turn Germany
into an agrarian state; however, other leaders elected
to dismantle the German war industry. For example,
they broke the large I.G. Farben industrial machine
into 3 smaller companies: Hoechst, Knoll (BASF),
and Bayer. All 3 now are major corporations, and
probably larger than the original business; and my
father was involved in this.

WCR: *What kind of lawyer was your father in
Manhattan?*

EDF: He practiced general law. Before going to law
school, he worked at W.R. Grace and Company.

WCR: *What was his role at Grace?*

EDF: My father started as the office boy for the

*This series of interviews is underwritten by an unrestricted grant from
Bristol-Myers Squibb.

†Baylor Heart & Vascular Institute, Baylor University Medical Center,
Dallas, Texas 75246.
‡Ochsner Clinic Foundation, New Orleans, Louisiana 70121.

president. At that time, Grace was a large shipping company in Latin America. During World War I, at the age of 21, my father was sent to Santos, Brazil, a major coffee exporting center, as manager. After 4 years, he returned to New York, attended law school at night and, later, started his own law practice. He married my mother in 1929. He joined the government in 1942, and we continued to live in New York until our family moved to Washington, DC, in 1943.

WCR: *Your father went to Washington, DC, before the rest of the family?*

EDF: Yes. Although he started with the Treasury Department in 1942, his work required that he travel throughout Latin America and work with a number of foreign banking institutions in New York. For this reason, we remained in New York.

WCR: *When did you grandparents come to the United States and were your parents second generation Americans?*

EDF: My grandparents came to New York in the late 1880s, so my parents were second generation Americans.

WCR: *When were your parents born?*

EDF: My father was born in 1896 and he died in 1982. My mother was born in 1900, and she died in 1994 in New Orleans. She spent her last 7 years living with us.

WCR: *What was your daddy like?*

EDF: He was a kindly, gentle-thinking person, very considerate of others, and very interested in reading and self-education. Love of family was of prime importance to him.

WCR: *You and your father were quite close?*

EDF: Yes, and he had a major influence on my life and my thinking.

WCR: *Were there lots of books around the house?*

EDF: Yes. We were surrounded by many books. My father and I loved to look up things together. We discussed a wide range of subjects, including politics, all the time. My father had a number of friends in Washington, DC, who often visited at our house. My brother and I were never excluded from their discussions. Dinner was another time for family talk and discussion.

WCR: *There was always a major interest in learning?*

EDF: Yes. Education was of prime importance to our family.

WCR: *Where were your father's parents born?*

EDF: They were born in what is now Poland. At the time it was the Austro-Hungarian Empire. Over the years it was part of the Ottoman Empire, Poland, Germany, or Russia. I recently visited my paternal grandparents' hometowns. My paternal grandfather was born in Rzeszów, a very small town at the time, and my paternal grandmother was born in Tarnov, about 35 miles away (although they had related to me when I was a child that they lived at a great distance from each other). Tarnov was the first town whose inhabitants were "relocated" to Auschwitz in World War II. While visiting Auschwitz several years ago, I observed an exhibit filled with suitcases. On one suit-

case was white adhesive tape with the maiden name of my grandmother. My maternal grandmother came from Riga, Latvia, and my paternal grandfather from a small town called Zneim in Russia. Of interest, his last name was Zneimer.

WCR: *Which law school did your father attend?*

EDF: New York Law School.

WCR: *When your father grew up, I gather there wasn't a lot of money around the house?*

EDF: Correct. There was food and shelter, but not a lot of extras.

WCR: *He went to college, too?*

EDF: No. Then, a college education was not necessary to enter law school.

WCR: *He went right from high school to law school?*

EDF: No. Following high school, he went to work for Grace. The president of Grace took my father "under his wing" and on his return from Brazil urged him to attend law school at night while working during the day.

WCR: *Your father was on his own at a relatively early age?*

EDF: Yes.

WCR: *How long did law school take him?*

EDF: Three years.

WCR: *How did your father join the government in 1942?*

EDF: He volunteered to join the government at the outset of World War II.

WCR: *How did he volunteer?*

EDF: Since he didn't serve in the military during the World War I while he was in Brazil, and was too old for the World War II, he approached people he knew in the Department of Treasury. With his background in law, economics, and the export/import business, they placed him in the Foreign Funds Control group, where he worked until the end of the war. For a short period after the war, he was with the War Assets Administration. He was then recruited by the Department of the Army to join General Clay's staff in Berlin.

WCR: *What kind of person was your mother?*

EDF: My mother was a devoted wife and mother. She finished high school and worked as a secretary after her graduation. She was very bright and had tremendous energy. She was very well read, and even in her dying years, she was a voracious reader. She was highly committed to the importance of education. My mother and father were very close and devoted to each other.

WCR: *It sounds like your home was a very pleasant one? There was not a lot of pressure on you to do well. That was taken for granted?*

EDF: There was no obvious pressure, but I guess that was expected. My mother always said, "You have an opportunity to get a higher education, so take advantage of it." She also balanced it with "this above all, to thine own self be true." As a natural consequence of the love that my brother and I had for our parents, we both worked hard in college and in medical school or law school.

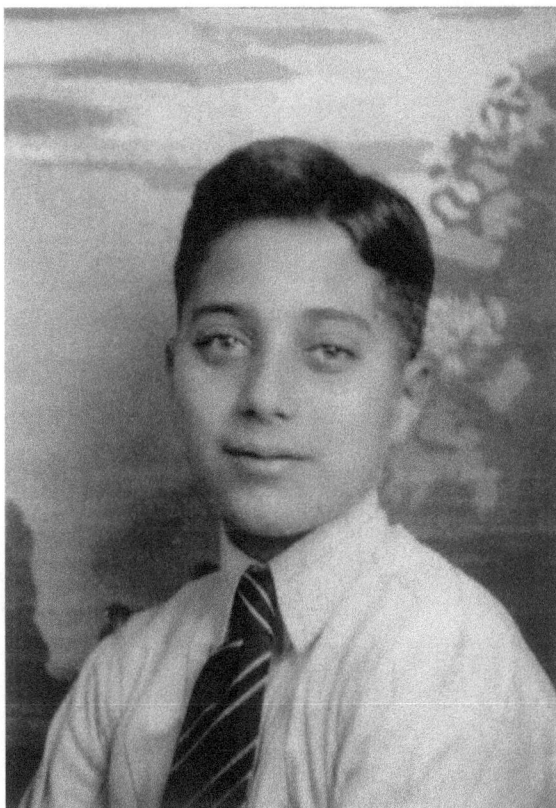

FIGURE 1. EDF at age 10, taken in a photo booth as a present for his mother.

WCR: *You were 12 when you came to Washington, DC. That meant that the first 6 grades you went to school in Brooklyn. Was that public school?*

EDF: Yes.

WCR: *What do you remember about grade school and New York?*

EDF: One thing that I remember is that the principal of our grade school was a high school teacher of my father. I had a lot of friends and relatives in New York. We had a large extended family there, since my mother had 5 siblings. My father had just 1 sister; 4 other siblings had died during the flu epidemic in 1918. When I was about 6 years old, my maternal grandmother lived with us until we moved to Washington, DC. Our entire family was always very devoted to each other.

WCR: *You lived in Washington, DC, until you were 16. So, you went to 7th through 11th grades there?*

EDF: Yes. Until 1948, when my father accepted his position in Berlin.

WCR: *How long were you actually in Berlin?*

EDF: We were in Berlin from February through August of 1948. Soon after our move to Berlin, the post-war troubles with the Soviet Union began, and, with the onset of the airlift, many civilian families were encouraged to return to the States. If you will remember, there were genuine concerns that the Cold War might get hot. So, we returned to the States in August 1948.

WCR: *You had already finished high school?*

EDF: Yes. I finished high school in Berlin, where I graduated from the Thomas A. Roberts School for American dependents in West Berlin. There were 8 American schools throughout Germany after the war; 1 was in Berlin. The Army provided the educators for the schools. You can imagine it was a unique learning (and living) experience; I thoroughly enjoyed it. Our graduation speaker was Robert Murphy, the political advisor to General Clay, and a friend of my father. He later became an ambassador and Assistant Secretary of the Department of State.

WCR: *Did you learn German during those few months there?*

EDF: No, not really. At the time I spoke very poor German. However, 35 years later, Sherry and I had an opportunity to visit Berlin. I hadn't been back since 1948. On that visit, we stopped by my former home, and through an interpreter, I asked the owner of the home whether I could show my wife their home. As soon as we walked into the house, I started speaking German even better than I had ever spoken before! Although I had studied a little German in college, I certainly surprised myself by my sudden transient fluency. It was a true Preustian experience!

WCR: *During high school and junior high school were there extracurricular activities that you participated in? Were you an athlete?*

EDF: I ran the mile in track. I also was the manager of the team. I played basketball after school and some baseball in Berlin; but I, certainly, was not an athlete.

WCR: *Were there any teachers in junior high school or high school who had a particular impact on you?*

EDF: There is no teacher who stands out during this period. However, 1 teacher, Bruce I. Schneider, who was both my high school shop and math teacher, did have a rather strong influence on me during my internal medicine training. After his high school teaching career, he attended medical school and eventually went to the National Institutes of Health (NIH) as an oncologist, I came to know him very well when he was my attending at DC General. I couldn't forget him. He had a withered finger, and the first time I was in the NIH Clinical Center we were on the same elevator. I recognized "Mr. Schneider" by his withered "pinky." When we got off on the same floor, I asked him, "Did you ever teach me shop?" He said, yes, and our friendship began. I was deeply impressed by his knowledge and his disciplined approach to teaching on daily rounds.

WCR: *After you came back from Berlin, where did you move? Where did your parents move?*

EDF: As soon as we landed in New York, I immediately went off to college. My parents moved to Washington, DC, in the Chevy Chase area.

WCR: *Your father started working where?*

EDF: He initially went with the Department of State, and several years later, he joined the Department of Commerce.

WCR: *He stayed in government?*

EDF: Yes.

FIGURE 2. EDF at age 17 at his graduation from high school in Berlin, Germany, in 1948.

FIGURE 3. EDF at age 19, in ROTC, at Washington & Jefferson College.

WCR: *Your parents lived in the Washington, DC, area for the rest of their married life?*

EDF: Yes.

WCR: *How did you decide to go to Washington and Jefferson College?*

EDF: When in Berlin, I had planned to attend college in Scotland while my family lived in Berlin, but the airlift changed those plans. I hurriedly had to find a college in the States. I wanted to attend a small liberal arts school with an excellent pre-medical program. I had heard of Washington and Jefferson College from a family member. It had only 1,100 students at the time, and was located in western Pennsylvania. It was known to have a first-rate pre-medical program.

WCR: *By the time you entered college you had already made up your mind to be a physician?*

EDF: Yes. I became interested in medicine as a pre-teen while still living in New York. While living in Washington, DC, before we moved to Berlin, I was further stimulated by *Dr. William B. Walsh*, who became a lifelong friend. He had just gone into practice with *Dr. Charles Geschicter* following his Naval service and his internal medicine training at Georgetown. While in practice, Bill Walsh started Project Hope in the 1950s, when he was able to obtain a hospital ship with the help of General Eisenhower. As you know, HOPE traveled the world administering health care to patients in underdeveloped areas. In brief, Bill Walsh stimulated further my interest of medicine. He gave me medical journals and books to read. Even later in

my career, in the 1980s, I entered into some programs with Bill and Project Hope while I was at Ochsner. We began joint programs in Costa Rica and Honduras, and we visited often, occasionally at HOPE's headquarters in Hopewell, Virginia.

WCR: *You met Dr. Walsh when you were 12 or 13 years of age?*

EDF: Yes. Our relationship began when I was a baby-sitter for his young children, who later became leaders in Project HOPE.

WCR: *Was there anybody in your extended family in New York—siblings of your mother or father who was a physician?*

EDF: No. I am the first physician in our family.

WCR: *Did your mother or father push you at all? You mentioned that they wanted you to be a professional person.*

EDF: They instilled in both my brother and me the importance of a higher education. My brother and I each selected a profession. It was always clear to me that medicine was the way I would go.

WCR: *Did schoolwork always come relatively easy for you?*

EDF: I think so. I studied. I don't remember working late hours doing homework. What I had to do, I did well and expeditiously. I enjoyed reading. Also, in high school, I was interested in music. I played piano, but not very well. I was interested in the Washington Senators, the major league baseball team.

WCR: *Did you and father go to baseball games together?*

EDF: Oh yes, at old Griffith Stadium on Georgia and Florida Avenues. I have very fond memories of those times.

WCR: *Who was the one who mentioned Washington and Jefferson College to you the first time?*

EDF: Probably my mother's sister. She had a friend who lived in Washington, Pennsylvania, and her son had graduated from that school.

WCR: *Where is Washington, Pennsylvania?*

EDF: It's in southwestern Pennsylvania, about 25 miles from Pittsburgh.

WCR: *You went to college how long and did you have any role models?*

EDF: I went 4 years. There I had 3 role models—2 were the professors of biology: Doctors *Clarence Dieter* and *Homer Porter*. They took great pride in the pre-med program. I excelled and related strongly with them. The third was a professor of psychology, *Dr. Frederick Swift*. I related with him more as a friend. He had a country home in New Hampshire and my brother and I visited with him there.

WCR: *How many students were in your senior class of college?*

EDF: Less than 400.

WCR: *How did you stand in your senior class?*

EDF: I was among the top in the class. I was always on the Dean's list.

WCR: *College was a good experience for you?*

EDF: Very good. I had many friends, some of whom I am still in contact with. The classes were always small and there was great opportunity to interact with faculty. There was the chance to take small discussion seminar courses, and these years of living away from home broadened me considerably.

WCR: *Was Washington and Jefferson College a private school?*

EDF: Yes. It is the oldest school west of the Allegheny Mountains. Its student body was all male; now it's coed. Many of the students were veterans of World War II, most of whom were very competitive, and many were interested in going to medical school. My college advisors suggested that I apply to 3 medical schools: the University of Maryland, Jefferson, and Temple. I was accepted first to the University of Maryland School of Medicine in my home state, and 1 week after my interview with the Dean, I made my choice immediately.

WCR: *How many students were in your medical school class?*

EDF: There were 100 men and 4 women.

WCR: *You entered medical school in 1952. How did medical school hit you? Were there any surprises, particularly at the beginning?*

EDF: Yes. It was far more competitive and difficult than I expected. I remember most that we had to take 126 hours of anatomy the first semester. That was almost a full-time course until Thanksgiving.

WCR: *Did you have any role models in medical school?*

EDF: *Theodore E. Woodward* was 1 of 2 professors who greatly influenced my life. He was the first full-time chairman of the Department of Medicine when I was a junior student. He had been a major consultant to the Army after World War II, when he worked with typhus and Rickettsial Disease in North Africa and Europe. He was my first Professor of Medicine on clinical rounds, and I turned to him for my first history and physical workup. Twenty years later, when I was a visiting professor at Maryland and spent a week with him at his home, he returned my workup to me. He asked me if I noted my grade and rhetorically asked me why I only received an A−. He then answered by saying that "nobody is perfect."

WCR: *Who else had an impact on you in medical school?*

EDF: In addition to Ted Woodward, *John C. Krantz*, the Professor and Chairman of Pharmacology. As students, we called Krantz's lectures "the hour of charm." He spoke beautifully, and was the author of our textbook of pharmacology. I related with him as a student, and asked whether I could work on one of his projects with him. Soon thereafter, *Dr. Bernard Brodie*, of the National Heart Institute (NHI), lectured to our class. Following his lecture, Dr. Krantz asked me to come forward and introduced me to Bernard Brodie. Dr. Brodie inquired whether I would like to spend the summer working at the Heart Institute with him or one of his associates. He subsequently placed me with *John Severinghaus*, an anesthesiologist who later worked with the Julius Comroe group at the University of California, San Francisco. He was in the early stages of developing the Severinghaus-Bradley electrode, as it was later termed. Bradley followed me after that first summer at the Clinical Center with the development of the electrode for measurement of blood gases. Most of my time with John Severinghaus was spent moving our lab from the NHI building to the new Clinical Center that was just completed, and, in working on the Van Slyke instrumentation for blood in gas analysis, which was later necessary to calibrate the electrode.

WCR: *It got you tuned in to research?*

EDF: Yes. It completely turned me on to academic medicine and research and introduced me to many people who today are leaders in American cardiovascular medicine. We had conferences in the Heart Institute every Friday afternoon. There I met many clinical associates—*Donald Fredrickson, John Oates, Leon Goldberg, Gene Braunwald*, and others directed by *Luther Terry* and *Robert P. Grant*. After returning to medical school from the NIH, I continued attending the Heart Institute conferences on Friday afternoons as a junior and senior medical student. I would cut school to drive in from Baltimore to attend. I usually sat near Bob Grant. One Friday, he said, "Do you know any students who might want to work with me next summer?" I returned, "Yes, I would." He said, "I knew you would." He was studying electrocardiograms of patients who had left bundle branch block but then went into normal ventricular conduction and then back into left bundle block. We reviewed every electrocardiogram at the nearby hospitals, including Georgetown, George Washington, Friedman's, DC General, and the Mt. Alto Veterans Administration hospitals. He spent at least 3 or 4 afternoons teaching me how to read electrocardiograms and spatial vector electrocardiography. He visited the "heart station" 2 or 3 afternoons at Georgetown Hospital where I spent most of my time, and I spent 2 afternoons with him at the Clinical Center. That's how I got to know him well. When I was ready to apply for housestaff training, he advised me to go to Boston. I told him that I preferred to be in Washington, DC, with Proc Harvey's program at Georgetown Hospital. Bob suggested that I go to the DC General Hospital's Georgetown program because there were good people there, including *Hugh Hussey*, the head of medicine, and then I could go on to Georgetown. During my application process, Doctor Hussey became Chairman of the Department of Medicine and Dean of the Medical School at Georgetown University.

WCR: *So you applied for training at DC General?*

EDF: Yes. My internship at DC General Hospital began in pediatrics, and therein lays an interesting story. During my pediatric rotation, I was assigned to a group of 2 to go to Senator Lyndon Johnson's office to work out a pay raise for our housestaff. (A bill to increase the housestaff stipends had already been turned down in the House of Representatives.) Since pediatrics was a slow service at that time, we were to be "lobbyists" in behalf of our housestaff. On our first visit, Lyndon Johnson taught the 2 of us how we could get the bill through. We were successful in obtaining a $1000 pay raise, from $1500 to $2500 annually. He accomplished this by putting it into the District of Columbia "Pawn Brokers" bill.

WCR: *How did Johnson impress you?*

EDF: In 1956, he was a very impressive and obviously powerful man who was the majority leader of the Senate. On entering his office, he was seated behind his desk with his very large shoes on the desk facing us. At his request, the 2 of us from DC General sat down and listened intently to our memorable personal lesson in the political process. Three years later (1959) I was driving from New York on the New Jersey Turnpike with my wife; we stopped at a Howard Johnson's; and there was Lyndon Johnson with his family holding "court" in a booth with a circle of people. Johnson saw us and said, "Hi, young man. Are you earning any more money than during your internship?"

WCR: *And how was the rest of your internship and residency at DC General?*

EDF: At DC General Hospital, Hugh Hussey, Chairman of the Department of Medicine, appointed me "acting" resident rather than an intern because an assistant medical resident had developed polio. Some of the best senior students were selected to be acting interns. Among them were *Tom Andriole*, now Chairman of the Department of Medicine at the University of Arkansas, and *Donald Massaro*, now head of the pulmonary division at Georgetown Hospital. Of the 12 regular interns, and later residents in my group on the Georgetown service, 10 of us became professors or

deans. At the end of my second year at DC General, Dr. Hussey, then Dean as well as Medicine Chair, suggested that I take a year of fellowship at Georgetown University with *John Rose*, the Chairman of the Department of Physiology (and, later Dean). On my first day of fellowship, John Rose instrumented a dog, and my job was to analyze the arterial pressure tracings during inspiration and expiration. At 5 P.M. that day, I sensed that I was going to spend a year doing just that. I went to the Dean's office, and explained to Dr. Hussey that I could not spend a year following the inspiration, expiration, and arterial pressure curves of dogs. He smiled patiently, and then called Ed Freis and said, "Ed, do you want to take a brash bright young fellow to work with you this year?" I started with Ed Freis and arranged my schedule so that I could also spend time during my third year with both Proc Harvey and Ed Fries to obtain further cardiovascular training. Thus, the 3 Georgetown professors that had the greatest impact on my future life were Hugh Hussey, Proc Harvey, and Ed Freis.

WCR: *What were the characteristics of Hugh Hussey that were significant to you?*

EDF: He was patient, understanding, an extremely knowledgeable clinician, and very interested in his housestaff and students. He was a remarkable mentor and played an active role in my immediate decision making and thinking about my future.

WCR: *What about Proctor Harvey?*

EDF: Proc was a kind, gentle, and most knowledgeable cardiovascular physician; he still is.

WCR: *That was 1957/1958?*

EDF: Right. I had met Proc first when I was with Bob Grant in 1954 and 1955 at NIH. I used to drive into Washington from Baltimore to attend Proc's Thursday night citywide conferences at Georgetown Hospital.

WCR: *Did you have an easy or a hard time deciding which specialty to enter? Did any of the specialties other than internal medicine appeal to you?*

EDF: I had a difficult time deciding. I was also interested in medical problems in OB/GYN and actually had acquired a residency in it at the University of Maryland before graduating, but changed my mind under the influence of Doctor Hussey.

WCR: *Hugh Hussey became the editor of the JAMA?*

EDF: Yes. He influenced me in switching my residency to Internal Medicine at Georgetown. I later visited him at his lovely apartment on Lakeshore Drive in Chicago when he was editor. He clearly was a mentor who profoundly influenced the course of my professional career.

WCR: *Tell me about Ed Freis. What was it about him and about systemic hypertension that appealed to you so much?*

EDF: He, too, is a patient teacher who was available to all who were interested. His philosophy was one that I have tried to continue in my training program. Like Freis, I like to give my fellows open reign to their work in our area of research. They can come into my office to discuss our studies and review our data and manuscripts at any time. Ed put me in contact with *Harold Schnaper*, his Assistant Chief of Medicine. Freis did his hypertensive and cardiovascular research with Schnaper and placed me in the radioisotope service, where I worked with the physicists and did the clinical research studies. We did our first work immediately after Taplan and Winters reported their initial work with radioisotope renography. We also measured skin and muscle flow with radioiodine and albumin. Then came the antihypertensive drugs.

WCR: *Ed Freis was the first to use chlorothiazide?*

EDF: Yes. He was among the first 2 investigators.

WCR: *That drug came out initially for heart failure?*

EDF: No. It was for the kidney. We worked first with guanethidine, a postsympathetic blocker, and published the first report on that. Ed Freis started working with chlorothiazide after *George Schreiner* at Georgetown had given it to a patient with the nephrotic syndrome, and the patient lost 17 pounds. It was used first as neither an antihypertensive drug nor a diuretic. Since it was a sulfonamide derivative, the drug was given to Schreiner as an antibiotic for renal infections. Ed was among the first to use chlorothiazide for hypertension. *Robert Wilkins*, at Boston University, was also using it. Wilkins and Ed Freis were racing to publish first the effects of chlorothiazide for hypertension. Wilkins published his article in the *Boston Medical Quarterly* and Ed published his in the *DC Annals* within days of each other. They both showed that chlorothiazide was both an effective diuretic as well as an exciting antihypertensive agent. Ed and I reported the first hemodynamic studies with chlorothiazide in *The New England Journal of Medicine*, and Ed became deeply interested in how the thiazide diuretics attenuated the antihypertensive characteristics of other antihypertensive drugs. Our studies had shown that the pressor responsiveness to norepinephrine was attenuated by chlorothiazide, and the agent also increased the antihypertensive action of one of the ganglion blocking drugs. That work was published in the *Journal of Clinical Investigation*, and, in my first year with Ed Freis, we published 11 papers on those and other exciting subjects. It certainly underscores the stimulation and excitement which he engendered in me.

WCR: *That was the third year after medical school?*

EDF: Yes.

WCR: *You really got turned on to research?*

EDF: Yes, very much so. During that year, Ed wrote his classic article entitled "Hemodynamics of Hypertension," published in *Physiologic Reviews*. Most of Ed's succeeding fellows (including myself) made their life careers from insights derived from this classic work. Ed took me out on his boat on the Chesapeake Bay 1 weekend that year where I read and discussed this paper with him. That really turned me on. I got interested in hemodynamics. *Jay Cohn*, who later trained with Freis, became interested in the role of blood volume, which he later championed; it was a major theme in Ed's paper. My first fellow at the Cleveland Clinic was *Bob Tarazi*, who got interested in the role of plasma volume and the veins in hypertension as well as in cardiogenic hypertension. These, too, were major themes in Freis' review, which we pursued together.

WCR: *You needed 1 more year of residency?*

EDF: Yes. I did that year at Georgetown Hospital, when I also worked with Ed and with Proc. That year I met *Sherry Fine* and we were married later that year.

WCR: *How did you meet your future wife?*

EDF: One of residents I related with at morning report with Ed Freis suggested that I call a particular young lady that he had recently met at a party.

WCR: *This was when?*

EDF: That was in January 1959.

WCR: *You were 28?*

EDF: Yes. I called her early in February. On our first date I concluded that she had to be my wife, and 9 months later we were married.

WCR: *What were the features that were so appealing to you about her?*

EDF: She was very attractive, intelligent, and interesting, and we had a great first date.

WCR: *What was she doing at the time?*

EDF: She was working at the Brookings Institution in Washington, DC. It was on Jackson Square across from the White House. At the time that I met her, she was a research assistant for a transportation economist working with the transportation infrastructure of underdeveloped countries. I spent a lot of early evenings waiting in front of the Brookings Institution to take Sherry home.

WCR: *What was her training in?*

EDF: She did her undergraduate work in political science at Alfred University, and then attended Duke University in Asian Studies. She later received her Masters degree in education.

WCR: *She was from where?*

EDF: She was from New York City.

WCR: *If it were not for Ed Freis, you would probably not have met Sherry?*

EDF: That's probably correct.

WCR: *Did Ed Freis suggest that you go to the Fort Knox medical research laboratory?*

EDF: Yes. At Fort Knox I was assigned to the circulation section following *Francis Haddy's* tour of duty. I did dog studies, leading to the publication of over a dozen articles in the *JCI*, *American Journal of Physiology*, and *Circulation Research* during those 2 years. We studied the effects of ions and endotoxin on vessel tone in the forelimb, kidney, coronary and mesenteric circulations; it was exciting and a new dimension of cardiovascular research for me. While I was still at Fort Knox, Haddy, who was then head of research at the VA Research Hospital and on the faculty at Northwestern University in Chicago, offered me a position. At the same time, Ed Freis invited me to return to Washington, DC as a VA clinical investigator at his VA hospital. I was concerned that if I went back with Ed Freis that I would not be venturing out on my own. So I opted to go to Northwestern as a Veterans Administration Clinical Investigator.

FIGURE 4. EDF at the US Army Medical Research Laboratory, Ft. Knox, Kentucky, 1961.

However, before I decided on Chicago, Haddy had left to become the Chairman of the Department of Physiology at the University of Oklahoma. So, once again I took over his laboratory and went on to obtain my Master's degree in physiology at Northwestern.

WCR: *How did you like Chicago?*

EDF: We loved living there. We then had 1 daughter, who was born in Fort Knox. It was after our first year in Chicago that we decided to look for a house and not live in the downtown area. Every potential house was an hour's drive each way to and from the hospital. This frustrated us, and at that point, quite coincidentally, our lives changed. *Harriet Dustan*, who worked with *Irvine Page* at the Cleveland Clinic, presented a paper at the Central Society on the dependence of volume in controlling pressure in patients on dialysis with end-stage kidney disease. I asked a question at the conclusion of her paper. She gave me a quick retort, but indicated that she was interested in talking with me after the session. When we met, she mentioned that Dr. Page and she were looking for a third physician on their staff and asked would I be interested in joining them. Page was a role model for me by his reputation; so I visited Cleveland later that month, and accepted their invitation to join the Research Division without even asking salary. Soon after my arrival at the Clinic, I initiated our first studies on the hemodynamics in hypertension. We had a clinical research service as part of our program project grant, and we studied every one of our hypertensive patients

together. Bob Tarazi soon joined us as a research fellow, and we divided our interests by mutual agreement: I took the hemodynamics; Tarazi studied plasma volume, and Dustan took the role of plasma renin activity. (In those days that meant measuring renin by rat bioassay while measuring pressure responses on a smoked drum.) We would never order anything on a patient unless all 3 of us agreed, so that we would not interfere with each other's studies. That went on for 5 years. "Dusty" referred to that time as "her halcyon days," and I refer to it as "my days in Camelot." Page was exciting and challenging.

WCR: *Were the 5 years in Cleveland "growing" years professionally?*

EDF: Yes, they sure were! They gave me the confidence that I could do independent clinical research and that I could obtain my own research funding. It refocused my interest in clinical investigation. I had spent 2 years doing animal studies at Fort Knox. At Northwestern, I also continued with my experimental dog studies, but I also inherited from Haddy at the VA, its role as one of the centers of the VA Cooperative Study. And, most fortunately, this kept me in touch with Ed Freis. I was one of the co-investigators of the VA Cooperative Study in the early years of this major groundbreaking series of studies.

WCR: *Why did you decide to leave the Cleveland Clinic if it was perfect?*

EDF: It was perfect in terms of the relationship among the 3 of us. About the time that Bob Tarazi joined the staff, Page retired, and I thought that I needed to be in a medical school. I received several offers. I was invited to Oklahoma by *Tom Bruce*, the head of cardiology, who had been part of *Richard Bing's* group at Wayne State. The chairman of medicine at the University of Oklahoma was *James Hammarsten*, a delightful person. The chairman of physiology at Oklahoma was *Gene Jacobson*, who had succeeded Haddy, and Gene worked part of the time in my lab at Fort Knox. Another fellow I knew, *Marion Cotton*, was chairman of pharmacology; his interest was with digitalis. I became professor of medicine, physiology and pharmacology at Oklahoma and initiated a "bridging" course between the 2 preclinical years and the 2 clinical years of medical school. The course focused on pathophysiology, and became the basis of my first textbook. I believe it was the first pathophysiology course in the country, and our textbook provided the basis for our course. So, at Oklahoma, I was able to work in clinical pharmacology, pharmacology, pathophysiology, physiology, and was also able to continue with the VA Cooperative Study with Ed Freis. Oklahoma, too, was 1 of the original centers of the cooperative study.

WCR: *How did Oklahoma City sit with you?*

EDF: By that time, we had 3 children. Larger cities were not where we wished to live. Sherry, who was from New York, preferred the smaller cities. We both liked Oklahoma City. In my initial visits to Oklahoma I was told that hypertension was not a problem there, especially in either the black or Indian populations. (That was obviously wrong and cemented my interest

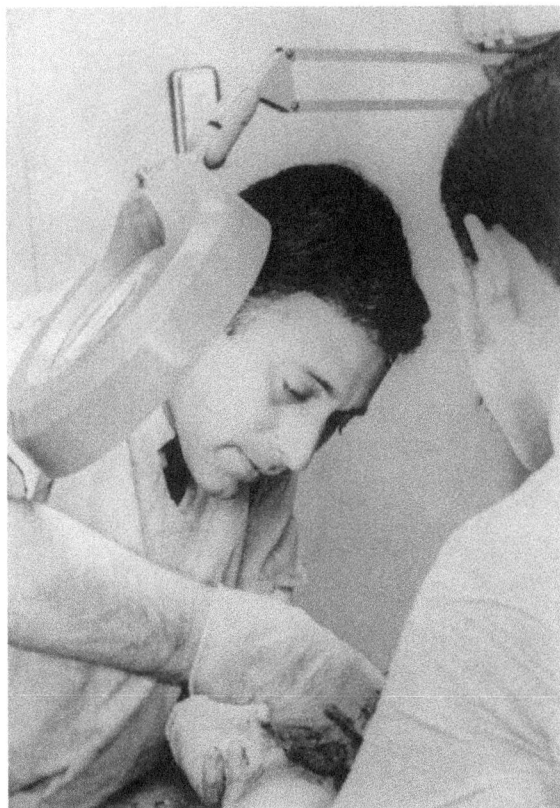

FIGURE 5. EDF and graduate student Marc A. Pfeffer in 1 of their first studies together at the University of Oklahoma Health Sciences Center, 1969.

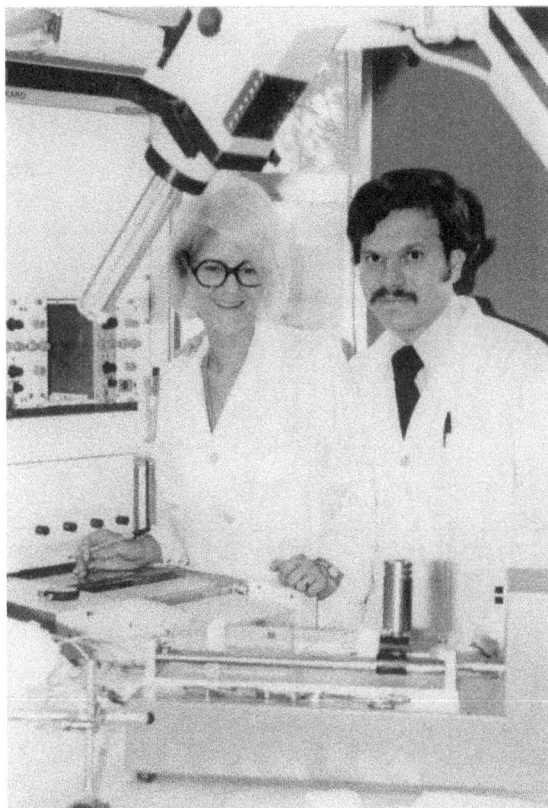

FIGURE 6. Janice M. Pfeffer and Marc A. Pfeffer soon after beginning their research career together with EDF in 1970.

in Oklahoma.) I soon set up a clinical hypertension program. After a year, Jim Hammarsten gave me a separate Section on Hypertension in the Department of Medicine. We had a very successful research program with large VA research support, and I had a couple of RO-1NIH grants. In addition, I headed the VA Cooperative Study at that Institution. At Oklahoma (and in Cleveland before) we were the first to study β blockers in this country for hypertension. It was very exciting. While there, I helped recruit *Solomon Papper*, who had been Chairman of the Department of Medicine in New Mexico and at the Medical College of Virginia before that. He came to Oklahoma as a Distinguished Professor in the VA Hospital program. We became very close friends, and, in our relationship, he helped me refine my philosophy about medical education.

WCR: *I remember 1 of your papers comparing the frequency of hypertension and its treatment at the university hospital, VA hospital, and at a couple of community hospitals in Oklahoma. It was a terrific paper.*

EDF: Thanks for your compliment. The VA and university hospitals did not fare as well as the practicing community hospitals. Hypertension was ignored by every facet of medicine, and in our study, published in *JAMA*, we pointed to the national problem of ignoring post-hospitalization treatment of hypertension, even if the disease was recognized in the individual patient while he or she was hospitalized.

William Middleton was Director of the VA nationally following World War II. During the war he had been the chief internist for the Department of Army in the European Theater of Operations. After the war, he was the VA Medical Director, and he was responsible for making VA hospitals part of universities, emphasizing the need for education and research programs. He often visited VA hospitals and gave conferences. He was a superb clinician, asking direct questions (in an Oslerian fashion) of the audiences. I met him first while I was with Ed Freis, and shortly after 1 of his visits to our VA hospital, he invited me to have lunch with him at the VA Central office. After he retired, he spent time 1 summer at the Muskogee (Oklahoma) VA Hospital, which was related with our University. I attended on occasion at Muskogee, and he visited with us at our home as well as our hospital.

WCR: *What things are you most proud of from your Oklahoma experience?*

EDF: Clearly, the first and foremost is my pride in the people I worked with and our joint investigative accomplishments. There were 2 people at the beginning of my doctoral mentoring experience at Oklahoma who provided great excitement to my academic life: *Janice Pfeffer* and *Marc Pfeffer*. They gave me the excitement and personal intellectual reward of watching them grow in their research accomplishments. Marc had just graduated from Rockford College and came to *Gene Jacobson's* Physiology Department. Marc's fiancé needed a job, and Gene

FIGURE 7. EDF and Sherry on summer vacation in Aspen, Colorado, 1972.

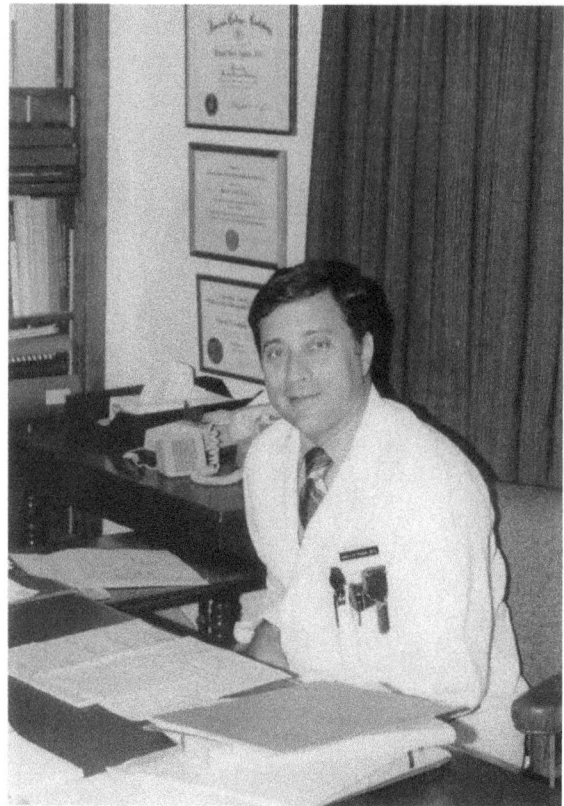

FIGURE 8. EDF in his office at the University of Oklahoma Health Sciences Center, 1974.

suggested that she work with me in my laboratory. Janice was superb and had a great mind. Marc, therefore, had at least 1 reason to join me as my graduate student during my first year at Oklahoma. This was the beginning of 34 years of truly close friendship. Jan pursued her graduate work with me after Marc, and I still think of them as our academic children. Jan died 2 years ago, and Marc and his children remain very much a part of our family. The second thing that was particularly exciting to me was establishing the pathophysiology course that led to 3 editions of the book while I was in Oklahoma.

A third aspect of my program was the clinical research, which has remained highly productive over the years. A number of other outstanding people who came through our program in Oklahoma included *Frank Dunn* and *Jose de Carvalho*. Dunn, from Scotland, initiated the first echocardiographic study in hypertension in our patients. Jose was extremely productive, and finally returned to Brazil. Frank and Joe came to New Orleans with me when we left Oklahoma. And, of course, there were a large number of research fellows from Japan, South America, and Europe who returned to productive faculty positions at their "home" universities. There were a number of fellows and families who came with me, including my secretary and her husband, when we moved our "shop" to New Orleans. We also moved 3 colonies (over 3,000) of our rats to Ochsner.

WCR: *How did the move to the Ochsner Clinic come about? That was 1976?*

EDF: Yes. In 1975, quite coincidentally, I was awarded an endowed chair at the University of Oklahoma, the George Lynn Cross Research Professorship. (*Dr. Cross* had been President of the University of Oklahoma, who wanted to build a school "whose academics the football team could be proud.") Shortly thereafter, the Ochsner Institutions made me an attractive offer to come to New Orleans. My philosophy of being at a large multispecialty clinic rather than at a university had to be readdressed. I thought if I could develop research and education as part-and-parcel of the Ochsner Clinic, that would be exciting. At the Cleveland Clinic, Irv Page didn't insist on the Research Division being part of the clinical area. He was more interested in the research program as an independent area; I was interested in clinical investigation, and I thought this was important were I to go to Ochsner. I believed that the fundamental and clinical research program in hypertension should be part of the hypertension section in the clinic. My responsibility in 1976 was to head education and research at the Ochsner Clinic Foundation as well as the Hypertension Division in the Clinic. Ochsner already had a superb graduate medical education program. In my first year, we developed our continuing medical education and allied health activities. We had a very good program in hypertension that continues to this day. *Dick Re*, *Franz Messerli*, and *Frank Dunn* soon came. We had fine and productive fellows. *Hector Ventura*

FIGURE 9. EDF interviewing Irvine H. Page for the AOA and National Library of Medicine at the CDC in Atlanta, 1978.

FIGURE 10. Louis H. Sullivan, MD, Secretary of the Department of Health and Human Services and EDF, Vice Chairman, Council for High Blood Pressure Research, on the occasion of Dr. Sullivan's address at the Council's Annual CIBA Award Dinner, 1987.

was 1 of the outstanding, and he now heads the education and research program of our Cardiovascular Department. As our Clinic grew, so did research and education. Dick Re soon headed our Hypertension Section and the Foundation's research program. I continued as head of our education programs, and I continue with these activities along with our hypertension research work. The institution awarded me the title of Alton Ochsner Distinguished Scientist and head of academic affairs, and about 4 years ago, while still editing the journal *Hypertension*, I stepped down from the head of academic affairs. I still continue with my regular patient care clinical activities, and research, as well as for directing our annual Alton Ochsner Award Relating Smoking and Health, and our CME and Allied health sciences programs.

WCR: *Ed, you've been here at the Ochsner Clinic*

Foundation for 27 years. You've been a major builder of this institution during that period of time. What accomplishments here are you most proud of?

EDF: I am most proud of our research and clinical programs in hypertension. The institution has nurtured and protected me so that I could maintain our clinical and basic research programs, my clinical activities, and participate in a number of national and international activities in the hypertension area. I have had a large number of research fellows from all over the world, and, who on their return to their home universities, take home the teaching of our excellent research and training program.

I have also been able to pursue my other interests, including my textbook on hypertension, cardiovascular medicine, pathophysiology, and on medical boards review. The latter was started in 1931 by *Harold Rypins*, and I assumed the editorship of Rypins in its 12th edition and have carried it through to the present 18th edition. This was the first textbook to prepare young physicians for state medical board licensure exams. When I assumed this editorship, it was a 1-volume text. It's now published in 3 parts: a clinical, basic sciences, and questions and answer volume. We also published monographs for each discipline as offshoots from these volumes. I have also enjoyed a number of committee responsibilities for major organizations. I was the Governor of Louisiana for the American College of Cardiology, and on the Board of Trustees of the College. I have always been extremely active with the Council for High Blood Pressure Research of the American Heart Association. Serving as Chairman of the Council and Editor-in-Chief of *Hypertension* were highlights of the service aspects of my academic career.

WCR: *You were editor of* Hypertension *in what years?*

EDF: From 1994 through 2002. I also was Chairman of the Council for High Blood Pressure Research from 1988 to 1990. I've been a member of the Joint National Committee for the National High Blood Pressure Education Program for the past 32 years and a member of all the JNC reports until this year.

WCR: *You've been on all 6 JNC committees?*

EDF: Yes. I enjoyed doing that work. Most of the national hypertension education programs throughout the world have modeled themselves after the hypertension program in the United States. Ed Freis' Cooperative Study's accomplishments stimulated Ted Cooper to start that program when Ted was Assistant Secretary for Health under Secretary Eliot Richardson. Eliot Richardson was interested in hypertension

FIGURE 11. EDF in office at the Alton Ochsner Medical Foundation, 1997.

FIGURE 12. EDF receiving Master of the American College of Physicians, 1994.

because a parent sustained a stroke from hypertension and died. Ted knew the importance of hypertension, and believed that a National Hypertension Education Program would be an ideal way to show Congress how the practice of medicine can be affected directly through research. I also served on the WHO committees on hypertension and cardiovascular disease for a number of years and have advised the VA. I have chaired several study sections for the NIH, and I was

on the first Food and Drug Administration advisory panel on cardiovascular, renal, and pulmonary drugs. I also chaired 3 Specialized Center of Research (SCOR) study section committees in hypertension and I just finished chairing a special NIH obesity committee.

WCR: *What are your day-to-day activities like now compared to your earlier years at Ochsner? What time do you wake up in the morning? What time do you get to the hospital? What time do you leave the hospital? What time do you get home? What time do you go to bed?*

EDF: Now I get up at 5:30 or 6 A.M. I'm usually at the hospital by 7:15 A.M. I see patients at least 3 or 4 days a week from 8:30 A.M. to noon. I spend the afternoons now going over research data and programs with our staff and fellows. I still do a lot of writing and editing. I used to do more at night at home. I still travel more than I should.

WCR: *What time do you leave the hospital as a rule?*

EDF: Now, I usually leave around 5 P.M. In the earlier days, I would get here about 7 A.M., and get as much done as I could before seeing patients. Then I would work probably to 7 P.M., go home, have dinner, and in the evening work probably until 2 A.M. I usually functioned well with 4 to 5 hours of sleep.

WCR: *How much sleep do you need now?*

EDF: I usually go to bed at 11 P.M. or midnight, but get up at the same time. Early on, I used to do my writing by hand. Now, I write on computer.

WCR: *How many trips do you take a year as a rule?*

EDF: Probably around 20.

WCR: *How have you worked the travel into your other agendas?*

EDF: With difficulty. I plan well in advance. I used to take more trips to Europe, South America, and Japan. It's difficult traveling in and out of New Orleans. Almost every trip we make, one must change planes more than once, and now there are fewer flights.

WCR: *How much time do you take off a year?*

EDF: We used to take 2 weeks vacation in the summer. We loved taking extended car trips with our children. Now, we take more 3- or 4-day weekend trips to visit with our children and grandchildren. Not infrequently our children join us on our summer vacations, and we enjoy spending the holidays, particularly Thanksgiving, with them.

WCR: *Tell me about your kids.*

EDF: We have 3 children. Our daughter Margie lives in Chicago.

She was born in 1962 in Fort Knox. Margie received her undergraduate degree from the University of Utah and her masters in training and development at Loyola University in Chicago. She has been in adult education at the Cooking and Hospitality Institute of

FIGURE 13. EDF receiving Award of Tribute by Tulane University School of Medicine from Dr. Hector O. Ventura, a former research fellow, 1999.

FIGURE 14. EDF attending the Award of Tribute dinner in 1999 as given by Tulane University School of Medicine, with Marc A. Pfeffer, Victor Dzau, and EDF (standing, left to right), and Sherry, Margie (daughter), and Tom Beckman (sitting, left to right).

Chicago. Now, she's in retail with a large company. Margie's husband teaches pastry and bread baking at the Hospitality Institute.

Lara was born in 1969. She received her college and master's degrees at Northwestern University in learning disabilities. And now she is a learning specialist at the Latin School of Chicago. She and her husband have 1 son, Jackson, the younger of our 2 grandchildren. Her husband is a human resources consultant. They live near Margie and Tom.

Our son Bruce is married to Rachel, a demographer. They live in Pennington, New Jersey, not far from Princeton. He graduated from the University of Chicago and then went to the Medical College of Wisconsin, where he was recruited by Bristol-Myers Squibb to work in their research laboratories. Now, he's working with 1

of the clinical research organizations that monitor human drug studies. His wife works at the University of Pennsylvania Medical Center as a consultant in biostatistics. They have 1 child, Maye, a 4-year-old girl.

WCR: *What do you do from a non-medical standpoint? You mentioned music was something you enjoyed.*

EDF: I enjoy music a great deal.

WCR: *What kind?*

EDF: Any kind, and I have a large and varied collection of musical recordings. I like the show tunes from the Broadway musicals. We have an excellent symphony orchestra in New Orleans, which Sherry and I like to attend regularly. Every summer we visit Aspen to attend their wonderful music festival. We used to go for a few weeks with the children, hiking, etc. Now, we spend a week or so attending the concerts, ballets, and plays, and we also do a lot of walking. Sometimes 1 or more of our children's families join us.

WCR: *When you get home at night, do you turn music on?*

EDF: I turn on music or the cable news, but I spend a lot of time listening to CDs.

WCR: *What kind of CDs?*

EDF: My favorites are operas, usually without words. I have a nice collection of them—I particularly enjoy the Italian operas. I also enjoy Beethoven and Bach.

WCR: *Do you read much outside of medicine?*

EDF: Yes. Primarily history and biographies. I particularly enjoy the presidents and other political leaders. Most recently, I read the *John Adams* book, and 1 on *James Madison* and *Jefferson*. I've probably read most of the books on *John Kennedy*, *Richard Nixon*, and *Harry Truman*. I've read a few of *Jimmy Carter's* books. I just completed *Thomas Bonner's* remarkable biography of *Abraham Flexner*. It is a "must" for anyone interested in the history of Academic Medicine in this country. Abraham Flexner, in my opinion, is 1 of the major figures in American (and world) medicine of the past 100 years. And, he wasn't a physician!

WCR: *Are you religious?*

EDF: In my own way I am, but I am not a regular "Temple-goer." I used to be much more active and served on our Temple board of trustees, but I had to reduce these activities because of my other professional time commitments.

WCR: *Do you go to synagogue during the holidays?*

EDF: Yes, and it is important for me to do this with our family.

WCR: *Are you a football or baseball fan? Do you like sports?*

EDF: Yes. I follow our football team on television.

FIGURE 15. Family reunion celebrating the new millennium (December 31, 1999) at Williamsburg, Virginia. *Left to right*, son Bruce with wife, Rachel Weinstein, daughter Lara and husband, John Bremen, and daughter Margie and husband, Tom Beckman.

FIGURE 16. EDF and Sherry at their favorite vacation spot in Aspen, 2002.

I'm a fair weather friend of the Saints. When in Oklahoma, I had to be an avid football fan.

WCR: *When you pick up the newspaper in the morning, what's the first section you read?*

EDF: The news section, but I go through the entire paper before leaving home.

WCR: *Ed, you've been in research nearly 45 years. As you look back over your career—research, mentoring, teaching, committee activities—what are the things you are most proud of?*

EDF: The young people who I have had an opportunity to influence has given me a feeling of real accomplishment. I believe that each generation builds upon the accomplishments of those before and that is the path of progress. I am proud of my research efforts, particularly those concerning hemodynamics and mechanisms of risk of target organ involvement in hypertension. In 1964, when we began our studies on the heart in hypertension, there were no clinical studies in that area. Left ventricular hypertrophy was not considered a risk until the Framingham study pointed it out. Bob Tarazi and I were the first to show decreases in cardiac mass with antihypertensive therapy. We found that short periods of antihypertensive treatment could decrease myocardial mass independent of pressure. The concept evolved that if high pressure or elevated cholesterol levels were lowered, cardiovascular risk would decrease. Everyone inferred that if ventricular mass decreased, cardiovascular risk would also diminish. We have focused our work in recent years on the question as to why decreasing the heart mass should decrease risk. The increased risk is not due to hypertrophy of the cell, per se, but to the associated myocardial ischemia, fibrosis, and apoptosis. Our studies have shown that the angiotensin-converting enzyme inhibitors, angiotensin receptor antagonists, and some calcium antagonists can prevent and reverse the disease in both heart and kidneys by reversing ischemia and by reducing fibrosis and apoptosis. More recently, we have found that the thiazide diuretics adversely affect the kidney, pathologically and hemodynamically. We are now determining whether agents that inhibit the local renin-angiotensin-aldosterone systems prevent these effects of the thiazides.

WCR: *What do you do on Saturdays and Sundays as a rule?*

EDF: Saturday nights we frequently go to concerts or visit with friends. On Sunday mornings, we enjoy reading *The New York Times*, our local newspaper, and the weekly news magazines, and watching the Sunday talk shows. In the afternoon I write. Occasionally, Sherry and I go to a movie. We also spend time on weekends as well as in the evening talking with our children and grandchildren over the telephone and having our grandchildren recognize our voices.

WCR: *Do you entertain much at home?*

EDF: Yes, with close friends. Sherry and I prefer small and informal gatherings rather than large social events.

FIGURE 17. Edward D. Freis, MD, and EDF on the occasion of Dr. Freis' 90th birthday celebration in Washington, DC, 2002.

quires a much longer commitment to their development and life academically. Mentoring needs to be encouraged; we must stimulate and reward these leaders of clinical research. This is our challenge!

WCR: *Ed, on behalf of the* AJC *readers, I want to thank you for your openness.*

EDF: Thank you. You have a remarkable technique of getting information from people. You get people to talk to you with ease. Your interviews are important for both practicing and academic cardiovascular physicians. People need to learn from others and from history. Unfortunately, many individuals fail to acknowledge the past and the accomplishments of others. We can learn much from our history and it is a clear basis for our future.

WCR: *Thank you, Ed.*

WCR: *Ed, how much time did you spend on* Hypertension *a week when you were Editor-in-Chief?*

EDF: The number of manuscripts increased from 617 to over 1,400 during my editorship. I would spend at least 2 to 3 hours a day. The journal rented space from Ochsner across from my regular office and that was a tremendous time saver.

WCR: *Ed, are you going to work forever?*

EDF: I will probably continue doing research for a few more years. I have just recruited 2 additional people on our research staff. I have committed myself to some new fellows, including 2 fellows of previous fellows (my "grand-fellows"). I want to start taking piano lessons, which I have not done in many years.

WCR: *Ed, you've lived in New York, Washington, DC, Berlin, Fort Knox, Chicago, Oklahoma City, and now New Orleans. Which of these cities did you enjoy the most?*

EDF: Each city has its own special strengths and memories. At present, we would say New Orleans since it is where we are now. For my work and colleagues, I would say Cleveland because of Page, Dustan, and Tarazi. Cleveland and Oklahoma were my rapid growth periods. In those days, I enjoyed each waking moment and slept only about 4 hours a day. If Chicago was not so cold, I probably would like to live there. But, obviously, living in New Orleans for the past 27 years has been satisfying, personally and professionally.

WCR: *Ed, is there anything you'd like to say that we haven't talked about?*

EDF: I'd like to speak to one area I think is important, and, that is the proper mentoring of younger colleagues. Faculties now do not have as much time as in the past for teaching and interacting with medical students, house officers, and fellows. We certainly need the newer mentoring grants from NIH. But, it is important to remember that an ideal mentor does not only stimulate the person while in training, but re-

Selected Publications of EDF Selected by EDF

8. Frohlich ED, Wilson I, Schnaper HW, Freis ED. Hemodynamic alterations in hypertensive patients due to chlorothiazide. *N Engl J Med* 1960;262:1261–1263.

10. Scott JB, Frohlich ED, hardin RA, Haddy FJ. Na$^+$, K$^+$, Ca^{++}, and Mg^{++} action on coronary vascular resistance in the dog heart. *Am J Physiol* 1961;201:1095–1100.

18. Frohlich ED. Local effect of adenosine mono-, di-, and triphosphate vessel resistance. *Am J Physiol* 1963;204:28–30.

28. Frohlich ED. Vascular effects of Krebs intermediate metabolites. *Am J Physiol* 1965;208:149–153.

41. Frohlich ED, Tarazi RC, Ulrych M, Dustan HP, Page IH. Tilt test for investigation of a neural component in hypertension and its correlation with clinical characteristics. *Circulation* 1967;36:387–393.

44. Frohlich ED, Tarazi RC, Dustan HP, Page IH. The paradox of beta- adrenergic blockage in hypertension. *Circulation* 1968;37:417–423.

48. Frohlich ED, Tarazi RC, Dustan HP. Hyperdynamic beta-adrenergic circulatory state: increased beta receptor responsiveness. *Arch Intern Med* 1969;123:1–7.

50. Frohlich ED, Tarazi RC, Dustan HP. Re-examination of the hemodynamics of hypertension. *Am J Med Sci* 1969;257:9–23.

58. Tarazi RC, Dustan HP, Frohlich ED, Gifford RW Jr, Hoffman GC. Plasma volume and chronic hypertension. Relationship to arterial pressure levels in different hypertensive diseases. *Arch Intern Med* 1970;125:835–842.

60. Frohlich ED, Kozul VJ, Tarazi RC, Dustan HP. Physiological comparison of labile and essential hypertension. *Circ Res* 1970;27:55–69.

61. Veterans Administration Cooperative Study Group on Antihypertensive Agents (member). Effects of treatment on morbidity in hypertension. II. Results in patients with diastolic blood pressure averaging 90 through 114 mm Hg. *JAMA* 1970;213:1143–1152.

65. Frohlich ED, Tarazi RC, Dustan HP. Hemodynamic and functional mechanisms in two renal hypertensions: arterial and pyelonephritis. *Am J Med Sci* 1971;261:189–195.

68. Frohlich ED, Tarazi RC, Dustan HP. Clinical-physiological correlations in the development of hypertensive heart disease. *Circulation* 1971;44:446–455.

73. Veterans Administration Cooperative Study Group on Antihypertensive Agents (member). Effects of treatment on morbidity in hypertension. III. Influence of age, diastolic pressure, and prior cardiovascular disease; further analysis of side effects. *Circulation* 1972;45:991–1004.

74. Pfeffer MA, Frohlich ED. Electromagnetic flowmetry in anesthetized rats. *J Appl Physiol* 1972;33:137–140.

81. Pfeffer MA, Frohlich ED. Hemodynamic and myocardial function in young and old normotensive and spontaneously hypertensive rats. *Circ Res* 1973;32:28–38.

85. Emery AC Jr, Whitcomb WH, Frohlich ED. "Stress" polycythemia and hypertension. *JAMA* 1974;229:159–162.

89. Pfeffer MA, Frohlich ED, Pfeffer JM, Weiss AK. Pathophysiological implications of the increased cardiac output of young spontaneously hypertensive rats. *Circ Res* 1974;34:235–244.

104. Adamopoulos PN, Chrysanthakopoulis SG, Frohlich ED. Systolic hypertension: nonhomogeneous diseases. *Am J Cardiol* 1975;36:697–701.

105. Chrysant SG, Frohlich ED, Adamopoulos PN, Stein PD, Whitcomb WH,

Allen EW, Neller G. Pathophysiologic significance of "stress" or relative poly-cythemia in essential hypertension. *Am J Cardiol* 1976;37:1069–1072.

106. Nishiyama K, Nishiyama A, Frohlich ED. Regional blood flow in normotensive and spontaneously hypertensive rats. *Am J Physiol* 1976;230:691–698.

108. Pfeffer MA, Pfeffer JM, Frohlich ED. Pumping ability of the hypertrophying left ventricle of the spontaneously hypertensive rat. *Cir Res* 1976;38:423–429.

121. Pfeffer MA, Pfeffer JM, Weiss AK, Frohlich ED. Development of SHR hypertension and cardiac hypertrophy during prolonged beta blockade. *Am J Physiol* 1977;232:639–644.

122. Dunn FG, Chandaratna P, de Calvalho JGR, Basta LL, Frohlich ED. Pathophysiologic assessment of hypertensive heart disease with echocardiography. *Am J Cardiol* 1977;39:789–795.

130. Veterans Administration-National Heart, Lung, and Blood Institute Study Group for Cooperative Studies on Antihypertensive Therapy: Mild Hypertension (member). Treatment of mild hypertension: preliminary results of a two-year feasibility trial. *Cir Res* 1977;25:180–187.

132. Tsuchiya M, Walsh GM, Frohlich ED. Systemic hemodynamic effects of microspheres in conscious rats. *Am J Physiol* 1977;233:617–621.

141. Dunn FG, de Carvalho JGR, Frohlich ED. Hemodynamic, reflexive, and metabolic alterations induced by acute and chronic timolol therapy in hypertensive man. *Circulation* 1978;57:140–144.

150. Trippodo NC, Walsh GM, Frohlich ED. Fluid volumes during onset of spontaneous hypertension in rats. *Am J Physiol* 1978;235:52–55.

154. Messerli FH, de Carvalho JGR, Christie B, Frohlich ED. Systemic and regional hemodynamics in low, normal, and high cardiac output in borderline hypertension. *Circulation* 1978;58:441–448.

155. Pfeffer MA, Ferrell BA, Pfeffer JM, Weiss AK, Fishbein MC, Frohlich ED. Ventricular morphology and pumping ability of exercised spontaneously hypertensive rats. *Am J Physiol* 1978;235:193–199.

158. Chrysant SG, Walsh GM, Kem DC, Frohlich ED. Hemodynamic and metabolic evidence of salt sensitivity in spontaneously hypertensive rats. *Kidney Int* 1979;15:33–37.

162. Chrysant SG, Danisa K, Kem DC, Dillard BL, Smith WJ, Frohlich ED. Racial differences in pressure, volume and renin interrelationships in essential hypertension. *Hypertension* 1979;1:136–141.

163. Dustan HP (chairman), Frohlich ED (co-chairman), Geller RG, Bevan RD, Bohr DF, Coleman TG, Frolich JC, Ganong W, Hawthorne EW, Kuchel O, et al. General recommendations of the Hypertension Task Force of the National Heart, Lung, and Blood Institute of the National Institutes of Health (Executive Summary). *Hypertension* 1979;1:150–151.

165. Pfeffer MA, Pfeffer JM, Dunn FG, Nishiyama K, Tsuchiya M, Frohlich ED. Natural biventricular hypertrophy in normotensive rats. I. Physical and hemodynamic characteristics. *Am J Physiol* 1979;236:640–643.

166. Messerli FH, de Carvalho JGR, Christie B, Frohlich ED. Essential hypertension in black and white subjects: hemodynamic findings and fluid volume state. *Am J Med* 1979;67:27–31.

168. De Carvalho JGR, Messerli FH, Frohlich ED. Mitral valve prolapse and borderline hypertension. *Hypertension* 1979;1:518–522.

169. Pfeffer JM, Pfeffer MA, Fishbein MC, Frohlich ED. Cardiac function and morphology with aging in the spontaneously hypertensive rat. *Am J Physiol* 1979;237:461–468.

172. Frohlich ED, Tarazi RC. Is arterial pressure the sole factor responsible for hypertensive cardiac hypertrophy? *Am J Cardiol* 1979;44:959–963.

181. Yamamoto J, Trippodo NC, Ishise S, Frohlich ED. Total vascular pressure-volume relationship in the conscious rat. *Am J Physiol* 1980;238:823–828.

189. Messerli FH, Frohlich ED, Dreslinski GR, Suarez DH, Aristimuño GG. Serum uric acid in essential hypertension: an indicator of renal vascular involvement. *Ann Intern Med* 1980;93:817–821.

191. Trippodo NC, Yamamoto J, Frohlich ED. Whole-body venous capacity and effective total tissue compliance in SHR. *Hypertension* 1981;3:104–112.

192. Messerli FH, Christie B, de Carvalho JGR, Aristimuño GG, Suarez DH, Dreslinski GR, Frohlich ED. Obesity and essential hypertension. Hemodynamics, intravascular volume, sodium excretion, and plasma renin activity. *Arch Intern Med* 1981;141:81–85.

197. Trippodo NC, Frohlich ED. Controversies in cardiovascular research: similarities of genetic (spontaneous) hypertension. Man and Rat. *Circ Res* 1981;48:309–319.

200. Dreslinski GR, Frohlich ED, Dunn FG, Messerli FH, Suarez DH, Reisin E. Echocardiographic diastolic ventricular abnormality in hypertensive heart disease: atrial emptying index. *Am J Cardiol* 1981;47:1087–1090.

211. Pegram BL, Ishise S, Frohlich ED. Effect of methyldopa, clonidine, and hydralazine on cardiac mass and haemodynamics in Wistar-Kyoto and spontaneously hypertensive rats. *Cardiovasc Res* 1982;16:40–46.

215. Frohlich ED. Hemodynamic factors in the pathogenesis and maintenance of hypertension. *Fed Proceed* 1982;41:2400–2408.

226. Frohlich ED. Achievements in hypertension: a 25-year overview. *J Am Coll Cardiol* 1983;1:225–239.

229. Ventura HO, Messerli FH, Oigman W, Dunn FG, Reisin E, Frohlich ED. Immediate hemodynamic effects of a new calcium-channel blocking agent (nitrendipine) in essential hypertension. *Am J Cardiol* 1983;51:783–786.

230. Reisin E, Frohlich ED, Messerli FH, Dreslinski GR, Dunn FG, Jones MM, Batson HM Jr. Cardiovascular changes after weight reduction in obesity hypertension. *Ann Intern Med* 1983;98:315–319.

231. Dunn FG, Oigman W, Sundgaard-Riise K, Messerli FH, Ventura HO, Reisin

E, Frohlich ED. Racial differences in cardiac adaptation to essential hypertension determined by echocardiographic indexes. *J Am Coll Cardiol* 1983;1:1348–1351.

236. Frohlich ED. Hemodynamics and others determinants in development of left ventricular hypertrophy: conflicting factors in its regression. *Fed Proceed* 1983;42:2709–2715.

237. Frohlich ED, Messerli FH, Reisin E, Dunn FG. The problem of obesity and hypertension. *Hypertension* 1983;5:71–78.

245. Dunn FG, Oigman W, Ventura HO, Messerli FH, Kobrin I, Frohlich ED. Enalapril improves systemic and renal hemodynamics and allows regression of left ventricular mass in essential hypertension. *Am J Cardiol* 1984;53:105–108.

247. Sesoko S, Pegram BL, Willis GW, Frohlich ED. DOCA-salt induced malignant hypertension in spontaneously hypertensive rats. *J Hypertens* 1984;2:49–54.

248. Frohlich ED, Messerli FH, Dunn, FG, Oigman W, Ventura HO, Sundgaard-Riise K. Greater renal vascular involvement in the black patient with essential hypertension. A comparison of systemic and renal hemodynamics in black and white patients. *Mineral Electrolyte Metabolism* 1984;10:173–177.

249. The Joint National Committee on the Detection, Evaluation, and Treatment of High Blood Pressure (member). The 1984 report of the Joint National Committee on detection, evaluation, and treatment of high blood pressure. *Arch Intern Med* 1984;144:1045–1057.

251. Ventura HO, Messerli FH, Frohlich ED, Kobrin I, Oigman W, Dunn FG, Carey RM. Immediate hemodynamic effects of a dopamine-receptor agonist (fenoldopam) in patients with essential hypertension. *Circulation* 1984;69:1142–1145.

255. Frohlich ED, Cooper RA, Lewis EJ. Review of the overall experience of captopril in hypertension. *Arch Intern Med* 1984;144:1441–1444.

265. Kobrin I, Oigman W, Kumar A, Ventura HO, Messerli FH, Frohlich ED, Dunn FG. Diurnal variation of blood pressure in elderly patients with essential hypertension. *J Am Geriatrics Soc* 1984;32:896–899.

267. Cambotti LJ, Cole FE, Gerall AA, Frohlich ED, MacPhee AA. Neonatal gonadal hormones and blood pressure in the spontaneously hypertensive rat. *Am J Physiol* 1984;247:258–264.

268. Frohlich ED. Clinical conference: hypertensive cardiovascular disease: a pathophysiological assessment. *Hypertension* 1984;6:934–939.

288. Trippodo NC, Januscewicz A, Pegram BL, Cole FE, Kohashi N, Kardon MB, MacPhee AA, Frohlich ED. Rat platelets activate high molecular weight atrial natriuretic peptides in vitro. *Hypertension* 1985;7:905–912.

290. Amodeo C, Kobrin I, Ventura HO, Messerli FH, Frohlich ED. Immediate and short-term hemodynamic effects of diltiazem in patients with hypertension. *Circulation* 1986;73:108–113.

291. Kobrin I, Frohlich ED, Ventura HO, Messerli FH. Renal involvement follows cardiac enlargement in essential hypertension. *Arch Intern Med* 1986;146:272–276.

292. Frohlich ED, Gifford R Jr, Horan M, Kaplan NM, Maxwell MH, Payne G, Roccella EJ, Shapiro AP, Weiss S, Bowler AE. Nonpharmacologic approaches to the control of high blood pressure. Report of the Subcommittee on nonpharmacologic therapy of the Joint National Committee on detection, evaluation, and treatment of high blood pressure, 1984. *Hypertension* 1986;8:444–467.

302. Tarazi RC, Frohlich ED. Is reversal of cardiac hypertrophy a desirable goal of antihypertensive therapy? *Circulation* 1987;75:113–117.

314. Dunn FG, Ventura HO, Messerli FH, Kobrin I, Frohlich ED. Time course of regression of left ventricular hypertrophy in hypertensive patients treated with atenolol. *Circulation* 1987;76:254–258.

315. Frohlich ED. Diuretics in hypertension. *J Hypertens* 1987;5:43–49.

319. Nunez BD, Frohlich ED, Garavaglia GE, Schmieder RE, Nunez MM. Serum uric acid in renovascular hypertension: reduction following surgical correction. *Am J Med Sci* 1987;294:419–422.

324. Frohlich ED (chairman), Grim C, Labarthe DR, Maxwell MH, Perloff D, Weidman WH. Report of the Special Task Force Appointed by the Steering Committee, American Heart Association, Vol. 5 of Recommendations of the Human Blood Pressure Determination by Sphygmomanometer. Dallas, Texas: AHA Publication No. 70–1005(SA), 1987, pp. i-34; see also *Hypertension* 1988;11:209–222.

332. The Joint National Committee on the Detection, Evaluation, and Treatment of High Blood Pressure. The 1988 Report of the Joint National Committee on detection, evaluation, and treatment of high blood pressure. *Arch Intern Med* 1988;148:1023–1038.

343. Frohlich ED. State of the art: The first Irvine H. Page Lecture: the mosaic of hypertension: past present, and future. *J Hypertens* 1988;6:2–11.

364. Frohlich ED. State-of-the-art: hemodynamic differences in black and white patients with essential hypertension. *Hypertension* 1990;15:675–680.

366. Frohlich ED, Sasaki O. Dissociation of changes in cardiovascular mass and performance with angiotensin converting enzyme inhibitors in Wistar-Kyoto and spontaneously hypertensive rats. *J Am Coll Cardiol* 1990;16:1492–1499.

379. Frohlich ED. Is reversal of left ventricular hypertrophy in hypertension beneficial? *Hypertension* 1991;18:133–138.

398. Chien Y, Frohlich ED, MacPhee AA, Pegram BL. Quinaprilat increases total body vascular compliance in rats with myocardial infarction. *J Cardiovasc Pharmacol* 1992;19:430–434.

403. Frohlich ED, Apstein C, Chobanian AV, Devereux RB, Dustan HP, Dzau V, Fauad-Tarazi F, Horan MJ, Marcus M, Massie B, et al. The heart in hypertension. *N Engl J Med* 1992;327:998–1008.

405. Frohlich ED, Sasaki O, Chien Y, Arita M. Changes in cardiovascular mass, left ventricular pumping ability, and aortic distensibility after calcium antagonist in Wistar-Kyoto and spontaneously hypertensive rats. *J Hypertens* 1992:10:1369–1378.

408. Joint National Committee on the Detection, Evaluation, and Treatment of Blood Pressure (member). The 1992 Report of the Joint National Committee on the detection, evaluation, and treatment of blood pressure (JNC-V). *Arch Intern Med* 1993;153:154–183.

409. Frohlich ED, Chien Y, Sesoko S, Pegram BL. Relationships between dietary sodium intake, hemodynamics and cardiac mass in spontaneously hypertensive and normotensive Wistar-Kyoto rats. *Am J Physiol* 1993;264:30–34.

424. Arita M, Horinaka S, Komatsu K, Frohlich ED. Reversal of left ventricular hypertrophy with different classes of drugs causes differing ventricular biochemical changes. *J Hypertens* 1993;11:354–355.

435. Komatsu K, Frohlich ED, Ono H, Ono Y, Numabe A, Willis GW. Glomerular dynamics and morphology of aged SHR: effects of angiotensin converting enzyme inhibitor. *Hypertension* 1995;25:207–213.

439. Ono H, Ono Y, Frohlich ED. Nitric oxide synthase inhibition in spontaneously hypertensive rats: systemic, renal, and glomerular hemodynamics. *Hypertension* 1995;26:249–255.

455. Ono Y, Ono H, Frohlich ED. Hydrochlorothiazide exacerbates nitric oxide blockades nephrosclerosis with glomerular hypertension in spontaneously hypertensive rats. *J Hypertens* 1996;14:823–828.

462. Frohlich ED, Arthur C. Corcoran memorial lecture: influence of nitric oxide and angiotensin II on renal involvement in hypertension. *Hypertension* 1997;29:188–193.

463. Nunez E, Hosoya K, Susic D, Frohlich ED. Enalapril and losartan reduced cardiac mass and improved coronary hemodynamics in SHR. *Hypertension* 1997;29:519–524.

472. The Joint National Committee on Prevention, Detection, Evaluation, and Treatment of High Blood Pressure (member). The Sixth Report of the Joint National Committee (JNC-VI) on prevention, detection, evaluation, and treatment of high blood pressure. *Arch Intern Med* 1997;157:2413–2446.

474. Francischetti A, Ono H, Frohlich ED. Renoprotective effects of felodipine and/or enalapril in spontaneously hypertensive rats with and without L-NAME. *Hypertension* 1998;31:795–801.

475. Susic D, Nunez E, Hosoya H, Frohlich ED. Coronary hemodynamics in aging spontaneously hypertensive (SHR) and normotensive Wistar-Kyoto (WKY) rats. *J Hypertens* 1998:16:231–237.

482. Susic D, Francischetti A, Frohlich ED. Prolonged L-arginine on cardiovascular mass and myocardial hemodynamics and collagen in aged spontaneously hypertensive rats and normal rats. *Hypertension* 1999;33:451–455.

484. Susic D, Varagic J, Frohlich ED. Pharmacologic agents on cardiovascular mass, coronary dynamics and collagen in aged spontaneously hypertensive rats. *J Hypertens* 1999;17:1209–1215.

486. Nakamura Y, Ono H, Frohlich ED. Differential effects of T- and L-type calcium antagonists on glomerular dynamics in spontaneously hypertensive rats. *Hypertension* 1999;34:273–278.

487. Frohlich ED. Risk mechanisms in hypertensive heart disease. *Hypertension* 1999;34:782–789.

488. Ono Y, Ono H, Matsuoka H, Fujimori T, Frohlich ED. Apoptosis, coronary arterial remodeling, and myocardial infarction after nitric oxide inhibition in SHR. *Hypertension* 1999;34:609–616.

504. Nakamura Y, Ono H, Zhou X, Frohlich ED. Angiotensin type 1 receptor antagonism and ACE inhibition produce similar renoprotection in L-NAME/SHR rats. *Hypertension* 2001;37:1262–1267.

507. Varagic J, Susic D, Frohlich ED. Coronary hemodynamic and ventricular responses to AT1 receptor inhibition in SHR interaction with AT2 receptors. *Hypertension* 2001;37:1399–1403.

513. Ono H, Ono Y, Takanohashi A, Matsuoha H, Frohlich ED. Apoptosis and glomerular injury after prolonged nitric oxide synthase inhibition in SHR. *Hypertension* 2001;38:1300–1306.

514. Susic D, Varagic J, Frohlich ED. Isolated systolic hypertension in elderly WKY's reversed with L-arginine and ACE inhibition. *Hypertension* 2001;38:1422–1426.

519. Zhou X, Ono H, Ono Y, Frohlich ED: N- and L-type calcium channel antagonistic effects on glomerular dynamics in L-NAME rats. *J Hypertens* 2002;20:993–1000.

BOOKS

4. Frohlich ED, ed. Pathophysiology: Altered Regulatory Mechanisms in Disease. 3rd Ed. Philadelphia: JB Lippincott Company, 1984:940.

11. Frohlich ED, ed. Preventive Aspects of Coronary Heart Disease. In: Brest AN, editor-in-chief. Cardiovascular Clinics. Philadelphia, PA: FA Davis, 1990:239.

12. Frohlich ED, Subak-Sharp G. In: Frohlich ED, ed. Take Heart! Cut Your Inherited Risks of Heart Disease. New York: Crown Publishers Incorporated, 1990:168.

45. Frohlich ED, ed. Hypertension: Evaluation and Treatment. Tokyo, Japan: Nankodo Co. Ltd, 2000:173.

46. Frohlich ED, ed. Rypins' Basic Sciences Review. 18th Ed. Philadelphia, PA: Lippincott Williams & Wilkins, 2001:810.

47. Frohlich ED, ed. Rypins' Questions & Answers for Basic Sciences Review. 18th Ed. Philadelphia, PA: Lippincott Williams & Wilkins, 2001:285 (w/CD Rom).

48. Frohlich ED, ed. Rypins' Clinical Sciences Review. 18th Ed. Philadelphia, PA: Lippincott Williams & Wilkins, 2001:441 (w/CD Rom).

EDITORIALS

24. Frohlich ED. Obituary—Solomon Papper, MD. *Am J Med* 1985;78:271–276.

25. Frohlich ED. In memoriam: Robert C. Tarazi, MD, 1925–1986. *Hypertension* 1986;8:vii-viii.

28. Frohlich ED. Cardiac hypertrophy in hypertension. *N Engl J Med* 1987;317:831–833.

48. Frohlich ED, Dustan HP, Bumpus FM. Irvine H. Page: 1901–1991. The celebration of a leader. *Hypertension* 1991;18:443–445.

64. Frohlich ED. Uric acid: a risk factor for coronary heart disease. *JAMA* 1993;270:378–379.

101. Frohlich ED. In memoriam: Harriet Pearson Dustan. *Hypertension* 1999;34:162–163.

114. Frohlich ED. In memoriam: Janice M. Pfeffer, PhD. *Hypertension* 2000;36:1.

127. Frohlich ED. Treating hypertension—what are we to believe? *N Engl J Med* 2003;348:639–641.

VALENTIN FUSTER, MD, PhD:
A Conversation With the Editor*

Dr. Valentin Fuster is Director of The Zena and Michael A. Wiener Cardiovascular Institute, Mount Sinai Medical Center; Richard Gorlin, MD, Professor of Cardiology; Vice-Chairman of Medicine, and Dean for Academic Affairs, Mount Sinai School of Medicine, in New York City. He was born in Barcelona, Spain, in 1943. His grandfathers and father were physicians, as is one of his brothers. He received his MD degree, first in his class, in 1967 from Barcelona University and after a straight medical internship at the university, moved to Edinburgh, Scotland, where he was a research fellow in cardiovascular diseases for 3 years. During this period, he received a PhD degree. In 1971 he moved to Rochester, Minnesota, and the Mayo Clinic, where he remained for 10 years, rising to the rank of Professor of Medicine at age 39. Then, he went to New York City as Chief of Cardiology at Mount Sinai School of Medicine for another 10 years. In 1991, he moved to Boston as Chief of Cardiology at the Massachusetts General Hospital; he returned to New York 3 years later to assume his present positions. His investigations, which have led to over 700 publications, have focused primarily on the roles of platelets and various clotting factors in producing atherosclerotic plaques. He was one of the first to appreciate the role of plaque disruption in the development of some acute coronary syndromes and to identify the elements leading to plaque rupture and the thrombogenic components of plaques. For his work he has received 7 honorary doctorate degrees, several outstanding research and teacher awards, and several major national leadership posts, including last year's presidency of the American Heart Association. He is a major figure in world cardiology, a wise human being, an outstanding teacher, an ideal mentor, and an extremely nice and good guy.

William Clifford Roberts, MD[†] **(Hereafter, WCR):** *I am speaking with Dr. Valentin Fuster in my office at Baylor University Medical Center (BUMC) on November 30, 1999. Dr. Fuster has just given a splendid lecture (8 to 9 A.M.) at Medical Grand Rounds here at BUMC and at 12:00 noon he will speak to the medical house staff on what lies ahead of them in the future. His visit to BUMC was made possible by an unrestricted grant from Bristol Myers Squibb. Dr. Fuster, could you discuss your growing up period, describe your mother and father, your siblings, and what it was like in Barcelona during the 1940s and 1950s?*

*This series of interviews are underwritten by an unrestricted grant from Bristol-Myers Squibb.

[†]Baylor Cardiovascular Institute, Baylor University Medical Center, Dallas, Texas 74246.

[‡]The Zena and Michael A. Wiener Cardiovascular Institute, Mt. Sinai Medical Center, New York, New York 10029.

Valentin Fuster, MD, PhD[‡] **(Hereafter, VF):** I was born in Barcelona in the region of Catalonia, Spain. In those years, the dictatorship of the Franco regime had a significant negative impact on the intellectual life of the country. In Catalonia, where the Catalan language is spoken, textbooks in the Catalan language were not allowed at the University. In medical school there was a significant clash between the dictatorship and the left-wing parties, particularly the Communist party; this clash was very tangible across the University campuses. Indeed, over the years many intellectual dissidents had to leave the country.

My father was a Physician and Professor of Psychiatry at the University of Barcelona. His practice was very focused on young people who were psychiatrically ill. It was an interesting combination: my father, a devoted student and devoted to the young people, and my mother, a completely optimistic, very positive person. Such a combination had a very positive influence on me. Another positive influence was my maternal grandfather, who had been the President of the University of Barcelona. He was a man absolutely dedicated to others. He was instrumental in the development of public school in rural areas, and he worked to make schools affordable to everybody. He also was a Professor of Therapeutics at the Medical School of Barcelona.

I attended Jesuit school for 9 years, but I was not completely happy there because their system was very strict. Nevertheless, the Jesuits gave me the methods and tools of how to approach any project. They were absolutely superb in the method of teaching. In retrospect, I feel that I was privileged to be educated in the Jesuit system. Intellectually, it was quite rewarding.

WCR: *How many brothers and sisters do you have?*

VF: Four.

WCR: *And where are you in the hierarchy?*

VF: I am the youngest. Thirteen years separated the oldest from the youngest (me). My oldest brother is a neuroscientist at UCLA; the second and third are economists; the fourth, my sister, is an administrator in a hospital.

WCR: *So there are 4 boys and 1 girl? I gather at that time your biggest meal was at 2:00 or 2:30 in the afternoon? What was life like growing up in your family?*

VF: I was very lucky. I grew after the Spanish Civil War and the Second World War had ended. I remember those growing up years very fondly. Our home was an attractive intellectual setting very critical of the Franco regime. After Franco died, Spain had an incredible miracle during the transition from a dictatorship to a democracy. Two factors were critical: (1) my generation had learned from the previous generation about the devastation of the civil war and the tragedy of human suffering. (2) The King of Spain took over

FIGURE 1. VF *(left)* with his family, his son Pablo, daughter Silvia, and wife, Maria, at the Cardona home in Catalonia, Spain, in 1981.

FIGURE 2. VF with former Secretary General of the UN Javier Perez de Cuellar, during the Investiture as Honoris Causa of the University of Valladolid (Spain) in 1998.

as a symbol after Franco had died and pulled together all the parties and established a dialogue. These 2 reasons explain why Spain had a smooth transition, and, eventually, an excellent economy.

WCR: *What years did the civil war occur?*

VF: 1936 to 1939. It was a very bloody war. Franco evolved triumphantly and moved Spain to a strict dictatorship, which had significant consequences intellectually. As I said, a large number of people from that generation—such as professors of universities—had to leave the country. They went to South America and to other European countries. When Franco died, many of these intellectuals (musicians, painters, artists, and so forth) from that generation came back.

WCR: *Your grandfather was President of the University of Barcelona during that war period?*

VF: No, before the war. My grandfather was not only the President of the University of Barcelona, but he was instrumental in developing the first University Hospital in Barcelona, which is called the Hospital Clinico. My grandfather had the philosophy that if you were lucky and had a certain talent you could transmit that in one way or another to a next generation. He had a major impact on me. Indeed, when I look at myself, what I really enjoy doing, what particularly excites me, is dealing with the young people, and trying to transmit something I learned.

WCR: *I gather you saw a lot of him growing up?*

VF: No, I didn't. But whether in the University or Medical School, I perceived some of his influence. It was then that I became interested in him and wrote his biography. Research for my book was where I learned about my grandfather.

WCR: *When did he die?*

VF: In 1923.

WCR: *So you never knew him at all? You never met him?*

VF: Correct. I never met him.

WCR: *But he was a hero to you?*

VF: Yes, he was.

WCR: *What about your father? Did he have a lot of impact on you?*

VF: Yes, he had influence in one aspect. As a psychiatrist he gave me absolute freedom. He gave his children the possibility of developing themselves. I sensed in him an incredible degree of respect for the development of a young person. I think that's why he was so successful as a psychiatrist of young people.

WCR: *What kind of influence did your mother have on you? What kind of person was she?*

VF: A very significant influence. My mother transmitted to us something that is quite important. She always saw the glass as "half full" rather than "half empty." My mother transmitted to us a high degree of positive thinking. To grow up in that environment was extremely exciting. The trust provided by our father regarding respect for our freedom, and then the degree of optimism of our mother, created a wonderful environment to grow up in.

WCR: *I gather your house growing up was an intellectual environment?*

VF: It was in many respects. The intellectual part actually came from my father. My father was a self-made individual. When he moved from legal medicine to psychiatry he went to Austria to study and then to Germany. He met with 2 gurus in psychiatry—Freud and Jung. Their 2 completely different philosophies had a significant impact on him in intellectual development. Indeed, what he transmitted to us was the sense of balance. He was not a dogmatic person in any way. He was very hard working. He was interested in history. He wrote a book on the history of psychiatry in Europe and he traveled to many libraries in Europe. I recall my father always writing at night.

WCR: *Both your father and grandfather (your mother's father) wrote a lot?*

FIGURE 3. VF with Dr. Richard Gorlin (left) and Dr. Randall Griepp (right) in 1996.

FIGURE 4. VF with his mother, father, and siblings at their home in Barcelona, Spain, in 1980.

VF: Yes. My grandfather wrote hundreds of documents about education, about the need to pay attention to young people. He believed that all citizens should have access to education. He was an advocate for education. My grandfather believed that the future of the country was dependent on education.

WCR: *What about your father's father?*

VF: My father's father was a very successful, charismatic, kind, down-to-earth general physician on the Spanish island of Majorca and later in Barcelona.

WCR: *So both of your grandfathers and your father were physicians? Were there other physicians in your family?*

VF: Yes. A brother of my mother was also a physician.

WCR: *Were there lots of books around your house growing up?*

VF: Yes. Full of books. As I said, my father was interested in history, particularly of the 18th and 19th century. He had a group of intellectual friends in Barcelona and they often met in our home for their "discussions."

WCR: *When you were in school before the university, I gather that you left home relatively early in the morning, but you came home for the feast at 2:30 P.M. or so? All of the family would be there?*

VF: Absolutely. This was the main meal of the day; it was at 2:30 P.M. We would return to the school at 4:30 P.M. and then leave school again at 7:30 P.M.

WCR: *What was that feast like? Did you all have debates and discussions around the table?*

VF: You have to understand the environment. My father had a Residential Psychiatric Clinic, which was under the administrative supervision of my mother. The conversations quite often focused on problems in the clinic. I was brought to understand the medical and the administrative environments by the conversations of my father and mother.

WCR: *What was your mother's background? Did she finish the University?*

VF: My mother completed high school and attended a finishing school. In Spain it was quite unusual in those years for women to go to the university. Today, it is different.

WCR: *Was there enough money that you did not need to worry about it when you were growing up?*

VF: I don't think so. Tennis was what I loved the most. I could only have 1 racquet at a time. I could not have 2 or 3 racquets simultaneously like my other teammates. My father gave us an incredible degree of freedom, but he was very strict in the financial area. I never had the sense of a life that was very easy. I did not see a lot of affluence. Our lives, however, were comfortable.

WCR: *When you were born in January 1943, how many people lived in Spain?*

VF: Probably 36 million.

WCR: *How many lived in Barcelona in 1943?*

VF: About 1 million people. Now it is 3 million.

WCR: *Did you walk to school?*

VF: Yes, I walked. It was half a mile from home to the school.

WCR: *Was the house of adequate size for your family? Did you have your own bedroom growing up?*

VF: Yes. Our house was really nice, located in Pedralbes, one of the nicest districts of Barcelona. It was a very attractive area to live in.

WCR: *You mentioned you played tennis and were a tennis champion?*

VF: We had a tennis court near our house. I always loved sports. I began to play tennis at age 8. At first I played on my own, but I later got into a tournament

FIGURE 5. VF with Dr. Dwight C. McGoon *(left)* and Dr. Richard Gorlin *(right)* during his investiture as endowed Professor at Mount Sinai Medical School in 1982.

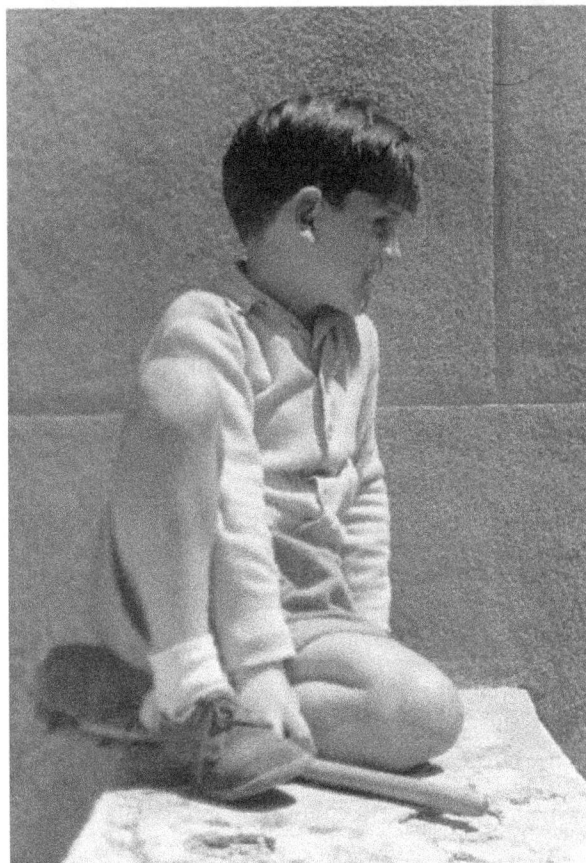

FIGURE 6. VF at age 5.

and did well. Then I was recruited by a larger club in Barcelona, and continued to do well. I was later recruited by the Barcelona Tennis Club, a club played in by the best tennis players in Spain. This was not very

far from our home. I began to play tennis vigorously and I was in the highest rank for my age. It was very exciting traveling and playing in tournaments. I began to think about the possibility of dedicating myself to tennis. I was selected for the Junior Spanish team. I was selected to play the Orange Bowl, which is like the equivalent of the Davis Cup for junior players (ages 16 to 18). At that time I went on vacation to Germany for a few weeks in the summer. When I came back the captain of the team said, "You are part of the Spanish team, but we think you should play a tournament with the others as they have been working very hard here; you will not have a problem." But I lost. I had played 4 hours a day for a few years—before school, after school. It was on that particular occasion of disappointment that I thought about the decision of whether or not I should quit. I decided to quit completely.

I then asked myself what would I do with the time? I was very attracted to nature, probably because of the area where I lived which was in the outskirts of Barcelona. I considered the possibility of studying agriculture, but the environment at home was medical and it was hard to escape the possibility of making a career decision in medicine. I told my father, "I am quitting tennis and I decided to study medicine." My father said to me, "If you study medicine, you have to be at the very top." A thousand people used to enroll at Barcelona Medical School, and only 150 passed the first year. In high school I had not been a good student, but my father's message was clear. I decided to focus and put 100% effort into my studies. I entered medicine full speed, working very hard, and I did well. In medical school I had a wonderful mentor. He was a tennis fan, perhaps considered the best physician in Spain; a general internist who wrote a standard textbook of Medicine for the Spanish-speaking countries. His name was *Pedro Farreras*. He said to me "To be a good physician you have to know the basics." The basics at that time were pathology. So I began every summer going to a different lab in England to learn pathology.

WCR: *This is while you were in medical school?*

VF: Yes. What was interesting was why I became a cardiologist. It is because Pedro Farreras, my mentor, had an acute myocardial infarction at age 45. He said, "I feel confident about my knowledge in most of the subspecialties, except cardiology. You should be a cardiologist." I agreed and that's how I became a cardiologist—because of his myocardial infarction.

Going back to tennis. I was working in Liverpool with *Professor Harold Sheehan*, a great pathologist (the Sheehan's syndrome). I was a third-year medical student. I recall the members of the staff being somewhat surprised about a medical student spending 2 months just looking at pathology specimens. I felt

FIGURE 7. Barcelona 1992. VF receiving the 1992 Andreas Grietnzig Scientific Award from the European Congress of Cardiology. His mother (age 89, present age 96) received a bouquet of flowers from the organizing committee.

Then I played tennis, and eventually bicycle riding. I always did something rather vigorously and enjoyed it.

WCR: *When did you take up cycling?*

VF: One of my brothers encouraged the cycling. I particularly enjoyed mountain biking, particularly in the summer. But I never took it seriously until about 7 or 8 years ago, when I decided cycling could combine my love of nature and my love of sports. I decided to go for the hardest, which was the Pyrenées or the Alps, a stage of the Tour de France. I have now done the Tourmalet 3 times. The Tourmalet is probably the most difficult mountain in Europe that you can do by cycling. Last year, I did it together with the Aubisque and the Aspen. These are 3 mountains that constitute 1 of the most difficult stages of the Tour de France. The problem I face is that I don't have much time to prepare myself every summer. I begin to train a couple of months before we go to Spain for 3 weeks. During those 3 weeks, I do about 50 miles a day training; it's lonely, but very, very exciting. Then, the last day, is the day of the "big ride" in the Pyrenées or the Alps.

WCR: *How high is the altitude that you have to cycle up to in the Tourmalet?*

VF: We are talking more than 7,000 feet at a 7% to 10% incline.

WCR: *How long does it take you to do it?*

VF: Usually, to do the 3 mountains nonstop, it takes about 7 or 8 hours. Many of my friends don't understand how I can do it. It is a matter of confidence. When you feel that you are getting exhausted, slowing for a few minutes usually restores confidence again. Our brain has incredible power to allow us to perform physically as well as mentally. The power to really "carry on" is a matter of confidence. Indeed, such experience with bicycling has served me in my professional career.

WCR: *It sounds like you have always been active. Have you always slept relatively a small amount?*

VF: I slept little from a very young age, even in my teens. It has less to do with the requirements of work or the need to accomplish things, than with one's own constitution. I sleep no more than 4 to 5 hours a day. Maybe what is happening to me is that I am constantly active mentally. For me to find 10 minutes when I have nothing to do is rare and these 10 minutes are very precious. I am constantly active. I am constantly excited about things—things that can be done, things that should be done, etc.

WCR: *How did your mother instill that sense of responsibility in you?*

VF: It came from both my mother and my father.

WCR: *What are some examples of that?*

VF: They told me "You always have to give, you should never expect to receive." "The world is full of injustice and if you are lucky you have an obligation to do something for others." This was constantly en-

lonely in the sense that there was no connection to the people around me. They there were not used to a young guy doing that. Coincidentally, a tennis tournament was organized among all the members of the Institute of Pathology. I thought this was my opportunity. I had quit tennis 3 years before, but I got a racquet and I beat everyone 6 to 0, 6 to 0. So when I finished, I became like some kind of a hero all of a sudden. In fact, Professor Sheehan called me and said he would like to work more closely with me and that he would be very happy to recommend me for any position I wanted in the United Kingdom. This is how he recommended me to go to the Royal Infirmary of Edinburgh and to work as a research fellow in the cardiology department with *Michael Oliver* and *Desmond Julian*. This recommendation would never have happened if I had not won that tournament. So tennis paid off, long term.

WCR: *You finished, what would be called in the USA, high school at age 18?*

VF: Yes.

WCR: *You entered the University of Barcelona immediately thereafter? You went directly into medical school from high school?*

VF: We had the so-called "pre-university year." When we finished high school we had a single year of pre-university. Then we went directly to medical school, 6 years of medical school.

WCR: *Did you have pay tuition to go to medical school?*

VF: Since it was a State run system, the tuition was low.

WCR: *When you were in high school, except for your last year, you didn't study too hard?*

VF: I was not a good student. I just enjoyed doing many other things.

WCR: *What sports did you play other than tennis?*

VF: Soccer. I was the captain of the soccer team when I studied with the Jesuits and I played very hard.

FIGURE 8. VF receiving the 1996 Principe de Asturias Award of Science and Technology, the highest award given to a Spanish-speaking scientist by the Prince of Spain.

forced in my upbringing. In a way I'm very ambitious, very hard working, but it is what I achieve that gives me the pleasure. It is not that I am going to be above somebody else. This doesn't give me pleasure at all. If I can do something that might be meaningful for somebody else, I put effort into it, and I feel satisfied. I was told of the importance of this attitude since a very young age. It has helped to have such "a very positive attitude" as my mother use to say.

WCR: *Valentin, your mother is still alive and 96 years old?*

VF: Yes. She is 96 and very active. She walks on the street every day.

WCR: *How old was your father when he died?*

VF: He was 85.

WCR: *He died in what year?*

VF: He died in 1985.

WCR: *Let me ask you about your medical school life. You mentioned that when you enrolled there were 1,000 medical students and after that first year the class size was cut down to 100?*

VF: I think it was 150 after 1 year and then 100 at graduation.

WCR: *I gather that you graduated number 1 in your class in medical school?*

VF: Yes.

WCR: *Did you enjoy medical school?*

VF: Yes, but I attended few lectures. I did it on my own. My mentor Pedro Farreras told me to get the best books available, to see patients, and to do research. This is what I did. By the time of the examinations, I had a global view, a combination of having read the best books that Dr. Farreras recommended for me (most were written in English, some in French), of

having dealt daily with patients, and also of having spent time in the Laboratory of Pathology research.

WCR: *You met Pedro Farreras before you started medical school?*

VF: Yes.

WCR: *He was also a tennis player. That's how you met him?*

VF: He played tennis very well. As I said before, we belonged to the same tennis club, and he decided to mentor me. He was an incredible mentor. I now constantly talk about mentorship to the young residents, fellows, and investigators. I regularly try to have meetings with the young physicians and scientists to encourage them to take advantage of mentorship. The problem with mentorship is that there are very few mentors who are able or willing to put effort into it.

I also had another mentor who was superb, *Desmond Julian*, in Edinburgh. Desmond was the pioneer of the coronary care units and I was his clinical fellow for 3 years. I was working there for my PhD thesis about platelet behavior, but I also saw patients with him. First, he told me how to examine a patient and how to use common sense in clinical judgment. Second, he showed me how to be humble. You cannot see patients and be dogmatic or arrogant. Desmond is a very talented person, and he is the one who actually encouraged me to come to the USA and spend some time here before going back to Spain. Another physician who was very valuable to my education was *Michael Oliver,* who gave me an insightful approach to methodology for clinical studies. I was lucky. I was well trained in pathology, I learned about thrombosis, and I had great teachers on the clinical side. When I moved to the Mayo Clinic, I was able to use all that

FIGURE 9. VF in 1997.

FIGURE 10. VF in 1998.

earlier training, from the more basic to the clinically applied. Mayo Clinic was ideal for me. I found it to be a very peaceful atmosphere, where I was able to expand investigationally and clinically.

WCR: *Let me go back for a moment to medical school. You rotated through the various services— medicine, surgery, gynecology, pediatrics, pathology, and psychiatry. You were obviously a good athlete. So many athletes go into surgery, it seems to me. Did you have an attraction for surgery, or was it easy for you to decide on medicine?*

VF: Intellectually, medicine was more attractive to me. The surgeons are quite able in "fixing" things rapidly. Somehow, I was always more attracted by a slower cognitive process of understanding pathogenesis and applying therapy. I have always been more attracted by the process that leads to somewhere than by just a decision to solve something quickly.

WCR: *After medical school you interned in medicine at the hospital connected to your medical school. Was that mandatory in Spain at the time?*

VF: Yes.

WCR: *Was that your sixth year?*

VF: No. Seventh. I had already been like a "volunteer" student intern for the previous 3 years. In other words, when I said to you that I didn't attend many lectures it was because I was working as a "volunteer"

student intern. After the 6 years of medical school, however, a formal internship of 1 year was mandatory.

WCR: *How did you decide to go to Edinburgh?*

VF: The decision was based on advice from my mentor. He told me "if you are going to do cardiology, you have 2 places to go—the National Heart Institute in London or The Royal Infirmary in Edinburgh." Bill, you might ask why not the USA. I thought the USA was very technologically advanced, and at that time I needed more of a solid foundation and the UK was able to provide that. I chose Edinburgh because my mentor said there I would be somebody who they would look after and who they would pay attention to. "If you go to a huge place like London, it will be more difficult for you to get the attention you need at your stage." Thus, I chose Edinburgh, and it was quite rewarding.

WCR: *When did you learn to speak English?*

VF: Do you think I'll ever learn?

WCR: *Yes.*

VF: The first language in Spain, of course, was Spanish, but the first foreign language we had to learn was French.

WCR: *That was in high school, early on?*

VF: Yes, we studied French for 5 years. I learned English by myself. I never had any formal teaching in English. When I was in medical school, some of the

FIGURE 11. VF and Pope John Paul II in Rome, Italy, in 1999.

FIGURE 12. VF climbing the Col de Tourmalet in France in August 1997.

FIGURE 13. Dinner of Past Presidents of the American Heart Association, New York, in 1999.

textbooks were in English, and reading them is how I learned English.

WCR: *When you went to Edinburgh were you surprised by the way medicine was practiced in Scotland?*

VF: I was impressed by the system, by the fact the patients had good, free, and rapid access to very good medicine. Nevertheless, I constantly heard complaints from physicians about how much the National Health Service was demanding from them and how poorly they were paid. Another complaint in UK was how difficult it was to have a position as a "Consultant." Otherwise, what I learned in the British system was that whether you were rich or poor, you were treated equally, and I believe, effectively. Later, I was lucky

to be part of a superb, integrated system at the Mayo Clinic. Thus, before I came to New York, Edinburgh provided me with the best educational research and clinical experience I ever had. At Mayo I had witnessed first-hand the best physician-patient integrated system anywhere.

WCR: *You got your PhD degree there?*

VF: Yes.

WCR: *What did you get that in?*

VF: I wrote the thesis on platelet factor 4. I developed technology for its identification as well as for assessment of platelet function. Specifically, I tried to evaluate whether circulating platelet factor 4 could identify patients who had a blood clot during acute myocardial infarction versus those who did not, a debate of that time.

FIGURE 14. VF and wife Maria in Edinburgh, Scotland in 1979.

FIGURE 17. VF at the Barcelona Tennis Club in 1958.

FIGURE 15. Mayo Clinic Cardiovascular Fellows—promotion in 1974.

FIGURE 18. Dr. Richard Gorlin and The Fuster's in 1988.

FIGURE 16. VF (second from left, bottom row) as captain of the soccer team (Jesuits), Barcelona, Spain, in 1955.

WCR: *Your PhD was actually awarded from University of Barcelona?*

VF: Yes, but the thesis was done at Edinburgh.

WCR: *Did you write any papers during medical school?*

VF: I wrote a biography of my grandfather, and a paper on language development. I was very interested

in the way children develop their cognitive and expressive aspects. I began writing medical papers after I was trained in Edinburgh.

WCR: *You became interested in thrombosis from the very beginning. How did that come about?*

VF: It came from a single event. Professor Sheehan was showing me a pathological slide when I was in Liverpool as a third-year medical student. I looked at the slide, not under the microscope, but against the light to see the overall picture. I saw a circle and inside was something red without structure. Under the microscope the red material still had no structure. He said, "Now is when you have to use electronmicroscopy." By electronmicroscopy, the material in the

FIGURE 19. Mount Sinai Cardiovascular Fellows with a few members of the staff—promotions in 1985.

slide was a platelet thrombus. The patient had died of coronary thrombosis. That day I became convinced that platelets were important in coronary thrombosis and coronary disease. That was in 1963 or 1964. That single slide led to my research career. That's why my thesis for the PhD was on platelets in myocardial infarction. This is how my interest in platelets, thrombosis, and, eventually atherosclerosis, developed.

WCR: *Pathology seemed to attract you early on?*

VF: Very much so. I think pathology at that time was probably what today would be molecular biology or genetics. It was so tangible. Pathology continues to be very attractive to me.

WCR: *Did you almost go into pathology, at least consider it?*

VF: Sure I did. In fact, I considered undertaking an investigational career. The heart attack of my mentor really led me to a different course. Harold Sheehan told me I should pursue investigational pathology and clinical cardiovascular medicine at the same time. This is why I always have been interested in the link between basic and experimental pathology with clinical cardiology. I have tried to pursue both in parallel.

WCR: *After your medical internship in Barcelona you went to Edinburgh and spent 3 years in cardiology?*

VF: Yes.

WCR: *Not only doing clinical work, but also research?*

VF: Research was about 75% of my time, while about 25% was clinical.

WCR: *How did you decide to go to the Mayo Clinic from there?*

VF: I wanted to spend some time in the USA to get a taste for US medicine. I was accepted by Gene Braunwald into his program in San Diego for 2 or 3 years of fellowship. But we then realized that I did not have a green card, which was necessary in order to work in California. A friend of mine from Spain was then being trained at the Mayo Clinic as a surgeon. He notified me that I could be considered for a fellowship at the Mayo Clinic without having a green card. I applied to Mayo Clinic, and they were extremely helpful. Harold Sheehan and Desmond Julian wrote letters of recommendation, and I was accepted. Although I was already trained or nearly so in cardiovascular diseases, I had to start all over again with an internship. I was allowed to do just 1 year in internal medicine and be eligible for the boards. I then had 2 full training years in cardiology.

WCR: *You went to the Mayo Clinic in 1971?*

VF: Yes.

WCR: *By 1974 they had asked you to stay on as a permanent staff member of the clinic?*

VF: Yes.

WCR: *It's my understanding that at least when you start there, you are seeing patients "x" number of segments a week?*

VF: Yes.

WCR: *Because you were doing so well in research, I gather you got progressively more time off from clinical duties?*

VF: Yes. The Chairman of Medicine at that time, *James Hunt*, a very strict person, said he would give me some time off from clinical duties for 1 year; after that only if I had obtained an NIH grant. I got an

American Heart Association (Minnesota) grant and also my first NIH grant. After the first year, I was a clinical consultant 60% of the time and 40% was devoted to research. *Robert Frye* at the Mayo Clinic became the Chairman of Cardiology. Bob taught me a lot of cardiovascular medicine. But, most importantly, he is one of the unique individuals I have seen in my career who was able to infuse significant confidence to the young students and physicians around him.

WCR: *For someone coming from warm Barcelona, the Mayo Clinic must have been quite a shock for you and your wife? How did that work out?*

VF: Yes. It was hard. The winters were hard for everybody. The Mayo, however, is a well-integrated system and a very "warm" environment. What you receive from the educational part overcomes all the difficulties of those winters.

WCR: *When did you get married?*

VF: The day before I left for Edinburgh, 31 years ago.

WCR: *Who is your wife?*

VF: My wife comes from a family in a small town near Barcelona. She studied nursing in Barcelona, sociology at the University of Minnesota, and eventually she did graduate work in medieval art history at Columbia University in New York.

WCR: *How did it come about that you were offered the position as Head of Cardiology at Mt. Sinai School of Medicine?*

VF: *Richard Gorlin* read my publications in the field of thrombosis. He was very intuitive. He knew that soon thrombosis was going to be a subject of paramount importance in the cardiovascular field. He gave me a call and said: "I want you to be head of cardiology at Mt. Sinai." My answer was negative since I was having a good time at Mayo. When I told my wife she said that my answer was too precipitous, since this would be a good opportunity for her to study art history in New York, which is what she wanted to do. Obviously, there are many reasons why one makes a move. My wife was very persuasive. Mt. Sinai Medical Center, with all the difficulties that I encountered when I arrived there, was a very human place. After a short while, I felt very supported. I was able to move forward and contribute to the development of a research and clinical environment that I feel very proud about. Richard Gorlin was a very loyal and strong supporter of my objectives. He was an advocate of academic excellence.

WCR: *Where did you move to in New York?*

VF: To Bronxville, a suburb of New York City. We had 2 children and we were concerned about their education. They went to an excellent public school.

WCR: *That commute was how long?*

VF: Thirty minutes each way.

WCR: *You were driving?*

VF: Yes. That gave me a chance to think and to listen to music. I didn't feel that that was a bad deal.

WCR: *You were at Mt. Sinai for 10 years? As you look back on those 10 years (1981 to 1991), what are you most proud of?*

VF: The integration of the academic full-time staff with the private attendings working there. My charge was to develop a strong full-time group, very academically oriented, and to preserve or even enhance the talents of the private physicians. The environment in cardiology at Mt. Sinai, then and now, has been extremely nice. We meet with the fellows almost daily for a teaching session in the morning. We have been very successful in obtaining NIH grants and fellowship funding. It is a very stimulating place to be right now.

WCR: *When you went there in 1981, how many cardiologists were on salary?*

VF: I would say probably 16 or 17. Now there are 36.

WCR: *And how many private cardiologists use the hospital?*

VF: About 40.

WCR: *So 40 in private practice and now 37 full time?*

VF: We are close to 40-40.

WCR: *Could you discuss a bit your 3-year sojourn to Boston, and how that came about and what you learned from it?*

VF: It was in the early 1990s when I had an offer to go to Spain, a very attractive offer that didn't crystallize. Then I was asked to be Head of Cardiology at the Massachusetts General Hospital. It was an attractive possibility. The job that was presented to me was to develop an academic enterprise. The Massachusetts General Hospital did not have any full-time cardiologists at that time. I had a good experience at Mt. Sinai in developing that. I took that offer as a challenge in an institution with a great reputation and associated with a top medical school. At the same time in New York I found myself very much pressed by patient care. Many patients demanding to be seen. I saw Boston as a good opportunity.

WCR: *You were getting a bit of burn out?*

VF: Yes, I was. That's really the fact. I thought Boston would be an opportunity to pursue my academic interests even more. It would be a great challenge. I was in Boston 3 years. My experience in Boston, in retrospect, was helpful and positive. What happened there is complex. Basically, I found a very incredibly talented group of people to work with. I'm talking about residents, fellows, and young investigators, very committed and very excited. But I also found that the support from the top for me to develop what I was told to develop was lacking. I ended up in a situation that was difficult because it was an expenditure of energy in trying to work in a system where you are not entirely sure you will be able to accomplish what you want. It would have been quite different if I had been supported as I had been told during my recruitment. That was not the case. When I decided to leave, it was painful. I probably made the most important and difficult decision of my life. Despite the nice position and the opportunities, and despite a strong support by the number of members of the staff, such as the outstanding *Dr. Roman DeSanctis*, I had an intuitive feeling. I thought I would be spending great part of my energy outside of my academic pursuits just trying to work on a system. What I wanted the system to be was not quite ready. Retrospectively, what I was advocating there is taking place now. I think I was a little bit too early. Modestly, I will say the system was not quite prepared for innovation.

WCR: *How did Mt. Sinai get you back?*

VF: They learned what was happening. *Dr. Jack Rowe*, CEO of Mt. Sinai, showed up in Boston and said, "You come to New York and we'll offer what you want." It was a kind of very supportive attitude. With him came *Randall Griepp* who was the Head of Cardiac Surgery at Mt. Sinai. I was offered to develop a Cardiovascular Institute, putting together all the clinical cardiovascular specialties, to develop strong basic and clinical research, and to report directly to the Dean and the CEO on most administrative, clinical, and research matters. The offer was very exciting because it gave me the opportunity to focus my energies into an academic purpose, and I took it. It helped that I was a known entity at Mt. Sinai, since I had been there previously for 10 years.

WCR: *What is a Cardiovascular Institute? Are you going to build the building, what does that mean?*

VF: We are all integrated. All the cardiovascular group—pediatrics, vascular surgery, cardiovascular surgery, cardiovascular radiology, adult cardiology, etc.—is all part of the Institute. For example, our present development of magnetic resonance imaging is not in conflict or in competition with the Department of Radiology since cardiovascular radiology is part of the Cardiovascular Institute. If cardiovascular radiology had been separated perhaps it might have been a problem. It is a new enterprise devoted to cardiovascular diseases. I meet once a week with the Head of Cardiothoracic Surgery, Randall Griepp, at 6:30 A.M. every Wednesday. We are all working together. I have seen the development of excitement among the staff, attendings, fellows, and investigators. Clinically, I have seen an increase in quality of care and an increase in effectiveness with shortening in the length of stay of the patients. The research is all integrated and federal funding is rapidly increasing. It is the modern way to do things. We have an outstanding Chairman of the Department of Medicine, *Barry Coller*, who is quite supportive. In fact, I serve as Vice-Chairman of Medicine and I report to Barry on matters that relate to educational programs and academic promotions.

WCR: *The residents in the Department of Medicine rotate through your service? And the vascular surgeons as well as the cardiovascular surgeons also?*

VF: Of course, the residents in Medicine rotate through Cardiology. We are now developing elective cross rotations with the cardiovascular surgeons and pediatric cardiologists. It takes a few years for this to evolve. It is just beginning.

WCR: *I believe I heard you indicate that you are going to build a separate building for the cardiovascular institute.*

VF: I am working on it now.

WCR: *Is that for research?*

VF: In part it will be for basic research, in part for experimental investigation, and in part for clinical trials and population studies. The administration of the medical school has approved such a large building, which will also entail other research activities. I am working very hard to bring it to fruition. It will be a mixed building, but the Cardiovascular Institute will occupy a part of it.

WCR: *Valentin, could you go through a typical day? I know you do a lot of different things, but what would a day for you be like? What time do you get up in the morning, get to the hospital, leave the hospital, and get back home?.*

VF: I wake up about 4:30 A.M.; I'm at the hospital at 5 A.M. From 5 to 7:45 A.M. I do my thinking, I work on academic matters, and I plan research projects. At 7:45 A.M. we have morning report where I meet with the fellows and medical staff. We discuss 2 clinical cases of interest until 8:30 A.M.. From 8:30 to 9:15 A.M. I see my hospitalized patients. From 9:15 A.M. to 7:30 P.M. can be divided into 3 parts (it changes from day to day in the week). One part involves research, another patients, and the third administration and meetings. I devote to research the hours early in the morning and then maybe 2 other hours a day in one way or another, such as meeting with our research group, meeting with or recruiting other people, analyzing data, etc. I have a very large load of patients, but I enjoy it. I try to see patients that have been referred by cardiologists if I can. I like complexity. I enjoy that. The rest is devoted to administration. I get home about 8:00 in the evening. We have dinner. From 9:00 to before midnight I work on something such as reading or editing my own movies.

WCR: *When do you show these movies? Who do you show them to?*

VF: Some friends come to my home and they want to see my latest movie, whether it is about themselves or about a particular city or occasion, such as the Olympic games in Barcelona. This weekend we will have old friends that we saw 20 years ago and then again 10 years ago. I had made movies of them, which I will edit without difficulty since I have sophisticated equipment and all movies are well classified and categorized.

WCR: *How did you get interested in movies?*

VF: I like the feeling of creating something on my own. Aside from making movies, sometimes I write poetry influenced by Rabindranath Tagore or philosophical assays— influenced by Teillard de Chardin. I enjoy every minute of what I do. I have many other interests—I love reading contemporary history such as Paul Kennedy's *Preparing for the Next Century*, and *Rise and Fall of the Great Powers* or Paul Johnson's *Modern Times* and *History of the Jews*.

WCR: *You now live in Manhattan, relatively close to the medical center, overlooking Central Park?*

VF: Pretty close.

WCR: *What do you and your wife do together?*

VF: For us there are 2 precious times. One is Saturday afternoon and the other is Sunday afternoon. On Saturday afternoons we go out, we visit a museum, have dinner somewhere in New York, and then we go to a movie or a play. This is something we both enjoy tremendously every week. On Sunday afternoon we spend the time at home. We review what went on during the week and also planning what is next. She's very active in the Foundation that we have established in her native town of Cardona, a medieval town near Barcelona. I try to be of some help in her town projects, which entail architectural preservation and cultural programs.

WCR: *What have you taken home from being President of the American Heart Association?*

VF: It has been a unique opportunity for creativity. First of all, the American Heart Association is a fabulous organization. I've never seen any organization with so many volunteers putting time, effort, devotion, and passion for a purpose. I'm talking about the volunteers at the level of the public, as well as physicians and scientists giving so much time. I am satisfied about what I tried to accomplish, and I hope I will see a continuation. I have worked very hard in trying to simplify the complexity of the organization and to enhance the role of the scientific councils, the root of the organization. I worked hard with other colleagues in trying to find ways to bring back young investigators to the American Heart Association. So, we are developing a "forum" for young investigators—Americans and non-Americans—where mentorship will be available. I have worked in trying to integrate the work of the American Heart Association with that of other organizations with similar purposes— Diabetes Societies, American College of Cardiology, European Society of Cardiology, NHLBI, CDC, etc. I have worked to establish of a way to enhance and simplify the health and science messages from the American Heart Association to the public. Finally, we are trying to enhance the international presence of the American Heart Association, particularly in developing countries.

WCR: *Your platter was already filled when you became President of the American Heart Association. How did you work that into your schedule?*

VF: It's method, prioritizing. If previously I had 1 day a week or about 52 days a year that I had to be out from the institution, during this year, I devoted most of these days to the American Heart Association. I was here in Dallas so many times! The commitment on weekends was the only negative part because it changed our lifestyle at home.

WCR: *What things have you accomplished that you are most proud of?*

VF: I am proud of the number of hours I have invested into teaching. From the research point of view, I am proud by the original contributions of our group to the understanding of the field of thrombosis and atherosclerosis, and perhaps to the development of the subspecialties "cardio-hematology" or "thrombo-cardiology." In addition, my original contributions to the understanding and natural history of dilated cardiomyocardiopathy and primary pulmonary hypertension perhaps went beyond to be "observational hobbies." The integration and environment created by the Cardiovascu-

lar Institute in New York is also important to me. Finally, I feel proud that, in spite of the commitments, I have continued to be a doctor. When I see a patient today, and I see many, I still feel the urge to know all the minutia. The higher the complexity of the case, the higher the "thrill" I experience, particularly if I am able to understand the problem and able to help.

From the point of view of the family we have 2 wonderful children. Both quite different. Our daughter is in the Graduate School of Design at Harvard, studying architecture. She's in the third year and is doing very well. Our son is a musician. He has been in Spain for 2 years and he's doing very well. I feel proud of both.

WCR: *What do you want to do in the future? What is your age now?*

VF: Fifty-six. Everything is now crystallizing. I want to see our research to succeed in a major way, and our young investigators. I'd like to see our Cardiovascular Institute to continue to progress towards a most attractive magnet for young people, towards an excellent integrated environment to work, and towards the highest quality and effective cardiovascular practice provided to all patients, regardless of their economical status. When I came back to New York about 5 years ago, I said to myself I needed 10 years to accomplish this dream. I hope it will come true.

WCR: *Valentin, you've been a delight to talk to. On behalf of not only me, of course, but the readers of* The American Journal of Cardiology, *thank you for pouring your soul out, so to speak, in such a free and open manner.*

VF: Thank you very much, Bill.

PLATELETS AND ANTITHROMBOTICS (EXPERIMENTAL)

5. Fuster V, Kazmier FJ, Cash JD, Bowie EJW, Owen CA Jr. Assay of platelet factor 4 in plasma. *Mayo Clinic Proc* 1973;48:103–106.
6. Fuster V. Platelet kinetics and effect of aspirin in chronically induced intravascular coagulation in dogs. *Thromb Diath Haemorrh 1974;60(suppl):371–376.*
8. Fuster V, Bowie EJW, Kazmier FJ, Owen CA Jr. Plasma platelet factor IV-like activity reflecting rate of platelet consumption in chronically induced intravascular coagulation in dogs. *Thromb Res* 1974;4:247–260.
14. Fuster V, Lewis JC, Kottke BA, Ruiz CE, Bowie EJW. Platelet factor 4-like activity in the initial stages of atherosclerosis in pigeons. *Thromb Res* 1977;10:169–172.
18. Didisheim P, Fuster V. The actions and clinical status of platelet suppressive agents. *Semin Hematol Today* 1978;15(i):55–72.
21. Linos A, Worthington JW, O'Fallon W, Fuster V, Whisnant JP, Kurland LT. Effect of aspirin on prevention of coronary and cerebrovascular disease in patients with rheumatoid arthritis. A long-term follow-up study. *Mayo Clin Proc* 1978;53(9):581–586.
33. Fuster V, Chesebro JH, Frye RL, Elveback LR. Platelet survival and the development of coronary artery disease in the young: the effects of cigarette smoking, strong family history, and medical therapy. *Circulation* 1981;63:546–551.
35. Fuster V, Chesebro JH. Current concepts of thrombogenesis. Role of platelets. *Mayo Clin Proc* 1981;56:102–112.
36. Fuster V, Chesebro JH. Pharmacologic effect of platelet inhibitor drugs. *Mayo Clin Proc* 1981;56:185–195.
37. Fuster V, Chesebro JH. Platelet-inhibitor drugs in management of arterial thromboembolic and atherosclerotic disease. Present recommendations. (Part III) *Mayo Clin Proc* 1981;56:265–273.
52. Chesebro JH, Clements IP, Fuster V, Elveback LR, Smith HC, Bardsley WT, Frye RL, Holmes DR Jr, Vlietstra RE, Pluth JR, Wallace RB, Puga FJ, Orszulak TA, Piehler JM, Schaff HV, Danielson GK. Platelet inhibitor drug trial in coronary artery bypass operation: benefit of perioperative dipyridamole and aspirin therapy on early postoperative vein graft patency. *N Engl J Med* 1982;307:73–78.
58. Chesebro JH, Fuster V. Platelet inhibitors in coronary artery bypass operations. *N Engl J Med* 1982;307(23):1453–1454.
69. Chesebro JH, Fuster V, Elveback LR, Clements IP, Smith HC, Holmes DR,

Bardsley WT, Pluth JR, Wallace RB, Puga FJ, Orszulak TA, Piehler JM, Danielson GK, Scchaff HV, Frye RL. Effect of dipyridamole and aspirin on late vein graft patency after coronary bypass operation. *N Engl J Med*1984;310:209–214.

94. Fuster V, Chesebro JH. Role of platelets and platelet inhibitors in aortocoronary artery vein graft disease. *Circulation* 1986;73(2):227–232.

137. Fuster V, Cohen M, Chesebro JH. Usefulness of aspirin for coronary artery disease. *Am J Cardiol* 1988;61:637–640.

160. Heras M, Chesebro JH, Penny WJ, Bailey KR, Badimon L, Fuster V. Effects of thrombin inhibition on the development of acute platelet-thrombus deposition during angioplasty in pigs. *Circulation* 1989;79:657–665.

162. Fuster V, Cohen M, Halperin JL. Aspirin in the prevention of coronary disease. *N Engl J Med* 1989;321:183–185.

167. Heras M, Chesebro JH, Webster M, Mruk J, Grill D, Badimon L, Fuster V. Prevention of thrombosis by recombinant hirudin during arterial angioplasty in pigs: comparison with heparin. *J Am Coll Cardiol*1989;13:77A.

168. Stein B, Fuster V, Halperin J, Chesebro JH. Antithrombotic therapy in cardiac disease: an emerging approach based on the pathogenesis and risk. *Circulation* 1989;80:1501–1513.

180. Stein B, Halperin JL, Fuster V. Prevention of left ventricular mural thrombosis and arterial embolism during and after acute myocardial infarction. *Coronary Artery Disease* 1990;1:180–189.

188. Heras M, Chesebro JH, Webster MWI, Mruk JS, Grill DE, Penyy WJ, Bowie EJW, Badimon L, Fuster V. Hirudin, heparin and placebo during deep arterial injury in the pig: the in vivo role of thrombin in platelet-mediated thrombosis. *Circulation* 1990;82:1476–1484.

244. Zoldhelyi P, Webster MWI, Fuster V, Grill DE, Gaspar D, Edwards SJ, Cabot CF, Chesebro JH. Recombinant hirudin in patients with chronic, stable coronary artery disease: safety, half-life, and effect on coagulation parameters. *Circulation* 1993;88(part 1):2015–2022.

269. Meyer BJ, Badimon JJ, Mailhac A, Fernandez-Ortiz A, Chesebro JH, Fuster V, Badimon L. Inhibition of growth of thrombus on fresh mural thrombus: targeting optimal therapy. *Circulation* 1994;90:2432–2438.

270. Meyer B, Fernandez-Ortiz A, Mailhac A, Falk E, Badimon L, Michael AD, Chesebro JH, Fuster V, Badimon JJ. Local delivery of r-hirudin by a double-balloon perfusion catheter prevents mural thrombosis and minimizes platelet deposition after angioplasty. *Circulation* 1994;90:2474–2480.

345. Vorchheimer DA, Fuster V. Oral platelet glycoprotein IIb/IIIa antagonists: the present challenge is safety. *Circulation* 1998;97:312–314.

349. Meyer BJ, Badimon JJ, Chesebro JH, Fallon JT, Fuster V, Badimon L. Dissolution of mural thrombus by specific thrombin inhibition with r-Hirudin. Comparison with heparin and aspirin. *Circulation* 1998;97:681–685.

357. Badimon JJ, Lettino M, Toschi V, Fuster V, Berrozpe M, Chesebro JH, Badimon L. Local inhibition of tissue factor reduces the thrombogenicity of disrupted human atherosclerotic under flow conditions. *Circulation*1999;99:1780–1787.

VASCULAR BIOLOGY

17. Fuster V, Bowie EJW, Lewis JC, Fass DN, Owen CA Jr, Brown AL. Resistance to arteriosclerosis in pigs with von Willebrand's disease: spontaneous and high cholesterol diet induced arteriosclerosis. *J Clin Invest* 1978;61:722–730.

19. Fuster V, Bowie EJW, Lewis JC. The von Willebrand pig as a model for atherosclerosis research. *Thromb Haemostas*1978;39:322–327.

51. Fuster V, Fass DN, Kaye MP, Josa M, Zinsmeister AR, Bowie EJW. Arteriosclerosis in normal and von Willebrand pigs: long-term prospective study and aortic transplantation study. *Circ Res*1982;51(v):587–593.

78. Fuster V, Lie JT, Badimon L, Rosemark JA, Badimon JJ, Bowie EJW. Spontaneous and diet induced coronary atherosclerosis in normal swine and swine with von Willebrand's disease. *Arteriosclerosis* 1985;5:67–73.

83. Steele PM, Chesebro JH, Stanson AW, Holmes DR Jr, Dewanjee MK, Badimon L, Fuster V. Balloon angioplasty: Natural history of the pathophysiologic response to injury in a pig model. *Circ Res* 1985;57(1):105–112.

88. Badimon L, Steele P, Badimon JJ, Bowie EJW, Fuster V. Aortic atherosclerosis in pigs with heterozygous von Willebrand's disease: comparison with homozygous von Willebrand and normal pigs. *Arteriosclerosis* 1985;5(4):366–370.

98. Badimon L, Badimon JJ, Galvez A, Chesebro JH, Fuster V. Influence of arterial damage and wall shear rate on platelet deposition. Ex vivo study in a swine model. *Arteriosclerosis* 1986;6(3):312–320.

105. Lam JYT, Chesebro JH, Steele PM, Dewanjee MK, Badimon L, Fuster V. Deep arterial injury during experimental angioplasty: relation to a positive Indium-111 labeled platelet scintigram, quantitative platelet deposition, and mural thrombosis. *J Am Coll Cardiol* 1986;8(6):1380–1386.

113. Fuster V, Griggs TR. Porcine von Willebrand's disease. Implications for the pathophysiology of atherosclerosis and thrombosis. *Prog Hemostas Thromb* 1986;159–183.

117. Lam JYT, Chesebro JH, Steele PM, Fuster V. Is vasospasm related to platelet deposition? Relationship in a porcine preparation of arterial injury in vivo. *Circulation*1987;75(1):243–248.

119. Rand JH, Badimon L, Gordon RE, Fuster V. Distribution of von Willebrand factor in porcine intima varies with blood vessel type and location. *Arteriosclerosis* 1987;7(3):287–291.

114. Badimon L, Badimon JJ, Rand R, Turitto VT, Fuster V. Platelet deposition

on von Willebrand factor deficient vessels: extracorporeal perfusion studies in von Willebrand's disease swine utilizing native and heparinized blood. *J Lab Clin Med* 1987;110:634–647.

145. Lam JYT, Chesebro JH, Fuster V. Platelets, vasoconstriction, and nitroglycerin during arterial wall injury: a new antithrombotic role for an old drug. *Circulation* 1988;78:712–716.

150. Badimon L, Badimon JJ, Turitto VT, Vallabhajosula S, Fuster V. Platelet thrombus formation on collagen type I: a model of deep vessel injury. Influence of blood rheology, von Willebrand factor and blood coagulation. *Circulation* 1988;78:1431–1442.

158. Badimon JJ, Badimon L, Galvez A, Dische R, Fuster V. High density lipoprotein plasma fractions inhibit aortic fatty streaks in cholesterol-fed rabbits. *Lab Invest*1989;60:455–461.

170. Badimon L, Badimon JJ, Turitto VT, Fuster V. Role of von Willebrand factor in mediating platelet-vessel wall interaction at low shear rate: the importance of perfusion conditions. *Blood* 1989;73:961–967.

175. Fuster V, Stein B, Badimon L, Badimon JJ, Ambrose JA, Chesebro JH. Atherosclerotic plaque rupture and thrombosis: evolving concepts. *Circulation* 1990;82(suppl II):47–59.

179. Badimon JJ, Badimon L, Fuster V. Regression of atherosclerotic lesions by high density lipoprotein plasma fraction in the cholesterol-fed rabbit. *J Clin Invest* 1990;85:1234–1241.

183. Ip JH, Fuster V, Badimon L, Cohen M, Badimon JJ, Chesebro JH. Syndromes of accelerated atherosclerosis: Role of vascular injury and smooth muscle cell proliferation. *J Am Coll Cardiol* 1990;15:1667–1687.

198. Badimon L, Badimon JJ, Lassila R, Heras M, Chesebro JH, Fuster V. Thrombin regulation of platelet interaction with damaged vessel wall and isolated collagen type I at arterial flow condition in a porcine model. Effects of hirudins, heparin and calcium chelation. *Blood* 1991;78:423–434.

200. Badimon JJ, Badimon L, Turitto VT, Fuster V. Platelet deposition at high shear rates is enhanced by high plasma cholesterol levels. Study in vivo in the rabbit model. *Arterioscle Thromb* 1991;11:395–402.

204. Fuster V, Badimon L, Badimon JJ, Ip JH, Chesebro JH. The porcine model for the understanding of thrombogenesis and atherogenesis. *Mayo Clin Proc* 1991;66:818–831.

218. Fuster V, Badimon L, Badimon JJ, Chesebro JH. Coronary artery disease: progression and acute coronary syndromes (Part 1). *N Engl J Med* 1992;326:242–250.

219. Fuster V, Badimon L, Badimon JJ, Chesebro JH. Coronary artery disease: progression and acute coronary syndromes (Part 2). *N Engl J Med* 1992;326:310–318.

262. Fernandez-Ortiz A, Meyer BJ, Mailhac A, Falk E, Badimon L, Fallon JT, Fuster V, Chesebro JH, Badimon JJ. A new approach for local intravascular drug delivery: iontophoretic balloon. *Circulation*1994;89:1518–1522.

264. Fernandez-Ortiz A, Badimon JJ, Falk E, Fuster V, Meyer B, Mailhac A, Weng D, Shah PK, Badimon L. Characterization of the relative thrombogenecity of atherosclerotic plaque components: Implications for consequences of plaque rupture. *J Am Coll Cardiol*1994;23:1562–1569.

265. Moreno PR, Falk E, Palacios IF, Newell JB, Fuster V, Fallon JT. Macrophage infiltration in acute coronary syndromes: implications for plaque rupture. *Circulation* 1994; 90:775–778.

267. Fuster V. Lewis A. Conner Memorial Lecture. Mechanisms leading to myocardial infarction insights from studies of vascular biology. *Circulation* 1994;90:2126–2146.

277. Falk E, Fallon JT, Mailhac A, Fernandez-Ortiz A, Meyer B, Weng D, Shah PK, Badimon JJ, Fuster V. Muramidase: a useful monocyte/macrophage immunocytochemical marker in swine of special interest in experimental cardiovascular disease. *Cardiovasc Pathol* 1994;3:183–189.

291. Stary HC, Chandler AB, Dinsmore RE, Fuster V, Glagov S, Insull W, Rosenfeld ME, Schwartz CJ, Wagner WD, Wissler RW. A definition of advanced types of atherosclerotic lesions and a histological classification of atherosclerosis: a report from the Committee on Vascular Lesions of the Council on Arteriosclerosis, American Heart Association. *Circulation*1995;92:1355–1374.

292. Falk E, Shah PK, Fuster V. Coronary plaque disruption. *Circulation* 1995; 92:657–671.

293. Falk E, Fuster V. Angina pectoris and disease progression. *Circulation*1995; 92:2033–2035.

298. Shah PK, Falk E, Badimon JJ, Fernandez-Ortiz A, Mailhac A, Villareal-Levy G, Fallon JT, Regnstrom J, Fuster V. Human monocyte-derived macrophages induce collagen breakdown in fibrous caps of atherosclerotic plaques: potential role of matrix-degrading metalloproteinases and implications for plaque rupture. *Circulation* 1995;92:1565–1571.

302. Fuster V, Falk E, Fallon JT, Badimon L, Chesebro JH, Badimon JJ. The three processes leading to post PTCA restenosis: dependence on the lesion substrate. *Thrombosis and Haemostasis* 1995;74:552–559.

309. Fuster V, Gotto AM, Libby P, Loscalzo J, McGill H. Task Force 1. Pathogenesis of coronary disease: the biologic role of risk factors. *J Am Coll Cardiol*1996;7:964–975.

315. Moreno PR, Bernardi VH, Lopez-Cuellar J, Murcia AM, Palacios IF, Gold HK, Mehran R, Sharma SK, Nemerson Y, Fuster V, Fallon JT. Macrophages, smooth muscle cells, and tissue factor in unstable angina. Implications for cell-mediated thrombogenicity in acute coronary syndromes. *Circulation* 1996; 94:3090–3097.

316. Moreno PR, Bernardi VH, Lopez-Cuellar J, Newell JB, McMellon C, Gold HK, Palacios IF, Fuster V, Fallon JT. Macrophage infiltration predicts restenosis after coronary intervention in patients with unstable angina. *Circulation* 1996; 94:3098–3102.

319. Toschi V, Gallo R, Lettino M, Fallon JT, Gertz SD, Fernandez-Ortiz A, Chesebro JH, Badimon L, Nemerson Y, Fuster V, Badimon JJ. Tissue factor modulates the thrombogenicity of human atherosclerotic plaques. *Circulation* 1997;95:594–599.

321. Fuster V, Fallon JT, Nemerson Y. Coronary thrombosis. *Lancet* 1996; 348(suppl I):S7–S10.

330. Fuster V, Fallon JT, Badimon JJ, Nemerson Y. The unstable atherosclerotic plaque: clinical significance and therapeutic intervention. *Thromb Haemostas* 1997;78(1):247–255.

346. Fuster V, Poon M, Willerson JT. Learning from the transgenic mouse: endothelium, adhesive molecules and neointimal formation. *Circulation* 1998; 97:16–18.

348. Gallo R, Padurean A, Toschi V, Bichler J, Fallon JT, Chesebro JH, Fuster V, Badimon JJ. Prolonged thrombin inhibition reduces restenosis after ballon angioplasty in porcine coronary arteries. *Circulation* 1998;97:581–588.

353. Badimon JJ, Fernandez-Ortiz A, Meyer B, Mailhac A, Fallon JT, Falk E, Badimon L, Chesebro JH, Fuster V. Different response to balloon angioplasty of carotid and coronary arteries: effects on acute platelet deposition and intimal thickening. *Atherosclerosis* 1998;140:307–314

355. Fuster V, Fayad ZA, Badimon JJ. Acute coronary syndromes: biology. *Lancet* 1999;353:SII5–SII9

356. Gallo R, Padurean A, Jayamaran T, Marx S, Roque M, Adelman S, Chesebro J, Fallon J, Fuster V, Marks A, Badimon JJ. Inhibition of intimal thickening after balloon angioplasty in porcine coronary arteries by targeting regulators of the cell cycle. *Circulation* 1999;99:2164–2170.

CORONARY DISEASE AND ANTITHROMBOTICS (CLINICAL)

9. Fuster V, Connolly DC, Frye RL, Danielson MA, Elveback LR, Kurland LT. Arteriographic patterns early in the onset of the coronary syndromes. *Br Heart J* 1975;37(12):1250–1255.

25. Fuster V, Frye RL, Kennedy MA, Connolly DC, Makin HT. The role of collateral circulation in the various coronary syndromes. *Circulation* 1979;59: 1137–1144.

40. Holmes DR Jr, Hartzler GO, Smith HC, Fuster V. Coronary artery thrombosis in patients with unstable angina. *Br Heart J* 1981;45:411–416.

80. Ambrose JA, Winters SL, Stern A, Eng A, Teichholz LE, Gorlin R, Fuster V. Angiographic morphology and the pathogenesis of unstable angina pectoris. *J Am Coll Cardiol* 1985;5(3):609–616.

82. Fuster V, Steele PM, Chesebro JH. Role of platelets and thrombosis in coronary atherosclerotic disese and sudden death. *J Am Coll Cardiol* 1985;5(6): 175B–184B.

89. Lapeyre AC III, Steele PM, Kazmier FJ, Chesebro JH, Vlietstra RE, Fuster V. Systemic embolism in chronic left ventricular aneurysm: incidence and the role of anticoagulation. *J Am Coll Cardiol* 1985;6:1233–1238.

91. Ambrose JA, Winters SL, Arora RR, Haft JI, Goldstein J, Rentrop KP, Gorlin R, Fuster V. Coronary angiographic morphology in myocardial infarction. A link between the pathogenesis of unstable angina and myocardial infarction. *J Am Coll Cardiol* 1985;6:1233–1238.

93. Ambrose JA, Winters SL, Arora RR, Eng A, Riccio A, Gorlin R, Fuster V. Angiographic evolution of coronary artery morphology in unstable angina. *J Am Coll Cardiol* 1986;7:472–478.

97. Meltzer RS, Teichholz LE, Visser CA, Fuster V. Intracardiac thrombi and systemic embolization: the role of two-dimensional echocardiography. *Ann Int Med* 1986;104:689–698.

112. Fuster V, Chesebro JH. Mechanisms of unstable angina. *N Engl J Med* 1986;315(16):1023–1025.

138. Fuster V, Badimon L, Cohen M, Ambrose J, Badimon JJ, Chesebro JH. Insights into the pathogenesis of acute ischemic syndromes. *Circulation* 1988; 77:1213–1220.

142. Ambrose JA, Monsen C, Borrico S, Gorlin R, Fuster V. Angiographic demonstration of a common link between unstable angina pectoris and non-Q wave acute myocardial infarction. *Am J Cardiol* 1988;61:244–247.

143. Ambrose JA, Tannenbaum M, Alexopoulos D, Hjemdahl-Monsen CE, Leavy J, Weiss M, Borrico S, Gorlin R, Fuster V. Angiographic progression of coronary artery disease and the development of myocardial infarction. *J Am Coll Cardiol* 1988;12:56–62.

181. Cohen M, Fuster V. Unstable angina: mechanisms and treatment. *Coron Artery Dis* 1990;1:166–169.

195. Cohen M, Adams PC, Hawkins L, Bach M, Fuster V. Usefulness of antithrombotic therapy in resting angina pectoris or non-Q-wave myocardial infarction in preventing death and myocardial infarction (A pilot study from the Antithrombotic Therapy in Acute Coronary Syndromes Group. *Am J Cardiol* 1990;66:1287–1292.

239. Ridker PM, Hebert PR, Fuster V, Hennekens CH. Are both aspirin and heparin justified as adjuncts to thrombolytic therapy for acute myocardial infarction? *The Lancet* 1993;341:1574–1577.

242. Fuster V. Coronary thrombolysis—a perspective for the practicing physician. *N Engl J Med* 1993;329:723–5.

246. Cohen M, Xiong J, Parry G, Adams PC, Chamberlain D, Wieczorek I, Fox KAA, McBride R, Chesebro JH, Fuster V. Prospectiv comparison of unstable

angina versus non-Q wave myocardial infarction during antithrombotic therapy. *J Am Coll Cardiol* 1993;22:1338–1343.

247. Fuster V, Dyken ML, Vokonas PS, Hennekens C. Aspirin as a therapeutic agent in cardiovascular disease. *Circulation* 1993;87:659–675.

258. Cohen M, Adams PC, Parry G, Xiong J, Chamberlain D, Wieczorek I, Fox KAA, Chesebro JH, Strain J, Keller C, Kelly A, Lancaster G, Ali J, Kronmal R, Fuster V. Combination antithrombotic therapy in unstable rest angina and non-Q-wave infarction in nonprior aspirin users: primary end points analysis from the ATACS trial. *Circulation* 1994;89:81–88.

259. Hirsh J, Fuster V. Guide to anticoagulant therapy. Part 1: Heparin. *Circulation* 1994;89:1449–1468.

260. Hirsh J, Fuster V. Guide to anticoagulant therapy. Part 2: Oral anticoagulants. *Circulation* 1994;89:1469–1480.

266. Schecter AD, Chesebro JH, Fuster V. Refractory Prinzmetal angina treated with cyproheptadine. *Ann Intern Med* 1994;121:113–114.

272. Goodman SG, Langer A, Durica SS, Raskob GE, Comp PC, Gray RJ, Hall JH, Kelley P, Hua TA, Lee RJ, Fuster V, for the Coumadin Aspirin Reinfarction (CARS) Pilot Study Group. Safety and anticoagulation effect of a low-dose combination of warfarin and aspirin in clinically stable coronary artery disease. *Am J Cardiol* 1994;74:657–661.

278. Cohen M, Parry G, Adams PC, Xiong J, Chamberlain D, Wieczorek I, Fox KAA, Kronmal R, Fuster V, and the Antithrombotic Therapy in Acute Coronary Syndromes Research Group. Prospective evaluation of a prostacyclin-sparing aspirin formulation and heparin/warfarin in aspirin users with unstable angina or non-Q wave myocardial infarction at rest. *Eur Heart J* 1994;15:1196–1203.

284. Braunwald E, Jones RH, Mark DB, Brown J, Brown L, Cheitlin MD, Concannon CA, Cowan M, Edwards C, Fuster V, Goldman L, Green LA, Grines CL, Lytle BW, McCauley KM, Mushlin AI, Rose GC, Smith EE, Swain JA, Topol EJ, Willerson JT. Diagnosing and managing unstable angina. *Circulation* 1994;90:613–622.

300. Cairns JA, Fuster V, Gore J, Kennedy JW. Coronary thrombolysis. *Chest* 1995;108(suppl.):401S–423S.

301. Hirsh J, Dalen JE, Fuster V, Harker L, Patrono C, Roth GJ. Aspirin and other platelet-active drugs: the relationship between dose, effectiveness, and side effects. *Chest* 1995;108(suppl.):247S.

308. Fuster V, Pearson TA (Co-Chairs). 27th Bethesda Conference: matching the intensity of risk factor management with the hazard for coronary disease events. *J Am Coll Cardiol* 1996;27:957–1047.

310. Pearson TA, Fuster V. Executive Summary. 27th Bethesda Conference: matching the intensity of risk factor management with the hazard for coronary disease events. *J Am Coll Cardiol* 1996;27(5):961–963.

318. Cohen M, Adams PC, McBride R, Fuster V, the Antithrombotic Therapy in Acute Coronary Syndromes Research Group. Prospective comparison of patient characteristics and outcome of non-prior aspirin users versus aspirin users with unstable angina or non-Q-wave myocardial infarction treated with combination antithrombotic therapy. *J Thromb Thrombol* 1997;4:275–280.

333. Mehta D, Curwin J, Gomes JA, Fuster V. Sudden death in coronary disease: acute ischemia versus myocardial substrate. *Circulation* 1997;96:3215–3223.

336. Hennekens CH, Dyken ML, Fuster V. Aspirin as a therapeutic agent in cardiovascular disease. A statement for healthcare professionals from the American Heart Association Writing Group. *Circulation* 1997;96:2751–2753.

346. Fuster V (principal investigator). Coumadin Aspirin Reinfarction Study. Randomized double blind trial of fixed low dose warfarin with aspirin after acute myocardial infarction. *Lancet* 1997;350:389–394.

347. Theroux P, Fuster V. Acute coronary syndromes: unstable angina and non-Q-wave myocardial infarction. *Circulation* 1998;97:1195–1206.

354. Cairns JA, Kennedy JW, Fuster V. Coronary thrombolysis. *Chest* 1998; 634S–657S.

358. Vorchheimer DA, Badimon JJ, Fuster V. Platelet glycoprotein IIb/IIIa receptor antagonists in cardiovascular disease. *JAMA* 1999;281:1407–1414

360. Grundy SM, Pasternack R, Greenland P, Smith S, Fuster V. Assessment of cardiovascular risk by use of multiple-risk-factor assessment equations: a statement for healthcare professionals from the American Heart Association and the American College of Cardiology. *Circulation* 1999;100:1481–1492.

361. Langer A, Fisher M, Claiff RM, Goodman S, O'Connor CM, Harrington RA, Fuster V. Higher rates of coronary angiography and revascularization following myocardial infarction may be associated with greater survival in the United States than in Canada. *Can J Cardiol* 1999;15:1095–1102.

IMAGING ATHEROSCLEROSIS—THROMBOSIS

27. Fuster V, Dewanjee NK, Kaye MP, Josa M, Metke MP, Chesebro JH. Noninvasive radioisotopic technique for detection of platelet deposition in coronary artery bypass grafts in dogs and its reduction with platelet inhibitors. *Circulation* 1979;60:1508–1512.

61. Pumphrey CW, Chesebro JH, Dewanjee MK, Wahner HW, Hollier LJ, Pairolero PC, Fuster V. In vivo quantitation of platelet deposition on human peripheral arterial bypass grafts using Indium-111-labeled platelets: effect of dipyridamole and aspirin. *Am J Cardiol* 1983;51:796–801.

64. Badimon L, Fuster V, Chesebro JH, Dewanjee MK. New "ex vivo" radio-isotopic method of quantitation of platelet deposition: studies in four animal species. *Thromb Haemost* 1983;50(3):639–644.

67. Wahner HW, Dunn WL, Dewanjee MK, Fuster V. Survival time and organ distribution of 111In-Oxine-labeled human platelets in normal subjects. *Nucl Med Biol* 1983;1:918– 921.

129. Badimon L, Turitto V, Rosemark JA, Badimon JJ, Fuster V. Characterization of a tubular flow chamber for studying platelet interaction with biologial and prosthetic materials. Deposition of 111Indium-labeled platelets on collagen, subendothelium, and expanded polyterafluoroethylene. *J Lab Clin Med* 1987;110: 706–718.

141. Vallabhajosula S, Paidi M, Badimon JJ, Le NA, Goldsmith SJ, Fuster V, Ginsberg HN. Radiotracers for low density lipoprotein biodistribution studies in vivo: technetium- 99m low density lipoprotein versus radioiodinated low density lipoprotein preparations. *J Nucl Med* 1988;29:1237–1245.

148. Weinberger J, Ramos L, Ambrose JA, Fuster V. Morphologic and dynamic changes of atherosclerotic plaque at the carotid artery bifurcation: sequential imaging by real time B-mode ultrasonography. *J Am Coll Cardiol* 1988;12:1515–1521.

282. Toussaint J-F, Southern JF, Fuster V, Kantor HL. 13C-NMR spectroscopy of human atherosclerotic lesions: relation between fatty acid saturation, cholesteryl ester content, and luminal obstruction. *Arterioscler Thromb* 1994;14:1951–1957.

296. Toussaint J-F, Southern JF, Fuster V, Kantor HL. T2-weighted contrast for NMR characterization of human atherosclerosis. *Arterioscler Thromb Vasc Biol* 1995;15:1533–1542.

306. Toussaint JF, LaMuraglia GM, Southern JF, Fuster V, Kantor HL. Magnetic resonance images lipid, fibrous, calcified, hemorrhagic, and thrombotic components of human atherosclerosis in vivo. *Circulation*1996;94:932–938.

313. Wexler L, Brundage B, Crouse J, Detrano R, Fuster V, Maddahi J, Rumberger J, Stanford W, White R, Taubert K. Coronary artery calcification: pathophysiology, epidemiology, imaging methods and clinical implications. *Circulation* 1996;94:1175–1192.

329. Toussaint JF, Southern JF, Fuster V, Kantor HL. Water diffusion properties of human atherosclerosis and thrombosis measured by pulse field gradient nuclear magnetic resonance. *Arterioscler Thromb Vasc Biol* 1997;17:542–546.

338. Vallabhajosula S, Fuster V. Atherosclerosis: imaging techniques and the evolving role of nuclear medicine. *J Nucl Med* 1997;38:1788–1796.

343. Toussaint J-F, Southern JF, Kantor HL, Jang I-K, Fuster V. Behavior of atherosclerotic plaque components after in vitro angioplasty and atherectomy studied by high field MR imaging. *Magn Reson Imag* 1998;16(2):175–183.

351. Fayad Z, Fallon JT, Shinnar M, Dansky HM, Poon M, Badimon JJ, Charlton SA, Fisher EA, Breslow JL, Fuster V. Noninvasive in vivo high resolution magnetic resonance imaging of atherosclerotic lesions in genetically-engineered mice. *Circulation*1998;98: 1541–1547.

367. Worthley SG, Heft G, Fuster V, Zaman AG, Fayad ZA, Fallon JT, Badimon JJ. Serial in vivo magnetic resonance imaging documents arterial remodeling in experimental atherosclerosis. *Circulation* 2000;101:586–589.

370. Fayad ZA, Nahar T, Fallon JT, Goldman M, Aguinaldo JG, Badimon JJ, Shinnar M, Chesebro JH, Fuster V. In vivo MR evaluation of atherosclerotic plaques in the humanthoracic aorta: a comparison with TEE. Circulation. 2000 (in press).

371. Fayad ZA. Fuster V, Fallon JT, Jayasundera T, Worthley SG, Helft GMD, Aguinaldo JG, Badimon JJ, Sharma S. Noninvasive in vivo human coronary artery lumen and wall imaging using black blood magnetic resonance. *Circulation* 2000 (in press).

376. Shinnar M, Fallon JT, Wehrli S, Levin M, Dalmacy D, Fayad ZA, Badimon JJ, Harrington M, Harrington E, Fuster V. The diagnostic accuracy of ex vivo magnetic resonance imaging for human atherosclerotic plaque characterization. *Arterioscler Thromb Vasc Biol.* 1999;19:2756–2761.

CARDIOMYOPATHY, PULMONARY HYPERTENSION

39. Fuster V, Gersh BJ, Giuliani ER, Tajik AJ, Brandenburg RO, Frye RL. The natural history of idiopathic dilated cardiomyopathy. *Am J Cardiol* 1981;47:525–531.

75. Fuster V, Steel PM, Edwards WD, Gersh BI, McGoon MD, Frye RL. Primary pulmonary hypertension: natural history and the importance of thrombosis. *Circulation* 1984;70(4):580–587.

84. Cohen M, Horowitz SF, Machac J, Mindich BP, Fuster V. Response of the right ventricle to exercise in isolated mitral stenosis. *Am J Cardiol*1985;55:1054–1058.

92. Cohen M, Edwards WD, Fuster V. Regression in thromboembolic type of primary pulmonary hypertension during 2 1/2 years of antithrombotic therapy. *J Am Coll Cardiol* 1986;7:172–175.

120. Cohen M, Monsen C, Francis X, Sherman W, Ambrose JA, Teichholz LE, Fuster V. Comparison of single plane videodensitometry-based right ventricular ejection fraction in right and left anterior oblique views to biplane geometry-based right ventricular ejection fraction. *J Am Coll Cardiol*1987;10:150–155.

123. Steele PM, Fuster V, Cohen M, Ritter DG, McGoon DC. Isolated atrial septal defect with pulmonary vascular obstructive disease: long-term follow-up and prediction of outcome after surgical correction. *Circulation* 1987;76:1037–1042.

147. Cohen M, Charney R, Hershman R, Fuster V. Reversal of chronic ischemic myocardial dysfunction after transluminal coronary angioplasty. *J Am Coll Cardiol* 1988;12:1193–1198.

233. Merino A, Hauptman P, Badimon L, Badimon JJ, Cohen M, Fuster V, Goldman M. Echocardiographic "smoke" is produced by an interaction of erythrocytes and plasma proteins modulated by shear forces. *J Am Coll Cardiol* 1992;20:1661–1668.

236. Sugrue DD, Rodeheffer RJ, Codd MB, Ballard DJ, Fuster V, Gersh BJ. The clinical course of idiopathic dilated cardiomyopathy: a population-based study. *Ann Intern Med*1992;117:117–123.

271. Dec GW, Fuster V. Idiopathic dilated cardiomyopathy. *N Engl J Med* 1994;331:1564–1575.

325. Kushwaha SS, Fallon JT, Fuster V. Restrictive cardiomyopathy, *N Engl J Med* 1997;336:267–276.

VALVULAR AND CONGENITAL HEART DISEASE

12. Fuster V, Danielson MA, Robb RA, Broadbent JC, Brown AL. Quantitation of left ventricular myocardial fiber hypertrophy and of interstitial tissue in human hearts with pressure and volume overload. *Circulation* 1977;55:504–508.

31. Fuster V, McGoon DECC, Kennedy MA, Ritter DG, Kirklin JW. Long-term evaluation (12 to 22 years) of open heart surgery for Tetralogy of Fallot. *Am J Cardiol* 1980;46:635– 642.

45. Fuster V, Pumphrey CW, McGoon MD, Chesebro JH, Pluth JR, McGoon DC. Systemic thromboembolism in mitral and aortic Starr-Edwards prosthesis: a long-term follow-up (10–19 years). *Circulation* 1982;66(suppl. I):157–161.

48. Danielson GK, Fuster V. Surgical correction of Ebstein's anomaly. *Ann Surg* 1982;196:499–504.

62. Chesebro JH, Fuster V, Elveback LR, McGoon DC, Pluth JR, Puga FJ, Wallace RB, Danielson GK, Orszulak TA, Piehler JM, Schaff HV. Trial of combined warfarin plus dipyridamole or aspirin therapy in prosthetic heart valve replacement: danger of aspirin compared with dipyridamole. *Am J Cardiol* 1983;5:1537–1541.

70. McGoon MD, Fuster V, McGoon DC, Pumphrey CW, Pluth JR, Elveback LR. Aortic and mitral valve incompetence: long-term follow-up: 10–19 years of patients treated with the Starr-Edwards prosthesis. *J Am Coll Cardiol* 1984;3(4):930–938.

165. Cohen M, Fuster V, Steele PM, Driscoll D, McGoon DC. Coarctation of the aorta: long- term follow-up and prediction of outcome after surgical correction. *Circulation* 1989;80:840–845.

285. Heras M, Chesebro JH, Fuster V, Penny WJ, Grill DE, Bailey KR, Danielson GK, Orszulak TA, Pluth JR, Puga FJ, Schaff HV, Larsonkeller JJ. High risk of thromboemboli early after bioprosthetic cardiac valve replacement. *J Am Coll Cardiol* 1995;25:1111–1119.

307. Prystowsky EN, Benson DW, Fuster V, Hart RG, Kay GN, Myerburg RJ, Naccarelli GV, Wyse G. Special report: management of patients with atrial fibrillation: a report for health professionals from the Subcommittee on Electrocardiography and Electrophysiology, American Heart Association. *Circulation* 1996;93:1262–1277.

331. Lengyel M, Fuster V, Keltai M, Roudaut R, Schulte HD, Seward JB, Chesebro JH, Turpie AGG. Guidelines for the management of left-sided prosthetic valve thrombosis. A role for thrombolytic therapy. *J Am Coll Cardiol* 1997;30:1521–1526.

BOOKS—EDITOR

Fuster V, ed. Diseases of the Heart (Enfermedades de Corazon). En el libro: Medicina Interna Pro Farreras-Rozman, 7a Edicion Edit Marin, Barcelona, 1972; 250–402; 1978 (9th edition); 1982 (11th Edition).

Brandenburg RO, Fuster V, Giuliani ER, McGoon DC, eds. Cardiology: Fundamentals and Practice. St. Louis, MO: Year Book Medical Publishers, 1987;1–1986; 1991 (2nd edition).

Fuster V, Verstraete M, eds. Thrombosis in Cardiovascular Disorders. Philadelphia, PA: W.B Saunders Company, 1992;1–565.

Fuster V, Ross R, Topol EJ, eds. Atherosclerosis and Coronary Artery Disease. Philadelphia, PA: Lippincott-Raven, 1996;1285–1297.

Fuster V, ed. Syndromes of Atherosclerosis. Correlations of Clinical Imaging and Pathology. Armonk, NY: Futura Publishing, 1996;1–558.

Fuster V, Alexander RW, O'Rourke, eds. Hurst's the Heart. 10th Edition. New York: McGraw Hill, in press.

Fuster V, ed. The vulnerable atherosclerotic plaque: understanding, identification and modification. American Heart Association Monograph Series, 1998.

Vestraete M, Fuster V, Topol EJ, eds. Cardiovascular Thrombosis. Philadelphia, PA: Lippincott-Raven 1998, 1–871.

Nash IS, Fuster V, eds. Efficacy of Myocardial Infarction Therapy—An Evaluation of Clinical Trials Evidence. New York: Marcel Dekker, 1999:1–493.

WALLACE BRUCE FYE III, MD, MA, MACC:
A Conversation With the Editor*

Bruce Fye was born in Meadville, Pennsylvania, on 25 September 1946 and grew up mainly in the Philadelphia area (Figure 1). He graduated from The Johns Hopkins University in Baltimore, Maryland in 1968 and from The Johns Hopkins University School of Medicine in 1972. At Hopkins, he was elected to Phi Beta Kappa and Alpha Omega Alpha. His internship and 2 years of medical residency were at the New York Hospital Cornell Medical Center. His fellowship in cardiology was at Johns Hopkins. During his fellowship Dr. Fye was selected as a Robert Wood Johnson Clinical Scholar. After completing his cardiology training, he received a Master's degree in medical history from Johns Hopkins. In 1978, Dr. Fye moved to Marshfield, Wisconsin, to create an echocardiographic laboratory at the Marshfield Clinic. Three years later, he became Chair of the Department of Cardiology there, and he remained in that position until 1999. In addition to his cardiologic practice, Dr. Fye has written extensively on the history of medicine, particularly related to cardiovascular disease and physiology. He has written 2 books and edited 3 others. He has written 26 chapters in various books and published approximately 275 articles, most of which were in peer-review journals. He has been very active in the American College of Cardiology (ACC) for 20 years and was the president of the ACC in 2002 to 2003. Dr. Fye is a internationally known medical historian and was president of the American Osler Society in 1988 to 1989. His book *American Cardiology: The History of a Specialty and Its College* (1996) won the William H. Welch medal of the American Association for the History of Medicine in 2000. That prestigious medal is awarded to the "sole investigator of a book of outstanding scholarly merit in the field of medical history published during the 5 calendar years preceding the award." In 2001, he moved to Rochester, Minnesota, to be Consultant in the Division of Cardiovascular Diseases of the Mayo Clinic and Professor of Medicine and Professor of History of Medicine at the Mayo Clinic College of Medicine. In addition to his practice, his writing, and his collecting and selling of medical books, he is a popular sought-after speaker. He has given approximately 200 lectures in various meetings and been the invited visiting professor to 36 major medical centers, mainly university medical centers, in the US. Additionally, he is a great guy, honorable in every way, and fun to be around. He and his lovely wife, Lois, are the parents of 2 wonderful daughters.

FIGURE 1. Wallace Bruce Fye during the interview (photo by WCR).

William Clifford Roberts, MD[†] **(hereafter WCR):** *Dr. Fye, it's a real pleasure to talk with you, and I'm grateful to you for your willingness to talk with me and therefore to the journal's readers. Could we start by my asking you to discuss your early upbringing, some of your earliest memories, your parents, and what it was like growing up in Pennsylvania?*

Wallace Bruce Fye, MD[‡] **(hereafter WBF):** I was born in September 1946 in Meadville, a small town in northwestern Pennsylvania that is the home of Allegheny College. My parents met there because they shared an interest in music. I can go back further than that. You just showed me a book about pellagra your father, Dr. Stewart Roberts, wrote in 1912 and that triggered a thought. If it were not for typhoid fever, I would not be here talking to you today. Although my mother's parents died before I was born, her father was born and raised on a farm outside of Meadville that had been in her family since about 1850, and still is. My mother's mother was born in Denmark in 1879, but she was orphaned when she was about 12 years

*This series of interviews is underwritten by an unrestricted grant from Bristol-Myers Squibb.

†Baylor Heart & Vascular Institute, Baylor University Medical Center, Dallas, Texas 75246.

‡Cardiovascular Division, Mayo Clinic, Rochester, Minnesota 55905.

FIGURE 2. WBF's mother Anne Schreck, Oberlin College 1936.

old. She and her 3 brothers crossed the Atlantic Ocean by themselves to be raised by an aunt and uncle in Bridgeport, Connecticut. What does this have to do with typhoid fever? Well, my mother's mother, after going through high school in Connecticut, somehow entered nurse's training at Meadville City Hospital in Pennsylvania. After graduating she cared for a farmer with typhoid fever. He survived, they were married, and my mother was born in 1913.

My mother went to a 1-room schoolhouse until she was in the ninth grade. In junior high, she became very interested in the piano. After graduating from high school in 1930, she went to the Oberlin Conservatory of Music in Oberlin, Ohio. This was at the beginning of the Great Depression, and I'm not sure how her family, a farm family, could afford to send her to Oberlin College. I know my mother worked in the college cafeteria to help pay the expenses. She graduated from Oberlin in 1936 with a major in organ and piano (Figure 2). She then got a part-time job as a church organist in Meadville and lived with her parents and her older brother on the farm. She also taught piano at the Pennsylvania College of Music, a private music school in Meadville. That was where she met my father, who played and taught violin.

My father was born and grew up in Oil City, Pennsylvania, in the heart of the "oil rich" part of northwestern Pennsylvania. His mother's family was

in the oil business in Venango County in the 1870s, but for a variety of reasons much of their wealth was gone by the early 20th century. My father played the violin in junior high and high school in Oil City. He went to Allegheny College in Meadville and got a bachelor's degree, graduating in 1936. He met my mother in Meadville 2 years later. My dad's first job was working as a teller in a very small bank in Conneaut Lake, Pennsylvania, a popular summer resort with a large lake and an amusement park. He earned $80/month in his first job, a significant amount of money during the Depression when many college graduates were out of work.

My dad helped pay his way through college and later supplemented his salary from the bank by playing violin. In college he organized an 11-member dance band called "Bruce Fye and the Alleghenians." This was at a time when there were a lot of dance bands and small orchestras in America. By 1940, he was working at the First National Bank in Meadville, and his dance band played at various events in northwestern Pennsylvania and northeastern Ohio. He was also concertmaster of the Meadville Symphony Orchestra.

When the US entered World War II, almost every able-bodied man either wanted or felt compelled to enlist in some branch of the armed services. My dad wanted very much to get into the Army Air Corps because he was infatuated with flying. He became a flight instructor and later a flight officer in the Army Air Corps Transport Command, also known as the Ferry Command. He flew fighter planes, including P-47s and P-51s, from the US to Brazil where they were sent by ship across the Atlantic to the front.

WCR: *When was your father born and when did he die?*

WBF: He was born in 1914 and died in 1983.

WCR: *And your mother?*

WBF: She was born in 1913 and died in 1986.

WCR: *When did your parents marry?*

WBF: They got married in 1939. By this time my dad was elected as the local representative of the American Federation of Musicians, and my parents spent their honeymoon in Kansas City where the union held its national convention in 1939.

WCR: *Your mother and daddy stayed in Meadville much of their lives?*

WBF: No. Actually, they lived several places. We moved about every 4 years until I went to college in 1964. Born in 1946, I was 1 of the first baby boomers, 1 of the *real* first baby boomers born about a year after most soldiers came back from World War II (Figure 3). In 1952, we moved to Mansfield, Ohio, where my dad was hired by Westinghouse to develop their consumer credit division (Figure 4). After 2 years he decided to return to banking. Expecting to leave Mansfield, he sold our house, and my mother and I spent the summer in a small cottage on Lake Erie, at a place called Geneva on the Lake. That's where I learned to swim. One funny thing I remember about learning to swim in Lake Erie was that the very coarse sand was filled with smooth pieces of colored glass, a

FIGURE 3. W. Bruce Fye Jr. holding WBF III 1946.

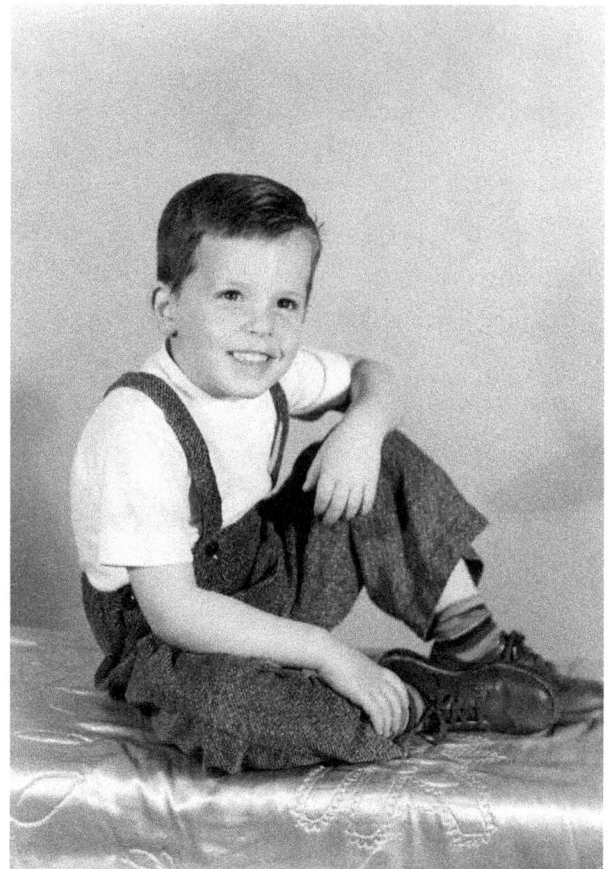

FIGURE 4. WBF at age 4, 1950.

result of so much trash being dumped in the lake. Another memory relates to the swimming instructor that taught about 40 of us to swim. She was a white-haired woman in her 60s who drove back and forth to the beach on a motorcycle.

After that summer, we moved back to Mansfield where my dad took a job as a branch manager of a bank. In 1955, after I finished the third grade, we moved to Springfield, Pennsylvania, where my dad took a job as branch manager for the Philadelphia National Bank. The late 1950s was an exciting time to live in the Philadelphia area because rock 'n' roll was just developing. My friends and I enjoyed the weekly "canteen" dances and went to a couple of rock 'n' roll shows in Philadelphia. At the end of seventh grade, my dad was promoted to regional manager of the Bucks County branches of the Philadelphia National Bank. We moved to Yardley, a scenic town along the Delaware River about 30 miles north of Philadelphia. Because we moved every 4 years when I was a kid, I learned how to make friends easily. This was espe-

cially important, because I was an only child. Actually, the reason I am an only child is that my mother almost died giving birth to me. Her labor lasted about 45 hours and was a miserable experience for both of my parents. That's why they decided not to have any more children.

WCR: *What was your mother like?*

WBF: This gets into the psychohistory that you do so well. Of course, I can answer that based on growing up with her and knowing her until she died in 1986, but I also have the benefit of detailed diaries she kept from age 15 until her mid-50s, and then more sporadically until she died. Her diaries were mostly fun to read, and they helped me understand her life through her own eyes. But there were times when she was clearly depressed. She was very popular in college and had lots of friends, but the diaries reveal that she lacked self-confidence. My mother was a very bright, kind, thoughtful and supportive person, but she was also an alcoholic. She started college just as Prohibition ended, and I assume she started drinking at Oberlin, but I don't know. Her drinking problem developed in an environment where people drank either at college or afterward. She apparently found it to be a liberating thing for her. On the other hand, looking at her from the outside, her alcoholism was anything but liberating. It led to social isolation. When I was about 8, she developed alcoholic hepatitis and nearly died. I don't remember much about that other than we had a housekeeper who lived with us for several months. She struggled with alcoholism throughout much of her life. There were periods when she was sober for many months, but it was a significant problem for her until her later years when she gained control over her alcoholism.

WCR: *Was your mother warm with you?*

WBF: Yes, very much so, and I felt great affection for her. But she was also very fragile. Her personality was very different when she was drinking. She was never a disheveled, unkempt, visibly drunk person, but her behavior, her voice, and her thinking were clearly different when she was drinking. It was very sad to see, and it confined my parents a good deal. They rarely socialized. On the few occasions they had guests for dinner, my mother would get so flustered that my dad would take over and do almost everything. There was so much tension in the air you could cut it with a knife. Probably the biggest thing was that I didn't have my friends and classmates over to my house. That was because it was unpredictable how my mother would be. My parent's house was not a place where friends congregated. We didn't have parties at our house. Despite her bouts with alcoholism my mother had several good friends wherever we lived. She was truly a warm and wonderful person, and made friends easily each time we moved. Church was always very important to her. She was very religious and very involved in church work. She was also very artistic. In addition to playing piano, she painted and made pottery.

WCR: *What was your father like?*

WBF: My dad was a very smart, ambitious, hard-working guy. He was also very intense, although he almost never got really angry. I'm a lot more driven and a little less intense. He cared very deeply for my mother and tried hard to help her in various ways. When I was in college she was being treated for alcoholism as an inpatient in a large psychiatric hospital near Philadelphia. Driving with my father to visit her once, I said to him, "Why do you stay married to her? Her alcoholism is such a problem. How can you deal with this?" He said something that was very sweet and compelling, "Because I really love her very much." He tried to make life easy for her, but I think part of the conflict was his intensity and her frailty in a sense. Still, I grew up in an environment that I don't think is all that unusual. Almost every family has its dysfunctional elements. For that matter, I don't think I have ever met anyone who isn't slightly eccentric in some way. I'm defining that very broadly, and I certainly believe that I'm eccentric. The uniqueness of individuals and their idiosyncrasies are what make people interesting in my opinion.

WCR: *Did you and your father get along?*

WBF: Yes, but there was some tension at times. He was very strict and rigid. I remember a few annoying situations. When I was a junior in high school, I was dating a girl that was my first true love, and we were supposed to go out 1 evening on a date. Well, it was very foggy, and my dad forbade me to drive because it was so foggy. That really aggravated the hell out of me. Saying the word "hell" brings back another memory of how strict he could be. Each summer I would spend a few days with my aunt, uncle, and cousins who lived on the farm where my mother grew up outside of Meadville. It was a lot of fun to visit and play with them and to work on the farm bailing hay and doing other chores. Like most farm families, there was a certain amount of swearing in the air. There was no swearing at all in my house. Once, when my dad came to pick me up at the farm, I said "God" in some context that had nothing to do with praying. He made me go straight to the car. That was pretty harsh I thought, and I know my cousins thought he was crazy to react like that to a single swear word that was part of their vocabulary.

Here are a couple of more examples of how rigid my dad was. I had a modest allowance, $5 a week when I was in junior high school. I had a paper route and in the summer I mowed lawns. My father set the price I could charge a neighbor to mow their lawn. The maximum was $1. This used to bug me because some of the lawns were fairly big and sometimes a person would offer to pay me $2, but my dad said I could only take $1. In retrospect, some of his rules that annoyed me at the time helped me develop a sense of responsibility. For example, he never let me go out and do pranks like soaping windows on "mischief night" before Halloween. He said it just made work for somebody else. He was absolutely right. At the time his rules seemed arbitrary and stifling. In other ways my parents were quite liberal with respect to letting me do things. They let me go into Philadelphia by myself when I was 13 years old. They were concerned about me because I was their only child. For example, my dad never wanted me to take a summer job that carried any risk. In college I had a friend die during the summer as a result of a construction accident.

WCR: *What was dinner like at your home with you and your parents?*

WBF: I really only remember the high school years. We sat at a small table in the kitchen and ate on fiesta ware that I got rid of in Arizona after my parents died in the 1980s. Our older daughter, Katherine, who now collects it, could kill me. When we lived in Yardley, my father was promoted to Vice President and eventually Senior Vice-President of the Philadelphia National Bank, and he commuted to Philadelphia by train each day. He left home around 7:00 A.M. and got home at about 6:30 P.M., so he had long days. My mother would prepare dinner each night. We had about 10 different things that most Americans had at that time—meat loaf, stuffed pork chops, hash, and so forth. When Swanson's TV dinners became popular, we ate those once or twice a week.

WCR: *What was the conversation at dinner?*

WBF: I honestly don't remember. I've read many of your interviews where people recall having deep and intellectual conversations with their parents about world events, and so forth. I don't remember that, although I know we didn't sit there in silence. Somewhere along the way, we started eating in a small den while we watched the evening news from 6:30 to 7:00 P.M. We also watched several popular television shows together, including Bilko, Jack Benny, Jackie Gleason, and Ed Sullivan. By the time he got home at night, my dad seemed to be burned out in a sense. He didn't have any real hobbies or activities at home besides reading magazines and an occasional book. On the other hand, he was very active in several local and regional civic organizations. In contrast, when I come home from work, I'm consumed by activity. I have so many things I want to do, whether it's research or writing or editing or working with the books. If I had 5 bodies, each one would be fully occupied, and I still wouldn't have time to pursue all of my interests. I have always had lots of hobbies, but they have almost all been individual pursuits, mainly collecting things.

WCR: *Did they push you in school or did you just automatically always make good grades?*

WBF: My parents expected me to do well in school, but they didn't push me to the point that I recall them being annoying. They worried I didn't study very much. It bothered them that I didn't study as much as they thought I should.

WCR: *You made good grades in high school and at Johns Hopkins University?*

WBF: I think I graduated twelfth in my class of about 500 in high school, but I didn't really work as hard as I could have or should have at that stage of my life. I wanted to get good grades, but I had lots of other interests. I had lots of friends, had lots of hobbies, was quite involved in music, and enjoyed dating. I didn't really know how to focus my energy at that point.

WCR: *Were there any teachers in junior high or high school who had impact on you?*

WBF: I think so, but there were no specific teachers that I remember as being truly influential mentors. Several of them had some influence on me, and most seemed to like me. One funny thing I remember is that I had the same teacher for fifth and sixth grades. In my final fifth grade report card she wrote that she would have me "bouncing around" again in her classroom the next year. She mentioned my smiling face and said I could do nice work when I settled down. Today, those behaviors would probably be labeled hyperactivity, but then I was perceived as a very social kid who enjoyed friends and didn't focus on my work as much as my teachers or parents thought I should. I think my teachers had a sense that I wasn't always working up to my potential. As I told you before, I didn't study that hard in high school. In terms of specific individuals, there was a teacher I remember in particular. He taught German and social studies in eighth grade. His name was *Samuel Rifkin,* and I think he came out of the ultra-liberal New York orbit. He was a very bright guy. He drove a couple of my classmates and me to Newark, New Jersey, to meet a family who had emigrated from Russia around 1959. That was a fascinating experience for us, hearing firsthand why they left Russia.

WCR: *Your parents were musicians, what instruments did you play?*

WBF: My mother was a piano teacher, and she started teaching me piano when I was about 5 years old. That was a huge mistake, because of a combination of my mother's temperament and my age. I had different interests and didn't want to practice or be taught by my mother. After 2 or 3 years I stopped taking piano lessons. When I was in the fourth grade, I started to play violin in the elementary school orchestra, and the next year I started to play tuba in the band. Although my dad was a full-time banker, he kept his musical interest up until we moved to Yardley in 1958. Before we moved to the Philadelphia area, he was concertmaster (a part-time job) of the Erie Symphony Orchestra, and *Jascha Heifitz,* one of the world's greatest violinists, was the guest artist. I have a photograph that Heifitz inscribed for my father. When we moved to Yardley, the junior high school did not have an orchestra, so I played the tuba in the concert band and sousaphone in the marching band. In high school, I also sang in the choir and played string bass in a jazz band and small jazz quartet. When I started college, I dropped all these activities to focus on studying.

WCR: *Other than music, how did you spend your free time as a child?*

WBF: I grew up before video games and computers, although we had a television quite early (1952) because my dad worked for Westinghouse. Most of the time when I wasn't playing outside with friends, I was busy collecting things. Many kids in the 1950s and 1960s were collectors, but I was a very serious, if somewhat unfocused, collector. I collected stamps, coins, butterflies, baseball cards, and comics. But my collecting life changed dramatically in the summer of 1960 when I was visiting my cousins on their farm in Meadville. I tagged along with my uncle and a cousin when they went to a country auction. Just after we arrived, they were auctioning off 2 big boxes of old books. I borrowed $2.50 from my uncle and got them. That was a critical catalyst for my interest in book collecting, and later my book collecting became the major driver of my interest in medical history, research, and writing.

WCR: *Were there any books in those boxes you were interested in?*

WBF: That's a good question. It shows the value of printed documents or letters when you are trying to do history. (Oral history, which you are an expert at and I've done quite a bit myself, is relying on people's memories to try to capture the story and get it right.) The main book of interest to me was an odd volume of a 2-volume set of books written by *James G. Blaine,* a member of congress and an unsuccessful candidate for president in the 19th century. He published a book called *Twenty Years of Congress* in 1884. I got volume one at the auction, but the challenge was to find the missing volume. I knew there were some second-hand bookstores in Philadelphia, so I went to several searching without success for the other volume. We lived in Yardley at the time, and there was a large bookstore, named Traver's Bookstore, on the main street in Trenton, New Jersey, just across the Delaware River. The first floor was devoted to new hard-cover books, and the basement was filled with paper-backs and textbooks. There was a long narrow corridor in the basement that contained several hundred old books, and I bought a few old books there in 1961, including a New York edition of Homer's *Odyssey* published in 1861 (exactly 100 years earlier) for 75 cents.

One day I asked the owner, a man in his 70s, where he thought I should go to find the missing volume of *Twenty Years of Congress*. I remember him saying something like, "Come with me young man." We got on the elevator on the first floor and went up. I had no idea that there were more books on the second and third floors of the store. This was a classic main street storefront in downtown Trenton, built around 1900. It was a very long and narrow building with 15-foot ceilings and large white globe lights that were in all old schools at that time. Well, when he opened the elevator door there was a huge dark space with tall windows at each end. He pulled the cords to a few lights and guided me to an area filled with old American history books. Not only did he have the missing volume, he had 4 sets of this 1884 book for $2.75 a set. I was absolutely hooked. Trying to find an odd volume of *Twenty Years of Congress*, I'd been guided to the book collector's equivalent of a forgotten gold mine. They had stopped selling the used and old books and closed off the top 2 floors years earlier, and it was obvious from the dust that almost no one ever visited the upper floors. Although I had already begun to collect old books, this was literally like hitting the mother lode. I was addicted.

WCR: *You were how old then?*

WBF: I was 14 at that time. While many of my friends were playing sports or doing other outdoor things, I began to spend every Saturday in this bookstore. My mother or my dad would drop me off at the store in the morning and pick me up when they closed. I probably spent 50 Saturdays in that place during my last 3 years in high school and saw only 7 or 8 people on those upper floors the entire time. Because they made no effort to sell those old and used books and had priced them years earlier, I found many bargains. Over the years I bought several hundred books from that bookshop, especially when they had a going-out-of-business sale in 1965. My early collecting interests were the Civil War, Abraham Lincoln, African exploration, and some literature. I have to emphasize that I was not a reader. In fact, the same fifth grade teacher who told my parents I would be in her class the following year said in my report card that one problem I had was that I didn't read enough library books. So I didn't buy those old books to read, I collected them. Many people build libraries from books they bought to read. I've filled libraries with books I wanted to have for one reason or another. Later, when I was in medical school, I began to buy books that I would eventually use as tools for my historical research and writing. For years, I have read books and articles regularly, but I read them for the facts they contain

rather than reading fiction or nonfiction books for pleasure.

WCR: *When your parents would take you to that bookshop in Trenton, what did you do for those 6 hours you were there?*

WBF: There were probably about 100,000 old and used books on those 2 floors. I would literally wander around the store, which was more like a warehouse, looking at the books. I'd try to decide over the course of many hours which ones I wanted. I was like a kid in a candy store, but a candy store that had so much stuff you couldn't believe it. Nobody else knew about it. It was little private nirvana. The biggest problem was that I had only a modest allowance, so I had to make choices.

WCR: *Just by having books, you get a little information by osmosis, don't you think? You have a general idea of what's in that book even though you haven't read all the pages.*

WBF: You are absolutely right. I know you are a very astute observer of the world of publishing. I've bumped into you many times at national meetings on publisher's row, where you are taking notes. Each year you publish an excellent synopsis of the new cardiology books. I agree that you can learn a great deal from books without reading them in their entirety. I learned a useful descriptive phrase from a world-renowned medical historian many years ago. He talked of "reading in" a book as opposed to reading a book.

WCR: *Other than the store in Trenton, New Jersey, where did you buy books when you were in high school and college?*

WBF: There was an annual library book sale in Langhorne, Pennsylvania, a small town near Yardley. I helped them organize the sale and picked up many bargains over the 3 or 4 years I went to that sale. That is where I got my first book related to medicine: Harvey Cushing's 2-volume Pulitzer Prize–winning *Life of Sir William Osler*.

WCR: *This was what year?*

WBF: About 1964, probably the summer after I graduated from high school. By that time I had been accepted as a premed student at Johns Hopkins. Another event, about the same time, demonstrates my passion for collecting lots of books as a teenager. My mother and I went to an auction in Princeton, New Jersey, because I saw a newspaper ad that mentioned the sale would include a large quantity of books. There was very little competition for the lot of 20 or so boxes of books, so I got them all for $25. The library included many books on religion, history, and travel among other things. By that time I owned about 2,000 books and had built shelves in our basement to hold them. When I was in college and medical school I also went to Goodwill Industry stores and used bookstores in the Baltimore area looking for interesting books at good prices.

WCR: *Did either of your parents collect books?*

WBF: My parents had books, but they were not collectors. They bought books to read, and they still had some of their college textbooks. Our house wasn't full of books, but there were books. My parents read for enjoyment and had accumulated a small library of fiction and nonfiction books typical of that era, but they were not avid readers. They weren't collectors either, so I don't know where I got that gene.

WCR: *What did your mother and father think about your book collecting?*

WBF: They were very supportive. My mother lent me the money to buy that big bunch of books in Princeton. They let me build lots of bookshelves in the basement. My dad helped me pack the books when we moved from Baltimore to New York City. They were always extraordinarily supportive with respect to my book collecting.

WCR: *When you were growing up, did your mother and daddy and you go on vacations in the summertime? Did you travel at all?*

WBF: Not very much. The main focus of travel was back to Meadville to visit my paternal grandmother and my 2 aunts, 2 uncles, and 4 cousins. That was my entire family. My grandmother was my only grandparent; the others died before I was born. She was born in Pennsylvania in 1889 and married a carpenter, Wallace Bruce Fye, in 1910. My father and I were named for him. My grandmother had crippling arthritis and was basically housebound from the time she was in her mid-60s. She lived with my dad's brother and his wife. She lived on the first floor of a 2-story house, and they lived on the second floor. They had no children. It was a curious sociological relation. My father was extremely successful in banking. His brother started college at Allegheny during the Depression, but he didn't finish because their father died in 1937 and the money ran out. He worked as a clerk in a lumber store and was a part-time musician. He took care of his mother.

There was an undercurrent of tension there because my father was so successful and his brother was not. It didn't play out visibly, but it was an undercurrent. In terms of vacations, I was expected to spend a couple of weeks with my grandmother every summer. At Christmas I was expected to go, generally just with my dad, across Pennsylvania to be with her. I think my dad thought of his mother as fragile, and as her only grandson, I was very special in her eyes. The irony is that she lived to be 93, and she died just a few months before my dad died. My grandmother was a very smart woman, and she was always very interested in my life and career. In 1968, when Lois and I got engaged, my grandmother gave me the engagement ring she got in 1910. It was a very nice diamond, and she wanted me to give it to Lois. You asked about vacations. Your course in Williamsburg reminds me of one of the few family vacations I took with my parents. We visited Williamsburg in about 1963, and we went to the Montreal Expo. We really didn't take family vacations. I'm not sure how much vacation my dad got. I'm sure he got at least 2 weeks, but this was way before modern era banking in terms of salaries and benefits for top-level executives.

WCR: *When you would go to Meadville, you'd sometimes go by yourself?*

WBF: It's interesting that you ask that question. In fact, when we lived in Springfield when I was in junior high, I flew by myself a few times from the Philadelphia airport to either Erie or Youngstown. My first commercial flight was in a DC-3, and that was pretty memorable. Because of their design when you got on a DC-3 you entered from the rear and walked up to your seat at about a 15-degree angle. I remember they gave us Canadian mints. Later, I thought it was a really big deal the first time I flew in a plane with 4 propellers. I also remember flying in a Constellation that had 3 tails. One time I was on the plane at the Philadelphia airport, and as we taxied out to the runway the stewardess came to collect the tickets. She got to me, and I didn't have my ticket. My dad still had it. They turned the plane around and went back to the gate, got my ticket, and off we went. How times have changed. My dad kept up his pilot's license after the war, and from the late 1940s until about 1955 he was a part owner of a small plane. Later, he would occasionally rent a plane and fly us back and forth to and from Meadville. I remember going across Pennsylvania in a single-engine plane in the winter during lousy weather. It was not a lot of fun. I was more risk adverse than my dad when it came to flying. He got a great thrill out of flying in World War II and flying little planes subsequently.

WCR: *When and how did you decide you wanted to be a doctor?*

WBF: I decided I wanted to be a doctor when I was in the 10th grade. One rather strange reason had to do with something my dad said to me when we were raking leaves. In Yardley, we had a moderate-sized yard with quite a few trees, including 4 apple trees. I hated doing yard work. Well, as I was raking leaves, my dad said something to the effect that "a bachelor's degree is not enough education these days." My immediate reaction was negative because as a ninth grader I was looking at 7 more years just to get through college. Nevertheless, he planted a seed in my mind that to be competitive during my lifetime I should get an advanced degree. At that point I didn't know what I wanted to do. I was considering engineering, which was a hot topic at that time because of the space program. At one point I seriously considered trying to get into the Air Force Academy. One thing that shifted me away from engineering was the introduction of the "new math." I did very well with the old math, algebra, and geometry through the 10th grade. The next year my school adopted the new math, and I was suddenly adrift in dense fog without a compass or a lighthouse. I was totally befuddled by it.

There was a weekly television show from Johns Hopkins at the time, and the news media carried lots of stories describing medical breakthroughs. I remember being very impressed by medical advances reported in magazines, newspapers, and television. Although my mother's mother had been a nurse, she died before I was born, and there were no doctors in my family. In fact, my interactions with doctors had been mostly unpleasant. As a kid I had lots of ear infections and got too many shots of penicillin to have very positive feelings about medicine. I also remember being scared to death of getting polio as a child in the early 1950s. Ironically, when I lived in Mansfield, Ohio, I was enrolled in the big Salk polio vaccine clinical trial. There was a lot of optimism in the air regarding medicine in the early 1960s. The polio vaccine worked and, suddenly, the fear of getting polio was erased. Antibiotics were available to treat infections. Heart surgery was producing many breakthroughs that were reported in *Life* magazine and the *The Saturday Evening Post*, magazines my parents got. I saw medicine as an exciting career, and my parents encouraged that notion. Whenever people have asked me why I went into medicine, my standard answer has always been that I like people. I've always enjoyed people, and clinical medicine provides many opportunities to interact with and help people.

WCR: *You entered The Johns Hopkins University as a premed in 1964. Say something about your college experience.*

WBF: I decided to apply to the premed program at Johns Hopkins University because of the reputation of the medical school. My fallback was Rutgers University. I don't know what gave me the confidence to think that I was going to get into one or the other. Fortunately, I got into Johns Hopkins. The strange thing is that when I got to Hopkins as a freshman in the fall of 1964, I found myself in a sea of premeds, and every one of us wanted to go to the Johns Hopkins Medical School. Many of us wondered out loud, "What the hell have we done?" The medical school took only about a dozen Hopkins undergraduates each year, and here I was with about 150 other premeds who would be competing with me for those precious spots.

One reason I became competitive was related to my freshman year roommate, *Bob Scheible*, a premed from Racine, Wisconsin. He was obsessed with 2 things: the Green Bay Packers and studying. He came to Baltimore in the fall of 1964 with all the Packer paraphernalia you can imagine. More importantly, he put the fear of God into me with respect to studying. In high school I did not have very good study habits. I didn't apply myself the way I did later on. As a freshman at Hopkins I saw how hard Bob studied, and I figured I had better do the same thing because we were surrounded by smart kids from all around the country. So Bob and I would eat breakfast in 5 minutes and rush off to class. We'd rush back to the dorm after class in the afternoon and start studying and eat dinner quickly in the cafeteria. Suddenly, I was transformed from someone who took studying casually into someone who took it so seriously it is almost comical in retrospect. I developed a work ethic at that point that has been characteristic of me ever since. It was a matter of developing self-discipline and being able to focus.

The other thing about college that helped shape my character was that Johns Hopkins University had an honor system we pledged to follow. In our high school honors classes, we didn't indulge in any heavy duty cheating, but several of us shared information when completing assignments. When I got to Hopkins and signed the honor code statement, a light switch was turned on. Intellectual integrity became an absolute for me. From that point on, I knew that absolutely everything I did, every single thing I did or didn't do, was up to me and me alone. It wasn't with any help from anyone else or any lack of commitment or desire. Whatever the output was, it was because I determined it.

Another thing happened during my freshman year at Hopkins that I will never understand. English writing was a required course for every Hopkins liberal arts undergraduate. For some unknown reason, I had that course waived. My SATs were very good, but they weren't close to perfect in English. It made no sense to me that I was excused from that requirement because I hardly knew the difference between an adjective and an adverb. As a result I avoided some interesting undergraduate courses because they required term papers. One factor that determined the courses I took at Hopkins was that premeds had to fulfill certain requirements, especially in the sciences. One requirement that blew a lot of premeds out of the water was physics. Hopkins, well known for its world-class medical school, also had a world-class engineering school. The university offered just 1 introductory physics course, and it was 6 credits a semester (12 credits). So, one tenth of your undergraduate grade point was determined by physics. All the premeds had to take this course. Many pre-engineering students came to that physics class armed with 2 slide rules in case 1 broke down. Needless to say, many of us premeds thought our career objectives were tied to getting at least a B in physics.

WCR: *You were in college from 1964 to 1968, a very turbulent time in America's history. How did this affect you?*

WBF: A traumatic event for all Americans at this time was the assassination of President Kennedy in November 1963. When the president was shot I was a senior in high school. They cancelled school, and I watched hours and hours of live television coverage of the assassination and the subsequent murder of Lee Harvey Oswald. During my college years the Viet Nam war kept escalating and the civil rights movement was gathering momentum. It was impossible to ignore the growing turbulence in our society during 1960s, although there was less student activism at Johns Hopkins than at many other campuses like Berkeley or the University of Wisconsin. During the Viet Nam war era I heard several government officials and political leaders speak at Hopkins because of Baltimore's proximity to Washington and *Dr. Milton Eisenhower, Dwight Eisenhower's* brother, was president of the university. Milton Eisenhower had been an influential figure in Washington in the 1930s and 1940s, long before his brother became a huge military figure and then president in 1952. After Dr. Eisenhower retired, I got to know him fairly well when I was a cardiology fellow and graduate student in medical history. During dinner at our home one evening, Dr. Eisenhower explained that before World War II, when he was in the Department of Agriculture, people used to refer to Ike as Milton's brother.

He laughed as he recounted how the hierarchy changed during WW II.

I saw President *Lyndon Johnson* speak twice at Johns Hopkins, in 1964 and in 1965. The first time he spoke, just before the election he stood on the steps of Gilman Hall, a huge brick building at Hopkins that is the centerpiece of the undergraduate campus. I got there very early and was in the front row. I was already somewhat of a political groupie as a freshman in college. According to the newspaper, there were about 7,000 people in the audience. The *Baltimore Sun* published a picture that showed me in the front row surrounded by students holding Johnson/Humphrey signs. At the end of his speech, the president bolted down the steps to shake hands with some of the crowd that was held back by a long rope. There was a Secret Service man standing right in front of me, who muttered under his breath, "Son of a bitch. There he goes again." What he was referring to, obviously, was that Lyndon Johnson was coming down to work the crowd. This was less than 1 year after Kennedy's assassination, and Johnson's Secret Service detail surely worried any time he got into a crowd. This is a somewhat embarrassing anecdote, but I shook the president's hand 4 times as he slowly made his way back to the helicopter that had landed near the campus tennis courts. He kept shaking hands all the way back to his helicopter that was several hundred yards from where he spoke. After shaking his hand the first time I backed out of the crowd, walked about 100 feet toward the helicopter and moved back into the crowd. I did this 2 more times. At that point I realized I was interested in the political process. But I wasn't in any of the student political organizations, mainly because I was working as hard as I could as a premed hoping to get into medical school.

Lyndon Johnson came back to Hopkins in the spring of 1965 and spoke in Schriver Hall, an auditorium that seated about 1,000 people. I got there very early and got a good seat. Although I saw the president deliver his speech, I didn't realize how important it was until about 2 years ago. I don't watch much TV, but I was channel surfing one evening and stopped on a documentary about the Viet Nam war. They showed a brief video clip of Lyndon Johnson giving that 1965 speech at Johns Hopkins. The thing that was bizarre was, while I was watching this clip from a speech Johnson gave almost 40 years earlier, there was about a 1-second shot of a few people in the audience, and I saw myself sitting there in a madras plaid sport coat. This prompted me to go to Google and search for "Lyndon Johnson—Johns Hopkins—1965." Not only could I read a transcript of the speech, I could watch and listen to the entire speech on my computer screen. He used the occasion to explain to the American people why we were in Viet Nam, and stated that we would stay there as long as it took to win. This anecdote reflects the power of the Internet, how we can find out and know things that otherwise would not be available. Thinking back to 1968, when I got my undergraduate degree from Hopkins, I remember how many of my classmates worried they would be drafted

if they didn't get into medical school. Fortunately, I was accepted at the Johns Hopkins School of Medicine and could continue on my career path toward becoming a doctor.

WCR: *You married Lois Baker during your first year of medical school. Where did you meet her?*

WBF: Lois and I were married in Baltimore in 1969. I met her in high school when I was a senior and she was a junior. We went to Pennsbury High School, a large public school near Yardley that had about 500 kids in each class. The way we met was total serendipity. She got the wrong homeroom and locker assignments, and for that reason her locker was just opposite mine. She has always had a beautiful smile, and I suspect that was one of the main things that made me notice her. Our first date was on Friday the 13th in December 1963, so we dated for 9 months before I went off to college in the fall of 1964. The next year Lois started nursing school at Washington Hospital Center in D.C. Her mother was a nurse, and her older sister had gone to nursing school at Washington Hospital Center. That's why Lois went there. We dated through my freshman year, when she was still in high school, and part of my sophomore year of college. Then, I think she got tired of dating a premed in Baltimore who studied all the time. She and her girl friends at Washington Hospital Center found themselves in a great social whirl between George Washington University, Georgetown, and the Naval Academy. As a result, we broke up for a couple of years. When I was a senior in college, I called her and suggested that we get back together. Happily, she agreed. We got married in May of 1969 during my first year of medical school. I have to give Lois great credit for her consistent support and encouragement over the years.

WCR: *You mentioned Lois' captivating smile. What other characteristics attracted you?*

WBF: First, I should mention that I had absolutely fallen head over heels for a girl the year before Lois and I met. When that girl broke up with me I was really devastated. It was a classic first true romance. After that I dated several girls once or twice, but when I met Lois I sensed there was something very special about her. She was quiet, thin, and attractive, but it was her personality that really won me over. Her smile and her laugh were very engaging. She was fun to be around.

WCR: *You started medical school at Johns Hopkins in 1968. What was medical school like for you?*

WBF: I really struggled with the basic sciences. I didn't like all the memorizing, and like many of my classmates I had difficulty seeing the relevance of some of the things we were expected to memorize in biochemistry and anatomy, for example. When I got to the clinical rotations I really hit my stride. I worked hard on those rotations, but I realized fairly early in my junior year that I was not interested in surgery or the surgical specialties. As I mentioned, Lois and I got married during my freshman year. By the time I was doing my clinical rotations she was head nurse in the obstetrical operating rooms at The Johns Hopkins

Hospital. It may seem strange, but I never delivered a baby in medical school. That was a conscious decision on my part. Basically, I knew I would never deliver a baby in practice, so I couldn't see any reason to subject some mother and her baby to my lack of experience.

WCR: *How did the OB/GYN faculty react when you said you didn't want to deliver babies?*

WBF: I don't think I ever actually said that I didn't want to deliver a baby. I just managed not to do it. There were others who wanted to deliver lots of babies, and they were happy to have more opportunities to do that.

WCR: *What about your other clinical rotations?*

WBF: I liked all my clinical rotations, but as I mentioned earlier, I decided to go into internal medicine during my junior year. In terms of pediatrics I remember the specific event that convinced me I didn't want to be a pediatrician. I was on call and admitted a little baby, maybe 6 months old, in the middle of the night. Obviously, I couldn't take a history from the baby, but I tried hard to examine him. Well, he shrieked and wriggled and squirmed around for the better part of a half-hour. That experience reinforced something I sensed about myself, that I am not a very patient person. This was in 1971, and doctors didn't have all the fancy imaging tests we now take for granted. Today's imaging tests have changed the approach to diagnosis dramatically. I didn't especially like surgery, and I didn't think I had the manual dexterity to get really good at it.

One of the main things that attracted me to internal medicine was the intellectual challenge of differential diagnosis. When I was a medical student from 1968 to 1972, a group of Hopkins faculty members (led by the chief of medicine *A. McGehee Harvey*) wrote 2 big internal medicine textbooks. One was a completely rewritten, multi-authored edition of William Osler's *Principles and Practice of Medicine*, and the other was a huge book titled *Differential Diagnosis*. I also thought the weekly Clinicopathologic (CPC) conferences were fascinating. The approach (that you know so well) is to have an internist try to come up with the right diagnoses based on the history, physical examination, laboratory tests, and x-rays. Of course, the pathologist always had the last word. I found those exercises very interesting, something like a Sherlock Holmes mystery.

WCR: *After spending 8 years at Johns Hopkins you started your internship at New York Hospital-Cornell Medical Center in New York City. How did you choose that program?*

WBF: Actually, I didn't. When I went to New York City for the interview, I met with *Alex Bearn*, the chief of medicine at New York-Cornell, and also with *Laird Myers*, the chief of medicine at Memorial Sloan-Kettering, across the street. The rumor among candidates for a medical internship at New York Hospital was that if both chiefs interviewed you, they really wanted you. It looked like an excellent program, but Lois and I weren't sure we wanted to live in Manhattan. My first choice was the Strong Memorial Hospital at the

University of Rochester, and New York Hospital was actually my fourth choice. As it turned out, it was an excellent (but very demanding) training program, and Lois and I enjoyed living in New York City. But it was quite a surprise when I opened the envelope that came on match day.

WCR: *You didn't apply to Hopkins?*

WBF: No. That was on purpose because I'd been there for 8 years, and I wanted to go somewhere else. Another factor was that the Hopkins internship had not gone to every third night call. I'd seen the house officers in action, and many of them looked exhausted. I thought, "I need more sleep than I'd get here." The great irony was the New York Hospital internship was supposed to be every third night call, but I ended up with 7 months of every other night call, because 2 interns dropped out and the timing of my rotations. Another thing that was different as an intern at New York Hospital compared with what I saw at Hopkins was who was around late in the evening. At Hopkins the medical wards seemed to be more crowded with interns, residents and students up to midnight or so. When I got to New York Hospital, it was pretty lonely at night when you were on call. There was a chain of supervision, but you weren't surrounded by people. You couldn't just turn to someone and ask what they thought about something. There was telephone contact with supervising residents and attending physicians, but you were expected to take responsibility for your patients.

This was also a time when New York Hospital was challenged because of a severe nursing shortage. As a result they closed 1 or 2 of the general medical wards. That decision created a huge furor among the medical house staff because those rotations were viewed as prime opportunities to learn. It caused a real brouhaha. There were six people from Hopkins in my internship group at New York Hospital, but we were spread out because there were about 30 interns. There were 3 assistant residents from Hopkins 1 year ahead of us. One of those residents drafted a letter to be sent back to Hopkins saying that they shouldn't send medical students to New York Hospital for internship because they had closed some of the medical wards. I was very busy with a sick patient in the coronary care unit when this resident came up to me and said, "Here, sign this! Everybody else from Hopkins is signing it." I read it, and it seemed pretty inflammatory. It didn't seem like a good thing to do, but I saw this list of names on there and figured I should sign it.

Well, there was a lot of fallout from that letter. *Tom Killip* was the head of cardiology at New York Hospital at the time, and he had some role in the residency training program. I remember going into Tom Killip's office and having a very uncomfortable chat about this letter. He more or less told me to write a letter of retraction. It was a very intimidating interaction, and I knew this thing was going to be a cloud over my head at New York Hospital unless I made some effort to salvage the situation. This situation taught me to be more politically astute about such things. I think this was one thing that affected my approach to decision-making and, eventually, my leadership style. You need to weight the risks and benefits of decisions and think about all the implications of your words and actions. The 3 years I spent at New York Hospital were exhausting and energizing, all at once. It was a very demanding training program and many of the patients were interesting and challenging. The house staff was very bright, and most of the attending physicians were excellent doctors.

WCR: *When did you decide to become a cardiologist?*

WBF: Lois recalls that during my coronary care unit rotation as an intern I came home and said, "I'll never be a cardiologist!" I don't remember saying that, but I do remember how exhausted I was during much of my internship. It was as an assistant resident that I became interested in cardiology. I liked cardiac physiology and auscultation although it took me a long time to get very good at it. That reminds me of a funny story about *Philip Tumulty*, the great white-haired general internist at Johns Hopkins, widely known for his skills as a diagnostician. As a junior medical student, I had a middle-aged woman with rheumatic heart disease. I listened and listened and listened to her precordium, but I couldn't sort out all the sounds and murmurs. When I left the patient's room I saw Dr. Tumulty sitting at the desk writing a note. I asked him if he would listen to my patient to help me understand what I was hearing. We went into her room, and he listened intently for a few minutes. When we got back to the nursing station he said, "Yes, there's a lot going on in there." He made some observations about the murmur of mitral stenosis, but I felt somewhat reassured that he didn't fully understand all of the complex auscultatory findings.

As I found cardiology increasingly interesting, many of the other subspecialties of medicine simply fell away. I didn't like gastroenterology. Nephrology was fairly new, and I'd seen patients on chronic dialysis who looked very pale and chronically ill. It didn't seem like nephrology was something that was going to engage me. I had rotated through Memorial Sloan-Kettering, a cancer hospital, and I had never seen such sick patients in my life. Although cancer chemotherapy seemed promising at the time, the advances in oncology during the last 30 years seem quite small compared with those in cardiology. I'd done quite a bit of neurology at Hopkins as a medical student and during electives, and I found it very interesting. In fact, some of the neurology staff at Hopkins really encouraged me to go into that specialty. During a rotation at Memorial Sloan-Kettering I got a call from *Guy McKhann*, the chief of neurology at Hopkins, offering me a spot that had opened up unexpectedly in their neurology residency. I thanked him for the offer, but I had decided on a career in cardiology by this point.

When I decided to become a cardiologist I applied to the fellowship programs at Yale, Penn, Duke, Hopkins, and maybe 1 or 2 other places. It surprised me how actively I was recruited by Hopkins because I had not done a cardiology elective as a medical student, and I didn't know any of the faculty very well. My main concern about going back to Hopkins for my fellowship was that I thought it would be too research oriented. I knew I wanted to be a clinical cardiologist. When I applied to Hopkins *Mike Weisfeldt*, who is just 6 years older than me, was a junior faculty member and director of the fellowship program and *J. O'Neal Humphries*, was head of the clinical service. Well, during a telephone conversation they both assured me that if I came back to Hopkins, they would respect that I wanted to be a clinician and didn't want to be plugged into someone's research project as a fellow passing through the lab. They were compelling; I thought Hopkins was a great institution, and Lois and I liked Baltimore, so I went back to Hopkins.

WCR: *Why were you so certain that you did not want to participate in cardiology research?*

WBF: That conclusion was based on 2 years of organic chemistry research I did as an undergraduate at Hopkins. I liked chemistry, and as a junior, I took a semester of organic chemistry research. The professor, *Alsoph Corwin*, was heavily involved with defense research earlier in his career. The area of research I was assigned to related to porphyrins. When I started that research, no one gave me any introductory reading or any real guidance in terms of the purpose of the research or how to go about it. Obviously, I should have asked more questions and sought direction. Despite the fact I really didn't understand much about what I was doing or was expected to do, I turned in reports that were somehow believed to justify an A. Although I wasn't especially interested in what I thought I was supposed to be doing, I was pragmatic enough to realize that 3 credits of A each semester for organic chemistry research had to be a good thing in terms of my chances of getting into medical school. But something far more important came out of those 3 semesters of feeling adrift in someone else's research project. I resolved I would never again spend time doing research on something that didn't interest me or that I didn't understand. From that point on, I knew I didn't want to be plugged into someone else's project as a trainee passing through, just picking something up where the last one left off. Eventually, this is how I decided to focus my research exclusively on medical history—and on topics that were of special interest to me.

WCR: *So, what happened with respect to research during your cardiology fellowship at Hopkins?*

WBF: Not long after starting my fellowship, I had an appointment to see Mike Weisfeldt, who was meeting with each first-year fellow to discuss what ongoing research project we wanted to work on during our training. It's important to emphasize that Mike was already an accomplished investigator, and he had a very strong personality. After Mike described the various research projects underway in the division, I said something like, "Wait a minute. Don't you remember our phone conversation when I said I didn't want to do that?" I reminded him that I wanted to be a clinical cardiologist and did not want to spend time as a transient in someone's ongoing research project. I remember that Mike was visibly annoyed. About 5

FIGURE 5. WBF and A. McGehee Harvey, Johns Hopkins 1977.

FIGURE 6. WBF and Mike Weisfeldt, 1996.

years ago, I told this story to my good friends *Paul Kligfield* of New York Hospital and *Jim Weiss* of Hopkins, when we were having a glass of wine one evening at one of the national meetings. Suddenly, as I was recounting this tense interaction that had taken place 25 years earlier, Jim Weiss blurted out, "I was there! Weisfeldt blanched. He just got white." I had forgotten that Jim was my faculty advisor, and it was certainly a surprise to have him recount that pivotal moment in my life from his perspective.

Even at that early stage of his career, Mike was an architect of academic careers, and he thought he knew what was best for his fellows. I am sure he thought he was helping us in terms of our careers, but this was one time I'm glad I had the courage of my convictions. I protested that I didn't want to do biomedical research, and reminded him that he knew that when he accepted me as a fellow. I believed I was right and that Mike knew it. I don't recall how the meeting ended, but I said something like, "If I have to do research as a cardiology fellow I would really like to do it in medical history." A few days later Lois and I left for a short vacation. During that brief time, it was announced that Mike was chosen to succeed *Richard Ross* as chief of the cardiology division.

When I got back from vacation there was a message that I should make an appointment to see Dr. Weisfeldt. I figured he was going to tell me I had to get involved in someone's laboratory or clinical research project, but it wasn't like that. Mike had discussed my situation with *Victor McKusick*, the new chief of medicine at Hopkins. Fortunately, Dr. McKusick had a deep interest in the history of medicine. He had written some historical papers earlier in his career and was very interested in Hopkins' history. He came up with a suggestion that turned out to be a win-win in terms of salvaging the discussion I had with Mike, who was now the chief of cardiology. The idea was to have me apply to be a Robert Wood Johnson Clinical Scholar. This new program was designed to encourage clinical trainees to get an advanced degree in a field such as health policy or economics to complement their traditional medical training. Hopkins was one of the first institutions to have a Clinical Scholars pro-

gram, and Victor and Mike wanted me to apply for a grant that would fund my clinical cardiology training and pay the tuition for a Master's degree in medical history. Mike has been a big supporter of my career ever since, and I view him as one of my main mentors (Figure 5).

Through another stroke of good fortune, *A. McGehee Harvey* became my preceptor. He had just stepped down as chief of medicine at Hopkins after holding that position since 1946. Beginning in 1973, Dr. Harvey focused almost all of his energy on historical research and writing and helping to develop the medical archives. *William Greenough*, an infectious disease specialist and director of the Hopkins Clinical Scholar's Program, encouraged me to ask Dr. Harvey if he would be willing to be my faculty advisor for my master's program in medical history. He said he would, and that was the beginning of a remarkable relationship and a pivotal phase of my career. Dr. Harvey was a legend at Hopkins and in the world of academic internal medicine. I had known him only casually as the William Osler Professor of Medicine whose teaching rounds on the wards were very formal and at times somewhat tense. There was quite a ritual before he appeared and during his teaching rounds. He could be thoroughly intimidating if the medical students or house staff didn't know their stuff. But he was totally different when I worked sone-on-one with him for 2 years. A wonderful mentor, we became very close (Figure 6). That may have been due, in part, to he and I sharing a real passion for medical history—something that most physicians care little about. He taught me many things about historical research and writing. I learned to dictate first drafts of papers that I then edited and edited and edited. He also taught me how to use library book carts with flat shelves to keep different projects organized, making it easier to research and write more than one study at a time.

WCR: *You are well known as a medical historian, where did that interest come from?*

WBF: More than anything, my deep commitment to researching and writing medical history is an outgrowth of my passion for collecting books. The dynamics aren't quite what you would imagine. People familiar with my publications might assume that I enjoyed history as a kid and took lots of history courses in college. That's not how it happened. I wasn't especially interested in history in high school or college. As a freshman at Hopkins I took the required survey course on the history of western civilization. During my junior year I took a course about the history of African-Americans, a new course Hopkins added in the context of the civil rights movement. It was very interesting because it looked at American history from a perspective that was totally new to me. I already had an interest in the Civil War, a popular topic in the 1960s because of the centennial of the conflict. By the time I was a junior in college I had several dozen books about the Civil War and Abraham Lincoln. Again, I have to emphasize I didn't really read those books. I collected them and looked at the pictures and read the captions. Nevertheless, it was really through the books that I truly got interested in history. For me book collecting and historical research have been like inseparable Siamese twins. If you took away one, would the other exist? I would say no. I think they are so intertwined it's like DNA strands. You can't take one away.

So, the medical history research and writing is a positive result of my bibliomania; by that I mean a state of mind in which my love of books got out of control (I became really obsessed with collecting books >40 years ago). I have often said that if I had become addicted to heroin when I became addicted to books I would have died about the same time as Janis Joplin and Jim Morrison. Luckily, my addiction was to books, things I could use for scholarly purposes. Eventually, when I began to focus my collecting on old medical books and medical history reference works, I used quite a few of them for research. But mainly it was about finding and acquiring old medical books—not reading them. Any passionate collector would understand this, but it seems strange to noncollectors.

WCR: *You collected many kinds of books in high school and college. When did you start to collect medical books?*

WBF: When I was a sophomore in college at Hopkins. There was a pizza place about a half-mile from the campus, and there was a used bookstore across the street. For me, it was the double pleasure of having a pizza and then spending time in the bookstore. It was owned by *John Gach*, a high-school graduate who is one of the world's experts on the history of psychology and psychiatry. He is very bright and learned about these subjects by focusing his business on them. John is about my age. Shortly after I met him in 1965, he encouraged me to start collecting medical books because I planned to be a doctor. That made a lot of sense, and he always had some interesting medical books and pamphlets. Because I didn't have a lot of spending money I began to trade nonmedical books I didn't want for medical books that I did. In that way I gradually built up a medical book collection and got rid of books that were out of scope. By the time I started medical school in 1968, I was really interested in collecting medical books. That interest was reinforced by the extraordinary medical history collection housed at the Welch Medical Library at the medical campus. The seventh and eighth floors of the medical library were filled with thousands of medical history books and pamphlets, and the rare book room was a remarkable place where the great classics of medicine were displayed in special cases. I found myself spending lots of time looking at old books.

WCR: *In addition to being an avid book collector, you have also been a bookseller. When did you start the book business?*

WBF: Well, I mentioned that I began trading nonmedical books for medical books with several Baltimore booksellers during medical school. There were many medical books and collections of reprints in that city because so many of the doctors at Hopkins had collected books, and their collections were dispersed when they died. Shortly before Lois and I moved to New York to start my internship in 1972, I ran an ad in the local newspaper saying that the following Saturday we would be selling about 2,000 books in our apartment for $2 or less each. More than 200 people came and went during that day. By the time it was over I had a big pile of 1- and 5-dollar bills and a lot fewer nonmedical books. We started the mail order book business In New York City later in 1972. As I mentioned earlier, my internship was grueling, but I had every other Saturday off. On many of those Saturdays I would take the subway to Union Square to visit the many used bookstores on Fourth Avenue, Broadway, and a few other streets near that subway stop. At the same time I ran a small box ad to buy medical books in a trade journal called the *Antiquarian Bookman's Weekly*. In response I got dozens of postcards, letters, and lists from people all over the country offering medical books for sale. It seemed that I had found a great way to buy medical books without even leaving our apartment.

Selling books in New York was more of a problem. Our apartment was too small to have many of my books there, so most of them were in my parent's basement in Yardley. We also didn't take our car to New York City. In Baltimore most of my books were in our apartment, and I could put 2 or 3 boxes of nonmedical books in my car and take them to booksellers who were willing to buy some of them or give me a credit toward purchases from their stock. Also, when we lived in New York I began to buy medical books for resale. Initially, I sold medical books only to other booksellers who specialized in this field. There were about a dozen medical book specialists in America, and Lois and I began creating small lists and catalogs of medical books for sale. Gradually, collectors who wanted to buy medical books learned about us and requested catalogs.

My bibliomania kept growing in the 1970s. Whenever Lois and I took a vacation, we always went to any old bookstores along the way. I'll tell you one funny story. In 1975, when we lived in New York, Lois and I drove around New England in our 1969 Camaro visiting bookshops. We had lists of booksellers, and as we traveled we checked the Yellow Pages for others not listed in book directories. One Sunday afternoon, driving through Connecticut, I stopped at a phone booth and found a listing for "The Old Mystic Bookshop." I called the shop on the chance it was open. A man answered the phone, and I asked if he had any medical books. He said no, but he did have about 40,000 used books. When we got to the shop it was in an old white clapboard house, and a man in his 70s came to the door. Just as we went inside, he asked if I was interested in psychology books. He led me to a back room and pointed to a wall filled from floor to ceiling with what he called psychology books.

Although many of the books in that room were on psychology, many were on physiology, especially neurophysiology. He had bought the library of *Walter R. Miles*, a psychologist who had been on the faculty at Yale and was interested in the physiologic aspects of behavior, vision, and other topics. It was a tremendous library that included several classic books such as a first edition of *Charles Sherrington's* 1906 monograph *Integrative Action of the Nervous System*. I couldn't believe how many interesting and important neuroscience and physiology books he had in his small shop. What made it even better is that he was very motivated to sell them and offered them to me for a few dollars a volume if I bought something like 200. Well, we filled the trunk and the back seat with boxes. The car was so full, Lois had to ride with her feet on a box on the floor in front of the passenger seat.

By this time I had figured out that the best way to buy the books I wanted was to sell books. As a collector I had to rely on the dozen or so medical booksellers for quotes or catalogs. As a book dealer I got lots of lists of medical books that general booksellers or so-called book scouts wanted to sell. Selling books was also a practical way to cope with my bibliomania. I could buy books I want for my personal collection. I could buy books for other people. I could buy 5 copies of a new medical history book if and when the publisher put it on sale, assuming I would later sell it to collectors for a few dollars more than I paid for it. If I had a copy of a specific book in good condition, I could buy a better copy and sell the lesser copy. If I found a copy that had a dust wrapper, I could buy that one and sell the one that didn't. If I saw a copy that was signed by the author, I could buy that one. In collecting terms, this process is called "trading up," and I've been doing it for >30 years. It explains why so many of the books in my personal collection are in fine condition and why quite a few are signed by the author. One question that sometimes comes up is how I decide what I collect and what I sell. It's actually quite simple. My main collecting interests are cardiology, William Osler, anatomic atlases, medical history, medical biography, and medical bibliography. I do not collect other subjects, and I sell books in areas I collect if I already have a copy in my personal collection. I also collect and sell engraved portraits and autographs of physicians and medical scientists.

One important thing to note is that the book business has always been kept totally separate from my professional life as a physician. I believed strongly that I wanted a firewall between my medical life that has always been in a group practice setting and my book life that has always been done on my time (nights, weekends, and during vacations). Moreover, the book business has always been strictly mail order. The time I devoted to the business was moderated by the fact that we had a secretary from 1978 to 2000 who handled all the inquiries as well as pulling, packing, and shipping the books.

After we left Marshfield in 2000 we downsized the business significantly, and Lois took over those responsibilities. All along I had the fun of hunting for the books on trips, looking through catalogs and doing a little research on the books I bought for resale to develop a short catalog description of each one. Basically, I would dictate a few sentences on each item that my secretary entered into a comprehensive computer program designed for booksellers. The brief descriptions I dictated were designed to provide a potential buyer with an idea of who the author was, what the book contained, and why it was collectable in a historical sense. Doing this for literally thousands of medical books over 3 decades, I learned a lot about the history of medicine. It's like a 1,000-piece puzzle or a huge patchwork quilt. I've got most of the edge pieces together and figured out the pattern because I've looked up the lives and contributions of most of the influential physicians, surgeons, and medical scientists who wrote books over the past 200 years.

WCR: *How many total books do you have?*

WBF: That's a tough question to answer because we've never counted them. Our computer database provides some help in estimating how many books we have, but there are many books that are not in the database. Also, the books fall into 3 main categories: those that are for sale, those that are part of my personal collections, and those that have not been cataloged or may move back and forth between the business stock and my collection. Over the years I've assembled an incredibly comprehensive reference collection numbering several thousand volumes. My personal cardiology collection includes well over 2,000 books and 10,000 offprints. Overall, I would estimate that there are about 25,000 books and at least that many pamphlets and offprints. Before we left Wisconsin we wholesaled almost 10,000 books and medical journal issues to make the move more manageable.

WCR: *Your passion for book collecting led to your deep interest in the history of medicine. As a Robert Wood Johnson Clinical Scholar at Hopkins you got a master's degree in medical history. How did that come about?*

WBF: I mentioned earlier that it was my reluctance to do traditional biomedical research as a first-year cardiology fellow at Hopkins that led Victor McKusick and Mike Weisfeldt to encourage me to apply for a Clinical Scholar grant. I haven't explained how I got so interested in historical research, except to say that my book collecting was a major stimulus. Like many things in my life a mixture of mentoring and serendipity was involved. As a college senior, I took a course taught at the medical school by *Louis Lasagna*, a pioneer of clinical pharmacology who also published articles and books about medical ethics and medical sociology. In 1968 he taught a seminar course open to undergraduates called *The Physician and Society*. Much of the course dealt with medical ethics. We talked about the ethics of abortion and other social issues that intersected with medicine.

A subject that came up in one of these sessions was euthanasia. This was in 1968, and I was still a premed undergraduate. When Dr. Lasagna said "euthanasia" I thought he was saying "youth in Asia," because our country was deeply involved in the Viet Nam war at the time. Suddenly, it became obvious he was talking about mercy killing—euthanasia—not youth in Asia. I had never heard the word and wasn't aware of the concept. We had to do a term study for this course, and I decided to write about contemporary attitudes about euthanasia. I did most of the research over spring vacation at the Princeton University library because it was about 15 miles from my home in Yardley. As a college senior, I had never been in a medical library. The research I did on contemporary attitudes toward euthanasia reflected a combination of popular, legal, religious, and philosophical views of the practice. I got a good grade on the study and continued to have an interest in the topic of euthanasia.

During my first year of medical school at Hopkins I decided to spend my elective quarter in the history of medicine researching the intellectual origins of the concept of active euthanasia. The Institute of the History of Medicine at Johns Hopkins has long been one of the premier programs in the history of medicine. *Owsei Temkin* (who died in 2003 at the age of 99) was one of the world leaders of medical history, but he became emeritus professor the year I started medical school. They had just hired a new professor from McGill University, *Lloyd Stevenson*. He had been dean at McGill, but his academic field was the history of medicine. Unlike Temkin, Stevenson was not a very inspiring lecturer. History of Medicine was a required course during lunchtime, and I recall sharing my classmates' dislike for memorizing names and dates in the history of medicine. In fact, I never liked memorizing much of anything.

Unlike my undergraduate study on contemporary attitudes about euthanasia, as a medical student I used the rich resources of the Johns Hopkins medical library. They had a huge collection of old medical books and journals and all the references necessary to find obscure medical articles published decades or centuries ago. As I looked through bibliographies and historical books and articles, I found that no one had ever written up on how this rather extreme concept of active euthanasia was introduced into medical thought. After reading dozens of articles written in the late 19th century, I discovered that the idea of active euthanasia was first described in detail in 1870 by *Samuel Williams*, a schoolmaster in Birmingham, England. He was a member of an amateur philosophical

group called the Birmingham Liberal Club. His published essay about active euthanasia reflected the influence of what came to be called social Darwinism. It also reflected that morphine, ether, and chloroform had recently been introduced into medical practice to treat or eliminate pain. In 1979, a decade after I did the research, I finally published a study that explained how this radical concept was introduced into medical thought.

WCR: *So you really liked the Institute of the History of Medicine at Hopkins and all the books they had there. Did you keep up your interest in medical history during the rest of medical school and during your residency?*

WBF: Only to a limited degree because of the clinical demands on my time. That's one reason my essay on the history of euthanasia was published a decade after I did the research.

WCR: *You got a master's degree in medical history. What did you have to do to get that degree?*

WBF: There were few required courses or seminars at the Institute of the History of Medicine in 1976 to 1978, when I was working on my degree. The main focus was researching and writing a thesis. The subject I first chose, and the topic I eventually settled on represent 2 more examples of serendipity. As a fellow member of the American Osler Society, you will appreciate this story. I began thinking about a topic for my thesis in 1976. A few years earlier *Jack McGovern* and *Chester Burns* edited a book entitled *Humanism in Medicine*, a series of essays about William Osler, the Canadian-born physician who was the first professor of medicine at Johns Hopkins. The book contained an essay on Osler's strong objection to expanding the full-time faculty system of medical education from the basic sciences to the clinical subjects, written by *Wilbert Davison*, the former dean at Duke. When I read that study I became fascinated with the dispute about the full-time system during the early decades of the 20th century and how the concept and its consequences influenced American medical education. So, I decided to write my thesis on the history of the full-time system of medical education.

During the 1976 meeting of the American Association for the History of Medicine I met *Richard Wolfe*, the rare books librarian and archivist of the Countway Library of the Harvard Medical School. Dick is one of the smartest and most energetic people I have ever met. In fact, he's as productive as you; he's your match. But he's got so many different interests. He's got an encyclopedic mind and knew the Harvard medical archives inside out. When we first met I mentioned I was interested in the history of the full-time faculty system of medical education. When I asked if the Harvard archives might have some good sources, it was as if I had plugged him into an electric outlet. Dick speaks in a very accelerated fashion, reflecting how fast he thinks. So he said in a rapid staccato fashion, "Full-time, full-time. *Henry Bowditch*. You've got to study the Bowditch papers. He was the first full-timer; he started full-time."

Henry Bowditch was a Harvard physiologist during the final 3 decades of the 19th century whose name is associated with the "All-or-None Law of Cardiac Contraction." Well, Dick Wolfe convinced me I had to go to Boston and look through the huge collection of Bowditch's letters and manuscripts. It turned out that there was so much rich and untapped manuscript material that I narrowed the subject of my master's thesis to Bowditch, how he became America's first full-time physiologist, and his impact on the professionalization of physiology and the reform of American medical education. Eventually, I incorporated material I had collected on other physiologists in my book *The Development of American Physiology: Scientific Medicine in the 19th Century* published by Johns Hopkins in 1986.

WCR: *You've talked about how you got interested in the history of physiology and scientific medicine. What was your clinical training in cardiology like at Hopkins?*

WBF: First, I should mention that I did 6 months of cardiology fellowship at New York Hospital-Cornell Medical Center during my year as a senior medical resident. That was an experimental program that allowed senior residents to focus on a subspecialty if he or she knew what they wanted to do at that point. My cardiology training at New York Hospital was devoted mainly to inpatient consultations and electrocardiographic interpretation. During the 2 years as a cardiology fellow at Hopkins (1975 to 1977), I did all the clinical rotations except that I traded off my second year cath lab rotation for more time in echo.

WCR: *What made you decide to emphasize echocardiography?*

WBF: Again, mentoring was an important part of that decision. I mentioned Mac Harvey's influence on my historical research and writing. My early interest in echocardiography was due mainly to the influence of *Nick Fortuin* at Hopkins. In 1975, Nick had just left the full-time faculty to go into practice in Baltimore, but he was still head of what was then called the Cardiographics Laboratory, reflecting its earlier focus on phonocardiograms and pulse tracings. Jim Weiss was the associate director of the lab at the time, and he also mentored me. He urged me to join the American Society of Echocardiography when it was formed, and I did. Nick Fortuin was a very gregarious, funny, and energetic guy who was also an excellent cardiologist. Early in my fellowship he sort of took me under his wing. It was also a very exciting time in echo. M-mode echo was a pretty new technique, and the echo tracings were often combined with phonocardiograms, pulse tracings, and apex cardiograms. I thought it was fantastic to be able to see murmurs and heart sounds printed out and timed with the motion of the valves displayed by echo. I said earlier how much I enjoyed cardiac physical diagnosis and cardiac physiology. Echo tied these things together. For example, an M-mode echo of the mitral valve showed how the leaflets behaved in mitral valve prolapse and mitral stenosis. Suddenly, the mystifying sounds of the heart became visual, and I could figure them out. In addition to Nick Fortuin and Jim Weiss, the technical staff in the echo lab were fun to be around.

FIGURE 7. Johns Hopkins Cardiology Division 1975-1976 (WBF, third row from bottom, third from left).

By the end of my first year of fellowship, I knew I wanted to focus my clinical cardiology career on echocardiography (Figure 7). I wasn't interested in invasive cardiology, a field that was growing very rapidly as a result of the recent invention of coronary artery bypass surgery. Most of the fellows gravitated to the cath lab. Only a few of us did not. *Pat Come* was 1 year ahead of me in cardiology and she, too, focused on echo. *Bernadine Healy* was a year ahead of me in the fellowship program, although she had already spent time at the National Institutes of Health working with you. I first met Bernadine when I was a senior medical student doing a subinternship at Good Samaritan Hospital, a private hospital affiliated with Hopkins. She was an assistant resident at the time and was tough as nails. I never had an unpleasant interaction with her, but I saw her tear into some of my classmates for one reason or another.

Another thing I took advantage of as a fellow at Hopkins were the specialty clinics. In addition to general cardiac clinic where I worked with Nick Fortuin and *Frank Davis*, an excellent cardiologist in private practice in Baltimore, I also participated in the obstetrics cardiac clinic where pregnant women with known or suspected heart disease were seen. A unique part of the Hopkins cardiology program that few fellows took advantage of was the adult congenital heart disease clinic run by *Helen Taussig*, a true pioneer in the field of pediatric cardiology. Although she was in her late 70s by this time, Dr. Taussig still saw a few patients she had cared for years and decades earlier. In some ways, her clinic was a living museum! She saw patients who had long outlived their predicted natural history or who had been operated on by *Alfred Blalock* or others.

WCR: *You left Hopkins in 1978 to join the Marshfield Clinic, a multispecialty group practice in Wisconsin. How did you decide to join that practice?*

WBF: During 1977 to 1978, I was an instructor in cardiology, but much of my time was devoted to completing my master's degree in medical history. By this time, Mac Harvey and I were really close, and I was under a lot of pressure from him to stay at Hopkins. I had studied the history of academic medicine for 2 years, and I knew I wanted to enter private cardiology practice and focus on echo. They didn't really need another full-time person in echo at Hopkins at this point, and I knew my research interest in medical history was not mainstream in terms of the likelihood of academic advancement. So, I decided that the best thing for me was to look for a job where I could develop an echo lab and practice cardiology with protected time for my historical research.

The Marshfield Clinic opportunity is another example of the powerful but unpredictable phenomenon of serendipity. In 1976 Nick Fortuin asked me to be an instructor in the introductory echocardiography course he taught at Hopkins twice a year. Cardiologists came from all over the country to take this brief course that included live patients. This was at the same time the American Society of Echocardiography was founded, and many practices were interested in adding echo to the services they provided. I remember how pleased Nick was that *Hughes Day*, the American pioneer of the coronary care unit movement, took his course. During one of these echo courses I met 2 doctors from the Marshfield Clinic, one was a pediatric cardiologist and the other was an adult invasive cardiologist. They wanted a tour of the history of medicine library, and when we walked there I remember them describing this big group practice in a tiny town in Wisconsin. I had never heard of the Marshfield Clinic and, at that point, I had no real interest in asking them about job opportunities there. Lois and I thought we would stay in the mid-Atlantic region, somewhere between Massachusetts and Virginia between the Atlantic Ocean and the western Pennsylvania border.

When the time came to look for a job, I was a very disciplined job seeker. I learned something from Mac Harvey, who had trained hundreds of medicine residents, that I still tell fellows when they are considering career alternatives. He said that job-hunting involves a spectrum that blends interests and opportunities. Obviously, the first decision is whether you want to stay in academics or enter private practice. I wanted to go into practice, but I wanted to join an academically oriented practice if I could find one. Mac Harvey's spectrum ranges from emphasizing what you want to do versus where you want to be. In other words, if you want to stay somewhere or you want to move to a specific location, you have to be open-minded about what you will do to stay in one place or go somewhere else. At the other end of the spectrum you define precisely what you want to do, and then you have to be very open-minded about where you'll go to do it. I knew my personality was at the latter end of the spectrum. I knew exactly what I wanted to do. I wanted to be a clinical cardiologist with a subspecialty in echo at a place that would support my research interest in medical history.

When I was considering job opportunities in 1977 I was proactive in a way you don't see very often

today. I ran an ad in a couple of journals and wrote to several state medical societies describing what I wanted to do. Cardiology in the mid-1970s was in an enormous growth phase. Echo and nuclear cardiology were still relatively new techniques, and invasive cardiology was growing like crazy in response to the introduction of coronary bypass surgery less than a decade earlier. There was a tremendous demand for cardiologists. I talked with people about different jobs, and I interviewed for a hospital-based position at the Berkshire Medical Center in Massachusetts. None of these opportunities was quite what I was looking for. Then, I got a letter from the medical director at the Marshfield Clinic, who expressed great interest in having me come and start an echo laboratory. He described the size and scope of the practice. I remember telling Lois I had found a great job, "too bad it's in Wisconsin."

This attitude reflected I was an east coast guy who was raised around Philadelphia and trained in Baltimore and New York City. But as Lois and I talked about it, the Marshfield job sounded intriguing, so we went to look at the clinic and the community. Lois was pregnant with our first child at the time, and that was significant part of the equation. She had loved both New York City and Baltimore. Now, we rationalized that Marshfield, a town of about 18,000 in rural central Wisconsin, really in the middle of nowhere, would be a great place to raise a family. When we visited we liked the people we met, and the Marshfield Clinic was a very impressive place.

Before I finally decided to take the Marshfield job, I ran into Tom Killip at Hopkins. By this time (1977) he had left New York Hospital and was chief of medicine at Evanston Hospital in Evanston, Illinois. Tom was doing a site visit at Hopkins relating to the Coronary Artery Surgery Study (CASS) trial. I asked him if he knew anything about Marshfield Clinic. He said he did, and that they had randomized more patients in CASS than any other center. That was a big boost. It made Marshfield seem like an academically oriented group practice. It was also challenging and exciting to be able to start an echo lab at a referral center that already had significant invasive cardiology and open-heart surgery programs. The few echoes performed at Marshfield in 1977 were interpreted by a senior radiologist interested in ultrasound.

WCR: *How did things go when you got to the Marshfield Clinic?*

WBF: When I went to Marshfield Clinic in 1978, I was idealistic and pretty naïve. The multispecialty group practice model seemed somewhat familiar because that is the way most academic medical centers functioned. At Marshfield the main focus was on patient care. They really needed more help in cardiology because they had had difficulty recruiting and retaining cardiologists and some other specialists because of their location and salary philosophy. In the early 1950s they established a salary plan that after 5 years every doctor was paid the same salary, no matter what their specialty. So pediatricians, heart surgeons, psychiatrists, and plastic surgeons all got paid the same salary after 5 years on staff. Most of my colleagues during fellowship knew all about the income potential of invasive cardiology in 1975. But that wasn't my interest. I wanted to be an echocardiographer and clinical cardiologist with an interest in historical research so I wound up in Marshfield, Wisconsin. As Lois and I had hoped, it turned out to be a phenomenal place to raise our kids. It also turned out to be an excellent place for me to develop my own particular interests.

I started there in July 1978 at $52,000, very close to their top salary at the time because they really wanted me. It turned out that I was walking into a firestorm about salaries because problems related to recruiting and retaining certain types of specialists had become critical. For the 22 years I was at Marshfield Clinic there were 22 years of fighting about salaries at this very democratic institution where the salaries of every specialty were voted on by the board every year. Also, the board was huge because every physician who was voted a full member of the group after a 2-year associate period became a member of the board. By the time I became a full member of the clinic in 1980 there were about 160 people on the board. We met once a month in the evening and discussed, debated, and voted on all sorts of things, from the most trivial issue to major decisions regarding acquisition of practices and major equipment purchases. There was an executive committee of 9 people including the officers. The president was elected every year. Any member of the board of directors was eligible to be president. The executive committee members were elected for a 3-year term and they could only serve two 3-year terms.

WCR: *All on the board were MDs?*

WBF: No. There were a few PhDs and some oral surgeons on the staff, but it was almost entirely made up of physicians and surgeons. Department and division elections were held every 2 years, and everyone got to vote, even the new associates. When I got there in 1978, Marshfield Clinic had a traditional sort of academic arrangement in terms of a department of medicine and subspecialty divisions. That changed for cardiology in 1979. One of the sore spots for all of the medical subspecialists was a thing called "number one call" which was a general medical call for nights and weekends that rotated among all of the general internists and medical subspecialists. This was before there were full-time emergency room physicians. Cardiology had been relieved of this call because they were so short staffed before I came.

When I arrived there was still far too much cardiology for the size of the division that consisted of 7 cardiologists. When our division argued that we should not have to return to this general medical call you can imagine the furor it caused. The only option that cardiology had to stay off that call was to become a separate department. We lobbied and argued for a year before the 2 committees that decided such things allowed us to become a separate department. It is important to understand that this structural change had no implications whatsoever in terms of our salaries.

We knew that it would be more difficult to recruit more cardiologists if they had to participate in general medical call, and that argument carried a lot of weight.

I was a very vocal proponent for cardiology becoming a separate department, and I was identified by several of the cardiologists as someone who could effectively lead our group. The governance and leadership structure of Marshfield Clinic was totally opposite that of academic centers. Marshfield was very democratic, and department and division chairs are elected every 2 years by a majority vote of all members of their group. I was elected chair of cardiology for the first time in 1981 and was re-elected 8 times, serving a total of 18 years. By the time I left Marshfield in 2000, I had hired every cardiologist who was practicing there. I enjoyed the administrative aspect of my life because I liked to solve problems and help move things forward. I enjoyed trying to build up the cardiology program there, but I spent far too much time and energy fighting for cardiology salaries. I always came well armed with data, and that infuriated some members of other divisions and departments. The data I showed reflected the dramatic growth of single-specialty cardiology groups, and that we were competing with academic centers and multispecialty groups for doctors and for patients. I believed deeply that a strong and stable cardiology department was in the best interest of the Marshfield Clinic. What agitated others was that a significant factor in achieving that goal was paying cardiologists higher salaries.

Lois and I developed some wonderful friendships in Marshfield, and we enjoyed living there very much, especially when we were raising our girls. The remote location and size of the town meant that I had more discretionary time than cardiologists elsewhere who commuted long distances and worked at several hospitals. I lived three quarters of a mile from work, and we still lived on the edge of the country. Marshfield was a community I have characterized lovingly as a town without social obligations and without social opportunities. No one belonged to the country club unless they really liked golf. The restaurant situation was always problematic because the population base was too small to support anything resembling a really good restaurant. Cross coverage was excellent in our group so when you were off, you were off. That meant I could spend most nights and weekends with my family, doing historical research and writing, and working with my books.

As I mentioned, my book collecting and book selling have had a very profound positive effect on my passion for medical history research and writing. My comprehensive medical history reference collection made it possible for me to publish so many historical papers as an independent scholar working in isolation. If I have a question I need to answer in the course of my research, I don't have to go to the library to look something up. I don't have to wait for the staff to get an old journal only to discover the article I requested isn't what I want. I can short-circuit all of that. In my own home, I can do my research at night and weekends and have instant access to most of the information I need. This has given me an enormous advantage over other medical historians, especially clinician historians. Today, most medical history is written by social historians, in part, because few physicians have the time to pursue serious historical scholarship.

WCR: *Your bibliography shows that you were a regular contributor of historical articles to* Circulation *in the 1980s. How did that come about?*

WBF: It was a combination of mentoring and serendipity. When *Burt Sobel* became editor of *Circulation* in 1983, he wanted to have a series that demonstrated the unforeseen practical consequences of basic research. He first invited *Julius Comroe* to write the essays because he had written many papers and a book about this very phenomenon—how all clinical advances can be traced back to dozens, if not hundreds, of small research projects and advances pieced together by a multitude of persons. But Comroe was ill and couldn't take on the assignment. Comroe recommended Mac Harvey, but he was consumed with several historical projects. Mac Harvey encouraged Burt Sobel to call me. This was in late 1982, and I'd been at Marshfield just 4 years. I'd been chair of cardiology for about a year, and our cardiology practice and the echo lab were growing. I was already working on my book on the professionalization of American physiology. I remember distinctly getting Burt's call. I knew who he was, but I'd never met him. He described his idea for a series that he envisioned in *Circulation* and explained he'd like to have an article every 3 months. I told him I didn't really think I could do it because I was so busy already. But as we were talking, I realized how stupid it would be to turn down a column in *Circulation*. So I said, "Okay. Let me understand a little bit better what you want and I'll try my best to do it." His initial notion was to have very crisp, very brief essays.

The first study I did for my "Preludes and Progress" series in *Circulation* was on Starling and his law of the heart. I found it difficult to compress into a short space how Starling got interested in cardiac physiology, what he did, and what effect it had on practice. This was back in the days when authors received lots of reprint requests. I had a sense that people were reading the articles. Burt placed them so they were the lead articles in *Circulation*. There were 13 of them over the course of 3 and 1/2 years. The first one was short. The only real criticism that I received on that series was when *Michael O'Rourke*, from Australia, wrote Burt a letter. Michael, who I came to know in later years, argued that my essay was superficial. I used that letter to convince Burt Sobel that I needed more pages for each essay. Basically, Burt responded by telling me to write longer papers if that was what it took to make the point. The average article wound up being 6 to 7 printed pages. I remember being incredibly disciplined about this. I had to do research to get these pieces together, but they gave me tremendous respect for deadlines. I worked extremely hard on them.

I really enjoyed researching and writing the Preludes and Progress series. This was the first time I really read carefully the research and clinical papers of scientists and physicians of the late 19th and early 20th centuries to see how they approached cardiovascular physiology and clinical practice. It was amazing how sophisticated some of the research was and surprising how long it often took for scientific advances to be translated into practice. One example that I thought was incredible related to the career and contributions of American physiologist *William Townsend Porter*. Like most first generation full-time American physiologists, he spent 3 years studying in Germany around 1890. While there, he wrote to one of his mentors at St. Louis University saying he knew he could practice medicine *or* he could be a physiologist, but if he tried to combine the 2, he thought he would be an amateur at both. I couldn't believe the content of this letter.

I was writing a book on the professionalization of physiology at the time, and I couldn't have imagined a more compelling letter in terms of arguing for full-time careers in the basic medical sciences. Lois was driving the car on a trip when I read a Xerox of this letter that I had received, and I said, "Wow! Listen to this." Porter moved from St. Louis to Boston to join Henry Bowditch's physiology at Harvard in 1893. His research focused on the coronary circulation by occluding the coranary arteries in dogs. He measured intracardiac pressure, evaluated the heart rhythm, and studied the pathology and histology of the myocardium in response to different amounts of time he occluded a coronary artery. Porter's experiments in the 1890s were remarkable because his long-forgotten publications had implications almost a century later when there was a tremendous amount of interest in myocardial preservation.

WCR: *You and Lois have 2 offspring. Tell me about them.*

WBF: We have 2 daughters. *Katherine Anne* was born at The Johns Hopkins Hospital on February 18, 1978. We didn't know whether the baby was a girl or a boy, but we knew a caesarian (C) section would be necessary because the baby was in the breach position. The C-section was scheduled for Monday morning, and Lois went into labor early Saturday morning. She was in labor for about 4 hours before they could start the C-section because there were some trauma cases going on and anesthesiologists were busy with those. Lois had been head nurse of the obstetrical operating rooms a few years earlier, and she knew her obstetrician very well because he was a chief resident when she worked there. Finally, they delivered our daughter while I was in the room. Lois and I nicknamed her "Lerty" for alert because her eyes were wide open when she was born. Our second child, *Elizabeth Jane* was born on June 1, 1981, at St. Joseph's Hospital in Marshfield. Because she was the first baby born in June in Wood County, Wisconsin, Elizabeth was the "June diary baby." There were more cows than people in Wood County at the time, so this was a big deal. We got a variety of things from local merchants to celebrate the event.

WCR: *What was Katherine like as a child and what is she doing now?*

WBF: Katherine was a very social child from the time she could walk and talk. She was smiley, friendly, and precocious. She never talked baby talk, in part because we never talked baby talk to our kids. Katherine spoke early and clearly, and adults found her incredibly engaging. She was a very self-assured and opinionated child, something that caught some of her friend's parents off guard. Still, she was very well liked and had lots of friends. Her sister, Elizabeth, was born when Katherine was 3. We have some great pictures of Katherine holding her baby sister minutes after we brought her home from the hospital. They bonded very quickly. Their personalities have always been very different, but they were (and are) very close. When Katherine was in elementary school she was very outgoing. On the other hand Elizabeth was quiet and shy. She didn't want to go to kindergarten. She didn't want to take ballet or perform. Elizabeth didn't want to do any of that. By the time she got to high school, however, Elizabeth had become very outgoing and self-confident. Both girls were involved in a lot of extracurricular activities, especially Elizabeth. She was elected class president for both her junior and senior years of high school and was junior prom queen. They both had several boyfriends over the years. That reminds me of a funny story.

In the mid-1990s I was very involved in the government relations activities of the American College of Cardiology. As a result I had gotten to know Congressman *David Obey* who represented our district in Wisconsin and chaired the powerful House Committee on Appropriations. Dave brought influential politicians and government officials to our district regularly. It turned out that First Lady *Hillary Clinton* was going to speak to about 250 people Dave invited to participate in a special event in Wausau, Wisconsin, the evening of February 18. Coincidentally, that was Katherine's 16th birthday. When I got an invitation to the event I said to Katherine, "I think you could meet the first lady on your 16th birthday." She said, "Why would I want to do that? I want to be with my friends." I said, "Katherine, think about it. If you spend that evening with your friends, it will blur with every other night you spent with your friends in high school. You'll never forget meeting the first lady." She thought about it for a moment and said she would go if her boyfriend could come along. I agreed, and the event was very energizing. Mrs. Clinton chatted with Katherine for a few moments as she greeted participants in the event. Later, Katherine received a great handwritten note from Hillary, "Happy 16th birthday, Katherine Fye from Hillary Rodham Clinton." She treasures that memento of an evening she almost missed.

After graduating from Marshfield Senior High School, Katherine went to Carleton College, in Northfield, Minnesota. Carleton is ranked fifth in the nation in *US News and World Report's* ranking of liberal arts colleges. In addition to having a great sense of humor, Katherine is very deliberate. In many ways she is very much like me. The way she chose Carleton is an example of how decisive she can be. One of my closest friends in

Marshfield had a daughter who was one of Katherine's best friends. He took his daughter to see several colleges and universities in the upper Midwest. Katherine decided to meet them in Northfield so she and her friend could visit Carleton together. When Katherine toured Carleton she decided immediately that she wanted to go there. She applied, was accepted, and loved it. She graduated from Carleton in 2000 with a major in English. She played bassoon in the orchestra and got very involved in birdwatching and natural history. President *Bill Clinton* was her graduation speaker, and he shook hands with each of the 400 or so graduates.

Katherine graduated from Carleton when I was transitioning from Marshfield Clinic to Mayo Clinic. When she moved back to Marshfield after graduation I was on a 3-month vacation sabbatical, something Marshfield physicians were eligible for after 20 years of service. We were building a house in Rochester, and I moved into an apartment there in early August. People would ask me if I had children, and I'd say "yes." When they asked me about them I would say, "Our older daughter graduated from Carleton and is pleasantly adrift." That's because Katherine didn't know what she wanted to do at that point. She lived at home for a year. During this time she decided to be an elementary teacher. She's always liked old people and little kids. Before she could apply to graduate school in elementary education she had to take several prerequisite courses. After taking some classes in Rochester she enrolled as a full-time student at the University of Minnesota. Katherine applied to the University of Michigan Graduate School in elementary education and got her master's degree and teaching certificate from there in 2003. She teaches first grade in Ypsilanti, Michigan, a distant suburb of Detroit near Ann Arbor. Her class is about 80% African-American and the other 20% is a mixture. She absolutely loves it.

WCR: *What about your younger daughter, Elizabeth?*

WBF: As I mentioned earlier, Elizabeth evolved from a shy little kid into a very self-assured, outgoing, and energetic teenager. Although Lois and I did not know it at the time, Elizabeth decided she wanted to be an actor when she was in elementary school. She did lots of play-acting with her friends and enjoyed dressing up in costumes and role-playing. Elizabeth says the thing that really convinced her she wanted to be an actor was a special 2-part TV production of *Alice in Wonderland*. The cast included many well-known comedians, actors, and stars like Carol Channing and Imogene Coca. The little girl who played Alice in this production had long, straight blond hair, and Elizabeth tells us that she said to herself after seeing that special, "I could to that. I want to be an actor." She didn't talk about it much for the next 2 or 3 years. She got parts in several school plays in junior high. By the time she got to high school Elizabeth was completely convinced she really wanted to be an actor. I saw all of the plays and musicals she was in during junior and senior high school. The one performance that convinced me how much talent and potential Elizabeth had was when she played Chava in *Fiddler on the Roof* as a senior in high school. She was remarkable, and many of our friends who had seen her in other productions were very impressed by this performance.

When Elizabeth was in the 10th grade she really wanted to go to a summer acting camp. I subscribed to the Sunday *New York Times*, and Lois found an ad in the back of the magazine for "Stage Door Manor," an acting camp in the Catskill Mountain area of New York where there were many vaudeville theaters in the 1950s and 1960s. Although I was reluctant to have Elizabeth get into the New York orbit at that point, she and Lois convinced me that is was okay. She went and absolutely loved it. The kids were mostly in senior high school, and they were all very serious about acting. In fact, several of them already had agents. Elizabeth felt at home with these kids, although she had grown up in dairy country with kids coming in off the farm to go to school with her. She went back to Stage Door Manor for a total of 3 summers and got lots of valuable experience there. She could certainly act and sing, and she was learning how to dance. Elizabeth was cast as the female lead in *42nd Street*, *On the 20th Century*, and *Bernarda Alba*. I remember very well when the owner of Stage Door Manor told Lois and me, "You've got a star on your hands."

WCR: *Where did Elizabeth go to college?*

WBF: That's an interesting question. I wanted Elizabeth to go to Carleton College because it's a great school, her sister was there and loved it, and Northfield was a small town just 3 hours from Marshfield. Elizabeth applied, was accepted, and started college there in the fall of 1999. She was in 3 theatrical productions as a freshman, but she was very frustrated because the other students in the plays viewed them as an extracurricular activity. On the other hand, Elizabeth wanted to be challenged and to feel she was learning skills that would help her compete in the tough field of acting. She didn't share those feelings with me at the time. But that changed suddenly and dramatically when Lois and Elizabeth picked me up at the Minneapolis airport when I returned from the summer 2000 American College of Cardiology board meeting.

We stayed at a hotel in Minneapolis that night and after dinner Elizabeth handed me a several-page letter describing how unhappy she had been at Carleton. The letter was filled with emotion and very compelling. In it, Elizabeth explained how much she wanted to be an actor and that Carleton was the wrong school for that goal. She wanted to go to New York University. She was going to apply to NYU, and that was that! I was really blown away by her letter. I decided I had to respect her ambition and support her career goal. Elizabeth did everything she said, and more. She applied to NYU, was accepted, moved to New York City, and graduated in 2003 with a major in drama and a minor in psychology. Dustin Hoffman, whose son was also at NYU, was their graduation speaker. She now lives in Greenwich Village in a fifth-floor walkup apartment with a close friend who is also an aspiring actor.

WCR: *It is supposed to be very hard to get work as an actor in New York City. How has she done?*

WBF: You are certainly right about it being a hard field to break into. I reminded her of that repeatedly during high school and college. As a senior at NYU, she was one of just a few students selected to perform before an audience of agents and casting directors. Several agents expressed interest in her, and she signed with Harden-Curtis Associates, a highly regarded firm. Although she graduated only 1 year ago, she appeared on *Law and Order: SVU* (ABC) with a speaking part about 3 months ago. She was also in 3 episodes of the soap opera *One Life to Live* (NBC). Recently, she was chosen to be part of the cast in a 6-week workshop devoted to developing a musical called *Good Vibrations*, based on the Beach Boys. The musical is scheduled to open on Broadway in 2005. Although she is not assured of a role in the Broadway production, the experience will be valuable. Acting is an extraordinarily tough profession. She auditions all the time. I see my passion, my drive, and my ambition in Elizabeth. In each kid, I see my intensity and other unique parts of me, but I also see a lot of Lois in both of them. They are very different, but they are great friends. Both girls are very close to their mom, and I feel that they are also very close to me, although I am almost always the one to say "Wait a minute" or "I don't think so." They have known for a long time to go to their mom if they want something.

One reason that Lois and I are so close to our girls is that they lost all 4 of their grandparents when they were very young. Lois's father died when he was 64, and her mother died when she was 68. My father died when he was 68, and my mother died when she was 73. So, by the time Katherine was 9 and Elizabeth was 5, they no longer had grandparents. The only way to rationalize the tragic and premature loss of our parents and their grandparents is to explain that I got to know my kids much better because they didn't have grandparents to visit during summer vacations and holidays. As a result, the 4 of us spent all of our vacations together, including 4 trips to Europe to hunt for books. During those trips we rode around in the same car and stayed in bed and breakfasts or small hotels. As a result I got to know my kids tremendously well.

WCR: *You mentioned your mother particularly was quite religious during your growing up stage. Do you go to church now? Has that been a part of your life?*

WBF: We do. We belong to the First Presbyterian Church in Rochester. We haven't been particularly active because in the 3 and 1/2 years that we've lived there we've been so incredibly busy with unique travel opportunities and obligations. When we lived in Marshfield, we attended church regularly. Lois was very involved in our church there. Part of it, too, was our kids. We thought it was important to have them firmly grounded. I'm sort of a spiritual person, but I'm not a deeply religious person. I liked going to church in Marshfield partly because it made me think about things differently, and I saw people I knew and liked in a different context. In Rochester I have less discretionary time because my days are somewhat longer,

FIGURE 8. Lois and WBF at 25th Johns Hopkins Medical School reunion, 1997.

FIGURE 9. WBF, Lois, Katherine, and Elizabeth, New York City, 2004.

my commute takes longer, and I have been traveling more on weekends. So when Sunday comes and I am home, I think, "Gosh, I've got to go to work tomorrow." I often start working on some historical project at about at 7:30 A.M. and work most of the day. It's a balancing act.

WCR: *Bruce, you were in Marshfield for how long?*

WBF: Twenty-two years.

WCR: *In that period of time your 2 girls were more or less raised. They had either gone to college or were about to go to college. You had a house that had the capacity to handle your huge book collection. You had been elected every 2 years as Chairman of the Department of Cardiology. You enjoyed your setup. You took off 1 month each year. You had a trip somewhere every month. Why did you elect to go to the Mayo Clinic?*

WBF: That was certainly the most spontaneous important decision I've ever made in my life. It was totally unexpected. Lois and I had not talked about leaving Marshfield. We enjoyed our life there, and had many very close friends. I found my work at Marshfield Clinic very satisfying, and I had enough time to pursue my historical and bookish interests (Figure 8). But frankly, as anyone who has been in a leadership or administrative position can understand, there comes a

time when you feel you've expended your energy and exhausted your resources in terms of trying to move the system, change policies, or have people see things your way. My biggest challenge during the 18 years I was chair was to try to build and maintain a strong cardiology department in a large multispecialty group practice against a significant salary gradient that attracted many cardiologists to join single specialty groups. Finally, I grew tired of lobbying for cardiology salaries in an institutional context where salary discussions took place in the open with literally hundreds of doctors in the audience.

I decided I no longer wanted to be chair of cardiology in early 1998, but as a result of tremendous pressure from my colleagues in cardiology I completed my ninth term that ended in January 1999. The following September, our younger daughter started at Carleton College, and our older daughter began her senior years there. We were suddenly empty nesters (Figure 9). Although we had lived in Marshfield for 22 years, we had lived in Manhattan for 3 years, Baltimore for 11 years, and had grown up around Philadelphia. We traveled a lot during our Marshfield years to make up for the lack of cultural attractions and restaurants in that small town. Lois was always enthusiastic about using our vacation time to go to interesting places, to eat in ethnic restaurants, and to enjoy the things we didn't have access to at home. But in terms of the decision to leave Marshfield, it is really hard to believe how quickly we made up our minds. We'd never really talked about leaving. We'd wondered where our close friends would eventually end up because a number of people clearly were going to move somewhere else when they retired.

Lois and I were sitting in our family room on a Saturday in the fall of 1999, and I said to her, "If I didn't have all these books, I'd seriously consider leaving." She said, "You can't let the books control your life." I said, "I'm calling Mayo on Monday" She said, "Good." It came absolutely out of the blue. There is no question that this brief conversation and the feelings it reflected were catalyzed by a few specific incidents at work that pushed me over the edge in terms of saying, "I don't need this aggravation any longer." For years various people around the country had approached me and asked if I would be interested in this position or that opportunity. My answer was always "no." I was quite content professionally, socially, and in every other way with Marshfield. But now, I felt differently. So, Monday morning I called Mayo Clinic and talked to *Jamil Tajik*, the division chair. I had known Jamil casually for 20 years and had gotten to know him better in recent years. He had invited me to speak on the history of American Cardiology to the Mayo Cardiovascular Society in 1996 and to speak at the 50th anniversary of cardiac catheterization at Mayo Clinic in 1997.

When I got him on the telephone, I said, "Jamil, this is Bruce Fye, and I'm thinking about options at this point in my career and wonder if you would have anything for me at the Mayo Clinic?" His response was very simple and straightforward. In fact it was a single word, "Fantastic!" It turns out that's a word Jamil uses frequently. Regardless, that 1 word was enough for me to know instantly that I was going to the Mayo Clinic. Of course I had to go through a very formal interview process. I was interviewed by about a dozen people, all the way up to *Hugh Smith*, a cardiologist, who I'd known for some time, and who was chair of the Mayo Clinic Board of Governors. I felt a certain kinship with several of the Mayo cardiologists because of my involvement with national cardiology organizations.

For example, *Bernard Gersh* sat beside me on the ACC Board of Trustees for at least 2 years because we were arranged alphabetically. Anyone who knows Bernard knows that he's very open about his feelings and opinions. He had been at Mayo Clinic for many years before he became chief of cardiology at Georgetown. When we sat together at ACC board meetings Bernard told me how things were changing at Georgetown. He kept telling me what a great place Mayo was, and eventually, he made up his mind to return there, a place he beleieved was as good as any medical center on the planet. So, Bernard planted this subliminal message in my brain.

When Lois and I had that brief and unexpected discussion about leaving Marshfield Clinic, my comment about calling Mayo Clinic was almost a reflex. That was the only place I considered. I am sure one of the reasons was that I knew and admired so many of the cardiologists there, but also I was accustomed to multispecialty group practice. Mayo Clinic is a unique blend of multispecialty group practice and academic medicine. As a result of my historical research, I had been a keen observer of academic cardiology and academic medicine in general for 25 years. Much of my research was related, from a historical and sociological point of view, to the various factors that contributed to the success or failure of patient careers, departments, and even entire institutions. Generally, success or failure depends on a blend of patient characteristics that exist in a specific institutional context and a larger social context. To use a colloquialism, I was pretty street-smart about academic medicine without ever having been in it. I knew from studying the history of academic medicine and from watching the careers of dozens of friends in academic cardiology that I was not interested in being in a traditional academic environment. Also, I'd heard so much about the Mayo Clinic because Marshfield used it as a benchmark for a variety of things.

WCR: *How far away from Marshfield is the Mayo Clinic?*

WBF: It's a 3-hour drive through rural southwestern Wisconsin and southeastern Minnesota. It's a pleasant and scenic drive.

WCR: *What was your interview for the job at Mayo Clinic like?*

WBF: Well, like most things at Mayo Clinic, it was a very structured and formal process. But it was a very comfortable process because of the dozen or so people who interviewed me, I knew most of them because of my involvement in the ACC and the American Heart Association. The most common question I was asked was, "Why do you want to come here?" My response was, "Why wouldn't I?" It seemed to be an ideal context for me given my clinical and research interests. I was also very familiar with the structure and philosophy of a large multispecialty group practice. Like Marshfield Clinic, Mayo Clinic is dedicated above all else to patient care. The main difference, from my point of view was Mayo's deep commitment to research and education. Marshfield Clinic had an academic veneer. It was fundamentally a practice, and there were very few incentives to do academic things—research, publish, or teach. People who did those things at Marshfield really wanted to do them. I thought this was a good thing in some respects, but those activities were undervalued at that institution during much of my career there.

Marshfield was a great place to practice, and I benefited greatly from the clinic's support of my historical interests during most of the time I was there. I was able to write 2 books because Marshfield had an educational sabbatical program. Every 7 years you could apply for 3 months off, and I used those sabbaticals to write the books based on research I had done over the previous several years. In 1999, I had another book in mind. I wanted to write a history of heart failure, but Marshfield's sabbatical program had changed. For financial reasons they decided that a physician would be allowed only 2 educational sabbaticals during their career at Marshfield. At the same time, protected time for research was harder to get, and that was very frustrating for me. My perception was that, compared with Marshfield Clinic's academic veneer, Mayo Clinic had 8 inches of solid oak in terms of academic environment. During the 4 years I have been in Rochester, Mayo has struggled with the many of the forces and fiscal challenges that have affected all other academic medical centers. Still, Mayo has huge resources and an enormous critical mass of talent. They have done better than most places, but that 8-inch-thick oak has been planed down to about 7 inches.

WCR: *Was that the right decision for you?*

WBF: Bill, there has never been a millisecond that I have thought it was anything other than the absolutely right decision. I've been blessed in so many aspects of my life and my career. I've been very fortunate. I admit I've had the courage of my convictions, and I've pushed my own agenda very hard on several occasions to get the protected time for research or to get concessions that I believed were necessary to build the Department of Cardiology at Marshfield.

WCR: *How much time do you get off now for your research?*

WBF: When I interviewed at Mayo, I made it very clear that my historical research and writing were an extraordinarily important part of me. It's been my academic identity for 25 years. It's why they knew me. It's why you know me. I believed that this was something I wanted to see expand rather than contract if I moved from Marshfield to Mayo. I asked to have 20% protected time for my historical research and writing and was told that was very acceptable given my track record of research productivity and publications in medical history. I've always had a variety of historical projects on the stove. I am usually researching and writing several things at a time. I must tell you, Bill, that 2 of the articles I'm proudest of were published in the *AJC*: a history of electrocardiography in which I made the point that *Willem Einthoven* published his study on the invention of the electrocardiogram in 1902 in Dutch, although most investigators erroneously cite his better-known study of 1903, published in German. The content of the papers is identical but few are aware of the earlier study, because it was published in a very rare "Festschrift" or celebration volume in honor of a Dutch professor. The second study that I published in *AJC* that I think is useful is a history of cardiac arrhythmias.

WCR: *What historical subjects are you researching now?*

WBF: Most of my energy is focused on researching and writing a book on the history of cardiology at Mayo Clinic. This is a huge project that will take several years to complete, because I am reviewing a vast amount of printed and archival material and conducting oral history interviews. The Mayo book is a natural extension of my book on American cardiology that looks at the development of our specialty at one very important and influential academic medical center.

WCR: *How did you decide to tackle what sounds like a very big project?*

WBF: I can't remember if it came up during the interview process or whether it was very shortly after I arrived, but *Jamil Tajik*, a very dear friend and 1 of the most incredible human beings I've ever known, started encouraging me to write a history of the Mayo cardiovascular division. As I thought about his suggestion, I realized how logical it would be for me to write a history of cardiology at Mayo Clinic. I have gotten very enthusiastic about it. For many decades one or more Mayo cardiologists has had a deep interest in the history of cardiology, beginning with *Fredrick Willius*, who founded the division in 1922. He published a book with *Thomas Keys*, a Mayo librarian, entitled *Cardiac Classics* in 1941. This is a great book that reprints part or all of about 50 classic publications on the heart from the time of William Harvey to the early 20th century. In 1948, Willius wrote a book entitled *A History of the Heart and Circulation* with *Thomas Dry*, a Mayo cardiologist originally from South Africa (a first-generation Bernard Gersh in terms of the South Africa-Mayo connection). Three additional volumes of Cardiac Classics were published in the 1980s by Mayo cardiologist *John Callahan*, Mayo librarian *Jack Key*, and Mayo cardiac surgeon *Dwight McGoon*. John Callahan started collecting materials for a history of cardiology at Mayo in the early 1990s, but he retired subsequently and was kind enough to pass his notes and copies of various documents on to me. So, I am building on a rich tradition of historical scholarship in the Mayo cardiovascular division.

The idea of writing the history of cardiology at Mayo is appealing to me for a number of reasons. When I started working there in the summer of 2000, I didn't know much about the history of the clinic or its cardiovascular division. The place was obviously a unique powerhouse of clinical talent and academic accomplishment. I thought researching and writing the history of cardiology at Mayo would be a good way for me to learn about the clinic in general. Recognizing that not everyone appreciates historical research and writing, I also thought my colleagues in cardiology would be more supportive of a major project that focused on their specialty and their institution. Finally, there is a very ironic aspect to my project on the history of Mayo cardiology. We spoke earlier about my mother's years at Oberlin College. I have her diaries, and in the volume for 1933 or 1934 she wrote something like, "My dear friend *Helen Clapesattle* is leaving Oberlin. Oh, how much I will miss her." I couldn't believe it, because Helen Clapesattle went on to write the definitive history of Mayo Clinic. Her book, *The Doctors Mayo*, was published by the University of Minnesota Press in 1941.

WCR: *You have also written >50 biographical articles for the series "Profiles in Cardiology." That's a lot of work. How did you get involved in that effort?*

WBF: *Willis Hurst* gave me that opportunity. I really got to know Willis after he became a member of the American Osler Society in the mid-1980s. Because you are also a member of the Osler Society, you know it is a small organization devoted to perpetuating the ideals of William Osler and stimulating interest in medical history and the medical humanities. In 1984, I was invited to edit a series of limited edition, leather-bound reprints of important books in the history of cardiology. I agreed and asked Willis Hurst to be a member of the editorial advisory board of The Classics of Cardiology Library, the name of the series. The first book published wasn't a reprint, it was a new book I edited, entitled *William Osler's Collected Papers on the Cardiovascular System*. This big book, >900 pages long, demonstrated that cardiology was one of Osler's main interests.

After this book appeared in 1985, Willis asked me to write a short biographical sketch of Osler for a new section, "Profiles in Cardiology," that would be a regular feature in *Clinical Cardiology*, a journal edited by *Richard Conti*. Willis liked my Osler article and encouraged me to write more biographical papers for the series. When the book *Profiles in Cardiology* was published in 2003, it included >200 biographies reprinted from the journal, and I had written 1/4 of them. Researching and writing those papers took a lot of time, but I learned a great deal about the history of cardiology from the effort. I am still writing profiles. Willis has been a very influential mentor over the years.

WCR: *You were President of the American College of Cardiology from March 2002 to April 2003. How did you handle that major responsibility as a Mayo Clinic cardiologist?*

WBF: When I interviewed at Mayo in the fall of

FIGURE 10. President George W. Bush *(second from left)* and WBF *(second from right)* at the American College of Cardiology meeting, Orlando 2001.

1999, I had not been formally elected vice president of the ACC. I knew the nominating committee had voted to submit my name to the Board of Trustees as their choice for vice president, with a term that would begin in March 2000, but Jamil Tajik did not know this when I called to ask about the possibility of me joining Mayo Clinic. During the interview process, I explained to the leaders of the Mayo cardiovascular division and to Hugh Smith, Chair of the Mayo Board of Governors, that it was very likely I would become president of the college in 2002. I knew that would be a huge responsibility, and I wanted to be sure Mayo Clinic would allow me the time necessary to focus my energy on the college during my presidential year.

When I started to work at Mayo Clinic in August 2000, I brought the ACC presidency up proactively with everyone who was in a position to help me figure out how to balance that important role with my responsibilities as a Mayo cardiologist (Figure 10). In addition to Jamil, *David Hayes*, who was then vice chair of the division, the echo leadership, and the division's executive committee were totally supportive. But Mayo Clinic is an enormous bureaucratic institution, and there are lots of rules regarding time away. I found myself in a quagmire of bureaucracy that fortunately I was able to navigate with help from Jamil and David as well as *Jim Seward*, director of the echo lab. I think it worked out very well for everybody involved—the Mayo Clinic, the ACC, and for me. I felt very good about the year because I was able to devote most of my time and energy to the college. This was partly due to the fact that I transferred the entire ACC presidential honorarium to the clinic and did not have a significant practice because I had just joined the institution. During the presidential year, I spent about 2/3 of my time doing ACC-related things and the rest interpreting echoes (Figure 11). After my term was over, I got involved once again in clinical cardiology practice, something I enjoy very much.

In 2003 David Hayes, who had succeeded Jamil Tajik as chair of the cardiovascular division, invited me to serve on the division's executive committee. It's a wonderful feeling to think that your colleagues perceive you can contribute something to what is already

FIGURE 11. WBF becomes President of ACC, accepting gavel from Doug Zipes, Atlanta 2001.

an incredibly sophisticated and robust division. The unique thing I brought to the division and its executive committee is a blend of 2 dimensions, time and space. I have a special understanding of how cardiology emerged and grew as a specialty because that has been the major focus of my research for >2 decades. In addition, thanks to the many wonderful opportunities I have had as a result of my various roles in the ACC, I have a sense of the issues that confront our specialty based on the experiences of colleagues across the country. Finally, having come to the Mayo Clinic after practicing elsewhere for 22 years, I bring the perspective of an outsider, someone who did not train and practice exclusively in Rochester.

WCR: *You really got involved in the college via the government relations committee?*

WBF: In fact, I got involved in the college because of my interests in books and history rather than government relations. That came later. The patient responsible for my first committee appointment in the ACC was a leading academic cardiologist named *Jim Warren*, who had been at Peter Bent Brigham, Emory, Duke, and Ohio State. With *Eugene Stead*, Jim was one of the early American pioneers of cardiac catheterization at Grady Memorial Hospital in Atlanta. Jim was also interested in medical history, and I met him through the American Osler Society. When he invited me to be a member of the ACC's library committee in 1987, I could never have imagined that I would become president of the college 15 years later. During the 1990s, I got progressively involved in the ACC, although I also served on several committees of the American Heart Association.

WCR: *What were some of the main things you did with the college?*

WBF: Along with several other cardiologists, I helped organize the Wisconsin chapter and began a 3-year term as Governor in 1993. That same year I was appointed to the ACC's Government Relations Committee. I found that experience very interesting, especially because there were so many important issues confronting cardiology and all of specialty medicine during the early and mid-1990s between the rapid growth of managed care and the Clinton health reform plan that sought to decrease the number of specialists. I chaired the government relations committee between 1996 and 1999, and that was one of the most interesting experiences of my professional life. In 1997 I was elected to the board of trustees.

WCR: *In addition to this and your other committee work, you wrote a history of American cardiology and the history of the ACC. That book was published in 1996, and then in 2002, you became president of the college. Your knowledge of the history of the college must have been far greater than anybody who has held that office.*

WBF: Well, I guess that is true, because I read every word of the verbatim transcripts of the meetings of the board of trustees and the executive committee from 1949 until the early 1990s. I also benefited greatly from interviewing 45 people on various aspects of the college's history and the history of American cardiology in general.

WCR: *What accomplishments as president of the ACC are you most proud of?*

WBF: When I was elected vice president in 1999, *Christine (Chris) McEntee*, the ACC's new CEO, asked me, "What do you hope to accomplish during your presidential year?" At that point I didn't really have any specific plans or an agenda for change. It was humbling to think that I would eventually be responsible for an organization that had thrived during its first 50 years. I did, however, think there were some issues that needed to be addressed with respect to cardiology in general. The main thing I hoped to influence during my term was the perception, widely held in the 1990s, that there were too many cardiologists. Despite this common wisdom, I knew many cardiologists around the country who were having trouble recruiting partners to help them cope with increasing workloads. At a personal level, I had great difficulty recruiting cardiologists to Marshfield during my 18-year tenure as chair. When I chaired the ACC's government relations committee, served on the board of governors, and researched my book on American cardiology, I recognized that a lot of factors were coming together that would result in a significant gap between demand for and supply of cardiologists.

Like most readers of *AJC*, I lived through the era of unchecked growth of managed care that pushed the gatekeeper model and the Clinton health reform proposal that demanded a reduction in the number of specialists. Throughout the 1980s and 1990s, there were many noisy debates about the mix of generalist physicians and specialists. During the early 1990s, several academic cardiology divisions were considering how to gain independence from the parent department of medicine to have greater autonomy and influence within their institutions. There was also tension around the perception that cardiologists in academic centers or multispecialty groups were being "taxed" excessively and were subsidizing other specialists.

The single specialty cardiology group phenomenon was extraordinarily powerful, and it distorted the salary structure. This led a lot of promising academic cardiologists to enter private practice. The thing that really took the wind out of the sails of the academic cardiology movement toward more autonomy was the managed care capitation model. The rhetoric in the mid-1990s was that profit centers would become cost centers, and there would be fewer patients and fewer dollars going to cardiologists because of the gatekeeper model. I wrote about all this in my book on American cardiology, and I delivered a plenary lecture on managed care and the cardiac patient at the 1997 annual meeting of the American Heart Association. That was a harsh talk in which I criticized many aspects of the aggressive for-profit managed care movement.

Getting back to your question about my term as ACC president, I'll say a few words about how I approached the workforce problem. When I told Chris McEntee I wanted to use ACC resources to gather evidence to support my belief that there was a growing shortage of cardiovascular specialists, she said what many people thought in 2000, "What are you talking about? There are too many cardiologists." I said, "No, I don't think so, and I'm going to try to prove it." So I appointed an ACC task force with representatives of the American Heart Association and the larger cardiology subspecialty societies. To gather data on the current and short-term markets for cardiologists, I designed a questionnaire that was sent to cardiology training program directors, senior cardiology fellows, a random sample of ACC fellows, and to recruiters.

Based on several hundred responses to our surveys, we concluded that there was a large unmet demand for cardiologists. We also used data from several other sources to demonstrate that the burden of cardiovascular disease would grow as the population was aging and successful treatments were keeping cardiac patients alive who would have died just a few years earlier. Another concern was that the number of first-year cardiology training slots fell by 20% between 1994 and 1999. Bethesda Conference 35 was devoted to work force, and the report and recommendations that resulted from that effort were approved by the ACC board of trustees. They were published in the *Journal of the American College of Cardiology* in July 2004.

A second thing I helped accomplish during my term as president was the creation of a new membership category for non-physician clinicians who are active members of a cardiac care team. These are nurse clinicians, physician assistants, and clinical nurse specialists whose practice focuses on the care of cardiac patients under the supervision of a cardiologist. When I first got involved in some of the discussions about this as president-elect, one of the older trustees said there had been discussions about this years earlier and there had been very little support for expanding the membership beyond physicians and surgeons. I was aware of that history, but I thought the time was right to revisit the issue, because so many cardiologists in academic or private practice settings now depended on these non-physician clinicians to help them deliver care on a day-to-day basis.

The team care model worked very well in cardiology at Marshfield. I thought these patients should have greater access to the college's excellent educational programs and products. After all, they need to know many of the things that clinical cardiologists need to know as they care for cardiac patients. I was pleased that the task force on the cardiac care team I appointed, led by *Gus Lambrew*, presented a report to the board that strongly supported the concept of creating a new membership category for these non-physician clinicians. At the last ACC board meeting I chaired, there was a unanimous vote to extend membership to these vital members of the cardiac care team. We changed the bylaws so the college is no longer strictly for physicians, although there is no question it is and will remain primarily a professional organization for doctors who are cardiovascular specialists.

Another thing I should mention in the course of this very candid and personal interview is something I told the trustees at the first board meeting I chaired. I told them I wanted to be remembered for urging them to "slow down and take a deep breath." That statement requires explanation for anyone not involved in the college leadership over the past few years. The college entered a new era when Chris McEntee was hired as executive vice president in 1998. She is a very bright and very ambitious person who energized the college. When I asked her what she wanted to accomplish at the college—after she asked me the same question—she told me that she wanted "to take the organization to the next level." Chris had a lot of ideas about the ACC and wanted to see several things change and change rather quickly. There is no doubt many things needed to change, but I found the pace unsettling. Several working groups and task forces were launched in the late 1990s, and many recommendations were sent to the board for their review and approval.

One major driver of change was the conviction held by some influential college leaders and staff members that the ACC should move quickly to launch a comprehensive series of innovative internet-based educational programs. Initially, it was proposed that the college build the infrastructure as well as supply the content for this ambitious project that some declared was the future of the ACC. A staff survey at about this time projected dramatic growth in the number of employees. These aggressive projections of staff growth were a major factor in the decision to close the learning center at Heart House. In addition, there were concerns that the college needed to offer learning center programs at other locations because the attendees at the Heart House programs were mainly from the northeast. I can't go into all the details, but I found myself in an increasingly awkward position of trying to slow things down when other leaders and Chris were trying to move forward quickly and decisively.

By nature, I am a person who is more inclined than most leaders to build consensus and move slowly, considering a variety of possible consequences. My leadership style was shaped in part by the very democratic nature of the Marshfield Clinic. As I said earlier, I was elected and re-elected chair of cardiology there 9 times. That doesn't happen unless you are a consensus builder and trusted to make decisions that are in the best interest of the majority. Every president of the college brings his or her personality and personal interests to the position. It must be very hard for the staff to adjust to a new president every year.

My predecessor as president of the college, *Doug Zipes*, is a brilliant and incredibly accomplished individual who has contributed tremendously to electrophysiology. I think he would agree with my perception that he is a very ambitious, driven, and a "let's do it now" kind of person. That is his leadership style, and it is part of the reason he has been so successful. During the year I was president-elect, there were times I felt like a passenger in a car going too fast for conditions. I'm sure part of this feeling related to my unique appreciation of the history and traditions of the college. I was also much less confident than some college leaders and staff that internet-based continuing medical education was going to replace the traditional forms of education that the college had developed in a few short years.

Although I didn't want to be stereotyped as a dinosaur whose feet were planted in the concrete of the past, unwilling to change or accept innovation, I really believed that too many things at the college were changing too quickly. I would have preferred to see how some of the new initiatives or approaches worked out before a whole new series of changes were recommended or implemented. There was a good deal of frustration and uncertainty among several academic cardiologists who had dedicated years to the college as educators or leaders. They didn't quite understand what was happening, why it was happening, and why they weren't asked for their opinions about changes they perceived would affect them directly in their roles as educators and program directors. I spent a lot of time during my presidential year listening to program directors who were frustrated about changes in the format of and publicity about live programs and the decision to close the learning center at Heart House.

The final thing I focused on as ACC president was the subject of my presidential address at the opening plenary session of the 2003 meeting in Chicago, a meeting that began just 10 days after President Bush

FIGURE 12. WBF in home library, Rochester, 2003.

launched the war against Iraq and during the SARS epidemic. Needless to say, the attendees at that ACC annual meeting were distracted by international events, and many international participants stayed home. My address, subsequently published as a lead article in *Journal of the American College of Cardiology*, was entitled "The Power of Clinical Trials and Guidelines, and the Challenge of Conflicts of Interest." It's the tension between funding to move science and knowledge forward and the sources of that funding. We now take clinical trials and practice guidelines for granted, although the whole paradigm that places so much emphasis on evidence-based medicine is only a few decades old. Cardiology is dependent on pharmaceutical and industry support for much of our clinical investigation. Clearly, industry has an agenda when they fund clinical trials. They are hoping to prove that their products are effective to increase their profits.

Industry depends on academics to help design and conduct these clinical trials, and they look to experts and opinion leaders to spread the word if the results of a trial demonstrate a benefit in terms of outcomes. The challenge is to be sure that bias does not creep into the process of reporting clinical trials, incorporating their findings into practice guidelines, and disseminating new knowledge gained from trials through educational programs and products. Nearly everyone is potentially conflicted to some degree at one level or another. I think it is important to acknowledge this and manage it through disclosure and other means. There is no doubt that a healthy academic-industry interface is vital for progress. Without this collaboration, much of

what we consider to be progress would grind to a halt. I think you have to be alert to potential bias when you read articles or listen to presentations. It's a subject that people and institutions that have a tremendous amount of power to influence public opinion and policy must reflect on.

Another thing in terms of the medical progress and economics is that there simply isn't enough money going forward to provide care, even to the people who are insured, let alone the 45 or so million Americans without health insurance. There are too many technologic advances already. There are too many things on the horizon. I don't know how the country is going to deal with it, but it is clear to me that the trajectory we are on with respect to discoveries and demographics is problematic. These are very exciting times in terms of all the advances, but these are also very challenging times. As a historian, it has been fun to research and write about how modern cardiology came to exist, and as a cardiologist it has been fun to practice during a time of remarkable advances in the diagnosis, treatment, and prevention of cardiovascular disease (Figure 12).

WCR: *Bruce, I would like to thank you on behalf of the Journal's readers and myself for this insightful interview. Thank you.*

WBF: It's been my pleasure. You've asked a lot of probing questions that brought back a lot of memories. I've told you before how helpful your detailed interviews of dozens of physicians will be for future historians interested in 20th century cardiology.

BEST PUBLICATIONS AS SELECTED BY WBF

Books

1. Fye WB, ed. William Osler's Collected Papers on the Cardiovascular System. Birmingham, Alabama: Gryphon Editions, 1985.
2. Fye WB. The Development of American Physiology: Scientific Medicine in the Nineteenth Century. Baltimore: The Johns Hopkins University Press, 1987.
3. Fye WB, ed. Classic Papers on Coronary Thrombosis and Myocardial Infarction. Birmingham, AL: Gryphon Editions, 1991.
4. Fye WB. American Cardiology: The History of a Specialty and its College. Baltimore, MD: The Johns Hopkins University Press, 1996.
5. Hurst JW, Conti CR, Fye WB. Profiles of Cardiology: A Collection of Profiles Featuring Individuals Who Have Made Significant Contributions to the Study of Cardiovascular Disease. Mahwah, NJ: Foundation for Advances in Medicine and Science, 2003.*

Selected Book Chapters

4. Fye WB. Growth of American physiology, 1850-1900. In: Physiology in the American Context, 1850-1940. Geison GL, ed. Bethesda, MD: American Physiological Society, 1987;2:47–65.
7. Fye WB. Acute myocardial infarction: a historical summary. In: Gersh BJ, Rahimtoola S, eds. Acute Myocardial Infarction. New York: Elsevier, 1990:1–13.
9. Fye WB. Albion Walter Hewlett: teacher, clinician, scientist, and missionary for "Pathologic Physiology" In: Howell JD, ed. Medical Lives & Scientific Medicine at Michigan, 1891–1969, Ann Arbor, MI: The University of Michigan Press, 1993:45–72.
10. Fye WB. A history of cardiac arrhythmias. In: Kastor JA, ed. Arrhythmias. Philadelphia: WB Saunders, 1994:1–24.
13. Fye WB. A historical perspective on atherosclerosis and coronary artery disease. In: Fuster V, Ross R, Topol E, eds. Atherosclerosis and Coronary Artery Disease. Philadelphia, PA: Lippincott-Raven, 1996:1–12.
15. Fye WB. Cardiovascular pharmacology: a historical perspective. In: Frishman WH, Sonnenblick EH, eds. Cardiovascular Pharmacotherapeutics. New York: McGraw-Hill, 1996:47–56.

*W. Bruce Fye contributed 57 biographies to this book.

24. Fye WB. William Osler's bibliomania. In: Barondess J, Roland CG, eds. The Persisting Osler III: Selected Transactions of the American Osler Society 1991–2000. Malabar: Krieger Publishing, 2002:67–78.

Selected Articles

4. Fye WB. The literature and history of internal medicine—an annotated bibliography. *Ann Intern Med* 1977;87:123–128.

7. Fye WB. Active euthanasia—an historical survey of its conceptual origins and introduction into medical thought. *Bull Hist Med* 1979:52:492–501.

9. Fye WB. Collecting medical books—practical and theoretical considerations. *Trans Coll Phys Philadelphia* 1979;1:305–323.

15. Fye WB. Echocardiography 1980: indications and usefulness. *Wis Med J* 1980;79:19–22.

19. Fye WB. Key references: history of cardiology. *Circulation* 1981;64:434–436.

21. Fye WB. Why a physiologist? The case of Henry P. Bowditch. *Bull Hist Med* 1982;56:19–29.

27. Fye WBS. Weir Mitchell: Philadelphia's "lost" physiologist. *Bull Hist Med* 1983;57:188–202.

31. Fye WB. Ernest Henry Starling: his law and its growing significance in the practice of medicine. *Circulation* 1983;68:1145–1148.

33. Fye WB. Sydney Ringer and the role of calcium in myocardial function. *Circulation* 1984;69:849–853.

34. Fye WB. Heparin: the contributions of William Henry Howell. *Circulation* 1984;69:1198–1203.

37. Fye WB. Coronary arteriography: it took a long time. *Circulation* 1984;70: 781–787.

38. Fye WB. Collecting medical books: challenges and opportunities in the 80s. *Bull NY Acad Med* 1985;61:250–265.

39. Fye WBH. Newell Martin: a remarkable career destroyed by neurasthenia and alcoholism. *J Hist Med Allied Sci* 1985;40:135–166.

41. Fye WB. Acute coronary occlusion always results in death: or does it? The observations of William T. Porter. *Circulation* 1985;71:4–10.

44. Fye WB. Cardiology in 1885. *Circulation* 1985;72:21–26.

45. Fye WB. Ventricular fibrillation and defibrillation: historical perspectives. *Circulation* 1985;71:858–865.

46. Fye WB. The delayed diagnosis of acute myocardial infarction: it took half a century! *Circulation* 1985;72:262–271.

55. Fye WB. Nitroglycerin: a homeopathic remedy. *Circulation* 1986;73:21–29.

56. Fye WB. H. Newell Martin and the isolated heart preparation: the link between the frog and open heart surgery. *Circulation* 1986;73:857–864.

60. Fye WB. T. Lauder Brunton and amyl nitrite: a Victorian vasodilator. *Circulation* 1986;74:222–229.

62. Fye WB. American contributions to cardiovascular medicine and surgery. Bethesda: National Institutes of Health, 1986.

63. Fye WB. The history of cardiology: a bibliography of secondary sources. Bethesda: National Library of Library Med, 1986.

66. Fye WB. Carl Ludwig and the Leipzig Physiological Institute. "A factory of new knowledge." *Circulation* 1986;74:920–928.

70. Fye WB. The literature of American internal medicine: a historical view. *Ann Intern Med* 1987;106:450–461.

88. Fye WB. The origin of the heart beat: a tale of frogs, jellyfish and turtles. *Circulation* 1987;76:493–500.

110. Fye WB. William Osler's departure from North America. The price of success. *N Engl J Med* 1989;320:1425–1431.

113. Fye WB. Austin Flint, 1812-1886. *Clin Cardiol* 1989;12:476–477.

132. Fye WB. Vasodilator therapy for angina pectoris: the intersection of homeopathy and scientific medicine. *J Hist Med Allied Sciences* 1990;45:317–340.

136. Fye WB. Medical authorship: traditions, trends, and tribulations. *Ann Intern Med* 1990;113:317–325.

145. Fye WB. The origin of the full-time faculty system: implications for clinical research. *JAMA* 1991;265:1555–1562.

159. Fye WB. Medical book collecting: a retrospect and a forecast. *New Jersey Med* 1992;89:835–841.

165. Fye WB. The history of medicine: an annotated list of key reference works. *Ann Intern Med* 1993;118:59–62.

167. Fye WB. A history of the American Heart Association's Council on Clinical Cardiology. *Circulation* 1993;87:1057–1063.

178. Fye WB. Disorders of the heartbeat: a historical overview from antiquity to the mid-20th century. *Am J Cardiol* 1993;72:1055–1070.

186. Fye WB. A history of the origin, evolution, and impact of electrocardiography. *Am J Cardiol* 1994;73:937–949.

229. Fye WB. Managed care and patients with cardiovascular disease. *Circulation* 1998;97:1895–1896.

241. Fye WB. Franz M. Groedel. *Clin Cardiol* 2000;23:133–134.

253. Fye WB. President's Page. Convocation address: the art of medicine. *J Am Coll Cardiol* 2002;39:1238–1241.

257. Fye WB. Cardiology workforce: there's already a shortage, and it's getting worse! *J Am Coll Cardiol* 2002;39:2077–2079.

258. Fye WB. Women cardiologists: why so few? *J Am Coll Cardiol* 2002;40: 384–386.

260. Fye WB. Cardiology and technology: an enduring and energizing partnership. *J Am Coll Cardiol* 2002;40:1192–1195.

264. Fye WB. Medical history: a valuable tool to help us frame the present and predict the future. *J Am Coll Cardiol* 2002;41:346–349.

265. Fye WB. The power of clinical trials and guidelines, and the challenge of conflicts of interest. *J Am Coll Cardiol* 2003;41:1237–1242.

271. Fye WB. Cardiology's workforce shortage: implications for patient care and research. *Circulation* 2004;109:813–816.

272. Fye WB, Hirshfeld JW, et al. Cardiology's workforce crisis: a pragmatic approach. Presented at the 35th Bethesda Conference, Bethesda, Maryland, October 17-18, 2003. *J Am Coll Cardiol* 2004;44:215–275.

273. Fye WB. The origins and implications of a growing shortage of cardiologists. *J Am Coll Cardiol* 2004;44:221–232.

W. BRUCE FYE, and *American Cardiology:* A Conversation With the Editor About the Author and His Latest Book*

William C. Roberts, MD[†] (hereafter called WCR): I am in Dallas, Texas, speaking by telephone with Dr. W. Bruce Fye in Marshfield, Wisconsin, on April 4, 1996. Bruce, before talking about your new book, could you provide the readers the background of how you got interested in medical history in the first place?

W. Bruce Fye, MD[†] (hereafter called WBF): Let me start at the very beginning. When I was a boy in the 1950s (I'm now 49), I collected baseball cards, comics, stamps, butterflies, and finally books. I bought 2 boxes of books at a county auction and that started it. When I started college at the Johns Hopkins University, I fell upon a book seller located about 1/2 mile from the campus. Over time he said, ''You know if you're going to medical school, you should start to collecting medical books.'' So I did. I started trading off some of my nonmedical books to get medical books. During my freshman year at Johns Hopkins Medical School, I spent my elective quarter in the History of Medicine Department, which was the first organized department of medical history in the country. That was my first formal exposure to the ''history of medicine.'' I didn't do anything with it during the next several years, but the book interest continued to grow, and I became more active in medical book collecting.

When I returned to Hopkins from the New York Hospital–Cornell Medical Center, where I did my internship and residency, I had a discussion with Mike Weisfeldt about what research I would do as a fellow in cardiology. I reminded him that he assured me if I came back to Hopkins I wouldn't have to do biomedical research because I didn't care to. I wanted to be a clinical cardiologist and I had exposure to basic organic chemistry research as an undergraduate at Hopkins and decided at that time that I never wanted to be involved again in something I didn't understand if I could avoid it. I told him I wanted to do research in history of medicine. Initially, it wasn't clear how that was going to play out, but the Robert Wood Johnson Clinical Scholars Program had just begun, and Mike Weisfeldt and Victor McKusick, the Chairman of the Department of Medicine at the time, arranged for this maverick kid, i.e., me, to obtain this support to do a master's program in the history of medicine department at Hopkins while completing my cardiology training.

• • •

WCR: So you obtained formal training in medical history during your 2-year fellowship in cardiology?

WBF: Right. I stayed a third year as a member of the faculty of cardiology to complete my master's degree in medical history.

• • •

WCR: And how many books have you collected?

WBF: I have my private reference collection, but I have also had a mail order book business since 1973. I've probably got nearly 40,000 volumes in house, but most of it represents the business stock.

• • •

WCR: Where do you keep all these books?

WBF: I have a big house with a big basement. I also put on an addition to the house recently. The basement looks like a library, and it just grows and grows, probably by about 1,500 books a year. The basement, which is 2,300 square feet, contains most of the books. The living room and the original family room, however, also have floor to ceiling bookcases on all 4 walls.

• • •

WCR: What did your parents do? Did they have a historical bent?

WBF: My father was a banker. He graduated from Allegheny College and ended his career as Senior Vice President of the Philadelphia National Bank. My mother was a graduate of Oberlin Conservatory of Music and taught piano during her young

W. Bruce Fye, MD.

*This interview is underwritten by an unrestricted grant from Bristol-Myers Squibb.

†From the Baylor Cardiovascular Institute, Baylor University Medical Center, Dallas, Texas 75246.

‡From the Department of Cardiology, The Marshfield Clinic, Marshfield, Wisconsin 54449.

married life, and then was a mother and home-maker for the rest of it. They both read books and had books, but neither one was a collector of things. I basically came from an educated, middle-class family that sort of had books around, but neither of my parents had any ''burning passion'' for either history or books. They had an appreciation of history, however.

WCR: Do you have siblings?

WBF: No. I'm an only child.

• • •

WCR: *American Cardiology* was your second major nonedited book?

WBF: That is correct. My first nonedited book was published in 1987, and was titled *The Development of American Physiology: Scientific Medicine in the 19th Century*. That book was an outgrowth of my master's thesis at Hopkins. The thesis dealt with Henry P. Bowditch, America's first full-time faculty member in the modern sense of the word, and a Harvard physiologist. I got interested in him because I was interested in medical education and particularly the full-time system of medical education. In looking at the origins of that, I fell upon Henry P. Bowditch, and decided that physiology was really the model in this country for the full-time faculty system. My master's thesis on Bowditch was about 250 pages long. I decided to synthesize the other pieces of the physiology story into that book. Fundamentally, my first book was a study of professionalization, of the origins of the full-time system, and it helped me understand a lot of the dynamics about current stresses and strains of academic medicine.

• • •

WCR: In that first book you got into the American Physiological Society and its development?

WBF: Right. One chapter deals with the development of the American Physiological Society.

• • •

WCR: So when you started looking into the origins of the American Heart Association and The American College of Cardiology (ACC) you had a background in how to handle that type of information.

WBF: That's right. I wouldn't claim it was a real sophisticated background because I didn't have access to nearly the wealth of archival material for the American Physiological Society that I did later for the ACC, but it's true I had written something on organizational history.

• • •

WCR: Let's focus now on your new book *American Cardiology*. I think it is a masterpiece and should be required reading for all cardiovascular specialists. How long did it take you to write this book?

WBF: I worked on it for 5 years. That included a 3-month sabbatical from the Marshfield Clinic, and I am given 20% of my time to do historical research. Most nights and weekends were spent working on this book. So a huge amount of time went into the project. It took 5 years given the fact that I have a medical life, an administrative life, a family life, and

a ''bookish'' life. But it was certainly a passion. It was the consuming primary activity, outside of my daily life at the Marshfield Clinic, for 5 years.

• • •

WCR: I gather that you interviewed many people in doing this book. Who was particularly helpful to you? What was ''your vision'' for this book? How did you begin?

WBF: I had never done oral history before. That idea really didn't come into my mind, at least that I can recall, but it came up when I was dealing with Bill Nelligan and Helene Goldstein in the earliest phases of the project. We were discussing ground rules. The first ground rule that I established was that there would be no editorial involvement on the part of the ACC or I would not take on the project. And they fully agreed. Bill Winters, when he was president of the ACC, was the one who suggested this project to me. He thought the book would be particularly timely because Simon Dack was soon to retire as editor of the *Journal of the American College of Cardiology* (formerly editor of *The American Journal of Cardiology*, which for 25 years was the official journal of the ACC), and Bill Nelligan was soon to retire as executive director (for 27 years) of the ACC. He believed that these 2 individuals particularly would have memories and insights that would be lost if someone didn't make an effort to capture them. It became obvious in the early discussions with Nelligan that oral history would be a natural part of the project. My first response was that I simply did not have time for that, but Nelligan insisted that no one else could do it. And I became convinced in the context of our conversation that he was right. Then I went off and got some tutoring in oral history and read a lot about it.

The next issue was who to interview. A lot of that was sort of serendipity. There were a few obvious people, such as Bill Nelligan, some former ACC presidents who had been in office at particularly important times, but the thing that was apparent to me soon was that I was going to run out of time. There were many other people who could have provided useful insights. In fact, you and I Bill once talked about that. The issue that arose was simply a logistical issue. If I was going to bring this thing to fruition, I was going to have to stop asking questions and start writing. Thus, there were a lot of people who would say, ''You should have talked to. . . .'' or ''You must talk to. . . .'' or ''Why did he bother talking to. . . .''—that kind of thing. As it evolved, it had a great deal to do with who was going to be at a certain place at a certain time and who I thought might have an especially interesting perspective on some event. I spoke to a fairly broad spectrum of individuals, all listed in the back of my book. I talked to the 2 physicians who started diagnostic cardiac catheterization, namely Richard Bing (He's still alive and still active.), and Louis Dexter, who has since died. I think most cardiologists assume that cardiac catheterization has been around a lot longer than it has. Grey Diamond, a person very influential with the college for a number of years and a very dynamic and energetic person, provided some especially good insights. There were a few sound bites that I heard in various interviews. They were sort of like ''Wow! That'll be in the book!'' Most interviews were more for background information and for general perspective. In fact, one of my concerns about the book is the way it will be received by those people who were interviewed and by those who were not interviewed. Their natural reaction is to go to the index and look for their names, and I'm afraid most won't find themselves there, because they were interviewed mainly for context and for background about how cardiology evolved. The book is the study of a discipline. It is not a series of biographical sketches.

• • •

WCR: Are you glad you did the book?

WBF: I am absolutely elated I had the opportunity to write this book. It was a tremendous opportunity and it became a consuming passion. It was something that I very much wanted *to do right*. I wanted to write a book that would not only appeal to members of a college or to cardiologists. I tried to write a book that would be of some interest to anyone curious about the evolution of specialized medicine in the 20th century. I hope it is viewed as a model for writing the history of a medical specialty. I tried to cover a wide range of topics, including various technological advances (particularly electrocardiography and coronary angiography which had such an enormous impact), socioeconomic factors, such as the growth of private insurance after World War II, and the development of the National Heart Institute, which poured vast amounts of money into academic medical centers, among others.

• • •

WCR: I was intrigued by your discussion of the electrocardiogram and how that really separated, at least initially, ''the heart specialist'' from general practitioners. And now today, the electrocardiogram takes a back step compared to the other instruments of precision that are available.

WBF: I think that's correct. The electrocardiograph really was the thing that people who had an interest in the heart rallied around. The electrocardiogram not only provided the physician with very useful information about the heart, it also served as a powerful signal to patients: ''Look, I'm a heart specialist because I've got this equipment that I know how to use, I know how to interpret what it produces, and that sets me apart.'' That's not a whole lot different from other types of specialists. Ophthalmology is really the paradigm of specialization, and it was launched by the invention of the ophthalmoscope. It is often a specific tool which at least initially defines an area of specialization. As technology progresses, the older tools are eclipsed by newer ones. The electrocardiogram is still fundamental to the evaluation of heart patients, but now it's joined, of course, by a vast number of other techniques to look at cardiac structure and function.

• • •

WCR: Bruce, how is your work week spent? How much time do you spend seeing patients, etc.?

WBF: I've been Chair of the Department of Cardiology at Marshfield Clinic since 1981, and there are 16 cardiologists. I spend about 25% of my time doing administrative tasks. I came to Marshfield in 1978 to start the echocardiography laboratory, so a good deal of my nonadministrative, nonhistory time is spent interpreting echocardiograms. The piece of time left over is spent in traditional, general consultative cardiology practice. Basically, I'm a clinical cardiologist and my time is spent in 4 areas: patient care, administration, echo reading, and research.

• • •

WCR: You obviously are what some would call ''an academic cardiologist'' and yet The Marshfield Clinic is not officially connected to a medical school. Is this correct?

WBF: Yes. We have both general and specialty practices at the clinic. We have a research foundation that's freestanding. Its budget is about $12 million. Medical students from the University of Wisconsin rotate through our clinic. We have our own residency training program. The thing that is really nice about The Marshfield Clinic is that if someone is interested in research or teaching, there is nothing keeping them from pursuing those interests. Yes, I am an academically oriented person who practices in basically a nonacademic setting, but I've not found that to be a problem. In part, because my research is unique to me. Although I don't require a large support staff, I do require sophisticated people, mainly librarians and secretarial support, but it's not the same as trying to organize a major research laboratory.

• • •

WCR: Why did you go to The Marshfield Clinic?

WBF: The job. My wife and I were both raised in Pennsylvania. I wanted to start or head up an echocardiography laboratory in a referral center. I was working with A. McGehee Harvey at Hopkins and he pressured me to stay there, but they didn't need anybody in echocardiography. I had 2 choices: either stay at Hopkins and reinvent myself as a general internist-type of cardiologist, or leave. I was looking for a specific type of position and Marshfield had a sophisticated cath and open heart surgery program, but they had a big void in echo. They needed someone to start their echocardiography program. I told my wife, ''I found a great job, too bad it's in Wisconsin.'' I had this parochial East Coast view that I wanted to practice somewhere between Massachusetts and Virginia and no further west than Ohio. The people we met in Marshfield convinced me what a great place it was, and I finally decided that it was the right place for me and my family. After 17 years, we both enjoy Wisconsin very much, except for the long, hard winters.

• • •

WCR: Has anybody been particularly influential in your career in medical history? You've mentioned

A. McGehee Harvey and Victor McKusick. Has anybody really tried to guide you along or have you been essentially on your own from the beginning?

WBF: I would say that I have been on my own. I have received very little direct help from others. I got into medical history research because I refused to be put into a square hole as a round peg. I did not care to conform to the academic model that "you are a fellow here, these are the projects that are underway, which one do you want to work on?" I didn't want to do that. I wanted to do something that I designed and thought through and brought to fruition. Mike Weisfeldt and Victor McKusick said "OK. We've got this guy and he's strong-willed. Is there something we can do to use his energy constructively and appropriately." They connected me to the Robert Wood Johnson Foundation and their Clinical Scholars Program. The Clinical Scholars Program funded my cardiology/medical history program that led to a masters degree.

Another defining moment for me in terms of my identity in the cardiological community as a historian was provided by Burton Sobel when he was editor of *Circulation*. Burt initially wanted Julius Comroe to write capsules of cardiologic history for a new section he wanted to start in *Circulation* called *"Preludes and Progress."* But Comroe was ill, in fact I think terminally ill when Burt approached him. Comroe told Sobel to ask A. McGehee Harvey to write the series. Burt called Mac Harvey but he was too busy with other things, and suggested that Burt call me. Harvey was my preceptor for my master's degree and we were very, very close. He respected what I did, and thought I was the logical person for Burt's series. When Burt called me, I remember telling him that I really didn't know how I could take this on. But in the midst of the conversation, I'm thinking, "This is insane. This guy is giving me a column in *Circulation*, there's no way I can turn this opportunity down." So I agreed to do it. The first piece was the worst one because I had an artificial length constraint. Burt wanted sort of a one-page punchline essay and I didn't know how to do that. I think Comroe could have done it, but I couldn't. That was the only essay that generated a critical letter. I told Burt, "If you had let me do it the way I wanted to do it, the criticism wouldn't exist" because the piece was fundamentally "superficial." He thereafter allowed me the freedom to write what I thought was necessary. That's when the essays became 6 or 7 editorial pages long with lots of references. These pieces appeared every third month for about 3 1/2 years, for a total of 13. Thereafter, at the national meetings, physicians would say to me, "Hey, I saw your paper!" Burt placed these pieces as the lead article of each issue, the first one the reader fell upon. Then as if that wasn't enough, he collected them together in a free-standing supplement. So I got even more "air time." For me, that was a big thing.

Then the physiology book came out in 1987. It didn't make a big splash because it concerned a narrow field. But nevertheless, the book got a number of very good reviews. Thus, I had a track record of writing a book on professionalization and writing all this stuff for history of cardiology in *Circulation*. I met Bill Winters in China in 1983, and he followed my historical publications with interest and he eventually asked me to write *American Cardiology*.

Those were the most important stages: somebody during my training that didn't snuff me out and say "shut up and get in the lab kid," and then The Marshfield Clinic allowing me 20% of my time for research. Additionally, living in a town of only about 18,000 has helped enormously. Being remote and isolated, I have few social obligations, unlike people that live in suburbia or urban areas where they might feel pressured to belong to the country club or pressured to take advantage of those cultural things, whether it be the opera or symphony or whatever, those things don't exist where I live. And also I've got a 5-minute commute. I live 7/10th of a mile from my office that is attached to a 500-bed hospital. Here's a statistic that blows people away when they think about commuting: If you commute 1 hour each way every day for 5 days, that's 10 hours every week, and if you multiply that by the 260 Mondays through Fridays of the 52 weeks of the year, that represents 3 months of 40-hour work weeks. Consequently, I have an enormous amount of discretionary time that most practitioners don't have. Although academics might have had that kind of discretionary time at one time, they certainly don't have it now. So I have passion for historical research and writing. And I have a wonderful reference library at my home. I have people around the world stimulating the interest further by saying, "Hey, I like that piece you wrote. Would you do this or something. . . ." Then, I have an extraordinarily tolerant wife and family.

• • •

WCR: Bruce, what is your day like? What time do you wake up in the morning? Get to the hospital? Go to bed at night?, etc.

WBF: I usually wake up between 5:30 and 6:00 A.M. I'm a morning person. I usually get to my office by 7:00 A.M. and I work hard all day long to get my work done so I can leave by 5 to 5:15 P.M. Then I go home and basically go down to my basement with the books. I'll surface for dinner and now and again to visit with my family. I can be interrupted, it makes no difference. Interruptions don't really phase me.

• • •

WCR: What time do you go to bed at night? How much sleep do you need?

WBF: Usually I go to bed around 11:00 P.M. I get around 6 or so hours of sleep each night.

• • •

WCR: Has medical history altered the way you practice? How has it influenced your day-to-day activity?

WBF: That's a very good and important question. I think it has influenced my attitudes and probably my behavior in a very real way. A sense of history humbles one; it provides a needed perspective; it emphasizes that we all have very finite lifespans. We have finite opportunities to contribute something, to learn things, and to sort of "touch" people. It has caused me to be very skeptical of dogmatic physicians. The smartest physicians in France, America, and England 150 years ago bled people for virtually any condition. And it wasn't because those doctors were stupid, it was because that was their view of how patients could be helped at that time. A lot of things we do to patients today will be looked at by physicians 100 years from now as very primitive, ill-advised, and possibly even harmful. Maybe cancer chemotherapy and coronary bypass will fall into one of those categories. Nevertheless, we are all locked in our era, in the time we live in, and we're limited to the technologies and approaches that are available to us. A healthy skepticism is very useful for doctors. Probably patients get better from things on their own a lot more than we'd like to acknowledge. That's why some historians have argued that in the 19th century it didn't make any difference what kind of practitioner—whether a homeopath or a regular doctor—one went to because medicines then available were as likely to cause harm as good. Most diseases then were self-limited or untreatable. I think I understand the dynamics of medicine a lot better than most people do because I have a sense of how we got to where we are. I understand the origins of academic medicine in this country, probably better than almost any Dean of any medical school because it's been a subject of interest and a research focus of mine for nearly 2 decades. I understand a lot of the tensions—the financial ones, the power struggles that exist—because I have studied professionalization. It's given me a lot of insight into the tensions that exist among individuals and institutions. That helps me as an administrator of a large clinical department in a practice context. I've written some things to try to give people clues from the historical record as to risks they face today. I'm very concerned about the devaluation of research and the pressures on researchers—the clinical researchers particularly—to devote more time to patient care to compete in managed care, a highly competitive environment.

• • •

WCR: I would recommend your new book to all cardiologists. Do you agree?

WBF: I hope people will go through the book, look at some of the graphs, maybe read 2 or 3 pages, and decide that it is interesting enough to stick with it. I hope that sociologists and politicians will read *American Cardiology*. Most people on Capitol Hill don't have the foggiest notion about how the National Institues of Health evolved, what specialty training is all about, and how it was created. We need to understand how we got to where we are. There are so many rash and radical things occurring each day. I'm concerned that if people don't understand how we got the good pieces of American medicine, they are not going to be able to effectively preserve them.

• • •

WCR: Bruce, do you have ambitions or desires to do things other than what you've already done before you call it quits?

WBF: I've been very content where I am because it allows me to do everything I like or want to do. I am very ambitious, but I am ambitious in a controlled sense. I think many positions that people take or have the opportunity to take are fairly unstable. They reflect on both the local institutional context and on the national context. I don't really have any grand plans to reinvent myself to be, for example, a full-time medical historian. I would not do that. I enjoy medical practice and medical administration too much to do that. I don't really have ambitions to be a foundation president or a medical school influential in some capacity because I just enjoy what I'm doing now too much. I think I would have to give up too much. If I had stayed at Hopkins, I never would have produced a fraction of the historical work that I have produced here. I think I've had an impact, both because of my interest and thank God, my ability, but mostly because of support and opportunities, from encouragement from people at the right time and at the right place. For example, your willingness to liberalize your page limits for my electrocardiogram article. That's the kind of support and encouragement I've gotten on multiple occasions. People who said, "Look, here's the ball—I'll watch you run with it!" That was what the ACC allowed me to do with this book and I think that's why the book is such a success from my point of view, i.e., in terms of what I had hoped for. There was no one who said, "Look, you've got to pay more attention to the former presidents—they're not going to be happy if they don't see themselves in the book," or people that said, "Look, you can't really get into the tensions between the 2 organizations; if you pull up the rug and look what's under there, it's going to make people uncomfortable!" My approach was to do this in the most honest, forthright fashion I could. Obviously, I could be criticized for putting my own spin on it, but I think that's inevitable when somebody writes something. You see the world through your own eyes. I've tried hard to look at a vast array of sources and talk to a diverse group of people to gain perspective, so I think the story is correct. It is a logical place to discuss the tensions between academic departments of internal medicine and academic divisions of cardiology. I think that's going to make some Deans and Chairs of Medicine uncomfortable as their division chiefs send their department heads xerographic copies of that section. I felt that issue was extremely important. That's the other thing you learn from history, that medicine and society are much more than are inevitable series of discoveries, like a relay race. I am a great believer in serendipity and being at the right place at the right time, and being sensitive to queues.

• • •

WCR: How much time do you spend away from home? How much time do you take off each year?

Do you use most of that "off time" working on a particular task of interest at the moment?

WBF: I take off about 3 or 4 weeks at a time in the summer. It's a time where I sort of disengage and spend time travelling with my wife and my family. In each of the last 5 years, we have traveled to Europe spending the days in bookshops hunting for medical books and the evenings together—high-quality family time. I am away from the clinic about once a month for various national activities or meetings during the other 11 months of the year. My colleagues have been very supportive of my historical research and my active involvement in the ACC and American Heart Association.

• • •

WCR: Is there anything that you would like to discuss that we haven't about your most recent book or about anything else?

WBF: I think people who read the book will be impressed how quickly things developed in cardiology, how the technologies came on-line, how quickly the field grew after World War II. Franklin Roosevelt died from complications of hypertension in 1944, before there were effective antihypertensive drugs. John F. Kennedy was elected President in 1960. In 1960, there were no coronary care units, coronary bypass surgery had not been invented, selective coronary angiography was being performed only at The Cleveland Clinic, cardiac valve replacement and implantable pacemakers were introduced that year, and cardiopulmonary resuscitation did not start until a year later. Think how different cardiology would be if radiologists, rather than cardiologists, performed coronary angiography. I talk about all this in the book. I guess all authors hope that their writings resonate with the reader's life and that the reader identifies with something in the book. If the book stimulates people to be more concerned about the current situation in medicine in this country and about the future, that's a bonus.

• • •

WCR: Bruce, can people obtain your book from Astra-Merck?

WBF: Astra-Merck purchased enough copies for every member of the ACC. Members of the ACC can get a copy directly from their Astra-Merck representative. Others can purchase the book directly from the ACC in Bethesda, Maryland, or from the Johns Hopkins University Press in Baltimore, Maryland.

• • •

WCR: Bruce, thank you. This interview will be followed by a list of your publications. I believe this list will be very helpful to some of the readership.

PUBLICATIONS OF W. BRUCE FYE

BOOKS

1. Fye WB. The Development of American Physiology: Scientific Medicine in the Nineteenth Century. Baltimore: The Johns Hopkins University Press, 1987.
2. Fye WB. Editor of William Osler's Collected Papers on the Cardiovascular System. Birmingham: Gryphon Editions, 1985.
3. Fye WB. Editor of Classic Papers on Coronary Thrombosis and Myocardial Infarction. Birmingham: Gryphon Editions, 1991.
4. Fye WB. American Cardiology: The History of a Specialty and Its College. Baltimore: The Johns Hopkins University Press, 1996.

BOOK CHAPTERS

1. Fye WB. Henry Pickering Bowditch: pioneer American physiologist and American educator. In: Barondess JA, et al, eds. The Persisting Osler: Selected Transactions of the First Ten Years of the American Osler Society. Baltimore: University Park Press, 1985:257–264.
2. Fye WB. Key references history of cardiology. In: Callahan JA, et al, eds. Classics of Cardiology. Malabar, FL: R.E. Krieger, 1983:3:614–616.
3. Fye WB, editor of Maude Abbott, Osler's Contributions to our Knowledge of Heart Disease in William Osler's Collected Papers on the Cardiovascular System, edited with introduction by W. Bruce Fye. Birmingham, AL: Gryphon Editions, 1985:xv–xxvii.
4. Fye WB. Growth of American physiology, 1850–1900. In: Gerald L. Geison, ed. Physiology in the American Context, 1850–1940. Bethesda, MD: American Physiological Society, 1987:47–65.
5. Fye WB. The Literature of internal medicine. In: Maulitz RC, Long DE, eds. Grand Rounds: One Hundred Years of Internal Medicine. Philadelphia: University of Pennsylvania Press, 1988:55–84.
6. Fye WB. The delayed diagnosis of myocardial infarction. In: It is Good to Know: Essays and Appreciations in Honour of the 90th Birthday of Dr. Harold Nathan Segall. Montreal, 1989:173–182.
7. Fye WB. Acute myocardial infarction: an historical summary. In: Gersh BJ, Rahimtoola S, eds. Acute Myocardial Infarction. New York: Elsevier, 1990:1–13.
8. Fye WB. Introduction: acute myocardial infarction: an historical summary. In: Fye WB, ed. Classic Papers on Coronary Thrombosis and Myocardial Infarction. Birmingham, 1991:ix–xxvi.
9. Fye WB. A history of cardiac arrhythmias. In: Kastor JA, ed. Arrhythmias. Philadelphia: WB Saunders, 1994:1–24.
10. Fye WB. Albion Walter Hewlett: teacher, clinician, scientist, and missionary for "pathologic physiology." In: Howell JD, ed, Medical Lives & Scientific Medicine at Michigan, 1891–1969. Ann Arbor: The University of Michigan Press, 1993:45–72.
11. Fye WB. William Osler's departure from North America. In: Barondess J, Roland CG, eds. The Persisting Osler II: Selected Transactions of the American Osler Society 1981–1990. Malabar: Krieger Publishing, 1994:245–257.
12. Fye WB. Acute myocardial infarction. In: Richard Lewis, ed, ACCSAP 1995–96. Bethesda: American College of Cardiology, 1995:2.3–2.35.
13. Fye WB. A historical perspective on atherosclerosis and coronary artery disease. In: Valentin Fuster, Robert Ross, and Eric Totpol, eds. Atherosclerosis and Coronary Artery Disease. Philadelphia: Lippincott–Raven Publishers, 1996:1–12.

ARTICLES (major ones only)

1. Fye WB. The literature and history of internal medicine—an annotated bibliography. Ann intern Med 1977;87:123–128.
2. Fye WB. Review. In: Waife SO, ed. Notable Medical Books from the Lilly Library, Indiana University. Bull Hist Med 1978;52:144–145.
3. Borenstein DG, Fye WB, et al. The myocarditis of systemic lupus erythematosus, association with myositis. Ann Intern Med 1978;89:619–624.
4. Fye WB. Active euthanasia—an historical survey of its conceptual origins and introduction into medical thought. Bull Hist Med 1979;52:492–501.
5. Fye WB. Echocardiography 1980—indications and usefulness. Wis Med J 1980;79:19–22.
6. Fye WB, Molina E. Right atrial angiosarcoma—echocardiographic diagnosis and surgical correlation. Johns Hopkins Med J 1980;147:111–116.
7. Fye WB. A primer on medical books. AB Bookmans Weekly 1981;67:3658–3696.
8. Fye WB. Key references: history of cardiology. Circulation 1981;64:434–436.
9. Fye WB. Medical history in Wisconsin. Wis Med J 1981;80:13–14.
10. Fye WB. Why a physiologist? The case of Henry P. Bowditch. Bull Hist Med 1982;56:19–29.
11. Fye WB. Henry Pickering Bowditch, pioneer physiologist and medical educator. Harvard Medical Alumni Bulletin 1983;57:46–49.
12. Fye WB. S. Weir Mitchell–Philadelphia's "lost" physiologist. Bull Hist Med 1983;57:188–202.
13. Fye WB. Librarians in the history of the health sciences: challenges and opportunities in the 80s. Watermark (Bulletin of the Association of Librarians in the History of Health Sciences) 1983;6:14–18.
14. Fye WB. Ernest Henry Starling: his law and its growing significance in the practice of medicine. Circulation 1983;68:1145–1148.
15. Fye WB. Sydney Ringer and the role of calcium in myocardial function. Circulation 1984;69:849–853.
16. Fye WB. Heparin—the contributions of William Henry Howell. Circulation 1984;69:1198–1203.
17. Fye WB. Medical history librarianship: an overview. AB Bookmans Weekly 1984;73:3365–3380.
18. Fye WB. Coronary arteriography—it took a long time. Circulation 1984;70:781–787.

19. Fye WB. Collecting medical books: challenges and opportunities in the 80s. Bull NY Acad Med 1985;61:250–265.

20. Fye WB. H. Newell Martin—a remarkable career destroyed by neurasthenia and alcoholism. J Hist Med Allied Sci 1985;40:135–166.

21. Fye WB. Acute coronary occlusion always results in death—or does it? The observations of William T. Porter. Circulation 1985;71:4–10.

22. Fye WB. Cardiology in 1885. Circulation 1985;72:21–26.

23. Fye WB. Ventricular fibrillation and defibrillation: historical perspectives. Circulation 1985;71:858–865.

24. Fye WB. The delayed diagnosis of acute myocardial infarction: it took half a century! Circulation 1985;72:262–271.

25. Fye WB. Nitroglycerin: a homeopathic remedy. Circulation 1986;73:21–29.

26. Fye WB. H. Newell Martin and the isolated heart preparation: the link between the frog and open heart surgery. Circulation 1986;73:857–864.

27. Fye WB. Coronary arteriography. Cardiology in Practice. 1986;3:57–62.

28. Fye WB. T. Lauder Brunton and amyl nitrite: a victorian vasodilator. Circulation 1986;74:222–229.

29. Fye WB. American contributions to cardiovascular medicine and surgery. Bethesda, National institutes of Health, 1986 (22 page pamphlet).

30. Fye WB. The history of cardiology: a bibliography of secondary sources. Bethesda, National Library of Medicine, 1986 (pamphlet).

31. Fye WB. An artificial heart operation in 1859. J Heart Transplant 1986;5:178.

32. Fye WB. Carl Ludwig and the Leipzig Physiological institute: "a factory of new knowledge." Circulation 1986;74:920–928.

33. Fye WB. The literature of American internal medicine: a historical view. Ann Intern Med 1987;106:450–461.

34. Fye WB. The origin of the heart beat: a tale of frogs, jellyfish and turtles. Circulation 1987;76:493–500.

35. Fye WB. William Osler. Clin Cardiol 1988;11:356–358.

36. Cowan MD, Fye WB. Prevalence of QTc prolongation in women with mitral valve prolapse. Am J Cardiol 1989;63:133–134.

37. Fye WB. William Osler's departure from North America. The price of success. N Engl J Med 1989;320:1425–1431.

38. Fye WB. James Hope. Clin Cardiol 1989;12:358–359.

39. Fye WB. Austin Flint, 1812–1886. Clin Cardiol 1989;12:476–477.

40. Fye WB. Pierre Mere Latham, 1787–1875. Clin Cardiol 1989;12:609–611.

41. Fye WB. William Osler's departure from North American—addendum. N Engl J Med 1989;321:1199.

42. Fye WB. T. Lauder Brunton, 1844–1916. Clin Cardiol 1989;12:675–676.

43. Fye WB. An older person's guide to cardiovascular health and disease. Dallas: American Health Association, 1989 (pamphlet).

44. Fye WB. Karel Frederik Wenckebach, 1864–1940. Clin Cardiol 1990;13:146–148.

45. Fye WB. William Henry Broadbent. Clin Cardiol 1990;13:62–64.

46. Fye WB. Allan Burns. Clin Cardiol 1990;13:301–302.

47. Fye WB. Charles James Martin. Dictionary of Scientific Biography 1990;18:597–599.

48. Fye WB. Vasodilator therapy for angina pectoris: the intersection of homeopathy and scientific medicine. J Hist Med Allied Sci 1990;45:317–340.

49. Fye WB. William Townsend Porter. Clin Cardiol 1990;13:585–587.

50. Fye WB. Thomas Bevill Peacock. Clin Cardiol 1990;13:447–448.

51. Fye WB. Giovanni Maria Lancisi, 1654–1720. Clin Cardiol 1990;13:670–671.

52. Fye WB. Medical authorship: traditions, trends, and tribulations. Ann Intern Med 1990;113:317–325.

53. Fye WB. Lazzaro Spallanzani. Clin Cardiol 1990;13:817–819.

54. Fye WB. The origin of the full-time faculty system: implications for clinical research. JAMA 1991;265:1555–1562.

55. Fye WB. Carl Ludwig. Clin Cardiol 1991;14:361–363.

56. Fye WB. The history of the full-time clinical faculty system. JAMA 1991;266:514.

57. Fye WB. The strictly full-time professor of medicine in an American medical school: Hopkins, not Michigan. JAMA 1991;266:2987.

58. Fye WB. J. Milner Fothergill. Clin Cardiol 1992;15:220–222.

59. Fye WB. Caleb Hillier Parry. Clin Cardiol 1992;15:619–621.

60. Fye WB. Medical book collecting: a retrospect and a forecast. N J Med 1992;89:835–841.

61. Fye WB. Cary F. Coombs. Clin Cardiol 1992;15:868–869.

62. Fye WB. Albion Walter Hewlett. Clin Cardiol 1993;16:76–78.

63. Fye WB. The history of medicine: an annotated list of key reference works. Ann Intern Med 1993;118:59–62.

64. Fye WB. René–Joseph–Hyacinthe Bertin. Clin Cardiol 1993;273–274.

65. Fye WB. A history of the American Heart Association's Council on Clinical Cardiology. Circulation 1993;87:1057–1063.

66. Fye WB. H. Newell Martin. Clin Cardiol 1993;16:631–632.

67. Fye WB. Richard Lower. Clin Cardiol 1993;16:757–758.

68. Fye WB. Disorders of the heartbeat: a historical overview from antiquity to the mid-20th century. Am J Cardiol 1993;72:1055–1070.

69. Fye WB. About the history of the discovery of the cardiac conduction system. Jpn Circ J 1993;57:1187–1189.

70. Fye WB. Henry Pickering Bowditch. Clin Cardiol 1994;17:221–222.

71. Fye WB. A history of the origin, evolution, and impact of electrocardiography. Am J Cardiol 1994;73:937–949.

72. Fye WB. Edward Jenner. Clin Cardiol 1994;17:634–635.

73. Fye WB. John Forbes. Clin Cardiol 1995;18:236–237.

74. Fye WB. Albrecht von Haller. Clin Cardiol 1995;18:291–292.

75. Fye WB. Arthur Cushny. Clin Cardiol 1995;18:360–361.

76. Fye WB. William Murrell. Clin Cardiol 1995;18:426–427.

77. Fye WB. Louis Faugeres Bishop. Clin Cardiol 1995;18:541–542.

78. Fye WB. Julien Jean César Legallois. Clin Cardiol 1995;18:599–600.

79. Fye WB. Henry Ingersoll Bowditch. Clin Cardiol 1995;18:685–686.

80. Fye WB. John Blackall. Clin Cardiol 1996;19:77–78.

ARTHUR GARSON, JR., MD, MPH:
A Conversation With the Editor*

Arthur Garson was born in New York City on February 14, 1949. He attended private schools in New York City until high school and then he went to Choate School in Wallingford, Connecticut. From there it was Princeton University where he graduated summa cum laude in 1970. His medical school was Duke University from which he graduated in 1974 having been elected to Alpha Omega Alpha. His internship and first-year residency in pediatrics also was at Duke University, and his 3-year fellowship in pediatric cardiology was at Baylor College of Medicine in Houston, Texas. After finishing his fellowship in 1979, he stayed on the faculty at Baylor College of Medicine, rising to the rank of Professor of Pediatrics and Professor of Medicine in 6 years. At one time, he was director of the electrocardiography laboratory, pacemaker clinic, and electrophysiology laboratory at Texas Children's Hospital in Houston. In 1988, he became Chief of Pediatric Cardiology at Texas Children's Hospital and Baylor College of Medicine. In 1992, he left for Durham, North Carolina, to be Associate Vice Chancellor for Health Policy and Chief of Pediatric Cardiology at Duke University Medical Center. In 1995, he returned to Houston to be Vice Chairman of Pediatrics for Strategic Planning at Baylor College of Medicine and Vice President of Texas Children's Hospital. In 1996, he became Senior Vice President and Dean for Academic Operations at Baylor College of Medicine. In 1999, Dr. Garson was President of the American College of Cardiology (ACC). In June 2002 he moved to Charlottesville, Virginia, to become Dean of the School of Medicine and Vice President of the University of Virginia, Charlottesville. He has published 8 books, 160 articles in peer-reviewed medical journals, 78 chapters in various books, 29 editorials, 5 public service pamphlets, and 30 invited articles in various medical journals. He is recognized as one of the elite pediatric cardiologists in the world. He and his lovely wife, Suzan, are the parents of 2 girls. They both are art lovers and cook with passion. He is also a nice guy and fun to be around.

William Clifford Roberts, MD[†] **(hereafter WCR):** *It is February 22, 2001, and Dr. Arthur Garson and I are in my home. Tim, I appreciate your willingness to talk to me and, therefore, to the readers of* The American Journal of Cardiology. *Could we talk a bit about your family, your parents, and siblings? What it was like growing up in New York City? What did your parents do?*

Arthur Garson, Jr., MD, MPH[‡] **(Tim) (hereafter TG):** Bill, it's an honor to be here, especially considering your previous interviewees. My parents were a South/North combination. My father was born in Atlanta, of parents who had come from Austria. After my father's parents got married, they decided to make brassieres for a living. My father was the oldest of 3 children who went to grade school in the early part of the century, just as the IQ test was created. He "pegged out" on the IQ test and nobody knew what to do with him. They kept promoting him through grade after grade such that he graduated from high school at age 10. His parents then enrolled him in Oglethorpe University in Atlanta. According to my father, he didn't get straight A's, but he made it through college in 4 years and graduated at age 14. He then went into his father's brassiere business. What else was a 14-year-old with a college degree going to do? He couldn't even drive! He spent the next 6 or so years selling bras door to door in Atlanta. Then he moved to New York to start the marketing end of what turned out to be the Lovable Brassiere Company. He then went off fairly shortly thereafter to World War II. He told amazing stories about being in the Army Intelligence. Some things have come out since in novels that he actually participated in—ways to fool the enemy. He married my mother in 1946 after coming back from the war. I was the child of his second marriage. He had a son and a daughter by the first marriage and my mother had a daughter by her first marriage. They were married for 50 years!

The Lovable Company became, in the 1960s, one of the largest, if not the largest, by sales, bra-producing companies in the world. The company, at one time, had factories in 18 countries. Our parents told my brother and me when we were teenagers that if we thought we might want to go into the bra business, we had to spend half of every summer working for the company. When I was 16 I learned how to cut patterns in Puerto Rico. My brother, who is 5 years older, had gone through that a few years earlier and cut the end of one finger off learning how to cut bras. I was a little more careful after he told me the tricks of the trade. Then I went to California and learned how to ship bras. I ended up in Atlanta in quality control, matching peach straps to peach hook and eyes to peach cloth, learning the right way to match colors. It was during that same summer, which was in the middle of college, that I thought maybe I wanted to be a physician, and I then worked in a laboratory in New York City at Mount Sinai. A gastroenterologist allowed me to round with him and to work in his basic science lab. I was able to see science, medicine, rounds, and bras in

*This series of interviews are underwritten by an unrestricted grant from Bristol-Myers Squibb.
†Baylor Heart and Vascular Center, Baylor University Medical Center, Dallas, Texas 75246.
‡Dean of the School of Medicine and Vice President, University of Virginia, Charlottesville, Virginia 22908.

FIGURE 1. TG wearing a bowtie at an early age.

the same summer and picked medicine instead of bras. Although I took some economics early at Princeton, I majored in biology. At Princeton I had to do a bachelor's thesis. It took up my entire senior year. I did animal research in college trying to figure out how to make peripheral nerves grow back faster, something that later had implications in my life.

WCR: *When was your father born and when did he die?*

TG: He was born in 1913 and died in 1998.

WCR: *And your mother?*

TG: She was born in 1924 and she is still alive. I can't evaluate a father that I respected and loved as I would a peer. He didn't spew Einstein-type equations at dinner. My favorite memory of him is his story of his going to lunch frequently in the 1950s with the president of Jockey Shorts. They were always trying to name their products, like Cross Your Heart bras. Jockey Shorts was trying to name their new boxer shorts because they had never made boxer shorts before. My father suggested "Grand Ballroom." He had a quick sense of humor. He was highly ethical (sometimes tough in the garment business) and ultimately logical.

WCR: *It sounds to me like your father was extremely successful in business. The Lovable Brassiere Company is a well-known company.*

TG: The Lovable Company was at its height just before the late 1960s. About the same time that many women quit wearing bras, the company had its own computer system installed and it made a complete switch over to the computer system in one day without running dual books. That was a drastic mistake. Their computer system failed. They were unable to track orders, to deliver, or to buy materials. We all learned from that experience. Every previous year it had gone well, but in the face of adversity it did not do well.

To fast-forward, why did I as the Chief of Pediatric Cardiology go get a degree in public health? Part of that degree was in business, not in epidemiology. I knew that pediatric cardiology was doing just fine at the time. Having watched the Lovable Company not do well in time of adversity stimulated me to go back to school to learn how to deal with business adversity and to anticipate and deal with problems. In the 1970s the Atlanta Lovable group bought out the New York group, including my father and brother. Later, the Atlanta group sold to Sarah Lee. Sarah Lee—brownies and bras.

WCR: *What is your mother like?*

TG: My mother was born in New York City and was refinement personified—elegant, caring. She taught us to do for others and give what we could of ourselves. She worked in an art gallery while I was a teenager.

WCR: *What was your home like? Were there a lot of books around the house?*

TG: There was a lot of art, and happily, I've got some of that, even some Magrittes! There was music. None of us played an instrument, but we had classical music playing when growing up. Our dinner conversations were mainly about business or their travels. My father did not take a business trip without my mother. They went to Russia and China very early. I guess that traveling would be my third hobby, after art and cooking. Our whole family likes to travel. My parents' traveling surely influenced me.

When I was in high school on the last day of a 17th and 18th century French painting course, the teacher showed slides of a recent Magritte exhibit in New York, and I discovered surrealism. I couldn't even spell it at the time. That was the beginning of my deep interest in art. During my first 2 weeks of cardiology fellowship in Houston, I went gallery hopping and came across a print I really liked. Although I didn't have any money, I asked the people in the gallery if I could work for them so I could purchase the print. I worked there for about a year on Saturdays during my first year of cardiology fellowship to buy the print. I've still got the print. Maybe some day we will own an art gallery.

Since medical school I've always been in the South. My brother and sisters are all in New York City. My brother is still in the bra business. One sister's husband had been president of CBS Sports. I learned a lot about sports from the 2 of them and from people behind the scenes with contacts in sports. My other sister is in the design business. We all learn a lot from each other.

WCR: *Was there anybody in high school or junior high school who had a major impact on you?*

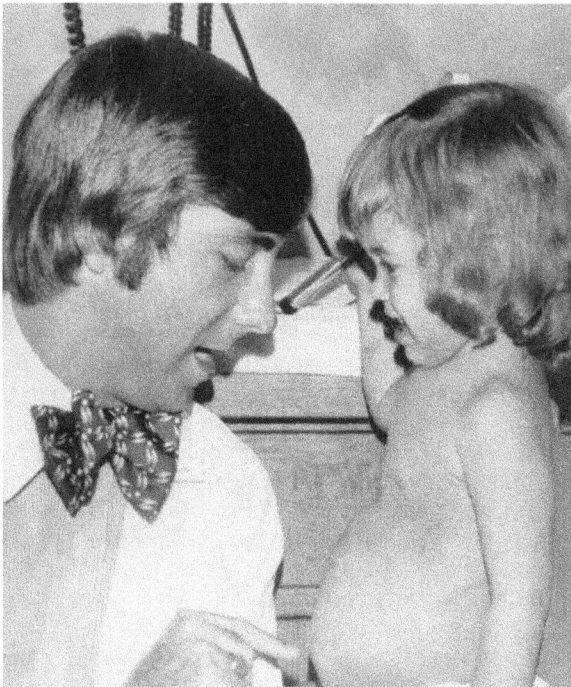

FIGURE 2. TG in medical school with the patient he would eventually follow the longest time.

TG: There were 2 and they were both physicians. It's fascinating to me that many people pursue careers because they meet individuals. One was our family doctor, an internist in the 1950s. He had a fair amount to do with the early use of insulin. My parents were out of the country when my appendix burst. He stepped in more like a surrogate parent while I was recovering. In discussions with him, I thought being a physician was a good thing to do. He gave me my first stethoscope when I went to medical school. The enclosed card said, "You will learn more if you listen to the patient without this stethoscope." I still have that card. The other physician is a surgeon who I watched operate for 2 or 3 summers in a row. He would make patients feel better by joking with them, talking on their level. Those 2—an internist and a general surgeon—were ultimately responsible for my going to medical school.

WCR: *Were there any teachers in junior high school or high school who had a major influence on you?*

TG: Yes. One was a biology teacher who made biology exciting. He made all of us draw an animal and it had to be art—no line drawing! The act of agonizing over that drawing brought biology to life. The other was an English teacher who was a classic thinker and challenged the way we all thought. I wrote many short stories in high school and college. Fortunately, the gene is there in our 17-year-old daughter.

WCR: *What extracurricular activities did you do in high school? Were you an athlete? Did you play sports?*

TG: I played tennis beginning at age 5. I played junior varsity tennis in high school and freshman squash at Princeton.

WCR: *You must have met a lot of people in college, both faculty and students. Did some of them have a major influence on you?*

TG: There was a musical comedy organization at Princeton called the Princeton Triangle Club that put on a musical comedy show each year. *Jimmy Stewart* and *Josh Logan* had been in that show. I was the business manager of the Triangle Club for 2 years, my sophomore and junior years. The squash coach told me, "You could either be on the varsity squash team or you can be in the Triangle Club. You can't do both." I stopped playing squash. To be a 19-year-old with a $100,000 budget trying to get 80 people around the USA to 13 different places was great. We gave shows in Chicago, Rochester, New York, Miami, etc. I put the whole tour together and a playbill (called a "Ploybill"), and a 33-rpm record. That was a fair amount to run as a college kid. Probably, the person who had the most influence on me was the one who got me interested in the Triangle Club. It was nearly a full time job for 2 years. The Triangle show toured over Christmas vacation. For 2 weeks, we went to about 12 different places, put on a show every night, then took a bus or a train to the next stop. Fortunately, we had a reading period at Princeton that was 2 weeks after Christmas vacation.

WCR: *You were in college what years?*

TG: From 1966 to 1970.

WCR: *You must have done very well academically in high school at Choate to get into Princeton. Why did you choose Princeton?*

TG: I've joked many times that my roommate went to Stanford. At the time I thought Stanford was a place in Connecticut. I got a great education at Princeton.

WCR: *How did you decide to go to Duke to medical school?*

TG: I applied initially only to eastern schools, including Columbia and Hopkins. I learned of the "new" Duke curriculum and was attracted to it. The Duke curriculum in the late 1960s included all of the basic science studies in the first year and all of the clinical work in the second year. The third and fourth years were electives. In my third year, I developed a mathematical model of tetralogy of Fallot—in 162-dimensional space. I also had the advantage of a "southern" father who did not make fun of my going to a school in the South. I had a roommate my first year at Duke who could not take the South. He left Duke and entered Harvard for his last 2 years. The Duke faculty and students were wonderful.

WCR: *Who influenced you in medical school?*

TG: *David Sabiston, Denton Cooley,* and *Michael DeBakey.* Their ability to do heart surgery, to actually do something visibly for patients, attracted me to the idea of being a heart surgeon. I started medical school wanting to be a heart surgeon. The chair of surgery at Duke was David Sabiston, who was clearly one of the greatest American surgeons, and he influenced me tremendously. He helped arrange a trip my first summer in medical school to Birmingham to spend time with *John Kirklin.* I had some great discussions with

Dr. Kirklin about cardiology and decided that summer to be a pediatric cardiologist, not a heart surgeon.

WCR: *After you had been in medical school for a while, were you secure that you had chosen the right profession for yourself? There were no second doubts?*

TG: I had no second doubts. I remember once at 4 A.M. carrying a cup of urine down 6 flights of stairs to look at it under the microscope, having just talked to my brother the night before who was in business making a great living and not carrying urine down 6 flights of stairs, wondering, "Have I missed something here?" And saying, "No." I've been delighted with medicine.

WCR: *I guess it is advantageous to decide what you want to do early in medical school. On the other hand, having difficulty in deciding what to do in medical school might allow you to look more thoroughly into each of the various specialties. In your junior and senior year, did you spend a lot of time in pediatric cardiology?*

TG: The summer between second and third year, I spent in Houston with *Dan McNamara* in pediatric cardiology at Baylor College of Medicine. Dan McNamara was my true mentor. He was gentle, smart, had a good sense of humor, and great values.

WCR: *How did you decide to do your internship in Durham at Duke rather than in Houston or elsewhere?*

TG: When I left Houston and entered my third year of medical school Dan said, "You have a spot here if you want it." Duke Pediatrics was excellent, so I stayed and did 2 years of pediatric training there.

WCR: *How did your training in pediatrics go at Duke? Did you enjoy it? Were you glad you picked that specialty?*

TG: Yes. It's interesting to think back. We tend to remember patients. My favorite patient died last year. I was a second-year medical student on the surgery rotation in 1968 and she had had 1 of the very first Mustard operations for transposition of the great arteries at Duke. I spent 13 straight nights at Duke Hospital with this child on the surgery rotation. I bonded with her and her parents. I wound up taking care of her and staying in touch with them forever.

WCR: *What attracted you to kids?*

TG: Kids are optimistic and don't get bogged down in being sick.

WCR: *When did you get married? What stage were you in at that time?*

TG: In 1979. I was in my first year on the faculty at Baylor College of Medicine in Houston. I had met my wife in Dallas. Just before we married, she was about to go into a masters program in social work to be a psychotherapist and she did. She is an adolescent psychotherapist. She is a gentle, genuinely nice person, and if I were an adolescent (or a husband!), I would put my total trust in her. We have built 3 houses together and have stayed married! We eventually built nearly the same house 3 times: Houston—Durham—Houston. The third one is a bit different, but they have all been galleries to live in. Fortunately, we have

FIGURE 3. TG and Suzan on their wedding day, August 4, 1979.

similar tastes in art and in houses or we would have destroyed each other by now.

WCR: *Did you enjoy your pediatric cardiology fellowship in Houston?*

TG: The most important event of my first year was back when it was not possible to put your name first on more than 1 abstract for the Annual Scientific Sessions of the ACC. *Paul Gillette* had already become a friend and mentor. We worked on a number of projects, and my name went first on the "atrial ectopic tachycardia" abstract. The abstract presented before mine was by a person who had written a book on pediatric electrophysiology, and the topic of his talk was that atrial ectopic tachycardia did not exist. After our 2 presentations, the moderator decided to have a joint discussion. Thus, the discussion was between this very senior investigator, who thought the entity did not exist, and me, a first-year cardiology fellow, who thought it did exist. That was the very first talk I had ever given. Somebody asked the question, "You said quinidine doesn't work for this arrhythmia. Why doesn't quinidine work?" I learned quickly the difference between "I don't know" and "Nobody knows." I knew I didn't know. *Ken Rosen*, who had already done a great deal of work in adult electrophysiology, stood up in the audience and said, "That's a stupid question. Nobody knows the answer to that." I was eternally grateful to Ken Rosen.

I was also hooked on pediatric electrophysiology. Shortly thereafter, I went to an adult electrocardiography course in Philadelphia taught by *Leonard Dreyfus*. The penny dropped—the electrocardiogram made sense. In the late 1970s there wasn't much out there about pediatric electrocardiography. Paul had done a lot of the very early catheter work in children. I became the surface electrocardiogram person and he became more of the intracardiac person. Very quickly we taught each other things. I learned innovation from him. At one point, we were extremely busy with large numbers of kids and young adults with arrhythmias from around the country and from around the world. He had the "slow service" of children with pacemakers and I had the "fast service" of children with tachycardias. We each had our assigned fellow and a nurse, and although a lot of times we made rounds together, we had 2 complete services in pediatric electrophysiology for about a year.

WCR: *How many papers did you write during your 3-year cardiology fellowship?*

TG: I wrote 2 books. The first book, written during my second year of fellowship, was on ways to analyze pediatric arrhythmias. The "child" of that book, the electrocardiogram book, which I wrote by myself, was written during my third year of fellowship and finished the first year we were married. My wife often sat patiently while I drew a lot of the electrocardiograms for that book. Paul and I published our first book together on electrophysiology in 1981. I don't know how many papers I wrote during my fellowship, but I guess about 20.

WCR: *Your fellowship was from July 1976 to July 1979. When did you meet your future wife?*

TG: Friday, September 13, 1978. We fondly remember "Friday, the 13th" in Dallas.

WCR: *How did that come about?*

TG: Some very good friends of mine, whom I had spent time with in Houston, moved to Dallas and I met her parents at a wedding. Everybody said, "The two of you need to get together." I flew to Dallas, and thereafter we had a whirlwind courtship because she was in Dallas and I was in Houston. Fortunately, Southwest Airlines had flights for $26.00 one way. We spent each weekend traveling back and forth.

WCR: *How long did you stay in Houston? When did you go back to Duke?*

TG: I became Chief of Pediatric Cardiology in Houston in 1988. I followed Dan McNamara. We had breakfast together every week for that whole next year. It was a wonderful transition time. I learned that I could honor him by continuing some of his initiatives and at the same time bring something a little different. I had spent growing up learning about money, worrying about economics, and I almost went into the business world. I was able to learn from the things that Dan did, and added a dimension to billing and collections.

As fortunes go, I had 2 collapsed disks necessitating neck surgery and came out of the operating room paralyzed. That certainly changed things.

WCR: *When was that?*

TG: In 1990. It was several months before I could move my arms at all. It was during that time that I enrolled into the Master of Public Health Program at the University of Texas in Houston. I couldn't write, I couldn't go to class, but they allowed me to do the whole degree by independent study. Of the 10 courses, 7 of them were in finance—macroeconomics, microeconomics, strategic planning, and health policy. What people say when you get a degree as an adult is probably correct: you change jobs. I really felt that I

wanted to do something different. Duke had been looking for a Chief of Pediatric Cardiology, and 1991 was the beginning of health care reform.

Again, back to a story of a patient, because that is the real reason I decided to get into policy. My first night on call, a blue baby with truncus arteriosus operated on that day at the age of 5 had a very rocky night, but she made it and I bonded with her and her family and followed her as she grew. About 10 years later, she developed atrial flutter but was well controlled on medication. She decided not to go to college. She finished high school but couldn't get a job in a medium-sized town in Texas. She had no disability, but as soon as she told potential employers that she had had heart surgery, she could not get a job. She was no longer covered by insurance. Her Medicaid ran out. She had wonderful—but not wealthy—parents. She had stopped refilling her expensive prescription at the same time as the funding disappeared. Several months later, she arrested at home and was resuscitated, but with severe brain damage. Paradoxically, now that she was "disabled," she was again covered by a government program.

My Master of Public Health thesis was on a cost–benefit analysis of a job-training program for adults with congenital heart disease (stimulated by this patient's inability to get a job). Trying to develop policy to provide healthcare coverage for her and the other uninsured led to my broader interest in policy. Duke was looking for someone who would be a medical person in policy because health care reform was coming. I did both. I was the Chief of Pediatric Cardiology and Associate Vice Chancellor for Health Policy. I was in Washington, DC, 2 or 3 days a week "lobbying" for medical schools. On the other days, I taught policy in Duke's Sanford Institute of Public Policy, and saw patients. It was a great few years. But, no health care reform. By that time, I was Vice Chairman of Pediatrics at Duke as well. I was busy, but still made a large number of outlying clinic trips; I learned to see patients very efficiently in those clinics—sometimes >10 new patients in an afternoon. I also spent time traveling around the state trying to bring Duke pediatric cardiology and pediatrics to those areas. I talked to doctors around the state to find out what they wanted and then would come back to Duke and try to make that happen. The best thing for Duke was that I recruited some outstanding people and they are still there. Rather than what I was able to do, it's what they were able to do.

WCR: *You increased the pediatric cardiology load a great deal during your tour there?*

TG: I increased the faculty, and then the size of the service increased. When I got there it was perhaps stable to decreasing, and it increased.

The Chairman of Pediatrics at Baylor recruited me back as Vice Chairman of Pediatrics and Vice President of Texas Children's Hospital for Quality and Outcomes. The next year he became the president of Baylor College of Medicine and he asked me to take the lead in developing a new strategy for the medical school. At the end of that year he asked me to become

FIGURE 4. The Garson family in 1999: (*from left to right*) Mother Patricia, sister Kathy, TG, sister Sue, brother Tom, and father Arthur.

the Dean for Academic Operations, and to direct the strategic planning process for the medical school—12 teams of faculty and staff, strategic planning, and then work with the departments to operationalize the strategy. At Duke, I tried to understand faculty at a departmental level and had started to develop some of these things that have now become affectionately known as "metrics." At Baylor in Houston, we fully developed a process—understanding at the faculty level, the departmental level, and the school level—to examine the efficiency and effectiveness of faculty members. The whole thing now has come to fruition at Baylor. We are now able to work with department chairs to help them understand their entire department in all these different dimensions and to set goals.

WCR: *What happened to your paralysis? What happened to your neck?*

TG: It has gotten better and better. I couldn't lift my arms to eat for several months. I still can't swim very far. It's well enough that nobody (including me) thinks about it anymore. I certainly learned a great deal about the healthcare system—perhaps most of all, what an administrative nightmare it is for parents. My biggest regret of this whole thing was that my youngest child was a year old and I couldn't pick her up for 6 months. I wanted to teach my kids to play tennis and I can't do that.

WCR: *What is your day-to-day life like? Do you sleep much? What time do you get up in the morning? What time do you get to the hospital? What time do you leave the hospital? What time do you go to bed at night? Give me a feel for that.*

TG: I get up at 5:45 A.M. I'm at the hospital by 6:45 A.M. unless it's a monthly meeting with the Chairman of Surgery and that's at 6:00 A.M. I get home about 7:00 to 7:30 P.M. My last meetings are usually over by 5:30 P.M., and then I try to clear my desk so that I can help my kids with their homework in the evenings. I have 2 girls. I generally don't take the 11-year-old and the 16-year-old shopping, but I can do homework with them, so this is important time for us. When I come home I'm theirs until they go to bed. I try to get work done before I come home so that we can eat dinner together, and then if they have homework, I'm the math and science guy and my wife is the history and English woman.

WCR: *You've gotten your 2 girls interested in art also, I presume?*

TG: Yes. The two of them have very different tastes. They know exactly what they like. I found that out when we did minor redoes of their rooms. At the poster store I said, "You can each buy 3 posters for your rooms." They each went through books and I watched what happened. One is much more drawn to photography and realism and one is much more drawn to Van Gogh. You learn about your children every day!

WCR: *What do you think your girls are going to do? They're very attractive young ladies.*

TG: Thank you. At present, the older one is a good writer. She writes poetry. She's done a lot of journalism. She went to Oxford last summer to study journalism. I suspect she will do something with the written word, but it may end up being the law. The younger one is interested in teaching and is just marvelous with people. She would make an outstanding teacher. That's where they are right now.

WCR: *I understand that you are an exquisite chef. How did you get interested in cooking? You don't look like you eat too much. How did that come about and what do you like to cook?*

TG: French food. I took a number of French cook-

FIGURE 5. The Garsons on the day TG became president of the ACC, March 1999: (*from left to right*) TG, Lauren, Kathleen, and Suzan.

ing courses while I was an intern and a resident. These things are never coincidences. When I met my wife to be, I learned that she too liked to cook, and she was a lot better cook than I was. Before we had kids we used to have a New Year's Eve party where we would cook for 150 people. We would start cooking and freezing at Thanksgiving. We'd borrow neighbors' freezers and essentially cook a buffet for 150. It's fun. It's creative. It's fun having people over and making an experience out of it. Not just eating but talking and thinking about the food and ways to make it better. It's been a great experience.

WCR: *That's become a social activity to have 2 or 3 couples over and you both cook for them?*

TG: Yes. It's funny what we've now gravitated to. My wife is much better at fixing desserts. I can't even read dessert recipes and understand what is going to be good. She is outstanding, very innovative with desserts. I'm better with the main courses.

WCR: *How have you been able to continue your 2 pediatric cardiology books?*

TG: There is the *Textbook of Pediatric Cardiology* and the arrhythmia book that Paul Gillette and I continue to edit. Fortunately, the 2 are staggered. The simple answer to the pediatric cardiology textbook is that *Tim Bricker*, who is the current Chief of Pediatric Cardiology at Baylor College of Medicine, is the real operating head of that book now. I give him tremendous credit for doing it. I keep trying to get him to put his name first. I cajole when people don't turn in their chapters, and I do the final edits.

WCR: *You can't turn the arrhythmia book over to someone else?*

TG: No, but right now Paul is the first editor of that book. The arrhythmia book has always been Gillette and Garson. I've just been asked to update/rewrite the electrocardiography book that I wrote myself, and I

will probably start doing that in the next couple of months.

WCR: *I am now in Dr. Arthur Garson's office at Baylor College of Medicine in Houston. It is February 28, 2002. The first occasion that Dr. Garson and I talked was in Dallas, February 22, 2001. It has taken slightly over a year for us to get back together. Tim, I apologize that we couldn't finish this interview the first time. It was my fault, not yours. We were just about to talk about your period as president of the ACC. Could you discuss the year preceding the presidency, the presidency, and the year afterward? What type of time commitment did that necessitate? How did you handle that position superimposed on your other duties? What did you take away from that presidency experience?*

TG: Being president of the ACC is an incredible honor. The year before the presidency was really one of expectation. That time commitment was probably 15% to 20% of my time away, but it entailed a lot of correspondence and learning the policies and priorities of the current and previous presidents. The immediate past president, president, president-elect, and vice president met by conference call monthly and in person so that the College had continuity in programs and in thought rather than any one president getting too far out on a limb on a certain policy.

The year of the presidency was a 35% to 40% time commitment. I set up a couple of hours every morning completely blocked out for the ACC. Anybody with ACC business could call, and anybody could get an answer immediately between 10:00 A.M. and 12:00 noon every day I was in town. Most of the time away was working for the ACC. The year was almost every positive superlative word you could come up with. It was the most fun, the most different, and the most enjoyable year I've had. I have nothing but positive things to say about that year.

The College found itself at a crossroads where a number of issues had come to the fore, one of which was a financial plan. We needed to make sure that the college was going to be fiscally successful, but creating simply a fiscal plan without other strategies seemed ludicrous. We created what we called "The Task Force for the 21st Century." *Mike Wolk* did a superlative job chairing that task force, which became the keystone of the year from the standpoint of having to rethink what we did. We did a "zero base" for the ACC. We considered whether the ACC was about advocacy, patient care, guidelines, or education, or all of them. We tested whether those were still the correct missions. We went through a number of possible scenarios. After all the testing, we came back and said, "Yes, those in fact are the things that we are about." Patient care means the guidelines and patient care performance measures and the science and art of patient care practice. There were 3 other task forces. It was a tough orchestration issue for the College staff to try to keep all the different task forces on track and moving, but, as the best staff in the world, they pulled it off. I think a lot of the ACC's operations of the past few years have been based on the reports of those task forces. The Board Effectiveness Task Force was chaired by *George Beller* and it caused us to look inward. For example, we changed the format of board meetings to deal with decisions using group process. Many of these improvements were taken to a high level the next year when George Beller became the ACC president. There was an Education Task Force, chaired by *Rick Nishimura*, that looked carefully at how we would educate cardiologists in the next 10 years. An entirely new format of electronic education was born out of that year, and it is now taking shape. In the Membership Task Force, chaired by *Spencer King*, advocacy became an extremely important topic. The task force asked: "How do we demonstrate the things that we are doing for the membership in advocacy, and how do we listen carefully to the members to know what they want to get done?"

WCR: *Is the average ACC member feeling that the $600 yearly ACC dues are worth the price? How would you respond to that?*

TG: Everything is a balance between cost and effectiveness. What the College does that individuals cannot do for themselves are the pieces that are the most difficult to show to the membership. It's unfortunate to have to talk about money, but when the Medicare payment rate went down this year, the College spearheaded an effort to get it reversed. Individual members can't do that. When there are individual chapters that are having trouble with either reimbursement or quality of care or practice guidelines in a state, the college is there to help. They help both locally and nationally to try to educate, and even negotiate, reversal proactively. Both the College and the American Heart Association spent a lot of time and a lot of money creating state-of-the-art practice guidelines that take a tremendous amount of support to keep

current. A guideline created in 1996 is not helpful in 2002. The guidelines and their derivatives, so-called performance measures, are indicators to individual physicians as to how they are doing with their own patients. Our higher education arena is now trying to create a whole new way a cardiologist can either call us on a Palm Pilot or on a personal computer. A whole panoply of answers to questions on arrhythmias to heart failure can now be done wirelessly with present-day technology. They range from looking up answers to questions, to getting mini tutorials for those taking the extracurricular courses, and making them available to those not in attendance. The dues are high. The usefulness side, however, is increasing. It's a balance. The membership tells us when they are feeling the pinch.

WCR: *What I'm asking, in a way, is for more details on the college's annual report. Is it possible to say out of the $600 dues, what amount goes into producing the* Journal of the American College of Cardiology; *what amount goes into the annual scientific sessions; what amount to influence legislature, nationally and statewide; what amount to prepare or update guidelines; what amount for the new computer-based programs? What specifically is the money being used for?*

TG: That is a great idea! The Board of Trustees gets it in minute detail. Accountability to the membership in the appropriate level of detail is a great idea. Different presidents have done that over the years in different formats.

WCR: *Did you take away anything from your presidency that has been useful to you in your subsequent endeavors?*

TG: Many things. The most important lesson that I took away is that organizations are not about organizations. They are about the leadership of that organization. The American Heart Association and the ACC got a lot closer during my presidency, in some small part because I was a friend of the president of the American Heart Association at that time. The leadership was incredibly congenial. Some mutual collaboration between the ACC and the subspecialty societies has also improved by person-to-person contact between the leaders of each organization.

The idea of spending a whole year quietly planning my plenary address, which was to propose a new health care system for the United States, was one of the most enjoyable experiences, if not the most enjoyable work-related experience, I've ever had. The address went through 19 drafts. I made proposals for the year 2010 that were purposely provocative in 2000. What I've learned since then is that there are a myriad of different approaches to getting this job done; the tough assignment is balancing cost, access, and quality. I was enormously gratified that the ACC board adopted principles for healthcare reform several months after my plenary. The first priority is coverage for all Americans by 2010. I have been working with a number of ACC members since that time on the uninsured. You can have a system that provides health care for everyone, that has high quality, but it's too expensive. The eventual goal must be to provide some variety of health care for every American by the year 2010. That goal does not tell us how to do it. Quality requires work. Quality is about better data and about better information systems. Doctors, above all, want to provide the highest quality for their patients, but they need to know what quality is without having to spend hours looking up the answer to a problem. The goal must be the highest possible quality where patients and physicians and other health-care providers work together for the patient's health. That goal is more achievable with greater electronic record keeping. This potential database will help us understand how to treat patients. We have had in our grasp for 5 to 10 years now the ability to understand how best to treat certain common diseases. That understanding hopefully will allow the disappearance of the very wide variation in treatment that exists now. I've called this "evidence-based, individually applied medicine." Perhaps in common diseases, 50% of people fit the perfect practice guidelines and 50% don't. The issue is how to take what you know from the practice guidelines and individually apply them because only 1 patient sits in front of you at a time. A whole new science must be developed to help make decisions on the basis of data that you can extrapolate to your individual patient. Hopefully with better data, doctors and patients can work together to provide only the care that is necessary and work together to prevent disease. The doctor can stress smoking less and weight loss—but the physician cannot make it happen.

Access to care is expensive. It's not simply a matter of "Do you work?" Only 17% of people who are uninsured are unemployed! The problem is that a lot of employed people make under $20,000 a year, and cannot afford the premiums. I hope within 10 years that there will be ways of knitting together different funding mechanisms such that a patient could be funded by Medicaid, the State Children's Health Insurance Program, Medicare, or different kinds of private insurance that will be seamless and electronically based. Now we have multiple systems and we spend a lot of money trying to prove whether somebody's actually covered. In the future we need to find better ways to make the costs go down. The current billing cost is 8% to 9%. Medicare is 3%. Medicare works pretty well. It costs less than half the other systems. If you took billing costs from 8% to 4%, you'd save $51 billion a year. We can do a lot to improve the system. We need a uniquely American solution—not a single payer.

WCR: *How did you keep your "home fires" burning brightly by spending nearly 50% of your time during your College presidency away from home?*

TG: Everybody kept his/her sense of humor. I didn't miss a day on the telephone with my family no matter where I was. I even rented a cell phone in Japan and I had a 6:00 A.M. (Japan time) conference call with my boss back home. E-mail and an 800 beeper allowed me to be "transparently available."

WCR: *How many trips did you take during your College presidency that were College-related?*

TG: I was out of the country 5 times and I probably took 10 other College-related in-country trips, not including the trips back and forth to Bethesda, Maryland, which were probably 6. Some presidents have traveled as much as once a week. I was on the lower end of that.

WCR: *I suspect that you spent more time with adult cardiologists during the year of your ACC presidency and the year on each side of that than you had in a long time. Did you notice much difference in the thinking of an adult cardiologist versus that of a pediatric cardiologist? It seems to me that adult cardiology is >90% coronary disease. A valve disease patient is exciting to an adult cardiologist. In pediatric cardiology you may see a child with a ventricular septal defect in one room, an atrioventricular canal defect in the next room, aortic valve stenosis in the next, etc. There's a great variety. Did you notice differences in approaches to problems by the 2 groups of specialists?*

TG: That year I dealt mainly with physicians about common problems, such as how to get educated, how to get reimbursed, and how to create guidelines, not about disease entities. I found a fair similarity in the approaches. Fortunately, when trying to come up with plans for advocacy, education, and guidelines, the constituencies were similar in their overall approach.

WCR: *How many pediatric cardiologists are there in the United States?*

TG: About 1,200 board certified.

WCR: *How many in the whole world?*

TG: Close to 3,000.

WCR: *How many babies are born each year in the United States with congenital heart disease?*

TG: About 26,000.

WCR: *How many new pediatric cardiologists do you need each year in the United States? Do pediatric cardiologists ever retire?*

TG: One retires per millennium! The whole workforce issue in pediatric cardiology is probably less complex than in adult cardiology, but not dissimilar in approach. "Are there enough?" is probably best figured out by the market. Are cardiologists finishing fellowships getting jobs? What is the usual waiting time to see a pediatric cardiologist? There's probably about the right number of pediatric cardiologists in the United States. The unknowable question is how are the diseases going to change? About 90% of the newborns with congenital heart disease survive to adulthood. Who is going to take care of those patients? If you say that pediatric cardiologists should take care of those patients, then you wind up saying that every year the patient population increases by 90% of the number of newborns with congenital heart disease. I believe that there probably should be specialists in adults with congenital heart disease who are adult cardiologists or pediatricians with special training. In the current system, many places combine an adult cardiologist and a pediatric cardiologist to help take care of adults with congenital heart disease. That arrangement is attractive for the pediatric cardiologist because he or she gets to continue to see their patient. It's not terribly efficient, however, for 2 physicians to care for 1 patient if 1 expert could do it. Depending on who takes care of the adult with congenital heart disease, one will have either a greater or a lesser need for pediatric cardiologists.

The entire field of risk factors for atherosclerosis in childhood is emerging. Management of this group of children to prevent coronary disease in the adult is just beginning. Then the question would be who is going to take care of those children? Would the adult cardiologist or internist take care of the 10-year-old with atherosclerotic risk factors? That's not going to happen. That's an area of pediatric cardiology that is likely to expand and probably should.

Then there is the fetus. As more and more work begins to occur in the fetus, there will be an increase of specialists within pediatric cardiology, neonatology, and surgery, who deal with the fetus as a separate patient population. Then if we go from the fetus to the gene, and deal with gene therapy, we have another group of specialists. All these new areas make it difficult to predict what will happen to the workforce. I believe there is going to be a physician shortage largely in medical specialties for adults in the next 5 to 6 years; we are starting to see it now. Adults with heart disease now stay alive longer, the prevalence of disease continues to rise, people are living longer, the baby boomers are getting older, all leading to a large increase in the number of patients with heart disease. It has been estimated that by 2030, the prevalence of patients with heart disease in the U.S. will double.

WCR: *You support the adult congenital heart disease clinics that* Joe Perloff *started and now* Carol Warnes *at the Mayo Clinic and others have?*

TG: Absolutely. I hope that there are specialists in adult congenital heart disease or more adult and pediatric cardiologists trained in both medicine and pediatrics. We will not have enough physicians to go around if we continue to have 2 physicians taking care of 1 patient, where 1 well-qualified physician would do.

WCR: *I understand that you have a congenital heart condition, namely mitral valve prolapse.*

TG: Correct. My father also had mitral valve prolapse.

WCR: *I understand that you had a mitral valve repair operation in 2001. Could you talk a bit about that and also what you learned about the health care system by actually going through that experience yourself?*

TG: I was obviously anxious about it, having watched enough people go through cardiopulmonary bypass and having friends remind me of how dangerous heart surgery is. I had surgery after Halloween but walked into a Halloween party and the topic of conversation was, "Gee, you're having heart surgery. Isn't it nice that most people make it through?" It was quite an ordeal just watching people's expressions. A number of my nonmedical friends thought that there was a significant chance I was going to die in that

operation, even though I knew better. I had to continue to tell them that this was an incredibly safe procedure. It was a shock to get on the scales on day 2 and find I weighed 40 pounds more than I did 2 days before the operation! A lot of crystalloid still stuck in my body. When people talk about a controlled ventricular rate and atrial flutter, they never experienced it. It is only controlled in words. I had atrial flutter for 4 days, and although it didn't make me dizzy, I could not concentrate on anything.

WCR: *What was your ventricular rate?*

TG: It varied from 60 to 120. I learned about caring nurses. I had the good fortune of having a couple of nurses who were really good human beings instead of automatons. I've learned to dispose of every bill. I decided until 6 months after surgery and the letter came from the collection agency that I would not pay much attention to the bills because they were contradictory. It's very difficult to tell who has paid what. I figured it would settle down. If I can't figure it out, think what the problem is for the non-educated.

WCR: *When was the day of the operation?*

TG: November 5, 2001.

WCR: *You are feeling fine now?*

TG: Perfect.

WCR: *Do you still have a precordial murmur?*

TG: I think not because my echo is perfect.

WCR: *You were symptomatic before the operation?*

TG: I was not.

WCR: *You were asymptomatic? It's hard to improve symptoms by a procedure when you are already asymptomatic?*

TG: Correct. I had mild pulmonary hypertension and a large left atrium.

WCR: *You were in sinus rhythm before the operation?*

TG: Yes.

WCR: *And you are in sinus rhythm again?*

TG: Yes. The other thing I learned medically is that a β blocker (I was on sotalol for awhile.) is not as benign as people would like to think. It's incredibly important, of course, that people take β blockers for certain diseases, after myocardial infarction for example. The side effects are probably more prevalent than we realize. That fact may have something to do with the decreased compliance.

WCR: *Did you have cardiac catheterization before you had mitral valve repair?*

TG: Yes.

WCR: *Why did you undergo catheterization?*

TG: To be certain my coronary arteries were fine. I never had left ventricular angiography or left-sided pressure measurements.

WCR: *You mentioned earlier that you had a hip operation about 12 years ago.*

TG: I had 2: April and August 1998.

WCR: *You've had 2 hip replacements?*

TG: Both hips.

WCR: *What was the matter with your hips?*

TG: It was something affectionately known as "disappearing hip," and nobody really knows its cause. I went from being asymptomatic to completely incapacitated in about 2 months. The first hip was the most incapacitating. The surgeon pointed out to me that radiographically the second hip looked just like the first hip and that it was going to do the same thing. I was getting ready to be president of the ACC. The second one was symptomatic but less symptomatic than the first one. The idea of being in the middle of the ACC presidency and having that kind of incapacitation was not good.

WCR: *Did you have cemented or non-cemented hips?*

TG: Cemented.

WCR: *And you have been asymptomatic since?*

TG: Yes.

WCR: *Who was your cardiac surgeon?*

TG: *Gerald Laurie.*

WCR: *Do you think cardiac surgeons who do congenital heart operations should limit their practice exclusively to congenital heart disease?*

TG: Surgeons are now accountable for outcomes. If a surgeon produces absolute top outcomes in both congenital and acquired heart disease, I would have no good basis to say that he or she should do only one. It's hard to believe, however, that outcomes of surgeons who do nothing but congenital heart surgery day in and day out will not be better than those who are not limited. It's hard to find a basis for mandating that restriction.

WCR: *Tim, I've never seen you when you didn't have on a bow tie. I wear these vertical ties and you wear the horizontal ties. Why do you wear a bow tie all the time?*

TG: I take it off to brush my teeth! The story goes back to the first day of Duke Medical School. The professor of neurology on the first or second day gave one of the greatest lectures that I'd ever heard. His introductory lecture made neurology absolutely clear. He had on a bow tie about the size of a battleship. While I did not become a neurologist, I did identify that if somebody that smart and that good could be a little bit different, I decided that was okay for me. It sort of stuck.

My mentor and good friend, Dan McNamara and I (when a second-year cardiology fellow) went to the National Institutes of Health to discuss a grant application to a new program before submission. On the plane, Dan said, "Now Tim, these are serious people. You better not wear a bow tie when you talk to them." I went out that evening and bought a regular tie and showed up the next morning for breakfast and he looked at me and said, "You look different. What is it?" I said, "I'm doing what you told me to do." He said, "What's that?" I said, "Look very carefully." He said, "Oh you need to put your bow tie back on." That was the last vertical tie I have bought.

WCR: *How much teaching do you do now?*

TG: I teach an 8-week seminar in the MBA program at Rice, and I teach medical students as well.

WCR: *Do you have to prepare a lot for them?*

TG: Yes. The format is pretty similar for both. It's one of those things where the questions remain the same but the answers change. Its purpose is to introduce the students to national health policy. My introductory talk is called "Myths, Truths, and Realities of Health Care." We go through headlines that may be true or false. For example: "Infant mortality is a good index of medical care. False. It's a good index of health care." Teaching keeps me on my toes. I also see pediatric cardiology patients regularly in the clinic. I teach in that clinic just like the other "docs."

WCR: *What is your recommendation now for the U.S. health care system? What would be the fairest system we could have in this nation? Why did the Clinton health care scheme fail so badly?*

TG: There are treatises on this. A number of issues happened simultaneously. National healthcare reform failed for a number of reasons. There were a lot of internal political reasons. There was no consensus on a single plan. If your constituents either were for no change or for a particular plan and there was no consensus, elected officials could end up not being reelected by staking themselves to a particular plan. Probably the single most important thing is that the United States didn't have the money to pay for a health care system that was going to cover the uninsured. The money simply was not there. This was the early 1990s when health care costs were rising tremendously, as they are again. There was talk about losing our competitiveness with Japan. We were attempting to say that if we had a unified health care system, we could save money. When all of the estimates came in, however, there was no money to be saved. People said, "The market can fix this cost problem with HMOs. We don't have to do anything nationally." It's not clear actually that HMOs cut costs; they cut payments. Premium growth went down from double digits in the early 1990s to single digits in the mid-1990s but they are now growing again. The American public demonstrated that they wanted to choose their physician and have high quality care; neither is cheap.

WCR: *Are HMOs dead in this country now?*

TG: The original principles of the health maintenance organization were reasonable. You have your own physician who understands what you do, who is not reimbursed directly for doing more tests, and who worries about prevention. Capitation, when applied to individual physicians, has problems. The ideal is to be reimbursed in a way that rewards the amount and quality of work done, without reward for simply doing more tests. I suspect that these concepts will remain. I believe that the idea of the distant medical director and the medical director's surrogates who approve or disapprove care will disappear as more and better information becomes available, and the information is available electronically. We may not want to call them HMOs, but there will still be health plans. There must be better integration of physicians and sites of care. That doesn't necessarily mean that hospitals and physician groups will own each other, but that communication, mainly electronic, will allow the rapid setting of appointments, of transferring records with appropriate confidentiality, etc. It makes sense to have a group of people—physicians, other practitioners, hospitals—accountable for quality, rather than saying it's at the individual physician level. At the physician or hospital level, there are all kinds of other things—hospital mortality, outcome measures—that are going to be more and more team-based.

WCR: *Tim, do you think private practice in the United States will die in the foreseeable future?*

TG: No. I believe the U.S., being entrepreneurial, being the greatest consumer and provider country in the world, will continue to develop private practice in new ways. How the physicians aggregate will likely change.

WCR: *What do you mean by medical care versus health care?*

TG: The old days were easier. Medical care was what doctors did and health care was everything else. As physicians have gotten more and more interested in prevention, the lines have become more blurred. On the health care end are the epidemiological problems of poor sanitation and famine. When a physician and a patient work together to stop smoking, that's borderline between medical care and health care. Infant mortality is related to the age at which the mother becomes pregnant. Many things go into infant mortality, but when a 12-year-old gets pregnant, infant mortality is higher than when a 25-year-old gets pregnant. That's health care's contribution to infant mortality. The neonatal intensive care unit is a medical care contribution to infant mortality.

WCR: *Tim, of all the professional activities—teaching, clinical investigation, book publishing, figuring out how to provide the highest quality health care efficiently—which are you most proud of so far?*

TG: The things you've described a lot of physicians can do. The things that you haven't described—sitting by a patient's bed through the entire night in a recovery room, balancing different infusions to try to allow that child to make it to the morning, and going back and forth every 30 minutes trying to keep parents informed, the extent to which I've done that well is probably the most satisfying of all.

WCR: *There are 125 medical schools in the U.S. Are they all going to survive?*

TG: I am highly optimistic about our medical schools' surviving for 2 reasons. We're responsible for producing innovation in patient care and we do that through the combined mechanism of research and teaching. Students keep faculty on their toes. Medical schools have gotten more accountable. Medical schools now know that if they are going to take care of patients, they have to do it in a way that is highly effective, highly efficient, and highly patient friendly. They are getting there. They are not there yet. Long waits to see physicians are unsatisfactory. In our own school, once patients get to physicians, patient satisfaction is extremely high, but there is less satisfaction getting through any bureaucratic system, whether it's private practice or a medical school. That aspect still needs a lot of work. We are getting more accountable as physicians. Medical school physicians are now

acting more like our private practice colleagues. The overall problem medical schools face now—and it is getting worse—is that the reimbursement for patient care is not increasing at a satisfactory rate; this year it is even decreasing. Research is very expensive. Our medical school, as do most, does not receive full reimbursement, even from the National Institutes of Health, for every research-related expense we have. Medical schools spend a fair amount subsidizing research. The National Institutes of Health are the best, but other granting agencies pay a lot less for indirect costs. The patient care enterprise is now less able to subsidize the research enterprise. The amount of time faculty now have for teaching has become squeezed because teaching is seen as something done while one either takes care of patients or while doing research. That has to change. Teaching is a profession, and teaching medicine needs to be viewed as a profession. We've got to work on that. The missions are interrelated. The good news is that we are holding ourselves more accountable for better patient care, for research productivity, for better teaching. We're all getting better at measuring ourselves and teaching ourselves how to do better.

The other reason medical schools are going to survive is because there is going to be a serious physician shortage in the next 5 to 10 years. The problem with predicting workforce is that it is not a straight line. It's not easy to extrapolate demand. The problem is not supply. It is demand as the diseases change and as the models for taking care of patients change. It is likely that as more and more sophisticated care is available, whether it is gene therapy or new devices, the interventional type of cardiologist or gene therapist cardiologist is not going to have enough time to deal with heart failure. There are going to be hybrid models in which a generalist cardiologist takes more and more care of what currently the most specialized cardiologists take care of and that the most specialized cardiologist in 5 to 10 years from now will have a lot of other things to do. Medical schools will be necessary, not only to turn out more physicians, but also to continue to provide the innovation as the curve of what we are able to do becomes more and more.

WCR: *How many medical students do you have here at Baylor College of Medicine?*

TG: We have 168 per class.

WCR: *Texas has 8 medical schools?*

TG: Yes.

WCR: *That's a lot of medical students coming out every year.*

TG: It is. Based on HMO productivity back in the early 1990s, the current workforce prediction was that we would have too many physicians now. Indeed, a glut of physicians was predicted. In certain specialties, shortages are already appearing—anesthesiology, gastroenterology, interventional cardiology, and electrophysiology. As soon as the spigot got turned a little toward off, a shortage appeared. We are probably pretty close right now to what we need. As the demand increases in the next 5 to 10 years, as we contrive to get better at keeping people with chronic disease alive and well, and as the baby boomers age, there will be a patient excess for the available physicians. And too many physicians aged 50 to 60 are saying that they are not going to practice more than another 3 years. Retirements of physicians have not been well figured into the workforce.

WCR: *Are your finishing pediatric cardiology fellows getting good job offers and multiple ones?*

TG: Absolutely.

WCR: *I understand that the same scenario is happening with the adult cardiology fellows?*

TG: That's right.

WCR: *Tim, as I look around your lovely office, I see 6 gorgeous paintings. I understand that you have a good many more in your home. I wonder if you could talk about your art hobby and collection?*

TG: My interest in art stems from my parents. We had a lot of art at home. My mother, for a period, worked at an art gallery. My own interest started in high school. I learned of Magritte in high school and I love his paintings. He painted the bowler-hatted man, very surreal, with the apple for a face. It turned out, unbeknown to me, that both my parents liked the same artist. He died in 1967 and in 1968 they bought 6 of his lithographs. They gave them to me for my twenty-first birthday. That was the start of my collection. I bought another of his lithographs at a gallery in Houston by working there on Saturdays for 10 months. Both my wife and I like to collect. Fortunately, we've run out of wall space and money simultaneously. We've built 3 houses that are fairly similar, but all of them have been lit as art galleries. We still very much enjoy, whenever we travel, going to as many galleries as we can. It's been fun to discover cities through their galleries. There are some amazing galleries in surprising cities—Anchorage, Alaska, and Sydney, Australia, for example, have rows and rows of interesting galleries. If I could afford all the impressionists, I would buy them. We have a number of post-impressionist artists.

WCR: *In your present position, I'm sure you have to go to a number of social activities. You're always trying to recruit financial support for the medical school and its activities. I suspect that you are always doing some type of faculty recruiting. How does your social schedule fit in with your professional and family activities?*

TG: I'd say about half of the nights of the week either I'm out or my wife and I are out. When I have an option, I try to go home first and help with homework.

WCR: *You are a very positive person. You've always got a smile on your face. I've never detected any negative aspects of you. It would seem to me that you are in an ideal position. You've got a lot of friends. You have a great capacity for friendship. You deal with other people quite reasonably and honorably. What are your future plans? You are still a very young man.*

TG: Staying in medical education and being in a medical school. The next 5 to 10 years in medical

education, trying to help people be innovative, is going to be extremely exciting. I also will continue to try to figure out how we can get health care coverage for everybody in the U.S. My wife and I would love to have a combination art gallery and French restaurant some time.

WCR: *Could you talk about your wife Suzan?*

TG: Suzan is an adolescent psychotherapist and really empathic with teenagers. She tells me she had a great adolescence and, therefore, she is able to be positive with the adolescents she counsels. She works 3 days a week. She does counseling largely for normal kids that bad things happen to, for example, teenagers who have congenital heart disease are psychologically affected by it or counseling for children of divorce. We have 2 great teenage girls, and I give her tremendous credit.

WCR: *How much time do you take off a year for a real vacation?*

TG: We take 4 days in December to go to New York to see my family, and we take 5 or 6 days in the summer to go somewhere. That's about the extent of pure vacation.

WCR: *Do you have a vacation house?*

TG: No.

WCR: *What do you do on Saturdays?*

TG: If I'm not spending time at the computer, or writing a paper, or preparing a talk, or doing homework with the kids, or preparing a dinner for a group of people, I like to read novels. I get tremendous relaxation spending 2 or 3 hours on a Saturday or a Sunday reading an escapist-type novel. I don't like medical novels.

WCR: *Do you have a lot of books around the house?*

TG: We do. We have a pretty good collection of art books, and I have a library in my study that is ceiling to floor. The novels that I've tried to keep are the ones that I might someday try to reread because they are well written. I remember the plot, but I might reread one just for the enjoyment of the words.

WCR: *How much do you entertain at home?*

TG: About once a month.

WCR: *Suzan likes that too?*

TG: Absolutely. Our 2 girls also like to cook, so sometimes all 4 of us cook together.

WCR: *I see a picture on your desk of your shaking hands with* President George W. Bush. *Do you know him pretty well?*

TG: I don't. I've met him once and that was at the ACC meeting. I know his head health policy advisor very well. I've spent a fair amount of time in discussions with the president's advisors, but little time with him.

WCR: *Is there anything that you'd like to talk about that we haven't touched on?*

TG: I don't think so. You've done great!

WCR: *Tim, thank you, not only on my behalf of course, but on behalf of the readers of* The American Journal of Cardiology.

Best Publications of TG Selected by TG (Numbered as in his CV)

Articles in Peer-Review Journals

9. Garson A, Nihill MR, McNamara DG, Cooley DA. Status of the adult and adolescent following repair of tetralogy of Fallot. *Circulation* 1979;59:1232–1240.

11. Garson A, Gillette PC. Junctional ectopic tachycardia in children: electrocardiography, electrophysiology, and pharmacologic response. *Am J Cardiol* 1979;44:298–302.

14. Garson A, Gorry GA, McNamara DG, Cooley DA. Decision analysis in tetralogy of Fallot. *Am J Cardiol* 1980;45:108–113.

19. Garson A, Kugler JD, Gillette PC, Simonelli A, McNamara DG. Control of late postoperative ventricular arrhythmias with phenytoin in young patients. *Am J Cardiol* 1980;46:290–294.

24. Garson A, Gillette PC, McNamara DG. Supraventricular tachycardia in children: clinical features, response to treatment and long-term follow-up in 217 patients. *J Pediatr* 1981;98:875–882.

30. Garson A, Gillette PC. Electrophysiologic studies of supraventricular tachycardia in children. I. Clinical-electrophysiologic correlations. *Am Heart J* 1981;102:233–250.

49. Garson A. Ventricular dysrhythmias after congenital heart surgery: a canine model. *Pediatr Res* 1984;18:1112–1120.

51. Garson A, Gillette PC, Titus JL, Hawkins EP, Kearney D, Ott D, Cooley DA, McNamara DG. Surgical treatment of ventricular tachycardia in infants. *N Engl J Med* 1984;310:1443–1445.

59. Garson A, Randall DG, McVey P, Smith RT, Moak JP, Gillette PC, McNamara DG. Prevention of sudden death after repair of tetralogy of Fallot: treatment of ventricular arrhythmias. *J Am Coll Cardiol* 1985;6:221–227.

60. Ott DA, Garson A, Cooley DA, McNamara DG. Definitive surgery for refractory cardiac tachyarrhythmias in children. *J Thorac Cardiovasc Surg* 1985;90:681–689.

62. Garson A, Bink-Boelkens, Hesslein PS, Hordof AJ, Keane JF, Neches WH, Porter CJ. Atrial flutter in the young: a collaborative study of 380 cases. *J Am Coll Cardiol* 1985;6:871–878.

65. Zipes DP, Cobb LA Jr, Garson A Jr, Gillette PC, James TN, Lazzara R, Rink L. Task Force VI: arrhythmias. *J Am Coll Cardiol* 1985;6:1225–1232.

70. Carpenter RJ, Strasburger JF, Garson A, Smith RT, Deter RA, Engelhardt HT. Fetal ventricular pacing for hydrops secondary to complete atrioventricular block. *J Am Coll Cardiol* 1986;8:1434–1436.

86. Zipes DP, Akhtar M, Denes P, DeSanctis RW, Garson A, Gettes LS, Josephson ME, Masson JW, Myerburg RJ, Ruskin JN, Wellens HJJ. Guidelines for clinical intracardiac electrophysiologic studies. *J Am Coll Cardiol* 1989;14:1827–1842.

93. Garson A, Perry J, Ott D, Gillette PC, Cooley DA. Supraventricular tachycardia due to multiple atrial ectopic foci: a relatively common problem. *J Cardiovasc Electrophysiol* 1990;1:132–138.

95. Garson A. Stepwise approach to the unknown pacemaker ECG. *Am Heart J* 1990;119:924–941.

99. Perry J, Garson A. Supraventricular tachycardia due to Wolff-Parkinson-White syndrome in children: early disappearance and late recurrence. *J Am Coll Cardiol* 1990;16:1215–1220.

101. Moss AJ, Schwartz PJ, Crampton RS, Tzivoni D, Locati EH, MacCluer J, Hall WJ, Weitkamp L, Vincent GM, Garson A, Robinson JL. The long QT syndrome: prospective longitudinal study of 328 families. *Circulation* 1991;84:1136–1144.

111. Towbin JA, Bricker JT, Garson A. Electrocardiographic criteria for diagnosis of acute myocardial infarction in childhood. *Am J Cardiol* 1992;69:1545–1548.

122. Dreyer WJ, Paridon SM, Fisher DJ, Garson A. Rapid ventricular pacing in dogs with right ventricular outflow tract obstruction: insights into a mechanism of sudden death in postoperative tetralogy of Fallot. *J Am Coll Cardiol* 1993;21:1731–1737.

123. Garson A, Dick M II, Fournier A, Gillette PC, Hamilton R, Kugler JD, Van Hare GF, Vetter V, Vick GW. The long QT syndrome in children: an international study of 287 patients. *Circulation* 1993;87:1866–1872.

127. Denfield SW, Kearney DL, Garson A. Developmental differences in canine surgical scars. *Am Heart J* 1993;126:382–389.

129. Garson A Jr, Allen HD, Gersony WM, Gillette PC, Hohn QAR, Pinsky WW, Mikhail O. The cost of congenital heart disease in children and adults: a model for multicenter assessment of price and practice variation. *Arch Pediatr Adolesc Med* 1994;148:1039–1045.

131. King SB III, Frye RL, Fuster V, Garson A Jr, Gay WA Jr, Popp RL. 25th Bethesda Conference: future personnel needs for cardiovascular health care. Task Force 2: academic health centers. *J Amer Coll Cardiol* 1994;24:290–295.

135. Martin AB, Perry JC, Robinson JL, Moss AJ, Garson A Jr. Calculation of QTc duration and variability in presence of sinus arrhythmia: a potential solution to a vexing problem. *Am J Cardiol* 1995;75:950–952.

136. Garson A, Wolk MJ, Morrin SB, Gold W, Dickstein M. Resource based relative valve scale for children: comparison of pediatric and adult cardiology work values. *Cardiol Young* 1995;5:210–216.

138. Epstein AE, Miles WM, Benditt DG, Camm AJ, Darling EJ, Friedman PL,

Garson A Jr, Harvey JC, Kidwell GA, Klein GJ, et al. Personal and public safety issues related to arrhythmias that may affect consciousness: implications for regulation and physician recommendations. A medical/scientific statement for the American Heart Association and the North American Society of Pacing and Electrophysiology. *Circulation* 1996;94:1147–1466.

140. Gajarski RJ, Towbin JA, Garson A. Fontan palliation vs. cardiac transplantation: a comparison of charges. *Am Heart J* 1996;131:1169–1174.

143. Garson A Jr, Kanter RJ. Management of a child with Wolff-Parkinson-White syndrome and supraventricular tachycardia: model for cost effectiveness. *J Cardiovasc Electrophysiol* 1997;8:1320–1326.

149. Speer ME, Lindsay S, Garson A Jr. Use of risk-adjusted outcome measures to determine cost-effectiveness and reduce variation of care using a practice guideline for children with asthma. *Dis Manage* 1998;1:227–233.

154. Garson A Jr. Arrhythmias and sudden death in elite athletes. American College of Cardiology, 16th Bethesda Conference. *Pediatr Med Chir* 1998;20:101–103.

155. Christiansen JL, Guccione P, Garson A. Difference in QT interval measurement on ambulatory ECG compared with standard ECG. *PACE* 1998;19:1296–1303.

157. Garson A, Strifert KE, Beck JR, Schulmeier GA, Patrick JW, Buffone GJ, Feigin RD. The metrics process: Baylor's development of a "report card" for faculty and departments. *Acad Med* 1999;74:861–870.

158. Steinwachs DM, Collins-Nakai RL, Cohn LH, Wolk MJ, Garson A. The future of cardiology: utilization and cost of care. *J Am Coll Cardiol* 2000;35:1092–1099.

160. Stewart MG, Jones DB, Garson A Jr. An incentive plan for professional fee collections at an indigent-care teaching hospital. *Acad Med* 2001;76:1094–1099.

161. Skorton DJ, Garson A Jr, Allen HD, Fox JM, Truesdell SD, Webb GD, Williams RG. Task Force 5: adults with congenital heart disease: access to care. *J Am Coll Cardiol* 2001;37:1193–1198.

162. Garson A. The U.S. healthcare system 2010: problems, principles and potential solutions. *Circulation* 2000;101:2015–2016.

Editorials

1. Garson A, Gutgesell HP, Pinsky WW, McNamara DG. The ten minute talk; organization, slides, writing and delivery. *Am Heart J* 1986;2:193–203.

2. Garson A. Dosing the newer antiarrhythmic drugs in children: considerations in pediatric pharmacology. *Am J Cardiol* 1986;57:1405–1407.

4. Garson A. The science and practice of pediatric cardiology in the next decade. *Am Heart J* 1987;114:462–468.

7. Garson A. The emerging adult with arrhythmias: management and financial health care policy. *PACE* 1990;13:951–954.

8. Garson A. Clinical research on children in the 1990s. *J Am Coll Cardiol* 1992;19:636–637.

9. Garson A. Health care policy for adults with congenital heart disease: the patient, the physician and society. *Circulation* 1992;86:1030–1032.

10. Garson A. Pharmaceutical policy and children: the time has come. *PACE* 1993;16:1064–1065.

11. Garson A. Health care in America 1993: myths, truths and realities. *Cardiol Young* 1993;3:408–411.

14. Garson A. The sinking of US healthcare legislation: What have we learned? *Acad Med* 1995;70:346–347.

16. Friedman RA, Garson A Jr. Implantable defibrillators in children: from whence to shock. *J Cardiovasc Electrophysiol* 2001;12:361–362.

ACC President's Pages

1. Garson A. Convocation address: Leadership: "We're going there with fire." *J Am Coll Cardiol* 1999;33:1432–1434.

2. Garson A. Personalizing continuing medical education. *J Am Coll Cardiol* 1999;33:1744–1745.

3. Garson A. The ACC and subspecialty societies: the beauty of the quilt. *J Am Coll Cardiol* 1999;33:2085–2086.

4. Garson A. The great circle: a target for better patient care. *J Am Coll Cardiol* 1999;34:294–295.

5. Garson A. What is advocacy doing for us? What can we do? *J Am Coll Cardiol* 1999;34:607–609.

7. Garson A. Performance measures and our "art." *J Am Coll Cardiol* 1999;34:1229–1230.

8. Garson A. The ACC Annual Scientific Session — a new meeting for the millennium. *J Am Coll Cardiol* 1999;34:1657.

9. Garson A. Integrating the Internet into your practice. *J Am Coll Cardiol* 1999;34:2139–2140.

10. Garson A. Health care coverage for adults with congenital heart disease: strong, steady steps. *J Am Coll Cardiol* 2000;35:255–256.

11. Garson A. Back to the future: part III. *J Am Coll Cardiol* 2000;35:535–536.

12. Garson A. Accountability 2000. *J Am Coll Cardiol* 2000;35:804–807.

13. Garson A. The U.S. healthcare system 2010: problems, principles and potential solutions. *J Am Coll Cardiol* 2000;35:1048–1052.

Public Survey

1. Garson A. The Future of Health Care. New York: Louis Harris and Associates, 1998.

White House Briefing Paper

1. Garson A, Eagle KE, Medicare Healthcare Quality Incentive. August, 2001.

Invited Articles

17. Garson A. How to measure the QT interval: measurement of repolarization: what is normal? *Am J Cardiol* 1993;72:14B–16B.
19. Hart EM, Garson A Jr. Psychosocial concerns of adults with congenital heart disease—employability and insurability. *Cardiol Clinics* 1993;11:711–715.
21. Maron BJ, Garson A Jr. Arrhythmias and sudden cardiac death in elite athletes. *Cardiol Rev* 1994;2:26–32.
26. Berman S, Bogdan J, Buchanan G, Curran J, Garson A Jr, Gross R, Halfon N, Lewak N, Nelson R. Guiding principles for managed care arrangements for health care of infants, children, adolescents and young adults. *Pediatrics* 1995; 95:613–615.
27. Garson A Jr. Teaching tomorrow's doctors to choose cost-effective care. *Managed Care* 1996;5:47–48.
31. Garson A, Levin SA. Ten 10-year trends for the future of healthcare: implications for academic health centers. *Ochsner J* 2001;3:10–15.

Books

1. Garson A, Gillette PC, McNamara DG. A Guide to Cardiac Dysrhythmias in Children. New York: Grune & Stratton, 1980.
2. Gillette PC, Garson A. Pediatric Cardiac Dysrhythmias. New York: Grune & Stratton, 1981.
3. Garson A. The Electrocardiogram in Infants and Children: A Systematic Approach. Philadelphia: Lea and Febiger, 1983.
4. Gillette PC, Garson A. Pediatric Arrhythmias, Electrophysiology and Pacing. New York: Grune & Stratton, 1990.
5. Garson A, Bricker JT, McNamara DG. The Science and Practice of Pediatric Cardiology (Vols 1–3). Philadelphia: Lea & Febiger, 1990.
6. Gillette PC, Garson A. Clinical Pediatric Arrhythmias. 2nd Edition. Baltimore: W.B. Saunders, 1999.
7. Garson A, Bricker JT, Fisher DJ, Neish SM. The Science and Practice of Pediatric Cardiology (Vols 1–2). 2nd Edition. Baltimore: Williams and Wilkins, 1998.

Book Series

1. Skorton DJ, Garson A. Congenital Heart Disease in the Adult. Baltimore: W.B. Saunders, 1995.

Book Chapters

1. Garson A, McNamara DG, Cooley DA. Tetralogy of Fallot in adults. In: Roberts W, ed. Cardiovascular Clinics. Philadelphia: FA Davis, 1979:341–364.
2. Garson A, McNamara DG. Postoperative tetralogy of Fallot. In: Engle MA, ed. Pediatric Cardiovascular Disease. Philadelphia: FA Davis, 1980:407–429.
3. Garson A. Supraventricular tachycardia. In: Gillette PC, Garson A, eds. Pediatric Cardiac Dysrhythmias. New York: Grune & Stratton, 1981:177–253.
4. Garson A. Ventricular dysrhythmias. In: Gillette PC, Garson A, eds. Pediatric Cardiac Dysrhythmias. New York: Grune & Stratton, 1981:295–360.
5. Garson A. Systematic interpretation of cardiac dysrhythmias in children. In: Leibman J, Plonsey R, Gillette PC, eds. Pediatric Electrophysiology. Baltimore: Williams and Wilkins, 1982:136–155.
9. Garson A. Sudden death in children. In: Morganroth J, Horowitz LN, eds. Sudden Death. New York: Grune & Stratton, 1985:47–56.
12. Garson A, Coyner T, Shannon C, Gillette PC. Systemic interpretation of the fully automatic (DDD) pacemaker electrocardiogram. In: Gillette PC, Griffin JC, eds. A Practical Guide to Cardiac Pacing. Baltimore: Williams and Wilkins, 1986:181–270.
13. Garson A, Smith RT, Moak JP. Invasive electrophysiologic studies in children. In: Horowitz LN, ed. *Cardiology Clinics*: Electrophysiologic Evaluation of Arrhythmias. Philadelphia: FA Davis, 1986;4:551–564.
14. Garson A. New antiarrhythmic drugs: treatment based upon "mechanism". In: Doyle EF, Engle MA, Gersony WM, Rashkind WJ, Talner NS, eds. Pediatric Cardiology. New York: Springer-Verlag, 1986:411–414.
16. Garson A. Electrocardiography. In: Anderson R, Macartney F, Shinebourne E, Tynan M, eds. Paediatric Cardiology. Edinburg, UK: Churchill Livingstone, 1987:235–317.
21. Garson A. Troubles du rhythme et de la conduction apres correction de la tetralogie de Fallot: rapports aves la mort subite. In: Kachaner J, Batisse A, eds. Progres en Pediatrie: Rhythmologie Pediatrique. Paris, France: Doin, 1987:141–149.
22. Garson A. Experimental and clinical findings in ventricular arrhythmias in the young. In: Aliot E, Lazzara R, eds. Ventricular Tachycardias. Boston: Martinus Nijhoff, 1987:134–152.
23. Garson A. Electrocardiography. In: Cole CH, ed. The Harried Lane Handbook. 11th ed. Chicago: Year Book Medical Publisher, 1987:64–74.
25. Garson A, Moak JP. Pediatric arrhythmias. In: Zipes DP, Rowlands DJ, eds. Progress in Cardiology. Philadelphia: Lea & Febiger, 1988:187–202.
30. Garson A, Gillette PC, Smith RT, Moak JP. Electrophysiology. In: Adams F, Emmanouilides GC, Riemenschneider TA, eds. Moss' Heart Disease in Infants, Children and Adolescents. 4th ed. Baltimore: Williams and Wilkins, 1989:154–156.
33. Garson A. Ventricular arrhythmias. In: Gillette PC, Garson A, eds. Pediatric Arrhythmias, Electrophysiology and Pacing. New York: Grune & Stratton, 1990:427–500.
34. Garson A. Chronic postoperative arrhythmias. In: Gillette PC, Garson A, eds. Pediatric Arrhythmias, Electrophysiology and Pacing. New York: Grune & Stratton, 1990:667–678.
35. Garson A. Chronic arrhythmias in children with a normal heart. In: Gillette PC, Garson A, eds. Pediatric Arrhythmias, Electrophysiology and Pacing. New York: Grune & Stratton, 1990:648–654.
36. Garson A. Arrhythmias and sudden death. In: Gillette PC, Garson A, eds. Pediatric Arrhythmias, Electrophysiology and Pacing. New York: Grune & Stratton, 1990:630–636.
58. Garson A Jr. Ventricular arrhythmias after repair of congenital heart disease: Who needs treatment? In: Hess J, Sutherland GR, eds. Congenital Heart Disease in Adolescents and Adults. The Netherlands: Kluwer Academic Publishers, 1992:147–154.
60. Garson A, Kanter RJ. Rate adaptive pacing in children: requirements and clinical application. In: Benditt DG, ed. Rate Adaptive Pacing. Cambridge, MA: Blackwell Scientific Publications, 1993:193–198.
64. Garson A. Abnormalities of cardiac rate and rhythm. In: Oski FA, DeAngelis C, Feigin RD, McMillan JA, Warshaw JB, eds. Principles and Practice of Pediatrics. 2nd ed. Philadelphia: J.B. Lippincott, 1994;88:1641–1645.
65. Garson A, Kanter RJ. Arrhythmias in congenital heart disease. In: Podrid PJ, Kowey PR, eds. Cardiac Arrhythmias: Mechanisms, Diagnosis, and Management. Baltimore: Williams and Wilkins, 1995:1131–1160.
69. Garson A. Electrocardiography. In: Garson A, Bricker JT, Fisher DJ, Neish SM, eds. The Science and Practice of Pediatric Cardiology. 2nd ed. Baltimore: Williams and Wilkins 1998;37:735–788.
70. Garson A. Evaluation of cost and effectiveness in pediatric cardiology. In: Garson A, Bricker JT, Fisher DJ, Neish SM, eds. The Science and Practice of Pediatric Cardiology. 2nd ed. Baltimore: Williams and Wilkins, 1998;136:2939–2944.
75. Garson A. Sudden death. In: Gillette PC, Garson A, eds. Clinical Pediatric Arrhythmias. 2nd ed. Baltimore: W.B. Saunders, 1999:287–292.
76. Garson. Abnormalities of cardiac rate and rhythm. In: Oski FA, DeAngelis C, Feigin RD, McMillan JA, Warshaw JB, eds. Principles and Practice of Pediatrics. 3rd ed. Philadelphia: J.B. Lippincott, 1999:1428–1432.
77. Garson A, Pinsky WW. Metrics: an academic report card in evaluating physician performance. In: Pinsky WW, ed. Enhancing Physician Performance: Advanced Principles of Medical Management. Tampa, FL: American College of Physician Executives, 2000:357–358.

BERNARD JOHN GERSH, MD:
A Conversation With the Editor*

Dr. Bernard Gersh was born in Johannesburg, South Africa, on October 2, 1941, and he grew up in Northern Rhodesia (now Zambia). His schooling was in South Africa. He graduated from the University of Cape Town with a degree in medicine in 1965 at age 24 and was awarded a Rhodes Scholarship the same year. After internship in Cape Town, he spent nearly 3 years at the University of Oxford and there began his research in cardiovascular disease, and was awarded a Doctor of Philosophy. He then returned to Cape Town to complete his training in internal medicine and in cardiology. He remained in Cape Town until 1978, when he moved to the Mayo Clinic, Rochester, Minnesota. His clinical investigations blossomed at the Mayo Clinic, where he remained until 1993 when he moved to Washington, DC, to become Chief of the Division of Cardiology at Georgetown University Medical Center. He has authored or coauthored over 350 articles in medical journals, 75 book chapters, and edited 6 books.

William Clifford Roberts, MD[†] **(Hereafter, WCR):** *I am talking with Dr. Bernard Gersh in his office at Georgetown University Medical Center in Washington, DC, on May 1, 1998. You have a most interesting background. I wonder if we might start by your discussing your upbringing in Zambia (previously Northern Rhodesia). I gather you were born in Johannesburg, South Africa. What were some of your earliest memories?*

Bernard John Gersh, MD[‡] **(Hereafter, BJG):** My father was born in 1906 in Jerusalem, but lived in Eastern Europe for a period as a little boy. In 1913, at the age of 7, he was brought to South Africa. My mother was born in what is now Lithuania and came to South Africa at age 3 or 4. My father was brought to South Africa by his great uncles after his father had died. His great uncles, around the turn of the century, were some of the early pioneers in what was then called Rhodesia. They were traders and also some of the first (if not the first) to have a cattle ranch in that part of the world. They went there by ox wagon.

They made a living trading along the Zambezi River in Rhodesia and also by collecting or driving cattle on to ranches where the cattle would be fattened up and eventually sold. My father, at age 18, went to work for my great uncle in Rhodesia, which was split off into Northern and Southern portions. Then, when in his 20s, he started his own business in what then was Northern Rhodesia and is now Zambia. The major

industry was copper mining, and the mines had been opened only a few years before my dad went into business on his own. It was a hard life, with few amenities in this rather remote mining town in the late 1920s. The mortality due to malaria was particularly high. He developed a diverse, and at least for that part of the world, a large private company that was involved in a number of different ventures. The reason I was born in Johannesburg, South Africa, was because my mother was from Johannesburg and there were no good hospitals in the area where we lived. She went back to her home for my birth. It took about 3 days on the train and then when I was a couple of weeks old she brought me back to our home in Northern Rhodesia.

WCR: *How far was Johannesburg from Northern Rhodesia where you lived?*

BJG: About 2000 miles. We lived in a pretty little town called Kitwe, which was 30 miles from the border of what was then the Belgian Congo. Its population was about 80,000. It was the center of one of the largest copper mines in the world. My dad had bought some ranches about 300 miles away in a beautiful part of the country where there was a lot of open bush and wildlife. As a consequence of exposure to this as a child, I remain very interested in wildlife (including birds) to this day. My dad learned to fly in the early 1930s. The reason was that the roads were terrible in that part of the world. There were no tarred roads and it would take forever to get anywhere in the rainy season. He needed to visit these ranches and he decided he would learn to fly. This was only 30 years or so after the Wright brothers' first flight. When he would come back from a trip he would fly around the house and my mom would get in the car and go and pick him up at the airport. This is one of my early memories. I can remember standing in the garden and see his plane circling. He told me that the navigation was simple. There was 1 railway line in Zambia that went from north to south. That railway line actually was destined to go from the Cape in South Africa to Cairo and all the development in Zambia was basically along the lines of rail. For navigation, my dad would find the railway line and fly down the railway line until they came to an appropriate station near one of the ranches and then they would fly around and look at the name on the station. If it was the right place he knew he had to turn left or right.

WCR: *How big is Northern Rhodesia. How wide is it? The railroad was going north and south. How far on either side of the railroad is the country?*

BJG: Zambia is quite a large country, which I suppose is about a thousand miles in width. It stretches from the border of Angola on the West to Malawi (previously Nyasaland) and Rhodesia (now Zimbabwe) on the east. The northern border of the

*This series of interviews was underwritten by an unrestricted grant from Bristol-Myers Squibb.

†Baylor Cardiovascular Institute, Baylor University Medical Center, Dallas, Texas 75246.

‡W. Proctor Harvey Teaching Professor of Cardiology, Chief, Division of Cardiology, Georgetown University Medical Center, Washington, DC.

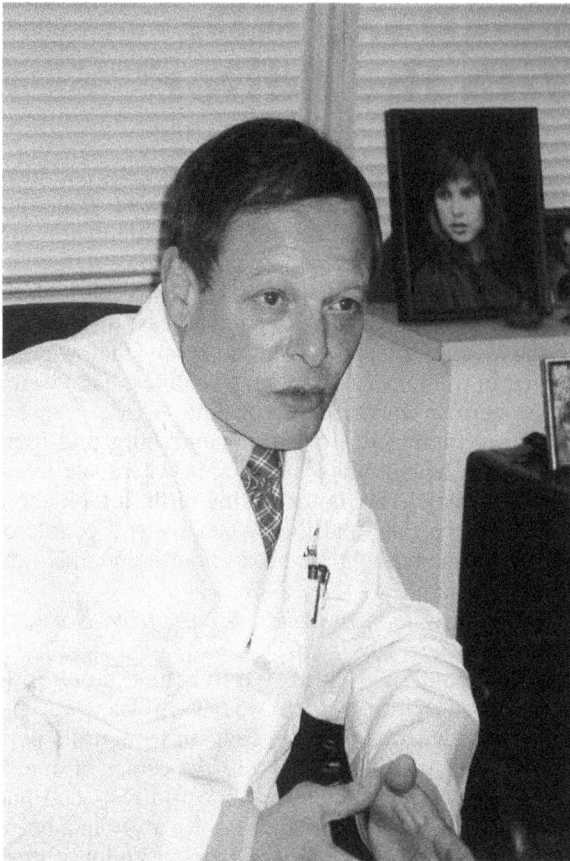

FIGURE 1. BJG during the interview in his office.

FIGURE 2. BJG during the interview.

country would be the Congo, and the far northeastern border is Tanzania. Despite its large size, it contains few people. When I grew up it was a British colony of about 2.5 million people, of which 80,000 were mainly expatriates from the United Kingdom and South Africa, working in the mines, and most of the remainder were British civil servants, working for the Colonial Government, in addition to a relatively small business and farming community. I do remember it as a great place in which to grow up, and that the mining town in which we lived had all the facilities for sports. My parents had 2 children, my sister and me, and she is 3 years younger. We both grew up under the English system of boarding schools, since the educational opportunities in our hometown were limited. I went away to prep school in Johannesburg when I was 11 and subsequently to a high school (Hilton College) near Durban in South Africa. My sister went to Salisbury (Harare) in Rhodesia at about the age of 10. It was generally accepted in that part of the world at that time that children were sent away to boarding school either in South Africa or England.

My main recollections of home were during month-long vacations from school. We went a long way away to school. Johannesburg was about a 4-day trip on the train from my home. My sister and I loved coming home for the holidays. I used to play every sport under the sun: cricket, rugby, squash, fish, ride horses. I learned to ride when I was about 8 or 9; it

was 15 or 20 years later that I learned how you put a bridle on a horse, which reflected my Colonial upbringing. I really liked Rhodesia, especially the bush.

WCR: *Somebody would put the saddle on the horse for you?*

BJG: That is correct, and you have to realize that it was a rather anachronistic colonial lifestyle, which was probably a lot better for the colonists than for the colonized. The English boarding school system was very rigorous and tough, and it was a highly disciplined environment. One certainly learned at an early stage to cope with homesickness and to become quite independent.

WCR: *Do you remember anything about World War II?*

BJG: The only thing I remember about World War II was going to an airport and seeing troops flying up to the desert. I must have been about 3 or 4 at the time. I have a vague recollection of my father in uniform, but I was only 4 when the War ended, and it may be that this recollection comes from a photograph.

WCR: *By 1952 you went away to school, except you were home 3 months of the year?*

BJG: One had 6 weeks' vacation around Christmas time and a total of about 3 months of the year at home. If your parents could afford it and wanted a better education for you, you had to go away. In our family, education was very important. It was hard to go away to boarding school at a relatively young age and the

FIGURE 3. BJG during the interview.

first year or 2 was not easy. Nonetheless, one's friends were in the same boat and in any event, the only option was to get on with it and learn how to cope. There are certain advantages to this type of education, particularly when the boarding school is close to the individual's home, so that they can come home on weekends. My 2 older children were educated in South Africa and were able to return to their mother for the weekends, whereas my 2 youngest children were educated in the USA at a nonboarding public school. On balance, I prefer the latter form of education, but do not regret having experienced the former.

WCR: *Did you wear a tie everyday?*

BJG: Yes. I wore a uniform with a tie. Sport was compulsory and I loved virtually all forms of sport, but I was not too strong in the arts.

WCR: *What were your parents like? You have spoken a good bit about your father. I gather he was quite successful.*

BJG: Dad was very successful. He was a completely self-made at a very young age. He was extremely bright and a good businessman who instilled in all of us the highest ethical standards. I am sure under different circumstances my father would have built an enormous organization. I am very close to my parents, surprisingly, given the distance. We have always remained close as a family, although I expect we would not do very well if we had lived in each other's houses all the time. My mom and dad now live in Worcester, Massachusetts, and we are still close. They immigrated to the USA when my dad was 87. My sister and brother-in-law live there also. My sister is married to an American.

My mom's family was very different. My mom came from an intellectual family. They had little money but were a huge and very close-knit family. They used to sit around the table and have great intellectual discussions and were very liberal and progressive. She is the youngest of 8 siblings. In my dad's family, the cousins were business people.

WCR: *Did you go in the plane with your father to visit the ranches?*

BJG: Rarely. I flew with him only once or twice, since he did not want me in the plane with him—I

suspect for safety reasons. By the time I was growing up, the roads were tarred and you could drive to the ranches. I used to go down to them with friends.

WCR: *Were you a hunter?*

BJG: I hunted very little. I love to fish. I regret that I only recently have become very interested in bird watching, because I was living in a place that was a paradise and I never looked at a bird. The only birds I saw as a kid were those I plugged with a 0.22. As a child, I was fascinated by all forms of wildlife and remain so to this day. My wife, who is from England, feels the same way, and like many other people who have spent time in that part of the world, I can think of nothing better than to spend all day sitting around a water hole watching the ever changing pageant of wildlife, including the birdlife that so characterizes Africa.

WCR: *I gather that your mother was quite educated?*

BJG: My mother was a nursery-school teacher. She was educated at a young age. She went up to this pretty rough mining town and she and my father made a great life for themselves. Socially, it was a spectacular place, because it was a prosperous area of the country. They left in 1970 when my father was 65 and went to Cape Town. By then the country had become independent and there really were very few options for a family business. He did not retire, but stayed involved in a number of things. My mom did a great job. She came from Johannesburg, the biggest city in South Africa. In the 1930s, when she married my dad, Zambia was pretty primitive.

WCR: *Did your father have much education? Did he go to university?*

BJG: At the age of about 13 he got a very high grade in a national examination called Junior Certificate, which was 2 or 3 years before he left school. This was what we called "form 8" and then you leave school in the 10th grade.

WCR: *He was in South Africa?*

BJG: Yes. There was no money, so my dad could not go to university. He did not want to be a clerk in some office, so he went up and joined his uncles in a wild part of the country. Apparently in the 1920s, the cattle sales which took place on the line of rail, gave rise to many interesting stories which were recounted in an article written by my father for the Northern Rhodesian Archives. They were a social event for people who led rather isolated lives in the bush, and after the sales, most of the time was spent drinking and playing poker until the early hours of the morning, waiting for the train to arrive. Apparently, many a time the train was held up, waiting for the end of the "jackpot" pool. My dad also wrote of an expedition that was led by one of my great uncles in the 1900s, consisting of wagons with armed horsemen and followers, which was sent into what was then Portuguese West Africa (Angola) in search for a reputed treasure which was never found, but they apparently had to fight their way through hostile tribesmen and then returned with most of the cattle lost and the wagons left behind. This sounds rather romantic, and they were certainly interesting days, but I am sure life was very hard.

When my sister and I grew up, we were not a family that sat around the dinner table and had structured conversations on what book we read this week or what political event was meaningful. My sister and I read voraciously at a young age, and were encouraged by my parents. I still do love to read. Probably because my dad did not get a chance to get a university education, education was very important to him and my mum. They were able to afford to have my sister and me educated extremely well, and I was sent to the best schools in South Africa. The virtue of really working hard and driving for excellence was in the family, but in sort of an understated way. There was never any reward if one of us became first in our class. My mum and dad always said they expected us to do our best and strong ethical principals were drilled into us at an early age. My dad ran his businesses that way. A great moment for my dad and mom was my receiving the Rhodes Scholarship. The irony was that they could have afforded to send me to Oxford, but they did not have to since the scholarship took care of that.

WCR: *Were you an athlete in high school?*

BJG: I matured late in a lot of ways and did better at University than at school. Games came easily to me, particularly ball games. I played competitive rugby at the university, competitive squash, a bit of cricket, all at a level good enough for me to get the Rhodes Scholarship.

WCR: *So you were fast?*

BJG: Yes, fast over a short distance. I was not fast over 200 or 300 yards. I ran very fast for the first 20 yards, unless I got caught by someone who weighed 150 pounds more than me. I felt then and still do now, that sport is an important part of life, and I personally liked being a player as well as following sport. I wish I had been bigger and heavier, which really would have helped me in the sports I enjoy the most, such as rugby. What I should probably have done was to concentrate more on one sport in which I could have reached a higher level, as opposed to playing just below the level I would have liked to have achieved, but in several sports. Nonetheless, I had a great time at University, enjoyed my sporting career, and it did result in life-long friendships which come from the camaraderie of playing on a team. Sport is an extremely important part of South African school and university life. Some people say it is overemphasized, but that is probably the case all over the world. I am very pleased that most of my children are interested in sport, and even one of my daughters, who is not interested in it, is actually very good at whatever athletic activity she takes on.

WCR: *Did anybody have an impact on you in high school? I gather you were a very good student, read at lot. Did studies come easy for you or did you have to work hard?*

BJG: Both. I had a checkered career academically. I did well in high school but never reached my full potential as I matured late. When I got to the university what happened to me was what happened to a lot of the Rhodesian and ex-boarding school kids. For the first time in life, I was relatively unrestricted. The boarding school discipline was tough and very rigid, and the school I was at was way out in the country on about 50,000 acres. The nearest girl's school was about 7 miles away. You could go and visit your girlfriends, but you had to run that distance and run back. We were in magnificently scenic country, but a long way from anywhere. It was great in that you could hike and ride and play any sport you wanted, but it was limited in other ways. When I got to University after all these years, suddenly there was freedom and the bright lights. As a consequence, I failed my first year in medical school, but was given the chance to repeat it, which is an option that is not available for the current generation of medical students. I really enjoyed the change from school to university, and Cape Town was a great city, but it did take me time to settle down and realize that life was not all play. I passed my first year after repeating it, and then midway during the second year, which was a very important year in which we did anatomy and physiology, I realized that if I did not buckle down I could again get into trouble, and I subsequently passed that year very comfortably. I then realized that I could accomplish a great deal more if I put my mind to it. Medical school in South Africa, as in many other countries, is a 6-year course without a preceding undergraduate degree. Something that did have a deep impact on me was that a very close friend, a partner in crime so to speak from where I grew up, was killed in a car accident with his girlfriend. It was a sad and sobering experience which made me sit down and take stock. I then settled down and started working consistently after that. The following year, the first clinical year and my fourth year in university, I realized that I really enjoyed medicine and that it was what I really wanted to do. We had half-year examinations and I went up to look at the results (you were ranked from 1 to 120) and somebody said there must be a mistake, because my usual position in the first 3 years was about 119. On the board, I was first. I never dropped below that again.

WCR: *For the fourth, fifth, and sixth years you led the class?*

BJG: Yes. In the final year, however, we were not given marked grades. There were 3 subjects: surgery, internal medicine, and obstetrics and gynecology. I got the class medals in 2 of the 3. It was a great year for me. It was a good year from a sporting standpoint also.

One event which did have an impact on me in high school was an illness I had during the final year. I remember waking up one morning and my joints were sore and stiff. I was taken to the hospital, and although they never made the diagnosis, I probably had a viral illness related to polio. I was in the hospital for about 6 weeks. I don't know whether I was paralyzed or whether it was just too painful to move my legs, but I do remember that I could not move. I was only 16 at the time. This event, probably more than anything else, convinced me to go into medicine. I remember waking up one night in the hospital around 2:00 A.M. and saying to myself, "This is ridiculous. I am going to walk." I managed to get myself up out of bed, but I could not get back into bed. The nursing staff were incredibly sympathetic. When I came out of the hospital I then had to go to physiotherapy and learn how to walk using the parallel bars. I still have very short Achilles tendons. Four weeks after leaving the hospital I had to write my high school finals. Basically, I had been out for the last 3 or 4 months and the high schools finals in South Africa are a national examination where everybody takes the same test. I did well in my high school finals or matriculation examination, but perhaps I did not achieve what I could have done had I not missed the last part of the school year. At that stage I really had not made up my mind about what I wanted to do, other than to go to Cape Town University. The provisional plan was for me to study accounting and general business. I actually think I would have been very happy going into my father's business, had times been different. Strangely enough, while recovering from my illness, I had a talk with a cousin of my father's, Dr. Jack Wilton, who was a surgeon in Johannesburg. I remember asking him "tell me about medicine" and realized at the time that I was already thinking about medicine as a profession. Before that we, as a family, had never really discussed medicine in my context, but I had had the opportunity to see doctors and nurses working in the hospital and I was both impressed and fascinated. I also was the recipient and survivor of excellent care. I remember Jack Wilton saying that I would never regret a career in medicine, and although I may have made the decision rather impulsively, I am extraordinarily pleased that I did do so, although I believe that I would have been happy in other occupations. Nonetheless, my early years at medical school were not auspicious, and it was only during the latter years, when I first came into contact with patients in the clinical years, that I realized that there was nothing that I wanted to do more than be a physician. I was recently talking to my mother, who feels that my illness really was a turning point, since it occurred just before I finished high school and thus precipitated the decision to embark upon a medical career.

WCR: *Could you describe what a day was like in high school? You wore uniforms, it was a very disciplined atmosphere, you got up at a certain time, went to bed at a certain time.*

BJG: It was a tough school. The more your parents paid for education, the tougher the school was. It was very much like boot-camp in the Army. It was an incredibly beautiful school. You could see the mountains in the distance. There would be a wake-up bell at about 6:30 A.M. You would get up, have a cold shower, and then go to what we called "prep," which was about an hour of school work. Then you would have breakfast and then be in class. We would break for lunch. Classes would end about 2:00 or 3:00 in the

afternoon. Sport was from 3:00 to 6:00 P.M. Rugby and cricket were compulsory, but you could play anything you wanted—tennis, squash, etc. About 6:00 in the evening you would shower and have dinner. There would be "prep" (homework) from 7:00 to 9:00. Lights out would be around 10:00 P.M. The school was all male. The food was just horrible, and even then there was not enough of it. Sundays they would kick you out of the school and you could go anywhere you wanted on the grounds. A couple of miles hike, about 2,000 feet down, was a big river called the Umgeni, where one could swim the rapids. The other big break in the day was Saturdays because you could play sport, and one went away on Saturdays to play against other schools. No one was really sorry to leave school at the end of 5 years. I learned some good lessons from the school system, but I enjoyed the University life a great deal more.

WCR: *You were in high school for 5 years?*

BJG: Yes.

WCR: *Did you have any mentors in high school?*

BJG: I thought the teaching was fairly average. No teacher really stood out or inspired me in either prep school or college. One of the coaches (a teacher who also coached) had an influence on me. I liked his attitude toward sports which was "give it your best and if you win fine, but if you don't, you have done your best." It was a school that had a tremendous history and incredible surroundings and has now become a great school, but at that point it had some problems.

WCR: *How many students were in your class?*

BJG: The whole school was 330 kids for 5 years. Sixty or 70 kids in each year. There were about 15 to a class.

WCR: *You went to prep school 2 years in Johannesburg before going to high school for 5 years?*

BJG: Yes. When I went to prep school that was a real adjustment. It was a different environment from a small town in Rhodesia.

WCR: *What did you study in high school?*

BJG: English, math, physics, chemistry, history, and a language.

WCR: *Did any subject stand out for you in high school?*

BJG: Nothing really stood out. I liked English and history. At prep school, the level of education was phenomenally high. I had virtually done my first year of high school at prep school before I started high school.

WCR: *Was it easy to get into medical school? You said 3 months before you decided to go to the University of Cape Town, you decided you were going to be a physician.*

BJG: It was a lot easier than it is now, and a lot easier than in the USA. I think there are a couple of things that stood me in good stead; I was a good student in a very good school. I did very well in my final examinations, given the fact that I was away sick for most of the last 4 months. I did not get as high marks as I would have liked to have had, but nevertheless they were good. In those days they put a little bit more stock in other activities such as being "an all-rounder," not just purely academic.

WCR: *So you were a good athlete in high school? You played all sports.*

BJG: I was okay. I was good, but not as good as I would have liked to have been, but I played a number of sports at a competitive level.

WCR: *Now you are at the university in this gorgeous, magnificent city of Cape Town. You are free for the first time and you are going to a coed school for the first time. You had never been to a coed school before. Although you liked studying a little bit, there were so many other enticements that the freedom almost blew you out.*

BJG: You said it! Studying was okay, but it was not nearly as much fun as were all the other things. I came close to blowing it.

WCR: *You had to repeat year one again, so it actually took you 7 instead of 6 years to get through the university, but by the time you were in your fourth year you became a star. Who influenced you in medical school? Did anybody take you under their wing?*

BJG: South Africa is not a touchy-feely country. Medical school and internship years were tough. It was not an environment where you evaluated your teachers. They evaluated you! Nonetheless, there were a number of people who really did make an impression on me. One was the Professor of Surgery, *Dr. Jannie Louw.* He was an inspiring but despotic character, a very fine surgeon, a great teacher, very tough taskmaster. I was captain of the medical school rugby team, and he was our patron and I got to know him quite well. He was one of the people responsible for my applying for the Rhodes Scholarship. I was fascinated by cardiac hemodynamics and by the heart as a pump. At that time there were 2 people at Cape Town who were really becoming known all over the world: one was Professor *Velva Schrire*, who was the Head of Cardiology. He was an absolutely brilliant man but a cold character in many ways. He trained with *Dr. Paul Wood* at the National Heart Hospital in London. He, together with *Chris Barnard*, developed the cardiovascular program at the University of Cape Town. I was impressed by that. In the late 1960s, Cape Town was one of the power houses of clinical cardiology in the world. The other individuals who made a great impression on me were *Dr. Louis Vogelpoel* and *Dr. Andre Swanepoel*, cardiologists now in private practice. Their publications were state of the art. Louis Vogelpoel first used amylnitrate to increase the intensity of precordial murmurs, such as in patients with pulmonic stenosis and tetralogy of Fallot. Another person who had an influence was *Dr. John Brock*, who was Chairman of Medicine and had been a Rhodes Scholar. We were very proud of the University of Cape Town. It still is a great university and the medical school has a terrific tradition. The standards were very high. Some of the best clinicians I have ever seen work there, including Professor Velva Schrire, Dr. Louis Vogelpoel, *Dr. Walter Beck*, in addition to some excellent, well-funded and well-published scientists. *Lionel Opie* has been a driving force in basic research

for over 25 years, and we have enjoyed a long association and collaboration on many fronts. I hope that in the new South Africa they continue to recognize what the University of Cape Town can offer to the country and to the continent, because it is a great institution which could be a beacon for the continent as a whole. The cardiovascular physicians at the University of Cape Town published prolifically from 1950 to 1980.

WCR: *How many were in your class?*

BJG: Approximately 180 students entered medical school. It was a 6-year school with no prior undergraduate training. Somewhere around 60 or so would not complete medical school, about 120 graduate every year. By the fourth year, the first of the clinical year, the attrition rate thereafter was very low.

WCR: *What did you take the first 2 years?*

BJG: The first year was physics, chemistry, botany, and zoology. The second year was a crucial year, anatomy and physiology. A group of 8 dissected the body. The third year included pathology and biochemistry among others. The fourth year was when one started seeing patients. What I loved right from the beginning in my second year was cardiovascular physiology. Guyton's *Textbook of Physiology* made an impression on me—it was a great book. In the clinical years I liked surgery the best. They taught it in such a logical crisp fashion. By the time I graduated I had decided I wanted to be a cardiac surgeon, which I felt was the ultimate thing. In those days, Barnard had just come back from the University of Minnesota. Even in the late 1950s, he published an operative mortality for tetralogy of Fallot of about 12%. The cardiac program at Cape Town was something the whole country was proud of. I knew Chris Barnard quite well. Another person who had an influence on me was his brother *Dr. Marius Barnard*. Marius had been in practice in Rhodesia and came back to do surgery. I used to work with him at his home. He was studying for his subspecialty boards and I was studying for my final exams.

My last year at the University was an extraordinarily satisfying and enjoyable year. I was very excited about medicine; excited over the fact that I was doing well, and in general it was a very successful time for me. I did particularly well in my favorite subjects, which were medicine and surgery. You know what it is like once one gets on a roll. I even did well in psychiatry and medical jurisprudence, topics I had very little interest in at the time. It was also a successful year for me from a sporting standpoint. I also became involved in a number of administrative activities within the University.

I wrote my finals in December, and 3 months earlier in September I had applied for the Rhodes Scholarship. My father asked if I had thought about it and I said "no," not with my prior record. Then I went and talked to Professor Louw and others at the University of Cape Town, and they all said that it was a good idea. The Rhodes Scholarship is a big deal in South Africa. I was the first guy from Zambia to get it. One week after I graduated I got a note saying I was short-listed. I had done very well on my final medical school exams. I went up for the interviews one week after I graduated. Then I was told I had won the Rhodes Scholarship. You have to be under 25 the day you take up residence at Oxford. I deferred the beginning of the Rhodes until after I did my internship, which was in surgery and medicine in Cape Town. That was a tough year. You had to do the internship in either surgery, medicine, or obstetrics and gynecology!! Internship was incredibly grueling and I learned a lot. The intern was the lowest person on the totem pole.

WCR: *Did you work every night, every other night, as an intern?*

BJG: One worked 2 nights out of 3. The system was that you would come in early morning, work that day and through that night and the next day. The second night you were on second call. That meant if they really got overburdened they could bring you in. The third night you were off.

WCR: *Did you live at the hospital?*

BJG: Yes. Everybody lived at the hospital.

WCR: *Did the hospital pay you anything?*

BJG: Not much. I don't remember what it was.

WCR: *Internship is a unique experience for all newly qualified physicians.*

BJG: Yes, I remember that on Saturday a party was always going on. Guys who had been up for 72 hours would attend and there was a certain camaraderie. The only criticism I would have of the internship was that it was very menial. Your job was to work up the patients. They would not even let you prescribe drugs. The resident ran the show. The resident was someone who could make your life very tough—you learned very quickly to follow orders.

WCR: *The resident was just 1 year above internship?*

BJG: No. They had the system of senior interns as well. The resident could be several years above the intern.

WCR: *Were there any women in your class of 120?*

BJG: Yes. There were quite a few. I can't remember the proportion, but there were a substantial number. Internship made one realize the hospital is a special place and that medicine is a special and unique discipline which demands accountability and responsibility. We have all made mistakes as interns and one never forgets them. I will never forget my last day of internship seeing the new interns come in and saying, "Guys, you have an interesting year ahead of you."

WCR: *I visited the University Hospital in Sydney, Australia, one time, and at 5:00 P.M. everyday in the doctor's lounge the hospital served beer. Doctors would come there and talk to each other and do a lot of consulting with one another over a bottle of beer. Did that happen at your hospital?*

BJG: It certainly happens in England. I don't remember how it worked in Cape Town. Alcohol may have been available in the doctor's quarters. Down the road was a pub where staff would go during off hours.

WCR: *So now you are ready to begin your time in Oxford?*

BJG: I had a problem. The Rhodes Trust really did not know what to do with a qualified physician. The average Rhodes scholar had done 3 years Bachelor of Arts Degree or Bachelor of Science Degree. Not only was I a physician, I had already completed my internship. I worried whether it was a mistake to have accepted the Rhodes, because I thought I was going back as a university student instead of getting on with medicine and a career. Generally, the award of a Rhodes scholarship is for 2 years, with the option for a third year if necessary, particularly if one is doing a higher degree, such as a Doctor of Philosophy. At that time, the Rhodes Trust insisted that Rhodes scholars start at the beginning of the academic year in September/October, but my internship finished in January 1967. I then left Cape Town for London and obtained a position as a research assistant at the National Heart Hospital, working for *Dr. Donald Longmore*, a cardiac surgeon, on animal models of cardiac transplantation. At that time, *Dr. Donald Ross*, who was originally from South Africa, was the senior surgeon at the National Heart Hospital, and the senior resident in cardiac surgery was *Sir Magdi Yacoub*. Magdi and I have remained in close contact since then. I enjoyed the 6 months in the animal laboratory, which also gave me the chance to use my hands, in addition to living in London.

In September, I went on to Oxford and loved the place from the first day. Because my education had been "very English," I felt totally at home. I also had a number of friends who were already at Oxford, and I also felt, as I do today, very comfortable with the United Kingdom. It was rather unusual to have a second chance to go back to a university and to lead the life of a student, scholar, and a "gentleman," as opposed to the real world of an internship. Oxford was a great experience, both intellectually and in terms of the people one met, and I would not have missed this for the world. These were among the best 3 years I have spent anywhere. I felt strongly, however, that I needed to achieve scholastically, because I was, in a way, giving up 2 to 3 years in a university setting, whereas many of my friends had already started to climb the clinical ladder. I initially started a Science Degree in Physiology, which was a traditional undergraduate course, with a mentor who would meet with me once a week and send one off to write an essay or other structured work. I tried this for 2 weeks, after which he and I sat down and agreed that this would not work. As a qualified physician, I soon realized that there was no way I could go back for an undergraduate degree, and, at that time, we decided that I would do a PhD or DPhil, using Oxford terminology. Unlike an American University, in which PhD students enter into a more structured program, at Oxford it was really up to the student to find a mentor. The other Rhodes scholar, who was in the same position as I was at that time, is my long-standing friend, *Dr. Philip Harris*, who is current Chief of Cardiology at St. Vincent's Hospital in Sidney, Australia.

Most of us were not that fortunate in finding a mentor initially, but I subsequently met *Dr. Cedric*

Prys-Roberts, who was a young anesthesiologist who was interested in cardiac ventricular function and contractility. He was setting up an animal laboratory with the objective of evaluating the effects of various anesthetics on ventricular function. At that time I had been strongly influenced by the work of *Dr. Ed Sonnenblick* on ventricular contractility (dP/dt/max), and I felt that this would be a good laboratory for me to work on cardiac function and at the same time to provide data on anesthetics for Dr. Prys-Roberts. I subsequently did my PhD in the Department of Anesthesia and the subject was "Ventricular Function and Hemodynamics in the Dog During Anesthesia." I was not particularly interested in the effects of anesthetics per se, but what I was interested in was using depressant anesthetics as a model to look at ventricular contractility and aortic input impedance, using a number of indices. Cedric Prys-Roberts, subsequently President of the Royal College of Anesthesiologists, and I set up that animal laboratory together, and it turned out to be a very satisfying and intellectually stimulating time.

Other people at Oxford at that time were *Dr. Peter Sleight,* who was a young consultant at the time, and we remain friends to this day. *Dr. Grant de Jersey Lee* did some great work. He was a very bright, eccentric Englishman. He worked on pulmonary input impedance and hemodynamics. I really enjoyed Oxford. I learned a lot. It taught me self-sufficiency. More formal instruction might have made it a bit easier and better. But at Oxford you did not get a lot of help, but you learned a lot of lessons and the end result was extremely rewarding.

WCR: *You were there 3 years?*

BJG: Two and a half years. At the end of my first year I was struggling to get my thesis off the ground and at that time did not have much data. The methodology was rather time consuming in that we had to develop ways of testing high fidelity pressure measurements. I became quite involved with the physics of pressure measurements. I wanted to measure dp/dt, but at that time we did not have catheter tip micromanometers and the development of high fidelity hydraulic pressure measurement was quite difficult. My first article was published in *Cardiovascular Research* and was entitled "Physical Criteria for the Measurement of Left Ventricular Pressure and Its First Derivative." I was indebted to a physicist, *Dr. Clive Hahn,* for much advice.

Although the first year was somewhat slow from the standpoint of data accumulation, it was nevertheless a great year and a learning experience, which was made more enjoyable by the ability to continue to be active from a sporting standpoint, in addition to the milieu of Oxford. My second year, from a research standpoint, was very productive in that we generated a great deal of data, and the end of that second year, I sat down for about 4 months and wrote the thesis. From start to finish, I completed the PhD in 30 months. Cedric Prys-Roberts taught me a great lesson that I have never forgotten. He wrote well, crisply and

tightly, but in addition he made me adhere to deadlines, a habit I have maintained to this day.

After finishing my PhD, I returned to Cape Town. By that time, I had 8 or 10 publications and had been giving talks at conferences around the UK. Professor V. Schrire, who was head of Cardiology at Cape Town, felt that I had been out of clinical medicine for some time and that I should become a senior intern again. Talk about being brought back to earth! Nonetheless, the next 6 months as a senior intern were incredible. I probably worked harder than I had ever worked before. Professor Schrire was quite a taskmaster, but the experience I gained in 6 months was extraordinary. My particular job was to work up the patients who were admitted to the Cardiology Service, most of them for cardiac catheterization. For reasons that were unclear, my fellow intern was fired and his workload was transferred to me. In spite of having a newborn son, I would get in early, admit about 10 patients a day, work them up, do the blood work, etc. The day ended about 10 o'clock at night. Professor Schrine would come to see the patients and usually give me a short tutorial about a particular patient. At the end of that period, I had accumulated an enormous experience in bedside cardiology and probably knew as much then as I did any time in my subsequent career. The 10 patients a day would include a few with rheumatic heart disease and 1 or 2 with adult congenital heart disease, hypertrophic cardiomyopathy, dilated cardiomyopathy, restrictive cardiomyopathy, constrictive pericarditis, etc. The variety and wealth of pathology was extraordinary.

Initially, I wanted to become a cardiac surgeon, but after finishing my PhD at Oxford I realized that if I was going to do cardiac surgery, I would have to spend the next 6 years in general surgery, which would be a long wait before I would be back in the cardiovascular field. Having just done 3 years of cardiovascular research, it appeared much more appropriate to do cardiology, and at the end of my senior internship at Groote Scheur Hospital in Cape Town, I had absolutely no doubt about deciding to become a cardiologist. I was not only excited about cardiovascular research, I was also enormously stimulated by the art of clinical cardiology, and by the fact that through the development of cardiac surgery, there was so much one could do for one's patients.

After completing my senior internship in Cardiology, I completed my medical residency in about 2 to 3 years and started the Cardiology Fellowship Program in Cape Town. In my second year as a Cardiology Fellow, one of the consultants went off on a sabbatical and I took his place in the coronary care unit, which was again a remarkable experience. Unfortunately, I was still paid as a Fellow, but I functioned as a consultant.

As a senior intern, I was taught a good lesson by Dr. Prys-Roberts. He wrote to me and said that my PhD thesis should generate at least 5 papers and that it was time for me to start writing them. I vacillated and was busy, a senior intern working very hard. In any event, I received another letter which really urged me to get the papers out, because he felt that they were not only important, but that the laboratory had been set up to do that in the first place. One month later, the first paper arrived and I noted that he was the first author and I was the second author. What he did was entirely fair and appropriate, since this reflected his time and effort on the project, but it was now time to write the second paper and I rapidly got the message. I subsequently wrote the second paper in a very short time, followed by the third and the fourth. This lesson is something which should be emphasized to fellows and residents. If one takes on a project, there is an obligation to complete it, and writing the paper is part of a debt that one owes to one's co-workers and to oneself.

I am very pleased that I completed the PhD. I believe that the particular subject of a thesis is not particularly important. It is the learning process. I realized very early on that I did not want to be a bench researcher for the rest of my life, but I learned many lessons in regard to the analysis of data; the accuracy of the methodology, how to read critically, and how to be objective, and to show initiative. What I also learned fairly early on was that although the methodology of my project was difficult, once the data started falling out, I found it fascinating. To this day, I have not ceased to be excited by data and the potential for the data to tell a story. Obtaining the PhD after the MD had changed my approach to research and clinical investigation. Additionally, Oxford is also a wonderful place in which to be.

WCR: *When did you get married?*

BJG: I got married my second year at Oxford. The rule at that time was that as a Rhodes Scholar you could not get married in your first year.

WCR: *So this was 1968?*

BJG: Yes. My first year I lived at the college. There was a club at Oxford called Vincent's Club, which was limited to 100 to 120 people and you had to be an active sportsman to join. It was a rather elite club and that is where we ate at night and spent most of our time. The great thing about Vincent's Club was that the members were from all over the world, about 50% postgraduate PhD students, and a third Rhodes Scholars. I met a lot of great characters from all parts of the UK there. It was a great society to live in, and I loved it. To this day I have friends in South Africa, New Zealand, Australia, and England whom I met at Oxford and we have remained close. Our wives also became friendly.

WCR: *It is now 1978 and you are 37 years old. How did you get to the Mayo Clinic? What were you thinking about doing?*

BJG: About the time of my divorce in 1975, I met *Dr. Charles Mullins*, who at that time was Chief of Cardiology in Dallas, shortly before Jim Willerson took the appointment. Charlie Mullins came to Cape Town on a sabbatical and was very impressed with the institution from a clinical standpoint. I believe he was also struck by the breadth of the clinical experience that I and other young consultants were having. At that time I was the youngest consultant in the institu-

tion. I ran the coronary care unit. One day a week I put in pacemakers. I spent 2 days a week in the cardiac catheterization laboratory, and we studied in the laboratory both adults and children. At that time, *Dr. Hein Wellens* had developed one of the first invasive electrophysiology programs in Holland and *Dr. Brian Kennelly*, who was then in Cape Town, but is now in Laguna Beach, took a sabbatical to work with Wellens. Dr. Kennelly was a superb clinical cardiologist who introduced invasive electrophysiology to Cape Town, and I started doing that as well. I think the variety impressed Charles Mullins, since not many cardiologists in the USA were as comfortable with a diverse spectrum, ranging from the coronary care unit, to infants, and invasive electrophysiologic studies. At Cape Town, we also catheterized the first patients who had heterotopic heart transplants. *Dr. Wally Beck*, who was Chief of Cardiology at that time, and I published the article in *The American Journal of Cardiology*. It took me 3 weeks to analyze the data, since no one previously had catheterized a patient with 2 hearts, which sometimes beat simultaneously and sometimes sequentially. It was fascinating to analyze the human dynamics in terms of completing preloads and afterloads.

Despite the huge variety of experience, I was getting unhappy in Cape Town. Schrire had died. It was a great job clinically, but I felt that my research training was going to waste. I was also frustrated from an academic standpoint, and Dr. Mullins felt that I would benefit from a few years in an academic institution in the USA. I felt that if I was really going to fulfill my academic potential I had to leave South Africa, and I wanted a change. My plan was to come to the USA for 5 to 10 years and generate papers and some research and then go back to South Africa. I interviewed at a number of centers in the USA, but I wanted to see the Mayo Clinic, which was famous in South Africa. Charlie Mullins, being an absolute gentleman, tried to recruit me to Dallas, but said that he knew *Bob Brandenburg* (at Mayo) and would pass my curriculum vitae on to him. Bob Brandenburg wrote me from the Mayo and said he had just stepped down as Chairman of Cardiology (it's a rotating chairmanship at the Mayo), but would pass my curriculum vitae on to Robert Frye. A day later, this guy, with an Oklahoma accent, called me and said he had heard I was coming to the USA to look at some jobs, and he wanted me to come and visit the Mayo Clinic. I arrived there in March having spent the previous 2 weeks on the West coast and in the South. When I arrived at the Mayo Clinic, it was cold and snowing. Late that evening, I told Bob Frye that if he offered me a job if I would take it. Two months later I was rounding in the coronary care unit in Cape Town, and he phoned me and said everything had gone through the usual channels and that I had a job at the Mayo Clinic.

By that time I was about to marry my current wife, Ann, an English girl who had lived for a couple of years in Mauritius, an island between South Africa and Australia in the Indian Ocean. She left her ex-husband, took her daughter, and came to Cape Town. She was a nurse and had worked in the cardiac surgical intensive care unit at Red Cross Children's Hospital in Cape Town where Chris Barnard did a lot of his work. I met her in Cape Town and we got married in November 1977. In February, I went to the Mayo Clinic to write my Minnesota license. My wife is an extremely adaptable person, who really enjoyed her life in Mauritius, which is somewhat of a tropical paradise. When I met her, she liked walking around barefoot with a flower in her hair—a real tropical beach girl. I remember well staying at the Kahler Hotel in Minnesota and looking out of the window at about 4 P.M. one afternoon when the temperature was something unbelievable. The wind was blowing and it was pitch dark, and all I could see was an individual walking across the road, bent over, looking 100 years old, but for all I know he was probably only 30. I called my wife, who was in Cape Town at the time (in mid-summer), and remember well telling her that "You have absolutely no concept of where you are coming to." At the time of that visit, I had been playing volley ball or body surfing in Cape Town and had fractured a scaphoid. It was mid-summer in Cape Town and I arrived at the Mayo Clinic with my arm in a cast and a deep tan. Apparently one of the cardiologists, with whom I subsequently became very friendly, went to Bob Frye and stated dogmatically "that this South African recruit would not last very long in Minnesota." We finally arrived in Rochester, Minnesota, in August 1978 and spent 15 years there. Initially, we were homesick. What I missed above all were the traditional South African or English sports, such as rugby and cricket and our friends. In any event, my 15 years at the Mayo Clinic were a fantastic experience. Although Rochester was an entirely different environment, it was one of those moves which turned out perfectly for both sides, in that the Mayo Clinic was good for me and I believe I was good for the Mayo Clinic. The institution may be the best run medical organization in the world. They have incredible resources. No better patient care is available anywhere in the world. Bob Frye, who had a huge influence on me, was a superb Chief of Cardiology and is a great friend.

WCR: *What made him so?*

BJG: He is just a fine individual. He is straight, honest, and blunt. He made it absolutely clear that if I wanted to write 100 papers that that was fine, good for me and good for the Mayo Clinic, but that it did not make me a better individual than someone else who was working just as hard seeing patients every day and not writing papers. The strength of the clinic is its need for individuals with different talents. He encouraged us to be productive academically, but we did not get paid for that, and you were not treated that differently. We all carried a heavy clinical load. You wrote and did studies because you wanted to. When I got to the Mayo Clinic it was like "Pandora's box," and I was a kid at the cookie counter. The Mayo Clinic has an incomparable medical records system and some unique, large databases. I had learned at an early stage

that I enjoyed analyzing data, and felt that I had the ability to ask of the database the correct questions, and to understand what could and could not be learned from a particular database. At a later stage, I had the chance to work on a number of multicenter trial writing committees, which brought me into association with *Dr. Eugene Braunwald.* It was interesting to see his reactions and excitement to the presentation of new data. Buried into a database are stories, and if the data are analyzed properly, one can tease out the message, and I find this exciting. It is somewhat like a voyage of discovery. The other great strength of the Mayo Clinic is its collegiality. Nothing in my professional experience has compared with this.

I developed some very good collaborative working relationships with people like *David Holmes, Rick Dishimura, Steve Hammill* in electrophysiology, *Hartzell Schaff* and *Gordon Danielson* (in surgery), *Bob Frye,* and *Hugh Smith.* Dr. Frye got me involved initially with case study and one thing led to another. *Ray Gibbons* was really a pioneer in measuring infarct size with sestamibi and I learned a lot about myocardial infarction. Before he left, I collaborated with *Valentin Fuster* on several diverse and quite important studies. It was just an enormously productive environment. I became director of the 2 coronary care units, but also I had to make a choice early on between (you could not do everything at Mayo like you could at Cape Town) electrophysiology, cardiac catheterization, or pacing. I decided to do pacing and electrophysiology and work in the coronary care units. After about 6 years I got a bit bored with pacing and wanted to spend more time with electrophysiology. I dropped the pacing and used almost 40% of my time doing electrophysiology.

I was at the Mayo Clinic at a very exciting time in cardiology. For a start, this was the early phase of the era of acute reperfusion therapy, which I have always found fascinating. To be in the coronary care unit in the early hours of the morning and to see what happens to the patient when the artery is opened, is unforgettable. It has been a stimulating experience to see the theoretical concepts translated into reality during my fellowship years and my early years as a consultant in Cape Town and at the Mayo Clinic. I also had the unique experience of working with some of the great cardiac surgeons of the modern era, like John Kirklin and Dwight McGoon, in analyzing the 25- to 30-year follow-up of the original series of patients with congenital heart disease repaired at the Mayo Clinic in the 1950s and early 1960s. The Mayo Clinic and Foundation is a great institution and my experience there was phenomenal. I am very proud of that association.

WCR: *What was your day like at the Mayo Clinic?*

BJG: It varied, depending upon what one was assigned to do for that particular week. If one was assigned to see outpatients, one would start fairly early in the day and one would be extremely busy until approximately 5 to 6 P.M. There were some similarities with private practice, in that if one fell behind and was unable to work efficiently, your schedule could come apart. The pressure of clinical practice at the Mayo Clinic is immense, but it is also unbelievably well organized and geared to an incredibly efficient delivery of patient care. It is extraordinarily efficient from the standpoint of both physician and patient, in that one could complete a very detailed workup within a short space of time. It was not the physician's job to run around looking for reports, x-rays, etc. This was all done for you.

If I was assigned to the electrophysiology laboratory, we would begin at about 8 A.M. and probably finish some time between 3 to 5 P.M. Thereafter, one would do inpatient and outpatient consultations, including the follow-up of patients who had perhaps been seen as an outpatient the previous week. There really was little time to waste. The Mayo Clinic placed a big emphasis on teaching, and if one was assigned to the hospital service or the coronary care unit, one would round from 8 A.M. to approximately noon, and from 12 to 1, it was customary to have lunch with the residents and to provide some didactic teaching from 1 to 2. In the afternoon, one would either see new patients who were admitted to the hospital, or one might go back to the office in the outpatient clinic and clean up whatever had to be done there. It made for a busy day. I suspect now that at the Mayo Clinic, as everywhere, the day has become even busier as physicians have to see more patients to generate the same revenue. At that time it was possible to sit down from 5:30 to 7 P.M. to do some academic work. I suspect that the clinical day has become longer there now as it is everywhere else.

WCR: *What time did you get there in the morning?*

BJG: It was only a 5-minute drive from home. I was usually at the clinic by 7 A.M., although I tend to be late-night person and I would rather get up later and go to bed late. I rarely go to bed before midnight. The other aspect of life at Mayo was that most days of the week there would be a conference. On Friday, we would have a clinical cardiology conference at 8:00 A.M. and Thursday would be the cardiac catheterization conference. The Mayo clinical conferences were fantastic. There would always be someone there who really knew what he/she was talking about. Facts dominated over anecdote. If there was an anecdote someone would turn around and say "We actually have looked at this and this is what we found," or what would come out of it would be "We should look at this." It was a very exciting place.

WCR: *What about Saturdays and Sundays?*

BJG: We did not see patients on Saturday or Sunday unless you were on the hospital service. Saturday morning was very much a working/teaching morning. There would usually be a fellows conference from 8:00 to 9:00 A.M., and then those of us who were involved academically would go downtown to the big Mayo Building and I would work until 1:00 P.M. in my office. I think John Kirklin, in the interview you did with him, alluded to the "Golden period" when he, *Jim DuShane, Howard Burchell*, and *David Donald*, got a lot done on Saturday mornings. On Sunday, I never went into the office, but I worked at home from about 4:00 to 7:00 P.M. I am very efficient with my time. I don't waste time, so if I had 15 minutes or so between cases I would work on a manuscript or I would read. I always reckoned you could read something useful in 15 minutes.

WCR: *How did somebody coming from warm Northern Rhodesia or Cape Town or Durban, South Africa, tolerate that severely cold weather?*

BJG: It was certainly an adjustment that was helped by the fact that I actually like snow, and the cold but crisp days with blue sky. Nonetheless, it is a very long, tough winter. One of the activities I miss is cross-country skiing on a wintery Sunday morning. *Dr. Hugh Smith*, who did a superb job running the Division of Cardiology and introduced it to the era of managed care after Bob Frye, and I spent many pleasant and strenuous hours cross-country skiing on one of the frozen rivers in winter. My whole family are very keen downhill skiers and our vacations, strangely enough, are usually spent skiing in the mountains, whereas one would think our natural inclination would have been to head South. I suspect, however, if the choice was purely up to my wife, more of our winter vacations would be spent next to an ocean, as opposed to heading west into the Rockies. We have twin daughters born in Rochester, and my stepdaughter lives in Minneapolis. When we moved to Washington, one of the twins' complaints was that there simply was not enough snow in the winter. Nevertheless, the winter was too long.

WCR: *You were very happy at the Mayo Clinic. I am sure you had other offers from other institutions in addition to Georgetown. What enticed you to move to Washington, DC, to be Chief of Cardiology at Georgetown University Medical Center?*

BJG: I had come to a crossroads professionally. I decided that maybe I should do something different. A part of me had always thought that I would like, at some stage, to be a Chief of a Cardiology Division at an academic medical center, and particularly in an institution where I would have the chance to build a program. The Mayo Clinic is an extraordinarily self-sustaining institution. No matter what the prestige of an individual, if he/she leaves, the Institution will carry on without missing a beat. At a smaller institution, one does have the opportunity to build, and that is both an attraction and a challenge. Approximately 5 or 6 years before I left the Mayo Clinic, the question came up in regard to whether I would go back to South Africa to 1 of the 2 major medical centers there. When I finally decided I had to make a decision, I realized that it was too late to return to South Africa because I had become a US citizen by then; 2 of my children were born in the States, and, furthermore, I was very happy both professionally and personally. I very much enjoyed being part of academic medicine in the USA. One of the attractions of Georgetown was that it is a university with great prestige, and under *Dr. W. Proctor Harvey* and *Dr. Charles Hufnagel*, cardiovascular medicine at that institution was at a pinnacle in the 1950s and 1960s. Nonetheless, during the 1980s and 1990s, the program was experiencing difficult times, but I did feel that there was the potential to rebuild it, given the underlying strength of the University, and its location in Washington, DC, which is one of the great cities of the world. Another factor was the presence of some excellent basic science in the cardiovascular area at Georgetown, including individuals such as *Ray Woosley* and *Martin Morad* in the Department of Pharmacology and a strong Research tradition at the Washington VA Hospital under *Ross Fletcher*. I have been at Georgetown now for 5-1/2 years and have not regretted the move at all, but it has been a difficult time for anyone to try to build in academic medicine, unless there are enormous resources at one's disposal. Academic medicine is certainly in turmoil at the moment. I suspect that the climate to build a strong cardiovascular program was much easier 15 years ago than it is now. It may not be something that can be done effectively other than at institutions with extensive resources.

There are 2 aspects of the Georgetown position that have been very satisfying. The year before I came the fellowship program did not match; it is now an excellent program and very competitive. It has been great to see that turn around. The other is to see recruited young faculty develop. We have some very good young cardiologists here, and it is satisfying to see them making their mark both nationally and even internationally. The greatest reward at this stage in one's career is to see others develop and mature, and this remains the case, even if one is a competitive individual as so many of us are. I cannot think of anything that would satisfy me more than to see young faculty develop and then move on to become leaders in their own right. Moving from the Mayo Clinic to Georgetown was very difficult. One can get complacent if you stay in a job for too long. To try something different is part of growing up. I have not regretted the move and the experience gained from it, and it has certainly not been easy during a time of declining resources.

WCR: *Have you found it easy or difficult to keep bright people in academic cardiology?*

BJG: Up until now, we have been able to keep the young faculty despite the financial and infrastructural pressures that prevail in academic medicine. I hope that some of our success in keeping faculty is because of my influence, but I am sure that the reputation and location of this excellent University play a part. We have a superb young faculty and a good balance of older, experienced individuals with national reputations. Academic medicine, however, is now under siege and the pressure continues to build to see more and more patients. There will be very little protected time. Until the recent potential increase in funding for NIH, grant funding was getting enormously difficult. We and others have faced some real threats in that the young investigator is truly an endangered species. I can understand why someone in their late 30s or early 40s, who appreciates that funding exists only to the 13th percentile or whatever, realizes that they have a family to support, and the institution cannot support them if they do not get grants. They give up, and we

are close to losing a generation of mentors because many people have given up being academic clinical investigators, since it is an occupation that is difficult to sustain. I hope that the new increased funding for NIH will address this problem, but there will be a lag time before this takes effect. If we expect young academic cardiologists to work as hard seeing patients as they do in private practice, and we cannot give them anything, such as protected time for research or academic travel, then they are not going to stay.

WCR: *Do you think we have too many cardiologists?*

BJG: I don't know. I have heard from some that we have too many, and from others that we don't have enough. It depends on how you define a cardiologist. If everybody with heart disease is going to be taken care of by a cardiologist, then maybe we don't have enough. Does everybody with hypertension need to be taken care of by a cardiologist? The answer is "no." There is an imbalance of cardiologists. In certain parts of the country, there are too many, and in many areas there are too few. We probably have too many interventional cardiologists in the USA, particularly given the evidence that individual and institutional volumes have a major impact upon outcome. This will become even more cogent as interventional cardiology becomes more complex with the expansion of devices.

WCR: *How big is your staff of cardiologists at Georgetown?*

BJG: We are 14 fulltime here at the Georgetown University Medical Center, Washington, DC, and also we have a very strong faculty at the Veterans Administration Hospital under Dr. Ross Fletcher. We also have a large number of part-time cardiologists.

WCR: *If you total everybody here at Georgetown University Medical Center in heart disease, you say 14 faculty, you add up the secretaries, technicians and so on, how many people are you talking about?*

BJG: I am not sure. It is difficult to give you an answer, because many of our people are employed by the hospital, some are employed by the faculty of medicine, and many of them are cross appointments. I am sure if one really added everyone up, there is an excess of 100 people working within the division of cardiology.

WCR: *Cardiology involves lots of procedures which are costly but profitable. Do you think cardiologists should be on salary?*

BJG: I have always been on salary, and I am very comfortable with that. Some physicians see a lot more patients than do others, and some surgeons do a lot more operations than others, and they deserve a higher salary, but how does one interpret this in an academic institution? In a university-type setting, a salaried system works best, but we need to develop an incentive-based system of reimbursement. What everyone struggles with is what do you classify as the incentive? Is it just numbers of patients seen or numbers of procedures performed? How do you reward someone who publishes even though they may not have a great deal of grant support, but the work is very good for the institution because they are analyzing the institution's data? How do you reward the person who works extremely hard at perhaps running the quality assurance program in an institution, which is a very important area, even if it does not lead to national recognition? An incentive-based system is good, but we must avoid a system whereby the only incentive is to do more procedures or see more patients. We have to find other incentives. How do you reward educators who play an essential role, not only for the institution, but for medicine in this country and for the next generation? How do you support young investigators with the potential to receive NIH or other grant support, but who need more time to develop before they can receive grant support?

WCR: *I suggest that most cardiologists who are chiefs of cardiology at the various university hospitals around the country, if not friends of yours, are acquaintances of yours. How much happiness is there among cardiology chiefs today in the various university hospitals in the USA?*

BJG: Not a great deal. Individuals in these positions are a lot less happy than they were in the 1980s. But, this applies to most positions in academic medicine. We're under tremendous pressures. We are being reimbursed less for what we do. There is less money to go around. Academic medical centers are having to reengineer themselves, and it is difficult. I am sure if you talk to chairmen of medicine they will say it was much more fun in the 1980s, the reason being that physicians were paid a lot more for less work. It is very easy to develop a program and enjoy doing it when the resources are there, but when they are not, you have to say "no" to people. It is much more fun to say "yes." It is a much more difficult job now and people are less happy, but it does not mean it does not have its rewards. It does.

WCR: *What do you do everyday? What time do you get to the hospital? What time do you go home at night?*

BJG: It varies, but I will often be in the hospital by 7:00 A.M. I have a 20-minute drive from my home in Bethesda, Maryland. When I don't have a 7:00 A.M. meeting, which I have twice a week, it will be closer to 7:30. I usually get home about 8:00 P.M.

WCR: *When you get home at night do you do any more medical work?*

BJG: I used to do a lot more work at home at night than I do now. Typically, when I was at the Mayo, I would start a little later. I would have dinner just after 8:00, and then I would often work from 9:00 to 10:30 or 11:00 P.M. I usually work on Saturday mornings and Sunday evening.

WCR: *You have had an impressive career. You are obviously a good physician, a good cardiologist. You have been highly productive, both clinically and academically. You have put together a lot of studies. What do you want to do now? Let's say you have 20 professional years left. What do you want to do?*

BJG: In terms of leisure, I love to ski. I am a keen fisherman and an enthusiastic but novice fly fisherman. I enjoy going to strange, out of the way places to spend a great deal of time and effort to catch a fish, which I will promptly put back into the river and release. Perhaps it is a throwback to our hunter-gatherer instincts. Other leisure activities which I enjoy are running, hiking, and since both of our daughters are good tennis players, I have spent a fair amount of time on the courts with them during the weekend. I am not the kind of person, however, who can devote a large amount of my time to hobbies or leisure activities, but I do read widely. I obviously read an enormous amount of medicine, but I mix this with fiction, history, wildlife, and a variety of other "reads."

I want to continue with an active clinical practice and I really enjoy academic cardiology. I want to remain both professionally and academically challenged. I enjoy analyzing data and I like to think that I practice evidence-based cardiology. I want to be part of generating that evidence and not just simply relying on data which is the work of others. So in response to your question, I plan to continue to do what I am doing now, and despite the pressures on cardiologists in terms of the delivery of health care, in many ways it is a more exciting time than it was 10 or 20 years ago. We are in the era of molecular biology, but one does not have to be a molecular biologist to learn to integrate the findings from the basic science laboratory into our clinical practice. We are also in an era when the natural history of disease is rapidly changing, which in itself is a fascinating opportunity for research. One example of this lies in the molecular genetics of hypertrophic cardiomyopathy. I believe within the next 5 years, this will be an integral part of our clinical practice. This is something that I learned from Dr. Gene Braunwald, who is as excited by data today as he probably was 30 years ago. What is important is to not remain static, and to appreciate the huge changes that are taking place and to modify our clinical practice and research directions accordingly.

I also learned a great deal from our studies on atrial fibrillation, dilated and hypertrophic cardiomyopathy, and coronary artery disease, which I subsequently integrated into my own day-to-day practice. I like to practice evidence-based medicine, but it is also challenging and stimulating to generate the evidence as opposed to simply relying on evidence provided by others. It has been said that evidence-based medicine is "perpetuating other people's mistakes instead of your own," but I disagree.

WCR: *Are you interested in being a Chairman of a Department of Medicine?*

BJG: Probably not, since my inclination and interests are primarily cardiovascular, both clinically and academically. I am very interested in cardiovascular disease, and probably not as interested in the other disciplines of internal medicine as perhaps I should be. I am not saying that I would not take the job as Chairman of Medicine, but it is not one of my priorities, at least at the present.

WCR: *What kind of relation have you had as head of the largest division of the Department of Internal Medicine with the Chairman of Internal Medicine? Do you have much contact?*

BJG: Yes. The Chairman of Internal Medicine here, *Dr. Paul Katz,* has only been in this position 6 to 9 months. We have a good relationship.

WCR: *You have more contact with the cardiovascular surgeons than you do with the chairman of medicine?*

BJG: In regard to one's day to day life, cardiologists have always had more contact with cardiovascular surgeons and pediatric cardiologists than with many of our colleagues in internal medicine. It is a function of how we practice on a daily basis. Nonetheless, I believe that the days of cardiology's breaking away and becoming a separate department are probably over and counterproductive. There are already enough pressures on academic medicine that fighting among ourselves will not achieve anything. Given the radical changes in health-care delivery, it may well be that a Department of Cardiology might not do as well on its own as opposed to being a part of the Department of Medicine or some other larger program. I believe that to some extent, some of the tensions between medicine and cardiology have dissipated, but there are still many aspects of the relationship that need to be worked out. We need a symbiotic relationship because the old system has gone, at least in most institutions, and it will simply not be possible for cardiology to continue to subsidize a department of medicine to the extent that this has been the case in the past, since the money from cardiology will simply not be sufficient to support the other divisions within of the department of medicine. It will therefore be necessary for other subspecialties in medicine to at least break even, although I believe it is appropriate for cardiology to help support some programs that have no chance of being economically viable.

To function efficiently, both clinically and economically, a division of cardiology needs to be part of a Clinical Cardiovascular Institute, that offers a seamless, integrated form of care. This does not mean that cardiology needs to break away from medicine, not at all. I would rather have my academic roots in a department of medicine than in department of surgery. We have to find a way to practice in such a way that patients flow from the cardiologist to a vascular surgeon or to a cardiac surgeon in a much more efficient mode than is usually the case. Places such as the Mayo Clinic and the Cleveland Clinic have that kind of organization already in place.

WCR: *Dr. Gersh, you have 5 children?*

BJG: One of my children is a step-daughter; 4 children are my own.

WCR: *Your children are how old?*

BJG: My step-daughter is 29. My son is 28. He lives in South Africa where he has established his own business. I have a daughter, aged 25, who graduated from the University of Cape Town and then she did a master's degree in creative writing at Columbia Univeristy in New York. She is living in New York and is a writer. Then, I have twin girls whose prom is tonight at Walt Whitman High School in Bethesda. They are almost 18. One is going to the University of Colorado, which probably tells you that she has inherited my love of skiing, as has the other. My other daughter is going to the University of Wisconsin at Madison. They are identical twins, but very different in many respects. One is interested in doing medicine, whereas the other has not the slightest interest; her major will be environmental studies.

WCR: *Have you been a good father?*

BJG: I am sure that, like many of us, I can be legitimately criticized. There is no doubt that I have not spent enough time with my children, and I regret that, particularly now that they are graduating from high school. My wife, Ann, has been fantastic in this regard. She is very close to our children as well as playing a wonderful role as a stepmother to my older children. Although like many of us, I did not spend enough time with my children, particularly when they were younger, I believe I have certainly been close to them, and they have certainly grown up well and I am very proud of them. I have been able to maintain quite close contact with my older children, although our relationship has been tested by the fact that they spent a lot of their youth in South Africa and we have been apart. While they were at school, we used to see each other 3 times a year, which is very much like the situation when I was growing up at boarding school. Every year for about 12 years, my son and I would spend a few days musky fishing at a small resort on the Canadian side of the Lake of the Woods—there are great memories that we both have of those times. The proof of the pudding is in the eating, and the entire family has remained close. The ties are there despite the distances.

WCR: *I see from your curriculum vitae that you have travelled quite extensively both in the USA and abroad during the last 15 years. How do you handle all the travel?*

BJG: As you know better than most, Bill, travel provides a unique opportunity to maintain close professional and personal contacts around the world. It is undoubtedly one of the benefits of a successful academic career, and it is a privilege to be invited to speak and to teach before one's peers, both nationally and abroad. The downside is the amount of work involved, and travel is disruptive. Nonetheless, the advantages certainly outweigh the disadvantages. I find planes extremely conducive to work, and use my time en route very productively. It is a great opportunity to write and to read without the distractions of a telephone. I also keep the time away to a minimum, although at times whenever my wife is with me, we may add on a few extra days of vacation.

WCR: *How much time do you take off a year for vacation?*

BJG: I generally take 2 weeks for pure vacation, but as I mentioned, we will often add a few days of vacation at the end of a professional trip, either when we go overseas or at the American College of Cardiology's ski meeting, at which I have frequently been on the faculty.

WCR: *You mentioned hobbies; skiing, bird-watching, fishing. You also mentioned that you try your best to do as much reading as you can in medicine as well* *as outside of medicine. Anything that you really would like to do, that you just do not have time to do?*

BJG: I run regularly, probably about 10 miles a week. One of the great things about Washington, DC, is that one can run virtually year-round, and the Chesapeake and Ohio Canal tow path along side the Potomac River is a magnificent place in which to run.

When I was in South Africa, I was a very keen squash player and played the game competitively, but unfortunately it was not played much in the Midwest when we first arrived. I would like to get back to playing squash again. Obviously, I would like to have more time for bird and wildlife watching, and this is something that we do when we are back in Southern Africa.

WCR: *It might be a little trite, but what do you like most about yourself? What are you most pleased with about Bernard Gersh?*

BJG: Outside of my professional accomplishments, I consider myself an honest person and I pride myself on a sense of accountability and ethical principles. I learned that from my father. If I agree to take on a task, I always complete it. From a professional standpoint, I am pleased with the fact that I have had a very wide training in a number of cardiovascular disciplines and like the fact that I am comfortable in many areas, such as acute and chronic coronary artery disease, electrophysiology, cardiomyopathies, arrhythmias, and some aspects of congenital heart disease. I owe this to the breadth of the training that I initially received in South Africa. I consider that I do practice evidence-based medicine, and that if I make a clinical decision, that I am doing it because I really know the data, including the limitations of the data. I like to feel that I know what I am doing and why and what the justification is for ordering a particular test or form of therapy, and that I do not just practice by anecdote and "gee whiz, I think it is a good idea." What is equally important is to understand that in some patients there are no data to support one's decision, and one has to act accordingly because it perhaps "is a reasonable idea." What I have also found very satisfying is when one can turn around and say "we did not know how to handle this problem, so we studied it, and this is what we found, and this is now what we do." It goes back to the practice of evidence-based medicine, but it is satisfying to feel that one has played some small role in generating some of the evidence.

I suppose I like the fact that I have wide interests and I can enjoy myself in many different ways, even if I seem to be so preoccupied professionally. I utilize time very efficiently and I am never bored and never at a loss for anything to do. Nonetheless, I do have the ability to switch off very quickly, so that I could be working until 10:30 at night and yet 5 minutes later may be buried in a book on a completely different subject.

WCR: *What do you want to be remembered for when you are gone?*

BJG: I would like someone to say that they saw me, at the age of 90, ski the bumps at Snowmass with great style and finesse, albeit very slowly. The fact that they would actually see this 90-year-old skiing down the bumps with his own knee joints in place would be great, particularly if his eyes could see the way down and his mind could find the path.

WCR: *Your father is 92? Is he healthy?*

BJG: He is physically very healthy, but his memory is not what it was and I find this difficult to accept. Nonetheless, he is very loved by his children and grandchildren, and is very much the family patriarch, and extraordinarily well taken care of by my mother.

WCR: *How old is your mother?*

BJG: My mother is 82 and is in great shape. Mentally she is in her 40s—always questioning us children, but also in her element cooking a family dinner, which is not bad considering that she grew up in a colonial society, surrounded by servants. My parents only emigrated to the States when my father was in his mid 80s and my mother in her mid 70s.

WCR: *Is there anything we have not discussed that you would like to discuss?*

BJG: I think I have already said too much.

WCR: *Dr. Gersh, on behalf of myself and the AJC readers, I want to thank you for your being so open and refreshing.*

BJG: I feel privileged to have been invited. I have enjoyed reading the other interviews.

WCR: *Thank you.*

BJG's Best Publications as Selected by Him

2. Reuben SR, Swadling JP, Gersh BJ, Lee G de J. Impedance and transmission properties of the pulmonary arterial system. *Cardiovasc Res* 1970;5:1–9.

4. Gersh BJ, Hahn CEW, Prys-Roberts C: Physical criteria for measurement of left ventricular pressure and its first derivative. *Cardiovasc Res* 1970;5:32–40.

5. Prys-Roberts C, Gersh BJ, Reuben SR, Schultz DL. The effects of halothane on the interactions between myocardial contractility, aortic impedance and left ventricular performance. I. Theoretical considerations and results. *Br J Anesthesia* 1972;44:634–649.

6. Gersh BJ, Prys-Roberts C, Reuben SR, Schultz DL. The effects of halothane on the interactions between myocardial contractility, aortic impedance and left ventricular performance. II. Aortic input impedance and the distribution of energy during ventricular ejection. *Br J Anesthesia* 1972;44:767–775.

7. Gersh BJ, Prys-Roberts C, Baker AB. The effects of halothane on the interactions between myocardial contractility, aortic impedance and left ventricular performance. III. Influence of stimulation of the sympathetic nerves, beta-adrenergic receptors and myocardial fibers. *Br J Anesthesia* 1972;44:995–1005.

9. Beck W, Gersh BJ. Left ventricular bypass using a cardiac allograft: haemodynamic studies. *Am J Cardiol* 1976;37:1007–1113.

10. Joffe HS, Rose AG, Gersh BJ, Beck W. Figure-of-eight circulation in thoracopagus conjoined twins with a shared heart. *Euro J Cardiol* 1977;6:157–166.

11. Forman R, Gersh BJ, Fraser R, Beck W. Haemodynamic observations in patients with the Lillehei aortic and mitral valve prostheses. *J Thorac Cardiovasc Surg* 1978;75:595–598.

13. Holmes DR, Gersh BJ, Maloney JD, Merideth J. Follow-up experience with permanent endocardial tined pacemaker electrodes. *J Thorac Cardiovasc Surg* 1980;79:565–569.

15. Fuster V, Gersh BJ, Giuliani ER, Tajik AJ, Brandenburg RO, Frye RL. The natural history of idiopathic dilated cardiomyopathy. *Am J Cardiol* 1981;47:525–531.

17. Gersh BJ, Bassendine M, Forman R, Walls RS, Beck W. Coronary artery spasm and myocardial infarction in the absence of angiographically demonstrable coronary obstructive disease. *Mayo Clin Proc* 1981;56:700–708.

20. Lloyd EA, Gersh BJ, Kennelly BM. The hemodynamic spectrum of "dominant" right ventricular infarction in 19 patients. *Am J Cardiol* 1981;48:1016–1021.

23. Holmes DR Jr., Osborn MJ, Gersh BJ, Maloney JD, Danielson GK. The Wolff-Parkinson-White syndrome: a surgical approach. *Mayo Clin Proc* 1982; 57:345–350.

24. Nishimura RA, Gersh BJ, Vlietstra RE, Osborn MJ, Ilstrup DM, Holmes DR.

Hemodynamic and symptomatic consequences of ventricular pacing. *PACE* 1982;5:903–910.

26. Miller FA, Seward JB, Gersh BJ, Tajik AJ, Mucha P Jr.. Two-dimensional echocardiographic findings in cardiac trauma. *Am J Cardiol* 1982;50:1022–1027.

30. Schaff HV, Gersh BJ, Piehler JM, Puga FJ, Danielson GK, Pluth JR. The morbidity and mortality of reoperation for coronary artery disease and analysis of late results with the use of actuarial estimate of event-free interval. *J Thorac Cardiovasc Surg* 1983;85:508–515.

32. Nishimura RA, Gersh BJ, Holmes DR, Vlietstra RE, Broadbent JC. Outcome of dual-chamber pacing for the pacemaker syndrome. *Mayo Clin Proc* 1983;58: 452–456.

33. Gersh BJ, Kronmal RA, Schaff HV, Frye RL, Ryan TJ, Myers WO, Athearn MW, Gosselin AJ, Kaiser GC, Killip T III. Long-term (5 year) results of coronary bypass surgery in patients 65 years old or older: a report from the Coronary Artery Surgery Study. *Circulation* 1983;68(suppl II):II-190–II-199.

34. Schaff HV, Gersh BJ, Pluth JR, Danielson GK, Orszulak TA, Puga FJ, Piehler JM, Frye RL. Survival and functional status after coronary artery bypass grafting: results 10 to 12 years after surgery in 500 patients. *Circulation* 1983; 68(suppl II):II-200–I-204.

35. Wood DL, Hammill SC, Holmes DR, Osborn MJ, Gersh BJ. Catheter ablation of the atrioventricular conduction system in patients with supraventricular tachycardia. *Mayo Clin Proc* 1983;58:791–796.

39. Hammill SC, Holmes DR, Wood DL, Osborn MJ, McLaran C, Sugrue DD, Gersh BJ. Electrophysiologic testing in the upright position: improved evaluation of patients with rhythm disturbances using a tilt table. *J Am Coll Cardiol* 1984;4:65–71.

41. Sugrue DD, Holmes DR, Gersh BJ, Edwards WD, McLaran CJ, Wood DL, Osborn MJ. Cardiac histologic findings in patients with life-threatening ventricular arrhythmias of unknown etiology. *J Am Coll Cardiol* 1984;4:952–957.

42. Fuster VF, Steele PM, Edwards WD, Gersh BJ, McGoon MD, Frye RL. Primary pulmonary hypertension: Natural history and the importance of thrombosis. *Circulation* 1984;70:580–587.

43. Schaff HV, Gersh BJ, Fisher LD, Frye RL, Mock MB, Ryan TJ, Ellis RB, Chaitman BR, Alderman EL, Kaiser GC, Faxon DP, Bourassa MG, and Participants in the Coronary Artery Surgery Study. Detrimental effect of perioperative myocardial infarction on late survival after coronary artery bypass. *J Thorac Cardiovasc Surg* 1984;88:972.

44. Evans RW, Manninen DL, Gersh BJ, Hart LG, Rodin J. The need for and supply of donor hearts for transplantation. *J Heart Transplant* 1984;4:57–62.

47. McLaran CJ, Gersh BJ, Sugrue DD, Hammill SC, Seward JB, Holmes DR Jr.. Tachycardia induced myocardial dysfunction. A reversible phenomenon? *Br Heart J* 1985;53:323–327.

49. Gersh BJ, Schaff HV, Vatterott PJ, Danielson GK, Piehler J, Orszulak T, Puga FJ. Results of triple valve replacement in 91 patients: perioperative mortality and long-term follow-up. *Circulation* 1985;72:130–137.

50. Gersh BJ, Kronmal RA, Schaff HV, Frye RL, Ryan TJ, Mock MB, Myers WO, Athearn MW, Gosselin AJ, Kaiser GC, Bourassa MG, Killip T III, and Participants in the Coronary Artery Surgery Study. A comparison of coronary artery bypass surgery and medical therapy in patients aged 65 years or older: a nonrandomized study from the CASS (Coronary Artery Surgery Study) Registry. *N Engl J Med* 1985;313:217–224.

52. Sugrue DD, Gersh BJ, Holmes DR Jr., Wood DL, Osborn MJ, Hammill SC. Symptomatic "isolated" carotid sinus hypersensitivity: natural history and results of treatment with anticholinergic drugs or pacemaker. *J Am Coll Cardiol* 1986; 7:158–162.

54. McLaran CJ, Gersh BJ, Osborn MJ, Wood DL, Sugrue DD, Holmes DR Jr.., Hammill SC. Increased vagal tone as an isolated finding in patients undergoing electrophysiologic testing for recurrent syncope: response to long-term anticholingeric therapy. *Br Heart J* 1986;55:53–57.

55. Gersh BJ, Fisher LD, Schaff HV, Rahimtoola SH, Reeder GS, Frater R, McGoon DC. Issues concerning the clinical evaluation of new prosthetic valves. *J Thorac Cardiovasc Surg* 1986;91:460–466.

58. Holmes DR, Davis KB, Mock MB, Fisher LD, Gersh BJ, Killip T, and Participants in the Coronary Artery Surgery Study. The effect of medical and surgical treatment on subsequent sudden cardiac death in patients with coronary artery disease: a report from the Coronary Artery Surgery Study. *Circulation* 1986;73:1254–1263.

59. Click RL, Gersh BJ, Sugrue DD, Holmes DR, Wood DL, Osborn MJ, Hammill SC. Role of invasive electrophysiologic testing in patients with symptomatic bundle branch block. *Am J Cardiol* 1987;59:817–823.

62. Shah P, Abelman W, Gersh BJ. Cardiomyopathies in the elderly. Bethesda Conference on Cardiovascular Diseases in the Elderly. *J Am Coll Cardiol* 1987;10:77A–79A.

63. Myers WO, Gersh BJ, Fisher LD, Mock MB, Holmes DR, Schaff HV, Gillispie S, Ryan TJ, Kaiser GC, and CASS Investigators. Time to first new myocardial infarction in patients with mild angina and three vessel disease comparing medicine and surgery: a CASS Registry study of survival. *Ann Thorac Surg* 1987;43:599–612.

64. Kopecky SL, Gersh BJ, McGoon MD, Whisnant JP, Holmes DR Jr., Ilstrup DM, Frye RL. The natural history of lone atrial fibrillation. A population-based study over three decades. *N Engl J Med* 1987;317:669–674.

66. McLaran CJ, Gersh BJ, Sugrue DD, Hammill SC, Zinsmeister AR, Wood DL, Osborn MJ, Holmes DR Jr.. The influence of clinical and electrophysiologic characteristics on late survival in patients resuscitated from out of hospital cardiac

arrest: a comparison of patients with and without coronary artery disease. *Br Heart J* 1987; 58:583–591.

67. Olson LJ, Edwards WE, McCall JT, Ilstrup DM, Gersh BJ. Cardiac iron deposition in idiopathic hemochromatosis: histologic and analytic assessment of 14 hearts from autopsy. *J Am Coll Cardiol* 1987;10:1239–1243.

68. Mullany CJ, Gersh BJ, Orszulak TA, Schaff HV, Piehler JM, Puga FJ, Illstrup D, Danielson GK, Pluth JR. Combined aortic and mitral valve replacement with tricuspid annuloplasty in 109 patients. Early results and late survival. *J Thorac Cardiovasc Surg* 1987;94:740–748.

69. Myers, WO, Gersh BJ, Fisher LD, Mock MB, Holmes DR, Schaff HV, Gillispie S, Ryan TJ, Kaiser GC, and Other CASS Investigators. Medical versus early surgical therapy in patients with triple-vessel disease and mild angina pectoris: a CASS registry study of survival. *Ann Thorac Surg* 1987;44:471–486.

74. Holt GW, Gersh BJ, Holmes DR, Vlietstra RE, Bresnahan JF, Reeder GS, Smith HC. The results of percutaneous transluminal coronary angioplasty in patients with early post infarction angina pectoris. *Am J Cardiol* 1988;61:1238–1243.

77. Kopecky S, Gersh BJ, McGoon MD, Mair D, Porter CJ, Ilstrup D, McGoon DC, Kirklin J, Danielson GK. Long-term prognosis for patients undergoing surgical repair of isolated pulmonary valve stenosis: follow-up at 20 to 30 yrs. *Circulation* 1988;78:1150–1156.

78. Huber KC, Gersh BJ, Sugrue D, Frye RL, Bailey K, Ritts RE. T-lymphocyte subsets in patients with idiopathic dilated cardiomyopathy and their relationship to duration of symptoms. *Int J Cardiol* 1988;22:59–66.

79. Oh J, Gersh BJ, Nassef A, Miller FA, Chesebro J, Holmes DR, Smith HC, Tajik AJ. Effects of acute reperfusion on regional myocardial function: serial two-dimensional echocardiographic assessment. *Int J Cardiol* 1988;22:161–168.

80. Hermanson B, Omenn GX, Kronmal RA, Gersh BJ, and Participants in CASS. Beneficial six-year survival outcomes from smoking cessation in older men and women with coronary artery disease: results from the CASS registry. *N Engl J Med* 1988;319:1365–1368.

82. Kontos GJ Jr., Schaff HV, Gersh BJ, Bove AA. Comparison of left ventricular function in patients with acute and chronic mitral regurgitation. *J Thorac Cardiovasc Surg* 1989;98:163–169.

83. Codd MB, Sugrue DD, Gersh BJ, Melton LJ III. Epidemiology of idiopathic dilated and hypertrophic cardiomyopathy in Olmsted County, MN, 1975–1984. *Circulation* 1989;80:564–572.

84. Roger VL, Ballard DJ, Hallett JW, Osmundson PJ, Puetz PA, Gersh BJ. Influence of coronary artery disease on morbidity and mortality after abdominal aortic aneurysmectomy: a population- based study, 1971-1987. *J Am Coll Cardiol* 1989;14:1245–1252.

85. Myers WO, Schaff HV, Gersh BJ, Fisher LD, Kosinski AJ, Mock MB, Holmes DR, Ryan TJ, Kaiser CC, and CASS Investigators. Improved survival of surgically treated patients with triple vessel coronary artery disease and severe angina pectoris: a CASS Registry Study. *J Thorac Cardiovasc Surg* 1989;97: 487–495.

86. Lemery R, Gersh BJ. Programmed ventricular stimulation during variant angina: report of a case. *PACE* 1989;12:1878–1883.

88. Hayes SN, Freeman WK, Gersh BJ. Low pressure cardiac tamponade: diagnosis facilitated by Doppler echocardiography. *Br Heart J* 1990;63:136–140.

89. Hammill SC, Trusty JM, Wood DL, Bailey KR, Vatterott PJ, Osborn MJ, Holmes DR, Gersh BJ. Asymptomatic nonsustained ventricular tachycardia: limited role for electrophysiologic testing. *Am J Cardiol* 1990;65:722–728.

91. Lavie C, Gersh BJ. Electrical and mechanical complications in acute myocardial infarction. *Mayo Clin Proc* 1990;65:709–730.

92. Mullany CJ, Darling GE, Pluth JR, Orszulak TA, Schaff HV, Ilstrup DM, Gersh BJ. Early and late results after isolated coronary artery bypass surgery in 159 patients aged 80 years and older. *Circulation* 1990;82:IV-229–IV-236.

93. Fay WP, Taliercio CP, Ilstrup DM, Tajik AJ, Gersh BJ. The natural history of hypertrophic cardiomyopathy in the elderly. *J Am Coll Cardiol* 1990;16:821–826.

94. Rogers WJ, Coggin CJ, Gersh BJ, Fisher LD, Myers WO, Oberman A, Sheffield TL, for the CASS Investigators. Ten year follow-up of quality of life in patients randomized to medicine versus coronary bypass graft surgery: the Coronary Artery Surgery Study (CASS). *Circulation* 1990;82:1647–1658.

96. Murphy JG, Gersh BJ, McGoon MD, Mair DD, Porter CJ, Ilstrup DM, McGoon DC, Puga FJ, Kirklin JW, Danielson GK. Long-term outcome after surgical repair of isolated atrial septal defect: Follow-up at 27 to 32 years. *N Engl J Med* 1990; 323:1645–1650.

98. Christian TF, Clements IP, Behrenbeck T, Huber KC, Chesebro JH, Gersh BJ, Gibbons RJ. Limitations of the electrocardiogram in estimating infarction size after acute reperfusion therapy for myocardial infarction. *Ann Intern Med* 1991; 114:264–270.

100. Vatterott PJ, Hammill SC, Bailey KR, Wiltgen CM, Gersh BJ. Late potentials on signal-averaged electrocardiograms and patency of the infarct-related artery in survivors of acute myocardial infarction. *J Am Coll Cardiol* 1991;17:330–337.

101. Thompson RC, Holmes DR Jr., Gersh BJ, Mock MB, Bailey KR. Percutaneous transluminal coronary angioplasty in the elderly: early and long-term results. *J Am Coll Cardiol* 1991;17:1245–1250.

102. Christian TF, Gibbons RJ, Gersh BJ. Effect of infarct location on myocardial salvage assessed by Tc-99M isonitrile. *J Am Coll Cardiol* 1991;17:1303–1308.

103. Christian TF, Behrenbeck T, Gersh BJ, Gibbons RJ. Relation of left ventricular volume and function over one year after acute myocardial infarction to infarct size determined by technetium-99m sestamibi. *Am J Cardiol* 1991;68: 21–26.

104. Pfeffer MA, Moyé LA, Braunwald E, Basta L, Brown EJ, Cuddy TE, Dagenais GR, Flaker GC, Geltman EM, Gersh BJ, et al, for the SAVE Investigators. Selection bias in the use of thrombolytic therapy in acute myocardial infarction. *JAMA* 1991;266:528–532.

105. Steingart RM, Packer M, Hamm P, Coglianese ME, Gersh BJ, Geltman E, Sollano J, Katz S, Moye L, Basta LL, et al, for the SAVE Investigators. Sex differences in the management of coronary artery disease. *N Engl J Med* 1991; 325:226–230.

108. Hibbard MD, Holmes DR, Bailey KR, Reeder GS, Bresnahan JF, Gersh BJ. Percutaneous transluminal coronary angioplasty in patients with cardiogenic shock. *J Am Coll Cardiol* 1992;19:639–646.

109. Rihal CS, Gersh BJ, Whisnant JP, Rooke TW, Sundt TM Jr., O'Fallon WM, Ballard DJ. Influence of coronary heart disease on morbidity and mortality after carotid endarterectomy: a population-based study in Olmsted County, Minnesota (1970-1988). *J Am Coll Cardiol* 1992;19:1254–1260.

110. Sugrue DD, Rodeheffer RJ, Codd MB, Ballard DJ, Fuster V, Gersh BJ. The clinical course of idiopathic dilated cardiomyopathy. A population-based study. *Ann Intern Med* 1992;117:117–123.

112. Cavender JB, Rogers WJ, Fisher LD, Gersh BJ, Coggin CJ, Myers WO, for the CASS Investigators. Effects of smoking on survival and morbidity in patients randomized to medical or surgical therapy in the Coronary Artery Surgery Study (CASS): 10-year follow-up. *J Am Coll Cardiol* 1992;20:287–294.

113. Grogan M, Smith HC, Gersh BJ, Wood DL. Left ventricular dysfunction due to atrial fibrillation in patients initially believed to have idiopathic dilated cardiomyopathy. *Am J Cardiol* 1992;69:1570–1573.

114. Lemery R, Smith HC, Schaff HV, Giuliani ER, Gersh BJ. Prognosis in rupture of the ventricular septum after acute myocardial infarction and role of early surgical intervention. *Am J Cardiol* 1992;70:147–151.

115. Bell MR, Gersh BJ, Schaff HV, Holmes DR, Fisher LD, Alderman EL, Myers WO, Parsons LS, Reeder GS, and Investigators of the Coronary Artery Surgery Study. The effect of the completeness of revascularization on long-term outcome of patients with three-vessel disease undergoing coronary artery bypass surgery: a report from the Coronary Artery Surgery Study (CASS) Registry. *Circulation* 1992;86:446–457.

116. Kishon Y, Oh JK, Schaff HV, Mullany CJ, Tajik AJ, Gersh BJ. Mitral valve operation in postinfarction rupture of a papillary muscle: immediate results and long-term follow-up of 22 patients. *Mayo Clin Proc* 1992;67:1023–1030.

118. Munger TM, Packer DL, Hammill SC, Feldman BJ, Bailey KR, Ballard DJ, Holmes DR, Gersh BJ. A population study of the natural history of Wolff-Parkinson-White syndrome in Olmsted County, Minnesota, 1953 through 1989. *Circulation* 1993;87:857–865.

119. Gibbons RJ, Holmes DR, Reeder GS, Bailey KR, Hopfenspinger MR, Gersh BJ, for the Mayo CCU and Cath Lab Groups. Immediate angioplasty compared with the administration of a thrombolytic agent followed by conservative treatment for myocardial infarction. *N Engl J Med* 1993;328:685–691.

120. Rumberger JA, Behrenbeck T, Breen JR, Reed JE, Gersh BJ. Non-parallel changes in global left ventricular chamber volume and muscle mass during the first year following transmural myocardial infarction in man. *J Am Coll Cardiol* 1993;21:673–682.

121. Bell MR, Holmes DR, Berger PB, Garratt KN, Bailey KR, Gersh BJ. The changing in-hospital mortality of women undergoing balloon angioplasty. *JAMA* 1993;269:2091–2095.

122. Murphy JG, Gersh BJ, Mair DD, Fuster V, McGoon MD, Ilstrup DM, McGoon DC, Kirklin JW, Danielson GK. Long-term outcome of patients undergoing surgical repair of Tetralogy of Fallot. *N Engl J Med* 1993;329:593–599.

123. Gersh BJ, Anderson JL. Thrombolysis and myocardial salvage: results of clinical trials and the animal paradigm; paradoxic or predictable? *Circulation* 1993;88:296–306.

125. McAllister B, Christian T, Gersh BJ, Gibbons R. Prognosis of myocardial infarctions involving more than 40% of the left ventricle. *Circulation* 1993;88: 1470–1475.

126. Thompson R, Holmes DR, Gersh BJ, Bailey K. Predicting early and intermediate term outcome of coronary angioplasty in the elderly. *Circulation* 1993;88:1579–1587.

127. Clements IP, Christian T, Higaro S, Gibbons R, Gersh BJ. Residual flow to the infarct zone as a determinant of infarct size after angioplasty. *Circulation* 1993;88:1527–1533.

129. Christian TF, Gibbons RJ, Hopfensberger MR, Gersh BJ. Severity and response of chest pain during thrombolytic therapy for acute myocardial infarction: a useful indicator of myocardial salvage and infarct size. *J Am Coll Cardiol* 1993;22:1311–1316.

131. Redfield MM, Gersh BJ, Bailey KR, Ballard DJ, Rodeheffer RJ. Natural history of idiopathic dilated cardiomyopathy: effect of referral bias and secular trend. *J Am Coll Cardiol* 1993;22:1921–1926.

132. Reeder GS, Bailey KR, Gersh BJ, Holmes DR, Christianson J, Gibbons RJ. Cost comparison of immediate angioplasty versus thrombolysis followed by conservative therapy for acute myocardial infarction: a randomized prospective trial. *Mayo Clin Proc* 1994;69:5–12.

134. Eagle KA, Rihal CS, Foster ED, Mickel MC, Gersh BJ, for the Coronary Artery Surgery Study (CASS) Investigators. Long-term survival in patients with coronary artery disease: importance of peripheral vascular disease. *J Am Coll Cardiol* 1994;23:1091–1095.

135. Coughlin SS, Gottdiener JS, Baughman KL, Wassermann A. Marx ES, Tefft

MC, Gersh BJ. Black-white differences in mortality in idiopathic dilated cardiomyopathy: the Washington DC Dilated Cardiomyopathy Study. *J Nat Med Assoc* 1994;86:583–591.

139. Shen WK, Hammill SC, Hayes DL, Packer DL, Bailey KR, Ballard DJ, Gersh BJ. Long-term survival after pacemaker implantation for heart block in patients aged >65 years. *Am J Cardiol* 1994;74:560–564.

140. Redfield MM, Gersh BJ, Bailey KD, Rodeheffer RJ. Natural history of incidentally discovered, asymptomatic idiopathic dilated cardiomyopathy. *Am J Cardiol* 1994;74:737–739.

141. Farkouh ME, Rihal CS, Gersh BJ, Rooke TW, Hallett JW Jr., O'Fallon WM, Ballard D. Influence of coronary heart disease on morbidity and mortality after lower extremity revascularization surgery: a population-based study in Olmsted County, Minnesota (1970–1987). *J Am Coll Cardiol* 1994;24:1290–1296.

142. Morris JJ, Rastogi A, Stanton MS, Gersh BJ, Hammill SC, Hartzell HV. Operation for ventricular tachyarrhythmias: refining current treatment strategies. *Ann Thorac Surg* 1994;58:1490–1498.

143. Tung RK, Win-Kuang S, Hayes, DL, Hammill SC, Bailey KR, Gersh BJ. Long-term survival after permanent pacemaker implantation for sick sinus syndrome. *Am J Cardiol* 1994;74:1016–1020.

144. Rihal CS, Eagle KA, Mickel MS, Gersh BJ. Surgical therapy for coronary artery disease among patients with combined coronary artery and peripheral vascular disease. *Circulation* 1995;91:46–53.

145. Gersh BJ, Chesebro JH, Braunwald E, Kirklin JW, Lambrew C, Passamani E, Solomon RE, Ross AM, Ross R, Terrin ML, Knatterud GL, and the TIMI-II Investigators. Coronary artery bypass graft surgery after thrombolytic therapy in the thrombolysis in myocardial infarction trial, phase II (TIMI-II). *J Am Coll Cardiol* 1995;25:395–402.

146. Rihal, CS, Davis, KB, Kennedy, JW, Gersh BJ. The utility of clinical, electrocardiographic, and roentgenographic variables in the prediction of left ventricular function. *Am J Cardiol* 1995;75:220–223.

148. Smith SC, Blair SN, Criqui MH, Fletcher GF, Fuster V, Gersh BJ, et al. AHA Medical/Scientific Statement-Consensus Panel Statement. Preventing heart attack and death in patients with coronary disease. *Circulation* 1995;92:2–4; *J Am Coll Cardiol* 1995;26:292–294.

149. Bell MR, Grill DE, Garratt KN, Berger PB, Gersh BJ, Holmes DR. Long-term outcome of women compared to men following successful coronary angioplasty. *Circulation* 1995;2876–2881.

150. Bell MR, Berger PB, Holmes DR, Mullany CJ, Bailey KR, Gersh BJ. Referral for coronary artery revascularization procedures following diagnostic coronary angiography: evidence for gender-bias? *J Am Coll Cardiol* 1995;25: 1650–1655.

154. Miller TD, Gersh BJ, Christian TF, Bailey KR, Gibbons RJ. Limited prognostic value of thallium-201 exercise treadmill testing early after myocardial infarction in patients treated with thrombolysis. *Am Heart J* 1995;130:259–266.

156. Williams JF, Bristow MR, Fowler MB, Francis GS, Garson A, Gersh BJ, Hammer DF, Hlatky MA, Leier CV, Packer M et al. ACC/AHA report guidelines for the evaluation and management of heart failure. Report of The American College of Cardiology/American Heart Association Task Force on Practice Guidelines [Committee on Evaluation and Management of Heart Failure]. *J Am Coll Cardiol* 1995;26:1376–1398; *Circulation* 1995;92:2764–2784.

157. Lamas G, Flaker G, Mitchell G, Smith S, Gersh BJ, Chuan-Chuan W, Moye L, Rouleau JL, Rutherford JD, Pfeffer MA, Braunwald E, for the SAVE Investigators. Effect of infarct artery patency on prognosis after acute myocardial infarction. *Circulation* 1995;92:1101–1109.

158. Cannan CR, Reeder GS, Bailey KR, Melton LJ, Gersh BJ. The natural history of hypertrophic cardiomyopathy: a population based study 1976–1990. *Circulation* 1995;92:2488–2495.

160. Simari RD, Bell MR, Pao TC, Gersh BJ, Ritman EL. The acute effects of delayed reperfusion following myocardial infarction: a 3D x-ray imaging analysis. Physiology and function from multidimensional images. *Proc SPIE Med Imag* 1996;2709:383–393.

162. Shaw LJ, Eagle KA, Gersh BJ, Miller DD. Meta-analysis of intravenous dipyridamole- Thallium-201 imaging (1994–1995) and dobutamine echocardiography (1991–1994) for risk stratification before vascular surgery. *J Am Coll Cardiol* 1996;27:787–798.

163. Shen W-K, Hammill SC, Munger TM, Stanton MS, Packer DL, Osborn MJ, Wood DL, Bailey KR, Curachi Y, Lo PA, Gersh BJ. Adenosine: potential modulator for vasovagal syncope. *J Am Coll Cardiol* 1996;29:146–154.

164. Shen WK, Hayes DL, Hammill SC, Bailey KR, Ballard DJ, Gersh BJ. Survival and functional independence after implantation of a permanent pacemaker in octogenarians and nonagenarians. *Ann Int Med* 1996;125:476–480.

165. Lamas A, Mitchell G, Flaker G, Smith Jr. S, Gersh BJ, Moye L, Braunwald E, Pfeffer M. Clinical significance of mitral regurgitation after acute myocardial infarction. *Circulation* 1997;96:827–833.

167. Dries DL, Domanski MJ, Waclawiw MA, Gersh BJ. Antithrombolic therapy is associated with a reduced risk of sudden cardiac death in patients with ischemic heart disease. *Am J Cardiol* 1997;79:909–913.

168. Wyse DG, Anderson J, Antman E, Cooper E, DiMarco J, Epstein A, Gersh BJ, Jenkins L, Saksena S, Sherman D, et al. Atrial fibrillation follow-up investigation of rhythm management—The AFFIRM Study design. *Am J Cardiol* 1997;79:1198–1200.

169. Eagle KA, Rihal CS, Mickel MC, Holmes DR, Foster ED, Gersh BJ. Cardiac risk of noncardiac surgery: Influence of coronary disease and type of surgery in 3,368 operations. *Circulation* 1997;96:1882–1887.

170. Huber KC, Gersh BJ, Bailey KR, Schaff HV, Hodge DO, Cha RH, Chesebro JH. Variability in anticoagulation control predicts thromboembolism after mechanical valve replacement: a 23 year population-based study. *Mayo Clinic Proc* 1997;72: 1103–1110.

171. Kawalsky DL, Garratt KN, Hammill SC, Bailey K, Gersh BJ. The impact of infarct artery patency and late potentials on late morality after acute myocardial infarction. *Mayo Clinic Proc* 1997;72:16–21.

172. Castillo P, Palmer C, Halpren M, Hatziande UE, Gersh BJ. Cost effectiveness analysis of thrombolytic therapy in acute myocardial infarction: a decision analysis model. *Ann Pharmacother* 1997;31:296–303.

173. Solomon, AJ, Gersh BJ. Managment of chronic stable angina: medical therapy, percutaneous transluminal coronary angioplasty and coronary artery bypass surgery. *Ann Intern Med* 1998;128:216–223.

174. Eagle KA, Rihal CS, Mickel MC, Holmes DR, Foster ER, Gersh BJ. Cardiac risk of noncardiac surgery; influence of coronary disease and type of surgery in 3368 operations. CASS Investigators and Michigan Heart Care Program. Coronary Artery Surgery Study. *Circulation* 1997;96:1882–1887.

Reviews, Invited Articles, Editorials

33. Kapoor W, Hammill SC, Gersh BJ. Diagnosis and natural history of syncope and the role of invasive electrophysiologic testing. *Am J Cardiol* 1989;63:730–734.

36. Wilson WR, Gersh BJ. Infective endocarditis: experimental and clinical developments, antimicrobial therapy and management of complications. *Curr Opin Cardiol* 1989;4:423–427.

39. Gersh BJ, Califf R, Loop FD, Akins C, Pryor DB, Takaro T. Coronary bypass surgery in chronic stable angina. *Circulation* 1989;79:I-46–I-59.

40. Califf R, Topol E, Gersh BJ. From myocardial salvage to patient salvage in acute myocardial infarction: the role of reperfusion therapy. *J Am Coll Cardiol* 1989;14:1382–1388.

43. Lavie C, Gersh BJ. Acute myocardial infarction: initial manifestations, management, and prognosis. *Mayo Clinic Proc* 1990;65:531–548.

44. Lavie C, Gersh BJ. Reperfusion in acute myocardial infarction. *Mayo Clin Proc* 1990;65:549–564.

54. Gersh BJ, Rihal CS, Rooke TW, Ballard DJ. Evaluation and management of patients with both peripheral vascular and coronary artery disease. *J Am Coll Cardiol* 1991;18:203–214.

71. Gersh BJ. The changing late prognosis of acute myocardial infarction: implications and mechanisms. *Eur Heart J* 1995;16:50–53.

75. Klein GJ, Gersh BJ, Yee, R. Electrophysiological testing: the final court of appeal for diagnosis of syncope? *Circulation* 1995;92:1332–1335.

83. Morillo CA, Klein GJ, Gersh BJ. Can serial tilt testing be used to evaluate therapy in neurally medicated syncope? *Am J Cardiol* 1996;77:521–523.

84. Reeder G, Gersh BJ. Modern management of acute myocardial infarction. *Curr Probl Cardiol* 1996;21:585–668.

95. Gersh BJ. Pathophysiology and treatment of single-vessel coronary artery disease. *Am J Cardiol* 1997;80:21–91.

97. Solomon A, Gersh B. Open artery hypothesis. *Ann Rev Med* 1998:63–74.

PAUL A. GRAYBURN, MD, on Percutaneous Mitral Repair With the MitraClip™ Device: A Conversation With the Editor

Paul A. Grayburn, MD[a,b,]*, and William C. Roberts, MD[a,b,c]

Paul Grayburn did his general cardiology fellowship under the tutelage of Dr. Anthony N. DeMaria at the University of Kentucky from 1984 to 1986, followed by a year of interventional cardiology training with Dr. David C. Booth. In 1988, he was recruited to the University of Texas Southwestern Medical School by Dr. James T. Willerson, where he served on the faculty for 15 years. During that time, he was director of the echocardiography laboratories at the University of Texas Southwestern and chief of cardiology at the Dallas Veterans Affairs Medical Center, where he also practiced interventional cardiology. In 2002, Dr. Grayburn moved to Baylor University Medical Center to accept the Paul J. Thomas Chair in Cardiology Research and Education. He has published more than 260 articles, mainly in peer-reviewed medical journals. He has served as an associate editor of *The American Journal of Cardiology* since 1997. He is on the editorial boards of *Circulation*, the *Journal of the American College of Cardiology: Cardiovascular Imaging*, and *Heart*. Dr. Grayburn currently serves on the Publications Committee for the Endovascular Edge-to-Edge Repair Study (EVEREST) II and the Core Lab Committee and Steering Committee of the Surgical Treatment for Ischemic Heart Failure (STICH) trial. He has held a National Institutes of Health K24 grant for mentoring junior faculty members and an R01 grant, "Functional Mitral Regurgitation in Ischemic Cardiomyopathy," for 3-dimensional transesophageal echocardiographic evaluation of the mechanisms of functional mitral regurgitation (MR) in the STICH trial. He has served on multiple committees for the American Society of Echocardiography, including the Task Force for Quantitation of Valvular Regurgitation. He is currently the principal investigator for the MitraClip (Abbott Laboratories, Abbott Park, Illinois) studies at Baylor Health Care System and co-investigator for the Cardiothoracic Surgery Network Trials on MR. Dr. Grayburn's background in interventional cardiology and echocardiography, including intraoperative transesophageal echocardiography during surgical mitral valve repair, give him a unique insight into percutaneous mitral valve therapies.

William Clifford Roberts, MD (hereafter Roberts): *Dr. Grayburn, I appreciate your coming to my house for our discussion. It is March 24, 2011. You have been involved with percutaneous mitral valve repair for a number of years?*

Paul A. Grayburn, MD (hereafter Grayburn): Yes, since 2002.

Roberts: *Let's go back to the surgeon, Ottavio Alfieri. He was the one who initiated attaching the margins of both anterior and posterior leaflets together in the center of the orifice to reduce the degree of MR operatively. When did that start?*

Grayburn: He first reported what is now known as the Alfieri operation in 1995.[1]

Roberts: *Paul, how did that procedure work out? He did quite a few cases himself, and a few other surgeons did a few cases but then they all quit doing them. Are long-term results available on that operative procedure?*

Grayburn: The Alfieri repair technique is performed infrequently. It is occasionally used as a last-ditch attempt to salvage a mitral valve repair and avoid mitral valve replacement for degenerative MR. For repair of functional MR, particularly in ischemic cardiomyopathy, it's usually not used, even though that is the group of patients for which Alfieri originally developed the technique. Alfieri's more recent data suggest that the suture technique works best if an annuloplasty ring is also inserted. Most of us are disappointed with the results of mitral valve repair of functional MR due to a dilated left ventricle regardless of technique.

Roberts: *When you say "functional MR," you mean that the mitral valve leaflets and chordae are anatomically normal.*

Grayburn: Exactly. Functional MR is thought to be a disease of the left ventricle.

Roberts: *For the Alfieri procedure to work, not only does the figure-8 suture have to be utilized, but a mitral ring must be utilized as well. That was his conclusion?*

Grayburn: Yes. Functional MR may be more complex. For example, not all patients with "functional" MR have a dilated annulus. In such patients, the Alfieri stitch might work well as a primary repair technique. Other patients have tenting of the leaflets towards the apex as the papillary muscles are pulled outward. Others have phenomenal discoordination of the ventricular septum and lateral wall, which may respond to a biventricular pacemaker. Some patients have combinations of these pathologies. Every patient with "functional" MR is a little bit different.

Roberts: *When you say pulling of a mitral leaflet by the papillary muscles, that's toward the apex such that the orifice is prevented from closing during ventricular systole because the ventricle has dilated both longitudinally and laterally?*

Grayburn: Correct. That is known as the Carpentier class 3B mechanism for MR: restriction of leaflet closure.

Roberts: *The percutaneous procedure for repairing or diminishing the quantity of MR started when and where?*

[a]Baylor Heart and Vascular Institute and Departments of [b]Internal Medicine (Cardiology) and [c]Pathology, Baylor University Medical Center, Dallas, Texas. Manuscript received April 13, 2011; revised manuscript received and accepted April 13, 2011.

*Corresponding author: Tel: 214-820-7500; fax: 214-820-7533.

E-mail address: paulgr@baylorhealth.edu (P.A. Grayburn).

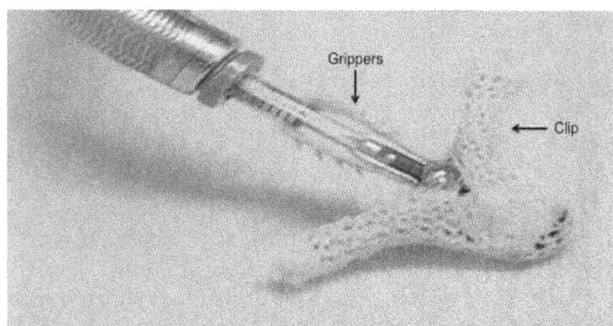

Figure 1. Close-up view of the MitraClip device. The cloth-covered clip is seen along with the grippers, which in this view are raised. After the leaflets are seen to insert into the clip, the grippers are released, pinching the leaflets between the clip and the grippers. Careful transesophageal echocardiographic guidance is required to visualize complete insertion of both leaflets.

Grayburn: I first got involved with it in November 2002, when I met with Jan Komtebedde, a veterinarian working for a company called Evalve, Inc. Evalve came up with a design for a metallic clip that could be placed percutaneously, pinning the anterior and posterior mitral leaflets together in the same manner as an Alfieri suture. Evalve developed the technique, and the device known as the MitraClip. The company recently has been purchased by Abbott Vascular.

Roberts: *What does the device look like? Can you describe it?*

Grayburn: The clip itself is made of cobalt chromium, and it has a polyester covering on it (Figure 1). It is delivered through a 24-inch sheath that tapers to 22Fr at the tip. It is inserted through a femoral vein and then advanced across the atrial septum. It has a steerable guide that allows one to orient the clip properly toward the mitral valve once the sheath is placed and the dilator removed. The clip is operated by a mechanism that sits outside the body.

Roberts: *That's after entering through the atrial septum?*

Grayburn: Correct. The whole procedure has to be guided by transesophageal echo (TEE). The procedure involves a complex interplay between a skilled interventionalist and a skilled echocardiographer to identify the anatomy properly and to place the clip in the proper position.

Roberts: *You started doing these at Baylor University Medical Center (BUMC) when?*

Grayburn: We did our first patient in 2006.

Roberts: *How many have you done subsequently at BUMC?*

Grayburn: We have now done 24 patients. We do them at both of the Baylor heart hospitals: downtown and at Plano.

Roberts: *Has it been difficult to recruit these patients?*

Grayburn: Yes and no. We get many referrals for the procedure. Of our last 112 patients referred for TEE to see if they are candidates for the clip, only 17 patients were eligible and received a clip. Many patients referred are excluded from the percutaneous procedure because their anatomy is not suitable for clip placement or they don't have enough MR to require a clip.

Roberts: *What are criteria presently for doing this percutaneous procedure?*

Grayburn: A typical patient with mitral valve prolapse would require that the MR jet be at the A2-P2 interface, basically in the center of the mitral coaptation line.

Roberts: *How many scallops are there in a normal mitral valve?*

Grayburn: There are 3 scallops in the posterior leaflet. The anterior leaflet does not have any. In addition to requiring that the middle scallop of the posterior leaflet or the corresponding segment of the anterior leaflet be involved, the width of the flail segment cannot be >1.5 cm, and the difference between the *flail gap*, which is how far apart the leaflets are, cannot be >1.0 cm.

Roberts: *The length of the leaflet is the distance from its attachment to the mitral annulus to the free margin?*

Grayburn: If a segment is flail, that flail segment cannot be >1.5 cm wide, or the clip would not be able to restore the integrity of the valve. We look for a narrow flail segment.

Roberts: *Are you looking at the length from the attachment of that leaflet to its free margin? You are not looking at the width of that leaflet according to its attachment to the mitral annulus?*

Grayburn: We look at both. The term *flail width* is the width of the segment along the commissure line from commissure to commissure.

Roberts: *That would correspond to the annular width.*

Grayburn: The other measurement is the distance from the free edge of the anterior leaflet to the free edge of the posterior leaflet. If it is too far apart, both leaflets cannot be grabbed by the clip.

Roberts: *The distance apart or gap has to be <1.1 cm.*

Grayburn: Yes.

Roberts: *That is in ventricular systole?*

Grayburn: Correct.

Roberts: *What is it normally in ventricular diastole?*

Grayburn: In ventricular diastole, when the leaflets are fully opened, it could easily be 3 to 4 cm. But that distance is not relevant, because the clip is deployed in ventricular systole, when the leaflets are close together.

Roberts: *How many patients have had this percutaneous procedure so far worldwide?*

Grayburn: At the present time, >3,000 procedures have been done worldwide. The clip is approved in Europe, so it is much easier to get the clip there, and it is being done a lot more commonly in Germany and Italy and other places in Europe than in the USA, where its use is still restricted by the FDA (US Food and Drug Administration). In the USA, the clip can only be used as part of a continuing-access registry or compassionate-use protocol.

Roberts: *What do you mean by "compassionate-use" protocol for this percutaneous procedure?*

Grayburn: After the randomized trial was completed, the FDA allowed a continuing-access registry that goes under the name REALISM (Real World Expanded Multicenter Study of the MitraClip System). The FDA allows 20 patients per month to be done in the USA. This is a common practice of the FDA. Their point is to allow investigators who have acquired skill in doing this procedure to maintain those skills until such time as the device can be approved.

Roberts: *That's 240 procedures for the year in the entire USA?*

Grayburn: Yes. More recently, the FDA has come out with a compassionate-use protocol so that certain patients who either are nonsurgical candidates or require an urgent or emergent use or just a use under a compassionate-care protocol are allowed. It's difficult to get that done, because it requires a series of letters and approvals from the company and the FDA. Nevertheless, those patients can also be done at the present time.

Roberts: *What patient with pure MR would you not consider for this procedure?*

Grayburn: The results of the EVEREST II trial have just been published.[2] This trial randomized patients with significant MR (3 to 4+) to the clip versus to surgery. Surgical repair was more effective at relieving MR, but the clip was safer than surgery. Surgery was more likely to end up with either no MR or only mild MR, whereas the clip more likely ended up with mild or moderate (1 to 2+ MR) (Figure 2). The major safety difference was that there was a marked reduction in need for blood transfusion with the clip as compared to surgery. The trade-off is that surgery provides a better chance of complete elimination of the MR, particularly in patients with mitral valve prolapse, but obviously surgery is more invasive and less safe. Certain patients definitely should go to surgery. Those would include patients who have need for other valve surgery, or they need coronary bypass surgery or a maze operation for concomitant atrial fibrillation. For a young patient with posterior leaflet prolapse, the surgical results are both excellent and durable. Our first patient with the clip is doing well 5 years later. There are a couple of patients followed 8 years after the clip insertion. The long-term durability of the clip, however, has not been proved yet. Patients at high risk for surgery might be perfect candidates for the clip because of its much less invasive nature.

Roberts: *Any degree of mitral stenosis would be a contraindication to percutaneous clip implantation?*

Grayburn: Correct.

Roberts: *One thing that Dr. Robert Bonow has stressed is that the average US cardiac surgeon, when a patient is sent for a mitral valve repair, has a greater chance of leaving the operating room with a mechanical prosthesis or bioprosthesis than a repair. The average cardiac surgeon is probably not very good at mitral valve repair for pure MR.*

Grayburn: The STS (Society of Thoracic Surgeons) database, upon which those data are derived, does not allow discrimination of the mechanism of the MR. Of course, some mitral valve replacements are necessary because of an unsuitable valve for repair. For example, it could have been a prior repair that failed and now a replacement is required, and the valve could not and should not have been repaired. However, I agree that most US cardiac surgeons have a low volume of mitral valve repairs and probably are not experts at doing that operation.

Roberts: *I understand that the average US surgeon does only about 10 valve operations a year. In EVEREST II, comparing mitral repair operatively to the percutaneous mitral clip, the surgeons involved have done a good number of mitral repairs.*

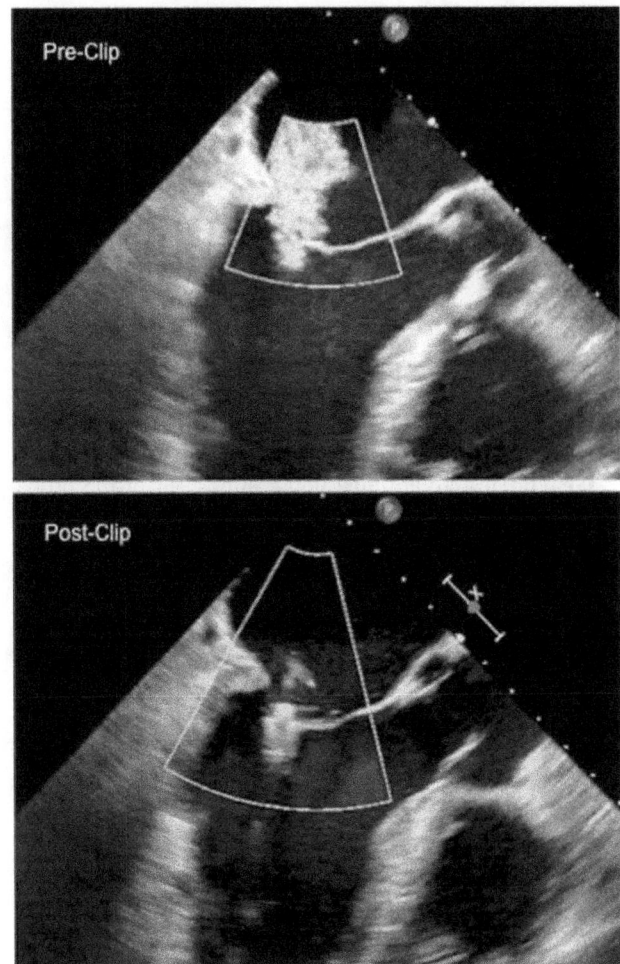

Figure 2. *(Top)* Transesophageal echocardiographic long-axis view showing a large color flow jet and proximal flow convergence before MitraClip placement. Transesophageal echocardiography was performed in the catheterization laboratory during the procedure. *(Bottom)* Same view immediately after MitraClip deployment. MR has been reduced to mild. The proximal flow convergence region has been abolished.

Grayburn: That's true. The quality of surgeons at the EVEREST II sites was very good, and they were selected specifically for having good operative results from mitral valve repair operations.

Roberts: *How many sites were involved in EVEREST II?*

Grayburn: There were 38 sites in the USA, although not all sites were particularly active.

Roberts: *How many patients will be in the EVEREST II analysis?*

Grayburn: The study was enrolled 279 patients: 184 randomized to the MitraClip and 95 to surgery. However, only 80 of the 95 patients randomized to surgery actually underwent surgery. Some patients randomized to surgery decided not to have it.

Roberts: *Did they have the clip instead?*

Grayburn: No, because they were randomized to surgery, they were supposed to have surgery, but something happened. Typically, they changed their minds.

Roberts: *What about the patients randomized to the clip? Did any of them prove to be unsuitable for the clip?*

Grayburn: Yes. Six patients randomized for the clip changed their minds.

Roberts: *All of the patients in EVEREST II could have had either procedure?*

Grayburn: Correct.

Roberts: The publication that appeared in *JACC* (*Journal of the American College of Cardiology*) on August 18, 2009, was an analysis of those patients who had the clip. There was no randomization in that study?

Grayburn: Yes. That was the EVEREST I study, which evaluated the safety and feasibility of the clip.[3]

Roberts: *The percutaneous clip procedure, I gather, is quite a long one, maybe 4 hours or so early on, about the same amount of time that the operative figure-of-8 edge-to-edge procedure takes. What is your experience at BUMC? How long does this percutaneous clip procedure take to do?*

Grayburn: We are now doing almost all of the procedures in <2 hours. Both EVEREST I and EVEREST II trials were done while the investigators were on their learning curve of the clip. We've gotten better in several ways: (1) we are better at identifying who can and who cannot have a successful result with the clip, and (2) we are faster and more proficient at placing the clip.

Roberts: *These studies are before you go to the operating room?*

Grayburn: Yes. The preoperative study is to determine whether a clip is a good idea or not. That's a part of the learning curve. There is another learning curve in the actual procedure. One thing we've learned is the actual site of the transseptal puncture is critical to being able to quickly and effectively deploy the clip. The atrial septum has to be punctured more posteriorly and superiorly than we normally do to give room to come down with the device in a coaxial manner on top of the mitral leaflets. Now, we spend a lot more time making sure we do the transseptal puncture correctly.

Roberts: *If you have a circular foramen ovale membrane, you don't try to hit it in the center or the top but as close to the bottom of that membrane as you can.*

Grayburn: Right, we want to stay as far posterior as we can to stay away from the aorta and superior to the mitral leaflets. We've recently done 3 cases with a device time of <60 minutes. That's not skin-to-skin but the time once the mitral valve clip is ready to be applied after the transseptal puncture. If the transseptal puncture is in the correct site the clip can be attached in both leaflets fairly quickly.

Roberts: *You use the TEE during the procedure?*

Grayburn: Yes.

Roberts: *One person manipulates the echocardiogram, and the other person puts in the device. Can you go through the procedure step by step?*

Grayburn: Sure. The patient is intubated in the lab by an anesthesiologist. The TEE probe is placed, and the mitral valve is again evaluated. Then the interventionalist puts in a venous sheath in a femoral vein. Early on, a full left-sided heart catheterization was done: ventriculogram and left atrial and left ventricular pressure measurements. Now few labs do a full left-heart catheterization. The first step is the transseptal puncture using a Brockenbrough needle under TEE guidance to make sure the location of the puncture is both superior and posterior. Then, a guidewire is placed in the left upper pulmonary vein and the transseptal system is removed. Then, the femoral vein is dilated to accommodate the large sheath. The MitraClip sheath system is then put in and advanced into the left atrium.

Roberts: *How wide is the mitral clip system?*

Grayburn: It is a 24Fr system which is 8 mm in diameter. The engineers will eventually, I suspect, make these instruments smaller. Once the sheath is placed, then the clip system is introduced into the sheath, being very careful to avoid any air bubbles.

Roberts: *The sheath is about 8 mm in width?*

Grayburn: Yes. The clip of course is smaller than 8 mm, so that it can go through the sheath. The guidewire is removed, and then the clip is introduced and advanced so that it is extending completely out of the sheath. This is done under TEE guidance to be sure that the tip of the clip is free in the left atrial cavity and not up against the wall, which could perforate. Once that clip is out of the sheath, we steer it down toward the mitral orifice. Medial-lateral and anterior-posterior steering is done to position the clip in the exact location of the MR jet. The clip is then opened, and its position is again checked to make sure it's where it should be. We also make sure that the clip is oriented perpendicular to the coaptation line. Then the clip is advanced into the left ventricular cavity, simultaneously checking to make sure the clip has not rotated. If a clip is placed, for example, at a 45° angle to the closure line, the MR might actually be worsened. Thus, great care is taken during this time to make sure the alignment of the clip and position of the clip relative to the MR jet is perfect. Then the clip is pulled back under TEE guidance. We want the anterior and posterior mitral leaflets to drop down into the center of the clip, and then little grippers are lowered to pin those leaflets together. Then, the clip is tightened and closed so the leaflets are coapted. Again, we check carefully under TEE guidance that the leaflets are inserted completely down into the clip and that the grippers are on top of them so we have good grasping. The grippers almost look like Velcro where they come down from above and pin the leaflets between the clip and the gripper (Figure 1). Then, the clip is closed and MR is evaluated to make sure it has been reduced.

Roberts: *How long are the clips from the end of the device? The ones that actually stay on the mitral leaflet.*

Grayburn: The clip has 2 sides, posterior and anterior, and each side is about 1 cm long.

Roberts: *You insert 1 clip per patient?*

Grayburn: A second clip can be inserted if needed. If significant MR remains on either side of the clip, then a second clip can be inserted adjacent to the first clip.

Roberts: *You indicated that the clip is placed where the jet is. The jet, however, might be eccentric in the orifice. How do you handle the eccentric jet? You don't always put these clips in the center of the mitral orifice?*

Grayburn: The device was designed initially to mimic the Alfieri stitch, which goes in the center of the mitral orifice. Nevertheless, a small triangular flail segment on the side one can be grasped with the clip. The idea is to put the clip wherever it needs to go. Again, this is carried out under TEE guidance so that one can put the clip right on top of the MR jet and hopefully eliminate it. If there is still a residual jet either medial or lateral to that first clip, a second clip can be inserted.

Roberts: *The central portion of the anterior mitral leaflet is devoid of chordae. Thus, a clip placed in the central portion of the anterior leaflet does not interfere with chordae, and it is usually a bit thicker than the posterior leaflet. A flail posterior leaflet which protrudes toward left atrium during ventricular systole is usually thicker than it ought to be. Probably, the thicker it is the easier it is to handle?*

Grayburn: Not necessarily. One potential contraindication to placing the clip would be markedly thickened leaflets, those too thick to fit into the clip. Markedly thickened or calcified mitral leaflets would be a contraindication to this procedure.

Roberts: *How thick can the combination of both anterior and posterior leaflets be to be inserted into the clip?*

Grayburn: We haven't specifically looked at that or developed specific criteria for that. If we think the leaflets are graspable and will sit down into the clip, well, that's it.

Roberts: *If a hospital or medical institution has physicians, such as yourself, that do these procedures, you attract more patients with pure MR probably than you would otherwise?*

Grayburn: Yes, that's true. We have had a number of patients referred for the clip who ended up having a mitral valve repair because we determined that that procedure was preferable in them to the clip. These patients may not have come to BUMC for an operative mitral repair had we not had the availability of the clip.

Roberts: *That same scenario is probably happening with the percutaneous aortic valve implantation without replacement.*

Grayburn: I think it is.

Roberts: *After you get the clip in place, are you always pleased? Sometimes do you wish that it had been placed a little further to the right or to the left? How often are you pleased with your performance?*

Grayburn: There have in fact been times on initial deployment that we have decided that we missed the jet origin either medially or laterally. One beauty of the clip system is that the clip can be released, repositioned, and redeployed. We have done that on several occasions. We have not had a failure at BUMC yet. All of our clips have reduced MR to 2+ or less. We have not had a clip detach or a clip embolize. There have been a handful of clips that have detached from 1 leaflet and subsequently not redeployed. These few patients have gone to surgery. One concern early on was that if a clip was unsuccessful, would surgical repair then be precluded? Argenziano and colleagues[4] demonstrated that mitral valves containing failed clips could still be repairable.

Roberts: *Of the mitral clip procedures done at BUMC, there have been no failures? You have not had to send any patient to surgery on an emergency basis or within a few weeks after the percutaneous procedure? You've done 24 cases at BUMC?*

Grayburn: Correct.

Roberts: *How many percutaneous mitral clip procedures do you have to do to "fulfill" the learning curve?*

Grayburn: We are just now examining that question. The learning curve varies according to the skill of the operator. By the time we had done 10 cases, we were quite confident that we knew what to do. But the learning curve involves more than 1 thing. First, it involves selecting the right patient. Second, it involves procedural details. We learned early that the site of the transseptal puncture is crucial.

Roberts: *The number 1 reason for not putting a percutaneous clip in a patient with pure MR, assuming that there is no dysfunction of the aortic valve or need for simultaneous coronary bypass grafting, is what?*

Grayburn: It's not having enough MR. Nearly 50% of the patients referred to me for evaluation do not have severe MR. Their echocardiogram was misinterpreted. They often did not have the quantitative measures that are recommended by the American Society of Echocardiography.[5] One difficulty with this whole area is that we are not as good as we think we are at grading the severity of MR echocardiographically.[6] Further quantitating the degree of MR once a clip is in place is even more difficult. When turning on a water hose, a steady flow comes out. If you then put your thumb over the nozzle of that water hose, it results in a massive spray. Once the clip is placed, a spraylike jet results, and it looks a lot worse on color Doppler than it looks on angiography. It looks a lot worse than it probably is. We have some difficulty grading the degree of MR after the clip is placed.

Roberts: *That's in the operating room?*

Grayburn: Both the operating room and subsequently.

Roberts: *Subsequently, by transthoracic or transesophageal echocardiography?*

Grayburn: Either one. The first patient that we did 5 years ago was a 46-year-old man on disability. He was unable to work. After we did the clip procedure in him, he got a job as a truck driver, and he still has it today. He's active and very happy. The core lab graded his MR as moderate (2+) after the clip. I was convinced that his MR was less than that because of how well he's done and because the left ventricular angiogram after clip placement showed no MR at all. Recently, I did a magnetic resonance imaging (MRI) study on him, and his regurgitant volume was 6 ml. In other words, his forward stroke volume and his total left ventricular stroke volume were essentially the same, confirming again that he did not have significant MR at all, even though the color Doppler jet looked as if he had significant MR. This is clearly a spray effect, analogous to putting your thumb over a water hose and creating a huge spray.

Roberts: *Should you do an MRI on every one of these patients postoperatively?*

Grayburn: I don't know that that's what we need to do, but I think we need to work hard at finding better ways of grading and quantifying MR after the clip and even before the clip.

Roberts: *You are one of the world's authorities on echocardiography. If you have difficulty reading the degree of MR in these patients after insertion of the clip, the elsewhere general echocardiographer must have a terrible time making a proper evaluation?*

Grayburn: There are some quantitative measures of MR that are supposed to be done and have been recommended by the American Society of Echocardiography,[5] but unfortunately, these measurements are not done routinely in many labs. I often see outside echocardiograms in which the color flow is turned on but none of the quantitative measurements have been done or even attempted. I think the quality of echocardiography that is done in a high-volume center that focuses on mitral valve disease and other valve disease is quite a bit different than what is done in the community. I strongly believe that we need to have centers of excellence in valvular heart disease where patients can come and know that they are going to be evaluated by very good clinicians with state-of-the-art echocardiography and MRI, if needed, with state-of-the-art surgeons who are experts in mitral valve repair. This is a team-interactive approach to determine what's best for the patients.

Roberts: *This procedure looks pretty reasonable to me, an outsider. On the other hand, the percutaneous aortic valve procedure for patients with aortic stenosis does not look nearly as reasonable to me. All patients you have done have 3+ or 4+ MR. Do you do this procedure on some asymptomatic patients?*

Grayburn: Yes.

Roberts: *What are criteria for the asymptomatic ones versus the symptomatic ones?*

Grayburn: There is debate here. There are no randomized control trials, but there are some studies from the Mayo Clinic, in particular, that suggest that patients with flail mitral leaflets have a poor prognosis even if they are asymptomatic, and, therefore, they should be operated.[7,8]

Roberts: *When you say "flail," that's just 1 portion of either posterior or anterior leaflet that is prolapsing into or toward left atrium during ventricular systole?*

Grayburn: With flail, there is loss of coaptation, and usually a torn chord is visible. These patients tend to have a worse prognosis than patients with MR but no flail leaflet. Some investigators believe that if a leaflet is flail in an asymptomatic patient, that should warrant operative repair. The guidelines also recommend that an asymptomatic patient with pure MR should be considered for surgery if there is evidence that the left ventricle is dilating or that the left ventricular ejection fraction has fallen below 60%. Also, the presence of pulmonary hypertension or atrial fibrillation might make operation more advisable in an asymptomatic patient.

Roberts: *New-onset atrial fibrillation or long-term?*

Grayburn: New-onset in particular.

Roberts: *And how much pulmonary hypertension?*

Grayburn: A right-sided heart catheterization would be recommended to measure pulmonary vascular resistance and left atrial pressure to determine how much of the pulmonary hypertension is from the MR.

Roberts: *In general, a pulmonary arterial systolic pressure >50 mm Hg would concern you?*

Grayburn: Yes.

Roberts: *How much does a mitral clip device cost? When the FDA approves this device, presuming that's going to happen, what is the speculation regarding cost?*

Grayburn: The current price that we pay for the clip is $18,000. That's a "clip package." It is the same cost if we put in 1 or 2 clips.

Roberts: *Is the company that presently is producing these devices going to have competition? Are there other companies trying to develop a similar device?*

Grayburn: There are a number of companies developing different techniques for repairing the mitral valve percutaneously. The devices vary from annuloplasty-type procedures to procedures that address the leaflets or the chords. Some companies have developed artificial chords that can be put in percutaneously for ruptured chordae. A number of companies have developed devices designed to shrink the mitral annulus. Most were developed as coronary sinus devices. I doubt that these devices are going to succeed, because of anatomical considerations. One computed tomographic study showed in almost 2/3 of patients that the coronary sinus overlapped a portion of the left circumflex coronary artery, so there is a risk of tying off or occluding this major artery with a coronary sinus cinching device. Other studies have shown that the coronary sinus is a centimeter or 2 cephalad to the mitral annulus, a distance too far away to shrink the annulus. Guided Delivery Systems (Santa Clara, California) has a device that goes into the left ventricle and attempts to cinch the mitral annulus from below. Other devices being developed try to pull the papillary muscles together and reposition them, because functional MR is a disease of left ventricular dilation. If the left ventricular cavity can be reduced in size, the amount of MR can be reduced.

Roberts: *I understand that the surgeon who started the edge-to-edge operation for pure MR said "that it worked only when you put a mitral ring in also." You are not putting a mitral ring in the patients in whom you are doing the percutaneous procedure. If you have a patient with chronic pure MR and a large annulus, that patient is not a candidate for the present percutaneous clip?*

Grayburn: That is generally correct. In the EVEREST I and EVEREST II trials, patients were excluded if they had a markedly dilated left ventricular cavity. The criterion was a left ventricular cavity diameter in peak systole >5.5 cm. Patients with these massively dilated ventricles and huge mitral annulae would not have been eligible for the MitraClip in those studies. I hear from my colleagues in Europe that they are using the MitraClip procedure in patients with markedly dilated left ventricles from ischemic cardiomyopathy.

Roberts: *That's functional MR?*

Grayburn: Yes. I was surprised, but I understand that they are achieving early success in these type patients. Surgery for functional MR utilizing an annuloplasty ring appears early to reduce the degree of MR, but later the MR worsens again. It is important to look at the specific mitral anatomy of each patient and determine what is best in each of them. In functional MR with a dilated left ventricle, sometimes just medical therapy reduces ventricular cavity size and decreases the amount of MR. Cardiac resynchronization therapy also may reduce the degree of MR. Functional MR appears not to be 1 disease but has several mechanisms, including annular dilatation, which may be either symmetrically dilated or asymmetrically dilated. Is there myocardial viability? Should the patient be revascularized? Is there a left bundle branch block? Should the patient get cardiac resynchronization therapy? Is this primarily tenting, and if so, would chordal cutting decrease the MR? Cutting the basal chordae may help relieve tenting and lessen the amount of MR. We must individualize each patient.

Roberts: *About 30 years ago, I was involved in a necropsy study in which we measured the circumference of mitral annulus as well as that of other valve annulae. The normal mitral annulus in adults is about 9 cm in circumference. In persons with ischemic cardiomyopathy or idiopathic dilated cardiomyopathy, the annulus is dilated but usually not more than about 2 cm. Thus, from 9 to 11 cm, about a 20% increase. In patients with mitral valve prolapse, in contrast, the mitral annulus circumference may increase to as much as 19 cm. In actuality, the only cases with huge annulae I have seen at autopsy are patients with mitral valve prolapse, particularly when associated with the Marfan syndrome. Have you encountered arrhythmias or conduction disturbances or atrial septal defect as consequences of this procedure? What complications have occurred?*

Grayburn: The complications that have occurred would be partial clip detachment, where the clip comes off 1 leaflet. So far, the clip has been detached from only 1 leaflet. If it becomes detached from both leaflets, embolism, of course, could be the consequence. At this point, I am aware of 37 patients who have undergone mitral surgery following percutaneous clip insertion, but not all of those cases were clip detachment; most were failures to completely relieve the MR. In 17 patients, the clip was not even deployed because of failure to reduce MR severity.

Roberts: *Or you didn't get the clip attached?*

Grayburn: If one does not get the clip attached, it can be removed. If the clip cannot be attached or if it does not relieve the MR, the clip can be removed completely and surgery performed. Another complication is return of the MR after the clip has been inserted. Surgery then would be necessary. There are obvious vascular complications that might occur with any catheterization procedure, including a groin hematoma or bleeding. The most feared complication is perforation of the heart with the clip hardware causing acute tamponade. Fortunately, that is rare.

Roberts: *That was mainly left atrial wall?*

Grayburn: Yes, mainly left atrial perforation either by the wire, which is a very stiff wire, or by the clip itself as it's coming out of the sheath. These patients are prone to atrial fibrillation anyway because of their mitral valve disease, but as far as I can tell, there is no increased frequency of atrial fibrillation or other arrhythmias from use of the clip.

Roberts: *And no conduction disturbances?*

Grayburn: Correct. The device does not go anywhere near the conduction system.

Roberts: *What if the patient has mitral annular calcium? Do you stay away from that? How do you handle those patients?*

Grayburn: On TEE, we determine the severity of mitral annular calcium and also subvalvular calcium at the tips of the papillary muscles or on the chordae. Excessive mitral annular calcium may prevent us from successfully deploying a clip.

Roberts: *How old are most of your patients?*

Grayburn: At BUMC, our patients have ranged from 30 to 91 years (mean 60).

Roberts: *Postoperatively or postprocedure, what drugs do you give these patients? How long are they in the hospital?*

Grayburn: If the procedure goes well without any complications, they go home the following day. All but 1 of our patients at BUMC has gone home the following day. That 1 patient had a groin hematoma and required transfusions and stayed 3 days in the hospital. Typically the patient arrives in the morning, gets the procedure done, and goes home the following morning.

Roberts: *Are they on heparin during the procedure?*

Grayburn: Yes. Once the transseptal puncture is done, heparin is started, and the activated clotting time is measured. We try to keep it above 250. Then we put them on aspirin and clopidogrel for 3 months postprocedure.

Roberts: *Have there been any emboli, not of the device, but an event interpreted as embolus in any of the patients late postop?*

Grayburn: Remember that these patients are also at risk for atrial fibrillation, so if someone were to have an embolic event, one would have to try to differentiate whether this was due to atrial fibrillation and a clot or whether it was related to the clip. It's pretty clear to me that it's not the clip. There has not been any description of a thrombus attached to the clip. The clip is very quickly covered by fibrous tissue, and in the cases that have gone to surgery after a clip, there is a very dense tissue fibrous grown over the clip. The clips appear to be nonthrombogenic.

Roberts: *Is there worry about too many interventionalists getting involved with this procedure when and if it is approved by the FDA?*

Grayburn: I think 1 of the key items that is going to be necessary to get FDA approval is to have a plan in place to limit this procedures to centers of excellence. Evalve does have such a plan in place.

Roberts: *Evalve is a company?*

Grayburn: Yes. This is going to be something very carefully watched. I think all companies involved in percutaneous valvular disease are quite aware of this problem. These devices must be restricted to hospitals that have high volume, expertise in all of the areas involved, including imaging, clinical cardiology, intervention, and surgery. If all interventionalists started doing this complicated procedure, the complication rate would be higher.

Roberts: *How many centers of excellence do we need in the USA for valvular heart disease?*

Grayburn: In my opinion, 50 would probably be sufficient. There needs to be some geographic diversity, but 50 centers of excellence with top-flight surgeons, top-flight cardiology teams should be sufficient.

Roberts: *Essentially 1 per state?*

Grayburn: More populous states will need more. The number may need to be 100.

Roberts: *How do you follow these patients after this procedure?*

Grayburn: The study protocol requires that they get an echocardiogram 1 day after the procedure.

Roberts: *That's transthoracic?*

Grayburn: Yes. Then another one at 1 month, and then we follow them every 6 months after that by echocardiography and clinical examination.

Roberts: *What is the latest follow-up so far?*

Grayburn: Eight years. There are a handful of patients now that have had the clip for 5 to 8 years.

Roberts: *Have any cardiovascular surgeons had a clip put in?*

Grayburn: Not that I am aware of, or rather none that will admit to it.

Roberts: *Paul, I think this has been very good. Is there anything else you'd like to discuss?*

Grayburn: No, I think it's been a wonderful time, and I appreciate the opportunity to speak with you.

Roberts: *Thank you!*

1. Fucci C, Sandrelli L, Pardini A, Torracca L, Ferrari M, Alfieri O. Improved results with mitral valve repair using new surgical techniques. *Eur J Cardiothorac Surg* 1995;9:621–626.

2. Feldman T, Foster E, Glower DG, Kar S, Rinaldi MJ, Fail PS, Smalling RW, Siegel R, Rose GA, Engeron E, Loghin C, Trento A, Skipper ER, Fudge T, Letsou GV, Massaro JM, Mauri L; the EVEREST II Investigators. Percutaneous repair or surgery for mitral regurgitation. *N Engl J Med* 2011;364:1395–1406.

3. Feldman T, Kar S, Rinaldi M, Fail P, Hermiller J, Smalling R, Whitlow PL, Gray W, Low R, Herrmann HC, Lim S, Foster E, Glower D; EVEREST Investigators. Percutaneous mitral repair with the MitraClip system: safety and midterm durability in the initial EVEREST (Endovascular Valve Edge-to-Edge Repair Study) cohort. *J Am Coll Cardiol* 2009;54:686–694.

4. Argenziano M, Skipper E, Heimansohn D, Letsou GV, Woo YJ, Kron I, Alexander J, Cleveland J, Kong B, Davidson M, Vassiliades T, Krieger K, Sako E, Tibi P, Galloway A, Foster E, Feldman T, Glower D; EVEREST Investigators. Surgical revision after percutaneous mitral repair with the MitraClip device. *Ann Thorac Surg* 2010;89:72–80.

5. Zoghbi WA, Enriquez-Sarano M, Foster E, Grayburn PA, Kraft CD, Levine RA, Nihoyannopoulos P, Otto CM, Quinones MA, Rakowski H, Stewart WJ, Waggoner A, Weissman NJ. Recommendations for evaluation of the severity of native valvular regurgitation with two-dimensional and Doppler echocardiography. *J Am Soc Echocardiogr* 2003; 16:777–802.

6. Grayburn PA, Bhella P. Grading severity of mitral regurgitation by echocardiography; science or art? *JACC Cardiovasc Imaging* 2010;3: 244–246.

7. Ling LH, Enriquez-Sarano M, Seward JB, Tajik AJ, Schaff HV, Bailey KR, Frye RL. Clinical outcome of mitral regurgitation due to flail leaflet. *N Engl J Med* 1996;335:1417–1423.

8. Grigioni F, Tribouilloy C, Avierinos JF, Barbieri A, Ferlito M, Trojette F, Tafanelli L, Branzi A, Szymanski C, Habib G, Modena MG, Enriquez-Sarano M; MIDA Investigators. Outcomes in mitral regurgitation due to flail leaflets: a multicenter European study. *JACC Cardiovasc Imaging* 2008;1:133–141.

JOSEPH CHOLMONDELEY GREENFIELD, Jr., MD: A Conversation With the Editor*

Dr. Joseph C. Greenfield, Jr., was born in Atlanta, Georgia, on July 20, 1931. I first met him, I believe, in 1947 when he was a junior at Henry Grady High School in Atlanta, and I was a sophomore. Dr. Greenfield was in the class with my brother. Joe had a reputation of being a good guy, he was popular with his classmates, he was smart, he was on the rifle team, and he collected butterflies. He went to Emory University for 3 years, where he was elected to Phi Beta Kappa, and then he went to Emory University School of Medicine where he graduated in 1956 and was a member of Alpha Omega Alpha. His internship and residency in medicine were at Duke University in Durham, North Carolina. From there, he spent 3 years in the National Heart Institute in Bethesda, Maryland, working in the laboratory of Dr. Donald Fry. He returned to Duke in 1962. A year later he was appointed Chief of the Cardiology Section at the Durham Veteran's Administration Medical Center. In 1981, he became Chief of the Cardiology Division at Duke University Medical Center, and in 1983 he became Chairman of the Department of Medicine of Duke University Medical Center. He continued in that post until 1995. He also continued as Chief of Cardiology until 1989. Since 1970, he has been Professor of Medicine, and since 1981 he has been the James B. Duke Distinguished Professor of Duke University.

Until age 50 (1981), Dr. Greenfield spent about 80% of his time in his research laboratory working with animal models. He and his colleagues conducted a series of seminal studies focusing on the heart's response to ischemia and how the coronary arteries responded to a variety of stressors. His research, which generally asked fundamental physiologic questions, led to publication of nearly 150 scientific articles, appearing mainly in the *Journal of Clinical Investigation*, *Journal of Physiology*, *Circulation Research*, and *Circulation*.

Shortly after Dr. Greenfield's return to Durham in 1962, he began reading electrocardiograms in the heart stations at both the Veterans Administration and Duke University Hospitals. That endeavor has continued until the present, including during the period of his chairmanship. He often interprets 1,000 electrocardiograms a week.

During his 12 years as Chairman, the Department of Medicine underwent explosive growth. Total faculty grew from 152 MDs and 21 PhDs in 1983 to 290 MDs and 45 PhDs in 1995. Research funding from the National Institutes of Health grew from 13.6 to more than 34 million, boosting the department's NIH ranking from 14th in the nation in total funding to the top 6; clinical billings went from nearly $19 to $76 million a year. Outpatient visits increased from 68,000 to 180,000; house staff grew from 95 to 145 physicians (US applicants for house staff positions grew from 600 to 1,200 a year); and fellowships went from 120 to 155. By the last of the Greenfield years, the department was recognized by *US News and World Report* as the third best internal medicine program in the United States. All of this growth occurred in the midst of difficult times for internal medicine in most parts of the country.

During his chairmanship, Greenfield made house staff and fellowship training a major priority not only for himself but for his entire department, with the goal of providing the best patient care anywhere. He considered the internship and residency years the most important part of the entire education, the time when one really learns to be a doctor. Greenfield created an exciting atmosphere for learning and achieving, and in doing so, this colorful and charismatic leader became almost a cult figure among those in the department. He both gave and received intense loyalty, and he was an extraordinary motivator and mentor.

Greenfield was always there for the house staff and faculty. He was gone no more than 10 days a year. He generally took morning reports 3 times a week; made general medicine attending rounds once or twice a week, and conducted "pizza rounds" every Friday night beginning at 11 P.M. or midnight. The latter was held in the departmental library; he would chat with the residents about patients, about their own families, and about what they needed to do better jobs. I doubt if any departmental chairman has been as much loved by his house staff and faculty as Joe Greenfield.

Greenfield is different from any other chairman I have met. His simple and small office is decorated by pictures of his hero, General Robert E. Lee, and an inspiring Civil War battle scene. Greenfield avoids social events, meetings ("Nothing was ever accomplished with more than 2 people in a room."), and trips. He rarely gives a talk. He has always driven to and from work in a truck. He is happy with his simple tastes, his unpretentiousness, his loyalties (to his family, colleagues, and institutions), his duties, his hobbies (Civil War, English-Pointer Birddogs, quail hunting, and butterflies), and his beliefs. We need more Joe Greenfields.

William C. Roberts, MD†(hereafter, WCR): *It is February 12, 1998, and I am in the office of Joseph C. Greenfield, Jr., in Durham, North Carolina. Joe, I appreciate your willingness to speak to me and the AJC readers. What I would like to do is start as early as you remember and try to learn where that spark to excel academically came from. Could you talk about*

*This series of interviews was underwritten by an unrestricted grant from Bristol-Myers Squibb.

†Baylor Cardiovascular Institute, Baylor University Medical Center, Dallas, Texas 75246.

FIGURE 1. JCG in his office.

your growing up in Atlanta, your parents and siblings, and who had major influences on you during those early days?

Joseph C. Greenfield, Jr.,[‡] **(hereafter, JCG):** I was born in Atlanta in 1931, and lived there until 1956. (We lived in Richmond for about 1 year, when I was age 5 or 6, and then returned to Georgia.) My early years coincided with the depths of the Depression. I was, for better or worse, an only child. My earliest memories to excel came from my mother, who was academically inclined. Her father, my grandfather, who died in 1935, was a Methodist minister who received a PhD from Yale. He spent most of his life teaching ancient languages at what was then Florida State Women's College, now Florida State University. He instilled in my mother a love for academic endeavors. He was a Latin scholar, and, of course, when I went to high school I was made to take 4 or 5 years of Latin, which I promptly forgot, but which probably did help by making me do something I despised. After he died, I spent a fair amount of time in Tallahassee, Florida, with my grandmother who was originally from North Carolina. Her father was a surgeon in the Army of Northern Virginia during the Civil War. (I still have his surgeon's manual.) My father was a graduate of Georgia Tech. In the Depression, civil engineers were not in demand, and he went first into the insurance business, and finally into banking, working at First National Bank of Atlanta. His father, an Atlanta businessman, was involved in the development of the Crippled Children's Hospital. I remember his mother very well. She was born near Atlanta and the stories I remember from her were mainly those involving her family in and after the Civil War. She had 2 brothers killed, and the 1 surviving brother, a physician, lived with them. Because of her, I developed a life-long interest in the Civil War. When I grew

up in Atlanta, many of the old Civil War trenches were still discernable, and I used to pick up "minie balls" on the school yard.

I had a very good education in the Atlanta public schools. The teachers that I remember in grammar school pushed us to excel. High school education for boys, at that time, in Atlanta consisted of 3 high schools: Boy's High, Tech High, and Commercial High. These were all public schools. The curriculum at Boy's High was designed to prepare for college. I had a wonderful education; the teachers really expected and demanded excellence. At that time, many of the classrooms were in old dilapidated wooden buildings heated with woodburning stoves. (We had a lot of fun putting firecrackers in them during class.) That experience made it clear to me that physical structure is not important in education. What we learned was dependent on the kind of people doing the teaching and what they demanded of us.

Another important factor in my growing up was World War II. I was 10 years old when Pearl Harbor was destroyed. The war affected our everyday life considerably with rationing, blackouts, and trying to help by collecting scrap, etc. My cousin was severely wounded in Germany and was hospitalized at Lawson Hospital near Atlanta. Weekly visits to him impressed on me the suffering associated with war.

During the summers while I was in high school and college, I worked in the pharmacology laboratory with Dr. Arthur Richardson, who was Chairman of Pharmacology at Emory University School of Medicine. I learned a lot and I enjoyed this research experience. At that time, Dr. C. Heymens from Belgium, who described the carotid sinus baroreceptors, was in the laboratory and I had a chance to interact with him. At Emory College, my primary mentor was Dr. Bell Wiley, a noted Civil War historian. At that time, you could enter medical school after 3 years, which I did, but during the summers while I was in medical school, I went back to college and got my AB degree in history. When I graduated from medical school, it became obvious to me that I was not going to be an historian, but my interest in history has continued.

I interned at Duke primarily because some of the house staff at Grady Hospital, who had graduated from Duke, told me that the training program was excellent. Obviously, Dr. Eugene Stead had a great influence on my life in demanding that the house staff enmesh ourselves in patient care. At that time, we worked 5 out of 7 nights sleeping in the hospital. It was not an ideal situation for family life, but we learned medicine.

As you remember, we were deferred from military service through medical school and house staff training. When I finished my training in internal medicine, I should have been placed on active duty under the

‡James B. Duke Distinguished Professor, Duke University, Durham, North Carolina 27710.

FIGURE 2. JCG during the interview

what was going on in the world, especially the World War.

WCR: *Where did you grow up in Atlanta? Where was your home located?*

JCG: It is about a mile from Emory University in Lennox Park.

WCR: *Were you close to your father? Did you hunt and fish with him?*

JCG: No. I did hunt with my great uncle, but my father was never a hunter or fisherman. He was a competitive pistol shooter and I went to a number of tournaments with him. Primarily because of his influence, I competed on the rifle team in high school.

WCR: *What about your mother?*

JCG: She was very much a stay-at-home person. Fortunately or unfortunately, raising me was almost her entire life.

WCR: *You were not a wealthy kid? How would you categorize yourself as far as opportunities that you had as a youngster versus some of your colleagues now?*

JCG: No, we were not wealthy, although we certainly were not destitute. We had a very difficult time financially in 1937 and had to live in Fayetteville, Georgia, with my grandmother. I went to a 1-room school and saw real poverty. I never will forget inviting a couple of my classmates to Sunday dinner; they ate so much they got sick. The lunch they brought to school each day was a cold potato. We did not have a lot when I grew up, but I did have an opportunity to go to college. I was expected to work, be it yard work or that type of thing, from an early age. My summers were spent working. I joined the Boy Scouts and got a lot out of that experience. I became an Eagle Scout, and again the drive to excel was very important. At that time Bert Adam's Boy Scout's Camp was right outside of Atlanta. I spent several weeks each summer there and got a lot out of the experience.

WCR: *Was your family religious?*

JCG: As I mentioned, my grandfather was a Methodist minister and my mother and I went to church every Sunday. My father was a Baptist. I am not sure he meant it to be particularly laudatory, but he described his mother as "an Admiral in the Lord's Navy." When he told her he was going to marry a Methodist she was absolutely convinced that "mixed marriages" would never work. When they baptized me but did not hold me under the water, she became so upset that she walked out. Although my father did not attend church regularly, my mother accompanied me to church weekly until I was perhaps 14 or 15 years old.

WCR: *Did you choose Emory to go to college because it was right there?*

JCG: It was near my house and at that time, cheap.

WCR: *You lived at home during college and medical school?*

JCG: Yes. I could walk, about a mile, to college. I was a member of Kappa Alpha (KA) social fraternity. That was a very important experience for me. When I entered college about half the class were returning World War II veterans. The other half were young

Berry Plan. I was very lucky in that I was accepted by the National Heart Institute at Bethesda, Maryland, to work with Dr. Bob Grant, an outstanding electrocardiographer. I joined the Public Health Service and went to work with Bob Grant. However, the day I arrived, Bob decided to become the Director of the National Heart Institute and left active research. I had to find a place to work and by sheer chance I found Dr. Donald Fry, who, I think, is one of the brightest and smartest people I have ever met. He had made a number of fundamental observations in both the mechanics of cardiac and pulmonary function. He was a superb individual and a very close friend. I was very lucky to have had the opportunity to work with him for 3 years. After completing my military obligations, I moved back to Duke and with Don's help and support developed my own research laboratory. We used a technique which we had developed to measure continuous cardiac output in patients. I became interested in studying the factors that regulate coronary blood flow and did most of my subsequent research work in this area.

WCR: *Let me go back a little bit. What was home life like for you when you were a youngster? You mentioned that your mother, in particular, was an intellectual person. What was it like sitting around the dinner table at night when you would come home from junior high school and high school?*

JCG: I grew up in what was the outskirts of Atlanta. (Now it's almost downtown.) I had the opportunity to do a lot of things outdoors, like hunting and fishing. A lot of our conversations were about these kinds of activities. We did not talk a lot about politics because my father hated Franklin Roosevelt so much that he would not talk about him. The kinds of conversations we had revolved mainly around day-to-day activities,

smart alecs like me who had just graduated from high school. The older members of the fraternity put pressure on us to excel. I found the KA fraternity very important in that regard.

WCR: *You started college in 1949 when the GI bill was flourishing?*

JCG: Yes. College was filled with people that had been in World War II.

WCR: *They were anxious to do well?*

JCG: They were not there to play or to see how they could waste time in college. They made sure that we did the same thing.

WCR: *So they upped the standards for you folks coming right out of high school?*

JCG: My first semester I made all As and then dropped off and made a couple of Bs the second semester; I was dressed down by the president of the fraternity for making poor grades.

WCR: *In what way was being in the social fraternity important to you?*

JCG: It was very important to me. The members in the upper classes made sure that I excelled in school.

WCR: *Although it was a social fraternity, the members placed a lot of emphasis on doing well scholastically. Who influenced you in college? In college you majored in history?*

JCG: I majored in history as I mentioned. Dr. Bell Wiley was the main teacher I remember.

WCR: *What about sciences? Were you always turned on by biology and chemistry?*

JCG: I did well in them, but I never really liked them as much as I liked history. Some of the best courses I took in college were seminar courses where I read selected books and then discussed them with the professors.

WCR: *When you went to college had you already made up your mind that you wanted to go to medical school?*

JCG: Yes. I was in the accelerated 3-year program.

WCR: *You were put into the medical school track right out of high school? You knew you were going to medical school when you entered college?*

JCG: Yes, if I could get in. It was very competitive at that time to get into medical school.

WCR: *It was difficult at that time because the medical school classes were small, and because all those veterans were increasing the competition?*

JCG: That is exactly right.

WCR: *You went to Emory and finished college in 3 years? You went 12 years before that to school?*

JCG: Right. I did not skip any grades.

WCR: *When you finished college you were 20?*

JCG: Yes. I started medical school in 1952 at age 20 after 3 years in college. I had not finished college when I began medical school, but went back to college in the summers and that allowed me to get the (AB) degree in history.

WCR: *So you finished medical school at age 24? Did anybody turn you on in medical school?*

JCG: We had some very good basic science teachers. Probably the instructor I remember the best was the Chairman of Pathology, Dr. Walter Sheldon. He

FIGURE 3. JCG during the interview.

was a superb teacher and demanded that we excel. In the clinical years, there were only a few full-time faculty. Thus, many of our clinical teachers were volunteers who were in private practice. Several of the major departments at the time did not have chairmen. Many of these volunteers and members of the Emory Clinic were really superb role models. Dr. Bruce Logue, an outstanding cardiologist, was by far the best. Most of our clinical training occurred at Grady Hospital. There were not a lot of senior physicians in that hospital. It was mainly run by house staff. We learned by doing without much instruction. Actually, this training complimented what was available at Duke. At Grady Hospital, we had been able to do anything with patients, but there was no one to teach us what to do. When I got to Duke I saw the flip side in that there were a lot of staff physicians in the hospital and we were more constrained in making decisions about patients.

WCR: *When you were in medical school did you have a problem deciding what kind of physician you wanted to be or was that relatively easy for you?*

JCG: Primarily because of Dr. Logue, I wanted to be a cardiologist from the day I first went on the wards. Like most medical students, I went through a very transient period when I wanted to be a surgeon. However, I found out very quickly that I could not stand in the same place for a long period of time. This fact ended that potential career.

WCR: *When you came to Durham, Duke University Medical Center, in 1956, Dr. Stead had been here for 7 or 8 years? Except for the 3 years you were at NIH, you have not left Duke? What do you remember about medical internship and residency at Duke? You have* *already mentioned that you lived at the hospital. You were essentially on call all the time?*

JCG: We were totally enmeshed in medicine; we learned a lot. Primarily, I learned to enjoy delivering patient care. We ate, breathed, and lived medicine continually. In this respect, I think the things that I really enjoyed the most, which is so hard to get in training now, is to have personal relationships with so many patients. We had plenty of time to talk to them. It is hard to believe in 1998, but the first patient I took care of with a heart attack was a bank executive from Greensboro, North Carolina, who happened to be driving through Durham when he developed chest pain. At that time, there was no special place to put acute cardiac patients. The standard approach for patients with heart attacks was to put them in bed, relieve the chest pain, and have them on complete bed rest for 6 weeks. This meant they had to be fed by the nurses for at least 3 weeks. After that they could sit in a chair by the bedside. They were anticoagulated not to prevent cardiac clotting, but to try to prevent the complications of thromboembolism that so frequently occurred. In the acute patient, it was a maxim that if you could not make the patient pain free, he was going to die. I remember giving this patient large doses of morphine to no avail. After about 12 hours, he looked at me and said "Where do I go from here?" and died. I could do nothing except watch him die. On the other hand, we did know both the patients and families and we became physicians in the sense that we were involved with these people. They were not just a disease that you treated and discharged in 48 hours. This was a wonderful experience that physicians in training cannot get anymore. Of course, I had the opportunity to be involved in most of the changes that have taken place in cardiology from the beginning. When I began my internship the care of patients with heart attacks was not much different from the way patients with acute myocardial infarction had been treated for the preceding 100 years.

WCR: *You finished your house officer training and your 3 years at NIH in 1962. That was the year before Jack Kennedy was assassinated? So, in 1962, the therapy of acute myocardial infarction in actuality was about the same as it had been for the previous 100 years.*

JCG: I don't remember the exact date when defibrillators became available. We did have primitive pacemakers at that time. Actually, I was involved at the NIH in putting in one of the very early pacemakers. Also, I was at the NIH when the transeptal techniques to do left heart catheterizations were perfected. Cardiac care units became fairly widespread about 1965. The one at Duke was opened in 1964. The basic care of patients with acute myocardial infarction had not changed until we had the opportunity to put them in one place. The reason that cardiac care units were opened was to take care of patients who needed to be defibrillated or to have symptomatic bradycardia treated.

WCR: *You had an internship and 2 years as a resident in medicine and then you had 3 years at the National Heart Institute?*

JCG: The cardiology boards gave me credit for the 3 years at NIH. I had no other formal training in cardiology.

WCR: *When you returned to Duke in 1962, you were a cardiologist as it was defined at that time?*

JCG: That's right.

WCR: *How did things go when you came back to Durham? You set up your laboratory at the Veterans Administration Hospital. You started reading electrocardiograms daily?*

JCG: When I arrived at the NIH, Dr. Robert Berliner asked me to be responsible for the Heart Station at the Clinical Center (the NIH Hospital) and I read electrocardiograms for the next 3 years. When I returned to Duke, I became responsible for the ECG interpretation at the VA, and in 1969 I took over the Heart Station at Duke Medical Center, which I have continued until the present. I really enjoy reading ECGs and teaching electrocardiography to trainees.

In the beginning my research was helped immeasurably by Dr. George Tindall, a neurosurgeon, who let me use his laboratory until I could equip a laboratory of my own. We collaborated on a number of studies of cerebral blood flow. It was difficult at first to get money for research funding, but soon thereafter the NIH funds became readily available. Frankly, it was very easy to get grants beginning about 1964 and for the next 20 years. I obtained a Career Development Award, which funded my salary, and an RO1 and a VA Merit Review Award funded the research.

WCR: *How did you focus on coronary blood flow, coronary circulation, myocardial perfusion? Was that drawn out of your experience with Donald Fry?*

JCG: Not really. Don Fry taught me to think like a physiologist and to study the mechanics of the heart. I really became interested in coronary blood flow by visiting Donald Gregg at the Walter Reed Hospital. He was the "Father" of coronary flow physiology. He had developed an electromagnetic flow meter which allowed the continuous measurement of coronary flow. I had done similar blood flow work in the aorta at NIH and I brought this technique to Duke.

WCR: *You went over to see Donald Gregg in Washington, DC, on your own? You were already interested in it? How did you like working in the dog lab? I guess you used dogs primarily when you were working at the NIH?*

JCG: Most of the experimental work we did was with unsedated dogs. Because of Donald Gregg's influence, I tried to work on conscious, unsedated animals in an attempt to mimic the human pathophysiology as closely as possible. We developed a number of techniques to measure the factors which control coronary blood flow distribution in a number of different physiologic situations (e.g., exercise and pathologic conditions; e.g., cardiac hypertrophy). I was extremely lucky, in that 8 excellent graduate students completed their PhD thesis work with me. Two of these students, Judith Rembert and Philip McHale, remained in the

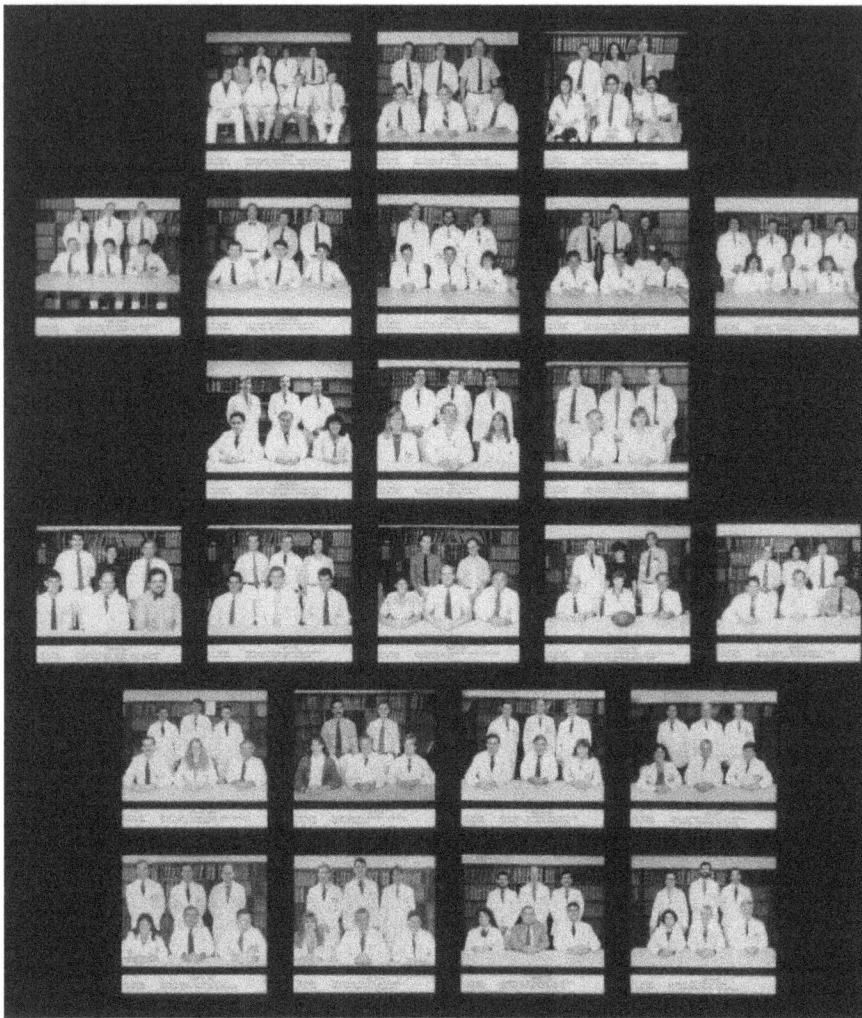

FIGURE 4 . Photographs of JCG with his chief residents and assistant chief residents at both Duke University Medical Center and the Veteran's Administration Medical Center during JCG's tenureship as Chairman.

laboratory and were largely responsible for our success in publishing high quality research.

WCR: *When you came back to Durham, North Carolina, from Bethesda, Maryland, you were entirely at the VA Hospital here?*

JCG: I had appointments at both Duke Hospital and at the VA Hospital, but I spent my day at the VA Hospital as Chief of Cardiology and doing research.

WCR: *When did you become Chief of Cardiology at the VA?*

JCG: 1963.

WCR: *How big was the division of cardiology in 1962, including your staff at the VA Hospital plus the staff at Duke University Medical Center?*

JCG: It would be a guess. There were no more than 15 senior staff physicians altogether.

WCR: *What is it today?*

JCG: About 52 full-time faculty.

WCR: *Just in cardiology?*

JCG: Yes.

WCR: *When you came back, I gather that you enjoyed teaching?*

JCG: Very much.

WCR: *You enjoyed taking care of sick people?*

JCG: Yes, but at the VA Hospital I was not the primary physician. The house staff actually took care of the patients and I functioned as a mentor or attending physician. I did not spend a lot of time in clinics seeing patients; I never did, as a matter of fact.

WCR: *You spent a lot of time in the laboratory at that time. That was the thing that was really turning you on then, I gather? You were enjoying this research and you were quite productive. When did it occur to you that maybe you would also like to be Head of Cardiology at Duke University Hospital? When is the first time that the idea of Chairmanship of the Department of Medicine was ever entertained by you?*

JCG: Very early on, I got a number of offers to look at academic positions, both as Chief of Cardiology and Chief of Medicine. The more I looked, the more I was happy with what I was doing. I primarily spent my day doing research and teaching. Thus, for a 20-year period, research in cardiovascular physiology and pathophysiology occupied more than 90% of my endeavors—I thought about research and little else. I really did not take a serious administrative job until 1981, when I became Chief of Cardiology at Duke.

FIGURE 5. JCG (second from left) with the 2 previous chairman (Drs. James B. Wyngaarden [center right] and Eugene A. Stead [far right]) and the present chairman (Dr. Barton F. Haynes [far left]).

Thus, I spent nearly 2 decades without any major administrative responsibilities. It could not have worked out better. When I did take an administrative position, I cut the scope of my research effort significantly so that a limited amount of high quality work could be maintained. This afforded me time for my duties. Many of my colleagues have tried to manage academic administrative positions and run a large research program—to the detriment of both.

WCR: *In actuality you were 50 years old when you became Chief of Cardiology, not only at the VA Hospital but also at Duke University Medical Center. What was it that turned you on to the potential usefulness of invasive cardiology? It is my understanding, for example, that you were the one that really made Duke Cardiology shift gears. You got all these patients, not only in this area, but all over the state, and set up the helicopter service. It seems to me you were quite a visionary. You were ahead of other people by a long shot in getting that done. As you reflect on it, what did you forsee that others did not at that time?*

JCG: We need to answer this question from a couple of directions. First, the primary mandate of this institution, Duke University Medical Center, as defined by Mr. Duke was to deliver health care to the patients of North and South Carolina. Duke Medical Center was not developed as a primary research institution. It was built to take care of patients, and to this day plays a major role in caring for indigent patients without compensation. We had been very successful in setting up referral patterns from an area within a 100-mile radius of Durham. It was very clear to me

that we could make a major impact on the health care of patients with coronary disease in this state. At the time, we certainly were doing bypass surgery, but really not large numbers. We were not doing angioplasty, although angioplasty was being done in a number of other institutions. Thrombolytic therapy was not available at that time. However, it was very clear to me that interventional techniques were going to be the future and we could help the institution grow as well as make a major impact on health care in this state.

I had an experience in 1982 with a neighbor, a lady in her early 60s, who came to the hospital with mild chest pain. When she arrived in the emergency room, she developed complete heart block, cardiogenic shock, and for all intents and purposes, would have died. One of our cardiologists, Dr. Jess Peter, took her immediately to the cardiac catheterization laboratory and did an emergency coronary angioplasty. She walked out of the hospital a few days later a well person. As a matter of fact, she lived another 14 years. Based on my experiences with the first patient I had as an intern (who died with an acute myocardial infarction and I could not do anything for him), and the experience with this lady (who for all intents and purposes was "dead," but walked out of the hospital 5 days later a well person), I knew that we needed to dramatically alter our approach to the treatment of patients with acute myocardial infarction. Since Durham is a small community, we needed to develop a mechanism of rapidly transporting patients to the hospital. Helicopters at that time were primarily used for patients with trauma. We had a major knock-down war with the hospital administration in making them understand that we knew we could get the acute cardiac patients referred. I don't know the actual data, but the first year 75% of the transports by helicopter were cardiology patients. The program was so successful that we dramatically increased the number of patients admitted for cardiac disease, increasing the number of cardiac catheterizations and patients undergoing bypass surgery. In so doing, we improved the health care of the people in this state. At this point, I need to recognize the work of several of my colleagues who were primarily responsible for this growth: Dr. Rob Califf, Director the Cardiac Care Unit, initiated many of the clinical trials of thrombolytic therapy; Dr. Richard Stack, Director of the Interventional Laboratory, developed a number of successful devices; and most importantly, Dr. Harry Phillips, who was largely responsible for the enormous increase in the number of cardiac patients referred to this institution.

WCR: *At the same time, as a byproduct, it also improved the image of this medical center across the*

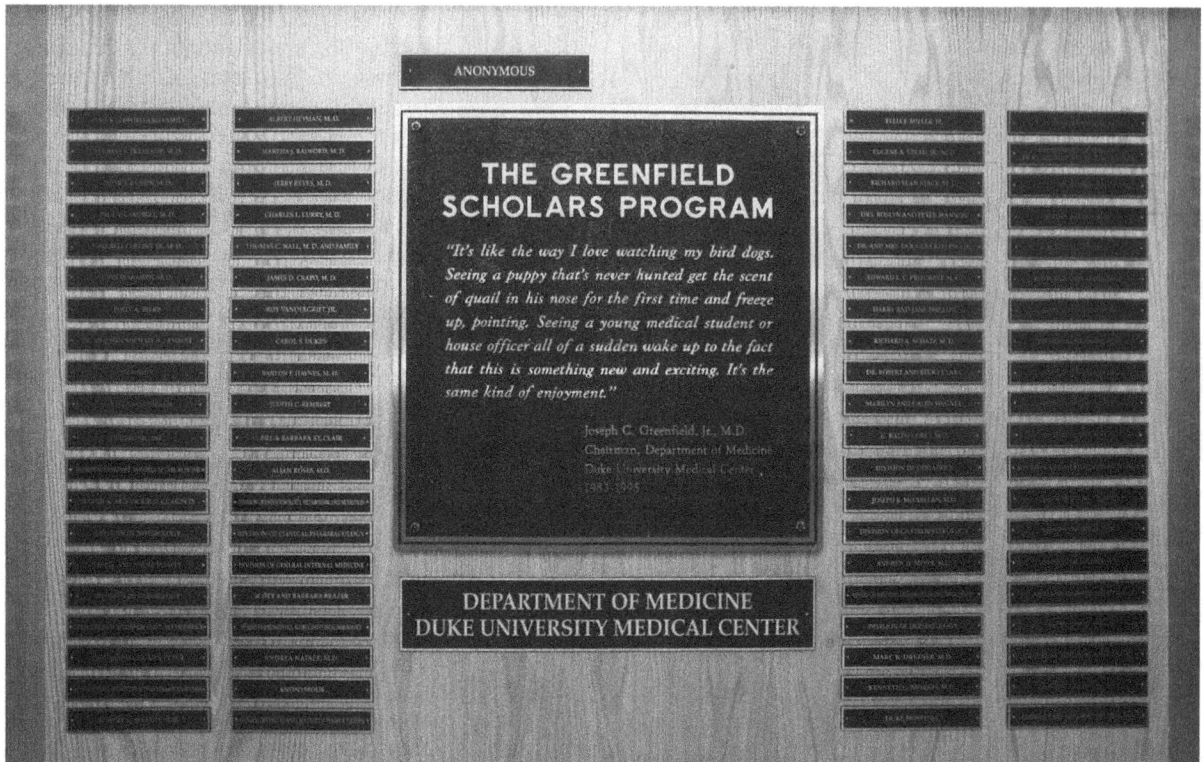

FIGURE 6. Photograph of the donors to The Greenfield Scholars Program, provided by JCG's colleagues in his honor. The program was initiated to provide salary support for the training of physician-scientists at Duke University Medical Center.

state, I suspect, enormously. You were paid for those procedures, so your Division of Cardiology must have been extremely well appreciated at that time by the medical center.

JCG: I'm not sure "appreciated" is the right word, but results were certainly recognized.

WCR: *You became Chief of Cardiology at Duke Medical Center in 1981 when you were 50 years of age. Then, low and behold, the next year you were offered the Chairmanship of Medicine here. How did that come about?*

JCG: Jim Wyngaarden, as you know, became the Director of the National Institutes of Health. There was a year's search, and basically it did not seem to be going anywhere. They had asked me to look at the job earlier and I really was not interested. The longer the search went it looked like things were going to deteriorate, so I talked to Dr. William Anlyan and was offered and accepted the position. It was kind of a defensive action. I did not think this place could keep going without a Chairman of Medicine; we were not making any headway without one.

WCR: *So you became Chairman of Medicine in 1983. You stayed Chairman until 1995. That is a 12-year period. What were your goals when you took that Chairmanship?*

JCG: To try to make absolutely certain that in every one of the medical subspecialties we excelled in patient care, in research, and in training. I have always viewed the Duke Medical Center as primarily a place to train specialists. Certainly, we have trained good general internists, but during my time, 90% of the

house staff that finished their internal medicine training went into a subspeciality. I think the thing I concentrated on as much as anything else was our house staff program, trying to get the best students we could, and to train them to be physicians. About half of those trainees also did their fellowships at Duke. The bulk of the people that we kept on the senior staff as clinicians came through our training program. From the outside we recruited primarily research-trained physicians. We did recruit a number of physician-scientists and the department became well funded from external sources such as the NIH. However, the main thing I concentrated on was making sure that the house staff program was the best it could be and that we delivered the best possible care we could.

WCR: *I understand, Joe, that you spent an incredible time with your medical house staff. You knew each one of them very well. Your door was always opened to them or to anyone else, I gather, on your staff, and, furthermore, you were always here. You were not traveling on the circuit.*

JCG: I tried to do 2 Visiting Professorships a year at the maximum. I went to the American Society for Clinical Investigation about every other year and I served on the American Board of Internal Medicine. That was it. I did not take any other jobs or anything else. I never was significantly involved in the committee work of American Heart Association, the American College of Cardiology, or other academic organizations.

WCR: *So you took a maximum of 3 or 4 trips a year. Therefore, you were here, you were accessible, and*

FIGURE 7. Photograph of JCG with one of his beloved bird dogs (Photography by Will & Denni McIntyre, McIntyre Photography, Inc., 3746 Yadkinville Road, Winston-Salem, North Carolina 27106.)

you were part of the house staff team in a way. You took morning reports?

JCG: I took morning reports every Monday and Wednesday and gave a clinical conference on Friday. Grand Rounds were held on Friday; I came in every Friday night to eat pizza with the house staff and to do 11:00 P.M. sign-out rounds with them. Many times these sessions went on to 2:00 in the morning.

WCR: *These 11:00 Friday night rounds, that was something you initiated. That had not gone on here before? What gave your that idea? What was your purpose?*

JCG: To try to get to know the house staff and also to make them understand that I was very interested in the quality of care they were delivering.

WCR: *That meant your whole medical house staff was here from 11:00 P.M. Friday night to whatever time you left Saturday morning?*

JCG: Just the ones rotating on the general medicine service at that time.

WCR: *So you had a relatively small group you could get to know?*

JCG: They usually would come from the VA Hospital also, at least those that were on call that night. I would say that on the average we would have 20 people there.

WCR: *You would bring the pizza?*

JCG: No. The department furnished the money and the house staff had a good time trying to get pizza as cheaply as possible.

WCR: *Would you actually make rounds or would you discuss patients?*

JCG: I initially started out doing the sign-out rounds with them. At Duke, we have a policy that the Chief Resident in medicine sees the new admissions every night. I initially did that and later on it became more of a social gathering.

WCR: *I understand you had a cardiology conference with the cardiology fellows and staff on Saturday morning.*

JCG: We did for a long time.

WCR: *You did at the time you were making these midnight rounds, and the cardiology conference started at 8:00 A.M.?*

JCG: Yes, that is right.

WCR: *Do you need much sleep?*

JCG: I am not a Napoleon. I can't get by on 3 hours, but I probably can get by on 5 without any real trouble.

WCR: *What do you usually do? What time did you wake up in the morning when you were Chairman of Medicine, Head of Cardiology, etc.?*

JCG: Six o'clock.

WCR: *What time do you go to bed?*

JCG: Midnight.

WCR: *What time do you come to the hospital?*

JCG: I had to be at the hospital at 8:00 A.M.

WCR: *You live on a farm?*

JCG: I have about 25 acres which is surrounded by a large tract of land, the Duke forest. A friend of mine built a log cabin and it is an ideal retreat. It is only a 5-minute drive from the hospital. I have a home in town, but I spend a lot of time at this place.

WCR: *I understand that your house staff had an incredible degree of loyalty to you and you instilled in them a tremendous loyalty to the Duke institution? What in you, as you examine yourself, gave you those characteristics to be such a mentor to all these young house officers?*

JCG: I think that I thoroughly enjoyed doing it. If you don't, you can't do it at all. I did enjoy trying to solve their problems and help them. The other thing is that I put myself in a position to have enough time to do it properly. I was not away from the institution very much, I was at Duke. I thoroughly enjoy hunting, quail hunting particularly. I have trained bird dogs all my life. There is nothing any more fun than seeing a young bird dog for the first time smell quail and really start doing what he was put on this earth to do. House staff and students are similar. The first time that you see them really get excited about medicine is a very rewarding situation.

WCR: *Once you took a house officer you sort of treated them as your kid in a way. You brought them along, made sure they got the fellowship they wanted, and they knew you would take care of them, but, at the same time, you apparently instilled in them to give their best. How did you do that? Everyone wants to get the best out of people who are under them, but apparently you did it?*

JCG: I think it was the obvious combination of carrot and stick, putting them where they could excel and making damn sure that they did. A major factor is peer pressure. The house staff did extremely well because they did not want their peers to see them not perform.

WCR: *You gave up cardiology after awhile? 1989?*

JCG: Yes.

WCR: *You were Head of the Division of Cardiology and the Department of Medicine simultaneously for about 6 years? Why did you keep cardiology?*

JCG: This sounds a little bit self-serving, but at that time, I really enjoyed cardiology more than medicine. Also, if you looked around the country, at that particular time, there was a lot of unrest among various cardiology divisions because they were supporting departments of medicine financially. There were a lot of arguments back and forth about cardiology's breaking off and being their own department. I just did not want to fight about finances with the Chief of Cardiology, because basically cardiology underwrote everything.

WCR: *What did you enjoy most about being Chairman?*

JCG: Developing people, be it house staff or young faculty.

WCR: *You enjoy being the mentor?*

JCG: Yes. Giving people opportunities and watching them to see how they do.

WCR: *Did anybody take care of you when you were coming along? Do you owe your career, in other words, to somebody who kept supporting you, or do you think primarily you are a self-made person professionally?*

JCG: I think Dr. Stead was that person. He mentored me in my early formative career and really tried to help me develop.

WCR: *You seem to be very loyal to your institution. Is that just the way you were put together or did you develop a love for Duke and instill that in others with time?*

JCG: Probably the latter is the way I was put together; I felt and still do feel, this institution did an enormous amount for me, gave me opportunities I could not have dreamed of having anywhere else. I owe back to them the kind of loyalty we talked about.

WCR: *I gather that while you were chairman you really upgraded the gastrointestinal, neurology, hematology-oncology, and cardiology divisions. Did you find that difficult in these arenas that you had not been in for 20 years essentially?*

JCG: I was lucky to pick very good people and I left them alone. I have always felt that the way you excel is to find the best person and then get the hell out of their way. That is what I did.

WCR: *It sounds like you have a good sense for talent. You sense it. What are you looking for in people that you want to surround yourself with?*

JCG: Bright people. I have always said that everyone around you should be smarter than you are. (In my case, that is pretty easy.) Above all, they need to be interested in developing other people's careers, not building everything for their own self-satisfaction. Any person, no matter how good they are profession-ally, but who are extremely self-centered and only interested in themselves will never build anything. I think the key thing is to try to find people who get a certain amount of enjoyment out of watching other people do well. I look for these characteristics more than anything else. Most of us get to where we are in medicine by being extraordinarily self-centered and looking after ourselves. That is one of the real failings in academic medicine. Not many people are interested in anybody else.

WCR: *What would be an example you would see in a house officer, somebody who is not trying to get credit for being clever or giving credit to others?*

JCG: Somebody who does extra work and does not complain about it or just covers for people and nobody even knows about it. That is the kind of person you are looking for.

WCR: *When you came on as Chairman of Medicine in 1983, how many faculty did you have at that time?*

JCG: Around 175: 152 MDs and 21 PhDs.

WCR: *When you stepped down in 1995, 12 years later, how many faculty did you have?*

JCG: It got up to about 250 MDs and 45 PhDs.

WCR: *How many house officers did you have in medicine most of the years?*

JCG: We usually had 45 to 50 interns, and about 35 or 40 junior and senior residents.

WCR: *And the total house staff?*

JCG: Somewhere in the neighborhood of 100 or 110. We also had an equal number of subspeciality fellows.

WCR: *One hundred to 110 house staff, 100 to 110 fellows in the various divisions, and then 250 or so faculty. You knew all those people?*

JCG: I would say I knew the faculty fairly well, knew the house staff well, about half the fellows came from the house staff, so I knew them, but it was very hard to know the fellows who had come from other places.

WCR: *If you traveled around a lot, there is no way you could remember the names of 500 people.*

JCG: No.

WCR: *If you add technicians in the Department of Medicine, secretaries, and financial people, you are talking about 1,000 folks?*

JCG: About 1,000.

WCR: *It has always amazed me how you seemed to have managed a huge department of medicine, a very large division of cardiology. Your office was always small. Your desk was always clean. Your door was always open. You must be very decisive and make these decisions, at least they have the appearance of being made quickly. I presume you have thought a lot about them before the decision was made.*

JCG: Several things enter into that. One of them is that I have never been impressed that any important decision was made with more than 2 people in the room. I think large meetings are a complete waste of time. The only reason to have such meetings is to convey what has already been decided. The reason for the small office is obvious. We don't have a lot of space at Duke, so I made sure I had an office that was

FIGURE 8. Photography of JCG surrounded by photos of his bird dogs, past and present. Dr. Greenfield displays the most recent addition to his collection of shotguns. Shortly before Greenfield stepped down from his chairmanship, he received a phone call late one afternoon from one of his faculty members, who had called to let him know that he and other departmental faculty would be meeting that night at a Durham restaurant to discuss a plan to begin charging the house staff for a statistics course that they would soon be required to take. Irate, incensed, absolutely livid that the faculty would even consider levying a fee on the house staff, Greenfield stormed off to the restaurant and barged into the meeting room. He was stopped short by the sight of about 40 or so grinning departmental faculty who had tricked him into a surprise dinner in his honor. They presented Greenfield with a rare, one of a kind, Purdy shotgun, that he had admired a few months earlier in a national hunting magazine. It is this gun that JCG displays in this photograph. The gun was made entirely by hand, with intricate carvings in both the stock and the metal. The shotgun is as much a work of art as it is a firearm. (Photography by Will & Denni McIntyre, McIntyre Photography, Inc., 3746 Yadkinville Road, Winston-Salem, North Carolina 27106.)

small and I had the cheapest desk available. When people would walk in and tell how cramped they were for space I would tell them to look at my office. If they wanted an expensive desk I would say "Fine, you write a check for the difference between my desk and yours and we will get you a bigger desk." It seemed to work very well. As far as keeping my desk clean, I have always had a big waste paper basket. I don't look at a lot of this stuff that comes through. I just throw it away.

WCR: *Joe, I understand you don't pay the best salaries in the country? What is your view on how much it takes to retain a good staff financially?*

JCG: I followed Dr. Stead's approach; try to balance the salary level and the unscheduled time. Thus,

a faculty member who works in a situation where patient responsibilities define their day completely made a higher salary. Faculty who are primarily doing research and can, to a large extent, dictate their own schedule, make less. Promotions come faster when faculty have the time to do more academic things. Many of my colleagues don't believe that is a fair approach. However, one thing is certain. The money generated by patient care activities underwrites a portion of the cost of doing research and allows some of the faculty the freedom to function as physician-scientists. That is how I arrived at faculty members' salary. A private institution like Duke simply can't compete salary wise with state institutions because our only sources of money are grants and what we get from patient care revenues. Endownments provide a trivial portion of the overall budget.

WCR: *When did you get married?*

JCG: I got married in 1955.

WCR: *That was immediately before you came to Duke? You married a lady from Atlanta?*

JCG: Yes. She was a technician I met at Grady Hospital. She was from Cochran, Georgia.

WCR: *You have 3 girls?*

JCG: Yes.

WCR: *Have you been a good daddy all these years?*

JCG: At least reasonably good. My oldest daughter has been severely retarded from birth. She lives with us and works everyday at a sheltered workshop and does extremely well. The second is a cardiologist in electrophysiology at Duke. The other is involved in developing the outreach programs at Duke.

WCR: *So they are all right here?*

JCG: Yes.

WCR: *Do you have grandchildren?*

JCG: No.

WCR: *Joe, what do you do in your spare time? I hear you like quail hunting?*

JCG: Right. I hunt and train bird dogs.

WCR: *How many dogs do you have now?*

JCG: Currently, I have probably 15.

WCR: *What kind of dogs are they?*

JCG: English pointers. At the present, all of my dogs are in Florida. They, like rich Yankees, winter in Florida and summer with me in North Carolina.

WCR: *Your quail hunting started when you were in Atlanta?*

JCG: It was very early, about age ten.

WCR: *I hear that you have gone to Africa to do some big game hunting. What was that like?*

JCG: Until recently, I had no interest in big game hunting. I hunted deer and turkeys a few times, but I did not enjoy it at all. The man I have hunted quail with in Florida since 1984 became a professional guide in Africa and he enticed me into going there for the first time in the summer of 1996. I went cape buffalo hunting in Tanzania. The mystique of this country captures you like nothing else; it is very hard to explain. I really enjoyed buffalo hunting. I got into a situation where we nearly got killed by a cape buffalo. Last year, I went to South Africa near Kruger Park where elephants have not been hunted in about 5 years. I had the opportunity to hunt bull elephant with a man whose father was a professional ivory hunter and who had spent the first 30 years of his life hunting elephants. This was by far the most emotional and rewarding experience I've had hunting.

WCR: *These adventures are new in your life?*

JCG: Brand new, like everything else, I seem to do things late.

WCR: *You were gone a little longer than usual for these trips?*

JCG: Sixteen days.

WCR: *Before 1995, you never did that.*

JCG: The longest I ever was gone was to Florida to hunt for 4 days at a time and then come back.

WCR: *During your major period of your Chairmanship you were gone 2 to 3 weeks a year at most?*

JCG: I did not take summer vacations at all, so the only time away was just when I hunted or went to an occasional meeting.

WCR: *You got interventional cardiology, acute care cardiology, going at this institution and expanded it over the state. How do you think angioplasty and stents and atherectomies and these invasive procedures are going to pan out with time?*

JCG: The initial clinical presentation of coronary disease, particularly acute myocardial infarction and unstable angina, has been dramatically improved by these techniques. Now we are able to really take care of people extraordinarily well, assuming you can intervene early enough after the onset of acute myocardial infarction. These procedures must be viewed as palliative, which may add an extra 10 years to life, but should never be considered, as many people do unfortunately, as curative. It is a mystery to me why coronary disease may progress very rapidly for reasons totally unknown, then not change for a long period of time, and then progress again. I still think there is a tremendous opportunity to do more positive things to improve the status of patients with coronary disease. What we are running up against, as always, is money. The initial manifestations of coronary disease have been moved primarily to the age group of 60 and 70 years of age. Who will pay for new treatment modalities? Certainly not Medicare. Does it cost less to die of cardiovascular disease or something else? This is a major issue as far as the cost of health care is concerned and there is no ready answer.

WCR: *Coronary bypass should be viewed the same way.*

JCG: Absolutely. It, too, is a palliative procedure.

WCR: *Joe, you seem to have a pretty good business mind. Your department during your chairmanship did quite well financially?*

JCG: We made a lot of money from clinical endeavors. For the last 3 years, we had problems with reimbursements going down, but we still did well.

WCR: *Where did your financial savvy come from?*

JCG: I was lucky to pick one of the best business managers in academic medicine, Paul Thacker. He is superb and he saved us all kinds of money.

WCR: *What is your advice for young doctors today? Managed care, how do you sense it now?*

JCG: There is one thing I always tell them, "Look, when you get your MD degree, no matter what happens you are going to eat, i.e., you are going to make enough money to live on, you don't have to worry about that. What you want to do is enjoy taking care of patients, get up in the mornings and be a physician. If you allow all the problems associated with health care reimbursements, managed care, etc., to become dominate in your thinking, it will destroy your effectiveness as a physician." Where I have a problem, is to try to honestly advise students who are interested in a basic research career as an MD, or even doing a lot of clinical research as an MD, and tell them that they are going to do well. This is very difficult because I am not sure myself. The physician-scientist, and I really believe in the concept of physician-scientist, is having a very difficult time. It is hard to talk people into going into a career where they are concerned about whether they can make a living.

WCR: *Joe, I gather there are 125 chairmen of medicine around the country. I suspect you are the only one who drives an old Chevy truck to work.*

JCG: 1991 is not too old.

WCR: *How did that come about?*

JCG: I started driving a pickup truck before pickup trucks were the in thing. I got my first one in 1964 as a hunting vehicle. To be candid, I needed to be able to haul dogs without having to smell them—thus, a truck's ideal.

WCR: *There are other chairmen across the country and I suspect you know most or at least many of them pretty well. Who have you respected enormously as a departmental chairman in medicine and why?*

JCG: Clearly, Dr. Stead was by far the best. However, chairmen such as Drs. Don Seldin, David Kipnis, Eugene Braunwald, Holly Smith, Frank Abboud, and Claude Bennett had that extra something special and were able to put together and maintain superb departments.

WCR: *It sounds to me like being a departmental chairman with so many people, the less selfish you are, as you have already mentioned, the better your department. It sounds to me like you can't think of yourself at all during this period of time.*

JCG: That is correct. You need to sublimate all of your own particular goals and enjoy watching your people excel.

WCR: *But at the same time, you were able to keep your lab going while chairman?*

JCG: From 1981 until the present, although funded reasonably well, we gradually decreased the scope of our work. I was able to continue to produce high quality research but at a much lower volume. I still have a Merit Review from the VA which will end in October 1998. It is very difficult to be competitive in research unless you concentrate almost entirely on research. I do most of my best work after waking in the morning by thinking about what I am going to do during the day. When you are chairman you are thinking about the department rather than what you are going to do in research.

WCR: *I understand that you have read hundreds of electrocardiograms every week at Duke University ever since you came back here in 1962. You must get to know a lot about people by reading electrocardiograms with them. Why have you done that? Is it because this is just a professional hobby for you?*

JCG: For a number of reasons: (1) it is the best way to know about every sick patient in the hospital automatically because they are going to have an electrocardiogram, and you can keep up with the clinical service; (2) I thoroughly enjoy it; and (3) the financial situation is such that nobody could accuse me of not pulling my weight because the professional fees more than pay my salary and always have.

WCR: *Although you have probably read more electrocardiograms than about anybody now, have you ever written a paper on electrocardiography?*

JCG: A few.

WCR: *That's it?*

JCG: I worked with Ray Bonner of IBM to develop a program for reading electrocardiograms. I thoroughly enjoyed this work and we wrote a couple of papers.

WCR: *Joe, you are 66 years old now? As you look back over your career, you have been a terrific scientist. You have been a loved teacher. You have been a mentor to numerous young physicians. You are responsible for a large number of their careers. You have lead one of the world's great departments of medicine, one of the world's best cardiology divisions. Your research has always been thought of to be on the highest level. What are you most proud of among all your endeavors?*

JCG: Probably the people I have interacted with and helped to develop their careers.

WCR: *When you get home at night do you do much medical work?*

JCG: No.

WCR: *You do it in the morning or at the hospital?*

JCG: Yes.

WCR: *Joe, does anything bother you about cardiology today?*

JCG: The thing that has distressed me the most has been the failure of the cardiology community to grasp the fact that they needed to develop criteria for the training of invasive cardiologists and to certify them. There are a significant number of inadequately trained invasive cardiologists (e.g., a large number of angioplasties in this country are done by physicians who do <30 a year.)

WCR: *Do you think we need all these cardiologists? Why at a center like this do you keep pouring out so many cardiologists?*

JCG: We are pouring out a few less, but I think it is an interesting question. I believe that when I get sick I want to see the best specialists possible to take care of me who understand my disease. It is very hard to prove that cardiovascular specialists are worthwhile, but we are beginning to get data now which shows what you knew to be true. If you have a heart attack and you are taken care of by a cardiologist, you are going to do better in terms of all the parameters than

FIGURE 9. Photograph of JCG behind the counter in the old-fashioned country store he has recreated on his farm in rural Durham County. The farm has long been a favorite retreat for Greenfield, who built this cabin a few years ago with the help of friends. (Photography by Will & Denni McIntyre, McIntyre Photography, Inc., 3746 Yadkinville Road, Winston-Salem, North Carolina 27106.)

if cared for by a noncardiologist. I don't subscribe to the notion that health care costs are going to be lowered by getting rid of specialists. Currently, a large portion of the health care dollar is going to support the administrative aspects of medicine, such as advertising, highly paid corporate executives, and a gaggle of administrators, but not to physicians. I have not seen that this new approach actually reduces overall health care costs. I am concerned that we are at a point where the ability to deliver first class care health care has been severely curtailed. Maybe the nation can tolerate this situation, but I think it is a shame. The other answer to your question is that Duke Medical Center is in a position to train excellent subspecialists better than most other institutions. It strikes me as ridiculous that we should reduce the number we train while others don't.

WCR: *What is your view on preventive cardiology in general? Cholesterol lowering, blood pressure lowering?*

JCG: It depends on what we are going to prevent. I am certain that if the general population were willing to comply and all the known risk factors for the development of cardiovascular disease were eliminated, the disease on the average would occur some-

FIGURE 10. Greenfield in his country store by the stove. (Photography by Will & Denni McIntyre, McIntyre Photography, Inc., 3746 Yadkinville Road, Winston-Salem, North Carolina 27106.)

FIGURE 11. Photograph of Greenfield showing his butterfly collection in his farm cabin. Greenfield began the butterfly collection as a young boy. He is still an occasional collector. He once caught a rare natural hybrid that he gave to the American Museum of Natural History. (Photography by Will & Denni McIntyre, McIntyre Photography, Inc., 3746 Yadkinville Road, Winston-Salem, North Carolina 27106.)

what later in life. Whether or not the number of people actually developing cardiovascular disease would be reduced is a moot question. Certainly people will live longer. On the other hand, it is axiomatic that in the long run death will not be prevented. Thus, preventative strategies are unlikely to lower health care costs. If anything, living after the age when Social Security and Medicare take over will drain the national coffers. One thing is certain, we are all going to die. It is not clear to me that dying of something other than cardiovascular disease is cheaper.

WCR: *Talk a bit about your research. From age 30 to 50 you were straight ahead. As you look back over your own work, the training of others in your laboratory, the standards you set, the demand for accurate reproducible data, how does it hit you now?*

JCG: I cannot really say that anything we ever did was of major importance, but we published a body of excellent, solid research which will stand the test of time. I am very proud of it.

WCR: *The research made you a better doctor, a better teacher?*

JCG: A better doctor and a better teacher, because of the necessity to understand what the scientific method is all about and what it takes to prove an hypothesis.

WCR: *I suspect that you could not have been a chairman of a department which is as research based as yours without having gained an enormous amount*

of confidence from the success of your own research work.

JCG: There are 2 parts to this issue: (1) you have to be able to talk about research to people doing research in order to gain their respect if they are going to work for you. You have to produce research on your own to really make them comfortable, and (2) I think it also enables you to pick out people that are likely to be productive in the research arena.

WCR: *A lot of people talk about how much they have learned on travels, but I gather that as you reflect on your basic lack of travel, you are very pleased that you did it your way rather than the other way.*

JCG: Yes.

WCR: *That would be your advice to any young physician?*

JCG: What you learn primarily from traveling is that you have a very good situation at home—you better get back to it.

WCR: *You have mentioned your hobbies (Civil War, hunting). I gather you have been a student of butterflies all your life? Do you have other hobbies?*

JCG: No. I still collect butterflies. I am not a lepidopterist, but I have a reasonable collection and have had some fun with it.

WCR: *How many do you have?*

JCG: I have no idea.

WCR: *Do you have a butterfly list like bird watchers have a bird list?*

JCG: Yes. I was able several years ago to catch a couple of hybrids which are not supposed to occur in the wild. They're in the American Museum of Natural History.

WCR: *I understand, Joe, that you are a student of the Civil War.*

JCG: I got this interest from both my grandmothers.

WCR: *Are you a collector of Civil War books?*

JCG: Yes.

WCR: *Are you a first edition collector?*

JCG: No. I am more interested in what's in the book than what it looks like.

WCR: *So you still do a lot of reading on that topic?*

JCG: Yes. Also, I have recently gone on a number of walking tours of Civil War battlefield sites.

WCR: *I noticed that when you were in college you were a history major. Did you focus in any particular area during that time?*

JCG: Primarily in American History.

WCR: *Do you think these hobbies, the ability to get away by hunting, the ability to engross yourself in a Civil War tale, to find a beautiful butterfly has made you a better doctor and a better person? Do they help you communicate much better with people you talk to? Do you think your being a straight-shooter, which is what you are, trying to be enormously fair with everyone, were major assets in making your 12 years as departmental chairman so successful?*

JCG: I don't think there is any question about it. Sure. People will work for you for a variety of reasons. If you can pay them well, most people will work for you no matter what kind of person you are. If you can't do that, you have to substitute a number of things and the things you mentioned are the things you substitute. Try to develop a milieu where they want to work and promote the feeling that you are really going to try to do the best you can to meet their needs.

WCR: *Joe, thank you. I think that was terrific. I appreciate your willingness to do this.*

JCG: Bill, I am very delighted. I feel honored.

JCG's BEST PUBLICATIONS AS SELECTED BY JCG

5. Greenfield JC Jr., Patel DJ. Relation between pressure and diameter in ascending aorta of man. *Circulation Res* 1962;10:778–781.
12. Fry DL, Griggs DM Jr., Greenfield JC Jr. Myocardial mechanics; tension-velocity-length relationships of heart muscle. *Circulation Res* 1964;14:73–85.
13. Hernandez RR, Greenfield JC Jr., McCall BW. Pressure-flow studies in hypertrophic subaortic stenosis. *J Clin Invest* 1964;43:401–407.
25. Greenfield JC Jr., Tindall GT. Effect of acute increase in intracranial pressure on blood flow in the internal carotid artery of man. *J Clin Invest* 1965;44:1343–1351.
27. Greenfield JC Jr., Fry DL. Relationship between instantaneous aortic flow and the pressure gradient. *Circulation Res* 1965;17:340–348.
40. Greenfield JC Jr., Tindall GT. Effect of norephinephrine, epinephrine, and angiotensin on blood flow in the internal carotid artery of man. *J Clin Invest* 1968;47:1672–1684.
43. Greenfield JC Jr., Harley A, Thompsson HK, Wallace AG. Pressure-flow studies in man during atrial fibrillation. *J Clin Invest* 1968;47:2411–2421.
47. Harley A, Starmer CF, Greenfield JC Jr. Pressure flow studies in man: an evaluation of the duration of the phases of systole. *J Clin Invest* 1969;48:895–905.
52. Ruskin J, McHale PA, Harley A, Greenfield JC Jr. Pressure-flow studies in man: effect of atrial systole on left ventricular function. *J Clin Invest* 1970;49:472–478.
62. Greenfield JC Jr., Rembert JC, Young WG Jr., Oldham HN Jr., Alexander J, Sabiston DC Jr. Studies of blood flow in aorta-to-coronary venous bypass grafts in man. *J Clin Invest* 1972;51:2724–2735.
63. Bonner RE, Crevasse L, Ferrer MI, Greenfield JC Jr. A new computer program for analysis of scalar electrocardiograms. *Comp Biomed Res* 1972;5:629–653.
70. Ruskin J, Bache RJ, Rembert JC, Greenfield JC Jr. Pressure-flow studies in man: effect of respiration on left ventricular stroke volume. *Circulation Res* 1973;48:79–85.
71. Starmer CF, McHale PA, Cobb FR, Greenfield JC Jr. Evaluation of several methods for computing stroke volume from central aortic pressure. *Circulation Res* 1973;33:139–148.
77. Bache RJ, Cobb FR, Greenfield JC Jr. Effects of increased myocardial oxygen consumption on coronary reactive hyperemia in the awake dog. *Circulation Res* 1973;33:588–596.
81. Bache RJ, Cobb FR, Greenfield JC Jr. Myocardial blood flow distribution during ischemia-induced coronary vasodilatation in the unanesthetized dog. *J Clin Invest* 1974;54:1462–1472.
86. Bache RJ, Ball RM, Cobb FR, Rembert JC, Greenfield JC Jr. Effects of nitroglycerin on transmural myocardial blood flow in the unanesthetized dog. *J Clin Invest* 1975;55:1219–1228.
88. Wesly RLR, Vaishnav RN, Fuchs JCA, Patel DJ, Greenfield JC Jr. Static linear and nonlinear elastic properties of normal and arterialized venous tissue in dog and man. *Circulation Res* 1975;37:509–520.
102. Rembert JC, Kleinman LH, Fedor JM, Wechsler AS, Greenfield JC Jr. Myocardial blood flow distribution in concentric left ventricular hypertrophy. *J Clin Invest* 1978;62:379–386.
105. Swain JL, Parker JP, McHale PA, Greenfield JC Jr. Effects of nitroglycerin and propranolol on the distribution of transmural myocardial blood flow during ischemia in the absence of hemodynamic changes in the unanesthetized dog. *J Clin Invest* 1979;63:947–953.
109. Fedor JM, Rembert JC, McIntosh DM, Greenfield JC Jr. Effects of exercise- and pacing-induced tachycardia on coronary collateral flow in the awake dog. *Circulation Res* 1980;46:214–220.
114. Schwartz GG, McHale PA, Greenfield JC Jr. Hyperemic response of the coronary circulation to brief diastolic occlusion in the conscious dog. *Circulation Res* 1982;50:28–37.
115. Schwartz GG, McHale PA, Greenfield JC Jr. Coronary vasodilatation after a single ventricular extra-activation in the conscious dog. *Circulation Res* 1982;50:38–46.
123. Stack RS, Phillips HR III, Grierson DS, Behar VS, Kong Y, Peter RH, Swain JL, Greenfield JC Jr. Functional improvement of jeopardized myocardium following intracoronary streptokinase infusion in acute myocardial infarction. *J Clin Invest* 1983;72:84–95.
136. Sadick N, Dubé GP, McHale PA, Greenfield JC Jr. Metabolic mediation of single brief diastolic occlusion reactive hyperemic responses. *Am J Physiol* 1987;253:H25–H30.
141. Bauman RP, Rembert JC, Greenfield JC Jr. Regional atrial blood flow in dogs: effect of hypertrophy on coronary flow reserve. *J Clin Invest* 1989;83:1563–1569.
147. Dubé GP, Bemis KG, Greenfield JC Jr. Distinction between metabolic and myogenic mechanisms of coronary hyperemic response to brief diastolic occlusion. *Circulation Res* 1991;68:1313–1321.
148. Bauman RP, Rembert JC, Greenfield JC Jr. Regional blood flow in the canine atria during exercise. *Am J Physiol* 1993;265:H629–H632.
151. Bauman RP, Rembert JC, Greenfield JC Jr. Uniform vascular reserve in canine atria and ventricles during rest and exercise. *Am J Physiol* 1995:H1578–H1582.

CASE REPORTS, EDITORIALS, AND CLINICAL REVIEWS

6. Platt AP, Greenfield JC Jr. Inter-specific hybridization between Limenitis Arthemis Astyanax and Archippus (nymphalidae). *J Lepid Soc* 1971;25:278–284.
21. Rozear MP, Massey EW, Horner J, Foley E, Greenfield JC Jr. R. E. Lee's Stroke. *The Virginia Magazine of History and Biography.* 1990;98:291–308.
28. Rozear MP, Greenfield JC Jr. "Let us cross over the river": The final illness of Stonewall Jackson. *The Virginia Magazine of History and Biography.* 1995;103:29–46.

Lazar John Greenfield, MD: An Interview With the Editor

Lazar John Greenfield, MD[a,*], and William Clifford Roberts, MD[b,c,d]

Lazar Greenfield was born in Houston, Texas, in 1934, and that is where he grew up. He attended public schools and then Rice University before graduating with honors from Baylor University College of Medicine in 1958. He trained in general and thoracic surgery at The Johns Hopkins Hospital from 1958 to 1966. During that period he also spent 2 years in the surgery branch of the National Heart Institute at the National Institute of Health. Following his training he went to Oklahoma City as Chief of the Surgical Services at the Veteran's Administration Hospital at the University of Oklahoma Medical Center. He was named a Markle Scholar and rapidly ascended the academic letter to become a Professor of Surgery in 1971. In 1974, Dr. Greenfield moved to Richmond, Virginia, to be the Stuart McGuire Professor and Chairman of the Department of Surgery at the Medical College of Virginia, Virginia Commonwealth University. He remained in that position until 1987 when he became the F.A. Coller Distinguished Professor of Surgery and Chairman of the Department of Surgery at the University of Michigan School of Medicine in Ann Arbor. He developed an outstanding department of surgery which rose to the national ranking of No. 4 in research awards from the National Institute of Health. After 15 years as chair, he retired from that responsibility and was appointed Interim Vice President for Medical Affairs and Chief Executive Officer of the University of Michigan Health System from 2002 to 2003. He then took a sabbatical at the Center for Medical Devices at the Food and Drug Administration the next year. He retired from the university in 2004 but remained as a consultant to the Medical Products Surveillance Network. From 2004 to 2011, he was editor-in-chief of *Surgery News*, the monthly publication of the American College of Surgeons. Dr. Greenfield has been highly productive in his career having published 128 book chapters, and more than 404 scientific articles in peer reviewed journals, as well as 2 major textbooks of surgery. He has served on the editorial boards of 15 scientific journals and on an NIH study section. He is best known for his development of an intra-caval filter device to prevent pulmonary embolism and the device bears his name. He has received many awards, including the Rene Leriche Prize, the Roswell Park Medal, and the Jacobson Innovation Award of the America College of Surgeons. Annual research awards in his name have been established by the Humera Society of the Medical College of Virginia, and the Section of Vascular Surgery of the University of Michigan. He is recognized as an expert in vascular surgery and has lectured extensively in the USA and abroad. He has been elected to membership in 51 scientific and professional societies and received honorary membership in 9 additional organizations. He has served as member and then President of the Lifeline Foundation and chair of the board of the American Surgical Association Foundation. As a fellow of the American College of Surgeons he served on the Board of Governors, the Advisory Council for Vascular Surgery, and as Vice President and President-elect. He has been elected President of the American Surgical Association, the American Venus Forum, the Society of Surgical Chairs, American Association of Vascular Surgery, International Federation of Vascular Societies and the Halsted Society. He has been a director of the American Board of Surgery and has served as chairman of the National ACGME-Residency Review Committee for Surgery. In 1995, Dr. Greenfield was elected to the Institute of Medicine of the National Academies of Science. He has been designated a Johns Hopkins Society Scholar and has received Distinguished Alumnus Awards from Rice University and Baylor University College of Medicine. He has been happily married to his wife, Sharon, since 1956. They have 3 children and 8 grandchildren. His oldest son is Professor and Chair of the Department of Neurology at the University of Arkansas. Additionally, Lazar Greenfield is a great guy.

William Clifford Roberts, MD (hereafter Roberts): *Dr. Greenfield, it is a pleasure to have the opportunity to talk with you. Your lecture* The Frank Kidd Jr., MD Annual Lectureship in Surgery *was wonderful. Could we begin by your describing a bit of your growing up in Houston, your parents, siblings? What the atmosphere was like in your home growing up?*

Lazar John Greenfield, MD (hereafter Greenfield): I have no siblings. My mother was divorced when I was a baby and we lived in my maternal grandfather's house. I grew up there. We raised chickens and pigeons in the backyard. When I was 6 years old, a squab fell out of the nest and was pounced upon by the chickens resulting in a lot of damage to its neck. I rushed over, picked him up and took him to my grandfather to see if he could help it. He looked at it and said, "We will eat him for dinner". I said "Oh no, we have to save him". He took a needle and thread, sewed up the neck of this little squab, and told me to take care of him. And I did. Eventually, I put him back in the nest and he grew up. I could always spot him because he never grew any feathers on the back of his neck. I was amazed that one could repair something back to health. That convinced me at an early age that I wanted to go into medicine and to become a surgeon.

Roberts: *What did your father do?*

Greenfield: I'm not sure. I never had any contact with him. He had been trying to start a filling station during the

[a]Professor and Chair Emeritus, University of Michigan, Department of Surgery, Ann Arbor, Michigan; [b]Executive Director, Baylor Heart and Vascular Institute, Baylor University Medical Center, Dallas, Texas; [c]Dean, A. Webb Roberts Center for Continuing Medical Education, Baylor Health Care Systems, Dallas, Texas; and [d]Editor in chief, *The American Journal of Cardiology* and *Baylor University Medical Center Proceedings*.

*Corresponding author: Tel: (520) 885-8692.

E-mail address: lazarg@med.umich.edu (L.J. Greenfield).

Depression, which was a tough time. They had gotten married in California and I think he went back to California.

Roberts: *What was your mother like? What was her name?*

Greenfield: Her maiden name was *Betty Greenfield*. She was very focused on education although she had been taken out of school in the sixth grade in order to work. She always wanted to get a higher education. Later in life she did go back for course work. She told me early on that if I wanted to be a physician I had to make good grades in school. She was a very talented pianist. Obviously, having me didn't do much for her career. She became a legal secretary. Although she continued to teach piano she never performed again. She was a bright woman who I think could have done well in terms of her own education if she had had the opportunity.

Roberts: *She never went to college?*

Greenfield: Correct. She got a degree from the Houston Conservatory of Music and as a graduate of the conservatory qualified to take courses at the University of Houston This was when I was in high school. No one in my family had gone to college. I was the first one.

Roberts: *What did your maternal grandfather do?*

Greenfield: He was in real estate. He had immigrated from what is now Israel at the age of 19. He had a grocery store and when my mom was growing up she worked in the store. He branched out from that one store and got into real estate. He was a successful realtor.

Roberts: *What was your relationship with your maternal grandmother? You were the only youngster with 2 grandparents and your mother?*

Greenfield: My mom was one of 7 siblings, 6 sisters and 1 brother. There were other women in the home but I was the only child. It was a traditional middle eastern family.

Roberts: *How many lived in the house you lived in?*

Greenfield: At different times there were 2 or 3 of them in the home. The sisters got married and moved out as I grew up.

Roberts: *Did you have a room of your own growing up?*

Greenfield: From time to time.

Roberts: *What was school like? Grammar school, junior high, and high school?*

Greenfield: I enjoyed school. I got a little bored so they jumped me in grades. There wasn't an enrichment program at that time so I was simply advanced. I was always 2 years younger than everyone else in class. That meant I had to learn to run fast because I usually got chased after school.

Roberts: *You were advanced? This happened in grammar school?*

Greenfield: Yes.

Roberts: *Were there any teachers who had considerable influence on you early on?*

Greenfield: When I got to junior high school, there were some teachers that took an interest in me, encouraged me to do projects, and helped me learn more about science.

Roberts: *Did you take to science? Did that come naturally?*

Greenfield: I loved it. I wanted to do research from an early age—asking questions and finding out about things.

Roberts: *You went to public schools? Were the schools close to your house?*

Greenfield: Yes. I walked to school.

Roberts: *Where did you live in Houston?*

Greenfield: I lived on San Jacinto Drive, which was in the MacGregor School District. It's not there anymore but it was a good area to grow up in. There were other kids in the neighborhood but I was alone a lot and became somewhat self-sufficient.

Roberts: *Being 2 years younger than all your classmates, was that scary?*

Greenfield: It was educational.

Roberts: *When you got into high school, did you play sports or what were your activities?*

Greenfield: I liked sports. I was small in size so it was hard to play football, but I was on the ROTC team. I had a great time in high school. The age difference wasn't as big a deal by then. My mother wanted me to get involved in performance activities, so I was a child actor. I was in several drama plays and that gave me access in high school to do things involving the variety shows as Master of Ceremonies.

Roberts: *You were a local celebrity?*

Greenfield: Not really. But I was popular.

Roberts: *Did learning come easy for you?*

Greenfield: Yes.

Roberts: *Did you read fast?*

Greenfield: I enjoyed reading. I read everything I could get a hold of. I was able to get books. My mother bought me adventure books and we had a set of encyclopedias. Money was in short supply so I had to get a job. I had one when I was 14 and got a driver's license early.

Roberts: *When you were 14, what grade were you in?*

Greenfield: I was in high school as a sophomore.

Roberts: *You graduated from high school at 16?*

Greenfield: Yes. I got into Rice University. At the time Rice was an institute with essentially all scholarships once you got accepted. It cost me $25 a year, an activity fee. I was very fortunate. I continued to work at a grocery store as a checker through college.

Roberts: *Was that just on the weekends?*

Greenfield: No, I worked during the week as well.

Roberts: *Did you consider other colleges or was Rice the only choice?*

Greenfield: It was my only choice. We couldn't afford for me to go anywhere else.

Roberts: *Did you live at home during college? How far was Rice from your home?*

Greenfield: By that time, my mother had wisely taken advantage of her real estate upbringing and got us into a duplex, and then a home located fairly close to Rice University. I was able to go by either bicycle or walking every day.

Roberts: *It was still just you and your mother? She never remarried?*

Greenfield: She did but after I had gone off to medical school.

Roberts: *Did you and your mother get along well?*

Greenfield: Yes. It was a good upbringing. I had some unruly episodes growing up, frustrated by having to work all the time. Early on I got sent to a ranch in West Texas for "attitude improvement". That was a good experience.

Roberts: *How old where you then?*

Greenfield: I was about 13.

Roberts: *What do you mean by "unruly?"*

Greenfield: At the time I was rebellious and my mother was having difficulty with me. She was working and didn't want me to be alone in the summertime, so she sent me out to this ranch in West Texas.

Roberts: *That was summertime? When you were living with all your aunts and grandparents and mother, what was dinner like? Did all of you eat together?*

Greenfield: No. It was strictly the middle-eastern approach — the men were fed at the table and then the women ate afterwards. I ate dinner with my grandfather and then my mother, her sisters and my grandmother would eat.

Roberts: *Were you religious? Did you go to synagogue?*

Greenfield: I went to Hebrew school but I was not particularly religious. I was indoctrinated, had my bar mitzvah at 13, and stayed connected.

Roberts: *Where there many Jews in your public schools?*

Greenfield: Yes, there was a comfortable number. I was in a Jewish high school fraternity and that was a source of a lot of good social interaction.

Roberts: *You mentioned that you did have some influential teachers in junior high and high school. Specifically who and how did they influence you?*

Greenfield: They encouraged me to not only look at science but to look at some of the better writers. I was given a book of Emerson's essays by one teacher. She encouraged me to read and develop more mature approaches to life. They were well aware that I was socially in a disadvantaged position because of my age. It was more difficult in junior high because I was much shorter than everyone else.

Roberts: *What did you major in at Rice?*

Greenfield: They had a pre-med curriculum. I was premed from the very beginning. After 3 years I wanted to go to medical school. I went across the street and applied to Baylor University College of Medicine but didn't hear from them. I heard a rumor that the dean at Rice was very unhappy with premeds planning to leave Rice before graduation. I applied to Tulane University and got accepted. I took my acceptance letter back to Baylor and requested an answer or I was going to Tulane. They admitted it was true that the dean had asked them not to notify me that I had been accepted. I was able to get into Baylor and the Rice dean eliminated the premed curriculum after that.

Roberts: *Basically Rice was or is an engineering school. Did you take a lot of engineering courses?*

Greenfield: No I did not. I got influenced more at Rice by my philosophy teacher, *Radoslav Tsanoff*, a wonderful man. I took as many of his courses as I could.

Roberts: *Did anyone else at Rice have an influence on you?*

Greenfield: I was there with friends that I had gone to high school with and that was very helpful to be in a group because I didn't live in a dormitory. We were "townees" and a little different from the rest of the students who boarded on campus.

Roberts: *Did any of your classmates at Rice become prominent in their elected fields?*

Greenfield: My best friend and best man at my wedding is a prominent internist in Houston.

Roberts: *How big was Rice when you were there?*

Greenfield: Our class was about 400. The entire school included probably 1,400 students.

Roberts: *In your graduating class, how did you rank?*

Greenfield: I never graduated. I had been on the Dean's list every year and with those good grades I was able to get into medical school after 3 years of college.

Roberts: *You skipped 2 grades in grammar school and 1 grade in college. Now, entering medical school, you are 3 years younger than most of your classmates?*

Greenfield: Yes, I was 19 when I entered medical school.

Roberts: *Were there any major surprises in medical school that you didn't expect?*

Greenfield: Not really. It was as much fun as I thought it would be. I loved it from the very beginning. I loved the cadaver dissection, and everything related to it.

Roberts: *How many were in your class?*

Greenfield: 83 students.

Roberts: *What year did you enter medical school?*

Greenfield: 1954.

Roberts: *And you were born in 1934?*

Greenfield: Right.

Roberts: *How did you come out in medical school?*

Greenfield: I did well. I was able to get involved early in research. The first summer I went to the chief of pharmacology to try to get a job doing research. He gave me an assignment to test some drugs. Then he promptly took off for Europe. I was on my own doing this research project all summer. I got it done, wrote it up, and got published.

Roberts: *Did you work outside also at the grocery store while you were in medical school?*

Greenfield: No. I was able to get some paying positions as a lab assistant when I got into surgery. I tried to make that surgical connection as quickly as I could. It took another year before I got that connection. I was given the opportunity to do some surgical research and to be paid as a laboratory assistant.

Roberts: *Did you have scholarship money while in medical school?*

Greenfield: No, but by then my mother had been saving money all along for me to go to medical school. Medical school tuition was a little over $800 a year.

Roberts: *Who had major influence on you in medical school?*

Greenfield: I got connected with *George Morris*, and worked with him on a variety of projects, both clinical and experimental. I did some work for *Dr. Michael DeBakey* although I didn't spend time with him personally. I was sewing grafts in animals as a junior medical student and really loved vascular surgery.

Roberts: *How much time were you spending on these research projects?*

Greenfield: Lots of time. I was doing the regular classes too. I was able to do some of the clinical projects while I was a junior.

Roberts: *By the time you finished medical school, you had how many publications?*

Greenfield: 12.

Roberts: *Did you feel the impact of Dr. DeBakey in everything you did even though you didn't spend time with him directly?*

Greenfield: Oh yes, and *Denton Cooley* also because he was in the department at that time. I was able to watch their interaction and to watch them operate. I scrubbed in as a student.

Roberts: *Was it pleasurable to operate with DeBakey?*

Greenfield: Not really. But it was instructive. Everything about the school was clearly supportive of surgery but the surgery training program sort of turned me off because it was a very hostile environment. It was a situation where there was a lot of blaming. There was not enough learning from what had happened to patients. I knew that I didn't want to train there. I was encouraged train elsewhere also by Denton Cooley. He encouraged me to go to Hopkins, which I subsequently did.

Roberts: *How did you like operating with him?*

Greenfield: I didn't get to operate with him. I just watched him.

Roberts: *The Hopkins surgical internship in 1958 only took 12 interns?*

Greenfield: They took 12 and finished 2. It was a steep pyramidal program.

Roberts: *You did the internship and then where did you go?*

Greenfield: I went to the NIH right after the internship.

Roberts: *But you had an understanding with Dr. Blalock that he would accept you back?*

Greenfield: No. There was no understanding. I just knew that I was going to the NIH and I was grateful for that opportunity because it took care of the selective service requirement. I assumed that if I did a good job at the NIH I would get to come back.

Roberts: *How did Hopkins hit you? You had grown up in Houston, your college and medical school were in Houston, and all of a sudden you are in Baltimore.*

Greenfield: By then I was married and my wife was pregnant when we moved to Baltimore. My concern was for my budding family as well as for what I was doing. We lived across the street from the hospital. The call situation was very rigorous — on call 24 hours a day, 7 days a week. I got a few hours off if my patients were doing well, which I was usually able do on weekends.

Roberts: *Alfred Blalock was chairman while you were there. Did you have much contact with him?*

Greenfield: Not a lot. But I did get to scrub as an intern a few times with him and he did call me in at the end of the year and offer me the opportunity to go to the NIH. I did that and had a terrific time there.

Roberts: *What did you like about NIH? You were with Andrew G. Morrow in the clinic of surgery in 1959-1961?*

Greenfield: I had a wonderful experience. I was able to spend a lot of time in the lab. I did some clinical work but because of my interest and because I was productive in the lab, he arranged it so that I could spend more time in the lab and that gave me a chance to work with *Jerry Austen* and *Paul Ebert*. Paul subsequently became my co-resident and we finished the program together at Hopkins. Paul and I had been interns together. He stayed on at Hopkins when I went to the NIH and then he came the next year.

Roberts: *You got married in 1956 and your wife's name is Sharon Bishkin. What were some features that attracted you to her and how did you happen to meet?*

Greenfield: She was dating a friend of mine and was younger than me. Still in high school when we began to date. Then she went to the University of Texas and won a beauty contest. I knew I had to make a move or otherwise I was never going to see her again. She went to secretarial school and worked for George Morris at Baylor.

Roberts: *She was able to complete how much college?*

Greenfield: Two years.

Roberts: *After you were married a couple of years, you had a baby?*

Greenfield: Yes. He is now Professor and Chair of Neurology at the University of Arkansas in Little Rock.

Roberts: *How did you let him get into neurology?*

Greenfield: It wasn't easy. I was amazed he became a physician. He was a philosophy major at Yale and I thought I'd be supporting him his whole life.

Roberts: *The experience at NIH kept you in the research arena. Do you know any other colleagues that had 12 publications by the time they had finished medical school?*

Greenfield: No.

Roberts: *How did you and Dr. Blalock hit it off?*

Greenfield: Very well. He was declining in health and activity over the years I was there, so I had more contact with *Frank Spencer* and *Hank Bahnson*. I was at a senior level in the program when Dr. Blalock stepped down and subsequently died. I was a senior resident the year that *Dr. George Zuidema* came to Hopkins.

Roberts: *What was the change in atmosphere at Hopkins when Dr. Zuidema came?*

Greenfield: It was difficult. Dr. Blalock had such a strong presence and had been such a good operating surgeon. Dr. Zuidema was young and I think it was a difficult transition for him too because of the resident's loyalty to Blalock. Also, the fact that it had been a cardiovascular program and now was changing to general surgery. It was a challenge for me just to find a job after I finished the program.

Roberts: *He couldn't help you from a cardiovascular standpoint. He wasn't interested?*

Greenfield: He didn't know me that well.

Roberts: *What year did he come to Hopkins?*

Greenfield: 1965.

Roberts: *How did it work out that you came to the University of Oklahoma?*

Greenfield: *John Schilling* was a visiting professor from the University of Oklahoma at Hopkins. He was the chair of surgery at Oklahoma. We met and got along very well. He seemed interested in me. There was another Hopkins product, *Rainey Williams*, already at the University of Oklahoma. It was an attractive opportunity.

Roberts: *You became immediately head of surgery at the VA Hospital.*

Greenfield: Yes. It was an interesting situation. I was a little anxious because this was an administrative job for which I had absolutely no training. Dr. Schilling told me not to worry that the secretary for the chief knew how everything worked in the VA and he was right. She taught me everything I needed to know about administration.

Roberts: *How many surgeons were on staff at the VA?*

Greenfied: I was the only fulltime surgeon. There were a lot of visiting surgeons who were practitioners in town who would attend but we had only 5 faculty members to staff 3 hospitals — a children's hospital, a university hospital and the VA hospital. I had responsibilities in the University Hospital as well. I even had some responsibilities at the Children's Hospital. It was an ideal environment. I got to do so many different things like trauma call. And I did the first kidney transplant in the state.

Roberts: *You were trained in general surgery and in cardiac surgery. You had no specific training in vascular surgery?*

Greenfield: Correct. There wasn't any at that time.

Roberts: *I gather that you gradually gave up cardiac surgery?*

Greenfield: Yes. As I got more involved in responsibilities for teaching general surgery residents, I found that if I was going to spend any time with them I had to be doing cases that general surgery residents would scrub on and those were the vascular cases.

Roberts: *Vascular is very exciting though. You are everywhere. How did you get into the inferior vena cava filter, which your name is attached to?*

Greenfield: Like a lot of things, that interest came from a bad outcome in patients. I had a young man who died after a motorcycle accident from massive pulmonary embolism. I had resuscitated him and performed an open pulmonary embolectomy but he didn't survive. It was a very frustrating experience. At the time I was working with a petroleum engineer, *Garman Kimmel*, on an entirely different problem. I was working on a technique to measure pulmonary surfactant. This was a hot topic because of the interest in the *wet lung syndrome*. We designed a device to measure surface tension which was the only way to do it at the time. This was before the biochemical approach had been developed. We got the device developed. (And sure enough the biochemistry technique came along to make that no longer necessary.) But this surfactometer was exquisitely sensitive to the presence of detergent in water and it became a very useful approach in public health for detecting it in water systems. The device was called the "Greenfield Surfactometer". So, when my patient

died it was terribly frustrating and I considered the possibility of a different approach to getting clots out of the lungs that would not require the use of a heart-lung machine. I asked Garman Kimmel if he could fashion a cup that I could screw on to the end of a catheter. At the NIH I had spent a lot of time getting catheters into the pulmonary artery. And I knew if I could get a cup on the end of a catheter I could use suction to grab a clot and potentially pull it out of the pulmonary circuit. He was able to develop and fashion a cup that I could screw onto the end of cardiac catheter. I did 10 cases in shock like that salvaging 7 of the 10 but 2 of them had recurrent emboli. At that point I was unhappy because I would have to take these sick patients and open them up to put a clip on the vena cava. That was the standard approach at the time.

Roberts: *Clip means totally occluding it or just narrowing it?*

Greenfield: No. This is a clip that compartmented the vena cava. It required a direct approach to put it on the vena cava. It was a big operation.

Roberts: *Compartmenting means what?*

Greenfield: It means pinching the vena cava down to a smaller diameter and having prongs that separate it into small channels. That was the "Miles-DeWeese Clip" that was the standard approach. I was talking to Mr. Kimmel about an alternative way to trap clots. He said that sounded a lot like the problem he had in the oil field with sludge because sludge in the pipelines gets into the valves and they have to dig them up. It is very labor intensive. They used a cone-shaped trap to capture the sludge and the pipeline stays open. He proceeded to show me geometrically what that meant. I thought that it was a great concept — what if we added some hooks, fashioned it out of wire, and figured out a way to put it into the inferior vena cava? He got his machinist to build one, made it out of stainless steel wire. We tested the concept in dogs for 2 years and there was evidence that it was working well. I persuaded the VA to allow me to begin to put them in patients. Then I presented the data on the use of the embolectomy catheter and the filters at a cardiology meeting in Dallas. That meeting was attended by *John Abele* from Meditech (subsequently became Boston Scientific). He was very interested in the catheter and wanted to come to Oklahoma City with me. At that time, the filter concept had been patented, not by me since I was a State employee, but by Mr. Kimmel. We worked out a deal where Meditech took the patent, and although I never got royalties, they agreed to pay for follow-up studies. I was primarily interested in following the patients and finding out what happened to the filters and to the trapped clots. The company agreed to do that.

Roberts: *That continued over many years?*

Greenfield: It continued about 23 years until the company changed hands and direction.

Roberts: *You developed that filter within 2 or 3 years after you came to the University of Oklahoma. How did the move to Richmond and the Medical College of Virginia (subsequently Virginia Commonwealth University) come about?*

Greenfield: While at OU I presented a lot of papers in various places, and I had also collaborated with a terrific basic scientist, *Lerner Hinshaw*. He was a world class investigator in the field of septic shock. We published a lot of papers together. At the time, I was getting visibility from our studies and for the cardiovascular articles. I got invited to look at some cardiac jobs which I really wasn't interested in. I wanted to stay more broadly based. Then the politicians in Oklahoma decided that the surgeons at the University were abusing the system and stealing money. They made some wild accusations and the dean didn't support his faculty. John Schilling resigned and left the institution and in that turmoil I got an offer to come look at the job at the Medical College of Virginia. I took that opportunity and accepted the chair of surgery.

Roberts: *That was what year?*

Greenfield: 1974.

Roberts: *At that time you were 39 years old?*

Greenfield: Yes.

Roberts: *How did you enjoy being chairman of a much larger department?*

Greenfield: It was a learning experience and interesting. I followed a very strong and charismatic leader, *David Hume*, who had flown his airplane into a mountain. It was a little difficult at the beginning but there were good people there and I was able to recruit and build that department. It was a very good experience.

Roberts: *When you came initially, how many full-time department members were there?*

Greenfield: I don't remember the exact number. It was not a large department, maybe 20+ faculty members but it included all the specialties.

Roberts: *When you left, how many were there?*

Greenfield: It had more than doubled in size.

Roberts: *After you had been there say 5 years and you were comfortable with the chairmanship and the program you had set up, how much teaching were you able to do weekly?*

Greenfield: I ran generally one or 2 conferences a week, had an hour a week with the students, and made rounds with the students. I was very much involved in the teaching program.

Roberts: *How many operations were you doing yourself during this period?*

Greenfield: I was operating generally 2 days a week.

Roberts: *When you were operating, what was your most common type cases?*

Greenfield: I was doing both thoracic and vascular cases. I started out doing some cardiac cases but then I got away from that and just stayed with thoracic and vascular.

Roberts: *You've always kept thoracic under your domain?*

Greenfield: I did for a number of years and then gave that up when I went to Michigan. I primarily did vascular cases in Michigan.

Roberts: *So let's say you were 45 years of age in Richmond. What was your typical day like? What time would you get up in the morning? What time did you leave the hospital? What was your evening like? What time did you go to bed?*

Greenfield: I was always at the hospital by 7:00 A.M. and usually ran conferences starting at 7:00 A.M.

Roberts: *You would get up at 5:30 A.M.?*

Greenfield: 5:30 to 6:00 A.M.

Roberts: *And the days you were operating, what were those days like?*

Greenfield: They were long days. I would usually get home by 7:30 or 8:00 P.M.

Roberts: *What about the days you didn't operate?*

Greenfield: I would still get home about the same time.

Roberts: *Did you enjoy teaching students?*

Greenfield: I did. That was the most rewarding part of it—finding talent and cultivating it.

Roberts: *Were you pleased with the support that your department received from the dean and others?*

Greenfield: It depended. The deanship changed a couple of times. Deans have different flavors and attitudes. Some were supportive and some were less supportive but I figured out how to make things work regardless of who was there.

Roberts: Your research work continued to flourish during that Richmond period.

Greenfield: Yes. I was able to continue activities in the lab.

Roberts: *How did you like Richmond?*

Greenfield: I liked Richmond. My kids had to make a significant adjustment then. It was a lot harder on them because I had taken them out of high school. Virginia is very much a Southern state. It is an inbred environment. Virginians are most interested in pedigrees. They want to know your lineage. It was hard on my kids. Like a lot of things it was a maturing experience. When they were told that if they wanted to succeed in any profession they had to stay in the state to go to college, they couldn't wait to get out and all ended up going out of state to college.

Roberts: *Where did they go?*

Greenfield: My oldest son went to Yale, my daughter went to Pratt in New York, and my youngest son went to Vanderbilt and then Emory Law School.

Roberts: *How did the Michigan opportunity come about?*

Greenfield: Again, it was tied to pressure at both ends. There was a change in deanship in Richmond that was difficult and unfortunate. The dean didn't like the department of surgery and wanted to extract as much out of it as possible. He made it very uncomfortable for me. When I got the call to come look at the job at Michigan, it was pretty easy to say "yes". Even though we had enjoyed living in Virginia, and had built a home there, the opportunity in Michigan seemed to be essentially moving from the minors to the majors. I saw a very significant opportunity to do more and have more influence in surgery there.

Roberts: *That's one of the great medical schools and universities in the USA?*

Greenfield: I think so.

Roberts: *You got to Ann Arbor Michigan in what year?*

Greenfield: 1987.

Roberts: *I bet you were very glad you had had the experience in Richmond before you got to Ann Arbor?*

Greenfield: Yes. It was very helpful. I was fortunate to work with a very strong chair of medicine, *Bill Kelly*. Everyone said he was scary to work with but I found him to be very cooperative. We figured out that we had a lot more to gain from working together than working against each other. We were able to do some things at the institution that I don't think either of us could have done individually.

Roberts: *He left in what year?*

Greenfield: It was just a few years after I got there that he went to Penn.

Roberts: *What were you most proud of during your 15 years at Richmond?*

Greenfield: At Richmond I was able to develop a training program that was very competitive. We were getting much better candidates into the program and a lot of them were headed for academic careers. Previously it had been essentially a community hospital type program. We were able to recruit strong faculty members and start a good trauma program for example.

Roberts: *What were the big differences between your department at the University of Michigan and that of the Medical College of Virginia?*

Greenfield: The resources were considerably better. The Michigan institution was very focused academically, and the community support was stronger. The reputation allowed us to recruit talent and good trainees to the program. I felt there were no limits. Over the years, we steadily strengthened the research program and became No. 4 in the country in research dollars from the NIH, which was light years from where it had been.

Roberts: *What did your budget just for the department of surgery reach?*

Greenfield: I would be guessing. It would be several million. We had a large faculty, over 110 full-time.

Roberts: *If you take 110 faculty, their assistants, lab technicians and other supporting people, how many employees were you talking about under your domain? Did you know all of the surgical faculty?*

Greenfield: It was several hundred. I did know all the surgical staff. I didn't have direct contact with all of them but I was aware of their expertise, what they were doing, and what their problems were. I maintained an open office,

essentially anyone could come in at any time. I tried to stay in touch. It was harder because the only people I could see on a regular basis were the section heads weekly. A lot of my management had to be through them.

Roberts: *What were your divisions?*

Greenfield: I had all the subspecialties too.

Roberts: *Everything under surgery, including ENT?*

Greenfield: No, ENT was separate.

Roberts: *Your department was similar to David Sabiston's at Duke University?*

Greenfield: Yes. When Sabiston did not get Dr. Blalock's job at Hopkins, he went to Duke.

Roberts: *Did you have time to operate very much at Michigan? This was a huge administrative ordeal.*

Greenfield: I still operated but generally only one day a week.

Roberts: *I suspect that was very good for the rest of the department?*

Greenfield: I hope so. It was important that I be there to defend turf and to keep track of what was happening.

Roberts: *You have been very active through the years in a number of surgical organizations — president of several. How much traveling were you doing in say 1995?*

Greenfield: I actually had more responsibilities away from the department in Richmond because I was on the board of surgery and on a study section for the NIH. I was spending a lot of time away while in Richmond and tried to control that a little bit more when I was at Michigan. I continued to travel while in Michigan but it was different.

Roberts: *It's amazing to me how you were been able to follow through on your inferior vena cava filter through decades. There are very few people who continued working in an area for 40+ years. How have you been able to do that?*

Greenfield: I was able to set up a support system — a group of people who would help me track those patients and set up a feedback loop so that we could get the patients interested in coming back for examinations and follow-up. Meditech supported that for a long time and that helped a great deal. It involved staff people to a great extent.

Roberts: *Lazer, are there topics that we have not discussed that you would like to do so?*

Greenfield: No, I think you have covered the pertinent aspects of my career very well.

Figure 1. Sharon and me from an event 10 years ago. We celebrated our 57th wedding anniversary in August 2013.

Figure 2. The editorial group from Greenfield's *Surgery Principles and Practice*. Now in its 5th edition with Mulholland as Editor in Chief.

Figure 3. Pictured with Dr. Mike DeBakey when he was Visiting Professor at Michigan.

Figure 4. Pictured with Dr. John Cameron (Hopkins) (L) and the late Dr. Alex Walt (Wayne State).

Figure 6. Introducing Dr. Diane Simeone who became the Greenfield Distinguished Professor of Surgery in 2007 at the University of Michigan.

Figure 5. Sharon and me enjoying another favorite recreation on the dance floor (1992).

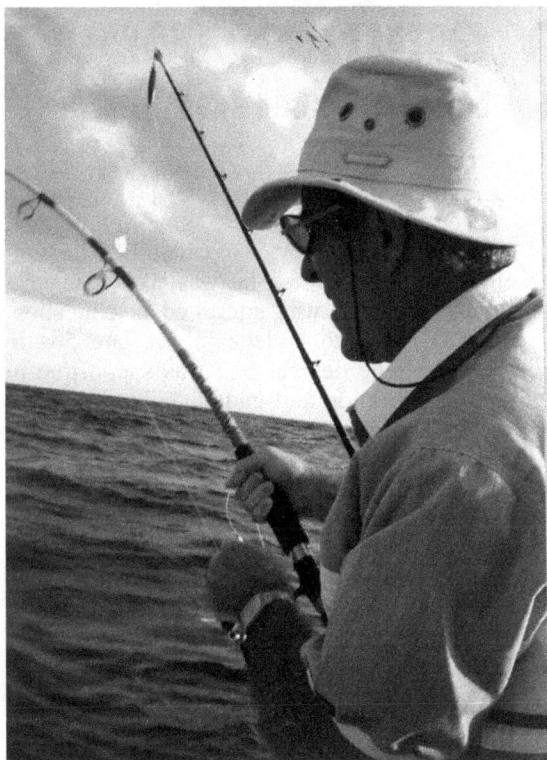

Figure 7. A fishing outing in New Orleans when I was a guest of their surgical society.

Figure 8. Another favorite pastime — fishing for barracuda in Florida (Dec' 2010).

SCOTT MONTGOMERY GRUNDY, MD:
A Conversation With the Editor*

Since 1981, Scott Grundy has been Director of the Center for Human Nutrition at the University of Texas Southwestern Medical Center in Dallas. He grew up in Memphis, Texas, went to Texas Technological College in Lubbock on a basketball scholarship, graduating in 1955 with honors, and then he went to Baylor College of Medicine in Houston, graduating in 1960 with both a Masters of Science and an MD degree. His research in lipids began as a medical student. After brief training in internal medicine and in pathology in Houston, he went to Rockefeller University in New York City, where he obtained a PhD degree in 1968. From there, he went to Phoenix, Arizona, as Chief of the Clinical Research Section of the National Insitute of Arthritis and Metabolism. From there, he went to the University of California-San Diego in 1973, where he remained for 8 years. Virtually his entire investigative career has been directed toward understanding atherosclerosis and preventing and arresting it. He was among the first to demonstrate the effectiveness of the statin drugs. His contributions to our knowledge of lipid metabolism have been enormous, and they have led to the publication of nearly 500 articles. Dr. Grundy has played a leading role in formulating the guidelines for using lipid-lowering therapy. He is also a splendid man with a good sense of humor and graciousness that makes him well liked by all fortunate enough to know him.

WILLIAM CLIFFORD ROBERTS, MD[†] (hereafter WCR): *I am talking with Dr. Scott Grundy in his conference room at the University of Texas Southwestern Medical Center on July 15, 1998. Dr. Grundy, I appreciate your willingness to talk with me so that the readers of* the American Journal of Cardiology *will get to know you better. I have been following your work for a long time. You are one of my heroes, so to speak, so I am really pleased to be here. I understand that you were born in Memphis, Texas, on July 10, l933. Is that where you grew up? Tell me about Memphis, Texas.*

SCOTT MONTGOMERY GRUNDY, MD, PhD[‡] (hereafter SMG): Bill, Memphis is a small town in the Panhandle of Texas. It is 90 miles southeast of Amarillo. When I grew up there, it was a town of about 5,000 people. It has since shrunk to about 3,500. It is a farming and ranching community. Mostly cotton and cattle feed are grown on surrounding farms, and cattle are raised on small ranches. It was a fine place for me to grow up. I lived there until I went away to college. My father, Allen Grundy, farmed and practiced law. We owned a farm 11 miles from town. Unfortunately,

*This series of interviews underwritten by an unrestricted grant from Bristol-Myers Squibb.
†Executive Director, Baylor Cardiovascular Institute, Baylor University Medical Center, Dallas, Texas 75246.
‡Director, Center for Human Nutrition, The University of Texas Southwestern Medical Center, Dallas, Texas 75235.

my father died when I was 10 years old. He was a good father for the time I knew him. My mother, Beulah Montgomery Grundy, also called Boodie, was a marvelous mother to me. She was well educated, studied constantly, and was interested in education. She even went back to college in her late 50s to complete her college degree. She was supportive of her childrens' education and undoubtedly played the major role in my early development, which set the stage for my later career.

WCR: *What do you remember about your daddy?*

SMG: Mainly, I remember going to the farm with him from time to time. He seemed to work hard, and I remember him dressed in work clothes. Although he practiced law, I was not much aware of this aspect of his life.

WCR: *Did he die young of heart disease?*

SMG: I believe not. There was no talk about a heart attack. He was admitted to our little hospital in Memphis. Something went wrong with him, and suddenly he died. Our family was never quite clear what went wrong. We never had a definite diagnosis to my knowledge.

WCR: *Was this his first illness?*

SMG: As far as I know, it was. He was 47 years old when he died. I believe he had been in fairly good health. In those days it probably was dangerous to go into a hospital. Maybe the same is true today.

WCR: *How many siblings did you have?*

SMG: I had 1 brother, Larry, 7 years older and a sister, Elizabeth, 2 years younger than I was.

WCR: *Your mother was really the one who brought you up?*

SMG: Definitely. She was the central person in my early life.

WCR: *Did she work?*

SMG: Not outside the home. She raised the kids. In those days, mothers usually didn't hold an outside job. We had aunts, uncles, and grandparents nearby. There was a strong family structure that was supportive, but demanding on my mother. She took on the task of keeping our extended family together and going. She also was an important member of the community, especially in her church. She remained in Memphis for her whole life. Most of her siblings left the town. She assumed the responsibility for caring for my grandparents in their later years.

WCR: *So your mother's and your father's parents grew up in the vicinity of Memphis, Texas, or close by?*

SMG: My grandfather on my mother's side, Steven Scott (S.S.) Montgomery (I am named for him), and his father, James Clowney Montgomery, came to the Texas Panhandle in 1889, and they actually organized the town of Memphis, which became the country seat of Hall County. My grandfather was born on a ranch

FIGURE 1. SMG at the time of the interview.

10 miles east of Sherman, Texas, in Grayson County. His early home was near a small town called White-wright, Texas. He told his grandchildren many wooly tales of his childhood there. His parents had come to Texas from Alabama, trying to escape unhappy lives after the Civil War. S.S. served as sheriff of Hall County from 1894 to 1898. He eventually became the President of the First National Bank of Memphis. He was a co-organizer, director, and elder of the First Presbyterian Church which came into being in 1900 (most of the other 13 original members were relatives). He was a pillar of the community until his death at age 94 in the 1960s. In 1891, S.S. married Lulu May Walters, who was a music teacher living in Vernon, Texas. S.S. and Lulu had 5 children, of whom my mother was the youngest. My grandfather was a most important person in my life from very early. After my father died, he served as the male figure in my life. Working with my mother, he took good care of me, and also inspired me to intellectual pursuits. His involvement with the Presbyterian Church, along with that of most of my relatives in Memphis, ensured my participation in church activities.

On my father's side, my grandfather was Joe Grundy. I didn't really know him; he died when I was a baby. Joe Grundy and his brother came to the Panhandle in 1889 from Kentucky; they settled in a small community called Newlin, which was about 10 miles south of Memphis. The Grundy brothers sold real estate and farmed. In the early 1890s Joe returned to Kentucky to fetch Lucinda (Cindy) Clack to be his

wife. They moved to Memphis some years later after my father was born. They too became regular members of the Presbyterian Church. Cindy, my grandmother, lived until the 1950s and died of "old age" in her 80s. In many ways she was my real "grandmother." She had a wonderful house, and usually our family had lunch (then called dinner) at her house every Sunday after church.

WCR: *Your mother and father knew each other growing up?*

SMG: My mother was born and raised in Memphis. My father moved there with his parents from Newlin. I don't know the circumstances of the meeting of my mother and father, but undoubtedly it was in the Presbyterian Church, which was at the center of social lives in those days. My father was 7 years older than my mother; he was born in 1896, and my mother in 1903. He went to the University of Texas in Austin, and during the First World War he was commissioned after schooling at Virginia Military Institute (VMI). He did not go to France, however, during the war.

WCR: *Your mother was the intellectual one. She stressed education.*

SMG: Yes. She had considerable schooling for a small town. She was in the very first class of the Hockaday school for women in Dallas, and in the early 1920s she attended Trinity College, which then was in Waxahachie, Texas. Trinity University was affiliated with the Presbyterian Church; it has since moved to San Antonio, Texas. However, the old school buildings that were Trinity are still in Waxahachie, but are used for some other purpose. My mother was never happy that she had not received her college degree, and in her late 50s, she went back to college, took courses, and obtained her degree.

WCR: *What did your older brother do?*

SMG: After he finished high school in Memphis, Larry went to college for about a year at the University of Texas in Arlington; then in 1943, he went into the Navy. At the end of World War II, he went to Baylor University in Waco, where he majored in chemistry. There he met Mary Alice Thompson, who was from Palestine, Texas, and they were married. After graduation and marriage, Larry and Mary Alice went to Oklahoma A&M, Stillwater, Oklahoma, where he received a masters degree in chemistry. Then he became a teacher at Clarendon Junior College in Clarendon, Texas. He taught there for several years before going to work with Phillips Petroleum Company, first in Borger, Texas and then in several other places, including Bartlesville, Oklahoma (the company's headquarters). While working at Phillips, Larry was offered a job on the East Coast; he and his family (wife and two children) moved to Boston, where he became the director of a factory making plastic items. After several years there, he was transferred to Maine. Later, he took a similar job with a larger company in New Jersey. Unfortunately, he became afflicted by chronic lymphocytic leukemia, and sadly, suffered for a long time before he died a couple of years ago.

WCR: *What has your sister Elizabeth done?*

SMG: After graduating from high school, Elizabeth went to college at West Texas State College in Canyon, Texas. Canyon is right outside of Amarillo. There she met and married Gene Murray. They have since lived in Canyon and have two sons. Both Elizabeth and Gene have taught in public schools. Elizabeth taught in Amarillo, Texas, and still does. Mainly, she has worked in special education with disadvantaged children. She spends almost full time thinking and planning how to improve educational techniques. She is a devoted teacher and has tremendous energy that is directed almost entirely to her teaching work. She has made many contributions to the public educational program in Amarillo. Her husband, Gene, taught in the Canyon school system for many years. However, he retired a little early so that he could pursue his creative and artistic interests. Gene is enormously talented, being both musically and artistically inclined. Although he has always been creative, his productivity mushroomed after his retirement. He plays a key role in planning, set and costume design, and singing in the Amarillo opera. Even more impressive is that the fact that he writes his own operas. Several of his operas, which are mostly of Western genre, have been produced in the Amarillo area. You will recall the story of the supposed landing of the unidentified flying object (UFO) in Roswell, New Mexico, in the 1950. Roswell has become the Mecca of the UFO crowd. Gene recently wrote an opera about this event, and it premiered in Roswell this summer. I am told it will become an annual event there. I have seen several of Gene's operas. They grasp the essence of the West and transform it into music.

WCR: *What was it like growing up in Memphis, Texas? Did you live in town?*

SMG: Yes, my family owned a farm and I used to go there with my father. I didn't like farm work, however. To me the work was boring, and early on, I knew I was destined not to become a farmer. You always had to worry about the weather and crops, and the worries were the same, year in and year out. There was nothing in farming that interested me. Instead, I stayed in town and did things there. I was mainly interested in sports. I liked school, and the combination of school, sports, and church largely made up my childhood and adolescence.

WCR: *You grew up in Memphis in the 1930s during the Depression?*

SMG: I was a small child in the 30s, but went to school in the 40s.

WCR: *Do you remember the Depression at all? Was it talked about?*

SMG: I remember it being talked about, but I don't recall any financial hardships. Instead, I remember the dust storms that occurred at that time. They are indelible in my mind. To me they are somehow linked to the Depression. There were days when one literally couldn't see across the street because the sand was so thick. This was not unusual. But I don't remember any money problems. We were never hungry or suffered in any way.

FIGURE 2. SMG at the time of the interview.

WCR: *You say you liked sports better than farming. What sports did you play?*

SMG: Baseball and basketball. I liked them both. One year while I was playing, our high school basketball team won the state championship. It was thrilling. Furthermore, I went to Texas Tech University on a basketball scholarship. I had more talent for basketball, but actually liked baseball better.

WCR: *What positions did you play in baseball in high school?*

SMG: Outfield and first base. I was in love with baseball. The essence of my feeling about baseball is caught in Ken Burn's recent video documentary of the American baseball experience.

WCR: *Did you like your studies in high school? Did you work hard?*

SMG: I did work hard, but school was easy. Sadly, high school work was not very demanding. Nevertheless, we had 2 or 3 exceptionally talented teachers who were inspirational and stimulating. They deserve credit for starting me off on the right track in academics.

WCR: *Which high school teachers had the greatest influence on you?*

SMG: There were 2 who inspired me academically. One was Elsie Guthrie, who was a brilliant English teacher. She would have made an outstanding college teacher. The other was Neville Wren. Miss Wren had been the Director of the Department of Chemistry at Lubbock High School, before moving back to Memphis to care for her elderly mother. Her taking a job in

FIGURE 3. SMG as a senior in high school.

FIGURE 4. SMG (far right) as a senior in high school on the championship basketball team.

Memphis High School was a stroke of luck for me. She gave me a solid foundation in chemistry (which I didn't have in other subjects), and this made college chemistry much easier for me.

WCR: *How many students were in your senior class in high school?*

SMG: About 38.

WCR: *So you graduated number 1 in your class of 38?*

SMG: I was either first or second.

WCR: *So you enjoyed your school work and worked hard?*

SMG: Yes, but it didn't challenge me. I realized how limited my education was when I got to Texas Tech and had to confront students from "big" cities like Lubbock and Dallas. It was obvious that they knew a lot more than I did, and it took me awhile to catch up.

WCR: *You mentioned your church activities in Memphis. What was it like? You went to Sunday school and church regularly? Maybe church dinners on Wednesday night?*

SMG: Right. Much of the social life in our town revolved around the churches, for our family, the Presbyterian Church. Our church had good ministers, and we also had regional programs for youngsters. Every summer I went off to church camp where we came into contact with some remarkable people, among whom were Presbyterian missionaries who worked in foreign countries. They would talk to with

us about the wonderful things they were doing and how they were saving lives as well as souls. Some told about their work in Africa, Asia, or parts of South America. Their stories broadened my outlook beyond the bounds of Texas.

WCR: *What were the effects of your early religious experiences on your later life?*

SMG: They were considerable, and in several areas. Presbyterians seem to intellectualize religion. Presbyterianism is a form of Calvinism, and it stresses a stern, intellectual commitment to God and mankind. Our religious studies were strong on church history, and they broadened my interests into history in general. To me, Calvinist theology has a strong philosophical bent, and readings in theology sparked what became a prolonged interest in the history of Western philosophy. These interests were heightened by contact with learned ministers from the regional Presbytery, and they have remained with me throughout life. In addition, my religious experiences and associations opened my eyes to the plight of mankind. Stories of missionaries vividly revealed to me the extent of human suffering throughout the world. These impressions undoubtedly had an impact on my thinking that influenced my later career decisions. I was less affected by religious dogma. In religion I was more inspired by Albert Schweitzer than by Billy Graham. The uncertainties of religious doctrine left me with little desire to try to save souls. Insight into human

FIGURE 5. SMG at graduate ceremonies at high school.

suffering had yet another influence with regards to my career. It created a barrier to pursuit of pure science that is not tangibly linked with human end points.

But all of this religious influence acted at a deeper level and came out later. My true preoccupation in high school was with sports, which didn't seem incompatible with the religious life. In fact, church on Sunday morning didn't keep me away from baseball games on Sunday afternoon. But I can assure you that in close basketball games we prayed earnestly for God to side with our team.

WCR: *So when you finished high school, you chose to go to Texas Tech. How far is Lubbock from Memphis?*

SMG: One hundred fifty miles.

WCR: *How did you choose to go to Texas Tech? I assume all your tuition was paid since you were on a basketball scholarship.*

SMG: Correct. I had to choose between TCU (Texas Christian University; Fort Worth) and Tech (Texas Tech). Although I went on an athletic scholarship, I made the decision on academics. For some reason, I thought Texas Tech was better academically.

WCR: *When you got to college, what happened?*

SMG: I started out spending much of my time on basketball practice, as required by the athletic scholarship. Fortunately, in retrospect, I was not a college-caliber player. After about one and a half years I came to realize that basketball held no future for me, so I began to get more serious about my studies.

WCR: *Can you tell me whether there were any long-term beneficial effects of your youthful experience with sports?*

SMG: One of my life-long characteristics has been an intense preoccupation with the subject of current interest to me. When I was involved in sports, it was serious business. As such, I found both baseball and basketball to be demanding and molding activities. They required mental and physical exertion and endurance. They also forced me to come to grips with my limitations. In addition, team sports reveal that success can only come through teamwork. Of great importance to me, competitive sports teach us to never give up; one can never tell when fortune may smile at the last moment, as it sometimes did for me. At least for me, intensive involvement with sports was a preparation for coping with adult life. I have come to see the wisdom of the inscription at the entrance to the athletic fields at West Point, that is, what is learned here will bear the fruits of victory "upon other fields, on other days." Without the experience gained from those long hours of exertion and competition in high school and college, I truly doubt that I would have been able to sustain the ups and downs of a lifelong career in research. Like the batter at the plate, in medical research there are many more outs than hits, and homeruns are few and far between.

WCR: *So you turned to academic work. What was your major?*

SMG: Chemistry.

WCR: *Your brother also majored in chemistry? Who had a scientific impact on your back in Memphis?*

SMG: My brother had an influence, as did my high school chemistry teacher, Neville Wren.

WCR: *Did Texas Tech provide well for you academically?*

SMG: Again, fortunately, Texas Tech was an excellent place for an education. They had wonderful teachers who took great interest in the students. My mind was opened up to a new world of learning, which went far beyond anything I was ever exposed to in high school.

WCR: *Did anybody at Texas Tech University have a major impact on you?*

SMG: There were 3 people in the Department of Chemistry who had the greatest influence. Margaret Stuart taught qualitative analysis. She was stern, but caring and committed. She took me on as a laboratory assistant. I remained her friend for the rest of her life. Joe Dennis was Chairman of the Department of Chemistry. He was extremely intellectual, an excellent teacher, and a good Presbyterian. He provided me with the fundamentals of biochemistry; fortuitously, I wrote a research paper for him: the biosynthesis of cholesterol. Robert Goodwin was the dean of Arts and Sciences, and later became president of Texas Tech. He taught me how to think about the reactions of organic molecules, but he did more than that—he gave me a solid grasp of the carbon backbone of the biological world. These 3 people were true role models. Other teachers at Texas Tech were excellent, particularly the science professors. After Texas Tech, I never had any problems with the academics of medical school. In fact, in medical school, I was scientifically way ahead of most of the other students.

WCR: *You went to college from 1951 to 1955, 4 years? How many students were at Texas Tech at that time?*

SMG: Five thousand.

WCR: *Did you live in the dormitories?*

SMG: I started out in the athletic dorm. That was an experience. I can assure you that the primary interest of most of my teammates was not academics. My view of college and professional athletes has been rather jaded ever since. However, the dorm kitchen fed us better than all the other students on campus—one plus.

WCR: *How tall are you?*

SMG: Six feet, 3 inches.

WCR: *How much did you weigh then?*

SMG: I weighed about 190 pounds, more than I do now. But it was all muscle then.

WCR: *After you gave up basketball, did they take your scholarship away?*

SMG: Of course. I had to come up with the tuition afterwards, but it was cheap enough.

WCR: *What is your assessment of your education at Texas Tech?*

SMG: In those days Texas Tech was quite strong in science and engineering. I tried to take full advantage of this strength. Not only did I receive a strong grounding in organic chemistry and biochemistry, I fell in love with these subjects. Thereafter, I always thought in molecular terms. I have since visualized biological processes as molecular events. I have no doubt that my experience at Texas Tech laid the foundation for my academic career. Upon entering medical school, I gravitated toward research and biochemistry. This love and understanding of molecular processes provided a balance to humanistic tendencies acquired through religious experience and made it unlikely that I would pursue a career in the routine practice of medicine.

WCR: *Where did you apply to medical school?*

SMG: At first I applied to two Texas schools: University of Texas Medical Branch at Galveston and Southwestern Medical School in Dallas. I was accepted at Galveston without an interview. I interviewed in Dallas at Southwestern, which was then housed in old U.S. Army barracks on Oak Lawn Ave. Parkland Hospital also used to be on Oak Lawn. When Baylor University College of Medicine moved to Houston from Dallas in 1943, there was no medical school in Dallas for awhile. Then an influential group of citizens organized Southwestern Medical School, which was later affiliated with the University of Texas. When I visited Southwestern and its barracks, I said to myself "This is a medical school?" But I was resigned to go there nonetheless.

WCR: *But you ended up at Baylor Medical School in Houston.*

SMG: At first I did not even apply to Baylor because tuition was $1,000 per year, and that was out of my reach. Then fate intervened. At Texas Tech, we had a pre-med club and one of our invited speakers

was James Schofield, Assistant Dean at Baylor. I sat next to him. Dr. Schofield was an aggressive recruiter of good students for Baylor. We chatted, and he asked why I had not considered Baylor. I said I couldn't afford to come to Baylor. He told me that perhaps Baylor could give me a scholarship ($500 per year), and he offered to pay my way to come to Houston for an interview. I got on the train and went to Houston. Baylor Medical College had a brand new building, quite a contrast to Southwestern's barracks. Several things attracted me to Baylor besides the scholarship and facilities. The fact that someone actually took a personal interest in me was appealing. Also, Baylor only had 3 examinations per year! The rest of the year you could study and prepare, but did not have to sweat out the every Saturday morning exams that I had been warned about at Southwestern and Galveston. Dr. Schofield also told me that Baylor fully intended to graduate all of its students, and would not flunk out a sizable portion of the class. I had heard tales of large numbers of students flunking out of the other schools in Texas. Being from a little town in the Panhandle, I was not filled with confidence in my abilities. So I chose Baylor to be on the safe side. I often reflect on this chance encounter with James Schofield and wonder how my life would have been different if I had not met him and had gone to Southwestern instead. Perhaps not so badly. I would have been a student of Dr. Donald Seldin! Not having been one of Dr. Seldin's boys has been one of the regrets of my life. Just look at the great researchers and teachers who grew up under him, Drs. Jean Wilson and Daniel Foster, for example, not to mention Joseph Goldstein.

WCR: *You had to come up with another $500 to go to Baylor.*

SMG: That wasn't too hard, particularly after I got married and my wife worked.

WCR: *Why did you take 5 years to graduate from medical school?*

SMG: I took an extra year and participated in their masters degree program. At Baylor, students could get a masters degree while going to medical school. They split their second year, and thus had half-time in research for two years to work on it. Many students who entered this program ended up in academic medicine. Some of them became quite well known. Providing research training for medical students was visionary on Baylor's part. I'm sorry we don't still use Baylor's model in our medical schools. We don't do enough to encourage our bright medical students to pursue research and academic careers.

WCR: *When you entered Baylor University College of Medicine in Houston in 1955, how many students were in your class?*

SMG: Ninety.

WCR: *How did you find medical school? Did you enjoy it?*

SMG. It was a tremendous experience. I enjoyed every minute of it. The teachers were terrific. Everything Dr. Schofield said was true. The faculty really supported the students. There was no undue pressure.

We studied hard, but I loved it. To me, Baylor was a fabulous place to receive a medical education.

WCR: *Who had an impact on you?*

SMG: It is not fair to single out individuals, because so many contributed. But 2 do stand out. One was Clark Griffith, Chairman of the Departments of Biochemistry at both Baylor and M.D. Anderson Hospital. He was a cancer biochemist of considerable renown. Strangely enough, despite his cancer interests, Dr. Griffith is the person who got me started in atherosclerosis research. When I entered the masters degree program, I decided to work with Dr. Griffith. He said to me one day that the Anderson-Clayton company wanted Baylor to do research on the potential of one of their products, lecithin, to prevent atherosclerosis. The company offered to buy the Biochemistry Department an analytical ultracentrifuge, which at that time cost $30,000, if Dr. Griffin would study the effects of lecithin on lipoproteins. This centrifuge was championed by John Gofman and his team at Berkeley. Gofman had recently "rediscovered" the serum lipoproteins and had developed a method for analyzing them with the ultracentrifuge. John Gofman was truly a genius, and deserves enormous credit—much more than he has received—for his contributions to the fields of lipoproteins and atherosclerosis. He clearly delineated very low-density lipoprotein (VLDL), low-density lipoprotein (LDL), and high-density lipoprotein (HDL) as separate lipoproteins. His methods of classifying lipoproteins are still used today. He also was prescient in predictions of the atherogenicities of the different lipoprotein species. Dr. Griffin asked me if I would like to work on this project for my masters degree. I agreed, was given complete control over the ultracentrifuge, and was allowed to follow my own interests. Incidentally, I found that feeding lecithin to rabbits doesn't improve their lipoproteins or prevent atherosclerosis. Of interest, I was taught to use the ultracentrifuge by researchers at the Air Base in San Antonio, who were measuring lipoproteins prospectively on West Point cadets and pilots. They ran thousands of samples, but unfortunately, none of their studies ever made it to the scientific literature.

WCR: *What did you learn in your lipoprotein research?*

SMG: I did naive studies on effects of solvent extractions in the attempts to get at the protein core of lipoproteins. In fact, this work resulted in several publications, although the tools were not available to do definitive work on the apolipoproteins. Of more substance was the observation that mental stress raises serum cholesterol and lipoprotein levels. There was a hint of this in the literature before, but I believe that I really nailed it down. Since the medical students had their exams every 3 months, the pressure would mount so that on the day of the exam, when they were in a state of panic, their cholesterol levels were much higher than in the relaxed period between exams. I reproduced this fluctuation several times over 2 years.

WCR: *So by the time you graduated from medical school you had written 10 papers?*

SMG: Yes.

WCR: *When you interview people now to work in your laboratory, do you always look to see if they published when in medical school?*

SMG: That is a plus, but unfortunately, we rarely see much evidence of student research because medical schools don't give their students a chance to be involved in research as Baylor did. I have tried to rekindle interest in the Baylor model, but with little success. In my view, a great opportunity is being missed.

WCR: *Who was the other influential person at Baylor?*

SMG: Michael E. DeBakey. Dr. DeBakey was previously interviewed by you for this series. He truly is one of my heroes. When I was in medical school, he was just an incredible man, almost superhuman, a person way beyond the ordinary in talents, skill, and knowledge. He was an inspiration to me, and still is. He was also working on atherosclerosis. Although he suggested to me that I should consider surgery as a career, and has continuously admonished me afterwards for my mistake, surgery was not to my taste. Nonetheless, he was supportive and helped me get funding for my research on atherosclerosis and lipoproteins. Dr. DeBakey taught me how to apply oneself to work and how to make things happen. He was incredibly good at making things happen; he, more than anyone, built Baylor into what it is today.

WCR: *When did you decide you liked research and that research is what you wanted to do?*

SMG: As I mentioned, the stage was set by my college studies, but my association with Dr. Griffith was the precipitating influence. In fact, when I finished medical school, Dr. Griffith wanted me to go straight into the Department of Biochemistry, which I did. However, I received another opportunity that gave me a boost in this direction. I was invited to work in the laboratory of Prof. Sune Bergstrom of the Karolinska Institute in Stockholm. This was made possible because of Sune Bergstrom's visits to the newly formed Lipid Research Center in Houston headed by Evan and Marjorie Horning. Dr. DeBakey was a strong supporter of this new center, and he obtained funding for me to spend a summer in Bergstrom's laboratory. Sune Bergstrom was a co-discoverer of prostaglandins, for which he received the Nobel Prize. Also, his laboratory was working on bile acids, which was the subject of my research with him and his group. This experience opened my eyes to how good research is actually carried out.

WCR: *That was immediately after you finished medical school?*

SMG: Yes, 1960.

WCR: *Who were you classmates in medical school.*

SMG: My best friend was Malcolm Daniel, now a cardiac surgeon in Chattanoga, Tennessee. Another close friend was George Noon, now a well-known cardiac surgeon who worked closely with Dr. DeBakey throughout his career. Another was Wayne Bardin who has had an illustrious research career in

FIGURE 6. SMG with E. H. Ahrens, Jr. *(left)*.

endocrinology at the National Institutes of Health and the Population Council of the Rockefeller Foundation.

WCR: *After you decided you did not want to be a surgeon, what did you decide you wanted to do?*

SMG: That is a good question. I could not decide immediately. I wanted to continue with research, but realized that I needed clinical training. So I gave up the Biochemistry position and started an internship in Internal Medicine. In a rotation on pathology, I met the new chairperson of pathology, Dr. Robert O'Neill, who was working on atherosclerosis. He convinced me to switch to a pathology residency and promised that I could work with him.

WCR: *Then the pathologist enticed you to come to the pathology department. How long were you there?*

SMG: A year.

WCR: *You did that so not much because you were interested in pathology, but in atherosclerosis and the new pathology figure was prominent in experimental atherosclerosis?*

SMG: That is exactly right. However, Dr. Griffith was not happy with this pathway and urged me to consider going to Rockefeller University to obtain a PhD. He used his influence to obtain an interview for me at Rockefeller.

WCR: *So you went to Rockefeller University in 1962?*

SMG: Yes, July 1962. Dr. Griffin made his last major contribution to my career by promoting this move.

WCR: *You stayed at Rockefeller University until what year?*

SMG: 1971.

WCR: *How did that work out?*

SMG: Rockefeller was even better than Baylor. The Rockefeller University at that time was absolutely at its peak. There were many famous scientists there. Detlev Bronk, the former President of the National Academy of Sciences, was its president. In the 1950s, at the request of David Rockefeller, Dr. Bronk had assumed direction of Rockefeller and had established

a graduate school. He also brought in many fine scientists. He changed the old Rockefeller Institute into a graduate university. When I reached Rockefeller, I was able to survey different laboratories and choose the one I wanted to work in. I was attracted to E.H. (Peter) Ahrens, Jr., who was doing outstanding work in lipid metabolism. He was a link to my interest in atherosclerosis. I continued to work with Pete Ahrens for almost 9 years, completing my PhD along the way.

WCR: *So you were doing basic research?*

SMG: No, not basic research. Pete Ahrens believed in clinical research; for him human research was basic research. He was committed to doing research in humans. In fact, he has been a strong advocate of clinical investigation for many years, and he certainly was influential in setting my research direction. I have focused on clinical research ever since. He deserves the credit for my being a committed clinical investigator.

WCR: *What you are doing now, in actuality, is similar to what you were doing at Rockefeller University in the 1960s?*

SMG: More sophisticated, but along the same lines.

WCR: *You also got some training in internal medicine and endocrinology while you were there. You were chief resident in the hospital?*

SMG: It was all research. After I finished my PhD, I went on the faculty. The Chief Resident at the Rockefeller Hospital was the person who coordinated all the clinical activities. It was not a training position.

WCR: *How many beds were in the Rockefeller University Hospital?*

SMG: Forty, when I was there.

WCR: *For both children and adults?*

SMG: Yes.

WCR: *Surgery?*

SMG: No, they were all research beds. Some beds were funded by NIH, and some by the Rockefeller University.

WCR: *Where is the Rockefeller University located?*

SMG: At 66th Street and York Avenue. It consists of a campus with several research buildings, including 1 hospital building.

WCR: *Where did you live in New York?*

SMG: East 77th Street and York Avenue.

WCR: *So you were close?*

SMG: Yes, I always walked to work. We didn't even own a car.

WCR: *Tell me about your training at Rockefeller.*

SMG: Rockefeller was the defining experience of my career. Working with Pete Ahrens taught me to carry out human research and lipid research. In addition, I was exposed to many of the renown biological scientists of our time. We had day-to-day contact with these great people. Rockefeller was an open society. We had a common dining room where everyone came for lunch. One could sit down with Nobel laureates and members of the National Academy of Sciences and chat with them any day. Some of the faculty I knew personally included Fritz Lipmann, Edward Tatum, Henry Kunkel, Gerald Edelman, Lyman Craig, Stanford Moore, William Stein, Maclyn McCarty, Alexander Bearn, Rene Dubos, George Palade, Christian DeDuve, Richard Shope, Rebecca Lancefield, Vincent Dole, Bruce Merrifield, and Payton Rous. When Payton Rous was a medical student, he contracted TB and took the cure on a ranch in the Panhandle of Texas; he used to reminisce with me about those times. Dr. Bronk insisted that the PhD students get special attention, and we had ready access to all of these people. Many of the PhD students were close friends. My best student friend at Rockefeller was Anthony Cerami, who has made marvelous contributions to many fields, including diabetes, immunology, and aging. I have maintained a close relationship with him ever since.

WCR: *You did not have to pay to be there. They paid you?*

SMG: Yes, they paid me. This made it possible for me to go there.

WCR: *Can you describe the work you did there in those 9 years?*

SMG: Let me say that my research was carried out in a very active laboratory. Some of the researchers in Dr. Ahrens' group were Norton Spritz, Jules Hirsch, Alan Hofmann, Gerald Salen, Tatu Miettinen, Robert Lees, and Jean Davignon. All of these researchers have become well known. My own research was focused on the development of the cholesterol balance method. This methodology aimed to define human cholesterol metabolism in quantitative terms. It measures how much cholesterol the body makes, how much is absorbed, and how it distributes throughout the body. It also measures the synthesis of bile acids, a product of cholesterol. Once the methods were worked out, we were able to study the effects of various nutrients and drugs on cholesterol metabolism. Pete Ahrens was one of the discoverers of the action of polyunsaturated fats to lower the blood cholesterol, and he wanted to know how polyunsaturated fats alter the body's cholesterol metabolism. However, at Rockefeller, the development of new methodology seemed to be an end-in-itself. In the rarefied atmosphere of this institution, new methods appeared to be even more important than new biological discoveries. My own research attempted to expand on methods to study cholesterol metabolism, including use of radioactive tracers to follow the pathways of cholesterol into and out of the body.

WCR: *What was a typical day like in 1965 when you were working in the lab at Rockefeller University?*

SMG: The research was so exciting I spent almost full time at work. Of course, New York offered many cultural opportunities, and we took some advantage of these, when time and money permitted. On a day-to-day basis, most people came to work at 9:00 A.M., and I often stayed until 7:00 or 8:00 P.M. Still, there was a leisure quality to the research. There was not a great deal of pressure to publish many papers, as there

is today. Grant funding was relatively easy to obtain. Also, Dr. Ahrens had plenty of grant money because he was a highly respected scientist. Our research was never restricted by lack of funds. We were given considerable freedom in our research. Rockefeller had the tradition of using the "sink or swim" method of training young scientists. Nevertheless, the pace was comfortable, but stimulating through exchange with many brilliant people. The situation was almost ideal, and in many ways, more civilized than in the current competitive environment.

WCR: *How many PhD students were there in each class?*

SMG: About 20.

WCR: *You and Ahrens became very close? How much older than you was he?*

SMG: Eighteen years. We certainly had a close personal relationship, and a productive relationship. Pete was meticulous, demanding of excellence, and continuously questioning. New findings had to be confirmed in 3 or 4 different ways. For me, he was a terrific mentor, and he gave me a strong foundation in clinical research.

WCR: *Here, you went from Memphis, Texas, to Lubbock, to Houston, and then to New York City. Except for your 3-month sabbatical in Sweden, had you ever been out of Texas, or Oklahoma, before going to New York?*

SMG: On only a couple of occasions.

WCR: *New York must have been mind boggling.*

SMG: Indeed. Before going to the big and bad city there was considerable anticipation and anxiety, but it turned out to be a fabulous place to live.

WCR: *When did you get married?*

SMG: After my first year in medical school.

WCR: *How did you meet your wife?*

SMG: I met her first briefly at summer church camp during high school. In fact, I first knew her brother, Harry Parker. The Parkers also were Presbyterians, and they lived in Tulia, Texas, a small town between Amarillo and Lubbock, Texas. Harry had a sister, Lois Parker. Although I knew her for several years, both in high school and college, my relationship with her only began to grow during my senior year in college.

WCR: *So Lois went to Texas Tech, too?*

SMG: She did.

WCR: *What did Lois do while you were in medical school?*

SMG: She taught special reading classes in the Houston public schools. Except for the time when she was raising our young children, she has spent her whole adult life teaching children with reading handicaps. She followed a career similar to that of my sister, Elizabeth, and has brought an untold number of children up-to-speed academically, so that they could compete successfully with other children.

WCR: *When you went to New York, did you have any children?*

SMG: We had one 4-month-old girl, Pamela. She was born in Houston in 1962.

WCR: *How could you leave Rockefeller University, where each day you were with the world's best scien-*

tists in an elegant place with good support? Your apartment was only a few blocks away, and there were great cultural opportunities and great professional stimulation. How did it come about that you went to Arizona?

SMG: Often I have asked myself this same question, but it was quite clear that several factors influenced me. Even though Rockefeller was a wonderful place to do research, its commitment to clinical investigation seemed limited. Clinical research at Rockefeller had gradually given way to basic research. Therefore, I came to believe that opportunities for clinical investigation would probably be greater in other institutions. I made an attempt to obtain a joint appointment with Cornell Medical school, but was unsuccessful. Rockefeller at that time, and maybe even now, although located side-by-side with Cornell, did not have much interaction or communication. Each maintained its institutional separateness. Other factors in my decision included the relatively low pay for research physicians and concerns about supporting and educating a family in New York City.

WCR: *But what led you to Phoenix?*

SMG: The Phoenix offer grew directly out of my research. In our cholesterol balance studies we found that people who took the triglyceride-lowering drug, clofibrate, excreted excessive amounts of cholesterol from the body. We therefore inquired about the mechanism and speculated that the excess cholesterol probably came through the liver and into the bile. I thought it would be important to prove this, so I developed a method to measure amounts of cholesterol passing through the biliary tree. It required passing a triple-lumen tube into the duodenum and using markers to estimate cholesterol flow from the bile into the duodenum. We found that patients taking clofibrate indeed had an excess of biliary cholesterol. About the same time, Dr. Donald Small in Boston made a seminal observation. He reported that people with cholesterol gallstones had what he called "supersaturated" or "lithogenic" bile (i.e., bile that carried more cholesterol than could be held in stable solution by the solubilizing lipids—bile acids and phospholipids). This discovery put the study of cholesterol gallstones on a scientific basis. Most gallstones are made out of cholesterol. It occurred to me that I could actually determine what causes lithogenic bile by measuring all of the lipids being secreted into bile. If so, I potentially could determine the causes of cholesterol gallstone formation. At Rockefeller, I perfected the technique of measuring biliary lipid secretion.

At the same time, it was discovered that a high proportion of all Pima Indians in Arizona developed cholesterol gallstones. The institute of NIH, now called the National Institute of Diabetes, Digestive Diseases, and Kidney (NIDDK), had decided to build a research facility in conjunction with a new referral hospital for the Indian Health Service in Phoenix. Moreover, the gastroenterology community was putting more pressure on NIH to have more research in their field. In part to placate this community, I suppose, it was decided to put more emphasis on the gallstone problem of the American Indians. NIDDK therefore built a 20-bed metabolic ward and a large laboratory facility on the top floor of the new facility. Dr. Robert Gordon, Clinical Director of NIDDK, offered to make me director of this new facility, provided I would concentrate on the gallstone problem. Enthusiasm for this project of course was an outgrowth of the work of Donald Small's work on lithogenic bile, but it also was prompted by the observation of Reno Vlalachivc and Leon Swell that Navajo Indians had a reduced pool size of bile acids. I believe that Donald Small is the person who recommended me to Bob Gordon. Because my future at Rockefeller seemed problematic, I felt this was a good opportunity to apply my new method for measuring biliary lipid secretion. I was offered the position of section chief, which Bob Gordon told me was equivalent to being a full professor. Whether this is true or not, I don't know, but I was ready to believe it. Anyway, I believe my decision was the right one. I took full advantage of the opportunity. The facility in Phoenix was outstanding. We had a research budget of 2 million dollars a year for research projects, and I have never had so much research money since.

WCR: *What did you discover in Phoenix?*

SMG: We found out why Indians develop gallstones. They have two defects in their biliary lipid metabolism. First, they oversynthesize cholesterol and pour this excess cholesterol into bile. This overproduction of cholesterol is secondary to obesity, which is common in Pima Indians. In addition, American Indians have an inherent defect in the regulation of bile acid synthesis that leads to a reduced pool of bile acids in the enterohepatic circulation. Thus, being overweight combined with a bile acid defect causes highly lithogenic bile and accounts for the high prevalence of gallstones. I was particularly proud of the fact that I discovered why American Indians in particular and obese people in general develop gallstones. This provides a physiological explanation for the long-known clinical phenomenon: fat, forty, female, and gallstones. The research also was a paradigm for our subsequent findings that the metabolic stress imposed on a background of latent genetic defects elicits various clinical metabolic disorders.

WCR: *So you were in Phoenix 2 years? You really did a lot in those 2 years?*

SMG: I was prepared for it.

WCR: *Did you ever go home during those 2 years?*

SMG: Not too often. We really worked hard. There was not a lot to do in Phoenix but work. We had a good team. NIDDK made a big investment there.

WCR: *How many people did you have in that operation?*

SMG: Four or 5 physicians.

WCR: *You went to San Diego-La Jolla, California, in January 1973?*

SMG: I would have been happy to have stayed in Phoenix because of the facilities and the opportunity. Shortly after I went to Phoenix, however, Dr. Daniel Steinberg, who had recently gone to the new medical school in San Diego, asked me if I would be chief of the metabolic section at the Veterans Affairs (then called Veterans Administration) Hospital, which was on the campus of the University of California, San Diego (UCSD). I told him that his offer was attractive, but I had just started in Phoenix. Dan said the VA Hospital was not completed, and he would hold the position for a couple of years. I visited and found La Jolla and UCSD to be terribly attractive. La Jolla is a beautiful city. Also, there was a terrific faculty at UCSD. Eugene Braunwald was chairman of Medicine there, and he had robbed the NIH of some of its best investigators when he set up the Department of Medicine. It did not take a lot of persuading for me to realize that even though Phoenix was a wonderful research opportunity and offered the chance to put my research on the map, it did not compare with San Diego as a place to build an academic career. I therefore moved to San Diego in 1973.

WCR: *How did it work out?*

SMG: Everything worked out very well. UCSD was a fine medical school. The only problem was a limitation in resources. The VA Hospital was cramped for research space, and this curtailed expansion of my research program. Also, potential sources of funding were limited mostly to NIH grants. I certainly am not complaining, however. The facilities were adequate, and we accomplished much research and published a large number of papers. The VA Hospital provided me with a metabolic unit that must have been one of the best in the country. We were able to keep up to 20 patients on that ward, which allowed us to carry out several studies simultaneously.

WCR: *It sounds like you kept patients on the metabolic ward for months if you wished?*

SMG: We could keep them as long as we wanted. The opportunities seemed unlimited. All my time in San Diego was satisfying. Overall, the medical school was outstanding. I had the chance to interact with many outstanding professors. Also, I was able to develop a close and wonderful relationship with Dan Steinberg. He was one of the giants in the lipid field, a tremendous associate, very supportive of me, and a great friend. I have nothing negative to say about my relationships at the VA Hospital or UCSD.

WCR: *Tell me about your research in San Diego.*

SMG: One phase of our research was on the metabolism of cholesterol and bile acids. I continued to study the mechanisms of formation of lithogenic bile and cholesterol gallstones. This work was done in association with research fellows and faculty colleagues. These included Henry Mok, Klaus von Bergmann, and Gary Hardison. Also, my associate from Rockefeller days, Alan Hofman, moved from the Mayo Clinic to UCSD, and we frequently discussed research issues. I believe that our research provided several new insights into the enterohepatic circulation of cholesterol and bile acids in humans. In particular, we better defined the influence of obesity on biliary lipid metabolism. At this time I also became involved in the National Cholesterol Gallstone Study, a multicenter trial to determine whether chenodeoxycholic acid would effectively dissolve cholesterol gallstones.

The study was headed by Dr. Leslie Schoenfield of Los Angeles, and was a model of a clinical trial. Although the trial was clinically negative, it engendered new approaches to the clinical management of gallstones.

WCR: *You also worked on the blood lipids, didn't you?*

SMG: Yes. We did many studies on the mechanisms of hypertriglyceridemia in humans. It appeared that most patients at the VA Hospital had elevated serum triglycerides. This observation led us to develop methods to determine rates of formation and catabolism of triglyceride-rich lipoproteins in humans. These methods required use of radioisotopes and we developed kinetic models to decipher metabolic parameters. In this effort, I collaborated with Dr. Virgil Brown and Dan Steinberg. Also, our team worked closely with investigators at NIH in Bethesda, Drs. Mones Berman and Loren Zech, as well as with Dr. Barbara Howard in Phoenix. Investigators in my own laboratory who worked on these problems included Drs. Antero Kesaniemi and Gloria Lena Vega, among others. At this time, I also developed collaborative studies with Drs. David Bilheimer, Fred Dunn, Joseph Goldstein, and Michael Brown at the University of Texas Southwestern Medical School. These collaborative metabolic studies probably paved the way for my move to Dallas. All in all, I believe our studies on metabolism of lipoproteins helped to define pathways and regulation of serum lipoproteins in patients with different forms of hyperlipidemia. In my view, our major observation in San Diego was that obesity leads to an overproduction of lipoproteins by the liver, and when obesity is combined with hereditary defects in catabolism of VLDL and LDL, patients will develop hypertriglyceridemia or hypercholesterolemia, respectively. It reinforced our paradigm of the interaction of obesity and genetics in the causation of metabolic disorders.

WCR: *What about your nutrition studies in San Diego?*

SMG: In this area I was fortunate, because I had the opportunity to work with Dr. Fred Mattson. Fred had been director of lipid research at Proctor and Gamble (P&G) for many years. I knew him from my Rockefeller days. He retired at an early age from P&G and moved to San Diego, where he became director of the Lipid Research Clinic laboratory at UCSD. Fred and I came up with the idea that monounsaturated oils (like olive oil) might be superior to polyunsaturated oils in lowering serum cholesterol levels. So we designed a study to test this hypothesis. I completed the study after I moved to Dallas.

WCR: *You found that monounsaturated fatty acids are in fact better for us than polyunsaturated fatty acids?*

SMG: Overall, they seem to be safer and just as effective.

WCR: *Effective in lowering LDL?*

SMG: Yes, our results indicated that they are as effective in lowering LDL. Also, they do not lower HDL, as polyunsaturates do when consumed in large amounts. There has been a long-term concern that excess polyunsaturated fatty acids might have detrimental effects, for example, promoting cancer, suppressing the immune system, and facilitating LDL oxidation. We believed that we circumvented these problems by going to monounsaturates. This form of unsaturated fatty acids has been consumed in large amounts as olive oil for centuries in the Mediterranean area. In Mediterranean countries, there is a low incidence of coronary heart disease, as shown by the 7-Country Study, as well as a low rate of cancer. We believed that there was a lot going for monounsaturates.

WCR: *If you are going to have to eat eggs, cook them in olive oil?*

SMG: If you are going to use fat in your diet, monounsaturates are the best kind.

WCR: *Do you eat a lot of olive oil in your home?*

SMG: We eat some. I don't use huge amounts of fat and oil, but olive oil is my favorite.

WCR: *Why is olive oil so expensive?*

SMG: Olive oil is expensive because of its taste and limited supply. Olive trees grow only in certain small areas of the world. Costs are increased more by the expense of production, preparation, and shipping. However, there are other sources of monounsaturates: canola oil and high-monounsaturated forms of safflower oil and sunflower oils. Later, when I was in Dallas, I worked with animal scientists at Texas A&M University to produce pork that was rich in monounsaturates.

WCR: *When you say polyunsaturates, what you in essence are saying is that the dominant component of that particular fatty acid is the polyunsaturated component. Some saturated and monounsaturated components are also there, but they are in the minority.*

SMG: Yes. Olive oil is roughly 75% monounsaturated. Our study has proved to be controversial, but we believe that monounsaturates are the best of the 3 fatty acids. The idea that polyunsaturates are the best, which was the predominant dogma in the 1960s and 1970s, has not fallen easily. Even much of my own research has been devoted to understanding how polyunsaturates lower cholesterol levels. However, it is now my opinion that we should limit intakes of polyunsaturates. We require small amounts in the diet, but not large amounts.

WCR: *If you give 100 people a fatty acid that is predominantly polyunsaturated or monounsaturated, you will lower the LDL in a lot of them, but in some of them, you don't lower it at all. Is that correct?*

SMG: If you control exactly what a person consumes on a metabolic ward, and you replace saturated with any type of unsaturated fatty acid, either poly or mono, most people will lower their LDL levels to some extent. However, the degree of lowering is quite variable. The reduction will range from 10% to 30%. Dr. Margo Denke, who has worked with me in Dallas, has done extensive research on the variation in diet responsiveness, and continues to work on this important issue.

WCR: *How do saturated fatty acids raise our LDL?*

SMG: That is a question that goes back to the beginning of my research with Pete Ahrens. We phrased the question differently in those days. We asked, "How do polyunsaturated fatty acids lower the cholesterol level?" That was the focus of our thinking then. It is generally now believed that saturated fatty acids raise the LDL levels, whereas other nutrients (polyunsaturates, monounsaturates, and carbohydrates) yield a "baseline" LDL level. These later nutrients do not actually lower LDL levels like cholesterol-lowering drugs. We still don't know the answer to this question from a biochemical viewpoint. The best evidence, however, suggests that saturated fatty acids suppress LDL-receptor synthesis, whereas other nutrients allow for a "normal" expression of receptors. Dr. John Dietschy and his group in Dallas have extensively studied this pathway in animal models.

WCR: *You must have loved living in La Jolla? Here you have lived in Memphis, Texas, Lubbock, Texas, Houston, Texas, New York City, Phoenix, Arizona, La Jolla, California, and now somebody is knocking on your door to return to Texas. How did that come about?*

SMG: Let me say that every move for me opened new doors and reinvigorated me. Each had a highly positive effect on me. The opportunity to come to Dallas was just plain good luck for me. There were influential people in the Dallas community who thought that medical schools are not paying enough attention to nutrition. They felt that the University of Texas at Southwestern in particular should teach medical students and young physicians more about nutrition, because good nutrition offers the best approach to preventing disease and prolonging life. Bill, I know that you hold this belief strongly yourself. Anyway, these people began to work on the medical school to try to get it to start a nutrition program.

WCR: *Who were the people? Have they been the big donors to the University of Texas Southwestern?*

SMG: That is what many of them are now. I might try to create a bit of history. The central persons are Mr. Peter O'Donnell, Jr. and his wife, Edith O'Donnell. They deserve enormous credit, not only for creating the nutrition program, but in addition for much of what Southwestern is today. They are primarily responsible for the creation of the Center for Human Nutrition, and I was fortunate to be chosen to be its first director in 1981. The O'Donnells made the initial endowment to the Center for Human Nutrition. The decision to create this Center was made by Dr. Kern Wildenthal, then dean of Southwestern, and Dr. Charles Sprague, Southwestern's president. The people who suggested my name to be the director of the Center were Drs. Joseph Goldstein and Michael Brown, who as everyone knows, work in the cholesterol field, too. At the time I came to Southwestern, they had already discovered the LDL receptor and were on their way to fame. The discovery of the LDL receptor is the most important discovery ever made in the lipoprotein field, and it rightly entitled Goldstein and Brown to the Nobel Prize in 1985. I believe that they thought I would bring good science to the Center

FIGURE 7. SMG (far right) with Peter O'Donnell, Jr. (far left), Mary Ann Cauldwell (center left), and Carolyn Bacon (center right).

for Human Nutrition, which was to be devoted to human research. In addition to these influential people, Dr. Ronald Estabrook has been a strong supporter of our Center. Also, the Veterans Affairs Medical Center in Dallas made a major commitment to our program by creating a metabolic ward for me to carry out clinical investigation.

Also, I must mention that many influential people in Dallas have been strong moral and financial supporters of our program. Mr. O'Donnell, in his wisdom, established a support group named the Friends of the Center for Human Nutrition. This group consists of almost 200 individuals or families in the Dallas area who are committed to yearly contributions to our Center. This group has been lead by such people as Vin Prothro, Charles Best, Carla Francis, Margo Perot, Lida Hill, and Rita Clements, Roger Horchow, Carolyn Bacon, and Dr. Philip Montgomery, just to name a few. Their support has provided a major financial underpinning to our Center.

WCR: *How does the Center for Human Nutrition fit into Southwestern Medical School?*

SMG: It provides space and financial resourses for faculty members who are working in the field of nutrition and related areas. Its major thrust is human research, and naturally I have turned its focus to cholesterol, lipids, lipoproteins, diabetes, and the prevention of atherosclerosis. Our Center's faculty members have established collaborations with many other investigators at Southwestern. We are very fortunate, because Southwestern Medical School is one of the world's foremost medical research institutions and it provides a rich environment for collaboration. We also work closely with the Department of Clinical Nutrition in the School of Allied Health Sciences.

WCR: *So you came to Dallas in 1981 at age 48. How much longer are you going to work?*

SMG: For several more years, I hope. Right now, the Center for Human Nutrition is at the peak of its productivity. Several of the Centers' faculty have matured into independent investigators in their own right.

Dr. Gloria Lena Vega is carrying out research on obesity and fatty acid metabolism and their role in hypertriglyceridemia. Dr. Kenny Jialal has developed a large program in antioxidants and their role in prevention of chronic disease. Dr. Margo Denke is working on the genetic and environmental basis of variation in diet responsiveness. Dr. Abhimanyu Garg is making seminal observations on genetic disorders of adipose tissue that may provide new insights into the problem of insulin resistance. Dr. Jonathan Cohen has started a large program in the study of human genetics and its interface with nutrition, particularly obesity. He has recently made key observations on genetic factors controlling HDL levels. Dr. Shailesh Patel has recently uncovered the genetic locus of a rare but important disorder in cholesterol metabolism. Dr. Nilo Cater is studying the effects of new nutritional approaches to lowering LDL levels, and Dr. Nicola Abate is investigating the genetic basis and metabolic consequences of insulin resistance, particularly as they are related to abnormalities in fat distribution. All of our faculty members are the mentors of research fellows who are being trained in our Center. My job now is to guide and support this sizable group of creative scientists, both faculty and research fellows.

WCR: *How many people do you have in the Center for Human Nutrition?*

SMG: We have 8 faculty, at least an equal number or more of research fellows, along with technicians, nurses, dietitians, and administrative assistants, for a total of about 35.

WCR: *When you started to medical school in 1955, you started right away investigating atherosclerosis and you have continued investigating that problem your entire career. Here you come from an area of the world, Texas, where you were surrounded by cows. I bet your daddy had cows on the farm.*

SMG: Yes. That is right. We even had a cow in town that I milked.

WCR: *So you were surrounded by bovine muscle, milk, butter, and cheese. Then you got into chemistry, and it sounds almost like the day you hit medical school or certainly the day you hit organic chemistry, that you started doing research. You have focused on the same problem for over 40 years.*

SMG: That is true.

WCR: *You have not dilly dallied here and yon; it was straight ahead on the same problem. You are labeled as a endocrinologist? What do you consider yourself?*

SMG: A metabolic nutritionist.

WCR: *The amount of training you had in internal medicine was limited. (That was not infrequent when you and I came along.) Your residency training was a small portion of your professional life. You were in* *research right away. (Incidentally, Eugene Braunwald was the same way.)*

SMG: The same was true of many people who trained at Rockefeller and the NIH. Most have medical school positions and some are chairpersons of departments of medicine. I have always felt insufficient in my training in internal medicine. This probably has impaired my ability to teach on attending rounds. I have been conscientious in trying to improve my knowledge in internal medicine. Through my attending experience at UCSD and Southwestern, I have learned a great deal.

WCR: *How much time do you spend on attending rounds?*

SMG: Six weeks a year in general internal medicine. Also, I see a large number of patients in our lipid clinic and on the metabolic wards.

WCR: *You have really done an enormous amount of work during these 40+ years. Of all of your contributions, which ones are you the most proud of? What work are you most pleased with? When you are gone, what do you want people to remember about you?*

SMG: In research, there are 3 areas. But first, let me say that since medical student days I have been working on the regulation of the blood cholesterol and lipoprotein levels. This has been the overriding theme of my research. I was convinced that abnormalities in lipoprotein metabolism and concentrations underlie much of the atherosclerotic process.

WCR: *What are the 3 areas?*

SMG: First, I am pleased with the work we have done to elucidate pathways of cholesterol and lipoprotein metabolism. Development of new techniques to study these pathways has been particularly gratifying. The most definitive first result of this effort was the discovery of the metabolic basis of cholesterol gallstone formation, which was the outgrowth of cholesterol balance methodology. It also established the paradigm of the interaction of obesity and genetics in causation of metabolic disorders.

Second, I am perhaps best known for our research in dietary fat. The optimal intake of dietary fat is such an important public health issue and any new information is both welcome and influential. I have been particularly rewarded for clarifying the role of monounsaturated fat in the diet. This effort has been influential in modifying dietary fat recommendations around the world.

Third, our group at Southwestern played an important role in the rejuvenation of the HMG CoA reductase inhibitors (statins) at the time when interest in these agents was dormant. The success of the statins in the treatment of hypercholesterolemia has been particularly satisfying. I might recount some of the interesting history of these drugs. This class of agent was discovered in Japan by Dr. Akira Endo, who was working for a pharmaceutical company. He discovered a drug, compactin, that lowered serum cholesterol in animals. Compactin then was shown to lower cholesterol levels in humans. Shortly thereafter, Merck followed the lead and developed a similar drug called mevinolin, now named lovastatin. Merck scientists also showed that mevinolin lowered cholesterol levels. However, neither drug was advanced further in development at this time. When I moved to Dallas, Joe Goldstein and Mike Brown were interested in the statins because they activated LDL receptor synthesis. I had many conversations with them about these drugs. At this time, Merck was not committed to developing mevinolin, and there were rumors that compactin caused cancer in animals. Moreover, conventional wisdom among drug companies was that cholesterol-lowering drugs were not financially viable.

There was one person at Merck, however, who was convinced of lovastatin's potential. This was Dr. Jonathan Tobert. I was able to work out an arrangement with Jonathan and Merck, such that I could apply for an IND (Investigational New Drug) from the FDA (Food and Drug Administration) to test lovastatin in humans. I got the IND and Merck provided us with the drug. This was 1982. Another investigator, Dr. Roger Illlingworth, from Portland, Oregon, had a similar arrangement. Dr. David Bilheimer and I tested lovastatin in hypercholesterolemic patients and found it to be extremely effective in lowering serum cholesterol levels. Goldstein and Brown were intimate advisors in these studies. We published our findings in 1983. Goldstein and Brown and others at Southwestern were influential in renewing interest in the statins at Merck. Thus, in my view, the Southwestern team played an important role in promoting the statins at a time when their future was in question. Subsequently, researchers in the Center for Human Nutrition did many different studies that revealed new, potential uses of statins in different forms of hyperlipidemia. Now, everyone knows how beneficial the statins are. They are being used in millions of people worldwide. Naturally, it is highly rewarding to have meaningfully participated at the beginning with these agents.

WCR: *This is a situation where you had to convince the pharmaceutical company rather than the pharmaceutical company's trying to convince a group of physicians?*

SMG: That is probably true. That, at least, is my perspective. You could talk to people at Merck and perhaps get a different perspective. Certainly, the person who bit the bullet at Merck was its chairman, Dr. Roy Vagelos. He is the one who took the financial gamble and he deserves an enormous amount of credit, going out on a limb and committing Merck to lovastatin at a time when it was not clear whether it would be profitable or not. I do, however, believe that the scientific work combined with enthusiasm from Southwestern was a significant factor in promoting the further development of this class of drugs. Whatever my contribution, the statins represent the greatest advance in line with my quest for better ways to regulate serum lipoprotein levels. Of course, other investigators have been seeking this holy grail. These lipoprotein investigators, starting with John Gofman and his associates, in truth, have been a small band of committed researchers with a dream that has been largely realized by the great advances of the past decade.

WCR: *You are talking about your most important contributions. You have named 3. Can you discuss your statemanship and education endeavors and treatment stands you have been involved in?*

SMG: This has been a gradual but increasing effort, starting first with the American Heart Association. In the early 1980s, I was the chair of the Nutrition Committee of the American Heart Association. In 1982, we produced a rationale statement for the American Heart Association's dietary recommendations. I was the senior author in this report, which set forth clearly the American Heart position about diet. I have continued to work with the American Heart Association ever since and have been chairperson of several committees: Cholesterol Task Force, Task Force on Risk Reduction, Prevention Committee, Arteriosclerosis Council, and Council on Scientific Councils. These committees have put out a series of statements on nutrition, treatment of hyperlipidemia, and other risk reduction strategies.

In 1986, I was appointed as the American Heart Association's representative to the newly formed National Cholesterol Education Program (NCEP) of the National Heart Lung and Blood Institute. I have participated one way or another in all of the NCEP's panel reports. I was chairperson of the second NCEP Adult Treatment Panel report (ATP II), which made recommendations for treatment of high blood cholesterol in adults. I have tried to be a spokesman for NCEP. Working on NCEP with Dr. James Cleeman, director of NCEP, and Claude Lenfant, Director of NHLBI, has been a joy. It also has been satisfying to me, because I believe that the NCEP and its affiliated organizations, including the American Heart Association, have had a major impact on the way people think about cholesterol. I recognize that the science underpinning of the cholesterol hypothesis has improved progressively in recent years, and this has helped to convince people about the importance of cholesterol in atherosclerosis, but science is not always immediately translated into clinical practice. For this reason, a lot of us, including yourself, Bill, promote cholesterol awareness and understanding through lectures and position papers. I sense that these efforts do have a major effect on attitudes about cholesterol and nutrition.

WCR: *Dr. Grundy, you have done a lot of work on triglycerides. I am sure you get the question a lot, "How important are triglycerides?" It seems to me that since your recommendations from the Adult Treatment Panel that the major focus should be on LDL cholesterol, you have had a lot to say about triglycerides. I wonder if you are changing your tune a bit on triglycerides?*

SMG: I still believe that priority should be given to LDL. LDL is the major atherogenic lipoprotein. Recent clinical trials bear out the benefit of LDL lowering. However, I do believe that the whole triglyceride area is very important. Our research has shown that high triglyceride levels are largely due to the interaction of obesity and latent genetic defects in triglyceride catabolism. There is growing evidence that trig-

lyceride-rich lipoproteins are atherogenic, similar to LDL. Moreover, high triglycerides are a good clinical indicator of insulin resistance, and insulin resistance is going to emerge as another major risk factor for heart disease. Also, high triglycerides usually are associated with low HDL cholesterol and small, dense LDL, both of which appear to be atherogenic factors. Therefore, high triglycerides are linked to atherogenesis through multiple pathways. It is a mistake for clinicians to ignore elevated triglycerides, but the clinical focus should be on associated risk factors as much as on high triglycerides, per se.

WCR: *What about measuring non-HDL cholesterol (total cholesterol minus HDL)? How does that fit versus having to have a fasting sample so you get a triglyceride value?*

SMG: We have been interested in the idea of combining LDL and VLDL into a single number, which is non-HDL. If VLDL is atherogenic like LDL, it seems reasonable to combine the two and let that be the target of treatment. However, some investigators feel that this takes the focus off LDL, which has been espoused by NCEP as the primary target of cholesterol-lowering therapy. Thus, for clinical purposes, it may be necessary to continue to separate LDL and triglycerides (or triglyceride-rich lipoproteins). LDL should still be the primary target of hyperlipidemia treatment, whereas elevated triglycerides can be managed separately.

WCR: *What is your day-to-day life like now? I know you spend a lot of time over here at work. What time do you get up in the morning? What time to do you go to bed at night? Can you describe a typical day?*

SMG: I usually get up about 6:30 A.M., do a little exercise, and read *The New York Times* and *The Dallas Morning News,* and get to work around 9:00 A.M. Often, I go to the VA Hospital directly from home and check on our activities there or see patients in the lipid clinic. Then I come to the medical school and try to work with the faculty on their plans, their research designs, their fundraising efforts, their manuscripts. This, plus correspondence and working on manuscripts, take up most of the afternoon. I spend considerable time with NCEP and the American Heart Association business, and this requires a lot of telephone work. Finally, I usually spend a couple of hours doing paperwork at home at night.

WCR: *What time do you leave the medical school?*

SMG: Between 7:00 and 8:00 P.M.

WCR: *So you are putting in about 10 to 11 hours at work? Then, you put in another couple of hours at home. What time to you go to bed?*

SMG: Eleven o'clock.

WCR: *So you get a reasonable night's sleep?*

SMG: Yes. I am not like Dr. DeBakey, who seemingly sleeps only about 4 hours. I wish I could do that, but I cannot.

WCR: *What about Saturdays and Sundays? Do you come in?*

SMG: Yes. I usually come to my office at 11:00 A.M. on Saturday and Sundays and work until 6:00 P.M. It might seem that I am a slave to work, but my work schedule is frequently interrupted by trips. I travel frequently to Washington for committee meetings (the NCEP and the Food and Nutrition Board), to the American Heart Association, for lipid symposia (like you do, Bill), and on visiting professorships. It is not unusual for me to be gone a couple of days a week.

WCR: *How many trips do you go on a year?*

SMG: Too many. I would say probably 25 or 30.

WCR: *Do you have hobbies outside of medicine?*

SMG: I would call them interests more than hobbies. I have a great interest in history and biography, and I read on these subjects every chance I get. I know a lot more about them than you might think. I used to read a good deal in the areas of general science, psychology, and philosophy, but my current interests are in history and politics. One of my "hobbies" is preparation for attending rounds by studying internal medicine. I do this to try to overcome by deficit in clinical training. I have developed a system of cards with case histories that I use for teaching medical students. In my attending periods, I try to spend extra time with the students alone.

WCR: *Although you went to college on an athletic scholarship, now you don't play golf, tennis, or run?*

SMG: I don't run. I walk and exercise at home, but don't participate in sports. I do occasionally watch sports on television, but I seem to have gotten the playing of competitive sports out of my system when I was young.

WCR: *You have how many children?*

SMG: Two, a daughter and a son.

WCR: *Pamela and Stephan? I know Pamela has written a book, because I have seen 1 of them. What does she do?*

SMG: Pamela went to Yale for college. She then worked as a journalist in Anniston, Alabama, for a couple of years. While in Anniston she conducted oral history interviews in a small, rural county. Her study, entitled *You Always Think of Home: A Protrait of Clay County Alabama* (University of Georgia Press, 1991), presented a Studs-Terkel style oral portraits of several dozen county residents. Then she left Alabama and entered graduate school at the University of North Carolina at Chapel Hill. Her PhD dissertation, *Learning to Win,* looked at the development of high school and college sports programs in North Carolina during the twentieth century. This thesis explored the way athletic competition became an integral part of the American educational system, and a key component of American culture. It describes the links that sports supporters drew between athletic programs and visions of a changing society. Pamela considered the roles that sports has played in creating communities, shaping ideas about men and women, and influencing the course of racial integration. Her thesis recounts several key moments in a heated and century-long debate over the direction and purpose of school athletics and how these debates reflect larger differences that are shaping American society.

WCR: *Is Pamela an athlete?*

SMG: She played tennis in high school, but not too much since.

WCR: *What about your son?*

SMG: Stephan is very literary and has written several books. He went to Southern Methodist University for college, and then to Cambridge University for his PhD. He is an expert on Germanic and Norse literature, legend, and society. His books generally take the form of historical novels or recounting of Germanic legends. They have been translated into German and are widely sold in Germany, England, and other European countries. They also are read in the United States. Stephan now lives in Ireland, which gives him ready access to European countries for his continuing research.

WCR: *How did Stephan get interested in these areas of study and writing?*

SMG: He has been reading and writing stories since he was very small. His Scandinavian heritage (on his mother's side) seemingly led him to an interest in the culture and religion of the Vikings, which in turn inspired him to retell the great stories of the North in his novels.

WCR: *What do you want to do for the rest of your professional career?*

SMG: I am extremely interested in research questions that we are currently addressing in the Center for Human Nutrition. My major interest right now is on "atherogenesis beyond LDL." A lot of the LDL problem we now understand and have largely solved, but I believe that other metabolic factors promote atherogenesis beyond an elevated LDL. One of these is the oxidation of LDL, which is the major interest of my colleague, Dr. Kenny Jialal. Other atherogenic factors are related to triglycerides, HDL, and insulin resistance. Most of the faculty members of the Center for Human Nutrition are working in one form or another on metabolism and genetics of lipoprotein and their relation to obesity, insulin resistance, and diabetes. I subsume this thrust under the term *metabolic syndrome.* This syndrome consists of the coexistence of multiple metabolic risk factors (dyslipidemia, hypertension, glucose intolerance, and a coagulation defects) in a single individual. I want to continue my efforts to better understand the origins and management of the *metabolic syndrome.* In my opinion the *metabolic syndrome* represents the product of the interaction of genetics and acquired factors.

WCR: *I guess you were behind the NIH's push to lower the body mass index to define obesity?*

SMG: That is partly true. Most doctors don't even know what body mass index is. I was on an NIH panel that just put out recent treatment guidelines on obesity. These have been controversial because some investigators have said that we are classifying almost all Americans as obese. In truth, there is an extremely high prevalence of obesity in the United States. All of our research tells us that even mild obesity when combined with latent genetic defects leads to several cardiovascular risk factors (the metabolic syndrome). Therefore, physicians need to make a mental link between excess body fat and cardiovascular risk. Control of obesity is the best way to reduce several cardiovascular risk factors at once.

WCR: *What is your body mass index?*

SMG: It is about 23. We call overweight a body mass index of 25 or greater. At this level the vast majority of people, except for a few muscular people, have excess body fat. However, another way to assess obesity is to measure the waist circumference. A large waist circumference is closely associated with insulin resistance and the metabolic syndrome.

WCR: *Why did the NCEP take obesity off the last list of risk factors?*

SMG: This requires a little explanation. Obesity is an important cause of all the metabolic risk factors like insulin resistance, hypertension, high triglyceride, high LDL, low HDL, and coagulation disorders. These are considered the primary risk factors and the effects of obesity on risk are largely mediated through these factors. Therefore, counting obesity per se as a risk factor may actually be counting it twice. Nonetheless, obesity is the underlying cause of several risk factors and, hence, is a contributing cause of cardiovascular disease. Obesity itself should be a direct target for treatment. This explains why the NIH has produced a separate guideline on the clinical management of obesity.

WCR: *You were the editor of the* Journal of Lipid Research *for 5 years. Did you enjoy that?*

SMG: It was a lot of work. Being editor is a rather thankless task in many ways. You make quite a few authors unhappy when you reject their papers. Still, it is stimulating and helps to keep you up to date. I felt that taking on the task was my responsibility to the lipid field, and particularly because Pete Ahrens was one of the founders of the journal. To me, becoming editor was some kind of obligation.

WCR: *What if somebody came along and offered you a deanship of a medical school? You have kept straight ahead with your research and have not been diverted off course. Are you ever tempted by other offers?*

SMG: I am just committed to my kind of research, and I do not intend to be diverted. It's as simple as that. First of all, I have built up a lot of experience in this area, and I can still apply that experience. This is particularly the case in helping younger investigators to develop their careers. I can do this job better than I could as being a dean. Other people are better qualified and trained for such positions.

WCR: *What advice do you give new, young researchers if they want to a career in medical research?*

SMG: My advise is "do it." Although we have been through some tough times with managed care and cutbacks in research funding, the future looks brighter. The country seems to be coming to the realization that we need a strong medical research base and the future of the health of the nation is going to depend on that, so there will be opportunities now.

I would like to make a special comment about clinical investigation as part of the medical research effort. I have the strong feeling that academic medicine does not put enough emphasis on clinical research. It is easier for faculty to advance academically doing basic science research than in clinical investigation. This is a mistake. Everyone agrees that medical practice should be evidence based. Evidence is derived from 4 types of research: basic research, epidemiology, clinical investigation, and clinical trials. Basic research provides the raw material for medical practice. Clinical investigation takes this knowledge and tests its potential application in patients. Finally, clinical trials test promising applications in large numbers of patients. Overemphasis on basic research at the expense of clinical investigation in medical schools creates an imbalance that impairs the full development of information required for evidence-based medicine. To a large extent, both medical schools and the NIH have abrogated their responsibilities in clinical research and clinical trials and have turned them over to the pharmaceutical industry. Although this industry has the responsibility to perform objective trials, its control of the funding and scientific questions leaves important gaps in our knowledge that can only come from extensive academic involvement in clinical research. One of my aims is to help to reestablish the balance in medical schools between basic research, clinical investigation, and clinical trials.

WCR: *As you look back, have you made any mistakes in your several moves, or have you spent too much time in one line of research that in retrospect you wished you had gone down another road?*

SMG: Perhaps the fundamental irreversible decision in my career was to do clinical research rather than basic research. Once that fundamental decision was made, it determined the course of my work. If I had chosen basic research, my career undoubtedly would have been totally different. I fully realize that there is a strong prejudice in the academic world in favor of basic research over clinical research, and I have paid a price in prestige. However, this disadvantage has been offset for me by my conviction that the academic world must seek a balance between basic and clinical research. Anyway, I can only guess at how my career might have been different if I had chosen basic research. I might have discovered something important, or perhaps I would have fallen by the wayside out of discouragement. I don't know.

WCR: *Is there anything, Dr. Grundy, you would like to discuss before we stop?*

SMG: I want to emphasize again how important my colleagues have been in supporting my career. I have not mentioned many associates whose names are on our joint papers, although their names will be listed in the bibliography that accompanies this interview. In addition, there have been a couple of people who have worked with me for many years who deserve special mention. Marjorie Whelan has been a long-term colleague and advisor. She was enormously helpful in establishing the metabolic units in Phoenix, San Diego, and Dallas. In Dallas, she has been the clinical coordinator of the Center for Human Nutrition, and she has been a vital interface with our patients, medical school administration, and donors. Her long-term contributions to our program have been tremendous. Another person who has given energy and stability to our research efforts is Dr. Gloria Lena Vega. She was the only scientist who moved with me from San Diego to Dallas, and she has contributed to every phase of the Center's work. I hope that this discussion makes clear that whatever accomplishments in the research area and public policy are attached to my name represent a team effort. I have been fortunate to be the spokesman for much of this united effort, but in no way should I be given primary credit for it.

WCR: *Scott, I want to thank you for sharing yourself and your thoughts with the readers of* The American Journal of Cardiology. *I appreciate your being so open.*

SMG: It was my pleasure.

SMG'S BEST PUBLICATIONS AS SELECTED BY HIM

6. Grundy SM, Griffin AC. Effects of periodic mental stress on serum cholesterol levels. *Circulation* 1959;19:496–498.

7. Grundy SM, Griffin AC. Relationship of periodic mental stress to serum lipoprotein and cholesterol levels. *JAMA* 1959;171:1794–1796.

13. Grundy SM, Ahrens EH Jr, Miettinen TA. Quantitative isolation and gas-liquid chromatographic analysis of total fecal bile acids. *J Lipid Res* 1965;6:397–410.

14. Miettinen TA, Ahrens EH Jr, Grundy SM. Quantitative isolation and gas-liquid chromatographic analysis of total dietary and fecal neutral steroids. *J Lipid Res* 1965;6:411–424.

15. Spritz N, Ahrens EH Jr, Grundy SM. Sterol balance in man as plasma cholesterol concentrations are altered by exchanges of dietary fat. *J Clin Invest* 1965;44:1482–1493.

16. Grundy SM, Ahrens EH Jr. An evaluation of the relative merits of two methods for measuring the balance of sterols in man: isotopic balance vs. chromatographic analysis. *J Clin Invest* 1966;45:1503–1515.

17. Grundy SM, Ahrens EH Jr, Salen G. Dietary beta-sitosterol as an internal standard to correct for cholesterol losses in sterol balance studies. *J Lipid Res* 1969;9:374–387.

18. Grundy SM, Ahrens EH Jr. Measurements of cholesterol turnover, synthesis and absorption in man, carried out by isotope kinetic and sterol balance methods. *J Lipid Res* 1969;10:91–107.

19. Grundy SM, Ahrens EH Jr, Davignon J. The interaction of cholesterol absorption and cholesterol synthesis in man. *J Lipid Res* 1969;10:304–315.

21. Grundy SM, Ahrens EH Jr. The effects of unsaturated dietary fats on absorption, excretion, synthesis, and distribution of cholesterol in man. *J Clin Invest* 1970;49:1135–1152.

26. Grundy SM, Ahrens EH Jr, Salen G, Schreibman PH, Nestel PJ. Mechanism of action of clofibrate on cholesterol metabolism in patients with hyperlipidemia. *J Lipid Res* 1972;13:531–551.

29. Grundy SM, Metzger AL. A physiological method for estimation of hepatic secretion of biliary lipids in man. *Gastroenterology* 1972;62:1200–1217.

30. Grundy SM, Metzger AL, Adler R. Mechanisms of lithogenic bile formation in American Indian women with cholesterol gallstones. *J Clin Invest* 1972;51:3026–3043.

32. Metzger AL, Adler R, Heymsfield S, Grundy SM. Diurnal variation in biliary lipid composition: possible role in cholesterol gallstone formation. *N Engl J Med* 1973;288:333–336.

33. Grundy SM, Duane WC, Adler RD, Aron JM, Metzger AL. Biliary lipid outputs in young women with cholesterol gallstones. *Metabolism* 1974;23:67–73.

34. Adler RD, Metzger AL, Grundy SM. Biliary lipid secretion before and after cholecystectomy in American Indians with cholesterol gallstones. *Gastroenterology* 1974;66:1212–1217.

36. Grundy SM. Effects of polyunsaturated fats on lipid metabolism in patients with hypertriglyceridemia. *J Clin Invest* 1975;55:269–282.

37. Bennion LJ, Grundy SM. Effects of obesity and caloric intake on biliary lipid metabolism in man. *J Clin Invest* 1975;56:996–1011.

38. Bilheimer DW, Goldstein JL, Grundy SM, Brown MS. Reduction in cholesterol and low density lipoprotein synthesis after portacaval shunt surgery in a patient with homozygous familial hypercholesterolemia. *J Clin Invest* 1975;56:1420–1430.

39. Grundy SM, Mok HYI. Chylomicron clearance in normal and hyperlipidemia man. *Metabolism* 1975;25:1227–1239.

43. Grundy SM, Mok HYI. Colestipol, clofibrate and phytosterols in combined therapy of hyperlipidemia. *J Lab Clin Med* 1977;89:354–366.

44. Grundy SM, Mok HYI. Determination of cholesterol absorption in man by intestinal perfusion. *J Lipid Res* 1977;18:263–271.

45. Bennion LJ, Grundy SM. Effects of diabetes mellitus on cholesterol metabolism in man. *N Engl J Med* 1977;296:1365–1371.

47. Mok HYI, von Bergmann K, Grundy SM. Regulation of pool size of bile acids in man. *Gastroenterology* 1977;73:684–690.

53. Bennion LJ, Grundy SM. Risk factors for development of cholelithiasis in man. *N Engl J Med* 1978;299:1161–1167.

57. Mok HYI, von Bergmann K, Grundy SM. Effects of continuous and intermittent feeding on biliary lipid outputs in man: application for measurements of intestinal absorption of cholesterol and bile acids. *J Lipid Res* 1979;20:389–398.

58. Zech LA, Grundy SM, Steinberg D, Berman M. A kinetic model for production and metabolism of very low density lipoprotein triglycerides: evidence for a slow production pathway and results for normolipidemic subjects. *J Clin Invest* 1979;62:1252–1273.

59. Grundy SM, Mok HYI, Zech LA, Steinberg D, Berman M. Transport of very low density of lipoprotein-triglycerides in varying degrees of obesity and hypertriglyceridemia. *J Clin Invest* 1979;63:1274–1283.

62. Bilheimer DW, Stone NJ, Grundy SM. Metabolic studies in familial hypercholesterolemia: evidence for a gene-dosage effect *in vivo*. *J Clin Invest* 1979;64:524–533.

66. Howard BV, Zech L, Davis M, Bennion LJ, Savage PJ, Nagulespuran M, Bilheimer D, Bennett PH, Grundy SM. Studies of very low density lipoprotein-triglyceride metabolism in an obese population with low plasma lipids: lack of influence of body weight or plasma insulin. *J Lipid Res* 1980;21:1032–1041.

71. Mok HYI, von Bergmann K, Grundy SM. Kinetics of the enterohepatic circulation during fasting in man: biliary lipid secretion and gallbladder storage. *Gastroenterology* 1980;78:1023–1033.

72. Sedaghat A, Grundy SM. Cholesterol crystals and the formation of cholesterol gallstones. *N Engl J Med* 1980;302:1274–1277.

74. Grundy SM, Mok HYI, Zech L, Berman M. Influence of nicotinic acid on metabolism of cholesterol and triglycerides in man. *J Lipid Res* 1981;22:24–36.

84. Beil U, Grundy SM, Crouse JR, Zech L. Triglyceride and cholesterol metabolism in primary hypertriglycerides. *Arteriosclerosis.* 1982;2:44–57.

103. Brunzell JD, Albers JJ, Chait A, Grundy SM, Groszek E, McDonald GB. Plasma lipoproteins in familial combined hyperlipidemia and monogenic familial hypertriglyceridemia. *J Lipid Res* 1983;24:147–155.

104. Wolf R, Grundy SM. Influence of weight reduction on plasma lipoproteins in obese patients. *Arteriosclerosis* 1983;3:160–169.

107. Wolf RN, Grundy SM. Influence of exchanging carbohydrate for saturated fatty acids on plasma lipids and lipoproteins in man. *J Nutr* 1983;113:617–620.

110. Bilheimer DW, Grundy SM, Brown MS, Goldstein JL. Mevinolin and colestipol stimulate receptor-mediated clearance of low density lipoprotein from plasma in familial hypercholesterolemia heterozygotes. *Proc Natl Acad Sci* 1983;80:4124–4128.

113. Bilheimer DW, Grundy SM, Brown MS, Goldstein JL. Mevinolin stimulates receptor-mediated clearance of LDL from plasma in familial hypercholesterolemia heterozygotes. *Trans Assoc Am Physicians* 1983;96:1–9.

115. Kesaniemi YA, Grundy SM. Influence of gemfibrozil on metabolism of cholesterol and plasma glycerides in man. *J Am Med Assoc* 1984;251:2241–2246.

116. Kesaniemi YA, Grundy SM. Dual defect in metabolism of very low density lipoprotein triglycerides in patients with type 5 hyper-lipoproteinemia. *JAMA* 1984;251:2542–2547.

119. Grundy SM, Bilheimer DW. Infuence of inhibition of 3-hydroxy-3methylglutaryl CoA by reductase by mevinolin in familial hypercholesterolemia heterozygotes: effects of cholesterol balance. *Proc Natl Acad Scin (USA)* 1984;81:2538–2542.

126. Bilheimer DW, Goldstein JD, Grundy SM, Starzl TE, Brown MS. Liver transplantation to provide low-density lipoprotein receptors and lower plasma cholesterol in a child with homozygous familial hypercholesterolemia. *N Engl J Med* 1984;311:1658–1664.

129. Vega GL, Beltz W, Grundy SM. Low density lipoprotein metabolism in hypertriglyceridemic and normolipidemic patients with coronary heart disease. *J Lipid Res* 1985;26:115–126.

130. Mattson FH, Grundy SM. Comparison of effects of dietary saturated, monounsaturated, and polyunsaturated fatty acids on plasma lipids and lipoproteins in man. *J Lipid Res* 1985;26:194–202.

132. Dunn FL, Grundy SM, Bilheimer DW, Havel RJ, Raskin P. Impaired catabolism of very low-density lipoprotein-triglyceride in a family with primary hypertriglyceridenia. *Metabolism* 1985;34:316–324.

133. Beltz WF, Kesaniemi YA, Howard BV, Grundy SM. Development of an integrated model for analysis of the kinetics of apolipoprotein B in plasma lipoproteins VLDL, IDL, and LDL. *J Clin Invest* 1985;76:575–585.

134. Kesaniemi YA, Beltz WF, Grundy SM. Comparisons of metabolism of apolipoprotein B in normal subjects, obese patients, and patients with coronary heart disease. *J Clin Invest* 1985;76:586–595.

135. Egusa G, Beltz WF, Grundy SM, Howard BV. Influence of obesity on the metabolism of apolipoprotein B in man. *J Clin Invest* 1986;76:596–603.

136. Vega GL, Grundy SM. Gemfibrozil therapy in primary hyper-triglyceridemia associated with coronary heart disease. *JAMA* 1985;253:2398–2403.

141. Grundy SM, Vega GL, Bilheimer DW. Influence of combined therapy with mevinolin and interruption of bile acid reabsorption on low-density lipoproteins in heterozygous familial hypercholesterolemia. *Ann Int Med* 1985;103:339–343.

142. Grundy SM, Vega GL, Bilhemier DW. Kinetic mechanisms determining variability in low-density lipoprotein levels and their rise with age. *Arteriosclerosis* 1985;5:623–630.

143. Grundy SM, Vega GL. Influence of mevinolin on metabolism of low-density lipoproteins in primary moderate hypercholesterolemia. *J Lipid Res* 1985;26: 1464–1475.

154. Vega GL, Grundy SM. In vivo evidence for reduced binding of low-density lipoproteins to receptors as a cause of primary moderate hypercholesterolemia. *J Clin Invest* 1986;78:1410–1414.

155. Grundy SM, Nix D, Whelan MF, Franklin L. Comparison of three cholesterol lowering diets in normolipidemic men. *JAMA* 1986;256:2351–2355.

159. Vega GL, Grundy SM. Treatment of primary moderate hypercholesterolemia with lovastatin (mevinolin) and colestipol. *JAMA* 1987;257:33–38.

166. Innerarity TL, Weisgraber KH, Arnold KS, Mahley RW, Krauss RM, Vega GL, Grundy SM. Familial defective apolipoprotein B-100: low-density lipoproteins with abnormal receptor binding. *Proc Natl Acad Sci* (USA) 1987;84:6919–6923.

171. Garg A, Grundy SM. Lovastatin for lowering cholesterol levels in non-insulin dependent diabetes mellitus. *N Engl J Med* 1988;318:81–86.

172. East C, Bilheimer DW, Grundy SM. Combination drug therapy for treatment of familial combined hyperlipidemia. *Ann Intern Med* 1988;109:25–32.

173. Grundy SM, Vega GL. Plasma cholesterol responsiveness to saturated fatty acids. *Ann J Clin Nutr* 1988;47:833–824.

177. Grundy SM, Florentin L, Nix D, Whelan MF. Comparison of monounsaturated fatty acids and carbohydrates for reducing raised levels of plasma cholesterol in man. *Am J Clin Nutr* 1988;47:965–969.

178. Bonanome A, Grundy SM. Effect of dietary stearic acid on plasma cholesterol and lipoprotein levels. *N Engl J Med* 1988;318:1244–1248.

179. Grundy SM, HMG-CoA reductase inhibitors for treatment of hypercholesterolemia. *N Engl J Med* 1988;319:24–33.

180. Garg A, Bonanome A, Grundy SM, Zhange Z-J, Unger RH. Comparison of a high monounsaturated fat diet in patients with non-insulin dependent diabetes mellitus. *N Engl J Med* 1988;319:829–834.

181. Uauy R, Vega GL, Grundy SM, Bilheimer DM. Lovastatin therapy in receptor-negative homozygous familial hypercholesterolemia: lack of effect on low-density lipoprotein concentrations or turnover. *J Pediatr* 1988;113:387–392.

183. Weisgraber KH, Innerarity TL, Newhouse YM, Young SG, Arnold KS, Krauss RM, Vega GL, Grundy SM, Mahley RM. Familial defective apolipoprotein B-100: enhanced binding of monoclonal antibody MB 47 to abnormal low-density lipoproteins. *Proc Natl Acad Sci USA* 1988;85:9758–9762.

186. Soria LF, Ludwig EH, Clarke HRG, Vega GL, Grundy SM, McCarthy BJ. Association between a specific apolipoprotein B mutation and familial defective apolipoprotein B-100. *Proc Natl Acad Sci USA* 1989;86:587–591.

191. Vega GL, Grundy SM. Comparison of lovastatin and gemfibrozil in normolipidemic patients with hypoalphalipoproteinemia. *JAMA* 1989;262:3148–3153.

193. Garg A, Grundy SM. High monosaturated fat diet for non-insulin-dependent diabetes mellitus. *N Engl J Med* 1989;320:536–537.

196. Grundy SM, Vega GL. Causes of high blood cholesterol. *Circulation* 1990;81:412–427.

198. Abbott WGH, Swinburn B, Ruotolo G, Hara H, Patti L, Harper I, Grundy SM, Howard BV. Effect of a high-carbohydrate, low-saturated fat-diet on apolipoprotein B and triglyceride metabolism in Pima Indians. *J Clin Invest* 1990; 86:642–650.

203. Beltz WF, Kesaniemi YA, Miller NH, Fisher WR, Grundy SM, Zech LA. Studies on the metabolism of apolipoprotein B in hypertriglyceridemic subjects using simultaneous administration of tritiated luecine and radioiodinated very low-density lipoprotein. *J Lipid Res* 1990;31:361–374.

205. Garg A, Grundy SM. Nicotinic acid as therapy for dyslipidemia in non-insulin-dependent diabetes mellitus. *JAMA* 1990;264:723–726.

209. Vega GL, Grundy SM. Primary hypertriglyceridemia with borderline high cholesterol and elevated apolipoprotein B concentrations. *JAMA* 1990;264:2759–2763.

216. Vega GL, Hobbs HH, Grundy SM. Low-density lipoprotein kinetics in a family having defective low-density lipoprotein receptors in which hypercholesterolemia is suppressed. *Arterioscler Thromb* 1991;11:578–585.

220. Grundy SM. Multifactorial etiology of hypercholesterolemia. Implications for prevention of coronary heart disease. *Arterioscler Thromb* 1991;11:1619–1635.

222. Denke MA, Grundy SM. Effects of fats high in stearic acid on lipid and lipoprotein concentrations in men. *Am J Clin Nutr* 1991;54:1036–1040.

226. Garg A, Grundy SM, Unger RH. Comparison of effects of high and low-carbohydrate diets on plasma lipoproteins, low-apoprotein and insulin sensitivity in patients with mild NIDDM. *Diabetes* 1992;41:1278–1285.

227. Wilson MA, Vega GL, Gylling H, Grundy SM. Persistence of abnormalities in metabolism of apolipoproteins B-100 and A-1 after weight reduction in patients with primary hypertriglyceridemia. *Arterioscler Thromb* 1992;12:976–984.

229. Gylling H, Vega GL, Grundy SM. Physiologic mechanisms for reduced apolipoprotein AI concentrations associated with low levels of high-density lipoprotein cholesterol in patients with normal plasma lipids. *J Lipid Res* 1992; 33:1527–1539.

231. Denke MA, Grundy SM. Comparison of effects of lauric acid and palmitic acid on plasma lipids and lipoproteins. *Am J Clin Nutr* 1992;56:895–898.

233. Jialal I, Grundy SM. Effect of dietary supplementation with alpha-tocopherol on the oxidative modification of low-density lipoprotein. *J Lipid Res* 1992;33:899–906.

235. Vega GL, Grundy SM. Two patterns of LDL metabolism in normotriglyceridemic patients with hypoalphalipoproteinemia. *Arterioscler Thromb* 1993;13: 579–589.

237. Gianturco SH, Bradley WA, Nozaki S, Vega GL, Grundy SM. Effects of lovastatin on the levels, structure, and atherogenicity of VLDL in patients with moderate hypertriglyceridemia. *Arteriocler Thromb* 1993;13:472–481.

238. Blades B, Vega GL, Grundy SM. Activities of lipoprotein lipase and hepatic triglyceride lipase in postheparin plasma of patients with low concentrations of HDL cholesterol. *Arterioscler Thromb* 1993;13:1227–1235.

242. Jialal I, Grundy SM. Effect of combined supplementation with a-tocopherol, ascorbate, and beta-carotene on low-density lipoprotein oxidation. *Circulation* 1993;88:2780–2786.

243. Arca M, Vega GL, Grundy SM. Hypercholesterolemia in postmenopausal women: metabolic defects and response to low-dose lovastatin. *JAMA* 1994;271: 453–459.

250. Abate N, Bruns D, Peshock R, Garg A, Grundy SM. Estimation of adipose tissue mass by magnetic resonance imaging: validation against dissection in human cadavers. *J Lipid Res* 1994;35:1490–1496.

254. Cohen JC, Wang Z, Grundy SM, Stoesz MR, Guerra R. Variation at the hepatic lipase and apolipoprotein AI/CIII/AIV loci is a major cause of genetically determined variation of plasma HDL cholesterol levels. *J Clin Invest* 1994;94: 2377–2384.

256. Abate N, Garg A, Peshock RM, Stray-Gunderson J, Grundy SM. Relationship of generalized and regional adiposity to insulin sensitivity in man. *J Clin Invest* 1995;96:88–98.

257. Mize C, Uauy R, Kramer R, Benser M, Allen S, Grundy SM. Lipoprotein-cholesterol responses in healthy infants fed defined diets from ages 1 to 12 months: comparison of diets predominant in oleic acid versus lenoleic acid, with parallel observations in infants fed a human milk-based diet. *J Lipid Res* 1995; 36:1178–1187.

258. Tato F, Vega GL, Grundy SM. Relation between cholesterol ester transfer protein activities and lipoprotein cholesterol in patients with hypercholesterolemia and combined hyperlipidemia. *Arterioscler Thromb Vasc Biol* 1995;15:112–120.

259. Tato F, Vega GL, Grundy SM. Bimodal distribution of cholesterol ester transfer protein activities in normotriglyceridemic men with low HDL cholesterol concentrations. *Arteriscler Thromb Vasc Biol* 1995;15:446–451.

269. Vega GL, Grundy SM. Hypercholesterolemia with cholesterol-enriched LDL and normal levels of LDL-apolipoprotein B. Effects of the step I diet and bile acid sequestrants on the cholesterol content of LDL. *Arterioscler Thromb Vasc Biol* 1996;16:517–522.

272. Abate N, Garg A, Peshock RM, Stray-Gunderson J, Adams-Huet B, Grundy SM. Relationship of generalized and regional adiposity to insulin sensitivity in men with NIDDM. *Diabetes* 1996;45:1684–1693.

274. Abate N, Garg A, Coleman R, Grundy SM, Peshock RM. Prediction of total subcutaneous abdominal, intraperitoneal, and retroperitoneal adipose tissue masses in men by a single axial magnetic resonance imaging slice. *Am J Clin Nutr* 1997;65:403–408.

276. Tato F, Vega GL, Grundy SM. Determinants of plasma HDL-cholesterol in hypertriglyceridemic patients: role of cholesterol-ester transfer protein and licithin cholesterol acyl transferase. *Arteriscler Thromb Vasc Biol* 1997;17:56–63.

279. Guerra R, Wang J, Grundy SM, Cohen JC. A hepatic lipase (LIPC) allele associated with high plasma concentrations of high density lipoprotein cholesterol. *Proc Natl Acad Sci USA* 1997;94:4532–4537.

284. Tato F, Vega GL, Grundy SM. Effects of crystalline nicotinic acid-induced hepatic dysfunction on serum low-density lipoprotein cholesterol and lecithin cholesterol acyl transferase. *Am J Cardiol* 1998.

285. Vega GL, Clark LT, Tang A, Marcovina S, Grundy SM, Cohen JC. Hepatic lipase activity is lower in African American than in white American men: effects of 5' flanking polymorphism in the hepatic lipase gene. *J Lipid Res* 1998;39: 228–232.

286. Nie L, Wang J, Clark LT, Tang A, Vega GL, Grundy SM, Cohen JC. Body mass index and hepatic lipase gene (LIPC) polymorphism jointly influence post heparin plasma hepatic lipase activity. *J Lipid Res* 1998;39:1–4.

287. Wang J, Freeman DJ, Grundy SM, Levine DM, Guerra R, Cohen JC. Linkage between cholesterol 7a-hydroxylase and high plasma low-density lipoprotein cholesterol concentrations. *J Clin Invest* 1998;101:1283–1291.

288. Mostaza JM, Vega GL, Snell P, Grundy SM. Abnormal metabolism of free fatty acids in hypertriglyceridemic men: apparent insulin resistance of adipose tissue. *J Intern Med* 1998;243:265–274.

DONALD CAREY HARRISON, MD: A Conversation With the Editor*

Don Harrison was born February 24, 1934, in Blount County, Alabama, located about halfway between Birmingham and Huntsville, and that is where he grew up. He graduated from Birmingham Southern College with a BS in chemistry in 1954 and from the University of Alabama School of Medicine in 1958. His internship and assistant residency in medicine were at the Peter Bent Brigham Hospital in Boston, and they were followed by a year of cardiology with Dr. Lewis Dexter. From 1961 to 1963, he was a clinical associate in the cardiology branch of the National Heart Institute in Bethesda, Maryland. In July 1963, he and his family moved to Palo Alto, California, were he was chief resident in medicine at Stanford University School of Medicine. Thereafter, he remained at Stanford, and in 1967, at age 32, he became chief of the division of cardiology. From 1972 until 1986 he was professor of medicine and the William G. Irwin Professor of Cardiology at Stanford University School of Medicine. He remained at Stanford until 1986, when he moved to Cincinnati as Senior Vice President and Provost for Health Affairs of the University of Cincinnati Medical Center and also as Professor of Medicine and Cardiology at the same university. In 2003, he retired from those positions but continues on a consultant status to that institution. During those 17 years while serving as the chief executive officer of the University of Cincinnati Medical Center and its affiliate relations, he also was a member of the university policy and planning committee, the final governing body for the university (Figure 1).

Thus, Dr. Harrison has had a distinguished career in cardiology and as the leader of a major university medical center. His publication list numbers nearly 600. Additionally, he has written or edited 7 books. He has traveled the world, giving presentations in most major centers on the planet.

For his many contributions, he has received a number of honors including an Honorary Doctor of Law degree at Birmingham Southern College (1995); President of the American Heart Association (1981 to 1982); recipient of the Gold Heart Award for the American Heart Association (1983); and Distinguished Alumnus, Birmingham Southern College (1984) and the University of Alabama Birmingham College of Medicine (1981). He has served on advisory committees and as consultants to a number of corporations in the US, including Hewlett Packard, Proctor and Gamble, and numerous venture capital firms. He is also the founder or co-founder of several venture companies and presently a partner in the Charter Life Science venture capital firm of Palo Alto and Cincinnati. Six patents have been issued in his name, and 6 are pending.

He and his lovely wife, Laura, are the parents of 3 and the grandparents of 8. Don is also a great guy and fun to be around. (Additionally I might add that he is a superb reviewer of manuscripts. I have sent him numerous manuscripts during my 23-year editorship of *The American Journal of Cardiology* and I am indebted to him for his always timely and perceptive reviews.)

William Clifford Roberts, MD[†] **(hereafter WCR):** *Don, I appreciate your willingness to talk to me and therefore to the readers of* The American Journal of Cardiology *about your personal and professional lives. We are in my home on November 13, 2005, at the time of the Annual Scientific Sessions of the American Heart Association. Dr. Harrison and I have been trying to arrange a time for this interview for about 3 years, and this is the first time we have been able to get together. Don, could we start by my asking you to talk about some of your early memories, where you were born, where you grew up, what your parents were like, your siblings and your home environs?*

Donald Carey Harrison, MD[‡] **(hereafter DCH):** Bill, I was born in North Central Alabama in a place called Forest Gap. Our home was 2 miles from any other house. I was born at home. My mother, who had lived in that part of the country for years, was a graduate of the high school which I later attended. She graduated in 1931. My dad's mother died while giving birth to his sister, and he was raised in an orphanage where he worked in the caretaker's house as a house boy. At about age 17 or 18, he started going to a gym and trained to become a boxer. He found a manager and became a professional boxer, and had about 40 fights all over the South, just before the Depression. He said he got his brains beat out for $100 many times. He fought as far North as Cincinnati. When the Depression came, there was no more money for prize fighting, so he became a hobo on a train and went to Nebraska to work in the wheat fields. Unfortunately, when he got there, he found that everyone else had gone to do that, too, and there were no jobs. He came back and his uncle, who had a delivery service for the Birmingham News, a major newspaper in the state, hired him and he delivered newspapers through out north Alabama. He often stopped at the café where my mother worked with her father and mother. They met there. They married and moved to Forest Gap. A year later, I was born, and my sister was born 3 years later. We lived at Forest Gap for about 3 years after I was born and then moved to Garden

---

* This series of interviews was underwritten by an unrestricted grant from Bristol-Myers Squibb.

† Executive Director, Baylor Cardiovascular Institute, Baylor University Medical Center, Dallas, Texas, 75246.

‡ Senior Vice President and Provost for Health Affairs Emeritus University of Cincinnati Medical Center Cincinnati, Ohio, 45267-0669.

Figure 1. DCH at the time of the interview. (Photo taken by WCR.)

City, 6 miles away in Culman County, where I grew up. During prohibition at Forest Gap, my father paid the Sheriff not to arrest him, so he was able to sell liquor and have gambling. People drove out from Birmingham to drink and gamble. It was a very remote place. I have 2 memories of it. I remember my sister being born when I was 3 years old, and I remember a large steam driven shovel working outside. When we moved to Garden City, my father had a brick house built, supposedly one of the nicest houses in town. It was on a hill and looked over the Mulberry Fork of the Warrior River. My dad moved there because prohibition had ended (in 1937) and Cullman County was 1 of 4 counties in the state that voted to be "wet," a southern term for allowing you to sell alcoholic beverages. It was also the only county in which you could sell alcohol on Sundays. My dad ran a tavern. People came from all over the state to buy beer. That is where I grew up. The town was small enough so that everybody knew everyone else and was related to them. We were probably some of the only strangers in that town.

WCR: *Garden City is half-way between Birmingham and Huntsville?*

DCH: Yes. It was on old Highway 31, the main north and south route until I-65 was built, and it missed Garden City which as a result dried up.

WCR: *When was your father born?*

DCH: In 1908, and he died in 1996 at age 88. My mother was born in 1912 and died in 1989 at age 78.

WCR: *Did you work in the tavern?*

DCH: Not until I was older. When World War II started, both my dad and mother went off to work. For 3 years, my sister and I lived with my maternal grandmother, who lived nearby. When my parents returned after the war, they went back into the tavern business, but the county had become "dry." Nevertheless, with certain maneuvers with the federal officials, they were able to sell alcohol. My dad never sold moonshine. He sold only bonded whiskey, so he was not bothered by the feds, but he was bothered by the state folks, who were always after him. I used to be very frightened that they were going to take him away, but they never managed to catch him. I worked at the pit bar-b-que operation of the tavern, and I cut the wood and helped prepare the "shoulders" to roast. After a few years my dad built a motel, the first Holiday Inn-like motel in the area. I was 16 and actually helped to build it. Two journeymen from Pennsylvania came through and said they knew how to build, so my dad hired them, and they built a motel. I worked in the motel a lot. We had a café in the motel. We only had 12 rooms in the motel, but I ran the front of the restaurant, while my mother and sister did all of the cooking, and my dad ran to motel part of it. I was in high school at this point. I had been able to drive since age 14. Regularly, I picked up all of the foods in Cullman after high school. I served breakfast in the café before I went to school, and all family members worked in the café in the evenings until we finished at about 9 P.M., and then we washed all the dishes by hand. Then I had to study after that, if I had studying to do.

WCR: *Where did you go to school?*

DCH: Garden City had a Junior High School for grades 1 to 9. I started when I was 6 years old. The school had been built by the Works Progress Administration (WPA), and it was a fairly nice school. I did very well in school. I was double promoted, meaning I made 2 grades at one time. I met Laura, my future wife, in Sunday school before we started grammar school. She and I were in the first grade together, and we were the only 2 students who were double promoted, so we finished high school at the same time. Garden City school had some reasonable teachers even although it was rural.

WCR: *Being double promoted means that you went from first grade to third grade?*

DCH: No. I went from first grade and then from second grade into fourth grade. It allowed me to finish high school when I was 16 years old.

WCR: *You and Laura met before you started school?*

DCH: Yes. We met in Sunday school at the Baptist church. My parents had a strange thing about Sunday school. Because they had been in the tavern business, they were really

Figure 2. April 1934. DCH at 6 weeks with mother, Sovola, and father, Walter Harrison.

Figure 3. DCH at 3 years old with new shoes.

shunned in the community, and we were looked down upon for that reason. Financially, we were better off than most people in the community. My folks didn't go to church, but they sent my sister and me to Sunday school, which was always a paradox to me and something that bothered me.

WCR: *When was your parents' tavern closed down?*

DCH: The motel was built when the tourist business was still very big. The motel opened in 1949 and I-65 came along in 1964.

WCR: *Was the motel adjacent to the tavern initially?*

DCH: It was on the same property. The tavern was torn down when the motel was built.

WCR: *What was your daddy like? Did you get a long well with him?*

DCH: My father and I got a long very well. He was a bit distant, but I would say he was persistent. He taught me to play baseball. My dad had been a good baseball player, and I was having a little trouble. He would hit the ball to me for hour after hour, making sure I could catch it. He was persistent about everything he did. I think that persistence came from his boxing days. He never wanted me to have anything to do with boxing. The day I was born, he went out

and burned all of his scrap books and boxing gloves, and he never told me about his boxing career until much later in my life. He didn't want me to get my brains beat out. My dad only went through the third grade in school, but he taught himself how to read, do math and how to write checks. My mother finished high school and was the top student in her class.

WCR: *Did your father have siblings?*

DCH: He had 2 brothers and 1 sister.

WCR: *Did they live in the community?*

DCH: No. He had lived in Birmingham, and 1 of his sisters was brought up by an aunt. He and the other 2 brothers, both older, grew up in an orphanage.

WCR: *Did your mother have an extended family?*

DCH: No. She had 1 sister who died in childbirth of puerperal fever, and one brother who spent 25 years in the Navy. That episode made my mother suspicious of doctors, and she did not want me to be a physician. She did not really forgive me for becoming a physician until I managed her medications during her last 6 or 7 weeks when she lived with us. She had pancreatic cancer. During that time she accepted that I was a physician, but, basically, all her life she didn't want me to be a physician.

WCR: *What was your mother's name?*

Figure 4. DCH on the way to school with sister, Ann, and barefooted, which is the way children went to school.

DCH: My mother's name was Sovola Thompson and my father's name was Walter Carey Harrison (Figure 2).

WCR: *When did they get married?*

DCH: They got married in 1933 and I was born the next year.

WCR: *What was your mother like?*

DCH: During my early years, my mother was the dominant figure in the family (Figure 3). She spent a lot of time reading to my sister and me. We had African-American maids who came out from Birmingham to help take care of us, because my mother worked with my father. Every night my mother read stories to us and really looked after us. She was very interested in our education, and she pushed us. My mother was my inspiration and the driving force behind my life in many ways. When I went away to college, and particularly when I made the decision to be pre-med, she had a terrible breakdown. She had some type of depression syndrome and had to be hospitalized and fed. She never totally got over that. One reason she never forgave me for being a doctor was because I think she resented not being able to go to college. In 1931, however, no one had any money where she grew up, and there was no way for her to go to any college. I think she really didn't want to get married, but my dad came along, and it was an opportunity to get out of the care of her family, and so she did.

WCR: *What did her parents do?*

DCH: Her dad was a coal miner and he moved yearly from

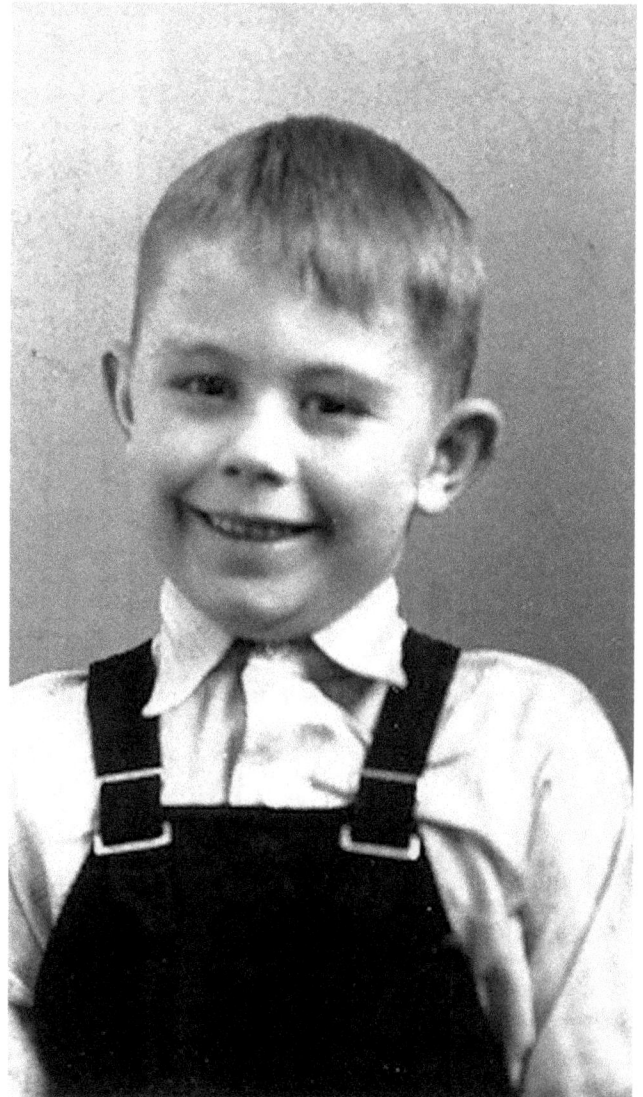

Figure 5. DCH school photograph for first grade.

place to place. She never had a place where she was settled. They went to Colorado for a while and then came back. He moved around Birmingham and around different counties in Alabama where coal mining was going on. My mother had an unhappy childhood. Her mother and father had separated, although they never divorced. I met her father only twice in my life.

WCR: *You said you met your future wife, Laura, before you started grammar school. What did her family do? Where did they live?*

DCH: They lived in the surrounding farm area of Garden City. Her dad was a farmer. He also did some butcher work at one of the local grocery stores. They were very poor. My family was relatively poor, but we were well off compared with most in the community of Garden City. Laura's family had no running water in the house until 1947. There was no electricity in her house for her first 6 or 7 years of school. Her dad raised some cotton and watermelons, but he had to borrow the money every year to buy the fertilizer. If the cotton crop wasn't good, they would barely make enough to

Figure 6. DCH at age 16. Baseball uniform for American Legion team.

make ends meet. We all went to school barefooted, because we started school in the middle of the summer (Figure 4). School started in early July, because we took a break for 6 weeks so kids could pick cotton. I could pick 200 pounds in a 12 hour day and was paid $6.00. I went to school in Garden City up to ninth grade, and then I went the Hanceville High School.

WCR: *How far was that from home?*

DCH: That was 6 miles from home. I rode a school bus, and then I started driving at the beginning of my junior year.

WCR: *What was your home like when you moved to Garden City into the house up on the hill?*

DCH: It was a nice house. We had indoor plumbing and a coal burning furnace and my sister and I each had our own bedroom. We were taken care of during our early years by African-American maids who told us ghost stories. I have very fond memories of them–Emma and Marilla. They told great scary ghost stories (Figure 5).

WCR: *I gather that you always did well in school.*

DCH: Yes. I was the valedictorian of my class in junior high, and I was the top person in my high school class. I was always competing with Laura who was not my friend then. She was always my biggest competitor. I have often said that the reason I succeeded was because I tried to keep up with her. In our sophomore and junior years in high school, the girls had virtually all the class officer positions. The senior year, 2 girls where nominated, and I was nominated to be class president. The girls' vote split and I became class president. My wife has never forgiven me for that.

WCR: *She was one of the girls nominated?*

DCH: Yes.

WCR: *How many students were in your high school senior class?*

DCH: Sixty seven graduated. The high school was a consolidated school consisting of students from all over the county. There was about 200 students in the entire school. I played football. I was a small guy, but I played guard, and I was captain of the football team my junior year. I was also on the baseball team, and we did very well (Figure 6). In the summers when we were not in school, we played the American Legion for Cullman. We were the State Champions in 1950. We played all over the state. My father helped me a lot. He was persistent and he pushed me to be persistent.

WCR: *What position did you play in baseball?*

DCH: Second base.

WCR: *Could you hit?*

DCH: Yes. I was the lead-off.

WCR: *So you were fast?*

DCH: I had a good eye to get on base and was good at getting rallies started.

WCR: *Were there any teachers in your junior high or high school who had a major impact on you?*

DCH: Yes. I had 2 teachers who really helped me a lot. Mrs. Lamont was my math teacher in high school, and she was a driving force, making me learn algebra and geometry. The other teacher was Mr. Holly, who was the civics and American government teacher, and he gave me a real appreciation for what this country was about. He was a dynamic teacher. Some teachers were not so excellent. The physics teacher in high school had only taken a summer course in physics at a junior college and never had any other training in physics. He gave me his physics college textbook about the third week in the course and said, "You know more about this subject than I do, so you use this textbook." I didn't get a very good grounding in high school physics.

WCR: *What about chemistry?*

DCH: I got a pretty good grounding in chemistry. I later majored in chemistry in college.

WCR: *It sounds like working much of the time that you learned how to do nearly everything. You learned how to cook, clean, cut wood, and fix things. A motel needs plenty of upkeep.*

DCH: Yes. I learned all kinds of things.

WCR: *You became a real fixer?*

DCH: I could fix almost anything.

WCR: *That must have helped you a bit in physics.*

DCH: It did later on. In college, I liked physics.

WCR: *In junior high and high school, did you have to study much or did it just come easy for you.*

DCH: Only occasionally would I have to do any studying. It all came easy for me in high school. We were tested all the time. Most people didn't have electricity until the Tennessee Valley Authority (TVA) brought it. Most of my classmates were so poor that they didn't have it. Many kids came bare foot to school, because they couldn't afford shoes. I had shoes, but preferred to go barefoot in the summer.

WCR: *Were there books around your house? Did your mother and daddy read the newspaper or magazines?*

DCH: Yes. They read the newspaper and took several

magazines, and there were always books. I had an aunt who worked in Washington, DC, and the Christmas gift from her would always be a stack of books. She was my great aunt. She was a single woman who worked as a secretary in 1 of the Department of State offices.

WCR: *What kind of books?*

DCH: At a younger age things like *Pinocchio* and later the series of the Brooks Brothers. *Billy Whiskers* was a favorite early book. As we advanced, she would send more advanced books.

WCR: *You didn't have family dinners at night because you were all working?*

DCH: The only time we did that was during the 3 years I lived with my grandmother during the war.

WCR: *Your grandfather wasn't there? It was just your grandmother, your sister and you?*

DCH: Yes. And also 1 of my cousins. My mother's sister (who died while giving birth) had a son who lived with my grandmother, my sister, and me. He was 2 years older than I was.

WCR: *Growing up, did you do any traveling or take any family vacations?*

DCH: Once we had a family vacation. We went to Ashville, North Carolina. My grandmother worked in a fancy hotel there, and because she did we got free rooms. We went to Mt. Mitchell and visited the Smoky Mountains. That was the only family vacation that I can remember.

WCR: *You said that your mother and daddy sent you and your sister to Sunday school, but they felt as though could not go to church.*

DCH: They didn't feel like they could go, nor did I think they had an interest in going.

WCR: *Did you study the Bible at all?*

DCH: Yes. We went to very fundamentalist Baptist churches. At age 12, you were supposed to be saved, and all my peers and school mates were saved that year, but I was quite skeptical of all of this, so I wasn't saved then. It took 2 years of pounding on me before I was saved. I was baptized in the Mulberry River by being dipped backwards 3 times, once in the name of the father, once in the name of the son, and once in the name of the Holy Ghost. We had to be a bit careful because few of those with me could swim.

WCR: *Did you do any fishing or hunting growing up?*

DCH: I did both. When about 8 years old, and living with my grandmother, I fished in a creek that ran into the Mulberry River, and when the river would rise the water came back up into the creek. I fished for Brem (Blue Gills) in the creek. As I grew older, I fished in the Mulberry River. We had trot lines with multiple hooks that ran across the river. I had a flat-bottom boat that we paddled and pushed with a pole in the river. I have fished all my life. My dad gave me a single-shot 22 rifle when I was 12 years old, and I was allowed to hunt, which I did on my own. I hunted for squirrels, which we ate. I became a pretty good shot. I shot only at their heads so I wouldn't damage the meat. On my fourteenth birthday, my father gave me a LC Smith double-barrelled shotgun and then I started hunting quail, rabbits, and doves.

WCR: *You didn't go hunting with your daddy?*

DCH: No. He did not hunt. He came looking for me when I got caught out after dark, sometimes back in the hollows of the hills. This was mountainous country where we grew up, and the creeks flowed down valleys where we would hunt. If I got caught out after dark, my dad would come find me. He was always quite angry at me when he would have to come after me. The worst experience I had was wandering into a group of people making moonshine. They pointed guns at me. This happened when I was about 15. I pleaded that I was lost and didn't know where I was and could never find my way back, and they let me go.

WCR: *You were in rattle snake, copperhead and water moccasin country. Did you ever see any of them?*

DCH: Yes. Several times when I was hunting, I came upon rattle snakes, and while fishing, cottonmouth water moccasins. We did a lot of frog gigging as well on the river. We would shoot the water moccasins at night with a rifle.

WCR: *Did you read fast as you were growing up?*

DCH: When learning to read, speed reading was taught. A problem I had later on was that I didn't learn to read phonetically. I learned to read whole sentences. I was a very fast reader, because that is the way we were taught to read. Speed reading as I do makes it difficult to read aloud. I found that I was always 3 sentences ahead of where I needed to be when I read aloud.

WCR: *When did the idea strike you that you might want to be a physician?*

DCH: It came about because of the local doctor in Hanceville. At that time they did a lot of testing of people for syphilis. They tested us for syphilis, and at the same time they did blood sugars on us. I had taken a large carbohydrate meal before having my blood sugar drawn and it was elevated. I thought I had diabetes. The local doctor then did a glucose tolerance test on me, and it was normal. He took a shine to me, and let me come to the hospital and make rounds with him. This was when I was a senior in high school and that experience stimulated my interest. When we had aptitude testing at the end of my senior year of high school, I tested strongly in science and other things that suggested medicine. I also tested strongly in law. My mother wanted me to be a lawyer. My mother's ambition was for me to be a lawyer, a politician, and eventually governor of Alabama, but I never met her goals for me. She hated the idea I would become a doctor.

WCR: *Neither your mother nor your father could advise you well on college since they had not gone.*

DCH: That's correct, but, there was never a question of my going to college. During my junior year in high school, I participated in the state wide oratorical contest, the winners of which would receive a college scholarship. A participant had to win in his/her school, district, county, region, and state. Although at 15 I was a real country boy compared with the rest, I won in my district. There were 5 girls and me.

They all gave much better memorized talks that I did. But the judges would take 1 sentence out of your speech and then you would have to give a 5-minute extemporaneous talk on it. I won on that count. The state competition was held at Birmingham Southern College. The stage looked so big. I competed against people who came from the big high schools of the larger cities. I took third place and as a result I got a scholarship to Birmingham Southern College. My mother had assumed that I would go to the University of Alabama in Tuscaloosa. She took me there, and we went around and then I went to Birmingham Southern College and really liked it. Although small, it was rated the best educational school in Alabama and still is. It was a good place. I chose to go there. I told my mother I would go there for the freshman year because of having the scholarship and then transfer to the University of Alabama. Of course, I never did.

WCR: *Did you get a scholarship for the other years?*

DCH: No. Tuition was only $400 annually then and my parents could afford that.

WCR: *How far was the campus from Garden City?*

DCH: Forty miles.

WCR: *How far is Huntsville from Garden City?*

DCH: About 40 miles.

WCR: *What was Southern Birmingham College like? How many people were in your class?*

DCH: The total number of students in the college was about 1,200 at that time. I finished in 3 years, because I went both summers. I had a tough time early on at Birmingham Southern, because most of the kids had come from prep schools or big name high schools in Birmingham area or elsewhere. Coming from a consolidated rural high school, I did not have the background and preparation they did. In first English class the students were asked to write an autobiographical sketch of our lives. My grade on the exercise was F. I had never previously made any grade under a B+. My advisor at the end of my first quarter in college said to me, "Son, if you don't do better, there is no chance that you will ever get into any medical school in the country." He worked with me. The English teachers had about 15 students in a class. They singled me out to work with me and did so at least an extra hour per week. It was a good place for me to go, and I got a great education. I majored in chemistry. By the time I finished, I was Phi Beta Kappa eligible but not inducted until later.

WCR: *What was the school like? Was it a private school?*

DCH: It was affiliated with the Methodist church. It was like a private school. It had great teachers and a wonderful educational program. The faculty worked a lot with students and had their best interest at heart. I have had a long-standing relation with that college subsequently. I gave the commencement address in 1996 and they gave me an honorary degree in Law. I have participated in many of their presidential programs and given money to support their activities.

WCR: *Where did you live in college?*

DCH: For nonfraternity men, the only dorm was an old Army barracks that had been built during World War II. That is where I lived for the first 2 years. By my last year, there they had built new dormitories for the girls and the boys moved into the old girls' dormitories.

WCR: *It sounds like you studied hard there.*

DCH: I studied very hard. I had to work really hard to keep up.

WCR: *How was it meeting the kids who had been to prep school and the other fancy schools as compared with your background?*

DCH: I was in awe of them as you might imagine. Just before going off to college my mother decided I needed a suit. She took me Birmingham—to Black's Department Store—and bought me a new suit. That was necessary for social affairs and new to me since I had not worn a suit before.

WCR: *Who were the teachers at Birmingham Southern College who had an impact on you?*

DCH: My advisor, *Dr. William Blair*, who was head of the Biology Department, my chemistry professor, and my advisor for my major, Dr. Bill Smithey. They were outstanding.

WCR: *It sounds like you had already decided on medicine before you got to college.*

DCH: Yes. I entered college as a premed student.

WCR: *That didn't please your mother too much, and then when you didn't transfer to University of Alabama in Tuscaloosa, that didn't please her either.*

DCH: No. Not at all.

WCR: *How did your father handle this?*

DCH: He never wanted me to be a lawyer. He wanted me to be a businessman and come back and get into the motel business with him. He actually bought property in suburban Birmingham (which I still own) to build a motel. He took it quite well, when I decided to go into medicine instead of doing that. He always admired what I did in medicine.

WCR: *What was the physician's name whom you met who did the glucose tolerance test on you?*

DCH: His name was *Dr. George Rowe*. He was a general practitioner.

WCR: *You made ward rounds with him?*

DCH: Yes. I made hospital rounds with him and sometimes went to his office with him during my last year of high school.

WCR: *Did he have children?*

DCH: He had 1 daughter but no sons.

WCR: *He sort of adopted you in a way.*

DCH: Yes. I really thought I was going to be a general practitioner. He had a nice house. He saw about 50 patients per day. Only later did I learn that he really wasn't very expert at some of the things he did.

WCR: *Did he do surgery?*

Figure 7. DCH football picture. Captain of the team junior year.

DCH: He did everything. But he wasn't very good at the surgery part.

WCR: *How did you decide to go to the University of Alabama Medical School at Birmingham (UAB)?*

DCH: My advisor, Dr. Blair said, "You are capable of going to medical schools other than UAB." UAB was a relatively new school. The first class entered in 1946, so by the time I went there in 1954 there had been few classes. The first graduating class was in 1950. He suggested that I apply to Emory, which I did. I also applied to the University of Pennsylvania and to Tulane. I went to an interview at the University of Pennsylvania. I was not accepted there. By that time I had also been accepted to UAB, and it was much less expensive to go to UAB, tuition being $200 per semester. I got a lot of encouragement to come to UAB and I did.

WCR: *Who was encouraging you?*

DCH: The faculty members at Birmingham Southern. *Mrs. Virginia Baxley*, the registrar at UAB, a very outgoing person, encouraged me via calls and letters to come to UAB, and said that I would do well there.

WCR: *How many were in your class?*

DCH: We started with 80 students and finished with 68.

WCR: *How many were in your graduating class at Birmingham Southern College?*

DCH: About 250.

WCR: *Where did you stand among them?*

DCH: In the top 5%.

WCR: *The faculty at Birmingham Southern must have been enormously pleased with you, because you needed tutoring when you first came, and then you ended up making Phi Beta Kappa. That is impressive.*

DCH: They helped me a lot.

WCR: *After the first year you were on your own?*

DCH: Yes. I studied hard most of the time, because I always took a heavy load. I did not do a lot of socializing. Laura went to what is now the University of North Alabama in Florence. She didn't go the first year after graduating from high school, because she didn't have the money to go to college. She worked as a high school secretary and then someone convinced her that she could go to college at Florence. At the time it was Florence State Teacher's College.

WCR: *When did you and Laura start going steady?*

DCH: At the end of high school. I asked her to be my date at the football banquet, which was in January or February of my senior year of high school (Figure 7). That was at the encouragement of a teacher, *Clair Mae Burkart*; I had no date and Laura's dad was very strict. He would not let her go out with boys. Somehow he knew me and let her go with me. We started going steady right away. In my first year in college I came home some weekends to work with my folks. She used to say that I used to come to visit her smelling like a French fried potato, because I had worked in the kitchen.

WCR: *How did you get back and forth between Birmingham and Garden City?*

DCH: I often hitchhiked back and forth. It was safe back then. My father knew several people who would leave Birmingham on Friday afternoons, and I also often came home with them. Often I got a ride back to Birmingham Southern on Monday mornings by a graduate student. I didn't come home every weekend, but I came home a lot.

WCR: *Were you in a fraternity?*

DCH: Yes. I was a Sigma Alpha Epsilon.

WCR: *Did you enjoy that?*

DCH: Not really. I didn't drink alcohol, and I didn't dance, having grown up in a Baptist environment. I started drinking a little bit in my fraternity at the time. My first year in the fraternity after my freshman year in college, I was elected to go to the National Convention which was in Chicago. We stayed on the campus of Northwestern University. I was 18 years old at the time. To go into the bars and the peep shows in Chicago you needed to be 21, so someone made cards for us to do that. Fraternity life was not a great thing for me.

WCR: *Did your mother and father drink much alcohol?*

DCH: Not a lot. They were never heavy drinkers. That had been a problem, however, with my maternal grandfather, who separated from my grandmother. He was a hot head and had mental problems. He was in the mental hospital for a while in Tuscaloosa after having beaten up a couple of guys with a baseball bat.

WCR: *How did you find medial school? You already had had a tremendous transition from Garden City to Birmingham Southern College. How was the transition from college to medical school?*

DCH: Medical school was relatively easy for me. It wasn't a hard transition for me. I had been well prepared, and by that time I knew how to study. I was better prepared than most of my classmates.

WCR: *How did you come out in medical school?*

DCH: I was first in my class every year!

WCR: *How old were you when you graduated from medical school?*

DCH: I was 24. I was younger than most of my classmates.

WCR: *Who had an impact on you in medical school?*

DCH: *Tinsley Harrison*. He was a tremendous teacher. I worked 2 summers doing research with him. I spent much time with him. I went to his house to work with him in the evenings. He did everything in the world to push me into a career in academic medicine. I was still planning to go back to Hanceville and be a general practitioner. It was Harrison who encouraged me to seek an academic career. He thought it great to take care of a single patient and to do research, but to teach an entire class of medical students allows dissemination of your views far beyond the medical school environment. He said a new idea can change the whole face of medicine. At night, we discussed such topics. He introduced me to *Bill Dock*, who gave a lecture at UAB. Harrison had me meet him at the airport. I got to have dinner with both of them.

The other person who influenced me was *Champ Lyons*, who was Chairman of Surgery. He wanted me to be a surgeon. During my senior year, I was an acting intern with him, because he didn't have an intern. He was a tough taskmaster. The day I was accepted at the Brigham (back then you got a telegram telling you if you were accepted), I was in the operating room with him, and the nurse came in and said, "There is a telegram for you from the Brigham Hospital asking you to accept an appointment as an intern." Lyons didn't even let me speak up. He told the nurse, "Tell them he accepts with pleasure." He had a great influence on my life.

WCR: *In what way?*

DCH: He convinced me that I was going to be a surgeon, when I went to the Brigham. He wanted me to do a year in internal medicine and then go into surgery. That was my plan when I went to the Brigham. Medical school was good for me. I grew up, did well, met a lot of people, and had good teachers. The physical diagnosis instructor, *Dr. Ledbetter*, was wonderful. He would take me to Hillman Hospital (the UAB wasn't much then), a concrete block building, where the medical and dental schools were located–the old Hillman Hospital, the Crippled Children's Clinic, and the Veteran's Administration Hospital. Then the UAB medical center occupied 4 blocks; now it occupies 55 square

blocks. He would take me into the dark dungeons of that hospital and bring patients in for me to do physicals on, and the patients had all kind of murmurs and pathology. I don't think he ever got permission. By the time I finished medical school I felt like a pretty accomplished doctor. In my junior year, I was an acting intern on wards where they had no interns. The 6 top students in the class were picked to work like interns. I did all kinds of medical things. These wards contained sick people. Some died every night. Sometimes I would search a textbook to find out what to do next.

WCR: *How did you break in with Tinsley Harrison initially?*

DCH: When starting my junior year, he asked if I would like to spend the summer working with him in his lab.

WCR: *What were Tinsley Harrison's characteristics that made him great?*

DCH: He had great enthusiasm and a great love of medicine. He had a way with patients. He could lay it all out to a patient, explain it to them, make them understand, and patients just worshiped him. We went to medical school then 6 days a week, and on Saturday we had a grand show (medical and surgical grand rounds) with Champ Lyons in surgery and Tinsley Harrison in medicine. They were both good showmen.

WCR: *What did Tinsley Harrison look like?*

DCH: He was 5 feet, 4 inches tall. He had big ears and walked with a jaunty step. He had all the enthusiasm in the world for whatever he was doing.

WCR: *What were the characteristics of Champ Lyons that were appealing to you?*

DCH: Champ was a stern task master who always promoted excellence. He had a work ethic that I admired. He came to the hospital at 4:30 A.M. and was still there at night. If patients needed to be operated on at night, he was there. He had come from the Mass General Hospital, where he had been chief resident. He had a great appreciation for the Mass General. Lyons wanted me to go to the Mass General and Tinsley wanted me to go to the Brigham.

WCR: *When you applied for an internship, did you apply to hospitals other than the Brigham?*

DCH: Yes. I applied to Barnes Hospital, St. Louis; Mass General and Boston City Hospitals in Boston, and to the University of Alabama in Birmingham.

WCR: *Your faculty encouraged you to do that?*

DCH: After I had gone to Boston for the intern interviews, Tinsley Harrison then tried to talk me into staying in Birmingham. This was after my Boston interviews. At the time of the Brigham interview, I was ill with a respiratory infection. At the end of my interview with 5 Brigham faculty, *George Thorn*, the chief of medicine there, told me, "Son, it has been nice to have you here. You come from a young medical school and you shouldn't be disappointed that you won't get a job here. Maybe there will be a place for you as a post doctoral fellow." I was crushed. I went to the Mass General to be interviewed the next day. They had 2 rounds of interviews. The first round was with 3 younger

Figure 8. Laura and DCH dressed for Christmas party 1978. One of many for the Cardiology Division at Stanford.

Figure 9. Laura and DCH with Howard Burchell in Los Altos home. Howard visited for 3 months each of 4 years.

faculty. *Roman DeSanctis* was 1 of them. The first thing said was, "This hospital has a great tradition. Those photographs there on the wall are some of the great physicians who have been here at MGH. Can you tell me anything about any of them?" I didn't know a single one of them. Nevertheless, I survived the first round of interviews. The second round was late in the evening and 6 applicants were interviewed together. We were asked ethical questions, such that you can take either of 2 sides. I was timid for that kind of interview. *Sam Barondes*, who later was my roommate at the Brigham and who I rotated with my first 2 years, said the interview was the most disgusting thing he had ever been through, and he didn't think they had learned anything about us. He said that we 6 interviewees were treated like children. (He had been first in his class at Columbia Medical School.) He was later called in by *Dr. Robert Loeb*, who said, "You have ruined our reputation. They will not take another medical student from Columbia at the Mass general for a long time after what you have done."

WCR: *How did Loeb find out about what Barondes had said?*

DCH: The Mass General folks called him. I went back

home to Alabama feeling very depressed about the Boston interviews. I then went to an interview at Barnes Hospital, which I liked. Because Tinsley was twisting my arm, I had filled out my preference form, putting UAB first and Barnes Hospital second, and I was going to leave the Boston hospitals out. Laura came to have dinner with me at the hospital where I was working and said, "You really want to go to Boston. No one will ever know if you are not accepted. Why don't you just put Boston first?" I redid the form, putting the Brigham first, Mass General second, Barnes third, and Alabama last. I got in the Brigham!

WCR: *What happened when you went to the Brigham and saw George Thorn?*

DCH: I reminded George Thorn later of that episode. When I arrived at the Brigham, it was a totally different story from the way they treated us as candidates. George Thorn had tea for us the first afternoon we were interns and told us how great we were because the 12 of us had been selected from the top medical schools and the top of everything, and they treated us like that the whole time we were at the Brigham. They built us up for careers in academic medicine and encouraged us to be excellent.

WCR: *That was 1958?*

DCH: Yes. I really enjoyed the Brigham. I believed, considered that although 6 of my fellow interns were all from Harvard, and that they probably knew more names of medical syndromes than I did, I knew a lot more about taking care of patients than they did, and I found that to be my liking. Living in Boston was a totally different experience. We lived in the slums of Back Bay. Laura worked as secretary for George Cahill.

WCR: *Laura graduated from University of North Alabama and then she came to Birmingham to work? When did you and Laura marry?*

DCH: We married the summer after she graduated in 1955. She graduated from college 1 year behind me, because she worked the first year after finishing high school. We married the summer after my first year of medical school (Figure 8).

Figure 10. DCH awarding Lew Dexter the Research Achievement Award as president of the American Heart Association 1982.

WCR: *Laura determined your career!*

DCH: In many ways she did.

WCR: *If you had not put Brigham first on your internship application, the chances are that you would not have gotten into NIH.*

DCH: That's right. She helped make that decision, too. I had an opportunity to go back to the Brigham or go to Stanford (Figure 9), when I was ready to leave NIH. *Gene Braunwald* said: "Go to one of those places and then come back with me as a staff member at NIH." People just didn't turn down being a senior resident at the Brigham. Stanford wanted me to be chief resident, because they were trying to institute the Brigham system. They wanted someone who knew the Brigham system, so I went to Stanford in 1963 after NIH. Laura made that decision, too. She said, "We have never been there. I've never been West of the Mississippi. Let's go to Stanford."

WCR: *You were at the Brigham for 2 years before you went to NIH. How did that work out? Were there any surprises during those first few weeks as an intern?*

DCH: Yes. Interns started a week before the senior residents came, and so we worked with the graduating senior residents. It was a little bit hectic. *Dave Nathan*, who had been at the NIH, was my senior resident. On a Saturday night, after I had been an intern for 5 days, I was trying to do a lumbar puncture on a patient, and Dave waltzes in and says, "Hello. I'm going to be your senior resident." I said, "Hello. Can you help me do this? I'm having trouble." He said, "I don't start until Monday." Working with Dave was great fun. All of my senior residents were fun: *Saul Rosenburg* became head of oncology at Stanford; Dave Nathan had a distinguished career at Harvard and was head of the Children's Hospital for awhile; *Bernie Landau* became head of biochemistry at Case Western Reserve; *Herb Levine* became chief of cardiology at Tufts, and *Stuart Bonderant*, one of my favorites, had an outstanding career at Indiana

and the University of North Carolina. Other than not being able to understand the Boston accent on the telephone, I had no problems. Bostonians also couldn't understand me because of my southern accent.

WCR: *In cardiology at the Brigham at that time, there was* Lewis Dexter, Dick Gorlin, Bernie Lown, and Sam Levine. *How do you interact with them?*

DCH: I had something to do with all of them. House officers took care of Sam Levine's patients on the private service, we read electrocardiograms with Bernie Lown, and we made rounds on cardiac patients with Dick Gorlin. After internship and first year residency, I spent my third year as a post-doctor fellow with Lew Dexter (Figure 10). During my first year residency there, I applied to NIH and was accepted to the National Cancer Institute, but I didn't want to do that. I wanted to go to the National Heart Institute, but I wasn't accepted there, so I went with Dexter instead. During that year, Lew Dexter told me that Eugene Braunwald was promoted and now had his own Cardiology Branch (he was no longer part of the Surgery Branch) and that he had an opening for someone. Dick Gorlin told me that I needed to get Dexter to call Braunwald, because they knew each other and a call from him would help me. Finally, Dexter did that. He called me into his office when he was talking to Gene on the phone and Gene said he was about ready to choose for the open position. He had interviewed about 25 other people, and asked if I would come down there tomorrow and interview with him. This was in 1961, just before the Kennedy inauguration. I flew down and spent a whole day with Gene. He told me what he wanted to do. He said, "We will be in touch." People who knew Gene told me that he never sent letters, but he called you if he accepted you. I didn't hear anything, and assumed that I wasn't going to get the job with him. I went to my postal box on Monday afternoon, and there was a note saying, "I've accepted you for the position. I will make arrangements to get you into the Public Health Service." That is all it said. The next morning, he called me and said, "We ought to get into this coronary sinus business and Dick Gorlin is the master of that. I want you to learn about it."

WCR: *How did Lew Dexter know Braunwald?*

DCH: Lew seemed to know everyone in cardiology. I presume that he was in some organizations with him. Gene was young at the time. He was only about 5 years older than I was.

WCR: *When did you decide to stay in internal medicine? You mentioned earlier that you intended to go into surgery after your internship.*

DCH: I never had a chance at all. About 6 weeks after I was at the Brigham, I was called in by George Thorn, who said, "We are choosing our residents for next year and you have 3 days to let us know if you want to be a resident or not." I didn't have time to think about being a surgeon at that point, and I liked internal medicine.

WCR: *Did you see George Thorn much as a house officer?*

DCH: Yes. We made rounds with George a lot.

WCR: *He recently died?*

DCH: Yes, he died at age 97 in 2004. He was not much of a clinician, but a great investigator.

WCR: *What made Sam Levine great?*

DCH: He always had the spark of a new idea. He was always explaining something. He was innovative and thinking of new ways in which things could be done. That is how we started getting people out of bed early after acute myocardial infarction. He got a chair on wheels and had the patient lifted out of bed into it after the third or fourth day.

WCR: *How did it work having 3 powerhouses in cardiology: Lew Dexter, Dick Gorlin, and Bernie Lown running 3 different services?*

DCH: There were some petty jealousies, but, by in large, things worked fairly well. Gorlin had trained with Dexter so he was pretty differential. Lown had been a fellow with Sam Levine and was more on the electrical side. Dexter was one of the earlier people in cardiac catheterization. He always felt slighted that he did not get the Nobel Prize after his work with congenital heart disease. The 3 got along pretty well.

WCR: *How did you and Laura like living in Boston?*

DCH: It was a totally new experience for us. As mentioned, Sam Barondes was a person with whom I rotated with. He introduced me around. Can you imagine a redneck from Alabama and a Jewish son of a rabbi from New York forming a bond and working together for 2 years? We also did some innovative research together. We went to Yale and learned some diagnostic techniques and applied them at the Brigham. He introduced me to a lot of good books, which I had not known in Alabama. Laura and I liked Boston, even although we lived in Back Bay. But everyone else lived that same way. Our pay as interns was $25 per month, so Laura worked until our first child was born at the end of that first year.

WCR: *How did you make it on that kind of money?*

DCH: We borrowed a little money from my dad for the first 2 years and then, for the year with Dexter, I got an American Heart Association Fellowship, which paid $5,500. I was one of the early American Heart Association postdoc Fellows.

WCR: *Did you take to the cold weather ok?*

DCH: Yes. We hated the snow, and there was a lot of it. Our second child was born just before we left Boston to go to NIH. Laura spent 8 days at the Boston Lying-Inn Hospital after Doug was born in the Richardson House. I had breakfast with her every morning in the hospital with silver service, a far cry from today's OB stays. We loved Boston. We were introduced to the theater. It was the first time we had ever been to live theater. We spent a lot of time at Harvard Square. We went to the Harvard Chapel for church and heard *Martin Luther King* and *George Buttrick*, its minister, a very famous man. We met a lot of very interesting people and finally learned to understand the Boston lingo.

WCR: *How did NIH work out for you?*

DCH: I had to work hard, but it was a great experience. Gene Braunwald was a wonderful person to work for.

WCR: *You came to NIH in July 1961?*

DCH: Yes. Early on Gene took me to see *Glenn Morrow*, the chief of the Surgery Branch. He said to Glenn, "This is going to be a remarkable person. He is going to be your cardiology consultant and will take care of your patients." Gene also told Glenn that he wanted him to do some work with me. Some of the best papers I wrote were with Glenn. He was a talented writer. During my days at NIH, I worked a lot with *Charles Chidsey*. We studied the autonomic nervous system as it affected the heart. During my second week at NIH, Gene said to me: "They have one of these drugs that blocks some of these receptors in the heart. I want you to find out about them." After a couple of weeks, Gene asked me if I had found out about them. I had written a letter to find out, but Gene told me to call and find out if we could get some of that compound. He said, "You don't write letters to this guy. You call him." Every Monday morning, we had a 4-hour meeting, and the group included *Dean Mason*, *John Ross*, Chuck Chidsey, *Tom Gaffney*, *Allan Goldblat*, myself, and Gene. There we layed out the week's research. At the NIH, I came in at 6:30 A.M. and made rounds with the surgical associates. Then I went to the laboratory and would kill about 24 rats by banging their heads against the sink and then I would cut their hearts out and place them in liquid nitrogen. I would then go to the dog lab and do 2 to 4 dogs. I would bring all of the samples back to Chidsey's lab, and then I would make rounds again at about 6 P.M. with the surgery group. We wrote manuscripts at night. I took statistics and math courses in the NIH night program. We worked everyday. Nina Braunwald told me once when at Gene's house on a Sunday night writing a study: "You guys have got to be crazy. It is a Sunday night and you are in here working. You are out of your minds." I learned a lot from Gene and Glenn.

WCR: *Were you the surgery consult the entire 2 years you were at NIH?*

DCH: Yes. I also read electrocardiograms when *Joe Greenfield* was on vacation. My previous training for reading electrocardiograms had been 1 month. Nevertheless, I did pretty well at it. I used to dove hunt with Joe at Potomac. We knew a farmer who had a millet field, and he let Joe and I hunt there. This is now all upscale residential. Gene caught me going out 1 day in the middle of the afternoon to go hunting. He wanted to know what in the world I was doing. I told him I would surely be back and work until midnight that night. Joe and I would sneak out some afternoons to go shoot doves.

WCR: *Where did you and Laura live in the Washington area?*

DCH: We lived on Ewing Drive in Bethesda, about 2 miles from NIH. I rode a bicycle most days to the NIH, because we only had 1 car.

WCR: *What were the characteristics of Gene Braunwald that made him such an inspiring leader?*

DCH: Gene had great insight on what the next big thing was going to be in cardiology and in medicine, and he had a lot of drive to get things done. He pushed people to their up-most to get things done. He had great insight into helping others analyze problems and how to solve them. He was an inspiration to get things done. I have a lot of drive, and there at NIH made the decision that I would stay in academics. I knew from my experience at the Brigham that what you did in the academic world was what made your career.

WCR: *Did you ever talk to Champ Lyons after leaving Birmingham?*

DCH: No. But, I did exchange letters with him.

WCR: *Before the 2 years were up at NIH, you had to decide whether you were going to go back to the Brigham Hospital or do something else?*

DCH: Yes. It was July 1962. I had a few calls from Saul Rosenberg at Stanford, who had been one of my residents. He said, "I'm starting a new program and I need housestaff. Would you like to come to Stanford and be chief resident?" I thought the idea was silly, and never thought of going to Stanford. Then one day I got a call from the Brigham and they said, "Are you coming back as a senior resident? We need to know in 1 week." The next hour I picked up the phone and called Saul Rosenberg and said, "The Brigham wants me to come back and I have to let them know in a week." He said, "Can you come out and see Stanford." I said, "Yes." He said, "When can you come?" I had already called the airline and learned that I could fly nonstop across the country to San Francisco. Rosenberg met me at the airport, took me home with him, and I spent 3 days there. There was a new chief of medicine, *Hal Holman*, and I liked him. Hal said there would be a job for me, although he didn't tell me much about what it was going to be. One thing he didn't tell me was that he didn't even consult the person running cardiology, namely, *Herb Hultgren*. On the plane back, I decided that I would return to the Brigham. I got back on the Friday, the day I was supposed to call the Brigham and let them know if I would be coming back. I called the office and no one was there. Over the weekend, I called Lew Dexter to talk to him about it. He said, "Don, you are nuts. You should go to Stanford. If you come back here you might get a small closet lab in about 5 years. You know how bad it is at Harvard. You should go to Stanford." I called Hal Holman and told him that I did want to come to Stanford, but I think that I should talk to the chief of cardiology. He said, "Well, he is in Peru now doing high altitude research. I can give you his phone number." I tried to reach him for 3 days and never got him, so I finally decided to go to Stanford. One should never try to reach the high Andes by phone. I was the first person in about 10 years to decline to go back to the Brigham.

WCR: *What did Braunwald think of your decision?*

DCH: Braunwald thought it was the right decision, because I needed to get 1 more year of residency to pass the boards. Gene said I could go and see what it was like, and then I could always come back and work for him.

WCR: *Did Laura go with you?*

DCH: No, not on the recruiting trip.

WCR: *So you left Bethesda after 2 vigorous years. By this time, you had a lot of publications and now you are at Stanford as chief resident. What was that like?*

DCH: I had not ever heard of someone's becoming chief resident at a place where they hadn't even been a house officer. Some house officers there, now senior residents, of course, wanted to be the chief resident. They had a little animosity about my coming in. Over time, I won them over. I worked with the interns a lot, and I examined every patient who came in. I spent a lot of time with Hal Holman, who was the chairman of medicine. He was not a great clinician. I knew almost as much general clinical medicine as he did. But it was a good year. Laura and I loved the weather, and we loved California. We lived in a rented house, because we thought we were going back to Bethesda. We had 3 kids by then, and they were growing up. I spent a lot of time at the hospital. I tried to go home to have dinner with the kids, but would always come back to the hospital afterwards. We lived only about 6 miles from the hospital.

WCR: *How big was the housestaff at Stanford at the time?*

DCH: There were 12 interns, 12 junior residents, and 6 senior residents. We also covered the program at the Palo Alto Veterans Administration Hospital.

WCR: *How did you and Herb Hultgren hit it off during your chief residency?*

DCH: Herb was gracious to me. He and Holman did not get along at all. They never talked. It was in January 1964 that Hal offered me a job as a faculty member. I was told that I needed to apply for a NIH grant. No one in cardiology there had a grant so, of course, I consulted Gene. I tried to figure out where I could do something to differentiate my research from Gene. Beta blockade was something that I had done a lot of work on, and there was potential in that area for me. I wrote a NIH grant, and Gene reviewed it for me and told me that I asked for too much money. But, I got almost $300,000 for my first year. Hal found an animal lab for me, but I shared it with hematology. The hematologists bled chickens. There were chicken feathers all over as I operated on dogs. There was 1 postdoc in cardiology, but he didn't work with me. I had, however, 5 medical students who had research experience work with me. They were in Stanford 5-year academic development track. One of them, *Walter Henry*, was a computer whiz, and he wanted to computerize the cath lab. *Joshua Lederberg*, who had an Advanced Research Projects Agency Network of the Defense Department room-size computers, let us use it. Henry later ended up at NIH. One student, *Denver Nelson*, who had worked in a physiology lab and had done work on isolated hearts at Iowa joined us. We borrowed equipment from the physiology teaching course, because we didn't have any money, and before my grant came through, we needed platinum electrodes. I took $55 of my own money and bought them. We had all the recorders we needed. We started studies on rat hearts during that year. A fellow, *Bob Griffin*, who had been a biochemist before medical school, also joined us. These were all great medical students. They were in a 5-year medical school program at Standord, and they were allowed to do a lot of research. They wanted to work with me to study the metabolic and hemodynamic effects of beta blockade. We looked at the effects of beta blockade on lipid metabolism. I also became, during the first year, associate director of the General Clinical Research unit and as a result also had a laboratory there. Gene visited during that first year, because I invited him to give a honorarium lecture. I had just finished several studies of the effects of beta blockers on arrhythmias in patients. I told Gene about the work, and as I took him to the airport he said, "If I were you I'd go home and write that work up quickly because I know some other people who are working on it." I went back home, called the medical students working with me, and we started writing that study that night. We sent it to the *New England Journal of Medicine* before the week was out. It was published. Then sometime toward the beginning of my first faculty year, my grant money came in.

Lee Langley, who was head of the training grant section at the NIH, shortly thereafter visited Stanford's physiology department. By then, I was giving lectures in physiology as well as in cardiology. Langley said, "I've noticed that you do not have a training grant in cardiology here at Stanford. I think you should apply for one." I put together a group of faculty to be members of a training group, because I had only medical students working with me. I got a few of the other faculty to help and I wrote a training grant, and we got 6 or 7 post docs. By this time, I was getting to be well-known nationally, so *Bob Petersdorf* tried to recruit me to Seattle at the end of 1965. He almost got me killed. I flew there. He picked me up in a brand new Ford Mustang, and we went to dinner and as he drove me to the hotel afterwards, he got on the wrong side of the road, and we were almost hit. About the same time, *Carl Moore* called me and asked me to look at the job in cardiology at Washington University. I will never forget my last Saturday morning meeting with him. He said, "You have done very well. For a young man I think you have written too many papers." I had never heard that in my life. I went back to Stanford, and Hal Holman said, "I'm going to make you head of cardiology." This was in early 1966. He waited a few months to do so. It was actually January 1967 when I became head of cardiology. I was 32 years of age. Herb Hultgren was asked to take a sabbatical. Herb was a well-known national figure in cardiology. *Norm Shumway*, the chief of cardiovascular surgery, supported my taking over totally, because he didn't think Herb was doing a good job of getting patients to Stanford. Not knowing exactly how to run a cardiology division, I visited a few big cardiology programs. I spent 3 days at the Mass General with *Ed Haber*, and then went to Hopkins to visit with *Dick Ross*, the chief there. I went back to Stanford and

began building a cardiology program. The first thing I did was start recruiting excellent post docs. By the third or fourth year of the program, I was competing effectively with the Brigham and the Mass General for post docs.

WCR: *You were chief of cardiology from 1967, age 32, to 1986, age 52. How did you enjoy those 20 years?*

DCH: We trained 179 fellows, and we added several faculty. We built a huge clinical program. Shumway was very supportive. I got a lot of national visibility because of the heart transplant program, and Shumway let me be on the national television press conferences with him. Some viewers said I stole the show, because I showed many pictures of cardiac outputs and other charts. But, I didn't. Shumway was the feature of the show. After that, I was asked to go to many places in the world to speak on cardiac transplantation and on work done on lidocaine, and blood levels, and computers. It was a hearty experience. We had a big clinical program. After a few years, over half of the admissions to the medical service were to cardiology. We built a great clinical program and a great research program.

WCR: *You were head of cardiology for 20 years. Twenty years in such an active place is a pretty good grind. There are not many heads of cardiology in academic centers who survive that long. I understand the longest serving cardiologist at a University Hospital in the US is* Bob Myerberg. *What was your day-to-day life like during your most active period? What time did you wake up at home, what time did you get to the hospital, leave the hospital, get home, go to bed?*

DCH: I got up 5:30 A.M. because I was jogged every morning—5 miles. I was at the hospital by 7:30 A.M. I took morning report for the cardiology service. I spent 2 afternoons in the clinic where I saw patients. I usually took 2-month rotations as a part of the in-patient service because, we would have between 15 and 30 patients in the hospital at any 1 time. Initially, I worked in the cath lab. I taught people how to do transseptal left-sided cardiac catheterization for the first 3 or 4 years, which I had learned at the NIH. I had been chief for about 2 years, when I got a call from a chief of medicine from Indiana and he said, "I have a young guy here who went to medical school at Hopkins, trained at Hopkins as a house officer, and he came back here to be a post doc with Charlie Fisch. He just doesn't want to do squid axons anymore and he has been sneaking off doing things with Harvey Feigenbaum." This was after I had received a second training grant at Stanford. The first one was a research one and the second one was more of a clinical one. He said, "I know that you just got a new training grant and this guy just wants to get away from Indiana. His name is Richard Popp. Do you think you can work him into your program?" I said, "Can you have him come out and see me?" Rich came and I asked him, "What do you need if I took you?" He said he needed an echocardiographic machine, and indicated that there were only 3 or 4 of them in the whole country at that point. I asked him how much one would cost, and it was something like $5,000. I went to the hospital and told them I had a new guy coming, and we needed to set up a new service because he has a machine that can measure how the heart moves and what valves were damaged. They said it would never work, and it would be a money loser for us. I looked at all of my grants, and found that I could buy $900 of technology without having to justify the purchase. I called up the people who made the echocardiograms, and we bought it piece by piece at $900 per piece. Rich came and we soon had an echocardiographic machine. I set up a lab with a separate budget to make it a money-making service for cardiology and continued to keep it separate from the hospital as long as I was head of cardiology. In all of this jocking for space and a separate service, I did make enemies. Anyway, it was a good time, I worked hard, and traveled a lot. I joined American Heart Association Scientific Sessions Committee in 1971 and was chairman from 1974 to 1977. Then I was on their research committee for 1 year, chairman of the publications committee for 4 years, then became president elect, and in 1982, became President of the American Heart Association. In the late 1970s, I became a candidate to be chair of medicine at about 20 institutions. I never considered any, except for the University of Pittsburgh and the University of Rochester. At one point, I was set on going to Rochester. There were division chief positions open at the time. Rochester promised me 2 new positions. I couldn't figure out how it was going to work, so I stayed at Stanford. Toward the end of my time, it was clear that I was not going to be chief of medicine at Stanford, because I had made too many enemies. The deanship came open, and I was one of the few internal candidates. I didn't get the job. *David Korn* got the job, and then I became restless to move somewhere else.

WCR: *During your cardiology peak period you mentioned the time you woke up in the morning. What time did you get home at night?*

DCH: In the summers, Laura brought the children to the Stanford student union, and we had dinner there. I didn't get home early Monday through Friday, but on the weekends I did try to spend time with my kids. We had a pool. I spent time camping with them. We took some rather long car trips. We took a month trip around the country in 1972, and went to all of the national parks in the west. In 1974, we took the family to Europe for a month. We did a lot of things as a family, but I worked long hours.

WCR: *Where did you live?*

DCH: We lived in Los Altos, which is next door to Palo Alto.

WCR: *How did the Cincinnati position come about?*

DCH: I was recruited to Michigan to be the Vice President of the medical school and head of the hospital. This was in 1984. They had been searching for a long time. I was on my way home from a trip to Europe and got called to come back for a third visit to meet with *Hal Shapiro*, the president of the University of Michigan. I had breakfast

with him on Sunday morning, and he offered me the job. I let people know at Stanford that I was considering it. We were building a cardiac research building at Stanford, and I had raised the money with Norm Shumway to build it. I thought, "Surely Stanford is going to offer me something to come back." But, I never heard anything from them. I went on to Europe, and then Harold Shapiro called me in New York and said, "We really want you because this is a great job." I hadn't heard back from Stanford, so I said, "Ok." The next day it was in all of the Detroit newspapers. I got back to Stanford and the Vice President of the University, the Dean of the Medical School, and *Ken Melman*, the chairman of the department of medicine, descended on me and said, "You have to stay and finish this building." I went through 10 days of agony because my appointment had not been presented to the Board of Regents at Michigan yet. It had been announced, and I re-nigged on them because Stanford wanted me to stay. It turned out to be a terrible mistake, because the Vice President, who was *Larry Crowley*, had to retire for health reasons as the senior Vice President. Ken Melmen was forced out over his plagiarism issue. *Dominic Purpura*, who was the Dean, had been dismissed at the "Saturday night massacre" that happens to Deans all of the time at Stanford. Shumway also had been part of the agreement for me to stay. They had promised me a heart institute, but all that fell apart. Here I had turned down the Michigan job, and things started to fall apart at Stanford. I had never taken a sabbatical, because something always came up every 7 years when it was available, so I decided to do that at the end of 1985. My first 6 months I stayed in California advising a Venture capital firm. They asked me to be the CEO of 1 company and the science advisor for another. After 6 months, I went to Israel to study the healthcare system there, because it interested me. I then went to Switzerland for 6 months. One of my patients had a villa, and it was a great place for us to settle.

While I was there, I got a call from *Bill Schubert* in Cincinnati. He was the head of the Cincinnati Children's Hospital, Chairman of Pediatrics, and chair of the search committee for a senior vice president. I had been mentioned as a candidate to become the senior vice president and provost. There was a new university president, and he was going to put all of the medical center, including the hospitals and health schools, under a senior vice president and provost. I couldn't spell Cincinnati! I returned to the states for a Bristol-Myers Squibb conference in New York City and thereafter visited Cincinnati. The president, *Joseph Steger*, looked like a reasonable guy and there were no huge problems. I thought it was an interesting opportunity. We had 2 other visits. Six weeks after my first visit, the President of the University called me and said, "I would like to offer you this job." By that time I learned of another scandalous matter. Someone had plagerized a lot of data for a lot of research studies and that involved the largest grant at Cincinnati. I was on my way to China at that point, and I asked if I could wait until I got back from the trip to look around a little more. He said, "Well, it sounds like you might not want the job if you let such minor issues as this cause you to waiver. If I don't hear back from you by 4 P.M., the offer is off." I called Laura and walked the floor for a while. I was unhappy at Stanford at this point, and I really wanted out. Joe Steger was not a very decisive person. It is the only time I had known him to be this decisive in his life, and it was with me that day. He said, "If you let a little thing like that upset you, you are probably not ready for this job because there are going to be many things to come up that will be as bad or worse." He was certainly right about that. I said that I would come.

I went on to China and came back at that time. I was the Program Chairman for the World Congress in Washington. We didn't have a house. We had bid on a couple of houses, but they fell through. We wanted to be close to the University, but we just couldn't find anything that didn't need to be rebuilt. We had just rebuilt our house in California, and Laura didn't want to do that again. I was in Washington, and I got a call from a real estate agent who said, "I found a house that is not on the market. It is probably a little more than you thought you wanted to pay. But, it is a wonderful house. It is an old house in the Indian Hills." She advised me to come look at it quickly, and I told her I could be in Cincinnati by about 5 P.M. that afternoon. She met me at the airport and took me out to see the house. It was wonderful and everything you would want in a house. It was 12,000 square feet, and built in an English Tudor style and on 7 acres of beautiful grounds. It was just beautiful. I called Laura and asked her when she could come. She took an overnight flight and came in by 9 P.M. and we made a bid by noon the next day. We sold our house in California and bought this one. We moved to Cincinnati in November 1986. It was a cold and rainy time, and we were lonely for a while. I was busy with work although. I went to work before daylight and came home late at night. The chief of surgery was also asking me to see patients. Laura had a bad cold and was sick and wanted to move back to California for awhile. When spring came it was great. Every job that I needed to fill was open. There was no director of the hospital, no dean of medicine, no chairman of medicine, no chair of OB, psychiatry and physiology so, I started recruiting. I did a Dean search for a year. I had *Ed Froelich, Tony Gotto*, and others, but they declined. They were not willing to take the risk. Finally, a faculty member who was head of research at the Children's Hospital, a brilliant guy, *John Hutton*, said, "I would like to be Dean." He had been at San Antonio and at the Rockefeller Institute. The president of the university said he was too quiet and that he would never be able to do the job. I said, "I want him as my Dean." He said, "Take him at your own risk." So, I did and John and I worked together for 15 years. He was Mr. Inside and I was Mister Outside. I did the community involvement while he ran the faculty. In research, we built a great place together. We went from $30 to $250 million in funding. We built $1 billion worth of buildings and renovations, 3 research build-

Figure 11. DCH with Robert Mondavi and wife Margrit.

ings, and we developed a great faculty. In my last year, we built a second campus about 45 miles north, where we built a clinical outpost, and now they are now building a hospital there. I stayed 17 years in that job. The average time is 5 years for this job. I had a lot to do with the Association of Academic Health Centers, where I was on the board for 6 years, and I was chairman for a year working closely with *Roger Bulger*.

WCR: *Your business experience must have helped you a great deal in this position?*

DCH: It did. I had a lot to do with the venture capital programs that looked at healthcare investments while I was at Stanford. One of the 2 companies that I told you about were looking at the immunological basis of atherosclerosis, and we had *Russell Ross* and Ed Haber on our advisory board. We did some good work. We made some monoclonal antibodies to plaque our idea was to image but we could never get enough isotope attached to be able to do that. The idea that plaque is a result of immunology has resurfaced. We spent 30 million dollars of venture capital money on this research. The other company I helped found and was head of the science advisory committee and later chairman of the board was EP Technology, and it developed all of the technology to do Wolff-Parkinson-White mapping and ablation. It became a very successful company, and we took it public. It was bought by Boston Scientific and is still a big division of Boston Scientific (Figure 11).

WCR: *How many patents do you have?*

DCH: I have 6 issued patents and 6 now in progress.

WCR: *Did you have to retire at Cincinnati or were you just tired?*

DCH: I was tired, and my wife said, "You stayed at Stanford too long, you are on top here, all of the things you wanted to get done you have done them and more, but you are tired and it is time that you step down".

WCR: *You stepped down in 2003?*

DCH: Yes.

WCR: You are 71 now, and you were 69 then?

DCH: Yes.

WCR: *How many nights per week during that time did you have to recruit or raise money?*

DCH: The first few years I did a lot because I was having people over all the time, and I was getting to know the community. I averaged about 3 nights per week.

WCR: *Did you work 12 hours a day?*

DCH: There were times I worked >12 hours. I soon built a team of people. I had a good capacity to give others responsibility and hold them accountable. One of the most valuable lessons I learned was that in a job like that process is important. I was a cardiologist, and I was used to dealing with people who had acute problems. If you didn't do something about it pretty quickly, patients would die. I wanted to run the medical center that way for a while, but I soon figured out that didn't work and that you had to go through a process to get things done. You had to lay things out. I didn't appoint a lot of committees. I appointed task forces that had a job to be done and when finished they disband. We managed to move a lot faster than committees. The other lesson I learned is to not compare how things were done at Stanford. I mentioned this several times during my first year. Someone said, "if you like Stanford so much why don't you go back?"

WCR: *What are you doing now?*

DCH: I am on several company boards in Cincinnati. I was on the SciMed board when it merged into Boston Scientific. I started 2 companies myself in Cincinnati. One was UMD, which stands for Uterine Muscle Dysfunction. Our first therapeutic program was for dysmenorrhea. I learned about the vaginal plexus that drains from the venus side of the upper part of the vagina into the uterus. I wrote a lot of patents around treatment of dysmenorrhea and we formed a company with venture funding. That company is still running and doing well. We also wrote a lot of other patents on vaginal drug delivery. I have 5 patents issued in that area and several that are pending. The second company was a follow-up to electrophysiology technology known as Atricure. We took this one public this year. It makes surgical instruments for ablation of atrial fibrillation using a minimally invasive technique. I am a co-founder of that one.

I also was asked to join a venture capital fund in California, Charter Life Science, in November 2003, shortly after I stepped down. I run the mid-West office. The big office is in Palo Alto, California. We are funding an early stage life science company. We are going to raise a new fund starting next year. I'm having fun.

WCR: *What is your day like now?*

DCH: I have 2 offices. I go to the University about 9 A.M. because I still have an office there and I am helping the person who replaced me. Since everything in Palo Alto starts at 10 A.M., I do a lot of video conferencing on the internet. We review companies. We have had 700 business plans submitted to us. It is harder to get a company funded than it is to get a grant. It is like going back to medical school, because I'm learning about different specialties like neurology, orthopedics and others. I have to read and learn about them and then go through the presentations that people make and then make judgments. I'm enjoying it. Most days I'm through by about 3:30 or 4 P.M.. I then go to the health club and then home. We try to spend the month of August at our house at Lake Tahoe. We go to San Francisco a lot because we have a time share on Nob Hill. My wife tries to visit all of the grand children at least once a quarter. I don't quite get there that much.

WCR: *Don, what in your multiple careers are you most proud of?*

DCH: Bill, this is a difficult question for one to answer about themselves in an objective way but I would highlight 3 things in my cardiology career about which I am quite proud of. The first of these is the training and direction I provided to my postdoctoral fellows during the 20 years that I was head of cardiology at Stanford. I have just reviewed the list and some of their accomplishments. During this period, there were 179 postdocs in our program over the 20 years. Eighty-two of them have gone on to academic careers; 10 have become heads of their cardiology units, and 1 was a chairman of medicine. In addition, 21 of them became entrepreneurs, either developing their own companies or developing the scientific and medical basis for a company and then becoming science advisors for the development of a company. And something of interest to you, 3 became editors of journals in their countries, England, Portugal and France. These postdoctoral fellows in their continuing careers have materially changed the practice of cardiology. I keep up with many of them, and when Laura and I travel we try to visit with them, invite them to dinners, and try to meet with groups in various cities. We have done that in Europe, in San Diego, in Montreal, in the San Francisco Bay Area, and elsewhere. Some of them even still call me for advice about their career. One axiom that I always told them was that if they wanted an academic career they needed to complete meaningful research and publish it in peer review journals, such as the *American Journal of Cardiology* and others. I had a favorite saying, "No one would know you east of Oakland if you did not publish the work that you have completed." This really kept them working hard and striving to publish.

Secondly, I am proud of my research accomplishments. It is always difficult to blow your own horn, but I believe there are a few areas of my research and publications that have helped move cardiology forward. These include the development of antiarrhythmic agents, especially lidocaine and several new antiarrhythmic drugs, the clinical use of beta blockers and the introduction of computers in cardiology to quantitatively document arrhythmias, ventricular function and structure, and echocardiology. I was one of the founders of the organization, Computers in Cardiology, which still goes forward today.

Thirdly, I am proud of being a cardiologist and the care I have provided to many patients from all over the world. At

Figure 12. DCH with Emir of Bahrain.

Stanford, I had a very large practice and even as the head of the medical center here in Cincinnati I continued to see patients. I cared for many patients with all varieties of heart disease throughout the US and from many foreign countries, such as Hong Kong, Bahrain (Figure 12), other middle eastern countries, even China. There was great satisfaction in providing expert cardiology care to these many patients. These are the accomplishments I made in cardiology. As you have pointed out I had a second career as an academic administrator.

WCR: *Would you highlight some of your accomplishments as an academic administrator at Cincinnati?*

DCH: In 1986, when I moved to the University of Cincinnati, my charge was to transform the Medical Center into a more academic and clinically relevant place. I worked in that job for 17 years, far longer than most administrators who direct academic medical centers. In fact, about 3 or 4 times as long. The accomplishments of which I am quite proud include so many elements that description would fill many pages. However, here are a few. During that tenure, the research funding for the entire medical center went from $30 million, when I arrived, to more than $250 million when I stepped down as head of the center. During the time we built over a billion dollars of new buildings or renovations of older buildings. This included 4 research buildings and the acquisition of 5 research buildings on the site of the original Merrill Dow Company, which I convinced the Aventis Company to give to the University. On that site we established a genome research institute and moved several large research programs from the main medical center campus to this site, about 10 miles away. I am also proud that we transformed clinical care and the development of University Hospital. For >100 years, the hospital affiliated with the medical school was known as Cincinnati General Hospital. About 10 years before my arrival its name had been changed and it had been rebuilt into University Hospital. When I arrived, we did a survey of the community and what

they thought of University Hospital. Almost 25% of people thought it was still the old General Hospital. We launched quite a campaign and after 2 years only 2% of people did not know that it was University Hospital. We rebuilt much of University Hospital, added a bed tower, new emergency rooms, new intensive care units, surgical units, and ultimately incorporated University Hospital into the Health Alliance of Greater Cincinnati of which I was one of the architects. We also developed new leadership in deans, department heads and faculty. One of the buildings that I managed to have built had *Frank Ghery* as the architect, and it was the first science building that he'd ever built. It was a real hit with the architectural community in Cincinnati. It was quite an experience working with him, and we became very good friends. Finally, I believe I transformed the image of the medical center and the internal attitudes of the faculty to have a more national and international outlook. The graduate programs increased almost exponentially, and the research productivity matured. I am quite proud of this stage of my career and the transformation of the medical center at the University of Cincinnati.

WCR: *You've had quite a career, are there other things you would like to mention?*

DCH: Yes, there are 2. Of course, I am quite proud of my family, my children and their spouses, 3 of whom are physicians, and my 8 grandchildren. They are now the highlight of my life, and I love to spend time with them.

I am also proud of my entrepreneurial activities. I have been the founder or co-founder of 6 companies in the life science area. Two have gone on to have initial public offerings, and they are now producing important medical products. Two were acquired by other companies and are active divisions, and 2 are still in their late development stage. Developing companies of this type is like raising children. They go through an early developmental stage like birthing, they mature into adolescence, usually with lots of problems, and finally if one persists and has a good idea and good intellectual property, they succeed in becoming adults. Over the past years I have had 6 patents issued, and I have 6 presently at the patent office being considered. This has been a new adventure for me and creating an idea that can be patented has great appeal, and I hope to be able to continue to generate good ideas.

WCR: *You have 3 offspring. Tell me about them.*

DCH: Our son, our oldest, Walter Douglas, is a general surgeon in Rocky Mountain, North Carolina. He is a member of the Boice Willis Clinic, which has about 80 doctors. His wife is a general internist, and they have 2 daughters. Our oldest daughter, Elizabeth (Beth) is married to Peter Hartzel. He was with Cummin engines for 13 years and then left and bought a business in California in security systems and gates. They lived in Beijing and Canterbury, England, for 3 years each, and they have 2 daughters. They live in San Carlos, California. Our youngest is Donna Marie, who is married to a high school classmate, David Marks, who is an interventional cardiologist at the Medical College of

Figure 13. Fishing trip with Irv Vrh showing large salmon caught by DCH.

Figure 15. Laura and DCH backpacking in the Sierra Nevada Mountains.

Figure 14. Laura and DCH on bike trip.

Figure 16. Laura and DCH with their entire family of children and grandchildren in the Galopogos celebrating 50th anniversary.

Wisconsin, Milwaukee. He followed my career almost exactly. After medical school at the University of California in San Francisco, he spent 6 years at the Brigham. They have 4 children.

WCR: *You have 6 grand daughters and 2 grandsons.*

DCH: Yes.

WCR: *It sounds like you still travel a lot.*

DCH: Not much overseas anymore. But I do travel a lot. Laura usually goes with me (Figure 13).

WCR: *How much vacation do you take now?*

DCH: I take breaks all of the time. We spent a month in Palo Alto last year, and 10 days in Galapagos with the whole family. Every year Laura and I take at least 1 organized bike trip (Figure 14). We took 1 to the islands off of Victoria, British Columbia, and rode for a week. We spend a month at Lake Tahoe, where we backpack with some of our grandchildren (Figure 15). This year is our 50th anniversary, so every month we have done something (Figure 16).

WCR: *What other hobbies do you have?*

DCH: Bike riding has become our biggest hobby. We ride 5 days a week, sometimes 50 miles.

WCR: *Do you take your own bike?*

DCH: No. When we go on these organized bike trips, they provide the bike and places to stay. We have done trips in France, Sicily, New England, and Hawaii in the past decade.

WCR: *What kind of bike do you have?*

DCH: I have 2 at Tahoe and 3 at home. I have a mountain bike, a road bike, and 2 hybrids.

WCR: *What do you do when you go home at night now?*

DCH: I cook with Laura. We watch movies. We have 8 symphony nights, 11 theater nights, and 8 Cincinnati Conservatory of Music, which is theater and musical things. We go out to eat a lot. We occasionally play chess together. We have learned not to get angry when the other one wins. We have had a little trouble with that, because we have always been competitive. Most recently we have been working Sudoku puzzles. I spend a fair amount of time keeping my wine cellar up. We generally do a couple of trips a year to the wine country.

WCR: *How long have you been bike riding?*

DCH: We started in California when the kids were young, but then gave it up for a few years. We really started in earnest about 12 years ago.

WCR: *Are you going to stay in Cincinnati?*

DCH: I think so. We made the decision not to go back to California, although we had invested money in a wonderful facility that was being built there by the Hyatt Corporation. It is on the Stanford campus and has every level of care. Thirty percent of the people going there are Stanford faculty who have retired.

WCR: *Is there anything that we haven't discussed that you would like to bring up?*

DCH: I told you about the book that I am writing. I didn't want the book to be about me. I am trying to illustrate the changes which have occurred in medicine in the 50 years of my career through patient stories, research stories, and so forth, to point out how things had changed in medicine. I had a famous patient die at NIH when there was no heart valves, and he had severe mitral regurgitation, *Frank Turgeon*. He was one of the photographers for the Nixon and Eisenhower campaigns. I also went through the story of how vaccines had changed. I told the story of how I was born at home and how chloroform was dripped on a cloth over my mother's face. There are many other stories in the book. I will publish it. When I started I talked to some people about publishing and they said there are 200,000 books produced every year, and only 5% are ever read by >1,000 people. I have it written, and it has now been edited.

WCR: *What is the name of it?*

DCH: One of the publishers I talked to wanted to call it *Healing Broken Hearts*, because I was a cardiologist who healed broken hearts, but also she made a point of my reconciliation with my mother when she was dying, and I healed my broken heart. The story about my mother is woven through the book.

WCR: *I understand that you have one of the finest wine cellars in the state of Ohio. Could you describe and discuss your love of wine and how you got into that activity?*

DCH: Having grown up in Alabama, I didn't even know what wine was. When we were in Boston some of my fellow interns had Saturday night parties with wine flowing. When we moved to Washington, I became aware of a store called Plain Old Pearsons. I used to buy wine from them. You could buy a case of French Rhone wine for $12. We used to drink wine only on the weekends, but we liked it a lot. When we first moved to Los Altos, there was a winery about 1 mile from our house, and I used to ride my bike over on the weekends and get a gallon of white wine and a gallon of red wine right out of the barrel. This was good wine. It was called Gemello's. It is still around. At that time we lived in the middle of the apricot orchards. Now there are all houses there. At one point, Los Altos was the apricot capital of the world. Not too long after I was there and started to see patients who headed winerys from Napa Valley and from Central Valley, I saw *Ernest Gallo*, who hated doctors but had the biggest winery. I also met *Robert Mondavi* on an airplane flying to Dallas. He later came to me for a heart evaluation. We became bossum friends, and I was asked to visit with he and his wife. They had a guest house, and we

would sample wines from his winery. I got to know a lot about Napa Valley wines because I visited many of the wineries. I had a small cellar in Los Altos. When we moved from Los Altos to Cincinnati, I carried with me out of my cellar about 60 cases of wine. The truck driver said if I'd like to take more I could. I went out and bought 20 more cases to take with me because I wasn't sure what wine would be like in Cincinnati.

When I got to Cincinnati I found in my house a false door in the basement. I opened the false door and there was a 6-foot safe door that needed to be opened. I got a safe cracker to open it, and found that it was a wine cellar for the family who had lived there during the prohibition. That explained the false door and the safe door. It was not very big. About 3 years after we were there I met a fellow who manufactured wine cellars. The next morning he brought one of his engineers over to see what I had. He came back with a plan for my cellar. He built it for me in 2 weeks. He said I could put about 4,500 bottles in there. I keep about 1,200 or 1,500 bottles there. It is temperature controlled and underground. I had Robert Mondavi come out twice for a dinner party. I was asked to be in the tasting group for the Cincinnati International wine festival to judge the wines and have for 15 years. We now have 120 wineries that submit wine for that. The funds support the public radio station and a number of charities. I collect a lot of different wines from California, New Zealand, Australia, France, Spain and Italy.

WCR: *How much wine do you drink?*

DCH: About two thirds of a bottle per night between Laura and me.

WCR: *Thank you, Don, for pouring your soul out here.*

DCH: I have enjoyed it. Thank you.

Best Publications by DCH as Selected by Him

Books

1. Harrison DC. Circulatory Effects and Clinical Uses of Beta-Adrenergic Blocking Drugs (monograph). Amsterdam: Excerpta Medica, 1972.

4. Miller HM, Harrison DC. Biomedical Electrode Technology: Theory and Practice. New York & London: Academic Press, 1974.

5. Harrison DC. Cardiac Arrhythmias: A Decade of Progress. Boston, GK Hall Medical Publishers, 1981. (*Dr. Harrison's comment: This book, which summarized presentations made by investigators from all over the world on arrhythmias held at Stanford University in 1980, is still used as 1 of the major text books on arrhythmias. It resulted as a follow-up to a conference that had been held in Denmark approximately 10 years earlier, in which I had participated. I was the organizer of this meeting and edited the text book that resulted.*)

Other Publications

7. Chidsey CA, Harrison DC, Braunwald E. Augmentation of the plasma norepinephrine response to exercise in patients with congestive heart failure. *N Engl J Med* 1962;267:650–654. (*Dr. Harrison's comment: In this article, we demonstrated the release of norepinephrine from the hearts of patients with congestive heart failure who were exercising. This represented some of the earliest work in understanding the hormonal responses of congestive heart failure in patients.*)

10. Harrison DC, Chidsey CA, Goldman R, Braunwald E. Relationship between the release and tissue depletion of norepinephrine from the heart by guanethidine and reserpine. *Circ Res* 1963;12:256–263. *(Dr. Harrison's comment: In this study, we demonstrated that drugs that were used to treat hypertension at that time had part of their action based upon the depletion of norepinephrine from the heart. This led to many other studies on how drugs that were used to treat hypertension really worked.)*

12. Harrison DC, Chidsey CA, Braunwald E. Studies on the mechanism of action of metaraminol (aramine). *Ann Intern Med* 1963;59:297–305.

15. Harrison DC, Goldblatt A, Braunwald E. Studies on cardiac dimensions in intact, unanaesthetized man. I. Description of techniques and their validation. *Circ Res* 1963;13:448–455.

16. Goldblatt A, Harrison DC, Glick G, Braunwald E. Studies on cardiac dimensions in intact, unanaesthetized man. II. Effects of respiration. *Circ Res* 1963;13:455–460.

17. Braunwald E, Goldblatt A, Harrison DC, Mason DT. Studies on cardiac dimensions in intact, unanaesthetized man. III. Effects of muscular exercise. *Circ Res* 1963;13:460–467. (Dr. Harrison's comment: These were physiologic studies that demonstrated cardiac function in unanesthetized patients. These studies were carried out by putting metal clips on the surface of the hearts during open heart surgery and studying their movements during a number of physiologic activities, such as respiration and exercise. These studies were carried out before echocardiography or quantitative angiography.)

20. Harrison DC, Sprouse JH, Morrow AG. The antiarrhythmic properties of lidocaine and procaine amide. *Circulation* 1963;28:486–491. (Dr. Harrison's comment: This is one of the articles of which I am most proud. Although it was known that lidocaine had membrane effects, its antiarrhythmic action had not really been demonstrated in patients. We demonstrated not only its antiarrhythmic properties but its electrophysiologic properties in the human heart in patients undergoing heart sugery. This led to the widespread use of lidocaine later as an antiarrythmic agent. Much of my subsequent work on antiarrythmic agents was stimulated by this early work at the NIH.)

25. Harrison DC, Braunwald E, Glick G, Mason DT, Chidsey CA, Ross J Jr. Effects of beta adrenergic blockade on the circulation, with particular reference to observations in patients with hypertrophic subaortic stenosis. *Circulation* 1964;29:84–98.

31. Harrison DC, Coggins CH, Welland FH, Nelson S. Mushroom poisoning in five patients. *Am J Med* 1965;38:787–792.

33. Harrison DC, Griffin JR, Fiene TJ. Effects of beta-adrenergic blockade with propranolol in patients with atrial arrhythmias. *N Engl J Med* 1965;273:410–415. (Dr. Harrison's comment: This was one of the earliest publications on the clinical use of beta blockers in the US. This paper helped me earn a promotion to an Assistant Professor at Stanford.)

36. Harrison DC, Griffin JR. Metabolic and circulatory responses to selective adrenergic stimulation and blockade. *Circulation* 1966;34:218–225. (Dr. Harrison's comment: This publication defined the metabolic and circulatory effects of β-adrenergic blockade with propranolol, the first clinically used β blocker in the US. It also stimulated me to write a book on the clinical research of several of our programs studying the adrenergic nervous system.)

40. Harrison DC, Kleiger RE, Merigan TC. Action of isoproterenol on heart cells in tissue culture. *Proc Soc Exp Biol Med* 1967;124:122–126.

48. Gianelly RE, Goldman RH, Treister B, Harrison DC. Propranolol in patients with angina pectoris. *Ann Intern Med* 1967;67:1216–1225.

50. Gianelly R, von der Groeben JO, Spivack AP, Harrison DC. Effect of lidocaine on ventricular arrhythmias in patients with coronary heart disease. *N Engl J Med* 1967;277:1215–1219. (Dr. Harrison's comment: This article was one of the first to use computers to quantitate arrhythmias in a coronary care unit and to utilize blood levels and pharmacokinetic studies of lidocaine as it affected the quantitation of arrhythmias. This again is one of my highlight papers, and one of which I am most proud. It was this paper than enhanced my world-wide reputation and allowed me to speak throughout the world. This served as the basis for using lidocaine for arrhythmias after myocardial infarction.)

52. Gianelly R, Mugler F, Harrison DC. Prinzmetal's variant of angina pectoris with only slight coronary atherosclerosis. *Calif Med* 1968; 108:129–131.

57. Henry WL, Crouse L, Stenson R, Harrison DC. Computer analysis of cardiac catheterization data. *Am J Cardiol* 1968;22:696–705. (Dr. Harrison comment: This was one of my first publications on the application of computers in cardiology. It carried out with excellent post-doctoral fellows who had experience with computers and from this we developed not only components for analyzing in an online fashion cardiac catheterization data but later ventricular function and echocardiographic interpretation. Most of the computer-based systems used today are just modifications of our work.)

61. Stinson EB, Dong E Jr., Schroeder JS, Harrison DC, Shumway NE Initial clinical experience with heart transplantation. *Am J Cardiol* 1968;22:791–803. (Dr. Harrison's comment: While the field of cardiac transplantation was largely the domaine of Norm Shumway, I and my post-doctoral fellows were instrumental in continuing to study these patients and understand how the heart functioned when there was no autonomic innervation of the heart. This, of course, was very important for making the reputation of cardiac surgery at Stanford and also in cardiology.)

74. Popp RL, Harrison DC. Ultrasound for the diagnosis of atrial tumor. *In Med* 1969;71:785–787.

75. Popp RL, Harrison DC. Ultrasound in the diagnosis and evaluation of therapy of idiopathic hypertrophic subaortic stenosis. *Circulation* 1969;40:905–914.

78. Harrison DC. New drugs in the treatment of angina. *N Engl J Med* 1969;280:895–896.

79. Finegan RE, Gianelly RE, Harrison DC. Aortic stenosis in the elderly. *N Engl J Med* 1969;281:1261–1264.

98. Popp RL, Harrison DC. Ultrasonic cardiac echography for determining stroke volume and valvular regurgitation. *Circulation* 1970;41:493–502. (Dr. Harrison's comment: Together with Richard Popp, we were among the first to use quantitation in echocardiography. We used what was known of angiograms to study stroke volume and valvular regurgitation. With 2-dimensional echocardiography, later this became even more quantitative.)

106. Harrison DC, Kerber RE, Alderman EL. Pharmacodynamics and clinical use of cardiovascular drugs following heart surgery. *Am J Cardiol* 1970;26:385–393.

122. Stenson RE, Constantino RT, Harrison DC. The interrelationships of hepatic blood flows, cardiac output, and blood levels of lidocaine in man. *Circulation* 1971;43:205–211. (Dr. Harrison's comment: This is one of the early studies that demonstrated the effects of cardiac output and hepatic blood flow on the metabolism of a drug such as lidocaine on which I had carried out many studies. This was really one of the early studies on pharmacokinetics with drugs and how cardiac function played a role.)

130. Graham AF, Schroeder JS, Daily PO, Harrison DC. Clinical and hemodynamic studies in patients with homograft mitral valve replacement. *Circulation* 1971;44:334–342.

133. Harrison DC, Ridges JD, Sanders WJ, Alderman EL, Fanton JA. Real-time analysis of cardiac catheterization data using a computer system. *Circulation* 1971;44:709–718. (Dr. Harrison's comment: This was one of our major publication on the use of computers in cardiology. The system which was developed for the cath labs still is widely used with very few changes in the original work that we did. It is being sold by many companies.)

151. Stenson RE, Crouse L, Harrison DC. Computer measurement of cardiac output by dye dilution: comparison of computer, Fick and Dow techniques. *Cardiovasc Res* 1972;6:449.

153. Harrison DC, Alderman EL. The pharmacology and clinical use of

lido-caine as an antiarrhythmic drug - 1972. *Mod Treatm* 1972;9: 139–175.

159. Zener JC, Hancock EW, Shumway NE, Harrison DC. Regression of extreme pulmonary hypertension following mitral valve surgery. *Am J Cardiol* 1972;30:820–826.

160. Alderman EL, Barry WH, Graham AF, Harrison DC. Hemodynamic effects of morphine and pentazocine differ in cardiac patients. *N Engl J Med* 1972;287:623–627.

173. Alderman EL, Matlof HJ, Wexler L, Shumway NE, Harrison DC. Results of direct coronary artery surgery for the treatment of angina pectoris. *N Engl J Med* 1973;288:535–539. *(Dr. Harrison's comment: This was a seminal paper demonstrating the effects of coronary bypass surgery on angina pectoris. We documented the physiologic and clinical effects and correlated them with increased coronary flow to ischemic segments of the heart.)*

175. Cannom DS, Graham AF, Harrison DC. Electrophysiologic studies in the denervated transplanted human heart: response to atrial pacing and atropine. *Circ Res* 1973;32:268–278. *(Dr. Harrison's comment: In this paper, we were able to demonstrate the electrophysiologic effects of pacing and atropine in patients who had transplanted hearts and no autonomic innervation. This was really the beginning of an electrophysiology program at Stanford.)*

189. Matloff HJ, Zener JC, Harrison DC. Idiopathic hypertrophic subaortic stenosis and heart block: cycle-to-cycle variation as a function of alterations in preload and afterload. *Am J Cardiol* 1973;32:719–722.

210. Cannom DS, Harrison DC. Detection of ventricular arrhythmias in real-time with a portable analog computer. *Am J Cardiol* 1974;33: 399–402.

211. Zener JC, Harrison DC. Changes in serum enzymes following intramuscular lidocaine. *Arch Intern Med* 1974;134:48.

212. Graham AF, Miller DC, Stinson EB, Daily PO, Fogarty TJ, Harrison DC. Treatment of refractory life-threatening ventricular tachycardia by surgery. *Am J Cardiol* 1974;32:909–912.

215. Cannom DS, Miller DC, Shumway NE, Fogarty TJ, Daily PO, Hu M, Brown B Jr., Harrison DC. The long-term follow-up of patients undergoing saphenous vein bypass surgery. *Circulation* 1974;49: 77–85.

219. Graham AF, Rider AK, Caves PK, Stinson EB, Harrison DC, Shumway NE, Schroeder JS. Acute rejection in the long-term cardiac transplant survivor: clinical diagnosis, treatment and significance. *Circulation* 1974;49:361–366. *(Dr. Harrison's comment: This was a major summary of the effects of acute rejection on cardiac transplant patients. This summarized >5 years of work for our program, which was then one of the only active ones in cardiac transplantation.)*

221. Popp RL, Brown OR, Silverman JF, Harrison DC. Echocardiographic abnormalities in the mitral valve prolapse syndrome. *Circulation* 1974;49:428–433.

222. Schroeder JS, Silverman JF, Harrison DC. Right coronary arterial spasm causing Prinzmetal's variant angina. *Chest* 1974;65:574–577. *(Dr. Harrison's comment: This was one of the first papers to demonstrate coronary spasm, and while it was published in a lesser known prestigious journal, it is frequently referred to as one of the early demonstrations of coronary spasms being important in variant angina pectoris.)*

223. Goodman DJ, Rossen R, Holloway EL, Alderman EL, Harrison DC. Effect of nitroprusside on left ventricular dynamics in mitral regurgitation. *Circulation* 1974;50:1025–1032. *(Dr. Harrison's comment: This was one of the earliest demonstrations that vasodilatation could alter valvular disease in patients with late stage heart failure. This concept has now been extended to many patients with congestive heart failure.)*

224. Alderman EL, Coltart DJ, Wettach GE, Harrison DC. Coronary artery syndromes after sudden propranolol withdrawal. *Ann Intern Med* 1974;81:625–627.

230. Lopes MG, Spivack AP, Harrison DC, Schroeder JS. Prognosis in

coronary care unit non-infarction cases. *J Am Coll Cardiol* 1974;228:1558–1562.

232. Coltart DJ, Berndt TB, Kernoff R, Harrison DC. Antiarrhythmic and circulatory effects of Astra W36095, a new lidocaine-like agent. *Am J Cardiol* 1974;34:35–41.

242. Collinsworth KA, Kalman SN, Harrison DC. The clinical pharmacology of lidocaine as an antiarrhythmic drug. *Circulation* 1974;50: 1217–1230.

258. Paaso BT, Harrison DC. A new look at an old problem: mushroom poisoning: clinical presentations and new therapeutic approaches. *Am J Med* 1975;58:505–509. *(Dr. Harrison's comment: This paper and number 31 are among my publications that are the most quoted. We studied patients with mushroom poisoning and defined 3 clinical phases of which are still widely used today among lay publications and other scientific publications. For many years I was consulted by physicians who had patients with mushroom poisoning.)*

260. Popp RL, Filly K, Brown O, Harrison DC. The effect of transducer placement on echocardiographic left ventricular dimensions. *Am J Cardiol* 1975;35:537–540.

266. Lopes MG, Fitzgerald J, Harrison DC, Schroeder JS. Diagnosis and quantification of ambulatory arrhythmias using an improved RR interval plotting system. *Am J Cardiol* 1975;35:816–823.

274. Alderman EL, Davies RO, Crowley JJ, Lopes MG, Brooker JZ, Friedman JP, Graham AG, Matlof HM, Harrison DC. Dose response effectiveness of propranolol for the treatment of angina pectoris. *Circulation* 1975;54:964–975.

277. Cannom DS, Rider AK, Stinson EB, Harrison DC. Electrophysiologic studies in the denervated transplanted human heart. II. Response to norepinephrine, isoproterenol and propranolol. *Am J Cardiol* 1975;36:859–866.

291. Ingham RE, Rossen RM, Goodman DJ, Harrison DC. Treadmill arrhythmias in patients with idiopathic hypertrophic subaortic stenosis. *Chest* 1975;68:759–764.

303. Bolen JL, Holloway EL, Zener JC, Harrison DC, Alderman EL. Evaluation of left ventricular function in patients with aortic regurgitation using afterload stress. *Circulation* 1976;53:132–139.

307. Harrison DC, Fitzgerald JW, Winkle RA. Ambulatory electrocardiography for diagnosis and treatment of cardiac arrhythmias. *N Engl J Med* 1976;294:373–380. *(Dr. Harrison's comment: This was an early use of ambulatory electrocardiography for studying and treating arrhythmias. For this, we used a computer to quantitate arrhythmias in 24 hour recordings in patients. This, I believe, is the first major publication on this subject.)*

309. Winkle RA, Alderman EL, Fitzgerald JW, Harrison DC. Treatment of recurrent symptomatic ventricular tachycardia. *Ann Intern Med* 1976; 85:1–7.

317. Winkle RA, Meffin PJ, Fitzgerald JW, Harrison DC. Clinical efficacy and pharmacokinetics of a new orally effective anti-arrhythmic, tocainide. *Circulation* 1976;54:884–889.

342. Mason JW, Winkle RA, Rider AK, Stinson EB, Harrison DC. The electrophysiologic effects of quinidine in the transplanted human heart. *J Clin Invest* 1977;59:481–489.

346. Berndt TB, Fitzgerald JW, Harrison DC, Schroeder JS. Hemodynamic changes at the onset of spontaneous vs. pacing-induced angina. *Am J Cardiol* 1977;39:784–788.

350. Bristow MR, Schwartz HD, Binetti G, Harrison DC, Daniels JR. Ionized calcium and the heart: elucidation of in vivo concentration response relationships in the open-chested dog. *Circ Res* 1977;41: 565–574.

359. Harrison DC, Meffin PJ, Winkle RA. Clinical pharmacokinetics of anti-arrhythmic drugs. *Progr Cardiovasc Dis* 1977;20:217–242. *(Dr. Harrison's comment: This was a summary paper outlining my experience with a number of anti-arrhythmic drugs particularly relating their pharmacokinetics to their antiarrhythmic actions. This review paper outlined many years of my work in this field.)*

362. Barry WH, Fairbank WM, Harrison DC, Lehrman KL, Malmivuo

JAV, Wikswo JP Jr. Measurement of the human heart vector. *Science* 1977;198:1159–1162.

380. Harrison DC, Meffin PJ, Winkle RA. Clinical pharmacology and anti-arrhythmic actions of tocainide. *Br Heart J* 1978;40:83–87.

381. Ricci DR, Orlick AE, Doherty PW, Cipriano PR, Harrison DC. Reduction of coronary blood flow during coronary artery spasm occurring sponta-neously and after provocation by ergonovine maleate. *Circulation* 1978;57:392–395.

384. Winkle RA, Meffin PJ, Harrison DC. Long-term tocainide therapy for ventricular arrhythmias. *Circulation* 1978;57:1018–1016.

386. Harrison DC, Fitzgerald JW, Winkle RA. Contribution of ambulatory electrocardiographic monitoring to antiarrhythmic management. *Am J Cardiol* 1978;41:996–1004.

392. Bristow MR, Thompson PD, Martin RP, Mason JW, Billingham ME, Harrison DC. Early anthracycline cardiotoxicity. *Am J Med* 1978;65: 823–832.

399. Anderson JL, Harrison DC, Meffin PJ, Winkle RA. Antiarrhythmic drugs: clinical pharmacology and therapeutic uses. *Drugs* 1978;15: 271–309.

415. Meltzer RS, Woythaler JN, Buda AJ, Griffin JC, Harrison DC, Martin RP, Popp RL. Two-dimensional echocardiographic quantification of infarct size alteration by pharmacologic agents. *Am J Cardiol* 1979; 44:257–262.

416. Sami M, Mason JW, Peters F, Harrison DC. Clinical electrophysiologic effects of encainide, a newly developed antiarrhythmic agent. *Am J Cardiol* 1979;44:526–532.

418. Harrison DC. Research related to noninvasive instrumentation. *Circulation* 1979;60:1569–1574.

432. Ginsburg R, Bristow MR, Harrison DC, Stinson EB. Studies with isolated human coronary arteries: Some general observations, potential mediators of spasm, role of calcium antagonists. *Chest* 1980;78:180–186.

437. Ginsburg R, Bristow MR, Stinson EB, Harrison DC. Histamine receptors in the human heart. *Life Sciences* 1980;26:2245–2249.

441. Sami M, Kraemer H, Harrison DC, Houston N, Shimasaki C, DeBusk RF. A new method for evaluating antiarrhythmic drug efficacy. *Circulation* 1980;62:1172–1179.

443. Orlick AE, Ricci DR, Cipriano PR, Guthaner DF, Harrison DC. Coronary hemodynamic effects of ergovine maleate in human subjects. *Am J Cardiol* 1980;45:48–52.

445. Baim DS, Rothman MT, Harrison DC. Improved catheter for regional coronary sinus flow and metabolic studies. *Am J Cardiol* 1980;46: 997–1000.

455. Schwartz JB, Jackson G, Kates RE, Harrison DC. Long-term benefit of cardioselective beta blockade with once-daily atenolol therapy in angina pectoris. *Am Heart J* 1981;101:380–385.

462. Kates RE, Keefe DLD, Schwartz J, Harapat S, Kirsten EB, Harrison DC. Verapamil disposition kinetics in chronic atrial fibrillation. *Clin Pharmacol Ther* 1981;30:44–51.

463. Sami M, Harrison DC, Kraemer H, Houston N, Shimasaki C, DeBusk RF. Antiarrhythmic efficacy of encainide and quinidine: validation of a model for drug assessment. *Am J Cardiol* 1981;48:147–156.

466. Samuelsson RG, Harrison DC. Electrophysiologic evaluation of encainide with use of monophasic action potential recording. *Am J Cardiol* 1981;48:871–876.

481. Kates RE, Harrison DC, Winkle RA. Metabolite cumulation during long-term oral encainide administration. *Clin Pharmacol Ther* 1982;31:427–432.

482. Clusin WT, Bristow MR, Baim DS, Schroeder JS, Jaillon P, Brett P, Harrison DC. The effects of diltiazem and reduced serum ionized calcium on ischemic ventricular fibrillation in the dog. *Circ Res* 1982;50:518–526.

485. Alderman EL, Hamilton KK, Silverman J, Harrison DC, Sanders WJ. Ana-tomically flexible, computer-assisted reporting system for coronary angiography. *Am J Cardiol* 1982;49:1208–1215.

500. Clusin WT, Buchbinder M, Harrison DC. Calcium overload, "injury" current, and early ischaemic cardiac arrhythmias—a direct connection. *Lancet* 1983;308:272–273.

504. Hughes EB, Zeman HD, Campbell LE, Hofstadter R, Meyer-Berkhout U, Otis JN, Rolfe J, Stone JP, Wilson S, Rubenstein E, Harrison DC, Kernoff RS, Thompson AC, Brown GS. Application of synchrotron radiation to non-invasive angiography. *Nucl Instr Methods* 1983; 208:665–675.

506. Effron MK, Harrison DC. Fibronectin: Cardiovascular aspects of a ubiquitous glycoprotein. *Am J Cardiol* 1983;52:206–208.

516. Rubenson D, Griffin JC, Ford A, Claude J, Reitz B, Knutti J, Billingham M, Harrison DC. Telemetry of electrophysiologic variables from conscious dogs: system design, validation, and serial studies. *Am Heart J* 1984;107:90–96.

523. Harrison DC. Is there a rational basis for the modified classification of antiarrhythmic drugs? In: Morganroth J, Moore EN, eds. Cardiac Arrhythmias: new Therapeutic Drugs and Devices. Boston, Martinus Nijhoff, 1985:36–40.

537. Harrison DC, Rapaport E, Thibault GE (chairpersons), et al. Workshop II: Cost containment issues in acute myocardial infarction and coronary management—points of view. *Am J Cardiol* 1985; 56(suppl):65C–69C.

540. Harrison DC. Antiarrhythmic drug classification: new science and practical applications. *Am J Cardiol* 1985;56:185–187.

552. Harrison DC, Kates RE, Q BD. Relation of blood level and metabolites to the antiarrhythmic effectiveness of encainide. *Am J Cardiol* 1986;58(suppl):66C–73C.

569. Harrison DC. Science for the 21st century: the coming biomedical revolution. "I: preparing for science in the 21st century (Harrison DC, Osterweis, M, and Rubin ER, eds.) The Association of Academic Health Centers, Washington, DC, 1991:3–9. *(Dr. Harrison's comment: As Chairman of the Board of the Association of Academic Health Centers, we sponsored conferences on the coming biomedical revolution. This was published as a monograph, and I think we early described what the next generations of research in medicine would be bringing to patient care.)*

572. Harrison DC. Counterpoint to the Sicilian gambit. Reasons to maintain the present antiarrhythmic drug classification. *Cardiovasc Res* 1992;26:566–567.

584. Signorello LB, Kennedy JA, Richmond RA, Sieu KL, Blot WJ, Harrison DC. Self-reported quality of life and health among Bjork-Shiley convexo-concave prosthetic heart valve patients. *J Heart Valve Dis* 2001;2:210–218.

585. Blot WJ, Ibrahim MA, Ivey TD, Acheson DE, Brookmeyer R, Weyman A, Defauw J, Smith JK, Harrison DC. Twenty-five year experience with the Bjork-Shiley Convexoconcave heart valve. *Circulation* 2005;111:2850–2857.

WATKINS PROCTOR HARVEY, MD:
A Conversation With the Editor*

Proc Harvey was born in Lynchburg, Virginia, on April 19, 1918. He grew up there as the youngest of 6 siblings. He graduated from Lynchburg (Virginia) College in 1939 and from Duke University School of Medicine in 1943. He interned in medicine at "The Brigham" Hospital in Boston and immediately thereafter went into the armed services. He returned in 1946 to "The Brigham" Hospital to complete his medical residency and his cardiology fellowship (under Dr. Sam Levine). He also was chief resident in medicine his final year at "The Brigham" and went directly from that position to chief of the division of cardiology at Georgetown University Medical Center in Washington, DC. He remained chief of cardiology there for next 35 years, retiring from that position, but not from cardiology, in 1985.

During his last year at "The Brigham," he published, with his mentor, Dr. Sam Levine, *Clinical Auscultation of the Heart*; it subsequently went through a second edition, and he is now working on a third edition. Dr. Harvey is best known as a magnificent teacher. He has directed the training of about 200 cardiology fellows, many of whom have subsequently been in prominent academic positions. He has received many awards for his achievements, including the Gold Heart Award of the American Heart Association, the Gifted Teacher Award of The American College of Cardiology, the Patrick Healy Award of Georgetown University, and the Distinguished Duke Medical Alumnus Award of Duke University School of Medicine. He has served as President of the American Heart Association and of several other medical organizations.

Proc has been a mentor to many, including me. He provided a platform for me in the Washington, DC, area as well as nationally, and I will always be indebted to him for that. Proc is a beloved physician and it's been an honor for me to be included among his friends.

William Clifford Roberts, MD† (Hereafter, WCR): *I am talking to Dr. Proctor Harvey in his office at Georgetown University Medical Center on December 30, 1999. This interview was started about a year ago, and unfortunately the first half of it was not recorded because of my pushing the button on the recorder the wrong way. Dr. Harvey, I appreciate your willingness to do this again. Let me start by asking you about your early memories growing up in Lynchburg, Virginia.*

Watkins Proctor Harvey, MD (Hereafter WPH): I was fortunate in having wonderful parents and a good home. I was the youngest of 6 children. There were 5

*This series of interviews was underwritten by an unrestricted grant from Bristol-Myers Squibb.
†Medical Director, Baylor Heart & Vascular Institute, Baylor University Medical Center, Dallas, Texas 75246.

FIGURE 1. WPH and his 4 brothers in Lynchburg, Virginia. WPH is the smallest of the boys and is at *bottom left*.

boys and 1 girl. My father had a good sense of humor. People would ask: "How many children do you have?" He would say, "I've got 5 boys and everyone has a sister." They'd say, "Oh my gosh, you've got 10 children?" My sister was the oldest. By the time I came along, I could do anything I wanted—go to bed when I wanted to, get anything in the kitchen I wanted, cook things for myself. I had independence. I played all sports, except baseball. We'd often play sports on the street in front of the house. It was a happy boyhood. During the depression, my father, as practically everybody did, had trouble making money. I knew he would give me anything if I'd just ask him for it, but I didn't want to do that because I knew he didn't have the money. He managed a tobacco warehouse. My father rose about 4 A.M., and went to the warehouse and greeted the arriving farmers who unloaded their tobacco. The tobacco was put in baskets and sold to buyers later that morning. In my senior year in high school, I got up with him, went to the tobacco warehouse, and made 15 cents an hour. I also worked in a filling station during the hard times. I learned a lot about cars. I also was an usher in a theater. I had a flashlight, wore a uniform, showed people to their seats, and helped them anyway I could. That's the first time I realized that you could have muscle cramps. At night, my calf muscles cramped (from the long standing). I also worked in a clothing store during holidays as a salesman. In the store I found I couldn't sell anything I didn't like. I remember people coming up and saying, "What do you think about this tie?" And I said, "You know, I really don't like it." And I would show them one I liked. A man came in (I think he was a doctor) once when our suits were on sale. He picked out 2 suits; 1 was expensive and the other was not. He said, "Which one do you like?" I said, "I like the less expensive one; you look better in it." I learned that if you are frank and honest with people and treat them like you want people to treat you, they liked you and came back. It was a good experience. My father died when I was 16.

WCR: *How old was he?*

WPH: He was 65. I remember his being in the hospital. He was unconscious and breathed loudly. He didn't recognize me. I remember lying there next to him and a direct blood transfusion was done from me to him.

WCR: *What was his problem?*

WPH: He had cancer. I believe it was pancreatic or one of the cancers that grow quickly. I needed to go to college because I graduated from high school at age 16. After graduation, I took some courses on typing and shorthand. Later, these techniques proved useful to me. I can still write things in Gregg shorthand. When it came time to go to college, I didn't have much money. A nice lady, who was very active in my church (Presbyterian), needed someone to chauffeur her. For 3 years I chauffeured her. She was like another mother to me. Initially, I took the streetcar and then a bus to go to Lynchburg College, which was in my hometown. This nice lady said, "I want you to take my car to college so that you get back earlier, so we can drive."

WCR: *What was her name?*

WPH: *SueSpeed Kirkpatrick.* She had had 1 son, but had lost him on Armistice Day in World War I. His best friend had been *Wiley Forbus*, who would come to see her. Forbus had trained at The Johns Hopkins Hospital and was one of the young group who moved to Duke University when it was a new medical school. I met him and I liked him. He was Professor of Pathology at Duke. My meeting him later played a role when deciding where to go to medical school. I could have gone to the Medical College of Virginia. I knew there was a new school at Duke and I liked Dr. Forbus, and therefore, thought it must be a good school. I applied to Duke Medical School, was accepted, and subsequently went there. As I look back, Bill, I'm glad that I didn't go to a big college after finishing high school. I just wasn't mature enough for that.

WCR: *How many students were at Lynchburg College when you went there?*

WPH: There were about 60 in my class, and maybe 200 in the whole school.

WCR: *You started college when you were 16 years old?*

WPH: No. I was 17. I finished high school at 16 and then the next year I enrolled in the college.

WCR: *Do you remember the population of Lynchburg in 1918 when you were born?*

WPH: I think it was about 30,000.

WCR: *As a young lad you could get yourself all over town with no problem?*

WPH: None at all. Taking buses, streetcars, and bicycles.

WCR: *What was the difference in age between you as the sixth child and the oldest one who was your sister?*

WPH: Seventeen years.

WCR: *You never lived with your sister?*

WPH: She was teaching kindergarten and first grade in Norfolk, Virginia, when my father died. She then came back to Lynchburg and taught the same lower grades in its schools. We were very close. She took an interest in everything I did. If I needed money she gave it to me. In medical school she sent me money even though she did not make much. That's when I realized that teachers were a major underpaid group in our country. She was a sweet and dedicated person. She was a saint! I talk about a 2-tier ratio, give/take. When a person's ratio of give and take is not 1, you've got problems. Hers was 10,000. I was fortunate in having family that was all together. My closest brother was 4 years older and the next older one was in his teens.

WCR: *Your father was actually 49 when you were born?*

WPH: Yes.

WCR: *What was your daddy like?*

WPH: Everyone liked him. He was a kind person. He would go out of his way to help other people. As a child there wasn't anything but love and respect for my dad. We got along well.

WCR: *What do you remember about your mother?*

WPH: She too was very kind and very intelligent. She went to college somewhere near Nashville, Tennessee, and then came to Virginia to teach. That's when she met my father. I just couldn't want for a better mother. After I finished my training and came to Georgetown, I was able to do some things for my mother. She stayed with my wife and me for periods. My sister developed cancer of the breast and lived only a couple of years after that. A regret in my life is that I was unable to have done as much for her as I would have liked because she died so young. There was nothing bad in my childhood except the death of my father. I couldn't have had a better upbringing as far as family values are concerned.

WCR: *Did your brothers stay in Lynchburg?*

WPH: One initially went to Texas to work for a manufacturer of jeans, then later to Minnesota, and finally he came back to Lynchburg. Subsequently, he moved to the eastern shore of Maryland. Another was in the insurance business and another worked for the telephone company. Another brother went to Virginia Tech, took ROTC there, and stayed in the military. He retired as a colonel in the Army. He commanded a battalion in Korea. Because he was much older than I was, we did few things together, but he certainly contributed to the family.

WCR: *Was there much stimulation around your home for scholarship?*

WPH: My parents believed in the importance of a good education. They certainly liked for the children to get good grades and were very pleased when we were on the honor roll.

WCR: *You graduated first in your class in high school?*

WPH: I don't remember if I was first or not. I was in the National Honor Society. I was president of my graduating class.

FIGURE 2. WPH while an intern at "The Brigham" in 1943.

WCR: *The reason you went to Lynchburg College was mainly financial?*

WPH: Yes.

WCR: *How many of the 5 siblings were able to go to college?*

WPH: Three of the 6 went to college.

WCR: *You essentially worked your way through Lynchburg College through the odd jobs and minimal living expenses?*

WPH: Yes. The tuition also was small. The tuition for medical school was $1,200 or $1,500 a year. I thought that was a lot of money. I have always believed that if anybody in this country wants an education, it's there, but you have to work for it.

WCR: *Were there any teachers who had a special influence on you in high school or at Lynchburg College?*

WPH: No. The first teacher who had a major influence on my own life was *Sam Levine* at The Peter Bent Brigham Hospital in Boston. I spent about 4-1/2 years with Sam Levine. I was closely associated with him when I was an intern, a senior assistant resident, and chief resident at The Peter Bent Brigham Hospital. That was a great experience.

WCR: *May I ask you more about Mrs. SueSpeed Kirkpatrick? It sounds in essence like you became her adopted son?*

WPH: I looked on her as a sweet person, like my mother. Her car was a 4-door Model A Ford. I would drive it to college and then to her house to take her for a ride. She would always take a friend. She must have been about 60 at that time. She had a little terrier named "Critter." He'd ride with me in the front and the 2 women rode in the back. We'd take drives to several beautiful areas close to Lynchburg. We took rides practically every day. The association with the older people was good for me, because I learned about older people. I learned that they liked to joke and kid around just like younger people.

WCR: *Proc, do you remember when Duke University Medical School started?*

WPH: My freshman class was the tenth class.

WCR: *So it must have started in 1929.*

WPH: Yes, somewhere around then. At that time Duke had a nationally ranked football team, known all over the country. Everybody on Saturday went to the football game, which I liked. Later, I hoped the school would be known for its academic excellence rather than for its football. That's the way it worked out. I was so fortunate in going to Duke. Years later when I received a Duke Alumnus Award, I was asked to respond. I said how I hoped Duke would become one of the top schools academically. It has.

WCR: *How did you come up with the money to go to medical school? You mentioned Wiley Forbus, a pathologist at Duke, who was the friend of the son of Mrs. Kirkpatrick.*

WPH: Both Dr. Forbus and Mrs. Kirkpatrick's son were overseas in World War I. Her son was killed on Armistice Day! His friend Wiley Forbus came at times to see Mrs. Kirkpatrick and that is how I got to meet him. I'd heard a lot about him. When I got to Duke I realized that he was one of the top pathologists in the world. He had described the Forbus aneurysm of the Circle of Willis. He ran a great department. In school at Duke I tended to avoid the professors. I guess I was afraid that they would ask me questions.

WCR: *How did you scrape up the money to go to medical school?*

WPH: One of my father's friends, Jack Adams, was a buyer for one of the tobacco companies. He purchased tobacco for his company at the auction in the tobacco warehouse where my father was the manager. He came to our home the night before my father's funeral and said, "What are you going to do next year?" I said, "I don't know. I'd like to go to college." Then he said, "Come see me." I knew what he meant. He was going to lend me money to go to Lynchburg College. I didn't need it, however, because I was able on my own to do it. But after I had been accepted into medical school, I knew I didn't have the money to go. I had gotten a small scholarship of $500 from the Lions Club or Kiwanis Club. I couldn't get the money from my family. The money just wasn't there. I had decided I was going to join the Air Force to become a fighter pilot. A friend of mine and I were going to join together. About that time, a friend reminded me that it was her uncle Jack Adams who had said, "Come see me." I went to see him. Jack Adams was an eccentric. The first time I met him was years before, when as a young boy at the summer farmers' market, I saw a puppy costing $5. I only had $3. I was standing there, and this man came up and said, "Go on and buy that puppy. I'll give it to you." And I asked my father about it and he said, "Oh, you take it. That was Jack, the bee man." He keeps bees. I had never met him before. I thought this man doesn't have much money and here he is giving me $5. I went and gave him my $3. He was a very wealthy man, but you would never have known it.

I thought that maybe he would lend me money to help pay for my medical school. That is when he said, "How much do you need? I'll take care of it." I turned over my life insurance to him. I had a $10,000 life insurance policy so that at least he would get paid. I was able to finish medical school, internship, and the Army service before beginning to pay him back. I saved every cent I made overseas, and when I returned I went to see him, thanked him, and repaid him. I said, "Now, Jack, I really appreciate what you have done, and I would now like to pay you back, including the interest." He said, "There is no interest." I then resolved to lend a worthy student money to go to school as Jack did for me (which I have done).

WCR: *You came from a small town of 30,000 and went to a relatively unsophisticated college. Your parents weren't in the sophisticated, wealthy group in town? When you got to Duke, you were entering a different realm for the first time in your life. How did you react to that?*

WPH: I was really anxious and nervous. There were about 70 of us in the class. At our first class gathering I remember having to sign something and my hands shook. Our class was small enough that we knew everybody. In anatomy there were 4 of us on each cadaver. There was a guy from Idaho. He was older and already balding. At our first session, he pulled the canvas cover off the cadaver and said, "If I was going to do an appendectomy, I would start right here." And he went through the details. I thought, "Oh my gosh, he can do an appendectomy." We called him the "Idaho sweet potato." A fellow from New York, while flipping his Phi Beta Kappa key on a chain, went up to a skeleton in the lab and named all the bones. All I knew about bones at that time was what the musical lyric said: "Dem bones, dem bones. The foot bone connects to the anklebone. The ankle bone connects to the leg bone, etc." Christmas came, and he wasn't there anymore. And the other one tried to detail everything without getting a broader picture, and he didn't last either. It wasn't that they lacked intelligence. Maybe they changed their minds about being doctors. The faculty at Duke was excellent, helpful, and made every effort to teach us and keep us in medical school.

WCR: *How many of the 70 graduated?*

WPH: Probably 60.

WCR: *Who influenced you in medical school? Was medical school a good experience for you?*

WPH: Yes, and I knew I was getting good medical training. There was no one person I strongly related to. All the teachers were good.

WCR: *Where did you live at medical school?*

WPH: I rented from a lady who took in boarders. I told her that I could work for my meals and bed. She said, "That will be fine." She always called me "Mr. Harvey." I would go to bed late, sometimes at 2 A.M., and get up at 4 A.M. to fire the furnace, and do other chores. I served at meals. The pace, however, was killing me. Finally, Dr. Forbus somehow learned of my predicament and said, "Look, borrow the money. Don't try to do this." The landlady thought I would bring her plenty of students to room and eat at her place.

WCR: *Proc, how did it come about that you interned at "The Brigham" Hospital?*

WPH: During my senior year in medical school I had a job working in Duke's beautiful medical library named after *Joshua Trent*, who had married one of the Dukes, and was a surgeon who died at a young age. He seemed to have been a brilliant fellow. The library was one of the prettiest I ever saw—everything was mahogany and leather. I worked in the library at night and on weekends. One Saturday night when in the library alone, I said to myself: "I have got to do something about internship." At that time no faculty person ever advised students about internships. Where would I go? I remembered that there was a famous doctor from Lynchburg who was at a hospital in Boston. There had been some things in the local newspaper about *Dr. Henry Christian*. I had met some of his sisters, who had lived several blocks from where I lived, but I had never met him. I said, "I know he is at a good place." I looked in Cecil's *Textbook of Medicine* and found a chapter by Henry A. Christian, Hersey Professor of Medicine at Harvard and Chief of Medicine at The Peter Bent Brigham Hospital. So I applied to The Peter Bent Brigham Hospital in Boston. I was told that I had to come to Boston and take an examination. I had no more than $50 to my name and it would cost me that to go there by train and back. A female physician intern 1 year ahead of me at Duke Hospital said, "I understand you've applied to The Peter Bent Brigham." I said "yes." She said, "You are wasting your time and money. There has never been a person from Duke who has gone there." Another person told me the same thing. I almost didn't go, but thought that I should at least try. I went up there, spending the only money I had. I had to take the exams at 3 Harvard Hospitals: Boston City, Peter Bent Brigham, and Massachusetts General. When doing so, I remember seeing a typical "old Boston"-type fellow, who was also applying, already getting gray, tweed coat and all. I remember thinking, "How can I compete against a person like this?" Fortunately, I got "The Brigham" Hospital internship. Then who should be on that same house staff but this fellow whom I had wondered if I could compete against. Later on in the year he had trouble keeping up with his records. I still remember hearing him back in another room dictating records of patients who had been there 2 months before. They gave him time off just to get caught up. And he was the one I was worried about! He was a wonderful person. We became close friends.

WCR: *Although Durham and Chapel Hill may be a little more sophisticated than Lynchburg, Boston was a lot more sophisticated and bigger than either Durham or Chapel Hill. How did you react to Boston?*

WPH: It was evening when I got off the trolley in front of the hospital. I walked up the stairs and saw the big columns at the entrance to The Peter Bent Brigham Hospital. I was scared. I think if someone had said, "Why are you coming here?" I would have turned around. There was a big foyer where a night clerk named Mack was in his booth. I told Mack my name. He called, "*Dr. C.B. Favour,*" the chief medical resident. Everyone called him "CB." He couldn't have been nicer. CB showed me my assigned room in the hospital. I quickly felt "at home." He later became the head of infectious disease.

WCR: *When in medical school, was it difficult or easy for you to decide what type of doctor you were going to be?*

WPH: I liked taking care of both children and adults. I felt that all doctors needed a basis in internal medicine. That is why I interned in medicine. When World War II came along, I could have gone either into pediatrics or into medicine, but pediatrics wasn't done in the Army. When in Medicine at Battey General Hospital in Rome, Georgia, I realized I was good at examining the precordium and other parts of the body, and that gave me a little boost in cardiology. From then on I knew I wanted to go back to The Peter Bent Brigham Hospital after the war for more training.

At "The Brigham" I liked that a lowly intern could dine in the dining room with all of the well-known faculty. You'd sit there and eat with the head of medicine or the head of surgery. I remember sitting there one day when I was an intern and the chief of surgery said something to *John Homans*. "John, it must be nice that you had a father who was such a well-known person." John said, "Hell, I didn't even know my father!" I remember thinking there's John Homans, the famous surgeon, and he didn't even know his father. His textbook on surgery was my favorite (easy to read and understand), and he was a delightful fellow ("down to earth," "an old shoe"). One Sunday morning on the private ward I was there going over patients and in walked *Howard Sprague*, of Sprague stethoscope fame from the Massachusetts General Hospital. He looked like he had just come out of Brooks Brothers, everything right in order. He had a new hat and a new suit on. He put his new hat up on the hook. Just about the same time Homans came in. He was wearing an old tweed sports jacket and everything "casual" (the opposite of Dr. Sprague). He said with his lisp: "Howard, how are you today?" He put his old beat up hat on a hook. Then they both went to their respective patients. I was still working on records. They both came back at the same time. Homans, who had a limp, looked up at the hat rack and said, "I don't know which hat is mine." He paused and

then took Sprague's hat, put it on, and, with a big mischievous grin, went out the door.

The intern/resident-faculty associations were most pleasant. The wives often came in on weekends to have Sunday dinner at the hospital. Also, we had a night dinner, cafeteria style, for the night personnel, and we were welcome, just like at home. Interns were not paid. We felt privileged to work for nothing! The pay was our education of excellence.

Bill, I don't remember in medical school or during my time at "The Brigham" anyone talking about money. Never! The talk was about our patients' problems and solutions and medical publications. (I later tried to do that at Georgetown.) It was a family atmosphere at "The Brigham." The faculty "cared." They took us under their wings. *Dr. George Thorn*, the chief of medicine, told us if we interned before we went off to war that there would be a place for us when we got back. There was.

WCR: *Your internship started in 1943 right after medical school. Was that July?*

WPH: I think it was February. We were supposed to graduate in June, but we graduated in February and didn't have any time off that preceding summer.

WCR: *You were on call every other night during your internship?*

WPH: Yes, every other night and every other weekend. It was the type of atmosphere that all the people you worked with were friends. It was a great group of people. Having been at Duke, we had been taught most procedures. I could do lumbar punctures, thoracentesis, peritoneocentesis, etc. In contrast, a lot of the Harvard boys had not had as much practical experience. That earlier practical experience gave me confidence that I could do well at "The Brigham." They were all bright, however, and they caught on quickly. They could all quote the medical literature. They would know the latest published article on everything. That forced me to read more. We talked constantly about what we were learning and the interesting patients. Grand rounds were focused on patients and every seat was filled. As chief resident, I was responsible for getting the patients and the speakers for grand rounds. It taught me how to run conferences, something that proved valuable when I went to Georgetown.

WCR: *Internship was just 9 months?*

WPH: Yes. It was World War II, and we were all in the same boat; everybody went to the Armed Services. I first went to Camp Barkley in Abilene, Texas. It was so cold in Boston. I said, "At least I'm going to a warm place." We arrived, however, in the worse snowstorm in Abilene, Texas, in 18 years! I had basic training at Camp Barkley and then was sent to Battey General Hospital in Rome, Georgia. It was pretty well known that if you didn't conform to things you would be sent overseas quickly. The commanding officer at a staff meeting one day said: "You men are using too much toilet paper." I couldn't believe it. He had his major, head of the Quartermaster Unit, get up and say how many sheets per day per person were permitted. (It was something like 18.) You were supposed to be

FIGURE 3. WPH as a captain in the Army in Angsburg, Germany, in November 1945.

at all social functions. I wasn't too happy there, and apparently my unhappiness showed.

WCR: *Where did you go overseas?*

WPH: It wasn't long before I was assigned to an air evac general hospital in Swindon, England, a railroad interchange. At times, we would get as many as 2,000 soldiers injured in combat 6 or 8 hours earlier. It was a wonderfully efficient system of moving those air-evac patients to the hospital. I was responsible for 3 wards, including a nurses ward (female), a chest ward, and a trenchfoot ward. We learned that external movement of the chest for chest injuries was preventative of chest fixation. We had these patients do exercises daily. We would put our hands on 1 side of the chest, lean on it, have the patient take a deep breath, and that would make the opposite side of your chest expand. We also learned that if the blood in the chest was not evacuated, the chest would become fixed by adhesions, which often led to thoracotomy with or without pneumonectomy. This was a busy time, but I was lucky because the chief of medicine, *Joe Turner*, had been a faculty member at Columbia University Hospital in New York. I learned a lot from him.

The worse experience overseas was during the Battle of the Bulge. Things were so bad it looked like the Germans would possibly win the war. We got orders not to discharge any previously injured, but now recovered, soldier so that he could get back to the front. Before that anybody injured would be shipped back to the USA. There was supposed to be a policy that physicians in a general hospital would exchange with other physicians on the front lines or at least ones in a combat group. Most of the time that did not happen, but it did happen with me. I was transferred to the Fourth Armored Division's lead tank division whose commander, Colonel McAuliffe, replied "nuts" to the German officer ordering "surrender." This helped in turning the tide in the Battle of the Bulge. I was the Battalion Aid Surgeon with the rank of Cap-

tain. This tank division was in the 3rd Army commanded by *General George Patton*. You could feel General Patton's influence throughout the division. He was a great leader. The war soon ended.

As a medical officer, I could do anything I wanted in the battalion as long as I took care of my responsibilities. I had a nice commanding officer who had just replaced Colonel McAuliffe. He even allowed me to drive a tank. These tanks had Packard engines and could go 45 miles per hour. There were 2 levers: if you pulled the right lever, the right track would slow so the tank turned to the right; if you pulled on the left lever, the tank would go to the left; if you pulled both levers, the tank would stop.

These were a great group of soldiers. I got to know them. I respected them. I ran my own makeshift hospital. Ordinarily, a sick patient who needed more advanced medical care or laboratory tests would be transferred from the battalion to the regiment medical unit. The soldiers did not want to leave our unit, pleading not to go. We set up a little hospital, maybe 8 beds (bunks). The men in the detachment were great nurses. If given a sulfa drug, they had to drink plenty of water. The patients were told to drink a certain number of canteens full of water each day. You would hear the "male army nurses" telling the patients to drink the water or they would knock their heads off. I was able to get some equipment and do lab work. I was not authorized to do that. I put it under "education for the soldiers." For a centrifuge, I put a string on the glass and whirled it around and the sediment would go to the bottom. I got supplies from a general hospital, including a microscope. We taught the men how to do smears and diagnoses. They were smart. It was a very cohesive and friendly group. No one wanted to leave. That was a great experience. It taught me that when you are alone you could go only so far. You look into the mirror and talk to yourself. At one time I referred someone to dermatology, but I was assigned to be the dermatologist! It also taught me what one can do on your own. I got so I could diagnose scabies from 10 feet away. They would burrow into the skin, defecate, cause itching, and they left little marks. I seldom sent these soldiers back to the regiment. They all wanted to stay here. We were able to treat most conditions ourselves.

Once while stationed in England, I had a patient with a very serious chest injury. I took this soldier to a hospital in England where *Dr. Dwight Harken*, a chest surgeon, worked. He had an excellent reputation for removing missiles, bullets, and shrapnel from the chest. When arriving at his hospital, he came up and welcomed us in his usual ebullient fashion. When seeing patients in his ward, we came to a patient who had fallen out of bed. Dr. Harken went on and on apologizing for this as if it was his fault. I told him that it could happen in any hospital. (After the war, Dr. Harken went to "The Brigham" Hospital where he was appointed Chief of Cardiovascular Surgery.) I was chief resident in medicine and a cardiac fellow with Samuel Levine at "The Brigham" when Harken did his first mitral finger fracture. Most patients died initially.

WCR: *Proc, how long were you in the Army?*

WPH: About 3-1/2 years. I was in Germany for 1-1/2 years of that time.

WCR: *Where were you in Germany?*

WPH: In Bavaria and in several other places.

WCR: *After you got out of the Army in 1946 you went directly back to "The Brigham" Hospital?*

WPH: Yes. When I returned to Boston I was not certain that Dr. Thorn was going to have a position for me. But, one was there.

WCR: *You didn't have correspondence with him. You just went back to "The Brigham"?*

WPH: That's right. That is when government-sponsored fellowships became available for the first time. There was one in cardiology, one in endocrinology, and one in hematology.

WCR: *When you went back to "The Brigham" Hospital in 1946 you must have been quite a bit more sophisticated than when you went there 3-1/2 years earlier? You could do about everything now. You remained at "The Brigham" for 4 years?*

WPH: Yes. I was at "The Brigham" until September 1950 when I moved to Washington, DC, to be the first head of cardiology at Georgetown University Medical Center.

WCR: *How did you and Sam Levine get to be such good friends? How did he get to be your major mentor?*

WPH: Sam had always wanted to produce a book of phonocardiograms of precordial murmurs and sounds. However, he never had anybody to do it. He mentioned his desire to me when I started in as the first fellow in cardiology at "The Brigham."

WCR: *That was right after you got out of the Army?*

WPH: Yes. I was very fortunate. I met *Irma* and then we decided to get married. I said something to her father and he said, "How much money are you making?" I said, "Five hundred dollars a year. But, next year I'm going to make $1,000." He said, "There are not many jobs that you can double your salary in a year!"

WCR: *When you returned to "The Brigham," you lived in the hospital again?*

WPH: Yes. There were rooms for the house staff. Each one had a room, and there was a chief resident's room.

WCR: *You were Sam Levine's first fellow?*

WPH: Yes. I was delighted to be with him because he was the one I picked out that I'd like to be like. I admired him as a man, as a father, and as a doctor. I liked the way he treated patients. I can still see his going into the big open ward with curtains between beds. (I believe there were 32 patients on each ward.) I can still see him with the woman who he had asked to sit up. She might have come from the poorest district in Boston. She'd sit up and he was just as kind to her as he would have been to *Arthur Fiedler*, the conductor of the Boston Pops Symphony Orchestra, who also was one of his patients. He straightened out her pillows before asking her to lie back again. That kindness and caring made an impression on me.

FIGURE 4. WPH with Irma on their wedding day.

I remember a patient with pernicious anemia. Sam Levine had been an intern on the same ward, and told the story that when he was an intern pernicious anemia was fatal and there was no specific therapy. Some patients were given blood transfusions but subsequently died. As residents, for those patients whose treatment was of no avail, we could try anything new that conceivably could be beneficial. Sam described a pernicious anemia patient, when he was an intern, who was dying but kept alive with blood transfusions. Liver abstract then became available, it was given to the patient, and it saved her life. I saw this same woman many years later when I was an intern (a lesson not to give up hope). *Minot* and *Murphy* received a Nobel Prize for their discovery of liver abstract to treat pernicious anemia. Dr. Murphy was on the staff of "The Brigham."

WCR: *As soon as you came out of the Army you became Sam Levine's fellow? After that year, despite the fact that you went back to the general medical wards, you kept seeing and working with Sam Levine?*

WPH: Yes, it was at least 4 years. It wasn't hard for me to do both. In fact, it helped me. As chief medical resident, I saw every patient admitted to the medical service of the hospital. I'd go over all of the new patients admitted before I went home at night.

WCR: *How big was The Brigham Hospital in 1946?*

WPH: It was about 100 medical and 100 surgical beds.

FIGURE 5. Photograph of WPH's mentor, Dr. Samuel A. Levine.

WCR: *About 200 beds. Did you work in the outpatient clinic then?*

WPH: Yes. We had a cardiac clinic every Wednesday and Sam ran it. As a Fellow you were a key person there. Shortly after returning to "The Brigham" and working in this clinic, I examined a sweet old lady. I asked her to tell me her problem. She said, "Doctor, I have spells." I was about to say "Tell me about them" when she said, "I'm having one now." Soon she said, "I'm having another one." I couldn't help but think, "Is this the real thing or can she call it at will?" I examined her then and sure enough she was correct and accurate; she had intermittent sinus pauses and temporary sinus arrest. I recorded it on both tape and phonocardiogram.

WCR: *In the Levine and Harvey auscultation book you recorded all the published phonocardiograms? You were at the hospital, essentially, all the time?*

WPH: Yes. *Rosalind Levine*, Sam's wife, was a sweet and wonderful lady and an artist. I got to know her well. She would sketch the rhythms. We showed her the rhythms on the electrocardiograms and she sketched them, and then we used the sketches in teaching.

WCR: *You collected all of those recordings in the first edition of the "Levine and Harvey" book on clinical auscultation of the heart?*

WPH: Yes. There are 2 editions. In the first one, a green book, I recorded all figures there. I also recorded all the phonocardiograms in the second edition, which had a blue cover and was several times bigger than the first edition.

Sam Levine demonstrated to me how to relax while working on Saturday afternoons. He would say, "Proc, I'm going to go take a snooze. Wake me in 20 minutes." He'd get on the examining table and he was "gone." In 20 minutes I would wake him up and he was then refreshed. I now do that myself. We couldn't help but develop a close bond. I showed him things he'd never seen before. He said, "I've always wanted

to do this." We started seeing the fruits that came from these recordings. For example, one was mitral stenosis. I heard an extra sound which we now know as the "opening snap". He had never paid attention to it. He'd say, "We will, keep looking for it." I brought him many other examples of that sound. We found that Wolfert and Margolis had described that sound a few years earlier, although it was not appreciated by others. They referred to a French physician who termed it "ouvre de la clachment."

Sam also was shown recordings and observations on variation of the intensity of the first heart sound in complete heart block and it was related to the PR interval recorded by electrocardiogram. If the PR was short, the first heart sound was loud; if the PR interval was prolonged, it was faint.

Sam Levine was invited to London to give a well-known lecture and I said, "What are you going to talk about?" "I'm going to tell them about the first heart sound in heart block and the opening snap in mitral stenosis. Things we're working on." I said, "Oh, they know all that." He said, "No, they don't." He went over, came back, and I asked him how things went. He was pleased with the reception of his lecture. He said they took him to the ward and asked him to tell the PR interval in a patient with first-degree heart block. He got it right on the button. Then they took him to another patient and he got it exactly right. They took him to another patient and he said, "No, that's enough." With a twinkle in his eye, he told me "I'm afraid that the next one I wouldn't do as well." He was an outstanding physician, and a dedicated, extremely intelligent, and "caring" man.

WCR: *When you were a fellow with Sam Levine, what was a day like?*

WPH: I started almost immediately collecting as many heart sounds and murmurs as possible. I asked the housestaff to call me any time, night or day, when they encountered a new or interesting auscultatory finding! I would see the patient, leave a note, and record a phonocardiogram. It was surprising and gratifying how quickly the collection grew. A large number of findings on auscultation today were unknown at that time. *Dr. Robert Gross*, the pioneer heart surgeon, was across the street at Children's Hospital. All of his adult patients came to "The Brigham" and I would examine them. (He was the first to close a patent ductus arteriosus. He did the first surgical correction of coarctation of the aorta. About the same time, Dr. Crawford independently performed the same operation in Sweden.) That was a great experience. I saw a wide variety of patients with heart problems. In fact, every heart patient in the hospital would likely be seen by both Sam Levine and me. I also saw all of Sam Levine's private patients.

WCR: *How did you like being chief resident under Dr. George Thorn?*

WPH: He was a very nice man. He treated everyone fairly and decently. He took morning report every day. I saw every patient that came into the medical service before the morning report. I had a wide experience. Mack was the operator at the phone booth which overlooked the emergency entrance and he would page you if needed. Mack would lean out of the window one level up and in a loud voice say: "chest" or "belly." If it was chest, the patient was sent to medicine; if it was belly, to surgery. We always laughed at that. You would work the patient up and go for the evening meal and sit and talk with everyone. I felt very much at home there.

WCR: *Was Sam Levine a great man?*

WPH: Yes. I also got to know *Paul White*. Years later, we had him at Georgetown as visiting professor and he was one of the nicest people you would ever meet, a real gentleman, and so was Sam Levine. They were the 2 best cardiologists in the world, and they both were in Boston. Levine was a better clinician and White was more attuned to the world. Paul White was the first person to go to Russia when the "iron curtain" was lifted. They let him come when no one else had been able to get in. They respected him and they knew he was there to do good. I got to know him and his wife *Ina*. They had 2 adopted children. I am sure that he never made much money. If you sent him a letter, he would write you back a handwritten letter. To show you the type man he was, once while in Florida, he rented a car and while driving in a rural area he saw a sign that said "Paul D. White, MD." He parked his car, went in, and after learning that Dr. White was busy, sat and waited. He did not tell the receptionist that he was the Paul Dudley White of Boston. He waited until the Floridian Dr. White had seen all his patients. Only then did he introduce himself and say his name was the same.

WCR: *How did you get to know Dr. Paul Dudley White so well that year?*

WPH: He had an annual course where I gave one lecture. *Dr. Tom Mattingly*, who later became President Eisenhower's physician, also took that course. I had never met him, but I was coming to Washington, DC, that summer and so was Tom. At that time he was a Colonel, and was coming to head cardiology at Walter Reed Army Hospital. I was a consultant in cardiology there. Tom Mattingly, whom I became very fond of, was like a little fox terrier. Bill, you knew him. He was a very fiery person. If he did not like something, you would know it right away. He put everybody on their toes at Reed. We became good friends, having mutual respect for each other. I used to go on the wards there and see patients at bedside. (Later, we had teaching conferences featuring patient presentations.) On one occasion, there was a note in the hospital chart signed by Colonel Mattingly. It said: "This is what Dr. Harvey would call such and such." I would not have called it that. So I wrote right under

Mattingly's note and said, "This is not what I would call it." We developed a mutual respect. He liked to give me a case as an unknown, get me out on a limb, hoping I would miss the diagnosis and then he would snip that limb off. It was good teaching for both me and those in attendance.

WCR: *You don't remember this, but I had an externship at Walter Reed Army Hospital between my junior and senior years in medical school (1957). While I was at Walter Reed Hospital, I was on the chest surgery service. I would go to Tom Mattingly's weekly cardiology conferences, and you came, and I remember your palpating the right side of the chest looking for the point of maximum impulse there as well as on the left side of the chest.*

WPH: They asked why I put both hands on the chest? I said, "If you had dextrocardia you will feel the point of maximal impulse over the right side, not the left." Tom Mattingly put cardiology at Walter Reed on the map. His people came out superb.

WCR: *Who were co-residents with you at "The Brigham"?*

WPH: Many who became well known. The surgeon *David Hume* was one. He later went to Richmond as Professor of Surgery of the Medical College of Virginia, and he developed the transplant program there. David Hume was chief resident in surgery when I was that in medicine. I saw many of his patients. He liked action, and that probably led to his death. Dave flew his own plane. On returning from a lecture on the West Coast, he crashed in bad weather in the mountains. He was a really good surgeon. "The Brigham" is where I learned to respect excellence in both medicine and surgery.

WCR: *Who was head of surgery there in the late 1940s?*

WPH: *Francis Moore*. He came from the Massachusetts General Hospital. He knew more about medicine, including metabolism, than most internists. He was instrumental in developing the transplant program at "The Brigham."

WCR: *Did you write much of the text in the 2 editions of the book with Sam Levine?*

WPH: In the first edition, I took all the tracings and I wrote some parts of it, but Sam did most of the text writing. In the second edition 10 years later I did the writing. After collecting phonocardiograms and text for the second edition, I took the manuscript to his home and we went over it. I would say with atrial septal defect that there was wide splitting of the second heart sound. Sam said, "How do you teach this?" I said, "By recording and actual listening. Also, you teach it with the knuckles of your hands striking a hard surface which imitate the sounds." I demonstrated that to him. He said, "Are you sure of that?" I said, "Yes." He then said, "Look the other way," which I did and he used his knuckles to test me. I was able to identify all correctly. I then said, "You look the other way," which he did. He too, was able to identify all of the sounds and accepted the importance of splitting of the heart sounds. He had paid no attention to the classification of gallops other than that they were either

FIGURE 6. WPH during his presidency of the American Heart Association.

systolic or diastolic. I knew that in diastole the S4 did not have the same significance as an S3 gallop. The systolic "gallop" was now the systolic "click" of mitral valve prolapse. I collected all these tracings, and he asked, "Was I was sure?" I said, "Yes."

The way the Wolff-Parkinson-White syndrome came about was the following. Paul White knew *Dr. Wolff* who was at the Beth Israel Hospital in Boston. Dr. Wolff told him he had seen some patients whose electrocardiogram showed a short PR interval, a wide QRS complex, and, frequently, associated supraventricular tachycardia. Dr. White also had observed a few similar patients. White also knew *Sir John Parkinson* in London. Parkinson also had several similar cases. Dr. White put these cases together and the result was the Wolff-Parkinson-White (WPW) syndrome. It was in 1950, at the Second World Congress of Cardiology in Washington, DC, that Dr. White introduced Dr. Wolff to Dr. Parkinson.

I remember Dr. Levine telling me that he had observed a few patients in his practice with episodic supraventricular tachycardia, a short PR interval, and a normal QRS complex. Frequently, the patient was a woman >30 years of age. Now everyone accepts the Lown-Ganong-Levine (LGL) syndrome: *Bernard Lown, Frank Ganong*, and *Sam Levine*. Bernard Lown followed me as the second fellow with Sam Levine. *Bill Schwartz*, who married Sam Levine's daughter, was the third fellow.

WCR: *I understand that Sam Levine took exquisite notes on his patients. Was that true?*

WPH: They were short notes on any little piece of paper that he had in his pocket. He wrote with a little "sawed-off" pencil he always carried with him. He told many anecdotes which I still remember—an excellent way of teaching. Now I do the same.

He took pleasure in showing me the contents of his doctor's bag, everything he used to examine his patients. A thoracentesis needle reminded him of a patient: he followed a little girl who lived close to his home in Newton Falls, Massachusetts, every day. She had acute rheumatic fever and developed myocarditis and pericarditis with pericardial effusion. He hoped that he would not have to tap her pericardial sac to remove the fluid. The effusion persisted, she showed no improvement, and he finally decided he had to remove the pericardial fluid. While getting his instruments out to have them sterilized at her home, he turned to the mother and asked how she thought her daughter was that day. The mother said she thought her daughter was "a little better." With that Sam immediately put the instruments back into his bag. The patient continued to get better from that point on. After hearing this anecdote several times, I almost felt like I had sort of done it, too. It taught me that the mother's observation on her child is so good and accurate that you had better pay attention. I have retold his anecdote when teaching many times.

Sam Levine was a complete doctor. He also was an expert on thyroid disease. He would admit a patient without indicating the diagnosis. If the housestaff did not pick it up they never forgot the diagnosis thereafter.

WCR: *Did he take care of patients without heart disease?*

WPH: No.

WCR: *Did you ever go to his private office to see patients?*

WPH: No. His secretary, however, would write notes to me concerning patients. (She was the worst speller I had ever seen.)

WCR: *Did you go to his home?*

WPH: Yes, many times. Some of the best cardiologists in Boston met once a month in their homes and presented work they were currently doing. Once, when the meeting was in Sam Levine's home, he asked me to present some of our studies on atrial flutter. Flutter waves produce varying PR intervals which cause changing intensities of the first sound. Atrial flutter, and this had never been described previously, produces a certain "PR" interval range: at short intervals the sounds are loud; at long intervals, the sounds are faint. In some patients, the flutter produces sounds that you can hear with your stethoscope. When I arrived, I was ready to show the material on a projector. I had a mental shock. The previous user had not replaced the electric cord. I passed around to this famous group of cardiologists the material I was supposed to show on the projector. Since, I always check the equipment before any conference. Sam was kind and understanding, however.

WCR: *When was it in your career that you realized you had such an exquisitely sensitive auscultatory ear?*

WPH: It was before I left "The Brigham." Colleagues there told me that. I did not believe them.

Then, when the book came out as I was leaving Boston, others began paying more attention.

WCR: *Did Sam Levine imitate the murmurs and sound like you do?*

WPH: He might imitate a faint aortic diastolic blow after examining a patient on the ward. I had not heard it until he did that. I realized starting then that if the sounds and murmurs could be imitated that learning would be easier. He imitated some murmurs but not to the extent that I do today. I saw what could be done by making the sounds. You can talk about sounds all your life. It is like a child learning the tick of a clock. You can say, this ticking has a certain frequency and decibels and rhythm, but cannot comprehend what you are talking about until you show the child an actual ticking clock, and then the learning is immediate.

The 200 or so who attend our annual course on auscultation and clinical heart disease all make "high pass" on hearing murmurs and sounds. Ours is the only such course in the world. We examine 150 to 200 patients during our course. Each participant of the course has a high fidelity ear phone to listen by means of infrared or FM radio transmission. Today, many physician assistants and nurses attend our course. Now, they often are the ones who do the initial work-ups of patients. That is okay. They are "sponges" and I welcome their coming. A nurse told me that she would see the patients first and then the doctor would. He might put his stethoscope on the patient to listen through the shirt or blouse (a real no, no), and then order tests.

WCR: *Proc, you met a young lady named "Irma" in Boston. How did that come about?*

WPH: I had an illness that I think was subclinical hepatitis. During it, I came home to Lynchburg, and while there I worked on the second edition of the Levine-Harvey book. I wrote the new text material and did all the lettering of the diagrams, among other things. I then went back to "The Brigham" Hospital for additional recuperation. One nurse who helped look after me when I was hospitalized introduced me to Irma. I liked her immediately. Later, I asked her for a date. She said "yes." Then I gave her a choice of going to the Boston College football game, which I hoped she would like to do, or going to the symphony. She said, "Let's go to the symphony." We still do. We often laugh about that.

Starting with *Dr. Henry Christian* years ago (he was the first Physician-in-Chief at "The Brigham"), no houseofficer could get married while a houseofficer at "The Brigham." No nurse was allowed to marry during her training. I was chief resident when Irma and I wanted to get married after dating for a year or so. I knew I had to get some rules changed, especially from the Director of Nursing. I decided to work from "the top down." I went first to my chief of medicine, Dr. Thorn, and said, "Dr. Thorn, Irma and I would like to get married." He said "wonderful, wonderful," a favorite saying of his. Then I went to *Dr. Norbert Wilhelm*, Medical Director, and said, "Dr. Wilhelm, I want to get married to one of the nurses. I have seen Dr. Thorn (who was his chief) and Dr. Thorn said,

'wonderful, wonderful'." So he said that it will be "wonderful." We then had to get permission from Irma's boss, the head of nursing. When I got to her and said that I had the permission of the key people, including her boss, Dr. Wilhelm, the Medical Director, I said, "They both said 'wonderful'." Thus, we broke that rule. Physicians today would not even know that that used to be the rule and what I did for them.

WCR: *Irma was from where originally?*

WPH: Nashua, New Hampshire, just across the border from Massachusetts.

WCR: *So you, a young fellow from Lynchburg, Virginia, married a Yankee girl, in 1949.*

WPH: Yes. I was 31, and she was 23. She likes the South. She was a beautiful girl, and still is.

WCR: *Proc, how did you get to know Henry Christian?*

WPH: There are all types of stories about him. He was a strict disciplinarian. He established the marriage rule. I was told that his feelings were hurt when he stepped down as Chairman of the Department of Medicine, when *Soma Weiss*, a brilliant man, replaced him. Unfortunately, Weiss died shortly thereafter after making his own diagnosis of ruptured intracerebral aneurysm. Some erroneously thought that Christian had not stayed "up to date," an accusation he resented. *Dr. Robert Monroe*, Dr. Christian's physician (and trained by Dr. Christian), told me one day: "I have told Dr. Christian to see some young people. He is going to give you a call." Sure enough, a couple of days later, Dr. Christian called and said: "I want you and your wife to come to Longwood Towers at 1:00 P.M. next Sunday for lunch." He did not say "can you come." We went over half-scared to death because I had heard all types of stories about him. At lunch, fruit was on the menu, both canned and fresh. We wanted the fresh, but before we could say so, he said we would all take the canned fruit. He was a delightful man. We then went back to his apartment. He had original paintings by some famous artists. His wife had developed mental changes, and she was in a nursing home. He was alone. We stayed probably until 5:00 P.M. He told us about many famous people in medicine. For example, he said this about a well-known physician, "You can't trust what he says." About others: "superb."

Later, I said, "Dr. Christian, as chief resident, we have housestaff come over to our apartment on Sundays for breakfast. We had a fourth floor walkup apartment on Queensbury Street (I paid $37.50 a month rent for the apartment.) Would you like to come?" He did and came over often thereafter. We then became even better friends. After a few times, he said, I want you to call me "Uncle Henry." I said, "Yes sir, Dr. Christian, I mean Uncle Henry." He enjoyed coming over with the younger people. We probably got him back to where he never would have gotten back to before without the contact with young physicians. He liked Irma. I remember her saying "Hold on to your fork, Uncle Henry," because we did not have much silverware. Later, at the meetings in Atlantic

FIGURE 7. WPH while teaching at Georgetown University.

dent. We were friends. Since Georgetown needed someone in cardiology, Rath told Jeghers that a friend of his was at "The Brigham" and that he is ready to go somewhere. Harold Jeghers came to see me. Jeghers came into the chief resident's room. I can still see him in a very comfortable leather chair with his feet up on the desk. He took his coat off. I liked him and I agreed to come to Georgetown to head up cardiology. He was a big man and his head slanted forward. He was called "the moose." Jeghers changed Georgetown quickly. The students at first rebelled a bit. They placed signs about: "The moose is watching you." It did not take long to break down the rebellion. We talked to the students about internships and genuinely tried to help them. *George Schreiner* also came several years later. *Lawrence Kyle* had already come as Head of Endocrinology. *John Curry*, who had been at the Boston City Hospital, came to head the pulmonary division. These changes turned the school around.

WCR: *You were attracted to the idea of coming back to Washington, DC, because it was close to Virginia?*

WPH: No. I could have gone to several places—California, Ohio, and Virginia. I was told by Jeghers that if I came to Georgetown to head cardiology that I would have a free hand. *Charlie Hufnagel* came at the same time to be Professor of Cardiovascular Surgery. It was purposeful that the 2 of us were invited to come. I remember Charlie's dog lab. It was a mess when he arrived—very discouraging. I remember someone coming up to him and saying, "Dr. Hufnagel, I don't know who is going to send you a patient, and if they send you one, who is going to diagnose the condition for you?"

The outpatient clinic was my responsibility. We had a woman there who was dying from severe aortic regurgitation and advanced heart failure. I had earlier presented some of his dogs at grand rounds at "The Brigham." These dogs ran around with plastic valves in their aortas. They looked healthy and happy. I had recorded phonocardiograms in a couple of them. I said to Charlie, "Why don't you put a valve in this patient?" He perked up and he did. The patient lived. That operation had never been done before. We were accused of putting foreign material into a patient. The newspapers said it was awful about the doctors at Georgetown putting "a cancer-causing plastic" in a patient. After placing the artificial plastic valve in the descending aorta, the ceramic-tiled operating room amplified the valve sounds. You could hear "click click, click click" sounds. They were pretty loud. Hufnagel closed the chest and you could still hear the loud sounds. I thought this would drive the woman

City, Irma and I met him and sat in one of the alcoves and chatted. I remember his saying, "the most common author we have today is et al." He hated multiple authorship articles. I agree with him.

Bill, you know there are usually only 2 or 3 people who really work on a manuscript. I always said at Georgetown, "We are not a paper mill. If something is good we report it and if possible, I want the youngest person on the manuscript to be the lead author." Anyone who has not really done anything is not included. I refused to put my name on something I really had not been a significant part of. It is so common today that a head of the department puts his name on everything. Christian edited Osler's *Textbook of Medicine* for several editions. I had heard that in one of them his foreword was, "Wisely or unwisely I have consulted no man in preparation of this textbook."

WCR: *How did the Washington, DC, move come about? How were you offered the head of cardiology at Georgetown?*

WPH: Harold Jeghers had just taken over from *Wallace Yater* as Head of Medicine at Georgetown. (Yater left to establish the Yater Clinic in Washington, DC.) *Charlie Rath* came to Georgetown from "The Brigham" as the hematologist when I was chief resi-

crazy. We had not thought of that because the dogs didn't seem bothered by the noise. That first night she was doing okay. I listened over her abdomen. The air in the stomach made the artificial valve sound like an alarm clock, and a cheap one at that. I put a sign at the foot of the bed saying, "Please do not discuss the sound of this valve with the patient." No one did, but 5 days later, I asked, "Does the sound of the artificial valve bother you?" She said, "No, it would bother me if I did not hear it." That is the way she took it. She lived about 6 years with the prosthesis. She died at a second operation. By this time, the original valve made less noise than when it was put in. She said she wanted her original valve back. She had some separation of the aorta at one attachment of the prosthesis. She worked in the hospital as an electrocardiographic technician. That helped because she would see other patients and say I have the prosthesis and am doing all right. One day after the first operation, she got in a cab and in a few minutes the cab driver cocked his head and listened. He then stopped the cab and listened more. Then he turned off the motor and listened again. He then got out of the car and looked under the hood. Then it dawned on her that it was her prosthetic valve that was making the noise.

Another story concerned a possible bomb going off in a movie theater in London. It had not been long after World War II. The patient at first did not realize why people seated near her started to leave the movie theater. She then realized that her prosthetic valve sounds were reminiscent of a bomb ticking during the war. Another patient with the prosthetic valve was presented at an American Heart Association meeting in California. He could back up against the wall, open his mouth, and the prosthetic valve sounds were clearly heard. Everybody there could hear it. Someone said, "Does the sound of that valve bother you?" He said, "No" then he paused and said, "At times it does. I like to play poker and when I get a good hand it may give my hand away." Another patient, with a sort of crazy sense of humor, took delight in going to a new doctor and saying I have something wrong with my throat. The loud valve sounds were easily heard without a stethoscope. One doctor after looking in his mouth and looking real puzzled said, "Son, are you being followed somewhere?" He said he was being followed at Georgetown Hospital. The doctor said, "Son, my advice to you is to go there as quickly as you can."

WCR: *Proc, when you came to Georgetown in 1950, were you on salary? Could you earn money from private practice?*

WPH: As I remember, I made $6,000 to $8,000 annual salary. I got $50 to go to Walter Reed Hospital, $50 to go to Bethesda Naval Hospital, and $50 to go to The Old Soldier's Home. I never made a lot of money. I was making $30,000 a year after being at Georgetown for quite a while. I was offered the Chief of Cardiology at the new University of Arizona School of Medicine in Tucson. I was also offered the Chairmanship of Medicine at the University of Miami. When I would get a good offer elsewhere, George-

town would then raise my salary a bit. I never had the usual type of private practice, but I did see patients in consultation with their own physician. I'd tell the patients that I would not follow them as a primary physician. "He referred you to me. Go back to your own doctor, and then if there is another problem, I will see you again." It worked.

WCR: *You were head of cardiology at Georgetown from 1950 to 1985, about 35 years. When you first came to Georgetown in 1950 did you have in mind what you wanted to create here or did that grow with you?*

WPH: That grew with me. All I wanted to do was excellent work and not compromise. At first, I had to do everything. There was only one other person I worked with, a man who had spent a year with the great *Frank Wilson* (of the University of Michigan in Ann Arbor, who taught electrocardiography to thousands). This person was a nice man with a loud belly laugh. I needed help and I thought he could work with me. He read the electrocardiograms. I quickly learned, however, that if I had him conducting a conference I had better be there to take it over. He was an alcoholic. He simply did not show up for many conferences. He would go for several weeks without reading the electrocardiograms. We covered for him. Then *Recep Ari* ("Reggie") came to Georgetown. Reggie came from Turkey via England and Vermont and then to Georgetown as a special fellow to learn electrocardiography.

WCR: *When did you take your first fellow in cardiology?*

WPH: It must have been 1951 or 1952.

WCR: *Your first fellow was Jack Stapleton. In the 35 years that you were head of cardiology, how many fellows did you have?*

WPH: I don't know the exact number, probably >200. What a group of great people! They have gone all over the country and had great influence. Initially, we got a $25,000 annual grant from the government to train cardiologists. A number of university training centers did that at the time. I would take 3 days a year for interviews. We would interview probably 75 top applicants and the other full-time faculty also interviewed them. We would grade them 1 to 6, 6 being the best. I looked for somebody with dedication, empathy, and teamwork—no prima donna. I think I know people. If I have any expertise, I can spot the right type of person. I would see a person who had the right qualities. I would say "Let's go to lunch and spend a little more time together." The opposite would be somebody who I knew was interested only in making a lot of money. This would come out quickly, and I would say, "Thank you for coming." I would not take anybody without his or her coming for an interview. I always told them that we did not have much money. Usually, the ones we took never asked what they would get paid. I told them that they needed to look on the fellowship as postgraduate medicine. We did not need them to run cardiology. If we can get more money, we will.

WCR: *When did you start your citywide Thursday night conferences from 8:00 to 10:00 at Georgetown Hospital?*

WPH: Almost 50 years ago.

WCR: *As you look back over your professional career, what accomplishments are you most proud of?*

WPH: I think the students and fellows. The payment was the pleasure of seeing them develop into a superb doctor. I do not look on a person who could make "all the money in the world" as the greatest success in life. Recently, I was asked to speak to our sophomore medical students for an hour on a subject of my choosing. Just before finishing I told them, "I hope you are not in medicine to make a lot of money. If that is the case, and if I were on the admission board, I would not let you in." I said, "What do you want when you end up your stay on this earth? Not money." I said, "Go to a resort in the middle of winter where people could not be without having been financially successful. There they are by a big pool or ocean with a cabana baking in the sun and often not swimming. You look at them and they don't look happy. There is no one laughing. They must be saying 'What is wrong? Here I have made it financially and I am not happy.' The answer is that to be what I call "successful" you have to contribute to society and you have the respect of your fellow men and women." The students all applauded. I felt good because I knew we still had fine young people and that spoke for them.

At Duke, as a senior medical student, I was once on the Kempner diet. The first dean at Duke, *Dr. Wilburt Davison*, had trained at Cambridge, and like most other faculty members was from the Johns Hopkins Medical School. Everyone loved the dean. He wrote a nice little book called *The Compleat Pediatrician*. Remember Isaac Walton's book—*The Compleat Angler*. (His book title was obviously a spin-off of his Cambridge University experience.) He was a lovable, balding, and overweight man with a mustache, and he smoked a pipe. I thought all deans were like him. On rounds we, including the Dean, all took little folding camp stools, sat by the crib, and then he would go over the case. (Don't stand when you can sit.) It was nice. I got bronchitis when a senior medical student (probably from one of the children) and I learned that the dean had had the same thing and that he took sulfathiazole. I reasoned that if the dean took it, it must be a good drug. That showed how naïve I was. I took sulfathiazole and it was not long before I became febrile and ached all over. I went to the dispensary and the doc on call was a classmate who advised that I take sulfathiazole. I said "no" because I believed that it was that drug that was making me feel so terrible. I had casts, red cells, white cells, and albumin in my urine. I had toxic nephritis from the drug. One faculty member, *Dr. Nicholson*, believed in a high protein diet for nephritis. *Dr. Kempner* believed in a low protein and low salt diet for nephritis. Although I hoped I would get Dr. Nicholson (because then I would get steaks), I got Dr. Kempner, who prescribed his rice diet with raisins and syrup but no salt and no protein. It tasted like paper. I was on that famous Kempner rice diet for

6 weeks. I learned a lot from him. He visited me everyday, and I looked forward to his coming to see me daily. I resolved that I would never have a patient who I did not see everyday. It was fortunate that I had Dr. Kempner because the worst thing I could have had was the high-protein diet. I learned he had patients who could not even read the big print of a newspaper, and after the rice diet, they could read the fine print. Subsequently, he added spinach to my diet, but it tasted just like all the other foods because there was no salt in it. When I started as an intern, I still had abnormal findings in my urine. I had no permanent residue, however.

We need to spend more time with patients. Never give a patient the impression that you don't have time for them. The chief technician of our echocardiography unit on returning from a visit to her gynecologist said, "I was up in the stirrups. The doctor came in and looked at his watch and said we have 5 minutes." I said, "Ruth, I am getting you another doctor. You don't want a doctor who has just 5 minutes for you." I refuse to see anybody in 5 minutes, which I could do. I don't want to be treated that way and I am not going to do it to others. I tell all students and house officers to take time with patients, and in this way you will practice proper medicine. That also saves the taxpayer money because proper examination allows diagnosis of an innocent murmur or mitral valve prolapse, for example, and then it is not necessary to have expensive laboratory tests.

I used to go to the State Department as a consultant in cardiology once or twice a week if I was in town. I often still take 60 to 90 minutes to see every patient. If told to take only 5 to 15 minutes to see a patient, I'd say, "You get somebody else." I try to impart that to those working with me. Take the time needed to carefully examine the patient! About 1 of 3 patients I see has a precordial murmur. Frequently, I see patients who have an innocent murmur. Most physicians do not know how to tell an innocent murmur from a significant one. I tell patients: "You have an innocent murmur. It doesn't mean anything." One patient remarked that she was pleased and then several moments later said: "Does that mean that I stand guilty?" And I said "yes."

WCR: *When you came to Georgetown medical center in 1950, how many medical students were there in each class then?*

WPH: One hundred. Now there are 200. I did not like the increase.

WCR: *You must be a bit disappointed with the way medicine has gone, managed care, and all. How do you think it is going to shake out 20 years from now?*

WPH: I don't know.

WCR: *You must also be a bit disappointed about the auscultatory skills of today's new physicians.*

WPH: In a report in *JAMA* several years ago, over 500 young doctors were given a test on 12 basic auscultatory findings. They averaged a score of 20 out of 100. Subsequently, a piece in *USA Today* was entitled, "Hear anything, doc?" It told about what they called the doctors' "lead ears"; how appalling it was.

FIGURE 8. WPH and Irma at Longwood Gardens, Pennsylvania, in 2000.

FIGURE 9. WPH's grandsons: Proctor Harvey Trivette (left) and Alex Trivette (right).

I was getting more upset as I read it, and then I realized that I had been saying the same thing for years. It is absolutely true. There are so many medical students and houseofficers coming out today who don't know how to examine a patient.

WCR: *Tell me about your children.*

WPH: I've been lucky that I had a wife like Irma and my children. The sad thing was losing 2 of our 3 children. I try to understand why 2 of our children died. I can't. One son died with cerebral palsy at the age of 5. Our son *Crick* was a "straight arrow." Everyone loved him. He had mitral valve prolapse. I think he is the only one who died suddenly of thousands of patients I've seen with mitral valve prolapse. Irma has mitral valve prolapse also.

WCR: *Does your daughter have it?*

WPH: No. She is a wonderful daughter (Janet), and married to a wonderful man (George), a radiation oncologist. Irma and I also have 3 great, loving grandsons.

WCR: *What is your age now? What projects are you working on now? Do you still come to the hospital every day?*

WPH: I'm 83. Oh yes, I come here daily. I've worked on numerous teaching projects and medical publications with *Dave Canfield* and *Doug Canfield* of Laennec Publishing. Anything I put out, I have a publisher. Laennec Publishing was formed for that purpose. Laennec invented the stethoscope. That is why we took that name. There are so many kind things that have been done for me. I'm proud of everything I've been tied up with in teaching and education.

WCR: *You've told many anecdotes about prominent individuals you have known through the years.*

WPH: I give a talk called "Anecdotes in Medicine." I tell about different people. For example, *George Marshall*, a great man, was our Chief of Staff in World War II. *General Tom Mattingly* told me that Marshall's wife had a bad rheumatic heart with many complications, including heart failure. The last thing Marshall wanted therefore was a rheumatic heart like his wife had. Then, apparently when Marshall was a Colonel, Dr. Mattingly told me that he too (Marshall) had a rheumatic heart, namely, mitral stenosis. The rheumatic heart had not been diagnosed previously. A soldier diagnosed with a rheumatic heart would ordinarily be out of the Army and certainly not brought up the ladder to the top levels. Here is a twist of fate. If Marshall had been discharged from the Army, we might not have won World War II. Marshall picked *Dwight Eisenhower* to lead the allied forces in Europe. Later, George Marshall was awarded the Nobel Peace Prize.

I know several anecdotes involving *Helen Taussig*. These anecdotes are particularly popular with a combined audience of lay and medical persons.

WCR: *Proc, I understand that you have some strong views on lawyers and malpractice?*

WPH: It is a national disgrace. This problem can be solved by doing away with frivolous medical and injury suits having contingency fees. Instead, for example, take 4 dedicated doctors, 4 dedicated lawyers, and 4 dedicated clergy, or other lay citizens for a panel of 12. A committee of these dedicated people should come up with a fair decision. This is needed! A woman in Chicago spilled coffee on herself in a fast-food restaurant and received 2 million dollars in damages. After a psychic got a magnetic resonance imaging study, he sued because the MRI caused a loss of his psychic powers—42 million dollars in damages. Recently, I saw TV spots featuring a bulldog-like man saying, "Don't let them get away with it. You have a doctor. We are open 24 hours a day."

WCR: *Proc, you're nice. You've certainly been good to me through the years. You have been my mentor. I want to thank you on behalf of the readers of* The American Journal of Cardiology *for pouring your soul out like this.*

WPH: It has been my pleasure.

HARVEY STANLEY HECHT, MD:
A Conversation With the Editor*

Harvey Hecht was born on May 24, 1943, in the Bronx in New York City, where he grew up. After graduating from Yeshiva University High School in New York, he went to Columbia College in New York City, graduating Phi Beta Kappa and Magna Cum Laude in 1964. He then went to the Albert Einstein College of Medicine and graduated in 1968. His internship and residency in internal medicine were at Lincoln Hospital of the Albert Einstein College of Medicine and Mt. Sinai Hospital, and his fellowship in cardiology was at Beth Israel Hospital in Boston, Massachusetts. After finishing his fellowship in 1973, he remained in Boston on the staff of Boston University School of Medicine. In 1974 he went to Frankfurt, Germany, as Chief of Cardiology of the 97th General Hospital of the US Army for 2 years. He then joined the faculty of University of California at Los Angeles, and after 7 years he went to the University of Southern California in Los Angeles, for a year. After 2 years in private practice in Los Angeles, he joined the staff of the San Francisco Heart Institute in 1985. In 1994, he moved to Phoenix, Arizona, to be the Director of Cardiac Imaging and Preventive Cardiology at the Arizona Heart Institute. Dr. Hecht has been the author of 46 articles published in peer-reviewed journals and 2 book chapters. He has been a major advocate of electron beam tomography and aggressive medical management of hyperlipidemia. He is the first and current President of the Society of Atherosclerosis Imaging.

William Clifford Roberts, MD[†] (hereafter, WCR): *Dr. Hecht, I appreciate your willingness to speak to me, and therefore, to the readers of* The American Journal of Cardiology. *This is July 14, 2000, and Dr. Hecht has just spoken at the weekly Cardiology Conference at Baylor University Medical Center. The title of his presentation was "The Usefulness of Electron Beam Tomography in the Treatment of Dislipidemias." Before getting into your topic, could you speak a bit about your upbringing, family, siblings, and schooling?*

Harvey Stanley Hecht, MD[‡] (hereafter, HSH): I grew up in the Bronx, New York City, in an Orthodox Jewish family. I have a sister. I went from parochial schools to Columbia University and from there to Albert Einstein College of Medicine. I did my internship and residency at Albert Einstein Medical Center and at Mount Sinai in New York. My cardiology

fellowship was in Boston, Massachusetts, at Beth Israel Hospital. Subsequently, I was in the Army in Germany for 2 years as a cardiologist. I then joined the faculty at the University of California at Los Angeles at the Wadsworth Veterans Administration Hospital. There, I ran the critical care unit and developed an interest in nuclear cardiology. Those were the early stages of nuclear stress testing. After 7 years at the VA Hospital, I spent a year at the University of Southern California running the nuclear cardiology section. I then was in private practice for 2 years in Los Angeles, met and married a wonderful woman, Dr. Deborah Bernstein, and moved to the San Francisco Heart Institute, where I spent 9 years with *Richard Myler* and *Simon Stertzer*, pioneers in coronary angioplasty. I ran the nuclear cardiology section there and also developed the stress echocardiography section. I published numerous papers both in nuclear cardiology and in stress echocardiography. We have 2 boys, Jared and Asher. Jared is now 13, an expert skier, tennis player, rock climber, and the National Scholastic chess champion. Asher, now 9, is the reigning Arizona chess champion, expert rock climber, artist with 3 gallery shows, irrepressible wit and, with his brother, a future Wimbledon doubles tennis champion.

I became disenchanted with treating patients with coronary artery disease after it was manifested by symptoms and developed an interest in prevention. I met *Robert Superko* at the Berkeley HeartLab and became very involved in extensive lipid analyses. Initially, I went to Robert Superko because I had a strong family history of coronary artery disease. I became impressed with his approach, which was a medically aggressive one. Superko was very much ahead of his time in terms of looking at factors other than low-density lipoprotein (LDL) cholesterol. After 9 years at the San Francisco Heart Institute, I went to the Arizona Heart Institute in Phoenix and became involved with *electron beam tomography* (EBT), formerly known as electron-beam computed tomography.

I went to Arizona—partly because of the job opportunity and partly because it was getting progressively more difficult to practice medicine in the Bay area. On arrival in Arizona, I initially was involved with the standard technology of nuclear stress testing and stress echocardiography, but then became involved with EBT. It was a technology that had been broached to me in San Francisco. It originated at Imatron in South San Francisco. The Imatron people visited us. We heard about it not via medical journals so much, but via advertising. At that time (10 or 12 years ago) there really wasn't much data about EBT. Imatron at the time made its case to the public, and a lot of physicians (especially cardiologists) took great umbrage at this and were angry that the public was

*This series of interviews are underwritten by a unrestricted grant from Bristol-Myers Squibb.

[†]Baylor Cardiovascular Institute, Baylor University Medical Center, Dallas, Texas 74246.

[‡]Director of Nuclear Cardiology and Stress Echocardiography, Director of Electron Beam Computed Tomography, and Director of Atherosclerosis Detection and Preventive Treatment Center, Arizona Heart Institute, Phoenix, Arizona 85006.

FIGURE 1. Harvey Stanley Hecht, MD.

offered a test which insurance did not pay for and for which there was not much supporting data. EBT didn't appeal to most cardiologists, who are more focused on intervention than prevention. The logic of EBT, however, was clear from the beginning—detecting plaque in the arteries for which the calcium was a surrogate.

WCR: *It's not actually a surrogate, it's a part of the plaque.*

HSH: Correct. The whole plaque is not imaged, just the calcified portion of it. The logic of its utility, both in terms of identifying patients at risk and in terms of using it to track plaque progression either in response to no treatment or to treatment, was very attractive. Nevertheless, EBT had to be substantiated by data. Appropriate data has accumulated over the last decade. There have been hundreds of peer-reviewed articles supporting the use of EBT. How do you use the data from EBT to impact coronary artery disease? This is where the attraction of advanced lipid testing became obvious to me. The best results in all the primary prevention trials have been reduction in event rates (cardiac death, nonfatal myocardial infarction) not exceeding 30% to 40%. What about the other 60% to 70%?

WCR: *But in the primary prevention trials using statins the LDL cholesterol did not get to <100 mg/dl. In other words, they had reductions from their baseline, but they didn't have ideal reductions.*

HSH: I agree, and I divide the response to that into 3 issues. (1) Did we do relatively poorly (i.e., 30% to 40%) because, as you're intimating, we did not reduce the LDL cholesterol low enough? (2) Are there known factors that we should be treating besides LDL cholesterol, including small dense LDL of which high-density lipoprotein (HDL) and triglyceride abnormalities are often the surface manifestation, lipoprotein (Lp(a)), homocysteine, etc.? (3) Perhaps there are causal agents about which we have no knowledge, no clue yet. I came to the conclusion that it's probably a combination of all 3. But, of course, this is yet to be proven. My approach, therefore, has evolved into an

aggressive medical one. The assumption we make is that every patient who has atherosclerosis has an identifiable abnormality which can be treated; to assume otherwise would be therapeutic nihilism. The other major issue, besides aggressive treatment, is aggressive identification of those people who are at particular risk. Correlating the results of EBT with standard lipid panels has demonstrated that the conventional approach recommended by the National Cholesterol Educational Program (NCEP) guidelines is inadequate in identifying those patients who are at particular risk. We looked at this issue in almost 1,000 patients who were asymptomatic and who had EBTs; approximately 55% of the middle-aged patients had calcified plaque and 45% had no evidence of calcified plaque. We found that had we used NCEP criterion to identify those patients who had plaque or who didn't have plaque, we would have been correct approximately 50% of the time, which is no better than a flip of a coin. To me, the fundamental flaw in the way we practice medicine nowadays in general and in preventive cardiology, in particular, is that we look at studies involving thousands of patients (the primary prevention trials or the Framingham study, for example) and we reach conclusions based upon average levels. Increased risk is assigned to a patient on the basis of the number and magnitude of their risk factors. It is an unwarranted leap of faith to extrapolate from a study involving thousands of patients to a single patient who may or may not have disease as predicted by those large studies. What EBT offered was an opportunity to make an accurate judgment for the individual patient as to whether or not he or she had calcified plaque without having to guess based upon whether or not they had an LDL cholesterol or an HDL cholesterol at a specified level, or a particular blood pressure, or whether other family members had heart disease, or whether the patient was or was not a smoker. Reaching conclusions based upon risk factors is simply a guess, sometimes educated, sometimes not. The EBT tells what the effect of all the risk factors are on that person's life and eliminates the guesswork.

WCR: *You are the first to correlate what is seen by EBT to the lipoprotein numbers and particle sizes, to Lp(a), and to homocysteine. Nobody else has this data. Is that proper?*

HSH: Yes.

WCR: *Where have you published your data?*

HSH: Our data was presented at the American Heart Association's Annual Scientific Sessions in Atlanta in November 1999.

WCR: *Is the manuscript in preparation?*

HSH: One manuscript is currently being reviewed by *The American Journal of Cardiology*. Another manuscript on EBT in women has been submitted to *The Journal of the American College of Cardiology*. A third manuscript looking at the LDL subclass profiles is in preparation.

WCR: *You are doing an EBT on everybody sent to you for a cardiovascular evaluation, irrespective of whether they have or do not have symptoms or other signs of myocardial ischemia?*

HSH: Most patients we see are self-referred and 99% of them have no symptoms. Patients with established coronary disease are in a different category; they may benefit by establishing a baseline calcium score which can then be re-evaluated over the years to judge the effects of secondary prevention efforts.

WCR: *Who do you do the lipoprotein analyses (number plus particle sizes), Lp(a), homocysteine, and chlamydia assessments on?*

HSH: We do a standard lipid profile on everyone, advanced lipoprotein analyses on those with plaque, and chlamydia titers only in those with EBT-demonstrated coronary calcium and no detectable lipid abnormalities.

WCR: *You do the EBT first?*

HSH: Yes.

WCR: *If there is zero coronary calcium, lipoprotein particle sizes are not determined?*

HSH: Correct. If they have a zero calcium score, I am much more conservative in my treatment. The purpose of EBT is to find patients who need aggressive drug therapy and to avoid drug therapy for those who do not need it. We're trying to get away from treating patients on the basis of their lipid numbers without demonstrating coronary disease.

WCR: *Suppose you have a healthy 65-year-old asymptomatic man with a total cholesterol of 220, LDL cholesterol of 150, HDL cholesterol of 35, and very low-density lipoprotein cholesterol of 35 mg/dl (triglyceride 175 mg/dl) and no coronary calcium by EBT. Do you treat that patient?*

HSH: I would treat that patient with diet and life style modifications. I would not put that patient on lipid-lowering drugs.

WCR: *If you take the same numbers, the same aged patient, and there is calcium by EBT, irrespective of what the calcium score is, would you treat that person?*

HSH: Yes. The presence of coronary calcium converts a patient from primary to secondary prevention, and therefore, I treat these patients.

WCR: *If you see calcium, you know they have atherosclerosis. They may not have symptoms from it, but they've got plaque.*

HSH: Correct.

WCR: *You do not treat numbers irrespective of calcium in plaque?*

HSH: Correct, unless the numbers are really high. For instance, if somebody has an LDL of 190 mg/dl and no coronary calcium, I treat that patient with lipid-lowering drugs. If the LDL cholesterol is 160 mg/dl, I do not treat that patient irrespective of the level of the HDL cholesterol. I will not treat it unless there is accompanying calcified coronary plaque.

WCR: *I understand that of the 10,000,000 or so people in this country with symptomatic myocardial ischemia, only 50% have ever been on a lipid-lowering drug. Of those on a lipid-lowering drug, the percent who reach goal, namely LDL ≤100 mg/dl, is about 20%. Have you found that telling people or showing people that they do indeed have plaque in*

their coronary arteries has served as a major stimulant to keep them on a lipid-lowering drug?

HSH: Absolutely. There was an abstract presented exactly to that effect. Compliance increases dramatically. When patients see calcium in their coronary arteries, they believe it and they are compliant. And I always present it to them as the proverbial bad news/good news situation. The bad news for the asymptomatic patient is that they indeed do have coronary disease. The good news is that they know about it now, they have not yet had a cardiac event, and they have a chance to alter their prognosis.

WCR: *It is my understanding that you not only use a lot of statin drugs, but that you also use a lot of niacin. Why do you do that?*

HSH: If you look for reasons to explain coronary atherosclerosis by EBT in patients who have subclinical disease, NCEP lipid values explain maybe 55% of the patients. Other factors, such as the sizes of the cholesterol molecules are important. LDL is composed of many subfractions, and patients who have a preponderance of small dense LDL as part of the atherogenic lipoprotein profile are at higher risk than those with larger LDL particles. This is an autosomal dominant inherited pattern present in at least 50% of women with established coronary disease, and almost the same percent of men. It increases the risk of having a heart attack threefold. Treating small dense LDL by increasing particle size has been associated with angiographic regression much more often than has been observed by lowering the LDL cholesterol number. LDL particle size of the smaller density is present in two-thirds of asymptomatic patients with coronary disease by EBT. By adding LDL particle size to our standard lipid measurements, the explanation for coronary disease increases from 55% to 75%.

Lp(a) is another inherited autosomal dominant abnormality associated with an increase of risk of coronary disease. Measuring this factor increases the explanation for EBT coronary disease to at least 85%, and this factor is also treatable. The drug of choice for lowering LDL cholesterol is a statin. The treatment for increasing LDL particle size and for lowering Lp(a) is niacin. It also is effective in increasing the cardioprotective component of the HDL, which can also be measured. Patients with a low HDL 2b2a component compared to the HDL 3 component may be at higher risk and the portion of HDL 2b can be increased by niacin without necessarily affecting a big increase in the total HDL.

WCR: *Statins have no effect on particle size?*

HSH: Statins have no effect on either LDL size or HDL size. Niacin is most effective. Fibrates also have an effect, but not as much effect as niacin, nor is it as advisable to combine a fibrate with a statin for fear of rhabdomyolysis.

WCR: *The chance of rhabdomyolysis is slightly greater with a fibrate plus a statin versus a statin plus niacin. I notice that you use 1,000 mg of niacin in some people and as much as 6,000 mg in other patients. Is the effect of niacin on LDL and HDL particle size and on Lp(a) levels dose related?*

HSH: Unfortunately, the effect from any given dose of niacin is absolutely unpredictable. We have some patients, who on 1,000 mg of niacin, totally correct their abnormalities—their HDL will go from 35 to 55; their triglycerides will plummet, and their particle size will normalize; some patients require 4,000 to 6,000 mg to accomplish the same effect.

WCR: *You use niacin with a relatively low dose of a statin drug, and you do that because of the effects it has on particle size and Lp(a) versus getting a further reduction in LDL by increasing the dose of the statin drug?*

HSH: That is absolutely correct. If I have a patient with diabetes and hypertension, I don't first treat the diabetes and then after getting that under control address the hypertension. I view abnormalities of total cholesterol LDL, abnormalities of particle size, and elevated Lp(a) as separate diseases. It makes no sense to first treat one to the desired level and then treat the other. If I have a patient with a high LDL, I use a statin. If that patient also has small dense LDL, as suggested by a low HDL and elevated triglycerides, I immediately start that patient on combination therapy (statin and niacin).

WCR: *You use niacin, not only to change particle size, but as a very good way to raise HDL and lower triglycerides?*

HSH: Absolutely. Niacin is extraordinarily potent in doing that, and when you increase the LDL particle size, the HDL invariably increases and the triglycerides decrease. Many patients who have seemingly normal-appearing HDL cholesterol and triglycerides nevertheless have the atherogenic lipoprotein profile. For instance, about 35% of patients who have HDLs in the 40 to 50 mg/dl range and triglycerides from 100 to 150 mg/dl levels (levels which most physicians consider normal) actually have the atherogenic lipoprotein profile with small dense LDL. Niacin increases the LDL particle size, will further increase the HDL, and decreases the triglycerides. The ideal profile is LDL 60, HDL 60, and triglycerides 60 mg/dl!

WCR: *What do you consider an elevated triglyceride?*

HSH: I get concerned with any triglyceride >100 mg/dl, especially in association with an HDL that is <50 mg/dl. That's a red flag that this patient may have small dense LDL.

WCR: *Do you consider any LDL cholesterol >100 mg/dl to be abnormal?*

HSH: I do in the presence of calcified plaque. Even though I can't cite data that indicates that lowering LDL from 105 to 60 is beneficial. If the patient has extensive calcified plaque, I believe the lower, the better.

WCR: *You are less likely to treat a person, even though the LDL, HDL, and triglyceride numbers are quite abnormal, if they don't have calcium by EBT?*

HSH: Correct.

WCR: *You're talking about persons over 50 years of age?*

HSH: Not only those patients.

WCR: *Suppose the patient is 35 and they have very bad numbers, but no calcium by EBT, you wouldn't ignore them then, would you?*

HSH: No, I wouldn't ignore them, I would strongly advocate dietary and lifestyle modification. If the LDL is >160 mg I would treat that patient with a statin. If the LDL is <160, the HDL low, and triglycerides high, I would use dietary and lifestyle modification first. If a patient has no calcified plaque, I don't feel compelled to institute drug therapy at an early age. I would repeat the EBT later and if the score is still 0, I still would not implement drug therapy. As soon as any calcified plaque appears, I will start a drug regimen. I feel safe with this regimen because the progression studies, albeit limited in number, have demonstrated that there is never a sudden burst of calcium. We know that as long as the calcified plaque burden remains low that the prognosis is excellent.

WCR: *You would agree that there are some people who have a lot of plaque without any calcium in the plaque?*

HSH: Yes, there are some. About 5% of patients who have cardiac events have zero calcium scores by EBT.

WCR: *Why do diabetics tend to have so much more calcium in their coronary arteries than nondiabetics of similar age and sex?*

HSH: I'm sure that the answer is multifactorial. The prevalence of small dense LDL is absolutely enormous in diabetics and is part of the cardiac dysmetabolic syndrome with elevated insulin levels, small dense LDL, high apoprotein B (this combination is a more powerful predictor of coronary disease and outcomes than the more traditional risk factors), and associated HDL and triglyceride abnormalities. How should these patients be treated? There is fear of using niacin in diabetics, but it is the most effective agent in treating the HDL, triglycerides, and small dense LDL in these patients. That the hyperglycemia will worsen in these patients is unlikely. In fact, hemoglobin A1C levels in patients on niacin is similar to that of similar aged patients not on niacin. Diabetics die of cardiac disease! That's the biggest killer.

WCR: *Or at least of vascular disease.*

HSH: Correct, but the cardiac component is the most responsible one. In the worst scenario even if niacin increased glucose levels, the insulin requirements could be increased. So what? If that is what you have to do to control the lipid abnormalities in diabetics, so be it.

WCR: *Are you saying that, with a few exceptions, most of the 15,000,000 diabetics in the USA should not only be on a statin drug, but they should also be on niacin?*

HSH: I would suspect that this would be the case. They should have their HDLs and triglycerides more closely observed and they should have their particle sizes measured and therapy instituted.

WCR: *Can you roughly assume that if the triglyceride level is >250, the HDL <40, the person is overweight, the blood pressure is elevated, and the* *blood sugar is 120 mg/dl, that the person has the metabolic syndrome?*

HSH: Yes, with 100% certainty.

WCR: *And therefore that person has an excess of small dense LDL versus the large buoyant LDL?*

HSH: Yes, absolutely.

WCR: *But you would nevertheless do lipoprotein particle size and Lp(a) as well as measuring the lipid numbers on that patient?*

HSH: I would. Measuring the LDL particle size is more important after treating the patient than before treatment begins. In the best of all possible worlds, measuring particle size before therapy allows one to better track it. Clearly, the test has some costs associated with it. If the patient who has the numbers you cited (the HDL <40 and triglycerides >200), you know the patient has small dense LDL. You can treat that patient with niacin without necessarily documenting particle size, but then how do you know when to stop?

WCR: *Niacin plus the statin.*

HSH: Plus the statin if there is an associated LDL abnormality. The American Diabetic Association now advocates that every diabetic should have a LDL <100 mg/dl. Every diabetic should be treated by secondary prevention standards. How do you know when the patient's particle size has increased? If the HDL goes from 35 to 45 and the triglyceride falls to 150, is that good enough? That is when you need to measure particle size, and if the patient has converted from the pattern B to a pattern A, fine. If not, then the dosage of niacin needs to be increased.

WCR: *There are not many places in the country where particle size is measured. I presume that you send the blood from your patients to the Berkeley Laboratory for these determinations?*

HSH: Correct.

WCR: *And those determinations include the lipid numbers, the lipid particle sizes, and Lp(a)?*

HSH: The ones that I measure routinely are the total, LDL, and HDL cholesterols, and the triglyceride, LDL particle size by graded gel electrophoresis, Lp(a), and homocysteine. When the triglyceride is <100 mg/dl the likelihood of having the small dense LDL is small, but the likelihood of having an inadequate amount of the cardioprotective HDL 2b may need to be evaluated. I use the HDL graded gel electrophoresis test when the triglyceride is ≤100 with a HDL of 45 to 65 and coronary calcium is present by EBT.

WCR: *What are the various portions of the HDL particles and which ones are important?*

HSH: The important subfractions are 2b,2a, and 3. The 2b component is the more cardioprotective one and the one most responsible for the reverse cholesterol transport.

WCR: *The Berkeley Laboratory, I presume, produces quite accurate values?*

HSH: Yes. They have extraordinary quality control, they have the most experience, and the largest number of articles validating their technology.

WCR: *Do you have a financial interest in that operation?*

HSH: No.

WCR: *Are there other laboratories in the country that measure particle size and do it accurately?*

HSH: Yes, there are. There are other technologies that are used, but they have not been validated against the gold standard of analytic ultracentrifugation as has the graded gel electrophoresis of the Berkeley lab.

WCR: *Which other labs do these measurements?*

HSH: I am aware of 2: *Lipomed* and *Atherotech* and each uses different techniques for the measurements which employ mathematical formulas to determine whether there is small, dense, or large buoyant LDL, but do not directly measure particle size and do not determine the percent distributions of the various subgroups, as does the Berkeley HeartLab.

WCR: *Why aren't there more laboratories in this country using the same technique that the Berkeley Laboratory uses?*

HSH: It's very difficult to do. It requires tremendous quality control. The gels used are difficult to prepare and maintain. It's very labor intensive.

WCR: *How much do these tests cost?*

HSH: They cost from $120 to $180.

WCR: *What do you get for that?*

HSH: You get the LDL particle size for $120; the HDL particle size costs $180.

WCR: *What about Lp(a)?*

HSH: The price is about $40. Measurement of Lp(a) is tremendously variable from laboratory to laboratory. If you track Lp(a) during niacin treatment, you must do the repeat tests in the same laboratory. Even if you do it in the same laboratory, unless it is an exceptional laboratory, there is tremendous variability.

WCR: *What blood do you send to Berkeley Laboratory?*

HSH: Plasma.

WCR: *Do you have to freeze it?*

HSH: No, just refrigerated. You send it off immediately.

WCR: *You send it by express mail and they get it the next day?*

HSH: Yes.

WCR: *Do you use niacin therapy very often as monotherapy or mainly as an add-on to statin?*

HSH: It is the unusual patient who has niacin as monotherapy in my practice for the following reason. I am impressed with the data suggesting that there may be a direct effect of statin on plaque stability independent of LDL lowering. If I have a patient with documented calcified plaque on EBT, small dense LDL, and elevated Lp(a), that patient gets put on niacin. If that patient has an LDL >100, that patient gets put on a statin. If the patient has an LDL <100 and extensive calcified coronary plaque, I put that patient on a statin drug. The LDL will be further lowered. Whether the patient will benefit from further LDL lowering or the direct effect of the statin on the plaque, I don't know. There are trials that are currently under way to determine whether lower is better.

WCR: *Your ideal is LDL = 60, HDL = 60, and triglycerides = 60 mg/dl?*

HSH: Yes.

WCR: *And that person is home free from an atherosclerotic standpoint.*

HSH: I would like to think that, but we've followed a number of patients with serial EBTs over a year and found that despite achieving absolutely beautiful numbers, similar to those or even better than those, there has been significant progression of their plaque burden. This further corroborates the notion that there is a major gap in our understanding of what is the intermediary between a given set of risk factors and the development of atherosclerosis.

WCR: *Or it could be that the values were quite different than that 5 or 10 years earlier or for a long period of time before the patient came to you. You don't know many of your patient's lipid numbers 10 years earlier, do you?*

HSH: That is true. Very few of them actually. Normalizing the patient's numbers later may not bring the process to a complete halt in the short term.

WCR: *If you take somebody at age 65 and you determine their lipid values, that's what those values are at the time you do the tests. They may or may not have been at that level 10, 20, or 30 years earlier. You just don't know. I've kept my lipid values for years, but I keep them at home so that I know what they are, but most people, of course, don't do that.*

HSH: That's true. I would like to think that lipid values are like cigarette smoking. Presumably, the increased risk of coronary disease disappears after a year of having stopped smoking. I would like to think that irrespective of what a patient's lipid values were before they came to see me, if I can normalize them over the course of the year, their past history will not lead to further progression. I make the assumption that any further progression is a result of inadequate efforts on my part or lack of understanding of what I need to do.

WCR: *I agree. If you have an asymptomatic person, no matter how much coronary plaque they have, at this moment in time, if you can keep the quantity of that plaque from increasing any further, that person should be okay.*

HSH: Right.

WCR: *Which form of niacin do you use and why?*

HSH: I always start my patients on *Niaspan*. The reason is because it is a once-a-day drug and once-a-day administration improves compliance. Niaspan is the only niacin preparation on the market which is efficacious in once daily dosing. Compared to the over the counter sustained release preparations, Niaspan has a lower incidence of hepatic abnormalities. There is no niacin preparation that is totally free of liver enzyme elevations. The 2 lowest ones are the immediate-release and the Niaspan. Compared to the immediate-release niacin, Niaspan also is much better tolerated. Because of the slow release of the niacin, flushing is considerably less with Niaspan than with the immediate-release form.

WCR: *You try to increase the dose of Niaspan to what?*

HSH: I start the patient on 500 mg a day for the first month and then increase it to 1,000 mg the next month. At that point, I remeasure the lipid parameters. When I get to the lipid goal, I stop. That's the dosage I will keep the patient on.

WCR: *How long do you keep the patients on aspirin when you initiate Niaspan therapy?*

HSH: Indefinitely.

WCR: *Do you use the 325-mg aspirin tablet?*

HSH: Ordinarily I prescribe a baby aspirin (81 mg) for patients with coronary calcium by EBT if they are not on niacin. The higher doses of aspirin are probably more efficacious in preventing flushing.

WCR: *How often do you do EBT on patients on cholesterol-modifying drug therapy?*

HSH: Once a year. I assess the cholesterol numbers at 2-month intervals until I have reduced the LDL to <100 with the statin and I improve the HDL, triglycerides, and particle size with niacin. Lp(a) is more difficult to treat than particle size. It usually requires much higher amounts of niacin, and sometimes I stop short of what I consider to be a good Lp(a) level because I don't want side effects that would force the patient to totally stop taking the niacin. I want them to at least reap the benefit of having corrected their HDL and triglycerides, even if I can't fully lower their Lp(a).

WCR: *What do you consider normal values for Lp(a)?*

HSH: Anything under 25. If the Lp(a) is >60 mg/dl, it is almost impossible to get it down to 25.

WCR: *Do you always give aspirin when you start a patient on niacin?*

HSH: I put all my patients with calcified plaque on aspirin irrespective of whether I put them on niacin or not. If they are on Niaspan, I tell them to take a 325-mg aspirin tablet in the evening at the time they take the Niaspan.

WCR: *You give niacin at bedtime?*

HSH: I do, because if they flush, hopefully they will sleep through it and be unaware of it.

WCR: *How well do your patients tolerate Niaspan? If you see 100 patients who you start on Niaspan, how many will still be on this drug a year later?*

HSH: About 90% of them, mainly because my patients are extremely motivated because they know they have calcified plaque on the EBT. Some patients are tempted to stop the medication at the first flush. I explain to them the importance of sticking with the drug because the flushing will often diminish over time. Sometimes I divide the Niaspan dose to twice or 3 times daily to increase tolerability.

WCR: *If you have somebody on 1,500 mg of Niaspan you might give him or her 500 mg with each meal?*

HSH: That's correct. If they don't tolerate it in a single dose, I'll divide the dose and find a regimen that's acceptable.

WCR: *Although you want it to be once a day, you don't always live by that.*

HSH: Correct. The only reason to give it once a day is for compliance purposes.

WCR: *What percent of your patients are only on a statin drug as monotherapy?*

HSH: A relatively small percent. Statins lowers LDL most effectively, but they are less effective than niacin in raising HDL and lowering triglycerides.

WCR: *Most of your patients are on both a statin drug and niacin?*

HSH: Correct.

WCR: *You give both the statin and niacin together at bedtime?*

HSH: Yes.

WCR: *Don't you think that giving them together would produce a larger hit on their liver compared to giving one upon arising and one at bedtime?*

HSH: That's possible, but I haven't seen anything to support that view.

WCR: *Do you do liver enzyme baseline determinations before you start somebody on niacin as well as a statin?*

HSH: Absolutely. We monitor both the liver enzymes and the lipids every time we see the patient.

WCR: *How often is that?*

HSH: I do them both every 2 months while I'm titrating. Once I get them to goal, I measure them at 6-month intervals. With niacin I also do a complete blood count because niacin can decrease the platelet count.

WCR: *You do liver enzymes every time you see the patient?*

HSH: Yes.

WCR: *Do you do a creatine kinase?*

HSH: No. If I have a patient on a statin and they have myalgia, irrespective of what their creatine kinase is, they are not going to take the drug. The moment they develop myalgias, I will stop that statin and start them on a different statin. I find one they can tolerate. If I've run out of statins and they have myalgias, I will then do a creatine kinase. If it is elevated, I will immediately stop the drug; if it is not elevated, I'll explain to the patient that they will benefit from a statin if they can tolerate the myalgias. I have no evidence that it will harm them other than causing discomfort. Then the patient has to balance the level of discomfort versus the potential benefit.

WCR: *Are you talking about an elevation 3 times normal or 10 times normal or 2 times normal or what?*

HSH: I've never seen a creatine kinase elevation in thousands of patients I've seen, but I know it happens.

WCR: *What do you tell your patients about side effects of a statin or niacin when you initiate therapy?*

HSH: I tell them that any medication can cause side effects. I tell them the most common side effects from niacin are flushing, itching, gastrointestinal distress, and diarrhea. For the statins, I tell them about myalgias, sleep disturbance, and appetite disturbance.

WCR: *Do you think there is really evidence for sleep disturbance with statins?*

HSH: Anecdotal. I've had a number of patients say, "Boy, I'm having nightmares." I stop the medicine and the nightmares go away. It's strictly anecdotal.

WCR: *The June 2000 issue of* Problems in Cardiology *was quite critical of EBT. Dr. Robert O'Rourke has been quite critical of EBT. Dr. Scott Grundy, in this town, has been an advocate of EBT and has used the phrase "We're as old as our arteries." How do you defuse the criticisms of EBT?*

HSH: There is a newly formed society called the *Society of Atherosclerosis Imaging*, which consists of representatives from the imaging community, particularly EBT, but also from magnetic resonance imaging and intravascular ultrasound, and prominent lipidologists and epidemiologists. We have addressed this issue in the form of a rebuttal statement press release, and more importantly, by guidelines published in the September 15, 2000, issue of *The American Journal of Cardiology*. The issues that Dr. O'Rourke and others (joint committee of the American Heart Association and The American College of Cardiology) have raised are mainly opinions of nonexperts on EBT, and they reflect a basic lack of understanding of the purpose of this technology. The critics of EBT have viewed it as unnecessary testing, as producing many false positives, as costly, and as a marketing tool for those institutions which have EBT. It must be understood that the purpose of EBT is not to get patients into the cardiac catheterization laboratory to demonstrate obstructive coronary disease. It is to keep patients out of the catheterization laboratory by detecting disease in its early stages, and therefore, prevent the sequelae of coronary narrowing. It is not about intervention; it is about prevention. The notion of false positives is erroneous and arises from the relatively low specificity of EBT for detecting obstructive disease, although recent data by Bielak (*Circulation*, July 2000) suggests that it is better for this purpose than previously realized. Nobody in the EBT community has ever advocated that it be used for determining degrees of coronary narrowing. There are many patients with very large plaque burdens who simply do not have significant coronary obstruction. Does that mean that they are not at high risk when there is heavy coronary calcium but insignificant coronary narrowing? That's absurd. That patient is at very high risk because of the extensive calcified plaque burden and associated soft plaque. EBT is not to be used as an equivalent of a stress test. Nobody has said it's to be used for that purpose. EBT actually exceeds the ability of nuclear stress testing to detect coronary disease. Nuclear stress tests only detect vessels that are already narrowed >50%, whereas EBT detects the very early stages of plaque formation. Also, there is no false-positive EBT for atherosclerosis. If calcium is detected, plaque is present.

There is an inadequate appreciation of the prognostic value of EBT and its value as a screening test. A recent World Health Organization report indicated that the USA was number 1 in expenditure per capita for health care, but number 37 in terms of the quality of the care delivered as determined by life span. We are much more interested in the USA in treating the disease and all its sequelae rather than in preventing it. EBT offers a wonderful opportunity to identify those patients that are at special risk, by its use as a screening tool. Paolo Raggi (*Circulation*, March 2000) showed that the yearly incident rate of coronary events in the presence of a zero calcium score was 0.1% per year, and that with a calcium score >400 (considered to be a high score), the annual event rate was 4.8%. That's a 45 times greater likelihood of having a coronary event if your score is >400 than if it is zero. The relative ability of conventional risk factors to predict a cardiac event over a 3-year period is at least 3 times less than that of coronary calcium detected by EBT in the same time period.

The current medical establishment and insurance company approach to EBT has created a 2-tiered system—those patients who can afford it will benefit from it; those who can't will suffer by not being adequately screened. In this country mammography is urged for all women over the age of 45 on an annual basis. And yet, coronary artery disease kills 8 times as many women every year as does breast cancer. It kills more women every year than men, and women are not screened for coronary artery disease using EBT. This test has been termed "the mammogram of the heart." The only reason that EBT has been advertised to the public is because without that nobody would benefit from this technology. The moment EBT is paid for by the insurance companies and endorsed by the physicians, advertising will cease. No insurance company pays for it now except in selected incidences when ordered by a physician to evaluate chest pain. It then may be reimbursed, depending upon the local carrier. In the asymptomatic population as a screening tool, it is not paid for by any third party.

WCR: *How much does EBT cost at your institution?*

HSH: It is $500.

WCR: *And how much does it cost around the country?*

HSH: Anywhere from $350 to $550. At our place it includes a lipid panel and a consultation with the cardiologist.

WCR: *A consultation with a cardiologist means what?*

HSH: The patient sits down with the cardiologist after the test and he or she goes over the results with the patient and discusses what needs to be done next.

WCR: *Do you do a physical examination?*

HSH: No.

WCR: *How much does a nuclear cardiologic stress test cost at your institution?*

HSH: Approximately $1,300. And the nuclear test is worthless for screening purposes.

WCR: *You can do 3 EBT tests around the country for 1 nuclear exercise stress test?*

HSH: Exactly. Rather than increase costs, EBT decreases costs because it tells you which asymptomatic patients need to go for stress testing. If the score is less than a certain level, it makes no sense whatsoever to do a stress test.

WCR: *What you are trying to do in a way is convert the medical dollar from diagnostic testing into therapeutic benefits?*

HSH: That is correct, and directed toward those patients whom you find to be at special risk and not waste the resources on patients who are not at a special risk.

WCR: *How much does the standard exercise stress test cost in your hospital?*

HSH: About $250.

WCR: *Your life before you started with EBT evolved around nuclear studies?*

HSH: That's right.

WCR: *Have you changed your viewpoint on them?*

HSH: I've totally changed my viewpoint on routine stress tests. I'm tired of seeing the consequences of coronary disease. I now direct my efforts towards preventing coronary disease. Even the nuclear people, of whom I am still one, do not advocate that stress testing be used as a screening test because the likelihood of having true positive results in an asymptomatic low prevalence population is quite low.

WCR: *You would admit that the standard exercise stress test is commonly used as a screening test by both internists and cardiologists in this country?*

HSH: Unfortunately it is.

WCR: *What you are saying is that the EBT test costs a bit more, but the answers you get from it are far more meaningful than those you get from the standard exercise test or a nuclear stress test?*

HSH: Absolutely. And there is a basic difference in philosophy. As I've said, any form of stress test is designed to detect the patient who already has significant obstructive coronary disease. It cannot detect the patient who is in the earlier stages of plaque formation, who does not yet have significant obstruction and yet may be at very high risk.

WCR: *Harvey, you are at ideal body weight and you are how old?*

HSH: Fifty-seven.

WCR: *How do you maintain such a straight body?*

HSH: Through considerable effort, including exercise and not eating very much.

WCR: *What do you do every day?*

HSH: I wake up about 5:30 or 6:00 A.M. and go biking through the hills around my home in Paradise Valley, Arizona.

WCR: *That is near Phoenix?*

HSH: Right. It is a suburb of Phoenix. I get most of my exercise through mountain biking. I play tennis 2 or 3 times a week. And I'm on the go all the time. I rarely sit down. There are times that I will see 40 patients in a day who have had an EBT.

WCR: *How many do you do a day at your institution?*

HSH: We do anywhere from 15 to 40.

WCR: *Do you run that operation?*

HSH: Yes.

WCR: *Were radiologists ever involved in EBT?*

HSH: Not at our institution. It has been strictly a cardiology-run operation from the beginning.

WCR: *How much did the machine cost?*

HSH: $1.8 million.

WCR: *If you are doing this at $500 a shot, you'll pay for that machine reasonably quickly?*

HSH: Unfortunately, this is another misconception. It is the rare EBT center that makes money because the costs associated with it are high. You need personnel, the cost of the machine is high, and a lot of money is spent on advertising.

WCR: *You advertise heavily in the Phoenix market.*

HSH: We do.

WCR: *How many sites in the USA have EBT?*

HSH: I think right now it is probably about 50 and it is increasing. Conventional CT scanners are either being retrofitted with the older models or the newer models are coming out with software packages that will give a calcium score. The problem with this technology is that it is neither as sensitive as EBT nor as reproducible.

WCR: *How long do these machines last?*

HSH: A long time. The original models have been around for 10 to 12 years and they are still functioning.

WCR: *Most patients with atherosclerotic coronary disease are overweight and many are obese. Do you get as good a scan in an obese person as you do in someone like yourself who is at ideal body weight?*

HSH: Not quite as good, but invariably a technically adequate scan. The more soft tissue you have to penetrate the less sharp the images will be. But it is the rare patient in whom you have any questions about whether or not there is significant calcium. If there are trivial amounts of calcium it may be confused with soft tissue.

WCR: *The reproducibility of EBT is what?*

HSH: It is to the point where any change of 5% or more in calcium volume (one of the measurements that accompanies the calcium score) is considered to be a significant change. Pfizer Pharmaceutical Company (New York, New York) has designed a study (The Belles trial) tracking postmenopausal women's response to different statins by using changes in their calcium volume to determine whether or not the drug has been successful in halting atherosclerosis.

WCR: *How is a Bronx boy getting along in the desert?*

HSH: Loving it. When I moved from San Francisco to Phoenix people said to me, "How could you do that? How could you leave San Francisco for the cowboy town?" It is simply not the case. Arizona, and especially Phoenix, have really matured. Phoenix has wonderful access to the outdoors, great restaurants, an enormous amount of culture, and for the sports aficionado, it has everything. It is also a fairly progressive medical community with the exception of the cardiologists who are as refractory to the concept of EBT there as they are anywhere else in the country.

WCR: *Where do you get most of your patients?*

HSH: Our patients come from self-referral. They hear the advertising and they come in for the test. Then, by word of mouth. Both patients and physicians who have had the test are invariably believers. I don't know of any naysayers who have had this test. We are seeing increasing numbers of patients referred by physicians. We would love to convert that to 100%. That is our ultimate goal.

WCR: *Have you had an EBT?*

HSH: I have and what I tell all my patients and colleagues is that it is okay to ask somebody if they had the EBT, but it's not okay to ask them what their score was.

WCR: *You are not going to tell me?*

HSH: I am not going to tell.

WCR: *Is there anything, Harvey, that I haven't asked you that you would like to discuss?*

HSH: Yes. The biggest health problem we face in the USA is coronary atherosclerosis. We have an opportunity in this country now to do 2 things: to reduce the mortality and the costs associated with it. They are: (1) identifying those patients at special risk and that can be accomplished by EBT; and (2) once identified, we need to refrain from focusing almost entirely on LDL, but evaluate these patients for all treatable lipid abnormalities, and then aggressively treat them.

WCR: *How did you initially get on the niacin bandwagon?*

HSH: This occurred through my exposure to Robert Superko at the Berkeley HeartLab.

WCR: *On behalf of the journal readers and myself I want to thank you, Harvey, for pouring your soul out, to speak to me and to our readers.*

HSH: It has been my pleasure.

HSH's BEST PUBLICATIONS AS SELECTED BY HSH

14. Hecht HS, Hopkins JM, Rose JG, Blumfield DE, Wong M. Reverse redistribution: Worsening of thallium-201 myocardiac images from exercise to redistribution. *Radiology* 1981;140:177–181.

27. Hecht HS, Shaw RE, Bruce T, Myler RK. Silent ischemia evaluation by exercise and redistribution tomographic thallium-201 myocardial imaging. *J Am Coll Cardiol* 1989;14:895–900.

30. Hecht HS, Shaw RE, Bruce TR, Ryan C, Stertzer SH, Myler RK. Usefulness of tomographic thallium-201 imaging for detection of restenosis after percutaneous transluminal coronary angioplasty. *Am J Cardiol* 1990;66:1314–1318.

36. Hecht HS, DeBord L, Shaw RE, Dunlap RW, Ryan C, Stertzer SH, Myler RK. Usefulness of supine bicycle stress echocardiography for detection of restenosis after percutaneous transluminal coronary angioplasty. *Am J Cardiol* 1993; 71:293–296.

37. Hecht HS, DeBord L, Shaw RE, Dunlap RW, Ryan C, Stertzer SH, Myler RK. Digital supine bicycle stress echocardiography: a new technique for evaluating coronary artery disease. *J Am Coll Cardiol* 1993;21:950–956.

45. Hecht HS, DeBord L, Sotomayor N, Shaw RE, Ryan C. Truly silent ischemia and the relationship of chest pain and ST segment change to the amount of ischemic myocardium: evaluation by supine bicycle stress echocardiography. *J Am Coll Cardiol* 1994;12:373–384.

LESLIE DAVID HILLIS, MD: A Conversation With the Editor*

David Hillis was born in Tyler, Texas, on November 25, 1945, and that is where he grew up. He attended public high school, where he was an all-A student and a star athlete in both football and baseball. He graduated from Columbia College in 1967 with a major in history, took a year of post-graduate work at the University of Texas, and graduated from Columbia University College of Physicians and Surgeons in 1972. His internship and residency in internal medicine was at Parkland Memorial Hospital of the University of Texas Southwestern Medical School, and the last of those 3 years he served as chief resident. His 3-year fellowship in cardiology was at the Peter Bent Brigham Hospital of Harvard Medical School. With that completed in 1978, he returned to Dallas, Texas, and joined the faculty of the University of Texas Southwestern Medical School as director of the cardiac catheterization laboratory, where he has been ever since. By 1988, he was a full professor of internal medicine, and 4 years thereafter he had an endowed chair. Currently, he is the James M. Wooten Chair in Cardiology, Associate Director of the Cardiology Division, and Vice Chairman of the Department of Internal Medicine. Dr. Hillis has written 323 publications, most of which are in peer-reviewed medical journals. In addition to his highly productive clinical work, he has received numerous outstanding teacher awards in both the cardiovascular division and in the department of medicine. He is a major force at his medical center. He has been the husband of *Nancy Addington Hillis* for 34 years. Additionally, he is a great guy.

William Clifford Roberts, MD[†] (hereafter, WCR): *I am in my home with Dr. Hillis and it is August 31, 2002. Dr. Hillis, I appreciate your willingness to talk to me and therefore to the readers of* The American Journal of Cardiology. *Could we start by my asking you to describe what it was like growing up in Tyler, Texas, what your parents and siblings were like, and some of your early memories?*

Leslie David Hills, MD[‡] (hereafter LDH): I was born and grew up in Tyler, a town with about 50,000 people at the time. (Now, it is about 75,000.) It is about 100 miles east of Dallas and about 50 miles from the Louisiana border. My parents, neither of whom had ever gone to college, were determined that their 3 children would be well educated, and they put a very high premium on being well educated. I am the youngest of 3 children; my sister is 5 years older and my brother is 3 years older than I am. Growing up in

FIGURE 1. LDH during the interview.

Tyler in the 1950's and early 1960's was built around a lot of outdoor activities—hunting, fishing, and sports (football, basketball, and baseball)—plus the incredibly high premium my parents placed on excellence in the classroom. I was captain of both my high school football team and baseball team. I attended Robert E. Lee High School, which at that time had not yet been integrated. There was a separate high school in town for people of color. (The Tyler schools integrated about 5 years after I had graduated.)

WCR: *What were your parents like? What did your father do? Did your mother work outside the home?*

LDH: My mother taught kindergarten in a private school, a circumstance that did not require that she have a teaching certificate, meaning that it didn't require that she have a college degree. My father for most of his adult life was a buyer for a local office supplies company. He did that work most of his adult life. Both my mother and father believed that the possibilities were limitless if one truly valued education and pursued it aggressively. No matter how modest one's background might be or how modest one's

*This series of interviews are underwritten by an unrestricted grant from Bristol-Myers Squibb.

†Baylor Heart & Vascular Institute, Baylor University Medical Center, Dallas, Texas 75246.

‡University of Texas at Southwestern Medical Center, Dallas, Texas 75390.

means might be, one could, in essence, do almost anything that one wanted to do if he/she studied diligently. They instilled that in us, not in a malignant or in an unmercifully demanding way, but in an incredibly supportive way. They were interested and very active supporters of everything we did, not only athletic activities, but also academic activities, and they were determined that we would be well educated and that we would go to college. All 3 of us ended up getting doctoral degrees. My brother is a physician in Tyler, and my sister has a PhD in English literature.

WCR: *Where did your mother and father grow up?*

LDH: My mother was born and grew up in Tyler. My father was born and grew up in Wylie, a small town north of Dallas and not far from McKinney. My mother was from a large family. After my mother and father married, they lived briefly on the Texas coast during the war, but by 1942 they moved to Tyler and remained there the rest of their lives.

WCR: *Where did they meet? Do you know?*

LDH: They were married in 1939. I am not sure when exactly or where they met.

WCR: *When did your father live?*

LDH: He was born in 1908 and died in 1969, which was during final exam week of the first year I was in medical school. He had been a heavy smoker and died from oat cell carcinoma of the lung.

WCR: *When did your mother live?*

LDH: She was born in 1916 and died in 1968. She died suddenly at age 51 of an intracerebral hemorrhage secondary to a ruptured berry aneurysm about a year-and-a-half before my dad died. I was then a senior in college.

WCR: *What was your mother like?*

LDH: She was very loving, very supportive, and incredibly generous with all 3 of us. Whatever we were interested in, she was interested in. As wide-ranging and as sometimes foolish as those things might be, whatever they were, she took as much interest in them as we did.

WCR: *What was your father like?*

LDH: He was also that way, but differently, in that he didn't show his emotions as much. He was more reserved, quieter, more deliberate, but generous with his time and incredibly interested in his children. For example, both my brother and I played football and baseball. My parents never missed one of our high school games. Sometimes that required driving 50 or 100 miles on a weekday when we would play in Lufkin or Nacogdoches or Texarkana. It was a family very much built around the 3 kids and built around the notion that our future was bright and unlimited. They were there in every way they could to support and encourage us and to help us to succeed.

WCR: *What was your home like?*

LDH: It was a modest home. My brother and I shared a bedroom. All 3 children shared a bathroom. My sister's room was directly across the hall from ours. We were encouraged and expected to spend time in the evenings studying and reading. Homework was the norm during all evenings. We always ate all of our meals together. Dinner in the evening was when dad got home from work, which was usually around 5:30 to 6 P.M.

WCR: *What were the conversations like around the dinner table?*

LDH: Almost all of them dealt with what was going on in our lives, what we were doing at school, not only with us, but also with our friends, both athletically and academically.

WCR: *Did your father or mother tend to dominate conversations?*

LDH: Probably my mother, simply because she was more verbal. She was more of a "talker" than dad. Both were involved, but probably my mother more than my dad.

WCR: *It sounds to me like both your mother and father were very intelligent people, although they didn't have the opportunity to go to college themselves. Did they read a lot? Were there many books around the house?*

LDH: There were. My mother read a lot more than my dad did. Both were very intelligent. My dad was extremely gifted mathematically. He could do fairly complicated arithmetic in his head. My mother was more interested in books and in reading, and she tried to impart that to us. She imparted it probably more to my sister than to my brother or me. My sister was an avid reader and still is, and has been ever since she was a teenager.

WCR: *Was your home a religious one?*

LDH: It wasn't highly religious. We went to a protestant church ("Disciples of Christ") probably 2 of every 3 Sundays. The church was a not huge part of our lives.

WCR: *When you sat down at the dinner table at night, did you say a blessing?*

LDH: Yes.

WCR: *Are you a regular church member now?*

LDH: No.

WCR: *And your wife?*

LDH: She belongs to a Methodist church here that she attends occasionally. I'm not a member of a church. I have fairly strong personal religious beliefs that I basically have chosen not to exercise through some formal structure like the church.

WCR: *Do you have a dog?*

LDH: No. We have a couple of cats. When growing up we always had dogs. Dogs were a part of our lives in Tyler for friendship and companionship.

WCR: *You mentioned hunting and fishing. Did you do a lot of that with your dad?*

LDH: Not with our dad. My brother and I hunted more than we fished. Most of the hunting we did was with shotguns, hunting small birds, doves in the fall, quail in the winter, nothing bigger than ducks. We fished for bass in the local lakes. I did a fair amount of it. I didn't do nearly as much of it as some of my friends did. With some of my friends, hunting was as much a part of their lives as going to school.

WCR: *Did your family go on vacations in the summertime?*

LDH: Occasionally. One thing we did almost as a ritual was to take a long weekend and go to the nearest city to watch major league baseball. Until about 1960, that was St. Louis, the nearest town to Texas with major league baseball, the St. Louis *Cardinals*. I have vivid memories of listening to St. Louis Cardinal baseball on KMOX radio in St. Louis. We could barely pick it up on our radio in Tyler. Then in 1960, Houston got a major league team, initially called the *Colt 45s*, then the *Astros*, and then our yearly trips to St. Louis turned into long weekend trips to Houston. Rather than being a 12-hour drive to St. Louis, it became a 4- to 4.5-hour drive to Houston. The reason we didn't travel otherwise was probably because there wasn't a lot of money to do so, and both my brother and I were heavily involved in baseball, and we were not anxious to take time off for a family vacation and miss baseball.

WCR: *David, you mentioned that you were captain of both your football team and your baseball team in high school. What position did you play?*

LDH: I played quarterback in high school and defensive back (cornerback) in college. We did not have a terribly good high school football team. I was an average high school football player. I was not a star. What I could do, probably better than others on the team, was pass. Those were the days, however, when high school football was not built around passing. We passed only as a last resort. I might throw 5 passes a game.

WCR: *Did you have a T-system?*

LDH: Yes.

WCR: *So you got every snap.*

LDH: Yes, I got every snap, but I usually handed it off to somebody else as soon as possible.

WCR: *Did you play defense at all in football in high school?*

LDH: No. I played only offense in high school. In college, I played predominantly defense.

WCR: *What position did your brother play?*

LDH: Steve initially was a quarterback, but during his senior year he played fullback. He was a very good football player. He was a much better football player than I was. He had several colleges looking at him seriously. He played 1 year for Tyler Junior College, and then he went to the University of Texas.

WCR: *It sounds like you were a pretty good pitcher in baseball?*

LDH: I was a much better baseball player than I was a football player. I had a couple of scholarship offers to play baseball in college, one at Rice, one at Texas A&M. I played baseball in the summers with a bunch of guys from East Texas who played for Texas, or Baylor, or Rice, or A&M. I also played baseball in college (Columbia University) and we had a very good baseball team. There were some very good baseball players, not only on our team, but also in the Ivy League in general. I pursued baseball with more tenacity than football, probably because I was better at it and I enjoyed it more. I played baseball every summer until my senior year in college.

WCR: *How did you become a pitcher?*

LDH: My brother was a catcher, but that had noth-

FIGURE 2. LDH on the pitcher's mound as a member of the Columbia University baseball team.

ing to do with my becoming a pitcher. I am left-handed. My father played baseball as a young man and he encouraged me to be a pitcher from the beginning.

WCR: *When you did not pitch, did you play?*

LDH: Sometimes I did. Occasionally, I would play the outfield or first base, but most of the time in high school I only pitched.

WCR: *Could you hit?*

LDH: Better than most pitchers, but not as good as most non-pitchers.

WCR: *Did you play basketball?*

LDH: Only recreationally. I never played on our high school team. I was never a particularly good basketball player.

WCR: *How big were you in high school?*

LDH: Six feet tall and 155 pounds.

WCR: *Were you fast?*

LDH: Yes. The one thing that helped me survive in playing college football was that I was very fast. I was fast relative to most of my teammates and our opponents.

WCR: *Did you ever run track?*

LDH: No.

WCR: *You don't know what you did the 100-yard dash or the 40-yard dash in?*

LDH: I have no idea.

WCR: *It sounds to me like you made all A's in junior high and high school and you were a star athlete. You must have been the talk of the town.*

LDH: I'm not sure that I was the talk of the town. Some of the terms that you use probably are stretching it a bit. I wouldn't call myself a star athlete. I was a good athlete by local standards and I did make almost all A's. I was in the top 10 in my high school class of about 220. In Tyler at that time, a number of people were better athletes than I was. Some of my teammates went to Southwest conference schools on football scholarships or on other scholarships. I was among them, but not among the very best.

WCR: *Were there any teachers in junior high school or in high school who had a particular impact on you?*

LDH: Yes. I had a magnificent American history teacher, *Bob Wyche*, in high school. He had the ability, as most really good teachers do, to make whatever subject he was teaching come alive. He had a particular interest in the Civil War, so we spent 80% of the semester talking about 4 years of history, 1861 to 1865, but we learned a lot. *Elton Chaney*, who taught geometry and trigonometry, also was a terrific teacher. He exuded enthusiasm, so it was hard not to become enthusiastic about his subject.

WCR: *Did your mother and/or father have an extended family in Tyler?*

LDH: My mother did. She had 1 brother and 3 sisters in Tyler, so there were a number of cousins. My mother was the youngest of 10 children. Because I was the youngest of her children, almost all of my cousins tended to be anywhere from 4 to 12 years older than me. The cousins were more my sister's and my brother's peer group than mine.

WCR: *Did your father have siblings?*

LDH: Yes. He had a brother who lived in Wylie, the town he had grown up in, and a half-sister who lived in Dallas. We saw them once or twice a year.

WCR: *I suspect that there are not many graduates of Robert E. Lee High School in Tyler who go to Columbia University. Columbia is a pretty expensive school. Did you get a scholarship to go there?*

LDH: Yes. At that time (1963), Columbia was going through a period when they were stressing geographic distribution. They made a concerted effort to recruit a student body, not only from the northeast or from the New York metropolitan area, but from all over the country. As a senior in high school at the time, I was all ready to go to Rice and play baseball. A guidance counselor at my high school called me one day and said there was a man from the Columbia admissions office who was driving through Texas, stopping at various high schools along the way. (The guidance counselor, in fact, had graduated from Columbia in the mid-1950's, having grown up in Amarillo, Texas.) The counselor called me to meet with him. I met with him, and he interested me enough that I applied. I was enjoying life and already had my future, so I thought,

planned as far as what I was going to do the next year. Nevertheless, I filled out the application, and I discussed it with my parents. Had it been left up to me, I probably never would have pursued it. The reason I pursued it was that my parents thought it was an opportunity of a lifetime. Although neither parent had gone to college and neither had lived outside of Texas, when their youngest son was given the opportunity to go to New York to college—even though I had in hand a full baseball scholarship to Rice or to A&M, such that my college would have cost them nothing—they thought this was an opportunity of a lifetime, despite the fact that it would cost them money and I would be moving far away. They thought that this was just the most exciting thing they had heard of. They really pushed me to apply to Columbia and then try to get financial help. The only time they ever went to Columbia University was to see me graduate from college. They did not have the money to make trips to New York.

WCR: *They never saw you play baseball or football at Columbia?*

LDH: They never did. When I came home at Christmas I would bring a suitcase full of film that the coaches gave me and we'd sit around at home (I would borrow the projector from the local high school football coach) in the evenings and watch all 10 football games. Baseball games weren't filmed, so they never saw a college baseball game. Within 18 months after I had graduated from college, both of them had died. They had a big vision of the world, even though their own world was not terribly large. They realized that there was a world out there that one should not be fearful of, and they encouraged all of us to be expansive in our ambitions.

WCR: *Your home sounds as if it was very pleasant and warm. There wasn't a lot of fussing or arguing going on?*

LDH: That's correct.

WCR: *Was there alcohol in your home?*

LDH: There was early on, but after my dad had some trouble with it, he abstained, beginning when I started in junior high on, and he never drank again.

WCR: *What kind of scholarship did you get from Columbia?*

LDH: At that time, several schools (Columbia among them) would give whatever amount of money one needed to make up the difference. My parents filled out a very detailed financial statement, and the university put that through some sort of a formula. They wanted to know what it would take to make up the difference. They usually would give you a combination of a grant, a scholarship, or a loan, plus they provided a part-time job working 10 to 15 hours a week for meal money. In my freshman year (this is in the days when dormitories were segregated by sex), the graduate women's dormitory at Columbia had a formally served dinner in the evenings, and my job that first year was to serve dinner in the women's dorm. In return, I got all of my meals in a little room off the kitchen.

WCR: *How did New York hit you? Here you were*

from a town of 50,000 people, and the furthest you had been away from home was St. Louis, Missouri.

LDH: I had never been to New York. I had only seen some photographs of the Columbia campus.

WCR: *How did you get up to Manhattan to begin your freshman year?*

LDH: By bus. I got on a Greyhound bus in Tyler and 48 hours later pulled into the Port Authority bus terminal in New York City.

WCR: *Was it understood when you went to Columbia that you would play both football and baseball?*

LDH: No, it was understood that I could do whatever I wanted. In my freshman year, I only played baseball. The institution, academically for me, being from a small town in Texas, was very intimidating. I thought that academically I would need all the time that I could possibly muster to survive, and so I didn't want, in the fall of that year, to do anything that would pull time away from studying. That was why I chose not do any extracurricular activities during that first semester.

WCR: *How did Columbia hit you? You were suddenly with a very sophisticated group of people, most of whom, I presume, had gone to private high schools.*

LDH: Probably half of my class was from the New York metropolitan area. They were bright and extremely motivated. All the Ivy League schools at that time were all male, except Penn and Cornell. Columbia was still all male and the women's college, Barnard, was across the street. I guess the answer to your question is that I was terrified.

WCR: *You were terrified of the potential difficulty of the academics or of the city?*

LDH: The city was very foreign, intimidating, but not terrifying. That's probably the right adjective for Columbia as well. I was intimidated at Columbia by my perception that my classmates and my dorm mates, and basically all of the people with whom I interacted were about 10 times smarter than I was.

WCR: *When you went to Columbia were you premed?*

LDH: No. I started out not knowing what I wanted to do and ended up majoring in history. I took some science courses, but I was not a premed. Academically, I had gone to a reasonably good high school, but I had some catching up to. I did that catching up predominantly during that first year. My grades during that first year were adequate, but they weren't nearly as good as they became during years 2, 3, and 4. Academically, I was behind, not hopelessly behind, but I had some work to do.

WCR: *You really applied yourself, particularly that first year?*

LDH: Yes, I did. I think for everyone going from high school to college that this is true. It's not unique to Columbia, but what struck me hardest and was most intimidating and difficult was just the huge amount of reading, at least relative to what I did in high school. It took a semester or 2 to become accustomed to that and to get up to speed.

WCR: *By the time you entered Columbia, had the*

thrill of learning become a part of your existence or did you sort of pick that up in college?

LDH: I more or less picked it up in college, but I have always and continue to be "intellectually curious." I am sure that was something that was instilled in me by my parents. My favorite courses in college were those that I took simply because they seemed interesting and stimulating. In my sophomore year, the course I enjoyed the most was one titled "Tolstoy and Dostoyevski." During that semester, we read about everything that both of them had written. It was 500 or 600 pages a week. But it was a magnificent course. At Robert E. Lee High School in Tyler I hadn't read a lot of Tolstoy and Dostoyevski. I had fulfilled my language requirement because I had taken Spanish in high school, so I had placed out of all but one semester of Spanish. As a junior, I decided it would be fun, interesting, and enlightening to take a language with a different alphabet. I still remember standing in the registration line to sign up to take Chinese, and, at the very last minute, I decided to take ancient Greek, which I did. I took 2 years of Greek, and in that second year we read *The Iliad* and *The Odyssey*—all of the Greek tragedies—and The New Testament. That was a fun thing to do. It was those kinds of things that were the most fun and had absolutely nothing to with science, and usually nothing to do with what I majored in. It had to do with things that I thought would be interesting. If you don't know much about something, the more you get into it, usually the more interesting it becomes.

WCR: *You took courses that both appealed to you and challenged you?*

LDH: Yes, and that broadened me.

WCR: *How big was Columbia University in 1963?*

LDH: At Columbia, the undergraduate part was, and still is, the smallest of the Ivy League schools. My college class was about 700 and now each college class is about 960 or 1,000. Harvard, Princeton, and Dartmouth are all about 1,200 to 1,300 per class.

WCR: *Do you have a handle on how you placed approximately among those 700 by the time you graduated?*

LDH: I made the Dean's List for the last 6 of my 8 semesters, throughout my sophomore, junior, and senior years. One had to have a B+ average to be on the Dean's List.

WCR: *Out of the 700, how many made the Dean's List?*

LDH: I don't have any idea. It was certainly not the days of grade inflation, that's for sure. There were a lot of "C's" flying around those days.

WCR: *You worked hard?*

LDH: Yes. I had the accelerator to the floor. I wouldn't say all the time, but most of the time I worked hard.

WCR: *I presume that you didn't have a lot of money to allow you to play around too much?*

LDH: I could do whatever New York offered that was either free or cheap. And there are a lot of things in New York that one can afford to do. You can go to a lot of museums without breaking the bank, and you could in those days buy standing room for most music performances of Broadway plays, opera, and the philharmonic. When I was in college, especially my freshman year, there was a group of us who loved going to Broadway shows (of course, I'd never seen one until I got there), but we couldn't afford the tickets. There is almost always one intermission at each Broadway show, and during the intermissions the theatergoers spill out onto the sidewalk in front of the theatre (these days it is usually people who are smoking). We would go down to the theatre district, and during the show intermissions, we would mingle with the people who had spilled out of the theater. When the bell would ring to call the people back into the theatre, we would also go in and stand at the back. I have seen the second act of every show on Broadway! I had no idea what went on in the first act, but it was a way of seeing the second act free.

WCR: *You had never been to an art gallery before you went to New York?*

LDH: Correct. Never!

WCR: *How did the New York culture strike you?*

LDH: "Foreign" is the right word to describe it. I had been to a few live performances or other cultural events. Our senior play in high school was about the extent of it. It was a whole new world for me. It was a world, until then, that I didn't know existed until I got there.

WCR: *It sounds like you flourished in it?*

LDH: I did. The first year was not pleasant, and I say that only because I felt inadequate intellectually and I felt "under the gun." I felt pressure. I felt basically vulnerable to not making it. That feeling of discomfort, of feeling, like you've "got to hack it" is not one that feels comfortable. Once I got through the first year, then I became convinced that if I stuck to my work and did my job that I wasn't going to flunk out, and I realized that I could make it.

WCR: *Did you have any thoughts during that first semester that maybe that baseball scholarship to Rice or A&M sounded pretty good after all?*

LDH: No. We had no telephones in our dorm rooms. To make an outside phone call, the pay phone in the lobby of the dorm had to be used. We could only afford for me to call home once a week, and I did so on Sunday evening. I remember vividly calling home those first few weeks and wishing (I had so much pride that I would never say to them "Can I come home?") that one of my parents, in a moment of weakness, would say, "Would you like to come home?" Had they asked that question, I would have said "Yes" and would have been on the next Greyhound bus out of there. But they were smart enough and insightful enough not to ask the question.

WCR: *You mentioned, David, that your parents went to Columbia only once during your time there. Did you go home occasionally?*

LDH: We had enough money for me to go to Columbia in September and to come home in June on the bus, and to fly back and forth at Christmas. I stayed in New York for the rest of the time. My roommate, who I had been assigned by total random drawing, was

from Fairfield, Connecticut (he is now a lawyer in Greenfield, Massachusetts). He and I roomed together all 4 years. He was a swimmer. A couple of Thanksgivings I spent with him and his family. His parents were kind of my surrogate parents while in college. Although my parents could not attend my college football or baseball games, my roommates' parents attended many of my baseball games! They would drive to Boston to see us play Harvard or to Hanover to see us play Dartmouth! Talk about a labor of love and devotion to some kid who wasn't even theirs.

WCR: *What were their names?*

LDH: Mr. & Mrs. Craig Barry. Craig, Jr, was their son.

WCR: *What was your pitching record in high school?*

LDH: I don't remember. It was good. In my senior year, the team that won the state championship came from Lufkin and it had a 35 and 1 win–loss record that year. Their one loss was to me. My pitching record in college was actually better than in high school. The only record I remember was 15 and 2, which represented my combined sophomore year in college in the spring and the summer season record when playing in a summer college league, and my earned run average was of 0.6/9 innings.

WCR: *Did you have a good fastball?*

LDH: Yes. I was going to say "incredibly good," but that's a bit boastful. I also had a very good curve ball.

WCR: *How fast could you throw the fastball?*

LDH: It was in the days before radar guns. I guess "fast enough," but I'm not sure how fast.

WCR: *When you were in high school, did you have jobs a lot?*

LDH: I worked in the summers usually. East Texas has oil and gas fields, and several summers I worked on drilling rigs. To drill an oil well you need huge amounts of water, and often within a few hundred yards of the oil well several teams drill water wells. I worked on those crews drilling water wells to support the oil wells.

WCR: *David, who on the faculty had an impact on you as an undergraduate at Columbia?*

LDH: Three professors, none of whom had anything to do with medicine. There was *Howard P. Davis*, a magnificent art history teacher. I took 2 courses from him—one on Italian Renaissance painting and one on Northern European painting. He was a phenomenal teacher of art, and I have vivid memories of how exciting he made those 2 subjects. He was a world expert on Giotto (the name of the course should have been "Giotto" because we spent the whole semester looking at every one of his paintings). In the Northern European course we studied mainly Jan Van Eyck. The teacher who taught Tolstoy and Dostoyevski was *Bob Belknap*, and he also was magnificent. He would stand in front of the class and read from the work by Tolstoy and Dostoyevski. His copy was in Russian. He would translate it into English as he was reading it himself in Russia. He was a magnificent teacher. *Jim Shenton*, a history teacher, also was magnificent.

WCR: *You filled in some of the holes you had not*

encountered in your first 18 years. There weren't many people back in Tyler with whom you could discuss these subjects.

LDH: There probably were, but I just didn't know who they were. They were not my football and base-ball-playing buddies.

WCR: *How did baseball work out at Columbia that first year?*

LDH: We had an undefeated team my freshman year. Back then, the freshman team didn't play a lot of games. We were 12 and 0. My sophomore year, we had our best team. The Ivy League for all minor sports played in a league called the "Eastern Intercollegiate League," which included the 8 Ivy League schools, plus Army and Navy. There were 2 or 3 members of our team who could have, had they wanted, played major league baseball, and all of them are now physicians. It was an unusual group of guys. There were a group of us who played baseball together and hung out together, and almost all of us went to medical school. When I was a sophomore, the shortstop on that team was *Archie Roberts*, who was all-Ivy League quarterback and is now a cardiothoracic surgeon in New Jersey. Had Archie decided to pursue baseball rather than football, unquestionably he would have played major league baseball. He was a magnificent shortstop and a left-handed hitter. But he wanted to play football, so he played with the *Cleveland Browns* for a couple of years when he was going to Case Western Medical School. We also had good teams the next couple of years, but not quite as good as during my sophomore year.

WCR: *You were in the starting rotation from the beginning?*

LDH: I was. There were 3 of us who were: 2 seniors and me. We didn't win the league, but we should have. We came in second or third that year.

WCR: *How many games would you play?*

LDH: We would play about 25 games each spring season. In those days we did not make a trip to Florida, which almost all of the northern schools now do, so it really wouldn't be very warm until the 1st of April. We played only in April and May.

WCR: *You'd start about 8 games?*

LDH: Yes, 8 or 9 games.

WCR: *You'd pitch the whole game?*

LDH: If I could. If I lasted.

WCR: *What was your record in the entire 4 years in college?*

LDH: I don't know. I've never thought about that.

WCR: *What kind of time commitment was baseball for you in college? You practiced, I presumed, every day?*

LDH: We practiced everyday for probably 2.5 to 3 hours. Most games were on Fridays and Saturdays, with a middle-of-the-week game in the New York area. The games away would be on Friday or Saturday. We started practicing indoors in February and went outdoors as soon as the weather allowed.

WCR: *You're talking about 28 hours a week.*

LDH: Yes, something like that, but it was something I enjoyed tremendously, and most of my teammates did as well.

WCR: *How did you decide to go out for football your sophomore year?*

LDH: I guess I missed it. A number of my friends played football, and I thought it would be fun to do, and by then I was academically confident that I could do it and that I would not suffer academically.

WCR: *I presume you went out for quarterback?*

LDH: I did, but that year Archie Roberts, a senior, was the quarterback and so I didn't play a lot until my senior year. My senior year I was a starting defensive back; one of the 2 cornerbacks. I missed 1 game that year due to an injury.

WCR: *How was the switch from quarterback to defensive back?*

LDH: In my case, it was pleasant. I remembered as a high school quarterback feeling lots of pressure to perform. (Texas high school football is big business, and the whole town would try to convince you that the whole town was riding on your shoulders.) I enjoyed playing football my senior year in college. It was probably the only time in my entire football career that I actually enjoyed playing. The pressure in high school made it uncomfortable, and even today, when I look at kids playing high school sports, I have mixed feelings about it. Learning to be an effective member of a team is something, however, that transcends sports—learning to deal with adversity and failure. Those are life lessons that hold you in good stead forever. I wish that one could impart those lessons in a less pressured environment. I lived in a state where high school football was a passion with lots of people. It's good to be passionate about something—but just not pathologically passionate.

WCR: *It sounds to me, David, that your 4 years of college were very successful. You made the honor role 6 of 8 semesters. You played on the first team in baseball from the very beginning, and you played 3 years of football. How did you decide that you wanted to become a physician? Did all of the other people with whom you were playing sports influence you in that regard? What happened?*

LDH: They did. There were a couple of things. My brother and I grew up in Tyler about 2 houses down from a physician, a urologist, named *Earl Clawater*. Dr. Clawater was very much a role model for both Steve and me. He was the person who first got us thinking about medicine. It was a great help that this bunch of football and baseball friends were guys intending to go to medical school, and all of them did. On baseball trips, for example, a lot of things like organic chemistry were being thrown around the bus. These were a bunch of smart, highly motivated, ambitious teammates and classmates.

WCR: *When did you decide in college that you were going to be premed?*

LDH: Probably about halfway through my junior year. I wasn't sure until then that I wanted to go to medical school. In my junior year I took inorganic chemistry, and in my senior year I took zoology.

FIGURE 3. The Hillis family: *left to right*, Steve (LDH's brother) and his wife, June; LDH and Nancy, Harriet (LDH's sister) and her husband, Jerome.

When I graduated from college, I went to graduate school for a year (in history) and during that year, I took organic chemistry, the science course I needed for medical school.

WCR: *When you actually graduated from Columbia, you hadn't finished your requirements for medical school?*

LDH: Correct, I had 1 more course to go. I had taken physics, zoology, and inorganic chemistry, but not organic chemistry.

WCR: *Did you play football or sports that post-graduate year?*

LDH: I spent that graduate year in Austin at the University of Texas. That's where I met my wife *Nancy*. She was a senior at Texas. We met in the spring and married August 31, after courting for only 4 months. We then went to New York, and I started medical school.

WCR: *How did the University of Texas fit you after 4 years at Columbia?*

LDH: The graduate courses I took were very good. They had a good history department, and the couple of the courses I took just for medical school purposes were adequate. A large state university, in general, is not as rigorous or as demanding as are smaller more intellectually demanding Ivy League schools. At any large state university you can work incredibly hard or you cannot work hard. I was in Austin knowing that I was going to medical school, and so I didn't find that I had to work terribly hard.

WCR: *Did you apply to medical school while you were in Columbia?*

LDH: Yes.

WCR: *They told you that you ought to complete this course?*

LDH: In mid-September, after being in Austin for only a week, I received a letter of acceptance to medical school at Columbia for the next year. Thus, I

had a whole year where all I had to do was pass organic chemistry. It was a great year.

WCR: *What were Nancy's characteristics that attracted you?*

LDH: She was a good student, a business major. (She has been a buyer for JC Penney all her working life.) She had and still has a magnificent sense of humor, and is an incredibly warm and kind person.

WCR: *She grew up in Highland Park in Dallas?*

LDH: Yes.

WCR: *During that year you must have come to Dallas a few times.*

LDH: We did. My mother died suddenly in January of that school year, so I tried to go to Tyler as often as possible to see my dad.

WCR: *That was a real shocker, wasn't it?*

LDH: It was, very much so.

WCR: *Did you apply to any medical school other than Columbia?*

LDH: Yes, I applied to Southwestern. That was the only other one.

WCR: *Did you get into Southwestern?*

LDH: I don't know. When I got admitted to Columbia, I withdrew my application from Southwestern. The person who interviewed me at Southwestern was *Dan Foster*, who is now the Chair of the Department (I am the Vice Chair). Dan now is one of my very closest friends and colleagues and, of course, that was at a time when I was a 22-year-old first-year graduate student, and Dan was in his late 30's. He's 15 or 16 years older than I am. He was a junior faculty member on the admissions committee at the time.

WCR: *Why did you get married after such a quick courtship?*

LDH: It just seemed like the thing to do. When you're young and foolish and as much in love as we were. . . . She had just graduated. We got married and then went to New York. I started medical school, and she started working for JC Penney. Their national buying office then was in New York, and 15 years later it moved to Dallas.

WCR: *That worked out well.*

LDH: It worked out very well.

WCR: *My mother used to give me little booklets of sayings by JC Penney. I loved them. How did medical school strike you? Other than the physician down the street from you when you were growing up, did you have any contact with hospitals or nurses or other physicians?*

LDH: No.

WCR: *In actuality, when you entered medical school, you didn't know much about doctors or what doctors really did?*

LDH: That's correct. Medical school was in some respects similar to college. I found medical school, especially the first year, to be intimidating and very demanding. Remember that I had not been a science major, and a lot of my medical school classmates had been. It was similar to college, in that I had some catching up to do. I managed to do it, but it took a lot of work.

WCR: *Did you have a scholarship to medical school?*

LDH: Yes, and loans also. By the time I graduated from college and medical school, I was in debt to the tune of several thousand dollars, but not nearly to the extent that young men and women are now. We paid it off in a few years.

WCR: *What were some early surprises for you in medical school? Were you intimidated by the quantity of work or by your perception that you were behind your classmates scientifically?*

LDH: Probably both, but more of the latter. I felt that their knowledge of science was much deeper and much more extensive than mine. What I had was qualitatively good, but it wasn't extensive. Up to that point, I had not thought about how necessary it was that I have an extensive knowledge of science.

WCR: *Why didn't you stay in New York for your postgraduate year rather than go back to Austin? Your return changed your life; it determined whom you married!*

LDH: Austin was cheaper. After all, I was a Texas resident, and I could go to the University of Texas at that time for $100 per semester. Columbia would have cost several thousand dollars per semester. It was 20 or 30 times more. The cost was the determining factor.

WCR: *What did your parents think when they came to New York to see you graduate?*

LDH: They were pleased, satisfied, and proud. I was the last of their 3 children to graduate from college, and that was a point of great pride for them. The college was small enough, so by the time I was a senior, I knew the dean and the major faculty members, and I introduced my parents to all of them. The dean told them what a terrific young man I was, and they believed him. It was a time when they saw things come to fruition.

WCR: *Who had impact on you in medical school?*

LDH: More than anyone was *Don Tapley*, an endocrinologist, and my attending physician when I was a third-year clerk on internal medicine. That third year of medical school on medicine was a life-determining experience.

WCR: *It was during that period that you decided on internal medicine?*

LDH: Yes and no. I still flirted with doing surgery. Even when I came to Dallas as an intern in medicine, it wasn't terribly unusual then to do a medicine internship and then a surgery residency. One of the places where a lot of trainees did that was Southwestern. When I came to Dallas as an intern, I wasn't sure what I wanted to do. I considered that I might go into surgery after a year of medicine. I wasn't convinced that I was going to be an internist, and certainly not convinced that I was going to be a cardiologist.

WCR: *What kind of impact did Dr. Tapley have on you?*

LDH: He, more than anyone else, was a role model and a clear thinker. He thought pathophysiologically. He possessed all of the things that all good physicians have—kindness, compassion, and a consideration of patients. He was an effective teacher, he was excited about medicine, and he wanted our experience in medicine to be good.

WCR: *He was on the full-time faculty at Columbia?*

LDH: Yes. Four or 5 years after I left, he became the dean of the medical school.

WCR: *How many were in your class at Columbia medical school?*

LDH: One hundred and fifteen.

WCR: *Did you and Nancy live close to the medical school?*

LDH: Nancy and I lived right across the Washington Bridge in Fort Lee, New Jersey, in the upstairs of a 2-story house. We had a yard and a Texas-like neighborhood. It was a 10-minute bus ride across the bridge and then a 10-minute walk down Fort Washington Avenue from the bus station to the medical school.

WCR: *When did you get a car?*

LDH: We had a car in New York, but we didn't use it much. We'd use it to go to the grocery store and for an occasional weekend trip.

WCR: *You must have had a car when you went to Austin?*

LDH: No, I didn't. I lived with a Columbia classmate who was at the Texas law school, and I borrowed his car occasionally.

WCR: *You didn't get your first car until you were 22?*

LDH: Correct.

WCR: *Did you enjoy medical school?*

LDH: I enjoyed the last 2 years. The first 2 years were a lot like college and not particularly pleasant. The third and fourth years were a lot of fun. It gradually changed the way college had.

WCR: *I gather that you concluded that you had made the right decision to become a physician?*

LDH: Even in the darkest days of medical school, I always felt like I'd made the right decision. At least by the third year, I felt that way. And I still feel that way; I'd do it again.

WCR: *Your older brother was where at this time?*

LDH: He graduated from Southwestern the same time that I finished my first year of medical school, and during my second year of medical school he was an intern at Parkland Hospital. In my last 2 years of medical school he was a general medical officer on an Air Force Base on the island of Crete in the Mediterranean. He spent 2 years there with his wife and his young son and daughter.

WCR: *How did you decide to do your internship in Dallas at Parkland Memorial Hospital? Did you apply to several places?*

LDH: I applied to only 2 places, Parkland and Columbia Presbyterian. My brother had raved about what a terrific medicine department Southwestern had. I came to Dallas as a fourth-year student and did a 2-month student internship (July and August) of my

FIGURE 4. LDH and his brother Steve, a urologist.

FIGURE 5. LDH and Donald W. Seldin, who was Chief of Medicine at the University of Texas at Southwestern Medical Center for 37 years, under whom LDH trained.

FIGURE 6. LDH and Dr. Daniel W. Foster, his close friend and the present Chairman of Medicine at the University of Texas Southwestern.

fourth year. I got to know some of the faculty and decided that indeed it was a terrific place. At that point, both Nancy and I were anxious to get back to Texas. I was told that if I applied to Parkland, that I would be one of their choices. At that time, *Dr. Jay Sanford*, the vice chair, ran their residency program, and *Dr. Donald Seldin* was the chair of the department.

WCR: *How did Nancy enjoy New York City?*

LDH: We both loved New York. The longer we lived there, the more we enjoyed it, and we still tremendously enjoy New York City. To enjoy New York, it helps to have money, and so our experience in New York now is different than it was when I was in medical school. She liked it then, but she likes it much more now because she is familiar and comfortable with it, and I am the same way.

WCR: *How did your medical internship at Parkland, beginning July 1972, work out?*

LDH: It was magnificent. College and medical school were good experiences. Being a medicine intern and a medicine resident in Dallas at that time was a life-changing experience for me. The department of medicine in Dallas at that time was an incredibly exciting and vibrant place. Dr. Seldin had been chair for 20 years, and he had built, what some people thought, was the best medicine department in the country; it was certainly one of the best, if not the best. Every section head was a young, vibrant, dynamic, enthusiastic physician-teacher. *John Fordtran* ran the gastrointestinal division; *John Dietschy* was with him. *Jim Willerson* had just arrived in the cardiology division. *Joe Goldstein* and *Mike Brown* had just arrived and Joe ran the genetics division, and he and Mike were getting their lab set up. *Jean Wilson* was there,

and he also was the editor of the *Journal of Clinical Investigation* (1972 to 1977). *Dan Foster* was there in endocrinology along with Jean Wilson. Those 3 years as in intern and resident were magical. It was magical because of all of these people who were incredibly good teachers. They had a presence. As an intern and resident, I saw them on the wards making rounds, teaching house staff, and students. They were good doctors. They were doing "cutting edge" research in their laboratories. It was an amazingly exciting place. Although college and medical school had been exciting, they did not compare to those 3 years as an intern and a resident.

WCR: *What made Donald Seldin a great chairman of the department of medicine?*

LDH: He was, and is, uncompromising in his insistence on excellence. He demands of himself, and of everyone around him, that they be the best, and there's not a lot of fluff. There's not a lot of praise or "pats on the back" unless they are really deserved. The value of his currency is incredibly high. That is, if Dr. Seldin tells you that you have done something well, take it to the bank. That means you've done it well. What makes him so special? I'll use a term that he would use. He has "good taste," and what he means by that is the ability to choose people well. You have to be able to look at them and not so much see them in what they're doing now, but see them in the potential of what they will be doing 5, or 10, or 20 years from now. I don't think that there is anyone that I've ever known who has the kind of taste that he has. He built this department with good taste. Over the course of 30 years he identified young people who he saw something in, and he was not bashful enough to plan their whole career, if they needed it planned and to bring them back into positions of leadership. He did that with Jean Wilson, John Fordtran, Dan Foster, Joe Goldstein, and me, and with numerous others. He planned my career, in that he told me where to go for my cardiology fellowship, and what I would be doing when I returned. He was not hesitant in doing that, and he did that with numerous other people.

WCR: *It must have been both a surprise and an honor to be selected by him as his chief resident after only an internship and 1 year of residency?*

LDH: In those days, that's the way Southwestern did it. The chief residents now spend an extra year. They are fourth-year house officers. In those days, the way the department operated was that there were 2 chief residents, the 2 Seldin believed were his 2 best senior residents. Doing it that way taught me a lot about leadership. My co-chief resident was *John Harper*, now a cardiologist here in Dallas. John and I were all of a sudden thrown into a situation where a third of the house staff we directed were our peers. They were house officers who we had been interns and first-year residents with. It teaches one a lot about leadership and about interpersonal skills to be their friend, and yet not be their friend if they need to be kicked in the rear or need to be disciplined in some way.

WCR: *How did you work that out?*

LDH: I worked it out probably similar to the way I work out things today. How do you get people to do things they don't want to do, or how do you get them to change their behavior? You cajole them, you prod them, you throw things at them, you scream at them. It's whatever works for them individually. Different people need different stimuli. For some it is just putting your arm around them and telling them that if they ever do that again, you will be profoundly disappointed, and that's enough. For others, it's looking them in the eye and telling them if they ever do that again that they better have a lot of life insurance.

WCR: *It is my understanding that many in those days were relatively fearful of Dr. Seldin? It sounds to me like you hit it off with Dr. Seldin right away. Is that proper?*

LDH: That is proper, but I, too, was incredibly fearful of him. We all were. And fear is not all bad. Fear served me well as a freshman in college and as a

freshman in medical school. The fear of not making it. It was fear of incurring his wrath. But it was no different than the fear I had with my parents; my biggest fear was that I would disappoint them, and my biggest fear with him was that I would say something or do something that was stupid, and he would look me in the eye and tell me it was stupid, and I know that would be disappointing to him. Did he throw charts at me and scream at me? I can't remember that he ever did that. There were all sorts of stories about what went on back in the 1950s and 1960s. He was demanding and he had very high expectations. What I didn't want to do was not meet those expectations!

WCR: *How many senior residents were with you your first year of residency?*

LDH: About 25.

WCR: *So you and John Harper were the 2 picked from 25.*

LDH: Correct.

WCR: *How did you get interested in cardiology?*

LDH: I think largely through Jim Willerson. Jim had arrived in Dallas about 6 months before I did. He had come from the Massachusetts General Hospital, where he had been a medical resident and cardiology fellow, and then a junior staff person for a few months. My first 2 months as an intern were spent in the coronary care unit with him as the attending. Jim, as he is today, was demanding and intense, but all in a good sense. He was a magnificent role model, and he turned me on to cardiology. It was the center of the universe from that point on for me. A lot of it had to do with Jim's enthusiasm, and his being such an incredibly good role model.

WCR: *What were your working hours like as an intern at Parkland Hospital in 1972?*

LDH: We were on every third night for the whole year, and we worked every day. We worked an average of 110 or 120 hours a week.

WCR: *You'd get to the hospital at what time?*

LDH: I've always been an early morning person. I would usually get there at 6:15 or 6:30 A.M. and start rounding by myself, seeing my patients. I would leave for home anywhere from 4 to 7 P.M.

WCR: *And the third night you were on, you were really on?*

LDH: Yes, you were cross-covering all of the other interns' patients, plus you were admitting new patients. So you were busy. Usually, I was able to get a couple of hours sleep, but sometimes it was none.

WCR: *David, I gather that during the course of that year and probably very early in the course of that year, you decided that internal medicine was the thing for you, not surgery.*

LDH: Yes, that's correct. That was largely through the excitement of Dr. Seldin and his department.

WCR: *How did it come about that you went to the Brigham and Women's Hospital (I guess it was Peter Bent Brigham at that time) for your cardiology fellowship?*

LDH: It wasn't complicated. About halfway through my first year of residency or 18 months after I came to Dallas, Dr. Seldin (I had already told him I wanted to do cardiology) said to me: "I want you to go and train with *Gene Braunwald*, because he is the best cardiologist in the world. After you've finished your fellowship with him, you will come back and join the faculty." He and Dr. Braunwald, both then and now, were extremely close friends. I never filled out an application for fellowship. I never had a letter of support. It was one phone call from Dr. Seldin to Dr. Braunwald, and literally in 2 minutes it was settled. I would do my fellowship at the Brigham and then return to Dallas and join the faculty. About a month later, Dr. Braunwald came to Dallas as a visiting professor and I met him for the first time. He said: "Welcome, glad to have you, and I'll see you in a year-and-a-half." It was agreed that I would go there for 3 years and then come back. Dr. Seldin asked at the very end of my chief residency year when I got ready to go to Boston, "Now in 3 years, you are going to come back and join the faculty. What position would you like?" We were sitting in his office, and I remember thinking to myself, "I've never seen a cardiac cath but my impression was that what went on in there was kind of neat." Naively, I said I would like to be the director of the cath lab. And he said: "OK." He said, "Then it's settled." When you get back in 3 years, you'll be the director of the cath lab. That's what happened.

WCR: *What characteristics do you think that Dr. Seldin noted in you that allowed him to say that you were one of the people of his "taste?"*

LDH: I've thought about that. The short answer is that I don't know. I should probably ask him. In my more egotistical moments, I would try to convince you that he saw some things in me that he saw in Jean Wilson, Joe Goldstein, Dan Foster, and John Fordtran, but that's a pretty select group. I'm not sure I'm in their league. What he may have seen was an excitement about medicine, a lot of intellectual curiosity, a tremendous amount of energy and commitment, and a willingness to work hard. At that stage, those were the things that I brought to the table. I was excited about what I was doing, what I wanted to do, and I was willing to work my butt off to try to make it happen. That's probably what he saw.

WCR: *It sounds like he liked you and that he just liked being around you?*

LDH: It was interesting. During the year as chief resident, we spent a lot of time together. Our present chief residents ask me sometimes what was most valuable or what was most fun, or what was most unique about the year as chief resident, and I think it was 2 things: one was learning leadership skills, and the other was the friendship that I developed with Dr. Seldin. I went from being a lieutenant in his department to beginning to develop a very strong friendship that has grown. He and I these days are extremely close friends. Nancy and I take trips with him and Ellen a couple of times a year, and have done so for several years. He has become much more than just a colleague; he's a genuine close friend. That began during that year as chief resident.

WCR: *How did Boston work out?*

LDH: It worked out great. I spent the first year

FIGURE 7. LDH and his wife Nancy.

working in an animal laboratory with *Peter Maroko*, who had come from San Diego in 1972 with Dr. Braunwald. Peter and Dr. Braunwald were working on myocardial infarct size in the very early days. Also, there was *Peter Libby*. When I got there in 1975, Dr. Braunwald had been at the Brigham for 3 years, and he had 2 very active animal labs. One was run by Peter Maroko and the other was run by *Steve Vatner*. Steve was doing chronically instrumented dogs and looking at sophisticated basic cardiovascular physiology. I spent the first 12 months with no clinical responsibilities working in Peter Maroko's lab, and then I began the clinical fellowship.

WCR: *How did you like the lab work?*

LDH: I liked it, I enjoyed it, but I missed patient contact. I was very busy and tried as best I could to be as productive as I could. I learned for the first time about the scientific method. The next 20 months were as a clinical fellow; I went back into the dog lab for my last 4 months of fellowship. Two-thirds of my clinical experience was in the cath lab.

WCR: *Did you have much contact with Braunwald?*

LDH: I did, especially during that year in the animal lab. We had weekly meetings with him, where we presented all our data to him. He was a very effective mentor. He kept very close touch with what was going on in the animal lab and made suggestions and critiqued data. He and I, at that point, also wrote some sizable papers together. Just writing papers with him was a real educational experience. Dr. Braunwald taught me to write scientifically. He's an incredibly good writer.

WCR: *Did you go to his house to work on papers?*

LDH: No, but I would sit down with him at his office. A lot of manuscripts got kicked back and forth with huge amounts of scribbling on them, and then each time less scribbling as it came back. We would go through 5 to 10 drafts of each manuscript.

WCR: *You had the experience of working with 2 of the very finest departmental chairmen of medicine in the last half of the 20th century: Seldin and Braunwald. How would you compare the 2?*

LDH: In many respects, they have different personalities. Dr. Seldin is much less reserved, and possesses more spontaneity. He's more talkative or "bubbly" than Dr. Braunwald.

WCR: *Would "charming" be a word?*

LDH: I think so, yes, although Dr. Braunwald is charming also. Their similarities are strong. They both demand excellence, and they do not compromise on that. They know when they see it. That is an important point. You could demand it, but if you didn't recognize it, then you might have a problem. They know what they want. They know what they don't want, and they have a pretty good feel for what it takes to get it; they expect it of themselves, and they expect it of those they work with. They are remarkably similar in that way. They are both very fair; they are both free of fluff. For both of them, the value of their currency is extremely high. If they compliment you and tell you that something is good, it really is good, because they are not just saying it. If it's not good, they won't say it, and I have a tremendous high regard for that. They're demanding of excellence, but in a very good way—in a nondestructive way. There's a lot of rigor, and I think rigor is good. I think people work best and do their best if things are rigorous.

WCR: *How would you sum up your experience of those 3 years in Boston? You had an opportunity to meet a lot of major figures in medicine, not just in cardiology, but in other areas as well. Was Tom Smith there?*

LDH: Tom was the chief of the division. *Bill Grossman* directed the cath lab, *Joe Alpert*, the coronary care unit, and *Peter Cohn*, the clinical service. The faculty was a terrific group of young people who were on their way up. My fellowship colleagues also were outstanding. They included *Blase Carabello, Elliot Antman, Josh Wynne,* and *Shelly Goldberg*. My time at the Brigham was professionally very satisfying and productive, and it armed me with what I was sent there to be armed with. They armed me with the skills to go back to Dallas and make the department better.

WCR: *Once you got back to Dallas, what happened?*

LDH: I was chief of the cath lab from the first day I walked in in July 1978, and I have been in Dallas at Southwestern ever since. I very much wanted to make the cath lab good in a number of ways. I wanted to make it a good place for people to learn and have the teaching in it be good. I wanted it to be my research laboratory. I saw the cath lab as an opportunity. It was an era when cath labs didn't have the demands placed on them that are there today, i.e., to crank out huge numbers of cases. When I was a fellow at the Brigham, we usually did 2 or 3 cases a day in each cath room, and each case lasted a couple of hours. Part of that was doing some research protocol. That's very much the way I wanted Dallas to be, and so what I tried to create was what I will term "an academic cath lab," a cath lab where one could take an extra 10 to 45 minutes to address a question worth answering. That's what I attempted to do from the time I arrived in 1978. I wanted it to be an exciting place for fellows to learn the technique and to learn physiology and to make it a place where we could do human investigation.

WCR: *Is it very difficult to do that anymore with so many coronary patients?*

LDH: Yes it is. The cath labs are overwhelmed, and the economics of hospitals these days usually don't allow a procedure that should last for only 30 minutes to last for 120 to 180 minutes. If you occupy the room for that period of time, somebody's got to pay for it. Twenty-five years ago, the hospital wasn't pounding its fist on the desk demanding that one pay for it. In 1978 and for the first 10 or so years after returning to Dallas, one could do just about anything that one wanted in the cath lab from a time perspective. As long as the patient had consented to it, as long as the internal review board had agreed to it, the hospital really didn't care whether the procedure lasted an hour or 2 hours, but now they do.

WCR: *Dr. Hillis, you've been at Southwestern for 24 years and during that time you've been highly productive. You have brought new knowledge about various cardiovascular conditions into the public domain. You have won numerous teaching awards from medical students, internal medicine house staff, and cardiology fellows as a superior, devoted, and caring teacher. You've been offered, at various institutions around the country, chiefships of cardiology and chairmanships of departments of internal medicine. You are a force at your medical center, not only in the department of medicine, but also in the entire hierarchy of the medical center. You have an endowed chair. You have served as chair of a number of committees to choose the chair of other departments and subdivisions. How has Southwestern been able to keep you through the years with these other opportunities frequently flying in your face?*

LDH: The short answer is because Southwestern and Parkland are very special places. The atmosphere of the medical center includes collegiality, camaraderie, and respect all the way from the most clinical of the clinical people to the most basic of the basic scientists. It is a remarkably friendly, supportive, and fun place to work. Surely, in other parts of the country or the world there must be other places like this. I credit a lot of that atmosphere to what Dr. Seldin created during his years as chair of the department of medicine. He was instrumental in building an institution where everybody involved was excited about being there, liked and respected their colleagues, and got along with them regardless of what they did. I have very deep friendships with Dr. Seldin, Dan Foster, *Bob Alpern* (the dean), and with numerous members of the medicine department and the cardiology division. In the past when I have been offered other positions, I have felt it impossible to leave because of those friendships and because of the atmosphere of the medical school. It is different than most other places.

When *Al Gilman* won the Nobel Prize in 1994, after that announcement was made that morning, there was a spontaneous "pep rally" in the big auditorium, where people from all over the campus showed up to celebrate with Al Gilman and his lab, the fact that he and Rodbell had just been awarded the Nobel Prize. Hundreds of people from all over the campus were there to celebrate the success of one of their colleagues rather than to mumble to themselves, "He's accomplished this, and I haven't, and what can I do to pull him down so I'll look better" or something like that.

It's an atmosphere of support that is largely due, or a substantial amount of it is due, to the atmosphere that Dr. Seldin began to create in the 1950s. So much of Southwestern revolves around Dr. Seldin. He had become chair of the department of medicine when he was 31 years old in 1951; in 1962, when he was in his early 40s, he was offered 1 of the 3 department of medicine chairs at Harvard. He had already been chairman at Southwestern for 10 years, and the school was getting better, but Southwestern wasn't yet a world-class institution. Obviously Harvard was. Finally, he decided not to go to Boston, but first he sat down with the regents of the University of Texas and he basically told them: "Southwestern will never be a world-class medical school unless the basic sciences are world-class. What I am asking from you is that in return for my staying at Southwestern, I want major resources to be earmarked for the basic sciences. Don't worry about the medicine department, the medicine department will do fine—we're doing OK and we will continue to do well. What I want you to do is pour all of the resources that you can garner into the basic sciences, because until that happens, no matter how good the medicine department is, this medical school will never be a great medical school." In other words, his request was totally selfless on his part. It would have been easy for him to demand a $25,000,000 endowment to stay in Dallas for the department of medicine. He didn't demand a dime for the department of medicine. What he demanded was that the other departments be made as good as the department of medicine. That kind of selflessness—an institution-wide priority rather than a department-wide priority—still exists today.

WCR: *What department was he offered at Harvard?*

LDH: He was offered the Blumgart Professorship and the Chair of the Department of Medicine at the Beth Israel Hospital in Boston.

WCR: *Do you think that Dr. Seldin basically is a bit of a rebel? Harvard was going to do well, whether he took that chair or not, whereas Dallas needed him. He was the visionary here and no matter how good he* would have been in Boston, Harvard would have continued to do well without him.

LDH: I think that's true. Why in the world in 1951 did he leave Yale and come to Dallas, when the medical school was a bunch of old army barracks? I think Dr. Seldin thought Dallas was an opportunity to build something that would be him, and that he could point at and say that this is something I had a significant part in doing, and that might not have happened at a place like Hopkins or Columbia or Yale or Harvard.

WCR: *Do you feel that your Texas heritage keeps you here? You were born in Tyler, you have been a major part of this medical center for 24 years, you have that competitive spirit to make this medical center great, which in turn makes Dallas better, and in turn makes Texas better. If you went off to the University of Iowa as chair of medicine, that's great, but was that what you were put on planet earth to do?*

LDH: Yes, I do. That's not unique to me by the way. People who did not grow up in Texas oftentimes have difficulty understanding the Texas mentality, but in my generation there was a feeling that Texas was a special place. It was the "can do" attitude among the people who lived here. I have it, and I know Jim Willerson has it. Jim has had numerous opportunities to go all over the country, but he has deep Texas roots, just like I do, and I think that is part of the reason he has stayed in Texas. Having been born and raised here, I feel the same way. That's not to say that I don't enjoy other parts of the country. I have numerous friends from elsewhere, but this is kind of where my heart is, and certainly professionally, Southwestern is where my heart is, and that was formed during those magical years of internship and residency.

WCR: *David, I'm fascinated by how you have survived so beautifully at Southwestern, and you are purely a clinical researcher. You're not in a dog lab. You're surrounded by molecular biologists and geneticists and yet you have brought new things out of a cardiac catheterization laboratory in the last 20 years, and most people haven't been able to be productive in that environment. At the same time, you're losing some very good clinical people. They've gotten a bit frustrated because they're not appreciated enough in a center that focuses on genetics and molecular biology. How are you going to work that out?*

LDH: I'm not sure I have an answer. This is not a problem unique to Southwestern. All top echelon medical schools are wrestling with this problem. Harvard, Hopkins, Duke, Washington University, University of California at San Francisco, etc., are places where oftentimes clinicians do not feel as appreciated or as rewarded as faculty in the basic science arena. I have never felt that way in my career at Southwestern. Why haven't I? I guess my answer would be leadership. Here's what I mean by that. I never felt as if I were a second-class citizen because I was doing clinical investigation rather than cloning genes, because the people for whom I worked—Jim Willerson as my divisional chief and then *Sandy Williams*, and Donald Seldin and then Dan Foster as my departmental chiefs—sent me the clear message that they highly valued what I was doing. The message they gave me was that they thought I was doing terrific work and that I should continue to do it. If there are clinicians who are doing clinical investigation and feel that they are second-class citizens, then we as the leaders of the institutions need to be better at convincing them that what they are doing is valued. It may be a leadership deficiency.

WCR: *What do you do as vice chair of the department of medicine at Southwestern?*

LDH: I run the house staff program. I am the program director of the internal medicine residency.

WCR: *And how many residents and interns do you have?*

LDH: A total of 142.

WCR: *Do you know all of them?*

LDH: I know all of them extremely well. Better than they wish I knew them, probably. I am in charge of choosing them. I am in charge of interviewing them. I don't interview all 350. We take 50 interns each year, and I am in charge of the interview process, I am in charge of choosing them, and I am in charge of running the residency program. Obviously, I have a lot of help from numerous people, but I am the program director for the residents. I chair, not all, but at least a good percentage of the search committees for divisional chiefs. Right now I am the chair of the search committee to choose a new chief of the hematology/oncology division. Our chief has just left. I also work on faculty development and faculty issues concerning interpersonal problems, things like that, and other things that Dan Foster asks me to do.

WCR: *What is your day like? What time do you get to the hospital now? Do you still run to work?*

LDH: I still run to work every day and I run home at night.

WCR: *How far is that?*

LDH: It is 3.5 miles each way, or 7 miles a day.

WCR: *Do you keep your clothes in a backpack?*

LDH: No, I keep clothes at work. The only thing that travels with me in a little fanny pack is my wallet and my keys. I awake at 5 A.M. and I walk out the door at about 5:15 with my T-shirt, shorts, and shoes on, and I walk through the door at Parkland Hospital at about 5:45. I shower, shave, get dressed, and then I start to work at 6:30. Since the day I joined the faculty 24 years ago, we have, every morning with the cath lab attendings (4 of us) and the fellows rotating in the cath lab, a session where we go over the previous day's catheterization cases, and we do that from 6:45 until 8 A.M.

WCR: *Do you go through every case done the previous day?*

LDH: Yes. We spend more time on some than others. We do about 5 cases a day on average. We talk at that conference about whatever it makes sense to talk about. We might spend 15 minutes talking about aortic stenosis if we catheterized a patient the previous day, and then talk about various issues related to that. Then we look at angiograms. The conference is aimed at the cath fellows, their time to sit down one-on-one with faculty.

WCR: *How many cardiology fellows do you have?*

LDH: We have 6 new ones each year.

WCR: *That means you have at least 18, plus you've got some fourth-year fellows?*

LDH: Yes.

WCR: *How many total cardiology fellows?*

LDH: Around 20.

WCR: *The cardiology division has how many faculty?*

LDH: About 35.

WCR: *And in the entire department of internal medicine?*

LDH: About 260.

WCR: *Your "bird list," so to speak, is 21 plus 142 plus 35 plus 260. That's the minimum?*

LDH: Yes.

WCR: *And you know people in other departments, too?*

LDH: I know a lot of people in other departments.

WCR: *And you've got secretaries and lab technicians, so your total "bird list" at Southwestern must approach 1,000.*

LDH: I'm sure it does. I'm not nearly as good as Dan Foster, who knows the janitors and the nurses' aides on each of the wards at Parkland Hospital. He knows everybody. It's that kind of a place. It's the kind of place where people speak to each other and know each other, and interact with each other very collegially.

WCR: *After the cardiology cath conference, what do you do?*

LDH: We start cath cases at 8. Some days I'm in the cath lab and some days I'm not. I'm there now for no more than 1 case a day. The other time I do administrative things for the department. I go to teaching conferences for the house staff a couple of days a week. Other activities include such things as reviewing manuscripts for journals, writing articles and book chapters, etc.

WCR: *Your major commitment to the division of cardiovascular medicine is the cardiac catheterization laboratory?*

LDH: Yes, but it is a little more than that because I round in the coronary care unit. There is 1 attending cardiologist for the 12-bed coronary care unit plus the same cardiologist for the 12- to 18-bed step-down unit, which totals about 25 to 30 patients on the service at any one time.

WCR: *You do that how much a year?*

LDH: I do that 6 weeks a year. I do it in 3, two-week blocks. It is an intense experience because you are the attending for 15 straight days. You have 1 fellow, 3 residents, 3 interns, and 1 to 3 fourth-year medical students.

WCR: *The rounding for that lasts how long?*

LDH: We start at 8 A.M. and it usually lasts most of the morning. During that 15-day period, there is hardly time for anything else. I enjoy that time, because if I'm going to be an effective program director for the residency program, I need to spend a lot of time interacting with house staff. I need to see them and watch them work. The coronary care unit is where I can do that best.

WCR: *Do you make ward rounds in general medicine?*

LDH: I do that 1 month a year.

WCR: *That's a pretty intensive activity also?*

LDH: Yes.

WCR: *You are responsible for most of the evaluations of the house officers?*

LDH: Yes, I am. I have a committee of faculty called the "Committee to Evaluate Clinical Competence," and that committee, which is made up of about 10 faculty, has regular monthly meetings to evaluate all of the house staff. If there are problems, they come to me, and I take care of them.

WCR: *What time do you usually leave the hospital?*

LDH: Anywhere from 5:30 to 7:00 P.M. I probably average about 6:15 or 6:30 P.M. I am home about 7 usually.

WCR: *What do you do at night these days as a rule?*

LDH: I usually watch the news on television and maybe some sporting activity. I usually go to bed at 9 o'clock. I need 8 hours of sleep. I'm only home for a couple of hours. I might go to bed at 9:30. I'm rarely awake at 10 P.M.

WCR: *What about Saturday and Sunday?*

LDH: We have a house staff conference on Saturday morning that I attend. Then, I'll usually work for an hour or 2 after that, and I get home around noon. I usually work about half a day on Sunday. Sunday is my favorite day, because I'm the only one in the office. The phone doesn't ring, no one interrupts me, my beeper doesn't go off, and I really get a lot of work done.

WCR: *Where's Nancy?*

LDH: Nancy, on Saturdays, usually does errands. On Sundays, until her mom died a few months ago, she spent time with her. Now, she usually visits relatives or takes care of other business, and I'm home by noon or 1 P.M. on Sundays.

WCR: *What hobbies have you continued?*

LDH: Besides running, I love to bicycle. I am an avid cyclist. I cycle on both Saturday and Sunday afternoons; I enjoy that tremendously.

WCR: *How many miles?*

LDH: Usually each day about 50. I usually cycle for about 3 or 3.5 hours on both Saturday and Sunday.

WCR: *Does Nancy cycle?*

LDH: No, she doesn't. I cycle with a group of friends. They are all medical school people. This afternoon I will cycle with Rick Lange, my close associate and good friend. Cycling is my passion in life now.

WCR: *Do you continue to read history?*

LDH: To some extent. The non-medical reading I do is in history, but I'm embarrassed to say, it is only 2 to 4 books a year, and that is usually on long trips.

WCR: *Are you interested in professional football?*

LDH: Not really. I enjoy college football, however. If professional football disappeared tomorrow, I would hardly care.

WCR: *You're not a golf or tennis player?*

LDH: I'm not. I used to play tennis, but I haven't played in 30 years, and I don't play golf.

WCR: *Do you continue to keep up with baseball?*

LDH: Not much. I watch it, but I don't have strong feelings about it. As I have gotten more into endurance-like sports, cycling and running, baseball has become less attractive to me, because I don't think baseball takes much endurance. It does take physical dexterity, but not the kind of endurance that basketball does.

WCR: *You've been running to work for 24 years?*

LDH: Yes.

WCR: *How fast do you run now?*

LDH: I probably run about an 8-minute mile now. I used to run 6-minute miles. In 1983, I came in 24th among about 4,000 runners in the White Rock Marathon.

WCR: *What was your time?*

LDH: It was 2:51 hours, which is about 6:30 minutes a mile.

WCR: *Do you run 10K's or marathons anymore?*

LDH: No.

WCR: *David, you and Nancy have a lot of friends in this town. Do you entertain a good bit?*

LDH: We eat out a lot, but we don't entertain at home a lot. We get together with friends at a restaurant or at their house, or occasionally at our house.

WCR: *How do you work out your travels? I'm sure you get a lot of invitations to give talks at various places. I expect you decline most of them.*

LDH: I do, yes.

WCR: *It sounds like you like staying home. You've got a lot of activities.*

LDH: Yes, I do.

WCR: *You mentioned that you and the Seldins take a couple of trips a year together. How do you work these travels out?*

LDH: We do enjoy traveling, but I always have mixed feelings about it, because I feel like I should be here doing my job. Nevertheless, we make time for them. We have enjoyed tremendously our trips with the Seldins, and we have done everything we can to go whenever these trips become available. Trips with the Seldins are usually for 7 to 10 days and always to Europe. That's where he likes to go and we end up in his favorite country, Italy.

WCR: *When you travel with the Seldins you've got a ready-made tour guide?*

LDH: We do. It's fantastic. It couldn't be better. He's a very learned and knowledgeable person about lots of things outside of medicine. He loves art, music, and history, and, if you believe in reincarnation, which I don't, I know he must have lived during the Italian Renaissance in Venice or in Florence or in Rome.

WCR: *Are you an opera buff?*

LDH: I'm not. I've gone to the opera numerous times, but I'm not an enthusiast about it like some of my friends are.

WCR: *Do you have music on in your house when you're home?*

LDH: No, usually not. We like it quiet.

WCR: *I hear that you're easy game for Dr. Seldin when it comes to ping pong?*

LDH: That's true. The year that John Harper and I were chief residents, we got into a discussion one day with Dr. Seldin when John and I were about to go over to the student union building at Southwestern at lunchtime to play ping pong. He started telling us about what a good ping pong player he was. John and I at the time were 27 years old and at or near the height of our athletic powers. Dr. Seldin was in his mid-50s and we started saying, "Yeah, yeah, yeah, tell us how great you were back in the old days" and he said, "Well, let's go play." We played and it wasn't even close; he destroyed us. I'm not exaggerating, and believe me we were not trying to lose; he hit shots with upspin and downspin and sidespin, and the scores ended up being something like 21 to 7 or 21 to 5. The tour-de-force at the very end was John Harper's splitting the rear-mid crease of his slacks wide open while lunging for a shot. He went back to Dr. Seldin's office with his tail between his legs, because he had to walk in such a way where you could see his underwear.

WCR: *You have about 200 medical students per class at Southwestern?*

LDH: That's correct.

WCR: *Two hundred per class and 163 house officers per year and 21 cardiology fellows per year. Your potential impact on a number of very bright people in this community is astounding.*

LDH: I really haven't ever thought about it, but that's pretty frightening.

WCR: *The number of physicians you know in this community and in the entire state must be very large. You can't go to many places where you don't know a number of doctors.*

LDH: That's very true.

WCR: *That must bring you a great sense of satisfaction.*

LDH: It does, absolutely.

WCR: *How knowledgeable now are you in the non-cardiologic subspecialties of medicine?*

LDH: Moderately knowledgeable. I attend several non-cardiologic teaching conferences each week for the medicine house staff and the students. Almost all of my continuing medical education in non-cardiology comes from those conferences. If you go to those conferences week in and week out, month in and month out, it is remarkable how well abreast you can stay on the important facts in each subspecialty. I go to 3 or 4 hours a week of house staff conferences that allow me to do that.

WCR: *You go to those conferences not for what you can get from them, but from what you can give to them?*

LDH: I would say both. We have a magnificent conference on Tuesdays at noon. It's called our potpourri conference, where the ward residents present in the course of an hour, 6 to 9 cases. The house officers call on whomever they want to in the audience—students, interns, faculty. Only 1 or 2 of the cases have to do with cardiology. That's where I do my learning about non-cardiology.

WCR: *Would they call on you for a hepatology case? Do they try to embarrass you?*

LDH: No, it's done in a very constructive way. They oftentimes call on people outside their specialty, and that's a good message to send to students and to house staff: that is, it's OK not to have the definitive answer. What you want to show them is that there is some logical thought process about how you approach a clinical problem.

WCR: *Do you think one of Dr. Seldin's characteristics that made him a great chairman, not only his "good taste" in picking people, but the fact that he was incredibly broad in his knowledge of medicine, not just in nephrology and metabolism, but the whole shebang?*

LDH: Yes, I think so. Absolutely. Even to this day, he's that knowledgeable. He has not only very broad non-medical interests, but also very broad medical interests. Dan Foster as chair of the department has continued that tradition. Dan is incredibly knowledgeable and skilled in all of medicine. It is important for the department chair to be that way.

WCR: *When will you retire?*

LDH: I don't know, but probably in the next 3 years.

WCR: *What are your goals from here on? You are 56 now?*

LDH: My goal is to continue to do what I'm doing and to enjoy it. I tremendously enjoy the job that I have and the things that it allows me to do. I enjoy playing a leadership role in the school and in the department, and I hope to continue to do that.

WCR: *If you were offered the chairmanship of medicine tomorrow, would you want it?*

LDH: I would take it. It would be intimidating to try to follow Dr. Seldin and Dan Foster because I think they have been, in their different ways, as good as one could possibly be.

WCR: *What makes Dan Foster a good chairman? He's quite different from you.*

LDH: He is different. He is demanding of excellence, uncompromising. He has magnificent interpersonal skills; he engenders loyalty and affection, and the respect of those with whom he works. The bond that he has with everyone in the department is quite remarkable, from the vice chair down to the secretaries. He knows them all and knows what their children do, and he knows what their problems have been. He is a quality human being who genuinely cares about the people who work in his department, and he is willing to do anything he can to help them to be successful.

WCR: *How much time do you take off a year?*

LDH: Probably 4 weeks total.

WCR: *Are most of those involved in some kind of medical activity?*

LDH: Probably half. Soon Nancy and I are going to Scotland for a week. We started doing that about 10 years ago. We go to Scotland at the end of the summer to get away from the Texas heat, and we go there just to enjoy being there.

WCR: *Where do you go?*

LDH: We go to a place about 2 hours north of Glasgow called Inverlochy Castle, which is a country house hotel. We enjoy going back there every year.

WCR: *You fly to Glasgow?*

LDH: We fly to Chicago and then to Glasgow, and then drive for 2 hours north of Glasgow.

WCR: *David, is there anything that we haven't discussed that you would like to talk about?*

LDH: The only other thing I would say is that whatever success I have had in Dallas is a testament to the people who we have talked about. It's also a testament to people like Rick Lange, who has been my colleague and close friend for 14 years. Rick is a magnificent person and physician and a magnificent colleague. If you ask Joe Goldstein and Mike Brown how their scientific marriage has prospered, I think each would tell you that they bring different things to the table. Rick and I bring different things, but they compliment one another. Rick has been an incredibly supportive good friend and colleague. I couldn't have asked for a better person to work with for 15 years.

WCR: *David, thank you for being so open. I'm sure the readers of this journal will enjoy getting to know you.*

LDH: Thank you, Bill. You're very kind to say that.

LDHs Best Publications as Selected by LDH

4. Hillis LD, Braunwald E. Myocardial ischemia. *N Engl J Med* 1977;296:971A–978;1034–1041;1093–1096.

10. Hillis LD, Braunwald E. Coronary artery spasm. *N Engl J Med* 1978;299:695–702.

26. Hirsh PD, Hillis LD, Campbell WB, Firth BG, Willerson JT. Release of prostaglandins and thromboxane into the coronary circulation in patients with ischemic heart disease. *N Engl J Med* 1981;304:685–691.

28. Johnson SM, Mauritson DR, Willerson JT, Hillis LD. A controlled trial of verapamil for Prinzmetal's variant angina. *N Engl J Med* 1981;304:862-866.

70. Winniford MD, Filipchuk N, Hillis LD. Alpha-adrenergic blockade for variant angina: a long-term, double-blind, randomized trial. *Circulation* 1983;67:1185–1188.

88. Nicod P, Rehr R, Winniford MD, Campbell WB, Firth BG, Hillis LD. Acute systemic and coronary hemodynamic and serologic responses to cigarette smoking in long-term smokers with atherosclerotic coronary artery disease. *J Am Coll Cardiol* 1984;4:96–971.

93. Winniford MD, Jackson J, Malloy CR, Rehr RB, Campbell WB, Hillis LD. Does indomethacin attenuate the coronary vasodilatory effect of nitroglycerin? *J Am Coll Cardiol* 1984;4:1114–1117.

98. TIMI Study Group. The Thrombolysis In Myocardial Infarction (TIMI) trial. Phase I findings. *N Engl J Med* 1985;312:932–936.

105. Hillis LD, Winniford MD, Jackson JA, Firth BG. Measurement of left-to-right intracardiac shunting in adults: oximetric versus indicator dilution techniques. *Catheter Cardiovas Diag* 1985;11:467–472.

107. Hillis LD, Firth BG, Winniford MD. Analysis of factors affecting the variability of Fick versus indicator dilution measurements of cardiac output. *Am J Cardiol* 1985;56:764–768.

108. Winniford MD, Kennedy PL, Wells PJ, Hillis LD. Potentiation of nitroglycerin-induced coronary dilatation by N-acetylcysteine. *Circulation* 1986;73:138–142.

111. Winniford MD, Wheelan KR, Kremers MS, Ugolini V, van den Berg E Jr, Niggemann EH, Jansen DE, Hillis LD. Smoking-induced coronary vasoconstriction in patients with atherosclerotic coronary artery disease: evidence for adrenergically mediated alteration in coronary artery tone. *Circulation* 1986;73:622–627.

113. Hillis LD, Firth BG, Winniford MD. Comparison of thermodilution and indocyanine green dye in low cardiac output or left-sided regurgitation. *Am J Cardiol* 1986;57:1201–1202.

117. Hillis LD, Firth BG, Winniford MD. Variability of right-sided cardiac oxygen saturations in adults with and without left-to-right intracardiac shunting. *Am J Cardiol* 1986'58:129–132.

120. Winniford MD, Jansen DE, Reynolds GA, Apprill P, Black WH, Hillis LD. Cigarette smoking-induced coronary vasoconstriction in atherosclerotic coronary artery disease and prevention by calcium antagonists and nitroglycerin. *Am J Cardiol* 1987;59:203–207.

124. Niggemann EH, Ma PTS, Sunnergren KP, Winniford MD, Hillis LD. Detection of intracardiac left-to-right shunting in adults: a prospective analysis of the variability of the standard indocyanine green technique in patients without shunting. *Am J Cardiol* 1987;60:355–357.

125. May DC, Popma JJ, Black WH, Schaefer S, Lee HR, Levine BD, Hillis LD. In vivo induction and reversal of nitroglycerin tolerance in human coronary arteries. *N Engl J Med* 1987;317:805–809.

135. TIMI Research Group. Immediate vs delayed catheterization and angioplasty following thrombolytic therapy for acute myocardial infarction. TIMI IIA results. *JAMA* 1988;260:2849–2858.

137. TIMI Study Group. Comparison of invasive and conservative strategies after treatment with intravenous tissue plasminogen activator in acute myocardial infarction: results of the Thrombolysis in Myocardial Infarction (TIMI) trial. *N Engl J Med* 1989;320:618–627.

138. Lange RA, Moore DM Jr, Cigarroa RG, Hillis LD. Use of pulmonary capillary wedge pressure to assess severity of mitral stenosis: is true left atrial pressure needed in this condition? *J Am Coll Cardiol* 1989;13:825–829.

140. Cigarroa RG, Lange RA, Williams RH, Bedotto JB, Hillis LD. Underestimation of cardiac output by thermodilution in patients with tricuspid regurgitation. *Am J Med* 1989;86:417–420.

143. Cigarroa RG, Lange RA, Williams RH, Hillis LD. Dosing of contrast material to prevent contrast nephropathy in patients with renal disease. *Am J Med* 1989;86:649–652.

145. Cigarroa RG, Lange RA, Hillis LD. Prognosis after acute myocardial infarction in patients with and without residual anterograde coronary blood flow. *Am J Cardiol* 1989;64:155–160.

146. Cigarroa RG, Lange RA, Hillis LD. Oximetric quantitation of intracardiac left-to-right shunting: limitations of the Qp/Qs ratio. *Am J Cardiol* 1989;64:246–247.

152. Lange RA, Cigarroa RG, Yancy CW Jr, Willard JE, Popma JJ, Sills MN, McBride W, Kim AS, Hillis LD. Cocaine-induced coronary artery vasoconstriction. *N Engl J Med* 1989;321:1557–1562.

156. Lange RA, Cigarroa RG, Hillis LD. Influence of residual antegrade coronary blood flow on survival after myocardial infarction in patients with multivessel coronary artery disease. *Coronary Art Dis* 1990;65:59–63.

157. Lange RA, Cigarroa RG, Wells PJ, Kremers MS, Hillis LD. Influence of anterograde flow in the infarct artery on the incidence of late potentials after acute myocardial infarction. *Am J Cardiol* 1990;65:554–558.

159. Lange RA, Cigarroa RG, Flores ED, McBride W, Kim AS, Wells PJ, Bedotto JB, Danziger RS, Hillis LD. Potentiation of cocaine-induced coronary vasoconstriction by beta-adrenergic blockade. *Ann Int Med* 1990;112:897–903.

161. Flores ED, Lange RA, Bedotto JB, Danziger RS, Hillis LD. Assesment of the sensitivity of hydrogen inhalation in the detection of left-to-right shunting. *Cathet Cardiovas Diag* 1990;20:94–98.

162. Flores ED, Lange RA, Cigarroa RG, Hillis LD. Effect of cocaine on coronary artery dimensions in atherosclerotic coronary artery disease: enhanced vasoconstriction at sites of significant stenoses. *J Am Coll Cardiol* 1990;16:74–79.

164. Hillis LD, Forman S, Braunwald E, and TIMI Phase II coinvestigators. Risk stratification before thrombolytic therapy in patients with acute myocardial infarction. *J Am Coll Cardiol* 1990;16:313–315.

174. Glamann DB, Lange RA, Hillis LD. Beneficial effect of long-term beta blockade after myocardial infarction in patients without anterograde flow in the infarct artery. *Am J Cardiol* 1991;68:150–154.

176. Brogan WC III, Lange RA, Kim AS, Mokiterno DJ, Hillis LD. Alleviation of cocaine-induced coronary vasoconstriction by nitroglycerin. *J Am Coll Cardiol* 1991;18:581–586.

183. Boehrer JD, Lange RA, Willard JE, Hillis LD. Influence of collateral filling of the occluded infarct-related coronary artery on prognosis after acute myocardial infarction. *Am J Cardiol* 1992;69:10-12.

187. Brogan WC III, Lange RA, Glamann DB, Hillis LD. Recurrent coronary vasoconstriction caused by intranasal cocaine: possible role for metabolites. *Ann Int Med* 1992;116:556–561.

191. Mokiterno DJ, Lange RA, Willard JE, Boehrer JD, Hillis LD. Does restoration of antegrade flow in the infarct-related coronary artery days to weeks after myocardial infarction improve long-term survival? *Coronary Artery Dis* 1992;3:345–346.

196. Boehrer JD, Moliterno DJ, Willard JE, Snyder RW II, Horton RP, Glamann DB, Lange RA, Hillis LD. Hemodynamic effects of intranasal cocaine in humans. *J Am Coll Cardiol* 1992;20:90–93.

197. Willard JE, Lange RA, Hillis LD. The use of aspirin in ischemic heart disease. *N Engl J Med* 1992;327:175–181.

198. Boehrer JD, Lange RA, Willard JE, Grayburn PA, Hillis LD. Advantages and limitations of methods to detect, localize, and quantitate intracardiac left-to-right shunting. *Am Heart J* 1992;124:448–455.

201. Boehrer JD, Glamann DB, Lange RA, Willard JE, Brogan WC III, Eichhorn EJ, Grayburn PA, Anwar A, Hillis LD. Effect of coronary angioplasty of late potentials one to two weeks after acute myocardial infarction. *Am J Cardiol* 1992;70:1515–1519.

203. Boehrer JD, Lange RA, Willard JE, Grayburn PA, Hillis LD. Advantages and limitations of methods to detect, localize, and quantitate intracardiac right-to-left and bidirectional shunting. *Am Heart J* 1993;10:33–36.

207. Brogan WC III, Grayburn PA, Lange RA, Hillis LD. Prognosis after valve replacement in patients with severe aortic stenosis and a low transvalvular pressure gradient. *J Am Coll Cardiol* 1993;21:1657–1660.

208. Boehrer JD, Moliterno DJ, Willard JE, Hillis LD, Lange RA. Influence of labetalol on cocaine-induced coronary vasoconstriction in man. *Am J Med* 1993; 94:608–610.

209. Moliterno DJ, Lange RA, Meidell RS, Willard JE, Leffert CC, Gerard RD, Boerwinkle E, Hobbs HH, Hillis LD. Relation of plasma lipoprotein(a) to infarct artery patency in survivors of myocardial infarction. *Circulation* 1993;88:935–940.

210. Glamann DB, Lange RA, Willard JE, Landau C, Hillis LD. Hydrogen inhalation for detecting intracardiac left-to-right shunting in adults. *Am J Cardiol* 1993;72:711–714.

215. Moliterno DJ, Lange RA, Willard JE, Boehrer JD, Hillis LD. Surgical restoration of antegrade flow in the occluded infarct artery improves long-term survival in patients with multivessel coronary artery disease. *Coronary Artery Dis* 1993;4:995–999.

221. Moliterno DJ, Willard JE, Lange RA, Negus BH, Boehrer JD, Glamann DB, Landau C, Rossen JD, Winniford MD, Hillis LD. Coronary artery vasoconstriction induced by cocaine, cigarette smoking, or both. *N Engl J Med* 1994;73:454–459.

222. Negus BH, Willard JE, Hillis LD, Glamann DB, Landau C, Snyder RW, Lange RA. Alleviation of cocaine-induced coronary vasoconstriction with intravenous verapamil. *Am J Cardiol* 1994;73:510–513.

223. Snyder RW II, Glamann DB, Lange RA, Willard JE, Landau C, Negus BH, Hillis LD. Predictive value of prominent pulmonary arterial wedge V waves in assessing the presence and severity of mitral regurgitation. *Am J Cardiol* 1994; 73:568–570.

226. Moliterno DJ, Lange RA, Gerard RD, Willard JE, Lackner C, Hillis LD. Influence of intranasal cocaine on plasma constituents associated with endogenous thrombosis and thrombolysis. *Am J Med* 1994;96:492–496.

231. Pirwitz MJ, Lange RA, Willard JE, Landau C, Glamann DB, Hillis LD. Use of the left ventricular peak systolic pressure/end-systolic volume ration to predict symptomatic improvement with valve replacement in patients with aortic regurgitation and enlarged end-systolic volume. *J Am Coll Cardiol* 1994;24:1672–1677.

233. Daniel WC, Lange RA, Willard JE, Landau C, Hillis LD. Oximetric versus indicator dilution techniques for quantitating intracardiac left-to-right shunting in adults. *Am J Cardiol* 1995;75:199–200.

239. Pirwitz MJ, Willard JE, Landau C, Lange RA, Glamann DB, Kessler DJ, Foerster EH, Todd E, Hillis LD. Influence of cocaine, ethanol, or their combination on epicardial coronary arterial dimensions in humans. *Arch Int Med* 1995;155:1186–1191.

243. Daniel WC, Pirwitz MJ, Horton RP, Landau C, Glamann DB, Snyder RW II, Willard JE, Wells PJ, Hillis LD, Lange RA, Page RL. Electrophysiologic effects of intranasal cocaine. *Am J Cardiol* 1995;76:398–400.

257. Vongpatanasin W, Hillis LD, Lange RA. Prosthetic heart valves. *N Engl J Med* 1996;335:407–416.

259. Daniel WC, Lange RA, Landau C, Willard JE, Hillis LD. Effects of the intracoronary infusion of cocaine on coronary arterial dimensions and blood flow in humans. *Am J Cardiol* 1996;78:288–291.

275. Pitts WR, Lange RA, Cigarroa JE, Hillis LD. Preoperative left ventricular peak systolic pressure/end-systolic volume ratio and functional status following valve surgery in patients with mitral regurgitation and enlarged end-systolic volumes. *Am J Cardiol* 1997;79:1493–1497.

276. Pitts WR, Lange RA, Cigarroa JE, Hillis LD. Cocaine-induced myocardial ischemia and infarction: pathophysiology, recognition, and management. *Prog Cardiovas Dis* 1997;40:65–76.

281. Pitts WR, Vongpatanasin W, Cigarroa JE, Hillis LD, Lange RA. Effects of the intracoronary infusion of cocaine on left ventricular systolic and diastolic function in humans. *Circulation* 1998;97:1270–1273.

284. Vongpatanasin W, Brickner ME, Hillis LD, Lange RA. The Eisenmenger syndrome in adults. *Ann Int Med* 1998;128:745–755.

301. Brickner ME, Hillis LD, Lange RA. Congenital heart disease in adults. *N Engl J Med* 2000;342:256–263;334–342.

312. Lange RA, Hillis LD. Cardiovascular complications of cocaine use. *N Engl J Med* 2001;345:351–358.

313. Rapp AH, Lange RA, Cigarroa JE, Keeley ED, Hillis LD. Relation of pulmonary arterial diastolic and mean pulmonary arterial wedge pressures in patients with and without pulmonary hypertension. *Am J Cardiol* 2001;88:823–824.

314. Rapp AH, Cigarroa JE, Lange RA, Keeley EC, Hillis LD. Hemodynamic characteristics and procedural outcome of patients with mitral stenosis and a depressed cardiac output. *Am J Cardiol* 2001;88:1212–1213.

320. Saland KE, Hillis LD, Lange RA, Cigarroa JE. Influence of morphine sulfate on cocaine-induced coronary vasoconstriction in humans. *Am J Cardiol* 2002; 90:810–811.

JEFFREY MICHAEL ISNER, MD:
A Conversation With the Editor*

Dr. Jeffrey Michael Isner was born in 1947 in Uhrichsville, Ohio, where he lived until high school when he and his family moved to Canton, Ohio. His college was the University of Maryland where he graduated magna cum laude, and his medical school was Tufts University in Boston. His internship in medicine was at his present hospital, and his residency in internal medicine and his fellowship in cardiology was at Georgetown University in Washington, DC. After spending 2 years in the Pathology Branch of the National Heart, Lung, and Blood Institute, he returned to Tufts University Medical Center in Boston where he rapidly rose to full Professor of Medicine and Pathology. In 1988 he moved from the New England Medical Center to St. Elizabeth's Medical Center in Boston to be Chief of Cardiovascular Research, and a few years later to be Director of the Human Gene Therapy Laboratory. Jeff Isner has been the leader of gene therapy for obstructive atherosclerotic arterial disease, and he has been a stimulus for many others to get involved in this area. His research has led to the publication of nearly 400 articles. I was fortunate to spend 27 months with Dr. Isner when he was at NIH. I knew after a short period that he was going places and certainly he has. Not only is he a splendid scientist and investigator but he also is a splendid physician and a wonderful guy. He also is an excellent story teller as this interview will demonstrate.

William Clifford Roberts, MD† (Hereafter WCR): *I am speaking with Dr. Jeffrey Isner in his office in Boston, Massachusetts, on July 29, 1998. Dr. Isner, I appreciate your willingness to talk to me and therefore the readers of* The American Journal of Cardiology. *Could you tell a bit about your early background—when and where were you born?*

Jeffrey Michael Isner, MD‡ (Hereafter JMI): I was born on December 11, 1947, in Uhrichsville, Ohio, where I lived until I was a freshman in high school, and then we moved to Canton, Ohio. My parents had moved to Ohio as a result of having to leave Nazi Germany. My parents were both born in southern Germany, Bavaria: my father, in a very small town outside of Nuremberg (Burghaslach) and my mother in a town called Bamberg. They had gone to high school there together but did not get married until 1940. They came to the USA in 1937. Initially, my father went to New York City, but soon moved to Cincinnati, Ohio, where there was a large German-Jewish community and where my father got a job.

Some of my uncles had already moved to Cincinnati and they got a job for him. He and my mother ultimately were able to get a retail store of their own to manage in Uhrichsville, Ohio. The small town was a major culture shock for them. My parents had grown up in a fairly affluent and sophisticated environment in Germany. My dad's family was very well off. They had a business that had been in the family for generations. Moving from there to a town in the middle of Ohio with a population of only 5,000 people with no other Jewish families was quite a change for them. Every time I had to make a change in my life I always related back to that. I thought if they could come from what they were used to and get used to starting out with nothing in an environment where they had to learn the language, the things I had to deal with were trivial by comparison.

WCR: *What years were your parents born?*

JMI: My dad was born in 1910, and my mother in 1916.

WCR: *Your father was about 27 when they came to the states. They had more or less grown up together I gather. What kind of education did your parents have?*

JMI: They both completed high school, but right at the point that they would have gone on to the equivalent of the university was the time when Jews were barred from any higher education in Germany. With all the events that happened subsequently, they never had an opportunity to attend a university.

WCR: *Their parents were quite educated? What did your grandparents do?*

JMI: Yes. I never knew any of my grandparents. They all had died before I was born. My mother's father had a successful textile business. He died in Germany when she was 9 years old. My paternal grandfather had a large clothing business. The others all escaped from Germany. My dad was able to get them out. They came after my parents came and subsequently died.

WCR: *Your parents got to Uhrichsville how long after they landed in the USA?*

JMI: Ultimately 1946. My dad came over in 1937, received his citizenship in 1942, and was immediately drafted to go into the Army. Almost as fast as he had escaped to the USA, he was back in Germany as part of the U.S. Army in a glider division. Early on his glider crashed and he was seriously injured. When my dad went back to Germany after he got out of the hospital he was assigned to a unit that trailed Patton's march through Europe after D-Day. He was actually assigned to a battalion that worked on securing the area he had grown up in Germany. They were taking care of the prisoners of war and one of his prisoners of war was his high school English teacher who had berated him for not learning to speak English. The

*This series of interviews are underwritten by an unrestricted grant from Bristol-Myers Squibb.

†Baylor Cardiovascular Institute, Baylor University Medical Center, Dallas, Texas 75246.

‡Professor of Medicine and Pathology, Tufts University School of Medicine, Boston, Massachusetts.

FIGURE 1. JMI during the interview.

teacher knew that my parents' family was anxious to get out of Germany. Subsequently, my dad was assigned as chaplain in General Eisenhower's headquarters and had the privilege of officiating at the rededication of the Frankfurt synagogue.

WCR: *Did he talk about the fact that he was a German and grew up as a German? Because he was Jewish he had to get out to survive. He came to the USA, acquired citizenship, and immediately was drafted into the US Army to fight his homeland. He must have had a great deal of mixed emotions about all that.*

JMI: No. I don't think they were mixed at all. I don't think there was any ambivalence. It was not difficult for my father and mother and other Germans in his situation to make a very quick turnabout in terms of their allegiance. They grew up being very loyal Germans. I heard the story many times about how one of my father's relatives kept saying, "Don't worry, there is no need to move, I have a commendation from having fought in the German Army during World War I and anybody with that particular honor was safe from persecution." My parents being younger perhaps did not have those biases. Sometimes when you are young you can see things a little more clearly. They said they recognized exactly what was happening. My parents also were very lucky. They got out unscathed. Almost everybody in their family got out unscathed, but they were subjected to much humiliation, which had a very clear-cut impact on their thinking.

I had a chance to go back to Germany with my mother about 10 years ago (My parents had always said they would never go back to Germany.) and give

a talk. I had heard so much about where my parents grew up, I thought this would be a great opportunity to see it firsthand through my mother's eyes. We went back to her home town. A couple of things were amazing: First, when arriving she called up her former best friend whom she had not seen for 40 years. She went to the store her family had owned and the lady said, "No, she is not working here today but you can call her." She agreed to meet my mother. My mom and I were sitting in a cafe and her friend walked in. She did not speak English so I could not understand their conversation. The amazing thing was these 2 people who had not talked to each other in 40 years, the greatest war in the history of mankind, and other unprecedented events had occurred in the interim, and they sat down and started talking like they had seen each other only the day before. The 2 of them talked nonstop for the next 90 minutes. I could not understand a word they said, but just watching the 2 of them was unbelievable.

Second, my mom showed me where the Jewish synagogue had been. It had been one of the great synagogues in Germany. I had seen hundreds of pictures of it but it had burned down. There was a little stone monument where it had been. You had to look underneath all the shrubbery to find the little monument. The father of a former friend of hers, Willie Lessing, had been arrested on Kristalnacht when the Nazis burned down many Jewish synagogues. They had taken him to the middle of the square while the synagogue was burning, and they had burned each of his eyes out. They then killed him there in the square. I think when my mom and dad saw things like that happening, it was not hard to make a decision about leaving and where their allegiance was going to be. She related this story to me as we were walking along the street near our hotel when she noticed a sign saying Willie Lessing Strasse. They had named a street after him.

The Mayor of Bamberg had arranged to have a tour guide show us around the city. My mom had other relatives who had been to Bamberg and the people there had tried to be very kind to any Jewish families' returning there. When we got to the hotel there were roses there for my mother, a necktie for me, and little books about the city. The Mayor had personally made available to my mother a young German woman to show us around the city. Bamberg was spared from the bombing. It received virtually no damage during the war. It is a beautiful classic old German city. The next morning a 24-year-old, gorgeous, blond, sophisticated, well-educated, charming German woman, who spoke perfect English, arrived to take us on a walking tour of the city. She spoke to my mom in German and English. I was wondering to myself about the apparent disconnect between what is now and what was then. As we were walking along I said, "Did you ever hear of someone named Willie Lessing?" She said, "Willie Lessing, Willie Lessing, there is a street here called Willie Lessing Strasse but, you know, I really don't know who that person was." My mom asked what she knew about Kristalnacht. She

FIGURE 2. JMI during the interview.

said those were the "schwarze yahren" (black years). She said she really did not know much at all about that time.

This was a woman who was clearly without prejudice. She was a lovely person. She obviously had a university education and yet she knew absolutely nothing about what was happening in Bamberg and other parts of Germany during the Nazi regime. When you have heard stories like that, where people had everything taken from them, were forced to leave not just their homeland but all of their valuable possessions that meant so much to them, and saw what happened to some of their friends, it is very understandable that when my parents came to the USA, Germany was in the past and they suddenly became proud Americans. When I would visit relatives in Cincinnati, some of the older German Jews who had emigrated to the USA still spoke in German much of the time. My parent's view was, "We are now in the USA, we are young, and this is where we are going to make our home. From now on we are Americans and there will be no German spoken in our house." I know virtually no German at all. It was never spoken in our house. When my parents took the pledge of allegiance they knew that the USA was what saved their lives, our families—parents, brothers and sisters. We were one of those families who could not buy a German car. You did not buy German products. It was a very clear break.

WCR: *Your mother and daddy came to the USA at the same time? How did they actually get out? Were they able to go to another country? This was 1937.*

JMI: Yes. They had a pretty straightforward exit. It was difficult for them to secure the appropriate papers.

They spent a couple of years trying to go through that process, but once they did they did not have to go to any unusual measures, they got on a boat and left. The problem was that they could not take anything with them. All of their personal property that was worth anything was left behind. My mother told me about some distant relatives who had tried to be clever about that and put valuables in their trunks and got caught and paid the consequences. My parents said they wanted to leave and left everything behind. They got on a boat and initially came to New York City.

WCR: *They got married not long after they landed in the USA?*

JMI: Yes.

WCR: *They must have had a sponsor from Cincinnati.*

JMI: They had a sponsor, Sol Wetzler, my mother's uncle, from New York; his son, Benjamin, was Chairman of the Democratic Party of New York State. My father moved to New York City first, my mother to upstate New York, and then both ultimately to Cincinnati.

WCR: *How long were they in Cincinnati? Your father was drafted pretty quickly after they got to Cincinnati.*

JMI: Yes.

WCR: *Was that 1942?*

JMI: Yes.

WCR: *He presumably got out of the Army in 1945?*

JMI: Yes. They remained in Cincinnati for a short period of time and then moved to Uhrichsville where my dad had a chance to have his own department store that he managed.

WCR: *How did he do after that? What kind of department store?*

JMI: Retail clothing. The good news was that to a large extent he was his own boss. It was his store. He did not want to stay in Cincinnati, although he had an opportunity to stay in the home office there. The jobs were pretty hard to find right after the war. Two of my uncles were working for a clothing company and my dad asked if he could go to work with them one day. He said he had nothing else to do. They told him that there was no job for him. Nevertheless, he went to work with them. Not having anything to do he walked into a room and started straightening things up. Suddenly, the owner walked in and asked what my dad was doing there and my dad said he had nothing else to do so he came to work with his brothers-in-law, found the room a mess, so he started straightening it up. The owner shook his head and gave my dad a job on the spot! My dad, however, wanted to be his own boss. To do that he had to move to Uhrichsville, Ohio, where he had his own store and some independence. When I was growing up I thought we were rich. There was never a time when I wanted for anything. We had a great family. My parents went out of their way to make things comfortable. My dad never made a lot of money during his life. He was paid very modestly. In retrospect, I now realize that. As kids, we had a great time. My sister and I thought we had everything we needed.

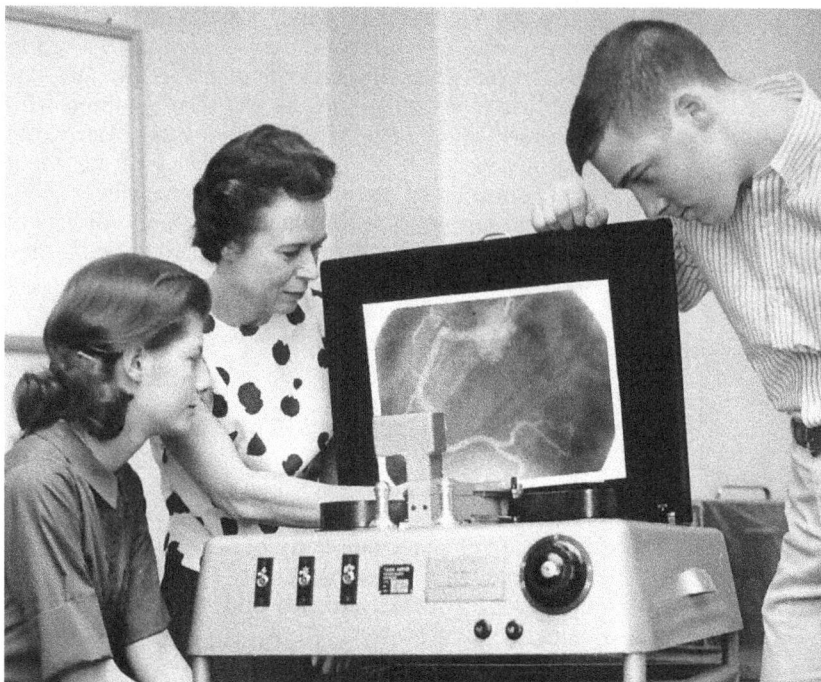

FIGURE 3. As an 11th-grade participant in Canton, Ohio High School Science Seminar, JMI *(left)* and classmate review cineangiogram performed earlier that day by Dr. Grace Hofsteter *(center)*.

WCR: *What year did your dad die?*

JMI: He died in 1976 when I was a first-year cardiology fellow.

WCR: *Is your mother still living?*

JMI: Yes.

WCR: *What is her age now?*

JMI: Eighty-two.

WCR: *What has happened to your mother in these last 23 years?*

JMI: She managed the department store after my dad died. My parents wanted us to move to a city that had a larger Jewish population and better schools so we moved to Canton when I was a freshman in high school. My dad had scouted out the area and found a place that did not have one of the stores and he convinced the guys in Cincinnati to open another one in Massilon, Ohio, near Canton. Massilon is big football territory. That is where Paul Brown used to coach high school before he went on to coach the Cleveland Browns. After my mom retired from managing the store, she moved to the Washington, DC, area where my sister and I were living.

WCR: *There were 2 of you, you and your sister?*

JMI: Yes.

WCR: *You are the oldest?*

JMI: Yes.

WCR: *You were born in 1947, and your sister?*

JMI: My sister was born 3 years later (1950).

WCR: *Although your mother and father were not able themselves to go to college it certainly sounds like they grew up in an educated family. It was just this unfortunate circumstance that prevented their going to college. What was home life like in Urichsville and Canton? Did your mother work?*

JMI: Yes. Both mom and dad worked in the store.

WCR: *So that is how she was able to become manager?*

JMI: Yes.

WCR: *What was it like at home? Did you discuss events of the day or your class work at dinner in the evening?*

JMI: First of all, it was an incredibly nurturing environment. For my parents, the family was absolutely everything. Kids were everything. Every time I ever met anyone who was a friend of my parents from as early as I can remember, the first words out of their mouths were we have heard all about you from your family. My mom had a hard time getting pregnant so by the time they had a couple of children they really felt lucky.

WCR: *They got married in 1940 and you were not born until 1947?*

JMI: Yes. They were both incredibly loving and generous people. I thought everybody was like that until I went away to college. I never really understood how exceptional it was until I started to meet friends and saw the other options. Above all, they had an unbelievable work ethic and they imparted that to my sister and me. Because what had happened to both my parents' having to start from scratch after coming to the USA, although they never complained, my dad and mom were insistent we get an education so that no matter what events occurred around us we had something that was exportable, something you could take with you that nobody could take away from you. A lot of our discussions at night were what we did in school? What did you learn? Because they had been subjected to this cataclysmic Holocaust they were also very much tuned into everything happening in the world politically. My dad went to his grave honestly believing that President Franklin Roosevelt had intervened personally to get his parents out of Germany. My dad had written hundreds of letters to Roosevelt to try to get his parents out while they were exploring all kinds of other avenues. When my grandparents actually got out, my dad was convinced it was because Roosevelt had personally intervened. There were a lot of discussions about politics and world events.

WCR: *When you grew up you were not around other family members? They were in Cincinnati, Ohio? How far was Cincinnati?*

JMI: A 3-1/2 hour ride. In those days people did not fly so much.

WCR: *The relatives you knew in Cincinnati were not your grandparents?*

JMI: Correct. They were aunts and uncles on my mother's side.

WCR: *So you knew nobody from your father's side?*

JMI: My father had one sister and she lived on Long Island. We visited her family there on occasion.

WCR: *What was the population of Uhrichsville?*

JMI: About 5,000 people.

WCR: *Canton was how far away?*

JMI: Forty-five minutes.

WCR: *What was the closest biggest city to Canton?*

JMI: Cleveland, about 90 minutes away.

WCR: *So you went to Cleveland periodically?*

JMI: We would go there to watch baseball or football games.

WCR: *Your school work was considerably well supported at home. I presume that you did extremely well academically in junior high and high school. Did you play sports?*

JMI: I played a lot of sports as I was growing up but I was never really good enough to make any of the school teams. That area was a hot bed of football in particular. Most time outside of school was spent playing sports. My father was a musician and had a great voice. He was a part-time cantor in a Jewish synagogue in upstate New York where we went once a year. It was a small community where one of my mother's brothers lived. The synagogue was not large enough to require a full-time compliment of cantor and rabbi throughout the year so my father would go once a year for the high holidays as the visiting cantor. He really loved music. My sister and I were never that receptive to it. We took piano lessons and trumpet lessons. I played in the band but I always preferred to be involved with sports. My parents were dead set against it. I wanted to play football and I was big enough and could have played. When we were growing up, one year I begged them to get me a football outfit. What they did was give me the whole outfit except the helmet. I think they figured I was smart enough not to go out and play without the helmet. They were not very supportive from that side of things. That was the only negative about my parents. As you know, I had a lot of interest in sports so I converted that to being a sports writer in high school and college.

WCR: *You wrote for your high school newspaper?*

JMI: Yes. When I got to college I was the associate sports editor of our college newspaper.

WCR: *Did anybody other than your family have much of an impact on your growing up?*

JMI: My mother and father had such a great impact and I regarded them with so much respect that it took a lot for anybody else to make much of an impression on me. They were so honest and hardworking. As a child and still to this day, I never saw any negative qualities about my parents. Thus, I always looked at other people by how they measured up to my parents. I don't remember any adult figure who had much of an impact on me until I was in high school.

In Canton, Ohio, they had a thing called the science seminar. The 4 high schools there organized this for students who excelled in science courses. It was structured so that every month they would have 50 to 60 students from the 4 high schools get together, and they would have speakers from different professions every month discuss what they did. After 6 months, each student was supposed to select someone as an advisor or mentor and go to where they worked and learn what they did. One speaker was a cardiologist, Grace Hofsteter. By the time I was in high school I was inherently curious about biology and already knew I wanted to be a doctor. There was a history of heart disease in my family. That is probably why I was always particularly curious about cardiology. She gave one of the talks and she was a wonderful woman. I talked to her about hooking up with her and she allowed me to do that. She was Mason Sones' first cardiology fellow at the Cleveland Clinic. There were a handful of women who did cardiac catheterization procedures at that time. She set up the first catheterization laboratory in Ohio outside the Cleveland Clinic. She had a great interest in pediatric cardiology as did Mason Sones. I would go out to Timken Mercy Hospital (where her cath lab was) every Wednesday after school. I watched her do cardiac catheterizations and then follow her around. It was oftentimes children or babies. (This was before the days of coronary bypass surgery.) A lot of it was valvular heart disease and congenital heart disease. With so few cath labs she had a large catchment area to draw from. I probably saw more pediatric cardiology during that year and one half than I saw in my entire career in cardiology. She would go over the angiograms with me and take me to see the baby and show me something on physical examination. There were occasional patients with coronary disease. I spent every Wednesday doing that. This was when I was in the 11th and 12th grades.

At the end of the science seminar you had to write what amounted to a paper or thesis. I spent a lot of time during my senior year in high school trying to work my way through books on congenital heart disease. I would go to her and ask her questions. In retrospect, when I think about how underpowered I was to try and understand any of this material, it is almost ludicrous, but I did learn. I still have this little paper that I wrote about tetralogy of Fallot, transposition of the great arteries, pulmonary atresia, etc. My job at the final meeting of the science seminar, along with the other students, was to give a 20-minute talk about what we had been doing. I practiced this talk at home the night before with my parents. I got to the end of it and my dad had this like glazed look in his eyes. I asked, "What do you think?" He said, "Jeff, I don't understand a single thing you said but it was the greatest talk I've ever heard."

Those meetings with Grace Hofsteter had a really major impact because she subsequently arranged for me to get a job working summers at the Cleveland Clinic for Mason Sones as his personal "gopher." In addition to that, she had an important impact on my choice as to what I was going to do. Most important of all, she was and is the most compassionate, honest, hardest working, best physician I have ever met in my entire career. For a long time she was the only cardiologist that Sones or any of the other staff at the Cleveland Clinic would accept catheterization films from without repeating the study before operation. Anytime you met anybody from the Cleveland Clinic and asked about Grace Hofsteter it was amazing the respect they had for her. She came from a Quaker background. Her sister was a missionary in India. The 2 of them were the most humble, self-effacing people I have ever met. She, to me, is still the model of what a doctor and certainly a cardiologist should be.

WCR: *Did you go up to her after her talk and ask if you could follow her around?*

JMI: Yes. I said I would like to see what you do and I am interested in going into medicine and being a cardiologist, although I don't really know what that meant. It would help me a lot to see what you as a cardiologist actually do. She was really happy to do it. She was incredibly generous with her time and everything else for the rest of my life.

WCR: *Were you and your sister close growing up?*

JMI: Yes. We have always been close.

WCR: *What does your sister do?*

JMI: My sister became a nurse and went on to get her masters degree in nursing. She was, for a period time before she had a family, working as a hematology oncology nurse at Georgetown University Hospital. More recently she has gone back to working in a radiology/oncology group associated with Georgetown. She has done very well. When I went back to do my fellowship at Georgetown and she moved to Washington, one of the people we had grown up with in Canton, Ohio, Bob Meister, was doing his residency at Georgetown. He introduced my sister to one of his fellow residents and he became her husband, Dick Robinson.

WCR: *What other activities in high school did you participate in that may have had an influence on you?*

JMI: When I was a junior in high school and became 16, I had to get a job. Both my sister and I had to work to have spending money. I got a job working as a carry-out boy at one of the local supermarkets. The job had an important impact on me. Early on, one of my first responsibilities was to clean the floor behind the meat counter after the store closed. This involved picking out all the meat that got stuck in the holes in the meat mat so that it would be clean the next day. I then had to clean out the toilets in the restrooms. After about 2 nights of that and after spending 8 hours on a Saturday carrying out groceries all day, just looking at the clock from the minute I got there until the minute I left, I said to myself that I had to be able to do something that I really loved for a job, because I could never ever spend the rest of my life wishing away the hours of the day. I thought about how people spend their entire lives working at jobs where they basically can't wait to be out of what they are doing. I thought that no matter how hard it might be, I had to do something that I loved.

WCR: *So that experience was a great stimulus to make you work hard in your studies.*

JMI: Yes.

WCR: *It sounds like you could have played sports, but that was something your parents knew did not have much of a future for you.*

JMI: Yes. That is a very nice way to put it.

WCR: *They sort of steered you to other paths. Is that proper?*

JMI: I think my wife would probably be a little more blunt about that, but I think that is accurate.

WCR: *Jeff, how did you go to the University of Maryland to college?*

JMI: This is going to be hard to believe. Both Dr. Hofsteter and Sones had gone to the University of Maryland Medical School. From both of them I heard about the University of Maryland, and so I decided that it was a place I was going to at least visit. Growing up in northeastern Ohio is nothing like living in Boston, where parents talk from the day the kids are born about what is the best Ivy League school their kids can get into. I did not know that much about Ivy League schools. Half of the schools I found out about when I went to medical school I had never even heard of before. I was naive about that. Where I went to school everybody was interested in football. I knew about every school in the country that had a good football team. Dr. Hofsteter and Dr. Sones talked me into visiting the University of Maryland. The medical school was in Baltimore and the undergraduate school was in College Park, Maryland. They had nothing to do with each other. My dad and I went up there. The place was one of the most beautiful campuses I had ever seen. It was a big school even at that time, about 27,000 students. I knew one of the kids there on the football team who was from close to where we grew up and I went to see him. He showed me the stadium and told me what a great time he was having there. We went there for what was supposed to be the interview. The lady told me there was almost no point in going through the interview because they took so few out-of-state students. I said I would take may chances and had the interview. Right after that I came out to the car where my dad was sleeping. He asked how it was and I told him I didn't know because they said they did not take many out-of-state students. I said it might have been a waste of time.

He suggested we go see what Washington was like. My dad had gotten us a hotel room to stay overnight in Washington, DC. That was the first time I had ever been to Washington, which was about 15 minutes from College Park. I thought it was the most spectacular place I had ever been—the White House, the Capitol, the Washington Monument, Arlington Cemetery. At that time they were building the Kennedy Center. I thought this was a great campus, a great football tradition here, 15 minutes away from a great city; what else did you need? The other thing was that I knew I wanted to go to medical school, and I knew that I was going to have to work hard to get into medical school because it was obviously very competitive. My thinking was that if I was going to have to work hard to get into medical school, then if I am going to have fun the fun has to be right there. I am not going to have time to go searching around for it. Here was a beautiful campus with 27,000 people, hundreds of great looking girls. I thought that would be a pretty good combination. My choice of a college was a little crazy but that is the way it happened.

Those were 4 years of my life that I would never ever trade for anything in the world. If I had to go back and do it over again, knowing a little more now than I did then, I would not change that decision for anything because I had a great time, made great friends that are still my best friends to this day. I grew up a lot socially and I grew academically as well. I was also sports writer for the school newspaper.

WCR: *Had you graduated first in your class in high school?*

JMI: I was 4th or 5th in my class of 200 students.

WCR: *When did you hear that you had been accepted at the University of Maryland?*

JMI: I think it was in the late winter or early spring in my senior year in high school.

WCR: *The number of students at the University of Maryland was 5 times larger than the town you grew up in. Canton had how many people?*

JMI: About 100,000.

WCR: *You mentioned you were a sports writer for the college newspaper. Did you do that right away or how did that come about?*

JMI: I was very lucky there. I happened to meet a couple of guys soon after I got there and joined a fraternity. Most in my fraternity were from out of state. There were not many people at Maryland at that time who came from out of state. We were all strangers in a way. This was a way to bond together. One guy who was a senior in the fraternity and was working for the school newspaper got me a job on the school newspaper covering varsity baseball and freshman basketball. I did that for a year and then got the job covering the varsity basketball team. Maryland's basketball team was not good in those days, but they were in the Atlantic Coast Conference so I got to go to every Atlanta Coast Conference (ACC) tournament during my sophomore, junior, and senior years. I had the same press credentials that the reporters from *The Washington Post* and *Baltimore Sun* had. I would sit there right beside Ken Denlinger from *The Washington Post* and the guys from the *Baltimore Sun*. It was a great "Walter Mitty" fantasy. I could pretend that I was a real genuine sports writer. At that time, Frank McGuire coached South Carolina; Vic Bubas, Duke; Dean Smith, North Carolina; and Norm Sloan, North Carolina State. I had the license, by virtue of the press pass, to go up and ask any of these guys anything I wanted. It was a great thrill.

When I was a senior one of my best friends had gone to high school with the son of the athletic director. We were sitting at the fraternity house one night and he said he had just talked to Jimmy Kehoe and he told me that his dad was going to announce the next day that Lefty Driesell was going to come to the University of Maryland from Davidson to be the head basketball coach. I ran back to the *Diamondback* (the name of our newspaper) office, and I called Lefty Driesell's home in North Carolina. He answered and I said, "This is the *Maryland Diamondback* calling and we want to confirm that you are going to be an-

nounced tomorrow as the next head basketball coach here." He started laughing and said "What, where did you hear this?" I said I could not reveal my source but I asked if he could confirm that and he started laughing again. He said, "No, I can't confirm that." I said, "Will you deny it?" He started laughing again and said, "I can't deny it either." I said, "Okay, we are going with the story tomorrow morning that you are going to be announced as the next coach here. Is there anything foolish about doing that?" He started laughing again and said, "You are getting me into trouble and I had better not say anything else." The next morning we ran the headline story on the front page of our school newspaper that Lefty Driesell was coming here to be the head basketball coach. This was the ultimate "Walter Mitty" episode. The next day, I was sitting there in the *Diamondback* office and I got calls from *The Washington Post* and *Baltimore Sun,* asking us how we had scooped them!

WCR: *So you wrote regularly during the basketball season?*

JMI: They played 27 games. I wrote almost daily about the team and then every night after the game I had to put a story together for the next morning about the game. I also was one of the writers covering the football team.

WCR: *So when you were in college, you wrote a lot of sports columns?*

JMI: I did, including one based on an interview with Red Auerbach. He was living in Washington when he was with the Celtics and he would come over and watch a lot of the basketball practices at Maryland. I got to interview him for about 2 hours and he was terrific.

WCR: *By the time you finished 4 years of college you knew how to produce an article quickly.*

JMI: I learned how to do that. I was not good at it initially. I am not a fast writer and I was slow initially. I got some lessons pretty quickly on how to do it faster.

WCR: *You got a degree in practical journalism?*

JMI: Yes, you could call it that. Interestingly, one of the other people on our newspaper at that time was Connie Chung. She was a year ahead of me. She, of course, was not doing sports.

WCR: *So that was a wonderful experience for you. It must have taken a lot of time to go to every one of those games, to write an anticipatory article before a game, describe the game, do interviews, etc.*

JMI: It took a lot of time, especially for a premed student. A lot of the students who were on the paper were journalism majors. This was part of their classes almost. For a premed student it was tougher. One of the most stupid things I ever did in my life was this: Maryland had the first black basketball player to play in the Atlantic Coast Conference. I came to college in 1965 and that year a black basketball player named Billy Jones started playing in Maryland, the first one in any of the ACC schools. I thought it would be good to do a story on what it was like to be the first black basketball player in the ACC, because when he went to North Carolina and South Carolina he had to put up

590   INTERVIEWS

FIGURE 4. Photograph of JMI's fellows at Saint Elizabeth's Hospital, Boston.

with a lot of guff and it was not easy for him. He was a great guy. I was so pressed for time, however, that instead of saying, "Let's go out and have a beer or let's sit down in the locker room after a game," the best way to do an interview, I called him from one of the pay phones on a Sunday night while I was studying at the library and said, "Hey Billy, this is Jeff Isner and I would like to talk to you about what it was like to be the first black basketball player in the ACC." You could imagine what a productive interview that was! It was the consequence of not having a lot of extra time.

WCR: *What did you major in college?*

JMI: Zoology. There were a certain number of required courses that you had to take as a pre-med student. It was a pretty rigorous and structured premed program. By the time I had taken all the required courses I had only to take about 2 more zoology courses to have a major in zoology. To be able to take some non-science courses, like art, history, music, and literature, I wanted to get the science major the most efficient way and zoology was the answer.

WCR: *It sounds like you were very busy in college. You were a member of a fraternity. You mentioned girls. Your social activities were pretty active. You were going down to Washington periodically. You were doing the newspaper column. I guess you kept all those columns?*

JMI: Yes. I still have a scrapbook.

WCR: *That was wonderful training for what you do now and have done in your professional career.*

JMI: There is no question about it. It really forced me, particularly that kind of writing, to be very efficient. I had a great high school English teacher, Esther Smith, who was one of the few teachers I still remember from either high school or college. She taught how to organize a coherent piece of writing. That was important to me. In college, writing with a deadline made me efficient, not only in how fast I could do it, but also in a limited amount of space. I am not saying this just because you are interviewing me, but the person who *really* taught me how to write was you. When I would sit there in your office the way you used to do it, I would bring in a draft and you would basically tear it apart and start from scratch. I watched how you put words together and how you edited things. That had a critical impact on my ability to write.

WCR: *Did some of your fellow students (you talked about great friendships you formed in college) have a significant impact on you? You said that still to this day they are your closest friends.*

JMI: One of my best friends, Bob Pincus, became the president of two banks in Washington. He was very successful, although no one would have predicted that on the basis of how he performed in college. My best friend in college and roommate for 4 years was Larry David, who subsequently became the co-developer, co-producer, and chief writer for the Seinfeld show. He and Jerry Seinfeld originated that show. I thought about this a lot after he won his first Emmy. When we were driving down to Florida for Spring break 1 year, there were 4 of us in the car, Larry, myself, 2 other guys. One of the other guys, Corey Blechman, also won an Emmy for writing the screenplay for *Free Willy*. I was thinking what were the chances of being in the car with 2 guys who ultimately go on to win Emmys? There were obviously some really creative people in our group. When I went out to visit Larry when the American Heart Association was held in Anaheim, Jim Symes (our Chief of Cardiovascular Surgery), Marianne Kearney (my chief technician), and I were given "walk-on" roles for one of the Seinfeld episodes.

Larry had previously spent a number of years doing standup comedy in New York City before he wrote Seinfeld. When I was working and living the life of an intern, feeling like the lowest person on the totem pole, one weekend I went down to visit Larry and he was living in a rundown apartment near Times Square. He was doing standup comedy with Robert Klein and others. He performed every Saturday night. I tagged along with him. He would go into 1 club and they would say "Oh, Larry, great to see you. We will get you on in about 5 minutes." He would wait and all of sudden someone else would walk in and Larry would not get the performance. By the time Larry would get on it would be about 12:30 A.M. and then no one would be there but a bunch of drunks. To go through that kind of rejection night after night made my life as an intern seem like a piece of cake.

WCR: *What did your parents say to you when you would send the newspaper columns home to them?*

JMI: They thought it was the greatest. If it had been up to my parents they would have been at the University of Maryland every weekend. They worked so hard to make sure their kids could go to school, and, frankly, that was another part of going to Maryland. My parents were in a financial situation where it was not so easy for me to qualify for a scholarship, but, on the other hand, if I went to a school that was more expensive it was going to be an incredible stretch for them. It turned out that Maryland was less expensive as an out-of-state student than going to Ohio State would have been as an in-state student. When I looked at that, I thought it would be a good deal for my

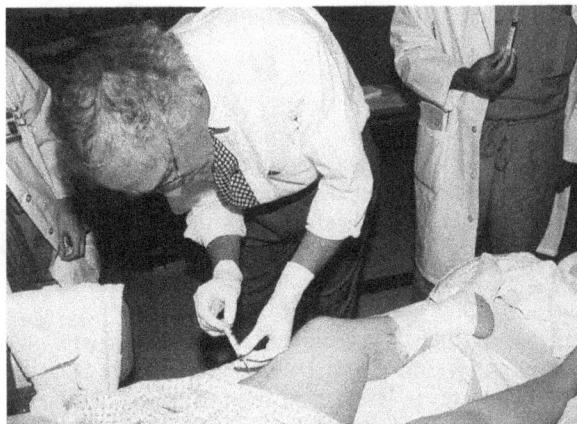

FIGURE 5. JMI performing intramuscular gene transfer for the first time in a patient with severe peripheral arterial obstruction.

parents, and, if I worked some, it would not be too tough for my family. They, as a result, wanted to hear every single detail about what was going on at the college because that was what they lived for, to send their kids to school.

WCR: *Did you have an automobile in college?*

JMI: No. I think I was probably the only kid in my fraternity that didn't. I never had a car until my senior year. I remember coming home at the end of final exams my junior year. My dad came to pick me up at the Cleveland-Hopkins Airport. I was exhausted. I just wanted to get to sleep and my dad took me out to this car, and I said, "Geez Dad, this is not your car." He said, "No, it's yours." I finally had a car my senior year!

WCR: *You made Phi Beta Kappa in college your junior year?*

JMI: Yes.

WCR: *You graduated magna cum laude?*

JMI: Yes.

WCR: *What does magna cum laude mean at the University of Maryland?*

JMI: I think it was based on your grade point average.

WCR: *It sounds like you worked extremely hard in college. You wanted to do well and your mission was to get into medical school. The sports writing sounds like it was something that after awhile you could not turn down. You could not give it up because it was providing too many opportunities and fun things. You were meeting people. You must have had a busy life in college. Did you sleep much?*

JMI: No. I remember coming home from the library when it closed at midnight. There was a sub shop where you would stop off to have a sub when you were getting ready to go to bed. Then you would come back and sit around with the guys before going to bed about 1:00 A.M. I was 1 of the few people in that fraternity who got up for an 8:00 A.M. class. Larry was my roommate and he never went to class. I was one of the few premeds in this fraternity and people always asked why I was studying so much?

WCR: *You lived in the fraternity house?*

JMI: Yes. I lived there until my senior year and then had an apartment off campus.

WCR: *Did anybody have an impact on you in college? It sounds like the college newspaper was very influential? What about teachers?*

JMI: When I look back on it, I don't know that there was any teacher that had a major impact on me. I knew I wanted to go to medical school so I did not need any kind of stimulus to study. I knew I had to get really good grades. One course which had an important impact on me was our honors course in science and philosophy that I was selected to take. That was perhaps the first time I ever encountered a truly Socratic type of teaching. We met at the professor's house. It started making me understand that there was a different way to think and approach things. We also had a good English Department and I read a lot of Southern writers like Falkner and Ellison. That was a great reprieve from all the science. I still have the books we had to read. I read relatively slowly, but part of that was due to my studying the author's writing technique as well as the content. That helped later on in terms of being able to write.

WCR: *How did you pick Tufts University School of Medicine?*

JMI: This was about as insightful as the way I picked Maryland to go to college. I loved being in the Washington, DC, area and I thought I wanted to be a practicing physician in that area. I wanted to go to Georgetown Medical School in Washington, DC. I applied to Georgetown and got in right away. I also had sent an application to the University of Maryland Medical School in Baltimore. I was asked to go to Maryland for an interview. I got to Baltimore a little bit late for the tour they were giving the interviewees. I was trying to find out where the tour was when I ran into the brother of one of my roommates at the University of Maryland who had just started his freshman year there. (He subsequently went on to be a very successful orthopedic surgeon in the Washington area.) He asked what I was doing there? I said I was there for an interview because I had applied to medical school. He asked if I was crazy, otherwise why would I want to spend 4 years in Baltimore. He said he was there because he had to be there. He said I could get into a lot of places. He said he had been in Boston the week before riding the MTA with a friend of his and that he must have fallen in love 15 times. He said if he were me that he would go to Boston to medical school. I wrote to Tufts and asked if it was too late to apply, and they said there was another month so I applied. I had never been to Boston or New England.

When I went to visit Tufts, one of the things they did on the tour of the medical school was to allow us to spend an hour with a former fellow of Dr. Proctor Harvey's, Dr. "Chris" Chrisitiello. The stethoscopes were set up and we listened to heart sounds. It was just by chance he happened to be doing it that day when I was there so I thought this was great since I wanted to go into cardiology. I was interviewed by one of the Associate Deans, Norman Grace. (He now has a place close to ours at the Cape, so I see him every weekend

there.) I don't remember much about the interview except that he asked what I imagined myself doing several years later. As a typical college student, I usually was thinking a maximum of about one day in advance. Certainly, I never got more than a year in advance. My role model as a doctor was Grace Hofsteter, a practicing physician. I said to him, "I don't know. I have not really thought that far in advance. I would be thrilled to get into medical school and I imagine that there are a lot of things you can do as a doctor and I am willing to consider all of them. The only thing I can tell you for sure that I have no interest in is academic medicine."

WCR: *Did you get a partial scholarship?*

JMI: Yes, and it was very partial. Tufts, even at that time, was one of the more expensive medical schools. I also got a very large loan. The only way that I would go to a place like Tufts was if I got that loan because I was very certain that I did not want my parents to have to pay for anything in medical school. I could have gone to Ohio State Medical School which was a lot less expensive, but I figured I would go to Tufts if I could get a combination of a scholarship and loans, so my parents would not have to pay for anything. I was able to ultimately pay for all my medical school. In those days there was a really great loan program. I worked all the way through medical school as a bartender and a waiter at a couple of the local pubs to make some extra money.

WCR: *Medical school was just like college for you. It was not the only activity you were doing during those 4 years.*

JMI: The only difference was that you really had to work at it to make sure it was not the only activity. It was very much different from college in the sense that all of a sudden you walked into a class where there were 120 clones of yourself. In my fraternity, I was one of the only premeds there, so everybody was doing something different from what I was doing. All of a sudden everybody was doing exactly the same thing. That was weird, and, moreover, all of a sudden from morning to night, all you studied was science. It was very monolithic. I took advantage of what was, at that point, a very liberal time at Tufts Medical School. This was during the Vietnam War. It was when a lot of universities and medical schools were starting to experiment with the pass/fail system. Tufts was one of the earliest to have a pass/fail system. I am not proud to say that I took full advantage of that. I was fortunately able to take a number of art courses and music courses at Harvard's night school just to do something different.

Nevertheless, I could say that the first 2 years of medical school were probably the 2 least enjoyable years of my entire academic learning experience or career. The first year I was there we had one of the worst snow storms in the history of Boston. All of a sudden, around November I thought I was in Siberia. It always snowed. I went to the medical library and got the names of 5 medical schools in southern California and actually wrote applications to transfer. It was also compounded by the fact that I barely had enough money to do much. Everybody I had graduated with at Maryland now had jobs and most were having a great time. They had enough money to enjoy themselves. Here I was 22 years old, living in a 2-man dorm room with hardly enough money to date. It was just not that much fun. Once we got into the clinics and started doing what I thought you came to medical school to do, however, then it became more fun. I then began spending more time going back and looking at material I learned in the first 2 years, since you could now see certain basic elements fit into what you were doing clinically. Then, as opposed to the first 2 years, I developed a voracious appetite for it.

WCR: *You obviously did not follow through on your applications to southern California medical schools.*

JMI: Probably inertia more than anything else. Once the Spring came and the snow melted and I could see signs of life it was different. I had a few good friends by then and we rented a place together for the next year. It seemed like I should stay.

WCR: *You worked harder the last 2 years than the first?*

JMI: Much harder.

WCR: *Who had an impact on you in medical school?*

JMI: The person who had the greatest impact on me in medical school was not on the faculty at Tufts, but was Mason Sones at the Cleveland Clinic. For 3 years I went back and worked directly for him in the summers. I was his personal gofer. He was such a unique guy, although always very controversial. People had very strong feelings regarding him one way or the other. To me he was the greatest. He was first of all one of the most honest people I have ever met. He was honest to a fault. There was not an ounce of "BS" about him. I just instinctively appreciated the fact that he was so very authentic. There was no agenda, no program—what you saw was what you got. Not only that, but 1967 was the first year I was at the clinic and that was the year that Rene Favalaro did the first coronary bypass operation. All of a sudden the whole face of 20th century cardiology completely changed. I was there as a premed and then a medical student— just awestruck by these gigantic first steps. I spent a lot of time in his office while some of the major figures in cardiology (At the time I did not know who they were but later on recognized the names.) were coming in there and I would sit there and watch and listen. Even as a totally unimportant, irrelevant medical student, Sones would spend an enormous amount of time with me. I would sit there at night and watch him go over angiograms. If anyone looks at enough angiograms, you can start figuring out what is going on. That was the time they were switching from doing the Vineburg procedure to coronary bypass. Soon I was comparing every other doctor I met to Sones. It was hard to find people who were achieving or changing medicine as much as he was. Frankly, it was hard to find people who were as unpretentious, down-to-earth, and brutally honest as he was.

For better or worse, Sones was the man who I ended up comparing a lot of my Tufts faculty to.

There were also people like Louis Weinstein who at that time was at the peak of his career. No matter what rotation I was ever on, I always tried to get over to go to his rounds because they were classics. He was a very inspiring figure. John Harrington, who at that time was one of several young outstanding nephrologists at the New England Medical Center, was very energetic and popular with the students. He took lots of time with the students. He is now the Dean of the Medical School. He encouraged me to keep academic medicine as a career option. And my cousin, Welton Gersony, also encouraged me to do an elective at Columbia-Presbyterian (Baby's) Hospital in New York City, where he was and still is Chief of Pediatric Cardiology. He made a very important impact on me.

WCR: *So you never changed your mind during medical school as to what you wanted to do. You wanted to be a cardiologist from those high school days?*

JMI: Right. I did, however, go through a period when I wanted to be a psychiatrist. Tufts had a great psychiatry department with a lot of young terrific guys. We had a lot of exposure to them during the first 2 years of medical school. That was the bright spot during the first 2 years of medical school. First of all, there were a lot of elements of English and history and drama. The psychiatrists would use all of that as part of their teaching. I loved that part of it. I spent 1 summer taking an extra elective in Boston doing psychiatry. One of the faculty helped me get a summer job at St. Elizabeth's Hospital in Washington, DC, doing psychiatry as part of the U.S. Health ("Co-Step") Program. I had a great mentor there named Steve Pechynic. When I had discussions with Sones about what I was going to do and I would tell him I wanted to be a cardiologist like he was, he said to me, "I think this is the frontier of cardiology, a great time to be a cardiologist, but it is not always going to be this way. I suspect that you should go into an area where people don't know anything. You ought to go into psychiatry. Those people are clueless. That is what I would do if I were your age." I spent a lot of time in psychiatry. I even went to London, United Kingdom, to do an elective at the Maudsley Hospital. I really thought, to my parents' great anxiety and concern, that I might be a psychiatrist!

WCR: *You got that out of your system by the time you entered the wards?*

JMI: Not entirely. I thought that I would take at least a year of medical internship, because even if I thought I was going to be a psychiatrist I thought it was important to do that. My desire to be a psychiatrist ended after I started my internship. I really loved the medical internship and from then on I knew I would be a cardiologist.

WCR: *How was class standing determined at medical school on a pass/fail system? Do you have any idea? Where did you stand?*

JMI: I have no idea. I guess the written evaluations were such that they ended up determining where you stood in your class but I had no idea where I was in my class.

FIGURE 6. JMI and wife Linda with sons Josh *(center)*, Matthew *(right)*, and daughter Jessica *(left)*.

WCR: *You are an athletic-appearing person. Did surgery appeal to you at all?*

JMI: What I loved about surgery was the locker-room atmosphere. I loved the fact that you would go into the operation saying "let's go get 'em." You would come out and say "That was great, let's go out and have a beer." Part of it was terrific. The camaraderie of the surgical team anytime of night, the tougher the better, the worse it got, was great. That part of it still appeals to me. Maybe that's why interventional cardiology appeals to me. What was missing, however, was the differential diagnosis. I don't want to say that internal medicine is more intellectual than surgery, but it was a different way of looking at things. The real deal in surgery was to do great surgery and less emphasis on the intellectual exercises of internal medicine. I liked that about internal medicine. One of my best friends in medical school, Chip Glassman, liked both surgery and medicine. He liked the operating room/locker room atmosphere even better than I did. He went off to be a urologist.

WCR: *Why did you pick St. Elizabeth's Hospital for your medical internship?*

JMI: A combination of things. I had made friends here. I had worked at St. Elizabeth's while in medical school because it was one of the Tuft's teaching hospitals. Some of the best times that I had had while I was in medical school were spent at St. Elizabeth's. It was an unusual hospital because there was a full-time academic faculty, and at the same time a large cadre of physicians who were in private practice. We saw large numbers of patients with myocardial infarction, pneumonia, sick-as-hell diseases, and at the same time there was still a very academic approach to how you took care of these patients. It was a great academic environment to learn how you take care of very sick people.

WCR: *When in medical school you paid your own way and what you could not pay you borrowed. You* *also worked during those 4 years. How many hours were you working a week?*

JMI: Probably 16 hours a week as a waiter or bartender.

WCR: *That is a lot of time while in medical school. When you were doing your internship I gather this is when you really decided you liked medicine, you liked being a doctor, and the internship was the hardest you had worked up to that point in your life. Who had an impact on your during the internship?*

JMI: My peers. It was a very strong house staff at that time including my own group. One of my colleagues and best friends, Barry Benowitz, went on to become an endocrinologist at the University of Utah; and a year ahead of me, Mike Jaker and John Dowling. Mike Jaker went on to be on the faculty at the New Jersey Medical School. John is now my personal physician and he also takes care of my friends, wife, and in-laws. He is now here on the staff. He gets an award every year for being one of the best physicians in Boston. I learned a lot from them. I still remember vividly specific patients where these guys would drill me because there was something I did not know or had not thought about. I can still remember walking with Mike Jaker down one of the corridors that I now walk down every day talking about the differential diagnosis on a patient we were going to see in the emergency room. They were enthusiastic, great teachers, just hungry to be on the front line. There were plenty of sick patients to take care of. The guys I was working with every day and every night were the ones I really learned a lot from.

The attending staff included Bernie Kosowsky, who had just become Chief of Cardiology. He took over from Tom Ryan who had just left to go to Boston University Medical Center. At that time his major interest was cardiac arrhythmias. He had worked with Tony Damato at Staten Island and also with Proctor Harvey at Georgetown. He spent a lot of time with medical students and house staff on arrhythmia interpretation and physical diagnosis. That was, of course, appealing to me as someone who wanted to go into cardiology. He pushed hard for me to go to Georgetown. Ken MacDonell, who at that time was Chief of the Pulmonary Division and Director of the Intensive Care Unit and is now the Chief of Medicine, simply made it fun to be a doctor. When I was a student and took an elective with him here, he would grab a bunch of students and take us over to hear the clinicopathologic conference at the Massachusetts General Hospital, or if there was a great speaker anywhere else in town, we would go hear the talk. People like Ken MacDonnell genuinely enjoyed practicing medicine. It was authentic and genuine. Not surprisingly, they were great teachers. They also made sure that anything you said you could back up with data. There was also Bob Flynn who was Chief of Neurology and subsequently became Chief of Medicine. He later became Director of Caritas Christi, the network of hospitals that St. Elizabeth's is part of. He was a spectacular neurologist. Rotations through his neurology division as well as Ken MacDonnell's pulmonary division were 2 of the most popular rotations at Tufts Medical School. Bob Flynn was a great teacher, a great diagnostician, and a very tough guy who would not put up with any BS at a time when long hair was in style. He was a great role model. Fred Stohlman, who was Chief of Medicine at that time, had just come from the NIH. They created a research department for him. He was the Editor of *Blood*. He had done seminal work on erythropoietin at NIH and had established a strong research group here in hematology. One of the young guys he had was Peter Quesenbury who was my very first attending here. He was a dynamic guy, hard core in the best sense of the word. He never stopped rounds when the clock stopped, but only after he had seen every patient. He would thoroughly discuss every differential diagnosis. He referred to every relevant article. When he was an attending, that is what his life was for that month. He was a tremendous teacher and subsequently went on to become Chief of Hematology at The University of Massachusetts Medical School. Lou Braverman, who was Chief of Endocrinology, was one of the editors of the major endocrinology textbook, and he also is now at the University of Massachusetts in Worchester, where he became Chief of Endocrinology. They were all outstanding teachers and physicians. At the end of that year, I knew reflexively how to deal with any patient that came across my path.

WCR: *You were very pleased at the end of your internship in the choice you had made?*

JMI: That year was one of the very best years I've ever had. Shortly after I finished the 2 years with you at the NIH, I came back to St. Elizabeth's to give Grand Rounds. I got up and said, "I know I am going to lose all credibility by saying this but the year of internship I spent here was 1 of the best years of my life." Of course, all the house staff started laughing. But it was really one of those years during which you worked hard and played hard. You did not have much time to play so when you played you played hard. I was living with a couple of female medical students who were best friends. We had a great house in Cambridge and there were parties there all the time. I left that year to go back to Washington because I thought that was where I wanted to live and went back there to do my residency.

WCR: *You went to Georgetown to do your first year residency and then your cardiology fellowship. You simply wanted to live in the Washington, DC, area.*

JMI: I really missed being in Washington and I missed my old friends. By that time, my Boston friends had scattered to do their internships. I started thinking where I wanted to go and what I wanted to do. I thought I really wanted to go back to Washington. Fred Stohlman, who was the Chief of Medicine

and good friends with Dudley Jackson, who was the Chief of Medicine at Georgetown, helped me go back.

WCR: *You had only 1 year of residency before you started your cardiology fellowship. How did you enjoy the Georgetown atmosphere?*

JMI: I thought it was great. At that time you spent about a third of your time at Georgetown, a third at Fairfax Hospital, and a third at the Washington Veterans Administration Hospital. It was a tremendous variety. Every setting was very different from the other. I loved being back in Washington. I lived in Glover Park and walked to work. It was a beautiful place to live. Before I went back to do a year of medical residency, I had already been accepted as a cardiology fellow. Georgetown had a great house staff at that time. It was an enriching place from a clinical standpoint.

WCR: *You had the 2 years of fellowship in cardiology. When did you start thinking that maybe you might like a career in academic medicine?*

JMI: The role model mentors at Georgetown were outstanding clinicians and teachers. I started to sense that their lives looked pretty interesting in terms of the teaching and what they were doing, plus it was about that time that I had kind of caught up educationally with what I had been exposed to at the Cleveland Clinic. I thought that was really exciting. Looking at what was happening—catheterization, angiography, bypass surgery—I now understood what was going on. I thought if I could somehow mix the practice of medicine with some of the other investigative possibilities that would be a lot of fun.

WCR: *How did you come to the National Institutes of Health?*

JMI: The chief resident when I was at Georgetown said to me, as I am sure he said to all the house staff, "Jeff, before you finish your residency you ought to write a paper." I said, "Why?" He said there was something good about having gone through that experience. The article is going to be forever and you will always have something. I took an elective with Phil Schein and Jack MacDonald, both of whom had come from the National Cancer Institute of NIH to start the cancer center at Georgetown. They were dynamic people. It was the only elective available to me. They said I had 1 choice, oncology or nothing. I signed up and it turned out to be an unbelievable month. I know I personally influenced 4 other friends who were house staff at either Georgetown or George Washington to also take the same elective month. None of them had any previous ideas about going into oncology and they all became oncologists. One of them went on to become Head of the AIDS Program at NIH. We had a patient who had an ovarian carcinoma with spontaneous peritonitis. I reported the case with MacDonald and Schein. That elective and experience of having written that paper made an important impact on me. I developed a different view of oncology, but not enough to want to change from going into cardiology.

WCR: *How did you come to NIH?*

JMI: About half way through my cardiology fellowship I decided I definitely wanted to go on to a career in academic cardiology. Rick Walsh, who was one of my fellow trainees, knew from the day he was born he wanted to be in academic medicine. We spent a lot of time talking about it. He was a great guy and is still one of my best friends. He became Head of Cardiology at the University of Cincinnati and just recently has taken over as Chief of Medicine at Case-Western Reserve. Jules Gardin was another good friend in our fellowship class who also wanted to go into academic cardiology, and he is now Chief at the University of California at Irvine. We all talked and concluded that if we were going into academic medicine that we needed to go somewhere where we could learn to do investigative work to complement the clinical orientation we had had in our fellowship. At that time you were coming to Georgetown for weekly pathology conferences. You were obviously a very charismatic teacher and had the ability to make pathology relate to what I was doing in clinical medicine. We also spent a month during our cardiology fellowship at the Armed Forces Institute of Pathology with Chip McAllister. I had a great time with him and got to see a tremendous variety of pathology. We also had a month at the NIH. All the Georgetown fellows rotated out to NIH for a month. Those were the glory days of the Cardiology Branch of the National Heart Institute. I found that environment heaven. People got paid to spend all day asking questions and getting answers. They also took care of patients. I thought what could be better. At the time, since all the fellows knew you, it was easy to come to your lab while we were rotating at the NIH. It seemed to be the place I wanted to be. I could stay in Washington. At the same time I could go to an environment that was wonderful and, as I thought about it, I thought the pathology, at least the way you were doing it, was something I could relate to. I could see how I could use this as an opportunity in academic medicine. It also seemed to me that you learned a lot from the pathology about how to do things clinically. The way you did the clinicopathologic correlations made sense clinically so it just seemed like a natural.

WCR: *You were obviously quite productive during those 2 years. How did it work out that you came back to Tufts?*

JMI: I was looking at a couple of different jobs. Then one day I was in Steve Epstein's office. We were talking and he happened to get a call from Dr. Sheldon Wolff, who had been at the NIH before he became Chief of Medicine at Tufts. Steve put his hand over the phone and said Shelly needs another cardiologist at Tufts and Steve asked me if I wanted to go there. I went the next week to meet Shelly. The hard part was that I did not want to leave Washington. At the same time, I knew that if I was going to do something on my own, having been trained by you to do cardiac pathology, it was almost imperative that I go away because I could not really do anything independently in Washington at that time. It seemed to me that this would be

a good thing to do at the time so that I could develop independence.

WCR: *You returned to Boston when?*

JMI: October 1979.

WCR: *You spread out in a lot of different areas. You did retain the pathology arena for a long time and you are still doing some of that but you got into the cath lab quickly.*

JMI: Part of the deal was the job I was looking at. (It seems naïve in retrospect.) I was absolutely intent on being able to work both in the cath lab and do cardiac pathology. We now joke about the standard "cath/path package." Of course, it was not standard at all. It did not exist. My thinking was that if you are working in a cath lab nobody is ever going to question that you are earning your living. Then you can take a little bit of a chance with the investigative part of what you want to do. With the jobs I was looking at I would only go there on the condition that I would have a joint appointment in pathology and I would spend roughly half my time doing cardiac pathology and the other half working in the cath lab from day 1.

WCR: *You started doing angioplasty quickly?*

JMI: At that point angioplasty had not yet been done in Boston! Shortly afterwards, however, Peter Block at the Massachusetts General Hospital and David Faxon at Boston University began performing coronary angioplasty. Just as I left the NIH I remember Sones telling me how he had just come back from a meeting with Grunzig and he was very excited about angioplasty. At that same time, Kenny Kent began doing it in Washington, DC. I remember a Thursday night conference at Georgetown at which Kenny Kent presented a patient of his who had angina 1 day and did not have it the next day. He opened the patient's shirt and no scars were on his chest. He said what do you think happened to this patient? It was the first angioplasty that had been done in Washington. I started doing angioplasty the first or second year I was back at the New England Medical Center. Everybody was learning it by doing it at that time.

WCR: *How did you get into lasers?*

JMI: After leaving the NIH and just after getting to Boston, angioplasty exploded. I was thinking to myself, "You dunce, why are you so stupid? First of all, you had the advantage of Sones' having gone over to meet with Grunzig in the earliest days of its development, and he tells you about it and you just pass it off and don't give it a second thought. Then Kenny Kent did it in Washington. So you had a second chance to get involved and you blew it again. This is the biggest thing that has happened since Sones did the first angiogram and Favalaro did the first bypass operation and you really blew it. So if something else comes along that looks like it is going to be angioplasty you better make damn sure you don't miss the boat this time." I was at a heart meeting session on angioplasty at the American Heart Association and George Abela presented a paper on some very simple studies that he had just done at Gainesville, Florida, in which they had used a laser to show that they could ablate plaque in coronary arteries in vitro. I thought, "Okay this is the next big thing coming along and I don't want to just ride this one. I want to be a conductor." It was obvious, however, that if you were going to do this you had to have a laser. I looked through the yellow pages in the telephone directory and tried to find out where I could get a laser. I could not find one anywhere. I figured if there were a laser in Boston that it would be at Massachusetts Institute of Technology. I called MIT and said I was a physician and wanted to meet someone who had a laser. They mentioned Fred Bowman. He did not have a laser but he said he would keep my name in mind if he found anyone who wanted to do something related to what I was talking about. Bowman was at a cocktail party and ran into Richard Clarke who was a Chemistry Professor at Boston University. Bowman called and told me about Richard Clarke who had a laser and worked on photosynthesis. Clarke was getting tired of doing that and was excited about what I was talking about and that I should give Clarke a call. I called Richard Clarke and he subsequently became one of my best friends. We hit if off right away. He is a great guy and one of the smartest people I have ever met. At the time I was single and he was single so we had almost unlimited time to work together. For me it was like going back to school again because I was learning about things I had never really paid much attention to before. It was a whole new vista and was the beginning of a great collaboration and a great personal friendship.

WCR: *Your bringing the laser along was really your initiation into investigative medicine. Isn't that correct?*

JMI: Yes, that is right.

WCR: *How is this laser going to work out as far as its usefulness in producing holes in the myocardium? Are you optimistic about it?*

JMI: I am not terribly optimistic about it. The NIH convened a panel in about 1983 when many of us were just beginning to work with lasers and cardiovascular disease. The panel was convened to try and help the NIH decide whether they should make an investment in this technology. I was assigned the job of giving a talk about what was then called "the Mirhoseini procedure." At that time, Mirhoseini was using a laser to create channels in the myocardium. Unfortunately, he was forced to do this in conjunction with bypass surgery. It was always impossible to decide whether it was the laser or bypass that was helping the patients. It was a procedure that everybody found intriguing. Many people were skeptical but nobody could dismiss it. It almost died on the vine and then subsequently it has had a rebirth. There have been a lot of interpretations about how this procedure works. Angiogenesis has been the latest interpretation of how this procedure works. I think it is hard to say. There have been so many things in interventional cardiology that defy logic. Even though balloon angioplasty was shown to be very effective, it took a long time to understand the mechanism of its effectiveness. Most interventionalists came to the conclusion early that they were not going to be concerned about how these things worked, but if they seemed useful, they could figure out the

mechanism later. As a result, there was a lot of empirical investigation. Enough effort is being applied to this right now that if it is effective we will know.

WCR: *Are you doing it now?*

JMI: No. We elected not to.

WCR: *Do you think it is going to work out from an intraarterial standpoint? Can you get enough holes in the myocardium intraarterially versus intraoperatively?*

JMI: I think so. I believe it still remains to be seen whether either the intraoperative or percutaneous approach will be definitive in terms of stand-alone therapy.

WCR: *Dr. Isner, you have become the leader in gene transfer angiogenesis. How did that come about?*

JMI: It was a combination of a couple of things. With lasers, we were very well funded by the NIH and had a very productive laboratory. We aimed at both applied research and basic research. When the lasers moved into the clinic, it became clear that it was going to be tough to continue to interest the NIH in funding fundamental laser-tissue interactions. That became painfully clear to me when we tried to renew a laser grant after having been very productive. It was around the time when cardiologists were starting to appreciate that there was something to be gained from molecular biology.

WCR: *This was what year?*

JMI: It was about 1989.

WCR: *You came to St. Elizabeth's in 1988?*

JMI: Yes. I had a couple of talented fellows from Canada, Guy Leclerc and Jeff Pickering, who came here funded by the Canadian Heart Association. They came to work on laser-tissue interaction. They got here and I said "You know what. I have news for you. I am not sure it is in your best interest or mine to pursue lasers further. Molecular biology is here for cardiologists and I think it would be good for both you and me if we got involved. We are going to learn this together." I was lucky enough that we had gotten one of our other laser grants renewed. I said, "We are going to use some of the support to bootstrap ourselves so that we can develop some expertise in molecular biology." I recruited a fellow from Bob Adelstein's lab at the NIH who helped us set up our laboratory. I sent Guy Leclerc off to Hubert Wolfe's lab to learn how to do in situ hybridization. Together, we started developing some rudimentary expertise in molecular biology. At the same time, we lacked a focus. What do we do with this?

At that time, directional atherectomy was beginning, and then we had access to plaques. Eric Topol was just starting the CAVEAT study. I was fortunate in that Eric subsequently became a very close friend and was able to arrange for us to be the core pathology laboratory for the CAVEAT study. By applying in situ hybridization and immunohistochemical techniques to these specimens from live patients, we figured we might learn a little more about the pathogenesis of atherosclerosis and, in particular, restenosis. Up to that time, studies of atherosclerosis and restenosis were limited to study of autopsied patients. All of a sudden, we could get "live" specimens! We took advantage. Also, in 1989 Betsy Nabel published her article in *Science* describing the ability to do arterial gene transfer in live animals. This was it. This was the perfect way to marry interventional cardiology and molecular biology. It gave us the focus we needed. We quickly got Betsy out here to give grand rounds and she was exceptionally generous in talking with us and bringing us up to speed on this whole new concept of gene transfer; she subsequently became a good friend. We also had a very close association at that time with Boston Scientific in terms of developing catheters for local drug delivery. Thus, we could marry what abilities we had in the animal lab to what we had learned in molecular biology. It also seemed like a great way to study both the elements responsible for restenosis and at the same time maybe use gene therapy as a means of developing a new way to approach restenosis.

The final piece was this. When we first had started using lasers in the clinic in the mid- to late 1980s, the initial investigations were in the peripheral arteries. At that time, we were doing these procedures at the New England Medical Center with the radiologists and the vascular surgeons with an absolute minimum amount of cooperation. As we started doing that work, we were forced to learn about peripheral vascular disease.

WCR: *When was that?*

JMI: 1986. When learning about the peripheral arteries and seeing how limited the therapeutic options were there, I developed an interest in this area. I saw a real opportunity to create an integrated program for the care of patients with peripheral vascular disease. One of the major reasons I came to St. Elizabeth's was an opportunity to establish from ground zero a true multidisciplinary group to include radiologists, vascular surgeons, and cardiologists. I was able to bring Kenny Rosenfield with me at that time who was one of our cardiology fellows at the New England Medical Center. Kenny helped start our peripheral vascular program, which was the first program of its kind in Boston and one of the very few in the country. We started seeing lots of patients with very severe peripheral arterial disease and most had failed surgery and were poor candidates for angioplasty; indeed, that is the only reason they were sent to us, that is as a last resort before amputation. I remember as a Georgetown fellow Helen Taussig's visit and her telling the story about how, as a woman coming out of Harvard Medical School, there had been very limited opportunities academically just because she was a woman. She was able to get a position on the faculty at The Johns Hopkins Hospital, but when she got there there was such prejudice that they told her, "Look, why don't you go take care of the blue babies because there is nothing that can be done for them anyway. There is nothing to lose by having you do that." I remember her saying how she was so angry about it that she said she was determined to find something that she could do for those "blue babies." The rest is history. She got involved with Blalock and did find something that could be done for those babies.

When I saw the patients with critical limb ischemia, I thought that this was the adult equivalent of the "blue baby." Everybody sends these cases because they say there is nothing else that can be done. When there is nothing left to be done, an opportunity arises to make a contribution! We had this large stable of patients with bad peripheral vascular disease. We were aware of Judah Folkman's long-standing campaign to neutralize the growth and metastasis of malignant tumors by neutralizing growth factors responsible for the growth of blood vessels that supported these tumors. If we could do the opposite, that is, promote blood vessel growth in these patients' legs, maybe it would be just enough to prevent amputation in them. About that time we were recruiting a new Chief of Cardiovascular Surgery here. I was at the beach at the Cape and ran into neighbors who talked about a friend of theirs in Montreal who is such a great guy and who wants to leave Canada. He was looking for a position in the USA and he is the greatest cardiovascular surgeon on the planet. (Of course, I figured this is the way my parents talked about me.) They said, "Would you mind if we have him get in touch with you?" I said, "Oh, yes sure." So he called me and his name is Jim Symes. He wanted to see what was going on and he sent me his CV. All of a sudden I find out that my friends on the beach were right! This guy, at least on paper, was a very productive academic cardiovascular surgeon. He was both a vascular surgeon and a cardiac surgeon. He came down to visit and turned out to be even better in person than he was on paper. He is a tremendously wonderful person and, again, he became another one of my very close friends. We were able to recruit him. After he got here I learned that he had worked with Vineburg as one of his trainees, and that procedure had stimulated his interest in angiogenesis. I told him of our idea to use growth factors to promote collateral vessel growth in these terrible peripheral vascular disease patients. He replied: "That is funny. We just talked recently to a guy from Genentech who said they had a new growth factor." We called up Genentech, and Napoleon Ferrara, who had identified vascular endothelial growth factor (VEGF), came shortly thereafter to Boston. We presented the idea to grow new blood vessels in the legs of these patients with terrible peripheral vascular disease. We could take advantage of some catheter-based techniques to introduce the protein. We also thought it might be possible to do this with gene therapy. We were starting to deal with a couple of different catheters in our lab. We already knew we could deliver a so-called reporter gene percutaneously via a couple of catheters we were working with. They gave us some material to try it out and Satoshi Takeshita immediately showed that the protein would work. However, we were unable to persuade Genetech to proceed with a clinical trial. We knew we could not make recombinant protein ourselves, but if gene therapy could be shown to work, we felt we could "manufacture" naked DNA in our own facility. We then decided to try doing that with gene therapy as well. An observation Douglas Losordo in our laboratory had made was to show that if a gene encoded for a protein that was secreted rather than a protein that remained within the cell, even so-called naked DNA (without viral vectors) could actually yield significant evidence of gene expression. It turned out that VEGF was a secreted protein, one of the only angiogenic growth factors at that time that was known to be secreted. We took advantage of all this to develop a gene therapy approach in the lab to grow collateral blood vessels in these patients with critical limb ischemia. Now for the first time we saw the goal line. That is how it all crystallized.

WCR: *You have moved from intraarterial peripherally to intramuscular peripherally. How have intramuscular injections worked out?*

JMI: We were being sent a lot of peripheral vascular patients, and in some of them we could not get access to the arteries of the leg because the atherosclerotic plaque was too extensive. We decided we needed another option. We thought perhaps we could take advantage of the intramuscular injection approach. In the lab, Yukio Tsurumi had documented that the intramuscular delivery was just as effective as the intraarterial delivery, so we decided to apply that route to patients. We first used the intraarterial approach on December 7, 1994, Pearl Harbor Day! We were very concerned that that was a day that would live in infamy again. That was when the lab was really cresting. After years of trying to put things together, we were ready to do cardiovascular gene therapy for the first time in a patient. We were tremendously excited. We thought we had a really clever way to do it. When we did the first intramuscular injection because we did not have anything else to offer the patient, I remember walking out of the room and thinking to myself, "You just did something that is about as close to voodoo as you could possibly get." The patient, a 37-year-old woman, had a huge ulcer in her lower leg, had been recommended to undergo below-knee amputation and she was on a "ton" of narcotic medicines for leg pain. They are looking to you as if you can provide some hope and you come in and do this kooky thing where you take a needle and do injections into the patient's leg, not having any idea where to place the needles.

WCR: *How many did you do?*

JMI: We did 4 injections.

WCR: *In the upper thigh?*

JMI: I got together with our vascular surgeon, Dr. Sy Razvi, and asked where he thought we ought to inject? He suggested above the knee and below the knee, at sites where we could palpate muscle and where we knew we were not going to injure a nerve, or find ourselves in an artery. We did a couple above the knee and a couple below the knee where we could palpate some good muscle. The next week the patient came back and when asked how she was doing she said, "There is something happening. I don't know what is going on but I can feel something happening." We figured this was a placebo effect. Two weeks later she came back again and said, "You know, I am telling you there is really something going on here."

At 3 weeks, she had a measurable increase in her ankle-brachial index, which we had had never seen in any patient who had intraarterial gene therapy. At 4 weeks, we did an angiogram and we saw new blood vessels. She had a marked improvement in her ankle-brachial index, and by 4 to 5 weeks we started to see the ulcer filling in. The leg pain also was lessening. We did a second round of injections and by about 4 weeks later her ankle-brachial index had gone from 0.3 to 0.6. (The published criteria for successful angioplasty or bypass surgery sequence is an increase in the ankle-brachial index of only 0.1.) This lady had increased from 0.3 to 0.6! One of our plastic surgeons, Dr. George Volpe, agreed that if the progress continued after her 8-week follow-up that she would be a candidate for a split-thickness skin graft. He went ahead and did that and low and behold the graft took. He said in the operating room, "You know this thing is bleeding like a stuck pig. You can leave. There is no question. Go home. I can tell you this graft is going to take." We still could not believe it but the graft started to heal perfectly. Sixteen weeks after the intramuscular injections, she had been successfully weaned from methadone, duragesic, percoset, and Elavil, all of which she had been taking for this pain. She went from being wheelchair bound to being completely ambulatory. She went back to work as a grade school science teacher by the next fall. By that time, we had tried the intramuscular injections in a couple of other patients and we were seeing a quantum leap in the improvement that the patients were experiencing. From that point on we did not do any more intraarterial gene therapy.

WCR: *That started what year?*

JMI: We started the intramuscular injections in 1996.

WCR: *How many injections do you do now?*

JMI: Currently, we are doing 8 injections at each setting. We do 2 or 3 treatment sessions.

WCR: *Are the injections painful at all?*

JMI: Not much. Most patients don't experience any significant discomfort. Rarely, a patient will take 2 tablets of Tylenol afterwards. For the most part, it is like getting your flu shots.

WCR: *You send them home quickly after that?*

JMI: Yes. We now do the injections as an outpatient procedure. They go home immediately afterwards.

WCR: *Who is paying for this?*

JMI: That is a good question. The insurance companies don't pay for it. We have done this thus far without industrial support so the hospital has absorbed a lot of the costs of this therapy. Dr. Michael Collins, our President and Chief Executive Officer, has been tremendously supportive.

WCR: *At first I gather you had a problem getting patients with peripheral vascular disease. Since your procedure has been so publicized and has been successful I gather getting patients is not a problem now?*

JMI: Getting patients is absolutely not a problem, although most patients we see are self-referred. Some are referred by cardiologists and internists. There is increasing public awareness of this procedure now.

WCR: *I gather that you have had few referrals from vascular surgeons?*

JMI: Very few are sent to us by vascular surgeons.

WCR: *What is the latest interval that you record an angiogram after the injections to see whether these new channels continue to stay open?*

JMI: We do no further angiograms after 1 year; our clinical follow-up is now out to 2 years.

WCR: *They are still looking good at that point? Now you are moving to the heart. What is happening there?*

JMI: Yes. We have adopted the approach for the heart that we used in the legs. Although early on we always thought we would do it by the intraarterial approach, we use the intramuscular route, whereby 100% of the DNA we are giving gets into the muscle. Not all of it gets into the cells but at least 100% of it is in the target tissue. We elected to take that approach for the heart and take advantage of the minimally invasive thoracotomy type of approach to deliver the gene that way. Jim Symes now has treated 14 patients. We began this in February 1998. Surprisingly, despite the fact that we started with a very low dose of the naked plasmid DNA, we have again seen some dramatic results. In fact, our early experience suggests that this may work better in the heart than it does in the leg, just as angioplasty surgery, or drugs typically do.

WCR: *Which cardiac patients are you now doing this procedure on?*

JMI: Currently, we are doing it in patients who are not candidates for any conventional treatment, including medical therapy, surgery, or angioplasty.

WCR: *This is the end of the line for them just like your peripheral vascular patients. Are you are optimistic about the heart?*

JMI: We have demonstrated both subjectively and objectively that it works in the heart. It is a matter of how broadly can you extend this therapy to the whole universe of patients with ischemic heart disease.

WCR: *You were the first to do this in the legs and the first to do it in the heart?*

JMI: It was by no means an individual effort. Ann Pieczek, Orit Manor, Marianne Kearney, Iris Baumgartner, Peter Vale, Guenter Rauh, Doug Losordo, and Jim Symes all made critical conditions. Work by Takayuki Asahara in our laboratory also led to the first clinical trial of gene therapy to prevent restenosis.

WCR: *Your office quarters, clinic and laboratory space is quite impressive. How big an operation do you have now? How many people do you have in your vascular medicine division here at St. Elizabeth's?*

JMI: Along with Kenny, Bob Schainfeld, and myself, we have 6 nurses, several technicians, several secretaries, and 3 fellows. It probably totals, together with our research group, about 45 people. That is 43 more than when I came!

WCR: *When you came here in 1988 there were 2 of you. Not only have you increased it multifold but the hospital has built you a wonderful setup.*

JMI: They have been very generous. It has been very important for us to have an area where we could bring all of our personnel together. Previously, we were scattered all over the hospital. We are now more efficient. The hospital was also very generous in giving us a superb physical plant for our research division, and the resources to recruit accomplished scientists like Ken Walsh, Vicente Andres, and Takayuki Asahara. The people in our research division work intimately with our clinical group, both in vascular medicine and in cardiology.

WCR: *You have taken your bench research directly to the patient. Your bench research was with an absolute goal line in mind from the beginning. You have acquired a tremendous amount of money from NIH and other sources to support all of these endeavors. How much grant money have you garnered since 1979?*

JMI: About $20 million.

WCR: *Each one of these protocols you fill out to get a grant looks like a book. It is a good thing you had to have all those sports-article deadlines.*

JMI: Never were any of those sports articles as oppressive to author as any of these grants.

WCR: *You have always been busy. You have never worked just 1 job or 1 task or 1 activity in your life. What is your life like now? What time do you get up in the morning? What time do you get to the hospital? What time do you leave the hospital? What time do you get home? What time do you go to bed? Can you describe a typical day?*

JMI: I usually get up about 4:45 A.M., which conveniently is the same time my wife gets up because she is a superb swimmer and swims 2 miles every morning before she gets the kids off to school. I usually try to work for a couple of hours at home. I try to do my writing in the mornings. I remember as a kid reading something from an article about Michael De Bakey where he said that early morning was always the most productive time of the day for him and it always stuck in my mind. When I get up early in the morning that is definitely the best time for me to write. I usually get to the hospital by about 8:00 A.M. Early on in my career when I was single, it was endless. I would stay here until I was done, which could mean eating at the hospital and staying late. Once I got married and had children, I always made it a priority to be home for dinner unless there were some unusual circumstances. I usually get home about 6:30 P.M., have dinner, spend some time with the kids, and work from about 9:00 to 11:30. I usually go to bed at 11:30 to midnight.

WCR: *What about on weekends?*

JMI: I typically have managed to get up and do some writing early on Saturday and Sunday mornings before everybody is up, and then have the rest of the day free for my family. On Sunday night I do some more work. Linda and I have had an agreement that I would do whatever traveling was required during the week. Weekends were a time we were all going to spend together, and for the most part I have tried to adhere to that. That post-dinner time and weekends are times committed to family.

WCR: *When did you get married, Jeff?*

JMI: I got married 13 years ago when I was 37.

WCR: *Jack Kennedy got married when he was 36 so you were 1 year after him. Your 3 children are how old now?*

JMI: Josh, Jessie, and Mathew are 12, 11, and 5.

WCR: *What are your goals, desires, or ambitions now? You are 50 years old and you have been going at it steadily, strongly, and competitively for a long time. What if somebody offers you the Chairmanship of Medicine or Chief Executive Officer of a developing company. How would you handle that?*

JMI: I said I would never go into academic medicine and that is where I have spent my life so I would never say never about anything. To me the thing that really motivated me more than anything else is a sense that I don't want to feel that I was just kind of passing through during this lifetime. I do not want to just be one more person that came and left. I always wanted to do something that could make a little difference. Certainly in medicine, after being exposed to Sones at the Cleveland Clinic and the things he had done, I thought if I ever had the opportunity to be able to do anything that could really change the way medicine is practiced, that is what I would like to do. It is still the way I feel. You need a certain amount of resources to be able to achieve things. For any opportunity to be attractive, it would have to provide a quantum leap in what I thought I could achieve.

WCR: *It is very exciting that you took an area of basic science and molded that into a therapy which was the only hope of these patients, and you started this endeavor only 10 years ago. When is this going to spread outside St. Elizabeth's Hospital?*

JMI: There are already other groups that are working in this area. We are nearing the end of the Phase I single center trial. My hope is that before the end of this year we will be into a Phase II multicenter trial that will involve other centers and hopefully with a catheter-based technique for doing the heart. I think the peripheral application is right now about as simplified as it can possibly get. I also hope the peripheral vascular work will soon be expanded to a multicenter basis.

WCR: *You hope to move away from the desperate person, particularly with peripheral vascular disease, to treat patients with less severe leg ischemia?*

JMI: That is the next logical place to go with this.

WCR: *Do you envision the application of this therapy to the myocardium as care for acute myocardial ischemia, such as unstable angina? It takes how long for the vessels to generate?*

JMI: That is really a great question. We have done a study in animals where we have treated acute limb ischemia. It worked in the animal model fairly effectively. Whether that could be used in the case of acutely ischemic myocardium is unknown. The gene expression takes probably 18 to 24 hours to begin. Although they develop quickly, the vessels still require days, maybe up to 14, to develop. As acute treatment, I would be more optimistic about the therapy applied to unstable angina than acute infarction.

WCR: *Chronically, from the heart's stand point, which patients do you envision this therapy to be used for?*

JMI: It certainly is going to be useful for patients who do not have any other therapeutic options. We can say that with confidence. Everything else is speculation. I don't think it is completely unrealistic that we might soon be in a situation where this might be a simple enough thing to do, that you could do a diagnostic catheterization on a patient, and, perhaps because they are not an ideal angioplasty or bypass candidate, you might go ahead and do an intramyocardial injection of the gene. If the patient is not unstable we can afford to watch the patient for a couple of weeks, and if they get better, angioplasty or bypass might be avoided. If it seems to be as benign as it appears to be from the earlier experiences, earlier application of gene therapy might be reasonable rather than using it as last-line therapy. It might be possible to set the clock back by 5 or 10 years. You may be buying the patient some important time, i.e., delay angioplasty or bypass and consequently the complications of each of these procedures.

WCR: *You would envision that it be given via catheter in the left ventricle?*

JMI: Right now that is the way I would envision it. It is something we know we can do because Peter Vale and Doug Losordo have already done it in our laboratory in non-human animals. We might be able to find some alternative approaches.

WCR: *Right now you have time for your work and your family and that is about it. You don't have any burning hobbies or do you?*

JMI: One good thing that came from my first 2 years of medical school in Boston was learning to sail—I did a lot of that before getting married. Subsequently, I have spent more time with hobbies the rest of the family enjoys more. We do a lot of skiing together. We play a lot of golf together. Other than socializing with friends that is probably the way we spend our time.

WCR: *So you try to keep the weekend to being a husband and a father like your parents?*

JMI: Yes. That was the model that my parents made for me. I think it was the model of Linda's parents. Our family is very important to both of us.

WCR: *Where is Linda from?*

JMI: She is from a wonderful family of 8 in Braintree, a suburb of Boston.

WCR: *Jeff, is there anything you would like to discuss that we haven't?*

JMI: When you were talking about people that have had an impact on me you did not give me the opportunity to discuss you. I thought I had an outstanding work ethic when I came to work for you. I remember the first weekend I was coming to work for you, having just finished my cardiology fellowship. It was the July 4th weekend. I remember coming to your office. I was with some friends and we had a place at Ocean City we were going to. I thought I would just drop by to say hello. I said, "I just wanted to say 'hi.' I am on my way to the beach." You had this kind of stunned look on your face. You came out with this big box of files of 150 patients who had died of rupture of the heart and said, "Maybe you can take these with you over the weekend and take a look at them." I remember walking out to the car and this girl I was with said, "What is that?" I said, "I got a little homework." We drove off to Ocean City with this box full of charts. I think you really turned it up a notch for me in terms of what was required to really achieve something and write well and think creatively. You used to make us look at all these cases and write down at the bottom of their file what is new about this case? That seemed like a pretty obvious thing but a lot of people don't look at it that way and as a result of that if I ever looked at a patient subsequently or if I ever looked at a research opportunity I started always looking at it that way. A lot of people who did not come from the experience I had in your lab never ever understood what it took to get something to the goal line. That was really an invaluable lesson.

WCR: *You are very generous in your comments, but you did not learn anything about what you are doing now from me.*

JMI: That may be true but I am not sure that without the experience I had in your lab I would be doing any of the things I am doing now.

WCR: *Jeff, I appreciate those generous comments. I appreciate your time. I am sure the readers of* The American Journal of Cardiology *will be enormously intrigued. Thank you.*

JMI: Thank you for the opportunity, Bill.

JMI's BEST PUBLICATIONS AS SELECTED BY HIM

6. Isner JM, Roberts WC. Right ventricular infarction complicating left ventricular infarction secondary to coronary heart disease. Frequency, location, associated findings, and significance from analysis of 236 necropsy patients with acute or healed myocardial infarction. *Am J Cardiol* 1978;42:885–894.

15. Isner JM, Sours HE, Paris AL, Ferrans FJ, Roberts WC. Sudden unexpected death in avid dieters using liquid-protein modified fast diet: observations in 17 patients and the role of the prolonged Q-T interval. *Circulation* 1979;60:1401–1412.

22. Isner JM, Kishel J, Kent KM, Ronan JA Jr, Ross AM, Roberts WC. Accuracy of angiographic determination of left main coronary arterial narrowing: angiographic-histologic correlative analysis in 28 patients. *Circulation* 1981;63:1056–1064.

36. Isner JM, Carter BL, Bankoff MS, Konstam MA, Salem DN. Computed tomography in the diagnosis of pericardial heart disease. *Ann Intern Med* 1982;97:473–479.

74. Deckelbaum LI, Isner JM, Donaldson RF, Clarke RH, Laliberte S, Aharon AS, Bernstein JS. Reduction of pathologic tissue injury using pulsed energy delivery. *Am J Cardiol* 1985;56:662–667.

77. Isner JM, Donaldson RF, Deckelbaum LI, Clarke RH, Laliberte SM, Ucci AA, Salem DN, Konstam MA. The excimer laser: gross, light microscopic, and ultrastructural analysis of potential advantages for use in laser therapy of cardiovascular disease. *J Am Coll Cardiol* 1985;6:1102–1109.

94. Isner JM, Estes NAM, Thompson PD, Nordin MR, Subramanian R, Miller G, Katsas G, Sweeney K, Sturner WQ. Acute cardiac events temporally related to cocaine abuse. *N Engl J Med* 1986;315:1438–1443.

95. Clarke RH, Isner JM, Donaldson RF, Jones G. Gas chromatographic-light microscopic correlative analysis of excimer laser photoablation of cardiovascular tissues. Evidence for a thermal mechanism. *Circ Res* 1987;60:429–439.

113. Steg PG, Gal D, Rongione AJ, DeJesus ST, Clarke RH, Isner JM. Effect of argon laser irradiation on rabbit aortic smooth muscle: evidence for endothelium-independent contraction and relaxation. *Cardiovasc Res* 1988;22:747–753.

115. Isner JM, Gal D, Steg PG, DeJesus ST, Rongione AJ, Halaburka KR, Slovenkai GA, Clarke RH. Percutaneous in vivo excimer laser angioplasty. *Lasers Surg Med* 1988;8:223–232.

117. Isner JM, DeJesus ST, Clarke RH, Gal D, Rongione AJ, Donaldson RF. Mechanism of laser ablation in an absorbing fluid field. *Lasers Surg Med* 1988;8:543–554.

120. Isner JM, Samuels DA, Slovenkai GA, Halaburka KR, Hougen TJ, Desnoy-ers MR, Fields CD, Salem DN. Mechanism of aortic balloon valvuloplasty. *Ann Intern Med* 1988;108:377–379.

139. Steg PG, Rongione AJ, Gal D, DeJesus ST, Clarke RH, Isner JM. Pulsed ultraviolet laser irradiation produces endothelium-independent relaxation vascular smooth muscle. *Circulation* 1989;80:189–197.

140. Chokshi SK, Moore R, Pandian N, Isner JM. Reversible cardiomyopathy associated with cocaine intoxication. *Ann Intern Med* 1989;111:1039–1040.

153. Isner JM, Rosenfield K, Kelly S, Losordo DW, DeJesus ST, Palefsky P, Langevin RE, Razvi S, Pastore JO, Kosowsky BD. Percutaneous intravascular ultrasound examination as an adjunct to catheter-based interventions: preliminary experience in patients with peripheral vascular disease. *Radiology* 1990;175:61–70.

163. Isner JM, Rosenfield K, Losordo DW, Rose L, Langevin RE Jr, Razvi S, Kosowsky BD. Combination balloon-ultrasound imaging catheter for percutaneous transluminal angioplasty: validation of imaging, analysis of recoil, and identification of plaque fracture. *Circulation* 1991;84:739–754.

164. Rosenfield K, Losordo DW, Ramaswamy K, Pastore JO, Langevin RE Jr, Razvi S, Kosowsky BD, Isner JM. Three-dimensional reconstruction of human coronary and peripheral arteries from images recorded during two-dimensional reconstruction of human coronary and peripheral arteries from images recorded during two-dimensional intravascular ultrasound examination. *Circulation* 1991;84:1938–1956.

173. Pickering JG, Weir L, Rosenfield K, Stetz J, Isner JM. Smooth muscle cell outgrowth from human atherosclerotic plaque: implications for the assessment of lesion biology. *J Am Coll Cardiol* 1992;20:1430–1439.

174. Mosseri M, Varticovski L, Fingert F, Chokshi S, Isner JM. In vitro evidence that myocardial ischemia resulting from 5-fluorouracil chemotherapy is due to protein kinase C-mediated vasoconstriction of vascular smooth muscle. *Cancer Res* 1993;53:3028–3033.

175. Gal D, Chokshi SK, Mosseri M, Clarke RH, Isner JM. Percutaneous delivery of low-level laser energy reverses histamine-induced spasm in atherosclerotic yucatan microswine. *Circulation* 1992;86:756–768.

176. Dietz WA, Tobis JA, Isner JM. Failure of angiography to accurately depict the extent of coronary arterial narrowing in three fatal cases of percutaneous transluminal coronary angioplasty. *J Am Coll Cardiol* 1992;19:1261–1270.

177. Leclerc G, Gal D, Nikol S, Kearney M, Weir L, Isner JM. Percutaneous arterial gene transfer in a rabbit model efficiency in normal and balloon-dilated atherosclerotic arteries. *J Clin Invest* 1992;90:936–944.

179. Losordo DW, Rosenfield K, Pieczek A, Baker K, Harding M, Isner JM. How does angioplasty work? Serial in vivo morphometric analysis of mechanisms of angioplasty in humans using intravascular ultrasound. *Circulation* 1992;86:1845–1858.

191. Pickering JG, Bacha PA, Weir L, Jekanowski J, Nichols JC, Isner JM. Prevention of smooth muscle cell outgrowth from human atherosclerotic plaque by a recombinant cytotoxin specific for the epidermal growth factor receptor. *J Clin Invest* 1993;91:724–729.

192. Losordo DW, Leclerc G, Gal D, Weir L, Takeshita S, Isner JM. Use of the rabbit ear artery to serially assess foreign protein secretion after site-specified arterial gene transfer in vivo: evidence that anatomic identification of successful gene transfer may underestimate the potential magnitude of transgene expression. *Circulation* 1994;89:785–792.

198. Gal D, Weir L, Leclerc G, Pickering JG, Hogan J, Isner JM. Direct myocardial transfection in two animal models: evaluation of parameters affecting gene expression and percutaneous gene delivery. *Lab Invest* 1993;68:18–25.

200. Isner JM, Rosenfield KR. Redefining the treatment of peripheral artery disease. Role of percutaneous revascularization. *Circulation* 1993;88:1534–1557.

205. Pickering JG, Weir L, Jekanowski J, Kearney M, Isner JM. Proliferative activity in peripheral and coronary atherosclerotic plaque among patients undergoing percutaneous revascularization. *J Clin Invest* 1993;91:1469–1480.

214. Takeshita S, Gal D, Leclerc G, Pickering JG, Riessen R, Weir L, Isner JM. Increased gene expression after liposome-mediated arterial gene transfer associated with intimal smooth muscle cell proliferation following vascular injury. *J Clin Invest* 1994;93:652–661.

217. Riessen R, Rahimizadeh H, Blessing E, Takeshita S, Barry JJ, Isner JM. Arterial gene transfer using pure DNA applied directly to hydrogel-coated angioplasty balloon. *Hum Gene Ther* 1993;4:749–758.

223. Takeshita S, Tsurumi Y, Couffinhal T, Asahara T, Bauters C, Symes JF, Ferrara N, Isner JM. Gene transfer of naked DNA encoding for three isoforms of vascular endothelial growth factor stimulates collateral development in vivo. *Lab Invest* 1996;75:487–502.

224. Takeshita S, Zheng LP, Brogi E, Kearney M, Asahara T, Pu LQ, Bunting S, Ferrara N, Symes JF, Isner JM. Therapeutic angiogenesis: a single intra-arterial bolus of vascular endothelial growth factor augments revascularization in a rabbit ischemic hindlimb model. *J Clin Invest* 1994;93:662–670.

225. Riessen R, Isner JM, Blessing E, Loushin C, Nikol S, Wight TN. Regional differences in the distribution of the proteoglycans biglycan and decorin in the extracellular matrix of atherosclerotic and restenotic human coronary arteries. *Am J Pathol* 1994;144:962–974.

234. Losordo DW, Rosenfield K, Kaufman J, Pieczek A, Isner JM. Focal compensatory enlargement of human arteries in response to progressive atherosclerosis: in vivo documentation using intravascular ultrasound. *Circulation* 1994;89:2570–2577.

238. Bauters C, Asahara T, Zheng LP, Takeshita S, Bunting S, Ferrara N, Symes JF, Isner JM. Physiologic assessment of augmented vascularity induced by VEGF in ischemic rabbit hindlimb. *Am J Physiol 267 Heart Circ Physiol* 1994;36: H1263–H1271.

239. Brogi E, Wu T, Namiki S, Isner JM. Indirect angiogenic cytokines upregulate VEGF and bFGF gene expression in vascular smooth muscle cells, while hypoxia upregulates VEGF expression only. *Circulation* 1994;90:649–652.

241. Isner JM. Vascular remodeling: honey, I think I shrunk the artery. *Circulation* 1994;89:2937–2941.

247. Bauters C, Asahara T, Zheng LP, Takeshita S, Bunting S, Ferrara N, Symes JF, Isner JM. Recovery of disturbed endothelium-dependent flow in the collateral-perfused rabbit ischemic hindlimb after administration of vascular endothelial growth factor. *Circulation* 1995;91:2802–2809.

248. Feldman LJ, Steg PG, Zheng LP, Chen D, Kearney M, McGarr SE, Barry JJ, Dedieu J-F, Perricaudet M, Isner JM. Low-efficiency of percutaneous adenovirus-mediated arterial gene transfer in the atherosclerotic rabbit. *J Clin Invest* 1995;95:2662–2671.

249. Takeshita S, Rossow ST, Kearney M, Zheng LP, Bauters C, Bunting S, Ferrara N, Symes JF, Isner JM. Time course of increased cellular proliferation in collateral arteries following administration of vascular endothelial growth factor in a rabbit mode of lower limb vascular insufficiency. *Am J Pathol* 1995;147: 1649–1660.

251. Asahara T, Bauters C, Pastore CJ, Kearney M, Rossow S, Bunting S, Ferrara N, Symes JF, Isner JM. Local delivery of vascular endothelial growth factor accelerates reendothelialization and attenuates intimal hyperplasia in balloon-injured rat carotid artery. *Circulation* 1995;91:2793–2801.

256. Brown DL, Hibbs MS, Kearney M, Loushin C, Isner JM. Identification of 92 kD gelatinase in human coronary atherosclerotic lesions: association of active enzyme synthesis with unstable angina. *Circulation* 1995;91:2125–2131.

265. Isner JM, Kearney, Bortman S, Passeri J. Apoptosis in human atherosclerosis and restenosis. *Circulation* 1995;91:2703–2711.

269. Asahara T, Chen D, Kearney M, Rossow S, Passeri J, Symes JF, Isner JM. Accelerated restitution of endothelial integrity in endothelium-dependent function after phVEGF165 gene transfer. *Circulation* 1996;94:3291–3302.

273. Namiki A, Brogi E, Kearney M, Wu T, Couffinhal T, Varticovski L, Isner JM. Hypoxia induces vascular endothelial growth factor in cultured human endothelial cells. *J Biol Chemistry* 1995;270:31189–31195.

274. Brogi E, Schatteman G, Wu T, Kim EA, Varticovski L, Keyt B, Isner JM. Hypoxia-induced paracrine regulation of vascular endothelial growth factor receptor expression. *J Clin Invest* 1996;97:469–476.

276. Isner JM, Pieczek RN, Schainfeld R, Blair R, Haley L, Asahara T, Rosenfield K, Razvi S, Walsh K, Symes JF. Early report: clinical evidence of angiogenesis after arterial gene transfer of ph VEGF165 in patient with ischemic limb. *Lancet* 1996;348:370–374.

281. van der Zee R, Zollman F, Passeri J, Lekutat C, Silver M, Isner JM. Vascular endothelial growth factor (VEGF)/vascular permeability factor (VPF) augments nitric oxide release from quiescent rabbit and human vascular endothelium. *Circulation* 1997;95:1030–1037.

286. Isner JM, Walsh K, Symes JF, Pieczek A, Takeshita S, Lowry J, Rosenfield K, Weir L, Brogi E, Jurayj D. Arterial gene transfer for therapeutic angiogenesis in patients with peripheral artery disease. *Hum Gene Ther* 1996;7:959–988.

287. Isner JM, Walsh K, Rosenfield K, Schainfeld R, Asahara T, Hogan K, Pieczek A. Arterial gene therapy for restenosis. *Hum Gene Ther* 1996;7:989–1011.

289. Tsurumi Y, Takeshita S, Chen D, Kearney M, Rossow ST, Passeri J, Horowitz JR, Symes JF. Direct intramuscular gene transfer of naked DNA encoding vascular endothelial growth factor augments collateral development and tissue perfusion. *Circulation* 1996;94:3281–3290.

292. Van Belle E, Tio FO, Couffinhal T, Maillard L, Passeri J, Isner JM. Stent endothelialization time course, impact of local catheter delivery, feasibility of recombinant protein administration, and response to cytokine expedition. *Circulation* 1997;95:438–448.

293. Van Belle E, Tio FO, Chen D, Maillard L, Chen D, Kearney M, Isner JM. Passivation of metallic stents following arterial gene transfer of ph VEGF165 inhibits thrombus formation and intimal thickening. *J Am Coll Cardiol* 1997;29: 1371–1379.

296. Couffinhal T, Kearney M, Witzenbichler B, Losordo DW, Symes JF, Isner JM. Vascular endothelial growth factor/vascular permeability factor (VEGF/ VPF) in normal and atherosclerotic human arteries. *Am J Pathol* 1997;150:1673–1685.

297. Kearney M, Pieczek A, Haley L, Losordo DW, Andres V, Schainfeld R, Rosenfield K, Isner JM. Histopathology of in-stent restenosis. *Circulation* 1997; 95:1998–2002.

303. Van Belle E, Chen D, Silver M, Bunting S, Ferrara N, Symes JF, Bauters C, Isner JM. Hypercholesterolemia attenuates angiogenesis, but does not preclude augmentation by angiogenic cytokines. *Circulation* 1997;96:2667–2674.

305. Asahara T, Murohara T, Sullivan A, Silver M, van der Zee R, Schatteman G, Isner JM. Isolation of putative endothelial progenitor cells for angiogenesis. *Science* 1997;275:964–967.

306. Tsurumi Y, Murohara T, Krasinski K, Chen D, Witzenbichler B, Kearney M, Couffinhal T, Isner JM. Reciprocal relation between VEGF and NO in the regulation of endothelial integrity. *Nature Med* 1997;3:879–886.

309. Murohara T, Horowitz JR, Silver M, Tsurumi Y, Sullivan A, Isner JM. Vascular endothelial growth factor/vascular permeability factor enhances vascular permeability via receptor tyrosine kinase Flk-1 mediated production of nitric oxide and prostacyclin. *Circulation* 1998;97:99–107.

313. Baumgartner I, Pieczek A, Manor O, Blair R, Walsh K, Isner JM. Constitutive expression of ph VEGF165 following intramuscular gene transfer promotes collateral vessel development in patients with critical limb ischemia. *Circulation* 1998;97:1114–1123.

324. Witzenbichler B, Asahara T, Murohara T, Silver M, Spyridopoulos I, Magner M, Principe N, Kearney M, Hu J-S, Isner JM. Vascular endothelial growth factor-C (VEGF-C/VEGF-2) promotes angiogenesis in the setting of tissue ischemia. *Am J Pathol* 1998;153:381–394.

325. Asahara T, Chen D, Takahashi T, Fujikawa K, Kearney M, Magner M, Yancopoulos GD, Isner JM. The Tie2 receptor ligands, angioprotein-1 and angiopoietin-2 modulate VEGF-induced postnatal neovascularization. *Circ Res* 1998;83:233–240.

326. Witzenbichler B, Maisonpierre PC, Yancopoulos G, Isner JM. Chemotactic properties of angiopoietin-1 and -2, ligands for the endothelial-specific receptor tyrosine kinase Tie2. *J Bio Chem* 1998;273:18514–18521.

328. Murohara T, Asahara T, Silver M, Bauters C, Masuda H, Kalka C, Kearney M, Chen D, Chen D, Symes JF, Fishman MC, Huang PL, Isner JM. Nitric oxide synthase modulates angiogenesis in response to tissue ischemia. *J Clin Invest* 1998;101:2567–2578.

329. Shyu K-G, Manor O, Magner M, Yancopoulos GD, Isner JM. Direct intramuscular injection of plasmid DNA encoding angiopoietin-1, but not angiopoietin-2, augments revascularization in the rabbit ischemic hindlimb. *Circulation*; in press.

330. Rivard A, Fabre J-E, Silver M, Chen D, Murohara T, Kearney M, Magner M, Isner JM. Age-dependent impairment of angiogenesis. *Circulation*; in press.

332. Couffinhal T, Silver M, Zheng LP, Kearney M, Witzenbichler B, Isner JM. Mouse model of angiogenesis. *Am J Pathol* 1998;152:1667–1679.

334. Isner JM, Baumgartner I, Rauh G, Schainfeld R, Blair R, Manor O, Razvi S, Symes JF. Treatment of thromboangitis obliterans (Buerger's Disease) by intramuscular gene transfer of vascular endothelial growth factor: preliminary clinical results. *J Vasc Surg;* in press.

NORMAN MAYER KAPLAN, MD: A Conversation With the Editor*

Dr. Norman M. Kaplan was born on January 2, 1931, in Dallas, Texas, where he grew up. He went to public high school and then to the University of Texas where he graduated from the pharmacy school in 1950 at age 19 and from the University of Texas Southwestern Medical School in Dallas in 1954. His internship and residency in medicine were at Parkland Memorial Hospital in Dallas. From there he served as Chief of the Endocrinology Service at Lackland Air Force Base in San Antonio, Texas, and from there he went to Bethesda, Maryland, where he was a research fellow in the Clinical Endocrinology Branch in the National Heart Institute. He returned to Dallas in 1961 as a faculty member at Southwestern Medical School where he became full professor in the Department of Medicine 9 years later. He headed the Division of Hypertension from 1977 until 1997. His research endeavors have focused primarily on therapy of systemic hypertension. He is an extremely popular lecturer who has spoken at numerous meetings all over the world. His book, *Clinical Hypertension*, first appeared in 1973, and the seventh edition appeared in 1998. That book is the most popular one on clinical aspects of hypertension ever produced.

William Clifford Roberts, MD[†] (hereafter, WCR): I am speaking with Dr. Norman Kaplan in his apartment complex in Dallas, Texas, on January 14, 1998. Dr. Kaplan, I would like to try to get to know you better as a person. I wonder if you might start by telling about your growing-up period. What was it like growing up in south Dallas? What were your parents like? I gather that they had a grocery store. Did they go to college? What about your siblings? When you were home at night after school, did you have some meaningful conversations around the table? I gather the synagogue played a major role in your growing-up period?

Norman M Kaplan, MD[‡] (hereafter, NMK): I was "a mistake." My mother and father had had 3 children and they thought they were finished. In the middle of the depression, when things were really bad, I came along. My mother rather jokingly commented to me that she tried to end the pregnancy by jumping off the flour barrel in the grocery store but it did not work. Despite that questionable beginning, I grew up in a very supportive family. My parents both came over in the early 1900s from the "old country": my father,

from white Russia and my mother, from Poland. They married in 1918 right after my father came back from being in the Army in World War I. They started a small grocery store close to the black ghetto area in south Dallas. I grew up in this small ramshackle grocery store with the attached living quarters. We were really poor, but never wanted. By having a grocery store we always had enough to eat. I never felt deprived. I was always carefully looked after by my father and mother. My father died suddenly, I assume from coronary artery disease, when I was 17. My mother was by far the matriarch of the family. She was the daughter of a Rabbi who was brought over here because many of the congregation that he had ministered to in a small community in Poland, about 80 miles from Warsaw, had come to Dallas. They decided they wanted their Rabbi from the old country to come over and they brought him with my mother and one of her siblings. Eventually, 6 other siblings, the whole family, came over. I think it happened to a lot of immigrants in those days that the first member or 2 who could afford the passage came over, and then as they made a little money they sent for the rest of them. They settled in Dallas in the early 1900s.

I was 7 years younger than my next sibling, my sister, and, therefore, I spent a lot of time by myself. My 2 older brothers are 9 and 11 years older than I am. I was sort of an independent but well-behaved little kid. I went to regular school and after hours to Hebrew school. The Hebrew school was every day, Monday to Thursday, and then, of course, synagogue on Friday night and Saturday, and Sunday school on Sunday morning. I spent a lot of time at our Orthodox synagogue.

Growing up, I was pretty much a loner. I had a few friends but pretty much took care of myself. I did very well in school. I basically made straight A's without any real effort and I was the salutatorian of my high school class. I was upset that I was not the valedictorian, but that was because I made a bad grade in typing. I never could type. I was doubly promoted and graduated from high school at age 16. I was socially a very backward kid. I did not date a lot or have a lot of friends, but I did begin to date the classmate who later became my first wife. When I went away to Austin to the University of Texas to undergraduate school at age 16, this was the first time I had ever really interacted with a lot of other young people my age. Becoming a member of a fraternity was a lifesaver for me and helped me form close friends, many of whom I still have. They have been very meaningful to me. It was an important formative time. I continued to date my first wife at the University and we married my freshman year in medical school, when I was only 19. I was in a big hurry. I am not sure why.

I got accepted at Southwestern Medical School

*This series of interviews are underwritten by an unrestricted grant from Bristol-Myers Squibb.

†Baylor Cardiovascular Institute, Baylor University Medical Center, Dallas, Texas 75246.

‡Department of Internal Medicine, University of Texas Southwestern Medical School, Dallas, Texas.

FIGURE 1. Photograph of Southwestern Medical School when NMK was a student, 1950-1954.

when I was 19. The decision to go into medicine was something I sort of fell into. My 2 older brothers had become pharmacists and they opened two drug stores. I thought that if I did not get into medical school I would become a pharmacist, so I took pharmacy as an undergraduate. I worked like a demon. I took 21 hours of courses each semester and went to school each summer. In 3 years I accumulated 144 hours of credit. If I had it to do it over I would never have gone into pharmacy, but would have taken liberal arts courses and gotten a good basic education.

Southwestern was a new and floundering medical school at the time. It had started during World War II after Baylor University College of Medicine moved from Dallas to Houston. Several Dallas physicians then started Southwestern Medical School, which initially was private. They built a little facility next to Parkland Hospital. By the time I got to medical school in 1950, it was about to go under. They almost lost their accreditation because *Tinsley Harrison*, who had been one of the primary strengths at the medical school, decided he had had enough of it and went back to Alabama, and *Carl Moyer*, a famous surgeon at that time, also left. In the late 1940s, the school did not have any significant financial support and was just about to go under when some people in Dallas exerted some influence on the state legislature and the University of Texas took it over in 1953 as its second medical branch, the first being the medical school in Galveston. At that same time, *Donald Seldin* who had just finished his fellowship in nephrology at Yale under *John Peters* and who was responsible for the future development of the school and who was my major mentor, became the Chairman of the Department of Internal Medicine. There were about 7 or 8 of us in the 1954 and 1955 classes of 100 students whom Seldin recognized as people he wanted to develop into his faculty. These included *Floyd Rector*, who subsequently went to San Francisco and was Chairman of the Department of Medicine there for the last few years; *John Fordtran*, who was not a student at South-

western but came here as a house officer, and subsequently became a leader of gastroenterology; *Dan Foster* who is now the Chairman of our department and a leading diabetologist; and *Jean Wilson* who became an outstanding endocrinologist; and *Charles Baxter* who became an outstanding burn surgeon. There were another 5 or 6 students who Seldin identified and he sent them all to the NIH. We are now talking about the late 1950s. For a young person who wanted to go into academic medicine, NIH was a necessity at the time. Seldin arranged with *Fred Bartter* to have me train as an endocrinologist at the NIH.

The medical school experience was a lot of fun. I never felt particularly threatened by what went on in medical school and I graduated tops in my class. I became Chief Resident at Parkland Hospital in 1957. I went into the Air Force for 2 years thereafter and spent 2 lovely years in San Antonio, having for the first time a little money to spend. We ended up with 4 daughters. I was a young Captain with a little money and a very easy job in the Air Force.

I then spent a year with *Fred Bartter* at NIH doing just bench laboratory research, studying the synthesis of aldosterone. I learned how to do the rather complex chromatographic isotopic assays for aldosterone and the rat bioassay for plasma renin activity. I got interested in aldosterone and renin as part of endocrinology. It was many years later that I really developed my primary interest in hypertension.

I came back to Southwestern in 1961 as an instructor, working as part of the endocrine group, which included *Leonard Madison*, *Roger Unger*, and *Don Seldin*, although he was primarily interested in the kidney. Gradually, as more younger investigators arrived, such as *Dan Foster*, *Jean Wilson*, and *Marvin Siperstein*, I got more interested in hypertension. When I came back from the NIH, Dr. Siperstein had joined the faculty and he worked with me for over a day in developing my first NIH grant. I had never put together a grant proposal and he had no interest in what I was doing. I was not planning to work with Dr. Siperstein, but Dr. Seldin asked him to help me put this together.

In those days, we had a rather small, probably 25-member, Department of Medicine, so all of us were close and collegial. Seldin, as the Chairman, went over every manuscript that any member of his department wrote and edited them extensively. He never put his name on them but he did spent a lot of time on manuscripts emanating from his faculty. We also had a fabulous series of sessions before any major society meeting where the research work was presented. As the faculty increased, the numbers of accepted abstracts also increased. We would spend 3 to 5 hours about 2 weeks before a meeting going over everyone's presentation. Seldin invariably detected flaws in the way the presentations had been put together or the slides composed. It was amazing; he would do this time after time. We were the people doing the work, we thought we knew everything on the subject, and had put it together logically. Yet, when we would present our work to the whole group, Seldin would stand up and say, "Look, this does not produce a logical sequence. You have to put it together this way, go from here to there instead of from there to here."

Southwestern Medical School was fortunate in having Seldin as the Head of Medicine. He began accumulating a faculty of young, bright, and imaginative people. You could go in and discuss problems with people who really were not working in your area because we were such a close group. It was a heady time for a young faculty person to be able to have those types of interactions, not only with the Chief, but also with other faculty. Today, the Department has over 200 members and it is very difficult to feel the same way. There are people here in our department now, where I have been for 38 years, who I don't even know. The close interrelationships made the foundation for my career.

I consider myself today mainly a communicator. I have done some good original work but most of what I have done and take most pride in is being able to take the work of others and put it together in a rational way that makes sense. I am not an elegant writer, but I try to keep it clear and simple. My major accomplishment is probably being able to look at a developing area, and, after much reading and listening, put together the information in a way that others can utilize meaningfully and apply to the care of patients. Maybe my rabbinical background, not only from my grandfather but from 5 generations of rabbis in my family before my grandfather, rubbed off a bit on me.

I have taken on through the years 3 major areas that have been contentious. The first was *primary aldosteronism. Jerome Conn*, at the University of Michigan, had put together the concept of the syndrome of aldosteronism due to a tumor of the adrenal gland in 1954. In the next 10 years, his group published a large amount of data on their experience with this syndrome. In 1964, Dr. Conn wrote in the *JAMA* that 20% of all hypertension was due to primary aldosteronism. I questioned this high frequency from the very beginning and began to accumulate data from patients in Dallas with hypertension and hypokalemia, the usual hallmarks of the syndrome. We measured aldosterone, we took tumors at autopsy (what we refer to now as "incidentilomas" but in those days were thought to be benign tumors of the adrenal gland) and measured the steroid synthesis in those tumors as well as in the tumors in patients who had the syndrome. We measured a whole variety of patients who had hypokalemia. Instead of finding a 20% frequency, we found <1% frequency of the syndrome among our hypertensive patients.

FIGURE 2. NMK in 1970.

My first national exposure was at the meeting of the Central Society for Clinical Research in Chicago in 1964 at the height of Dr. Conn's prominence from primary aldosteronism. When presenting for the first time before a major group (maybe 1,000 people) in Chicago with Jerome Conn sitting on the front row, I indicated that primary aldosteronism was not as common as he had claimed. He said it was simply a matter that we weren't looking at the right place and in the right manner. It turned out that I was closer to the truth than he was. Because Dr. Conn had become the world's authority in this area at the University of Michigan in those days, it is very possible that 20% of all their hypertensives did have the syndrome because the patients were being drawn there from all over the world. This is a phenomenon that happens in every disease that has been initially described by a new investigator. When physicians recognize new syndromes they accumulate such patients, funneling them into their own investigative area.

The same thing happened with renovascular hypertension and a number of forms of secondary hypetension. We must be cautious about the claims that come from investigators who describe a new syndrome. Because of the referral patterns they oftentimes recognize their problem much more frequently than is true in the general population. In those days, maybe less so today, there would be few laboratories that could study a described disease. These patients would come from far away places to be studied by a particular investigator. That is what happened with Dr.

Conn. At that time Ann Arbor was literally one of the few places in the world where the assays for aldosterone and renin could be done. I think Conn's mistake was that he interpreted his own experience to be applicable to the rest of the world.

The second thing I got involved with was *renin* and what it meant. *John Laragh*, who has been one of the original thinkers in the field of hypertension for the last 30 years, started in the early 1970s to look at the relation of plasma renin to hypertension. All the work that he and his group have done on the renin assay, on how to perform the assay, and what it means for diagnosis, prognosis, and treatment were all important contributions. But again I think John had blinders on. His experience, wherein renin was very important in diagnosis and in assessment of therapeutic responses, he felt applied to everyone where it obviously did not. Back in the early 1970s, I began to publish papers on the relation of renin measurements and other aspects of the renin-aldosterone system to the prevalence, prognosis, and therapy of hypertension. The years since that time have shown that John overstated his evidence although he still believes that renin plays a very important role in the diagnosis of hypertension, in the decision as to what its prognostic indications are, and in making therapeutic choices. The plasma renin level is important; it does add a great deal in the diagnosis of some low renin states, like primary aldosteronism, and in high renin states, like renovascular disease, but in most (>90%) hypertensive patients, renin assays do not give much additional information. It is now done relatively infrequently.

The third area concerns the *relation of calcium to blood pressure*. Dr. *David McCarron* of the University of Oregon was the strong advocate for calcium supplements to lower elevated blood pressure, claiming that calcium had a major impact on blood pressure. We found that calcium supplements lowered blood pressure only minimally, and we were one of the first to question this whole relation. Today, it is generally recognized that calcium supplements play a minimal role in lowering blood pressure.

I have been one who has questioned the implications of other people's work, but I have also made a few original observations, including some of the original work on mechanisms of the control of aldosterone synthesis (This was work I started at the NIH and continued here in Dallas for a few years.), on ways of assessing renin status via various clinical tests, and the mechanisms of oral contraceptive-induced hypertension. We described the "angiotension infusion test" which was an indirect way of assessing renin status. It was not a difficult procedure, but it was quickly supplanted by the ability to measure renin in a peripheral blood sample. The angiotensin-infusion test has been used, however, by obstetricians to detect early manifestations of preeclampsia.

In 1973, I published a book on hypertension. At that time, there was only one book on hypertension and it was by Sir George Pickering from Oxford, England. There were no journals devoted to hypertension. Pickering's book was wonderful, but his latest (second) edition was 8 years earlier (1964). I decided it was time for another book and I decided to do it by myself. At that time, single-authored books were not rare. The first edition was published by MEDCOM, a company in New York started by 2 young entrepreneurs. The book had a lot more illustrations and a lot more fancy layout than most books that were being published in those days. This first edition was reasonably successful. The latest edition, the 7th, appeared in 1998, 25 years after the first. The first printing of this latest edition by Williams & Wilkins was for 50,000 copies. The 6th edition was translated into 7 languages (Japanese, Chinese, Spanish, French, Italian, Russian, and Greek) and I was just informed that the 7th will be translated into Turkish and Polish. It makes me very proud that the book has been so well accepted. The Japanese particularly seem to love my book and I have become sort of a "guru" of hypertension in Japan. All 7 editions are single-authored except for the 1 chapter on childhood hypertension which has been written by my friend, *Dr. Ellen Lieberman*. A third or more of my time is occupied with keeping up with the literature for the next edition of this book. I would not maintain as much of an interest, for instance, in pregnancy hypertension if I did not need to include that area in the next edition. I am 67 years old and fortunately in good health so I hope to continue the book by doing all this reading and synthesizing. I hope there will be an 8th edition, but I am not so sure after that.

WCR: Let me go back a little bit. You have talked about mentors during your training, Donald Seldin, for example. Could you go back to your early childhood? You mentioned that your home or living quarters were next to the grocery store. Your next oldest sibling sister was 7 years older than you were. I presume you worked in the grocery store a good bit. What was life like on a day-to-day basis then?

WMK: In looking back, it was a lonely experience. I remember every afternoon after coming home from grammar school that I would throw a tennis ball up against the wall as my primary extracurricular activity. I also went to Hebrew school every afternoon. We did not have television. There was not much else to do. I was a fairly avid reader. I went to the library, located about 6 blocks from home, often. I did not have a lot of close relatives or friends that I was growing up with. We also tended to be very separate, being a member of the Jewish community. My mother, who was very Orthodox, wanted my older brothers and me to become rabbis. None of us did. She was very protective of us in a very gentile world, and she wanted and insisted that we practice our Orthodox/Jewish beliefs. We were a reasonably close family and as long as my mother was alive and well the family got together on all of the Jewish holidays and festivals. At Hebrew School, I did relate to other young Jewish kids in the community, but I don't remember any of them living anywhere near where I was. Most of them came from more affluent areas. Although south Dallas in those days was not a wealthy area, most people had established small stores and began to move up in the world. Most Jews lived in an

FIGURE 3. NMK teaching in 1982.

area of south Dallas which is today a very affluent area for African-Americans.

When I was around 12 or so there was a group called Young Judea, young Jewish kids who were looking to support Israel, which, of course, was not yet in existence. I remember as a kid collecting money, usually nickels and dimes, every Sunday morning at the delicatessen on Forest Avenue. They would let us out of Sunday School an hour early so we take a little blue box for the Jewish National Fund.

Maybe the fact that I have stayed pretty much a single investigator, written a single authored book, does reflect on the fact that when growing up I was pretty much by myself and did not have a lot of these nurturing relationships with a lot of other people.

WCR: I gather neither your mother nor father went to college?

NMK: Correct. I felt my mother was knowledgeable in the Jewish religion and in Jewish affairs. She was smart, but she was not an educated woman. She came to the USA and Dallas at about age 8 and did go to the public schools, but not beyond high school. My father came over at about age 14 years from "White Russia" near Kiev. He was an uneducated man, but he could read. Although he practiced as an Orthodox Jew he did not have the knowledge and the background that my mother did, having grown up with her father as a rabbi. My mother was educated in Jewish religious beliefs and prayer and such, but not in the outer world. I was 16 when I went to a symphony for the first time. It was my first exposure to anything outside of movies. But I never felt deprived. I thought we had every-

thing we needed and I did. I went to school with good clothes on, but I used to walk or hitch rides. We did not have an automobile. My father never did have a car. He drove a wagon with a horse until about 1940, and after that items were delivered to the grocery store. The first few years when I was at the University of Texas I had a bicycle. That was my way of getting around Austin. It was only when I was a senior in college and planning to come back to Dallas to enter medical school that I convinced by mother that I needed a car, and she, I think, went and borrowed some money to help me buy my first automobile. Coming out of that I guess has made me a little bit more aggressive about money than I would have been otherwise. Maybe that is one of the reasons I do so much lecturing and writing for the honoraria, although my faculty salary is obviously enough to keep me in good shape.

WCR: Your living quarters, being adjacent to the grocery store, must have been relatively small? Did you have a room of your own? Did you always room with your sister or one of your older brothers? Did you work in the grocery store there?

NMK: I slept with my mother and father in a bed next to theirs when I was a little kid. I remember that we had a black woman who was sort of a nanny to me during the daytime. She raised me as much as anybody because my mother and father were working in the grocery store. Apparently, I kept drinking out of a bottle until I was about 3 years old. I remember dropping the bottle and getting a real bawling out and

FIGURE 4. NMK in 1985.

then I decided that it was time to quit. I did work in the grocery store, mainly straightening out the shelves.

The second World War was a traumatic time because my mother had a lot of family left back in Poland. I remember vividly listening to the radio about what was going on in Europe and my mother's being very disturbed by the fact that Poland had been overrun quickly.

WCR: It sounds like school, whether grammar school, high school, college, or medical school, flowed very easily for you. Did your mother or father encourage you in school? Did they support your academic endeavors vigorously? Were your brothers and sisters similarly good students as you were?

NMK: I never had a lot of pressure put on me. When growing up, it seemed natural to excel in school. My strict Jewish Orthodox background encouraged me to learn all I could about Judism and religious practices. I don't remember ever being told that I should go to medical school. It just seemed something that sort of happened without any particular outside motivation. It must have been part of an ingrained attitude that being a good student and accomplishing something was expected. I don't ever recall being told that I didn't do well and should have made an A instead of a B. My academic achievements seemed to be self motivated or it came from sources that I never really identified. That whole attitude about reading and studying was just a natural assumption that my mother made and her children followed.

WCR: Were there any teachers in high school that had an impact on you?

NMK: A Mrs. Melson. She taught English literature. She motivated me to really work and go beyond what was expected. I remember having gone to the library and picking up books to read because of her

encouragement. She was about as tough a teacher as I remember having.

Forest High School, in those days, had about one third Jewish kids. The remainder were non-Jewish Caucasian since it was a segregated school. I encountered little overt anti-Semitism. I was nurtured by having a very strong Jewish family and my friends were almost entirely Jewish.

At the University of Texas as a student in the school of pharmacy, there was little special motivation provided. Although I did very well and came out with whatever honors you get from the University, it was not a place where I was stimulated. If I were able to go back, and, as I did with my children, I would have taken many liberal arts courses. In those days the University of Texas was very inexpensive. All 6 of my children, 4 by my first marriage and 2 stepchildren, went to the University of Texas. Two of my daughters, who subsequently became physicians, went through what was called Plan B at the University which was a group of 600 students considered special and brought into an intense liberal arts education. I wish that I had had that exposure.

WCR: It was expected that you would go to college. Your 2 brothers had gone off to pharmacy school. I gather your sister did?

NMK: In those days girls were not expected to do what the boys did. My sister went for only about 2 semesters to SMU, then quit, and got married. She was working as a secretary.

WCR: Do all 3 of your siblings now live in Dallas?

NMK: Yes. My father passed away early at about age 55 when I was 17. None of us knew of his having any medical problems. He died suddenly after having had chest pain. My mother lived 84 years. She was active until she was 80, serving as a cashier at my brother's drug store.

WCR: I gather that not only were you receiving your education at public high school but the Hebrew education you were receiving at the synagogue was a very important aspect of your education. I gather you learned to speak Hebrew fluently and your siblings as well. Could you discuss that briefly?

NMK: The speaking of Hebrew is something I never really picked up. I could read it and I could understand it pretty well, but in Dallas it is difficult to maintain your fluency. It did, however, play an important role in my life. When I was a junior medical student in Dallas in 1952, a friend of my family had a son who was going to have his Bar Mitzvah, and to do that the child has to stand up and read a part of the Bible in Hebrew. This kid did not know how to read Hebrew and he wanted to have the ceremony so they asked me if I would teach their kid how. I did and for about 5 years I supported myself and my family by teaching Jewish kids how to do their Bar Mitzvah. I would go out to their homes and charge $4.00 per hour to give these lessons. Four dollars an hour in 1954 or 1955 was a lot of money. I would make probably at the end of the week $25 to $30 from these lessons. That was a sizable part of our income.

I have always tried to maintain a reasonably close

Jewish identity. We have become, as has been true for a lot of Jewish people in the USA, less and less Orthodox. My wife and I now attend a conservative and occasionally one of the reform temples in Dallas. We have always tried to maintain a pretty close identity to the Jewish community. I have served, for example, on the board of the Dallas Jewish Federation. I was the first President of the Dallas Memorial Center for the Holocaust.

About 1964 I got involved in some Dallas Public School politics. This was right after the Kennedy assassination and Dallas was going through a major search of its own consciousness because many of us felt that Dallas had become somewhat reactionary in its attitude about a lot of things. About 6 weeks before the Kennedy assassination, Adlai Stevenson had come to Dallas and was spat on when speaking at SMU. There was a lot of antigovernment feelings in Dallas, which was sort of a "redneck haven." The public schools were woefully inadequate and underfunded. We had no kindergartens, no vocational education, no bilingual education. The teachers were paid at the very bottom of the level of teacher pay. Our tax base was very low. The whole system was run by what we referred to in those days as "the Dallas oligarchy," a small group of downtown businessmen, mainly bankers and insurance executives. They did things in Dallas because they were good for business. For instance, the integration of the schools, which had to be done because the courts were pressing all the school systems, was done without any agitation whatsoever. The reason was because the business community did not want to have Dallas look like Little Rock. Therefore, they passed an ordinance that prohibited 3 or more people getting together without the police being able to disperse them. Public protests consequently were prevented.

In early 1964, I happened to go to a meeting called by a few people to do something about our public schools. At the meeting, I spoke up and said, "We have to get organized. If we are going to change anything, we have to take over the school board." The school board was elected by the whole city in 1 at-large election. We decided that we would start a group of citizens trying to influence the vote for the Dallas School Board. We started an organization called the League for Educational Advancement in Dallas. *Dr. Richard Crout* (who later ran the FDA) and I were among those who started this organization and I was president for the first 4 years. In the next 5 to 7 years we really took over the Dallas school system by electing a group of outstanding citizens to the Dallas School Board, including Dan Foster who is now Chairman of our Department of Medicine. We got rid of the superintendent, who had been there for 24 years, and had been running it as a tight oligarchy. We brought in a young man, who, would you believe, came from the federal government, a native Texan named Nolan Estes, and he took over the Dallas School System. Subsequent to that a lot of changes came and a lot of improvements were made. Then we were forced by the courts to integrate the Dallas

School System and that resulted in busing. Virtually all the improvements we made in the Dallas School System were destroyed by the public antagonism to the idea of busing. Busing, though it accomplished integration, polarized the community. Even people who wanted to work to improve the public school system took their kids out of public schools and put them in private schools. This happened over much of the country. It unfortunately was a major detriment to the attempts that good citizens were making to try to upgrade the public schools. Eventually in Dallas, the minority populations (Hispanics and African-Americans) became the majority in the Dallas public schools. The white citizens fled to the suburbs. I was involved with the school system for about 10 years (1965-1975). Because of the integration of the school system much of the support that we had engendered from the general community was dissipated. Unfortunately, busing destroyed this amalgam that we had of citizens wanting to do what we had to do to improve the public school system.

I have considered myself a good liberal Democrat all these years. That has become a rare bird in Dallas, which is a very Republican community.

WCR: Dr. Kaplan, let me go back a little bit. I am intrigued by your growing up. When you were in high school, did you participate very much in extracurricular activities? Were you in the band? Did you play an instrument? Did you participate in sports?

NMK: I did play some tennis. I had begun to play tennis when I was in my young teens and I got to be fairly good. I lettered in tennis at Forest High School my senior year. I got involved in the debate team. That may have had a considerable influence on my latter public speaking abilities because we did have that same woman, Mrs. Melson, as the sponsor of the debating team. We debated once a week after school. I think that may have also helped sharpen my communicative skills. I was asked to run for the presidency of the senior class. I came up against a tall handsome WASP who promised that if he were elected that he would allow people to chew gum and get out of school an hour early, both of which obviously were totally irrelevant, but he got elected by a landslide. I was gangly and not very outgoing.

WCR: How did you get back and forth to the University of Texas?

NMK: Hitchhiking. In those days it was safe. Every 6 to 8 weeks when I came home or returned to college I made a sign and went out on the highway. The sign said, "Ride to Dallas or Ride to Austin." I had no problem. I probably was able to get back and forth as fast as you could drive. I was an ordinary looking kid with a little suitcase. I don't think I ever paid and I never flew on an airplane. I did get into a fraternity in Austin, likely because my older brother was a founding member. I think that played a major role in my social development, getting in with a group of somewhat more mature and socially advanced young men, and also some veterans. We did have some of the older guys who had come back from the Army under the GI Bill of Rights.

FIGURE 5. NMK at the time of the interview.

My mother sent me $100 a month to live on, for room, board, and books. Occasionally, I ran out of money and sent postcards (that my mother saved) that said, "Mom, please send me $7.50 so I can get a haircut and get my bicycle tire fixed." I waited tables at one the women's dorms to add to my income, and also to be able to get free meals. I worked all through college as a waiter at the LittleField Dorm. I was entranced by a lot of the young women and I certainly had not seen so many women up close in one place in all my life.

WCR: You and your high school girlfriend went to the University of Texas at about the same time?

NMK: Yes.

WCR: You got married at age 19?

NMK: We got married about 4 or 5 months after I came back to Dallas, after entering medical school.

WCR: Did you work during medical school? Was that a financial burden for you?

NMK: Fortunately, my wife worked as the secretary for the Rabbi at Temple Emmanuel, Levi Olin, who later became a member of the Board of Regents at the University of Texas. She supported me during medical school. I added to our income by teaching Hebrew to the Bar Mitzvah kids. During the first 2 summers, when we were out of school, I worked as a pharmacist in my brother's drug store.

WCR: When you finished medical school in 1954, you were debt free?

NMK: Yes. I then started internship at Parkland Hospital and it paid $25.00 a month, plus meals and laundry. My wife again supported me when I was a

house officer. We had our first child delivered the day before I graduated. I gave the Regent a cigar as he handed me my diploma. We had 4 daughters between 1954 and 1960. Two of them have become doctors, the other 2 are married to businessmen. Each of the 4 have children, and they have provided me with 9 grandchildren. I went into a second marriage 22 years ago and took on 2 stepsons who are out in California. My wife on her side has 4 grandchildren so between us we have 13 grandchildren. We are planning a large Passover together in April in Santa Fe, where we have a little house, with 12 adults and 13 grandchildren. We don't get together as a single family very often. I see the kids mainly when I travel to give talks. One daughter is an infertility obstetrician at Emory (Atlanta), and one daughter is a psychiatrist at the University of Cincinnati Medical School. Both of them married physicians who are on the same faculties. One daughter is in real estate in Austin with her husband, and 1 is in Detroit, Michigan, married to a real estate developer.

WCR: Other than Dr. Seldin, who mentored you in medical school and during your house officer period?

NMK: There was *Abraham Braude*, who came here as one of the very first appointees that Dr. Seldin made as Head of Infectious Disease. Abe Braude was a very gentle but tough investigator and teacher. As a second year resident, he took me under his wing and I did a little research project with him, and it resulted in my first publication. Abe had a strong influence; he encouraged me to become an academic physician. Beyond that, I think I got a lot of encouragement from my fellow residents, because as Seldin took over the department and developed it, we had a good group of bright young people. When I was at the NIH, 4 or 5 of these fellow house officers were also there. He was sending them up to NIH and to other places. He sent John Fortran to Boston to work with Franz Ingelfinger in gastroenterology. At the time there were only 12 to 18 interns and residents in Medicine. Today there are about 40 each year.

Parkland was and still is a great teaching hospital. I am very proud of the way Parkland has developed through the years and has become one of the premier teaching hospitals in the country. Dallas has continued to support Parkland in a very outstanding way. *Dr. Ron Anderson*, who has been our Chief Executive Officer, I think is an outstanding person. As is common now in a lot of places, we have opened up about 12 community outpatient facilities where people are now able to get their primary care and only come to Parkland when they get sick and need to be hospitalized or need to be seen by a specialist.

WCR: When you left your chief residency in 1958 and went into the military (San Antonio), you had actually not had any subspecialty training? I gather when you went to Lackland Air Force Base you were Head of Endocrinology and Metabolism there? Was that something you sought or how did that come about? You wrote several papers during your military experience?

FIGURE 6. NMK at the time of the interview.

NMK: That was almost luck. *Dr. Arthur Grollman* was Head of Experimental Pharmacology at the medical school. He was one of the outstanding people in experimental medicine. He had developed the process of measuring cardiac output by using the Fick principle about 1920. He also developed peritoneal dialysis as an experimental tool to keep dogs alive after he had excised their kidneys. Arthur was a true loner, very critical, and a very tough investigator. He wrote the standard textbook on pharmacology that was used countrywide for a long time. Arthur was also a Brigadier General in the Air Force Reserves and at that time he was the major consultant to the Air Force for endocrinology. When I was a third year resident I started some projects with Dr. Leonard Madison and Dr. Seldin as my mentors on diabetic nephropathy on rats. I had also done a couple of studies on insulin passing through the liver under the direction of *Dr. Leonard Madison*. So as a third year resident I got involved in some research projects that related to endocrinology, mainly to diabetes. I was deferred by the Berry Plan until completion of my residency.

In 1958 when I completed my residency, I went into the Air Force. I was assigned to the SAC Headquarters in Omaha, Nebraska. I looked on the map and saw where Omaha was and I realized I did not want to go there. I had never really worked with Dr. Grollman but I had been told that he was somebody that the Air Force respected. I went to Arthur: "Dr. Grollman, can you help me get a better assignment in the Air Force?," and he said "No problem." He picked up the phone, talked to somebody in Washington, and I was reassigned to Lackland Air Force Base and appointed

the Head of Endocrinology there. They were looking for a young doctor who was trained in endocrinology. This was a consultant hospital for the entire Air Force and patients were referred there from all over the world. I had not had a lot of formal training in endocrinology. Once I wrote down that my interest was endocrinology, even though I had no Boards or fellowship specific to that field; when I arrived there they appointed me head of Endocrinology. We took care of all the diabetic and the thyroid patients. There were many young outstanding physicians who came into the Air Force at that time. There was *Roscoe Robinson* who became the Dean at Vanderbilt, retiring just last year, *Bill Ord*, a cardiologist who helped develop the program for space medicine, and *Steve Boehring* who became the Dean of Indiana Medical School. We saw literally 100s of patients with pituitary problems, because this was the primary neurosurgery hospital where they did most of the neurosurgery for the entire Air Force. Even though I was the Chief I really was not that well trained, but I was able to manage, and learned a lot.

WCR: How did it come about that you went to the National Heart Institute at the National Institutes of Health in Bethesda, Maryland? I gather you were there just one year under Fred Bartter?

NMK: That arrangement was made by Dr. Seldin.

WCR: That was the first experience you had, I gather, doing basic laboratory research. Did you enjoy that? How did that impact you in later years?

NMK: I learned the techniques. I did not particularly appreciate or enjoy the laboratory bench type of work. I did it and I think we did some good work which was published in the *Journal of Clinical Investigation*, but it was not the sort of thing I felt I really wanted to do long term. I was much more interested in the clinical aspects from the beginning. At the Clinical Center (the NIH Hospital) there were lots of patients under Dr. Bartter's supervision with Addison's disease, postural edema, calcium abnormalities, hypertension and, of course, Bartter's syndrome of juxtaglomerular hyperplasia. Bartter was a very eclectic endocrine investigator, interested in a lot of different problems. Once or twice a week we would make rounds on the patients that were in the Clinical Center under his direction, and it was a very eye-opening experience for a young clinical investigator. Bartter was an excellent researcher. He was very quiet and soft spoken, and when making rounds with him you had to bend over and try to catch what he was saying. Bartter was not a good teacher but he was a wonderful investigator. He was very tough and very critical about his work. I certainly accepted that as a necessary requirement to become an academic physician.

When I came back to Dallas I immediately set up the steroid assays that I had learned at the NIH and got involved in aldosterone. That led very quickly into looking for primary aldosteronism clinically. We continued some studies on the basic mechanisms of steroid production of aldosterone synthesis, but then that became less and less of my interest. I became more and more clinically oriented.

WCR: So although you sort of got started as an endocrinologist, you evolved into a systemic hypertension expert. How did that come about? When did you realize that this is the thing you wanted to focus on?

NMK: I was interested in aldosterone and renin and was asked to see patients who had problems with endocrine hypertension. Then one day I said to myself, "I don't need to be another one of the general endocrine people here because we have a lot of them around." *Charlie Pak* had come down here from the NIH where he had worked with Bartter and he took over the calcium area at the medical center. Siperstein, Unger, Madison, Foster, and Wilson were all there involved in diabetes. I decided to focus on hypertension and I opened the hypertension clinic. We started as a branch of endocrinology, and became a separate division of hypertension in the mid-1970s. Through the years we have had only 1 to 3 fellows and 1 or 2 faculty people. I never tried to develop a large group of people. That might be considered a fault because we were not able to attract big grants but I did maintain my NIH sponsorship through research grants for about 20 years. I did not get involved in large projects. Beginning in the 1970s and going on until now my interest has really been in the larger area of clinical hypertension. I focus more on the endocrine forms of hypertension, but I realize that is only 1% of the entire hypertension picture. I gradually looked at areas other than the endocrine one.

WCR: Could you describe what being an intern was like in 1954 or being a Chief resident in 1958 compared to the training schedules of today. Did you work every other night?

NMK: Those were the days when house officers were expected to work hard and not get paid very much. We always had good supervision. Dr. Seldin and the other members of the faculty made rounds with us every day. We had a lot of good conferences. Even in those days when there were relatively few house officers and few faculty, it was a fairly intense academic environment. We did a lot of work on our own. I recall some nights taking care of bad heart failure patients and various and sundry serious problems where I did not feel terribly adequate. Gradually, the house officers became a much more sophisticated group and we became a very strong academic department, but in those early times occasionally it got a little scary for having to deal with problems without a lot of ancillary help. You were expected to get help if you needed it and to go to the library. We did not have Medline searches then. I recall going to the library in the middle of the night to try to find out how to deal with a patient's problems.

It was a heady time here because things were just blossoming. New people were being brought in. *Carlton Chapman* was brought in as the Head of Cardiology. He later became President of the American Heart Association, President at Dartmouth. One of the things Dr. Seldin maintained for his 35 years as the Head of the Department of Medicine was that you had to do research. You could not just be a member of his

FIGURE 7. NMK at the time of the interview.

department unless you had a laboratory doing some kind of research. It was not required that it be bench research. Now, of course, the Department has changed. We now have a Department of General Medicine where the members are primarily taking care of patients, but that is a response to the managed care explosion to keep the medical school solvent. For many years, the medical faculty had very little contact with private patients. That was one of the reasons why we have a very good town-grown relationship. The members of the community of physicians in Dallas never looked upon the medical school faculty as competing with them. We are now competing with everyone else for patients.

WCR: When you were in medical school did you have a easy or difficult time deciding that you wanted to be an internist?

NMK: As a junior student, I thought I wanted to become either a pediatrician or a psychiatrist, but then Dr. Seldin grabbed me one day and said, "I'd like for you to go into internal medicine." His presence and what was happening in the Department of Medicine influenced me. Because I was still not absolutely secure about going into internal medicine, I decided to take a rotating rather than a straight medicine internship. By the time I started the internship, however, I was certain that I wanted to be an internist.

WCR: You became a full-time faculty member in 1961, and a full professor by age 41 in 1970. In the late 1960s, 1970s, and 1980s you started traveling a lot. You became recognized as a splendid teacher. I have participated in a few programs with you around the world and you are appreciated as the world's hypertension guru. You got your book going in 1973 and I gather you realized right away that this was a tremendous opportunity to have a worldwide impact. Let's say it's 1980. What were your daily activities like at that time? What time did you wake up in the mornings? What time did you get to work? When were you doing most of your writing? Do you do your writing with a pencil and paper or do you write on a computer? Do you dictate? Did you do most of that at home or did you do it at work? What time did you go to bed at night?

NMK: I have never been able to work in my office at the medical school. I have always done my writing and lecture preparing almost entirely at home where I've always had an office. I have done every bit of my writing with pencil and paper. I have the computers now, but I don't use them for this purpose. I still am not very good at it. If only I had passed typing in high school I think my whole future would have been different! I do work long and hard hours but likely no longer or harder than most academicians. We do a fair amount of traveling. Whenever I go to a nice place like Japan I take my wife and we do some vacationing at the same time. I don't recall taking a trip, maybe 1 or 2, through these years that was not medically related. Obviously, its very fortunate that somebody is paying for my travel. I have over the years accepted lectureships and professorships and have gone almost all over the world. I believe I am accepted here at our school as the hypertension person but I think I don't get the adoration and the acclaim that I get when I go elsewhere. I guess that is oftentimes true. You are probably more of a guru outside of your own home than you are at home.

It has been a very good life. I guess I am lucky that I picked hypertension because after all that is the most common disease that we all deal with; the most common indication for prescription drugs. I have enjoyed the travel very much. I obviously overdo it. I guess I am also lucky in having at the medical school the ability to take patients only as a consultant. I have not been the primary doctor for these patients so that I can get away without interfering with the care of the patients. I did not start it off purposely that way. I see 4 to 8 new consult patients a week on average. That is what I do in addition to the patients at Parkland that I deal with as a teacher. In the private realm, I see these patients sometimes for weeks or months, but follow them now mainly by phone and fax. They send me their home blood pressure readings and I give them advice. They don't have to come back frequently to have their blood pressures monitored. I see these patients and then send them back to their primary doctor which means I can go away to Japan for 10 days without the necessity of maintaining contact with a lot of sick people. I also find that the airplane is a wonderful place for me to write because there is nobody interfering.

WCR: I presume you never took summer vacations when you were growing up. When you went away to Austin to college was that the first time you had ever really been outside of Dallas, Texas? When was the first time you were outside of Texas, for example? Have you been given a hard time at the Medical School for traveling a lot? I put you in top rank among medical educators that I have witnessed personally. I have seen how hard you work at these places and how beneficial it is to Dallas, Texas, as well as to your medical school. Could you comment on that? Did your lack of travel in childhood make travel more exciting to you as an adult? Has your lack of money as a youngster made the seeking a dollar bill possibly a little more attractive as you have gotten older?

NMK: I think without question those influences must be playing a role. I remember the thrill of going to Galveston for a family vacation as a teenager. The first time I went out of Texas was for my fraternity's national convention when I was 18. Seeing the rest of the world has been enjoyable for me. I think my primary motivation has been the fact that I am being asked to do what I consider to be a legitimate part of an academic career, which is to lecture and participate in meetings and symposia. For me, lecturing and writing have become the primary purpose of my academic life. I don't have a lab anymore. Since I realized about 15 years ago that after having done that for 20 years, lab research was really not my primary interest.

Beyond the desire to teach, there is no question that getting the honoraria and the acclaim as you go to various and sundry places as a visitor has been a major influence on my willingness to do this. I also appreciate the fact that I must have a basic psychological insecurity when people ask me to do something, I have a hard time saying no, even if its not a matter of money or acclaim. I am asked to go down to San Antonio to the medical school and give a lecture to their class where I don't get anything but travel expense, and I would hardly ever say that I can't do it.

I don't think in looking back that my relationships with my kids and family were affected very much by it because I really did not get into this until the kids were grown and had left home. I attend on the inpatient medical services taking 1 or 2 rotations a year, which means about 3 months time when I don't go away, unless it is something like a major committee meeting of the Joint National Committee. When I am asked to have a conference with house staff or students I always make myself available. I do appreciate the fact that I would be doing a lot more in the way of patient contact if I were to stay in Dallas more rather than traveling.

The book has become quite successful and has also added significantly to my income, but even if I didn't make anything from that book I believe I would still work on it. I guess my bibliography has now gotten up close to 500 and most of those are things that people have invited me to do: to participate in supplements, symposia, etc. The ones that are on my basic investigative work probably are no more than 100. The rest have been invited in one way or another.

WCR: Dr. Kaplan, you have already mentioned how many people in the USA and around the world have systemic hypertension, an incredibly common occurrence. It is my understanding that possibly 60 million Americans have systemic blood pressures >140/90 mm Hg. You have already mentioned that you wrote the drug therapy section of the Joint National Committee Report. What you say about treatment of hypertension has an incredible impact, an effect not only on physicians but on profits to pharmaceutical companies. What you say can sway a lot of people whether or not, for example, to use calcium antagonists versus beta blockers versus ACE inhibitors. How do you handle this potential power? Do you think it is ethical for you in this power position to invest in pharmaceutical companies' stock, for example?

NMK: I recognize that what I say may have a goodly amount of influence upon the market at large and pharmaceutical sales of antihypertensives. It poses a challenge for me. I hope that I am not influenced by that sort of thing. In the Joint National Committee Report we did make a statement about the use of calcium antagonists that recommends broadening their use, but it was based upon a very good randomized controlled trial that was published in *Lancet* and had been presented earlier.

I know that there are people who have been very concerned about the calcium antagonist controversy. I have written favorable comments about calcium antagonists. I would believe, however, that has not been influenced by the fact that I have received honoraria from pharmaceutical companies that manufacture or market calcium antagonists, because I also receive honoraria from pharmaceutical companies that market every other class of antihypertensive drug. I don't have any particularly special relation with companies that market calcium antagonists. I try to be objective. I can't say that I have no bias, but, on the other hand, when I see the evidence that an α-blocker drug is good for lipids and insulin sensitivity, then I will write papers and talk about the usefulness of α blockers, whether they are being sponsored by one of the companies that make α blockers or not.

I am very careful when I present talks under the sponsorship of a pharmaceutical company. I also will not accept honoraria from pharmaceutical companies that market drugs that I do not approve or do not use. I have no problem in talking under the sponsorship of a β-blocker marketer, because as part of my talk, which is generally on all general aspects of treatment, I will say something nice about β blockers. Similarly, if I am talking under the auspices of an ACE inhibitor marketer, I will indicate that there are particular places where ACE inhibitors are useful drugs. I would not say only negative things about drugs marketed by a company that has asked me to give a talk under their auspices, but I do believe that my presentations are as unbiased as I can make them. I try to be very careful to maintain my integrity. I don't think I have given a talk on the treatment of hypertension in the last 10 years, where I have not emphasized the importance of non-drug therapy, lifestyle change, because I consider that to be a very important aspect of the treatment of hypertension. There is nobody marketing those lifestyle changes. I also recognize that I am there under the sponsorship of a pharmaceutical company, and, therefore, I am going to say something about the products that this particular company makes, hopefully putting them in proper prospective which may include mention of adverse effects.

When I am asked to give a grand rounds at a medical school, and many of these are being sponsored by pharmaceutical companies, I rarely even do that much, because I assume that when I am asked to give a grand rounds it will be totally without any particular appreciation or attention to one pharmaceutical company's drugs. In those situations where I am presenting in an academic setting, my presentations are almost without any particular mention of one pharmaceutical company's products or another. Obviously, if I am talking about the drug treatment of hypertension I am talking about a variety of pharmaceutical companies' products and there is no way out of that.

WCR: You have been an advocate of non-drug treatment of hypertension for a long time. You seem to weigh less now than you did at one time in your life. You look quite healthy. What are you doing for your own health so that your blood pressure doesn't go up and your blood cholesterol levels don't get too high?

NMK: I try to live a life of moderation. I work out most every day, even when I am on the road. I believe that exercise is absolutely critical to good cardiovascular health and I practice what I preach. That is my way of keeping my weight under control, because part of travel is that you eat more than you do at home. I try to drink a little bit of alcohol on a regular daily basis. We keep a bottle of wine in our icebox and when I go out for a dinner I always have a glass or 2 of wine. I am a real believer in the protective effects of small amounts of alcohol. I eat a reasonably careful diet. I rarely have red meat or eggs. I think I follow the American Heart Association's guidelines of what is called the prudent diet, try to keep my weight under control, exercise regularly, drink a little bit, try to stay as unstressed as I can, although I admit I am a type A—but a happy type A. I am not one who is resentful or hostile. I taught Dean Ornish in Sunday School so he is someone I do relate to but I think his regimen is more than most patients will accept. I have not yet put myself on a statin drug because my cholesterol is only a little above 200 and since I don't have any other risk factors I figure I'm safe. But I recall some of your writings of a few years ago when you recommended that these drugs be much more widely advocated. I think time has actually proved you to be right. I thought you were a little bit wild at the time you were telling everybody to go on a statin, but I think we are all coming around to that because these drugs are so remarkably effective.

WCR: You talked about the "deadly quartet" and you popularized that syndrome: increased blood pressure, increased triglyceride levels, increased insulin, and increased upper body fat. That seems to put a lot of different things together. Could you comment on your analysis of that?

NMK: Actually other people, *Gerald Reaven* at Stanford and others, had talked about this syndrome, the insulin resistance syndrome, but in 1989 I gave a grand rounds here because of increasing awareness that hypertension was related to insulin resistance. I did extend the work of other people and I used that term first. I am not particularly proud of the "deadly quartet" as a term. Again, I don't think I made any original contributions to our understanding of this. I keep looking around America and we are so fat. You go to Japan and there is almost nobody overweight and they have one sixth as much coronary disease as we do. I clearly believe it has to be the lifestyle and the avoidance of obesity that makes the difference between our populations.

WCR: Dr. Kaplan, have you made any mistakes in your professional career? Is there anything you wish you had done that you did not do or certain things you did do that you wished you hadn't done?

NMK: I probably was a little bit too aggressive in attacking the aldosterone and the renin issues, but I have tried to be as objective and unbiased as I can be. I would have done more investigative work at our medical school, and been more actively involved in some projects with other associates in doing collaborative research. I headed the Hypertension Division at the medical school for about 18 years. *Ron Victor*, a bright young investigator, has recently replaced me. He is the prototype of the collaborative type of investigator. He has all kinds of people working with him. He is the kind of young man that I think if I were to go back I would try to emulate, doing collaborative work with other people to broaden the impact. The lecturing, writing, and teaching—I don't think I would want to change much of that. That is something I have enjoyed and I hope that I have been able to have a positive impact. I hope that I have been accepted as a relatively unbiased and objective person.

WCR: You talked about your being a loner as a child. In most of your publications you are usually the first author or the sole author. That can hardly be done today. When you started focusing on hypertension there was not anybody else to talk to. Now hypertension is being attacked by endocrinologists, cardiologists, nephrologists, etc. It has always bothered me that cardiologists as a group have ignored systemic hypertension. How do you get cardiologists interested in high blood pressure? They see oodles of patients with coronary disease, some of whom have hypertension.

NMK: I think part of it is because cardiologists have become so technologically oriented. There is nothing you really need to do that involves a catheter or an invasive procedure in the evaluation and management of patients with hypertension. Hypertension is a low technology area. For most patients all you have to do is take the blood pressure, take a good history and physical, get a little lab work, and start treating. I would hope that things are changing with cardiologists because of the recognition that heart failure, the most common indication for admission to general hospitals, is in large part the result of hypertension. The aging population with this tremendously high frequency of heart failure is forcing cardiologists to take a more active role in the earlier aspects of the disease so that they can treat the hypertension to prevent future heart failure.

Preventative cardiology has really never been a very popular aspect of medical care. Prevention is something that managed care operations might aggressively promote and pay for, and yet, when you spend an hour talking to a patient about the need for exercise and diet and all the other things, they don't pay any more than if you spend 5 minutes doing your regular office visit. I don't think it is true just of cardiologists. I think the same thing could be said of most areas. As specialists, we tend to deal primarily with the end results of problems that occur in patients.

WCR: What are your plans from here on? What do you want to accomplish now?

NMK: I have not thought about that seriously, although I did decide that now that I have gotten beyond age 65, I don't need the administrative hassling, so I voluntarily dropped the divisional Chiefship, although it was never a big responsibility of my life. I also wanted to make room for a younger person who I felt would be much better in expanding research on hypertension at our school. I am very pleased and satisfied with my current life situation. I would love to be able to continue to write, lecture, and see patients. I am very happy with the prospect of continuing to deal with hypertensive patients. I won't ever quit that. But I never wanted to be a full-time practitioner just dealing with patients. I like the balance between patient responsibilities as a consultant physician, the ability to write and lecture, and travel that I am now doing. I think it is a very pleasant and very productive mix that I am very pleased to be able to continue, and as long as my health holds out, as long as people want to hear me and read what I write, I think I will keep doing what I am doing now.

WCR: You must have gotten some opportunities to join one pharmaceutical company or another through the years? You have obviously declined those offers. It seems to me that there are more and more physicians, however, who have moved into the pharmaceutical arena in recent years and they had pretty good academic careers going for them. Could you comment on that?

NMK: I have had opportunities. I would immediately lose the one thing I probably want more than anything else, which is the general respect as an unbiased objective commentator on the whole area of hypertension. I want to maintain my independence. My current situation keeps me as independent as I want to be, and, therefore, I have resisted all the temptations that have been made available to me to take on these higher paying but more limiting kinds of work.

WCR: Could you comment just a moment on your television show, "Here's to Your Health", which I gather you received an Emmy nomination. You did that for about 4 years, 1984-1988.

NMK: It was fun. Actually it was something that was started by our local PBS station in cooperation with the medical school. *Dan Foster* was the first commentator on this program. Subsequent to that *Al Roberts* took it on. Then they asked me do it and I did for 4 years. I did enjoy very much being a ham in front of the screen. I understand they were being shown on 300 different stations, all through the PBS system. The Emmy nomination for daytime television came as a surprise. That was the first time that PBS had ever been nominated. I was beat out that year by Phil Donahue. It was sort of an ego trip but I do believe in public communication and making people aware. We talked about all sorts of things: depression, epilepsy, osteoarthritis, hypertension, coronary disease, etc., and got some good people to come to Dallas and we did some traveling to interview people elsewhere. It became so expensive that after awhile they could not justify continuing. I think that television has not provided good health information to the public. I don't know why but perhaps the public just does not want to look at such programming, unless its ER. I know we have some commentators on national television that give little snips, like Tim Johnson on ABC. I really wonder why we can't do a better job of that, but obviously we can't and so far commercial television has never bought into it.

WCR: Dr. Kaplan, are you concerned about the changes in health care delivery in the USA?

NMK: We are all going through the major revolution of managed care. I am obviously concerned as I am sure every academician is about the continued support of medical education and indigent patient care. We do a good job of it in Dallas but it is a strain on the taxpayers. There are >40 million Americans without their own health insurance. We are the only industrialized country in the world without a national health scheme of some sort. I am enough of a realist to realize that the federal government oftentimes messes things up and we can't have a solitary national health scheme, but the idea of single payer of health care is appealing to me. Take Canada as a good example of the way we ought to look at the future of providing adequate health coverage for our population. I think they have recognized that there has to be tax based on income to provide health care and then let the government stand away and let practitioners take care of their patients without other interference. I wish the Clinton attempt 4 years ago had been better thought out because there were some very good aspects of it. I believe, however, that a monolithic federally controlled health care system would not be appropriate. A single payer to raise the funds to provide health care and insure the entire population seems to me to be a very rational thing.

WCR: Although we are a big country, Dr. Kaplan, with 268 million people, do we really need 125 medical schools? We have 8 in the state of Texas. Granted Texas is the second largest state in the country, but are we producing too many physicians? A hungry doctor it seems to me is one of the most dangerous humans walking around.

NMK: Yes. I have been a firm believer for a long time that any time you put a doctor out there, he or she is going to generate enough business to make a good living. I think that has been well shown. The more physicians, the more hospital beds you have, the more they are utilized. We have to cut down on the number of specialists and we have to increase the number of primary care physicians. The concept of managed care's providing a gatekeeper to bring people into appropriate medical care is absolutely correct. I have no inherent bias against managed care. As a consequence, we get swamped at Parkland Hospital in the emergency room everyday with people who don't have a primary care provider and don't have any insurance. The number of doctors clearly has to be controlled and we do have to try to ensure an adequate number of primary care physicians. Cutting back on the number of specialists makes good sense.

WCR: Dr. Kaplan, I have enjoyed our conversation, and I appreciate your sharing a bit of your life and your views with the AJC readers.

NMK: My pleasure, Bill.

BEST PUBLICATIONS OF NMK SELECTED BY NMK

10. Kaplan NM, Bartter FC. The effects of ACTH, renin, angiotensin II and various precursors on biosynthesis of aldosterone by adrenal slices. *J Clin Invest* 1962;41:715–724.

15. Kaplan NM, Silah JG. The angiotensin infusion test: a new approach to the differential diagnosis of renovascular hypertension. *N Engl J Med* 1964;271:536–541.

16. Kaplan NM, Silah JG. The effect of angiotensin II on the blood pressure in humans with hypertensive disease. *J Clin Invest* 1964;43:659–669.

19. Kaplan NM. The biosynthesis of adrenal steroids: effects of angiotensin II, ACTH and potassium. *J Clin Invest* 1965;44:2029–2039.

22. Kaplan NM. Hypokalemia in the hypertensive patient: with observations on the incidence of primary aldosteronism. *Ann Intern Med* 1967;66:1079–1090.

23. Kaplan NM. The steroid content of adrenal adenomas and measurements of aldosterone production in patients with essential hypertension and primary aldosteronism. *J Clin Invest* 1967;46:728–734.

25. Jose A, Kaplan NM. Plasma renin activity in the diagnosis of primary aldosteronism. *Arch Intern Med* 1969;123:141–146.

27. Jose A, Crout R, Kaplan NM. Suppressed plasma renin activity in essential hypertension: roles of plasma volume, blood pressure, and sympathetic nervous system. *Ann Intern Med* 1970;72:9–16.

32. Saruta T, Saade GA, Kaplan NM. A possible mechanism for hypertension induced by oral contraceptives: diminished feed-back suppression of renin release. *Arch Intern Med* 1970;126:621–626.

38. Saruta T, Cook R, Kaplan NM. Adrenocortical steroidogenesis: studies on the mechanism of action of angiotensin and electrolytes. *J Clin Invest* 1972;51:2239–2251.

46. Kaplan NM. The prognostic implications of plasma renin in essential hypertension. *JAMA* 1975;231:167–170.

51. Kaplan NM, Kem DC, Holland OB, Kramer NJ, Higgins J, Gomez-Sanchez C. The intravenous furosemide test: a simple way to evaluate renin responsiveness. *Ann Intern Med* 1976;84:639–645.

53. Kaplan NM. Renin profiles: the unfulfilled promises. *JAMA* 1977;238:611–613.

54. Kaplan NM, Kramer NJ, Holland OB, Sheps SG, Gomex-Sanchez C. Single-voided urine metanephrine assays in screening for pheochromocytoma. *Arch Intern Med* 1977;137:190–193.

73. Ram CVS, Garrett BN, Kaplan NM. Moderate sodium restriction and various diuretics in the treatment of hypertension: effects of potassium wastage and blood pressure control. *Arch Intern Med* 1981;141:1015–1019.

79. Kaplan NM, Simmons M, McPhee C, Carnegie A, Stafanu C, Cade S. Two techniques to improve adherence to dietary sodium restriction in the treatment of hypertension. *Arch Intern Med* 1982;142:1638–1641.

85. Kaplan NM. Mild hypertension—when & how to treat. *Arch Intern Med* 1983;143:255–259.

98. Kaplan NM. Dietary salt intake and blood pressure. *JAMA* 1984;251:1429–1430.

125. Kaplan NM, Carnegie A, Raskin P, Heller JA, Simmons M. Potassium supplementation in hypertensive patients with diuretic-induced hypokalemia. *N Engl J Med* 1985;312:746–749.

134. Kaplan NM, Meese RB. The calcium deficiency hypothesis of hypertension: a critique. *Ann Intern Med* 1986;105:947–955.

143. Meese RB, Gonzalez DG, Casparian JM, Ram CVS, Pak CM, Kaplan NM. The inconsistent effects of calcium supplements upon blood pressure in primary hypertension. *Am J Med Sci* 1987;294:219–224.

156. Kaplan NM. Maximally reducing cardiovascular risk in the treatment of hypertension. *Ann Intern Med* 1988;36–40.

161. Kaplan NM. Calcium entry blockers in the treatment of hypertension. Current status and future prospects. *JAMA* 1989;262:817–823.

171. Kaplan NM. The deadly quartet: upper body obesity, glucose intolerance, hypertriglyceridemia and hypertension. *Arch Intern Med* 1989;149:1514–1520.

214. Khoury AF, Kaplan NM. Alpha-blocker therapy of hypertension. An unfulfilled promise. *JAMA* 1991;266:397–398.

233. Kaplan NM. The appropriate goals of antihypertensive therapy: neither too much nor too little. *Ann Intern Med* 1992;116:686–690.

235. Khoury AF, Sunderajan P, Kaplan NM. The early morning rise in blood pressure is related mainly to ambulation. *Am J Hypertens* 1992;5 (6 Pt 1):339–344.

250. Kaplan NM. Management of hypertensive emergencies. *Lancet* 1994;344:1335–1338.

251. Kaplan NM. Alcohol and hypertension. *Lancet* 1995;345:1588–1589.

252. Kaplan NM. Difficult to treat hypertension. *Am J Med Sci* 1995;309:339–346.

270. Kaplan NM. Gifford R W JR. Choice of initial therapy for hypertension. *JAMA* 1996;275:1577–1580.

272. Kaplan NM. Anxiety-induced hypertension. *Arch Intern Med* 1997;157:945–948.

DEAN JAMES KEREIAKES, MD: A Conversation With the Editor*

Dr. Dean J. Kereiakes was born in Louisville, Kentucky, in January 1953. He grew up in Cincinnati, Ohio, and was an all-city football player in high school. He graduated from the University of Cincinnati Magna Cum Laude in 3 years and from the University of Cincinnati College of Medicine first in his class in 1978. His training in internal medicine was at the University of California in San Francisco and at the Massachusetts General Hospital in Boston. His fellowship in cardiology was at the University of California in San Francisco. Thereafter, he returned to Cincinnati soon becoming director of cardiovascular intervention and later of the Cardiovascular Center at the Christ Hospital. Despite being in private practice following completion of his training he has published nearly 100 articles in peer review medical journals. He has participated in numerous multicenter interventional trials with his friends Eric Topol and Robert Califf. Most recently, he was instrumental in combining 5 cardiology groups into 1 in his community. Dean in my view is the Denton Cooley of Cardiology. He has performed over 18,000 cardiac catheterization procedures including >6,000 coronary angioplasties since 1984.

William Clifford Roberts, MD†（hereafter WCR）: *I am speaking with Dr. Dean Kereiakes in my office at Baylor University Medical Center on 14 July 1998. Dr. Kereiakes has just given a lecture at Medical Grand Rounds. Dr. Kereiakes, I would like to get to know you as a person. Could you describe some of your earliest memories? I gather that you were born in Louisville, Kentucky, but grew up in Cincinnati, Ohio. Could you describe your family: your mother, father, siblings, etc.?*

Dean James Kereiakes, MD‡（hereafter DJK）: My mother and father were both first-generation Greek Americans and were the son and daughter of Greek immigrants. My father did not speak English when he started school and he put himself through school on scholarships. He became a PhD in radiation physics and arguably the most prominent radiation physicist in the USA. He was president of the American Association of Physicists in Medicine and received every award available in radiation physics including the RSNA Gold Medal Award and the AAPM Coolidge and Gold Medal Awards. My mother is a more prototype ethnic Greek mother who was committed to the kids and the family. The drive to be a professional and well educated was always there. This is very typical of many ethnic subgroups in this country where early in

life it is instilled in the children that they should be a professional and that education is the pathway for the future. There was never any question in my mind that I would be a physician. I gave some consideration to being a lawyer early on, but that did not last long. There was always the drive and incentive to be a professional, to be in control of one's own destiny. I have a brother who is an ear, nose, and throat surgeon. He was trained at Massachusetts Eye and Ear and also was a graduate of the University of Cincinnati Medical School. I have 2 sisters. One entered law school but did not finish, and has 6 children. The other sister has a Master of Business Administration, works part time, and has 3 children. Both are wonderful mothers. One married a radiologist and the other one married a businessman.

WCR: *What was your father and mother like? Were you very close to both of them? What kind of impact did your parents have on you?*

DJK: My father worked very hard and I can remember him dropping us off at church on Sundays and going to his office to work. Although he was not around as much as other fathers, he never missed one of my football games. He would fly in from out of town to watch me play in a football game in high school. It meant a lot to me that he had that commitment, although he was quite busy in his profession and he traveled a fair amount. Mom was always there.

WCR: *Financially, your family did well?*

DJK: My parents offered us every opportunity. They were not wealthy by any stretch of the imagination. They were of moderate means. Yet, they put us in a position that we had every opportunity. In my lifetime, I will never make the same quantum leap they made from first generation to providing their children with the opportunities to be educated anywhere in the world.

WCR: *Where were you in the hierarchy among the 4 siblings?*

DJK: I am the oldest.

WCR: *In junior high school and high school I gather that you always made excellent grades?*

DJK: I made good grades until the middle of high school and then I started to apply myself more. My mission in high school was to play football. In high school, I always said that I was going to college and then medical school, but my real excitement in high school was playing football. I finished 4th in my high school class and was an all-city football player. It was not until college that I started to really apply myself. I expressly went to college with the intent of getting out in 3 years and going to medical school.

WCR: *How many were in your high school class?*

DJK: About 200.

WCR: *Was this a public school?*

DJK: Yes.

*This series of interviews was underwritten by an unrestricted grant from Bristol-Myers Squib.

†Executive Director, Baylor Cardiovascular Institute, Baylor University Medical Center, Dallas, Texas 75246.

‡Director, The Carl and Edith Lindner Center for Clinical Cardiovascular Research, The Christ Hospital, Cincinnati, Ohio 45219.

WCR: *What did you play in football?*

DJK: Linebacker and offensive guard.

WCR: *So you were a 60-minute man?*

DJK: I played both offense and defense.

WCR: *How much did you weigh in high school?*

DJK: I trimmed down from 235 to 225 as a senior.

WCR: *How much do you weigh now?*

DJK: Usually 170 pounds.

WCR: *How tall are you?*

DJK: I was 6'1" before the disc operation.

WCR: *In your home, did you sit around the dining room table and have intellectual discussions? Was it an intellectual home?*

DJK: It was intellectual to the extent that my parents expected us to do well in school. A "B" was tolerable, "Cs" were not tolerable. "As" were rewarded. We were motivated to make As and distinguish ourselves academically. There was a lot of subliminal influence or pressure to excel in school and to participate in school activities.

WCR: *Did you have any mentors in high school who had an impact on you?*

DJK: The person that stands out for me in high school was my football coach who was a very reserved, thoughtful, intelligent and surrogate father figure to many of the guys on the team. He was somebody who I still think of as a physician and still call "coach."

WCR: *Were you interested in your studies in high school?*

DJK: To be honest with you I was not interested in studying in high school.

WCR: *Did you play sports other than football?*

DJK: I played some baseball and track. I threw the shot and discus in track because I was a big guy, "a weight man," as they called it.

WCR: *Why did you pick the University of Cincinnati for college?*

DJK: As the oldest child of a first-generation Greek family, it was pretty well defined that I would stay in town for college. They made it easy for me to attend college at the University of Cincinnati, such as providing tuition. My father was a full professor of Radiology in the medical school and is currently Professor Emeritus. I went to the University of Cincinnati tuition free. I was able to commute from home for the first part of the first year.

WCR: *So you lived at home?*

DJK: I lived at home and commuted for half of my first year of college.

WCR: *When you went to college you decided not to play sports. You wanted to finish in a hurry? Three years? Why did you have this urgency?*

DJK: I felt I wanted to reach or attain my goal of being a physician as quickly as possible because in the future if I wanted to distinguish myself it would be as a physician and not as a football player. I figured the shortest tract to that would be best for me.

WCR: *How did it come about that you focused on medicine? When you went to college right out of high school you knew you wanted to be a physician?*

DJK: Yes. I went to college with the express intent of short tracking.

WCR: *How did you know you wanted to be a physician? How did that come about?*

DJK: Most of the associates my father had as Professor of Radiology were physicians. I perceived the level of admiration and respect that he had for those individuals which included the late *Ben Felson*, the father of American radiology, *Charles Barrett*, and *Eugene Sanger*. These men were pillars in radiology on a national and international level. These are people I associated with when I was a child. I admired and aspired to be like them. After high school I worked in the operating room at Cincinnati General Hospital as an orderly. I did this for 2 summers, and I really got to see from an orderly's perspective surgical procedures and training of the residents. *William Altemeier* was the Chief of Surgery and was a very prominent American surgeon. I learned a lot about what it meant to be a physician and the level of commitment it required. I saw the hours that were being put in by the surgical residents and the staff, and instead of being discouraged it actually stimulated me more. At the time I wanted to be a cardiac surgeon.

WCR: *That was when you were in high school and college?*

DJK: Yes.

WCR: *How did your father get involved with the Department of Radiology at the University of Cincinnati?*

DJK: I was born at Fort Knox, Kentucky, and my dad was a research physicist for the government. He was actually involved with the early non-orbit space flights. Gene Sanger was developing a radioisotope laboratory at the University of Cincinnati, and he recruited my dad to come to Cincinnati about 1958. He stayed at the University of Cincinnati until he retired. He spent his entire career in academic radiology and radiation physics. He is now 74 years old.

WCR: *Is he a PhD?*

DJK: Yes.

WCR: *Where did he get that degree?*

DJK: The PhD was at the University of Cincinnati.

WCR: *Was that after he got there?*

DJK: This was in his original training where he met my mother before we went to Louisville. He grew up in Bowling Green, Kentucky. He came to the University of Cincinnati to get his postgraduate training and through the Greek Orthodox Church he met my mother. They got married and he went back to Fort Knox as a research scientist for the government. When they came back to Cincinnati, the incentives were Eugene Sanger and my mother's family which was in Cincinnati.

WCR: *What year was your father born?*

DJK: He was born in 1924, and my mother, in 1931.

WCR: *You were born in 1953.*

DJK: Yes, January 8, 1953.

WCR: *You are how old now?*

DJK: Forty-five.

WCR: *Did you enjoy college?*

FIGURE 1. DJK during the interview.

DJK: Yes. I was in Sigma Alpha Epsilon fraternity and it was socially an interesting time for me. I used to cram for exams. I was the president of the fraternity after my second year of college. I learned how to interact with various people from various walks of life and backgrounds. That experience was valuable for me to improve my interpersonal skills. It was important to me to learn how to lead, govern, or influence other individuals.

WCR: *What did you major in in college?*

DJK: Biology. I got my degree after my first year in medical school. They accepted me into medical school after 3 years in college. I had a 3.9 grade point average and was active in campus activities, vice-president of the interfraternity counsel, and president of the fraternity. When asked, "What will you do if we don't take you in medical school this year?" I said I thought I could go to Harvard or Yale. They said "okay."

WCR: *Did you get a scholarship to medical school as well as to college?*

DJK: Yes. The arrangement for full professors at the University of Cincinnati was full tuition including graduate school.

WCR: *How did you like medical school?*

DJK: Very much. Medical school was the first time in my life that I really applied myself academically. I tried about as hard as I could both physically and emotionally. It was the right place and the right time. At the University of Cincinnati if you were a very motivated and driven student, you could get a lot of responsibility. As an acting intern, for example, I felt I really made judgment decisions in taking care of patients. I was supervised but because I was given more responsibility I was more comfortable with the responsibility of direct patient care when I subsequently went to my internship than some of my fellow interns

WCR: *Who had a major impact on you in medical school?*

DJK: One person who was really a confidant, who helped me a lot in medical school, and who encouraged me to apply to his alma mater, the Peter Bent Brigham Hospital, was *John Vestor,* an endocrinologist and Director of Research at the Good Samaritan Hospital, one of the hospitals connected with the University of Cincinnati. John Vestor also encouraged me to apply to the University of California San Francisco.

WCR: *Did you do any research in medical school?*

DJK: Another individual in medical school who influenced me and is now involved in the Food and Drug Administration was *Ray Lipicky,* a neurophysiologist. I learned a great deal about ion transport, and basic cellular electrophysiologic mechanisms, and voltage clamping from him. At the time, I changed from wanting to be a cardiac surgeon to wanting to be a cardiac electrophysiologist. That was in 1978 in the very early phases of that subspecialty of cardiology. I acquired an appreciation for basic cellular mechanisms.

WCR: *How many students were in your medical school class?*

DJK: One hundred ninety-two.

WCR: *You graduated first in your class?*

DJK: Yes.

WCR: *How many of those students were women?*

DJK: Probably 40%.

WCR: *You graduated in 1978?*

DJK: Yes.

WCR: *You had your choice essentially of which internship you wanted?*

DJK: The two I wanted were the University of California San Francisco (UCSF) and the Massachusetts General Hospital (MGH). They had the top 2 programs. I was really enthralled by UCSF. I interviewed there. It was a thriving intellectual institution. The Department of Medicine was chaired by *Holly Smith* who had a profound influence on my career. After an interview with *Jim Naughton,* who was the assistant Chief of Medicine and a renal specialist, I remembered saying to myself that I wanted to be there. I never thought I would get in there even though I was first in my class. It was everything I could have wanted.

WCR: *How many fellow interns were in medicine there?*

DJK: About 25 in straight medicine.

WCR: *You were at UCSF for your internship and first year of residency?*

DJK: Yes. During the first year of residency I asked Holly Smith if I could go to being a senior resident at MGH. He said, "If you will come back here and be my chief resident I will fix that for you." So I said "okay." He picked up the phone and called *Alexander Leaf. Steve Osterle* was a medical resident at the MGH and was short-tracking to his fellowship in cardiology at Stanford. I took his spot as a senior resident. I did my senior year heavily loaded with cardiology electives. I really wanted to get a sense and feel for the cardiology training at the MGH. It allowed me to preview where I would fit as a cardiology fellow and determine whether I wanted to go there or stay at UCSF.

WCR: *Who had an influence on you during your internship and your first year residency at UCSF? You mentioned Holly Smith. What kind of impact did he have on you?*

DJK: He had a profound impact. He is very thoughtful. He is one of the great statesmen of American medicine. He is both a clinician and a scientist, and he has compassion. Here is a man at the pinnacle of his profession, editing multiple textbooks, chairman of a department, the largest single NIH grant recipient, the largest single Howard Hughes grant recipient at the time, and he is compassionate. You learn a lot from watching a person like that. He is a Southern gentleman. He is a remarkable human being. I often think about him and *Kanu Chatterjee*, who also had a profound influence on me. I would follow Kanu around on coronary care unit rounds. Even if it added time or conflict to my schedule, I would try to follow him around as much as I could. I was literally in Kanu's back pocket. He has many of the same qualities as Holly Smith—a gentleman, thoughtful, analytic. When I approach a problem today, whether it is political or clinical, I often stop and imagine myself being Kanu Chatterjee or Holly Smith and think how they would approach the issue. Probably, the greatest compliment anyone can give another is to want to emulate those individuals 25 years later.

WCR: *How much contact did you actually have with Holly Smith?*

DJK: A lot. I got along with him extremely well. I would go sit in his office. I remember when Topol applied for internship at UCSF, I went into his office and told him this kid from Rochester, New York, was a star. I had done a 6-week elective in Rochester, New York, when I was a senior in medical school. I worked with *Marshall Leischman* and *Arthur Bauman* for 6 weeks. That is where I met *Eric Topol*. He was a junior medical student. We were on the same service and got along very well. A year later, he was walking through the hallway at the San Francisco General Hospital interviewing. After talking with him, I went right into Holly Smith's office and said I could vouch for him personally. I had a great relationship with Holly Smith and called him "Chief." To this day, I consider him a personal friend.

WCR: *You must have interacted with him a great deal when you were chief resident. Did he make ward rounds or do morning report.*

DJK: Yes. He alternated morning report with Naughton. As Holly's chief resident, I had a remarkable experience. Part of my appreciation for basic science research was the fact that at Holly's request, I would ask individuals like *Herb Boyer, J. Michael Bishop*, and *Harold Varmus*, all Nobel laureates, to speak to the house staff. Herb Boyer was the guy who first spliced DNA and founded Genentech. These are some of the most powerful figures in American sci-

FIGURE 2. DJK during Medical Residents Conference at Baylor University Medical Center.

ence. I would call and say, "I am Holly's chief resident and Holly would like for you to come down and present to our house staff on your work." We got to sit there as house staff and watch these individuals draw on a blackboard what would subsequently become Noble Prize winning experiments. It was almost like a religious experience for me. It was very exciting to see this, even though I am not a basic scientist. It helped me have a mind set to want to apply basic science in clinical practice and to look for ways to do that.

WCR: *Who were some of your fellow house officers at UCSF?*

DJK: *Rob Califf* and I were interns together; Eric Topol was our intern (I often joked that is the last time Eric ever worked for us.); *Michael Cayman*, who is now the Director of Research at Eli Lilly and a cardiologist; *Fred Moray*, who was ahead of us, and is one of the top electrophysiologists in the country; *Allan Guerci* was Director of the Coronary Care Unit at Hopkins for years and now he is Director of Research at St. Francis, a large private institution; and *Marcus Wharton*, a basic electrophysiologist at Duke; *Dennis Wahr* and *Larry DiCarlo* in Ann Arbor, Michigan. The group was called the *Moffitt Mafia*.

WCR: *At the UCSF you not only were influenced by Drs. Smith and Chatterjee, but your fellow house officers apparently had considerable impact on you.*

DJK: Yes. It was remarkable. There were 6 or 7 interns who were both MDs and PhDs. Several are now Chairmen of Departments of Medicine.

WCR: *Why did you want to go to the MGH considering your superb experiences at the UCSF?*

DJK: Before committing myself to a cardiology fellowship at the UCSF and literally locking myself in for a total of 6 years or more at 1 institution, I wanted to preview or sample what another institution had to offer. Since these were my first 2 choices for medical training, I got consumed with the idea that I wanted to train at both places. When I bounced that idea off Holly Smith he said he would make me a deal. If I would come back and be his chief resident he would see to it that I was a senior resident at the MGH. I had an opportunity to work with *Roman DeSanctis*, a gentleman and a great clinician. My co-senior residents at the MGH have continued to be my friends.

WCR: *I gather that you were not a national or international traveler during your high school and college years. Going out to San Francisco for the first time must have been an eye-opening experience for you.*

DJK: Hitting both coasts at age 25 was a fantastic experience for a mid-Westerner. In some ways I felt like a Hillbilly going to the big city. I could never have had the same experience if I had stayed in the Midwest.

WCR: *The same experience in what way?*

DJK: Exposure to the talent. Exposure to clinical talent, the research talent, the concepts. All the stimulation made it a remarkable experience to be in either the UCSF or the MGH.

WCR: *How did Boston hit you after having been in San Francisco for a couple of years?*

DJK: Boston was much more compact. I really enjoyed it. Several senior residents took me to a Harvard hockey game, a Boston Celtics game, and a Boston Red Sox's game. I got to experience Boston. It was a tremendous social experience in addition to being very busy clinically.

WCR: *How did your fellow house officers at the MGH take you? I would presume there are not many people who walk into the MGH as a senior medical resident having completed an internship and senior residency elsewhere.*

DJK: At times I probably was perceived as being a bull in a china shop. If I had to go back and do it over again I probably would have softened my approach. I would say that openly to everyone of those guys. MGH is a very clinical program. At the MGH they often did things clinically because that was the way they did it. At UCSF they often did things because that was the way it was supposed to be done based on basic science or animal research. For example, if I had a patient with noncardiogenic pulmonary edema at the Moffit Hospital, I would go upstairs to the Cardiovascular Research Institute and sit down with *Norman Staub* (Mr. Noncardiogenic Pulmonary Edema) who had devised animal models for creating an alveolar-capillary membrane defect. I would talk to him about the pathophysiology of this problem. I think the access to the basic scientists was greater at UCSF. At the Cardiovascular Research Institute you had renal, pulmonary, and cardiovascular physiologists all there. If you were inquisitive, which I was, wanting to read about the pathophysiologic mechanisms of everything, it was like being in a candy shop. I would go around and actually go seek out these individuals and talk to them about the basic pathophysiologic mechanisms of the disease process, which I found incredibly stimulating and very helpful in my understanding of the disease and treatment. I felt the MGH was much more of a clinical program, higher volume overall. My choice of cardiology fellowships influenced these factors in addition to Kanu Chatterjee, *Melvin Cheitlin*, and *Bill Parmley* (tremendous teachers and individuals). These were the reasons I went back to USCF for my cardiology fellowship.

WCR: *When did you decide you wanted to be a cardiologist?*

DJK: I think I made that decision the first or second year of house staff training. I can remember being a senior resident at MGH when they gave the first intracoronary streptokinase. I happened to be at the right place at the right time. There was a transformation in cardiology at that time from a diagnostic subspecialty to a therapeutic subspecialty. I was there at the time of the transition. I also was one of the first fellows in angioplasty. I was recruited by *Richard Myler* and *Simon Stertzer*. I spent half a year with them and half a year with *John Simpson* at Sequoia Hospital in 1984. After agreeing to go with Myler and Stertzer, Eric Topol was looking for a place to train in angioplasty. In an academic institution like The Johns Hopkins, he felt there was little opportunity to get his hands on an angioplasty catheter. There was a line waiting for a limited number of patients to train on. I told Eric they had 10 to 30 angioplasties a week in San Francisco and it is a great place for him to be. When he came to San Francisco, I would drive him every morning to the San Francisco Heart Institute where the 2 of us were "fellows." There we met *Barry George*, a tremendous clinical talent. Barry was a great operator even as a fellow. We were 3 of the foursome that founded the Thrombolysis and Angioplasty in Myocardial Infarction (TAMI) trial study group. We would sit around in the fellow's room at the San Francisco Heart Institute, and would call up Rob Califf at Duke. We devised the protocol for the TAMI I trial, which was a trial of the interaction of tissue plasminogen activator and balloon angioplasty. We were 4 young guys who wanted to do clinical research. The concern Califf had at the time was whether or not clinical research could be extended into the private sector. Barry George was going to Riverside Methodist in Columbus and I was going to Christ Hospital in Cincinnati. The TAMI I trial study group subsequently evolved into the TAMI 1-9 Trials, GUSTO, CAVEAT, IMPACT, EPIC, and EPILOG. All of these major trials evolved out of a nucleus of the TAMI trial I study group. This began the shift for clinical research to be done in large part in private institutions. Before that time, most clinical research was done in university-based academic institutions. What we proved in TAMI I was that high-quality and high volume clinical research could be done in the private sector. Now the success of programs like Duke Clinical Research Institute rest in their recruitment of patients from the private sector.

WCR: *You did your training in angioplasty and interventional work in the private sector with Richard Myler, Simon Stertzer, and John Simpson?*

DJK: Yes. During the 6 months I worked with John Simpson, I put the electric motor (motor drive unit) on his directional coronary atherectomy (DCA) catheter. The first DCA catheter was a hand crank device. I wrote a paper on angioplasty of chronic total occlusions, 76 consecutive cases. He gave me the watch I am now wearing for Christmas in 1984. At the time I made less than $16,000.00 a year. I certainly could not have afforded this watch. I have never gotten another watch.

WCR: *What kind of watch is it?*

DJK: It's a Rolex. It was given to me and engraved by John Simpson after I was a fellow with him in coronary angioplasty.

WCR: *How much did your watch cost Simpson?*

DJK: About $2,600 at the time. My wife and daughter (in a stroller) later saw the watch in a jewelry store, and determined that it was equivalent to a fourth or a third of my entire income that year.

WCR: *Why do you think he gave you the watch?*

DJK: I did 2 things for Simpson. I transformed his DCA catheter into a more functional device with high revolutions applied to the cutting mechanism. Second, I wrote one of the first manuscripts from that group. He saw the need to have somebody do clinical research and publish their clinical experiences.

WCR: *How did you return to Cincinnati after your fellowship?*

DJK: I was going to go to the University of Michigan. As I mentioned, Fred Morady, Larry DiCarlo, and *Dennis Wahr* went to Michigan. These were all UCSF people. I was recruited by *Bert Pitt* and *Bill Kelly.* I thought Michigan was a great place. At the time, however, we had a newborn and Ann Arbor was far away from any of our families. It was my wife's desire to be near one of the families because she knew I would be gone so much. She did not want to go to Ann Arbor. She probably made the right decision for me. I immediately told my friend Eric Topol what a great academic job Michigan was and how you could be financially rewarded in the structure developed by Bill Kelly. The rest was history. Topol went there and the TAMI trial study group came out of Duke and Michigan later.

WCR: *You went back to Cincinnati after completion of your cardiology fellowship?*

DJK: I was interested in interventional cardiology and the bulk of interventional procedures were done in the private sector. Within 3 years from the time I entered practice I was doing over 1,400 cath lab procedures a year. It was highly unlikely that I could have gone to any academic university-based program in the country and averaged 1,400 or more procedures a year for the first decade that I was in practice. This was a great opportunity. In the first 10 years I did 15,000 procedures.

WCR: *You started at Cincinnati in January 1985?*

DJK: Yes.

WCR: *Since that time you have done how many catheterizations?*

DJK: Between 17,000 and 18,000 cath lab procedures.

WCR: *How many angioplasties?*

DJK: Roughly 5,000 to 6,000.

WCR: *What enticed you to go back to Cincinnati?*

DJK: I had an opportunity to join *Charles Abbottsmith* who was the Chief of Cardiology at the Christ Hospital. He was a very astute clinician, a very technically proficient operator, and he was very supportive of me. He was absolutely the right person at the right time. His ego did not get in the way of having a young guy come in who had a lot of new ideas and brought in new technology. He was completely supportive and fully participating in those interests. In addition, I was influenced by another individual in Cincinnati who I had kept in contact with. I had been in school with the son of *Carl Lindner*, a financier in Cincinnati. When I was in California training, he had visited me on a couple of occasions and asked me what kind of equipment we needed to do complex coronary interventions. Christ Hospital was perceived in the community as a heart hospital largely because of expertise in coronary bypass surgery. Angioplasty was relatively underdeveloped at the time. *Jack Cook*, chief executive officer of Christ Hospital at that time, called me to say that Carl Lindner bought the equipment I had specified for the best possible catheterization laboratory. The message was loud and clear that Christ Hospital was the logical place for me to go.

WCR: *When did you get married?*

DJK: In 1981. It was right before I started the chief residency in Holly Smith's department.

WCR: *Your wife was from where?*

DJK: Anne grew up in Redwood City, California. Her father, *Ben Sugar*, was the Chief of Surgery for about 25 years at Sequoia Hospital which was where John Simpson went. Sequoia was a small private hospital with a tremendous cardiovascular service.

WCR: *How did you meet your future wife?*

DJK: Anne was a nurse at UCSF. She became head nurse in the coronary care unit for Kanu Chatterjee and we worked together there. Since our first child was born, she has committed herself to the success of the family. Her support and understanding have been boundless and have been the key to any success we have achieved. It has not been easy but she has always been there, to hold everything together.

WCR: *You have how many children?*

DJK: Four.

WCR: *What years were they born?*

DJK: 1984, 1986, 1987, and 1990.

WCR: *Girls and boys?*

DJK: The oldest is a girl and then 3 boys.

WCR: *Here you are back in Cincinnati January 1985, and you say 3 years later you are doing 1,400 caths a year?*

DJK: Yes. Angioplasties and caths combined.

WCR: *So you must have never been home.*

DJK: Anne spent countless hours as a "single parent." I worked all the time. I would go in on weekends,

FIGURE 3. DJK with his family.

whether it was DCA, eximer laser, stents. Part of the growth was perceived quality of care, and part was the advantage of access to new technology.

WCR: *Let's say your third year back. What was your life like on a day-to-day basis. What time were you getting up in the mornings?*

DJK: I got up at 5:00 A.M. every morning. I start rounds at 5:30 at the hospital.

WCR: *Is that then, now, or both?*

DJK: I get up now between 5:00 and 5:30 every morning and usually I am at the hospital before 6:00. I am running about half hour behind where I used to run for more than a decade. I started in the cath lab at 7:00 A.M. every day and did between 5 and 10 procedures. I went to the office every day, back to the hospital, and did consults every day until 7:00 to 9:00 at night. This was the first decade I worked at Christ Hospital. Then, on Sunday mornings I would write papers. I never really took vacations. I would travel with the family and I would get up at 4:30 or 5:00 in the mornings and write for 4 or 5 hours and then go do something with the family, but I never lost the incentive. It is quite a physical impediment to be that clinically involved and still write original manuscripts.

WCR: *What time were you going to bed? You got home about 8:00 P.M.*

DJK: Usually I am in bed by 10:00 or 11:00 and get up at 5:00.

WCR: *So you get 6 or 7 hours of sleep.*

DJK: I try to get 6 hours of sleep.

WCR: *You can go okay on that?*

DJK: I do all right. I can't sleep in the mornings anymore. One of the biggest problems of crossing time zones is that my eyes pop open at the equivalent of 5:00 A.M. I don't have to use an alarm clock.

WCR: *You had gathered in your group 5 cardiologists, and then in the 1990s you combined your group with others. How did that come about?*

DJK: I needed more focus in my life and in my practice. I felt that cardiology was going to go in the

anytime. It did not matter. At night time I would sleep in the intensive care unit or in labor and delivery. Cardiologists at that time were not doing primary or rescue angioplasty very much for myocardial infarction. I did primary angioplasty for acute myocardial infarction beginning immediately after I arrived back in Cincinnati.

WCR: *When you first went back to Cincinnati it was just you and Charles Abbottsmith? How did your partners come in? How did that get going?*

DJK: We got busier and busier and we literally worked all the time. We brought in another interventional cardiologist, *Tom Broderick,* who is an exceptional talent. We then brought in a noninterventionalist, *Robert Toltzis,* and another interventionalist, *David Whang,* in rapid fire. This is over a period of several years because of the growth of the practice, almost unmanageable growth. In part it was driven by technology. We had access to new technologies,

direction of increasing subspecialization among cardiologists. For example, in 1992 and 1993 I knew that there would eventually be a board exam offered in interventional cardiology, much like there is for electrophysiology. There are also certification exams now in noninvasive testing like echocardiography and electrocardiography. I felt like a jack of all trades is a master of none. In an effort for me to obtain more focus on intervention, clinical research, and writing, 3 years ago I construed a concept, a blueprint for a large group of cardiologists with a limited number of interventionalists. I believed that volume would drive proficiency and efficiency. I also felt that the business of medicine was organizing and we could either continue to compete with each other or we could organize ourselves in a fashion that would enhance the quality of care we provided. We had a number of cardiologists give up angioplasty for the betterment of the whole group.

WCR: *How many cardiologists are you talking about?*

DJK: Originally there were 18. There will be 28 as of August 1, 1998.

WCR: *This merger of these 5 groups into 1 came about what year?*

DJK: The merger was conceived October 1995. It was on the drawing boards for 11 months before that.

WCR: *How did you actually bring these groups together? Did you join together gradually 1 group at a time or all at the same time?*

DJK: It was a simultaneous merger of 5 competing groups.

WCR: *How did you do it? Did you call up the chief of each group?*

DJK: I called the senior partner in each group, including my senior partner Chuck Abbottsmith, who represented the Christ Hospital group. I told them the business of medicine is organizing. We will never have more influence than we do now. We can either wait and see what happens, make defensive moves, react, and maybe compete with each other, or we can make an offensive move in the same direction as our profession to increase subspecialization. Second, all the other issues relative to managed care have been dealt with very effectively by the preemptive move we made.

WCR: *Was it difficult to bring this about?*

DJK: There were some individuals who did not want to give up angioplasty. Most patients and hospitals would be better served if there was just 1 cardiology group in the medical center. With 1 group you may have more leverage or influence to make more uniform volume credentialing, more uniform practice patterns, and better adherence to practice guidelines that conform the care of different physicians so that you reign in outliers for cost and negative outcomes. It is very hard in a large hospital organization that has multiple smaller competing groups with variable volume credentialing, numbers of procedures per operator per year, variable practice patterns, and little or no adherence or enforceability of practice guidelines to quality assure and conform the care given to patients.

In this "new era of medicine" we are responsible for producing a product that has well-defined boundaries, that are reproducible. This includes outcomes and costs within defined confidence intervals. Business people have no problem with the concept of a reproducible product. That is how we have to represent ourselves. Our move was in the direction of standardizing our product whether it was outcomes through angioplasty, cost per procedure, or length of stay per diagnosis. I could control that better with 8 individuals doing 2,500 coronary angioplasties this year and I could layer in various practice guidelines to further enhance performance.

WCR: *What you are saying in essence is that with 1 large group you can set standards of excellence for cardiology in that particular institution, whereas if there are 5 separate groups of cardiologists using the same hospital there is no way to control standards.*

DJK: You can try. As a director of cardiovascular services in an institution like that, you will have to meet with them literally on a monthly or quarterly basis to enforce practice guidelines for the physicians and critical care pathways for the ancillary personnel.

WCR: *When you combined the cardiologists together into 1 group from these 5 groups, there were 25 cardiologists, and in the new setting only 8 did angioplasty. How many were doing angioplasty before?*

DJK: Fifteen.

WCR: *So you eliminated angioplasty from at least 7 operators? How did you entice them to give up something they presumably liked very much to do and was extremely profitable to them?*

DJK: Implicit in the success of that effort was the concept behind the financial remuneration of the partners in our group that hard work is rewarded whether it is in the cath lab or out of the cath lab and that everyone's time is valuable in taking care of the "whole patient." We designed a relative value unit (RVU) system for all of the tasks we do as cardiologists. This was a consensus decision of the first 19 partners. We divided the income among the shareholders or partners equally for 70% of the income after overhead for the group, and the other 30% is divided based on the individual's RVU production. It turns out that 3 of the top 6 earners out of the current 29 in the group do not do coronary intervention. They are very busy clinical cardiologists. We specifically rewarded the access of new patients into the practice because the life blood of the group lies in its patient base. We weighted the relative value of a new patient consult similar to that of a left-sided heart catheterization. Our clinical cardiologists, even the noninvasive cardiologists, are very motivated to bring in new patients. This strategy has an intrinsic gatekeeper capacity that has been extremely attractive to the payers in our area. They have sought us out because we have a financial remuneration system that rewards non-laboratory cardiac care and does not incentivize the performance of procedures. Remarkably, it has worked out that procedural volume is growing rapidly because of the influx of new patients into the group. Rewarding the clinical cardiologists for seeing new patients has resulted in a dramatic rise in procedural volume for the group, even though the financial structure would appear to discourage the performance of procedures. We had a growth in the first 2 years of 24% in angioplasty volume, and in 1997 to 1998 that growth will be even greater.

WCR: *If you bring a new patient into the group you are essentially paid the same as if you did a left-sided cardiac catheterization.*

DJK: Correct.

WCR: *What is your relationship with the University of Cincinnati? Your hospital is within a mile of the University Hospital? You are a Clinical Professor of Medicine at the University of Cincinnati. Do you teach at the university?*

DJK: We have a separate house staff training program that is accredited at the Christ Hospital and we have university-based residents from multiple subspecialties rotating through the Christ for clinical experience. I am a Professor of Clinical Medicine at the University of Cincinnati and my involvement in teaching is both for house staff on campus at the Christ Hospital and I make teaching rounds when I am covering our group's clinical service at the University. On weekends, I occasionally make formal Medical Intensive Care Unit and Coronary Care Unit teaching rounds at the University for house staff and fellows when our group is on that service. Partners in our group are the Director of the Coronary Care Unit and the Director of the Cardiac Catheterization Laboratory at the University. The bulk of the clinical service at the University is cared for by our private group. I envision an integration of the fellowship training program at the University of Cincinnati with that of the Christ Hospital.

WCR: *You have a cardiology fellowship at the Christ Hospital now?*

DJK: No. The cardiology fellowship program is at the University of Cincinnati and we have internal medicine training programs at both.

WCR: *Do we have too many cardiologist in this country?*

DJK: One of the reasons I think there is a perception that there are too many cardiologists in this country is that they are all trying to do the same thing. We probably don't need to have so many low-volume angioplasty operators. There should be a limited number of individuals who do interventional procedures and the other cardiologists who are not involved in interventional procedures could do more clinical work. There has been a lack of incentive for doing more clinical work because the dollar has been tied to doing the procedures. Although it may be less desirable to be perceived as somebody who does not do "the whole package," the reality of the situation is that good doctors who subspecialize and work closely together will be more efficient and more proficient than any one doctor trying to do the whole package, no matter how good that one doctor is or how hard he/she works. I am living proof of that statement.

WCR: *At Baylor University Medical Center, to have coronary angioplasty privileges, a minimum of 150 angioplasties must be done in a 2-year period to get recertified for the following 2 years. I understand, Dr. Kereiakes, that you have some data showing that efficiency and outcomes are better if you use 200 angioplasty procedures per operator per year than if you use a cutoff point of 75 annually. Can you expand on that?*

DJK: I can. Prior to the formal conception of our present group, 15 of the cardiologists did angioplasty and each averaged 120 procedures annually, well above the 75 annually required at Baylor University Medical Center. The composite outcome of death, Q-wave myocardial infarction, and emergent revascularization in 1997 was reduced by 56% in our group with 8 cardiologists doing angioplasty compared to 1995 when 15 did it. Each one of the subcomponents of that outcome, namely emergent reangioplasty, emergent bypass surgery, and death, has been cut in half. The composite complications are now down to 1.6%. Optimal outcomes in coronary intervention are achieved if individual operator volumes exceed 200 annually. That is why we picked 200 as a minimum volume threshold for credentialing in our group.

WCR: *Dr. Kereiakes, I understand that you don't do cardiac catheterization every day. You do it 3 times a week. During the 3 days that you work in the cath lab now, describe, if you would, what your day is like; how many procedures do you do?*

DJK: One benefit of a large group is some days out of the lab. The interventionists in our group work 3 days a week in the lab. On the lab days, you start at 7:00 A.M. You do cases you have referred to yourself electively from your 2 clinical days where you see outpatients in an office setting and you do all cases referred in from two thirds of the group who are noninterventional cardiologists. You work from 7:00 A.M. usually until 5:00 or 6:00 P.M. in the cath lab, procedure after procedure. I have averaged about 10 procedures a day when I am in the lab. For more than a decade, however, I worked in the lab every day, Monday through Friday, and frequently on Saturdays. It is useful to have break days out of the lab. Patients should have access to you in some capacity for a consultative process. I am in the office twice a week. All our interventionalists function in this manner.

WCR: *How does your 2 days out of the lab actually workout?*

DJK: I see about 20 patients every Wednesday and Thursday mornings. On Wednesday and Thursday afternoons, starting 2 years ago, I do clinical research in the Lindner Center for cardiovascular research. With that commitment of 2 half days a week there has been an exponential increase in funding for clinical research and in publications from our group.

WCR: *Are any of your other 28 cardiologic colleagues participating in research? Is your research mainly part of other multicenter studies around the country?*

DJK: All of our group enroll patients in clinical research trials. Several of them actively solicit trials. Several of our group members have co-authored publications in multicenter research trials. Actually, being first author in writing up clinical research trial results has largely been left to me. Holly Smith said after writing his first paper that it was like, "Giving birth to barbed wire." It was one of the most difficult things he had ever done. Anyone who has become facile with writing papers knows that it gets easier over time but it is a learning process. Most individuals never cross that threshold where they become more comfortable with it.

WCR: *How do you write papers? Do you write them with pencil and paper or do you dictate or what do you do?*

DJK: I usually write an outline with a #2 pencil and yellow pad and I dictate the first draft. For me, most of the references I know in my head or I have my office staff do a literature search and I hang the references on the draft much like ornaments on a Christmas tree. I know what I want to say. I had the benefit of learning from Kanu Chatterjee who taught me that what you are really doing in writing a paper, even a peer-reviewed scientific paper, is telling a story. You have to make an outline of the story you want to tell. The story is what the data tells you. Once I get a rough draft, then I modify it multiple times. Sometimes, I set it down for a week and come back to it and am appalled at what I wrote a week before and make modifications.

WCR: *I like your comment about outline. When I was in college I was an English major and some of my English teachers kept encouraging me to outline before I wrote. I virtually never did in college but when I reached NIH and I realized that my paycheck was dependent on my pen then I learned what an outline really meant. I outline every paragraph now. Until recently I wrote with a pencil on a yellow pad. I dictate some now but when I dictate the piece goes through a lot more drafts.*

DJK: I am always trying to be more productive. Having good ancillary personnel is enormously helpful and I am fortunate here. I need to get more computer literate.

WCR: *Let me ask about vacations, time off, hobbies, things for the future. You have 27 partners now. How much time to you take off a year?*

DJK: I don't know that I have really taken a true vacation ever. There may be a day that I don't do some work if I am traveling with my family, but, unfortunately, even then I find some ways to write, to focus on clinical research or upcoming presentations. Over the last couple of years, since the conception of the new group, I have traveled much more academically and learned a great deal. I have worked in cath labs in Europe, given symposia in Europe, and interacted with international physician groups. There is a lot we physicians in the USA can learn from them.

WCR: *How many trips do you actually go on in a year now?*

DJK: I limit my trips to, at most, 2 each month. It seems like I am always between being on call and being out of town.

WCR: *How much are you on call?*

DJK: In our group we take both clinical calls and interventional calls. In our large group, it is common-place to do a dozen urgent or emergent procedures over a weekend. It is not uncommon to spend nights in the hospital.

WCR: *With 8 interventionalists you are on call at least once a week?*

DJK: We are all on call approximately once a week in some capacity.

WCR: *So you spend a lot of time at work. You have 4 youngsters. What kind of father are you?*

DJK: You asked me about objectives for the future. The future, unfortunately, is coming much too quickly. My oldest will be a freshman in high school this fall. If I had to pick objectives for the future it would be to (1) spend more total time with my children, and (2) to spend more quality time with them. It is one thing to be in the vicinity; it is another to be focused on them. I found I have been guilty of letting my profession and my work distract me and take my focus off the kids, even at times when I have been physically present with them. I think focus is personal discipline. I have to try to make myself a better father. I am amazed at the rapidity with which they are growing up. We still have little ones. I try to make it to their sporting and school events, but still I don't think that is really being a good father, just showing up at events. I try to spend one-on-one time, actually take them out to dinner and be in a situation where we have to talk. It is amazing how they won't talk much at first but after you are there for an hour or so they become chatterboxes. All kinds of things come out. It is really a wonderful experience to go one on one and spend a couple of hours of time where I am not being distracted by work.

WCR: *You are 45 years old. You have done 18,000 cardiac catheterization procedures. You have formed a large practice group. You have a nice relationship with the medical school a mile away. You have 4 children. Your mother and father are still living and are living in Cincinnati. You've been financially well rewarded these past 14 years. What are your professional ambitions from this point as you see them now versus your personal ambitions?*

DJK: Eric Topol and others have asked me why I maintain the volumes I do in the cath lab. It is not money at this point. It is credibility. If you ask any of the top volume interventionalists in the country who publish they will tell you the same thing. When we present data to our colleagues, they know that we really do the work. I still see myself working in the lab, although my wife does not want me working in the lab, frankly. There probably is little reason for me to continue working in the lab to the extent that I do. Our group is set up so that I could do as well financially if I were not in the lab. I could transition myself into a noninterventional cardiologist and eventually I may do that. It would be a logical ambition to be chief of a program. I would like to not have to leave Cincinnati to do that. I like to write. At a time in a comparable career where most of my colleagues that I came out of training with have their fellows write the papers, I am still writing first-author papers because I like to do it. For the first time in my career I have had a little time to do it. I have 2 half days a week where I can actually run a clinical research center and I have had more focus on writing. I would like to continue writing, probably want to teach more, and do it in a fashion so that such an effort is rewarded within my group structure, and still be a clinical cardiologist. I don't see myself retiring from clinical cardiology, because it is what I do. I like taking the responsibility for making clinical decisions. I don't foresee in the immediate future stepping out of the cath lab because of the access to technology that it has given me. Being an original investigator of most of the new interventional technologies over the last decade has given me credibility among my peers.

WCR: *You seem to me to be like Denton Cooley, who has performed more cardiac operations than anybody in history. He is 76 years old and is still doing about 15 cases a week. You keep up the pace that you are doing now, by age 65 you too will have an enormous number of cardiac catheterization procedures.*

DJK: Although my numbers are down in the new group, I still do over 1,000 procedures a year. I was gone 72 days last year traveling (giving lectures, task force committees, American College of Cardiology, American Heart Association committees, etc.). Dr. Braunwald just asked me to serve on the committee to rewrite the guidelines for unstable angina. These things are not financially rewarding but they provide an opportunity to positively influence the care of patients everywhere.

WCR: *You have said that clinical investigation is profitable. What does that mean?*

DJK: There are 2 sides of this coin. Clinical investigation enhances patient care. Some clinicians don't get that. It clearly enhances the product of care as measured by outcomes and costs. Clinical investigation provides algorithms for care that are enforceable "guidelines," because the clinical research protocols are followed by clinical research nurses. In an efficient clinical research organization where overhead is held down and "tithings" to various institutions are limited, clinical research can be extremely profitable. There has been an explosion of interest around this country in taking clinical research vehicles public, having initial public stock offerings, and buying clinical investigation sites. We have been approached a half dozen times already. People want to buy our research site or a portion of it because of the quality of the research and the volume of it. The pharmaceutical companies in the future may ratchet down reimbursement for the performance of clinical research. But right now, the reimbursement in clinical research is very good. It is easy to make a profit. Our overhead is kept low in the Lindner Center. When doing clinical research at the university, our overhead was at least 10% more and resources were much less efficient. That does not mean we are not going to do clinical research at the university. In private settings, you may use a percentage of your funds to support a fellowship program, or

some type of medical education program. We put 10% of the funds earned and received into a fund that was matched by the hospital, producing a symbiotic relationship between the research center and the hospital. That fund exceeds several million dollars at this point.

WCR: *There is a lot of superb information coming out of the mass-volume private nonuniversity medical centers, such as yours and the Washington Hospital Center. Is clinical research going to be able to exist well in the university setting in the future? Will they have enough patients to do it?*

DJK: Two things will be an issue in a university setting. One will be the patient volume, and the second will be the overhead, the cost structure for providing the services. I think that clinical research can be done in a university setting, but it takes somebody who is ingenious and somebody who is resilient in trimming the cost of the product. The time has come and gone when pharmaceutical companies are willing to pay an exorbitant premium to a university-based research organization. At this time they are more willing to go to the clinical research organizations who can link and network multiple private centers and provide much more cost-efficient service. Clinical research at university settings is going to die unless bright individuals are able to produce a competitive product at a good price. There is some premium to be paid for the academic moniker, but that premium is not going to be 40% to 50% greater than having the same research done by private networks of investigational sites. We have an infrastructure within our center of research coordinators who screen patients and research nurses. The litmus test will be if we can grow from 4 to 5 million to 10 or 15 million and still manage to be efficient. That is going to be the challenge.

WCR: *Dr. Kereiakes, let me ask you about the quality of cardiologic care delivered to patients by private, nonuniversity groups, such as yours, versus that delivered in the better-than-average or average university medical centers in this country.*

DJK: First, our group is the clinical service, in essence, at the University of Cincinnati. Second, the size of the group does not necessitate that you are going to have an efficient organization. Our group has dedicated subspecialists, like our interventional core, that can achieve better outcomes, shorter lengths of stay, lower costs per procedure, than a smaller organization. This is done through a process of individual operator volume credentialing, practice guidelines for the physicians, and implementing critical care pathways for the ancillary medical personnel. Those are the 3 steps that I think are crucial to producing a streamlined reproducible product —high level volume credentialing, practice guidelines, and critical care pathways. We may be more effective in doing that in the private sector. Our group has been on both sides of the street. Outcomes are good at both sites. Some will argue that anytime you have a training program, medical practice becomes less efficient. I am not sure that is entirely right. Training programs are sometimes a scapegoat.

WCR: *You have been in the private arena now for 14 years doing a huge volume of cardiologic catheterization laboratory procedures. That has produced for you a considerable income. Is there resentment of that feature in you by the University cardiology groups?*

DJK: I feel that on a national level, particularly among the hard-core, prototype academicians, there has been a reluctance to embrace the private practitioner. Those of us in the private sector who have done a lot of procedures and also had academic pursuits have at times felt resentment. There was more resentment previously than there is now.

WCR: *What about interests outside medicine?*

DJK: I have been collecting wine for about 3 years and I have a cellar in my home. Unfortunately, it is the only hobby I have outside medicine. I try to spend any time I have outside of medicine with my family.

WCR: *Do you read much outside of medicine?*

DJK: I did. I read in bursts. I had a disc operation 7 years ago and in a week I think I read 10 novels.

WCR: *You mentioned a disc operation. Is that an old football injury or is that too many cardiac catheterizations?*

DJK: I think it is probably too many cardiac catheterizations. It is probably a congenital predisposition, which has been exasperated by wearing heavy lead aprons, bending over patients, and doing high volumes of procedures. Several of us interventionalists have been disabled by multiple disc operations.

WCR: *What do you see for the future in cardiology, let's say the year 2008? What is cardiology going to be like in 10 years?*

DJK: Coronary intervention will be transformed to an outpatient procedure with the miniaturization and increased user friendliness of interventional technology, particularly stenting. Stenting is not going to go away, because it efficiently provides a predictably good result. Stenting in my group is now exceeding 80% of all our coronary interventions. With the advent of third-generation stents, which can be put through catheters literally the size of a diagnostic catheter, a move toward the outpatient arena will occur in the next several years.

WCR: *What do you see as the future of coronary bypass surgery?*

DJK: Coronary bypass surgery is not going to go away. We are all palliating a disease process. Minimal invasive bypass surgery clearly has a role. To do an arterial graft of a single major vessel may profoundly influence survival. There will be more of an interface between partial revascularization with angioplasty, and partial revascularization with minimally invasive surgery.

WCR: *Do you use a lot of statin drugs?*

DJK: Yes. Our group had an independent audit of our use of statin drugs in a high volume cardiologic practice. Even among the interventional cardiologists, there was considerable variability in applying current standards. It is only by guideline driving it and tracking adherence to guidelines that you can really quality assure the care that you give in a large group.

WCR: *If Eli Lilly or another company asked you to come in as a major player in their organization, how would you respond to that?*

DJK: I am not currently interested in doing that. I have been asked to interview as Director of Cardiovascular Research at major pharmaceutical corporations but I don't want to leave "hands on" application of clinical research.

WCR: *Are you recommending a physician career for your young children at this point?*

DJK: I was impressed that you have a son who is a cardiovascular surgeon. If you ask my kids if they want to go into medicine, it's "no." Their friends' dads are chief executives of banks and other major corporations like Proctor and Gamble, etc. None of those guys have the intrusion into their personal life to the same extent that a busy physician does. None of them have the same amount of personal sacrifice nights, weekends, or holidays, as physicians. The inability to go anywhere without being tied to a pager takes its toll. When you take care of patients and you don't have fellows and junior faculty, when you are *the* care provider, the intrusion in your personal life can be overwhelming.

WCR: *Is there anything Dean that you would like to discuss that we have not discussed?*

DJK: I am really thankful to you Bill for asking me to come here. My first response when you called was that I didn't think I had much to offer. My career has not been a traditional academic one. What I have tried to do in my career is to integrate clinical research into every day clinical practice, to apply new technologies, and to quality assure the care product through clinical research protocols and practice guidelines.

WCR: *Dean, thank you for pouring out your views on so many different topics and for letting us get to know you better.*

DJK's Best Publications as Selected by Him

2. Kereiakes DJ, Morady F, Ports TA. High degree atrioventricular block after radiation therapy. *Am J Cardiol* 1983;51:1233–1234.

3. Kereiakes DJ, Herfkens RJ, Brundage BH, Webb RW, Gansu G, Lipton MJ. Computerized tomography in chronic thromboembolic pulmonary hypertension. *Am Heart J* 1983;106:1432–1436.

4. Kereiakes DJ, Ports TA, Finkbeiner W. Cardiac involvement in Henoch-Schonlein purpura: results of endomyocardial biopsy. *Am Heart J* 1984;107:382–385.

5. Kereiakes DJ, Naughton JL, Brundage BH, Schiller NB. The heart in diabetes. *West J Med* 1984;140:593–593.

7. Kereiakes DJ, Morady F, Heath D, Parsons T, Scheinman MM. Sudden death during ambulatory electrocardiographic monitoring: importance of morphologic confirmation to establish cause of death. *Am J Cardiol* 1984;53:1403–1404.

8. Kereiakes DJ, Parmley WW. Myocarditis and cardiomyopathy. *Am Heart J* 1984;108:1318–1326.

9. Kereiakes DJ, Chatterjee K, Parmley WW, Atherton B, Kereiakes AS, Spangenberg R. Improvement in left ventricular functions with intravenous and oral MDL 17043 in patients with congestive heart failure: hemodynamic and clinical evaluation in 38 patients. *J Am Coll Cardiol* 1984;4:884–889.

10. Kereiakes DJ, Viquerat C, Lanzer P, Botvinick E, Chatterjee K, Parmley WW. Mechanisms of improved left ventricular function following intravenous MDL 17043 in patients with severe chronic heart failure. *Am Heart J* 1984;108:1278–1284.

11. Viquerate C, Kereiakes DJ, Morris DL, Daly P, Wesman M, Hoyle M, Parmley WW, Chatterjee K. Alterations in left ventricular function, coronary hemodynamics and myocardial catecholamine balance with MDL 17043: a new inotrope-vasodilator agent in patients with severe heart failure. *J Am Coll Cardiol* 1985;5:326–332.

13. Kereiakes DJ, George BS, Stertzer SH, Myler RK. Percutaneous transluminal coronary angioplasty of left internal mammary artery grafts. *Am J Cardiol* 1985;55:1215–1216.

14. Kereiakes DJ. Myocardial infarction in the diabetic patient. *Clin Cardiol* 1985;8:446–450.

15. Kereiakes DJ, Selmon MR, McAuley BJ, McAuley DB, Sheehan DJ, Simpson JB. Angioplasty in total coronary artery occlusion: experience in 76 consecutive patients. *J Am Coll Cardiol* 1985;6:526–533.

19. Simonton CA, Daly P, Kereiakes DJ, Sata H, Modin G, Chatterjee K. Survival in severe heart failure treated with the new non-glyosidic, non-sympathomimetic oral inotrope agents. *Chest* 1987;92:118–123.

20. Kereiakes DJ, Abbottsmith CW, Callard GM, Flege JB. Emergent internal mammary artery grafting following failed percutaneous transluminal coronary angioplasty: use of transluminal catheter reperfusion. *Am Heart J* 1987;113:1018–1020.

21. Chatterjee K, Kereiakes DJ, Viquerat C, Podolin R. Improved left ventricular function with enoximone in patients with severe congestive heart failure: the potential mechanisms. *J Am Coll Cardiol* 1987;40:37C–41C.

22. Topol EJ, Califf RM, Kereiakes DJ, George BS, and the TAMI Study Group. The Thrombolysis and Angioplasty in Myocardial Infarction (TAMI) Trial. *J Am Coll Cardiol* 1987;10:65B–74B.

23. Topol EJ, Califf RM, George BS, Kereiakes DJ, Abbottsmith CW, Candela RJ, Lee KL, Bertrum P, Stack RS, O'Neill WW, and the Thrombolysis and Angioplasty in Myocardial Infarction (TAMI) Study Group. A randomized trial of immediate versus delayed elective angioplasty after intravenous tissue plasminogen activator in acute myocardial infarction. *N Engl J Med* 1987;317:581–588.

25. Topol EJ, George BS, Kereiakes DJ, Candela RJ, Abbottsmith CW, Stump DC, Boswick J, O'Neill WW, Stack RS, Califf RM, and the TAMI Study Group. Comparison of two dose regimens of intravenous tissue plasminogen activator for acute myocardial infarction: results of a multicenter trial of 2 dose regimens. *Am J Cardiol* 1988;61:723–728.

27. Kereiakes DJ, Topol EJ, George BS, Abbottsmith CW, Stack RS, Candela RJ, O'Neill WW, Califf RM, and the TAMI Study Group. Emergency coronary artery bypass surgery preserves global and regional left ventricular function after intravenous tissue plasminogen activator therapy for acute myocardial infarction. *J Am Coll Cardiol* 1988;11:899–907.

28. Topol EJ, Califf RM, George BS, Kereiakes DJ, Rothbaum D, Candela RJ, Abbottsmith CW, Pinkerton CA, Stump DC, Collen D, Lee KL, Pitt B, Kline EM, Boswick JM, O'Neill WW, Stack RS, and the TAMI Study Group. Coronary arterial thrombolysis with combined infusion of recombinant tissue-type plasminogen activator and urokinase in patients with acute myocardial infarction. *Circulation* 1988;77:1100–1107.

31. Topol EJ, Califf RM, George BS, Kereiakes DJ, Lee KL, and the TAMI Study Group. Insights derived from the Thrombolysis and Angioplasty in Myocardial Infarction (TAMI) Trials. *J Am Coll Cardiol* 1988;12:24A–31A.

32. Kereiakes DJ, Topol EJ, Califf RM, George BS, Abbottsmith CW, Stack RS, Candela RJ, O'Neill WW, Anderson LC, and the TAMI Study Group. Favorable early and long term prognosis following coronary bypass surgery therapy for myocardial infarction: results of a multicenter trial. *Am Heart J* 1989;118:199–206.

35. Topol EJ, George BS, Kereiakes DJ, Stump DC, Candela RJ, Abbottsmith CW, Aronson L, Pickel A, Boswick JM, Lee KL, Ellis SG, Califf RM, and the TAMI Study Group. A randomized controlled trial of intravenous tissue plasminogen activator and early intravenous heparin in acute myocardial infarction. *Circulation* 1989;79:281–286.

36. Ellis SG, Topol EJ, George BS, Kereiakes DJ, Debowey D, Sigmon KN, Pickel A, Lee KL, Califf RM. Recurrent ischemia without warning: analysis of risk factors for in-hospital ischemic events following successful thrombolysis with intravenous tissue plasminogen activator. *Circulation* 1989;80:1159–1165.

37. Califf RM, Topol EJ, George BS, Kereiakes DJ, Aronson LG, Lee KL, Martin L, Candela R, Abbottsmith CW, O'Neill WW, Pryor DB, Stack RS, and the TAMI Study Group. One-year outcome after therapy with tissue plasminogen activator: report from the Thrombolysis and Angioplasty in Acute Myocardial Infarction (TAMI) trial. *Am Heart J* 1990;119:777–785.

42. Kereiakes DJ, Weaver WD, Anderson JL, Aufderheide T, Martin LH, Anderson LC, Martin JS, Feldman T, Gibler WB, Teichman SL, McKendall G, Sherrid M. Time delays in the diagnosis and treatment of acute myocardial infarction: a tale of eight cities. *Am Heart J* 1990;120:773–780.

45. Muller DWM, Topol EJ, George BS, Kereiakes DJ, Aronson LG, Lee KL, Abbottsmith CW, Ellis SG, Califf RM, and the TAMI Study Group. Two-year outcome after angiographically documented myocardial reperfusion for acute coronary occlusion. *Am J Cardiol* 1990;66:796–801.

46. Kereiakes DJ, Topol EJ, George BS, Stack RS, Abbottsmith CW, Ellis S, Candela RJ, Harrelson L, Martin LH, Califf RM, and the TAMI Study Group. Myocardial infarction with minimal coronary atherosclerosis in the era of thrombolytic reperfusion. *J Am Coll Cardiol* 1991;17:304–312.

47. Gibler WB, Kereiakes DJ, Dean EN, Martin L, Anderson L, Abbottsmith CW, Blanton J, Blanton D, Morris JA, Gibler CD, Erb RE. Prehospital diagnosis and treatment of acute myocardial infarction: a north-south perspective. *Am Heart J* 1991;121:1–11.

49. Mark DB, Sigmon K, Topol EJ, Kereiakes DJ, Pryor DB, Candela RJ, Califf RM. Identification of acute myocardial infarction patients suitable for early hospital discharge after aggressive interventional therapy: results from the TAMI registry. *Circulation* 1991;83:1186–1193.

50. Sane DC, Stump DC, Topol EJ, Sigmon KN, Clair WK, Kereiakes DJ,

George BS, Stoddard MF, Bates ER, Stack RS, Califf RM, and the TAMI Study Group. Racial differences in responses to thrombolytic therapy with recombinant tissue-type plasminogen activator. *Circulation* 1991;83:170–175.

54. Kereiakes DJ, Califf RM, George BS, Ellis S, Samaha J, Stack R, Martin L, Young S, Topol EJ, and the TAMI Study Group. Coronary bypass surgery improves global and regional left ventricular function following thrombolytic therapy for acute myocardial infarction. *Am Heart J* 1991;122:390–399.

55. Sane DC, Stump DC, Topol EJ, Sigmon KN, Kereiakes DJ, George BS, Mantell SJ, Macy E, Collen D, Califf RM. Correlation between baseline plasminogen activator inhibitor levels and clinical outcome during therapy with tissue plasminogen activator for acute myocardial infarction. *Thromb Haemost* 1991;65:275–279.

60. Tenaglia AN, Quigley PJ, Kereiakes DJ, Abbottsmith CW, Phillips HR, Tcheng JE, Rendall D, Ohman EM. Coronary angioplasty performed with gradual and prolonged inflation using a perfusion balloon catheter: procedural success and restenosis rate. *Am Heart J* 1992;124:585–589.

63. Kowalenko T, Kereiakes DJ, Gibler WB. Prehospital diagnosis and treatment of acute myocardial infarction: a critical review. *Am Heart J* 1992;123:181–190.

65. Kereiakes DJ, Gibler WB, Martin LH, Pieper KS, Anderson LC, and the Cincinnati Heart Project Study Group. Relative importance of emergency medical system transport and the prehospital electrocardiogram on reducing hospital time delay to therapy for acute myocardial infarction: a preliminary report from the Cincinnati Heart Project. *Am Heart J* 1992;123:835–840.

67. Popma JJ, DeCesare NB, Pinkerton CA, Kereiakes DJ, Whitlow PL, King SB, Topol EJ, Leon MB, Ellis SG. Quantitative analysis of factors influencing late lumen loss and restenosis after directional coronary atherectomy. *Am J Cardiol* 1993;71:552–557.

70. George BS, Voorhees WD, Roubin GS, Fearnot NE, Pinkerton CA, Raizner AE, King SB, Holmes DR, Topol EJ, Kereiakes DJ, Hartzler GO. Multicenter investigation of coronary stenting to treat acute or threatened closure after percutaneous transluminal coronary angioplasty: clinical and angiographic outcomes. *J Am Coll Cardiol* 1993;22:135–143.

72. Kleiman NS, Ohman EM, Califf RM, George BS, Kereiakes DJ, Aguirre F, Bates E, Schaible T, Topol EJ. Profound inhibition of platelet aggregation with monoclonal antibody 7E3 Fab following thrombolytic therapy: results of the TAMI 8 pilot study. *J Am Coll Cardiol* 1993;22:381–389.

76. Granger CB, Califf RM, Young S, Candela R, Samaha J, Worley S, Kereiakes DJ, Topol EJ. Outcome of patients with diabetes mellitus and acute myocardial infarction treated with thrombolytic agents. *J Am Coll Cardiol* 1993;21:920–925.

77. Ryan TJ, Bauman WB, Kennedy JW, Kereiakes DJ, King SB, McCallister BD, Smith SC, Ullyot DJ. Revised ACC/AHA guidelines for percutaneous transluminal coronary angioplasty: a report of the American College of Cardiology/American Heart Association Task Force on Assessment of Diagnostic and Therapeutic Cardiovascular Procedures. *J Am Coll Cardiol* 1993;22:2033–2054.

84. Tcheng JE, Ellis SG, George BS, Kereiakes DJ, Kleiman NS, Talley JD, Wang AL, Weisman HF, Califf RM, Topol EJ. Pharmacodynamics of chimeric glycoprotein IIb/IIIa integrin antiplatelet antibody fab 7E3 in high-risk coronary angioplasty. *Circulation* 1994;90:1757–1764.

86. Boehrer JD, Kereiakes DJ, Navetta FI, Califf RM, Topol EJ. Effects of profound platelet inhibition with c7E3 before coronary angioplasty on complications of coronary bypass surgery. *Am J Cardiol* 1994;74:1166–1170.

88. Tcheng JE, Harrington RA, Kottke-Marchant K, Kleiman NS, Ellis SG, Kereiakes DJ, Mick MJ, Navetta FI, Smith JE, Worley SJ, Miller JA, Joseph DM, Sigmon KN, Kitt MM, duMee CP, Califf RM, Topol EJ, for the IMPACT Investigators. Multicenter, randomized, double-blind, placebo-controlled trial of the platelet integrin glycoprotein IIb/IIIa blocker integrelin in elective coronary intervention. *Circulation* 1995;91:2151–2157.

89. Aufderheide TP, Kereiakes DJ, Weaver WD, Simoons M, Gibler WB. Planning, implementation, and process monitoring for prehospital 12-lead ECG diagnostic programs. *Prehospital and Disaster Medicine* 1996;11:162–171.

90. Kereiakes DJ, Kleiman NS, Ambrose J, Cohen M, Rodriquez S, Palabrica T, Herrmann HC, Sutton JM, Weaver WD, McKee DB, Sax FL. A randomized, double-blind, placebo-controlled dose ranging study of MK-383 platelet IIb/IIIa blockade in high risk patients undergoing coronary angioplasty. *J Am Coll Cardiol* 1996;27:536–542.

91. Kereiakes DJ, Sketch MH Jr, Ohman EM, for the Perfusion Catheter Study Group. Perfusion balloon angioplasty in patients with complex coronary lesion morphology. *J Invas Cardiol* 1995;7(suppl B):4B–9B.

95. Kereiakes DJ. Percutaneous transcatheter therapy of aorto-ostial stenoses. *Cathet Cardiovasc Diagn* 1996;38:292–300.

96. Barsness GW, Ohman EM, Califf RM, Kereiakes DJ, George BS, Topol EJ. The thrombolysis and angioplasty in myocardial infarction (TAMI) trials: a decade of reperfusion strategies. *J Invas Cardiol* 1996;9:89–115.

97. Kereiakes DJ, Essell JH, Abbottsmith CW, Broderick TM, Runyon JP. Abciximab-associated profound thrombocytopenia: therapy with immune globulin and platelet transfusion. *Am J Cardiol* 1996;78:1161–1163.

98. Kereiakes DJ, Runyon JP, Kleiman NS, Higby NA, Anderson LC, Hantsbarger G, McDonald S, Anders RJ. Differential dose-response to oral xemilofiban following antecedent intravenous abciximab administration for complex coronary intervention. *Circulation* 1996;94:906–910.

99. Kereiakes DJ, Kleiman N, Ferguson JJ, Runyon JP, Broderick TM, Higby NA, Martin, Hantsbarger G, McDonald S, Anders RJ. Sustained platelet glycoprotein IIb/IIIa blockade with oral xemilofiban in 170 patients following coronary stent development. *Circulation* 1997;96:1117–1121.

100. Ohman EM, Kleiman NS, Gacioch G, Worley SJ, Navetta FI, Talley JD,

Anderson HV, Ellis SG, Cohen M, Sprigg D, Miller M, Kereiakes D, Yakubov S, Kitt MM, Sigmon KN, Califf RM, Krucoff MW, Topol EJ. Combined accelerated tissue-plasminogen activator and platelet glycoprotein IIb/IIIa integrin receptor blockade with integrelin in acute myocardial infarction: results of a randomized, placebo-controlled, dose-ranging trial. *Circulation* 1997;95:846–854.

102. The EPILOG Investigators. Platelet glycoprotein IIb/IIIa receptor blockade and low-dose heparin during percutaneous coronary revascularization. *N Engl J Med* 1997;336:1689–1696.

103. The IMPACT-II Investigators. Randomized placebo-controlled trial of effect of eptifibatide on complications of percutaneous coronary intervention: IMPACT-II. *Lancet* 1997;349:1422–1428.

108. Kereiakes DJ, Broderick TM, Whang DD, Anderson L, Fye D. Partial reversal of heparin anticoagulation by intravenous protamine in abciximab treated patients undergoing percutaneous intervention: rationale, safety, and clinical outcomes. *Am J Cardiol* 1997;80:633–634.

111. Ferguson JJ, Kereiakes DJ, Adgey AAJ, Fox KAA, Hillegass WB, Pfisterer M, Vassanelli C. Safe use of platelet GP IIb/IIIa inhibitors. *Am Heart J* 1998;135:S77–S89.111.

117. Kleiman NS, Lincoff AM, Kereiakes DJ, Miller DP, Aquirre FV, Anderson K, Weisman HF, Califf RM, Topol EJ. Diabetes mellitus, glycoprotein IIb/IIIa blockade, and heparin: evidence for a complex interaction in a multicenter trial. *Circulation* 1998;97:1912–1920.

128. Kereiakes DJ, Lincoff AM, Miller DP, Tcheng JE, Cabot CF, Anderson KM, Weisman HF, Califf RM, Topol EJ. Abciximab therapy and unplanned coronary stent deployment: favorable effects on stent utilization, clinical outcomes and bleeding complications. *Circulation* 1998;97:857–864.

130. Kereiakes DJ, Kleiman NS, Ferguson JJ, Masud AZ, Fitzgerald G, Broderick TM, Abbottsmith CA, Anderson LC, Anders RJ, Dreiling RJ, Hantsbarger GL, Bryzinski B, Topol EJ. Pharmacodynamic efficacy, clinical safety and outcomes following prolonged glycoprotein IIb/IIIa receptor blockade with oral xemilofiban: results of a multicenter placebo controlled randomized trial. *Circulation;* in press).

131. Kereiakes DJ. Preferential benefit of platelet glycoprotein (GP) IIb/IIIa receptor blockade: specific considerations by device and disease state. *Am J Cardiol* 1998;81A:49D–54E.

133. Bhatt DL, Lincoff AM, Kereiakes DJ, Tcheng JE, Godfrey N, Califf RM, Topol EJ. Reduction in the need for unplanned stenting with the use of platelet glycoprotein IIb/IIIa blockade in percutaneous coronary intervention. *Am J Cardiol* 1998;82:000–000.

134. Dove JT, Jacobs AK, Kennedy JW, Kereiakes DJ, Kern MJ, Kuntz RE, Popma JJ, Schaff HV, Smith SC, Williams DO. ACC/AHA Task Force Committee for PTCA Guidelines. *Circulation;* in press.

135. Ghaffari S, Kereiakes DJ, Lincoff AM, Kelly TA, Timmis GC, Kleiman NF, Ferguson JJ, Miller DP, Califf RM, Topol EJ, for the EPILOG Investigators. Platelet glycoprotein IIb/IIIa receptor blockade with abciximab reduces ischemic complications in patients undergoing directional coronary atherectomy. *Am J Cardiol;*1998;82:7–12.

136. Baim DS, Midei M, Linnemeier T, Schreibwer T, Cox D, Kereiakes DJ, Popma JJ, Robertson L, Prince R, Lansky AJ, Cutlip DE, Ho KKL, Kuntz RE, for the ASCENT Investigators. A randomized trial comparing the Multilink stent to the Palmaz-Schatz stent in de novo lesions. *Circulation;* in press.

137. Kereiakes DJ. Oral platelet GP IIb/IIIa inhibitors. *Coron Artery Disease;* in press.

138. Gibler WB, Wilcox RG, Bode C, Castaigne AD, Delooz H, Elich D, Fox KAA, Kereiakes DJ, Rupprecht H, Topol EJ. Prospective use of GP IIb/IIIa receptor blockers in the emergency department setting. *Ann Emerg Med;* in press.

SPENCER BIDWELL KING, III, MD:
A Conversation With the Editor*

Spencer King is a Professor with the Department of Medicine (Cardiology), Emory University School of Medicine, Atlanta, Georgia, and Director of the Andreas Gruentzig Cardiovascular Center of Emory University. He grew up mainly in Macon, Georgia, attended public schools, and then graduated from Mercer University in Macon in 1959. He then went to the Medical College of Georgia in Augusta, where he graduated in 1963. His internship was at Walter Reed General Hospital in Washington, DC, and his training in internal medicine and in cardiology was at Emory University in Atlanta. After practicing a year and a half in Denver, Colorado, he returned to Emory as Director of the Cardiac Catheterization of Emory University Hospital. In 1980, he was instrumental in bringing Andreas Gruentzig to Emory University Hospital. Spencer King has been a major player in interventional cardiology since its beginning. He is the author of over 300 publications in medical journals, and the author or editor of 6 books, all of which involve interventional cardiology. At present, he is also President of The American College of Cardiology and Chairman of the subspecialty board on interventional cardiology. He is also a nice guy.

William Clifford Roberts, MD[†] (hereafter, WCR): *I am speaking with Dr. Spencer King in his home in Atlanta, Georgia, on December 3, 1998. Spencer, I appreciate your willingness to talk to me, and, therefore, the readers of* The American Journal of Cardiology. *I wonder if we might start by your talking about some of your earlier memories. I gather you were born in Charleston, South Carolina, May 12, 1937. How long did you live there? What were your mother and daddy like and did you have brothers and sisters?*

Spencer Bidwell King, III, MD[‡] (hereafter, SBK): Bill, I was born in Charleston because my mother was from "low-country" South Carolina and we were living in a small community in western North Carolina. My father was Chairman of the History and the Political Science Departments and Associate Dean of a small college called Mars Hill College. There was only 1 physician in that town.

WCR: *What town was it?*

SBK: Mars Hill, North Carolina. To be born we had to go back to Charleston. I was born in Riverside Infirmary in Charleston.

WCR: *How far is Mars Hill from Charleston?*

SBK: Mars Hill was 20 miles north of Asheville. It is way up in the mountains of North Carolina, probably 250 miles from Charleston. My father was a history professor and my mother was the music instructor at Mars Hill College. She taught string music. I have 2 sisters: Jan is 3 years younger, and Margaret is 8 years younger.

WCR: *Where were your father and mother from originally?*

SBK: My mother was from South Carolina. Her family goes back to some of the first settlers, an old Huguenot family that came over during the persecution of the Huguenots about 1720. Another side goes back to the early English settlers, so there are both French and English in my blood. My father came from the western part of Georgia. His father was a Baptist minister. At one point he was in charge of the state Baptist church, and had an office in the Flat Iron Building in downtown Atlanta. My dad went to Boys' High School in Atlanta.

WCR: *Your father grew up mainly in Atlanta?*

SBK: My father grew up not only in Atlanta but also in Blakely in southwest Georgia. Then he went to Darlington School to finish up and lived with an uncle for a while, because the Blakely schools were not so good. My grandfather, being a Baptist minister, was pretty migratory. They lived in Atlanta for 2 or 3 years, but he grew up in a number of places. My mother grew up in Beaufort, South Carolina. After college, she went to the New England Conservatory of Music and then to Julliard as a violinist. She taught violin until 1998, at age 92, when she died.

WCR: *Is your father living?*

SBK: No. He died in 1977 at age 73.

WCR: *Your father majored in history, I presume, in college?*

SBK: No, my father wanted to be a journalist in college. He went to Mercer University and when he got out in the late 1920s, he got a job teaching in Blue Eye, Missouri. He took his sister out there and he told a lot of funny stories about that place. His sister tried to teach all the children poems by Sidney Lanier, Georgia's beloved poet, because she thought that was always what you had to learn in school. The kids in Missouri could not figure out what the song of the Chattahoochee was all about. He taught there for awhile and then went to Michigan and Vanderbilt for graduate work. He got a master's degree at Vanderbilt, and a PhD at the University of North Carolina in history and political science. He taught at Mars Hill College, and then in 1946 came to Macon, Georgia, to be Chairman of the History Department.

WCR: *You were 9 years old in 1946?*

SBK: Yes.

WCR: *Can you describe your early schooling?*

SBK: During my early education I went to 7 different grammar schools in 7 years. We moved from Mars Hill to Chapel Hill while my dad was getting his PhD. Then we moved to Macon right after World War II.

*This series of interviews are underwritten by an unrestricted grant from Bristol-Myers Squibb.
†Baylor Cardiovascular Institute, Baylor University Medical Center, Dallas, Texas 75246.
‡Director, Andreas Gruentzig Cardiovascular Center, Emory University, Atlanta, Georgia 30322.

FIGURE 1. SBK during the interview.

All my high school was in Macon. I then went to Mercer University in Macon. I literally walked to school from grade school through college.

WCR: *What was growing up like in Macon? You went to public schools all the way to college?*

SBK: Yes. Lanier High School was a boys' high school, a military high school, even though it was public. We wore uniforms 3 days a week. The boys went to 1 high school and the girls went to another high school. This was before integration, so there was a black high school in Macon where boys and girls went to school together. The white kids had to go to separate high schools. Settling in Macon was very important in my development because having come out of such a gypsy-like life through grade school I probably had a bit of insecurity. When I started the boys' high school, I benefited from the fact that a number of the teachers there had been students of my father, and I probably was helped along by some very important people who got me into some positions of leadership in junior high. It helped to build my confidence. The high school was terrific. It was a cross section of that town of 50,000 to 60,000. At least we saw all the white kids in town. Every socioeconomic level was involved. The fact that it was an all boys school, of course, probably warped me as far as being confident with women. In any case, it was very worthwhile. We had a group of outstanding students and teachers. The teachers were challenging and many

were superb. Most of what I learned I learned in high school.

WCR: *You mentioned you had several leadership positions in various organizations in junior high and high school. What were they?*

SBK: In junior high, my homeroom teacher, a history teacher who had studied under my father, picked me out of the class to run for the class presidency. I lost and ended up being the vice-president, but it made me feel better about myself. In my second year of junior high school they selected me most likely to succeed for some reason. In high school you got your rank in your senior year depending on what you had done in academics, military, and sports. There were actually 10 captains of the 10 companies. I was the last person to make captain. I got 1 of the companies. Maybe because I was the last one, I was probably more committed to the job than anybody else. We ended up winning all the awards, the best company, which was a big thing in high school.

I played football in junior high, but not in senior high school. I ran track. I was involved in various organizations. We had fraternities in high school and I was president of my fraternity. For some reason I tended to migrate toward leadership positions. It must have been because I had some need to do that.

WCR: *What did you do in track?*

SBK: I hated to run, so I never ran anything more than an 880, but the thing I was the best in was the discus. I was probably the world's smallest discus thrower, but I came in third in the state meet at Grady High in Atlanta. I weighed about 160 pounds, but I studied the form of a guy name *Fortune Gordine* who was the Olympic record holder for many years. There were no videotapes to watch, but I had still photographs of every position you get into to throw the discus. I practiced and learned how to throw the discus. Other people were largely just muscling it out there. I won most of the meets. In the region there was a guy named *Smokey White* from Thomaston, Georgia, who was a great big guy who played football and must have weighed about 230 pounds. In the region meet I beat him, and afterwards he asked how I did that. After the meet was over I said, "Okay, come over here and I will show you." The first time he threw it about 10 feet further than my winning throw! I also threw the Javelin, but I was not very good at it. On the high school baseball team was a centerfielder with a terrific arm. I talked him into joining the track team. His name was *Theron Sapp*. He ended up breaking the state record in the Javelin. He went on to become the "man who broke the drought." Georgia Tech had beaten Georgia 7 years in a row, but Theron Sapp was the fullback and *Dan Magill* who wrote a lot of stories about him, featured him in the *Constitution* as "the man that broke the drought." I got him into track, but he was a wonderful football player. He played for the Philadelphia Eagles for several years.

WCR: *Your high school was a power in athletics. You frequently won the state football championship and most everything else.*

FIGURE 2. SBK during the interview.

SBK: We won the football championship 6 or 7 times. When I first started high school, there had been 30 state basketball championships and Lanier had won 15 of them.

WCR: *How many students were in Lanier High School?*

SBK: The senior high school was grades 10, 11, and 12, and it consisted of about 1,200 boys. The junior high had about 1,000 students.

WCR: *What was homelife like when you were in junior high and high school? It sounds like both your mother and father were intellectuals. Did your mother teach at Mercer, too?*

SBK: No. She taught private music lessons and also taught music in public schools in Macon.

WCR: *What was it like when you all had dinner at night? Did you have intellectual discussions?*

SBK: I had an immense respect for both my parents. My father was probably something like I am. He came home late and went back to the office often and was kind of a workaholic. He was immensely respected. I related equally well to both of them. I remember a lot of conversations with other people around. I was never really a history buff in those days, but I absorbed a lot of it from my father. I heard what he was doing. He was an author as well. I listened to what he was doing. People came to visit him. I remember one time *Allen Dulles* came to visit. I sat on our porch with Allen Dulles hearing him tell about brain-washing techniques and how the Communist Chinese were able

to do it. I heard a lot about politics. I learned a lot about issues that my father was involved in. He was a radical on historic preservation. He was trying to save Wesleyan College in Macon at one time. He wrote an article for a weekly Macon paper and included a picture of the original building of Wesleyan College (the first woman's college in America) before it had been changed during the Victorian era. He wanted it restored, but Wesleyan was in a bit of financial difficulty. They wanted to sell the property because they had already moved the main campus out of town. He led a campaign to try to undo that. He was instrumental in getting historic markers throughout the state. He worked a lot in Atlanta at the Archives. His career went from political science, American history, Southern history, to Georgia history. He kept becoming more specialized. He authored a number of books, including the textbook published in 1955 that most kids read in Georgia history. It was used for another 20 years.

WCR: *What was the name of it?*

SBK: *Georgia History.* There were 3 authors, *Coulter* and *Saye* of the University of Georgia, and my dad. Something I learned from him then that probably colored my character thereafter was that in that book he wrote a chapter on *Eugene Talmadge* and the reaction to the 1954 Brown-vs-Board of Education decision. The chapter concerned the impact of the decision for integration in the state. His manuscript went to the publisher. In those days, and probably still today, there was an oversight committee of the Department of Education in the state. That committee, in reviewing the manuscript, deleted all reference to Brown-vs-Board of Education after he had seen the final proof. This was all taken out and censored. I remember he was extremely upset about the idea that academic freedom was being impinged upon by the state, because they thought it was not politically correct to talk about those kinds of things. It was a liberal household for Macon, Georgia. My father had been in Michigan and my mother had had her education in Boston and New York. We were products of the South for sure. My father was a Southern historian and knew everything about the Civil War. They both taught me tolerance and, in fact, I grew up as a social liberal in terms of race relations. In 1962, after I had gone to medical school, the church on the Mercer Campus, admitted an African student. My father had been chairman of the Deacons. Some people took offense at this African coming to the church. There was a whole series of events that took place that resulted in the firing of the pastor of the church along with the music director and others. My father led the charge to try to hold it together. His reaction to the whole thing was to try to mediate the situation, to try to save the church, but finally when they fired the people, he and my mother resigned from the church. This illustrates the kind of household I grew up in. There was a lot of concern about the problems we were going through in the 1950s and in the 1960s. I was influenced by them in terms of race relations.

FIGURE 3. SBK in 1939 with his father, Spencer B. King Jr., and his mother, Caroline King.

WCR: *It sounds like you felt your father's presence when he was in a room.*

SBK: Yes, without question. He was very engaging, very personable, and was the person in charge of the family and the extended family. He was the oldest of 7 children. His father, a Baptist minister, had been pretty stern. My father was not that way at all, but he was definitely in charge of everything in terms of taking responsibility.

WCR: *Did his brothers and sisters, your uncles and aunts, live in the Macon area? Did you see them often?*

SBK: Yes. Several of them lived in Americus, Georgia, where my grandfather retired from the ministry. Growing up, I would get on the bus and go down Highway 49 to Americus and visit my aunts, uncles, grandparents, and cousins. My father's only brother lived in Atlanta. He was chairman of the State brotherhood of Baptists. One sister lived in Washington, DC. Her husband was with the Commerce Department. One lived in Alabama, and the rest of them lived in Americus. Those were some of the most enjoyable experiences when I was 11 to 13 years old. I had a cousin who was 5 years older who rebuilt old jalopies. I remember one day going out to a race track in Americus. He had a 1934 Ford coupe that was souped up and he was going to race it in the stock-car races.

I was probably 13 at the time. I got into the car with him, whom I trusted implicitly, and we started going around this heavily banked dirt track. We came into one of the curves with the car wide open, the car left the track and rolled and landed right side up. My recollection was that I had no fear whatsoever. I thought he was totally in charge. I looked over at him and he was in a state of shock. Neither of us were hurt.

WCR: *What about your mother? Did you also go to South Carolina? Did she have brothers and sisters?*

SBK: Yes. She had 2 sisters. One sister, who lived in Beaufort, was married to a man who owned a large number of vegetable farms on St. Helena's Island. Her other sister taught at the University of North Carolina at Greensboro. We often went to Beaufort for visits and that was great fun. The cousins there lived in huge antebellum houses. It was quite an event to go there. One of my cousins, who still lives in Beaufort, had a small Cessna airplane. We flew with my sister and a cousin and landed on a beach at Hilton Head. I remember walking the dunes and exploring the virtually uninhabited Hilton Head beach when I was about 7 or 8 years old. Two of his children, my cousins, are now cardiologists in Myrtle Beach, South Carolina.

WCR: *It sounds like religion was an important factor in your home.*

SBK: Yes it was. Both of my parents came from strong religious backgrounds.

WCR: *What do your sisters do?*

SBK: My sister, Jan, is a physical therapist. She studied at the Medical College of Virginia and went to Denver, where she worked in rehabilitation at Children's Hospital. When she was about 30 years old she went to Germany and worked at the University of Heidelberg Spinal Cord Rehabilitation Center. When she returned, she met a Swedish/American man on a ski lift in Aspen, married him shortly thereafter, and they have lived happily ever after. They have 2 children and live in Chicago. She still practices physical therapy and he owns a ventilation equipment sales company. My youngest sister, Margaret, graduated from Mercer University in Macon with a degree in sociology. Living in Macon, she enjoys full time community involvement. Her husband, Rob, is a very successful orthodontist and they have one daughter who is a senior in high school.

WCR: *What made you decide to go to Mercer? It was certainly convenient and I presume the price was right?*

SBK: Lanier High School actually was oriented toward Georgia Tech. My son went to Westminster and at Westminster you heard about Princeton. At Lanier, particularly if you were good in science, you heard about Georgia Tech. There was never any talk about people going anywhere out of state to college in those days. One classmate went to West Point, and maybe one other classmate went to a college in the North. I probably would have chosen Georgia Tech had we been able to afford it, but Mercer was free tuition for me. When I finished high school, I could go anywhere I wanted as long as it was Mercer. It was an excellent decision, because it was a small school with

FIGURE 4. SBK throwing discus. He finished third in the state of the Georgia in 1955.

very personal attention where you could test your wings. The faculty was and still is very responsive toward the students. There were no teaching assistants. I probably resented that I was not going off to Georgia Tech for a few minutes, but I got over it.

WCR: *It did not bother you that your father was chairman of a major department there?*

SBK: I steered away from his courses. I never took a course from him. I don't remember being really concerned about my father's being on the faculty.

WCR: *Did both of your sisters go to Mercer?*

SBK: Yes.

WCR: *Where did your father go to college?*

SBK: He went to Mercer. He received a master's degree at Vanderbilt, some graduate work at Michigan, and his PhD at the University of North Carolina.

WCR: *Where did your mother go?*

SBK: She went to a college called Due West College for Women in Due West, South Carolina, later called Erskine College. She then went to the New England Conservatory of Music in Boston, where she got another degree in music. Then, she went to Julliard and Columbia where she studied violin.

WCR: *Your mother played the violin?*

SBK: She was a violinist. She and another woman started violin in the public schools in Macon. She also started the youth orchestra in Macon, and it was a catalyst for the Macon Symphony Orchestra. She was one of the charter members of the symphony and played into her 80s.

WCR: *Do you play a musical instrument?*

SBK: She tried everything on me. I took piano lessons, played a horn for awhile in the junior band, and an e-flat alto horn. I don't play anything now. I grew up listening to people learning to play the violin, which probably damaged me permanently.

WCR: *What about your sisters?*

SBK: Yes. They both played piano and cello or violin.

WCR: *Were there a lot of books in your home?*

SBK: Yes. There were a lot of books on history. I still have a great many of them, like a complete volume of messages of the Presidents from George Washington through Teddy Roosevelt.

WCR: *It sounds like your father could talk about almost any subject you brought up?*

SBK: Yes. He was certainly no expert in the field of science, but in history and political science and politics he was an authority.

WCR: *How did Mercer University affect your development?*

SBK: I lived at home during college. I walked about 4 blocks to college. It might seem like an extension of high school to some people, but it was really a total immersion in terms of activities. I was a typical college student, very interested in the fraternity, parties and girls, as well as studies. I was in Sigma Alpha Epsilon (SAE) at Mercer. I had been a good student in high school and was determined to be a good student in college, but I really did not know what I wanted to do. I took pre-med courses with a major in biology and a minor in chemistry. I also took a lot of liberal arts courses, including psychology, philosophy, religion, literature, but not much history. I also continued my high school military program because Mercer had an ROTC program and that paid a scholarship as well. I was successful in that, and in my senior year I became the commander of the ROTC unit at Mercer. It was pre-Vietnam and people were paying a lot of attention to the military. We trained in the summers at Fort Benning. I went into the reserves after college and remained in the Army Reserves through medical school. Those experiences probably influenced where I ended up interning in medicine.

WCR: *Did your parents push you to make good grades in school or was it simply expected of you?*

SBK: It was expected. It was subliminal. I don't recall ever being chastised for not making good

FIGURE 5. Cadet Colonel SBK Commander of Mercer ROTC Unit in 1959.

grades, although I did not always make good grades. In a small community, the teachers knew my family and it would have been a major embarrassment if I had not done well. I did feel pressure to make good grades but never directly. I never recall having been lectured by either parent about doing well in school.

WCR: *Was learning easy for you or did you have to work at it?*

SBK: It has never been terrifically easy. I think I had to work reasonably hard. I did not really feel driven to be the number 1 in my class in high school or college and I never was in medical school, either. I felt like I had do well, but I did not really feel compelled to be the top dog academically.

WCR: *You say you majored in biology with a minor in chemistry in college. You obviously were getting a scientific background. Was there anybody in your family who was a physician?*

SBK: The only people in my family who were even connected to medicine go way back. My great-grandfather had been the pharmacist's mate at Andersonville Prison during the Civil War. This man was responsible for trying to get medical supplies for the prisoners and for the people working at Andersonville. He was totally unsuccessful. There was probably no medicine to do them any good anyway. He was a quasi-medical person. My grandmother's uncle was a

purveyor of patent medicines. He made something called Dodson's Liver Tone and ionized yeast. He sold this out West before the turn of the century. In Cripple Creek, Colorado, many years ago, I found a shop that had a Dodson's Liver Tone bottle that had been brought up out of a privy.

I had no role model for medicine. In fact, I did talk with my father about majors and what I was doing. I remember him saying at one point when I told him I might want to go to medical school, "The chemistry major will be good because you can be a chemist if you don't get into medical school." I did not have any connections and did not know what getting into medical school was all about. I did not really make up my mind to do medicine until my junior year in college. Recently, I found the letter offering me a place at the Medical College of Georgia. That was a very important letter in my life. As it turned out, I was 1 of the first 2 people they took, but maybe that was because I went for an early interview.

WCR: *When you were growing up did your family go on vacations in the summertime?*

SBK: Growing up as the son of a history professor at Mercer in the 1940s and 1950s, meant having little excess money. We never felt the least bit poor, but in retrospect we were skidding along. We were always dealing with the people in town who seemed to be the most influential, but the truth is my father made a very paltry salary. The only vacations we ever took were to visit relatives. I recall going to Cherokee, North Carolina, one time. My father had an original Cherokee poem which he thought was a unique document that he wanted to learn about. We went to Cherokee for a vacation and to find somebody who could read Cherokee. We found an old man who was hammering out a canoe. He could read Cherokee and we got very excited and got him to stop what he was doing. My father handed him this old piece of paper with a message written in Cherokee. I remember he started reading it and he said, "In the beginning God created heaven and earth." It was the first chapter of Genesis translated into Cherokee. The joke was on us. We rarely went to the beach. We went to visit the relatives in South Carolina, and we went to Americus, Georgia, to visit my father's relatives.

WCR: *All the traveling you have done subsequently was new to you?*

SBK: Yes. When we moved to Macon, I was 10 or 11 and would hop on the bus to go visit relatives in Americus. We did not have a car at that time. My bicycle was my transportation. I went everywhere that a bicycle could go in and out of Macon. Growing up now, kids are driven everywhere. When I was 12 or 13 in Americus, my cousin, who had once rolled the car with me in it, had a friend with a small Piper Cub plane. We went out to Sumpter Field in Americus, got in the plane, cranked the prop, and flew up to an airfield near Macon. I got out and climbed the fence by a peach-packing plant and hitchhiked a ride home at age 12 or 13. That did not seem like such a radical thing to do. Of course I did not tell my parents that I had flown.

WCR: *When you decided in your junior year that you wanted to go to medical school, did you apply to any place other than the University of Georgia at Augusta?*

SBK: I applied only to the Medical College of Georgia. I did get an application form from Emory.

WCR: *How many were in your senior class at Mercer?*

SBK: Mercer had about 1,000 students at that time, so there were about 200 in the senior class. Thirteen of us went to medical school. Twelve of us went to the Medical College of Georgia. One went to Emory. The tuition at Georgia was about $600.00 for the whole year, and I had a state scholarship to pay that.

WCR: *You went to Augusta and started medical school in 1959?*

SBK: Yes.

WCR: *Did you have any mentors in college or high school that had an impact on you?*

SBK: I had a lot of mentors in high school. I mentioned a teacher in junior high, *Mr. Bell*, the teacher who picked me to run for class president. There was nothing democratic about it. He just picked me to be the representative. In high school, my French teacher, Russell Floyd, a very gentle man who commanded great respect through mechanisms yet unknown to me, was influential because he taught me there are elements of leadership that don't require dogmatism or forcefulness. He commanded respect by who he was. I had a physics professor who allowed us to explore on our own and encouraged us to investigate. I remember several of us sitting in the back row of the physics class talking about electricity, motors, AC and DC generators. We raised the issue of whether we could build a generator without brushes and reverse the usual AC/DC type generators. He gave us a challenge to do that. One of my classmates, *Richard Brubaker*, who truly was brilliant, and I got back on the blackboard and over a period of a couple of days drew off a scheme for developing this generator and designed it backwards. The difference between Richard and me is that I was very proud of developing this plan for the generator. Richard, on the other hand, went home and a few weeks later came back with a working model. Richard subsequently became Chief of Ophthalmology at the Mayo Clinic. I had a lot of classmates who were really superb. Richard was probably first in his class at Harvard Medical School. Another man in my class was *John Grinolds*, who went to West Point. He ended up being tops at West Point and the first graduate to join the Marine Corps. He was probably in line to be Commandant of the Marine Corps, but retired as a 2-star general. He is currently President of The Citadel. Another, *Frank Chew*, was the Treasurer of Delta Airlines. There were a host of other high school classmates who became physicians, lawyers, and entrepreneurs.

In college, there were several extremely influential teachers. One was *Otis Knight*, who was the Psychology Professor and a renaissance man who knew everything about everything. He taught me the investigative approach to science. My biology professor, *Graden Ware*, was just a great friend and mentor. I spent a great deal of time with him since I was a biology major. I loved to dissect cats, and find out what made them tick.

WCR: *Had you had science courses other than physics in high school?*

SBK: I had physics, chemistry, and biology in high school. The physics and chemistry teachers were superb.

WCR: *When in college, what were some of your extracurricular activities?*

SBK: I used to be a disc jockey at station WBML in Macon. The reason was I was one of the few people in Macon without a severe accent who could do "radio talk." I would say, "This is the red-headed ranch hand coming to you from WBML high above Mulberry Street Lane in beautiful downtown Macon." Of course it was the second floor of a real estate office overlooking an alley. During the summers, I worked every night and then I worked on Saturday night late. I did a kind of "makeout" show on Saturday nights. Sunday morning I opened the station with the gospel quartet time and played Montovani in the middle of the afternoon.

WCR: *How did you get started there?*

SBK: The station advertised that they needed an announcer. I auditioned and got the job.

WCR: *You were how old?*

SBK: I started when I was about 19. I did that through college. This was when rhythm and blues was big, and we had this guy named "King Bee" who did the rhythm and blues, and I was the straight guy. I did the announcing, read the news, did the station promotions. When he finished up, I played the pop music later at night. It was great. He was a promoter of "R&B" shows and was a friend of Little Richard who was from Macon and had made it big by 1957. King Bee wanted to bring Little Richard to town to do a show and we called him (Richard Pennyman) in Hollywood, California. I asked if I could get him signed up for a fraternity dance as well. When I got him on the phone, he agreed to come, but he said I could not tell anyone because it would violate his contract. I went back to campus and told everybody. I was now the big man on campus getting Little Richard to come there. The city council got wind that he was coming and they had him on some trumped up morals charge or something, so they blocked his coming back to Macon to do the show. My stock on campus went from sky high to the basement in 2 days.

WCR: *How many hours did you work a week at the radio station?*

SBK: I worked about 20 hours a week. This was 1 of my extracurricular activities in college. I was also in charge of booking the bands. When I went to medical school, they told me I had to sign up the band for the Freshman Brawl, the party after the freshman anatomy course. I called a man I knew at Mercer who was doing this for the Phi Delta Theta fraternity. This guy had gotten into this professionally, so he said he would send me a band called *Guitar Johnny Jenkins* and it would cost $150.00. I said we could scrape that

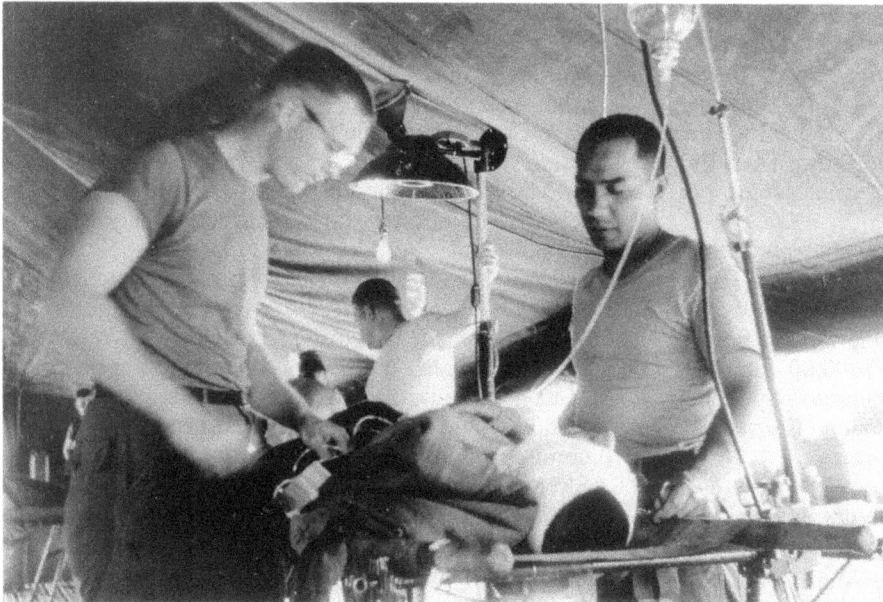

FIGURE 6. Captain SBK, commander of medical company at CuChi, Vietnam, and Dr. Richard Tesoro, attending a wounded soldier.

up for the party. A couple of days later he called and said he wanted to send a singer also. I said, "We are paying $150.00 and that is tops." He said, "Look, the guy needs the practice. I will send him for free." So I said, "Okay, send him over." It was *Otis Redding*. We had no idea who Otis Redding was, because this was before he made his big name. His was a side of town which we had obviously missed in high school.

WCR: *Was there alcohol in your home as you were growing up? Were your mother and father teetotalers?*

SBK: Yes, more or less. They occasionally had a glass of wine if offered.

WCR: *Your basic attitude on life has always been very positive?*

SBK: My attitude is that nice things have happened to me and they are not necessarily deserved. I feel that I was lucky to get a lot from my parents. I feel very much that things usually go well. I don't know if that influences what happens to you or not, and it is not what I have developed on purpose.

WCR: *Your father was Head of the Department of History at Mercer from 1946 to 1977 when he died?*

SBK: Yes.

WCR: *Did you mother move to Atlanta after he died?*

SBK: No. She stayed in their home in Macon until about 2 years ago, when she sold it and moved into a home in a retirement village in Macon.

WCR: *So you began medical school at the University of Georgia in Augusta in 1959? How did that go?*

SBK: It was a typical first year of medical school. I don't remember being terribly thrilled with everything. I did like some aspects of it. I enjoyed anatomy a great deal. I very much enjoyed physiology. This was the first time I had lived away from home. I was on my own for the first time. I lived in a house with several other people. There were no dorms at that time at medical school. I was not terrific at managing my time. I had a lot of fun. I was influenced by some

people in medical school. *William F. Hamilton*, the physiologist who was getting up in years, was the Chairman of the Physiology Department and he is the reason I am in cardiology. He approached everything the way I had learned to do it. In math I never memorized a formula. I tried to figure it out from scratch and tried to take everything back to the root. Dr. Hamilton had built many of the physiologic measuring devices in the department. He was the first person to measure blood pressure accurately with manometers. His place in medical history is not well recognized, but he was a major pioneer. He wrote a little red physiology book. The joke about the book was that when you saw any concept in it that was wrong, you should just wait another 5 or 10 years and it would be proved right again. He was a great influence, and I knew I liked physiology. I did not like biochemistry very much. It was too much memorizing. I still don't, but I put up with it. Clinically, I worked with *Virgil Sydenstricker*, who was another giant of the past who had been so important at the end of World War II during the Marshall Plan and the renutrition of Europe. He became a hematologist, self-taught, and knew virtually everything that you could know about hematology in those years. He was semi-retired and was at the Veterans' Administration Hospital, and I worked with him on electives when possible.

WCR: *You enjoyed medical school?*

SBK: Yes, very much.

WCR: *How many were in your class?*

SBK: One hundred. We started with 96 men, 4 women. We finished with probably about 90.

WCR: *Did you have a hard time deciding what specialty you wanted? You interned in medicine. Was that a difficult decision? You seemed to like anatomy.*

SBK: At one time, I considered orthopedics. My mother had a great friend in Washington who was the Chief of Physical Medicine at DC General. I said

FIGURE 7. SBK with his mother (midright) and 2 sisters.

something to her about orthopedics and she looked at me and said, "No, you have to go into medicine. That is crazy." Somehow I did not discuss it anymore, but I thought that was probably right and agreed with her. However, when I finished med school, I was not 100% sure about medicine. I had an Army obligation hanging over me because of the ROTC scholarship. I decided to do a rotating internship and was accepted at Walter Reed in Washington and interned there without any really preconceived idea. I enjoyed all the rotations. It was a spectacular year. That was 1963 to 1964 when a lot of people were having to go into the Army. Therefore, we had a terrific cadre of faculty there. It was as good as any internship I think you could ever imagine. *William Schwartz* was there in nephrology; *Kevin Berry,* in gastroenterology; *Thomas Mattingly* had just finished as Chief of Cardiology. *Mel Cheitlin* was there and *Gabe Gregoratos* was a fellow.

WCR: *Did you like surgery*?

SBK: Yes, I enjoyed surgery, but I was never tempted to do a surgery residency. I viewed surgery as purely mechanical. I had a prejudiced view about surgeons in that they were not thinkers.

WCR: *How did you do in medical school in the class of 90 or so graduating students*?

SBK: I did reasonably well.

WCR: *You were pleased with your internship*?

SBK: I was delighted with the way my internship turned out. In fact, we were so enthralled with the quality of the teaching at Walter Reed that of the 31 interns who were there, all 31 applied for fellowships in the Army. About 16 applied to medicine residencies. They gave only 2 at Walter Reed. One recipient was an outstanding man, who recently completed an army career, and the other one was a West Point graduate. The rest of us did not get Walter Reed, but some of us were offered residencies elsewhere in the Army. Some took it, but I didn't. I elected to go in a different way at that point. There were terrific experiences at Walter Reed. During that year I helped the orthopedic surgeon with an injection into Dwight Eisenhower's shoulder. I saw *Omar Bradley* as a patient. *Douglas MacArthur* came down, 6 months after his "Old soldiers never die" speech, and he was jaundiced, frail, and admitted with a suspected diagnosis of carcinoma of the head of the pancreas. He ended up being operated on. I assisted the chief of anesthesia during the operation. They opened him up and found that his pancreas was fine, but that he had a common duct stone that had been ignored for months. He had developed cirrhosis secondary to the stones. He had bleeding varices. They tried to stop those postoperatively. Finally, he strangulated an inguinal hernia and died. The whole thing was medical neglect. He was an incredible character. When I read about him in history I can see him. Every time one went into his room, no matter how sick he was, he would get out of bed and offer you a seat. He had to be in charge. The day Kennedy was assassinated, I was scrubbed with the Surgeon General on a thyroid operation. Somebody came into the room and said, "*General Heaton*, the President has been shot and they need you right away." He left the room and we were left to finish the operation. That night I was the officer of the day in the emergency room and I talked to the ambulance drivers as they went out to Andrews Air Force Base to pick up Kennedy's body. They thought they would bring it to the Armed Forces Institute of Pathology. They came back and said the Navy got there first and put him in a Navy ambulance and took him to the National Naval Medical Center in Bethesda, Maryland.

One night they brought in about 15 to 20 soldiers from Korea with hepatitis for Ward 35. I was supposed to work them up. I remember sitting there with all these people at 2:00 A.M. saying, "Okay, here is your history. Anybody object to this?"

WCR: *You went right into the armed services after internship*?

SBK: Yes. When I asked the assignment people, they said they had a plan to send me to Ranger school and then to lead a quasi-medical team for intelligence gathering in Laos. I said, "I just got married while I was an intern, and I am not really ready to go and crawl around in the bushes." I asked what else could I do. I said I would not do an Army residency if I could not do it at Walter Reed. This fellow joked and said, "What do you want a honeymoon?" I said, "Yes, that would be great." He said, "Do you want to go to

FIGURE 8. SBK with his family: SBK IV (left), Susan Gail King (midleft), and Gail King (midright) at lake home in North Georgia Mountains in 1997.

Hawaii?" He sent me to the 25th Division at Schofield Barracks, Hawaii. I was going there for 2 years, but as it turned out after a year I was called in one day (I was working in the outpatient clinic and by that time I really liked cardiology so I was reading all the electrocardiograms and seeing all the dependents), and the guy said, "We are transferring you to company D. Because you are the ranking officer, you will be the commander of company D." The next day they told my executive, my first Sargent, and me that they wanted everybody in our unit to dye their underwear green. I turned to my first Sargent who had been in Korea and said, "What does this mean?" He said, "It is not good news." About 2 weeks later we were on a boat headed out of Honolulu harbor for Vietnam. My company was picked to be the medical support for this separate brigade to try to interdict the Ho Chi Minh trail out of Cambodia. We were sent off into a place called Hobo Woods (the Iron Triangle was the general area) where the Viet Min movement had started 20 years before. It had always been under Viet Cong control. My bride, of course, stayed in Honolulu. About 2 days out at sea I asked the brigade commander: "Do you know what happened to the commander of this unit before you picked me?" He replied, "He heard about this and wrote his congressman and got out of it."

WCR: *What did you do in Vietnam?*

SBK: In Vietnam, we had a unit that was made up of 2 infantry battalions, a mechanized battalion, and some support groups, and one of those support groups was my medical company. We landed in landing boats. We charged through the surf like we were in the movies. There was no fighting there. We went to a place near Saigon which was being shelled at the time. We dug fox holes and spent a week getting ready to go out to where we were going to end up. I flew out in a helicopter that had been put together onsite. I watched them uncrate it. They put the thing together and this

fellow who looked like a Boy Scout got in and cranked it up and said "Get in." I got in with them and we flew ahead of the convoy of our group and landed. A company from the 1st Division was trying to secure the perimeter for us so we could land. I spent the first day helping the doctor from the 1st Division take care of people. Our group came in later that day and set up the headquarters. Immediately after we set up, 1 of our helicopters came and fired a pod of rockets prematurely right into our command post, so I spent that day trying to patch people up and get them evacuated. That was my introduction to Vietnam.

I spent the next half year there at Cu Chi and surrounding areas wondering what the heck I was doing there and having extremely ambivalent feelings. This was before there was a lot of reaction in this country to what was happening in Vietnam. I thought it was a hopeless situation from the outset. There was no morale problem among the troops. We were totally surrounded and could not get out to anything. People worked very hard, and I learned a great deal about people and what they can do under pressure. I found that people who had been the most destructive in a garrison situation in Hawaii became some of the most productive people there when given a job. You take somebody who is a social misfit and put him in a situation like that and give him a job and responsibility and he may flower. Other people, who had been very respectable back in the States, just fell apart. It was an interesting education for me.

WCR: *How long were you in Vietnam?*

SBK: I was there for 6 months. My time was then up in the Army. I mustered out and came to Emory.

WCR: *How did you decide to come to Emory?*

SBK: Before I went to Vietnam I had decided that I wanted to do medicine and cardiology. I went on an East Coast trip—Boston, New York, Washington, and Atlanta. At Emory, I went to both Emory University Hospital and to Grady Memorial Hospital. At Emory

Hospital I met *Bruce Logue* and *Ed Dorney* and talked to a couple of the fellows and got very excited about the opportunity to work with Bruce Logue and that group. *Willis Hurst* offered me a residency position in medicine. Thus, I came to Emory for my medical residency and stayed on for cardiology. I was aimed at cardiology from the day I arrived. I did a lot of electives in cardiology and worked in the cath lab when I was a junior resident for a period of time.

WCR: *Who had a major impact on you during your residency?*

SBK: Bruce Logue above anybody else. I hate to single out people. *Woody Cobbs*, Ed Dorney, and *Bob Franch*, and of course, Willis Hurst also had tremendous influence. I was Bruce Logue's fellow for 1 year. He was a man who taught by example. It was difficult to pin down what he did. I tried to absorb what he was doing and to learn to think through problems by separating the wheat from the chaff. I learned to take care of patients. Although Bruce never joined the American College of Cardiology, I am giving him a presidential citation in March 1999.

WCR: *What were Bruce Logue's characteristics that were so attractive to you?*

SBK: Incredibly intelligent. He could really smell out what was going on. I remember one day while we were walking down a hospital corridor, he looked at a radiograph on a light box, just passed it, had never seen the patient, saw that the left heart border was prominent in this child. The lung fields were clear. He looked up and said "absence of the left pericardium." That's what it was. He would do things like that. He was not an organized person, but he was incredibly intuitive and just went to the meat of the problem trying to find what he could do to help the patient. When a resident, I was standing one day with a fellow named *Bob Tally*. We had a patient who had a pericardial effusion. The patient had been doing fine, but the nurse called and said the patient was mildly dyspeniac. I mentioned that to Dr. Logue, we started walking down the hall and ran into Ed Dorney and said a couple of words to Ed. Within milliseconds, Dr. Logue blew by us like a rocket and said "He will be dead before you get there." We got there and he was just about dead. He was tamponading. You could absorb so much from Logue's experiences without his being structured at all. He was probably a lot more structured than I thought.

WCR: *Did you spend much time in the cath lab during your years as a cardiology fellow?*

SBK: Yes. I spent an entire year in the cath lab with Bob Franch who had the only cath lab at the Emory campus at that time. We studied only children with congenital heart disease and adults with valvular heart disease. We never did a coronary arteriogram. Bob Franch, at that time, was the number 1 referrer to the Mayo Clinic for the federal congenital surgery program. That was our regional place for crippled children. We saw a lot of congenital heart disease. In fact, when I finished the cardiology fellowship I thought of myself as sort of a pediatric cardiologist, because I had cathed maybe 200 infants and children by that time.

WCR: *You went to Denver after your 2-year fellowship at Emory to do what?*

SBK: When I finished the cardiology fellowship, I decided I really wanted to get into coronary work even though I had not done any coronary arteriograms. Bypass surgery had come in 1969. It looked like this was going to be an important thing. I started looking for places to go. There were not many places doing coronary angioplasty then. Northwestern in Chicago wanted somebody to run the cath lab. I visited the University of North Carolina in Chapel Hill, but none of these places were doing coronary surgery. The Cleveland Clinic and Milwaukee were the main places where coronary bypass was being done. I went out to visit my sister in Colorado, and while there I visited the University of Colorado Medical school to see what was going on. *Jack Vogel* was running the cath lab at the time. I sat down at lunch with him and asked what the situation was at the school. He said *Gil Bount* does not even believe in coronary artery disease much less have an interest in coronary arteriography or surgery. I asked about other hospitals in Denver and he said, "There is a cardiologist on every street corner." And then he added, "There is *Fred Schoonmaker* from Duke who came a year ago and is doing tons of coronary angiograms." I jotted down his name and went to my sister's to give him a call. It turned out that we knew a lot of people in common. He had trained with *Eugene Stead*. Fred had been at St. Luke's Hospital, a private hospital, in Denver for just over a year. He found out that I had trained at Emory with Bruce Logue and that I knew how to cath. He was particularly interested in the fact that I had done a lot of congenital heart disease work. I then visited him. It turned out that they were doing probably the third largest number of coronary bypass operations in the country at that time. I saw this as an opportunity to really learn something about coronary arteriography and bypass surgery. I went to work with Fred. He had already started using a different catheter. He was trying to use a single catheter to do coronary arteriograms. The reason we started doing that was because Adams and Abrams had reported a series of patients who had embolic complications from coronary arteriograms. We thought this was a problem of picking up the thrombus at the femoral puncture site, passing it up to the heart, and this was not happening with the *Sones* technique. We thought that it would be nice if we could do the Sones technique from the leg. We began to use different catheters, first Sones catheter, and then a multipurpose catheter made by Cordis. We finally became proficient with this multipurpose technique. Fred is the person who first did it. We collected all the patients and I finally put the paper together and it was published in *Circulation*.

Working with the surgeons, we learned that vein grafts seemed to have a high frequency of renarrowing. We could not figure out what the surgeons were doing wrong, so we took them all to Milwaukee to watch *Dudley Johnson* and found that our surgeons were overdilating the vein grafts. They would take out the saphenous veins and put clips on the end and then forcibly inject saline into the vein checking for leaks. Johnson was very gently injecting blood into the conduit and not over extending it. That was the only thing we could see that was done differently, and so they tried to do it Johnson's way. All of a sudden the early graft stenoses was going away. We had a lot of interesting times working directly with the surgeons trying to perfect bypass surgery. I had been there for about 18 months when Willis Hurst or Bruce Logue called saying that maybe coronary bypass was going to be very useful and Emory needed that to get started with coronary arteriography. They offered me a chance to come back and I took it.

WCR: *You set up the second cath lab there?*

SBK: Right. We set up the first cath lab in the hospital at Emory. There was a cath lab at Grady Hospital. They brought in surgeons who had done coronary bypass. *Ellis Jones* came 6 months after I did. That was when bypass surgery really took off at Emory.

WCR: *Were there difficulties in setting up the catheterization laboratory at Emory Hospital?*

SBK: When I went back to Emory there was a lot of discussion about how the cath lab would be structured, whether it would be in medicine or radiology. Before coming to Emory, I wrote a long letter saying that I would come under these conditions, a, b, c, d. One condition was that the lab had to be within the Department of Medicine. I got a letter back saying that *Dr. Heinz Weens*, the Chief of Radiology, said there was no way x-ray equipment was going to be in any department except radiology, and that if we started a cardiac cath lab in the hospital it had to be within radiology. The lab where I had worked with Bob Franch was in a research building. It was a freestanding lab under the auspices of the Dean. I made certain demands and it turned out they did not agree to any of them. They said I could come to Emory, but that I had to do the procedures jointly with a radiologist. I finally took a look at the situation, talked to Dr. Logue, he said to come and we would work it out. Without contract or letter of understanding, I accepted an appointment in medicine and radiology. *Pete Sones* was the radiologist. He was assigned to work with me and during the first case, I said, "Pete, hand me this; Pete, hand me that." We finished the case and I said, "Well, Pete, tomorrow we have another case." He said, "You are not going to see me. I am not going to stand here and hand you things." Thus, the radiology connection ended after 1 case. The lab was in radiology and it stayed there. I used the lab half a day and he used it the other half. Eventually, when we had more cases, I used it the whole day. Finally, they said they were building a new wing and needed to build some new cath labs. About mid-1975 a new wing was built and we developed the cath lab suite.

WCR: *By the late 1970s, bypass operations were flying.*

SBK: We were on the side of bypass, offering something over and above medical therapy. We wrote a little bit about that. We did a lot of work with the surgeons. We got very interested in trying to measure outcomes. We bought the first echo machine at Emory Hospital and added it to my office. There was also an interest in trying to measure what was happening with nuclear techniques. Because of our radiology connection, we were able to start a nuclear medicine operation in the cath lab using nuclear ventriculography. All these things were eventually taken over by other people and expanded. The pediatric part of it withered on the vine as the pediatricians began to hire cath people at Egleston Children's Hospital.

WCR: *How many caths were you doing at the peak?*

SBK: In the peak time, probably 800 to 1,000.

WCR: *How much time do you spend in the cath lab now?*

SBK: When I am in Atlanta, I am in the cath lab probably half the time, but I am only in Atlanta now about half the time this year. I do less than 200 interventional cases each year now. Most of my colleagues do more.

WCR: *What is the most you were doing when you were in Atlanta more?*

SBK: The most interventional cases I have done in a year is around 600.

WCR: *How many diagnostic caths do you estimate you have now done?*

SBK: Diagnostic caths must be >10,000.

WCR: *How many invasive angioplasty procedures?*

SBK: Interventional procedures are in the neighborhood of probably 6,000.

WCR: *It is my understanding that you were the one who enticed or suggested that* Andreas Gruentzig *come to Emory. How did that work out?*

SBK: I met Andreas in Miami Beach when he was presenting a poster of the dog experiments showing that a balloon could be inflated in a dog artery to break a constricting ligature and restore the normal pressure dynamics across the artery. I did not think much of it at the time. I could not imagine that this was going to work knowing what you had taught us about the pathology of arteries. I could not imagine that you could do this and an artery not just shatter. After that, I invited him, after he had done his first human cases, to a meeting of the South Atlantic Cardiovascular Society in Kiawah Island, South Carolina. This was a meeting that was composed of people from 5 Southeastern states, half cardiologists and half cardiovascular surgeons. We always had 1 outside speaker. I was in charge of organizing this particular meeting. Someone wanted us to have Gruentzig come, and I invited him. We got to know him on a personal level. I began to go to Zurich along with many other people. In January 1980 we were on a train in Switzerland going to a postcourse party following 1 of Andreas' demonstration courses. He sat down beside me and started telling me about the difficulties he was having in Zurich developing angioplasty the way he wanted. He was not given enough time in the cath lab. He wanted to leave. I asked what he was going to do, and he said he was either going to Germany or to the USA. He said if he could get a job as a professor in Germany he would go there, otherwise, he was coming to the USA. I asked where he was going. He said, "The Cleveland Clinic has been interested in me. That is probably the place that is most famous for heart surgery, and this might be a good place to go and develop angioplasty." He also mentioned that both Harvard and Stanford had made some overtures. I said, "What do you want to do?" He said, "Well, I want a couple of things: First, to develop the technique and make sure that I nurture it through this development period (there are going to be a lot of things happening and they will happen in the USA), and second, I want to be a professor." I said, "Where are you going to work?" He said he thought he would go to Cleveland. At that time Cleveland did not have a medical school. I said, "You can't be a professor at Cleveland. It is not a medical school." He said, "Oh, is that right?" That was all that transpired then, but after a while it became a real battle between Cleveland and Emory. We both worked on his Visa and his license. We brought him to Atlanta and tried to show him all the houses and nicer things. We introduced him to surgeons and told him they were not really evil people. Eventually, he decided to come to Emory. Many things were important. Probably the fact that we were able to get him a Visa and a license before the Cleveland Clinic played a role.

WCR: *He came to Emory in 1980?*

SBK: Yes.

WCR: *He was killed when?*

SBK: 1985. Almost exactly 5 years later.

WCR: *Did your number of angioplasty cases increase rapidly after he came?*

SBK: Yes. *John Douglas* and I had been doing angioplasty since June 1980. He came and started with us in late October or early November 1980, and we had done about 30 cases when he arrived. He, of course, was the leader of the interventional group then. I was Director of the Cardiac Catheterization Laboratory, and we needed a job title for him. He pointed this out quite forcibly and we created the title, "Director of Interventional Cardiovascular Medicine," for him. That might be where the term "interventional cardiology" originated. He was the leader of the world in terms of angioplasty and how it developed. He projected a very conservative image towards angioplasty, however. He was very aggressive in trying to treat patients with difficult problems. He would not shy away from anything, but he was very conservative in trying to avoid complications. Andreas did about 2,000 cases before his death.

WCR: *Technically, he was really superb?*

SBK: He was technically superb, but more than that, he would think through the case and try to predict the problems, and try to anticipate how to get out of trouble. With the equipment available then, every case was a real tour de force.

WCR: *After he died, did the number of cases continue to increase at Emory?*

SBK: They continued to increase through the 1980s. We ended up eventually at Emory University Hospital doing in the neighborhood of 1,600 to 1,900 coronary angioplasty cases per year. At Crawford Long Hospi-

tal, our other Emory hospital, the cases also began to build. Currently, between the 2 Emory hospitals, about 3,400 angioplasty cases per year are done.

WCR: *How many people are doing angioplasty at Emory now?*

SBK: We have 12 faculty who do coronary angioplasty.

WCR: *Since 1980, you have been involved in many multicenter studies, several of which you designed. You have built this huge database in cardiovascular disease at Emory. You have done a lot of publishing. As you look at all this now, what are you most pleased with?*

SBK: I am most pleased with our attempt at least to somewhat shepherd interventional cardiology. My early years in cardiology were largely focused on coronary artery disease but concentrated on surgical approaches. I really don't feel that I changed my interest when angioplasty came on the scene. I am still thinking in the same direction, increasing blood to myocardium. Our main contributions perhaps have been in trying to bring interventional cardiology up to a reasonable standard. Of the things I hope to be the proudest of is the development of the board certification in interventional cardiology. In its early development, angioplasty was a technique that was added on to what any person in the cath lab was already doing. Currently, we still have a large number of cardiologists performing procedures as a part of their general cardiology practice, and that will continue, and many of those do a superb job. As the field becomes more and more complex, it will ultimately be best served by people concentrating on interventional cardiology as their main activity, and that will mean fewer cardiologists doing angioplasty. In the future, interventional cardiologists will not only have the technical expertise to perform the procedures, but will also be very knowledgeable regarding alternative therapies for vascular disease.

WCR: *When is the first examination going to take place?*

SBK: On November 3, 1999.

WCR: *How many people will take that exam?*

SBK: We are guessing about 2,000. It will be available to people who have concentrated on interventional cardiology, whether they have trained formally or not. It will be available in the future for cardiologists who take approved ABIM-ACGME training in interventional cardiology.

WCR: *You are hopeful within a reasonable period of time that only people who are board certified in interventional cardiology will be doing the angioplasty procedures?*

SBK: I don't know that it will be only those people. With the acute interventions being needed, there will be a need for coverage. There will be a need for some people who do not perform enough procedures to really qualify or who do not have the board examination to still perform procedures. That is a local credentialing issue, and I predict that that will go on for many years to come. The added board certification is the opportunity to develop a cadre of people who can be certified as experts in the field. They should know in depth the field of interventional cardiology as it goes beyond balloons, stents, angiogenesis, improved preventive and stabilization methods, and all kinds of new developments in the future.

WCR: *How many coronary angioplasties do you have to do a year to be really good at it?*

SBK: This has been studied, and some people get good with fewer and some people take longer. There is no good answer for that. There is a correlation between volume and success rates. *Steve Ellis*, in a meta-analysis, found that a number of cases associated with good outcomes required a volume of about 70 per year, but for the more complex cases there was no break in the curve. The more people did, the better they were at it in the very complex cases up to a level of about 200. These numbers are not very important in the long run. What is important is that cardiologists involved in it are focused on the field as a major part of their activity. The board may help get away from the numbers by certifying people who achieve expertise. It is clear that doing only occasional angioplasties is inadequate to maintain expertise.

WCR: *Spencer, could we discuss your work habits, not this year, while you are also President of The American College of Cardiology, but back 2 or 3 years. What time do you get up in the morning? What time do you get to the hospital? What time do you leave the hospital? What time do you get home?*

SBK: I get up between 6:00 and 6:30 A.M. and get to the hospital between 7:00 and 7:30. I am pretty much at the hospital all day. I eat a limited breakfast. I sometimes eat lunch. About half the time I forget it. I am usually there until about 7:00 P.M. on an average day. I am trying to train myself to leave sooner than that, but I have a difficult time doing it. I have a lot of help from my wife, Gail, helping me to learn how to do that.

WCR: *What about weekends? Do you go in?*

SBK: I try not to go in on weekends. If I am on call, I certainly go, but I am making an effort not to go. It is a rare weekend, however, that I don't either go in or bring work home. There are just too many things hanging.

WCR: *Where do you do most of your writing?*

SBK: I do most of my writing at home. It is very difficult to do any writing in the office. There are too many distractions.

WCR: *Do you dictate or do you actually write paper and pencil?*

SBK: It depends on what it is. For a review, I may just dictate and then edit. For most things, I write it out first.

WCR: *You met Gail when and where?*

SBK: I met Gail when I was in medical school. She was a nursing student. We got married 1 month after beginning my internship.

WCR: *Where is she from?*

SBK: Savannah, Georgia.

WCR: *Does she have brothers and/or sisters?*

SBK: She has 2 brothers. One lives in Savannah and is a Fire Captain. Her other brother is with Delta Airlines in Montana.

WCR: *You have 2 children?*

SBK: Yes.

WCR: *What do they do?*

SBK: Our son, Spencer, is a philosophy graduate of Haverford College. He is very interested in philosophy, but he is not doing it professionally. He is currently doing remodeling construction, remodeling houses. He is also a musician. Our daughter currently lives near Hendersonville, North Carolina. She has been running a girls' camp. She is a sociology graduate of Connecticut College and is an outdoors sociologist. She worked for a number of years with juvenile offenders in outdoor survival experiences. She has taught in Africa, trekked for a winter in Nepal, and worked with the Mother Theresa house in Calcutta and Delhi. Right now, she is applying to a masters program in social work.

WCR: *Your kids are how old?*

SBK: Spencer is 31; Susan is 29.

WCR: *Have you been a pretty good daddy?*

SBK: I am an excellent daddy. My attendance has not always been what it should have been. When I am around, I am pretty decent. They are wonderful children and are interested in things other than medicine. I got over that very early. Probably, at some point, I hoped one of them would go into medicine, but now I would be shocked if they did because it is not their interest.

WCR: *Could you talk a bit about your Presidency of The American College of Cardiology? How have you enjoyed that position? Have there been surprises? What have you learned from this endeavor?*

SBK: I have enjoyed it immensely. The biggest surprise this year is the fact that our executive vice-president, who of course runs Heart House, resigned at the end of last year. We had to hire a new one and it was going to come on my watch. My biggest surprise is how smoothly that has gone and what a terrific job *Chris McEntee* has done as Executive Vice-President. It has been an extremely rewarding year so far. The activities of the College are a bit overwhelming both in education and in the advocacy arena. We have to work with private payers, with people on the Hill, with agencies such as the Food and Drug Administration, the Nuclear Regulatory Commission, and HICFA. The staff are the best of any health organization. It has been a tremendous amount of fun working with them. We see some challenges for the College.

The College's primary mission has been education and that remains true although we think we have to change the way education is done. We are not sure how long or big a role huge meetings will play in the future. We certainly can contend with those, but we think there are other ways to do it, and we are getting very active in electronic media and the internet. We have now entered an arrangement with a group that is going to put out medical cardiology news to physicians on a daily downloaded basis, like the Bloomberg network. This is an organization called *Medcast*. The

College will be their supplier of cardiology information. We are adding on some fulltime people to generate that content. Cardiology has become fragmented, and this is a place that the College has to wade in as people become more subspecialized into electrophysiology, interventional, pediatrics, heart failure, and so forth. There is the temptation for those groups go their own way. A major responsibility of the College is to recognize the subspecializaties and provide educational opportunities that take that into account. Giving depth to the experience of interventional cardiologists, for instance, while at the same time keeping them in the mainstream of cardiology is critical, because their patients need a physician who is also educated in secondary prevention, who also knows about heart failure, and who knows something of electrophysiology and the rest of cardiology. We have instituted in this coming year, a program in interventional cardiology that will precede The American College of Cardiology's annual meeting. Our plans for future years are to add on other subspecialty areas. Next year, it will be echocardiography, and clinical cardiology will also have a separate session going on. We are going to try to accommodate to this subspecialization by providing in-depth education in those subspecialty areas, while at the same time understanding that the cardiologist must remain, for the sake of the patient, knowledgeable about cardiology in general. One goal I have is to strengthen the subspecialty societies. It may sound paradoxical, but the College can play a role in strengthening those subsocieties, while they support and maintain a close affiliation with the College.

Another major responsibility of the College is in the advocacy arena. We have a very strong and effective lobbying group to get legislation passed. There are more and more concerns relative to reimbursement and what physicians have to do to document their evaluation and management of patients. Although the College is the leader in setting standards and recommending guidelines, there is a growing cookbook mentality when documentation rules do not have adequate professional input. We think this is a threat to quality care in the long run. The College is entering into a number of collaborative efforts on performance measures, quality of care, and doing this in collaboration with The American Heart Association, The American College of Physicians, and The American Medical Association. The College has to get even more aggressive in the advocacy arena. Whether this goes all the way to forming a political action committee, which would change the character of the college, is a point for open debate. Circumstances may dictate that the College take an even stronger stand to protect the profession and our patients.

WCR: *Do you think angioplasty is going to be here for a very long time?*

SBK: Microinterventional techniques are going to be here. Both the surgeons and the cardiologists will be doing these. The borders will blur over time, but less and less invasive procedures certainly will occur. The interventional techniques are going to be with us a long time. We have an aging population. Our mar-

velous successes in primary and secondary prevention, not withstanding, we still have a lot of people getting into trouble. I would be delighted if interventional cardiology was not necessary 20 years from now, but I suspect it will still be very important. As patients get older, and as they have multiple revascularization procedures, we end up with a lot of patients who are suffering, and there is not yet much to be done about them. The new techniques perhaps involving plaque stabilization and microimaging and angiogenesis through various means may be other areas where the interventional cardiologists will be very active in the future. The other place the interventional cardiologist is going, of course, is into the peripheral circulation. This is an area that is contentious with the radiologists and sometimes vascular surgeons. I don't think it should be. We should follow the admonition of Gruentzig, that whoever is trained in something should be allowed to do it. Therefore, we must insist on proper training. At Emory, we have formed a vascular center bringing together radiology, vascular medicine, vascular surgery, and cardiology into 1 organization to treat peripheral vascular disease.

WCR: *Do you do peripheral arterial work?*

SBK: No. We do have 2 people in our cardiology group and several in the cardiac and vascular radiology and vascular surgery groups, all of whom do these procedures.

WCR: *How much of your time now does the Presidency of The American College of Cardiology occupy?*

SBK: It takes about more than 50% of my time. It is a huge commitment.

WCR: *Is that time mainly for travel, or how much work when you are at home do you have to do with the College each day?*

SBK: I have a dedicated College fax machine at my office. I have my E-mail from the College coming into my office. I get stacks of E-mail and faxes every day, and I am every day in communication with the College. The travel involves many things, numerous trips to Heart House, to the Hill, to government agencies, the AMA, the ACP, chapter meetings to represent the College, international societies, the European and Asian-Pacific societies, the World Congress of Cardiology, plus a number of national societies.

WCR: *Spencer, do you have hobbies outside of medicine?*

SBK: I am a lousy golfer, but I enjoy it a lot.

WCR: *Do you play much?*

SBK: I don't play much. When I am out of town, I play, but hardly ever when I am in town. We go to Hawaii a couple of times a year to a place there and I play a lot when I am there.

WCR: *How much time do you take off a year?*

SBK: I camouflage it very well. I think I take a lot. Gail thinks I don't take any because her definition of taking time off is going on a trip without slides or an agenda book and that seldom happens. If you add it up, I get plenty of rest and relaxation, albeit almost all of it is in conjunction with a meeting. I hope, for my sake, that I will be able to change that and do something that does not involve slides in the near future. We have a cabin on a beautiful lake in the mountains. I hope we can spend more time there.

WCR: *When this College activity is over, what are you going to substitute for it? What are you going to fill that vacuum with?*

SBK: I am not completely sure. I have been very interested in clinical research, and I think I am helpful in clinical research. I am chairing a number of multicenter trials, and perhaps I can play more of a role there. Our unit at the Gruentzig Center is involved in many trials and in a lot of preclinical research as well. We have an excellent group of people doing that, and I enjoy working directly with them in animal research as well as in clinical research. I see myself being much more heavily involved in that way. What I will be doing in the immediate future is exactly what I am doing now, but more of it because I won't have the other responsibilities.

WCR: *You have no interest in being Chairman of a Department of Medicine?*

SBK: I visited 3 places to look at Chief of Cardiology and Chief of Medicine jobs, and I did not agree to go further with it. They were superb places, but I realized that probably I had more on my plate than I could handle in interventional cardiology, and perhaps the best thing to do was to stick with that and not try to get into being a division chair or a Chief of Medicine.

WCR: *Do you use a lot of the statin drugs?*

SBK: We use statins in almost every patient we identify with coronary artery disease, unless we find a lipid abnormality that is better treated with something else or not responsive to statin. We are extremely aggressive. I think the interventional cardiologist has an enormous opportunity and responsibility at a vulnerable time in the patient's presentation to jump on board with good education and to initiate therapy for lipid abnormalities at the time he/she sees them. Virtually everybody with coronary disease should be on good lipid management.

WCR: *Do you think the problem with restenosis after angioplasty is going to be solved?*

SBK: It has been a long road. There are some encouraging signs. Our own work with radiation has taught me that restenosis is a wound-healing phenomenon that can be inhibited the way other excessive would healing, such as keloid formation, is. Several studies seem to be pointing in the direction of radiation's being helpful, and we are very enthusiastic. On the other hand, there may be other things that are going to be helpful, such as antioxidants and drugs targeted at platelet-derived growth factor (PDGF) receptors. There is a good opportunity to control restenosis beyond what a stent can do. Stents obviously have had an impact but when you get restenosis within the stent it is an even bigger problem. I anticipate that we will eventually solve the restenosis problem.

WCR: *Is there anything you would like to discuss that we have not touched on?*

SBK: We have not discussed our work in defining the outcomes of angioplasty versu coronary surgery.

We just completed an 8- to 10-year follow-up of the Emory Angioplasty versus Surgery Trial. I think most will find it interesting and food for thought about long-term outcomes of more recent therapeutic innovations. The stent versus surgery trials will decrease reintervention, but the importance of secondary prevention cannot be overemphasized. *Bill Weintraub,* who heads our clinical outcomes research unit, has asked us to help with a trial involving very aggressive prevention measures. Bypass Angioplasty Revascularization Investigation II (BARI II) and a planned National Heart, Lung, and Blood Institute study are being developed to take advantage of powerful but underutilized medical approaches.

WCR: *Spencer, thank you, this has been wonderful and I appreciate your willingness to pour your soul, so to speak, to the readers of the AJC.*

SBK: It's been good visiting with you, Bill. I hoped I haven't bored you too much.

SBK'S Best Publications as Selected by Him

Books:
1. King SB III, Douglas JS Jr. Coronary Arteriography and Angioplasty. New York: McGraw-Hill 1984:478.
2. Vogel JHK, King SB III, editors. Interventional Cardiology: Future Directions. St. Louis: Mosby 1992:527.
3. Serruys PW, Strauss BH, King SB III, editors. Restenosis After Intervention With New Medical Services. Amsterdam: Kluwer Academic, 1992:504.
4. Vogel JHK, King SB III, editors. The Practice of Interventional Cardiology. Second Edition. St. Louis: Mosby 1993:718.
5. King SB III, Douglas JS Jr, editors. Atlas of Interventional Cardiology. Philadelphia: Current Science, Vol. XIII; 1997:275.

Published Articles:
1. King SB, Franch RH. Production of increased right to left shunting by rapid heart rates in patients with tetralogy of Fallot. *Circulation* 1971;44:265–271.
4. Dunaway M, King SB, Hatcher CR, Logue RB. Disabling supraventricular tachycardia of Wolff-Parkinson-White syndrome (type a) controlled by surgical A-V block and a demand pacemaker after epicardial mapping studies. *Circulation* 1972;45:522–528.
6. King SB, Mansour KA, Hatcher CR, Silverman ME, Hart NC. Coronary artery spasm producing prinzmetal angina and myocardial infarction in the absence of coronary atherosclerosis. *Ann Thorac Surg* 1973;16:337–343.
9. Schoonmaker FW, King SB. Coronary arteriography by the single catheter percutaneous femoral technique. *Circulation* 1974;50:735–740.
14. Logue RB, King SB, Douglas JS. A practical approach to coronary artery disease with special reference to coronary bypass surgery. *Curr Probl Cardiol* 1976;2:1–54.
19. Cobbs BW, King SB. Ventricular buckling: a factor in the abnormal ventriculogram and peculiar hemodynamics associated with mitral valve prolapse. *Am Heart J* 1977;93:741–758.
20. Morris D, King SB, Douglas JS, Hatcher CR, Jones EL, Wickliffe C. Hemodynamic evaluation of the porcine xenograft aortic valve. *Circulation* 1977;56:841–844.
45. Douglas JS, King SB, Jones EL, Craver JM, Bradford JM, Hatcher CR. Reduced efficacy of coronary bypass surgery in women. *Circulation* 1981;64:11–16.
46. Douglas JS, King SB, Craver JM, Jones EL, Hatcher CR, Bradford JM. Factors influencing risk and benefit of coronary bypass surgery in patients with diabetes mellitus. *Chest* 1981;80:369–372.
47. Kutcher M, King SB, Douglas JS, Craver JM. Constrictive pericarditis following coronary bypass surgery. *Am J Cardiol* 1982;50:742–748.
53. Ischinger T, Gruentzig AR, Hollman J, King SB, Douglas JS, Meier B, Bradford J, Tankersley R. Should coronary arteries with less than 60% diameter stenosis be treated by angioplasty? *Circulation* 1983;68:148–154.
57. Douglas JS, Gruentzig AR, King SB III, Hollman J, Ischinger T, Meier B. Percutaneous transluminal coronary angioplasty in patients with prior coronary bypass surgery. *J Am Coll Cardiol* 1983;2:745–754.
66. Thornton MA, Gruentzig AR, Hollman J, King SB, Douglas JS. Coumadin and aspirin in prevention of recurrence after transluminal coronary angioplasty: a randomized study. *Circulation* 1984;69:721–727.

70. Meier B, King SB, Gruentzig AR, Douglas JS, Hollman J, Ischinger T, Galan K, Tankersley R. Repeat coronary angioplasty. *J Am Coll Cardiol* 1984;4:463–466.

72. Bredlau C, Roubin GS, Leimgruber PP, Douglas JS, King SB, Gruentzig AR. In-hospital morbidity and mortality in elective coronary angioplasty. *Circulation* 1985;72:1044–1052.

73. Anderson HV, Roubin GS, Leimgruber PP, Douglas JS, King SB, Gruentzig AR. Primary angiographic success rates of percutaneous transluminal coronary angioplasty. *Am J Cardiol* 1985;56:712–717.

74. Leimgruber PP, Roubin GS, Anderson HV, Bredlau C, Whitworth H, Douglas JS, King SB, Gruentzig AR. Influence of intimal dissection on restenosis after successful angioplasty. *Circulation* 1985;72:530–535.

89. Anderson HV, Roubin GS, Leimgruber PP, Cos WR, Douglas JS, King SB, Gruentzig AR. Transstenotic pressure gradient measurements during percutaneous transluminal coronary angioplasty. *Circulation* 1986;73:1223–1230.

90. Leimgruber P, Roubin GS, Hollman J, Cotsonis GA, Meier B, Douglas JS, King SB, Gruentzig AR. Restenosis after successful coronary angioplasty in patients with single-vessel disease. *Circulation* 1986;73:710–717.

97. Whitworth HB, Roubin GS, Hollman J, Meier B, Leimgruber PP, Douglas JS, King SB, Gruentzig AR. Effect of nifidepine on recurrent stenosis after percutaneous transluminal coronary angioplasty. *J Am Coll Cardiol* 1986;8:1271–1276.

99. Gruentzig AR, King SB, Schlumpf M, Siegenthaler W. Long-term follow-up after percutaneous transluminal coronary angioplasty: the early Zurich experience. *N Engl J Med* 1987;316:1127–1132.

105. Roubin GS, Robinson KA, King SB, Gianturco C, Black A, Brown JE, Siegel RJ, Douglas JS. Early and late results of intracoronary arterial stenting after coronary angioplasty in dogs. *Circulation* 1987;76:891–897.

116. Detre K, Hulobkov R, Kelsey S, Cowley M, Kent K, Williams D, Myler R, Faxon D, Holmes D, Bourassa M, Block P, Gosselin A, Bentivoglio L, Leatherman L, Dorros G, King SB. Percutaneous transluminal coronary angioplasty in 1985–1986 and 1977–1981. The National Heart, Lung and Blood Institute Registry. *N Engl J Med* 1988;318:265–270.

119. Ellis SG, Roubin GS, King SB, Douglas JS, Shaw RE, Stertzer SH, Myler RK. In-hospital cardiac mortality following acute closure after percutaneous transluminal coronary angioplasty—analysis of risk factors from 8207 procedures. *J Am Coll Cardiol* 1988;11:211–216.

120. Black AJR, Anderson HV, Roubin GS, Powelson SW, Douglas JS, King SB. Repeat coronary angioplasty: correlates of a second restenosis. *J Am Coll Cardiol* 1988;11:714–718.

122. Talley JD, Hurst JW, King SB, Douglas JS, Roubin GS, Gruentzig AR, Anderson HV, Weintraub WS. Clinical outcome 5 years after attempted percutaneous transluminal coronary angioplasty in 427 patients. *Circulation* 1988;77:820–829.

123. Robinson KA, Roubin GS, Siegel MD, Black AJ, Apkarian RP, King SB. Intra-arterial stenting in the atherosclerotic rabbit. *Circulation* 1988;78:646–653.

124. Black AJ, Roubin GS, Sutor C, Moe N, Jarboe JM, Douglas JS, King SB. Comparative costs of percutaneous transluminal coronary angioplasty and coronary artery bypass grafting in multivessel coronary artery disease. *Am J Cardiol* 1988;62:809–812.

128. Roubin GS, Douglas JS, King SB, Lin S, Hutchinson N, Thomas RG, Gruentzig AR. Influence of balloon size on initial success, acute complications, and restenosis after percutaneous transluminal coronary angioplasty: a prospective randomized study. *Circulation* 1988;78:557–565.

130. Ryan TJ, Faxon DP, Grunnar RM, Kennedy JW, King SB, Loop FD, Peterson KL, Reeves TJ, Williams DO, Winters WL. Guidelines for percutaneous transluminal coronary angioplasty—a report of the American College of Cardiology/American Heart Association Task Force on assessment of diagnostic and therapeutic cardiovascular procedures. *J Am Coll Cardiol* 1988;12:529–545.

138. Ellis SG, Shaw RE, Gershony G, Thomas R, Roubin GS, Douglas JS Jr, Topol EJ, Stertzer SH, Myler RK, King SB. Risk factors, time course and treatment effect for restenosis after successful percutaneous transluminal coronary angioplasty of chronic total occlusion. *Am J Cardiol* 1989;63:897–901.

140. Black AJR, Namay DL, Niederman AL, Lembo NJ, Roubin GS, Douglas JS Jr, King SB III. Tear or dissection after coronary angioplasty. Morphologic correlates of an ischemic complication. *Circulation* 1989;79:1035–1042.

141. Ellis SG, Roubin GS, Wilentz J, Douglas JS Jr, King SB III. Effect of 18-24 hour heparin administration for prevention of restenosis after uncomplicated coronary angioplasty. *Am Heart J* 1989;117:777–782.

142. Liu MW, Roubin GS, King SB III. Restenosis after coronary angioplasty. Potential biologic determinants and role of intimal hyperplasia. *Circulation* 1989;79:1374–1387.

151. Ellis SG, Fisher L, Dushman-Ellis S, Pettinger M, King SB III, Roubin GS, Alderman E. Comparison of coronary angioplasty with medical treatment for single-and double-vessel coronary disease with left anterior descending coronary involvement: long-term outcome based on an Emory-CASS registry study. *Am Heart J* 1989;118:208–220.

156. Lembo NJ, Black AJR, Roubin GS, Wilentz JR, Mufson LH, Douglas JS Jr, King SB III. Effect of pretreatment with aspirin versus aspirin plus dipyridamole on frequency and type of acute complications of percutaneous transluminal coronary angioplasty. *Am J Cardiol* 1990;65:422–426.

157. Roubin GS, King SB III, Douglas JS Jr, Lembo NJ, Robinson KA. Intracoronary stenting during percutaneous transluminal coronary angioplasty. *Circulation* 1990;81(suppl IV):IV-92–IV-100.

159. Liu MW, Roubin GS, Robinson KA, Black AJR, Hearn JA, Siegel RJ, King

SB III. Trapidil in preventing restenosis after balloon angioplasty in the atherosclerotic rabbit. *Circulation* 1990;81:1089–1093.

177. Lembo NJ, King SB III, Roubin GS, Black AJ, Douglas JS Jr. Effects of nonionic versus ionic contrast media on complications of percutaneous transluminal coronary angioplasty. *Am J Cardiol* 1991;67:1046–1050.

182. Rab ST, King SB III, Roubin GS, Carlin S, Hearn JA, Douglas JS Jr. Coronary aneurysms following stent placement: a suggestion of altered vessel wall healing in the presence of anti-inflammatory agents. *J Am Coll Cardiol* 1991;18:1524–1528.

188. Ivanhoe RJ, Weintraub W, Douglas JS Jr, Lembo NJ, Furman M, Gershony G, Cohen CL, King SB III. Percutaneous transluminal coronary angioplasty of chronic total occlusions: primary success, restenosis, and long-term clinical follow-up. *Circulation* 1992;85:106–115.

190. DeMaio SJ, King SB III, Lembo NJ, Roubin GS, Hearn JA, Bhagavan HN, Sqoutas DS. Vitamin E supplementation, plasma lipids and incidence of restenosis after percutaneous transluminal coronary angioplasty (PTCA). *J Am Coll Nut* 1992;11:68–73.

192. Hearn JA, Donohue BC, Ba'albaki H, Douglas JS, King SB III, Lembo NJ, Roubin GS, Sqoutas DS. Usefulness of serum lipoprotein (a) as a predictor of restenosis after percutaneous transluminal coronary angioplasty. *Am J Cardiol* 1992;69:736–739.

195. Santoian EC, King SB III. Intravascular stents, intimal proliferation and restenosis. *J Am Coll Cardiol* 1992;19:877–879.

197. Karas SP, Gravanis MB, Santoian EC, Robinson KA, Anderberg K, King SB III. Coronary intimal proliferation after balloon injury and stenting in swine: an animal model of restenosis. *J Am Coll Cardiol* 1992;20:467–474.

200. Ghazzal ZMB, Hearn JA, Litvack F, Grobenberg T, Kent KM, Eigler N, Douglas JS, Jr., King SB III. Morphological predictors of acute complications after percutaneous excimer laser coronary angioplasty. Results of a comprehensive angiographic analysis: importance of the eccentricity index. *Circulation* 1992;86:820–827.

208. Weintraub WS, Kosinski A, Brown CL III, King SB III. Can restenosis after coronary angioplasty be predicted from clinical variables? *J Am Coll Cardiol* 1993;21:6–14.

210. Weintraub WS, King SB III, Jones EL, Douglas JS, Craven JM, Liberman HA, Morris AC, Guyton RA. Coronary surgery and coronary angioplasty in patients with two vessel coronary artery disease. *Am J Cardiol* 1993;71:511–517.

211. Weintraub WS, Ghazzal ZMB, Douglas JS Jr, Liberman HA, Morris DC, Cohen CL, King SB III. Long-term clinical follow-up in patients with angiographic restudy after successful angioplasty. *Circulation* 1993;87:831–840.

215. Santoian EC, Schneider JE, Gravanis MB, Foegh M, Tarazona N, Cipolla G, King SB III. Angiopeptin inhibits intimal hyperplasia after angioplasty in porcine coronary arteries. *Circulation* 1993;88:11–14.

216. King SB III, Schlumpf M. Ten-year completed follow-up of percutaneous transluminal coronary angioplasty: the early Zurich experience. *J Am Coll Cardiol* 1993;22:353–360.

217. Schneider JE, Berk BC, Gravanis MB, Santoian EC, Cipolla GD, Tarazona N, Lassegue B, King SB III. Probucol decreases neointimal formation in a swine model of coronary artery balloon injury. A possible role for antioxidants in restenosis. *Circulation* 1993;88:628–637.

219. Weintraub WS, Brown CL, Liberman HA, Morris DC, Douglas JS Jr, King SB III. Effect of restenosis at one previously dilated coronary site on the probability of restenosis at another previously dilated coronary site. *Am J Cardiol* 1993;72:1107–1113.

220. Hearn JA, King SB III, Douglas JS Jr, Carlin SF, Lembo NJ, Ghazzal ZMB. Clinical and angiographic outcomes after coronary artery stenting for acute or threatened closure after percutaneous transluminal coronary angioplasty. Initial results with a balloon-expandable, stainless steel design. *Circulation* 1993;88: 2086–2096.

221. Ryan TJ, Bauman WB, Kennedy JW, Kereiakes DJ, King SB III, McCallister BD, Smith SC Jr, Ullyot DJ. ACC/AHA Task Force Report. Guidelines for percutaneous transluminal coronary angioplasty. *J Am Coll Cardiol* 1993;22: 2033–2054.

225. Baim DS, Kent KM, King SB III, Safian RD, Cowley MJ, Holmes DR, Roubin GS, Gallup D, Sternkist AR, for the NACI Investigators. Evaluating new devices. Acute (in-hospital) results from the new approaches to coronary intervention registry. *Circulation* 1994;89:471–481.

233. King SB III, Lembo NJ, Weintraub WS, Kosinski AS, Bornhart HX, Kuther MP, Alaznaki NP, Guyton RA, Zhao X-O, for the EAST Investigators. A randomized trial comparing coronary angioplasty with coronary bypass surgery. *N Engl J Med* 1994;331:1044–1050.

234. Weintraub WS, Boccuzzi SJ, Klein JL, Kosinski AS, King SB III, et al. Lack of effect of lovastatin on restenosis after coronary angioplasty. *N Engl J Med* 1994;331:1331–1337.

238. King SB III, Lembo NJ, Weintraub WS, Ivanhoe R, Cedarholm JC, Stillabarog ME, Tally JD, DeMaio SJ, O'Neill WW, Frazier JE III, Cohen-Bernstein L, Robbins DC, Brown CL, Alexander RW. Emory angioplasty vs surgery trial (EAST): design, recruitment, and baseline description of patients. *Am J Cardiol* 1995;75:1C–23C.

239. Nunes GL, Sgoutas DS, Redden RA, Sigman SR, Gravanis MB, King SB III, Berk BC. Combination of vitamins C and E alters the response to coronary balloon injury in the pig. *Arteriosclero Thromb Vasc Biol* 1995;15:156–165.

242. Waksman R, Robinson KA, Crocker IR, Gravanis MB, Cipolla GD, King SB III. Endovascular low-dose irradiation inhibits neointima formation after coronary artery balloon injury in swine. A possible role for radiation therapy in restenosis prevention. *Circulation* 1995;91:1533–1539.

247. Waksman R, Robinson KA, Crocker IR, Gravanis MB, Palmer SJ, Wang C, Cipolla GD, King SB III. Intracoronary radiation before stent implantation inhibits neointima formation in stented porcine coronary arteries. *Circulation* 1995;92:1383–1386.

252. Weintraub WS, Mauldin PD, Becker E, Kosinski AS, King SB III. A comparison of the costs of and quality of life after coronary angioplasty or coronary surgery for multivessel coronary artery disease. Results from the Emory Angioplasty versus Surgery Trial (EAST). *Circulation* 1995;92:2831–2840.

253. Waksman R, Robinson KA, Crocker IR, Wang C, Gravanis MB, Cipolla GD, Hillstead RA, King SB III. Intracoronary low-dose B-irradiation inhibits neointima formation after coronary artery balloon injury in the swine restenosis model. *Circulation* 1995;92:3025–3031.

255. Ghazzal ZMB, Burton E, Weintraub WS, Litvack F, Rothbaum DA, Klein L, King SB III. Predictors of restenosis after excimer laser coronary angioplasty. *Am J Cardiol* 1995;75:1012–1014.

266. King SB III. Angioplasty from bench to bedside to bench. *Circulation* 1996;93:1621–1629.

267. Zhao X-Q, Brown BG, Stewart DK, Hillger LA, Barnhart HX, Kosinski AS, Weintraub WS, King SB III. Effectiveness of revascularization in the Emory Angioplasty versus Surgery Trial. A randomized comparison of coronary angioplasty with bypass surgery. *Circulation* 1996;93:1954–1962.

276. Hodakowski GT, Craver JM, Jones EL, King SB III, Guyton RA. Clinical significance of perioperative Q-wave myocardial infarction: the Emory Angioplasty Versus Surgery Trial. *J Thorac Cardiovasc Surg* 1996;112:1447–1454.

280. Ellis SG, Weintraub W, Holmes D, Shaw R, Block PC, King SB III. Relation of operator volume and experience to procedural outcome of percutaneous coronary revascularization at hospitals with high interventional volumes. *Circulation* 1997;96:2479–2484.

281. King SB III, Barnhart HX, Kosinski AS, Weintraub WS, Lembo NJ, Petersen JY, Douglas JS Jr, Jones EL, Craver JM, Guyton RA, Morris DC, Liberman HA, and the EAST Investigators. Angioplasty or surgery for multivessel coronary artery disease: comparison of eligible registry and randomized patients in the EAST trial and influence of treatment selection on outcomes. *Am J Cardiol* 1997;79:1453–1459.

286. King SB III and the RESTORE Investigators. Effects of platelet glycoprotein IIb/IIIa blockade with tirofiban on adverse cardiac events in patients with unstable angina or acute myocardial infarction undergoing coronary angioplasty. *Circulation* 1997;96:1445–1453.

288. Savage MP, Douglas JS Jr, Fischman DL, Pepine CJ, King SB III, Werner JA, Bailey SR, Overlie PA, Fenton SH, Brinker JA, Leon MB, Goldberg S, for the Saphenous Vein De Novo Trial Investigators. Stent placement compared with balloon angioplasty for obstructed coronary bypass grafts. *N Engl J Med* 1997;337:740–747.

289. King SB III. Is it important how one dies? Questions for planning future revascularization trials. *Circulation* 1997;96:2121–2123.

303. Weintraub WS, Stein B, Kosinski A, Douglas JS, Jr., Ghazzal ZMB, Jones EL, Morris DC, Guyton RA, Craven JM, King SB III. Outcome of coronary bypass surgery versus coronary angioplasty in diabetic patients with multivessel coronary artery disease. *J Am Coll Cardiol* 1998;31:10–19.

304. King SB III, Yeh W, Holubkov R, et al, for the NHLBI PTCA and NACI Investigators. Balloon angioplasty versus new device intervention: clinical outcomes. A comparison of the NHLBI PTCA and NACI Registries. *J Am Coll Cardiol* 1998;31:558–566.

309. King SB III, Williams DO, Chougule P, Klein JL, Waksman R, Hilstead R, Macdonald J, Ardesham K, Crocker IR. Endovascular B-radiation to reduce restenosis after coronary balloon angioplasty. Results of the beta energy restenosis trial (BERT). *Circulation* 1998;97:2025–2030.

310. King SB III, Ullyot DJ, Basta L, et al. Task Force 2: Application of medical and surgical interventions near the end of life. *J Am Coll Cardiol* 1998;31:917–949.

312. Gibson CM, Goel M, Cohen DJ, et al, for the RESTORE Investigators. Six month angiographic and clinical follow-up of patients prospectively randomized to receive either tirofiban or placebo during angioplasty in the RESTORE trial. *J Am Coll Cardiol* 1998;32:28–34.

320. King SB III. The development of interventional cardiology. *J Am Coll Cardiol* 1998; 31:Suppl. B:64–88.

JOHN WEBSTER KIRKLIN, MD:
A Conversation With the Editor*

I first met John Kirklin in 1969 when he was 52 years old. The occasion was a committee which had been formed to unify the nomenclature and coding of cardiovascular disease in children. That committee met on several occasions, and thus, I had an opportunity in a small room to witness John Kirklin in action. I remember being enormously impressed with the quiet precision with which he stated his views. There was never any doubt what his views were on a particular topic, but his manner was gentlemanly and persuasive without being overbearing. Of course, I had been fascinated by his rapid rise to fame at such a young age at the Mayo Clinic, and his essentially capturing cardiac surgery at that famous institution in his early 30s, and then within about 10 years becoming the first Chairman of Surgery there. His move to Alabama in 1966 when he was 49 years old was both a surprise to me and a fascination for me. I wondered why a man at the peak of his influence at a world famous institution would leave to move to a relatively impoverished state and to a medical center that was anything but the Mayo Clinic at the time. It was not long, however, before patients from all over the world were coming to Birmingham and young physicians were knocking on his door to train in his department. His high volume of publications continued after his coming to Birmingham, and it was not long before the Medical Center at the University of Alabama in Birmingham was well known all over the world.

Then in February 1978 I had another encounter with John Kirklin, and it had a lasting impact on me. A year earlier The American College of Cardiology had asked me to direct a course at their newly built Heart House, and I suggested one on the multidisciplinary approach to congenital heart disease. Jesse Edwards, Mary Ellen Engle, Sam Kaplan, and John Kirklin participated. During the 3 days of the meeting, 21 specific congenital cardiovascular malformations were discussed with either Jesse Edwards or myself describing morphologic features, either Mary Ellen Engle or Sam Kaplan describing the clinical, roentgenographic, electrocardiographic, and echocardiographic features, and John Kirklin discussing operative treatment and results. The malformations reviewed in this course included such topics as atrial septal defect, ventricular septal defect, aorticopulmonary defects, isolated pulmonic stenosis, tetralogy of Fallot, aortic isthmic coarctation and interruption, aortic valve stenosis, aortic valve atresia and other hypoplastic left heart syndromes, discreet and tunnel subaortic stenosis, supravalvular aortic stenosis, cardiac malpositions, transposition complexes, origin of both great arteries from the right ventricle, asplenia and polysplenia syndromes, pulmonic valve atresia with intact ventricular septum, tricuspid valve atresia, congenital mitral regurgitation and mitral valve prolapse, anomalous origin of one or both major coronary arteries, left ventricular inflow obstruction, the Epstein malformation, persistent truncus arteriosus, vascular rings, and congenital aortic regurgitation. John Kirklin presented his data with numbers and results for each of these specific anomalies. The science and precision of his presentations were overwhelming. Any observer at that conference could appreciate the desire for precision and quantitation sought in every aspect of his life by John Kirklin. I thought that 3-day conference personified the essence of this man. He brought that precision and conciseness to the operating room, to the intensive care unit, and to life in general. John Kirklin is the greatest scientific cardiac surgeon of this century and his contributions will continue to be influential many decades after he is gone.

William Clifford Roberts, MD[†] (hereinafter, WCR): *Dr. Kirklin, what I would like to try to learn from you is what gave you that desire to excel far above the pack. I wonder if you could start by talking about your parents. What it was like growing up in Muncie, Indiana? Did you have brothers and sisters? What do you remember from very youngest times?*

John Webster Kirklin, MD[†] (hereinafter, JWK): Well, what drove me, I suppose, is *the lure of the unknown*. Maybe that is what everybody says, but that is a very conscious appeal to me. What is not known has always made me curious, challenged me. As far as growing up, I don't remember very much about Muncie, Indiana, because my family left there when I was about 8 years old and my father accepted a position as a radiologist at the Mayo Clinic. I really grew up in Rochester, Minnesota. I don't have any outstanding memories of that era, at least related to medicine, except that when I left to go to college at the University of Minnesota the one thing I was pretty sure of was that I did not want to be a doctor. At the University of Minnesota, those 4 years were very formative to me in a lot of ways. I don't know exactly why, maybe just my age, or whatever it was, but I came under the influence of a biochemist named, Gortner, a great guy, not very well-known today, probably long ago dead, but he taught biochemistry at the University of Minnesota out on what was called "the farm" campus, not really part of the main university. He was a great man and had a reputation with all great chemists. The people in the Department of Chemistry and also in the Department of Physics at the University of

* This series of interviews are underwritten by an unrestricted grant from Bristol Myers Squibb.

† Baylor Cardiovascular Institute, Baylor University Medical Center, Dallas, Texas 75246.

‡ Department of Surgery, Division of Cardiovascular Surgery, University of Alabama School of Medicine, Birmingham, Alabama 35294-0007.

FIGURE 1. Photograph of JWK during the interview (by WCR).

Minnesota really attracted me. I liked what they did and what they taught. I suppose those years shaped me as much as anything else. Plus, the first year at Harvard Medical School, there was a guy named, A. Baird Hastings, teaching biochemistry. I spent the summer between the first and second years of medical school in Boston working in the laboratories of that department with Logan. I stayed with a couple of friends of mine, Bill Christiansen, and another from Michigan, Bill Vandorlaan, who became a well-known endocrinologist on the West coast. No doubt I was enormously enamored by those sciences and I suppose I developed a little bit of snootiness, intellectual arrogance, if you will, just a little, not a lot but a little, just enough to make me want to be different than most physicians. That is probably what started it.

WCR: *Did you have brothers and sisters?*

JWK: I had one sister, 4 years younger than me, and she is now dead. No brothers.

WCR: *You were the only boy and you were the older of the 2 siblings. Was there medicine in your family other than your father?*

JWK: No, there wasn't, and my father did not bring his work home. There was not much talk about medicine around the house. By the time I was beginning to finish at the university and was interested in medicine, I spent a lot of time with my father and watched him work, watched the operations and all that. Before that I had not particularly paid much attention to the Mayo Clinic.

WCR: *What was home life like in Minnesota. When your father came home, I presume his hours were relatively regular, did you'll sit around the dining table at night and have discussions on this or that topic? Was it an intellectual environs that you grew up in?*

JWK: Not particularly. I have a little trouble separating that period from later periods, but I don't think it was a particularly intellectual environment. I always was great in school. It was very easy for me. I got great grades and they all liked that, but there really wasn't much intellectual format.

WCR: *When you were in high school, did you play sports?*

JWK: Not competitively. I played the usual stuff kids play, tennis, basketball, a little bit of baseball, but never competitively.

WCR: *You were sort of a small guy.*

JWK: Yes, I was a small guy and still am. In college I weighed only 130 pounds.

WCR: *Why did you decide to go to the University of Minnesota to college? What were you planning to major in when you went off to college?*

JWK: I went to the University of Minnesota because a lot of my friends were going to Dartmouth, Harvard, Yale, and all of that, and I decided I wouldn't try, I would go to the university. I don't think any of my friends from Rochester went to the University of Minnesota when I did. It was a big school, much bigger now, but it was even then a huge university—easy to get lost in the mob. I figured if I made it there, I could make it anyplace.

WCR: *So you enjoyed the challenge of a big environs. You must have liked your home to want to go only 100 miles or so away to college.*

JWK: I am not sure that had much to do with it. I didn't go home very much.

WCR: *You were born in 1917. You went off to college in 1934?*

JWK: Yes, and I graduated from Harvard Medical School in 1942. I spent 4 years in college and 4 years in medical school. I graduated from the University of Minnesota in 1938.

WCR: *So that was in the midst of the depression. Were you conscious of the depression going on in the USA in Minnesota as a youngster?*

JWK: I was conscious of it, but I think one of the many things my father did for me was to shield me from it. He never talked about money, never complained about money, never said he had to borrow money to help me go to school, all of which he did, but he never discussed it with me. He just shielded me from that world.

WCR: *So you sort of took it for granted that you could go wherever you wanted and your family was supportive of that.*

JWK: Absolutely. My father played no role in where I went. He said, ''That is up to you.''

WCR: *What do you remember about college? Did you enjoy it? Did you have a good time?*

JWK: I had a wonderful time. I was the student manager of the football team for 4 years. At that time, the University of Minnesota football team was the greatest in the country, national champions for 3 years. I traveled with the team, and I adored every second of that football job. It is perhaps my fondest memory of the university. I also graduated with a lot of degrees, along with Phi Beta Kappa, and I liked that, but that was easy for me. I spent long hours on that dumb football manager's job.

WCR: *What did you do? What did "student manager" mean?*

JWK: As the freshman and sophomore manager, you were just an equipment "scuff pup." You picked up the footballs and shoulder pads after the players were done and put them away. In the junior and senior years, it was a white collar job and a very nice job, because you got to know the players, the coaches, you traveled with the team. It was fun.

WCR: *So you learned something about management during that period of time.*

JWK: The team had a great coach, a fellow named Bernie Berman. Nowadays most people do not remember him, but he was great by any standard. I enjoyed knowing him a lot.

WCR: *Have you kept up with some of the football players and coaches?*

JWK: Only, Bud Wilkinson. He was also in the same fraternity. He was one year ahead of me in school, and of course, he was a great football player. I knew him quite well.

WCR: *What did you major in in college?*

JWK: I think I majored in psychology because I could get to all those classes and still be the manager of the football team. I think I had 2 minors: 1 in biochemistry and 1 in abnormal psychology.

WCR: *So you went to the University of Minnesota without the intention of going to medical school. What made you switch to medicine?*

JWK: I don't know Bill. I suppose deep in my heart I always wanted to but would not let it surface. I don't know, just all of a sudden I wanted to go to medical school, and I wanted to go to Harvard Medical School.

WCR: *Why did you choose Harvard?*

JWK: I don't know. It was said to be hard to get into. Perhaps that was one reason. I don't really know. It had a great reputation. I asked around in Rochester, and everybody thought Harvard was a pretty good school.

WCR: *So you went off to Boston in 1938, having lived in a relatively small town (Rochester) and in a relatively large town (Minneapolis). Was Boston agreeable to you once arriving as a 21 year old?*

JWK: Yes.

WCR: *In medical school, did you find the teaching good? Was it better than it was at the University of Minnesota? Were you impressed with the way they taught or were you a bit disappointed?*

JWK: Neither. I was impressed with the people primarily.

WCR: *Your student colleagues or the faculty?*

JWK: I really meant the faculty, but the student colleagues were outstanding also. Many of them were my best friends for many, many years after that. The faculty was highly impressive. For example, in our freshman years, there were Saturday morning courses and one morning early in the year there was a course in wound healing given by Robert E. Gross, and when he walked in the room and had talked for a few

minutes, there were 100 cardiac surgeons in the audience. A lot of people like that had a profound impression on all of us.

WCR: *So you eventually went up and trained with him?*

JWK: Yes, right after I got out of the Army.

WCR: *Who had the biggest impact on you in medical school?*

JWK: Robert Gross, no question about it.

WCR: *How long was it after you entered medical school that you decided that "by golly, I am going to be a surgeon"?*

JWK: I don't know. I suppose I always wanted to be a surgeon. Maybe the glamour of it.

WCR: *Did you always like to work with your hands? Did you like to build things when you were a youngster.*

JWK: A little bit but I don't think anymore than anybody else. Not particularly.

WCR: *When you were in medical school, did you do any research?*

JWK: Yes, I spent one summer in the biochemistry laboratories.

WCR: *You enjoyed that?*

JWK: I did.

WCR: *You went 4 years to medical school, although the war had started in your senior year.*

JWK: The accelerated programs had not quite begun. The 999 internship program was in effect at that time.

WCR: *Who were some of your classmates in medical school that have done very well?*

JWK: There are so many, and one was Hans Zinsser. I can't think but there were a bunch of them. John Merrill, perhaps, was one of the best known. Some of them were surgeons. A few of them were heart surgeons.

WCR: *How many were in your class at Harvard?*

JWK: I think 110.

WCR: *Were you number 1 in your graduating class?*

JWK: I think so.

WCR: *Were you number 1 when you graduated from the University of Minnesota as far as you could tell.*

JWK: I was in a very small top percent.

WCR: *Did you have to study hard to make those grades or did they seem to come easy for you.*

JWK: Easy, I think.

WCR: *Here you were in Boston, you had the Brigham Hospital, the Massachusetts General, and you in 1942 decided to intern at the University of Pennsylvania. What was behind that decision?*

JWK: Sitting here thinking back, I suppose I was just sort of contrary. I did not want to follow the herd. Everybody said, "You've got to intern in Boston. It is the only place in the world." I knew it was not the only place in the world so I decided to go somewhere else.

WCR: *How did you like the University of Pennsylvania Hospital? Was that what you wanted after you got there?*

FIGURE 2. Photograph of JWK during the interview (by WCR).

JWK: It was a rotating internship. The Boston internships were all straight internships. I was interested in a rotating internship. I don't know why, but I was.

WCR: *During your year in Philadelphia, was there anybody who really had an impact on you?*

JWK: Perhaps 2 people, Jonathan Rhodes was there. Remember now that this was during World War II and a lot of those people were off to the war. Dr. Rhodes was there. Then there was a guy who was an assistant resident in medicine named Franklin Murphy. I don't know if you ever knew him, but he became a very famous person. He went to the University of Kansas as the Dean and then maybe as the vice-president. Then he went to California to the new school in Los Angeles, UCLA, built around a fancy new hospital. He went out there where he became the Chancellor. Then he went to become the CEO of the Times/Mirror Corporation. He was a high-school all-state halfback. A very unusual guy who I got to know pretty well, and who I enjoyed a lot. He had a big impact on me.

WCR: *Even though you decided to take a rotating internship, you always knew you wanted to go into surgery.*

JWK: Absolutely.

WCR: *In retrospect, were you glad you did the rotating internship?*

JWK: Surely.

WCR: *Most of your classmates took a straight medicine or straight surgical internship? So you were sort of a rebel in your choice? In other words, not many people from Harvard Medical School went for rotating internships.*

JWK: No, no one had for a long time.

WCR: *What did your colleagues, your classmates, and the faculty at Harvard think about this, the top fellow in the class taking a rotating internship?*

JWK: I don't know and I didn't care.

WCR: *Why did you decide to leave Philadelphia after 1 year to go to the Mayo Clinic?*

JWK: It was the 999 era, and you took a 9-month internship, then you had to commit to another 9 months or be willing to be drafted. I just decided to go back to Rochester for 9 more months, rather than staying in Pennsylvania. I did not think it was all that great, and I was anxious to get started with a surgical career, so I decided to go back to Rochester to do a surgical residency.

WCR: *Had you known a good number of the surgery faculty at the Mayo Clinic through your father? Would they come over to your house?*

JWK: No, not so much. I knew most of them, a little, not very well.

WCR: *When you got back there you liked it right away? You were pleased you made the change?*

JWK: Fairly pleased. I was disappointed in having to spend so much time on the medical service, but other than that I was pleased. I was happy.

WCR: *Did you get to do enough operating yourself right away or not?*

JWK: No, the Mayo Clinic does not work that way or it didn't then. It does now. I was just learning and excited about everything. I met my wife.

WCR: *You met your wife there? Your wife is a physician? At what stage was she?*

JWK: She came there as a resident in medicine at the same time I came as a resident in surgery.

WCR: *That was April 1943. When did you get married?*

JWK: In December 1943.

WCR: *You met and 6 months later you were married? Has your wife practiced while you have been married or not?*

JWK: Don't forget this was World War II. I went off to the service, knew I was going to go to a U.S. place for awhile so she decided she would go with me. She was pregnant at the time, and our child was born in an Army Hospital. Then, when I finished the service, we went back to Rochester. We had 2 children by then so she was pretty busy. She never finished her training, but when we came to Birmingham she began to work again, not as a practicing physician but in various clinics.

WCR: *So at age 26 in December 1943, you got married. Where did you go in the Army? What did you do those 27 months?*

JWK: I was a neurosurgeon!

WCR: *Where were you?*

JWK: The reason is that I had enough general surgical training to get a B medical occupational specialty in surgery but not an A. When I went in the service it was just at the time of the landing on the Normandy beaches, the Spring of 1944. The Army had a massive number of head injuries, peripheral nerve injuries, so they took some of us who had some general surgical training, not enough to be qualified general surgeons, sent us to neurosurgical school, sent me back to Philadelphia for 5 weeks, then we were neurosurgeons. For $2\frac{1}{2}$ years I practiced neurosurgery in the U.S. Army.

WCR: *Where were you?*

JWK: I was in Springfield, Missouri, at a place called O'Reilly General Hospital.

WCR: *You spent your full time there other than the 5 weeks or so in Philadelphia.*

JWK: I had just joined one of those auxiliary surgical teams as the war came to a close. I had just been assigned to go to the Pacific as the war ended.

WCR: *That must have been an exciting experience to learn a new specialty.*

JWK: I operated day and night, every day of the week practically. Worked under a wonderful man named Francis Murphy who was a neurosurgeon in Memphis. He is now dead. I got a lot of experience. It was a wonderful experience.

WCR: *You were the prime operator in no time flat. You were doing craniotomies, etc.*

JWK: Mostly peripheral nerve injuries, some sympathectomies, a few craniotomies, not many. Those people usually did not live to get there.

WCR: *Your period in the Army was in actuality a period of surgical training for you?*

JWK: Absolutely.

WCR: *So when you went back to the Mayo Clinic, it was almost like you had had a continual surgical residency since you began essentially in July 1943? You went back to the Mayo Clinic after the Army in October 1946. As a resident you only had 2 more years of training in surgery officially there at the Mayo Clinic. Is that correct?*

JWK: I went back to the Mayo Clinic primarily to spend a little time before I could go back to Boston to work with Dr. Gross for 6 months, which I did in 1948.

WCR: *The first 2 years back at the Mayo Clinic you were doing essentially general surgery. Did you do much chest surgery in that period? When you finished the Mayo Clinic did you feel comfortable in chest surgery?*

JWK: I felt comfortable with surgery in general. I had fantastic experience in the Army so I knew my way around the extremities, the neck, and then with my subsequent training at the Mayo Clinic, I was really a general surgeon. I did hysterectomies and so on.

WCR: *So during the 2 years of residency at the Mayo Clinic you were operating all you wanted to? Then in 1948 you went to the Children's Hospital for 6 months? What was that like.*

JWK: It was a great, great experience, primarily, I suppose, because of Dr. Gross, who was a fabulous surgeon, even in retrospect.

WCR: *When you say fabulous, do you mean technically, exquisitely, precise or what?*

JWK: Technically, an exquisite surgeon with a good mind, and just a great man.

WCR: *Was he the best surgeon technically you had encountered?*

JWK: I think so. We used to sit around at night with notebooks (I wished I had saved them), drawing all the things we could do if we could ever get inside the heart. In 1948, I had tons of drawings about fixing ventricular septal defects and repairing tetralogies, fixing mitral valves, all ready once we could get into the heart. It was interesting.

WCR: *Were these discussions with Gross?*

JWK: No, with colleagues, other residents.

WCR: *You were sort of off on your own in many of these many mental exercises before the pump came along.*

JWK: After I got back to Rochester, a fellow named Jesse Edwards was there and he was a very important component in that sort of internal operating. I learned about cardiac pathology from Jesse.

WCR: *When you went to work for Robert Gross for these 6 months, were you the only fellow with him?*

JWK: No, I was the junior resident technically. I had to wait for a spot, because, of course, everybody wanted to work with him. So I was a junior resident and the first rotation I was on was neurosurgery for I think 2 months, but the rest of the 6 months I spent scrubbing with Dr. Gross and doing a few hernias.

WCR: *In actuality you would have taken the 6 months with Robert Gross anytime during that 3-year period after you went back to the Mayo Clinic, when the slot opened up?*

JWK: I arranged that when I was still in the Army. It was very hard to get a job with him.

WCR: *When you worked with Gross, you were the first assistant? Did he let you do any cases as primary operator?*

JWK: I don't think I did any with him. I did a lot of cases at Children's as the primary operator, but I don't think I did with Gross.

WCR: *You enjoyed operating with him? How was he in the operating room? Did he talk or chat or was he totally focused on the job he was doing?*

JWK: The answer to that question is best answered by the following: I would pass him in the halls frequently, of course, and sometimes he would see me coming down the hall and he never said a word, so I did not say anything to him either. Sometimes I would pass him and he would stop and chat, so I got along great with him, because I think I knew how to get along with him. If he did not want to talk, I wouldn't. It was the same in the operating room. He would sometimes talk about the election of the Mayor of Boston, how lousy he was. Other times he would go 2 or 3 cases and not say a word, so I did not say anything either.

WCR: *So you figured out when to keep you mouth shut and when to converse with him. You felt parallel or in communication with him.*

JWK: I felt totally comfortable with him.

WCR: *Did he invite you to his house? Did you become friends with his wife and 2 daughters?*

JWK: Not close friends, but friends.

WCR: *When you left after those 6 months, did you consider him the best you had thus far encountered?*

JWK: Yes, and I was lucky enough to somehow keep crossing his path and seeing him. I sort of thought I had a special relationship with the guy.

WCR: *What were his work habits like? What time did he get to the hospital?*

JWK: Bill, I don't know. It just seems to me he was always there. I think he must have come early, but he was not a slave to the business by any means. He enjoyed living a lot. He was just a great guy to me, but not for everybody. A lot of people did not like him.

WCR: *You felt very comfortable that when he operated on people they were getting the best at that time. Was he an arrogant man?*

JWK: Many people would say so. He was not my definition of arrogance.

WCR: *He was still a pretty young fellow at that time. How did he rise so quickly up there.*

JWK: He closed a ductus while, his boss, Dr. William E. Ladd, was out of town. He became famous overnight. Dr. Gross was a senior resident. Gross did the ductus, the kid survived, and Gross was famous.

WCR: *From that point on people came directly to see Gross? How did Ladd react to all of that?*

JWK: Dr. Ladd was quite an old man by then. He was still fully active, but he retired within a few years. I think he had retired by 1948 when I was there. Dr. Gross was the Professor. There was not much time for Dr. Ladd to react. People said he did not like it very well, and he raised hell when he got back to work after the famous ductus, but what could he do. When you have a famous pupil, what can you do?

WCR: *Then, you went back to the Mayo Clinic and you had another year. Were you still in training for another year?*

JWK: Yes, I interrupted my training there to be with Dr. Gross.

WCR: *In actuality when you went back to the Mayo Clinic you were doing the same thing you were doing before, continuing your residency in general surgery.*

JWK: Yes. It was not until January 1950 that I became a member of the staff with full operating privileges.

WCR: *You knew they were going to ask you to join the staff, but you did not know that when you went back for that final year?*

JWK: No.

WCR: *So at age 31 years old, you are a member of the surgical staff of the Mayo Clinic. At that time were there boards in thoracic surgery?*

JWK: In thoracic surgery, yes, but not in cardiac surgery.

WCR: *You took your boards in general and then in thoracic surgery? Once you went on the faculty, you were doing more thoracic than you were doing general or not?*

JWK: Fifty/fifty perhaps. That was sort of the manner of living at that time. That is what everybody did.

WCR: *Up until that point, you had not published any articles in medical journals?*

JWK: I had published 1 article the summer in medical school while working in biochemistry. I published 2 or 3 articles while doing neurosurgery in the Army.

FIGURE 3. Photograph of JWK during the interview (by WCR).

WCR: *Here you are the 31-year-old new faculty person. Was anybody smothering you or looking over your shoulder or were you sort of on your own?*

JWK: I was for sure on my own, but I had a guy named Jim Clagett, and his predecessor, Dr. Harrington, who were senior thoracic surgeons at the Mayo Clinic, who were very good to me, totally supportive, very helpful, could not have been better.

WCR: *Clagett was how old then?*

JWK: I would guess 40.

WCR: *You mentioned when we started this discussion that what drove you was your curiosity, your desire to figure things out, to learn new things, to make innovations. Did you know Gibbon in Philadelphia when you were in that city?*

JWK: No, he was away with the U.S. Army or Navy. Also, he worked at Jefferson, a different hospital.

WCR: *So, when did you get wind of Gibbon's working on a heart/lung machine?*

JWK: I am not sure, Bill. All I can remember is that in 1952, at the Surgical Forums of the American College of Surgeons, Dr. Gross was presiding, and Dr. Gibbons gave a paper about his experience with dogs, and he said, "I think we are soon going to use this on people." That is when I suppose I really became conscious of it. Up until that time, I did mainly 2 operations at the Mayo Clinic: lymph node biopsies and mitral commissurotomies. That is what I did most everyday. Once in a while a gastric resection or colon resection, mitral commissurotomies, a new exciting operation, and sometimes a hernia.

WCR: *So you were the Mayo Clinic mitral commissurotomy person. How did you capture that? That was an exciting thing. Clagett did not want to do that?*

JWK: No, he didn't. Bob Glover had been trained at the Mayo Clinic. I knew him quite well, and somehow or another things were much easier being that I knew Dr. Bailey quite well. I knew Dwight Harken, of course. I had known him in Boston. We used to remark about his working in the dog lab doing this stuff. Mitral commissurotomy was sort of like the back of my hand to me. Before I had ever done one I had learned a lot about it, heard about it, lived and breathed it. It was exciting. There were only a few places in the world doing this. Mayo Clinic had plenty of cases so I did them.

WCR: *You enjoyed being in the heart?*

JWK: Sure. Absolutely.

WCR: *What was the first creative, innovative thing you did at the Mayo Clinic?*

JWK: I don't know the answer to that. I right away found myself in the middle of probably the most exciting group of people I had ever worked with, Howard Burchell, Earl Wood, Jesse Edwards, David Donald, and less well-known, but an experimental surgeon, Jim DuShane, and with that group of people, life was just terribly exciting. I think together we did a hell of a lot of innovative things. It is hard to take them apart, but we published tons of papers, and everyday was something new and exciting.

WCR: *Gibbon closed an atrial septal defect in 1953?*

JWK: Yes, it was in 1953. I can remember very well the period when that was done. My life in that era began when I was sitting talking to Earl Wood, who had just come back from an autopsy done by Jesse Edwards on a patient of Howard Burchell's who I had operated on by the closed method, a patient with pulmonary stenosis and a severe subvalvular (infundibular) obstruction. Earl Wood said: "You know, you are never going to do any better until you get inside that heart and look at it." I said, "Yes, I guess so." I was depressed, of course, about losing somebody. I think we decided that day to move ahead. "Okay, that is what we are going to do," we said. That was 1952, and Gibbon did not do his first successful case until 1953. We made a trip around the country then. Howard didn't go, Jesse didn't go, Earl went part of the time. I went all the time. Dave Donald went. We visited Gibbon's place. We visited Dewey Dodderal in Detroit and Bill Mustard in Toronto. Dodderal's pump looked like a car engine. He was a well-known thoracic surgeon, well-known for working experimentally with a machine built by General Motors. Gibbon was working with his machine which looked like an IBM computer because it had been built by IBM. Bill Mustard was working with monkey lungs as an oxygenator. Nobody was doing any clinical work. I suppose if I have any great, good luck it is that I am very impatient with people talking vaguely and promising, "We are fixing to get ready to do that." So, I decided to hell with it, we needed to do it, not just sit around talking about it or doing it on dogs. I had already had about a year and one-half in the dog lab with a simple pump oxygenator. We got permission from Gibbon and IBM to build essentially their machine. It was different from the General Motors one, but a little similar, quite a bit better. When we had it, we used it.

WCR: *When did you first use it?*

JWK: March 1955, and every year on that day I still get a letter from Howard Burchell, including 1996, 1997, and I'm sure I will get one in 1998. He is a special guy.

WCR: *Did you see Howard Burchell, Jesse Edwards, Earl Wood, a lot?*

JWK: Everyday practically.

WCR: *When you were at the Mayo Clinic, it is my understanding you operated every other day. So 1 week you operated 3 days, the next week 2 days.*

JWK: That came into effect while I was there, but it was not that way initially. You operated every other day including Saturday.

WCR: *So it became 3 days a week. Did you like that?*

JWK: It was okay. It was all I knew.

WCR: *The days you were not operating, you were seeing patients you were going to operate on the next day?*

JWK: Plus, working in the experimental laboratory.

WCR: *After the first pump operation, I gather that open heart surgery by you just absolutely took off, and each year the number of cases increased.*

JWK: So did the length of the waiting period. It became over a year sometimes. I will tell you a little story about that period, about Russell Brock, because you probably knew him and know that he was a very difficult, tough guy. I forget what day we did the first operation, let's say it was a Tuesday, and Tuesday night Dr. Varco called me from Minneapolis (We all knew each other quite well.) so, among other things, he said, "We have a visitor who would like to come down and talk to you." I said "That is fine, who is it?," and he said, "Russell Brock." He wanted to know if we were going to do another case, and I said, "Yes, we are going to do one Thursday." Russell came down Wednesday from Minneapolis and said, "Now, I guess you are going to do a case tomorrow." I said, "We are." He said, "I won't come to the operation." I said, "You have to, you are most welcome." He said, "No, I think there will be concern over a famous visitor." I said, "You will be most welcome." He said, "I want to sit in the gallery someplace where I won't be conspicuous, I don't want to bother you." He came and sat and did not open his mouth, just sat there. Absolutely the most consideration to a young surgeon that you can imagine. Most people don't think that about Russell Brock, but that is the way he was. That was a great period and, of course, it was a period when nobody knew the indications and so on. I saw a lot of patients that nobody knew whether they should be operated on or not. That is the reason I saw Howard Burchell, Jim DuShane and all those people quite a lot.

WCR: *So most of the conditions of the patients having cardiac operations using cardiopulmonary bypass had never been operated on before. You could not read about these conditions in the library because no one had operated on them before. You were oper-*

ating so much you could not put all the new innovations together at once.

JWK: We published them pretty much as they occurred.

WCR: *What was life like on a day-to-day basis. Your bibliography, no question, just sky rocketed during that period of time.*

JWK: The work ethic in southern Minnesota is enormous. Everybody works very hard. You don't survive through the winter if you don't work hard and plan ahead. We sort of reflected the area. You had to plan, work hard, "no rest for the wicked." We all worked very hard. We would get to work at 5:30 in the morning. It was an exciting, terribly busy, wonderful time.

WCR: *What time would you leave the hospital at night as a rule?*

JWK: As a rule, I don't know, but often it was 10:00 or 11:00 P.M.

WCR: *You were living at that hospital during that period. How did you write your manuscripts? Did you dictate, did you write them in pencil?*

JWK: I wrote them in pencil.

WCR: *When would you do most of your writing?*

JWK: Probably on the weekends and nonoperative days. I don't remember exactly, but I am almost sure that is when it was.

WCR: *It must have been a loss when Jesse Edwards left in 1960.*

JWK: It was a big loss. Actually, however, he never really left. Even to this day he goes back pretty frequently.

WCR: *At least you did not see him on a day-to-day basis. You found him very helpful, particularly early on, in your getting familiar with the inside of the heart?*

JWK: Extremely helpful. One day I asked Jess, "Where is the bundle of His?" He said, "I am not sure, but I'll tell you a person who does know and that is Maurice Lev and you should go see him." The next day I got on an airplane and went down to Miami to see him. I cannot say too much positive about Jess Edwards' influence on all of us. He was just a very important member of a small group.

WCR: *You were the first and I gather the only one to use the pump there early on, 1955 or 1956. Did anybody else at the Mayo Clinic do cases using cardiopulmonary bypass early on. I gather that Dwight McGoon did not come until later?*

JWK: Dwight came in 1958. A fellow named Bunky Ellis, who went to Boston about a year after I left, came and he did some of the cases.

WCR: *In 1964 you became Chairman of the Department of Surgery at the Mayo Clinic. How did that work out?*

JWK: I wanted it badly. There had never been a Chairman of a Department before. Everybody was equal among kings.

WCR: *Really. You were the first Chairman of Surgery at the Mayo Clinic.*

JWK: I think that is true. It became more and more obvious to me that the Surgery Department needed a Chairman. That was a very important period for me. I totally changed the residency system, became a member of the Board of Governors, so I had some voice in the overall clinic policy. It was an added challenge.

WCR: *But it was good preparation for what came later, I presume, or did you already know what you wanted to do?*

JWK: No, I didn't. I was too busy to know what I wanted to do the next year. I was just too busy, too happy, too faced with problems needing solutions which required a lot of thought and effort. I had no idea of leaving the Mayo Clinic until about 1965 when I began to get invitations to various places who wanted a Professor of Surgery. I thought about it. I had a second son, Jim, who was a state champion springboard diver, and he did not want to leave until after his senior year. For one reason or another, I stayed there, even after I began to be bitten by that bug, until 1966.

WCR: *Why did you get bitten? Here you were on the Board of Governors, the Chairman of the Department of Surgery. Were those things going to run out? I mean, you weren't going to be on the Board of Governors forever?*

JWK: No, but they were not about to run out. "What else could I do?" I asked myself.

WCR: *How did the University of Alabama come about? I am sure you had plenty of offers to a lot of different places. At the time you received an offer from the University of Alabama at Birmingham (UAB), I guess cardiology was quite good at the UAB.*

JWK: It was pretty good. The main thing about the UAB was that there was not much here.

WCR: *So that just aroused your competitive spirit?*

JWK: Not quite exactly. Even though I had been terribly busy, operating, and thinking about things, doing special studies, all the time in my mind, I suppose, I was formulating a lot of opinions about how things should be done, what should determine the number of residents that a hospital takes, how a surgical program really should be run, should the residents just be turned free to operate willy-nilly or should they never operate or something in between. What were the appropriate arrangements between people, financial arrangements, everything, and it was time for me to do an experiment, so I came to the UAB. I have never said it that way before but that is really it.

WCR: *So you wanted to see if you could pull off what you had formulated in your mind as an ideal Department of Surgery?*

JWK: My interests were not strictly in the Department of Surgery. They were in the UAB. It was the entire medical center.

WCR: *So you thought you would have an institutional impact as well as a departmental impact?*

JWK: I was sure I would. At least, I hoped I would.

WCR: *How did it actually come about. Did you receive a letter from the Dean or President or Provost from UAB? What were the details?*

JWK: Do you remember a man named Joe Reeves? Joe was there. He called me, and that is the way I first knew about it. They had invited Frannie Moore (Boston) to be their external advisor and he called me. That is the way I got started.

WCR: *Joe Reeves called you and said "come on down here and visit us."*

JWK: He said, "We need a new Professor of Surgery." Dr. Lyons had died of a brain tumor, suddenly, unexpectedly. So they suddenly needed a new chairman.

WCR: *Here you were, having grown up in and now living in Rochester, Minnesota, with relatively brief spans in Minneapolis and Boston, and suddenly you are looking at a spot in the deep South. When you came down to Birmingham to look things over, what happened? How did you react? All these buildings that I see here now were not here then.*

JWK: No, they weren't here. I knew what I was getting into. I came down here a few times. I knew it would be really tough, very difficult. All of my friends in Rochester said, "How in the world can you go down there with their attitude about the blacks?" Nobody in Rochester knew anything about blacks. A big surprise is that I was able to continue my cardiac surgical life at the same pace as in Rochester, found new colleagues, good colleagues. The patients came.

WCR: *When you came down here the first time, did you say "no, I don't want to get into this" or did you keep investigating?*

JWK: I said to them and to myself, "I need to know more about this." I think I came down 3 times.

WCR: *When you decided to come here, you came not only as Chairman of the Department of Surgery with yourself being Director of the Division of Cardiovascular Surgery, you also came as Chief of the Medical Staff. You must have come down here with the authority to carry out all the objectives that you had formulated in your mind that you wanted to do if you had a department you could make your own. In other words, did you have hiring and firing rights of people in the intensive care unit? Did you have control over the nursing service in surgery?*

JWK: Bill, I did not organize any of that ahead of time. I figured if I couldn't hack it by being there, I couldn't. I figured I could get the authority just because I have always been successful in getting it when I wanted it, and when I wanted it I went after it and got it. I ended up with a whole lot of authority, but no more than I had had at the Mayo Clinic.

WCR: *It sounds to me like you just wanted a fresh challenge. You had conquered about all there was to conquer at the Mayo Clinic. You were now still at a young age, 47, Chairman of the Department of Surgery, already full Professor for 7 years, on the Board of Governors at the Mayo Clinic. Is Jim your oldest or middle child?*

JWK: Middle, we have 3 children.

WCR: *Is the third one a boy or girl?*

JWK: Girl.

WCR: *So you have boy, boy, girl. So your third one was a junior in high school when you left Roch-*

ester. *So 1 more year and they are gone to college. The kids were soon to be gone.*

JWK: My wife was perhaps a little restless in Rochester, because she is a very bright person, was AOA in medical school, and I think she never urged me to stay or leave, but she was favorable to moving.

WCR: *Where was your wife from? Where did she grow up?*

JWK: The state of Washington.

WCR: *So she is a Northwesterner. Where did she go to medical school?*

JWK: Buffalo.

WCR: *She came to Buffalo to go to medical school. Where did she go to college?*

JWK: She went to college at Washington State for her first year and then the University of Oregon.

WCR: *When you came to the UAB, I presume, you changed faculty a good bit, you changed house staff a good bit, relatively rapidly. All of a sudden a flock of patients were coming from all over the world to the UAB. Overnight the whole medical center changes. So everybody was happy. Now what did you find your biggest challenge? Here you are studying patients after operations. When did you get into evaluating who should be operated on, when, timing the procedures, the statistical analyses that you brought into the evaluation. How did this evolve?*

JWK: I think the way everything evolves. You attract colleagues dependent on the environment you build. I was very lucky. I think it must have been 1969 or 1970 when a young man named Gene Blackstone walked into my office and wanted an internship. He has been here ever since and he is a genius, literally.

WCR: *He wanted a surgery internship? Where had he gone to medical school?*

JWK: The University of Chicago.

WCR: *So he walked into your office. I figured you had recruited him. How did you know he was a genius?*

JWK: He walked into my office and said, "I want an internship." I said, "Well, you have to apply through the internship committee, the national mechanism was operating then." He said, "I am not eligible for that." I thought, "Oh God, here is another guy that flunked out of medical school." I said, "Why aren't you eligible?" He said, "Well, I graduated 2 years ago." I said, "What have you been doing since?" He said he had been working with ... He named off the famous people at the University of Chicago. I said, "Have you been getting a Ph.D.?" He said, "No, I didn't have time." So Gene was already a very exceptional person, and as he worked as an intern, it was really obvious he was an exceptional person. He owed the Army/Air Force some time which he then gave to them, came back here, and has been here ever since. He is right next door, and we work very closely together and have for 25 years.

WCR: *Does he operate?*

JWK: No, he is not a surgeon. He is an investigator. He told me, "I don't want to be a surgeon. I want to be an investigator, and I figure the place to do that

is in the Department of Surgery where the action is.''
I figured he was right.

WCR: *He learned statistics on his own.*

JWK: No, at the University of Chicago he worked
under Paul Meier for a year or 2.

WCR: *You were no slouch in the stuff at that time
yourself.*

JWK: We pooled our efforts and there happens to
be a statistician here who is very special, very unique.
I am of the opinion that you will go any place and you
will find a few special people. There were a few
special people here and that made it possible.

WCR: *When you came to the UAB, rather than
operating every other day, you started operating every
day. Is that right?*

JWK: That is true.

WCR: *What was your typical day like after you
had been here 2 or 3 years.*

JWK: I would get up at 4:30 in the morning, work
for an hour at home on something, a book, a paper, or
something like that, come to work, operate maybe
until 1:00 or 2:00.

WCR: *You would get to the hospital at what time?*

JWK: Seven o'clock.

WCR: *But you had been up since 4:30 more or
less. What time would you walk into the operating
room.*

JWK: Seven-thirty. I never liked walking in when
someone else was preparing the patient.

WCR: *Did you do the thoracotomy?*

JWK: Yes, on the first case. Not necessarily on the
next one. We had a lot of wonderful residents.

WCR: *Why did you want to do that? Not many
Chairman of Departments that are cardiac surgeons
do thoracotomies anymore, do they?*

JWK: No, not many people accomplish what I
have done either. Maybe there is a correlation. It is
just that I suppose I am at the same time both confident and fearful. I just want to remember how to
pound in the nails and saw the lumber, and I don't
want to be in a position where I can't survive by
myself, requiring an entourage around me. I never
wanted to be in that position.

WCR: *So on your typical day, you would arrive at
the hospital at 7:00 A.M. You had been up for a couple
of hours before that. First case at 7:30. So how many
patients were you operating on each day at UAB?*

JWK: Not so many a day, maybe 3.

WCR: *So your operations were finished as a rule
by 1 or 2:00 P.M.*

JWK: Usually, but, you know, there is always the
exception that goes until 7:00 or 8:00 P.M.

WCR: *Most days you had some time to take care
of certain administrative tasks later in the afternoon.*

JWK: Administrative, research, data analysis,
things like that.

WCR: *What time would you leave the hospital as
a rule?*

JWK: Usually after dark 7:30, 8:00 o'clock.

WCR: *Were you any good after you got home?*

JWK: No.

FIGURE 4. Photograph of JWK during the interview (by WCR).

WCR: *Did you have a cocktail when you got
home?*

JWK: Usually.

WCR: *Would you do something else or would you
go to bed early?*

JWK: Go to bed early. Both my wife and I enjoy
music a lot so we usually sit down in the living room
and put on a CD or record and have a drink and talk
for a while, eat dinner, not do much after that.

WCR: *You were pretty good when you woke up in
the mornings, but not once you got home at night.*

JWK: I almost never worked at home at night.

WCR: *Now when your kids were young you did
not get home until 10:00 or 11:00 P.M.*

JWK: Too often.

WCR: *What kind of Daddy were you, are you?*

JWK: Probably not very good.

WCR: *When your son Jim was in the diving meets,
you were there?*

JWK: Always.

WCR: *What do your other 2 children do?*

JWK: My oldest son was interested in track. He
ran the 440 in high school. I would always go to that.
Our daughter Helen did the usual things young girls
do, ballet schools. She plays the violin. My wife is a
pianist, not a concert pianist but a serious one. Helen
has fulfilled her desires in that regard. Helen lives in
Gainesville, Florida, where her husband is a professor
of English. She plays in the Jacksonville Symphony.
She is a very talented gal.

WCR: *What does your older son do?*

JWK: He went to Dartmouth College, graduated
with all the honors, went to Harvard Law School
where he lost a little interest in excelling. Then he was
offered a position in a prestigious law firm in New
York which he took, but after about 6 or 8 years, he
became disenchanted with work, very introspective,

tried to commit suicide at one point, ultimately divorced his wife (they have 2 kids), married another woman, still lives in New York. I think he has gotten his act somewhat together now, not at a high level. Maybe he didn't like it there in some way. I don't totally understand. He is different and perhaps when you asked if I was a good father probably not. If I had been, that probably should not have happened to young John. But life unfolds in strange directions.

WCR: *You stepped down as Chairman of the Department of Surgery in 1982, and as Director of the Cardiothoracic Division in 1985. You kept operating. When did you stop operating?*

JWK: I am not sure. Anne, my secretary could tell us, but it must have been about 1990.

WCR: *Why did you stop operating. You look healthy, vigorous.*

JWK: I always knew I would sometime. I have always known that. You may remember Professor E. J. Zerbini, who was a great surgeon in Sal Paulo, Brazil. We all watched him operate long after he should have stopped. I never wanted that to happen to me. I thought the Mayo Clinic plan at that time was a bit too rigorous, no reason to stop at 65 or something just because you reached that age if you were still fit. But I began to wonder if I was doing as good a job as someone else could have done, and you can only live with that so long and then you quit.

WCR: *Did you feel a difference. You are 79 and will be 80 this year. You didn't stop operating until you were 71?*

JWK: Probably.

WCR: *Did you feel at 70 that you were as good as at 40?*

JWK: I probably was better at 70 because I knew more, had more good sense, more experience. Technically, I don't think there is much deterioration. I thought I still did a good job and I always promised myself (I am not sure I hit it exactly) that I would quit before people began to think I needed to.

WCR: *So you were operating and all of a sudden, boom. You said, "This is it."*

JWK: One day I walked out and I have never been back.

WCR: *Are you glad you did that?*

JWK: Yes, I am glad I did it. I am sorry the time came, but I am glad I did it.

WCR: *How many operations do you figure you have done in your life?*

JWK: 10,000, something like that.

WCR: *You mentioned in your book your group did 50,000 operations. How did the book,* Cardiac Surgery, *come about?*

JWK: You remember what you wrote about that, that it would never have a second edition? That is the reason we brought out a second edition! I don't know exactly when I began thinking about a book, but whenever it was, I was in South America at a meeting where Brian Barratt-Boyes was and somehow we found out that each of us was thinking about writing a book. I said to Brian "why don't we do it together?"

He was never in love with the idea, still isn't, but we did it, and I think it was better for having done so.

WCR: *The first edition was 1988. You said in all of the chapters that both of you contributed to each chapter. If you initiated one, you sent it to him and vice versa. You both participated in each of those chapters. Each chapter is really an in-depth discussion of the topic of that particular chapter. You not only provide your own experiences but those that you considered worthwhile. How did you do all that literature work?*

JWK: I suppose we had a little bit of help but mostly we did it ourselves. Besides, Bill, it may be difficult today, but we knew everybody, we talked to everybody, we visited everybody, so, therefore, we remembered their articles very well because you could see the guy in the paper. I think we just knew the field terribly well. We lived in it.

WCR: *How long did it take to do the book?*

JWK: Three or four years.

WCR: *What was your work pattern like? Would you work on that book in the mornings? You were still operating then.*

JWK: I did the first book primarily at home in the mornings. The second edition was done mostly at the university, because that is where I had some help and the whole thing to look at.

WCR: *You wrote out your first draft in pencil? You did not dictate?*

JWK: Very little. I must say I can always tell when someone has dictated a paper.

WCR: *I actually like your reference way with the alphabet, then the number, and, as you say, if you want to later on, you can plug a reference in without having to change every lousy number in the whole shebang. Now that system has not taken off very well. Has anybody else copied you there? I think it is very reasonable. I admire your innovation here.*

How did you like being Editor of the Journal of Thoracic and Cardiovascular Surgery?

JWK: As one editor to another, I actually enjoyed it. I resented to some extent the time it took. As you well know, it takes a huge amount of time, but it was made worthwhile, I thought, by the 5% or 10% of papers that I positively, very favorably improved by being editor, by the people we sent them to, by the decisions we made when they came back, by the suggestions we made to the authors. I think we did a worthwhile job. You must feel that way.

WCR: *How much time did you spend on it?*

JWK: A lot. As I recall, it bridged the period between when I was operating and when I wasn't. So in a way, it was a refuge for using the time that was set free by not operating. I spent a lot of time on it.

WCR: *In retrospect, are you glad you waited to do that magnificent book until you were 71 years of age? So many people do books at age 40. You could not have had as many original contributions, it seems to me, if you had done that way back.*

JWK: I could not have for sure. It seemed a natural time.

WCR: *I think Dwight McGoon's foreword was the*

most beautiful I have ever read in a book. When you were operating, what was your favorite operation? If you could do just 3 operations and that was it, which ones would they have been?

JWK: I suppose the tetrology because it was so varied and so much of it. We lived to create a lot of that stuff. The knowledge maybe as much as the technique.

WCR: *Did you do a lot of switch operations for complete transposition or not?*

JWK: I don't think I ever did that. I was beginning to back away when the arterial switch came along. I am very familiar with it, however.

WCR: *Do you think there will ever be another surgeon that will do the whole gamut like you have done?*

JWK: No. I don't know why, but partly because it is not the fashion. But Dr. Gibbon once said to me, "Kirklin, I am not interested in fashion."

WCR: *It must have been very exciting to see your operative schedule and have these exciting cases lined up one after the other: tetralogy with varying degrees of right ventricular outflow obstruction, then pulmonic valve atresia with ventricular septal defect, then mitral valve replacement, then a coronary bypass for example. Did you like doing the coronary bypass operation?*

JWK: Yes. I think it is very exciting. It is not an easy operation. Everybody does so many of them, I guess they are good, but yes, I thought it was an interesting operation.

WCR: *Can you describe the atmosphere of your operating room? What was it like to be in your operating room when you were doing a tetralogy case, for example?*

JWK: Well, I didn't like the music on, never did, never will. I think it is a distraction to everybody, anytime during the procedure. If I were the patient I wouldn't want anybody, the circulating nurse, or anybody else distracted. This is very serious business, all compacted into a short period of time. At the same moment, people don't perform well if their tension gets too high so you have to break it a little bit. I think it is a very exciting orchestra to be able to conduct. That is the way I tried to play it. Everyone was responsible for everything else. The anesthesiologist was responsible for the "rib spreader" being in properly, and I was held responsible for the endotracheal tube, in a way shared responsibility, a very exciting experience, much more exciting than to be a solo. It is great to forge a group that really acts as one, all for the same purpose.

WCR: *Did you talk much during the operations?*

JWK: I was not silent like Robert Gross. It is not my nature, but I am not terribly talkative. Some people talk every second. I think I talked a fair amount especially once the critical part was over.

WCR: *How did you relax your help, so to speak?*

JWK: Very important maneuver. I think I did it by knowing them quite well, by being sure I knew their names, always, I didn't forget them, and by some little joke or brief report of some sort, half-kidding, half-

serious. One has to do that. The people have to like working if they are going to give that extra little bit that once in a while is required.

WCR: *If one of your patients, lets say, bled postoperatively and you had gone home, did you come back?*

JWK: Usually. Almost always.

WCR: *Did you follow your patients postoperatively? You saw them everyday?*

JWK: Well, I wouldn't say I saw them everyday by the 5th, 6th, or 7th day, but early on I always saw them daily and I saw them before they went home.

WCR: *How were you able to get such good follow-up on all the patients you operated on? You couldn't see them.*

JWK: Just like everybody, plain hard work. We organized a whole bunch of people out there. We spent our money that way instead of taking it home.

WCR: *Do we have too many cardiac surgeons? How is the number going to be cut down?*

JWK: Well, one of the things I am very proud of is that when I came down here eons ago, I set about talking to people, getting information, to see how many new surgeons we needed rather than deciding how many residents we took by the amount of work to be done at the hospital. I figured the state of Alabama needed about 1 new cardiac surgeon every 5 to 8 years, something like that. I was not popular for my thinking and talking that way, but that is what needed to be done. We just overproduced ourselves. I believe it was because the hospital needed to dictate the number of residents rather than society.

WCR: *It seems to me that surgeons today don't get the kind of experience that you had. You grew up on the aorta and esophagus and all the rest of it. You mastered the congenital challenges, valve replacements, the whole gamut. Ninety percent of cardiac operations today are bypasses. Now the congenital heart surgeons are not doing any of the other stuff.*

JWK: That is why I didn't go to the Boston Children's Hospital when I had a chance to go. You never did that yourself. You moved freely through the field of cardiac pathology. It must have been the same reason.

WCR: *More fun that way.*

JWK: It is more fun that way. Absolutely more fun. More exciting, more stimulating.

WCR: *As you look back, did you make any mistakes.*

JWK: Sure, 100's. I think I always tried to identify them and prevent them in the future, but sure I made mistakes.

WCR: *You always analyzed what you were doing? How do you relax?*

JWK: My wife and I had been married about 3 or 4 years and it was very apparent what lay ahead and we would grow further and further apart. I was working all the time. She had the kids to worry about. So we decided we had to find something we could do together that was outside, that was a little dangerous, a little exciting, so we bought a couple of horses. She and I have been riding ever since. Her horse got unruly and she was dislodged from the saddle and broke her hip about 5 or 6 years ago. I still ride 3 times a week.

WCR: *Where do you live here?*

JWK: We built a house outside of town 30 years ago, and we still live there.

WCR: *Do you have acreage to ride on your property?*

JWK: No, I keep the horses boarded out.

WCR: *So, where you board them is where you ride? How long does it take you to get into work from where you live?*

JWK: Not very long. That was a prime consideration. I had to be able to get into work in 10 or 15 minutes. Somebody's bleeding, I need to get there. Now it takes a little longer because it has all built up around us, but where we lived originally south of town, it was in the booneys.

WCR: *Did you play a musical instrument when you were a boy?*

JWK: I used to play the piano some.

WCR: *What are you most proud of that you have been able to accomplish in your professional and personal careers?*

JWK: I think there must be a missing part in me somewhere because I never feel very proud of anything, happy with it, but not particularly proud of it. There is something inside me that makes me take it apart and say I could have done that a little better. I am relatively proud of my contributions to the cardiothoracic world. I am relatively proud of that. I would be disappointed if it had not included clinicians and pathologists. I think we contributed a little but we learned a lot from you. I think I am pleased, maybe not proud of the fact that I have been able to continue to concentrate on details, not be satisfied with just a broad picture. I am proud of the work we have done, but I wish we could have done more and better.

WCR: *The precision.*

JWK: The precision, I think, is the key to everything—in your head, you hands, and everything.

WCR: *Did you do much teaching of medical students when you came to the UAB?*

JWK: I did. Early on every afternoon for an hour I went down to one of the surgical wards where the students were. I was interested in that because I found out very early that the caliber was just as good here as it was where I had come from, but that their early education wasn't, and I found it quite interesting to inquire as to why. It was because of the desperate economic conditions in Alabama between World War I and World War II. It was just pitifully poor. I could only learn all that by really working with the students. Then, I had been here for 6 or 8 years when this epidemic came through of students grading the faculty. I spent zero time after that teaching medical students. Not because they graded me poorly, but I didn't like the idea.

WCR: *How many medical students are there at the UAB.*

JWK: I am not sure—100 I am tempted to think about in every class.

WCR: *The surgery housestaff and fellows in cardiothoracic surgery have been reduced. You need to start cutting down the numbers of medical students.*

JWK: It is a difficult problem. The world today is full of enormous problems. You must think so too. You are thoughtful about things and much of the world today is not very thoughtful. It seems to react more than anything.

WCR: *In the 50 years you have been in medicine and surgery, what surgeons do you really admire?*

JWK: Stanley Crawford. Maybe his is the first name that comes to mind. I had an enormous amount of respect, admiration and love for this man, all those things for Stanley Crawford. He was a great surgeon. Stanley stayed a generalist although he was the world's best when it came to the aorta, and he was also a superb abdominal surgeon. He was probably my greatest hero.

WCR: *You never worked with him?*

JWK: Never, but I somehow got to know him very well, spent a fair amount of time watching him operate. He would come up to Rochester ever so often. There are a lot of great surgeons. I shouldn't really single him out, but that is the name that comes to my mind when one asks about great surgeons.

WCR: *Do you think operating on some portions of the aorta, like the descending thoracic, is a bit more difficult than say aortic valve replacement or a mitral valve replacement?*

JWK: Absolutely. Very difficult.

WCR: *You can't make any mistakes in the aorta.*

JWK: No, and everything is more difficult. The exposure is more difficult, control of the bleeding is more difficult, the diseases are more difficult. There is nothing like an aortic dissection to challenge a surgeon. I think it is a tough, tough area and Stanley was just a master.

WCR: *You must be enormously pleased to have your son follow in your footsteps.*

JWK: I don't know Bill. I never felt particularly pleased, I liked it. The thing I like best is the story about it. He went to Ohio State because they had a great diving coach for college. In his third year, he called me to say, "I think I want to go to medical school." I said, "What?" He said, "Now, I even want to go to Harvard." I said, "That is nice, but you have to be more than wanting to. Why did you call." He said, "Well, I wanted a piece of advice." This was a first. He said, "Should I continue to dive next year? If I continue to dive I am risking not getting into Harvard. I think I will get into medical school some place, but I want to go to Harvard." I said, "Why?" He said, "It is supposed to be the best. If I can't dive, I think I probably can." I told him to go ahead and dive, and he nevertheless got into Harvard. He never dived again after beginning medical school because he was busy studying. Yes, I am proud of him. He has picked a very tough area, cardiac transplantation. I like it better than if he were doing something else, being a lawyer or business man or something.

WCR: *What is on the horizon out there in cardiac surgery? Jim is how old now?*

JWK: Fifty. Does not seem possible.

FIGURE 5. Photograph of JWK during the interview (by WCR).

WCR: *So he has 20 years more of operating.*

JWK: Fifteen, he says.

WCR: *Let's pick a 30-year-old surgeon. What is a 30-year-old cardiovascular surgeon today going to be doing at 55?*

JWK: I am sure things we have not thought about. I am afraid the world around him will limit his repertoire. I am afraid it will, and the reason I think that's bad is that he wants to do as well as he could on whatever he is doing as if he had a little more broad continuing experience. It is no good to be broadly trained and then thereafter do some little deal. People are still people and patients with heart trouble sometimes have trouble with their feet and so forth. I don't know. I think "where is medicine as a whole going to be?" It is very hard to see. I am guessing you and I have lived through the best years.

WCR: *You have interviewed a lot of people through the years, you have picked people to surround you that have obviously done very well on their own. When you pick a person to be a surgery resident or staff person, this is your person, what are you looking for? What characteristics are absolutely essential for you to find out about?*

JWK: I don't agree with the statement I am about tell you completely, but it is a little close. There was a surgeon at the Mayo Clinic called John Waugh, a great surgeon. John used to say, "I can tell you who is going to be a good surgeon by walking down the hall with him." I think there is a little truth to that. In other words, it is a very intuitive plus an analytical thing. I don't think there is any correct answer to the question, and I am not sure I have followed a consistent path. I was disappointed ever so often, but in general I think you just have to pay close attention to details, especially concentrating on the whole person. I can't answer that any other way.

WCR: *How do you handle a person you interview, looks like this person comes with a good record in medical school or further back than that, and low and behold you take him on your service and his hands are atrocious. You just know you don't want this person operating on anybody. How do you handle that type situation?*

JWK: It is difficult. I think the worst solution maybe is to tell him/her that. The best solution is if one can somehow find things that not only he is good at, but he likes, that are outside the operating room, gradually pushing him in that direction so he seems to have made the decisions himself. Often these people are aware of that after a while. They are not ignorant. So I think you just do your best to steer them, encourage them in other directions, for which they have more influence.

WCR: *When you were making the intensive care unit very technologically sophisticated, was that happening elsewhere around the country? You were ahead of the game there by a long shot. Is that not correct?*

JWK: As a matter of fact when we presented a paper at The American Surgical Association a long time ago, Jim Maloney from Los Angeles got up and showed a picture of a distressed child in the intensive care unit, and said "now that picture tells you more than all of this analytical approach could possibly have." I guess I could not have possibly disagreed with anything more. I think we were the first people to automate an intensive care unit, to bring computers into it. We were the first people ever to even have an intensive care unit. Cardiac surgery units were the first intensive care units. I am proud of that. I don't know if I am pleased with it. I think it was a good and correct thing to do. It does not mean you have to forget to smell things, feel things, does not mean that at all. It does not mean you are not a good clinician. It just means you are better if you have some information.

WCR: *It puts science and precision into it. Would you say that the desire to put precision and science* *into everything you do has been maybe your outstanding contribution?*

JWK: I hope so. I sincerely hope so.

WCR: *How would you state that?*

JWK: Just the way you did.

WCR: *You mentioned analyzing the minutia, the details, and when you started measuring pressure in pulmonary arteries, nobody else was measuring this. This is 1 simple example, so to speak.*

JWK: Probably congenitally I was lucky. I just always had a desire to have quantitative information. Information, wherever possible, rather than vagueness. Somehow it was just the way I came. I think the results kept getting better and better because of it.

WCR: *Were there some days in the operating room you were just a lot better than others?*

JWK: I am sure that is true.

WCR: *You had 2 cups of coffee before you walked into the operating room or you had zero?*

JWK: Never. I drank a cup of coffee at breakfast. I never drank coffee before I went in or between cases, not because it makes me jittery but because it just puts you a little bit on edge. You loose the serenity that is necessary for good decision making.

WCR: *May I ask what your life is like socially? Do you have a lot of friends here?*

JWK: I suppose many people think of us as loners, my wife and I. We have friends. She has friends that I don't know that she plays tennis with. I think we each have friends but we are not great socializers.

WCR: *You enjoy the quietness of the home when you are away from the hustle/bustle. Do you take off much?*

JWK: Probably less than most people.

WCR: *When you were operating so much, did you go on vacations?*

JWK: Always. We usually went for several relatively short times rather than 1 long time. We did not go on round-the-world cruises. We would go for a week or so, some place with the kids or later on by ourselves.

WCR: *You felt that a very useful thing to do?*

JWK: Absolutely. For a lot of reasons.

WCR: *You obviously get a lot of invitations to give talks and so on. You must have had to limit that a great deal.*

JWK: I did. I always felt that people who were talking a lot ended up without much to talk about. I did try to limit it.

WCR: *Is there anything that you would like to put in the record, so to speak, Dr. Kirklin, or discuss anything that we have not touched on?*

JWK: Gee, I think we have talked about most everything. I can't think of anything we have left out.

WCR: *Sir, it was a pleasure.*

JWK's best publications selected by JWK among his 750 articles in medical journals

12. Kirklin JW, McDonald JR, Harrington SW, New GB. Parotid tumors: histopathology, clinical behavior, and end results. *Surg Gynecol Obstet* 1951;92: 721–733.

22. Kirklin JW. Surgical treatment of mitral stenosis. *Proc Staff Meet Mayo Clin* 1952;27:357–360.

23. Kirklin JW, Burchell HB, Pugh DG, Burke EC, Mills SD. Surgical treatment of coarctation of the aorta in a ten week old infant: report of a case. *Circulation* 1952;6:411–414.

25. Knight CD, Kirklin JW. Abdominal incisions in infants. *Surgery* 1952;32: 689–695.

26. Kirklin JW, Openshaw CR, Tompkins RG. Surgical treatment of infundibular stenosis with intact ventricular septum: report of a case. *Ann Surg* 1953;137: 228–231.

27. Connolly DC, Lev R, Kirklin JW, Wood EH. The problem of isolated valvular versus infundibular pulmonic stenosis with particular reference to cardiac catheterization data and records obtained at the time of operation. *Proc Staff Meet Mayo Clin* 1953;28:65–71.

31. Kirklin JW, Jampolis RW. Intrapericardial dissection in left pneumonectomy for bronchiogenic carcinoma. *J Thorac Surg* 1953;25:280–285.

38. Kirklin JW. Surgical treatment of anomalous pulmonary venous connection (partial anomalous pulmonary venous drainage). *Proc Staff Meet Mayo Clin* 1953;28:476–479.

41. Kirklin JW, Connolly DC, Ellis FH Jr, Burchell HB, Edwards JE, Wood EH. Problems in the diagnosis and surgical treatment of pulmonic stenosis with intact ventricular septum. *Circulation* 1953;8:849–863.

45. Clagett OT, Kirklin JW, Edwards JE. Anatomic variations and pathologic changes in coarctation of the aorta: a study of 124 cases. *Surg Gynecol Obstet* 1954;98:103–114.

49. Silver AW, Swan HJC, Kirklin JW. Demonstration by dye dilution techniques of preferential flow across atrial septal defects from right pulmonary veins and inferior vena cava. *Fed Proc* 1954;13:138.

50. Lev R, Connolly DC, Kirklin JW, Wood EH. The immediate hemodynamic effects of mitral commissurotomy during surgery. *Surg Forum* 4:13–17.

52. Mears TW, Kirklin JW, Woolner LB. The fate of patients with alveolar-cell tumor of the lungs. *J Thorac Surg* 1954;27:420–424.

55. Fletcher G, DuShane JW, Kirklin JW, Wood EH. Aortic-pulmonary septal defect: report of a case with surgical division along with successful resuscitation from ventricular fibrillation. *Proc Staff Meet Mayo Clin* 1954;29:285–293.

62. Connolly DC, Kirklin JW, Wood EH. The relationship between pulmonary artery wedge pressure and left atrial pressure in man. *Circ Res* 1954;2:434–440.

68. Kirklin JW, Swan HJC, Wood EH, Burchell HB. Anatomic, physiologic, and surgical considerations in repair of interatrial communications in man. *J Thorac Surg* 1955;29:37–49.

70. Jones RE, Donald DE, Swan HJC, Harshbarger HG, Kirklin JW, Wood EH. Apparatus of the Gibbon type for mechanical bypass of the heart and lungs: preliminary report. *Proc Staff Meet Mayo Clin* 1955;30:105–113.

71. Donald DE, Harshbarger HG, Hetzel PS, Patrick RT, Wood EH, Kirklin JW. Experiences with a heart-lung bypass (Gibbon type) in the experimental laboratory: preliminary report. *Proc Staff Meet Mayo Clin* 1955;30:113–115.

72. Kirklin JW, McDonald JR, Clagett OT, Moersch JH, Gage RP. Bronchogenic carcinoma: cell type and other factors relating to prognosis. *Surg Gynecol Obstet* 1955;100:429–438.

76. Kirklin JW, Allen EV, Odel HM, Shick RM. Atherosclerosis and thrombosis of the distal part of the abdominal aorta: clinical and surgical considerations. *Circulation* 1955;11:799–805.

77. Kirklin JW, DuShane JW, Patrick RT, Donald DE, Hetzel PS, Harshbarger HG, Wood EH. Intracardiac surgery with the aid of a mechanical pump-oxygenator system (Gibbon type): report of 8 cases. *Proc Staff Meet Mayo Clin* 1955;30:201–206.

83. Clagett OT, Kirklin JW, Ellis FH Jr. Surgical treatment of coarctation of the aorta. *Surg Clin North Am* 1955;35:937–946.

90. Ellis FH Jr, Kirklin JW. Anomalous pulmonary venous connection. *Surg Clin North Am* 1955;35:997–1004.

97. Shepherd JR, Callahan JA, DuShane JW, Kirklin JW, Wood EH. Coarctation of the aorta with patent ductus arteriosus opening at the coarctation. *Am Heart J* 1955;50:225–236.

102. Kirklin JW, Daugherty GW, Burchell HB, Wood EH. Repair of the partial form of persistent common atrioventricular canal: so-called ostium primum type of atrial septal defect with interventricular communication. *Ann Surg* 1955;142: 858–862.

105. Ellis FH Jr, Kirklin JW, Callahan JA, Wood EH. Patent ductus arteriosus with pulmonary hypertension. *J Thorac Surg* 1956;31:268–282.

106. Kirklin JW, Ellis FH Jr, Wood EH. Treatment of anomalous pulmonary venous connections in association with interatrial communications. *Surgery* 1956; 39:389–398.

109. DuShane JW, Kirklin JW, Patrick RT, Donald DE, Terry HR Jr, Burchell HB, Wood EH. Ventricular septal defects with pulmonary hypertension: surgical treatment by means of a mechanical pump-oxygenator. *JAMA* 1956;160:950–953.

114. Kirklin JW, Weidman WH, Burroughs JT, Burchell HB, Wood EH. The hemodynamic results of surgical correction of atrial septal defects: a report of 33 cases. *Circulation* 1956;13:825–833.

118. Fuquay MC, Carey LS, Dahl EV, Kirklin JW, Grindlay JH. Myocardial revascularization: a comparison between internal mammary and subclavian-artery implantation in the dog. *Surg Forum* 1956;6:211–215.

120. Silver AW, Kirklin JW, Wood EH. Demonstration of preferential flow of blood from inferior vena cava and from right pulmonary veins through experimental atrial septal defects in dogs. *Circ Res* 1956;14:413–418.

121. Kirklin JW, Donald DE, Harshbarger HG, Hetzel PS, Patrick RT, Swan HJC, Wood EH. Studies in extracorporeal circulation. 1. Applicability of Gibbon-type pump-oxygenator to human intracardiac surgery: 40 cases. *Ann Surg* 1956; 144:2–8.

122. Donald DE, Harshbarger HG, Kirklin JW. Studies in extracorporeal circulation. II. A method for the recovery and use of blood from the open heart during extracorporeal circulation in man. *Ann Surg* 1956;144:223–227.

123. Becu LM, Fontana RS, DuShane JW, Kirklin JW, Burchell HB, Edwards JE. Anatomic and pathologic studies in ventricular septal defect. *Circulation* 1956; 14:349–364.

124. Cooley JC, Kirklin JW. The surgical treatment of persistent common atrioventricular canal: report of 12 cases. *Proc Staff Meet Mayo Clin* 1956;31: 523–527.

127. Kirklin JW, Ellis FH Jr, Barratt-Boyes BG. Technique for repair of atrial septal defect using the atrial well. *Surg Gynecol Obstet* 1956;103:646–649.

132. Kirklin JW, Harshbarger HG, Donald DE, Edwards JE. Surgical correction of ventricular septal defect: anatomic and technical considerations. *J Thorac Surg* 1957;33:45–47.

138. Kirklin JW, Patrick RT, Theye RA. Theory and practice in the use of a pump-oxygenator for open intracardiac surgery. *Thorax* 1957;12:93–98.

147. Berkson J, Harrington SW, Clagett OT, Kirklin JW, Dockerty MB, McDonald DJ. Mortality and survival in surgically treated cancer of the breast: a statistical summary of some experiences of the Mayo Clinic. *Proc Staff Meet Mayo Clin* 1957;32:645–670.

148. Theye RA, Patrick RT, Kirklin JW. The electro-encephalogram in patients undergoing open intracardiac operations with the aid of extracorporeal circulation. *J Thorac Surg* 1957;34:709–716.

149. Sturtz GS, Kirklin JW, Burke EC, Power MH. Water metabolism after cardiac operations involving a Gibbon-type pump-oxygenator. 1. Daily water metabolism, obligatory water losses, and requirements. *Circulation* 1957;16: 988–999.

150. Sturtz GS, Kirklin JW, Burke EC, Power MH. Water metabolism after cardiac operations involving a Gibbon-type pump-oxygenator. II. Benign forms of water loss. *Circulation* 1957;16:1000–1003.

152. Harshbarger HG, Kirklin JW, Donald DE. Studies in extracorporeal circulation. IV. Surgical techniques. *Surg Gynecol Obstet* 1958;106:111–118.

159. Kirklin JW, McGoon DC. Surgical technique for repair of high ventricular septal defects. *J Thorac Surg* 1958;35:584–590.

161. Kirklin JW, Silver AW. Technic of exposing the ductus arteriosus prior to establishing extracorporeal circulation. *Proc Staff Meet Mayo Clin* 1958;33:423–425.

163. Berkson J, Clagett OT, Dockerty MB, Harrington SW, Kirklin JW, McDonald JR. Treatment of breast cancer: the question of "selection." *Lancet* 1958;2:516–518.

165. Heath D, Helmholz HF Jr, Burchell HB, DuShane JW, Kirklin JW, Edwards JE. Relation between structural changes in the small pulmonary arteries and the immediate reversibility of pulmonary hypertension following closure of ventricular and atrial septal defects. *Circulation* 1958;18:1167–1174.

168. Kirklin JW, Ellis FH Jr, McGoon DC, DuShane JW, Swan JHC. Surgical treatment for the tetralogy of Fallot by open intracardiac repair. *J Thorac Surg* 1959;37:22–46.

169. McGoon DC, Swan JHC, Brandenburg RO, Connolly DC, Kirklin JW. Atrial septal defect: factors affecting the surgical mortality rate. *Circulation* 1959;19:195–200.

177. DuShane JW, Kirklin JW. Selection for surgery of patients with ventricular septal defect and pulmonary hypertension. *Circulation* 1960;21:13–20.

179. Kirklin JW. Surgical treatment of ventricular septal defects. *Am J Cardiol* 1960;5:234–238.

181. McGoon DC, Miff EA, Theye RA, Kirklin JW. Physiologic studies during high flow, normothermic, whole body perfusion. *J Thorac Cardiovasc Surg* 1960;39:275–287.

182. DuShane JW, Weidman WH, Brandenburg RO, Kirklin JW. Differentiation of interatrial communications by clinical methods: ostium secundum, ostium primum, common atrium, and total anomalous pulmonary venous connection. *Circulation* 1960;21:363–371.

185. Kirklin JW, Payne WS. Surgical treatment of tetralogy of Fallot after previous anastomosis of systemic to pulmonary artery. *Surg Gynecol Obstet* 1960;110:707–713.

186. Lyons WS, DuShane JW, Kirklin JW. Postoperative care after whole-body perfusion and open intracardiac operations: use of Mayo-Gibbon pump-oxygenator and Browns-Emmons heat exchanger. *JAMA* 1960;173:625–630.

189. Savard M, Swan HJC, Kirklin JW, Wood EH. Hemodynamic alterations associated with ventricular septal defects. In: Congenital Heart Disease. Washington: American Association for the Advance of Science, 1960:141–164.

190. Levin MB, Theye RA, Fowler WS, Kirklin JW. Performance of the stationary vertical-screen oxygenator (Mayo-Gibbon). *J Thorac Cardiovasc Surg* 1960;39:417–426.

194. Uihlein A, Theye RA, Dawson B, Terry HR Jr, McGoon DC, Daw EF, Kirklin JW. The use of protound hypothermia, extracorporeal circulation and total circulatory arrest for an intracranial aneurysm: preliminary report with reports of cases. *Proc Staff Meet Mayo Clin* 1960;35:567–578.

196. Kirklin JW, Payne WS, Theye RA, DuShane JW. Factors affecting survival after open operation for tetralogy of Fallot. *Ann Surg* 1960;152:485–493.

198. Beck W, Swan JHC, Burchell HB, Kirklin JW. Pulmonary vascular resistance after repair of atrial septal defects in patients with pulmonary hypertension. *Circulation* 1960;22:938–946.

199. Kirklin JW, McGoon DC, DuShane JW. Surgical treatment of ventricular septal defect. *J Thorac Cardiovasc Surg* 1960;40:763–775.

201. Kirklin JW, Devloo RA. Hypothermic perfusion and circulatory arrest for surgical correction of tetralogy of Fallot with previously constructed Potts-anastomosis. *Dis Chest* 1961;39:87–91.

205. Kirklin JW, DuShane JW. Repair of ventricular septal defect in infancy. *Pediatrics* 1961;27:961–966.

207. Kirklin JW, Devloo RA, Weidman WH. Open intracardiac repair for transposition of the great vessels: 11 cases. *Surgery* 1961;50:58–66.

209. Kirklin JW, Dawson B, Devloo RA, Theye RA. Open intracardiac operations: use of circulatory arrest during hypothermia induced by blood cooling. *Ann Surg* 1961;154:769–776.

213. Taylor LM, Theye RA, Devloo RA, Kirklin JW. Patterns of acid-base changes during surgical convalescence. *Surg Gynecol Obstet* 1962;114:97–101.

216. Theye RA, Kirklin JW, Fowler WS. Performance and film volume of sheet and screen vertical-film oxygenators. *J Thorac Cardiovasc Surg* 1962;43:481–488.

218. Moffitt EA, Kirklin JW, Theye RA. Physiologic studies during whole-body perfusion in tetralogy of Fallot. *J Thorac Cardiovasc Surg* 1962;44:180–188.

219. Kirklin JW, Payne WS. Tetralogy of Fallot. In: Benson CO, Mustard WT, Ravitch MA, Synder WH Jr, Welch KJ, eds. Pediatric Surgery. Chicago: Yearbook Medical Publishers, 1962:462–471.

220. Kirklin JW, Theye RA. Whole-body perfusion from a pump oxygenator for open intracardiac surgery. In: Gibbon JH Jr, ed. Surgery of the Chest. Philadelphia: WB Saunders, 1962:694–707.

224. Rehder K, Kirklin JW, Theye RA. Physiologic studies following surgical correction of atrial septal defect and similar lesions. *Circulation* 1962;26:1302–1311.

228. Payne WF, Theye RA, Kirklin JW. Effect of carbon dioxide on rate of brain cooling during induction of hypothermia by direct blood cooling. *J Surg Res* 1963;3:54–57.

233. Theye RA, Kirklin JW. Physiologic studies following surgical correction of ventricular septal defect. *Circulation* 1963;27:530–540.

235. Theye RA, Kirklin JW. Physiologic studies early after repair of tetralogy of Fallot. *Circulation* 1963;28:42–52.

241. Theye RA, Kirklin JW. Vertical film oxygenator performance at 30°C and oxygen levels during rewarming. *Surgery* 1963;54:569–572.

242. Kirklin JW, Theye RA. Cardiac performance after open intracardiac surgery. *Circulation* 1963;28:1061–1070.

243. Michenfelder JD, Kirklin JW, Uihlein A, Svien HJ, MacCarty CS. Clinical experience with a closed-chest method of producing profound hypothermia and total circulatory arrest in neurosurgery. *Ann Surg* 1964;159:125–131.

244. Sturridge MF, Theye RA, Fowler WS, Kirklin JW. Basal metabolic rate after cardiovascular surgery. *J Thorac Cardiovasc Surg* 1964;47:298–307.

247. Albertal G, Swan HJC, Kirklin JW. Hemodynamic studies two weeks to six years after repair of tetralogy of Fallot. *Circulation* 1964;29:583–592.

252. Kirklin JW, Harp RA, McGoon DC. Surgical treatment of origin of both vessels from right ventricle including cases of pulmonary stenosis. *J Thorac Cardiovasc Surg* 1964;48:1026–1036.

254. Rastelli GC, Weidman WH, Kirklin JW. Surgical repair of the partial form of persistent common atrioventricular canal, with special reference to the problem of mitral valve incompetence. *Circulation* 1965;31,32:I-31–I-35.

257. Rastelli GC, Ongley PA, Davis GD, Kirklin JW. Surgical repair for pulmonary valve atresia with coronary-pulmonary artery fistula: report of case. *Mayo Clin Proc* 1965;40:521–527.

258. Rastelli GC, Ongley PA, Kirklin JW. Surgical correction of common atrium with anomalously connected persistent left superior vena cava: report of case. *Mayo Clin Proc* 1965;40:528–532.

260. Frye RL, Kincaid OW, Swan HJC, Kirklin JW. Results of surgical treatment of patients with diffuse subvalvular aortic stenosis. *Circulation* 1965;32:52–57.

263. Kirklin JW, Wallace RB, McGoon DC, DuShane JW. Early and late results after intracardiac repair of tetralogy of Fallot: 5-year review of 337 patients. *Ann Surg* 1965;162:578–589.

273. Rastelli GC, McGoon DC, Ongley PA, Mankin HT, Kirklin JW. Surgical treatment of supravalvular aortic stenosis. *J Thorac Cardiovasc Surg* 1966;51: 873–882.

276. Mielke JE, Hunt JC, Maher FT, Kirklin JW. Renal performance during clinical cardiopulmonary bypass with and without hemodilution. *J Thorac Cardiovasc Surg* 1966;52:229–237.

278. Rastelli GC, Kirklin JW, Titus JL. Anatomic observations on complete form of persistent common atrioventricular canal with special reference to atrioventricular valves. *Mayo Clin Proc* 1966;41:296–308.

280. Hoeksema TD, Wallace RB, Kirklin JW. Closed mitral commissurotomy: recent results in 291 cases. *Am J Cardiol* 1966;17:825–828.

286. Cartmill TB, DuShane JW, McGoon DC, Kirklin JW. Results of repair of ventricular septal defect. *J Thorac Cardiovasc Surg* 1966;52:486–499.

296. Daicoff GR, Brandenburg RO, Kirklin JW. Results of operation for atrial septal defect in patients 45 years of age and older. *Circulation* 1967;35,36(suppl I):I-143–I-147.

297. Woods JE, Taswell HF, Kirklin JW, Owen CA Jr. The transfusion of platelet concentrates in patients undergoing heart surgery. *Mayo Clin Proc* 1967;42:318–325.

298. Rastelli GC, Kirklin JW. Hemodynamic state early after replacement of aortic valve with ball-valve prosthesis. *Surgery* 1967;61:965–971.

303. Reid DJ, Digerness S, Kirklin JW. Intracellular fluid volume in surgical patients measured by simultaneous determination of total body water and extracellular fluid. *Surg Forum* 1967;18:29–30.

305. Woods JE, Kirklin JW, Owen CA Jr, Thompson JH Jr, Taswell HF. Effect of bypass surgery on coagulation-sensitive clotting factors. *Mayo Clin Proc* 1967;42:724–735.

307. Reid DJ, Digerness S, Kirklin JW. Changes in whole body venous tone in surgical patients. *Surg Gynecol Obstet* 1967;125:1212–1216.

309. Kiser JC, Ongley PA, Kirklin JW, Clarkson PM, McGoon DC. Surgical treatment of dextrocardia with inversion of ventricles and double-outlet right ventricle. *J Thorac Cardiovasc Surg* 1968;55:6–15.

311. Kirklin JW. The tetralogy of Fallot, Caldwell Lecture, 1967. *Am J Roentgenol Radium Ther Nucl Med* 1968;103:253–266.

317. Sheppard LC, Kouchoukos NT, Kurtts MA, Kirklin JW. Automated treatment of critically ill patients following operation. *Ann Surg* 1968;168:596–604.

318. Reid DJ, Digerness SB, Kirklin JW. Changes in whole body venous tone and distribution of blood after open intracardiac surgery. *Am J Cardiol* 1968;22:621–623.

322. Hightower BM, Barcia A, Bargeron LM Jr, Kirklin JW. Double-outlet right ventricle with transposed great arteries and sub-pulmonary ventricular septal defect: the Taussing-Bing malformation. *Circulation* 1969;49,50(suppl I):I-207–I-213.

325. Breckenridge IM, Digerness SB, Kirklin JW. Validity of concept of increased extracellular fluid after open heart surgery. *Surg Forum* 1969;20:169–171.

327. Shepard RB, Kirklin JW. Relation of pulsatile flow to oxygen consumption and other variables during cardiopulmonary bypass. *J Thorac Cardiovasc Surg* 1969;58:694–702, 718–720.

333. Breckenridge IM, Digerness SB, Kirklin JW. Distribution volume, equilibration time, and exponential analysis of 82Br after open intracardiac operations. *Ann Surg* 1970;171:583–589.

337. Breckenridge IM, Digerness SB, Kirklin JW. Increased extracellular fluid after open intracardiac operation. *Surg Gynecol Obstet* 1970;131:53–56.

341. Kirklin JW. Systems analysis in surgical patients with particular attention to the cardiac and pulmonary subsystems (Macewen Memorial Lecture). Glasgow: University of Glasgow Press, 1970.

345. English TAH, Digerness SB, Kirklin JW, Karp RB. Pulmonary capillary blood volume and lung water in pulmonary edema. *Surg Gynecol Obstet* 1971;132:93–100.

347. Kouchoukos NT, Barcia A, Bargeron LM, Kirklin JW. Surgical treatment of congenital pulmonary atresia with ventricular septal defect. *J Thorac Cardiovasc Surg* 1971;61:70–84.

359. Kouchoukos NT, Kirklin JW, Sheppard LC, Roe PA. Effect of elevation of left atrial pressure by blood infusion on stroke volume early after cardiac operations. *Surg Forum* 1971;22:126–127.

362. Kirklin JW. A university department of surgery. *Am Surg* 1971;37:706–712.

368. Kouchoukos NT, Doty DB, Buettner LE, Kirklin JW. Treatment of postinfarction cardiac failure by myocardial excision and revascularization. *Circulation* 1972;45,46(suppl I):I-72–I-78.

372. Bargeron LM Jr, Karp RB, Barcia A, Kirklin JW, Hunt D, Deverall PB. Late deterioration of patients after superior vena cava to right pulmonary artery anastomosis. *Am J Cardiol* 1972;30:211–216.

377. Kirklin JW. Replacement of the mitral valve for mitral incompetence. *Surgery* 1972;72:827–836.

378. Stewart S III, Edmunds LH Jr, Kirklin JW, Allarde RR. Spontaneous breathing with continuous positive airway pressure after open intracardiac operations in infants. *J Thorac Cardiovas Surg* 1973;65:37–44.

379. Kirklin JW, Pacifico AD. Surgery for acquired valvular heart disease. *N Engl J Med* 1973;288:133–140, 194–199.

385. Ceballos R, Kirklin JW. Long-term anatomical results of intracardiac repair of tetralogy of Fallot. *Ann Thorac Surg* 1973;15:371–377.

388. Pacifico AD, Kirklin JW. Surgical repair of complete atrioventricular canal with anterior common leaflet attached to an anomalous right ventricular papillary muscle. *J Thorac Cardiovasc Surg* 1973;65:727–730.

392. Kirklin JW. Evaluating the results of cardiac surgery (Lewis A. Conner Memorial Lecture). *Circulation* 1973;48:232–238.

393. Archie JP, Kirklin JW. Effect of hypothermic perfusion on myocardial oxygen consumption and coronary resistance. *Surg Forum* 1973;24:186–188.

394. Pacifico AD, Bargeron LM Jr, Kirklin JW. Primary total correction of tetralogy of Fallot in children less than 4 years of age. *Circulation* 1973;48:1085–1091.

397. DuShane JW, Kirklin JW. Late results of the repair of ventricular septal defect on pulmonary vascular disease. In: Kirklin JW, ed. Advances in Cardiovascular Surgery. New York: Grune & Stratton, 1973:9–16.

407. Wisheart JD, Archie JP, Kirklin JW, Tracy WG. Myocardial blood flow and oxygen consumption in man early after valve replacement. *Circulation* 1974;49:933–942.

408. Sapsford RN, Blackstone EH, Kirklin JW, Karp RB, Kouchoukos NT, Pacifico AD, Roe CR, Bradley EL. Coronary perfusion versus cold ischemic arrest during aortic valve surgery. A randomized study. *Circulation* 1974;49:1190–1199.

409. Parr GVS, Kirklin JW, Pacifico AD, Blackstone EH, Lauridsen P. Cardiac performance in infants after repair of total anomalous pulmonary venous connection. *Ann Thorac Surg* 1974;17:561–573.

411. Kouchoukos NT, Kirklin JW, Oberman A. An appraisal of coronary bypass grafting (presented by Dr. Kirklin as Sixth Annual George C. Griffith Lecture). *Circulation* 1974;50:11–16.

414. Pacifico AD, Kirklin JW, Bargeron LM Jr, Soto B. Surgical treatment of common arterial trunk with pseudotruncus arteriosus. *Circulation* 1974;49,50(suppl II):II-20–II-25.

419. Parr GVS, Blackstone EH, Kirklin JW. Cardiac performance and mortality early after intracardiac surgery in infants and young children. *Circulation* 1975;51:867–874.

430. Fox LS, Kirklin JW, Pacifico AD, Waldo AI, Bargeron LM Jr. Intracardiac repair of cardiac malformations with atrioventricular discordance. *Circulation* 1976;54:123–127.

432. Blackstone EH, Kirklin JW, Bradley EL, Dushane JW, Appelbaum A. Optimal age and results in repair of large ventricular septal defects. *J Thorac Cardiovasc Surg* 1976;72:661–679.

439. Parr GVS, Kirklin JW, Blackstone EH. The early risks of re-replacement of aortic valves. *Ann Thorac Surg* 1977;23:319–322.

440. Stephenson LW, Kouchoukos NT, Kirklin JW. Triple-valve replacement: an analysis of 8 year's experience. *Ann Thorac Surg* 1977;23:327–332.

446. Pacifico AD, Kirklin JW, Blackstone EH. Surgical management of pulmonary stenosis in tetralogy of Fallot. *J Thorac Cardiovasc Surg* 1977;74:382–395.

447. Castaneda AR, Kirklin JW. Tetralogy of Fallot with aorticopulmonary window. Report of 2 surgical cases. *J Thorac Cardiovasc Surg* 1977;74:467–468.

452. Kirklin JW, Bargeron LM Jr, Pacifico AD. The enlargement of small pulmonary arteries by preliminary palliative operations. *Circulation* 1977;56:612–617.

458. Laws HL, Kirklin MK, Diethelm AG, Hall J, Kirklin JW. Training and use of surgeon's assistants. *Surgery* 1978;83:445–450.

460. Berger TJ, Kirklin JW, Blackstone EH, Pacifico AD, Kouchoukos NT. Primary repair of complete atrioventricular canal in patients less than 2 years old. *Am J Cardiol* 1978;41:906–913.

461. Katz NM, Kirklin JW, Pacifico AD. Concepts and practices in surgery for total anomalous pulmonary venous connection. *Ann Thorac Surg* 1978;25:479–487.

464. Alfieri O, Blackstone EH, Kirklin JW, Pacifico AD, Bargeron LM Jr. Surgical treatment of tetralogy of Fallot with pulmonary atresia. *J Thorac Cardiovasc Surg* 1978;76:321–335.

473. Gale AW, Arciniegas E, Green EW, Blackstone EH, Kirklin JW. Growth of the pulmonary anulus and pulmonary arteries after the Blalock-Taussig shunt. *J Thorac Cardiovasc Surg* 1979;77:459–465.

474. Blackstone EH, Kirklin JW, Pacifico AD. Decision-making in repair of tetralogy of Fallot based on intraoperative measurements of pulmonary arterial outflow tract. *J Thorac Cardiovasc Surg* 1979;77:526–532.

479. Kirklin JW, Conti VR, Blackstone EH. Prevention of myocardial damage during cardiac operations. *N Engl J Med* 1979;301:135–141.

480. Kirklin JW, Blackstone EH, Pacifico AD, Brown RN, Bargeron LM Jr. Routine primary repair vs two-stage repair of tetralogy of Fallot. *Circulation* 1979;60:373–386.

482. Blackstone EH, Kirklin JW, Bertranou EG, Labrosse CJ, Soto B, Bargeron LM Jr. Preoperative prediction from cineangiograms of postrepair right ventricular pressure in tetralogy of Fallot. *J Thorac Cardiovasc Surg* 1979;78:542–552.

483. Kirklin JW. A letter to Helen. *J Thorac Cardiovasc Surg* 1979;78:643–654.

493. Bharati S, Kirklin JW, McAllister HA Jr, Lev M. The surgical anatomy of common atrioventricular orifice associated with tetralogy of Fallot, double outlet right ventricle and complete regular transposition. *Circulation* 1980;61:1142–1149.

500. Kouchoukos NT, Oberman A, Kirklin JW, Russell RO Jr, Karp RB, Pacifico AD, Zorn GL. Coronary bypass surgery: analysis of factors affecting hospital mortality. *Circulation* 1980;61(suppl I):I-84–I-89.

504. Rizzoli G, Blackstone EH, Kirklin JW, Pacifico AD, Bargeron LM Jr. Incremental risk factors in hospital mortality rate after repair of ventricular septal defect. *J Thorac Cardiovasc Surg* 1980;80:494–505.

506. Fuster V, McGoon DC, Kennedy MA, Ritter DG, Kirklin JW. Long-term evaluation (12 to 22 years) of open heart surgery for tetralogy of Fallot. *Am J Cardiol* 1980;46:635–642.

508. Kirklin JW. The replacement of cardiac valves. *N Engl J Med* 1981;304:291–292.

509. Chenoweth DE, Cooper SW, Hugli TE, Stewart RW, Blackstone EH, Kirklin JW. Complement activation during cardiopulmonary bypass: evidence for generation of C3a and C5a anaphylatoxins. *N Engl J Med* 1981;304:497–503.

513. Kirklin JK, Blackstone EH, Kirklin JW, Stewart RW, Pacifico AD, Bargeron LM Jr. Management of the cardiac subsystem after cardiac surgery. In: Parenzan L, Crupi G, Graham G, eds. Congenital Heart Disease in the first 3 months of life. Medical and Surgical Aspects. Bologna, Italy: Patron Editore, 1981:33–41.

519. Kirklin JK, Blackstone EH, Kirklin JW, McKay R, Pacifico AD, Bargeron LM Jr. Intracardiac surgery in infants under age 3 months: incremental risk factors for hospital mortality. *Am J Cardiol* 1981;48:500–506.

520. Kirklin JK, Blackstone EH, Kirklin JW, McKay R, Pacifico AD, Bargeron LM Jr. Intracardiac surgery in infants under age 3 months: predictors of postoperative in-hospital cardiac death. *Am J Cardiol* 1981;48:507–512.

537. Katz NM, Blackstone EH, Kirklin JW, Pacifico AD, Bargeron LM Jr. Late survival and symptoms after repair of tetralogy of Fallot. *Circulation* 1982;65:403–410.

538. Fox LS, Blackstone EH, Kirklin JW, Stewart RW, Samuelson PN. Relationship of whole body oxygen consumption to perfusion flow rate during hypothermic cardiopulmonary bypass. *J Thorac Cardiovasc Surg* 1982;83:239–248.

540. Bergdahl LAL, Blackstone EH, Kirklin JW, Pacifico AD, Bargeron LM Jr. Determinants of early success in repair of aortic coarctation in infants. *J Thorac Cardiovasc Surg* 1982;83:736–742.

541. Blackstone EH, Kirklin JW, Stewart RW, Chenoweth DE. Damaging effects of cardiopulmonary bypass. In: Wu KK, Rossi ED, eds. Prostaglandins in Clinical Medicine. Cardiovascular and Thrombotic Disorders. Chicago: Year Book Medical Publishers, 1983:355–369.

558. Ceballos R, Soto B, Kirklin JW, Bargeron LM Jr. Truncus arteriosus. An anatomical-angiographic study. *Br Heart J* 1983;49:589–599.

563. Kirklin JW, Blackstone EH, Kirklin JK, Pacifico AD, Aramendi J, Bargeron LM Jr. Surgical results and protocols in the spectrum of tetralogy of Fallot. *Ann Surg* 1983;198:251–265.

564. Treasure T, Naftel DC, Conger KA, Garcia JH, Kirklin JW, Blackstone EH. The effect of hypothermic circulatory arrest time on cerebral function, morphology, and biochemistry. An experimental study. *J Thorac Cardiovasc Surg* 1983;86:761–770.

566. Kirklin JK, Westaby S, Blackstone EH, Kirklin JW, Chenoweth DE, Pacifico AD. Complement and the damaging effects of cardiopulmonary bypass. *J Thorac Cardiovasc Surg* 1983;86:845–857.

572. Fox LS, Blackstone EH, Kirklin JW, Bishop SP, Bergdahl LAL, Bradley EL. Relationship of brain blood flow and oxygen consumption to pertusion flow rate during profoundly hypothermic cardiopulmonary bypass. An experimental study. *J Thorac Cardiovasc Surg* 1984;87:658–664.

575. Kirklin JW, Blackstone EH, Pacifico AD, Kirklin JK, Bargeron LM Jr. Risk factors for early and late failure after repair of tetralogy of Fallot, and their neutralization. *J Thorac Cardiovasc Surg* 1984;32:208–214.

577. Stefanelli G, Kirklin JW, Naftel DC, Blackstone EH, Pacifico AD, Kirklin JK, Soto B, Bargeron LM Jr. Early and intermediate-term (10 year) results of surgery for univentricular atrioventricular connection (''single ventricle''). *Am J Cardiol* 1984;54:811–821.

578. Cleveland DC, Kirklin JK, Naftel DC, Kirklin JW, Blackstone EH, Pacifico AD, Bargeron LM Jr. Surgical treatment of tricuspid atresia. *Ann Thorac Surg* 1984;38:447–457.

590. Pacifico AD, Naftel DC, Kirklin JW, Blackstone EH, Kirklin JK. Ventricular septation within the spectrum of surgery for double inlet ventricles. *J Jpn Assoc Thorac Surg* 1985;33:593–601.

591. Kirklin JK, Kirklin JW, Pacifico AD. Homograft replacement of the aortic valve. *Cardiol Clin* 1985;3:329–341.

593. Blackstone EH, Kirklin JW. Death and other time-related events after valve replacement. *Circulation* 1985;72:753–767.

597. Kirklin JK, Blackstone EH, Zorn GL Jr, Pacifico AD, Kirklin JW, Karp RB, Rogers WJ. Intermediate-term results of coronary artery bypass grafting for acute myocardial infraction. *Circulation* 1985;72(suppl II):II-175–II-178.

602. Kirklin JK, Chenoweth DE, Naltel DC, Blackstone EH, Kirklin JW, Bitran DD, Curd JG, Reves JG, Samuelson PN. Effects of protamine administration after cardiopulmonary bypass on complement, blood elements, and the hemodynamic state. *Ann Thorac Surg* 1986;41:193–199.

610. Ferrazzi P, McGittin DC, Kirklin JW, Blackstone EH, Bourge RC. Have the results of mitral valve replacement improved? *J Thorac Cardiovasc Surg* 1986;92:186–197.

612. Quagebeur JM, Rohmer J, Ottenkamp J, Tuis T, Kirklin JW, Blackstone EH, Brom AG. The arterial switch operation. An eight-year experience. *J Thorac Cardiovasc Surg* 1986;92:361–384.

614. Kirklin JW, Pacifico AD, Blackstone EH, Kirklin JK, Bargeron LM Jr. Current risks and protocols for operations for double-outlet right ventricle. *J Thorac Cardiovasc Surg* 1986;92:913–930.

618. Kirklin JK, Blackstone EH, Kirklin JW, Pacifico AD, Bargeron LM Jr. The Fontan operation: ventricular hypertrophy, age, and date of operation as risk factors. *J Thorac Cardiovasc Surg* 1986;92:1049–1064.

622. Kirklin JK, Pacifico AD, Kirklin JW. Intraventricular tunnel repair of double outlet right ventricle. *J Cardiac Surg* 1987;2:231–245.

623. Sand ME, Naftel DC, Blackstone EH, Kirklin JW, Karp RB. A comparison of repair and replacement for mitral valve incompetence. *J Thorac Cardiovasc Surg* 1987;94:208–219.

631. Coles JG, Kirklin JW, Pacifico AD, Kirklin JK, Blackstone EH. The relief of pulmonary stenosis by a transatrial versus a transventricular approach to the repair of tetralogy of Fallot. *Ann Thorac Surg* 1988;45:7–10.

632. Castaneda AR, Trusler GA, Paul MH, Blackstone EH, Kirklin JW, and the Congenital Heart Surgeons Society. The early results of treatment of simple transposition in the current era. *J Thorac Cardiovasc Surg* 1988;95:14–27.

644. Shimazaki Y, Maehara T, Blackstone EH, Kirklin JW, Bargeron LM Jr. The structure of the pulmonary circulation in tetralogy of Fallot with pulmonary atresia. *J Thorac Cardiovasc Surg* 1988;95:1048–1058.

645. Kirklin JW, Blackstone EH, Shimazaki Y, Maehara T, Pacifico AD, Kirklin JK, Bargeron LM Jr. Survival, functional status, and reoperations after repair of tetralogy of Fallot with pulmonary atresia. *J Thorac Cardiovasc Surg* 1988;96:102–116.

647. Blackstone EH, Shimazaki Y, Maehara T, Kirklin JW, Bargeron LM Jr. Prediction of severe obstruction to right ventricular outflow after repair of tetralogy of Fallot and pulmonary atresia. *J Thorac Cardiovasc Surg* 1988;96:288–293.

659. Kirklin JW. Reply to the editor on early primary repair of tetralogy of Fallot. *Ann Thorac Surg* 1988;46:711.

663. Kirklin JW, Naftel DC, Blackstone EH, Pohost GM. Summary of a consensus concerning death and ischemic events after coronary artery bypass grafting. *Circulation* 1989;79(suppl I):I-81–I-91.

671. Fernandez G, Costa F, Fontan F, Naftel DC, Blackstone EH, Kirklin JW. Prevalence of reoperation for pathway obstruction after Fontan operation. *Ann Thorac Surg* 1989;48:654–659.

678. Fontan F, Fernandez G, Costa F, Naltel DC, Tritto F, Blackstone EH, Kirklin JW. The size of the pulmonary arteries and the results of the Fontan operation. *J Thorac Cardiovasc Surg* 1989;98:711–724.

681. Kirklin JK, Naltel DC, Blackstone EH, Kirklin JW, Brown RC. Risk factors for mortality after primary combined valvular and coronary artery surgery. *Circulation* 1989;79(suppl I):I-185–I-190.

682. Kirklin JK, Pacifico AD, Kirklin JW. Surgical treatment of prosthetic valve endocarditis with homograft aortic valve replacement. *J Cardiac Surg* 1989;4:340–347.

686. Kirklin JW, Fernandez G, Fontan F, Naftel DC, Ener A, Blackstone EH. Therapeutic use of right atrial pressures early after the Fontan operation. *Eur J Cardiothorac Surg* 1990;4:2–7.

688. Kirklin JW, Blackstone EH, Kirklin JK, Pacifico AD. Predicting the degree of relief of the pulmonary stenosis of atresia after the repair of tetralogy of Fallot. *Semin Thorac Cardiovasc Surg* 1990;2:55–60.

693. Fontan F, Kirklin JW, Fernandez G, Costa F, Naltel DC, Tritto F, Blackstone EH. Outcome after a ''perfect'' Fontan operation. *Circulation* 1990;81:1520–1536.

705. Kirklin JW, and the ACC:AHA Task Force Subcommittee on Coronary Artery Bypass Graft Surgery. Guidelines and Indications for the coronary artery bypass graft operation. *Circulation* 1991;83:543–589, 1125–1173.

712. Kirklin JW, Blackstone EH, Shimazaki Y, Kirklin JK, Mayer JE Jr, Pacifico AD, Castaneda AR. Morphologic and surgical determinants of outcome events after repair of tetralogy of Fallot and pulmonary stenosis. A two-institution study. *J Thorac Cardiovasc Surg* 1992;103:706–723.

713. Shimazaki Y, Blackstone EH, Kirklin JW, Jonas RA, Mandell V, Colvin EV. The dimensions of the right ventricular outflow tract and pulmonary arteries in tetralogy of Fallot and pulmonary stenosis. *J Thorac Cardiovasc Surg* 1992;103:692–705.

720. Crawford ES, Kirklin JW, Naftel DC, Svensson LG, Coselli JS, Safi HJ, Hess KR. Surgery for acute ascending aortic dissection: should the arch be included? *J Thorac Cardiovasc Surg* 1992;104:46–59.

722. Kirklin JW, Blackstone EH, Tchervenkov CI, Castaneda AR, and the Congenital Heart Surgeons Society. Clinical outcomes after the arterial switch operation for transposition. Patient, support, procedural, and institutional risk factors. *Circulation* 1992;86:1501–1515.

723. Walters HL, Digerness SB, Naftel DC, Waggoner JR, Blackstone EH, Kirklin JW. The response to ischemia in blood perfused vs. crystalloid perfused isolated rat heart preparations. *J Mol Cell Cardiol* 1992;24:1063–1077.

PETER RUSSELL KOWEY, MD: a conversation with the editor

Peter Russell Kowey, MD, and William Clifford Roberts, MD

Peter Kowey was born in Norristown, Pennsylvania, January 4, 1950, and that is where he grew up. He graduated from Bishop Kendrick High School in June 1967 as Salutatorian and received a Presidential Scholarship to St. Joseph's College in Philadelphia where he graduated in May 1971, Cum Laude with a BS in Biology and was a member of the Alpha Sigma Nu honors program. From there he went to the University of Pennsylvania in Philadelphia for medical school graduating in 1975. His internship in internal medicine was at the Milton S. Hershey Medical Center, Philadelphia, in Hershey, Pennsylvania, and his fellowship in cardiology was at the Harvard University School of Public Health and Peter Bent Brigham Hospital in Boston, finishing in June 1981. His major mentor was Dr. Bernard Lown. After completing his cardiology fellowship, he returned to Philadelphia, joining the Medical College of Pennsylvania as director of the coronary care unit and of the cardiac arrhythmia service. He rose to full Professor of Medicine and Pharmacology by 1990. He became chief of the division of cardiovascular diseases of the Mainline Health System, Bryn Mawr, Lankenau and Paoli Memorial Hospitals in 1999 and has remained in that position to the present. He also occupies the William Wykoff Smith Chair in Cardiovascular Research. From 1990 until the present he is also Professor of Medicine and of Clinical Pharmacology at Jefferson Medical College of The Thomas Jefferson University in Philadelphia. He was Clinical Professor of Medicine at MCP/Hahnemann/Drexel University College of Medicine from 1992 - 2003. He also serves as president of The Heart Center of Lankenau, Bryn Mawr, and Paoli Memorial Hospitals.

Throughout this 30-year period since finishing his training Dr. Kowey has been a prominent researcher primarily in the area of cardiac arrhythmias and conduction disturbances and these investigations have led to over 300 publications, mainly in peer-reviewed medical journals. He has been the recipient of numerous grants through the years in support of his research. He has been an *ad hoc* consultant to numerous pharmacologic and device companies. Through the years he has received numerous awards for his research and leadership accomplishments. He has edited or authored 11 books including 2 novels, one entitled *Lethal Rhythm* and the other, *Deadly Rhythm*. Dr Kowey has been on numerous advisory boards particularly with the Federal Drug Administration and also numerous monitoring boards of major multi-center studies. Dr. Kowey is the happy husband of Dorothy Freal Kowey and they have 3 very successful daughters. Dr. Kowey is also a wonderful human being who possesses a great sense of humor, a wonderful storytelling ability, and is a star speaker at most of the meetings where he presents. It was a real pleasure getting to know Dr. Kowey and I hope the readers feel the same way.

WILLIAM CLIFFORD ROBERTS, MD (hereafter **ROBERTS**): *Dr. Kowey, I really appreciate the opportunity to talk with you. Peter is here in Dallas and in my office and*

this is 19 November 2013. Dr. Kowey is in Dallas for the Annual Scientific Sessions of the American Heart Association and we were fortunate to get him to come to Baylor University Medical Center to give Grand Rounds earlier this morning and he graciously agreed to allow this conversation in my office thereafter. He is also giving a 12 noon presentation to the Baylor cardiology group. Peter, may we start by my asking you to talk about your early life, where and when you were born, your parents, and your siblings so we all can get a feel of your early life.

PETER RUSSELL KOWEY, MD (hereafter **KOWEY**): First of all thank you for the opportunity to sit and chat with you. I have enormous respect for the work you have done with the AJC over the last many years. I think these interviews are important to provide a perspective about people who have been laboring in this field. Our fellows and young faculty know very little about the people who have gone before them.

I was born January 4, 1950, in Norristown, Pennsylvania, a small town about 20 miles west of Philadelphia. My father was Lebanese. My paternal grandparents had emigrated from Beirut, Lebanon. My mother was Italian and her parents had emigrated from Naples, Italy. Both of my parents were extraordinarily hard-working people. They both dropped out of high school - my mother in the tenth grade and my father in the ninth. My mother's mother had died and she had to take over the role of mother for her younger siblings. My paternal grandfather sold fruit and vegetables off the back of a pick-up truck in the Philadelphia suburbs, and he needed my father to drive the truck for him. That's how my father became a truck driver, which was his occupation for the next 45 years.

ROBERTS: *What was your father's name?*

KOWEY: Peter Sarkis Kowey. Sarkis is a common name in Lebanon. Sarkis was a fourth century saint who is revered in Lebanon.

ROBERTS: *When was he born?*

KOWEY: He was born in 1921.

ROBERTS: *Is he still alive?*

KOWEY: He died in 1995 from diabetes.

ROBERTS: *Did he have it when he was young or older?*

KOWEY: When he was older. He was obese and didn't take good care of himself. He developed pretty severe macro-vascular disease.

ROBERTS: *What was your mother's name?*

KOWEY: My mother's name is Edith Adeline Sagrantz. All four of my grandparents came through Ellis Island and their names were severely altered. Kowey is actually "Khoui", and Sagrantz is "Sicoronza." My grandfather had a particularly bad experience when he arrived and they asked his name. Boutros is a name that goes back several generations in my family. So he memorized the English translation and said "Peter." But Lebanese people have a hard time with the "p" sound so it came out "Beter." The clerk recorded his last name as "Beter." My grandfather then said Joseph, thinking they next wanted his middle name, but that was recorded as his first name. So, he became Joseph Beter. When my father was born, he had to be named Peter in the tradition of the family, so for several years my father was known in his hometown as Peter Beter. Fortunately for me, he changed his name back to something like the Lebanese when he was married, and he became Peter Sarkis Kowey. I was given the middle name of Russell because I had two uncles by that name.

ROBERTS: *When was your mother born?*

KOWEY: 1920.

ROBERTS: *Is she still alive?*

KOWEY: No, she died in 2004 from progressive supranuclear palsy.

ROBERTS: *So neither your mother nor your father finished high school? Do you have siblings?*

KOWEY: I have one younger brother, Richard Brian Kowey. He was born in 1958.

ROBERTS: *What does he do?*

KOWEY: He is an executive vice president for a gas company. A very successful businessman and a real good guy.

ROBERTS: *Does he still live in the Philadelphia area?*

KOWEY: He lives about 20 miles north of Philadelphia.

ROBERTS: *Does he have children?*

KOWEY: He has 2 daughters, Erin and Emily.

ROBERTS: *What was home like as you were growing up?*

KOWEY: I think it was terrific. We lived in a blue-collar neighborhood, in a very modest house. My parents didn't have much money, but they were warm, engaging people. They were also very bright and they had a strong opinion about the value of education. They were completely and utterly convinced that my brother and I had to get as good an education as possible. They spent a lot of time helping with homework and encouraging us to do well in school.

ROBERTS: *Both your father and your mother or mainly your mother?*

KOWEY: My father was on the road a lot, being a truck driver.

ROBERTS: Eighteen-wheeler?

KOWEY: Yes. The funny thing is I was a truck driver. When I was in college he got me a job driving a truck during the summer.

ROBERTS: *It's hard to get drivers I understand.*

KOWEY: Back then there wasn't driver training like there is now. But I loved it. It was great getting out on the road on your own, especially in nice weather. I made a lot of money too, as a card-carrying Teamster.

ROBERTS: *So your parents were born here?*

KOWEY: Yes. They both were born in or near Philadelphia.

ROBERTS: *Did you know your grandfather?*

KOWEY: I knew my paternal grandfather and grandmother. But both of my mother's parents died before I was old enough to know them.

ROBERTS: *Your father's father was born in Lebanon. What was his name?*

KOWEY: He was Boutrus Khoui and as I said, he became Joseph Beter, born in the 1890s and he passed away in 1970.

ROBERTS: *And your paternal grandmother?*

KOWEY: Katherine Farhatley Khoui, and she also was born in the 1890s. She passed away in 1986.

ROBERTS: *As you were growing up, your father may or may not have been at the dining room table each night?*

KOWEY: He frequently was on the road.

ROBERTS: *It was often early on just you and your mother? Your brother came along 8 years later. What did you talk about?*

KOWEY: I remember it being pleasant. There was a lot of discussion about what I was doing at school. There was a high priority to get my schoolwork done, not that I couldn't go out and play after school. But I remember that homework always got the priority. We were one of the first families on the block to get a television set. My mother and I would watch some television before I went to bed. I remember watching the little black-and-white screen. My mom was a very warm person, great cook, and very nurturing. We had a good relationship.

ROBERTS: *Home life was pleasant?*

KOWEY: I don't remember it being onerous or burdensome in any way. She had a really good knack for getting me to do what I was supposed to do without slamming her fist on the table. I was spanked but rarely.

ROBERTS: *You and your father got along also?*

KOWEY: Yes we did. He was a bit more distant, due to his work but we had a good relationship. Sports were one of the ways we communicated because he was a big Philadelphia sports fan and made me into one as well. A lot of our conversations over the years had to do with how the Eagles or Phillies were doing.

ROBERTS: *Did you go to those sporting events with him?*

KOWEY: Yes. Some of my most vivid memories from childhood are going to Connie Mack stadium to see the Phillies or Franklin Field to see the Eagles.

ROBERTS: *Did you go on vacations?*

KOWEY: Yes. My dad got 2 weeks' vacation every year and during one of those weeks, we went to Wildwood, New Jersey. That was our big vacation.

ROBERTS: *What did you do there?*

KOWEY: We stayed at a boardinghouse, went to the beach every day, and the boardwalk at night for the amusement rides. Pretty standard Jersey shore stuff but we enjoyed it immensely. My mother's sister and her husband would bring their two girls, and we had a blast.

ROBERTS: *When you were growing up, you, did you go on big vacations across country? Or did you stay close to home?*

KOWEY: The only time we left Philadelphia was to visit an aunt in Florida every few years. We took this big pilgrimage by car to see her in Orlando. Never flew anywhere. First airplane ride was during my medical residency.

ROBERTS: *You didn't have a lot of money but you had enough for you to think your childhood was pleasant?*

KOWEY: Yes. Recently, my hospital asked me to visit my old stomping ground in Norristown. We get patients from that area and they thought it would be good PR to have me out in my old community to talk about my childhood in a commercial. So I went with a film crew to my old house. I hadn't been there in a long time and was amazed at how tiny it was. In my mind, we had a large backyard, but it was really not much bigger than your conference room. I remember spending hours throwing baseballs up against the garage wall, and shooting hoops on a basket my father nailed up on the wall of our house. I had enormous fun in that backyard and in the stone covered, narrow back alley behind our house, but in reality, it was a very modest place.

ROBERTS: *In grammar school, did you enjoy going to school?*

KOWEY: I did. I went to a Catholic grade school for 8 years, which was within walking distance of our house, about half a mile. The first few years, my mother would walk me to school, but then I would walk myself. I had nuns for teachers. I have very vivid memories of their discipline techniques. For example, there were 106 children in my first grade class with one nun, who was somewhere between 80 and 100 years old. She kept that class perfect. Nobody talked because if you did, you were immediately struck. Not hard, but firmly. And the other thing I remember is the way we sat in that classroom; there were 10 rows of 10 seats, and then there were 6 people who didn't get a full desk. The way you were seated was by your grades. So the top kids in the class got to sit in the first rows and the kids with the lowest grades were in the last rows. It was that way through grade school; every class had the same arrangement. Never any question about who was doing the best. It was cruel, but it did provide strong motivation to work hard. We graduated about 70 of those 100 kids and I keep up with a small number of my classmates.

ROBERTS: *Do you remember the names of all your grammar school teachers?*

KOWEY: They were all Sister something. Sister Mary Thomas, Sister Anna Theresa. I remember most of them quite well.

ROBERTS: *Did any of them have an extraordinary effect on you?*

KOWEY: I took piano lessons when I was in grade school. The sisters who taught me music had the biggest impact because I spent a lot of time with them. But I would say they were all extraordinary. These were women who had given up their lives essentially to teach us. They weren't all highly skilled, but they were totally dedicated and gave their time unselfishly.

ROBERTS: *And you felt it?*

KOWEY: Yes.

ROBERTS: *Did you have a piano at home?*

KOWEY: Yes. After I took lessons for a couple of years I was bugging my parents about getting a piano. It was a big deal because it cost a lot of money. The piano that we were looking at cost about $800, which back then was 4 weeks of my fathers' salary or more. It was a tough decision for them. But they finally bought it and delivery day was one of the best days of my life. I practiced on that piano for hours.

ROBERTS: *You really enjoyed music. Were you a natural at it? Were you good at it?*

KOWEY: Not really. I realized after 8 years of taking piano lessons that I didn't have much musical talent. I learned because I worked at it. I played the trumpet and French horn in high school, and the organ in church, but I never excelled. But the experience has given me a great appreciation of excellent music.

ROBERTS: *Do you sing?*

KOWEY: I took vocal lessons. Whenever I sing in the shower, my wife will tell me that whatever my parents spent on vocal lessons was a waste. I'm afraid she is correct, as she usually is.

ROBERTS: *Where did you get your great storytelling ability from? Was your mother a good storyteller?*

KOWEY: She was excellent. She loved to tell stories about growing up and her family experiences. I have a very large extended family. My mother had 13 siblings, my father had 7, and each of the siblings had lots of children, so I had an enormous number of cousins. I still can't keep track of all of them. When we had large family gatherings, all the cousins would sit around and ask my mother to tell stories about her years in Bridgeport, the tiny town where she grew up, just over the bridge from Norristown. She told great stories, down to the little details. I admired her for that. I think that was probably the seed.

ROBERTS: *What would be a story she would tell?*

KOWEY: She told many stories about her father. He was kind of a nasty person who disciplined them harshly, like locking them out of the house if they didn't get home on time, even in bad weather. But he was also an interesting character. He sold ice cream off the back of a truck for a living. We have a picture of him with the truck. What I found out recently from one of my older cousins was that my grandfather made an enormous amount of money and no one could figure out how. Turns out he was probably a bootlegger. The ice cream was a front. He would be selling ice cream to kids on one side of the truck and on the other side he would be selling hooch to adults.

ROBERTS: *How old was your mother when she found out how he made his money?*

KOWEY: She never found out. It was my cousin who discovered the story, long after my mother passed away.

ROBERTS: *What about your father, was he a good storyteller?*

KOWEY: No, he was pretty quiet and kept his emotions to himself. He was a worker. My work ethic comes from him. At any given time, my father would have 3 or 4 jobs. He fixed television sets back when TVs had tubes and were easy to repair. He used to service and grease cars and trucks on the side. He would fix appliances. Then he bought some old houses, fixed them up, and rented them out. He liked to be busy.

ROBERTS: *He was an entrepreneur.*

KOWEY: He was the breadwinner and took it very seriously. I remember a conversation I had with him. We were talking about families. He said, "I don't like to hear crap about 'loving your family.' You love your family by supporting them. Your job when you get married and have kids is to go out and make money for them and to get them a good education. That's showing your love." That conversation had a major impact on me. I have spent my career making sure that whatever I do, there are funds for the mortgage, food on the table and money for tuition payments.

ROBERTS: *That's good. Were your mother and father a close couple?*

KOWEY: They were very close. They were each other's best friends and they had a great relationship. A lot of it came from adversity. My father's parents did not want my father to marry my mother. She was Italian, and they wanted him to marry an Arab, like them. A lot of his siblings didn't really care for my mother either. My parents were insistent, got married and loved each other to the day they died.

My father didn't get drafted because he had asthma. He couldn't get into the service but he worked in a shipyard as his service requirement. He did not make much money back then. They lived in a tiny apartment and had no frills. I think that experience brought them closer together.

ROBERTS: *When they were both at home, which doesn't sound as if it happened a lot, what was it like?*

KOWEY: It was terrific. Because since my father wasn't home much, when he was home it was a celebration. One of his favorite things would be to bring something home from wherever he had been to cook. Like when he went to Maryland, he would bring back crabs. He might arrive home in the middle of the night because his run ended late. He would wake us all up, have the pot on the stove with the water boiling, and we would throw the crabs in and have a feast at 3:00 am in the morning. It was an event. When he left we were sad, and when he came home we were elated. I remember well the ebb and flow of our emotions.

ROBERTS: *You entered the ninth grade, what did you do after the first 8 years in school?*

KOWEY: I went to the local Catholic high school, *Bishop Kenrick*. Again, nuns and priest dominated as the teachers, but it was a pretty ordinary high school existence. I played intramural team sports but not too many because I was in the band. I was also on the debate team and a few other clubs.

ROBERTS: *Were there any teachers in high school who had a particular influence on you?*

KOWEY: Mr. Murray, an English teacher, was the director of the debate team. He taught me a tremendous amount about presenting in public. It has helped me in my career to speak comfortably in front of people. I'm not intimidated, and I think it was due at least partially to my experience on that debate team.

ROBERTS: *What did he do? What did he teach you?*

KOWEY: He taught English, but what he taught me was how to stand up in front of a group of people and present an argument that is cogent. Not to just fire facts at people but to build a story so people buy into your point of view. It was a debate society so you wanted people to be convinced. It worked. We had a great debate team and were the champions of the Catholic league several times. But a lot of it was because Mr. Murray was good at making us understand how to present arguments. It was a very good education. A number of my teammates became successful lawyers. Not a big surprise.

ROBERTS: *You would have been a great lawyer.*

KOWEY: My wife says that. She is a lawyer and she says that we goofed. She would have been a much better doctor because she is more compassionate. I like to argue and should have been the lawyer in the family.

ROBERTS: *How did Mr. Murray learn so much about teaching how to debate?*

KOWEY: He had been with the school for several years and director of the debate society for so long that he had learned a good deal. He was one of those naturally smart guys. I remember he was a chain smoker. Those were the days when you could smoke right in front of everybody. He died of lung cancer several years after I graduated. Too bad, he was a great guy.

ROBERTS: *Did you work during high school?*

KOWEY: I worked part-time for Mack Truck selling truck parts. I worked in the parts department one afternoon during the week, Saturday morning, and during the summer.

ROBERTS: *You always had some spending money in your pocket.*

KOWEY: Had to because it wasn't coming from anywhere else. My parents weren't stingy but just didn't have much to give.

ROBERTS: *Did you enjoy your work?*

KOWEY: I really think that my ability to connect with patients is because I spent a lot time with people at different socio-economic levels through my life. I dealt with truck drivers and laborers a lot. When I see such people as patients, I don't feel like I'm talking down to them. I understand where they're coming from. That's why I encourage kids to work during their schooling. It's not just for the money. You get exposed to other ideas and people and it's a valuable life experience.

One bad outcome from that experience is that I acquired a foul mouth. I was hanging around people who spoke that way and it stuck. I don't curse too often now, but when I'm on the golf course and hit a bad shot, it can get pretty nasty.

ROBERTS: *Did learning come easy for you in school or did you have to work at it?*

KOWEY: I think it came pretty easy. I worked hard but I don't remember having to struggle to learn things.

ROBERTS: *Were there books around your house? Did your mother encourage you read?*

KOWEY: Another big purchase that we made and that was a big decision for my parents was the World Book Encyclopedia. I was dying for those books. They finally bought a set and spent a lot of time reading them.

ROBERTS: *You probably read them all, didn't you? How old were you then?*

KOWEY: I would have been probably around fifth or sixth grade.

ROBERTS: *Learning appealed to you?*

KOWEY: Yes.

ROBERTS: *When you were talking about college, were you one of the first ones in your extended family to go to college?*

KOWEY: The very first.

ROBERTS: *Who gave you information on colleges?*

KOWEY: I have a great story about that. It was October of my senior year and I got a letter from St. Joseph's University. I knew St. Joe's was a great place, and that they had a good basketball team. I knew where the school was, but had never been there. The letter said, "Congratulations. You have been awarded a Presidential Scholarship to St. Joseph." Back then, the principals of Diocesan high schools in Philadelphia were allowed to allocate scholarships to the major Catholic colleges in Philadelphia. My principal learned that I was interested in St. Joe's, and, without telling me about it, gave one to me. I hadn't even applied to the place. My father came home that evening and I showed him the letter. He said that's fantastic and that is where you're going. I said I hadn't even seen the place. He said to get in the car and he drove me 20 miles into Philadelphia, circled around the campus 2 or 3 times and said, there now, you've seen it. And that's where you're going. I reminded him that I hadn't even applied. So he finds the admissions office, which is closed, and starts knocking on the door until an elderly priest came to the door. My father asked for an application and told me to fill it out in the car. He took it back to the Jesuit, got back in the car and said, "Congratulations - you've found your college." And that was my college interview and selection experience.

ROBERTS: *That was early on in the year?*

KOWEY: This was in October of my senior year of high school.

ROBERTS: *So your high school principal knew you were bright. You were the only one recommended for St. Joe's. And it was a full scholarship?*

KOWEY: I think it was a half scholarship. It was a substantial amount of money and my father was crazy for it.

ROBERTS: *You attended St. Joe's for college? It was 20 miles away from home? Did you live on campus? Did you have your own car?*

KOWEY: I commuted for the first 2 years. I have to laugh because my father who fixed cars made sure he got me a car to drive to Philly, but it was really a clunker. It was an old Oldsmobile Cutlass and I used to literally pray it wouldn't break down while I was driving to St. Joe's, especially on exam days. I was never really sure I would make it. When it did stop working, my father and I would patch it up and get me back on the road.

ROBERTS: *How long did it take to drive to college?*

KOWEY: About an hour with traffic.

ROBERTS: *An hour each way?*

KOWEY: Yes.

ROBERTS: *How did medicine come into the equation?*

KOWEY: For as long back as I can remember, I told people I wanted to be a doctor. I've tried to understand where that came from. We had a family doctor who I just idolized, named *James Barthold*. He was a primary care doctor with an office but he had no nurse, no appointments and no fancy equipment. He wore a suit and used a beautiful fountain pen. His office was nicely furnished, but the most important thing was two English Spaniels that were in his waiting room. I loved those dogs. I would ask to go to the doctor so I could see them. I think I got so enamored with

Dr. Barthold — I thought he was so cool — that I began to tell people I was going to be a doctor. There was no other place it could have come from. Nobody in the family or nobody we knew or none of our friends - nothing else that I can trace it to.

ROBERTS: *Did you have many illnesses growing up?*

KOWEY: Nothing serious. Measles, mumps, that kind of stuff but I was a healthy kid.

ROBERTS: *But you liked him too, he was a good guy.*

KOWEY: He didn't talk to me a lot but I just admired him. He was so confident and reassuring when my parents would go into his office. They always came out feeling as if something good had happened after he took care of them or me or my brother.

ROBERTS: *What was your implication when you say "he always wore a suit and had a nice pen" that he used? What did that do to you?*

KOWEY: I just admired the whole show. I thought he had put it all together and had figured out how to be a good doctor and how to portray himself as a professional and as a highly principled person who was really concerned about his patients.

Years later, when I was in college, I had a summer job as an orderly in our local hospital. I had to shave and prep the male patients before their surgeries. One day I got a list of the patients I had to shave and one of them was Dr. Barthold who was having a gallbladder operation. I almost lost it I was so nervous. I went to his room and he remembered me. It was crazy. We had a conversation catching up on my family and his. I got to tell him I was going to medical school and how he had influenced me. I never saw him after that. He died a few years later. I was grateful for the closure.

ROBERTS: *What did you do in college, other than travel back and forth from home? Were you involved in any activities?*

KOWEY: I was a biology major and a member of the biology club, and the pre-med honor fraternity. Most of my activities were science related. I played a lot of tennis and worked out with the team. I also played golf.

ROBERTS: *Your father liked golf?*

KOWEY: Yes he did. He was a terrible golfer, but he loved the game. It gave him a chance to hang out with his friends.

ROBERTS: *Did you take up tennis before college?*

KOWEY: Yes. Played some in high school and then in college. I wasn't good enough to actually be on the competition squad.

ROBERTS: *You look like you were a good athlete. Did you run fast?*

KOWEY: I liked playing any sport. I was a good shortstop in Little League. I didn't hit well but had a good glove and arm.

ROBERTS: *Have you kept exercising through the years? Still play tennis and golf?*

KOWEY: Yes.

ROBERTS: *What's your handicap?*

KOWEY: 11 or 12. It depends on the time of year.

ROBERTS: *How tall are you?*

KOWEY: 5'8".

ROBERTS: *What's your weight?*
KOWEY: 170.
ROBERTS: *College was quite an experience for you. That was the first time you were really out of the home.*
KOWEY: The last 2 years I got into an apartment, which I shared with 3 other pre-med guys. We lived off campus. This did not make my father happy. He thought I was wasting money because I could still have lived at home.
ROBERTS: *Were you paying for it?*
KOWEY: Most of it. They were helping out a bit.
ROBERTS: *You did work all through college?*
KOWEY: I did.
ROBERTS: *With the auto parts job initially?*
KOWEY: Yes, mostly delivering truck parts. Then I had all different types of jobs — soda canning factory, boxing soda cans for delivery. I worked in a steel mill one summer because that paid very well. The goal was to make as much money as possible during the summer. I had jobs pretty much through college.
ROBERTS: *When did you realize you were smart?*
KOWEY: Probably sometime in college. It dawned on me after my second or third year that I was going to be okay.
ROBERTS: *How did you do in college? Were you graded conservatively? What year did you enter college?*
KOWEY: 1967. I had a pretty rugged freshman year and didn't do as well as I thought I would. Inorganic chemistry was tough and I had a calculus course that I just didn't nail. My GPA after my first year was about 3.0, which wasn't going to cut it for medical school. I don't know what happened to make me switch gears but I didn't get another B. I pretty much aced the next 3 years.
ROBERTS: *What did you do different?*
KOWEY: I remember studying a bit harder, being able to game the system a little bit better. Not just putting the time in but knowing how to maneuver things and study efficiently. I wasn't just picking gut courses because I took all the usual pre-med stuff but I got on a roll.
ROBERTS: *Where there any teachers/professors in particular that had a prominent influence on you?*
KOWEY: The guy who ran the biology department was *Louie Marks* and he was a real character and looked a lot like Groucho Marx. He was a feisty guy. He really ran a tight ship. His goal was to get as many of the premed biology majors into medical school as he reasonably could. He did an amazing job. Katie Nash taught us comparative anatomy and was a wonderful person too. She was a former Ms. Maryland. She taught us when she was in the fifties, but she was still gorgeous. We all loved her even though she was a tough grader and her course very demanding.
ROBERTS: *How good a college/university is St. Joe's?*
KOWEY: It's an excellent Jesuit educational experience. It's not a large place but the Jesuits have a great tradition of emphasizing reading, writing, and thinking. The basics. So when you graduate, you have the tools to achieve. I am on the board of The College of Arts and Sciences now at St. Joe's and spend a lot of time there, including doing a little teaching and mentoring pre-med students.

ROBERTS: *What is the student body when you were there?*
KOWEY: There were about 400 people in our graduating class.
ROBERTS: *The entire school was how many?*
KOWEY: Two thousand. Up to about 4,000 these days, but still a pretty small school.
ROBERTS: *When you graduated, do you know what your ranking was in your class?*
KOWEY: Pretty sure I was in the top 25.
ROBERTS: *If it hadn't have been for your freshman year you would have really been up there. How did you go about getting into medical school? Who was your advisor then?*
KOWEY: Dr. Marks was our principal advisor. We all applied to the same places in Philly— Penn, Jefferson, Hahneman, Temple, and Penn State. Everyone applied to all those schools.
ROBERTS: *You got into Penn? Were there many that got into Penn?*
KOWEY: 35 people from St. Joe's applied to medical schools my year. There was a lot of interest because it was an automatic deferment, which meant no Viet Nam for those of us with low draft numbers. One guy got into Hopkins and Harvard, five of us got into Penn, and everyone else got into other schools in Philly. It was an amazing year, very smart class.
ROBERTS: *How did Penn hit you?*
KOWEY: I was in an accelerated curriculum in which we did basic sciences in one year before starting our clinical rotations in our second year.
ROBERTS: *You got put into the accelerated group from college?*
KOWEY: The whole class was in the accelerated program. The goal was to get us all in the clinic early, and have a lot of time to go back to do electives in either the basic sciences or in the clinic.
ROBERTS: *How many were in your class at Penn?*
KOWEY: About 150.
ROBERTS: *So what happened? Was medical school what you thought it was going to be like? Was there any major surprises? Did you find it a major step up from college?*
KOWEY: It was a major step-up from college, and it was a difficult for me. I remember the first several months of medical school being very intimidating. I was anxious about fitting in at such a sophisticated and advanced institution. But after a few months, I began to realize that I was fine academically. I had been well prepared and totally competitive with the students in my class. By the second semester of the first year, I was feeling better about being there. I also had a very positive experience at the Radcliffe Infirmary in Oxford between my second and third years of medical school. I did well on that demanding clinical rotation with Professor Paul Beeson as my attending, and I became much more confident about my clinical abilities.
ROBERTS: *You started medical school in 1971? Who paid for your medical school?*
KOWEY: My father wanted me to go to Penn State —Hershey because the tuition was a fraction of Penn's

tuition. He couldn't understand why I chose Penn. Penn State was $700 a year and Penn was $3,000. He said he would pay what Hershey charged and I would have to make up the difference, which meant grants, loans, and working.

ROBERTS: *Did you get some scholarships?*

KOWEY: Probably got half in scholarship and the rest was grants and loans.

ROBERTS: *In medical school you lived near the campus?*

KOWEY: I got an apartment near the art museum in Philadelphia because my two roommates were going to Temple Medical School. They were friends from college. We decided to get someplace in-between our two schools.

ROBERTS: *Who had extraordinary impact on you in medical school?*

KOWEY: There were a number of psychiatrists who had an impact on me in medical school. They were not psychoanalysts but neurobiologists who were interested in neurochemistry and membrane physiology. I did some research and got interested in the chemical basis of psychiatric disease. Believe it or not I planned to do a psychiatry residency at Penn. I had to do a year of medicine first. I picked Hershey since it was close. It was a new medical school and an interesting hospital.

I arrived at Hershey and was assigned in my second month to the coronary care unit with an every other-night rotation. My two attending physicians were Barbara Roberts and Robert DeJoseph, just out of their training and very enthusiastic. I spent three months with them attending and was completely and utterly seduced into cardiology, especially arrhythmia management. I went to the Chairman of Medicine, Graham Jeffries, and asked him if I could stay and do three years of medicine so I could apply for cardiology fellowships. He said fine.

ROBERTS: *Hershey Pennsylvania at that time was a brand new medical school.*

KOWEY: Yes.

ROBERTS: *That was really the first time you had been away from home?*

KOWEY: Yes, first time out of Philly.

ROBERTS: *How did that hit you?*

KOWEY: Hershey was a small town. There wasn't much to do so the residents bonded. It was one of the most collegial experiences of my medical career. I still keep in touch with many of them. We hung out together and became involved with each others' families. I enjoyed it.

ROBERTS: *When you were in medical school, did you have a hard time as you rotated through specialties deciding what you wanted to do?*

KOWEY: Yes I did. I liked everything I saw. But I the assignments that interested me the most by far were the psychiatric rotations. I was terribly interested in behavioral medicine as it related to physiology. I became convinced that psychiatric diseases are biochemically mediated. It was just a question of figuring out how.

ROBERTS: *Maybe that brought you more into drugs that you have subsequently been on?*

KOWEY: I perceived that the heart was going to be easier to study than the brain. That we were going to learn a

whole lot more about the biochemistry of the heart and how drugs affect the heart than we would about the brain. The heart is a lot more accessible to study and much less complex than the brain. It was the same idea; I just switched organs.

ROBERTS: *Was there any other experiences in medical school that had a lasting impact on you?*

KOWEY: I discovered in medical school that I liked procedures, I like to use my hands. I discovered that cardiac procedures were fun. It was a different way of interacting with the patient. The other thing I developed was a deep appreciation of literature and how it influences our field.

ROBERTS: *You knew before medical school was over that you didn't want to go into private practice?*

KOWEY: I think that was pretty clear to me even before medical school.

ROBERTS: *You said you got involved in research in medical school with neuropsychiatrists but you didn't publish any manuscripts. When was your first publication?*

KOWEY: In my cardiology fellowship.

ROBERTS: *How did you get your cardiology fellowship?*

KOWEY: Barbara Roberts had trained at the Brigham. She and I had several conversations about where to look for fellowships. I was pretty sure that I wanted to do electrophysiology at that point. I was interested in cardiac rhythm problems after my coronary care unit rotation. But this was happening just as electrophysiology was getting started. Hein Wellens had just published his experience with programmed stimulation of the heart, so the discipline was in its infancy. There were only a few places in the country where you could go and have any expectation of getting training in electrophysiology — Penn, Duke, Stanford, Indianapolis, and the Brigham. I applied to those programs. I didn't get into Duke or Stanford. I interviewed with Doug Zipes at Indianapolis and didn't get accepted. I enjoy giving him a hard time about that.

I was getting very nervous after multiple denials but finally got that positive phone call from *Bernard Lown* and Tom Graboys at the Peter Bent Brigham. I guess it was February of my second year of residency.

ROBERTS: *This was what year?*

KOWEY: February 1977.

ROBERTS: *You started in July 1977?*

KOWEY: I started in July 1978. Back then you applied for fellowship during the second year of your residency.

ROBERTS: *At that time, Braunwald went to the Brigham in 1972. What kind of program did Bernie Lown have at the Brigham in 1978?*

KOWEY: There were several services at the Brigham. *Richard Gorlin* and *Ed Sonenblick* had departed for New York. Lew Dexter was still there, but Gene Braunwald had really established himself at the Brigham before I got there. Lown had labs and offices in the Harvard School of Public Health but he had a large clinical service at the Brigham. So there was the Braunwald fellowship and the Lown fellowship. Many Braunwald fellows spent some time on the Lown service and the Lown fellows rotated on the Brigham clinical services. Most of my catheterization and echocardiography training was on the Brigham services. My research and arrhythmia training was with Lown. In many ways, I got the best of both worlds.

ROBERTS: *Tell me about Bernie Lown. I went on a trip with him when he was head of a delegation to study sudden death in Moscow about 1972. He was an absolute charmer. How did that work out for you?*

KOWEY: If you asked me to pick the person who had the greatest impact on my professional life, it would have to be Dr. Lown. He is one of the most fascinating people I've ever met. He was brilliant but personable, conversant - able to talk to almost anybody — patients or presidents. But the thing that made the biggest impression on me was his clinical skills. He is simply a master clinician. He is an amazing doctor. The most striking thing about him is his intuition at the bedside. He was able to arrive at the truth, even with what all of us thought was pretty superficial evidence. An astounding talent.

ROBERTS: *He had trained with Sam Levine?*

KOWEY: Yes.

ROBERTS: *Did you have any contact with Sam Levine?*

KOWEY: Sam passed away before I got to Boston. But we spent a lot of time talking about him. Lown was Sam Levine's fellow and partner for decades. They were more father-son than colleagues. I have a copy of one of Dr. Levine's original textbooks. It is page after page of commentary about patients. There are no tables, no figures, just information about patients he had seen. He had a photographic memory of all of the patients he had ever cared for. He taught Lown to be a master cardiologist.

ROBERTS: *How much time did you spend with Bernie Lown? Did you make rounds with him? He had a substantial private practice, right?*

KOWEY: Yes he did. We had two rotations with Dr. Lown. The first was on the clinical service at the Brigham. For 3 months we rounded with Dr. Lown daily. The other rotation was in his private office. We were assigned to the office rotation for 3 months. It was pretty intense.

ROBERTS: *What do you mean by intense?*

KOWEY: He is very demanding. If he asked a question, you had better know the answer because he does not suffer fools. Dr. Lown would also make the fellows write his notes. My first reaction to that idea was decidedly negative. But I was surprised to discover that it was fine and completely within the spirit of our relationship because we were literally at his knee. He was teaching me even as he was dictating his note. It was an extraordinary experience. I've never seen anything like it in medicine. It was an apprenticeship in every sense of the term.

ROBERTS: *Who were you fellow colleague fellows when you were there with Lown?*

KOWEY: Rodney Falk, Jeff Matos, and Betty Corrigan were the other three in my year. Peter Friedman, Elliot Antman and Bill Colucci were Braunwald fellows at the same time.

ROBERTS: *Was it a 3-year program at that time?*

KOWEY: It was a 2-year but most of us ended up spending more time there.

ROBERTS: *How did you get into electrophysiology?*

KOWEY: I was captivated by the whole idea that you could observe arrhythmias on the body surface. I fell in love with electrocardiography. I thought it was the coolest thing I'd ever seen. That you could record somebody's heart rhythm on the body surface, analyze it, and diagnose arrhythmias was fantastic. Then you had the opportunity to put catheters inside the heart and record arrhythmias and learn even more. You could even stimulate the heart to arrhythmia, administer drugs, and observe the effects of the drugs on electrical properties. It put everything together — anatomy, physiology, pharmacology, pathology. I fell in love.

ROBERTS: *How did you start doing EP procedures?*

KOWEY: It was during my first year of fellowship with Dr. Lown. Phil Podrid, who became one of my best friends, had just finished his own fellowship and was doing catheter procedures at the Brigham. They took place in the Levine Cardiac Unit in a small procedure room. We carried a homemade stimulator from the dog lab. We used a single right ventricular catheter, induced ventricular arrhythmias, placed the patient on an antiarrhythmic drug, and determined its effectiveness in suppressing inducability.

ROBERTS: *Did Bernie Lown do any of those procedures himself?*

KOWEY: No, he never did the invasive procedures himself.

ROBERTS: *But he knew what was going on in there?*

KOWEY: He would come in and observe and tell us what he thought. .

ROBERTS: *When did you leave Boston? You were there 3 years?*

KOWEY: I left at the end of 1981.

ROBERTS: *And you came back to Philly?*

KOWEY: I did. It was a tough decision. I had a couple of offers to stay in Boston. I considered an advanced fellowship at MGH. But my parents were still in Philly. My whole family was in Philly. I thought it was important to go back. I went to the Medical College of Pennsylvania, which was a medical school in Philadelphia. It doesn't exist anymore. It got absorbed into Hahnemann. They wanted me to start a program in electrophysiology. It was an opportunity to build something from scratch.

ROBERTS: *How long were you there? That's a big private hospital.*

KOWEY: Yes it was. It was a private medical school hospital. I was there 9 years.

ROBERTS: *But you had a lot of patients there.*

KOWEY: It was cool because they allowed me to build an electrophysiology practice from scratch. Over those 9 years that's exactly what I did. The only other established program in Philadelphia at that time was Penn.

ROBERTS: *But you started moving around in Philadelphia so after those first 9 years where did you go?*

KOWEY: I moved once to Lankenau in 1990. That was it. I've been there ever since.

ROBERTS: *But you've had appointments at Hahnemann?*

KOWEY: Correct. MCP was absorbed into Hahnemann-Drexel so that was where the Hahnemann appointment came from.

ROBERTS: *But physically you didn't move?*

KOWEY: No. I never spent any time at Hahnemann or any other school.

ROBERTS: *When you went to Lankenau where did that name come from?*

KOWEY: John D. Lankenau was a German entrepreneur and in 1860 he opened a hospital for German-Americans in Philadelphia called "The German Hospital." In 1861, it was commandeered by the Union for wounded soldiers. It reverted back to the German Hospital after the war but shortly thereafter was named The Lankenau Hospital after its founder. In 1955, it was moved to where it is now, the former grounds of the Overbrook Country Club. It is situated one block west of the Philadelphia city line.

ROBERTS: *What was the advantage/disadvantage to that?*

KOWEY: No wage tax. That's a big advantage in hiring nurses, and staff who work at the hospital. It's a perfect location at the top of the Main Line. We are right next to several nice residential areas so we have a wonderfully diverse demographic.

ROBERTS: *How big of a hospital is it?*

KOWEY: About 380 beds.

ROBERTS: *When you were there in 1990, why did you go there?*

KOWEY: Leonard Dreifus was the chief of cardiology and he was retiring. So Len actually called me and asked me if I would be interested in looking at the job. Initially, I wasn't interested because it wasn't a university hospital. But it was a large teaching hospital and it had its own fellowship. Len had built a beautiful basic electrophysiology laboratory. I had a basic lab that I knew I could transfer there. Most importantly, they didn't have much clinical electrophysiology. It was an opportunity for me to bring my clinical practice there, to continue my research and help with the fellowship program. It had all the components I was looking for. Plus I didn't have to move from Philly, which made my family happy.

ROBERTS: *Where do you live?*

KOWEY: I live in Bryn Mawr, which is ten minutes west of Lankenau.

ROBERTS: *When did you start dating and how did you meet your wife?*

KOWEY: I'm in my second marriage. My first wife and I met in college when I did that operating room orderly job. She was an operating room student nurse. We met, got married and had one beautiful daughter.

ROBERTS: *You were married in medical school?*

KOWEY: Yes, after the second year. We divorced after about 7 years of marriage. It was a relatively amicable divorce. We both realized that we wanted to go in different directions. She lives in North Carolina now and is still an OR nurse. We are friends and keep in touch. I met my present wife when I was at the Medical College of Pennsylvania. She was the head nurse of the coronary care unit. That was in 1982.

ROBERTS: *You weren't single very long in between those marriages?*

KOWEY: No, I divorced in 1981 and remarried in 1986.

ROBERTS: *What is your wife's name?*

KOWEY: Dorothy Freal Kowey.

ROBERTS: *Now, she is a lawyer now?*

KOWEY: Yes. She got tired of being a CCU nurse administrator. She went to law school but didn't like the law so much. Now she is a potter and very good at it.

ROBERTS: *At home? Or does she have a studio?*

KOWEY: We have a studio in our house. She also does stuff at our local arts center. She was a Fine Art major at Penn and then realized she couldn't make a living doing that so that's why she went to nursing school. Now she's back to art. She's a pretty extraordinary person for whom I have great respect.

ROBERTS: *You have a daughter by your first marriage and another daughter by Dorothy and Dorothy has a daughter from a previous relationship?*

KOWEY: Yes. Our youngest is an adopted daughter. So I have a biological daughter and Dorothy has a biological daughter and together we have an adopted daughter. It's truly a "modern family" unit.

ROBERTS: *How did you do that?*

KOWEY: When my daughter went to college, we were still relatively young and we didn't want an empty nest. We had some difficulties getting pregnant so we decided to adopt. Dorothy was in legal practice at the time. Her secretary came in one day crying because her son's girlfriend was pregnant and they weren't able to keep the baby. She asked if we might want to adopt the baby. We jumped at it, and that's how we adopted our daughter, Olivia.

ROBERTS: *Your children's names are what?*

KOWEY: The oldest is Susan Kealy, born 1969; the middle one is Jaime Shean, 1977, and the last is Olivia Kowey, 1990. Olivia is in Law School. Susan and Jaime are practicing attorneys.

ROBERTS: *So when you all get together, what's it like?*

KOWEY: I tell lawyer jokes. I always try to find one that stick pins in them but they don't care. They just ignore their silly father. Susan is a Trust and Estate Lawyer in Boston, and Jaime is in California and does credit law. My son-in-law in Boston is on the law faculty at Boston University and my middle daughter's husband is an intellectual property and patent attorney. And we are blessed with six beautiful grandchildren.

ROBERTS: *Peter, what is your day like right now? What time do you get up in the morning?*

KOWEY: I'm up at 4:30 in the morning. I make sure our dogs do their business and are settled. We have three Portuguese Water Dogs who like to crawl back into bed with my wife after I get up. Then I exercise on an elliptical trainer and rowing machine for about 30 to 45 minutes. I then shower and dress and I am at my desk before 6:00 am. Between 6:00 and 8:00 I try to do something creative. If possible, I try to get some work done on one of my novels. Once I get to 8:00, things get pretty hectic. The components of my days are similar but one day is never completely like the last. Two days a week I see patients. I have a lot of administrative meetings since I run the Division. I have a fair number of research meetings with my staff about various projects. I do a fair amount of consulting so teleconferences are dispersed through the day. I have a teaching responsibility for the fellowship and residency at Lankenau but I also have a faculty appointment at Jefferson so some of my teaching time is at Jefferson downtown. Every day is a menagerie of things that are all set up for me ahead of time by my amazing secretaries. Donna and Roe have been with me for decades and have kept me on a very even keel.

ROBERTS: *When do you leave the hospital at night?*

KOWEY: I rarely leave later than 6:00. Since I don't see my wife in the morning, I feel strongly about getting home and spending time with my family. I don't do dinner meetings or symposia very often. I try really hard to preserve some quality time with my wife—and my dogs, of course.

ROBERTS: *Do you do work at night?*

KOWEY: No. I did when I was younger but now that my day starts so early, I am pretty used up after dinner. So we just relax, I have a Scotch, and we put our feet up and watch something on TV. I can afford to do that because I work very efficiently during the day. I work at my desk while I have a small lunch. No time is wasted.

ROBERTS: *How many staff do you have in cardiology at Lankenau?*

KOWEY: I'm the head of cardiology for Main Line Health which has 4 hospitals in the system. There are about 100 cardiologists within the system. I'm administratively responsible for those cardiologists.

ROBERTS: *Do you make those appointments or do you just approve them?*

KOWEY: We have a fulltime faculty at Lankenau that I have more control over. The other hospitals are mostly private practice and they hire as they wish. All staff privileges and faculty appointments come through me.

ROBERTS: *How many cardiologists are at Lankenau?*

KOWEY: There are about 30.

ROBERTS: *How many fellows do you have?*

KOWEY: Sixteen. (Three-year fellowship and 4 per year). We usually have 2 interventional fellows and 2 electrophysiology fellows.

ROBERTS: *How many administrative, laboratory and other staff do you have?*

KOWEY: I'd have to sit down and count. Just say a whole lot.

ROBERTS: *Do you know most of them?*

KOWEY: I know almost everybody because I've been there so long. In fact I still have people that I brought with me from MCP. My personal secretary, Donna, has been with me for 32 years. Most of my staff is very senior, and very good.

ROBERTS: *Going through your CV I've never seen a list of consulting as long as yours. My own view is that physicians and pharmaceutical companies need to work together more rather than less. Your list impresses me rather than an opposite view of it. How did you get involved with evaluating so many drugs?*

KOWEY: First of all, I completely agree with what you just said. The only way to advance therapeutics is with industry support. Nearly every important therapeutic intervention in medicine has come with industry support. Even ideas that start in academic laboratories eventually need industry backing. Development is just too expensive. If industry is going to do a good job, they need help. That's a very important part of what I do.

ROBERTS: *When was your first appointment to the FDA?*

KOWEY: 1984. I was just a pup. Two years out of training. When I was a fellow I had worked with Public Citizen, a healthcare advocacy group in Washington run by Sid Wolfe. We published an article about unnecessary pacemakers and it got noticed. I actually ended up testifying about overutilization of pacemakers at a Senate Subcommittee meeting. Sid nominated me to be on the Cardiorenal Advisory Committee as the consumer nominated representative. I honestly had no idea what I was doing. I got to the first meeting and was so naïve. I opened my mouth and said something incredibly stupid. Ray Lipicky ran that division back then and he just let me have it. Remember, this was a public hearing of a new drug application and he basically destroyed me—and I deserved it. I quickly realized that this was a very important assignment and that I had to be better prepared. I started to really get into it. We would get these huge boxes of information to be reviewed prior to the meetings and the data were very interesting, as were my colleagues. *Bert Pitt, Ray Woosley, Craig Brater, Milton Packer, Lloyd Fisher, Jeremy Ruskin, Craig Pratt* were all members of that committee. They were great. We would have meetings 4 to 6 times a year. They asked me to come back for a second term and I continued on for 10 years. I was also on the FDA CV device committee for 4 years. Then I rotated off and as soon as I did, I started getting calls from drug and device companies asking if I would consult for their company. That's what started it. I agreed. I knew the ropes and could help them with their development programs. We got a lot of clinical trials started that way and a lot of drugs approved.

ROBERTS: *How much do you travel?*

KOWEY: I have made a real conscious effort to stay out of airports. I do a fair amount of traveling in the northeast corridor but I don't like being away for long periods. The nice thing about living in Philly, not that it was planned, is that we are close to Boston, Washington, New Jersey, Delaware, and New York, where almost all pharmaceutical companies have offices. So it's usual for me to get where I need to be by car, or train.

ROBERTS: *You see patients 2 days a week? Is that a morning or afternoon?*

KOWEY: It's usually all day.

ROBERTS: *You still have quite a big practice?*

KOWEY: Yes I do.

ROBERTS: *Do you do EP procedures anymore yourself?*

KOWEY: No, I gave that up several years ago.

ROBERTS: *Was that hard to give up?*

KOWEY: I thought it was going to be hard. I was sad initially but it freed me up and I was so happy about getting out from underneath what was a crushing schedule. I realized I was hurrying through procedures trying to beat the clock to get to a meeting. My partners love it because I feed them a lot of cases and they enjoy procedures.

ROBERTS: *Are you on salary?*

KOWEY: Yes. Straight salary.

ROBERTS: *No matter how many patients you see?*

KOWEY: I am paid for patient care as well as the administrative stuff. I convinced our Administration that a straight salary was best for me, that I didn't need any incentives. I wasn't going to stop seeing patients or sit on my hands.

ROBERTS: *That's nice. You've done a lot of investigative work through the years, what contribution that you've made are you most proud of?*

KOWEY: One of my first projects when I started at MCP was the implantable defibrillator. I got to know Mirowski very well and he agreed to let us implant the original device. Toby Engel and I actually put in the third device in the world in 1982. Sinai in Baltimore was first, Stanford second and then us. We stayed on the vanguard and produced several important papers about that new technology. We were really in on the ground floor.

I've also had a hand in the development of several drugs that are being used in cardiovascular medicine. I helped in various stages in the development of those drugs. For example, IV amiodarone was one of our most important projects. The oral formulation was approved in the 1980's but we had to spend several additional years on the development of the intravenous formulation. Mel Scheinman and I directed the clinical trial work that eventually got the drug through the FDA regulatory process. There are a lot of other examples of antiarrhythmic drugs, drugs for other cardiac indications, and most recently the novel oral anticoagulants. I am very proud of helping to get those drugs out to patients who need them.

ROBERTS: *You and Ray Woosley. Anyone else?*

KOWEY: Jim Reiffel, Jerry Naccarelli, Craig Pratt and a few others have worked hard in this space. It is challenging to say the least.

ROBERTS: *Have you been offered head of any pharmaceutical company just out of curiosity?*

KOWEY: No one has ever offered one to me formally. I've had people assess my level of interest, but I've had none.

ROBERTS: *No interest?*

KOWEY: No. I like what I'm doing. I never wanted to ascend the academic ladder, and I never wanted to go into industry. I've always wanted to see patients and be a cardiologist. The best thing about what I've been able to do is preserve my practice for 30 years and at the same time do lots of other interesting things. There is no other job that would have allowed me to do that.

ROBERTS: *Is cardiology at Lankenau a separate department or are you in the Department of Medicine?*

KOWEY: We are in the Department of Medicine.

ROBERTS: *As a division of cardiology?*

KOWEY: That's correct.

ROBERTS: *Do you have much contact with whoever is chairman?*

KOWEY: Yes. The guy who has been chairman for the past 20 years just stepped down and was replaced with another Infectious Disease physician. I have had good relationships with both of them. They have been very nice about leaving me alone because it works. We went from an averaged sized good cardiovascular program when I started to an immense program. We have tripled our revenue generation. We just built a $500 million Heart Pavilion on our campus. It's been a successful cardiovascular program because I've had a clear vision of what I wanted to do. A lot of my success was predicated on the idea that I wasn't leaving, I wasn't looking to become a dean or a president of a pharmaceutical company.

ROBERTS: *Do you take vacations?*

KOWEY: I take time away for different reasons. In the summertime we take a couple of weeks off to go to our lake house in the Poconos, my favorite spot in the world. I get a lot of my writing done up there. But other than that it's more in the flow of where meetings are being held. My wife will come along and we will spend an extra day or two at a nice place. We go out of our way to travel to see our grandchildren. We have three in California and three in Boston. They are the love of our lives. I am a sucker for lecture invitations in either place.

ROBERTS: *How did you get into the novel writing?*

KOWEY: The Jesuits in college encouraged us to use our right brain. They thought it was good for bio majors to take courses in other areas and I loved creative writing. I never pursued it. I knew that I could write well but I never had the motivation until I was in a court room defending a cardiologist in a malpractice case in 2004. A young woman who had long QT syndrome and had not been properly diagnosed died suddenly. The family sued everyone who had ever seen her including the cardiologist. The patient's husband was a multimillionaire. He was on the stand testifying how much he missed his wife and didn't know how he was going to live without her or who was going to take care of their children. None of it was true but nobody could tell the jury because it was prejudicial. I was furious because I knew the facts. To vent my spleen, I decided to write a story about the case. I had a yellow pad and pencil and I started scribbling. Once I started writing I just couldn't stop. I was like a maniac. I wrote the first draft in a few months but it was terrible. I still have that draft and can't believe I wrote something so stupid and prejudicial. The characters and scenes were poorly drawn. So I took some courses and started working on cleaning it up and it got better, with help from some friends. I finally managed to find a publisher. *Lethal Rhythm* was a success. There was a lot of excitement about it and the publisher agreed to a second book, *Deadly Rhythm*. My third book will be titled *Empty Net* and should be out next year. It's been so much fun. I've had an opportunity to meet some interesting people including a few who might be able to help to make the books into a TV series or movie. I've met people all over the country — publishers, literary types I never would have known. I've learned a tremendous amount.

ROBERTS: *When do you write?*

KOWEY: Early morning generally, but I try to carve out a few hours to write whenever I can.

ROBERTS: *If you get up at 4:30am, what time do you go to bed?*

KOWEY: No later than 10:30p

ROBERTS: *So 6 hours is normal for you and you feel good on that amount?*

KOWEY: Yes. I take a 20 minute nap every day in my office. It's essential. I never go out to lunch. I sit at my desk, have a small lunch, and then stretch out on the floor with a pillow. I wake up spontaneously and feel terrific.

ROBERTS: *So you and Tommy Edison….*

KOWEY: He almost never slept at night. He would work 4 hours and nap for a short time and then start working again. I just take one nap. If I don't get that nap when I'm at work, I'm dead. My afternoon is ruined. The phone gets turned off and my secretary knows what is going on. I recommend naps to my patients, especially my elderly patients. There is a good reason for siestas.

ROBERTS: *You were born in 1950. You are stepping down from your cardiology chiefship when?*

KOWEY: In about $1\frac{1}{2}$ years.

ROBERTS: *You are 63 now?*

KOWEY: I'll be 65 when I step down.

ROBERTS: *But you don't have to step down? That is a voluntary move on your part?*

KOWEY: I've been chief for 25 years and I think it's time for someone else to take over. I think if I went longer I would just get stale and I think it's time for somebody with new ideas to take over the reins. I'm going to stick around. I'm not leaving but I'll be part time. I'll support my successor because I want him/her to be successful. I think there comes a time in everyone's life when it's time to step aside.

ROBERTS: *What do you want to do after your retirement?*

KOWEY: Whatever I want to do. That's the goal: to wake up and plan the day with my wife. I want to write more, continue to do consults, and research. I'll still see patients, just not as many. I want to get out from under the administrative meetings and be more independent.

ROBERTS: *Do you do much malpractice testifying? I'm sure you are called all the time.*

KOWEY: I get lots of phone calls. I take cases selectively. I have a low threshold for taking a look but I'm rarely in the courtroom. I only take cases about which I feel strongly. Fortunately, if I write a strong opinion, the cases generally don't go to court. But I will go if I have to.

ROBERTS: *Doug Zipes does a good bit of cases, doesn't he?*

KOWEY: Yes. There are a few excellent people who do it selectively, like Doug, Eric Prystowsky, and Bob Myerburg. I feel obligated to do it because I think there are clearly cases wherein physicians have been taken advantage or where they haven't really done anything wrong and deserve to be defended.

ROBERTS: *What do you think Obamacare is going to do to your activities?*

KOWEY: I'm so far along in my career that I don't think it's going to have a major impact on me personally. There is potential for Obamacare to turn cardiology on its head. The end game of Obamacare is a capitated environment. There will be a fixed allotment per year per life and the ACO will be allowed to spend the money any way it chooses. But when the money runs out that will be it. If that happens, fee-for-service cardiology will vanish and we will no longer value people who do lots of procedures the way we do today. It will turn the world upside down. I think that is a good thing because we are doing way too many procedures and we over utilize technology and underutilize people's brains. It's going to be painful transition but I think that's where we need to head.

ROBERTS: *What do you think about all the expensive procedures that physicians and surgeons do? What's going to happen to them?*

KOWEY: I think as a society we are going to have some tough decisions as to how we allocate them. We're not going to be able to do as many and there will have to be some mechanism put into place to select patients who are most likely to benefit because we just can't go on the way we are. We just don't have enough money. Technologic advances continue, in the drug and the device side of cardiology without much regard for the cost issues. We are creating an amazing tension between what we can do and what we might be allowed to do. I can't bring any new technology or treatment into our hospital anymore without first being able to sit down and explain to an administrator what it's going to cost, what it's going to replace, and how much money it's going to generate. This includes new drugs, devices, and diagnostic procedures. They all have to be justified economically. In the old days if you wanted something new, you went out, bought it, and that was it. We're going to see progressively more scrutiny.

ROBERTS: *There are a lot of hospitals in Philadelphia, medical schools and some of those are going to close in relatively near future.*

KOWEY: I wouldn't say near future but I think there's certainly going to have to be an adjustment. As we get into less bed utilization and less technology, there are a number of hospitals that are going to have difficulties. Hard to say at this point when that will happen and which ones will be the losers, but I think that there is going to have to be some consolidation. You are right about Philadelphia being a very tough environment, especially in cardiology. We have way too many cardiologists. We have more Electrophysiologists in the Philadelphia metropolitan region than the United Kingdom.

ROBERTS: *How do you keep track of that?*

KOWEY: It isn't easy. We used to train our competition. Fortunately, more of our trainees are heading out to practice in other parts of the country.

ROBERTS: *You put that in the contracts?*

KOWEY: No, that wouldn't be fair to them. We did try to put a hold on our electrophysiology fellowship for a couple of years and not train people, and we were told that we would lose our accreditation.

ROBERTS: *What about 4 cardiology fellows per year, that's a lot.*

KOWEY: We are not the largest program in Philadelphia. I think we are sized well. You need to have a critical number of trainees to maintain the quality of the program.

ROBERTS: *What's your view on the new statin guidelines?*

KOWEY: It amazes me as a trialist that people can come out with a whole new paradigm without any new data. There were no new data that generated this guideline reformation. Guidelines are like that—based on a lot of opinions. As far as I'm concerned it's a tempest in a teapot. I think doctors will continue to measure lipids and disperse medicine based on an objective laboratory measurement not based on a risk score. I hope the new guidelines don't choke off lines of research. There are several new drugs coming along that will help us treat patients at risk. Guidelines don't necessarily do us a whole lot of good. They are not the standard of care but they are interpreted as such, and help lawyers when they sue doctors. Doctors aren't fully aware of what's in the guidelines. There are at least six or seven AF guidelines that are all different from each other. So which one are you supposed to pay attention to? I think we are going overboard with them. I'm still going to measure cholesterols and LDLs and give statins if they are elevated.

ROBERTS: *What do you do for fun?*

KOWEY: My wife says I have ADHD but I do a lot of different things. I play golf and tennis, and ski — downhill and cross-country. We like to sail and bike too. We have three Portuguese waterdogs that need a lot of exercise. We are total dog nuts. I like taking walks through the woods with the dogs. My daughters have kept me interested in a lot of things. Our youngest daughter is attending law school in Philadelphia now and finds great restaurants and shops for us to go to. We love to spend time with the grandchildren. They range in age from14 down to 6, and are continuously amusing. We have a very busy life but a happy one.

ROBERTS: *Is your daughter in Philadelphia?*

KOWEY: No she is in California.

ROBERTS: *And your second daughter?*

KOWEY: Dorothy's daughter is in Boston.

ROBERTS: *How far is your lake house from your home?*

KOWEY: One hour and 40 minutes, 92.6 miles. It's a terrific place on Lake Naomi. It's a developed community with a lot of amenities and our house is set back off the lake in the woods. It's heaven.

ROBERTS: *Are you religious?*

KOWEY: I was raised a Catholic. I was an altar boy and did all the Catholic stuff growing up. But somewhere along the way I lost the Catholic thing. I still believe there is a lot of what the Catholics teach that's important but we don't go to church. The ritual does nothing for me.

ROBERTS: *Peter is there anything you'd like to talk about that we haven't touched on?*

KOWEY: No, I think you did an amazing job of covering things. I'm at an interesting point in my life. We spend so much time at the beginning of our careers organizing what we are going to do. We thought it was complicated and it was, but we had a single goal: medicine. This part of our lives is even more complex because we have so many wonderful choices. What are you going to do when you are not the chief, or running a department? We have to make good choices. I'm looking forward to this time of my life and excited about organizing things, for me, for my patients and, most importantly, for my family.

ROBERTS: I think this has been terrific. Thank you.

Figure 1. Peter Kowey, age 3 with father and mother in Norristown, PA (1953)

Figure 2. Peter Kowey, age 15 with parents and brother Rick (1965)

Figure 4. Opening of CCU at Medical College of Pennsylvania (1985)

Figure 5. Parents 50th wedding anniversary (1992). *Left- to-right*: Peter, Dorothy, Peter S. Kowey (father), Edith A. Kowey (mother), Katie (sister-in-law) and Rick (brother)

Figure 3. ACC induction held in New Orleans (1983) with Dorothy

Figure 6. Dr. Kowey and Dorothy at Heart Ball in Philadelphia (2002)

Figure 7. Boating on Lake Naomi with his dogs, Mitten and Buffy (2006)

Figure 8. Dr. Kowey at Heart Rhythm Society book signing (2013)

BEST PUBLICATIONS OF PETER RUSSELL KOWEY SELECTED BY PETER RUSSELL KOWEY, MD, LISTED BY THE NUMBER IN HIS CURRICULUM VITAE:

4. Kowey PR, Friedman PL, Podrid PJ, Zielonka J, Lown B, Wynne J, Holman BL. Use of radionuclide ventriculography for assessment of changes in myocardial performance induced by disopyramide phosphate. *Am Heart J* 1982;104:769−774.

8. Kowey PR, Verrier RL, Lown B, Handin RI. Influence of intracoronary platelet aggregation on ventricular electrical properties during partial coronary artery stenosis. *Am J Cardiol* 1983;51:596−602.

16. Kowey PR, Eisenberg R, Engel TR. Sustained arrhythmias in hypertrophic obstructive cardiomyopathy. *N Engl J Med* 1984;310: 1566−1569.

43. Zukerman LS, Friehling TD, Wolf NM, Meister SG, Nahass G, Kowey PR. Effect of calcium-binding additives on ventricular fibrillation and repolarization changes during coronary angiography. *J Am Coll Cardiol* 1987;10:1249−1253.

45. Kowey PR, Friehling TD, Marinchak RA, Kline RA, Stohler JL, Yeager LA. The case for explantation of the automatic implantable cardioverter-defibrillator. *Am J Cardiol* 1987;59:1210−1211.

48. Kowey PR, Friehling TD, Marinchak RA, Sulpizi AM, Stohler JL. Safety and efficacy of amiodarone. The low-dose perspective. *Chest* 1988;93:54−59.

55. Kowey PR, Fisher L, Giardina EG, Leier CV, Lowenthal DT, Messerli FH, Pratt CM. The TPA controversy and the drug approval process. The view of the Cardiovascular and Renal Drugs Advisory Committee. *JAMA* 1988;260:2250−2252.

64. Luketich J, Friehling TD, O'Connor KM, Kowey PR. The effect of beta-adrenergic blockade on vulnerability to ventricular fibrillation and inducibility of ventricular arrhythmia in short- and long-term feline infarction models. *Am Heart J* 1989;118:265−271.

69. O'Connor KM, Friehling TD, Kowey PR. The effect of thromboxane inhibition on vulnerability to ventricular fibrillation in the acute and chronic feline infarction models. *Am Heart J* 1989;117:848−853.

71. Kowey PR, Waxman HL, Greenspon A, Greenberg R, Poll D, Kutalek S, Gessman L, Muenz L. Value of electrophysiologic testing in patients with previous myocardial infarction and nonsustained ventricular tachycardia. Philadelphia Arrhythmia Group. *Am J Cardiol* 1990;65: 594−598.

74. Pratt CM, Brater DC, Harrell FE Jr, Kowey PR, Leier CV, Lowenthal DT, Messerli F, Packer M, Pritchett EL, Ruskin JN. Clinical and regulatory implications of the Cardiac Arrhythmia Suppression Trial. *Am J Cardiol* 1990;65:103−105.

85. Messerlia FH, Kowey PR, Grodzickic T. Sublingual nifedipine for hypertensive emergencies (Letters to the Editor). *The Lancet* 1991;338: 881.

96. Kowey PR, Taylor JE, Rials SJ, Marinchak RA. Meta-analysis of the effectiveness of prophylactic drug therapy in preventing supraventricular arrhythmia early after coronary artery bypass grafting. *Am J Cardiol* 1992;69:963−965.

112. Hernández M, Taylor J, Marinchak R, Rials S, Rubin A, Kowey P. Outcome of patients with nonsustained ventricular tachycardia and severely impaired ventricular function who have negative electrophysiologic studies. *Am Heart J* 1995;129:492−496.

121. Kowey PR, Levine JH, Herre JM, Pacifico A, Lindsay BD, Plumb VJ, Janosik DL, Kopelman HA, Scheinman MM. Randomized, double-blind comparison of intravenous amiodarone and bretylium in the treatment of patients with recurrent, hemodynamically destabilizing ventricular tachycardia or fibrillation. The Intravenous Amiodarone Multicenter Investigators Group. *Circulation* 1995;92: 3255−3263.

122. Scheinman MM, Levine JH, Cannom DS, Friehling T, Kopelman HA, Chilson DA, Platia EV, Wilber DJ, Kowey PR. Dose-ranging study of intravenous amiodarone in patients with life-threatening ventricular tachyarrhythmias. The Intravenous Amiodarone Multicenter Investigators Group. *Circulation* 1995;92:3264−3272.

131. Grossman E, Messerli FH, Grodzicki T, Kowey P. Should a moratorium be placed on sublingual nifedipine capsules given for

hypertensive emergencies and pseudoemergencies? *JAMA* 1996;276: 1328–1331.

134. Kowey PR, Dalessandro DA, Herbertson R, Briggs B, Wertan MA, Rials SJ, Filart RA, Marinchak RA. Effectiveness of digitalis with or without acebutolol in preventing atrial arrhythmias after coronary artery surgery. *Am J Cardiol* 1997;79:1114–1117.

135. Kowey PR, Marinchak RA, Rials SJ, Filart RA. Intravenous amiodarone. *J Am Coll Cardiol* 1997;29:1190–1198.

142. Brandspiegel HZ, Marinchak RA, Rials SJ, Kowey PR. A broken heart. *Circulation* 1998;98:1349.

143. Volgman AS, Carberry PA, Stambler B, Lewis WR, Dunn GH, Perry KT, Vanderlugt JT, Kowey PR. Conversion efficacy and safety of intravenous ibutilide compared with intravenous procainamide in patients with atrial flutter or fibrillation. *J Am Coll Cardiol* 1998;31: 1414–1419.

146. Rials SJ, Xu X, Wu Y, Marinchak RA, Kowey PR. Regression of LV hypertrophy with captopril normalizes membrane currents in rabbits. *Am J Physiol* 1998;275(4 Pt 2):H1216–1224.

151. VanderLugt JT, Mattioni T, Denker S, Torchiana D, Ahern T, Wakefield LK, Perry KT, Kowey PR. Efficacy and safety of ibutilide fumarate for the conversion of atrial arrhythmias after cardiac surgery. *Circulation* 1999;100:369–375.

156. Reiffel JA, Kowey PR. Generic antiarrhythmics are not therapeutically equivalent for the treatment of tachyarrhythmias. *Am J Cardiol* 2000;85:1151–1153, A10.

165. Yan GX, Kowey PR. ST segment elevation and sudden cardiac death: from the Brugada syndrome to acute myocardial ischemia. *J Cardiovasc Electrophysiol* 2000;11:1330–1332.

169. Xu X, Rials SJ, Wu Y, Salata JJ, Liu T, Bharucha DB, Marinchak RA, Kowey PR. Left ventricular hypertrophy decreases slowly but not rapidly activating delayed rectifier potassium currents of epicardial and endocardial myocytes in rabbits. *Circulation* 2001;103:1585–1590.

171. Meng X, Mojaverian P, Doedée M, Lin E, Weinryb I, Chiang ST, Kowey PR. Bioavailability of amiodarone tablets administered with and without food in healthy subjects. *Am J Cardiol* 2001;87:432–435.

177. Kowey PR. The unnecessary pacemaker controversy revisited. *Pacing Clin Electrophysiol* 2002;25:269–271.

189. Medina-Ravell VA, Lankipalli RS, Yan GX, Antzelevitch C, Medina-Malpica NA, Medina-Malpica OA, Droogan C, Kowey PR. Effect of epicardial or biventricular pacing to prolong QT interval and increase transmural dispersion of repolarization: does resynchronization therapy pose a risk for patients predisposed to long QT or torsade de pointes? *Circulation* 2003;107:740–746.

191. Kowey PR, Kocovic DZ. Cardiology patient pages. Ambulatory electrocardiographic recording. *Circulation* 2003;108:e31–e33.

193. Yan GX, Lankipalli RS, Burke JF, Musco S, Kowey PR. Ventricular repolarization components on the electrocardiogram: cellular basis and clinical significance. *J Am Coll Cardiol* 2003;42:401–409.

197. Pepine CJ, Handberg EM, Cooper-DeHoff RM, Marks RG, Kowey P, Messerli FH, Mancia G, Cangiano JL, Garcia-Barreto D, Keltai M, Erdine S, Bristol HA, Kolb HR, Bakris GL, Cohen JD, Parmley WW; INVEST Investigators. A calcium antagonist vs a non-calcium antagonist hypertension treatment strategy for patients with coronary artery disease. The International Verapamil-Trandolapril Study (INVEST): a randomized controlled trial. *JAMA* 2003;290:2805–2816.

201. Yan GX, Joshi A, Guo D, Hlaing T, Martin J, Xu X, Kowey PR. Phase 2 reentry as a trigger to initiate ventricular fibrillation during early acute myocardial ischemia. *Circulation* 2004;110:1036–1041.

204. Kowey PR, Yannicelli D, Amsterdam E. COPPA-II Investigators. Effectiveness of oral propafenone for the prevention of atrial fibrillation after coronary artery bypass grafting. *Am J Cardiol* 2004;94: 663–665.

208. Joshi AK, Kowey PR, Prystowsky EN, Benditt DG, Cannom DS, Pratt CM, McNamara A, Sangrigoli RM. First experience with a Mobile Cardiac Outpatient Telemetry (MCOT) system for the diagnosis and management of cardiac arrhythmia. *Am J Cardiol* 2005;95: 878–881.

228. Pritchett EL, Kowey P, Connolly S, Page RL, Kerr C, Wilkinson WE; A-COMET-I Investigators. Antiarrhythmic efficacy of azimilide in patients with atrial fibrillation. Maintenance of sinus rhythm after conversion to sinus rhythm. *Am Heart J* 2006;151:1043–1049.

230. Olshansky B, Kowey PR, Naccarelli GV. Fast-track training of non-electrophysiologists to implant defibrillators: is it needed? *Pacing Clin Electrophysiol* 2006;29:627–631.

237. Rothman SA, Laughlin JC, Seltzer J, Walia JS, Baman RI, Siouffi SY, Sangrigoli RM, Kowey PR. The diagnosis of cardiac arrhythmias: a prospective multi-center randomized study comparing mobile cardiac outpatient telemetry versus standard loop event monitoring. *J Cardiovasc Electrophysiol* 2007;18:241–247.

239. Singh BN, Connolly SJ, Crijns HJ, Roy D, Kowey PR, Capucci A, Radzik D, Aliot EM, Hohnloser SH; EURIDIS and ADONIS Investigators. Dronedarone for maintenance of sinus rhythm in atrial fibrillation or flutter. *N Engl J Med* 2007;357:987–999.

245. Guo D, Young L, Patel C, Jiao Z, Wu Y, Liu T, Kowey PR, Yan GX. Calcium-activated chloride current contributes to action potential alternations in left ventricular hypertrophy rabbit. *Am J Physiol Heart Circ Physiol* 2008;295:H97–H104.

255. Dorian P, Al-Khalidi HR, Hohnloser SH, Brum JM, Dunnmon PM, Pratt CM, Holroyde MJ, Kowey P. Shock Inhibition Evaluation with Azimilide Investigators. Azimilide reduces emergency department visits and hospitalizations in patients with an implantable cardioverter-defibrillator in a placebo-controlled clinical trial. *J Am Coll Cardiol* 2008;52:1076–1083.

257. Laughlin JC, Kowey PR. Dronedarone: a new treatment for atrial fibrillation. *J Cardiovasc Electrophysiol* 2008;19:1220–1226.

262. Patel C, Yan GX, Kocovic D, Kowey PR. Should catheter ablation be the preferred therapy for reducing ICD shocks?: Ventricular tachycardia ablation versus drugs for preventing ICD shocks: role of adjuvant antiarrhythmic drug therapy. *Circ Arrhythm Electrophysiol* 2009;2:705–711; discussion 712.

263. Kowey PR, Dorian P, Mitchell LB, Pratt CM, Roy D, Schwartz PJ, Sadowski J, Sobczyk D, Bochenek A, Toft E; Atrial Arrhythmia Conversion Trial Investigators. Vernakalant hydrochloride for the rapid conversion of atrial fibrillation after cardiac surgery: a randomized, double-blind, placebo-controlled trial. *Circ Arrhythm Electrophysiol* 2009;2:652–659.

272. Al-Khatib SM, Calkins H, Eloff BC, Packer DL, Ellenbogen KA, Hammill SC, Natale A, Page RL, Prystowsky E, Jackman WM, Stevenson WG, Waldo AL, Wilber D, Kowey P, Yaross MS, Mark DB, Reiffel J, Finkle JK, Marinac-Dabic D, Pinnow E, Sager P, Sedrakyan A, Canos D, Gross T, Berliner E, Krucoff MW. Planning the Safety of Atrial Fibrillation Ablation Registry Initiative (SAFARI) as a Collaborative Pan-Stakeholder Critical Path Registry Model: a Cardiac Safety Research Consortium "Incubator" Think Tank. *Am Heart J* 2010;159:17–24.

277. Kowey PR, Reiffel JA, Ellenbogen KA, Naccarelli GV, Pratt CM. Efficacy and safety of prescription omega-3 fatty acids for the prevention of recurrent symptomatic atrial fibrillation: a randomized controlled trial. *JAMA* 2010;304:2363–2372.

282. Kowey PR. How much has malpractice litigation altered the care of cardiac rhythm patients? *J Cardiovasc Electrophysiol* 2011;22: 488–489.

285. Kowey PR. A piece of my mind. The silent majority. *JAMA* 2011;306:18–19.

291. Kowey PR, Crijns HJ, Aliot EM, Capucci A, Kulakowski P, Radzik D, Roy D, Connolly SJ, Hohnloser SH; ALPHEE Study Investigators. Efficacy and safety of celivarone, with amiodarone as calibrator, in patients with an implantable cardioverter-defibrillator for prevention of implantable cardioverter-defibrillator interventions or death: the ALPHEE study. *Circulation* 2011;124: 2649–2660.

297. Kowey PR, Naccarelli GV. The Food and Drug Administration decision not to approve the 110 mg dose of dabigatran: give us a way out. *Am J Med* 2012;125:732.